AMERICAN POPULAR SONGS

From the Revolutionary War to the Present

AMERICAN POPULAR SONGS

FROM THE REVOLUTIONARY WAR

TO THE PRESENT

EDITED BY

DAVID EWEN

RANDOM HOUSE

NEW YORK

First Printing
© *Copyright, 1966, by David Ewen*
All rights reserved under International
and Pan-American Copyright Conventions.
Published in New York by Random House, Inc.,
and simultaneously in Toronto, Canada,
by Random House of Canada Limited.
Library of Congress Catalog Card Number: 66-12843
Manufactured in the United States of America
by The Haddon Craftsmen, Inc., Scranton, Pennsylvania
Typography by Betty Anderson

Foreword

David Ewen is unquestionably the most prolific writer on music of all time. His more than fifty books cover practically every angle of the art, both serious and popular. This monumental volume of reference to the songs that are literally "of the American people" must be considered as important as any of his undertakings in the service of music.

Mr. Ewen himself explains in his Introduction the principles governing his selection of materials. He is entirely justified in assuming a truly national, perhaps even international, popularity for any song that has sold a million or more copies of sheet music or records (or both), and readers may often be surprised at the titles representing a perhaps unsuspected commercial success.

But there are other reasons for including in such an encyclopedia some songs that may have been previously unknown to the average listener. Some are included because they were the first or last works of their writers and therefore of historic if not necessarily musical interest. Some represent the first or perhaps most significant steps toward fame and fortune on the part of their creators. Others may assume a practical importance because of the part they played in establishing the careers of their composers or lyricists or both, or in serving as vehicles toward stardom for their interpreters, male or female, including bandleaders and instrumentalists as well as singers.

The anecdotes and inside information included in many of Mr. Ewen's discussions of individual numbers offer some astonishing and widely differing revelations. Often the birth of a popular song may well deserve the label of "inspiration," almost confirming the common belief that music springs spontaneously and quite unexpectedly from the brain or the emotions of its creator. Then again one may discover a story of laborious and painstaking effort in the slow development of a basic idea of words or tune into a finished product of ultimately universal appeal. In a surprising number of cases, a song was born

v

as the result of a mere chance remark or some apparently insignificant incident of otherwise prosaic daily life.

Above all, this is an encyclopedia of *songs*. Our popular songwriters come to life through the words and music that they wrote, not through a mere listing of biographical details. A study of the titles alone is often sufficient for the suggestion of the normal or exceptional development of careers in an art that is still a mystery to a large proportion of the American public. This encyclopedia is not merely a book of reference, to be used for the refreshment of memory, the evocation of nostalgia or the settlement of bets. It is a volume that can be treated as vital reading matter, to be enjoyed in large sections at a time or by skipping about from the familiar or unfamiliar song titles to the personalities that lie behind them. It is truly a collection of facts that read like fiction.

The time is now long past when apologies have to be made for the serious treatment of popular songs. They are accepted today as a type of urban folk music, quite as important in their way as the rural folk music that has always been treated with respect, particularly when the material has passed the test of time and become what is known as a "classic." There are classics of popular as well as serious music (the songs of Stephen Foster are an outstanding example) and it may well be argued that some of the best of today's popular songs (especially the highlights of modern musical comedy) might easily outlive much of the difficult and dissonant music of our time.

It is no longer news that popular music, even at its worst, is likely to express the manners, customs and habits of everyday people more accurately, and certainly more entertainingly, than a contemporary and scholarly "art" music possibly could. It may be done in obvious, often naïve, terms, but it expresses fundamental truths nevertheless. (There is something disquieting in the thought that the current craze for "rock 'n' roll" is in line with this recognized phenomenon!)

When we were a very young country, fighting wars of liberation and creating a political system for the future, our popular songs were naturally of the patriotic and political type, with a national rather than an individual appeal. Nor did we hesitate to borrow the melodies from otherwise unpopular England, as in the case of "Yankee Doodle," "Free America" and "The Star-Spangled Banner" itself. It might be noted in passing that many of the songs associated with later wars were actually non-militant in character and merely happened to become popular during the period of conflict. This applies to "Dixie's Land," "A Hot Time in the Old Town Tonight" (Spanish-American War) and "Tipperary," "The Long, Long Trail" and "K-K-K-Katy" of World War I. (World War II was definitely a mechanized, non-singing war.)

As our civilization spread westward, songs of the pioneering type naturally became popular, including also nostalgic songs of home and family, such as the classics of Stephen Foster, James C. Bland and others. With the increasing importance of transportation, our song-writers gradually covered that field, starting with horse-drawn vehicles and progressing through railroads and steamships to the bicycle, the automobile and eventually the airplane.

The so-called "Gay Nineties" (perhaps better characterized as "naïve") represented American life in a slow, casual, unhurried stage, with emphasis on largely artificial sentimentality. Popular songs had to tell a story, dealing necessarily with frustrated love and self-pity, with the waltz an almost automatic form of musical expression.

The early years of the twentieth century expressed a protest against such leisurely living and music, and our popular songs gradually developed the excitement of "ragtime" (meaning syncopation) and ultimately the elaborate embellishments of jazz. When the First World War came to an end, we had a decade of rebellion against all convention, reflected in the unrestrained music of the period, and not far removed from the barbaric tendencies of modern times.

Meanwhile very few of the details of American life escaped the attention of our songwriters. They gave musical expression to the clothes we wore, the games we played, the slang we talked, the dances we danced (including such animal imitations as the turkey trot, grizzly bear, fox trot and bunny hug), and what we ate and drank. National disasters and tragedies were celebrated in song, as were spectacular news events of a happier type. It has been estimated that more than five hundred pieces of music were written about Abraham Lincoln, mostly following his assassination. George Washington was also honored by many songs and instrumental numbers, of which the best known today is "The President's March," with the words beginning "Hail, Columbia, happy land." Lindbergh's flight across the Atlantic encouraged the publication of over a hundred songs, all now practically forgotten, including one by George M. Cohan.

Humor and love have been staples of our popular-song literature through the years, the former most frequently appearing in nonsense syllables, a technique that goes back to the madrigals of Elizabethan days, to whose "hey-nonny-nonny" our songwriters have added a "hot-cha-cha." Hardly a year passes without its novelty hit of the nonsensical type. Meanwhile our sentimental ditties have progressed from the straightforward statement, "I love you," to such indirect approaches as "If I loved you," "This *can't* be love because I feel so well," and *"They say* that falling in love is wonderful." The subject is still Love, explicit or implied.

From the primitive yet effective expression of human emotions to the even more effective sophistication of such an approach is a long step in the history of civilization. It is perhaps significant that the names most frequently encountered in this encyclopedia are those of men who combined an instinctive grasp of human realities with a highly organized technical skill. One does not have to be musically or verbally illiterate to write a Tin Pan Alley hit, much less a Broadway production number.

The American popular song is direct, perhaps obvious, in its appeal, but it is basic in its subject matter and generally sincere in its expression of recognized truths. There is every reason to welcome such a book as David Ewen's *American Popular Songs*.

S I G M U N D   S P A E T H

Summer, 1965

CONTENTS

CONTENTS

Introduction

American Popular Songs: from the Revolutionary War to the Present
is the first attempt to provide a comprehensive, alphabetical guide to
the songs Americans have sung and loved down the years. Over 3,600
such songs are listed, beginning (alphabetically) with "Aaron Slick
from Punkin Crick" and ending with "Zizzy, Ze Zum, Zum," and
running (chronologically) from "Yankee Doodle" and "The Girl I
Left Behind Me" in 1765 to the "Ballad of the Green Berets" early in
1966. The names of the composers and lyricists, the circumstances
surrounding the writing of the song, the basic facts of its performance history, the major productions on stage or screen where the
song was heard, best-selling recordings—in short, all historically
accurate material that is of general interest and all relevant information about America's most famous popular songs have been included
wherever possible.

Most of the songs in this encyclopedia are "standards"—a standard
being the popular-music equivalent of a classic in serious music:
music that has stood the test of time; that gives promise of perma-
nency in the repertory. A good many songs, while not standards, are
of historical, social or political interest; others, while forgotten today,
were immensely popular in their own day. For these reasons they
might invite curiosity for source material, and for these reasons they
have been included. A certain amount of space has been allotted to
rock 'n' roll, and its progenitors. I do not know if any of these numbers has a chance of survival, but I do know that this song style has
dominated the popular-music literature of over a decade and cannot
be ignored.

To make this volume more useful, the editor has included the
listing of over 140 each of composers and lyricists, and over 300 each
of musical comedies and motion pictures, with cross references to
their principal songs. This book also embraces succinct special ar-

ticles of special interest in the field of popular songs: Motion Picture Academy Awards; the Hit Parade; "Grammy" Awards; Gold Record Awards; the histories of ASCAP and BMI. In addition, the appendix has three listings that will prove valuable and informative: the all-time Hit Parade, a personal selection by this editor of what he considers to be the greatest song successes since 1765; a complete list of the all-time best sellers among popular recordings (single disks); and a listing of American performers, past and present, and the songs with which they are identified.

The title reveals the scope of the volume. To begin with, this is a source book of "songs." A song, by definition, comprises words and music and is intended for the voice. Instrumental compositions, therefore (say, numbers like David Rose's "Holiday for Strings," however popular), have no place here—except in those instances where, while they originated as instrumentals, they have become songs by virtue of the fact that lyrics were subsequently added to the melody ("Blue Tango" or "Nola," for example).

This, then, is a book of "popular" songs—that is, songs that have had mass circulation through popular media; the kind of song that was born in the theater and on the motion-picture screen; the kind of song that flourished in Tin Pan Alley. Jazz and the folk song—each of which is immensely rich in its own right and well deserving of cultivation in a similar way—are not discussed.

Nevertheless, a certain amount of flexibility has been tolerated. For one thing, America's national ballads are represented even though, strictly speaking, these do not conform to our definition of a popular song. These patriotic songs are included because when first written this was the popular music of the country. Beyond this, the popular song has through the years gathered unto itself, and made a part of itself, many songs that have sprung up in other fields: art songs, for example. Songs like Carrie Jacobs Bond's "Perfect Day" or Ethelbert Nevin's "The Rosary" started out as vocal concert numbers, but they have so often been given by popular performers through popular media that the editor deemed it desirable to list them in this volume. Similarly, there are a handful of jazz items ("Twelfth Street Rag" and "When the Saints Go Marching In" are examples) and folk tunes (say, "Home on the Range" or "On Top of Old Smokey") which are now so often regarded as popular songs that their inclusion appeared essential.

The encyclopedia, while confined to American songs, has also been somewhat flexible in incorporating several European song hits. In the main this was done where the song has become at least partially American through the addition of English lyrics and/or through its popularization by American performers through American media. However, European song hits that have not thus become partly

Americanized are avoided—however popular these numbers may have become in this country. This is the reason why those formidable song hits, written, popularized and sung by the Beatles from England, cannot be found in this book.

Material for this volume has been gathered over a period of many years: from attendance at stage and motion-picture performances; from personal associations with the country's foremost composers and lyricists; from listening to records; and most particularly from research into specialized fields for the preparation of various histories, source books and authorized biographies. Nevertheless, this book could hardly have been possible without the generous co-operation of many people all over the country—too many to list here by name: popular composers and lyricists, most of whom have been consulted for first-hand information and to check on gathered data; publishers, recording companies, motion-picture executives, Broadway producers and performers; organizations like ASCAP and BMI; libraries, and authorities on popular music. To all of these I would like here and now to express my apology for bombarding them so persistently with requests for needed material, and my most profound gratitude for the magnanimous spirit that motivated their ready and valuable responses.

D. E.

AMERICAN

POPULAR SONGS

Aaron Slick from Punkin Crick, a motion-picture musical starring Alan Young, Dinah Shore and Robert Merrill (Paramount, 1952). Songs by Ray Evans and Jay Livingston. *See:* Marshmallow Moon; My Beloved.

The Aba Daba Honeymoon, words and music by Arthur Fields and Walter Donovan (1914). A nonsense song about a monkey honeymoon. It was introduced by Ruth Roye at the Palace Theatre in New York in 1914, then popularized by her during her fourteen-week engagement in that theater. It was revived in the motion-picture musical *The King of Jazz,* starring Paul Whiteman and his orchestra (Universal, 1930). Jane Powell sang it in the non-musical motion picture *Two Weeks with Love* (MGM, 1950). In 1951 the MGM recording by Debbie Reynolds and Carleton Carpenter sold a million disks.

The A.B.C.'s of Love, words and music by George Goldner and Richard Barrett (1956). Popularized by Frankie Lymon and the Teenagers in a Gee recording.

Abdul Abulbul Amir, a pseudo-Oriental nonsense song of unknown authorship and date. Frank Crumit, who made a successful Victor recording in the 1920s, published the song as his own in 1928. But it is more probably of English origin from the time of the Crimean War. The song was a favorite of American soldiers during World War I, usually with improvised off-color lyrics.

About a Quarter to Nine, words by Al Dubin, music by Harry Warren (1935). Introduced by Al Jolson in the motion-picture musical *Get into Your Dance* (First National, 1935). He revived it on the soundtrack of the motion-picture musical *The Jolson Story* (Columbia, 1946).

Abracadabra, words and music by Cole Porter (1944). Introduced by June Havoc in the musical *Mexican Hayride* (1944).

Absinthe Frappé, words by Glen MacDonough, music by Victor Herbert (1904). Introduced by Harry Davenport in the operetta *It Happened in Nordland* (1904). It was interpolated in the motion-picture musical *The Great Victor Herbert* (Paramount, 1939).

Academy of Motion Picture Arts and Sciences Awards ("Oscar"). An annual award instituted in 1928 for distinguished contributions to the screen.

These musical productions (or productions with significant song interpolations) received Oscars as the year's best motion picture: *The Broadway Melody,* 1929; *The Great Ziegfeld,* 1936; *Going My Way,* 1944; *An American in Paris,* 1951; *Gigi,* 1958; *West Side Story,* 1961; *My Fair Lady,* 1964; *The Sound of Music,* 1965.

An annual song category was introduced in 1934. The first recipient was "The Continental."

The following songs received Oscars after 1934: Lullaby of Broadway, 1935; The Way You Look Tonight, 1936; Sweet Leilani, 1937; Thanks for the Memory, 1938; Over the Rainbow, 1939; When You Wish Upon a Star, 1940; The Last Time I Saw Paris, 1941; White Christmas, 1942; You'll Never Know, 1943; Swinging on a Star, 1944; It Might as Well Be Spring, 1945; On the Atchison, Topeka and Santa Fe, 1946; Zip-a-Dee-Doo-Dah, 1947; Buttons and Bows, 1948; Baby, It's Cold Outside, 1949; Mona Lisa, 1950; In the Cool, Cool, Cool of the Evening, 1951; High Noon, 1952; Secret Love, 1953; Three Coins in a Fountain, 1954; Love Is a Many Splendored Thing, 1955; Whatever Will Be, Will Be, 1956; All the Way, 1957; Gigi, 1958; High Hopes, 1959; Never on Sunday, 1960; Moon River, 1961; Days of Wine and Roses, 1962; Call Me Irresponsible, 1963; Chim Chim Cheree, 1964; *Shadow of Your Smile*, 1965.

Accent on Youth, words by Tot Seymour, music by Vee Lawnhurst (1935). Title song of a motion picture starring Sylvia Sidney and Herbert Marshall (Paramount, 1935).

Ac-cent-tchuate the Positive, words by Johnny Mercer, music by Harold Arlen (1944). Introduced by Bing Crosby in the motion-picture musical *Here Come the Waves* (Paramount, 1944), then popularized by him in a Decca recording. It was interpolated in the background music of the motion picture *Blue Dahlia*, starring Alan Ladd and Veronica Lake (20th Century-Fox, 1946).

This was one of the last songs which Mercer and Arlen wrote for *Here Come the Waves*—the initial idea coming to them during an automobile drive. After talking over one or two subjects, Mercer reminded Arlen of a spiritual-like tune he [Arlen] had been humming continually. When Arlen began singing it to him, Mercer remarked irrelevantly: "You've got to accentuate the posi-

tive"—a line that had somehow stuck in Mercer's mind since his boyhood days in school. Arlen now sang his spiritual-like melody, fitting in the line "you've got to accentuate the positive." By the time they drove to the studio they had most of the song written. "It must really have pleased John," Arlen remarked. "It was the first time I saw him smile."

Ace in the Hole, words and music by Cole Porter (1941). Introduced by Mary Jane Walsh, Sunny O'Dea and Nanette Fabray in the musical *Let's Face It* (1941). It was popularized in night clubs by Tommy Lyman.

Adams, Lee, lyricist. *See:* Strouse, Charles.

Adams and Liberty (or, The Boston Patriotic Song), words by Robert Treat Paine to the British melody "To Anacreon in Heaven" (1798), the same tune subsequently used for "The Star-Spangled Banner." "Adams and Liberty" served as a Presidential campaign song for John Adams.

Adamson, Harold, lyricist, born Greenville, New Jersey, 1906.

See: McHugh, Jimmy.

See also: An Affair to Remember; Around the World; Did I Remember?; Everything I Have Is Yours; Manhattan Serenade; My Resistance Is Low; Time on My Hands.

Adelaide's Lament, words and music by Frank Loesser (1950). Introduced in the musical *Guys and Dolls* (1950) by Vivian Blaine, who repeated her performance in the motion-picture adaptation of the musical (MGM, 1955).

As originally conceived by Loesser, this number was intended to be the lament of a strip-tease artist who is perpetually catching cold through overexposure to the elements. But in an attempt to make the character of Adelaide more sympathetic, Loesser finally decided to make her the victim of psychosomatic woes—the consequence of having her impending marriage to a gambler, Nathan Detroit, continually postponed.

Moss Hart once remarked in a

radio interview that he considered this lament one of the most original and effective musical-comedy numbers he had ever heard.

Adler, Richard, lyricist and composer, born New York City, 1923.

See (In collaboration with Jerry Ross): Even Now; Everybody Loves a Lover; Heart; Hernando's Hideaway; Hey, There; Rags to Riches; Steam Heat; There Once Was a Man; Two Lost Souls; Whatever Lola Wants; You're So Much a Part of Me.

See also: Another Time, Another Place; Cocoa Bean Song; The Newspaper Song; Nothing More to Look Forward To; Ordinary People; The Strange Little Girl; Teasin'.

An Affair to Remember (or, Our Love Affair), words and music by Harold Adamson and Leo McCarey, music by Harry Warren (1957). Theme song of a motion picture of the same name starring Deborah Kerr (20th Century-Fox, 1957). It was introduced on the soundtrack under the titles by Vic Damone and popularized by his recording for Columbia.

After All, You're All I'm After, words by Edward Heyman, music by Arthur Schwartz (1933). Introduced by Bing Crosby in the motion-picture musical *She Loves Me Not* (Paramount, 1934).

After Sundown, words by Arthur Freed, music by Nacio Herb Brown (1933). Introduced by Bing Crosby in the motion-picture musical *Going Hollywood* (Paramount, 1933), and popularized by him in a Decca recording. This song was not only largely responsible for the box-office success of this movie, it was also a significant force in making Bing Crosby a Hollywood singing star for the first time, placing him among the first ten leading box-office attractions in 1933.

After the Ball, words and music by Charles K. Harris (1892). This sentimental ballad was the first song to sell five million copies of sheet music. Through the years it is believed to have earned several million dollars for its composer.

When Harris wrote "After the Ball" he was still a neophyte, both as a composer and as a publisher. He had already written a few songs which he himself had published in Milwaukee. Then, in 1892, he paid a visit to Chicago. There, attending a ball, he saw a young couple quarrel and separate. The thought suddenly leaped to his mind, "many a heart is aching after the ball." Back in Milwaukee, Harris developed the idea into a ballad comprising three sixty-four-bar verses and three thirty-two-bar choruses. The story line ran as follows. An old man explains to his niece why he never married. Many years earlier a serious misunderstanding had arisen between himself and the girl he loved. At a ball, he had seen her kissing a stranger. Without waiting for an explanation, he left the ball, never to see her again. Only many years later, when it was too late, did he discover that the man she had kissed was her long-lost brother.

The ink not yet dry on his manuscript, Harris induced Sam Doctor, a vaudevillian, to introduce the ballad. Doctor did so in Milwaukee in 1892. During his performance he forgot his lines, and the song proved a fiasco. Harris now turned it over to J. Aldrich Libby, a singing star in the musical extravaganza *A Trip to Chinatown,* then playing in Milwaukee. Harris paid Libby $500 and a share in the song's royalties to interpolate the ballad in that extravaganza (an early example of "payola"). The song was used in the second act, set in San Francisco's Chinatown. Wearing an evening suit and white tie, Libby stepped before the footlights and delivered the ballad, even though it had no possible relation to the plot or setting. Not a sound was heard in the audience after he had completed the first verse and chorus. "I was ready to sink through the floor," Harris later recalled in his autobiography. "He then went through the second verse and chorus, and again complete silence reigned. I was making ready to bolt, but my friends . . . held me tightly by the arm. Then came the third verse and chorus. For a full minute the audience again remained quiet, and then broke loose with applause. . . . The entire audience arose and, standing, applauded wildly for five minutes."

M. Witmark and Sons, a leading Tin Pan Alley publisher, offered to buy the song for $10,000, but Harris preferred to gamble on it himself. A few days after the sheet music was ready, Oliver Ditson, the Boston music shop, sent in an order for 75,000 copies. Harris had to go out and buy a printing press to meet the order. Before long, orders came pouring in from all over the country. The ballad's popularity grew by leaps and bounds when Helene Mora, "the female baritone," included it in her vaudeville act; also when, in 1893, John Philip Sousa featured it prominently in a band arrangement at the World Exposition in Chicago. (The ballad became so popular with Sousa's audiences that henceforth he rarely gave a concert without playing it either on the program or as an encore.) Before the year of 1893 was over, Harris was using every available press in Milwaukee to meet the seemingly insatiable demand.

After You Get What You Want You Don't Want It, words and music by Irving Berlin (1920). It was revived by Marilyn Monroe in the motion-picture musical *There's No Business Like Show Business* (20th Century-Fox, 1955).

After You've Gone, words by Henry Creamer, music by Turner Layton (1918). Popularized by Al Jolson at the Winter Garden and by Sophie Tucker in vaudeville. Louis Armstrong scored his first major success in New York with this number, performing it at Connie's Inn in 1929; he also recorded it at that time for Okeh. The song was also a Benny Goodman specialty. Benny Goodman's Quartet played it on the soundtrack of a motion picture produced by Walt Disney, *Make Mine Music* (RKO, 1946). It was also

interpolated in several motion pictures. Among these were *Unholy Partners*, starring Edward G. Robinson (MGM, 1941); *For Me and My Gal* (MGM, 1942); *Atlantic City* (Republic, 1944), sung by Constance Moore; and *Some Came Running*, starring Frank Sinatra, Dean Martin and Shirley MacLaine (MGM, 1958), sung by Shirley MacLaine and a male trio.

Again, words by Dorcas Cochran, music by Lionel Newman (1948). Introduced by Ida Lupino in the motion picture *Roadhouse* (20th Century-Fox, 1949). Vic Damone revived it in 1954 in a Mercury recording that sold a million disks. The song was then heard in two non-musical motion pictures: *Island in the Sun*, starring Harry Belafonte and Joan Fontaine (20th Century-Fox, 1957), and *Best of Everything*, starring Hope Lange and Stephen Boyd (20th Century-Fox, 1959).

Ager, Milton, composer, born Chicago, Illinois, 1893.

See (Lyrics by Jack Yellen): Ain't She Sweet?; A Bench in the Park; Forgive Me; Happy Days Are Here Again; Happy Feet; Hard Hearted Hannah; I'm the Last of the Red Hot Mamas; I Wonder What's Become of Sally; Lovin' Sam; Who Cares?; A Young Man's Fancy.

See also: Auf Wiedersehen, My Dear; Could I, I Certainly Could; Crazy Words, Crazy Tune; Everything Is Peaches Down in Georgia; Freckles; I'm Nobody's Baby; Ten Pins in the Sky.

Ah, But Is It Love?, words by E. Y. Harburg, music by Jay Gorney (1933). Introduced in the motion-picture musical *Moonlight and Pretzels*, starring Mary Brian and Leo Carrillo (Universal, 1933).

Ahlert, Fred E., composer, born New York City, 1892; died New York City, 1953.

See (Lyrics by Edgar Leslie): Lovely; The Moon Was Yellow.

See (Lyrics by Roy Turk): The Free and Easy; I Don't Know Why; I'll Get By; Love, You Funny Thing; Mean to Me; Walking My Baby Back

Home; Where the Blue of the Night Meets the Gold of the Day; Why Dance?

See (Lyrics by Joe Young): I'm Gonna Sit Right Down and Write Myself a Letter; Sing an Old Fashioned Song; You Dropped Me Like a Red Hot Penny.

See also: I Gave You Up Just Before You Threw Me Down.

Ah, Sweet Mystery of Life (or, The Dream Melody), words by Rida Johnson Young, music by Victor Herbert (1910). One of Herbert's most successful songs, introduced by Orville Harrold in the operetta *Naughty Marietta* (1910). It served there as a kind of leitmotif—the pivot on which the plot spun: the heroine had heard a fragment of the song in a dream and offered to marry the one who could finish the melody for her, a task ultimately accomplished by the hero. In the motion-picture adaptation of the operetta (MGM, 1935), it was sung by Jeanette Mac-Donald and Nelson Eddy. The song was interpolated in the motion-picture musical *The Great Victor Herbert* (Paramount, 1939), sung by Allan Jones.

Ain't Dat a Shame?, words by John Queen, music by Walter Wilson (1901). A coon song classic that served as the inspiration for such subsequent coon songs as "Bill Bailey, Won't You Please Come Home" and "What You Goin' to Do When the Rent Comes 'Round?"

Ain't It a Shame?, words and music by Antoine "Fats" Domino and Dave Bartholomew (1955). Popularized by "Fats" Domino in an Imperial recording. Pat Boone's recording for Dot was also a best seller, and marked the beginning of his remarkable singing career.

Ain't It Funny What a Difference Just a Few Hours Make?, words by Henry Blossom, music by Alfred G. Robyn (1903). Introduced by Raymond Hitchock in the musical *The Yankee Consul* (1904).

Ain't Misbehavin', words by Andy Razaf, music by Thomas "Fats" Waller and Harry Brooks (1929). In-troduced by Louis Armstrong (then recently come to New York) in the all-Negro revue *Hot Chocolates* (1929). Armstrong credits this appearance as the beginning of his international fame. His 1929 Okeh recording (one of his first after coming to New York) has become a jazz classic.

Recalling how he came to write the song, Andy Razaf told an interviewer: "I remember one day going to Fats's house on 133rd Street to finish up a number based on a little strain he'd thought up. The whole show was complete, but they needed an extra number for a theme, and this had to be it. He worked on it for about forty-five minutes and there it was—'Ain't Misbehavin'.'"

The song was interpolated in several motion-picture musicals. These include *Stormy Weather* (20th Century-Fox, 1943), performed by Ada Brown and "Fats" Waller; *You Were Meant for Me* (20th Century-Fox, 1948), sung by Dan Dailey and chorus and danced to by Dan Dailey and Jeanne Crain; and *Gentlemen Marry Brunettes* (United Artists, 1955), sung by Alan Young, Jane Russell and Anita Ellis, the last of whom was dubbed in on the sound-track for Jeanne Crain.

"Fats" Waller's recording for RCA Victor was a best seller. He adopted the number as his theme song.

Ain't She Sweet?, words by Jack Yellen, music by Milton Ager (1927). This song was one of the rare instances in the Ager-Yellen collaboration in which the melody came before the lyric. The number was introduced by Paul Ash and his orchestra at the Oriental Theatre in Chicago. Within a week the song was a hit. It was further popularized in vaudeville by Eddie Cantor, Sophie Tucker and Lillian Roth. In Eddie Cantor's act (at the Orpheum Theatre in Los Angeles) a cute, shy little blond girl walked across the stage as he delivered the number; she was the then still unknown Sally Rand. In time the song sold over a million copies of sheet music. It was interpolated in the motion-picture musical *You Were Meant for Me* (20th Century-Fox, 1948), sung by Dan Dailey and chorus, and as a choral episode in the non-musical motion picture *Picnic,* starring Kim Novak and William Holden (Columbia, 1956).

An't That a Shame? See: Ain't It a Shame?

Ain't We Got Fun?, words and music by Richard A. Whiting (1921). Introduced by Arthur West in the revue *Satires of 1920.* It was then popularized in vaudeville by Ruth Roye. It was interpolated in several motion-picture musicals. These included Gus Kahn's screen biography *I'll See You in My Dreams* (Warner, 1951); *On Moonlight Bay* (Warner, 1951); *By the Light of the Silvery Moon* (Warner, 1953), sung by Doris Day and Gordon MacRae; and *The Eddie Cantor Story* (Warner, 1954), sung on the soundtrack by Eddie Cantor.

Akst, Harry, composer and lyricist, born New York City, 1894; died Los Angeles, 1963.

See (Lyrics by Lew Brown): Stand Up and Cheer; Taking Care of You.

See (Lyrics by Benny Davis): Baby Face; Dearest, You're the Nearest to My Heart; A Smile Will Go a Long, Long Way; Why Don't They Let Me Sing a Love Song?

See (Lyrics by Sam M. Lewis and Joe Young): Dinah; Revenge.

See also: Am I Blue?; Anima e Core; Guilty; May I Sing to You?

Alabamy Bound, words by Bud De Sylva and Bud Green, music by Ray Henderson (1925). Popularized by Eddie Cantor and by Al Jolson. It sold over a million copies of sheet music. It was interpolated in the motion picture *Broadway,* starring George Raft and Pat O'Brien (Universal, 1942), and in Jane Froman's screen biography *With a Song in My Heart* (20th Century-Fox, 1952).

"Alabamy Bound" was the last song Nora Bayes sang in public. This took place in 1928 at a benefit performance at the Bowery Mission House in New York. Four days later she was dead.

Alexander, Don't You Love Your Baby No More?, words by Andrew B. Sterling, music by Harry von Tilzer (1904). Von Tilzer got the idea for this coon song by watching the blackface vaudeville team of McIntyre and Heath and by overhearing a chance remark. An episode in the McIntyre and Heath act that always provoked laughter was the moment when McIntyre called Heath "Alexander." After that performance, while standing in the lobby, von Tilzer overheard a Negro lady asking her beau, "Don't you love your baby no more?" The addition of the name "Alexander" to this comment at once appeared to von Tilzer as ideal song material, and he relayed his thought to his favorite lyricist. The song soon became popular in vaudeville and minstrel shows. In all probability this number was the stimulation Irving Berlin needed for writing "Alexander's Ragtime Band."

Alexander's Ragtime Band, words and music by Irving Berlin (1911). In 1910 Berlin had written a ragtime song called "Alexander and His Clarinet," undoubtedly inspired by Harry von Tilzer's highly successful coon song "Alexander, Don't You Love Your Baby No More?" Dissatisfied with his own effort, Berlin put his song aside. Then, in 1911, elected a member to the Friars' Club in New York, Berlin was invited to appear as performer in the Friars' annual *Frolic.* For this occasion Berlin decided to write a special number. He salvaged the lyrics of "Alexander and His Clarinet" and joined them to a ragtime tune he had found in his well-stocked trunk, calling the hybrid product "Alexander's Ragtime Band."

He himself never did get around to introducing the number at the Friars' *Frolic.* Instead he submitted it to Jesse Lasky (later the motion-picture executive), then producing vaudeville shows on Broadway. Lasky turned it down. Soon after that the Columbia Burlesque, also on Broadway, used it, but nobody then paid much attention to it.

Emma Carus was the one who first made it popular—in a vaudeville theater in Chicago. "If we were John D. Rockefeller," reported an unidentified Chicago newspaperman after hearing Miss Carus sing "Alexander's Ragtime Band," "or the Bank of England, we should engage the Coliseum and get together a sextet including [Enrico] Caruso. . . . After the sextet sang it about ten times we should, have as a finale, have Sousa's Band march about the building, tearing the melody to pieces with all kinds of variations."

Eddie Miller, Helen Vincent, Ethel Levey and Sophie Tucker were some other vaudevillians who started to use the number in their acts. In a few months' time the sheet music sold over a million copies, and in a year the song became the most widely sung, played and danced-to "ragtime" number to come out of Tin Pan Alley.

Though it was the most successful "ragtime" song ever written—and the one number above all others that made America syncopation-conscious —"Alexander's Ragtime Band" is not a ragtime tune at all. Except for the word "ragtime" in the title—and for the single use of syncopation on the word "just" in the chorus—this song is basically a march tune with interpolations of bugle calls and a quotation from Stephen Foster's "Swanee River."

The song was used in, gave the title for, and played a basic part in the story of, a motion-picture musical (20th Century-Fox, 1938), sung there by Alice Faye. It was revived in the motion-picture musical *There's No Business Like Show Business* (20th Century-Fox, 1954), where it was used in an elaborate production number set in different countries and sung by Ethel Merman, Dan Dailey, Mitzi Gaynor, Donald O'Connor and Johnny Ray. A recording for Decca made by Al Jolson and Bing Crosby has become a collector's item due to their ad-lib remarks, including a favorite Jolson exclamation, "You dawg!"

The repeated accusations that one of the lines in the lyric was "war-mongering" led Berlin, early in 1965, to change "so natural that you want to go to war" into "so natural that you wanna hear some more." He explained: "The alternate line is available for anyone who doesn't want to sing the original."

Alexander's Ragtime Band, a motion-picture musical starring Tyrone Power and Alice Faye (20th Century-Fox, 1938). The songs were all Irving Berlin standards.

See: Alexander's Ragtime Band; Cheek to Cheek; Everybody's Doin' It; How Deep Is the Ocean?; International Rag; Oh, How I Hate to Get Up in the Morning; Ragtime Violin; Remember?; Say It with Music; Some Sunny Day.

Alice Blue Gown. *See:* In My Sweet Little Alice Blue Gown.

All Aboard for Blanket Bay, words by Andrew B. Sterling, music by Harry von Tilzer (1910). Sigmund Spaeth described this hit number of the early 1910s as a "kid song."

Allah's Holiday, words by Otto Hauerbach (Harbach), music by Rudolf Friml (1916). Introduced by Edith Day and chorus in the operetta *Katinka* (1915).

All Alone, words and music by Irving Berlin (1924). One of several ballads written under the inspiration of Berlin's dramatic love affair with Ellin Mackay, whom he married in 1926. The song was interpolated in the *Music Box Revue of 1923*, where it was popularized by Grace Moore, then making her Broadway debut. Grace Moore and Oscar Shaw sang it to each other on a darkened stage, each seated at a telephone at opposite ends of the stage.

All Alone (or, Hello Central, Give Me 603), words by Will Dillon, music by Harry von Tilzer (1911). Introduced in vaudeville, where it became one of the first numbers to utilize a telephone on the stage.

All Alone Monday, words by Bert Kalmar, music by Harry Ruby (1926). Introduced by Marie Saxon, Jack Whiting and chorus in the musical *The Ramblers* (1926). In the Kalmar and Ruby screen biography *Three*

Little Words (MGM, 1950), it was sung by Gale Robbins.

All at Once You Love Her, words by Oscar Hammerstein II, music by Richard Rodgers (1955). Introduced by William Johnson and Judy Tyler in the musical play *Pipe Dream* (1955).

All by Myself, words and music by Irving Berlin (1921). One of Berlin's most successful ballads up to that time, selling over a million copies of sheet music, a million and a quarter phonograph records and over one hundred and fifty thousand piano rolls. The song was revived by Bing Crosby in the motion-picture musical *Blue Skies* (MGM, 1946).

All by Myself, words and music by Antoine "Fats" Domino and Dave Bartholomew (1955). Popularized by "Fats" Domino in an Imperial recording.

All Coons Look Alike to Me, words and music by Ernest Hogan (1896). One of the earliest and most successful coon shouts, it made its author famous both as a songwriter and as a performer. Hogan introduced it in vaudeville, Rupert Hughes describing his rendition as "simply fascinating" because of its "impudent determination to keep out of key and out of time." Later in his life Hogan (a Negro) deeply regretted having written the song, now feeling it was demeaning to his race. Actually, except for the use of the term "coon" in the title, there is little in the song to slander the Negro people: the heroine of the song is merely saying she is indifferent to being jilted by her suitor, since all men, i.e., coons, look alike to her. A recording of this song was made as early as 1897— by Len Spenser for the Universal Phonograph Company, then owned and operated by the Tin Pan Alley firm of Joseph W. Stern & Co.

Allegheny Moon, words and music by Al Hoffman and Dick Manning (1956). Popularized by Patti Page in a Mercury recording that sold a million disks.

Allegro, a musical play with text and lyrics by Oscar Hammerstein II. Music by Richard Rodgers. Starring John Battles, Roberta Jonay and Anamary Dickey (1947). Original cast recording (RCA Victor).

See: A Fellow Needs a Girl; The Gentleman Is a Dope; So Far.

Allen, Robert, composer and lyricist, born Troy, New York, 1924.

See (Lyrics by Al Stillman): Can You Find It in Your Heart?; Chances Are; Enchanted Island; Home for the Holidays; If Dreams Come True; It's Not for Me to Say; Moments to Remember; No, Not Much; Teacher, Teacher; There's Only One of You; Who Needs You?; You Alone.

See also: Come to Me; Everybody Loves a Lover; I Never Felt More Like Falling in Love; Song for a Summer Night; To Know You Is to Love You; A Very Special Love.

All 'er Nothin', words by Oscar Hammerstein II, music by Richard Rodgers (1943). A comedy number introduced by Celeste Holm and Lee Dixon in the musical play *Oklahoma!* (1943). In the motion-picture adaptation of the musical (Magna Theatre, 1955), it was sung by Gloria Grahame.

Alley Cat, words and music by Frank Bjorn (1962). Popularized by Bent Fabric in an Atco recording.

Alley Oop, words and music by Dallas Frazier (1960). Popularized by the Hollywood Argyles in a Lute recording.

Allez Vous En, Go Away, words and music by Cole Porter (1953). Introduced by Lilo (in her Broadway debut) in the musical *Can-Can* (1953).

All for One, One for all. *See:* The March of the Musketeers.

All for You, words by Henry Blossom, music by Victor Herbert (1915). Love duet from the operetta *The Princess Pat* (1915), introduced by Joseph R. Lertora and Eleanor Painter. It was interpolated in the motion-picture musical *The Great Victor Herbert* (Paramount, 1939), sung by Allan Jones and Mary Martin.

All God's Chillun Got Rhythm, words and music by Gus Kahn, Walter Jurmann and Bronislau Kaper (1937). Introduced by Allan Jones in the

Marx Brothers' motion-picture extravaganza *A Day at the Races* (MGM, 1937).

All I Do Is Dream of You, words by Arthur Freed, music by Nacio Herb Brown (1934). Introduced by Gene Raymond in the motion-picture musical *Sadie McKee* (MGM, 1934). It was revived by Debbie Reynolds in the motion-picture musical *Singin' in the Rain* (MGM, 1952). In the motion picture *The Affairs of Dobie Gillis* (MGM, 1953), it was played under the titles; it was then sung in the film by Debbie Reynolds and Bobby Van.

All I Have to Do Is Dream, words and music by Boudleaux Bryant (1958). Popularized by the Everly Brothers in a Cadence recording.

All I Need, words by Fred Ebb, music by John Kander (1965). Ballad introduced by Liza Minnelli in the musical *Flora, the Red Menace* (1965).

All in Fun, words by Oscar Hammerstein II, music by Jerome Kern (1939). Introduced by Frances Mercer and Jack Whiting in the musical *Very Warm for May* (1939).

All I Remember Is You, words by Eddie De Lange, music by James Van Heusen (1939). Introduced by Tommy Dorsey and his orchestra, whose RCA Victor recording helped to popularize it.

All I Want for Christmas Is My Two Front Teeth, words and music by Don Gardner (1946). Introduced by the Satisfiers on Perry Como's radio show. It was popularized in 1948 by Spike Jones and his City Slickers in an RCA Victor recording.

All I Wants Is My Black Baby Back, words by Tom Daly, music by Gus Edwards (1898). Gus Edwards' first song hit. At that time Edwards knew so little about musical notation that he had to get Charles Frohman to write the melody down for him. The song was introduced in vaudeville by The Newsboy Quintet, of which Edwards was a member.

All My Life, words by Sidney D. Mitchell, music by Sammy H. Stept (1936). Introduced in the motion picture *Laughing Irish Eyes*, starring Phil Regan and Evelyn Knapp (Republic, 1936). The song was revived in the motion picture *Johnny Doughboy*, starring Jane Withers (Republic, 1942).

All My Love, words by Mitchell Parish, music by Paul Durand, the melody based on Ravel's *Bolero* (1950). Popularized by Patti Page in a best-selling Mercury recording.

All of a Sudden My Heart Sings. *See:* My Heart Sings.

All of Me, words by Seymour Simons, music by Gerald Marks (1931). Introduced in the non-musical motion picture *Careless Lady*, starring John Boles and Joan Bennett (Fox, 1932). Frank Sinatra interpolated it in the motion picture *Meet Danny Wilson* (Universal, 1952), and made a recording for Capitol which became one of his best sellers up to that time. Gloria De Haven sang it in the motion picture *Down Among the Sheltering Palms* (20th Century-Fox, 1953).

All of You, words and music by Cole Porter (1955). Introduced by Don Ameche in the musical comedy *Silk Stockings* (1955). In the motion-picture adaptation of the musical (MGM, 1957), it was sung by Fred Astaire, and danced to by Astaire and Cyd Charisse.

All or Nothing At All, words and music by Jack Lawrence and Arthur Altman (1940). Frank Sinatra's recording with the Harry James orchestra for Columbia in 1940 did only moderately well when first released. But with Sinatra's meteoric rise to fame in 1943, this recording was revived—to sell over a million disks. The song was interpolated in several motion pictures, including *Weekend Pass*, starring Noah Beery and Martha O'Driscoll (Universal, 1944), and *This Is the Life*, starring Donald O'Connor (Universal, 1944).

All Quiet Along the Potomac Tonight, celebrated Civil War ballad, words by Lamar Fontaine, music by John Hill Hewitt (1864). Hewitt dedicated his song to the "unknown dead of the present revolution."

The phrase, "all quiet on the Potomac tonight" was widely circulated in the press during the period of inactivity following the Battle of Bull Run. Hewitt's song is believed to have been based on an incident in which the lyricist himself had been involved. Lamar Fontaine was a member of the Second Virginia Cavalry. After completing his duty as guard, Fontaine turned over the post to his best friend, John Moore. As Moore stirred the coals, flames leaped up to reveal his position. An enemy picket on the opposite bank of the Potomac picked him off and killed him. As he saw his friend lie dead at his side, Fontaine happened to notice a newspaper nearby with the headline: "All Quiet Along the Potomac Tonight." The next day Fontaine wrote the five stanzas of a poem in which he had his friend recall nostalgically his wife and child the very moment he was killed. The popularity of this ballad during the Civil War led some commanding officers to prohibit the use of campfires during guard duty.

All 'Round My Hat, words by John Hansell (J. Ansell, Esquire), music arranged by John Valentine (1838). A comedy dialect song popularized by Jack Reeve. It was the ancestor of, and the inspiration for, the more familiar number, published in 1917, "Round Her Neck She Wore a Yellow Ribbon."

All She'd Say Was "Umh Hum," words and music by King Zany, MacEmery, and Van and Schenck (1920). Introduced by Van and Schenck in the *Ziegfield Follies of 1920*.

All Shook Up, words and music by Otis Blackwell and Elvis Presley (1957). Introduced and popularized by Elvis Presley in an RCA Victor recording that sold over a million disks.

All the King's Horses, words by Edward Brandt and Howard Dietz, music by Alec Wilder (1930). Introduced by Margaret Lee in the revue *Three's a Crowd* (1930).

All the Things You Are, words by Oscar Hammerstein II, music by Jerome Kern (1939). One of Kern's greatest ballads, introduced by Hiram Sherman, Frances Mercer, Hollace Shaw

and Ralph Stuart in the musical *Very Warm for May* (1939). "Original in its intervallic structure and subtle and magical in its enharmonic changes," wrote this editor in his biography of Kern, " 'All the Things You Are' was written by Kern more for his own artistic satisfaction than to woo a public, since he himself was convinced it could never become popular. Yet, after its appearance, it became one of Kern's hardiest successes in the sale of sheet music and records."

"All the Things You Are" was the only song used in *Broadway Rhythm* (MGM, 1944), the motion-picture adaptation of *Very Warm for May*. The song was also used in Kern's motion-picture biography *Till the Clouds Roll By* (MGM, 1946) and in the motion-picture musical *Because You're Mine* (MGM, 1952).

All the Way, words by Sammy Cahn, music by James Van Heusen (1957). Introduced by Frank Sinatra in the motion-picture biography of Joe E. Lewis, *The Joker Is Wild* (Paramount, 1957). The song received the Academy Award, while Sinatra's recording for Capitol sold over a million disks.

"The song was written to dramatize Joe E. Lewis's loss of voice," James Van Heusen explained to this editor, "and the big jump musically at the end of the second bar to the middle of the third bar was specifically designed to be difficult for him to sing, and he was supposed to break down dramatically."

All This and Heaven Too, words by Eddie De Lange, music by James Van Heusen (1939). Title song of a motion picture starring Bette Davis (Warner, 1939).

All Through the Day, words by Oscar Hammerstein II, music by Jerome Kern (1946). Introduced by Larry Stevens, Cornel Wilde and Louanne Hogan (the last singing on the soundtrack for Jeanne Crain) in the motion-picture musical *Centennial Summer* (20th Century-Fox, 1946).

All Through the Night, words and music by Cole Porter (1934). Introduced by Bettina Hall and William

Gaxton in the musical comedy *Anything Goes* (1934). Bing Crosby sang it in both motion-picture adaptations of the musical comedy (Paramount, 1936 and 1956).

Almost, words by Jack Lawrence, music by Stan Freeman (1964). Introduced by Karen Morrow in the musical *I Had a Ball* (1964).

Almost in Your Arms (Love Song from Houseboat), words and music by Jay Livingston and Ray Evans (1958). Introduced by Sophia Loren in the non-musical motion picture *Houseboat* (Paramount, 1958), where it was sung on the soundtrack by Sam Cooke.

Almost Like Being in Love, words by Alan Jay Lerner, music by Frederick Loewe (1947). Introduced in the musical play *Brigadoon* (1947) by David Brooks and Marion Bell. In the motion-picture adaptation of the musical (MGM, 1954), it was sung by Gene Kelly.

Alone, words by Arthur Freed, music by Nacio Herb Brown (1935). Introduced by Kitty Carlisle and Allan Jones in the Marx Brothers' motion picture *A Night at the Opera* (MGM, 1935). It was interpolated for Judy Garland in the motion picture *Andy Hardy Meets a Debutante* (MGM, 1940) and was revived in the motion-picture musical *Born to Dance* (MGM 1942).

Alone Together, words by Howard Dietz, music by Arthur Schwartz (1932). Introduced by Clifton Webb and Tamara Geva in the musical *Flying Colors* (1932).

Along the Rocky Road to Dublin, words by Joe Young, music by Bert Grant (1915).

Along with Me, words and music by Harold Rome (1946). Introduced by Paula Bane and Danny Scholl in the topical revue *Call Me Mister* (1946). Harold Rome explained to this editor: "This song started out as a love song to an old jalopy that the soldier has left behind him. Since love conquers satire, it turned into a straight love ballad by the time it was finished."

The Alphabet Song. *See:* "A" You're Adorable.

Alter, Louis, composer, born Haverhill, Massachusetts, 1902.

See (Lyrics by Sidney D. Mitchell): A Melody from the Sky; Twilight on the Trail; You Turned the Tables on Me.

See also: Come Up and See Me Sometime; Dolores; Do You Know What It Means to Miss New Orleans?; I'm One of God's Chillun; Isn't Love the Grandest Thing?; Manhattan Serenade; My Kinda Love; Overnight; Rainbow on the River; The Sky Fell Down.

Alvin's Harmonica, words and music by Ross Bagdasarian (1959). Popularized by Ross Bagdasarian (using the pseudonym of David Seville) in a Liberty recording.

Always, words and music by Irving Berlin (1925). One of several successful ballads written under the stimulus of Berlin's dramatic romance with Ellin Mackay, whom he married in 1926. Berlin presented his wife with all the rights to this song as a wedding gift. The song was revived by Deanna Durbin in the motion picture *Christmas Holiday* (Universal, 1944), where it played an important part in the story. This is one of five songs by Berlin which the composer himself regards as his special favorites, the others being "Easter Parade," "God Bless America," "Show Business" and "White Christmas."

Always in the Way, words and music by Charles K. Harris (1903). This sentimental ballad about a neglected child was Harris' last song success, even though he lived and composed for another quarter of a century.

Always Take Mother's Advice, words and music by Jennie Lindsay (1884).

Always True to You in My Fashion, words and music by Cole Porter (1948). The title was taken from Ernest Dowson's poem *Cynara*. The song was introduced by Lisa Kirk in the musical *Kiss Me, Kate* (1948). Ann Miller and Tommy Rall sang it in the motion-picture adaptation of the musical (MGM, 1953).

Amapola (Pretty Little Poppy), a popular Spanish song, music by Joseph M. Lacalle, English lyrics by Albert

Gamse (1940). The song with English lyrics was introduced by Deanna Durbin in the motion picture *First Love* (Universal, 1939). In 1941 Jimmy Dorsey's recording for Decca (with Helen O'Connell and Bob Eberle doing the vocal) sold over a million disks, to become his first major disk success. The song was interpolated in the motion-picture musical *The Fleet's In* (Paramount, 1942), performed by Jimmy Dorsey and his orchestra. It was also interpolated in the motion picture *Saddle Pals*, starring Gene Autry (Universal, 1947).

America, patriotic ballad, words by Samuel Francis Smith to the melody of the British national anthem, "God Save the King" (1832).

Smith was a student at the Andover Theological Seminary when Lowell Mason, distinguished American music educator, turned over to him several volumes of songs and hymns. He wanted Smith to write a song for a children's choir and for this purpose to use one of the melodies from these books. Smith tells the rest of the story: "On a dismal day in February, 1832, turning over the leaves of one of those music books, I fell in love with the tune, which pleased me by its simple and natural movement. . . . Observing at a glance that the German words were patriotic, I was instantly inspired to write a patriotic hymn of my own. Without attempting to imitate them, or even to read them throughout, I seized a scrap of waste paper and began to write. In half an hour, I think, the words stood upon it, substantially as they are sung today. I had not thought of writing a national hymn. I laid the song aside and nearly forgot I had made it."

Smith did not know that he was using "God Save the King," since that melody in his song book bore the German title, "Heil, Dir im Siegerkranz." "I wrote the hymn to suit the meter, which instantly appealed to me. I was not too versed in non-American music and was therefore taken completely by sur-

prise later when I was accused of being pro-British because I had used the tune."

Smith's patriotic ballad was sung for the first time by a children's choir at the Park Street Church in Boston on July 4, 1832. (Parenthetically: one of the members of that choir was Edward Everett Hale, aged ten.) Words and music were published for the first time in 1832 —in Lowell Mason's collection *The Choir, or Union Collection of Church Music.*

It was not long before "America" was being sung at patriotic rallies, in schools and at picnics. It became particularly popular during the Civil War, sung at war rallies, memorials, meetings and funerals, as well as in army camps and on the field of battle.

As Smith had originally written it, the ballad had only four verses. But from time to time he kept on adding new stanzas for special occasions. Two of these, long forgotten, were found and revived by the National Education Association in 1933.

In 1914 Smith's son presented the manuscript of "America" to the library of Harvard University. In accepting the gift, the librarian wrote: "This is one of the most precious bits of original manuscript which any American library could desire to own. From both a sentimental and patriotic viewpoint, it certainly ranks among our nation's most honored documents."

America, I Love You, a popular patriotic song, words by Edgar Leslie, music by Archie Gottler (1915). It achieved wide circulation just before and during World War I. It was revived by Alice Faye and John Payne in the motion-picture musical *Tin Pan Alley* (20th Century-Fox, 1940).

Americana, an intimate, sophisticated revue, mounted in 1926, 1928 and 1932. J. P. McEvoy was responsible for all the books and some of the lyrics for the three productions. Songs were contributed by various composers and lyricists, including Louis Alter, Irving Caesar, Con Conrad, George and Ira Gershwin, Jay Gorney and E. Y. Harburg, among others. Among the stars who appeared in the three productions were Roy Atwell, Lew Brice, Charles Butterworth, George Givot, J. Rosamond Johnson, Helen Morgan, George Tapps and Rex Weber.

See: Brother, Can You Spare a Dime?; The Lost Barber Shop Chord; My Kinda Love; Sunny Disposish.

American Beauty Rose, words and music by Hal David, Redd Evans and Arthur Altman (1950). Popularized by Frank Sinatra in a Columbia recording.

The American Hero, words by Nathaniel Niles, music by Andrew Law (1775). A song of the American Revolution, one of the earliest of exclusively American authorship. Niles wrote his lyrics, which he described as a "Saphick Ode," to a melody which Andrew Law had previously used for "Bunker Hill." "The American Hero" was no spirited battle song, but a melancholy ballad reflecting the somber spirit of the colonists when they realized they were involved in a life-and-death struggle with the British.

An American in Paris, a motion-picture musical starring Gene Kelly and Leslie Caron (MGM, 1951). It received the Academy Award. The score was made up of song standards by George and Ira Gershwin. George Gershwin's tone poem *An American in Paris* was used for an extended ballet sequence.

See: By Strauss; Embraceable You; I Got Rhythm; I'll Build a Stairway to Paradise; Nice Work If You Can Get It; Our Love Is Here to Stay; 'S Wonderful; Tra-la-la.

The American Society of Composers, Authors and Publishers (ASCAP). An organization founded in 1914 to protect the financial interests of composers, lyricists and publishers, whose popular songs were then being played in public places without compensation. The first officers of ASCAP were: George Maxwell, president; Victor Herbert, vice-president; Glen MacDonough, secretary; John Golden, treasurer. At its incep-

tion ASCAP numbered twenty-two publishers and one hundred and seventy composers and lyricists.

With Nathan Burkan as attorney, a suit was instituted against Shanley's Restaurant in New York for copyright infringement: the unauthorized performance of selections from Victor Herbert's operetta *Sweethearts* by the restaurant orchestra. Judge Learned Hand decided against the plaintiff, maintaining that musical performances in public places were not done for profit since no admission was charged. The Court of Appeals confirmed this decision. But on January 22, 1917, the Supreme Court reversed it. Justice Oliver Wendell Holmes said in part: "If music did not pay, it would be given up. If it pays, it pays out of the public's pocket. Whether it pays or not, the purpose of employing it is profit, and that is enough."

Many more legal battles had to be fought and won by ASCAP over a period of years to make the Supreme Court decision workable. In time, however, hotels, restaurants, cabarets and theaters signed up with ASCAP for the rights to use music by ASCAP members, paying an annual fee through special licenses. In 1921 ASCAP (now numbering one hundred and sixty-three members) earned $80,000; by 1922 this annual income passed the two-hundred-thousand-dollar mark. Movies became licensees in 1924, radio half a dozen years after that.

By 1962 ASCAP grossed over $35,000,000 from forty thousand licensees, and represented seven thousand composers and lyricists and more than two thousand publishers. A complex method was evolved for the distribution of the income. A computation was made of the number of performance-hours for each ASCAP song heard each day through all the media of public consumption. Top rating was given to those composers and lyricists whose songs accumulated the greatest number of performance-hours. Each of the top beneficiaries—Irving Berlin, Cole Porter, Richard Rodgers

And So to Sleep Again, words and music by Joe Marsala and Sunny Skylar (1951). Popularized in a best-selling Mercury recording by Patti Page.

And That Reminds You. *See:* My Heart Reminds You.

And the Angels Sing, words by Johnny Mercer, music by Ziggy Elman (1939). Popularized in an RCA Victor recording by Benny Goodman and his orchestra, with vocal by Martha Tilton and trumpet solo by Ziggy Elman. Benny Goodman and his orchestra, with Ziggy Elman, played it on the soundtrack of the motion-picture musical *The Benny Goodman Story* (Universal, 1956), where it was also sung by Martha Tilton.

And the Green Grass All Grew Around, words by William Jerome, music by Harry von Tilzer (1912).

And This Is My Beloved, words and music by Robert Wright and George "Chet" Forrest, melody based on the Nocturne from Borodin's second String Quartet (1953). Introduced by Doretta Morrow, Richard Kiley, Alfred Drake and Henry Calvin in the operetta *Kismet* (1953).

Angela Mia, words by Lew Pollack, music by Erno Rapee (1928). Theme song of the motion picture *Street Angel* (Fox, 1928).

Angel Child, words by Benny Davis and George Price, music by Abner Silver (1922). Introduced in the revue *Spice of 1922,* then popularized by Eddie Cantor.

Angel Face, words by Robert B. Smith, music by Victor Herbert (1919). Introduced by Ada Meade in the musical comedy of the same name (1919).

Angel Face, a musical comedy with book by H. B. Smith. Lyrics by Robert B. Smith. Music by Victor Herbert. Starring John E. Young and Jack Donahue.

See: Angel Face; I Might Be Your Once in a While; Someone Like You.

The Angelus, words by Robert B. Smith, music by Victor Herbert (1913). Prayer introduced by Christie MacDonald (as she listens to the tones of the Angelus) in the operetta *Sweethearts* (1913). In the motion-picture adaptation of the operetta (MGM, 1938), it was sung by Jeanette MacDonald and Nelson Eddy.

Anima e Core (or, With All My Heart and Soul), an Italian popular song, music by Salve d'Esposito, introduced by Ferruccio Tagliavini in the Italian motion picture of the same name. English lyrics by Mann Curtis and Harry Akst (1953). The English song was introduced in a revue, John Murray Anderson's *Almanac* (1953), and was popularized by Eddie Fisher in an RCA Victor recording.

Animal Crackers, a musical comedy with book by George S. Kaufman and Morrie Ryskind. Lyrics by Bert Kalmar. Music by Harry Ruby. Starring the Four Marx Brothers (1928).

The motion-picture adaptation starred Lillian Roth with the Four Marx Brothers (Paramount, 1930). Only three songs were used from the original score, supplemented by the interpolation of two standards.

See: Collegiate; Hooray for Captain Spalding; Some of These Days; Watching the Clouds Roll By.

Animal Crackers in My Soup, words by Ted Koehler and Irving Caesar, music by Ray Henderson (1935). Introduced by Shirley Temple in the motion picture *Curly Top* (20th Century-Fox, 1935).

Anka, Paul, composer and lyricist, born Ottawa, Canada, 1941.

See: Diana; I'm Just a Lonely Boy; The Longest Day; Put Your Head on My Shoulder; Teddy; You Are My Destiny.

Annabelle, words by Lew Brown, music by Ray Henderson (1923).

Annie Doesn't Live Here Anymore, words by Joe Young and Johnny Burke, music by Harold Spina (1933). When the song was brought to the attention of Guy Lombardo, he did not know if it was intended to be a comic number or a sad one. Nevertheless he was sufficiently intrigued with it to introduce it with the Royal Canadians and to help popularize it.

Annie, Get Your Gun, a musical comedy with book by Herbert and Dorothy Fields. Lyrics and music by Irving Berlin. Starring Ethel Merman and Ray Middleton (1946). Original cast recording (Decca).

The motion-picture adaptation starred Betty Hutton and Howard Keel (MGM, 1950). It utilized virtually the entire stage score. Soundtrack recording (MGM).

See: Anything You Can Do; Doin' What Comes Natur'lly; The Girl That I Marry; Moonshine Lullaby; Show Business; Sun in the Mornin'; They Say It's Wonderful; Who Do You Love, I Hope?; You Can't Get a Man with a Gun.

Annie Lisle, words and music by H. S. Thompson (1860). Celebrated ballad of the Civil War period. The tune was subsequently used by various colleges for their school songs, the most notable being that of Cornell University, "Far Above Cayuga's Waters."

Anniversary Song, words by Al Jolson, music by Saul Chaplin based on a melody from J. Ivanovici's *Danube Waves* (1946). Introduced by Al Jolson on the soundtrack of the motion-picture musical *The Jolson Story* (Columbia, 1946). This song proved the "sleeper" of the production. Within a brief period it sold over a million disks in Jolson's recording for Decca, and for several weeks running it was represented on the Hit Parade. Jolson sang it once again on the soundtrack of the motion picture *Jolson Sings Again* (Columbia, 1949).

Anona, words and music by Robert A. King (1903). This number, in the pseudo-Indian style then so popular in Tin Pan Alley, was King's first hit song. It was introduced in vaudeville by Mabel McKinley, niece of the martyred President. She was sometimes erroneously credited as its composer.

Another Autumn, words by Alan Jay Lerner, music by Frederick Loewe (1951). Introduced by Tony Bavar in the musical play *Paint Your Wagon* (1951).

Another Op'nin', Another Show, words and music by Cole Porter (1948). Opening musical number in the musical play *Kiss Me, Kate* (1948), where it was introduced by Annabelle Hill and chorus. The number was also used in the motion-picture adaptation of the musical (MGM, 1953).

Another Time, Another Place, words and music by Richard Adler (1961). Love ballad introduced by Sally Ann Howes in the musical play *Kwamina* (1961), and popularized by Robert Goulet in an RCA Victor recording.

Another Time, Another Place, words and music by Jay Livingston and Ray Evans (1958). Introduced in the motion picture of the same name, starring Lana Turner and Barry Sullivan (Paramount, 1958), and popularized by Don Cherry in a Columbia recording.

Answer Me, My Love, a German popular song, music by Gerhard Winkler, English lyrics by Carl Sigman (1953). The English song was popularized by Nat King Cole in a Capitol recording in 1954.

Any Kind of Man, words by Rida Johnson Young, music by Rudolf Friml (1918). Introduced by the then still unknown Mae West in the operetta *Sometime* (1918).

Any Old Place with You, words by Lorenz Hart, music by Richard Rodgers (1919). The first Rodgers and Hart song to get published commercially, and the first to be heard on Broadway. It was sung by Eve Lynn and Alan Hale in the musical *A Lonely Romeo* (1919), where it was an interpolation. Richard Rodgers told this editor: "What I earned from both the publication and the performance couldn't buy a suit; but the appearance of one of my songs in a Broadway show was certainly a big moment in my life."

The lyrics were most unusual for 1919 in their urbanity and sophistication ("I'll go to hell for ya, or Phil-a-del-phia, Any old place with you"). The music was distinguished by the secondary seventh chords in the harmony, and structurally by the use of a thirty-two-bar verse and a sixteen-bar chorus which reversed the then general procedure of a sixteen-bar verse and a thirty-two-bar chorus.

Any Old Port in a Storm, words by Arthur J. Lamb, music by Kerry Mills (1908).

Any Place I Hang My Hat Is Home, words by Johnny Mercer, music by Harold Arlen (1946). Introduced by Robert Pope in the musical play *St. Louis Woman* (1946).

Anything Goes, words and music by Cole Porter (1934). Title song of the musical comedy (1934), where it was introduced by Ethel Merman. She also sang it in the first motion-picture adaptation of the musical (Paramount, 1936); Mitzi Gaynor sang it in the second version (Paramount, 1956). It was interpolated orchestrally in Cole Porter's screen biography *Night and Day* (Warner, 1946).

Anything Goes, a musical comedy with book by Guy Bolton, P. G. Wodehouse, Howard Lindsay and Russel Crouse. Lyrics and music by Cole Porter. Starring Ethel Merman, William Gaxton and Victor Moore (1934).

There were two motion-picture adaptations. The first starred Bing Crosby and Ethel Merman (Paramount, 1936). Six songs were used from the Broadway score, together with several numbers by various lyricists and composers. The second adaptation starred Bing Crosby, Mitzi Gaynor and Donald O'Connor (Paramount, 1956). Together with the hit songs from the stage score, Porter's "It's De-Lovely" was interpolated; in addition, there were three new numbers by Sammy Cahn and James van Heusen.

See: All Through the Night; Anything Goes; Blow, Gabriel, Blow; I Get a Kick Out of You; It's De-Lovely; You're the Top.

Anything You Can Do, I Can Do Better, words and music by Irving Berlin (1946). Introduced by Ethel Merman and Ray Middleton in the musical *Annie, Get Your Gun* (1946). In the motion-picture adaptation of the musical (MGM, 1950), it was sung by Betty Hutton and Howard Keel.

Any Time, words and music by Herbert Happy Lawson (1921). A minor hit when first published, it became a major song success when revived thirty years later. Eddie Fisher's recording for RCA Victor in 1951 sold over a million disks.

Anytime Is the Time to Fall in Love, words by Elsie Janis, music by Jack King (1929). Introduced by Lillian Roth and Buddy Rogers in the motion-picture musical *Paramount on Parade* (Paramount, 1929). Buddy Rogers also sang it in the motion-picture musical *Along Came Love* (Paramount, 1931).

Any Way the Wind Blows, words by By Dunham, music by Marilyn and Joe Hooven (1959). Introduced by Doris Day in the non-musical motion picture *Please Don't Eat the Daisies* (MGM, 1959).

Any Way You Want Me (That's How I'll Be), words and music by Aaron Schroeder and Cliff Owens (1956). Popularized by Elvis Presley in an RCA Victor recording.

Anywhere I Wander, words and music by Frank Loesser (1952). Introduced by Danny Kaye in the motion-picture musical *Hans Christian Andersen* (Goldwyn, 1953).

Applause, a motion-picture musical starring Helen Morgan (1930). The score was primarily made up of standards.

See: Smiles; That's My Weakness, Now; What Wouldn't I Do for That Man; Yaka Hula Hickey Dula.

Apple Blossoms, an operetta with book and lyrics by William Le Baron based on Alexandre Dumas' romance *A Marriage of Convenience.* Musical score shared by Victor Jacobi and Fritz Kreisler. Starring Wilda Bennett and John Charles Thomas, with Fred and Adele Astaire in subsidiary roles (1919).

See: The Letter Song; Little Girls, Goodbye; Who Can Tell?; You Are Free.

An Apple for the Teacher, words by Johnny Burke, music by James V. Monaco (1939). Introduced in the motion picture *The Star Maker,* starring Bing Crosby (Paramount, 1939). Gene Autry sang it in the motion picture *The Last Round Up* (Columbia, 1947).

April in Paris, words by E. Y. Harburg, music by Vernon Duke (1932). Introduced by Evelyn Hoey in the revue *Walk a Little Faster* (1932), where it attracted little attention. Among the critics, H. T. Parker of Boston proved an exception by writing: "'April in Paris' is worthy, in place and kind, of that city in spring. There is a catch in the throat from it—if one has too many memories." The song first became successful in intimate *boîtes* of New York's East Side. Marian Chase, a society chanteuse, recorded it for Liberty; and it was this disk that was largely responsible for establishing the popularity of the song on a permanent basis. "'April in Paris,'" wrote Isaac Goldberg in a letter to Duke, "is one of the finest musical compositions that ever graced an American production. If I had my way, I'd make the study of it compulsory in all harmony courses."

The song provided the title for a motion picture (Warner, 1953), where it was sung under the titles by Doris Day.

April in Portugal, a popular Portuguese song ("Coimbra" or "Avril in Portugal"), music by Paul Ferrão, English lyrics by Jimmy Kennedy (1953). In the United States this song originated as "The Whispering Serenade," and was introduced with that title by Georgia Carr in a Capitol release. After that the number was popularized as an instrumental under its original title of "April in Portugal" in a best-selling Capitol recording. At this point the publishing house of Chappell contracted Jimmy Kennedy to write a new lyric, with which it proceeded to become a hit song.

April Love, words by Paul Francis Webster, music by Sammy Fain (1957). Introduced by Pat Boone and Shirley Jones in the motion picture of the same name (20th Century-Fox, 1957). Pat Boone's recording for Dot sold over a million disks.

April Showers, words by Bud De Sylva,

music by Louis Silvers (1921). Introduced by Al Jolson in the Winter Garden musical extravaganza *Bombo* (1921). The song became a Jolson specialty. He sang it on the soundtracks of the motion-picture musicals *The Jolson Story* (Columbia, 1946) and *Jolson Sings Again* (Columbia, 1949); his Decca recording in 1946 sold over a million disks.

The song provided the title for, was played under the titles of, and was sung by Jack Carson, Ann Sothern and Bobbie Ellis in the final scene of a motion-picture musical (Warner, 1948). Jeanne Crain sang it in the motion picture *Margie* (20th Century-Fox, 1946).

April Showers, a motion-picture musical starring Jack Carson and Ann Sothern (Warner, 1948). Most of the score was made up of standards, but several new numbers were written by Kim Gannon and Ted Fetter, and Kim Gannon and Walter Kent.

See: April Showers; Carolina in the Morning; Every Little Movement Has a Meaning of Its Own; It's Tulip Time in Holland; Pretty Baby.

Aren't We All?, words by Bud De Sylva and Lew Brown, music by Ray Henderson (1929). Introduced by Janet Gaynor and Charles Farrell in the motion-picture musical *Sunny Side Up* (Fox, 1929). It was also interpolated in the motion picture *Holy Terror,* starring George O'Brien and Sally Eilers (Fox, 1931).

Aren't You Glad You're You?, words by Johnny Burke, music by James Van Heusen (1945). Introduced by Bing Crosby in the motion picture *The Bells of St. Mary's* (RKO, 1945).

Aren't You Kind of Glad We Did?, words by Ira Gershwin, music by George Gershwin (1946). Introduced by Betty Grable and Dick Haymes in the motion-picture musical *The Shocking Miss Pilgrim* (20th Century-Fox, 1946).

Ira Gershwin discloses that the song had been written in the early 1930s, the lyric at that time concerned with a penniless young couple willing to take a chance on getting married. That song had not been written for any specific show, and a spot for it was never found. But Ira Gershwin liked the tune, and in working on *The Shocking Miss Pilgrim* (with a posthumous score by George Gershwin), he adapted a new set of lyrics for it "changing it from an Epithalamium of the Depression to a mid-Victorian colloquy."

Are You Going to the Ball This Evening?, words and music by Joseph P. Skelly (1881). A comedy ditty popularized in vaudeville by Tony Pastor.

Are You Having Any Fun?, words by Jack Yellen, music by Sammy Fain (1939). Introduced by Ella Logan in the *George White Scandals of 1939*.

Are You Lonesome Tonight?, words by Roy Turk, music by Lou Handman (1926). It was revived in 1960 by Elvis Presley, whose RCA Victor recording sold over a million disks.

Are You Makin' Any Money?, words and music by Herman Hupfeld (1933). Introduced by Lillian Miles in the motion-picture musical *Moonlight and Pretzels*, starring Mary Brian and Leo Carrillo (Universal, 1933).

Are You Really Mine?, words and music by Al Hoffman, Dick Manning and Mark Markwell (1958). Popularized by Jimmie Rodgers in a Roulette recording.

Are You Sincere?, words and music by Wayne Walker (1957). Popularized in 1958 by Andy Williams in a Cadence recording, one of Williams' first disk successes.

Arlen, Harold, composer, born Hyman Arluck, Buffalo, New York, 1905.

See (Lyrics by Ira Gershwin): The Man That Got Away; You're a Builder Upper.

See (Lyrics by E. Y. Harburg): Cocoanut Sweet; The Eagle and Me; Evelina; Happiness Is a Thing Called Joe; I Could Go On Singing; I Got a Song; Life's Full of Consequences; Lydia the Tattooed Lady; Over the Rainbow; Right as Rain; Song of the Woodman; Take It Slow, Joe; T'morra', T'morra'; We're Off to See the Wizard of Oz; You're a Builder Upper.

See (Lyrics by Ted Koehler): As Long as I Live; Between the Devil and the Deep Blue Sea; Get Happy; Happy as the Day Is Long; I Gotta Right to Sing the Blues; Ill Wind; I Love a Parade; I've Got the World on a String; Last Night When We Were Young; Let's Fall in Love; The March of Time; Stormy Weather.

See (Lyrics by Johnny Mercer): Ac-cent-tchu-ate the Positive; Any Place I Hang My Hat Is Home; Blues in the Night; Come Rain or Come Shine; Hit the Road to Dreamland; Legalize My Name; Let's Take the Long Way Home; My Shining Hour; One for My Baby; That Old Black Magic; A Woman's Prerogative.

See also: Fun to Be Fooled; Hooray for Love; I Never Has Seen Snow; It Was Written in the Stars; The Morning After; A Sleepin' Bee; So Long, Big Time; Sweet and Hot; Two Ladies in de Shade of de Banana Tree.

Arm in Arm, words and music by Meredith Willson (1963). Introduced by Janis Paige in the musical *Here's Love* (1963).

Armorer's Song, words by Harry B. Smith, music by Reginald de Koven (1891). Introduced by Eugene Cowles in the operetta *Robin Hood* (1891).

The Army Air Corps Song, words and music by Robert M. Crawford (1939). Crawford, then a member of the music faculty of Princeton University, wrote this song for a competition conducted by *Liberty* magazine in 1939. He won the first prize of $1,000. Not until three years after that did he become a member of the Air Force, when he served as Major in the Air Transport Command. During World War II the song achieved popularity as the Army Air Corps hymn. It was used as a recurrent theme in the Moss Hart stage production dedicated to the Air Corps, *Winged Victory* (1943), and was also used extensively in the motion-picture adaptation of this production (20th Century-Fox, 1944).

Army Blue. *See:* Aura Lee.

Around the World, words by Harold Adamson, music by Victor Young

(1956). Theme song of the Michael Todd motion-picture extravaganza *Around the World in Eighty Days* (United Artists, 1956). The number became one of the leading song hits of 1956–1957, with best-selling recordings by Victor Young and his orchestra for Decca, Eddie Fisher for RCA Victor, Jane Morgan for Kapp, Bing Crosby for Decca and Nat King Cole for Capitol.

Arrah Go On (I'm Gonna Go Back to Oregon), words by Sam M. Lewis and Joe Young, music by Bert Grant (1916). It was revived in the motion-picture musical *The Dolly Sisters* (20th Century-Fox, 1945).

Arrividerci Roma (or, Goodbye to Rome), a popular Italian song, music by R. Rascel, English lyrics by Carl Sigman (1955). The song with English lyrics was introduced by The Three Suns in an RCA Victor recording, then was popularized by Georgia Gibbs in a Mercury recording. Mario Lanza sang it in the motion-picture musical *The Seven Hills of Rome* (MGM, 1956).

Arthur Murray Taught Me Dancing in a Hurry, words by Johnny Mercer, music by Victor Schertzinger (1942). Introduced by Betty Hutton in the motion-picture musical *The Fleet's In* (Paramount, 1942). This is the song and the picture with which Betty Hutton first became successful with her rough-and-ready delivery.

Artificial Flowers, words by Sheldon Harnick, music by Jerry Bock (1960). Introduced by Ron Hussmann in the musical *Tenderloin* (1960). Before that show opened, the song became successful through Bobby Darin's recording for Atco.

Artillery Song. *See:* The Caissons Go Rolling Along.

Artists and Models, an annual Broadway revue which opened in 1923. Subsequent editions were mounted in 1924, 1925, 1927, 1930 and 1943. Among the composers and lyricists contributing songs were Harry Akst, Harold Atteridge, Phil Charig, Benny Davis, J. Fred Coots, Al Goodman, Sigmund Romberg, and Jean Schwartz. The stars included Phil Baker, Frank Fay, Jane Froman, George Hassell, Ted Lewis and Jack Pearl.

Three motion-picture musicals used the title of *Artists and Models.* They were: *Artists and Models* (Paramount, 1937); *Artists and Models Abroad* (Paramount, 1938); and *Artists and Models* (Paramount, 1955). The first two starred Jack Benny in all-star casts; the third, Dean Martin and Jerry Lewis. Various composers and lyricists contributed songs to these three productions, including Ted Koehler and Burton Lane, Leo Robin and Frederick Hollander, Leo Robin and Ralph Rainger, Jack Brooks and Harry Warren.

See: Innamorata; Promenade Walk; Stop, You're Breaking My Heart; Whispers in the Dark.

ASCAP. *See:* American Society of Composers, Authors and Publishers.

Ascot Gavotte, words by Alan Jay Lerner, music by Frederick Loewe (1956). Introduced by the ensemble as a production number in the musical play *My Fair Lady* (1956). It was also featured as a production number in the motion-picture adaptation of the musical (Warner, 1964).

Ask the Man in the Moon, words by J. Cheever Goodwin, music by Woolson Morse (1891). Introduced by De Wolf Hopper in the musical extravaganza *Wang* (1891).

Asleep in the Deep, words by Arthur J. Lamb, music by H. W. Petrie (1897). A song of the sea, a favorite of bassos (due to its low register), glee clubs and barber-shop quartets. It was introduced by Jean Early with the Haverly Minstrels at the McKivers Theatre in Chicago in 1898. The song became a hit after words and music had been published as a supplement to the *New York Journal and Advertiser* on December 18, 1898. This number was responsible for initiating a cycle of popular songs about the sea.

As Long As I Live, words by E. Y. Harburg, music by Harold Arlen (1934). Introduced by Lena Horne (then sixteen years old) and Avon

Long in the Cotton Club revue *Parade* in 1934.

As Long As There's Music, words by Sammy Cahn, music by Jule Styne (1944). Introduced by Frank Sinatra in the motion-picture musical *Step Lively* (RKO, 1944).

As Long As the World Rolls On, words by George Graff, Jr., music by Ernest R. Ball (1907).

As the Girls Go, words by Harold Adamson, music by Jimmy McHugh (1948). Introduced by Bobby Clark (and girls) in the musical of the same name (1948).

As the Girls Go, a musical comedy with book by William Roos. Lyrics by Harold Adamson. Music by Jimmy McHugh. Starring Irene Rich and Bobby Clark (1948).

See: As the Girls Go; I Got Lucky in the Rain; You Say the Nicest Things.

As Thousands Cheer, a musical comedy with book by Moss Hart. Lyrics and music by Irving Berlin. Starring Marilyn Miller, Clifton Webb and Ethel Waters (1933).

See: Easter Parade; Heat Wave; Not for All the Rice in China; Suppertime.

As Time Goes By, words and music by Herman Hupfeld (1931). Introduced by Oscar Shaw and Frances Williams in the musical *Everybody's Welcome* (1931). The song became only moderately successful after Rudy Vallée recorded it for RCA Victor. Then the song was revived in the motion picture *Casablanca,* starring Humphrey Bogart and Ingrid Bergman (Warner, 1942). Sung by Dooley Wilson, it served as a recurrent musical theme basic to the story development. The song now proved so popular that RCA Victor revived the old Rudy Vallée recording, which went on to become a best seller. The reason a new disk version of the song could not be released was because at that time the American Federation of Musicians had instituted a ban against all recordings.

As Years Go By, words by Charles Tobias, music by Peter De Rose, melody based on Brahms' Hungarian Dance No. 4 (1947). Introduced

in the screen biography of the classical composer Robert Schumann—*Song of Love,* starring Robert Walker and Katharine Hepburn (MGM, 1947). It was the only popular song in a score otherwise devoted to the classics.

As You Desire Me, words and music by Allie Wrubel (1932). It was popularized a number of years after publication in recordings by Tony Martin for Mercury and the Ink Spots for Decca.

At a Georgia Camp Meeting, a cakewalk classic, words and music by Kerry Mills (1899). It originated in 1897 as an instrumental two-step. The song was popularized in vaudeville by the song and dance team of Genaro and Bailey. Whenever this duo presented a coon song, it would introduce a brief strut before repeating the chorus. In their rendition of "At a Georgia Camp Meeting" they extended this strut into an elaborate dance routine; and it was with this routine, and with this song, that the cakewalk came into existence.

Mills wrote "At a Georgia Camp Meeting" as a reaction to coon songs and coon shouts which he felt were demeaning to the Negro people. He decided to write a Negro song of his own, and for this purpose he used the subject of a religious camp meeting in the South. After several publishers had turned down his composition, Kerry Mills formed the publishing house of F. A. Mills to issue the number himself. He peddled the sheet music to the stores and was personally responsible for getting Genaro and Bailey to present it in their act.

A-Tisket, A-Tasket, words and music by Ella Fitzgerald and Al Feldman (1938). A song that helped catapult Ella Fitzgerald to fame in night clubs, and in a Decca recording with Chick Webb that sold over a million disks. The memory of a nursery rhyme learned in childhood led Ella Fitzgerald to write the song. It was interpolated in the motion-picture musical *Two Girls and a Sailor* (MGM, 1944).

Atlantic City, a motion-picture musical

starring Constance Moore (Republic, 1944). The score was made up of standards.

See: After You've Gone; Ain't Misbehavin'; By the Sea; Mister Gallagher and Mr. Shean; Nobody's Sweetheart Now; On a Sunday Afternoon.

At Last, words by Mack Gordon, music by Harry Warren (1942). Introduced by Glenn Miller and his orchestra in the motion-picture musical *Sun Valley Serenade* (20th Century-Fox, 1941). Glenn Miller and his orchestra repeated this performance in the motion-picture musical *Orchestra Wives* (20th Century-Fox, 1942).

At Sundown, words and music by Walter Donaldson (1927). It sold over two million disks in various recordings of the late 1920s. Both Jimmy Dorsey and Tommy Dorsey made successful recordings in the early 1930s, the former for Capitol, the latter for RCA Victor. The song, therefore, was prominently featured in the screen biography of the Dorseys—*The Fabulous Dorseys* (United Artists, 1946). The song was also a Ruth Etting favorite. This is the reason why it was interpolated in her screen biography *Love Me or Leave Me* (MGM, 1955), sung by Doris Day. The song was also heard in the motion pictures *The Bells of Capistrano*, starring Gene Autry (Republic, 1942), and *Music for the Millions*, starring Margaret O'Brien and Jimmy Durante (MGM, 1944).

At the Codfish Ball, words by Jack Yellen, music by Lew Pollack (1936). A musical description of a piscatorial ball used as a production number in the motion picture *Captain January*, starring Shirley Temple (20th Century-Fox, 1936).

At the Hop, words and music by J. Medora, A. Singer and D. White (1957). Introduced in the motion picture *Let's Rock* (Columbia, 1958). Popularized by Danny and Juniors in an ABC Paramount recording.

Auf Wiedersehen, words by Herbert Reynolds, music by Sigmund Romberg (1915). This waltz was Romberg's first successful song in his first successful operetta. It was introduced by Vivienne Segal (in her Broadway debut) and Cecil Lean in the operetta *The Blue Paradise* (1916). In Romberg's screen biography *Deep in My Heart* (MGM, 1954), it was sung by Helen Traubel.

Auf Wiedersehen, My Dear, words and music by Al Hoffman, Ed Nelson, Al Goodhart and Milton Ager (1932).

Aunt Hagar's Blues, words by J. Tim Brymn, music by W. C. Handy (1920). It originated as an instrumental blues. The song was interpolated in J. Tim Brymn's revue *Put and Take* (1921). The song was subsequently interpolated in the motion picture *Hi, Good Lookin'*, starring Harriet Hilliard and Roscoe Karns (Universal, 1944).

Aura Lee, words by W. W. Fosdick, music by George R. Poulton (1861). It was adopted as the graduating-class song at West Point in 1865, with new words, and entitled "Army Blue." Since then it has become a favorite of barber-shop quartets. It was revived in the non-musical motion picture *Come and Get It*, starring Edward Arnold, sung by Frances Farmer and used in the background music as a recurrent theme (Samuel Goldwyn, 1936). It was interpolated in the motion picture *The Last Musketeer*, starring Rex Allen (Republic, 1952). As a West Point song it was presented by a chorus on the soundtrack, under the titles, in the non-musical motion picture *The Long Grey Line*, starring Tyrone Power (Columbia, 1955). Elvis Presley, in collaboration with Vera Matson, borrowed the melody for the popular song "Love Me Tender" in 1956.

Au Revoir, But Not Goodbye, Soldier Boy, words by Lew Brown, music by Albert von Tilzer (1917). It became popular in vaudeville as the draft began calling up Americans during World War I.

Au Revoir, Pleasant Dreams, words by Jack Meskill, music by Jean Schwartz (1930). It became popular as Ben Bernie's signing-off theme song on his radio program.

Autumn in New York, words and music by Vernon Duke (1935). Introduced as the finale to the revue *Thumbs Up* (1935). Like Duke's "April in Paris," this song had to wait a number of years before achieving recognition, which came mainly through a recording by Louella Hogan.

Autumn in Rome, words by Sammy Cahn, music by Paul Weston (1954). Based on a theme from the score by Alessandro Cicognini for the non-musical motion picture *Indiscretion of an American Wife*, starring Jennifer Jones and Montgomery Clift (Columbia, 1954).

Autumn Leaves, a popular French song ("Les Feuilles mortes"), melody by Joseph Kosma. It was made popular in Paris by Juliette Greco and interpolated in the French motion picture *Les Portes de la Nuit.* English lyrics by Johnny Mercer (1955). A recording executive for Capitol contracted Johnny Mercer to write American lyrics for this French melody. Twelve recordings were made in 1950 by such artists as Bing Crosby and Jo Stafford, none successful. Then in 1953 Roger Williams recorded it as an instrumental for Kapp that sold a million disks. In the non-musical motion picture *Autumn Leaves,* starring Joan Crawford (Columbia, 1956), it was sung on the soundtrack at the beginning and end of the film by Nat King Cole.

Autumn Serenade, words by Sammy Gallop, music by Peter De Rose (1945).

Avalon, words and music by Al Jolson and Vincent Rose (1920). Introduced and popularized by Al Jolson at the Winter Garden. An infringement of copyright suit was brought against this song by the publishers of Puccini's operas, G. Ricordi. Ricordi maintained that the melody of "Avalon" had been lifted bodily from the aria "E lucevan le stelle" from *Tosca.* On January 28, 1921, Ricordi's attorneys enlisted the aid of a piano, violin and trumpet— together with a phonograph record —to prove their case. Puccini and his publishers were awarded damages of $25,000, with all future royalties of "Avalon" to be confiscated. A small recording company which had gambled its assets in manufacturing and promoting "Avalon," convinced it would become a major hit, had to go out of business.

Benny Goodman and his orchestra played "Avalon" on the soundtrack of the motion-picture musical *The Benny Goodman Story* (Universal, 1956).

Away Down South in Heaven, words by Bud Green, music by Harry Warren (1927). Introduced and popularized by Fred Waring and his Pennsylvanians.

"A," You're Adorable (or, The Alphabet Song), words and music by Buddy Kaye, Fred Wise and Sidney Lippman (1948). Popularized in 1949 in best-selling recordings by Jo Stafford and Gordon MacRae for Capitol, and by Perry Como with the Fontane Sisters for RCA Victor.

B

The Babbitt and the Bromide, words by
Ira Gershwin, music by George
Gershwin (1927). Patter song introduced by Fred and Adele Astaire in
the musical *Funny Face* (1927).
The contrapuntal writing in the accompaniment to the verse and the
addition of a lively polka after the
chorus are of special musical interest. Ira Gershwin regards this as one
of his finest lyrics. It is the only song
lyric included in Louis Kronen-
berger's *Anthology of Light Verse*
(1934). The song was interpolated
for Fred Astaire and Gene Kelly in
the motion picture *Ziegfeld Follies*
(MGM, 1946).

Babes in Arms, words by Lorenz Hart,
music by Richard Rodgers (1937).
Title song of a musical comedy
(1937), introduced by Mitzi Green,
Alfred Drake and Ray Heatherton.
In the motion-picture adaptation of
the musical (MGM, 1939), it was
sung by Judy Garland, Mickey
Rooney, Betty Jaynes, Douglas Mc-
Phail and chorus.

Babes in Arms, a musical comedy with
book by Lorenz Hart and Richard
Rodgers. Lyrics by Lorenz Hart.
Music by Richard Rodgers. Starring
Mitzi Green and Alfred Drake
(1937).

The motion-picture adaptation
starred Judy Garland and Mickey
Rooney (MGM, 1939). Hit songs
from the stage score were supplemented by songs by Arthur Freed
and Nacio Herb Brown and by E. Y.

Harburg and Harold Arlen.

See: Babes in Arms; Good Morn-
ing; I Cried for You; I Wish I Were
in Love Again; Johnny One Note;
The Lady Is a Tramp; My Funny
Valentine; Way Out West; You Are
My Lucky Star; Where or When.

Babes in Toyland, a musical extravaganza with book and lyrics by Glen
MacDonough. Music by Victor Herbert. Starring William Norris,
George W. Denham and Mabel Barrison (1903).

There were two motion-picture adaptations. The first starred Laurel
and Hardy (MGM, 1934). Here the
basic stage score was used with an
interpolation of "Who's Afraid of the
Big Bad Wolf?" The second adaptation (Buena Vista, 1961) was a
Walt Disney production starring Ray
Bolger, Ed Wynn and Tony Sands.
The principal songs of the stage
score were used.

See: I Can't Do This Sum; Never
Mind, Bo-Peep; Toyland; Who's
Afraid of the Big Bad Wolf?

The Babies on Our Block, words by
Edward Harrigan, music by David
Braham (1879). Introduced in the
Harrigan and Hart musical extravaganza *The Skidmore Fancy Ball*
(1879). The melody used effective
quotations from several old Irish
tunes. This song is believed to have
influenced the writing of "The Sidewalks of New York."

Baby (You've Got What It Takes),
words and music by Murray Stein

and Clyde Otis (1959). Popularized by Brook Benton and Dinah Washington in a Mercury recording in 1960.

Baby Face, words by Benny Davis, music by Harry Akst (1926). Introduced by Jan Garber, whose RCA Victor recording (with Benny Davis doing the vocal) was a best seller. It provided the title for, was played under the titles of, and was used as a recurrent theme in the background music for a non-musical motion picture starring Barbara Stanwyck (Warner, 1933). Al Jolson sang it on the soundtrack of the motion-picture musical *Jolson Sings Again* (Columbia, 1949). Art Mooney's recording in 1948 for MGM sold a million disks.

Baby, It's Cold Outside, words and music by Frank Loesser (1948). Loesser wrote this number for performances at private parties, never intending it for general public consumption. In 1948, however, he interpolated it in his score for the motion picture *Neptune's Daughter* (MGM, 1949), where it was introduced by Esther Williams and Ricardo Montalban (and repeated as a comedy reprise by Red Skelton and Betty Garrett). It received the Academy Award.

Babylon Is Fallen, words and music by Henry Clay Work (1863). Work's second Negro song, written at the request of his publishers (Root and Cady), who wanted a sequel to his popular Negro number "Kingdom Coming," issued one year earlier. Work's inspiration for "Babylon Is Fallen" came from the then recent decision to recruit Negro soldiers into the Union Army. In Negro dialect, the song promoted the cause of Abolition strongly.

Baby's Birthday Party, words and music by Ann Ronell (1931). This was Miss Ronell's first hit song, popularized by Rudy Vallée and by Guy Lombardo and his Royal Canadians over the radio and on records. This number has since become famous as a piano novelty.

Baby Shoes, words by Joe Goodwin and Ed Rose, music by Al Piantadosi (1916). Popularized in vaudeville by performers of sentimental ballads.

Baby, Take a Bow, words by Lew Brown, music by Jay Gorney (1934). Introduced by Shirley Temple (in her screen debut) in the motion-picture musical *Stand Up and Cheer* (Fox, 1934).

The three-year-old Shirley Temple was on the Fox set during the shooting of *Stand Up and Cheer*. While some of the music from that film was being recorded, Shirley began to do a number of dance steps. She was noticed by a director, who hurriedly scribbled the words of "Baby, Take a Bow" on the back of an envelope. He asked her to learn the lines at once. Little Shirley then performed the song with such aplomb that an awed hush descended on the crowded, busy set. Harold Lloyd, who happened to be present, broke the silence with the exclamation: "By God, here's another Jackie Coogan!" Shirley was signed to a contract then and there, and given a starring role in *Stand Up and Cheer*. Her appearance in this film, and her performance of "Baby, Take a Bow," catapulted her into one of the greatest successes ever enjoyed in films by a child star.

Baby, Talk to Me, words by Lee Adams, music by Charles Strouse (1960). Introduced by Dick Van Dyke in the musical *Bye Bye Birdie* (1960). He repeated his performance in the motion-picture adaptation of the musical (Columbia, 1963).

Baby, the Rain Must Fall, words by Ernie Sheldon, music by Elmer Bernstein (1964). Title song of a motion picture starring Steve McQueen and Lee Remick (Columbia, 1964). It was popularized by Glenn Yarborough in a best-selling RCA Victor recording in 1965.

Baby, Won't You Please Come Home?, words and music by Charles Warfield and Clarence Williams (1919). Jimmy Lunceford's recording for Columbia has become a jazz classic. The song was interpolated in the motion picture *That's the Spirit,* starring Peggy Ryan and Jack Oakie (Universal, 1945), and it was successfully revived in the early 1960s by Jerry Vale in a best-selling Columbia recording.

Bacharach, Burt F., composer, born Kansas City, Missouri, 1928.

See (Lyrics by Hal David): Here Am I; Magic Moments; My Little Red Book; Love Can Break a Heart; Send Me No Flowers; The Story of My Life; What's New, Pussycat?; Wives and Lovers.

Back, Back to Baltimore, words by Harry H. Williams, music by Egbert Van Alstyne (1904). One of the composer's earliest successes, popularized in vaudeville and minstrel shows.

The Back Bay Polka, words by Ira Gershwin, music by George Gershwin (1947). Introduced by the Outcasts (a quartet representing a painter, a female lexicographer, a composer and a poet, who expressed their views on Boston) in the motion-picture musical *The Shocking Miss Pilgrim* (20th Century-Fox, 1947). Like the other songs in this film, this one was adapted from manuscripts left by George Gershwin at the time of his death a decade earlier.

Back Home Again in Indiana. *See:* Indiana.

Back Home in Tennessee, words by William Jerome, music by Walter Donaldson (1915). A song identified most often with the State of Tennessee. It was its composer's first hit—written before he had ever set foot on Southern soil.

Back in Your Own Back Yard, words and music by Al Jolson, Billy Rose and Dave Dreyer (1927). Popularized by Al Jolson, who revived it on the soundtrack of the motion-picture musical *Jolson Sings Again* (Columbia, 1949). It was also interpolated in the motion picture *Silver Spurs,* starring Roy Rogers (Republic, 1943).

Bagdad, words by Anne Caldwell, music by Victor Herbert (1912). Introduced by David C. Montgomery and chorus in the operetta *The Lady of the Slipper* (1912).

Bagdad, words by Harold Atteridge, music by Al Jolson (1918). Introduced by Al Jolson in the Winter Garden extravaganza *Sinbad* (1918).

Bajour, a gypsy musical comedy with book by Ernest Kinoy based on articles in *The New Yorker.* Lyrics and music by Walter Marks. Starring Chita Rivera and Herschel Bernardi (1964). Original cast recording (Columbia).

See: Living Simply; Love Line; Must It Be Love?

Baker Street, a musical comedy with book by Jerome Coopersmith based on stories by A. Conan Doyle. Lyrics and music by Raymond Jessel and Marian Grudeff. Two additional songs by Sheldon Harnick and Jerry Bock. Starring Inga Swenson, Martin Gable and Fritz Weaver (1965). Original cast recording (MGM).

See: Finding Words for Spring; I'd Do It Again; Letters; A Married Man; What a Night This Is Going to Be.

Bali Ha'i, words by Oscar Hammerstein II, music by Richard Rodgers (1949). Introduced by Juanita Hall in the musical play *South Pacific* (1949). She repeated her performance in the motion-picture adaptation of the musical (20th Century-Fox, 1958).

Rodgers was dining at Joshua Logan's apartment when Hammerstein arrived with the lyrics of "Bali Ha'i." Rodgers looked at the typewritten sheet for a moment. He then pushed aside the cup of coffee in front of him and started writing. In about half an hour he had the song completely written. He never had to change a single note.

Ball, Ernest R., composer, born Cleveland, Ohio, 1878; died Santa Ana, California, 1927.

See (Lyrics by J. Keirn Brennan): Dear Little Boy of Mine; Goodbye, Good Luck, God Bless You; Let the Rest of the World Go By; A Little Bit of Heaven; She's the Daughter of Mother Machree; Turn Back the Universe.

See (Lyrics by George Graff, Jr.): As Long as the World Rolls By; Isle o' Dreams; Till the Sands of the Desert Grow Cold; When Irish Eyes Are Smiling.

See also: I'll Forget You; In the Garden of My Heart; In the Shadow of the Pyramids; Love Me and the World Is Mine; Mother Machree; My Heart Has Learned to Love You; Will You Love Me in December as You Do in May? You Planted a Rose in the Garden of Love.

For Ernest R. Ball's screen biography, see *When Irish Eyes Are Smiling*.

The Ballad of Davy Crockett, words by Tom Blackburn, music by George Bruns (1954). Introduced by Fess Parker in *Davy Crockett*, a television production by Walt Disney which was also released as a full-length motion picture (Buena Vista, 1956). Bill Hayes' recording for Cadence in 1955 sold about a million and a half disks. Fess Parker's recording for Columbia and Tennessee Ernie Ford's recording for Capitol the same year each sold about a million disks. In all, about ten million disks were sold of twenty-three different recordings. The song was also recorded abroad in a dozen different languages, including some twenty different versions in France alone; in Japan it was a best seller.

The Ballad of Rodger Young. *See:* Rodger Young.

The Ballad of the Alamo, words by Paul Francis Webster, music by Dimitri Tiomkin (1960). Introduced by a chorus in the motion picture *The Alamo*, starring John Wayne, Richard Widmark and Laurence Harvey (United Artists, 1960), and popularized by Marty Robbins in a Columbia recording.

Ballad of the Green Berets, words and music by S/Sgt. Barry Sadler (1966). Hit song about the Vietnam war, introduced and popularized by Sadler in a best-selling RCA Victor recording.

Ballerina, words by Bob Russell, music by Carl Sigman (1947). Popularized by Vaughn Monroe in a best-selling recording for RCA Victor. The song

was successfully revived in 1955 by Nat King Cole in a Capitol release.

Ballin' the Jack, words by Jim Burris, music by Chris Smith (1913). A ragtime dance number whose lyrics made no attempt to explain what is meant by "ballin' the jack." It was introduced in vaudeville in 1913 by Billy Kent and Jeanette Warner (sometimes described as the creators of the fox trot). Eddie Cantor, who sang it for the first time, in vaudeville, in Houston, Texas, first made it popular; it became one of his earliest song specialties. When the song was revived in the motion-picture musical *For Me and My Gal* (MGM, 1942), it found a place on the Hit Parade. Danny Kaye featured it in his one-man shows, in a Decca recording and in his motion picture *On the Riviera* (20th Century-Fox, 1951). The song was also interpolated in the Dean Martin–Jerry Lewis farce *That's My Boy* (Paramount, 1951). During the craze for the twist, Chubby Checker popularized a twist version.

Bambalina, words by Otto Harbach and Oscar Hammerstein II, music by Vincent Youmans and Herbert Stothart (1923). Hit song about an eccentric country fiddler who enjoyed confusing his dancers by stopping suddenly in the middle of his rendition. The song was introduced by Edith Day and a female chorus in the musical comedy *The Wildflower* (1923).

The Banana Boat Song (or, Day-O), words and music by Erik Darling, Bob Carey and Alan Arkin (1956). A calypso number introduced by the Tarriers in a Glory recording. It was further popularized in 1957 by Harry Belafonte, whose RCA Victor recording sold a million disks. It was interpolated in the motion picture *Calypso Heat Wave*, starring Johnny Desmond (Columbia, 1957).

Bandana Days, words and music by Eubie Blake and Noble Sissle (1921). Introduced by Arthur Porter and chorus in *Shuffle Along* (1921), the first successful Broadway all-Negro revue.

The Band Played On, words by John

E. Palmer, music by Charles B. Ward (1895). The song was inspired by the popularity of German brass bands in the streets of New York. It was introduced by Charles B. Ward at Hammerstein's Harlem Opera House in 1895. It was then successfully promoted by the New York *World*, which published words and music besides publicizing the song in its columns. This was the first instance in Tin Pan Alley history when a popular song was successfully exploited by a newspaper.

Palmer once told an interviewer that he wrote this song at the suggestion of his sister. He was in his apartment listening to the sounds of a German brass band in the street below when his sister made a move to close the window. He stopped her by saying, "Let the band play on." It was then that his sister suggested using this phrase for a song. After completing both words and music, and failing to get a publisher, he happened to sing it *sotto voce* in the presence of Charles B. Ward, a vaudevillian. Then and there Ward bought the rights to the song, revised it slightly, took full credit as its composer, then published it himself under the imprint of the New York Music Company. He not only introduced it, but used his influence to get other vaudevillians to use it. Since the song sold over a million copies of sheet music, Ward realized a fortune from its publication; but its real author, Palmer, earned nothing but the pittance originally paid him.

The song was interpolated for James Cagney and Rita Hayworth in the non-musical motion picture *The Strawberry Blonde* (Warner, 1941); after the final scene the words were flashed on the screen for a community sing. It was sung by Denis Morgan in the non-musical motion picture *Cattle Town* (Warner, 1952).

The Band Wagon, a revue with book by George S. Kaufman. Lyrics by Howard Dietz. Music by Arthur Schwartz. Starring Fred and Adele Astaire and Helen Broderick (1931).

There were two motion-picture adaptations. The first was named *Dancing in the Dark* after its principal song, and starred William Powell and Betsy Drake (20th Century-Fox, 1949). Three songs were used from the stage score, with the interpolation of an earlier Dietz-Schwartz number, "Something to Remember You By." The second motion-picture adaptation retained the original title of the revue (MGM, 1953) and starred Fred Astaire and Cyd Charisse, with India Adams singing on the soundtrack for Cyd Charisse. Together with several of the hit numbers from the stage production, the score included songs from earlier Dietz-Schwartz stage musicals, with a new Dietz-Schwartz song, "That's Entertainment." Soundtrack recording (MGM).

See: Dancing in the Dark; I Guess I'll Have to Change My Plan; I Love Louisa; Louisiana Hayride; New Sun in the Sky; Something to Remember You By; That's Entertainment; You and the Night and the Music.

The Banks of the Dee, words by John Tait to the tune of the Irish song "Langolee" (c. 1767). One of America's earliest sentimental ballads. It described a Scotchman's farewell to his lass as he makes ready to join the British troops embarking for the American colonies. This song became popular during the Revolutionary War.

The Barkleys of Broadway, a motion picture musical starring Fred Astaire and Ginger Rogers (MGM, 1948). Songs by Ira Gershwin and Harry Warren, with the interpolation of "They Can't Take That Away from Me" by George and Ira Gershwin.

See: My One and Only Highland Fling; They Can't Take That Away from Me.

Barney Google, words by Billy Rose, music by Con Conrad (1923). A comedy number inspired by a popular newspaper cartoon. Conrad wrote it for Eddie Cantor, who introduced it in 1923, but the song is more generally identified with Olsen and Johnson. Billy Rose convinced Olsen and Johnson to use the song in their vaudeville act by devising a routine for them in which they capered up and down the aisles of the theater in the costume of a horse, while another actor, resembling Barney Google of the cartoons, served as the jockey. This song, and this routine, became so popular that they helped make Olsen and Johnson vaudeville headliners.

Barney, Take Me Home Again, words by Arthur W. French, music by George W. Brown (c. 1875). It served as the model for Thomas P. Westendorf in the writing of the more enduring ballad "I'll Take You Home Again Kathleen" in 1876.

The Battle Cry of Freedom, a celebrated Civil War ballad, words and music by George Frederick Root (1863). Root's inspiration came from the announcement on May 3, 1861, that President Lincoln had issued an appeal for forty more Army regiments and additional seamen for the Navy. "Immediately," Root later recalled, "a song started in my mind, words and music together. . . . I thought it out that afternoon and wrote it the next morning." The song had hardly been written when the Lombard Brothers, a singing attraction then specializing in war songs, came to the publishing house of Root and Cady in search of new material. They seized upon "The Battle Cry of Freedom" and introduced it the same day at a war meeting held in front of the courthouse in Chicago. By the time they had finished three verses, the audience joined in singing the chorus. A few days later the Hutchinson Family opened a war rally in Union Square, New York, with a rendition of "The Battle Cry of Freedom." The enthusiasm of the audience led the Hutchinsons to repeat the song several times.

Throughout the Civil War this ballad proved a powerful factor in maintaining the morale of Union soldiers. A young, unidentified soldier wrote during the war: "The tune put as much spirit and cheer into the army as a splendid victory.

Day and night you could hear it by every campfire and in every tent. Never shall I forget how these men rolled their lines." President Lincoln also recognized its value, by writing to Root: "You have done more than a hundred generals and a thousand orators. If you could not shoulder a musket in defense of your country, you certainly have served her through songs."

The ballad never lost its popularity. A thousand voices sang it loud and clear at the Republican Presidential convention in 1867 as part of a successful maneuver to create the proper atmosphere in which to nominate General Ulysses S. Grant. When, in 1896, money was raised for a Root monument in Chicago, ten thousand gathered at the Coliseum to hear Jules Lombard, now an old man, sing the ballad he had helped to introduce.

In 1897 Charles A. Dana, editor of the New York *Sun*, wrote: "George Root did more to preserve the Union than a great many brigadier generals, and quite as much as some brigades."

The Battle Hymn of the Republic, words by Julia Ward Howe to the melody of "John Brown's Body," which, in turn, had been taken from "Glory, Hallelujah" generally credited to William Steffe (1862).

Mrs. Howe—poet and philanthropist—was visiting Washington, D. C., in December, 1861, when she was invited to nearby Virginia to witness a review of Union troops. A sudden enemy attack compelled these troops to rush back to camp. En route they sang patriotic and war songs, one of them being "John Brown's Body." Reverend James Freeman Clarke, a member of Mrs. Howe's party, urged her then to write new war lyrics for the rousing melody of "John Brown's Body." She wrote them that night in her room at the Willard Hotel in Washington, D. C. "I scrawled the verses almost without looking at the paper," she later recalled. "Having completed the writing, I returned to bed and fell asleep, saying to myself, 'I like this better than most things I have written.' " Her poem was first published in the *Atlantic Monthly* in February, 1862, the title of "The Battle Hymn of the Republic" having been suggested to her by the editor. Mrs. Howe received a payment of five dollars for her poem. Almost immediately the verses were reprinted throughout the North. It became the poem of the hour. To the melody of "John Brown's Body" it was sung at war rallies, in army camps and on the field of battle.

Long after the Civil War was over, Mrs. Howe wrote: "The wild echoes of that fearful struggle have long since died away, and with them all memories of unkindness between ourselves and our Southern brethren. But those who once loved my hymn still sing it. I hope and I believe that it stands for what our whole country now believes in—in the sacredness of human liberty."

When, toward the end of her life, Mrs. Howe received an honorary degree of Doctor of Letters from Brown University, she was described as an "author, philanthropist, mother, friend of the slave, and the . . . singer of the battle hymn of freedom."

A Columbia recording of "The Battle Hymn of the Republic" by the Mormon Tabernacle Choir of Salt Lake City with the Philadelphia Orchestra in 1959 sold a million disks.

The ballad made front-page news twice in January of 1965. On January 20 it was sung by the Mormon Tabernacle Choir at President Johnson's Inauguration, immediately following the Inaugural Address. Several Southern members of the Joint Congressional Committee on Inaugural Ceremonies at first objected to this choice, maintaining that it was "a Union song." But the choir director persisted, arguing that "people have loved it wherever we have sung it" and that "it's connected with our country and has a stirring message." He won out.

Ten days later the ballad was sung in London at St. Paul's Cathedral, during the funeral services for Sir Winston Churchill. An erroneous report was at first circulated that this was done at the wish of Sir Winston himself. However, this was not the case. The ballad had been selected by Lady Churchill and members of the Churchill family in honor of Churchill's American mother.

The Battle of New Orleans, words and music by Jimmy Driftwood, melody based on an 1815 fiddle tune "The Eighth of January," celebrating Andrew Jackson's victory at New Orleans (1959). Popularized by Johnny Horton in a Columbia recording which received a "Grammy" from the National Academy of Recording Arts and Sciences as the best country and Western recording of the year. Another "Grammy" was presented to the song itself, as the best of the year in its field.

The Battle of the Kegs, words by Francis Hopkinson to the tune of "Yankee Doodle" (1778). A humorous song of the American Revolution. Hopkinson wrote the words to satirize the experiment of David Bushnell in sending powder-filled kegs down the river to destroy British ships anchored off Philadelphia. On seeing the floating kegs, the British fired wildly at them—an incident that Hopkinson found so comical that he wrote a set of mocking verses, beginning with the lines: "Gallants, attend, and hear a friend, /Trill forth harmonious ditty;/ Strange things I'll tell, which late befell,/In Philadelphia city."

Baubles, Bangles and Beads, words and music by Robert Wright and George "Chet" Forrest, melody based on themes by Borodin (1953). Introduced by Doretta Morrow in the operetta *Kismet* (1953). It was popularized by Peggy Lee in a Decca recording.

Be a Clown, words and music by Cole Porter (1948). Introduced by Judy Garland and Gene Kelly in the motion-picture musical *The Pirate* (MGM, 1948).

Beale Street Blues, words and music

by W. C. Handy (1917). Originally published in Memphis, Tennessee, under the title "Beale Street." The number proved a favorite with many jazz musicians, including Jack Teagarden, whose rendition was famous. It was sung by Mitzi Gaynor in the screen biography of Eva Tanguay, *The I Don't Care Girl* (20th Century-Fox, 1953). Danny Thomas' song "Bring Back Our Beale Street Blues" was written when Beale Street, in Memphis, Tennessee, was renamed Beale Avenue.

Beans, Beans, Beans, words by Elmer Bowman, music by Chris Smith (1912).

Be Anything (But Be Mine), words and music by Irving Gordon (1952). Popularized by Eddy Howard in a Mercury recording.

Beat Me Daddy, Eight to the Bar, words and music by Don Raye, Hughie Prince and Eleanor Sheehy (1940). Boogie-woogie tune introduced by Will Bradley and his orchestra (vocal by Ray McKinley) in a Columbia recording, then further popularized by Freddie Slack in a Capitol release.

Beau James, a motion-picture biography (with songs) of New York City's Mayor James J. Walker, starring Bob Hope as Jimmy Walker (Paramount, 1957). The score was made up of standards.
   See: Happy Days Are Here Again; Manhattan; The Sidewalks of New York.

Beautiful Dreamer, words and music by Stephen Foster (1864). Foster's last sentimental ballad, written a few days before his death.

Beautiful Eyes, words and music by George A. Whiting and Carter De Haven, music by Ted Snyder (1909). Interpolated in the musical *Mr. Hamlet of Broadway* (1908).

Beautiful Lady in Blue, words by Sam M. Lewis, music by J. Fred Coots (1935). Introduced in 1936 by Jan Peerce over the radio on the Chevrolet Hour.

Beautiful Love, words by Haven Gillespie, music by Victor Young, Wayne King and Egbert Van Alstyne (1931). It was interpolated for

Allan Jones in the motion-picture musical *Sing a Jingle* (Universal, 1944).

Beautiful Ohio, words by Ballard MacDonald, music by Robert A. King, using the pseudonym of Mary Earl (1918). A waltz first issued as a piano instrumental, and in that form became popular in vaudeville as an accompaniment to "allez oop" acrobat acts. Later in 1918 Ballard MacDonald wrote lyrics for it. As a vocal number, "Beautiful Ohio" achieved one of the largest sheet-music sales in the 1910s, over five million copies.
   When King wrote this waltz he was a salaried employe in Tin Pan Alley, in the publishing house of Shapiro, Bernstein. "Beautiful Ohio" was one of the songs he submitted under the terms of a contract in which he was required to write four songs a month, which then belonged outright to the publishing house. Even though the publishers were not legally bound to do so, they paid King royalties on "Beautiful Ohio" amounting to $60,000.

Be-Bop Baby, words and music by Pearl Lendhurst (1957). Popularized by Ricky Nelson in an Imperial recording in 1958 that sold about a million disks.

Be Careful, It's My Heart, words and music by Irving Berlin (1942). Introduced by Bing Crosby in the motion-picture musical *Holiday Inn* (Paramount, 1942); the song was then used in that picture for an effective dance routine by Fred Astaire and Marjorie Reynolds.

Because I Love You, words and music by Irving Berlin (1926). The last of the autobiographical love ballads written during the composer's dramatic romance with Ellin Mackay, whom he married in 1926.

Because of You, words by Arthur Hammerstein, music by Dudley Wilkinson (1940). It became popular a decade after publication upon being interpolated in the non-musical motion picture *I Was an American Spy,* starring Ann Dvorak and Gene Evans (United Artists, 1951). It was also used in the background music for the motion picture *Let's Make It Legal*, starring Claudette Colbert (20th Century-Fox, 1951). It occupied the Number One spot on the Hit Parade eleven times, the second largest number of first-place representations by any song in the history of that radio program. Tony Bennett's Columbia recording in 1952 sold a million disks and became his first major recording success.

Because They're Young, words by Aaron Schroeder and Wally Gold, music by Don Costa (1960). Popularized by Duane Eddy in a Jamie recording.

Because You're Mine, words by Sammy Cahn, music by Nicholas Brodszky (1951). Title song of a motion picture (MGM, 1952), where it was introduced by Mario Lanza, who made a successful recording for RCA Victor.

Because You're Mine, a motion-picture musical starring Mario Lanza and Doretta Morrow (MGM, 1952). Title song by Sammy Cahn and Nicholas Brodszky, with various standards interpolated in the score.

See: All the Things You Are; Because You're Mine; You Do Something to Me.

Because You're You, words by Henry Blossom, music by Victor Herbert (1906). Introduced by Neal McCay and Aline Carter in the operetta *The Red Mill* (1906).

Bedelia, words by William Jerome, music by Jean Schwartz (1903). Interpolated in the musical *The Jersey Lily* (1903), where it was introduced and popularized by Blanche Ring in her first Broadway starring role. This number is a rare instance in which one songwriter pays tribute to another ("I'll be your Chauncey Olcott"). The sheet-music sale in the early 1900s exceeded three million copies. The song was interpolated in the motion-picture musical *The Eddie Cantor Story* (Warner, 1954).

Beep, Beep, words and music by Carl Cicchetti and Donald Claps (1958). Popularized by The Playmates in a Roulette recording.

Beer Barrel Polka, a popular Czech song, music by Jaromir Vejvoda, English lyrics by Lew Brown (1934). It was interpolated in the musical *Yokel Boy* (1939). Will Glahe's recording for RCA Victor and the recording of Sammy Kaye and his orchestra for Columbia then helped to popularize the song into a sheet-music sale exceeding half a million copies. It was interpolated as a piano interlude in the non-musical motion picture *From Here to Eternity*, starring Montgomery Clift and Deborah Kerr (Columbia, 1954).

Before I Gaze at You, words by Alan Jay Lerner, music by Frederick Loewe (1960). Introduced by Julie Andrews in the musical play *Camelot* (1960).

Before I Met You, words by P. G. Wodehouse, music by Jerome Kern (1918). Introduced by Vivienne Segal and Carl Randall in the Princess Theatre production of *Oh, Lady, Lady!* (1918).

The Begat, words by E. Y. Harburg, music by Burton Lane (1947). Introduced by Lorenzo Fuller, Jerry Laws and Lewis Sharp in the musical play *Finian's Rainbow* (1947).

Begin the Beguine, words and music by Cole Porter (1935). A Porter classic introduced by June Knight in the musical *Jubilee* (1935). Porter's inspiration came from the rhythms of a native dance witnessed at Kalabahi in the Dutch East Indies. Porter played the song for the first time anywhere to Moss Hart, his collaborator on *Jubilee*, aboard the *Franconia* during a round-the-world cruise. "I had reservations about the length of the song," Hart later confessed. "Indeed, I am somewhat ashamed to record that I thought it had ended when he was only halfway through playing it."

"Begin the Beguine" made little of an impression in *Jubilee*. The song probably would have been completely forgotten, and would have remained in the discard indefinitely, but for a recording by Artie Shaw and his orchestra (in an arrangement by Jerry Gray). In 1936 Shaw was contracted by RCA Victor to make recordings on the Bluebird label. He was advised to make a swing version of Friml's "Indian Love Call" as his first disk. Shaw consented but only on the condition he be permitted to do the then unknown "Begin the Beguine" on the flip side. "I just happened to like it," he later explained, "so I insisted on recording it at this first session, in spite of the recording manager, who thought it a complete waste of time and only let me make it after I had argued it would make at least a nice quiet contrast to the 'Indian Love Call.'" Artie Shaw's recording sold two million disks, becoming one of the largest-selling instrumental recordings by an American band in recording history. "That recording of that one little tune, 'Begin the Beguine,'" Shaw went on to say, "was the real turning point in my life."

"Begin the Beguine" was one of two of Cole Porter's favorites among his own songs, the other being "Love for Sale." In 1963 it was selected by ASCAP as one of sixteen numbers in its all-time Hit Parade during its half century of existence. "Begin the Beguine" was interpolated in several motion pictures, including the Cole Porter screen biography *Night and Day* (Warner, 1946), sung by Carlos Raminez, and *Broadway Melody* (MGM, 1940).

Bei Mir Bist Du Schoen (Means That You're Grand), a Yiddish popular song, music by Sholom Secunda, English lyrics by Sammy Cahn and Saul Chaplin (1937). This was Sammy Cahn's first song hit, popularized in a Decca recording by the Andrews Sisters. It was sung by Priscilla Lane in the motion picture *Love, Honor and Behave* (Warner, 1938).

This song is reputed to have earned three million dollars; but Sholom Secunda had received only thirty dollars in all, the sum for which he had sold out his rights as composer. When the copyright expired in the early 1960s, Secunda reacquired the rights and made a new deal with the publishing company whereby he would henceforth participate in the royalties.

Be Kind to Your Parents, words and music by Harold Rome (1954). Introduced by Florence Henderson and Lloyd Reese in the musical *Fanny* (1954).

Believe What I Say, words and music by Johnny and Dorsey Burnette (1958). Popularized by Ricky Nelson's recording for Imperial.

Bell Bottom Trousers, a bawdy sea chantey of unknown authorship with new lyrics by Moe Jaffee (1944). Vincent Lopez and his orchestra helped make the new version a major song success in 1945; a best-selling recording was made for RCA Victor by Tony Pastor and his orchestra (vocal by Tony Pastor and Ruth McCullough).

Belle, Belle (My Liberty Belle), words and music by Bob Merrill (1951). Popularized by Guy Mitchell in a Columbia recording.

The Belle of New York, an operetta with book and lyrics by Hugh Morton. Music by Gustave Kerker. Starring Edna May and Harry Davenport (1897).

See: She Is the Belle of New York; They All Follow Me.

Belle of the Ball, words by Mitchell Parish, music by Leroy Anderson (1951). Popularized as an instrumental in a Decca recording by Leroy Anderson and his orchestra.

Bells Are Ringing, a musical comedy with book and lyrics by Betty Comden and Adolph Green. Music by Jule Styne. Starring Judy Holliday and Sydney Chaplin (1956). Original cast recording (Columbia).

The motion-picture adaptation starred Judy Holliday and Dean Martin (MGM, 1960). It utilized the basic stage score.

See: Just in Time; Long Before I Knew You; The Party's Over.

The Bells of St. Mary's, a motion picture with interpolated songs starring Bing Crosby and Ingrid Bergman (RKO, 1945). The score included "Aren't You Glad You're You," a new number by Johnny Burke and James van Heusen.

See: Aren't You Glad You're You.

Be My Life's Companion, words by Bob Hilliard, music by Milton De Lugg (1951). Popularized by the Mills Brothers in a Decca recording and by Rosemary Clooney in a Columbia recording.

Be My Little Baby Bumble Bee, words by Stanley Murphy, music by Henry I. Marshall (1912). Introduced by the Dolly Sisters in the *Ziegfeld Follies of 1911*. It was interpolated in the motion-picture screen biography of Ernest R. Ball, *When Irish Eyes Are Smiling* (20th Century-Fox, 1944); in the motion-picture musical *By the Light of the Silvery Moon* (Warner, 1953), sung by Doris Day and Russell Arms; and in the motion-picture musical *The Eddie Cantor Story* (Warner, 1954), sung on the soundtrack by Eddie Cantor.

Be My Love, words by Sammy Cahn, music by Nicholas Brodszky (1949). Introduced by Mario Lanza and Kathryn Grayson in the motion picture *The Toast of New Orleans* (MGM, 1952). Lanza's recording for RCA Victor sold about two million disks—becoming the only "Red Seal" classical release to achieve a hit-song status with disk jockeys. "By the time the picture played the neighborhood houses," wrote Joseph Pasternak, the motion-picture producer of *Be My Love*, "the song was one of the most phenomenally successful songs of the postwar period." Lanza adopted it as his theme song on his TV program, the Coca-Cola Hour. The song was interpolated by Connie Francis in the motion-picture musical *Looking for Love* (MGM, 1964).

Ben Bolt (or, Oh, Don't You Remember?), words by Thomas Dunn English, music by Nelson Kneass (1848). English wrote his poem for N. P. Willis, editor of the New York *Mirror*, without receiving any payment. There were two earlier musical settings of this poem before Kneass, a minstrel, wrote the one that became famous. Kneass confessed he borrowed his basic tune from an old German song. "Ben Bolt" was interpolated in productions of George Louis Du Maurier's *Trilby*, as the song performed by the hypnotized heroine under the spell of Svengali, the hypnotist.

A Bench in the Park, words by Jack Yellen, music by Milton Ager (1930). It was written for the Brox Sisters, who introduced it in the motion-picture musical *King of Jazz* (Universal, 1930).

Bend Down, Sister, words by Ballard MacDonald and Dave Silverstein, music by Con Conrad (1931). Introduced by Eddie Cantor in the motion-picture musical *Palmy Days* (United Artists, 1931).

Ben Franklin in Paris, a musical comedy with book and lyrics by Sidney Michaels. Music by Mark Sandrich, Jr. Starring Robert Preston as Benjamin Franklin (1964). Original cast recording (Capitol).
See: Hic, Haec, Hoc; Look for Small Pleasures; To Be Alone with You; When I Dance with the Person I Love.

The Benny Goodman Story, a motion-picture musical biography of Benny Goodman, starring Steve Allen as Goodman, with Donna Reed (Universal, 1956). Benny Goodman and his orchestra were heard on the soundtrack with such other all-time jazz greats as Gene Krupa, Teddy Wilson, Ziggy Elman, Lionel Hampton and Kid Ory. The score was made up primarily of Benny Goodman favorites.
See: And the Angels Sing; Avalon; China Boy; Goody Goody; Jersey Bounce; Let's Dance; Memories of You; Moonglow; S-h-i-n-e.

Berlin, Irving, composer and lyricist, born Israel Baline, Temun, Russia, 1888.
See: Snyder, Ted.
See also: After You Get What You Want; Alexander's Ragtime Band; All Alone; All by Myself; Always; Anything You Can Do; Be Careful, It's My Heart; The Best Thing for You; Blue Skies; Call Me Up Some Rainy Afternoon; Change Partners; Cheek to Cheek; Count Your Blessings; A Couple of Song and Dance Men; A Couple of Swells; Crinoline Days; Doin' What Comes Natur'lly; Dorando; Easter Parade;

Empty Pockets Filled with Love; Ephraham; Everybody's Doin' It; Everybody Step; A Fella with an Umbrella; The Girl of My Dreams; The Girl That I Marry; Give Me Your Tired; God Bless America; Goodbye, Beckie Cohen; Grizzly Bear; Happy Holiday; Heat Wave; He's a Devil in His Own Home Town; The Hostess with the Mostes' on the Ball; How Deep Is the Ocean?; How Many Times Have I Said I Love You?; I Left My Heart at the Stage Door Canteen; I'll See You in C-U-B-A; I Love a Piano; I'm a Vamp from East Broadway; I'm Puttin' All My Eggs in One Basket; International Rag; I Poured My Heart into a Song; Is He the Only Man in the World?; Isn't This a Lovely Day to be Caught in the Rain?; I Threw a Kiss in the Ocean; It's a Lovely Day Today; It's a Lovely Day Tomorrow; I Used to be Color Blind; I've Got My Captain Working for Me Now; I Want to Go Back to Michigan; Lady of the Evening; Lazy; Let Me Sing and I'm Happy; Let's Face the Music and Dance; Let's Have Another Cup o' Coffee; Let's Take an Old Fashioned Walk; A Man Chases a Girl; Mandy; Marie; Marie from Sunny Italy; Meat and Potatoes; Moonshine Lullaby; The Night Is Filled with Music; Nobody Knows and Nobody Seems to Care; Not for All the Rice in China; Oh, How I Hate to Get Up in the Morning; Opera Rag; Orange Grove in California; Pack Up Your Sins; Paris Wakes Up and Smiles; The Piccolino; Play a Simple Melody; A Pretty Girl Is Like a Melody; The Pullman Porters on Parade; Puttin' on the Ritz; Ragtime Jockey Man; Ragtime Violin; Reaching for the Moon; Remember; Russian Lullaby; Sadie Salome; Say It Isn't So; Say It with Music; Sayonara; Shaking the Blues Away; Show Business; Slumming on Park Avenue; Snooky Ookums; Soft Lights and Sweet Music; Somebody's Coming to My House; Some Sunny Day; The Song Is Ended; Stop the Rag; Sun in the Mornin'; Suppertime; Syncopated Walk; Take Off a Little Bit; Tell Me a Bedtime Story; Tell Me, Little Gypsy; That Mesmerizing Mendelssohn Tune; They Like Ike; They Loved Me; They Say It's Wonderful; This Is a Great Country; This Is the Army; This Is the Life; This Year's Kisses; Top Hat, White Tie and Tails; What'll I Do?; When I Leave the World Behind; When I Lost You; When My Dreams Come True; When the Midnight Choo Choo Leaves for Alabam; White Christmas; Who Do You Love, I Hope?; Woodman, Woodman, Spare That Tree; The Yam; You Can't Get a Man with a Gun; You Can't Make Your Shimmy Shake on Tea; You'd Be Surprised; You Keep Coming Back Like a Song; You're Just in Love.

Bernadine, words and music by Johnny Mercer (1957). Title song of the motion picture (20th Century-Fox, 1957), sung by Pat Boone, whose Dot recording was a best seller.

Bernstein, Leonard, composer, born Lawrence, Massachusetts, 1918.

See (Lyrics by Betty Comden and Adolph Green): I Get Carried Away; Lonely Town; Lucky to Be Me; My Darlin' Eileen; New York, New York; Ohio; A Quiet Girl.

See (Lyrics by Stephen Sondheim): I Feel Pretty; Maria; Tonight.

Beside a Babbling Brook, words by Gus Kahn, music by Walter Donaldson (1923).

Bess, You Is My Woman Now, words by Ira Gershwin and Du Bose Heyward, music by George Gershwin (1935). Love duet in the American folk opera *Porgy and Bess* (1935), introduced by Todd Duncan and Anne Brown. In the motion-picture adaptation of the opera (Columbia, 1959), it was sung on the soundtrack by Robert McFerrin (for Sidney Poitier) and by Adele Addison (for Dorothy Dandridge).

Best Foot Forward, a musical comedy with book by John Cecil Holm. Lyrics and music by Ralph Blane and Hugh Martin. Starring Rosemary Lane, Nancy Walker and June Allyson (1941).

The motion-picture adaptation starred Lucille Ball and William

Gaxton (MGM, 1943). It utilized the basic stage score.

See: Buckle Down, Winsocki.

The Best I Get Is Much Obliged to You, words and music by Benjamin Hapgood Burt (1907). A coon song sometimes identified as "Much Obliged to You" or "All I Get Here Is Much Obliged to You" or by the opening phrase of its chorus, "It's Mighty Strange."

The Best Is Yet to Come, words by Carolyn Leigh, music by Cy Coleman (1959). Introduced by Tony Bennett in a Columbia recording.

The Best of Everything, words by Sammy Cahn, music by Alfred Newman (1959). Title song of the nonmusical motion picture starring Hope Lange and Stephen Boyd (20th Century-Fox, 1959), where it was sung under the titles by Johnny Mathis.

The Best Thing for You, words and music by Irving Berlin (1950). Introduced by Ethel Merman and Paul Lukas in the musical *Call Me Madam* (1950). In the motion-picture adaptation of the musical (20th Century-Fox, 1953), it was sung by Ethel Merman and George Sanders.

The Best Things Happen While You're Dancing, words and music by Irving Berlin (1954). Introduced by Danny Kaye (and danced to by Danny Kaye and Vera-Ellen) in the motion-picture musical *White Christmas* (Paramount, 1954).

The Best Things in Life Are Free, words by Bud De Sylva and Lew Brown, music by Ray Henderson (1927). Introduced by Mary Lawlor and John Prince in the musical *Good News* (1927). Mary Lawlor repeated this performance in the 1930 motion-picture adaptation of this musical (MGM), while June Allyson and Peter Lawford sang it in the 1947 screen version (MGM). The song provided the title for the screen biography of De Sylva, Brown and Henderson (20th Century-Fox, 1956), and was sung in the opening scene before the titles by Gordon MacRae, Ernest Borgnine, Sheree North and Dan Dailey, and in the finale by Sheree North.

The Best Things in Life Are Free, a motion-picture musical biography of De Sylva, Brown and Henderson (20th Century-Fox, 1956). Gordon MacRae was starred as De Sylva, Dan Dailey as Henderson and Ernest Borgnine as Lew Brown. The score was made up of De Sylva, Brown and Henderson standards.

See: The Best Things in Life Are Free; The Birth of the Blues; Black Bottom; Broken Hearted; Button Up Your Overcoat; Just a Memory; Lucky Day; Sonny Boy; This Is the Missus; Without Love; You're the Cream in My Coffee; You Try Somebody Else.

Betty Co-ed, words and music by J. Paul Fogarty and Rudy Vallée (1930). A college song popularized by Rudy Vallée over the radio and in an RCA Victor recording. The song provided the title for and was used prominently in a motion picture starring Jean Porter, Shirley Mills and William Mason (Columbia, 1946).

Between the Devil and the Deep Blue Sea, words by Ted Kochler, music by Harold Arlen (1931). Introduced by Bill Robinson in *Rhythmania* (1931), a night-club revue produced at the Cotton Club in Harlem, in New York.

Bewitched, Bothered and Bewildered, words by Lorenz Hart, music by Richard Rodgers (1940). Introduced by Vivienne Segal in the musical *Pal Joey* (1940). In the motion-picture adaptation of the musical comedy (Columbia, 1957), it was sung first by Rita Hayworth, then by Frank Sinatra.

When *Pal Joey* was first produced in 1940, "Bewitched, Bothered and Bewildered" did not become popular. This was due mainly to the fact that at that time it could not be heard over the radio—ASCAP, in its dispute with the networks, having banned from the airwaves all music by its members. After the show closed on Broadway, the song was heard in Paris in a French translation ("Perdu dans un rêve immense d'amour"), to become one of the city's big song hits. It began to be heard in the United States in the late 1940s, and in 1950 it reached the top spot in the Hit Parade. Columbia Records now decided to issue a recording of the entire *Pal Joey* score in 1951. This in turn led to the Broadway revival of *Pal Joey* in 1952, which enjoyed the longest run of any musical revival in Broadway history. "Bewitched, Bothered and Bewildered" now became a standard.

Beyond the Blue Horizon, words by Leo Robin, music by Richard A. Whiting and W. Franke Harling (1930). Introduced by Jeanette MacDonald in the motion picture *Monte Carlo* (Paramount, 1930). She revived it in the all-star motion picture *Follow the Boys* (Universal, 1944). This song was said to be one of President Kennedy's favorite standards.

Leo Robin informed this editor: "In the picture (*Monte Carlo*), Jeanette MacDonald sang the song in the compartment of a moving train, and through the window, shots of peasants are seen in the field singing in harmony with her solo. The orchestration imitated the rhythm of the rails and other train effects. It was the talk of the movie industry at the time."

Bibbidi, Bobbidi, Boo, words and music by Mack David, Al Hoffman and Jerry Livingston (1948). Introduced in the Walt Disney full-length animated production *Cinderella* (RKO, 1949) sung on the soundtrack by Verna Felton. It was popularized by Perry Como in an RCA Victor recording.

The Bible Tells Me So, words and music by Dale Evans (1955). An inspirational song introduced by Roy Rodgers and Dale Evans, but popularized by Don Cornell in a Coral recording.

A Bicycle Built for Two. *See:* Daisy Bell.

Bidin' My Time, words by Ira Gershwin, music by George Gershwin (1930). An ensemble number in the style of a hillbilly song. It was introduced by the Foursome (a cowboy quartet also playing the harmonica, jew's harp, ocarina, and tin flute), in the musical comedy *Girl Crazy* (1930). The song was featured in the 1943 motion-picture adaptation of the musical comedy (MGM) and was interpolated in the George Gershwin screen biography *Rhapsody in Blue* (Warner, 1945). It was also sung by a male quartet in the motion-picture musical *The Glenn Miller Story* (Universal, 1953). In *When the Boys Meet the Girls,* a screen remake of *Girl Crazy* (MGM, 1965), it was sung by Herman's Hermits.

The two verses, four lines each, are amusing for the way in which they quote popular song titles or catch phrases in verses by other lyricists, such as "singing in the rain," "swingin' down the lane," "cryin' for the Carolines," and "tiptoe through the tulips."

Big Bad John, words and music by Jimmy Dean (1961). A popular song in the style of a folk ballad. Dean was scheduled to cut four sides in a recording session in Nashville, Tennessee, in 1961. Since he had only three songs ready and needed a fourth he wrote it on a plane en route to Tennessee. His hero was a six-foot-five, bronco-busting Paul Bunyan type. Dean's recording for Columbia sold over two and a half million disks, receiving the Gold Record Award in 1961.

The Big Black Giant, words by Oscar Hammerstein II, music by Richard Rodgers (1954). An extended narrative describing an audience as it appears to the performer on the stage. It was introduced by Bill Hayes in the musical *Me and Juliet* (1954).

Big Broadcast of 1936, a motion-picture musical starring Bing Crosby, Ethel Merman and others (Paramount, 1935). Songs by Leo Robin and Richard A. Whiting, Leo Robin and Ralph Rainger, Dorothy Parker and Ralph Rainger.

See: I Wished on the Moon.

Big Broadcast of 1938, a motion-picture musical starring Bob Hope (in his screen debut) and Shirley Ross (Paramount, 1937). Songs mainly by Leo Robin and Ralph Rainger.

See: Thanks for the Memory.

Big D, words and music by Frank Loesser (1956). A tribute to the city of Dallas, Texas, in the style of a popular song of the 1920s. It was introduced by Shorty Long and Susan Johnson in the musical play *The Most Happy Fella* (1956).

Big Girls Don't Cry, words by Bob Crewe, music by Bob Gaudio (1962). Popularized by the Four Seasons in a Vee Jay recording.

A Big Hunk o' Love, words and music by Aaron Schroeder and Sid Wyche (1959). Popularized by Elvis Presley in an RCA Victor recording that sold over a million disks.

The Big Hurt, words and music by Wayne Shanklin (1959). Popularized by Toni Fisher in a Signet recording.

Big Man, words and music by Glen Larson and Bruce Belland (1958). Popularized by the Four Preps in a Capitol recording.

The Big Movie Show in the Sky, words by Johnny Mercer, music by Robert Emmett Dolan (1949). A satire on small-time graft in a big-time state, introduced by Danny Scholl in the musical comedy *Texas, Li'l Darlin'* (1949).

The Big Sunflower, words and music by Bobby Newcomb (c. 1866). One of the most famous songs to come from the minstrel show. It was popularized by Billy Emerson, one of the greatest minstrels of all time, who made it his theme song. Whenever he sang it he would wear a huge sunflower in his lapel and perform a comical swagger between verses and a clog dance after the chorus.

The Bilboa Song, a German song, music by Kurt Weill, English lyrics by Johnny Mercer (1951). The Weill song, with German lyrics, appeared originally in his opera *Happy End* (1929). With the English lyrics it was popularized in America in a Columbia recording by Andy Williams.

Bill, words by P. G. Wodehouse, music by Jerome Kern (1927). Introduced by Helen Morgan in the musical play *Show Boat* (1927). She also sang it in the 1936 motion-picture adaptation of the musical (Universal), while Ava Gardner sang it in the 1951 screen version (MGM). Ida Lupino sang it in the motion-picture musical *The Man I Love* (Warner, 1947). Gogi Grant sang it on the soundtrack for Ann Blyth in the motion-picture musical *The Helen Morgan Story* (Warner, 1957).

"Bill" was an interpolation in *Show Boat.* It was written in 1918 for Vivienne Segal and the Princess Theatre production *Oh, Lady, Lady!* It was dropped from that show before opening night. Wodehouse and Kern then tried to fit it into *Sally* for Marilyn Miller. Her voice proved too small for it, and once again the song had to be discarded. When Kern first auditioned Helen Morgan for *Show Boat* he realized that his long-neglected ballad had found its interpreter; as a result "Bill" was inserted into *Show Boat,* even though the lyrics for all the other songs were the work of Oscar Hammerstein II.

Because "Bill" is the only lyric in *Show Boat* not by Hammerstein, the latter has often been erroneously identified as its author. Hammerstein made repeated attempts to set the record straight. For the 1946 revival of *Show Boat* he had a special note inserted in the program to give Wodehouse full credit. It read: "I am particularly anxious to point out that the lyric for the song 'Bill' was written by P. G. Wodehouse. Although he has always been given credit in the program, it has frequently been assumed that since I wrote all the other lyrics for *Show Boat,* I also wrote this one, and I have had praise for it which belonged to another man."

Bill Bailey, Won't You Please Come Home?, words and music by Hughie Cannon (1902). An early ragtime classic.

Bailey was a member of the vaudeville team of Bailey and Cowan, who died in Singapore in 1966. He often protested that the story about the writing of this song was fiction—the story being that locked out of his apartment by his wife one night, Bailey got the price for a hotel room from Cannon, a song-and-dance man; that Cannon assured him the wife would forgive; that this episode gave Cannon the idea for his ragtime number.

It was introduced by John Queen, a minstrel, in *Town Topics,* a show produced in Newburgh, New York. The song achieved such popularity that a deluge of Bill Bailey songs flooded the market ("I Wonder Why Bill Bailey Don't Come Home," "Since Bill Bailey Came Back Home" and so forth). The song has remained a favorite with many top-flight entertainers of a later generation, including Jimmy Durante, Ella Fitzgerald, Della Reese and Eddie Jackson. Bobby Darin's recording for Atco in 1960 was a best seller.

Bimbombey, words and music by Mack David, Hugo Peretti, and Luigi Creatore (1958). Popularized by Jimmie Rodgers in a Roulette recording.

Bingo Eli Yale, words and music by Cole Porter (1910). A football song written while Porter was still a Yale undergraduate; it is still popular in the college world.

Bird Dog, words and music by Boudleaux Bryant (1958). Popularized by the Everly Brothers in a best-selling Cadence recording.

A Bird in a Gilded Cage, one of the most successful sentimental ballads of the early 1900s, words by Arthur J. Lamb, music by Harry von Tilzer (1900). Von Tilzer agreed to write the music for Lamb's lyrics on the condition that his words made it perfectly clear that the unhappy girl in the song was the millionaire's wife, *not* his mistress. It is therefore paradoxical to learn that Harry von Tilzer first tested his song in a brothel. When he noticed the tearful reaction of some of the girls he remarked: "Now I know I have a hit, if even these ladies can weep over my song."

This was the first song by von Tilzer after he had become a partner in the publishing firm of Shapiro, Bernstein. It sold over two million copies. In 1902 von Tilzer wrote a sequel, "The Mansion of Aching Hearts," another substantial hit.

"A Bird in a Gilded Cage" was interpolated in the non-musical motion picture *Ringside Maisie,* starring Ann Sothern (MGM, 1941), and in the motion-picture musical *Coney Island* (20th Century-Fox, 1943).

The Bird on Nellie's Hat, words by Arthur J. Lamb, music by Alfred Solman (1906).

The Birth of Passion, words by Otto Hauerbach (Harbach), music by Karl Hoschna (1910). A minor-key waltz introduced by Jack Gardner and Lina Abarbanell in the operetta *Madame Sherry* (1910).

The Birth of the Blues, words by Bud De Sylva and Lew Brown, music by Ray Henderson (1926). Introduced by Harry Richman in a production number in the *George White Scandals of 1926.* This scene pointed up a battle between the blues and the classics, a compromise being reached at a climactic point with the presentation of an excerpt from Gershwin's *Rhapsody in Blue.* The song was the inspiration for a motion-picture musical, also named *The Birth of the Blues* (Paramount, 1941), for which Bing Crosby sang the number under the titles; within the movie itself the song was used for a production number as the climax to the story. The song was also heard in several later motion-picture musicals. These included *Painting the Clouds with Sunshine* Warner, 1951); *The Jazz Singer* (Warner, 1953), sung by Danny Thomas; and the screen biography of De Sylva, Brown and Henderson, *The Best Things in Life Are Free* (20th Century-Fox, 1956), sung by Gordon MacRae and danced to by Sheree North.

"The Birth of the Blues" was one of sixteen numbers selected by ASCAP in 1963 for its all-time Hit Parade during its half century of existence.

The Birth of the Blues, a motion-picture musical starring Bing Crosby and Mary Martin (Paramount, 1941). The score was made up primarily of standards.

See: The Birth of the Blues; By the Light of the Silvery Moon; Cuddle Up a Little Closer; Memphis

Blues; My Melancholy Baby; St. Louis Blues; Waiting at the Church; Wait Till the Sun Shines, Nellie.

Black and Blue (or What Did I Do to Be So Black and Blue?), words and music by Harry Brooks and Thomas "Fats" Waller (1929). Introduced in the all-Negro revue *Hot Chocolates* (1929). It became an Ethel Waters specialty, who made an outstanding recording of it for Columbia in the late 1920s.

Blackbirds of 1928, one of the most successful all-Negro revues produced on Broadway, with book and lyrics by Dorothy Fields. Music by Jimmy McHugh. Starring Bill Robinson and Adelaide Hall (1928).

See: Diga, Diga, Doo; I Can't Give You Anything But Love, Baby.

Blackbirds of 1930, an all-Negro revue, with book and lyrics by Flourney Miller and Andy Razaf. Music by Eubie Blake. Starring Ethel Waters, Buck and Bubbles and Jazzlips Richardson (1930).

See: Dinah; Memories of You; You're Lucky to Me.

Black Bottom, words by Bud De Sylva and Lew Brown, music by Ray Henderson (1926). Introduced by Ann Pennington in the *George White Scandals of 1926.* George White had helped devise the dance routine for the *Scandals* by hitting upon the effective opening steps for Miss Pennington while listening to Henderson play him the song in his apartment. The phrase "black bottom" probably referred to the muddy bottom of Suwanee River, the dance movements apparently suggesting the dragging of feet through mud. Alberta Hunter is the one officially credited with actually inventing the dance, which was copyrighted in 1926. However it was the De Sylva, Brown and Henderson song (and Ann Pennington's accompanying dance) that made the "Black Bottom" a social dance fad throughout the United States in 1926.

The song was interpolated by Sheree North in the screen biography of De Sylva, Brown and Henderson, *The Best Things in Life Are Free* (20th Century-Fox, 1956).

Black Coffee, a blues, words by Paul Francis Webster, music by Sonny Burke (1948). Introduced by Sarah Vaughan in a Musicraft recording but popularized in a best-selling recording by Ella Fitzgerald for Verve. Peggy Lee also recorded it successfully for Capitol.

The Black Crook, a musical extravaganza often singled out as America's first musical comedy, with book and lyrics by Charles M. Barras. Music (mainly adaptations) by Giuseppe Operti (1866).

See: You Naughty, Naughty Men.

The Blacksmith Blues, words and music by Jack Holmes (1952). Published originally in 1950 under the title "Happy Payoff Days." It was reissued under its definitive title in 1952 when it was popularized by Ella Mae Morse in a recording for Capitol.

Blame It on the Bossa Nova, words and music by Cynthia Weil and Barry Mann (1962). A lament about the effects of the bossa nova dance craze in 1962, popularized in 1963 in a best-selling recording for Columbia by Eydie Gormé.

Bland, James A., composer and lyricist, born Flushing, New York, 1854; died Philadelphia, Pennsylvania, 1911.

See: Carry Me Back to Old Virginny; De Golden Wedding; In the Evening by the Moonlight; In the Morning by the Bright Light; Oh, Dem Golden Slippers.

Blane, Ralph, composer and lyricist, born Broken Arrow, Oklahoma, 1914.

See (In collaboration with Hugh Martin): Boy Next Door; Buckle Down, Winsocki; Have Yourself a Merry Little Christmas; Love; Pass that Peace Pipe; The Trolley Song.

See also: My Dream Is Yours; The Stanley Steamer.

Bless 'Em All, an English popular song with words and music by Jimmie Hughes and Frank Lee, new American lyrics by Al Stillman (1941). It was introduced in the United States by the Jesters in a Decca recording and interpolated in two non-musical motion pictures in 1941 and 1942, *Marine Raiders* and *Captains of the Clouds.* It was successfully revived in the early 1950s, interpolated in the motion picture *Chain Lightning,* starring Humphrey Bogart and Eleanor Powell (Warner, 1950). In the non-musical motion picture *Betrayed,* starring Clark Gable and Lana Turner (MGM, 1954), it was used in the background music as a recurrent theme and whistled by a chorus in the final scene. The song was successfully recorded by Jane Morgan for Kapp.

Bloomer Girl, a musical comedy with book by Sig Herzig and Fred Saidy, based on an unproduced play by Dan James and Lility. Lyrics by E. Y. Harburg, Music by Harold Arlen. Starring Celeste Holm and Joan McCracken (1944). Original cast recording (Decca).

See: The Eagle and Me; Evelina; I Got a Song; Right as Rain; T'morra', T'morra'.

Blossom, Henry, lyricist, born St. Louis, Missouri, 1866; died New York City, 1919.

See: Herbert, Victor.

See also: Ain't It Funny What a Difference Just a Few Hours Make?

Blossom Time, an operetta based on the life of Franz Schubert, with book and lyrics by Dorothy Donnelly adapted from a German operetta *Das Dreimaederlhaus.* Music by Sigmund Romberg based on melodies by Franz Schubert. Starring Bertram Peacock as Schubert, with Olga Cook (1921).

See: Song of Love; Tell Me Daisy.

Blow, Gabriel, Blow, words and music by Cole Porter (1934). Introduced by Ethel Merman in the musical *Anything Goes* (1934). Miss Merman repeated her performance in the 1936 motion-picture adaptation of the musical (Paramount), while Mitzi Gaynor sang it in the 1956 motion-picture version (Paramount).

Blowin' in the Wind, words and music by Bob Dylan (1962). A popular song in the style of a folk ballad devoted to the problem of civil rights and integration. Though introduced and first popularized by Bob Dylan, it achieved its greatest success through a Warner recording by Peter, Paul and Mary, which received "Grammy" Awards from the National Academy of Recording Arts and Sciences in 1964 for the best performance by a vocal group and also as the best folk recording.

Blow Out the Candle, words and music by Phil Moore (1952). Popularized by Jane Wyman in a Decca recording. This is one of the songs with which Dorothy Dandridge first won night-club fame at La Vie en Rose in New York.

Blow the Smoke Away, words by Will M. Hough and Frank R. Adams, music by Joe E. Howard (1906). Introduced in Chicago in the musical *The Time, The Place and The Girl* (1907).

Blue Again, words by Dorothy Fields, music by Jimmy McHugh (1930). Introduced by Evelyn Hoey in the musical *The Vanderbilt Revue* (1930), but popularized by Guy Lombardo and the Royal Canadians.

The Blue and the Gray (or, A Mother's Gift to Her Country), words and music by Paul Dresser (1900). A ballad inspired by the Civil War.

Blue Bell, words by Edward Madden, music by Theodore F. Morse (1904). A hit song of the early 1900s popularized in vaudeville. It was revived a generation later in the motion-picture musical *The Jolson Story* (Columbia, 1946).

Blueberry Hill, words and music by Al Lewis, Larry Stock and Vincent Rose (1940). It was sung by Gene Autry in the motion picture *The Singing Hill* (Republic, 1941) and was first popularized by Glenn Miller and his orchestra (vocal by Ray Eberle) in a Bluebird recording. The song, however, became even more popular in 1957 through an Imperial recording by "Fats" Domino that sold a million disks. The song has also become a Louis Armstrong specialty.

Blue Bird of Happiness, words by Edward Heyman, music by Sandor Harmati (1934). Introduced by Jan Peerce in a stage production at the Radio City Music Hall in 1934.

Blue Hawaii, words by Leo Robin, music by Ralph Rainger (1937). Introduced by Bing Crosby in the motion-picture musical *Waikiki Wedding* (Paramount, 1937).

Blue Heaven (or, The Desert Song),
words by Otto Harbach and Oscar
Hammerstein II, music by Sigmund
Romberg (1926). Introduced by Vivienne Segal and Robert Halliday in
the operetta *The Desert Song* (1926).
In the 1929 motion-picture adaptation of the musical (Warner), it
was sung by John Boles and Carlotta
King; in the 1943 screen adaptation
(Warner), by Dennis Morgan and
Irene Manning; and in 1953 (Warner), by Gordon MacRae and Kathryn Grayson.

Blue Is the Night, words and music by
Fred Fisher (1930). Introduced in
the motion picture *Their Own Desire* (MGM, 1930).

The Blue Juniata, words and music by
Marion Dix Sullivan (1844). A ballad inspired by a river in Pennsylvania.

Blue Mirage (Don't Go), a German
popular song ("Fata Morgana"), music by Lotar Olias, English lyrics by
Sam Coslow (1955). Introduced in
the United States as an instrumental by Guy Lombardo and his Royal
Canadians in a Decca recording.

Blue Monday, words and music by
Antoine "Fats" Domino and Dave
Bartholomew (1957). Introduced by
"Fats" Domino in the motion-picture
musical *The Girl Can't Help It* (20th
Century-Fox, 1956), and popularized
by his best-selling recording for Im-
perial.

Blue Moon, words by Lorenz Hart, music by Richard Rodgers (1934). The
only Rodgers and Hart song to become a hit without first being introduced in a stage or screen musical.
It was first called "The Prayer," intended for a motion picture starring
Jean Harlow. Discarded from that
production, it was rewritten as "The
Bad in Every Man" and sung by
Shirley Ross in the non-musical motion picture *Manhattan Melodrama,*
starring William Powell, Myrna Loy
and Clark Gable (MGM, 1934). After
that it was subjected to a third revision and provided with the new
and now definitive title of "Blue
Moon." As such it was published by
Robbins as an independent number.
It achieved the largest sheet-music

sale of any Rodgers and Hart song
up to that time. The song was then
interpolated in several motion pictures. Among them were the Rodgers
and Hart screen biography *Words
and Music* (MGM, 1948); *Malaya,*
starring Spencer Tracy and James
Stewart (MGM, 1949), where it was
sung by Valentina Cortesa; *East
Side, West Side,* starring Barbara
Stanwyck and Ava Gardner (MGM,
1950); Jane Froman's screen biography *With a Song in My Heart*
(20th Century-Fox, 1952), sung on
the soundtrack by Miss Froman;
Rogue Cop, starring Robert Taylor
(MGM, 1954), where it was heard
as a piano interlude; and the Italian
motion picture directed by Federico
Fellini, *8½* (1963). In 1961 the song
achieved a million-disk sale through
Elvis Presley's recording for RCA
Victor. The Colpix recording by the
Marcels that year was also successful.

The Blue Paradise, an operetta with
book by Edgar Smith based on a
Viennese operetta by Leon Stein
and Bela Jensbach. Lyrics by Herbert Reynolds. Music by Sigmund
Romberg. This was Romberg's first
successful operetta. Starring Vivienne Segal (in her Broadway debut),
with Cecil Lean and Cleo Mayfield
(1915).
See: Auf Wiedersehen.

The Blue Room, words by Lorenz Hart,
music by Richard Rodgers (1926).
Introduced by Eva Puck and Sam
White in the musical comedy *The
Girl Friend* (1926). The song proved
so popular that it made a huge box-
office success of *The Girl Friend,*
which had started off rather badly.
The song was interpolated in the
screen biography of Rodgers and
Hart, *Words and Music* (MGM,
1948), and in the non-musical motion picture *Onionhead,* starring
Andy Griffith (Warner, 1958).

The Blues I Love to Sing, words by
Bob Miley, music by Duke Ellington
(1927). Ellington's first song hit.

Blues in the Night, words by Johnny
Mercer, music by Harold Arlen
(1941). Mercer and Arlen had originally written this number for a

motion picture to be called *Hot Nocturne*. This production had a jail scene, and in one of the cells a Negro was singing the blues. Arlen set out to write a blues that not only fit the scene, but the performer as well—William Gillespie. The finished song proved so effective that the producers decided to change the title of their picture to that of the Mercer-Arlen number (Warner, (1941).

The song was a hit even before the motion picture was released, with Jimmy Lunceford making a best-selling recording in which the song was given in two contrasting styles. Jerome Kern felt so strongly that this song deserved the Academy Award (which had gone that year to Kern himself for "The Last Time I Saw Paris") that he went to work to get the Academy bylaws changed. After 1941, therefore, only songs written specifically for the screen were eligible—a ruling that would have eliminated "The Last Time I Saw Paris" from Academy competition in 1941.

"Blues in the Night" was interpolated in the Broadway revue *Star and Garter* (1942), and was sung by John Garfield in the motion picture *Thank Your Lucky Stars* (Warner, 1943).

Blue Skies, words and music by Irving Berlin (1927). Introduced by Belle Baker in the musical *Betsy* (1926), where it was an interpolation. Al Jolson sang it in *The Jazz Singer* (Warner, 1928), and it was interpolated in the motion-picture musical *Glorifying the American Girl* (Paramount, 1929). It provided the title for a motion-picture musical (MGM, 1946), in which it was sung by Bing Crosby. The song was also featured in the motion-picture musical *White Christmas* (Paramount, 1954).

Blue Skies, a motion-picture musical starring Bing Crosby and Fred Astaire (MGM, 1946). All the songs were by Irving Berlin, most of them standards, but some new. Original cast recording (Decca).

See: All by Myself; Blue Skies; A

Couple of Song and Dance Men; Everybody Step; Heat Wave; How Deep Is the Ocean?; I'll See You in C-U-B-A; I've Got My Captain Working for Me Now; Not for All the Rice in China; Puttin' on the Ritz; Russian Lullaby; This Is the Army, Mr. Jones; You Keep Coming Back Like a Song; White Christmas.

Blue Star, words by Edward Heyman, music by Victor Young (1955). Theme song of the television series *Medic*, introduced over TV in 1955, then popularized in a Capitol recording by Les Baxter and his orchestra.

Blue Suede Shoes, words and music by Carl Lee Perkins (1956). It was first popularized by Carl Perkins in a Sun recording. It was then interpolated for Elvis Presley in the motion picture *G. I. Blues* (Paramount, 1956). Presley's RCA Victor recording sold over a million disks.

Blue Tail Fly (or, Jim Crack Corn), words and music by Dan Emmett (1846). A classic of the minstrel shows, said to have been one of President Lincoln's song favorites. It was revived in the Broadway musical *Sing Out, Sweet Land* (1944).

Blue Tango, an instrumental composition by Leroy Anderson, with added lyrics by Mitchell Parish (1952). Anderson's instrumental version was the first of its kind ever to achieve first place on the Hit Parade, where it was represented fifteen weeks, seven times in the Number One spot. For almost a year it was also a leading favorite on juke boxes throughout the country. Its sale of over two million disks in several different recordings represents one of the composer's greatest recording successes; one of the best-selling of these releases was by Leroy Anderson and his orchestra for Decca.

Blue Velvet, words and music by Bernie Wayne and Lee Morris (1951). Popularized by Tony Bennett, and revived in 1963 by Bobby Vinton in an Epic recording.

B.M.I. *See:* Broadcast Music Incorporated.

De Boatman's Dance, words and music by Dan Emmett (1843). Introduced at the Bowery Amphitheater in New York on February 6, 1843, by the Virginia Minstrels, of which Dan Emmett was a member. The program then described it as "a much admired song in imitation of the Ohio Boatman." The song was often used after that in minstrel shows for lively scenes in which minstrels impersonated Negro boatmen on the Ohio River.

Bobby Socks to Stockings, words and music by Russell Faith, Clarence Wey Kehner and R. di Ciccio (1959). Popularized by Frankie Avalon in a Chancellor recording.

Bob White (Watcha Gonna Swing To-night?), words by Johnny Mercer, music by Bernard Hanighen (1937). Popularized in a Decca recording by Bing Crosby and Connee Boswell.

Bock, Jerry, composer, born New Haven, Connecticut, 1928.

See (Lyrics by Sheldon Harnick): Artificial Flowers; Dear Friend; Far From the Home I Love; Fiddler on the Roof; Grand Knowing You; Ice Cream; Little Tin Box; Matchmaker, Matchmaker; Politics and Poker; She Loves Me; Sunrise, Sunset; Till Tomorrow; To Life.

See also: Mr. Wonderful; Too Close for Comfort.

Body and Soul, words by Edward Heyman, Robert Sour and Frank Eyton, music by John Green (1930). It was a European hit before it became successful in the United States. Green had written it as special material for Gertrude Lawrence; he was her piano accompanist at that time. She took the unpublished manuscript to England where she sang it over BBC. The broadcast was heard by Bert Ambrose, then one of London's most popular bandleaders, who played it and made it a hit; he also recorded it in England. Max Gordon, a Broadway producer, then secured the American rights to the song for his revue *Three's a Crowd* (1930), in which it was sung by Libby Holman and danced to by Clifton Webb and Tamara Geva. Since then the song has become a standard. It has been interpolated in several motion pictures. Ida Lu-

pino sang it in *The Man I Love* (Warner, 1946); it served as the theme melody for a non-musical motion picture starring John Garfield, also named *Body and Soul* (MGM, 1947); and it was played on the soundtrack by Carmen Cavallero for the motion-picture musical *The Eddie Duchin Story* (Columbia, 1956).

Bojangles of Harlem, words by Dorothy Fields, music by Jerome Kern (1936). Introduced by Fred Astaire in the motion-picture musical *Swing Time* (RKO, 1936).

Boll Weevil, words and music by Antoine "Fats" Domino and Dave Bartholomew (1956). Popularized by "Fats" Domino's recording for Imperial.

Bombo, a musical extravaganza with book and lyrics by Harold Atteridge. Additional lyrics by Bud De Sylva. Music by Sigmund Romberg, with various interpolations of songs by other composers and lyricists. Starring Al Jolson (1921).

See: April Showers; California, Here I Come; I'm Goin' South; Toot, Toot, Tootsie; Yoo Hoo.

Bonanza, words and music by Jay Livingston and Ray Evans (1959). Theme song from the TV series *Bonanza*.

Bon Bon Buddy, words by Alex Rogers, music by Will Marion Cook (1907). Popularized in vaudeville by the Negro team of Williams (Bert Williams) and Walker.

Bond, Carrie Jacobs, composer and lyricist, born Janesville, Wisconsin, 1862; died Hollywood, California, 1946.

See: I Love You Truly; Just A-Wearyin' for You; A Perfect Day.

Bongo, Bongo, Bongo. *See:* Civilization.

The Bonja Song, an instrumental composition published anonymously (1818), to which lyrics were subsequently added by R. C. Dallas. It is with this number that the banjo is believed to have first become popular as an accompanying instrument for Negro songs.

Bonne Nuit, Good Night, words and music by Jay Livingston and Ray Evans (1951). Introduced by Bing

Crosby in the motion-picture musical *Here Comes the Groom* (Paramount, 1951).

The Bonnie Blue Flag, words by Annie Chambers-Ketchum, music by Henry Macarthy (1862). A song favorite of the Confederate states during the Civil War. The lyrics traced the events leading to secession; the melody was based on an old popular Irish tune, "The Jaunting Car." The song was introduced in New Orleans in 1861 by Henry Macarthy, then adopted by the Confederate soldiers throughout the Southland as their favorite war song.

Boo Hoo, words by Edward Heyman, music by Carmen Lombardo and John Jacob Loeb (1937). Several years before he helped to write "Boo Hoo," Carmen Lombardo had completed a kind of stein song called "Let's Drink." He played the tune one day to John Jacob Loeb, a young songwriter, who suggested bringing in Eddie Heyman for some new lyrics. Heyman complied with "Boo Hoo" and Loeb helped Lombardo rewrite the melody. "Boo Hoo" was introduced in 1936 by Guy Lombardo and his Royal Canadians, who made it so popular that it achieved a place on the Hit Parade for seventeen weeks. The song was interpolated in the non-musical motion picture *Dead End,* starring Humphrey Bogart and Joel McCrea (Samuel Goldwyn, 1937).

Born to Dance, a motion-picture musical starring Eleanor Powell and James Stewart (MGM, 1936). Lyrics and music by Cole Porter.

See: Easy to Love; I've Got You Under My Skin.

Born Too Late, words by Fred Tobias, music by Charles Strouse (1958). Popularized by the Poni Tails in an ABC Paramount recording.

Botch A Me, an Italian popular song ("Ba-Ba-Baciama Picina"), by R. Morbelli and L. Astore, introduced in the Italian motion picture *Una Famiglia Impossible.* English lyrics and American adaptation by Eddie Y. Stanley (1952). The American song was popularized by Rosemary Clooney in a Columbia recording.

The Boulevard of Broken Dreams, words by Al Dubin, music by Harry Warren (1933). Introduced by Constance Bennett in the motion picture *Moulin Rouge* (United Artists, 1934). It was revived by Tony Bennett in a successful Columbia recording.

Bouquet of Roses, words by Steve Nelson, music by Bob Hilliard (1948). Popularized by Eddy Arnold in an RCA Victor recording.

Boutonniere, words by Bob Hilliard, music by Dave Mann (1950). Popularized in 1951 by Mindy Carson in a Columbia recording.

The Bowery, words by Charles H. Hoyt, music by Percy Gaunt (1892). Introduced by Harry Conor in the musical extravaganza *A Trip to Chinatown* (1892). In presenting this number, Conor impersonated a rube from the sticks who finds himself on the Bowery surrounded by drunks and thieves.

The song was not part of the score of *A Trip to Chinatown* when that extravaganza first opened. With business slow at the box office, Gaunt decided to interpolate "The Bowery" in the production, even though it had no possible relevance in a play with a San Francisco setting. After Conor had gone through the six verses and choruses of the song, the audience erupted into such a storm of approbation that he had to begin from the beginning and do it all over again.

"The Bowery" helped stimulate business for *A Trip to Chinatown,* which in time achieved what was then a record run of 650 performances. "The Bowery" was also one of the first songs from any American stage production to prove a best seller in sheet-music sales, selling several hundred thousand copies.

The Boy Next Door, words and music by Ralph Blane and Hugh Martin (1944). Introduced by Judy Garland in the motion-picture musical *Meet Me in St. Louis* (MGM, 1944).

The Boys from Syracuse, a musical comedy with book by George Abbott based on Shakespeare's *A Comedy of Errors.* Lyrics by Lorenz Hart. Music by Richard Rodgers. Starring Jimmy Savo and Teddy Hart (1938).

The motion-picture adaptation of the musical comedy starred Joe Penner, Allan Jones and Martha Raye (Universal, 1940). It used six of the principal songs from the stage score.

See: Falling in Love with Love; Sing for Your Supper; This Can't Be Love.

Boy, What Love Has Done to Me, words by Ira Gershwin, music by George Gershwin (1931). Introduced by Ethel Merman (in her Broadway debut) in the musical *Girl Crazy* (1931).

A Boy Without a Girl, words and music by Sid Jacobson and Ruth Sexter (1959). Popularized by Frankie Avalon in a Chancellor recording.

Braham, David, composer, born London, England, 1838; died New York City, 1905.

See (Lyrics by Edward Harrigan): The Babies on Our Block; Danny by My Side; I Never Drink Behind the Bar; The Last of the Hogans; Locked Out After Nine; Maggie Murphy's Home; The Mulligan Braves; The Mulligan Guard; My Dad's Dinner Pail; Paddy Duffy's Cart; Poverty's Tears Ebb and Flow; The Skidmore Fancy Ball; The Skidmore Guard; The Skidmore Masquerade; Sweet Mary Ann.

Branigan's Band, words by Charles A. Burke, music by W. F. Wellman, Jr. (1877). A popular marching song made famous at Wood's Museum in New York by Lydia Thompson, star of the Lydia Thompson British Blondes.

Brazil, a Brazilian samba ("Aquarelo do Brasil"), music by Ary Barroso, English lyrics by Bob Russell (1939). The song, with English words, was interpolated in several motion pictures. These included the Walt Disney full-length animated production *Saludos Amigos* (RKO, 1942); *The Gang's All Here,* starring Alice Faye and Carmen Miranda (20th Century-Fox, 1943); *Jam Session* (Columbia, 1944); *Brazil,* starring Tito Gui-

zar (Republic, 1944); and *The Eddie Duchin Story* (Columbia, 1956).

Breaking in a Brand New Heart, words by Jack Keller, music by Howard Greenfield (1961). Introduced and popularized by Connie Francis in an MGM recording.

Break the News to Mother, words and music by Charles K. Harris (1897). The idea for this sentimental ballad came to the composer while he was witnessing *Secret Service,* the famous stage melodrama starring William Gillette. In one of its most poignant scenes, a wounded drummer boy in the Confederate army whispers to the Negro butler at his plantation, "Break the news to Mother." The day after he had seen this play, Harris completed the first verse and chorus of his ballad. "Try as I might," he later recalled, "I could not think of a second verse or a climax for the song. How to end the song with a punch puzzled me. While in a barber's chair a thought came to my mind in a flash and I cried out, 'I have it! I'm going to kill him!' The barber who was shaving me at the time became very much startled when he heard this remark and thought I had lost my reason. . . . I was in a hurry to leave, and in less than two minutes was out of the chair, much to the relief of the barber. I had the last verse."

When Harris first sang his ballad to his brother, the latter insisted it could not possibly be a success. "There has been no war since 1865," Harris' brother reminded him, "and memories of that conflict are fast fading away. Another war is a long way off. So why in heaven's name have you written a war song?"

Realizing the validity of this argument, Harris put his song aside. One day, when Paul Dresser visited Milwaukee, and heard Harris sing this ballad to him, he said, "Charles, you have a big hit there, as big as my own 'Wabash.'"

The Spanish-American War gave Harris the timeliness the ballad needed. Harris reissued it, and it became a sensational success, a favorite with soldiers on the field of battle and with civilians at home. When first sung to a regiment about to leave for the front, "Break the News to Mother" made such a deep impression that many soldiers broke down and wept. Another and livelier tune had to be substituted hastily.

The ballad was interpolated in the motion-picture musical *Wait Till the Sun Shines, Nellie* (20th Century-Fox, 1952).

Breathless, words and music by Otis Blackwell (1958). Popularized by Jerry Lee Lewis in a Sun recording.

Breeze (Blow My Baby Back to Me), words by Ballard MacDonald and Joe Goodwin, music by James F. Hanley (1949).

The Breeze and I, an American popular-song adaptation of Ernesto Lecuona's "Andalucia" by T. Camerata, with lyrics by Al Stillman (1940). Popularized in 1940 in a best-selling recording by Jimmy Dorsey and his orchestra for Decca. It was interpolated in several motion pictures, including *Cuban Pete,* starring Desi Arnaz (Universal, 1946), and *On the Riviera* (20th Century-Fox, 1951).

Breezin' Along with the Breeze, words and music by Haven Gillespie, Seymour Simons and Richard A. Whiting (1926). Popularized by Al Jolson. It was interpolated in the motion-picture musical biography of Nora Bayes, *Shine On, Harvest Moon,* starring Ann Sheridan and Dennis Morgan (Warner, 1944). Danny Thomas sang it in the motion-picture musical *The Jazz Singer* (Warner, 1953). It was also heard in the motion-picture musical *The Helen Morgan Story* (Warner, 1957), sung on the soundtrack by Gogi Grant (for Ann Blyth).

Brennan, J. Keirn, lyricist, born San Francisco, California, 1873; died Hollywood, California, 1948.
See: Ball, Ernest R.

The Bridge of Sighs, words by Thomas Hood, music adapted by Edward L. White (1846). One of the most famous numbers in the repertory of the Hutchinson Singing Family.

The Bridge of Sighs, words and music by James Thornton (1900). One of its composer's most celebrated sentimental ballads.

Bridget, words and music by Cole Porter (1910). Cole Porter's first published song.

Brigadoon, a musical play with book and lyrics by Alan Jay Lerner. Music by Frederick Loewe. Starring David Brooks, George Keane and Marion Bell (1947). Original cast recording (RCA Victor).

The motion-picture adaptation starred Gene Kelly, Van Johnson and Cyd Charisse (MGM, 1954). The most significant songs from the stage score were used. John Gustafson sang on the soundtrack for Jimmy Thompson. Soundtrack recording (MGM).

See: Almost Like Being in Love; Come to Me, Bend to Me; From This Day On; The Heather on the Hill; I'll Go Home with Bonnie Jean; Love of My Life; There But for You Go I; Waitin' for My Dearie.

Bring Back My Blushing Rose, words by Gene Buck, music by Rudolf Friml (1921). Introduced by Mary Eaton in a production number in the *Ziegfeld Follies of 1921.*

Bring Back My Bonnie to Me, words and music credited to Charles E. Pratt, using the pen names of J. T. Woods for the lyrics and H. J. Fuller for the melody (1882). The song was based on "My Bonnie," which appeared in William H. Hills' *Student Songs* (1881), without identifying the author. The demand for this song led Pratt to adapt it and reissue it as his own composition.

Bring Back My Daddy to Me, words by William Tracey and Howard Johnson, music by George W. Meyer (1917). This ballad became popular during World War I just as the draft was beginning to convert American civilians into soldiers.

Bring Back My Golden Dreams, words by Alfred Bryan, music by George W. Meyer (1911).

Bring Back Those Minstrel Days, words by Ballard MacDonald, music by

Martin Broones (1926). A nostalgic recollection of old-time minstrel shows, introduced in the musical *LeMaire's Affairs* (1926).

Broadcast Music Incorporated (BMI), a rival organization to ASCAP (the American Society of Composers, Authors and Publishers), for the protection of the financial interests of composers, lyricists and music publishers.

BMI came into existence in 1940 during a bitter struggle between radio networks and ASCAP over license fees. When, in 1940, the radio networks refused to meet the demands made by ASCAP during negotiations for a new five-year contract, demands which the networks regarded as outrageous, ASCAP withdrew the music of all its affiliated members from the airwaves. This boycott lasted about a year. In the fall of 1941 a compromise was finally reached whereby ASCAP and the radio networks signed a new five-year contract (renewable at its expiration for an additional five years) for an annual fee far below that which ASCAP had originally demanded.

Thus made forcefully aware of the way in which ASCAP could control the programs of all radio broadcasts, the networks had meanwhile formed Broadcast Music Incorporated (BMI) to produce music of its own for radio broadcasting. It set out to acquire "performing rights from independent writers and publishers," as it explained in one of its first brochures, and to collect "license fees from the organizations which perform music for profit." It further explained that "except for operating expenses and a reasonable reserve, BMI pays all of the money it collects to the composers and publishers whose music is performed," determining the payments "on the basis of the performance of music on thousands of independent stations as well as on countrywide networks."

BMI was officially launched in 1940, with Neville Miller as president; Sydney M. Kaye, first vice-president; M. E. Tompkins, vice-president and secretary; and Charles Lawrence, treasurer. In its first year of operation it had several hundred affiliates to whom it distributed in excess of half a million dollars from its income of $1,500,000 from license fees. The organization grew by leaps and bounds, as more and more lyricists, composers and publishers—some of them newcomers—were drawn into its orbit. Less than a quarter of a century after its founding, BMI could boast that more than eight thousand writers and six thousand publishers were affiliated with it; that it had twenty thousand licensees in the United States and Canada; that it distributed about ten million dollars a year in performance payments.

In its initial year BMI authors and publishers produced a number of hit songs, among which were "The Breeze and I," "I Hear a Rhapsody," "You Are My Sunshine" and "It's a Big, Wonderful World."

The following are some of the hit songs by BMI lyricists, composers and publishers since 1940: The Ballad of Davy Crockett; Brazil; Canadian Sunset; Come On a-My House; Don't Be Cruel; Eighteen Yellow Roses; Hound Dog; I Don't Want to Set the World on Fire; Never on Sunday; Paper Doll; Pistol Packin' Mama; Rag Mop; Ricochet; Sixteen Tons; Tennessee Waltz; Tico Tico; Why Do Fools Fall in Love?; Young at Heart; Your Cheating Heart.

Broadway Melody, words by Arthur Freed, music by Nacio Herb Brown (1929). Title song of the motion-picture musical (MGM, 1929), introduced by Charles King. It was used for a production number, sung by Gene Kelly, in the motion-picture musical *Singin' in the Rain* (MGM, 1952).

Broadway Melody, the first successful talking and singing musical (MGM, 1929), and the first musical to win the Academy Award as the best motion picture of the year. Starring Charles King, Bessie Love and Anita

Page. Songs by Arthur Freed and Nacio Herb Brown, with an interpolation of George M. Cohan's "Give My Regards to Broadway."

See: Broadway Melody; Give My Regards to Broadway; You Were Meant for Me; The Wedding of the Painted Doll.

Broadway Melody of 1936, a motion-picture musical starring Jack Benny, Eleanor Powell and Robert Taylor (MGM, 1935). Songs by Arthur Freed and Nacio Herb Brown.

See: Broadway Rhythm; My Lucky Star.

Broadway Melody of 1940, a motion-picture musical starring Fred Astaire and Eleanor Powell (MGM, 1939). Songs by Cole Porter, old and new.

See: Begin the Beguine; I Concentrate on You; I've Got My Eyes on You.

Broadway Rhythm, words by Arthur Freed, music by Nacio Herb Brown (1935). Introduced by Eleanor Powell in the motion-picture musical *Broadway Melody of 1936* (MGM, 1935).

Broadway Rhythm (screen musical). *See: Very Warm for May.*

Broken Hearted, words by Bud De Sylva and Lew Brown, music by Ray Henderson (1927). Published as an independent number, then popularized in vaudeville by Belle Baker. It was used as a recurrent theme in the non-musical motion picture *Roxie Hart,* starring Ginger Rogers (20th Century-Fox, 1943). About thirty years after its publication it was revived by Johnnie Ray in a successful recording for Columbia. In the motion-picture biography of De Sylva, Brown and Henderson— *The Best Things in Life Are Free* (20th Century-Fox, 1956)—it was sung by Gordon MacRae and Ernest Borgnine.

Broken Hearted Melody, words by Hal David, music by Sherman Edwards (1959). Popularized by Sarah Vaughan's Mercury recording that sold a million disks.

The Broken Record, words and music by Cliff Friend, Charles Tobias and Boyd Bunch (1935).

Brooks, Jack, composer and lyricist, born Liverpool, England, 1912.

See: Am I in Love?; Innamorata; Ole Buttermilk Sky; That's Amore; You Ain't Talking to Me; You Wonderful You.

Brooks, Shelton, composer and lyricist, born Amesburg, Ontario, Canada, 1886.

See: Darktown Strutters' Ball; Honey Gal; Some of These Days; There'll Come a Time; You Ain't Talkin' to Me.

Brother, Can You Spare a Dime?, words by E. Y. Harburg, music by Jay Gorney (1930). Introduced by Rex Weber and a male chorus in the revue *Americana* (1932). It became an unofficial theme song of the depression years. It was interpolated in the non-musical motion picture *Embarrassing Moments,* starring Chester Morris (Universal, 1934).

Brotherhood of Man, words and music by Frank Loesser (1961). A satirical paean to universal brotherhood, introduced by Robert Morse, Rudy Vallée, Charles Nelson Reilly and Paul Reed in the musical *How to Succeed in Business Without Really Trying* (1961).

Brown, Lew, lyricist, born Odessa, Russia, 1893; died New York City, 1958.

See: Akst, Harry; Henderson, Ray; Stept, Sam H.; Von Tilzer, Albert.

See also: Baby, Take a Bow; Beer Barrel Polka; I'd Climb the Highest Mountain; Last Night on the Back Porch; Oh, Ma-Ma; Seven or Eleven; Shine; That Old Feeling; Then I'll Be Happy.

For the screen biography of De Sylva, Brown and Henderson, see *The Best Things in Life Are Free.*

Brown, Nacio Herb, composer, born Deming, New Mexico, 1896; died San Francisco, California, 1964.

See (Lyrics by Arthur Freed): After Sundown; All I Do Is Dream of You; Alone; Broadway Melody; Broadway Rhythm; The Chant of the Jungle; Good Morning; I've Got a Feeling You're Fooling; Love Songs of the Nile; The Moon Is Low; My Lucky Star; A New Moon Over My Shoulder; The Pagan Love Song; Should I?; Singin' in the Rain; The

Wedding of the Painted Doll; We'll Make Hay While the Sun Shines; When Buddha Smiles; The Woman in the Shoe; Would You?; You Were Meant for Me.

See also: Eadie Was a Lady; Paradise; Turn Out the Light; You're an Old Smoothie; You Stepped Out of a Dream.

Brown Eyes, Why Are You Blue?, words by Alfred Bryan, music by George W. Meyer (1925).

Brown October Ale, words by Harry B. Smith, music by Reginald de Koven (1890). A drinking song introduced by W. H. MacDonald in the operetta *Robin Hood* (1890).

Brush Up Your Shakespeare, words and music by Cole Porter (1948). Comedy number about the efficacy of being familiar with Shakespeare, introduced by Harry Clark and Jack Diamond in the musical play *Kiss Me, Kate* (1948). In the motion-picture adaptation of the musical (MGM, 1953), it was sung by Keenan Wynn and James Whitmore.

Bryan, Alfred, lyricist, born Brantford, Ontario, 1871; died Morristown, New Jersey, 1948.

See: Fisher, Fred; Meyer, George W.

See also: The Country Cousin; I Didn't Raise My Boy to Be a Soldier; Ireland Must Be Heaven; I Was So Young; Joan of Arc; Oui, Oui, Marie; When the Bees Are in the Hive; Winter.

The Bubble, words by Otto Hauerbach (Harbach), music by Rudolf Friml (1913). Introduced by Emile Lea, Burrell Barbaretto and Mana Zucca in the musical *High Jinks* (1913).

Buck, Gene, lyricist, born Detroit, Michigan, 1885; died Manhasset, Long Island, 1957.

See: Hirsch, Louis A.; Stamper, Dave.

See also: Bring Back My Blushing Rose; The Love Boat.

Buckle Down, Winsocki, words and music by Ralph Blane and Hugh Martin (1941). A semi-satirical football song introduced by Tommy Dix, Stuart Langley and chorus in the musical *Best Foot Forward* (1941). It was heard in the motion-picture

adaptation of the musical (MGM, 1943), and was interpolated in the non-musical motion picture *The Guy Who Came Back,* starring Paul Douglas and Linda Darnell (20th Century-Fox, 1951).

Buffalo Gals. *See:* Lubly Fan.

Bull Dog, a Yale football song, with words and music by Cole Porter (1911). Porter wrote it while attending Yale as an undergraduate. It was reprinted in the *New Yale Song Book* (1918). It was sung by a chorus in Cole Porter's screen biography *Night and Day* (Warner, 1946).

The Bully Song (or, The New Bully), words and music by Charles E. Trevathan (1896). Introduced by May Irwin in the musical *The Widow Jones* (1895). She created a sensation with it and forthwith established herself as one of the leading exponents of the "coon shout," besides becoming identified as "the stage mother of ragtime." Describing her performance, a writer for the New York *Sun* remarked in the mid-1890s: "Miss Irwin starts the song, her admirable dialect and spirit creating immediately the atmosphere that is needed to make it a success." May Irwin told a reporter in 1897: "I think any success that I may have had with this song is the result of intuition rather than anything else."

Though the sheet music credited Trevathan as the creator of both the music and the lyrics, there is serious doubt whether he actually wrote the song. Trevathan himself conceded that he had heard Mama Lou sing it at Babe Connors' place in St. Louis. Then, while en route from St. Louis to Chicago, Trevathan kept playing the tune on his guitar. May Irwin, who was a fellow passenger on that train, "heard me," as Trevathan later told an interviewer, "and asked me what the name of it was. I didn't know, and when she wanted to hear the words as I had heard them at Connors' joint, I pointed out that they weren't fit for the ears of a lady." Nevertheless she insisted on hearing it, then was so taken with it that she had him write it down for her—which he did with improvised and expurgated lyrics.

Burke, Johnny, lyricist, born Antioch, California, 1908; died New York City, 1964.

See: Johnston, Arthur; Monaco, James V.; Van Heusen, James.

See also: Annie Doesn't Live Here Anymore; Misty; Scatterbrain; Wild Horses.

Burke, Joseph A., composer, born Philadelphia, Pennsylvania, 1884; died Upper Darby, Pennsylvania, 1950.

See (Lyrics by Benny Davis): Carolina Moon; Oh, How I Miss You Tonight; Yearning, Just for You.

See (Lyrics by Al Dubin): Dancing with Tears in My Eyes; For You; The Kiss Waltz; Painting the Clouds with Sunshine; Tip Toe Through the Tulips.

See (Lyrics by Edgar Leslie): A Little Bit Independent; Moon Over Miami.

See also: In the Valley of the Moon; Rambling Rose.

A Bushel and a Peck, words and music by Frank Loesser (1950). Introduced by Vivian Blaine in a nightclub scene in the musical *Guys and Dolls* (1950). She repeated her performance in the motion-picture adaptation of the musical (MGM, 1955).

But Beautiful, words by Johnny Burke, music by James Van Heusen (1947). Introduced by Bing Crosby in the motion-picture musical *The Road to Rio* (Paramount, 1947).

But in the Morning, words and music by Cole Porter (1939). Introduced by Bert Lahr and Ethel Merman in the musical *Du Barry Was a Lady* (1939).

In her autobiography, Ethel Merman reveals that at the first few performances of *Du Barry Was a Lady* the song did not go over well. "It was all about the things you can do at night but in the morning you don't feel like doing them. So we 'hoked it up' by giving the impression that we were breaking each other up—which means giving each other uncontrollable giggles and laughter which are not in the book and which look impromptu—but we did it every night the same way and the audience loved it."

But Not for Me, words by Ira Gershwin, music by George Gershwin (1930). Introduced by Ginger Rogers (in her first Broadway starring role) in the musical *Girl Crazy* (1930). Later in the play, Willie Howard (playing the comic role of Gieber Goldfarb) used the song to demonstrate his gift at mimicking the singing styles of such popular artists as Rudy Vallée and Maurice Chevalier. The song was heard in all three of the motion-picture adaptations of the musical comedy (RKO, 1932, MGM, 1943, and MGM, 1965); in the 1943 adaptation it was sung by Judy Garland and in 1965 by Connie Francis and Harve Presnell. The song provided the name for a motion picture starring Clark Gable (Paramount, 1958), where it was used as a recurrent theme in the instrumental background and was sung on the soundtrack under the titles by Ella Fitzgerald. Miss Fitzgerald's recording for Verve received a "Grammy" from the National Academy of Recording Arts and Sciences for the best female solo vocal performance on disks in 1959.

Butterfly, words and music by Bernie Lowe and Kal Mann (1957). Popularized by Charlie Gracie's recording for Cameo, and by Andy Williams' recording for Cadence.

Buttons and Bows, words and music by Jay Livingston and Ray Evans (1948). Introduced by Bob Hope and Jane Russell in the motion picture *The Paleface* (Paramount, 1948). The song received the Academy Award. Dinah Shore's recording for Columbia sold over a million disks. Bob Hope's recording for Capitol was also a best seller. It was interpolated as a choral episode in the non-musical motion picture *Sunset Boulevard,* starring Gloria Swanson and William Holden (Paramount, 1950).

Button Up Your Overcoat, words by Bud De Sylva and Lew Brown, music by Ray Henderson (1928). Introduced by Zelma O'Neal and Jack Haley in the musical *Follow Thru* (1929). They repeated this performance in the motion-picture adaptation of the musical (Paramount, 1930). The song was interpolated in the motion-picture biography of De Sylva, Brown and Henderson, *The Best Things in Life Are Free* (20th Century-Fox, 1956).

By a Waterfall, words by Irving Kahal, music by Sammy Fain (1933). Introduced by Dick Powell and Ruby Keeler in the motion-picture musical *Footlight Parade* (Warner, 1933).

Bye, Bye, Baby, words by Leo Robin, music by Jule Styne (1949). Introduced by Carol Channing and Jack McCauley in the musical *Gentlemen Prefer Blondes* (1949). It was sung by Marilyn Monroe and chorus in the motion-picture adaptation of the musical (20th Century-Fox, 1953).

Bye Bye Birdie, a musical comedy with book by Michael Stewart. Lyrics by Lee Adams. Music by Charles Strouse. Starring Dick Van Dyke and Chita Rivera (1960). Original cast recording (Columbia).

The motion-picture adaptation starred Dick Van Dyke, Bobby Rydell and Janet Leigh (Columbia, 1963). It used the hit songs of the stage score. Soundtrack recording (RCA Victor).

See: Baby, Talk to Me; Kids; A Lot of Livin' to Do; Put on a Happy Face.

Bye, Bye, Blackbird, words by Mort Dixon, music by Ray Henderson (1926). First popularized by Eddie Cantor, then served as the theme song in vaudeville for Georgie Price. The song was featured in several motion pictures. These included: *Rainbow Round My Shoulder* (Columbia, 1952), sung by Frankie Lane; *River of No Return* (Columbia, 1954), sung by Marilyn Monroe; and *The Eddie Cantor Story* (Warner, 1954), sung on the soundtrack by Eddie Cantor.

Bye, Bye, Blues, words and music by Fred Hamm, Dave Bennett and Chauncey Gray (1930). It became the signature of Bert Lown and his Hotel Biltmore Orchestra.

Bye, Bye, Love, words and music by Felice Bryant and Boudleaux Bryant (1957). Popularized by the Everly Brothers in a Cadence recording, their first successful release.

By Jupiter, a musical comedy with book by Richard Rodgers and Lorenz Hart, based on Julian F. Thompson's *The Warrior Husband.* Lyrics by Lorenz Hart. Music by Richard Rodgers. This was the last musical comedy by Rodgers and Hart. Starring Ray Bolger and Benay Venuta (1942).

See: Careless Rhapsody; Everything I've Got Belongs to You; Nobody's Heart Belongs to Me; Wait Till You See Her.

By Myself, words by Howard Dietz, music by Arthur Schwartz (1937). Introduced by Jack Buchanan in the musical *Between the Devil* (1937). Judy Garland sang it in the motion-picture musical *I Could Go On Singing* (United Artists, 1963). This is Dietz's own favorite among his lyrics.

By Strauss, words by Ira Gershwin, music by George Gershwin (1936). A satire on the Viennese waltz, introduced by Gracie Barrie and Robert Shafter (then danced to by Mitzi Mayfair) in the revue *The Show Is On* (1936). It was revived in the motion-picture musical *An American in Paris* (MGM, 1951), sung by Gene Kelly, Oscar Levant and George Guetary.

By the Beautiful Sea, words by Harold Atteridge, music by Harry Carroll (1914). It was introduced in vaudeville by the Stanford Four and plugged to success in Coney Island amusement places by a chorus of boys in sailor suits hired by the publisher. It was then interpolated in the revue *The Passing Show of 1914,* sung by Muriel Window. The song was also interpolated in the motion-picture musicals *The Story of the Castles* (RKO, 1939) and *Coney Island* (20th Century-Fox, 1943). It was sung by Constance Moore in the motion-picture musical *Atlantic City* (Republic, 1944), and by a girls' chorus in the motion picture *Some Like It Hot* (United Artists, 1959).

By the Light of the Silvery Moon,

words by Edward Madden, music by Gus Edwards (1909). Introduced in vaudeville by Georgie Price (then a child star) in the Gus Edwards revue *School Boys and Girls*. For this number, Price was seated in the audience to serve as a singing stooge. Lillian Lorraine sang it successfully in the *Ziegfeld Follies of 1909*. After Florenz Ziegfeld's death, and with the reopening of the Ziegfeld Theater in 1933, Gus Edwards (on the stage) introduced Lillian Lorraine in the audience. He invited her to come to the stage and sing again "By the Light of the Silvery Moon." She delivered the opening measures, then broke into sobs and was unable to finish the song.

The song provided the title for and was sung by Doris Day and Gordon MacRae in a motion-picture musical (Warner, 1953). It was interpolated in several other motion pictures. Among these were: *Ruggles of Red Gap*, starring Charles Laughton (Paramount, 1935); *The Birth of the Blues* (Paramount, 1941); *Sunbonnet Sue* (Monogram, 1945); *The Jolson Story* (Columbia, 1946); and *Always Leave Them Laughing*, starring Milton Berle (Warner, 1949).

By the Light of the Silvery Moon, a motion-picture musical starring Doris Day and Gordon MacRae (Warner, 1953). The score was made up of standards.

See: Ain't We Got Fun?; Be My Little Baby Bumble Bee; By the Light of the Silvery Moon; The Chanticleer Rag; If You Were the Only Girl in the World; Just One Girl; Meet Me in St. Louis; Your Eyes Have Told Me So.

By the River Sainte Marie, words by Edgar Leslie, music by Harry Warren (1931). Popularized by Kate Smith. She featured it on her opening radio program over CBS on May 1, 1931. The song was interpolated in the motion picture *Swing in the Saddle*, starring Jane Frazee (Columbia, 1944).

By the Saskatchewan, words by C. M. S. McLellan, music by Ivan Caryll (1910). Introduced by John E. Young, Ida M. Lewis and chorus in the operetta *The Pink Lady* (1911).

By the Watermelon Vine, Lindy Lou, words and music by T. S. Allen (1904). Popularized in vaudeville and minstrel shows in the early 1900s. It was revived by John Payne, Alice Faye and Jack Oakie in the motion-picture musical *Hello, Frisco, Hello* (20th Century-Fox, 1943).

C

Cabin in the Sky, words by John Latouche, music by Vernon Duke (1940). Introduced by Ethel Waters and Dooley Wilson, with the Rosamond Johnson Choir, in the musical fantasy of the same name (1940). Ethel Waters repeated her performance with Eddie "Rochester" Anderson in the motion-picture adaptation of the musical (MGM, 1943).

Cabin in the Sky, a musical fantasy with book by Lynn Root. Lyrics by John Latouche. Music by Vernon Duke. Starring Ethel Waters, Todd Duncan and Katherine Dunham (1940).

The motion-picture adaptation starred Ethel Waters, Lena Horne and Louis Armstrong (MGM, 1943). Several hit songs were used from the stage production with some new numbers by E. Y. Harburg and Harold Arlen.

See: Cabin in the Sky; Happiness Is a Thing Called Joe; Honey in the Honeycomb; Life's Full of Consequences; Taking a Chance on Love.

Ça, C'est L'Amour, words and music by Cole Porter (1957). Introduced by Taina Elg in the motion-picture musical *Les Girls* (MGM, 1957). It was popularized by Tony Bennett in a Columbia recording.

Caesar, Irving, lyricist, born New York City, 1895.

See: Gershwin, George; Henderson, Ray; Youmans, Vincent.

See also: Crazy Rhythm; If I Forget You; Is It True What They Say About Dixie?; Just a Gigolo; Saskatchewan; Someone Will Make You Smile; That's What I Want for Christmas; Umbriago; Under a Roof in Paree; What Do You Do Sundays, Mary?

Cahn, Sammy, lyricist, born New York City, 1913.

See: Styne, Jule; Van Heusen, James.

See also: Autumn in Rome; Because You're Mine; Bei Mir Bist du Schoen; Be My Love; The Best of Everything; I'll Never Stop Loving You; I Should Care; It's a Woman's World; Melancholy Rhapsody; Pete Kelly's Blues; Shoe Shine Boy; Teach Me Tonight; Wonder Why?; Written on the Wind.

The Caissons Go Rolling Along (or, The Caisson Song), song of the United States Artillery, words and music by Edmund L. Gruber (1908). Gruber, a West Point graduate of the class of 1904, wrote this number while serving as a first lieutenant in the Artillery Corps in the Philippines. John Philip Sousa made a band arrangement in 1918 called *The Field Artillery March,* which helped to popularize the song; this arrangement was introduced by Sousa and his band at a Liberty Loan concert at the Hippodrome in New York in 1918. Because of the success of this adaptation, Sousa was for a time erroneously credited as the composer of the song.

The Cakewalk in the Sky, a coon shout,

words and music by Ben Harney (c. 1896). This was the first song in which the lyrics as well as the music were in a ragtime rhythm. It was introduced and popularized in vaudeville by Ben Harney.

Calcutta, words by Lee Pockriss and Paul J. Vance, music by Heino Gaze (1960). The Dot recording by Lawrence Welk and his orchestra in 1961 sold a million disks, and received the Gold Record Award.

Caldwell, Anne, lyricist, born Boston, Massachusetts, 1867; died Hollywood, California, 1936.

See: Kern, Jerome.

See also: Bagdad; I Know That You Know.

California, Here I Come, words by Al Jolson and Bud De Sylva, music by Joseph Meyer (1924). Interpolated by Al Jolson in the extravaganza *Bombo* during its road tour in 1923. Jolson sang it in the motion-picture musical *Rose of Washington Square* (20th Century-Fox, 1939) and on the soundtracks of *The Jolson Story* (Columbia, 1946) and *Jolson Sings Again* (Columbia, 1949). His Decca recording in 1946 sold a million disks. The song was heard in several other motion pictures. These included *Lucky Boy,* starring George Jessel (Tiffany Stahl, 1929), and the screen biography of Jane Froman, *With a Song in My Heart* (20th Century-Fox, 1952).

Calling to Her Boy Just Once Again, words and music by Paul Dresser (1900). A sentimental mother ballad introduced by Dick José.

Call Me Darling, a German popular song ("Sag' mir Darling"), by Bert Reisfeld, Mart Fryberg and Rolf Marbet. English lyrics by Dorothy Dick (1931).

Call Me Irresponsible, words by Sammy Cahn, music by James Van Heusen (1963). The song was originally written in 1955 for Fred Astaire, for a projected motion picture *Papa's Delicate Condition.* At that time the picture and the song were abandoned. Seven years later the motion picture was reintroduced into the production schedule of Paramount as a starring vehicle for Jackie Gleason. Though songs were to be dispensed with, a last-minute decision was made by the producer to have Gleason sing "Call Me Irresponsible." The song received the Academy Award. It was popularized in numerous recordings in 1963, most notably by Jack Jones for Kapp and Frank Sinatra for Reprise.

Call Me Madam, a musical comedy with book by Russel Crouse and Howard Lindsay. Lyrics and music by Irving Berlin. Starring Ethel Merman (1950). Original cast recording (Decca).

The motion-picture adaptation also starred Ethel Merman (20th Century-Fox, 1953). The basic stage score was used.

See: The Best Thing for You Is Me; The Hostess with the Mostes' on the Ball; It's a Lovely Day Today; They Like Ike; You're Just in Love.

Call Me Mister, a revue with book by Arnold Auerbach and Arnold B. Horwitt. Lyrics and music by Harold Rome. Starring Jules Munshin and Betty Garrett (1946). Original cast recording (Decca).

The motion-picture adaptation starred Betty Grable and Dan Dailey (20th Century-Fox, 1951). Three songs were used from the stage score, with several new numbers by Mack Gordon and Sammy Fain and others.

See: Along with Me; The Face on the Dime; Military Life; South America, Take It Away.

Call Me Savage, words by Betty Comden and Adolph Green, music by Jule Styne (1964). Introduced by Carol Burnett and Dick Patterson in the musical *Fade Out—Fade In* (1964).

Call Me Up Some Rainy Afternoon, words and music by Irving Berlin (1910). One of the earliest Irving Berlin hits in which both the words and the music were written by Berlin.

Call of the Canyon, words and music by Billy Hill (1940). Introduced by Gene Autry in the motion picture of the same name (Republic, 1942).

Several of the big name bands of the 1940s helped to popularize it, including those of Tommy Dorsey, Glenn Miller and Guy Lombardo. Tommy Dorsey's recording for RCA Victor and Glenn Miller's for Bluebird were best sellers.

Calypso Melody, words and music by Larry Clinton (1951). Popularized by David Rose and his orchestra in an MGM recording.

Camelot, words by Alan Jay Lerner, music by Frederick Loewe (1960). Title song of the musical play (1960), in which it was introduced by Richard Burton and Julie Andrews. This song, in the original cast recording, was a particular favorite of President John F. Kennedy. Mrs. Kennedy revealed to an interviewer: "The song he loved most came at the very end of this record. The lines he loved to hear were: 'Don't let it be forgot, that once there was a spot,/For one brief shining moment that was Camelot.' " These same lines, spoken by Richard Burton, were used on the soundtrack in the closing scene of the motion-picture tribute to President Kennedy exhibited at the Democratic Presidential Convention in Atlantic City in August 1964.

Camelot, a musical play with book by Alan Jay Lerner based on T. H. White's *The Once and Future King*. Lyrics by Alan Jay Lerner. Music by Frederick Loewe. Starring Julie Andrews, Richard Burton and Robert Goulet (1960). Original cast recording (Columbia).

See: Before I Gaze at You Again; Camelot; Follow Me; How to Handle a Woman; If Ever I Would Leave You; Simple Joys of Maidenhood; What Do Simple Folk Do?

De Camptown Races (or, Gwine to Run All Night), a nonsense song with words and music by Stephen Foster (1850). Introduced by the Christy Minstrels, it became a favorite with minstrel troupes everywhere. During the Lincoln-Douglas Presidential campaign in 1860, supporters of Lincoln used the tune for a parody whose refrain opened with the lines: "We're bound to work all night, Bound to work all day, I'll bet my money on the Lincoln hoss, Who'll bet on Stephen A?"

Canadian Capers, words and music by Gus Chandler, Bert White and Henry Cohen (1915). It was revived by Doris Day in the motion-picture musical *My Dream Is Yours* (Warner, 1949).

Canadian Sunset, words by Norman Gimbel, music by Eddie Heywood (1956). Popularized by two recordings, each of which sold a million disks: that of Hugo Winterhalter and his orchestra for RCA Victor and that of Andy Williams for Cadence, Williams' first successful release.

Can Anyone Explain? (No! No! No!), words and music by Bennie Benjamin and George Weiss (1950). Popularized by the Ames Brothers in a Coral recording.

Can Broadway Do Without Me?, a comedy number with words and music by Jimmy Durante (1929). Introduced by Durante in the musical *Show Girl* (1929).

Can-Can, a musical comedy with book by Abe Burrows. Lyrics and music by Cole Porter. Starring Lilo and Peter Cookson (1952). Original cast recording (Capitol).

The motion-picture adaptation starred Frank Sinatra, Shirley MacLaine, Maurice Chevalier and Louis Jourdan (20th Century-Fox, 1960). The principal songs from the stage score were used with several earlier Cole Porter standards. Soundtrack recording (Capitol).

See: Allez-vous En; C'est Magnifique; Come Along with Me; I Love Paris; It's All Right with Me; Just One of Those Things; Let's Do It; Live and Let Live; You Do Something to Me.

Candy, words by Mack David, music by Joan Whitney and Alex Kramer (1944). Popularized by Johnny Mercer, Jo Stafford and the Pied Pipers in a Capitol recording.

Candy and Cake, words and music by Bob Merrill (1950). Popularized by Arthur Godfrey in a Columbia recording and by Mindy Carson in an RCA Victor recording.

Candy Kisses, words and music by George Morgan (1948). Introduced and popularized by George Morgan in a Columbia release and further popularized by Georgia Gibbs in a Mercury recording. It was interpolated in the motion pictures *Loving You* (Paramount, 1949) and *Down Dakota Way*, starring Roy Rogers (Republic, 1949).

Can I Forget You?, words by Oscar Hammerstein II, music by Jerome Kern (1937). Introduced by Irene Dunne in the motion-picture musical *High, Wide and Handsome* (Paramount, 1937).

Can I Steal a Little Love?, words and music by Phil Tuminello (1956). Introduced in the motion picture *Rock, Pretty Baby*, starring Sal Mineo (Universal, 1957), and popularized by Frank Sinatra in a Capitol recording.

Can It Be Possible?, words by Jack Lawrence, music by Stan Freeman (1964). Introduced by Richard Kiley, Luba Lisa, Steve Roland and Buddy Hackett in the musical *I Had a Ball* (1964).

Can't Get Out of This Mood, words by Frank Loesser, music by Jimmy McHugh (1942). Introduced by Ginny Simms in the motion picture *Seven Days Leave* (RKO, 1942).

Can't Help Falling in Love (With You), words and music by Hugo Peretti, Luigi Creatore and George Weiss (1961). Introduced by Elvis Presley in the motion-picture musical *Blue Hawaii* (Paramount, 1961), and popularized by him in an RCA Victor recording that sold a million disks and received a Gold Record Award in 1962.

Can't Help Lovin' Dat Man, words by Oscar Hammerstein II, music by Jerome Kern (1927). Introduced by Helen Morgan, Norma Terris, Howard Marsh, Aunt Jemima and Allen Campbell in the musical play *Show Boat* (1927). Though this number was played in a fast tempo in the show, to set the mood for an effective dance, it has become popular as a torch song—a tradition initiated

by Helen Morgan in night clubs.

In the 1936 motion-picture adaptation of the musical (Universal), it was sung by Irene Dunne; in the 1951 screen version (MGM), by Ava Gardner. In the Jerome Kern screen biography *Till the Clouds Roll By* (MGM, 1946), it was sung by Lena Horne; in *The Helen Morgan Story* (Warner, 1957), by Gogi Grant on the soundtrack (for Ann Blyth).

Can't Help Singing, words by E. Y. Harburg, music by Jerome Kern (1944). Introduced by Deanna Durbin and Robert Paige in the motion-picture musical of the same name (Universal, 1944).

Can't We Be Friends?, words by Paul James, music by Kay Swift (1929). A torch song introduced by Libby Holman in the *Little Show* (1929). It was interpolated as an orchestral episode in the motion-picture musical *The Man I Love* (Warner, 1946) and as a piano episode in the non-musical motion picture *Backfire* (Warner, 1950), starring Edmond O'Brien and Gordon MacRae.

Can't Yo' Heah Me Callin', Caroline?, words by William H. Gardner, music by Caro Roma (1914). Its composer's greatest song hit, written to a "pseudo-Negro lyric."

Can't You See It?, words by Lee Adams, music by Charles Strouse (1964). Introduced by Sammy Davis in the musical *Golden Boy* (1964).

Can You Find It in Your Heart?, words by Al Stillman, music by Robert Allen (1956). Popularized by Tony Bennett in a Columbia recording.

Carefree, a motion-picture musical starring Fred Astaire and Ginger Rogers (RKO, 1938). Songs by Irving Berlin.

See: Change Partners; The Night Is Filled with Music; The Yam.

Careless Hands, words and music by Bob Hilliard and Carl Sigman (1949). Popularized by Sammy Kaye and his orchestra in a best-selling recording for RCA Victor and by Mel Tormé in a successful Capitol release.

Careless Rhapsody, words by Lorenz Hart, music by Richard Rodgers (1942). Introduced by Constance

Moore and Ronald Graham in the musical *By Jupiter* (1942).

The Carioca, words by Gus Kahn and Edward Eliscu, music by Vincent Youmans (1933). Introduced by Fred Astaire and Ginger Rogers in the first of their singing-dancing film classics, *Flying Down to Rio* (RKO, 1933). Though this number inspired an unforgettable dance routine by Fred Astaire and Ginger Rogers, Astaire was not at first satisfied with his work. "I was under the impression," he later recalled in his autobiography, "that we weren't doing anything particularly outstanding in 'The Carioca.' I had thrown in a few solos, too, in the limited time given me, but I never expected that they would register so well. However, everything clicked."

Carissima, words and music by Arthur Penn (1905). Introduced in the musical *The Red Feather* (1903). After getting published, the song entered the repertory of many vaudeville headliners between 1905 and 1907.

Carmen Jones, a musical play, Negro adaptation of Georges Bizet's opera *Carmen* with the music entirely by Bizet presented without alterations and with only minor deletions. Text and lyrics by Oscar Hammerstein II. Starring Muriel Smith and Muriel Rahn, alternating as Carmen, and Luther Saxon and Napoleon Reed, alternating as Joe (1943). Original cast recording (Decca).

The motion-picture adaptation starred Dorothy Dandridge, Harry Belafonte and Diahann Carroll (20th Century-Fox, 1954). It utilized the stage score.

See: Dat's Love; Dere's a Café on de Corner; Dis Flower; My Joe; Stan' Up and Fight.

Carmichael, Hoagy, composer, born Bloomington, Indiana, 1899.

See (*Lyrics by Frank Loesser*): Heart and Soul; Small Fry; Two Sleepy People.

See (Lyrics by Johnny Mercer): How Little We Know; In the Cool, Cool, Cool of the Evening; Lazy Bones.

See (Lyrics by Mitchell Parish):

One Morning in May; Star Dust; Washboard Blues.

See (Lyrics by Paul Francis Webster): Doctor, Lawyer, Indian, Chief; The Lamplighter's Serenade.

See also: Georgia on My Mind; I Get Along Without You Very Well; Ivy; Lazy River; Little Old Lady; My Resistance Is Low; The Nearness of You; Ole Buttermilk Sky; Riverboat Shuffle; Rockin' Chair.

Carnival, a musical play with book by Michael Stewart based on material by Helen Deutsch from the motion picture *Lili.* Lyrics and music by Bob Merrill. Starring Anna Maria Alberghetti (1961). Original cast recording (MGM).

See: Love Makes the World Go Round.

Carolina in the Morning, words by Gus Kahn, music by Walter Donaldson (1922). Introduced by Willie and Eugene Howard in the revue *The Passing Show of 1922.* When Donaldson wrote this successful number, he had never paid a visit to either North or South Carolina. The song was interpolated in several motion-picture musicals. These included *The Dolly Sisters* (20th Century-Fox, 1945), sung by Betty Grable and June Havoc; *April Showers* (Warner, 1948), sung by Robert Alda, Ann Sothern and Bobbie Ellis; and Gus Kahn's screen biography *I'll See You in My Dreams* (Warner, 1951), sung by Patrice Wymore.

Carolina Moon, words by Benny Davis, music by Joseph Burke (1928). Popularized by Guy Lombardo and the Royal Canadians. It was adopted by Morton Downey as his radio theme song.

Carousel, a musical play with book by Oscar Hammerstein II based on Ferenc Molnar's play *Liliom.* Lyrics by Oscar Hammerstein II. Music by Richard Rodgers. Starring Jan Clayton and John Raitt (1945). Original cast recording (Decca).

The motion-picture adaptation starred Gordon MacRae and Shirley Jones (20th Century-Fox, 1956). It utilized the basic stage score. Soundtrack recording (Capitol).

See: If I Loved You; June Is Bustin' Out All Over; Soliloquy; What's the Use of Wond'rin'?

Carousel in the Park, words by Dorothy Fields, music by Sigmund Romberg (1944). Introduced by Maureen Cannon in the musical *Up in Central Park* (1945). In the motion-picture adptation of the musical (Universal, 1948), it was sung by Deanna Durbin and Dick Haymes.

Carrie (or Carrie, Marry Harry), words by Junie McCree, music by Albert von Tilzer (1909). A ragtime song popularized in vaudeville by Sophie Tucker.

Carroll, Harry, composer, born Atlantic City, New Jersey, 1892; died New York City, 1962.

See (Lyrics by Ballard MacDonald): On the Mississippi; There's a Girl in the Heart of Maryland; The Trail of the Lonesome Pine.

See also: By the Beautiful Sea; I'm Always Chasing Rainbows.

Carry Me Back to Old Virginny, words and music by James A. Bland (1878). Introduced by George Primrose and his minstrels, after which it became a favorite with minstrel troupes everywhere.

The composer was inspired to write this ballad by looking at the peaceful setting of a plantation on the James River in the Tidewater section of Virginia, near Williamsburg. This had also been the stimulation for Bland's earlier song success "In the Evening by the Moonlight." Paying a return visit to this spot in 1878, Bland was suddenly reminded of a chance remark made to him by a girl student while he was attending Howard University in Washington, D. C. She was describing to him a dream that, she said, carried her back to her home "in old Virginny." Bland, in writing his ballad, transferred the girl's thoughts to a colored man's wish.

The song was adopted as the official one for the State of Virginia in 1940. Six years later, when Governor William A. Tuck of Virginia dedicated a tombstone for Bland at Merion, Pennsylvania, he said: "James Bland put into ever-ringing verse and rhyme an expression of feeling which all Virginians have for their state. 'Carry Me Back to Old Virginny' tells in inspiring song the innate patriotism and love of native heath of all our people, white and Negro alike."

Carry Me Back to the Lone Prairie, words and music by Carson Robinson (1934). A popular tune in the style of a cowboy folk song, introduced by James Melton in the motion-picture musical *Stars Over Broadway* (Warner, 1935).

Caryll, Ivan, composer, born Felix Tilken, Liège, Belgium, 1861; died New York City, 1921.

See: By the Saskatchewan; Goodbye, Girls, I'm Through; Kiss Waltz; My Beautiful Lady; Oh, Oh, Delphine; Venus Waltz.

Casey Jones, words by T. Lawrence Seibert, music by Eddie Newton (1909). Probably the most celebrated popular or folk song about the railroad.

The hero of this ballad was John Luther Jones, who acquired the nickname of Casey because he came from Cayce, Tennessee. On Sunday evening, April 29, 1900, he substituted as engineer for a sick friend on the Cannonball Limited out of Memphis, Tennessee. Near Vaughn, Mississippi, Jones was the fatal victim in a train crash. "Scalded to death by the steam," says the ballad, he died "with his hand on the throttle." He forthwith became a symbol of heroism in railroading. In 1947 a monument was erected on his grave at Mount Calvary Cemetery in Jackson, Tennessee. The inscription reads: "To the memory of the locomotive engineer whose name as Casey Jones became part of the folklore of the American language." Another plaque quoted two lines from the song: "For I'm gonna run her till she leaves the rail, Or make it on time with the southern mail."

The song was popularized in vaudeville by the Leighton Brothers. It was interpolated for Gene Autry in the motion picture *Sunset in Wyoming* (Republic, 1941), and was

heard in the Broadway musical play
Sing Out, Sweet Land (1944).

Castle of Dreams, words by Joseph
McCarthy, music by Harry Tierney,
the melody adapted from Chopin's
Minute Waltz (1919). It was introduced by Bernice McCabe and ensemble in the musical *Irene* (1919).
In the motion-picture adaptation of
the musical (RKO, 1940), it was
sung under the titles by a chorus
and used as a recurring theme in
the background music.

The Cat and the Fiddle, a musical
comedy with book and lyrics by
Otto Harbach. Music by Jerome Kern.
Starring Odette Myrtil, Georges
Metaxa and Bettina Hall (1931).

The motion-picture adaptation
starred Ramon Novarro and Jeanette MacDonald (MGM, 1934). The
basic stage score was used.

See: I Watch the Love Parade;
The Night Was Made for Love;
Poor Pierrot; She Didn't Say Yes;
Try to Forget.

Cat Ballou, words by Mack David,
music by Jerry Livingston (1965).
A popular song in the style of a
Western folk ballad. It was sung by
Nat King Cole and Stubby Kaye
throughout the non-musical motion-
picture satire of the same name
starring Jane Fonda and Lee Marvin
(Columbia, 1965), to comment on
the action in the story. The ballad
was further popularized by Nat King
Cole in a Capitol recording, one of
his last.

Catch a Falling Star, words and music
by Paul J. Vance and Lee Pockriss
(1958). Popularized by Perry Como,
whose RCA Victor recording sold
over a million disks. It received a
"Grammy" Award from the National
Academy of Recording Arts and
Sciences for the best solo male performance on disks that year, and a
Gold Record Award.

Cathy's Clown, words and music by
Don and Phil Everly (1960). Introduced and popularized by the
Everly Brothers in a Warner recording.

Centennial Summer, a motion-picture
musical starring Cornel Wilde,
Jeanne Crain and Linda Darnell

(20th Century-Fox, 1946). Songs by
Oscar Hammerstein II and Jerome
Kern, and by Leo Robin and Jerome
Kern. This was Kern's last score.

See: All Through the Day; In Love
in Vain.

A Certain Smile, words by Paul Francis
Webster, music by Sammy Fain
(1958). Title song of a non-musical
motion picture starring Rossano
Brazzi and Joan Fontaine (20th
Century-Fox, 1958). The song was
introduced in that movie by Johnny
Mathis and was popularized by
him in a best-selling recording for
Columbia.

C'est Magnifique, words and music by
Cole Porter (1953). Introduced by
Lilo (making her American debut)
and Peter Cookson in the musical
comedy *Can-Can* (1953). In the
motion-picture adaptation of the
musical (20th Century-Fox, 1960), it
was sung by Frank Sinatra.

C'est Si Bon, a French popular song,
music by Henri Betti, English
lyrics by Jerry Seelan (1950). It
was first popularized by Johnny Desmond in an MGM recording. This
is the song with which Eartha Kitt
achieved success for the first time
—at the Village Vanguard in New
York's Greenwich Village, and in an
RCA Victor recording in 1953. She
wrote in her autobiography: "'C'est
si bon,' people would say when they
saw me walking down the street or
in the restaurant. I felt wanted. I
was getting the love I wanted. . . .
I was getting it the hard way, for I
had to constantly prove myself in
order to maintain it."

The song was interpolated in the
non-musical motion picture starring
Audrey Hepburn and Gary Cooper,
Love in the Afternoon (Allied
Artists, 1957).

Chain Gang, words and music by Sol
Quasha and Herb Yakus (1956).
Popularized by Bobby Scott in an
ABC Paramount recording. The song
was successfully revived in 1960 by
Sam Cooke in an RCA Victor re-
cording.

Chances Are, words by Al Stillman,
music by Robert Allen (1957).
Popularized by Johnny Mathis in

a best-selling Columbia recording.

Change Partners, words and music by Irving Berlin (1938). Introduced by Fred Astaire and Ginger Rogers in the motion-picture musical *Carefree* (RKO, 1938).

Changing Partners, words by Joe Darion, music by Larry Coleman (1953). Popularized by Patti Page in a best-selling recording for Mercury.

Chanson d'Amour, words and music by Wayne Shanklin (1958). Introduced by Art and Dotty Todd in an Era recording, and popularized in a Dot recording by the Fontane Sisters.

Chantez, Chantez, words by Albert Gamse, music by Irving Fields (1957). Introduced and popularized by Dinah Shore on her television program.

The Chanticleer Rag, words by Edward Madden, music by Albert Gumble (1910). Hit ragtime tune of the 1910s, successfully revived by Doris Day in a production number in the motion-picture musical *By the Light of the Silvery Moon* (Warner, 1953).

Chant of the Jungle, words by Arthur Freed, music by Nacio Herb Brown (1929). Introduced by Joan Crawford in the non-musical motion-picture *Untamed* (MGM, 1929).

Charade, words by Johnny Mercer, music by Henry Mancini (1963). Title song of a non-musical motion picture starring Audrey Hepburn and Cary Grant (Universal, 1963). The song was popularized by Jack Jones in a Kapp recording, and by Sammy Kaye in a Decca recording emphasizing a strong beat.

Charleston, words and music by Cecil Mack and Jimmy Johnson (1923). Introduced in the all-Negro revue *Runnin' Wild* (1923), where it served to introduce a new dance that became a fad throughout the United States in 1923 and 1924. At Roseland, in New York City, a Charleston marathon in 1924 dragged on for almost twenty-four hours. The *George White Scandals of 1925* featured a huge production number in which the Charleston was performed by Tom Patricola and sixty girls. The song was also used for a period-piece production number in the motion-picture musical *Tea for Two* (Warner, 1950).

Charley, My Boy, words by Gus Kahn, music by Ted Fiorito (1924).

Charlie Brown, words and music by Jerry Leiber and Mike Stoller (1959). Popularized by the Coasters in an Atlantic recording.

Charmaine, words by Lew Pollack, music by Erno Rapee (1926). One of the earliest successful motion-picture theme songs. It was written to exploit the silent motion picture *What Price Glory?*, starring Edmund Lowe and Victor McLaglen (Fox, 1926). The success of this song was responsible for the widespread use of theme songs for motion pictures in the late 1920s and early 1930s. The melody was interpolated in the background music of the screen remake of *What Price Glory?* (20th Century-Fox, 1952), where it was used as a recurrent theme.

The song was also revived in 1952 by Mantovani, who recorded it with his strings for London. A Cleveland disk jockey, Bill Randle, plugged this recording into a million-disk seller. This recording of "Charmaine" marked the beginning of Mantovani's success as a recording and performing artist besides starting a vogue for lush string-oriented recording groups.

Chattanooga Choo Choo, words by Mack Gordon, music by Harry Warren (1941). Introduced by Glenn Miller and his orchestra in the motion-picture musical *Sun Valley Serenade* (20th Century-Fox, 1941). It subsequently became one of Glenn Miller's biggest hits both over the radio and on RCA Victor records, his 1941 release selling over a million disks. The song was interpolated in the non-musical motion pictures *The Big Lift*, starring Montgomery Clift and Paul Douglas (20th Century-Fox, 1950), and *Don't Bother to Knock,* starring Marilyn Monroe (20th Century-Fox, 1952), and it was sung by Dan Dailey in the motion-picture musical *You're My Everything* (20th Century-Fox, 1949).

Chattanoogie Shoe Shine Boy, words and music by Harry Stone and Jack Stapp (1950). It was interpolated in the motion picture *Indian Territory,* starring Gene Autry (Columbia, 1950). Red Foley's Decca recording and Bing Crosby's recording on the same label were best sellers.

Check and Double Check, a motion picture starring Amos 'n Andy (Freeman F. Gosden and Charles F. Correll) of radio fame (RKO, 1930). Songs by Bert Kalmar and Harry Ruby (their first motion-picture score). Additional songs by Irving Mills and Duke Ellington.
See: Three Little Words.

Cheek to Cheek, words and music by Irving Berlin (1935). One of Berlin's greatest commercial song successes. It was introduced by Fred Astaire and Ginger Rogers in the motion-picture musical *Top Hat* (RKO, 1935). The song was interpolated in the motion-picture musical *Alexander's Ragtime Band* (20th Century-Fox, 1938).

"I arranged a romantic flowing type of dance to fit the situation in the picture," Fred Astaire recalled in his autobiography, "and we took special pains to try for extra-smooth smoothness." Complications, however, set in with Ginger Rogers' costume, which was made up of innumerable feathers. While Astaire and Rogers were performing to the music of "Cheek to Cheek," the feathers began shedding, creating a veritable storm. "They blinded Fred," wrote Hermes Pan, the choreographer, "and got in his nose and made him sneeze. After about an hour he gave up. The next morning . . . the dress designer assured us it would be okay. But the feathers kept flying, and later in the afternoon Fred threw up his hands. He was white with anger. . . . Finally the designer agreed to spend all night sewing each feather into place, and on the third day, though a few feathers still flew, we were able to shoot the dance." In spite of this problem, the dance came off beautifully and, together with the song, became the highlight of the picture.

Cheerful Little Earful, words by Ira Gershwin and Billy Rose, music by Harry Warren (1930). Introduced by Hannah Williams in the revue *Sweet and Low* (1930). The song brought Hannah Williams featured billing in the show and a certain measure of temporary stage fame before her marriage to Jack Dempsey.

Cherokee, words and music by Ray Noble (1943). This was one of Ray Noble's leading song hits. It was popularized by Charlie Barnet and his orchestra, who interpolated it in the motion-picture musical *Jam Session* (Columbia, 1944).

Cherry Pink and Apple Blossom White, a French popular tune, music by Louiguy (no first name given), English lyrics by Mack David (1951). The song became popular in 1955 mainly through the RCA Victor recording by Perez Prado and his orchestra, and the Coral recording by Alan Dale. It was used as the theme song for the motion picture *Underwater,* starring Jane Russell and Gilbert Roland (RKO, 1955). It was revived in 1961 in a best-selling recording by Jerry Murad and his Harmonicats for Columbia.

Chester (or, Let Tyrants Shake Their Iron Rod), words and music by William Billings (1778). One of the earliest popular songs in America, sometimes described as "the Marseillaise of the Revolutionary War."

A friend of Samuel Adams and Paul Revere, and a passionate advocate of the revolution, Billings set himself the task of writing war songs to inflame the fighting spirit of the colonists. He fashioned war lyrics to a number of his own psalm and hymn tunes from his *New England Psalm Singer* and *The Singing Master's Assistant.* "Many of the New England soldiers . . . who were encamped in southern states," said the *Musical Reporter,* "had his popular tunes by heart and frequently amused themselves by singing them in camp to the delight of all those who heard them."

The most famous of these war songs by Billings was "Chester," whose melody came out of *The Singing Master's Assistant* (1776). "Chester" was sung by troops in camp and on the march to battle, a powerful influence in maintaining morale. In his *History of Popular Music*, this editor wrote: "The stately melody, even rhythm and formal cadences of Billings' old psalm seem to us not particularly appropriate for a war message with ringing accents. Nevertheless, the strains of 'Chester' reverberated throughout the colonies and proved to be . . . influential propaganda. . . . It is America's first great war song."

The twentieth-century American composer William Schuman used the melody of "Chester" for two symphonic works: *William Billings Overture* (1943) and *New England Triptych* (1956).

Chestnuts Roasting on an Open Fire (or, The Christmas Song), words by Robert Wells, music by Mel Tormé (1946). Introduced by Mel Tormé but popularized by Nat King Cole in a Capitol recording.

Cheyenne, words by Harry H. Williams, music by Egbert Van Alstyne (1906). A successor to "Navajo," by the same writers, which in 1903 had helped to start a vogue for songs about American Indians.

Chi-Baba, words and music by Mack David, Al Hoffman and Jerry Livingston (1947). Popularized by Perry Como in an RCA Victor recording.

Chicago (That Toddling Town), words and music by Fred Fisher (1922). Popularized in the 1920s in vaudeville. It was used in the background music as a recurrent theme for two non-musical motion pictures: *Little Giant,* starring Edward G. Robinson (Warner, 1933), and *Beyond the Forest,* starring Bette Davis (Warner, 1949). It was also played under the titles and used in the final scene of the non-musical motion picture *Roxie Hart,* starring Ginger Rogers (20th Century-Fox, 1943), a screen adaptation of the stage play *Chicago.* The song was heard in several screen musicals, including *The Story of the Castles* (RKO, 1939); the Fred

Fisher screen biography *Oh, You Beautiful Doll* (20th Century-Fox, 1949); and the Jane Froman screen biography *With a Song in My Heart* (20th Century-Fox, 1952).

A recording by Tommy Dorsey and his orchestra for RCA Victor in the late 1930s was a best seller.

Chili Bean, words by Lew Brown, music by Albert von Tilzer (1920).

Chim Chim Cheree, words and music by Richard M. Sherman and Robert B. Sherman (1964). Introduced by Dick Van Dyke in the Walt Disney musical fantasy *Mary Poppins* (Buena Vista, 1964). It received the Academy Award.

China Boy, words and music by Dick Winfree and Phil Boutelje (1922). It became a Benny Goodman specialty in the 1930s. The Benny Goodman Trio played it on the soundtrack of the motion-picture musical *The Benny Goodman Story* (Universal, 1956).

Chinatown, My Chinatown, words by William Jerome, music by Jean Schwartz (1906). Interpolated in the revue *Up and Down Broadway* (1910). It was subsequently heard in a number of motion pictures, including: *Bright Lights,* starring Frank Fay and Dorothy Mackaill (First National, 1931); the Ted Lewis screen biography *Is Everybody Happy?* (Columbia, 1943); *Jolson Sings Again* (Columbia, 1949), sung on the soundtrack by Jolson; and *The Seven Little Foys* (Paramount, 1955), sung by Bob Hope.

Chin Chin, a musical fantasy with book by Anne Caldwell and R. H. Burnside. Lyrics by Anne Caldwell and James O'Dea. Music by Ivan Caryll. Starring David Montgomery and Fred Stone (1914).

See: Goodbye, Girls, I'm Through.

The Chipmunk Song (or, Christmas Don't Be Late), words and music by Ross Bagdasarian (1958). Popularized by David Seville (pseudonym for Bagdasarian) in a Liberty recording that received "Grammys" from the National Academy of Recording Arts and Sciences as the "best recording for children" and the "best comedy performance" of the year. It was further popularized by the Chipmunks in a Liberty recording. The song has since become a Yuletide favorite.

The "Chipmunks" was a David Seville creation. He simulated chipmunk voices by increasing or decreasing the speed of a tape recording. Four such tapes were superimposed on the final recording, three of supposedly chipmunk voices, and the fourth of Seville's. "The Chipmunk Song" marked the birth of the Chipmunks. The idea came to Seville in September of 1958 in a novelty recording simulating animal or insect voices. "I recorded the song with half-speed little voices (my own) and sang an introduction in my normal speech voice. When I finished the first recording, the voices sounded like butterflies, or mice, or rabbits—but most of all they sounded like chipmunks."

Chloe, words by Gus Kahn, music by Neil Moret (1927). Successfully revived in a parody by Spike Jones and his orchestra in a novelty RCA Victor recording in the early 1940s, which included shrieks, pistol shots and ringing doorbells.

Choo Choo Train, a French popular song ("Le Petit Train"), music by Marc Fontenay, English lyrics by Jack Lawrence (1953). The English-language song was popularized by Doris Day in a Columbia recording.

Christmas in Killarney, words and music by John Redmond, James Cavanaugh and Frank Weldon (1950). Popularized by Dennis Day in an RCA Victor recording.

The Christmas Song. *See:* Chestnuts Roasting on an Open Fire.

Cinderella, a full-length Walt Disney animated cartoon (RKO, 1949). Songs by Mack David, Al Hoffman and Jerry Livingston.

See: Bibbidi-Bobbidi-Boo.

Cinderella, a musical production for TV, with book by Oscar Hammerstein II based on the famous fairy tale. Lyrics by Oscar Hammerstein II. Music by Richard Rodgers. Starring Julie Andrews and Jon Cypher. It was telecast over the CBS network (1957). Original cast recording (Columbia).

See: Do I Love You?; In My Own Little Corner; Ten Minutes Ago.

Cindy, Oh Cindy, words and music by Bob Barron and Burt Long, adapted from a Georgia sea chantey (1956). Introduced by Vince Martin, but popularized by Eddie Fisher in an RCA Victor recording.

A Circus World, words by Ned Washington, music by Dimitri Tiomkin (1965). Title song of a non-musical motion picture starring John Wayne (Paramount, 1965). It was popularized by Andy Williams in a Columbia recording. It received the Golden Globe Award from the Hollywood Foreign Press Association as the best song of the year.

Ciribiribin, an Italian popular song, music by A. Pestalozza, English lyrics by Rudolf Thaler (1909). Grace Moore revived it in her motion picture *One Night of Love* (Columbia, 1934). It then became a favorite in her repertory; she rarely gave a concert without featuring it either on the program or as an encore. Harry James' recording for Columbia in 1939 sold over a million disks.

Civilization (or, Bongo, Bongo), words and music by Bob Hilliard and Carl Sigman (1947). It was interpolated in the revue *Angel in the Wings* (1947), where it was introduced by Elaine Stritch. It was popularized by the Mills Brothers and by Danny Kaye with the Andrews Sisters, each in a best-selling Decca recording.

The Clapping Song (Clap Pat, Clap Slap), words and music by Lincoln Chase (1965). Popularized by Shirley Ellis in a best-selling Congress recording.

Clap Yo' Hands, words by Ira Gershwin, music by George Gershwin (1926). Introduced (and danced to) by Harland Dixon in the musical comedy *Oh, Kay!* (1926).

Ira Gershwin points out in *Lyrics on Several Occasions* that there were two curious things about the title of this song. One was that the title does not appear at all in the song itself: in the chorus it is heard as "clap-a-yo'-hands." Another curiosity is that "there is no attempt to wind up the lyric with a verbal twist or variation; words of the refrain's first section are repeated in the last." Ira Gershwin then goes on to explain that the number was written basically as a "stage tune for dancing, vocally carrying a one-minded invitation to join the jubilee. So the better part of lyric valor was to avoid any verbal change which might impede the song's exhortatory momentum before the dance."

When the song was first heard by a number of Gershwin's friends, Arthur Caesar (brother of the lyricist, Irving) objected to the line "on the sands of time you are only a pebble." He insisted that pebbles were never found on the sands. The Gershwin friends decided to do some research on this matter, went out to the beach and actually found a pebble. The line stayed in.

The song was interpolated in the George Gershwin screen biography *Rhapsody in Blue* (Warner, 1945).

Clarke, Grant, lyricist, born Akron, Ohio, 1891; died California, 1931.

See: Everything Is Peaches Down in Georgia; He'd Have to Get Under; If He Can Fight Like He Can Love; I Love the Ladies; My Little Bimbo Down in Bamboo Isle; Ragtime Cowboy Joe; Second Hand Rose; There's a Little Bit of Bad; Weary River.

Clementine, words and music credited to Percy Montrose (1884). When first published it bore the title of "Oh, My Darling Clementine." A year later it was reissued as "Clementine." On this occasion the author of words and music was identified as Barker Bradford. The song was revived in a swing version in the early 1960s by Bobby Darin in a best-selling Atco recording.

Cleopatterer, a comedy number with words by P. G. Wodehouse, music by Jerome Kern (1917). Introduced by Georgia O'Ramey, in the musical *Leave It to Jane* (1917). In the screen biography of Jerome Kern, *Till the Clouds Roll By* (MGM, 1946), it was sung by June Allyson.

Climb Every Mountain, words by Oscar Hammerstein II, music by Richard Rodgers (1959). An inspirational song introduced by Patricia Neway in the musical play *The Sound of Music* (1959). It was also sung in the motion-picture adaptation of the musical (20th Century-Fox, 1965).

Close As Pages in a Book, words by Dorothy Fields, music by Sigmund Romberg (1944). Introduced by Wilbur Evans and Maureen Cannon in the musical *Up in Central Park* (1945). In the motion-picture adaptation of the musical (Universal, 1948), it was sung by Deanna Durbin and Dick Haymes.

Close to My Heart, words by Andrew B. Sterling, music by Harry von Tilzer (1915).

The Coal Black Rose, author of words and music unknown (c. 1827). One of the earliest popular songs about the Negro. It was first made famous by the Negro minstrel George Washington Dixon, in Albany, New York, in or about 1827. One early published edition credited White Snyder as composer and lyricist, but this has not been accepted by subsequent research.

Coax Me, words by Andrew B. Sterling, music by Harry von Tilzer (1904). Popularized in vaudeville by Lottie Gilson, who used to sing it provocatively to the men in the front row.

Cobb, Will D., lyricist, born Philadelphia, Pennsylvania, 1876; died New York City, 1930.

See: Edwards, Gus.

See also: Goodbye, Dolly Gray; There's a Girl in This World for Everybody; Waltz Me Around Again, Willie; Yip-I-Addy-I-Ay.

A Cockeyed Optimist, words by Oscar Hammerstein II, music by Richard Rodgers (1949). Introduced by Mary Martin in the musical play *South Pacific* (1949). In the motion-picture adaptation of the musical (20th Century-Fox, 1958), it was sung by Mitzi Gaynor.

Cocktails for Two, words by Arthur Johnston, music by Sam Coslow (1934). Introduced in the motion picture *Murder at the Vanities*, starring Carl Brisson (Paramount, 1934). It was interpolated in the motion picture *Ladies' Man,* starring Eddie Bracken (Paramount, 1947). The novelty RCA Victor recording by Spike Jones and his orchestra in 1944 sold a million disks; it included the sounds of hiccups and shattering cocktail glasses.

Cocoa Bean Song, words and music by Richard Adler (1961). Opening number in the musical play *Kwamina* (1961), where it was introduced by Robert Guillaume, Scott Gibson, Gordon Watkins and ensemble.

The Cocoanuts, a musical extravaganza with book by George S. Kaufman. Lyrics and music by Irving Berlin. Starring the Four Marx Brothers (1925).

The motion-picture adaptation starred the Four Marx Brothers with Mary Eaton and Oscar Shaw (Paramount, 1929). The stage score was dispensed with and supplanted by a new number by Irving Berlin.
See: When My Dreams Come True.

Cocoanut Sweet, words by E. Y. Harburg, music by Harold Arlen (1957). A lullaby introduced by Adelaide Hall and Lena Horne in the musical *Jamaica* (1957).

The Coffee Song (or, They've Got an Awful Lot of Coffee in Brazil), words by Bob Hilliard, music by Dick Miles (1946). It was introduced as a production number in the stage show at the Copacabana night club in New York. Frank Sinatra's recording for Columbia was his first to sell a million disks. The song and Sinatra became so inextricably associated with each other that when at one public appearance Sinatra came to the stage with a cup of coffee, the audience understood the implication and gave him an ovation.

Cohan, George M., composer and lyricist, born Providence, Rhode Island, 1878; died New York City, 1942.
See: Forty-Five Minutes from Broadway; Give My Regards to Broadway; Goodbye, Flo; Harrigan; Hot Tamale Alley; I Guess I'll Have to Telegraph My Baby; I'm a Popular Man; I Want You; I Was Born in Virginia; Life's a Funny Proposition After All; Mary's a Grand Old Name; Nellie Kelly, I Love You; Over There; So Long, Mary; The Songs that Maggie Sings; There's Something About a Uniform; When a Fellow's on the Level; When We Are M-A-Double-R-I-E-D; When You Come Back; Why Did Nellie Leave Home?; The Yankee Doodle Boy; You're a Grand Old Flag; You Remind Me of My Mother.

For the screen biography of George M. Cohan, see *Yankee Doodle Dandy* (Warner, 1942).

Cold, Cold Heart, words and music by Hank Williams (1951). Introduced and first popularized in an MGM recording by Hank Williams. Tony Bennett's recording for Columbia in 1952 sold a million disks. It was sung on the soundtrack (for George Hamilton) by Hank Williams, Jr., in the motion-picture biography of Hank Williams, *Your Cheatin' Heart* (MGM, 1964).

Coleman, Cy, composer, born New York City, 1929.
See (Lyrics by Carolyn Leigh): A Doodlin' Song; Firefly; Hey, Look Me Over; I've Got Your Number; Little Me; Pass Me By; Witchcraft; You Fascinate Me; Young at Heart.
See also: The Other Side of the Tracks; Real Live Girl.

Collegiate, words and music by Moe Jaffe and Nat Bonx (1925). Introduced by Fred Waring and his Pennsylvanians (wearing collegiate outfits during the performance). The song was subsequently interpolated in several motion pictures. These included *The Time, The Place and The Girl,* starring Betty Compson (Warner, 1929); *Animal Crackers* (Paramount, 1930); and *Margie* (20th Century-Fox, 1946).

Colt .45, words by Douglas Hayes, music by Hal Hopper (1958). Theme song of the television series of the same name, introduced in 1958.

Columbia, the Gem of the Ocean, a patriotic ballad, words and music generally credited to Thomas à Becket (1843).

In 1843 David T. Shaw, a singer at the Chestnut Street Theatre in Philadelphia, asked Thomas à

Becket, an actor and musician, to write a patriotic song for a theatrical benefit at the Chinese Theatre in Philadelphia. As a point of departure for Becket, Shaw offered him several lines which he himself had scribbled on a piece of paper. "I found them ungrammatical and so deficient in measure as to be totally unfit to be adapted to music," Becket later explained. "We adjourned to the house of a friend and there I wrote the first two verses in pencil, and composed the melody on the piano. On reaching home, I added a third verse, wrote the introductory and terminating portions, made a fair copy in ink and gave it to Mr. Shaw with the request that he should neither give away nor sell a copy of the work."

Shaw's performance was a tremendous success. A number of weeks later, while visiting New Orleans, Becket came across a printed copy of the song. The publication claimed that David T. Shaw was its composer and lyricist, and that T. à Becket was only the arranger. Becket came to the publisher with a vigorous protest. "I purchased the original copy in pencil, and claimed the copyright which [the publisher] admitted, at the same time making severe comments upon Mr. Shaw's deception."

Becket now made arrangements with a Philadelphia publisher to issue the song under his own name. But it was now Becket's turn to come in for censure, since many accused him of having plagiarized an English song by Stephen Joseph Meany, "Britannia, the Pride of the Ocean." Becket, however, stoutly insisted that he, and he alone, wrote "Columbia, the Gem of the Ocean."

Comden, Betty, lyricist, born New York City, 1915.

See: Bernstein, Leonard; Styne, Jule.

See also: The French Lesson.

Come Along, My Mandy, an English ragtime song by Tom Mellor, Alfred J. Lawrence and Harry Gilford, adapted for American consumption with new lyrics by Nora Bayes and Jack Norworth (1907). Introduced by Nora Bayes in the musical *The Jolly Bachelors* (1910). Sigmund Spaeth pointed out that this number was a "high spot in a long line of 'Mandy' songs, besides influencing a number of 'Candy' and 'Sugar' ditties still to come."

Come Along with Me, words and music by Cole Porter (1953). Introduced by Hans Conried and Erik Rhodes in the musical *Can-Can* (1953). In the motion-picture adaptation of the musical (20th Century-Fox, 1960), it was sung by Shirley MacLaine.

Come Back, My Honey Boy, to Me, words by Edgar Smith, music by John Stromberg (1900). Introduced in the Weber and Fields extravaganza *Fiddle-Dee-Dee* (1900). It was sung at John Stromberg's funeral in 1902.

Come Back to Me, words by Alan Jay Lerner, music by Burton Lane (1965). Ballad introduced by John Cullum in the musical *On a Clear Day You Can See Forever* (1965) and popularized by Johnny Mathis in a Mercury recording.

Come Dance with Me, words by George Blake, music by Dick Leibert (1958). Introduced by Mario Lanza in the motion-picture musical *Seven Hills of Rome* (MGM, 1958) and successfully recorded by him for RCA Victor. Frank Sinatra also made a best-selling recording of this song for Capitol, which received a "Grammy" from the National Academy of Recording Arts and Sciences in 1959 as the best vocal performance on disks that year.

Come Down, Ma Evenin' Star, words by Robert B. Smith, music by John Stromberg (1902). This was the composer's swan song. It was introduced by Lillian Russell in the Weber and Fields extravaganza *Twirly Whirly* (1902).

The manuscript of this song was in the composer's pocket when he was found dead in his New York apartment in July, 1902, apparently the victim of suicide. When Lillian Russell started singing the number on opening night of *Twirly Whirly,* she broke down and was unable to continue. It thereafter became her song of songs. In 1912, when Weber and Fields were temporarily reunited in *Hokey Pokey*, Lillian Russell sang "Come Down, Ma Evenin' Star" to a deeply moved audience. The song was interpolated in the motion pictures *Broadway to Hollywood*, starring Alice Brady (MGM, 1933), and in Chauncey Olcott's screen biography *My Wild Irish Rose* (Warner, 1947).

Come Fly with Me, words by Sammy Cahn, music by James Van Heusen (1958). Title song of a Frank Sinatra recording album for Capitol. It then provided the title for a motion picture starring Dolores Hart, Pamela Tiffin and Karl Malden (MGM, 1963), sung on the soundtrack under the titles by Frankie Avalon.

Come, Go with Me, words and music by C. E. Quick (1957). Popularized by the Del Vikings in a Dot recording.

Come Home, Father, words and music by Henry Clay Work (1864). Its composer's most famous Temperance song. It is the plea of a child to his father to come home from the saloon to the bedside of a dying son. It was introduced in the melodrama *Ten Nights in a Barroom* by Timothy Shay Arthur, and was subsequently heard frequently at Temperance meetings. It received satirical treatment in a production number, sung by a chorus, in the motion-picture musical *Cruisin' Down the River* (Columbia, 1953).

Come, Josephine, in My Flying Machine, words by Alfred Bryan, music by Fred Fisher (1910). It was introduced in vaudeville by Blanche Ring, who made a historic recording of it for Victor in the early 1910s. The song was revived in the motion-picture musical *The Story of the Castles* (RKO, 1939), and in the screen biography of Fred Fisher, *Oh, You Beautiful Doll* (20th Century-Fox, 1949).

Come On-a My House, words and music by Ross Bagdasarian and William Saroyan (1950). William Saroyan, the Pulitzer Prize-winning play-

wright, and his cousin Ross Bagdasarian were making an automobile trip across New Mexico in 1949 when they decided to write this popular song as a lark. Saroyan interpolated it in an off-Broadway production of his play *Son* (1950), and it was recorded by Kay Armen. Then Mitch Miller, recording director of popular music at Columbia, convinced Rosemary Clooney to record it, though she doubted seriously if this was her type of song. Her release in 1951 became her first major disk success, selling over a million copies. Mitch Miller conceived an unusual effect in this recording by using a harpsichord to accompany Miss Clooney.

Come On, Papa, words by Edgar Leslie, music by Harry Ruby (1918). When first issued, this song became so popular in vaudeville that Ruby had to write another song like it ("And He'd Say Oo-La-La" in collaboration with George Jessel) so that Jessel might use it in his act in competition with vaudevillians on the same bill featuring "Come On, Papa." The latter was heard in the screen biography of Ruby and Kalmar, *Three Little Words* (MGM, 1950).

Come Out, Come Out, Wherever You Are, words by Sammy Cahn, music by Jule Styne (1944). Introduced by Frank Sinatra in the motion-picture musical *Step Lively* (RKO, 1944).

Come Prima (or, For the First Time), an Italian popular song, music by M. Panzeri, English lyrics by Buck Ram (1958). The Italian song was introduced by Domenico Modugno. With English lyrics, the song was popularized by Tony Dalardo in a Mercury recording.

Come Rain or Come Shine, words by Johnny Mercer, music by Harold Arlen (1946). Introduced by Ruby Hill and Harold Nicholas in the musical play *St. Louis Woman* (1946). This song is unusual in that it has no introductory verse; also it begins in one key and ends up in another. The original-cast Capitol recording of *St. Louis Woman*, in which it appears, has become a collector's item.

In *Happy with the Blues*, Edward Jablonski describes how the song was written. Arlen was toying with the song idea, then played it for Mercer. "Mercer liked the tune, even came up with a fitting opening line, 'I'm gonna love you, like nobody loved you,' after which he paused for a moment. Into the brief silence Arlen jokingly injected 'come hell or high water,' to which Mercer reacted with 'of course, why didn't I think of that. . . . Come rain or come shine.' Before Mercer went home that night they had the song complete."

Comes Love, words by Charles Tobias and Lew Brown, music by Sam Stept (1939). Introduced by Phil Silvers and Judy Canova in the musical *Yokel Boy* (1939). The song was interpolated in the motion-picture adaptation of the musical, starring Joan Davis (Republic, 1942). Kate Smith helped make the song popular in a Columbia recording. It then became a favorite of several big-name bands, including those of Jimmy Dorsey, Benny Goodman and Harry James.

Come Softly to Me, words and music by Gary Troxel, Barbara Ellis and Gretchen Christopher (1959). Popularized by the Fleetwoods in a Dolphin recording.

Come, Take a Trip in My Airship, words by Ren Shields, music by George Evans (1904). One of the earliest popular-song successes about air transportation; its writing was stimulated by the successful flight of the Wright brothers at Kitty Hawk. The song was first popularized in vaudeville by Ethel Robinson.

Come Tell Me What's Your Answer, Yes or No, words and music by Paul Dresser (1898). It was revived in Dresser's screen biography *My Gal Sal* (20th Century-Fox, 1942).

Come to Me, words by Peter Lind Hayes, music by Robert Allen (1957). Introduced on a television production of the same name, then popularized by Johnny Mathis in a Columbia recording.

Come to Me, Bend to Me, words by Alan Jay Lerner, music by Frederick Loewe (1947). A madrigal introduced by Lee Sullivan in the musical play *Brigadoon* (1947). In the motion-picture adaptation of the musical (MGM, 1947), it was sung on the soundtrack by John Gustafson (for Jimmy Thompson). This song is said to be one of Loewe's own favorites among his creations.

Come Up and See Me Sometime, words by Arthur Swanstrom, music by Louis Alter (1933). The phrase "come up and see me sometime" was popularized in the movies by Mae West. The song it inspired was introduced by Lillian Roth in the motion-picture musical *Take a Chance* (Paramount, 1933).

Come Where My Love Lies Dreaming, words and music by Stephen Foster (1855). One of Foster's most celebrated sentimental ballads on a subject other than a Negro. It originated as a part song for soprano, alto, tenor and bass. It was played at Foster's funeral by the Allegheny Citizens Brass Band.

Comin' In on a Wing and a Prayer, words by Harold Adamson, music by Jimmy McHugh (1943). The idea for the song came from a letter by Sonny Bragg, an Air Force pilot and former football star. He told McHugh of a close call he had had on a mission to North Africa when "we came in on one engine and a prayer." The song was introduced by Eddie Cantor at an Air Force base. It became popular during World War II, with a sheet-music sale in excess of a million copies.

Comme Si, Comme Sa, words and music by Joan Whitney and Alex Kramer, based on a popular French melody by Bruno Coquatrix, "Clopin-Clopant" (1949). It was popularized in successful recordings by Frank Sinatra for Columbia and Tony Martin for RCA Victor.

Comrades, words and music by Felix McGlennon (1887). Introduced and popularized in vaudeville by Helene Mora "the female baritone."

Concerto for Two (or, A Love Song), words by Jack Lawrence, music by

Robert C. Haring based on a theme from the first movement of Tchaikovsky's First Piano Concerto (1941). Popularized by Claude Thornhill and his orchestra in a Columbia recording.

Coney Island, a motion-picture musical starring Betty Grable and George Montgomery (20th Century-Fox, 1943). The score combined standards with several new numbers by Leo Robin and Ralph Rainger.

See: A Bird in a Gilded Cage; By the Beautiful Sea; Cuddle Up a Little Closer; Who Threw the Overalls in Mrs. Murphy's Chowder?

A Connecticut Yankee, a musical comedy with book by Herbert Fields based on Mark Twain's *A Connecticut Yankee in King Arthur's Court.* Lyrics by Lorenz Hart. Music by Richard Rodgers. Starring William Gaxton and Constance Carpenter (1927).

The song "To Keep My Love Alive" was written by Rodgers and Hart for the 1943 Broadway stage revival.

The motion-picture adaptation starred Will Rogers and Maureen O'Sullivan (Fox, 1931). The hit songs of the stage score were used.

See: I Feel at Home with You; On a Desert Island with Thee; My Heart Stood Still; Thou Swell; To Keep My Love Alive.

Connie's Hot Chocolates, an all-Negro revue with book and lyrics by Andy Razaf. Music by "Fats" Waller and Harry Brooks. Starring Jazzlips Richardson, Eddie Green and Margaret Sims (1929).

See: Ain't Misbehavin'; Black and Blue.

Conrad, Con, composer, born New York City, 1891; died Van Nuys, California, 1938.

See (Lyrics by Benny Davis): Lonesome and Sorry; Margie.

See (Lyrics by Herb Magidson): The Continental; Here's to Romance; Midnight in Paris; A Needle in a Haystack.

See (Lyrics by Billy Rose): Barney Google; You've Got to See Mama Every Night.

See also: Bend Down, Sister; Champagne Waltz; Crazy Feet; Way

Down Yonder in New Orleans; Ma, He's Making Eyes at Me; Memory Lane; Oh, Frenchy; Palesteena; You Call It Madness, But I Call It Love.

Consolation, words by Edward Madden, music by Theodore F. Morse (1908).

The Continental, words by Herb Magidson, music by Con Conrad (1934). Introduced by Fred Astaire and Ginger Rogers in the motion-picture musical *The Gay Divorcee* (RKO, 1934). This song (an interpolation in a Cole Porter score) became the first to win the Academy Award.

The Convict and the Bird, words and music by Paul Dresser (1888). One of Dresser's earliest publications, and one of his first successful sentimental ballads.

Coon, Coon, Coon, words and music by Leo Friedman (1901). When first published it was advertised as "the cleverest coon-comique ever issued, full of catchy melody and funny lines that combine to make it the hit of the season." It became popular both in vaudeville and in minstrel shows.

Coots, J. Fred, composer, born Brooklyn, New York, 1897.

See (Lyrics by Benny Davis): Cross Your Fingers; I Still Get a Thrill Thinking of You; Why?; Why Don't They Let Me Sing a Love Song?

See (Lyrics by Sam M. Lewis): Beautiful Lady; For All We Know; One Minute to One.

See also: I Want to Ring Bells; Love Letters in the Sand; Me and My Teddy Bear; A Precious Little Thing Called Love; Promenade Walk; Santa Claus Is Coming to Town; Time Will Tell; Two Tickets to Georgia; You Go to My Head.

Copper Canyon, words and music by Jay Livingston and Ray Evans (1949). Title song of a non-musical motion picture starring Hedy Lamarr and Ray Milland (Paramount, 1950). It was popularized by Teresa Brewer in a Coral recording.

Coquette, words by Gus Kahn, music by John Green and Carmen Lombardo (1928). This was Green's first published song, written during the summer of 1927 when, while still a student at Harvard, he was doing arrangements for Guy Lombardo and the Royal Canadians. Gus Kahn got the title from the Broadway play *Coquette*, which starred Helen Hayes in 1927. The song was introduced by Guy Lombardo and the Royal Canadians over the radio in 1927, and their Columbia recording later the same year was a best seller. The song was interpolated in the motion picture *Cockeyed Cavaliers*, starring Bert Wheeler and Robert Woolsey (RKO, 1934).

Cosi Cosa, words by Ned Washington, music by Bronislau Kaper and Walter Jurmann (1935). Introduced by Allan Jones in the Marx Brothers motion-picture extravaganza *A Night at the Opera* (MGM, 1935).

Coslow, Sam, lyricist, born New York City, 1902.

See: Johnston, Arthur.

See also: Blue Mirage; Sing, You Sinners; True Blue Lou; True Confession.

Count Every Star, words by Sammy Gallop, music by Bruno Coquatrix (1950). Popularized by Hugo Winterhalter and his orchestra in a best-selling RCA Victor recording.

The Country Cousin, words by Alfred Bryan, music by Vincent Youmans (1920). Youmans' first published song. It had been inspired by a motion picture of the same name starring Elise Hammerstein.

Count Your Blessings, words and music by Irving Berlin (1952). Introduced by Bing Crosby and Rosemary Clooney in the motion-picture musical *White Christmas* (Paramount, 1954). It was popularized by Bing Crosby in a Decca recording and by Eddie Fisher in a recording for RCA Victor. The song was represented thirteen times on the Hit Parade in 1954.

A Couple of Song and Dance Men, words and music by Irving Berlin (1945). Introduced by Fred Astaire and Bing Crosby in the motion-picture musical *Blue Skies* (MGM, 1946).

A Couple of Swells, words and music by Irving Berlin (1947). Introduced by Fred Astaire and Judy Garland in the motion-picture musical *Easter Parade* (MGM, 1948).

Covered Wagon Days, words and music by Will Morrisey and Joe Burrows (1923). A pioneer attempt at writing a motion-picture theme song. It was created to exploit a silent motion picture classic, *The Covered Wagon* USA, 1923). The song was also interpolated in the musical *The Newcomers* (1923).

Cover Girl, a motion-picture musical starring Rita Hayworth and Gene Kelly (Columbia, 1944). Songs by Ira Gershwin and Jerome Kern.

See: Long Ago and Far Away; Sure Thing.

Cow Cow Boogie, words by Don Raye, music by Gene De Paul and Benny Carter (1941). Popularized in a Capitol recording by Ella Mae Morse and Freddie Slack; this was the first successful release by the then newly formed recording company. Ella Mae Morse sang it in the motion-picture musical *Reveille with Beverly*, starring Ann Miller (RKO, 1943).

Cradle's Empty, Baby's Gone, words and music by Harry Kennedy (1880). A sentimental ballad about the death of an infant. It enjoyed considerable popularity in the early 1880s, particularly "among the shop girls of this city," as the New York *Herald* commented on November 9, 1884. The song was suddenly driven into oblivion by the outbreak of an epidemic in New York City in the middle 1880s that caused a large infant mortality.

Crazy Feet, words and music by Sidney D. Mitchell, Con Conrad and Archie Gottler (1930). Introduced by Dixie Lee in the motion-picture musical *Happy Days*, starring Warner Baxter, Charles Farrell, Janet Gaynor and numerous guest artists (Fox, 1930).

Crazy Heart, words and music by Fred Rose and Maurice Murray (1951). Popularized in a Decca recording by Guy Lombardo and the Royal Canadians. Hank Williams' recording for MGM in 1952 was also a best seller.

The Crazy Otto Rag, words and music by Edward R. White, Mack Wolfson,

Hugo B. Peretti and Luigi Creatore (1955). Popularized in a Decca recording by Crazy Otto and in a Dot recording by Johnny Maddox.

Crazy Rhythm, words by Irving Caesar, music by Roger Wolfe Kahn and Joseph Meyer (1928). It was written for Ben Bernie, who introduced it with his orchestra. It was then interpolated in the musical *Here's Howe* (1928). It was heard in several motion pictures, including the musicals *You Were Meant for Me* (20th Century-Fox, 1948) and *Tea for Two* (Warner, 1950).

Crinoline Days, words and music by Irving Berlin (1922). Introduced by Grace La Rue in the *Music Box Revue of 1922.* Robert Baral explains: "As she sang, she rose slowly via an elevator, her hoop skirt getting fuller and wider until the final yard came out of the trap to engulf the entire stage."

Croce di Oro (or, Cross of Gold), words by Bob Haring, music by Kim Gannon (1955). Popularized by Patti Page in a Mercury recording.

Cross Over the Bridge, words and music by Bennie Benjamin and George Weiss (1954). Popularized by Patti Page in a Mercury recording that sold over a million disks.

Cross Your Fingers, words by Arthur Swanstrom and Benny Davis, music by J. Fred Coots (1929). Introduced by Shirley Vernon and Milton Watson in the musical *Sons o' Guns* (1929).

Cross Your Heart, words by Bud De Sylva, music by Lewis E. Gensler (1926). Introduced by Mary Lawlor, Clarence Nordstrain and chorus in the musical *Queen High* (1926).

Cruisin' Down the River, a motion-picture musical starring Dick Haymes and Audrey Totter (Columbia, 1953). The score was made up mainly of standards.

See: Come Home, Father; Cruising Down the River; Pennies from Heaven; She Is More to Be Pitied than Censured; Sing, You Sinners; There Goes that Song Again.

Cruising Down the River, words by Eily Beadell, music by Nell Tollerton (1945). An English popular song introduced in London by Lou Preager. In the United States it was popularized in 1949 in two best-selling recordings: Blue Barron and his orchestra for MGM and Russ Morgan and his orchestra for Decca. It provided the title, was sung by a chorus under the titles, and was used as a recurring melody in the background music of a motion-picture musical (Columbia, 1953).

Cry, words and music by Churchill Kohlman (1951). Popularized by Johnnie Ray, whose Columbia recording sold a million disks. The song started a vogue for wailing ballads.

Cry Baby, words and music by B. Russell and V. Meade (1963). Popularized by Garnett Mims' recording for United Artists.

Cryin' for the Carolines, words by Sam M. Lewis and Joe Young, music by Harry Warren (1930). Interpolated in the motion-picture adaptation of the Rodgers and Hart musical *Spring Is Here* (First National, 1930), sung by the Brox Sisters. It was popularized by Guy Lombardo and the Royal Canadians over the radio.

Crying, words and music by Roy Orbison and Joe Melson (1961). Popularized by Roy Orbison in a Monument recording.

Crying in the Chapel, words and music by Artie Glenn (1953). Introduced by the composer's son, Darrell Glenn, but popularized by the Orioles in a Jubilee recording and by June Valli in an RCA Victor recording. Elvis Presley's recording for RCA Victor in 1965 was a best seller.

Crying in the Rain, words and music by Howard Greenfield and Carole King (1961).

Cry Me a River, words and music by Arthur Hamilton (1953). Popularized in 1955 by Julie London in a Liberty recording—her first successful release. She sang it in the motion picture *The Girl Can't Help It* (20th Century-Fox, 1958).

The Cry of the Wild Goose, words and music by Terry Gilkyson (1949). Popularized in 1950 by Frankie Laine in a Mercury recording that sold over a million disks. It was also interpolated in the motion picture *Saddle Tramp* (Universal, 1950).

Cry, the Beloved Country, words by Maxwell Anderson, music by Kurt Weill (1949). Introduced by Frank Roane and chorus in the musical play *Lost in the Stars* (1949).

Cuban Love Song, words by Dorothy Fields, music by Jimmy McHugh and Herbert Stothart (1931). Introduced by Lawrence Tibbett in the motion picture of the same name (MGM, 1931). Jimmy McHugh informed this editor: "For the recording, I had Tibbett make a harmony record of himself (overdubbed), and on the screen it showed the real Tibbett as a soldier and his image as a ghost standing beside him. This was the first multiple recording in record history."

The Cubanola Glide, words by Vincent P. Bryan, music by Harry von Tilzer (1909). An early ragtime classic, and one of the first successful popular tunes about social dancing, antecedant of songs about the grizzly bear, bunny hug, turkey trot, and so forth. Sophie Tucker was supposed to sing "The Cubanola Glide" in the *Ziegfeld Follies of 1909*, but the number was dropped from the show before it reached New York. She then helped to make it famous in vaudeville. Harriet Raymond sang it in the musical *The Girl from Rector's* (1910). The song was interpolated for Alice Faye in the motion picture *Fallen Angel* (20th Century-Fox, 1945).

La Cucaracha, a Mexican folk song, English lyrics by Stanley Adams (1934). The song, with English words, was introduced in the nonmusical motion picture *Viva Villa,* starring Wallace Beery (1933). It was subsequently interpolated in the motion picture *Romance of the Rio Grande,* starring Cesar Romero (20th Century-Fox, 1941). Hawley Ades made a fox-trot arrangement of "La Cucaracha," which, in an adaptation by Juan Y. D'Lorah, was introduced in the motion picture *La Cucaracha* (1934).

Cuddle Up a Little Closer, words by

Otto Hauerbach (Harbach), music by Karl Hoschna (1908). This was Harbach's first hit song—in his first produced show. It was introduced by Alice Yorke, in the operetta *The Three Twins* (1908). Though it achieved considerable success in that production, it was not originally written for it. Hoschna had first conceived this melody for a vaudeville sketch. When *The Three Twins* was in rehearsal he decided to use it in its score, with new lyrics by Harbach. The song has been heard in several motion pictures. These include *The Story of the Castles* (RKO, 1939); *The Birth of the Blues* (Paramount, 1941), sung by Mary Martin; the Ted Lewis screen biography *Is Everybody Happy?* (Columbia, 1943); *Coney Island* (20th Century-Fox, 1943), sung by Betty Grable; and *On Moonlight Bay* (Warner, 1951), sung by Gordon MacRae. It was used in the background music for the closing scene of the nonmusical motion picture *Tall Story,* starring Anthony Perkins and Jane Fonda (Warner, 1960).

A Cup of Coffee, a Sandwich and You, words by Billy Rose and Al Dubin, music by Joseph Meyer (1925). It was interpolated for Gertrude Lawrence and Jack Buchanan in the London musical production *Charlot's Revue of 1926* during its visit to New York.

Cupid and I, words by Harry B. Smith, music by Victor Herbert (1897). Hit waltz from operetta *The Serenade* (1897), where it was introduced by Alice Nielsen. It was in this production, and primarily with this number, that Alice Nielsen first became a star.

The Curse of an Aching Heart (or, You Made Me What I Am Today, I Hope You're Satisfied), words by Henry Fink, music by Al Piantadosi (1913). A carry-over of the 1890 vogue for sentimental balladry into the 1910s. Though often sung in all seriousness in its own day, the song also achieved considerable popularity as a parody of sentimental ballads. "It is still a sure laugh-producer," said

Sigmund Spaeth, "among the intelligentsia."

The Curse of the Dreamer, words and music by Paul Dresser (1899). Dresser wrote this ballad, originally entitled "The Curse," after his wife, May Howard, a burlesque queen, deserted him. He sought her out in her hotel room, where he sang it to her and through it effected a temporary reconciliation. After they had separated for good, Dresser rewrote the ballad, adding a happy ending and renaming it "The Curse of the Dreamer." It became one of his most successful ballads.

D

Daddy Has a Sweetheart and Mother Is Her Name, words by Gene Buck, music by Dave Stamper (1912). This number was placed in the *Ziegfeld Follies of 1911* for Lillian Lorraine. A. L. Erlanger, an investor in the *Follies* at the time, did not like Miss Lorraine, and both the star and the song had to be deleted from that production before opening night. Lillian Lorraine introduced the song at the Oscar Hammerstein Victoria Theatre in New York in 1911, in an act which Gene Buck directed and for which he helped design the set. The song was an enormous hit, starting a sheet-music sale that passed the million-copy mark. Meanwhile, Ziegfeld apologized to Buck for having removed the song from the *Follies*. It was interpolated in the *Ziegfeld Follies of 1912*, once again sung by Lillian Lorraine.

Daddy Long Legs, words by Sam M. Lewis, music by Harry Ruby (1919). A song inspired by the silent motion picture of the same name starring Mary Pickford.

Daddy's Little Girl, words by Edward Madden, music by Theodore F. Morse (1905).

Daddy Wouldn't Buy Me a Bow-Wow, words and music by Joseph Tabrar (1892). A comedy number enabling the performer to indulge in amusing baby talk. It was introduced in vaudeville by Joseph Tabrar, but became famous after Vesta Victoria, the English comedienne, sang it at Tony Pastor's Music Hall in New York.

Daddy, You've Been a Mother to Me, words and music by Fred Fisher (1920). It was interpolated in the Fred Fisher screen biography *Oh, You Beautiful Doll* (20th Century-Fox, 1949).

Daisies Won't Tell, words and music by Anita Owen (1908). The only hit song by its author. It is now remembered primarily for the opening phrase of the chorus, "Sweet bunch of daisies."

Daisy Bell (or, Bicycle Built for Two), words and music by Harry Dacre (1892). When Dacre, an English popular composer, first came to the United States, he brought with him a bicycle, for which he was charged duty. His friend (the songwriter, William Jerome) remarked lightly: "It's lucky you didn't bring a bicycle built for two, otherwise you'd have to pay double duty." Dacre was so taken with the phrase "bicycle built for two" that he decided to use it in a song. That song, "Daisy Bell," first became successful in a London music hall, in a performance by Kate Lawrence. Tony Pastor was the first one to sing it in the United States, at his own Music Hall. Its success in America began when Jennie Lindsay brought down the house with it at the Atlantic Gardens on the Bowery early in 1892. A good deal of the song's popularity was due to the fact that in 1892 the bicycle was becoming popular with women, having just been made easier and safer to handle.

Damn Yankees, a musical comedy with book by Douglass Wallop and George Abbott based on Wallop's novel *The Year the Yankees Lost the Pennant*. Lyrics and music by Richard Adler and Jerry Ross. Starring Stephen Douglas, Gwen Verdon and Ray Walton (1955). Original cast recording (RCA Victor).

The motion-picture adaptation starred Tab Hunter and Gwen Verdon (Warner, 1958). It used the principal numbers from the stage score. Soundtrack recording (RCA Victor).

See: Heart; Two Lost Souls; Whatever Lola Wants.

Damsel in Distress, a motion-picture musical starring Fred Astaire and Joan Fontaine (RKO, 1937). Songs by George and Ira Gershwin.

See: A Foggy Day; I Can't Be Bothered Now; Nice Work If You Can Get It; Stiff Upper Lip.

Dance, My Darlings, words by Oscar Hammerstein II, music by Sigmund Romberg (1935). Introduced by Nancy McCord (and ensemble) in the musical *May Wine* (1936).

Dance with a Dolly (with a Hole in Her Stockin'), words and music by Terry Shand, Jimmy Eaton and Mickey Leader, melody adapted from Cool White's 1844 song hit "Lubly Fan" (1940). Popularized by Russ Morgan and his orchestra in a Decca recording and interpolated in the motion picture *On Stage, Everybody*, starring Peggy Ryan (Universal, 1945).

Dance with Me, Henry (or, The Wallflower), words and music by Johnny Otis, Hank Ballard and Etta James (1955). Popularized by Georgia Gibbs in a best-selling Mercury recording. A rhythm and blues version, named "The Wallflower," was recorded by Etta James for Modern.

Dancing in the Dark, words by Howard Dietz, music by Arthur Schwartz (1931). One of the most successful songs by Dietz and Schwartz. It was introduced by John Barker in the revue *The Band Wagon* (1931),

and then was danced to by Tilly Losch.

One day, while *The Band Wagon* was being rehearsed, Schwartz felt a need in the production for a "dark song . . . somewhat mystical, yet in slow, even rhythm." The following morning he had the whole melody down on paper.

Artie Shaw's recording for RCA Victor in 1941 sold a million disks. The song subsequently provided the title, was sung on the soundtrack under the titles, was used as a recurrent theme in the background music, and was featured by Betsy Drake in a production number of a motion-picture musical (20th Century-Fox, 1949). In the motion-picture musical *The Band Wagon* (MGM, 1953), it was used as background music for an effective dance by Fred Astaire and Cyd Charisse.

Dancing in the Dark (screen musical). *See: The Band Wagon.*

Dancing on the Ceiling, words by Lorenz Hart, music by Richard Rodgers (1930). Written for the Ziegfeld production *Simple Simon* (1930), but dropped before that show opened in New York. The song was finally introduced in London by Jessie Matthews and Sonnie Hale in the musical *Evergreen* (1930). They repeated their performance in the English-made motion-picture adaptation of this musical (Gaumont British, 1935).

Dancing with Tears in My Eyes, words by Al Dubin, music by Joseph A. Burke (1930). Written for the motion picture *Dancing Sweeties* (Warner, 1930), but not used there. Published as an independent number, it became one of the major song hits in 1930.

Danger! Heartbreak Ahead, words and music by Carl Stutz and Carl Barefoot (1954). Popularized by Jaye P. Morgan in an RCA Victor recording.

Danke Schoen, words and music by Berthold Kaempfert (1963). Popularized by Wayne Newton in a Capitol recording.

Danny by My Side, words by Edward Harrigan, music by David Braham (1896). Hit song from the last of

Edward Harrigan's stage extravaganzas, *The Merry Malones* (1896). When the fiftieth anniversary of the opening of the Brooklyn Bridge was celebrated on May 24, 1933, Governor Alfred E. Smith of New York sang "Danny By My Side." The song had particular relevance during this celebration by virtue of its opening line, "The Brooklyn Bridge on Sunday is known as lovers' lane." Governor Smith then told a reporter that he deeply regretted the fact that apparently everybody else had forgotten this song.

Dapper Dan (The Sheik of Alabam'), words by Lew Brown, music by Albert von Tilzer (1921).

Dardanella, words by Fred Fisher, music by Felix Bernard and Johnny S. Black (1919). A syncopated fox trot with a recurring bass pattern, later known as "boogie." The song enjoyed enormous success. In less than a year after its publication it sold a million and a half copies of sheet music and almost a million records. The very first recording—for Victor by Ben Selvin's Novelty Orchestra—sold about a million disks, believed to be one of the first pressings to do so. As lyricist and publisher, Fred Fisher is believed to have earned over a million dollars from this number.

"Dardanella" originated as a piano rag entitled *Turkish Tom Tom*, a composition by Johnny S. Black. Impressed by its infectious rhythm, Fred Fisher suggested that Black add a chorus. When Black did so, Fisher wrote the lyrics, now naming and publishing the number as "Dardanella." At this point, Felix Bernard, a vaudevillian, came forward with proof that the basic melody was his, and that he had turned it over to Black. Fisher paid Bernard $100 for his interest in the music. After the song began reaping a financial harvest, Bernard sued Fisher, claiming he had been duped into accepting a mere pittance for his rights. He lost the suit. A far more significant lawsuit involved "Dardanella" and Jerome Kern's

"Ka-lu-a." This is discussed in the section on "Ka-lu-a."

"Dardanella" was interpolated as a piano episode in the non-musical motion pictures *Baby Face*, starring Barbara Stanwyck (Warner, 1933), and *Stella Dallas*, starring Barbara Stanwyck (Samuel Goldwyn, 1934), and in the Fred Fisher screen biography *Oh, You Beautiful Doll* (20th Century-Fox, 1949).

Darin, Bobby, composer and lyricist, born Walden Robert Cassotto, New York City, 1936.

See: Dream Lover; Eighteen Yellow Roses; If a Man Answers; Splish-Splash; That Funny Feeling; A True, True Love.

Dark Moon, words and music by Ned Miller (1957). Popularized by Gale Storm and by Bonnie Guitar in separate Dot recordings.

The Darktown Strutters' Ball, words and music by Shelton Brooks (1917). A ragtime classic popularized by Sophie Tucker in vaudeville. It was interpolated in several motion pictures. Among them were *The Story of the Castles* (RKO, 1939); *Broadway*, starring George Raft and Pat O'Brien (Universal, 1942); *The Dolly Sisters* (20th Century-Fox, 1945); and the Texas Guinan screen biography *Incendiary Blonde* (Paramount, 1945).

This song is one of sixteen selected by ASCAP in 1963 for its all-time Hit Parade during its half century of existence.

Darling, Je Vous Aime Beaucoup, words and music by Anna Sosenko (1935). Theme song of Hildegarde, written by her manager. It was introduced and popularized by Hildegarde in night clubs and in a recording for Decca. The most successful recording, however, is that of Nat King Cole for Capitol, which sold a million disks.

Darling Nelly Gray, words and music by Benjamin Russell Hanby (1856). This song is said to have had almost as great an impact in arousing sympathy for Negro slaves in pre-Civil War America as *Uncle Tom's Cabin*. The lyrics described the death of

Joseph Selby, a fugitive slave, in an Ohio station of the Underground Railroad. With his dying breaths he bids farewell to his beloved Nelly Gray, who had been snatched from his arms back in Kentucky.

Hanby wrote his ballad while attending Otterbein College in Westerville, Ohio. He mailed his manuscript to Oliver Ditson, the Boston publisher. The first Hanby knew that his song had been published was when one day he heard it performed at a concert.

Darn It, Baby, That's Love, words and music by Joan Edwards and Lyn Duddy (1950). Introduced by Bill Norvas and Phyllis Cameron in the intimate revue *Tickets Please* (1950).

Darn That Dream, words by Eddie De Lange, music by James Van Heusen (1939). Introduced by Benny Goodman and his orchestra in the musical *Swingin' the Dream* (1939) — a musical and "swing" version of Shakespeare's *A Midsummer Night's Dream*.

Dat's Love, words by Oscar Hammerstein II, music being the "Habanera" from Georges Bizet's opera *Carmen* (1943). Introduced on alternate nights by Muriel Smith and Muriel Rahn (and chorus) in the musical play *Carmen Jones* (1943). In the motion-picture adaptation of the musical (20th Century-Fox, 1954), it was sung by Dorothy Dandridge.

The Daughter of Rosie O'Grady, words by Monty C. Brice, music by Walter Donaldson (1918). This is the song which for half a century identified the younger Pat Rooney. He introduced it at the Palace Theatre in New York in 1919, accompanying his rendition with a waltz clog that became his trademark. This dance has since sometimes been erroneously credited to his father, the first Pat Rooney, a popular vaudevillian of the gaslight era. The song "The Daughter of Rosie O'Grady" provided the title for a motion-picture musical starring June Haver (Warner, 1950), where it was sung by Gordon MacRae.

David, Hal, composer and lyricist, born

New York City, 1921.

See: Bacharach, Burt F.

See also: American Beauty Rose; Broken Hearted Melody; Magic Moments; My Heart Is an Open Book.

David, Mack, lyricist, born New York City, 1912.

See: Bibbidi-Bobbidi-Boo; Bimbombay; Candy; Cat Ballou; Cherry Pink and Apple Blossom White; Chi-Baba; A Dream Is a Wish Your Heart Makes; The Hanging Tree; Hush, Hush, Sweet Charlotte; I Don't Care if the Sun Don't Shine; It Only Hurts for a Little While; It's Love, Love, Love; It's a Mad, Mad, Mad, Mad World; Love Has Many Faces; Moon Love; My Own True Love; Sunflower; La Vie en Rose; Walk on the Wild Side.

Davis, Benny, lyricist, born New York City, 1895.

See: Akst, Harry; Burke, Joseph A.; Coots, J. Fred.

See also: Angel Child; Goodbye, Broadway, Hello, France; I'm Nobody's Baby; Indiana Moon; Make Believe; Say It While Dancing; There Goes My Heart.

Davy Crockett. *See:* The Ballad of Davy Crockett.

The Dawn of Love, words by Otto Hauerbach (Harbach), music by Rudolf Friml (1912). Introduced by Emma Trentini in Rudolf Friml's first operetta, *The Firefly* (1912).

Day After Day, words by Howard Deitz, music by Arthur Schwartz (1932). Introduced by Clifton Webb in the musical *Flying Colors* (1932).

This is the song that gave Doris Day her stage name. She made her first modest appearances as a singer by using the name of her birth— Doris Kapplehoff. Auditioning for Barney Rapp, the bandleader, she sang "Day After Day." Rapp hired her as his band vocalist but suggested she use a stage name. She selected the name of "Day" because of the song she had sung.

The Day Before Spring, a musical comedy with book and lyrics by Alan Jay Lerner. Music by Frederick Loewe. This was the first musical-comedy success by Lerner and

Loewe. Starring Bill Johnson and Irene Manning (1945).

See: God's Green World; I Love You This Morning; My Love Is a Married Man.

Day In, Day Out, words by Johnny Mercer, music by Rube Bloom (1939). A favorite of big name bands of the early 1940s, including those of Tommy Dorsey and Artie Shaw.

Day-O. *See:* The Banana Boat Song.

Days of Wine and Roses, words by Johnny Mercer, music by Henry Mancini (1962). Title song of a motion picture starring Jack Lemmon and Lee Remick (Warner, 1962). It was sung under the titles by Andy Williams, who made a best-selling recording for Columbia. The song received the Academy Award. In 1964 it was also the recipient of "Grammy" Awards from the National Academy of Recording Arts and Sciences as the best song of the year, and as the best recording; the latter was that of Henry Mancini and his orchestra for RCA Victor.

The Day the Rains Came, a French popular song ("Le Jour où la Pluie Viendra"), music by Gilbert Becaud, who introduced it in Paris. English lyrics by Carl Sigman (1957). The song, with English lyrics, was popularized by Jane Morgan in a recording for Kapp.

Dearest Enemy, a musical comedy with book by Herbert Fields. Lyrics by Lorenz Hart. Music by Richard Rodgers. This was the first musical-comedy success by Rodgers and Hart. Starring Charles Purcell and Helen Ford (1925).

See: Here in My Arms.

Dearest, You're the Nearest to My Heart, words by Benny Davis, music by Harry Akst (1922). Introduced in Atlantic City, New Jersey, by Paul Whiteman and his orchestra, who then popularized it in other public appearances and in a Victor recording.

Dear Friend, words by Sheldon Harnick, music by Jerry Bock (1963). Introduced by Barbara Cook in the musical *She Loves Me Not* (1963).

Dear Heart, words by Jay Livingston and Ray Evans, music by Henry Mancini (1965). Title song of a motion picture starring Geraldine Page and Glenn Ford (Warner, 1965), where it was sung under the titles by a chorus. The song was popularized in a Columbia recording by Andy Williams and by Jack Jones in a Kapp recording.

Dear Hearts and Gentle People, words by Bob Hilliard, music by Sammy Fain (1949). The title comes from a phrase found scribbled on a piece of paper in Stephen Foster's pocket when he died. Bing Crosby's Decca recording in 1950 sold a million disks. Dinah Shore's recording for Columbia was also a best seller.

Dearie, words and music by Clare Kummer (1905). Introduced and popularized by Sallie Fisher in the musical *Sergeant Brue* (1905).

Dearie, words and music by Bob Hilliard and Dave Mann (1950). Popularized in a Decca recording by Ethel Merman and Ray Bolger.

A Dear John Letter, words and music by Billy Barton, Billy Liebert and Charles "Fuzzy" Owen (1953). Popularized in a Capitol recording by Jean Shepard and Ferlin Husky.

Dear Little Boy of Mine, words by J. Keirn Brennan, music by Ernest R. Ball (1918). Popularized in vaudeville by sopranos and tenors. Blanche Thebom sang it in the screen biography of Ernest R. Ball, *When Irish Eyes Are Smiling* (20th Century-Fox, 1944).

Dearly Beloved, words by Johnny Mercer, music by Jerome Kern (1942). Introduced by Fred Astaire in the motion-picture musical *You Were Never Lovelier* (Columbia, 1942).

Margaret Whiting (then not yet a professional singer) was the first to try out this song. She did it at Kern's home on Whittier Drive in Beverly Hills, from a lead sheet; Kern accompanied her at the piano. She was in such awe of the composer that she could not speak a word when her performance ended. Kern understood the silence. "I guess you like it, even though you don't say so," Kern said. "If you didn't like it, you would not have been able to sing it so well."

Dear Old Girl, words by Richard Henry Buck, music by Theodore F. Morse (1903). Its large sheet-music sale in 1903 and 1904 saved the publishing house of Howley, Haviland and Dresser from bankruptcy.

Dear Old Rose, words by Jack Drislane, music by George W. Meyer (1912).

December and May (or, Mollie Newell, Don't Be Cruel), words by Edward B. Marks, music by William Lorraine (1893). This was Edward B. Marks' first song. It was also one of the earliest "December-May" songs in American popular music. It was introduced by Lydia Yeamans at Tony Pastor's Music Hall in 1893, where she scored such a success that from then on, and for the next quarter of a century, she kept it in her repertory. Tony Pastor was so fond of this number, and of Miss Yeamans' rendition, that whenever she appeared at his Music Hall he insisted she include it in her act.

De De Dinah, words and music by Peter De Angelis (1958). Popularized by Frankie Avalon in a Chancellor recording.

Deep in a Dream, words by Eddie De Lange, music by James Van Heusen (1938). Introduced and first popularized by Russ Morgan and his orchestra.

Deep in My Heart, words by Dorothy Donnelly, music by Sigmund Romberg (1924). Introduced by Howard Marsh and Ilse Marvenga in the operetta *The Student Prince* (1924). In the motion-picture adaptation of the operetta (MGM, 1954), it was sung on the soundtrack by Mario Lanza (for Edmund Purdom). Lanza also recorded it in a best-selling RCA Victor release. The song provided the title for, was heard under the titles of and was interpolated in Romberg's screen biography (MGM, 1954).

Deep in My Heart, a motion-picture musical biography of Sigmund Romberg. Starring José Ferrer as Romberg, with Merle Oberon and an all-star singing cast that included Helen Traubel, Vic Damone, Tony Martin, Howard Keel and others (MGM, 1954). The score was made up of Sigmund Romberg standards. Soundtrack recording (MGM).

See: Auf Wiedersehen; Deep in My Heart; I Love to Go Swimmin' with Wimmen; It; Lover, Come Back to Me; Mr. and Mrs.; Road to Paradise; Serenade; Softly as in a Morning Sunrise; Stout Hearted Men; When I Grow Too Old to Dream; Will You Remember?; Your Land and My Land; You Will Remember Vienna.

Deep in the Heart of Texas, words by June Hershey, music by Don Swander (1941). An audience-participation song—the audience joining with handclapping at the end of each of several phrases in the chorus. The Columbia recording by Horace Heidt and his orchestra sold over a million disks. The song was interpolated in numerous motion pictures. Among these were *Heart of the Rio Grande,* sung by Gene Autry (Republic, 1942); *Hi, Neighbor,* starring Jean Parker (Republic, 1942); *Thirty Seconds Over Tokyo,* starring Spencer Tracy and Van Johnson (MGM, 1944); *I'll Get By* (Warner, 1950), where it was sung by Dennis Day; *Rich, Young and Pretty* (MGM, 1951), where it was sung in French by Wendell Corey; the screen biography of Jane Froman, *With a Song in My Heart* (20th Century-Fox, 1952); *How to Marry a Millionaire,* starring Marilyn Monroe (20th Century-Fox, 1953); and *Teahouse of the August Moon,* sung by Glenn Ford, Eddie Albert and Marlon Brando (MGM, 1957).

The Bluebird recording by Alvino Rey and his orchestra in 1942 was a best seller.

Deep Purple, words by Mitchell Parish, music by Peter De Rose (1939). It originated in 1934 as a piano composition; one year later Domenico Savino arranged it for orchestra. Its success, however, came only after Mitchell Parish had provided it with lyrics. It was popularized by Larry Clinton and his orchestra, and by Bing Crosby in a Decca recording. The song returned in a best-selling release in 1963 in an Atco recording by Nine Tempo.

Babe Ruth, the home-run king, loved this song so deeply that on each of his birthdays, during the last decade of his life, he had Peter De Rose sing it for him.

De Koven, Reginald, composer, born Middletown, Connecticut, 1859; died Chicago, Illinois, 1920.

See (Lyrics by Harry B. Smith): The Armorer's Song; Brown October Ale; Do You Remember Love?; Moonlight Song; Oh, Promise Me.

De Lange, Eddie, lyricist, born Long Island City, New York, 1904.

See: van Heusen, James.

See also: Moonglow; Solitude; A String of Pearls.

Delicado, a Brazilian popular song, with melody by Waldyr Azevedo, English lyrics by Jack Lawrence (1952). Popularized by Percy Faith and his orchestra in a Columbia recording.

Delicious, a motion-picture musical starring Janet Gaynor and Charles Farrell (Fox, 1931). Songs by George and Ira Gershwin, their first original score for the screen.

See: Delishious.

Delightful to Be Married. *See:* It's Delightful to be Married.

Delishious, words by Ira Gershwin, music by George Gershwin (1931). Introduced by Janet Gaynor and Charles Farrell in the motion-picture musical *Delicious* (Fox, 1931). This was the first song hit by George and Ira Gershwin written directly for the screen. It was subsequently interpolated in the George Gershwin screen biography *Rhapsody in Blue* (Warner, 1945).

De Paul, Gene, composer, born New York City, 1919.

See (Lyrics by Johnny Mercer): Jubilation T. Cornpone; Namely You; When You're in Love.

See also: Cow Cow Boogie; Irresistible You; Mister Five by Five; Teach Me Tonight.

De Pullman Porters' Ball, words by Edgar Smith, music by John Stromberg (1901). Hit song from the Weber and Fields musical extravaganza *Hoity Toity* (1901). It was introduced there by Fritz Williams, in his first appearance as a regular performer at the Weber and Fields Music Hall.

Dere's a Café on de Corner, words by Oscar Hammerstein II, the melody being the "Seguidille" from Georges Bizet's opera *Carmen* (1943). Introduced on alternate nights by Muriel Smith and Luther Saxon and by Muriel Rahn and Napoleon Reed in the musical play *Carmen Jones* (1943). In the motion-picture adaptation of the musical (20th Century-Fox, 1954), it was sung by Harry Belafonte and Dorothy Dandridge.

Der Fuehrer's Face, words and music by G. Oliver Wallace (1942). Comedy song of World War II, the only hit to lampoon Hitler. The song was written for a Donald Duck animated cartoon, *In Nutzy Land,* whose title was changed to that of the song because of the latter's sudden success. This number was popularized by Spike Jones and his City Slickers in a best-selling RCA Victor recording that sold over a million and a half disks and established the popularity of Spike Jones and his madcap band for the first time.

The song was a last-minute choice by the recording executives to fill the second side of Spike Jones' recording of "I Wanna Go Back to West Virginia." Spike Jones recorded "Der Fuehrer's Face" in two different ways, one with a trombone mocking each mention of Hitler, and the other with a rubber "razzer" creating the effect of Bronx cheers. Convinced that the latter effect was the superior, Jones made a trip from California to New York to convince the Victor executives to use the Bronx-cheer version; upon his arrival he learned that this was also the version favored by the Victor people.

De Rose, Peter, composer, born New York City, 1900; died New York City, 1953

See (Lyrics by Mitchell Parish): Deep Purple; The Lamp Is Low; Lilacs in the Rain.

See (Lyrics by Charles Tobias): As Years Go By; Love Ya; Somebody Loves You; When Your Hair Has Turned to Silver.

See also: Autumn Serenade; Have You Ever Been Lonely?; I Just Roll Along; Muddy Water; Wagon Wheels; Who Do You Know in Heaven?

Desert Song. *See:* Blue Heaven.

The Desert Song, an operetta with book by Frank Mandel. Lyrics by Otto Harbach and Oscar Hammerstein II. Music by Sigmund Romberg. Starring Vivienne Segal and Robert Halliday (1926).

There were three motion-picture adaptations. The first starred John Boles and Carlotta King (Warner, 1929). It utilized the basic stage score. The second starred Dennis Morgan, Irene Manning and Bruce Cabot (Warner, 1943). Five songs were used from the stage score, with interpolations of several new numbers by Jack Scholl and Sigmund Romberg among others. The third version starred Kathryn Grayson and Gordon MacRae (Warner, 1953). It utilized the basic stage score.

See: Blue Heaven; It; One Alone; The Riff Song.

De Sylva, Bud, lyricist, born George Gard De Sylva, New York City, 1895; died Hollywood, California, 1950.

See: Gershwin, George; Henderson, Ray; Youmans, Vincent.

See also: April Showers; California, Here I Come; Cross Your Heart; Eadie Was a Lady; If You Knew Susie; I'll Build a Stairway to Paradise; I'll Say She Does; I Won't Say I Will; A Kiss in the Dark; Look for Save Your Sorrow for Tomorrow; This Is the Life; Whip-poor-will; Wishing; Yankee Doodle Blues; You Are My Lucky Star; You're an Old Smoothie; Yoo Hoo; You Ain't Heard Nothin' Yet.

For the screen biography of De Sylva, Brown and Henderson, see *The Best Things in Life Are Free.*

Devoted to You, words and music by Boudleaux Bryant (1958). Popularized by the Everly Brothers in a best-selling Cadence recording.

Diamonds Are a Girl's Best Friend, words by Leo Robin, music by Jule Styne (1949). Introduced by Carol Channing in the musical *Gentlemen Prefer Blondes* (1949). It was with this song, in this production, that Carol Channing first became a star. Brooks Atkinson in the *New York Times* described her performance in the role of Lorelei Lee, and her rendition of "Diamonds Are a Girl's Best Friend," as "the most fabulous comic creation of this generation." In the motion-picture adaptation of the musical comedy (20th Century-Fox, 1953), this number was sung by Marilyn Monroe and Jane Russell.

Diana, words and music by Paul Anka (1957). This was Anka's first published song, and his first recording; the latter, for ABC Paramount, sold over a million disks and for thirteen consecutive weeks was the best-selling recording in the country. Over a six-year period, there were over three hundred recordings made of this song in twenty-two countries, with a total sale in excess of ten million disks. This song was inspired by a frustrated love affair between Anka (then aged fifteen) and a girl named Diana, three years his senior, in Anka's native Ottawa.

Diane, words by Lew Pollack, music by Erno Rapee (1927). Theme song of the motion picture *Seventh Heaven* (Fox, 1927), in which Janet Gaynor won the Academy Award.

The Dickey Bird Song, words by Howard Dietz, music by Sammy Fain (1947). Introduced by Jeanette MacDonald, Ann E. Todd, Eleanor Donahue and Jane Powell in the motion picture *Three Daring Daughters* (MGM, 1948). Freddy Martin and his orchestra made a successful recording for RCA Victor.

Did I Remember?, words by Harold Adamson, music by Walter Donaldson (1936). This was the last song sung by Jean Harlow in motion pictures, in *Suzy* (MGM, 1936).

Did You Close Your Eyes When We Kissed?, words and music by Bob

Merrill (1957). Introduced by Gwen Verdon and George Wallace in the musical play *New Girl in Town* (1957).

Did You Ever See a Dream Walking?, words by Mack Gordon, music by Harry Revel (1933). Introduced by Jack Haley in the motion picture *Sitting Pretty* (Paramount, 1933).

Dietz, Howard, lyricist, born New York City, 1896.

See: Schwartz, Arthur.

See also: All the King's Horses; The Dickey Bird Song; The Love I Long For; Moanin' Low.

Diga Diga Doo, words by Dorothy Fields, music by Jimmy McHugh (1928). Introduced by Adelaide Hall (in her Broadway debut) in the all-Negro revue *Blackbirds of 1928*, the first Broadway score by Miss Fields and McHugh. In presenting the song, Adelaide Hall was supported by a bevy of girls dressed in two-piece red-sequin costumes with red feathers to typify Zulus; the song was followed by an effective corybantic. Lena Horne sang it in the motion-picture musical *Stormy Weather* (20th Century-Fox, 1943).

Dig You Later. See: Hubba, Hubba, Hubba.

Dinah, words by Sam M. Lewis and Joe Young, music by Harry Akst (1925). Introduced by Ethel Waters in a revue at the New Plantations night club in New York during the summer of 1924. This is probably the first instance in which a hit song came out of a night-club production.

In her autobiography, Ethel Waters wrote: "Harry Akst and Joe Young asked me if I'd try a new one they'd written. And they sang it themselves for me, doing it fast and corny. 'Is that the way you want me to sing it?' I asked. Akst and Young looked at each other. 'Why not sing it your own way?' they said. . . . So that day I took the song home and worked on it."

Ethel Waters subsequently sang it in the revues *Africana* (1927) and *Blackbirds of 1930*. Her recording for Columbia has become a jazz classic. Louis Armstrong's early Okeh recording is also a prime fa-

vorite with jazz enthusiasts. Meanwhile, Eddie Cantor interpolated it in the musical comedy *Kid Boots* (1923). The song was also heard in the motion-picture adaptation of the Friml operetta *Rose Marie* (MGM, 1936) and in the motion picture *Broadway*, starring George Raft and Pat O'Brien (Universal, 1942).

When Dinah Shore (née Fanny Rose Shore) made her first radio appearance, in Nashville, Tennessee, she opened her first show with "Dinah." This is the reason why she assumed for herself the first name of Dinah.

Dinah (Stromberg). See: Kiss Me Honey, Do.

Dinner at Eight, words by Dorothy Fields, music by Jimmy McHugh (1933). Theme song of the motion picture of the same name starring John Barrymore and Jean Harlow (MGM, 1933). The song was introduced at Graumann's Chinese Theatre in Hollywood by Frances Langford on a coast-to-coast radio broadcast. The song reached the top spot in the Hit Parade in 1933.

Dipsy Doodle, words and music by Larry Clinton (1927). A nonsense song made famous by Larry Clinton and his orchestra. It was interpolated in the non-musical motion picture *Since You Went Away*, starring Claudette Colbert and Joseph Cotten (MGM, 1944).

Dirty Hands, Dirty Face, words by Edgar Leslie, music by James V. Monaco (1923). Popularized by Al Jolson, who sang it in his first motion-picture success, *The Jazz Singer* (Warner, 1928).

Dis Flower, words by Oscar Hammerstein II, the music being "The Flower Song" from Georges Bizet's opera *Carmen* (1943). Introduced on alternate nights by Luther Saxon and Napoleon Reed in the musical play *Carmen Jones* (1943). In the motion-picture adaptation of the musical (20th Century-Fox, 1954), it was sung by Harry Belafonte.

Dixie (or, Dixie's Land), words and music by Dan Emmett (1860). Though now famous as a Civil War ballad of the Confederacy, "Dixie" was written for a minstrel show, as a "walk-around." It was introduced by the Bryant Minstrels at Mechanics Hall in New York on April 4, 1859.

Emmett tells the story of how he came to write the song. "One Saturday night, in 1859, as I was leaving Bryant's theater where I was playing, Bryant called after me. 'I want a walk-around for Monday, Dan.' The next day it rained and I stayed indoors." At this point Emmett might have added that while searching for some idea for a walk-around he commented critically to his wife on Northern weather. "I wish I was in Dixie," he remarked nostalgically. "Suddenly," continued Emmett, "I jumped up and sat down at the table to work. In less than an hour I had the first verse and chorus. After that it was easy. When my wife returned I sang it to her. 'It's all about finished now, except the name. What shall I call it?' 'Why, call it "I Wish I Was in Dixie Land,"' she said. And so it was."

Undoubtedly, Emmett had heard the word "Dixie" during his travels in the Southland, since it had there become a favorite synonym for the South before the Civil War. But the origin of the word is still subject to controversy. Some believe it may have been a convenient contraction for "Mason and Dixon Line" but this is doubtful. Most (and these include the Webster Dictionary and the Encyclopaedia Britannica) derive the word from "dixie," a term used for a ten-dollar bill issued by the Citizens' Bank of Louisiana and circulated throughout the South; the French population of New Orleans inevitably referred to "ten" as "dix." But whatever the origin of the word may be, there is little question that it is mainly due to Emmett's song that "Dixie" has come to identify the South for Northerners ever since the Civil War.

As introduced by the Bryant Minstrels (of which Emmett was a member) the song was the background music for a lavish spectacle showing the gay side of life among Southern slaves. The first part of the song was enacted by a number of comedians; the second part was sung by the entire company. "It made a tremendous hit," Emmett continues, "and before the end of the week everybody in New York was whistling it." Minstrel shows everywhere borrowed the melody for their own walk-around. Publication of the lyrics in numerous broadsides was followed by the issue of the complete song in New York; the publishing house of Peters, having bought it outright from Emmett for $500, released it under the title "I Wish I Was in Dixie's Land." Songsters and newspapers reprinted it. Numerous adaptations and parodies were circulated. By August 10, 1861, the New York *Clipper* was able to call the song "one of the most popular compositions ever produced. . . . [It] had been sung, whistled and played in every quarter of the globe." The New York *Commercial Advertiser* also took note of its popularity by saying: " 'Dixie' has become an institution, an irrepressible institution in this section of the country."

The first Southern performance of "Dixie" took place at Charleston, South Carolina, in December of 1860 in a minstrel show produced by Rumsey and Newcomb. But the Southern popularity of this song dates from the time when it was used as march music for a company of Zouaves in a production of *Pocahontas* at the Variétés Theatre in New Orleans in March of 1861. With Susan Denim at the head, the Zouaves came out in full regalia, singing lustily, "I Wish I Was in Dixie's Land." The audience proved so enthusiastic, seven encores had to be given. Then a New Orleans publisher issued a pirated edition that sold thousands of copies. Confederate soldiers took over the melody for new martial lyrics and adopted it as a favorite war song. It was heard in war camps, on the march, on the field of battle. In *Three Months in the Confederate Army*, Henry Hotze quotes a Confederate soldier as follows: "It is marvelous with what wildfire rapidity this tune 'Dixie' has spread over the whole South." Just before General Pickett made his charge at Gettysburg, he ordered that "Dixie" be played to sustain the morale of his troops. After Appomattox, President Lincoln remarked that since the North had conquered the South it had also acquired "Dixie" as part of the spoils of war. As a testimony to his own enthusiasm for this song, President Lincoln at that same time requested the band outside the White House to play it for him.

Dixie, a motion-picture musical starring Dorothy Lamour and Bing Crosby (Paramount, 1943). Songs by Johnny Burke and James Van Heusen.

See: If You Please; Sunday, Monday and Always.

Dixieland Band, words by Johnny Mercer, music by Bernard Hanighen (1935). A "narrative song" originally recorded for RCA Victor by Benny Goodman and his orchestra. It was subsequently popularized by Bing Crosby in a Decca recording and by Johnny Mercer in a Capitol recording.

The Dixieland Volunteers, words by Edgar Leslie, music by Harry Ruby (1918). Introduced by Eddie Cantor in Baltimore, Maryland, during the run there of the *Ziegfeld Follies of 1918.* The local critic reported that Cantor's rendition "tore down the house."

Dixon, Mort, lyricist, born New York City, 1892; died Bronxville, New York, 1956.

See: Warren, Harry; Woods, Harry.

See also: Bye, Bye, Blackbird; Fare Thee Well, Annabelle; The Lady in Red; Mr. and Mrs. Is the Name; That Old Gang of Mine.

Doctor, Lawyer, Indian Chief, words by Paul Francis Webster, music by Hoagy Carmichael (1945). Introduced by Betty Hutton in the motion-picture musical *Stork Club* (Paramount, 1945), and further popularized by her in a best-selling recording for Capitol.

Do, Do, Do, words by Ira Gershwin, music by George Gershwin (1926). Introduced by Gertrude Lawrence in the musical comedy *Oh, Kay!* (1926). It was interpolated in the motion-picture musical *Tea for Two* (Warner, 1950), where it was sung by Doris Day and Gordon MacRae; it was also heard in *The Helen Morgan Story* (Warner, 1957).

Do, Do, My Huckleberry Do, words by Harry Dillon, music by John Dillon (1893). A nonsense song that became a staple in the repertory of the vaudeville team of the Dillon Brothers.

Does Your Heart Beat for Me?, words and music by Howard Johnson, Mitchell Parish and Russ Morgan (1936). Introduced and popularized by Russ Morgan and his orchestra. It then became their theme song.

Doggie in the Window. *See:* That Doggie in the Window.

Do I Hear a Waltz?, words by Stephen Sondheim, music by Richard Rodgers (1965). Title song of a musical (1965), introduced by Elizabeth Allen.

Do I Hear a Waltz?, a musical comedy with book by Arthur Laurents based on his play *The Time of the Cuckoo.* Lyrics by Stephen Sondheim. Music by Richard Rodgers. Starring Elizabeth Allen and Sergio Franchi (1965). Original cast recording (Columbia).

See: Do I Hear a Waltz?; Moon in My Window; Stay; Take the Moment; Two by Two.

Do I Love You?, words and music by Cole Porter (1939). Introduced by Ethel Merman and Ronald Graham in the musical *Du Barry Was a Lady* (1939). The song was also heard in the motion-picture adaptation of the musical (MGM, 1934), and was sung by Ginny Simms in the Cole Porter screen biography *Night and Day* (Warner, 1946).

Do I Love You? (Because You're Beautiful), words by Oscar Hammerstein II, music by Richard Rodgers (1957). Introduced by Julie Andrews and Jon Cypher in the television production of *Cinderella* (1957).

Doin' the Uptown Lowdown, words by Mack Gordon, music by Harry Revel

(1933). Introduced in the motion-picture musical *Broadway Thru a Keyhole*, starring Constance Cummings, Texas Guinan and Paul Kelly (United Artists, 1933).

Doin' What Comes Natur'lly, words and music by Irving Berlin (1946). A comedy number introduced by Ethel Merman in the musical *Annie, Get Your Gun* (1946). "When she [Ethel Merman] made her entrance in the first scene," wrote Maurice Zolotow, "garbed in an old dirtied-up piece of red flannel tied with a rope, black stockings, moccasins and a brace of quail tied to the strings—and proceeded to warble 'Doin' What Comes Natur'lly'—she created a rustic character on the Broadway stage that may live in people's minds as long as Joseph Jefferson's portrayal of Rip Van Winkle."

In the motion-picture adaptation of the musical (MGM, 1950), it was sung by Betty Hutton.

Do It Again, words by Bud De Sylva, music by George Gershwin (1922). Introduced by Irene Bordoni in the musical *The French Doll* (1922), where it was an interpolation. The lyrics are amusing for their suggestive double-entendres; this is the reason why the song was long banned from the airwaves. The music is unusual for its cross rhythms and shifting harmonies. The song was interpolated in the George Gershwin screen biography *Rhapsody in Blue* (Warner, 1945), and in *The Helen Morgan Story* (Warner, 1957).

Dolce Far Niente, words and music by Meredith Willson (1960). Introduced by Tammy Grimes and Mitchell Gregg in the musical *The Unsinkable Molly Brown* (1960).

The Dolly Sisters, a motion-picture musical biography of the famous stars of revues and musical comedies, starring Betty Grable and June Haver as the sisters (20th Century-Fox, 1945). The score was mainly made up of standards, but several new songs by Mack Gordon and James V. Monaco were included.

See: Arrah Go On; Carolina in the Morning; The Darktown Strutters' Ball; Give Me the Moonlight, Give Me the Girl; I Can't Begin to Tell You; I'm Always Chasing Rainbows; Oh, Frenchy; On the Mississippi; The Sidewalks of New York; Smiles.

Dolores, words by Frank Loesser, music by Louis Alter (1941). Introduced by Frank Sinatra and Tommy Dorsey and his orchestra in the motion-picture musical *Las Vegas Nights* (Paramount, 1941). This song received an award from ASCAP in 1941.

Domino, a French popular song, music by Louis Ferrari, English lyrics by Don Raye (1951). Popularized by Tony Martin in an RCA Victor recording.

Domino, Antoine "Fats," composer and lyricist, born New Orleans, Louisiana, 1928.

See: Ain't It a Shame?; All by Myself; Blueberry Hill; Blue Monday; Boll Weevil; Goin' to the River; I Can't Go On; I Lived My Life; I'm in Love Again; I'm Walkin'; It's You I Love; Love Me.

Donaldson, Walter, composer and lyricist, born Brooklyn, New York, 1893; died Santa Monica, California, 1947.

See (Lyrics by Gus Kahn): Beside a Babbling Brook; Carolina in the Morning; For My Sweetheart; Love Me or Leave Me; Makin' Whoopee; My Baby Just Cares for Me; My Buddy; My Sweetie Turned Me Down; That Certain Party; Yes, Sir, That's My Baby.

See (Lyrics by Edgar Leslie): Kansas City Kitty; On Behalf of the Visiting Firemen; Romance.

See (Lyrics by Sam M. Lewis and Joe Young): How Ya Gonna Keep 'Em Down on the Farm?; I'll Be Happy When the Preacher Makes You Mine; My Mammy; You're a Million Miles from Nowhere.

See also: At Sundown; Back Home in Tennessee; The Daughter of Rosie O'Grady; Did I Remember?; Georgia; In the Middle of the Night; Just Like a Melody Out of the Sky; Little White Lies; My Best Girl; My Blue Heaven; Sam the Old Accordion Man; Seven or Eleven; What Can I Say After I Say I'm Sorry?; Where'd You Get Those Eyes?; You Didn't Have to Tell Me; You're Driving Me Crazy.

The Donkey Serenade, words by Bob Wright and George "Chet" Forrest, music by Rudolf Friml and Herbert Stothart (1937). The song was based on "Chansonette," words by Sigmund Spaeth, music by Rudolf Friml (1923), which in turn was derived from an early Friml piano piece, *Chanson.* "The Donkey Serenade" was an interpolation in the motion-picture adaptation of the Friml operetta *The Firefly* (MGM, 1937), sung by Allan Jones, who made a best-selling recording for RCA Victor.

Donna, words and music by Ritchie Valens (1958). Popularized by Ritchie Valens in a Del-Fi recording.

Donnelly, Dorothy, lyricist, born New York City, 1880; died New York City, 1928.
 See: Romberg, Sigmund.

Do Not Forsake Me. *See:* High Noon.

Do Nothin' Till You Hear from Me, words by Bob Russell, music by Duke Ellington (1943).

Don't, words and music by Jerry Leiber and Mike Stoller (1958). Popularized by Elvis Presley, whose RCA Victor recording sold over a million disks.

Don't Be Angry, words and music by Napoleon Brown, Fred Madison and Rose Marie McCoy (1955). Popularized in a Savoy recording by Nappy Brown and in a Mercury recording by the Crew Cuts.

Don't Be Angry with Me, Darling, words by W. L. Gardner, music by H. P. Danks (1870). This was Danks' first song hit. During World War II it was sung as "Don't Be Angry with Me, Sergeant."

Don't Be Cruel, words and music by Otis Blackwell and Elvis Presley (1956). Popularized by Elvis Presley, whose RCA Victor recording sold seven million disks.

Don't Blame Me, words by Dorothy Fields, music by Jimmy McHugh (1933). Introduced by Jeanette Loff in the musical *Clowns in Clover* (1933). The song was popularized by Walter Wolfe King in Chicago. It was subsequently sung by Vic Damone in the motion picture *The Strip* (MGM, 1951), and by Constance Towers in the motion picture *Bring

Your Smile Along (Columbia, 1955).

Don't Bring Lulu, words by Billy Rose and Lew Brown, music by Ray Henderson (1925). It was revived by a children's chorus in the non-musical motion picture *Belles on Their Toes,* starring Myrna Loy and Jeanne Crain (20th Century-Fox, 1952).

Don't Come Running Back to Me, words and music by Sid Tepper and Roy C. Bennett (1964). Popularized by Nancy Wilson in a Capitol recording.

Don't Ever Leave Me, words by Oscar Hammerstein II, music by Jerome Kern (1929). Introduced by Helen Morgan in the musical *Sweet Adeline* (1929). It was sung by Irene Dunne in the motion-picture adaptation of the musical (Warner, 1935).

Don't Fence Me In, words and music by Cole Porter (1944). A popular number in the style of a cowboy folk song. It was written in the 1930s for a motion picture that was never released, *Adios Argentina.* The song was finally introduced by Roy Rogers in the motion-picture musical *Hollywood Canteen* (Warner, 1944). Roy Rogers sang it again in the motion picture *Don't Fence Me In* (Republic, 1945). Kate Smith helped make the song a major hit in 1944 in her radio broadcasts; so did Bing Crosby in a Decca recording with the Andrews Sisters that sold over a million disks. The song achieved the top spot of the Hit Parade in 1944 for several weeks running. It was interpolated in Cole Porter's screen biography *Night and Day* (Warner, 1946).

Don't Forbid Me, words and music by Charles Singleton (1956). Popularized by Pat Boone in a best-selling Dot recording in 1957.

Don't Forget 127th Street, words by Lee Adams, music by Charles Strouse (1964). A comic and at times bitter commentary on life in New York's Harlem, introduced by Sammy Davis and Johnny Brown (then used for a production number) in the musical *Golden Boy* (1964).

Don't Get Around Much Anymore, words by Bob Russell, music by Duke Ellington, melody derived from his instrumental composition *Never

No Lament (1942). Introduced by Duke Ellington and his orchestra in an RCA Victor recording. The song became popular mainly through Jimmy Savo's burlesque treatment in vaudeville and night clubs.

Don't Give Up the Old Love for the New, words and music by James Thornton (1895).

Don't Give Up the Ship, words by Al Dubin, music by Harry Warren (1935). Introduced by Dick Powell in the motion-picture musical *Shipmates Forever* (First National, 1935). The number was subsequently adopted as the official song of the United States Naval Academy.

Don't Hold Everything, words by Bud De Sylva and Lew Brown, music by Ray Henderson (1928). Introduced by Alice Boulden in the musical *Hold Everything* (1928).

Don't Let It Bother You, words by Mack Gordon, music by Harry Revel (1934). Introduced by Fred Astaire and Ginger Rogers in the screen musical *The Gay Divorcee* (RKO, 1934).

Don't Let the Stars Get in Your Eyes, words and music by Slim Willet, Cactus Pryor and Barbara Trammel (1952). Popularized by Perry Como in an RCA Victor recording that sold a million disks.

Don't Marry Me, words by Oscar Hammerstein II, music by Richard Rodgers (1958). Introduced by Miyoshi Umeki (in her Broadway debut) and Larry Blyden in the musical *Flower Drum Song* (1958). In this production the song was followed by a buck-and-wing dance by Larry Blyden. In the motion-picture adaptation of the musical it was sung by Miyoshi Umeki and Jack Soo (Universal, 1961).

Don't Put Me Off a Buffalo Any More, words by William Jerome, music by Jean Schwartz (1901).

Don't Rain on My Parade, words by Bob Merrill, music by Jule Styne (1964). Introduced by Barbra Streisand in the musical *Funny Girl* (1964).

Don't Sit Under the Apple Tree (with Anyone Else But Me), words by Charles Tobias and Lew Brown, music by Sam H. Stept (1939). The melody was originally used for a lyric entitled "Anywhere the Bluebird Goes." As "Don't Sit Under the Apple Tree" it was introduced in a farmyard scene in the musical *Yokel Boy* (1939). In the motion picture *Private Buckaroo* (Universal, 1942), it was sung by the Andrews Sisters, whose Decca recording was a best seller in 1942. Best-selling recordings by Kay Kyser for Columbia and Glenn Miller for RCA Victor further popularized the song, which was a particular favorite of G.I.s during World War II.

Don't Stay Away Too Long, words and music by Al Hoffman and Dick Manning (1955). Popularized by Eddie Fisher in an RCA Victor recording.

Don't Sweetheart Me, words by Charles Tobias, music by Cliff Friend (1943). Interpolated in the motion picture *Hi, Beautiful,* starring Martha Driscoll (Universal, 1944).

Don't Take Your Love from Me, words and music by Henry Nemo (1941). It was introduced by Mildred Bailey.

Don't Tell Her That You Love Her, words and music by Paul Dresser (1896).

Don't You Know?, words and music by Bobby Worth, the melody based on "Musetta's Waltz" from Puccini's opera *La Bohème* (1959). Popularized by Della Reese in an RCA Victor recording, her first release.

A Doodlin' Song, words by Carolyn Leigh, music by Cy Coleman (1958). Popularized by Peggy Lee in a Capitol recording.

The Door of My Dreams, words by Otto Harbach and Oscar Hammerstein II, music by Rudolf Friml (1924). Introduced by Mary Ellis and chorus in the operetta *Rose Marie* (1924). In the first motion-picture adaptation of the operetta (MGM, 1936) it was sung by Jeanette MacDonald; in the second (MGM, 1954), by Ann Blyth.

Dorando, words and music by Irving Berlin (1908). This was the first Irving Berlin song for which he wrote both the words and the music. (Earlier song efforts were confined to lyrics exclusively.) "Dorando" was written on a commission from a vaudeville entertainer who wanted a topical number for his act. Berlin complied with a series of verses (without melody) about a marathon runner named Dorando then much in the news. The vaudevillian turned down the finished product. Berlin now tried selling it as a lyric for a popular song. Ted Snyder, recently become head of the newly founded publishing house, the Seminary Music Company, offered to pay $25 for it on condition that the words had a melody. Berlin proceeded to dictate a tune to an arranger in Snyder's office. "Dorando," published by Seminary, started an association between Berlin and Ted Snyder which resulted in Berlin's first song hits, many of them with lyrics by Berlin to Ted Snyder's music.

Do Re Mi, words by Oscar Hammerstein II, music by Richard Rodgers (1959). A popular song with melody built on the ascending steps of the diatonic scale. It was introduced by Mary Martin and a group of children in the musical play *The Sound of Music* (1959). Julie Andrews and a children's chorus presented it in the motion-picture adaptation of the musical (20th Century-Fox, 1965).

Do the Clam, words and music by Wayne, Weissman and Fuller (1964). Introduced by Elvis Presley in the motion-picture musical *Girl Happy* (MGM, 1965), and popularized by him in a best-selling recording for RCA Victor.

Do the New York, words and music by J. P. Murray, Barry Trivers and Ben Oakland (1931). Introduced in the first-act finale of the *Ziegfeld Follies of 1931* by Harry Richman.

Do They Miss Me at Home?, words and music by S. M. Grannis (1852). Though written and published eight years before the outbreak of the Civil War, this ballad achieved its greatest popularity during that conflict. Numerous parodies were then circulated both in the North and the South. These included "Do They Pray For Me at Home?," "Oh, We Miss You at Home" and "Yes, We Think of Thee at Home."

Down Among the Sheltering Palms, words by James Brockman, music by Abe Olman (1915). It provided the title of and was featured in a motion picture starring Mitzi Gaynor, William Lundigan and Gloria De Haven (20th Century-Fox, 1953). It was sung by a girls' chorus on the soundtrack in the motion picture *Some Like It Hot* (United Artists, 1959).

Down Among the Sugar Cane, words by Avery and Hart, music by Richard C. McPherson, using the pen name of Cecil Mack, and Chris Smith (1908). This was Chris Smith's biggest song hit up to that time.

Down Argentine Way, a motion-picture musical starring Carmen Miranda (in her screen debut), Don Ameche and Betty Grable (20th Century-Fox, 1940). Songs by Al Dubin and Jimmy McHugh, and others.
See: South American Way.

Down by the Old Mill Stream, words and music by Tell Taylor (1910). One of the leading hit songs of the decade, selling in excess of two million copies of sheet music. Sigmund Spaeth noted that with present-day audiences this song is particularly popular in renditions accompanied by elaborate burlesque gestures. "The climax," explained Spaeth, "comes when the girl's age, 'sixteen,' is counted out on the fingers. 'Old' is open to various dramatic interpretations, but 'mill' and 'stream' are fairly obvious in their suggestion for action."

Down in Dear Old New Orleans, words by Joe Young, music by Con Conrad and Whidden (1912). This was Con Conrad's first published song. It was introduced by Rae Samuels, "the blue streak personality," in the *Ziegfeld Follies of 1912.*

Down in Jungle Town, words by Edward Madden, music by Theodore F. Morse (1908). It became a favorite with barber-shop quartets.

Down in Poverty Row, words by Gussie L. Davis, music by Arthur Trevelyan (1895). This was Gussie Davis' biggest song hit up to that time. It was introduced and popularized by Bonnie Thornton at Allen's Bal Mabile in New York.

Down in the Depths, words and music by Cole Porter (1936). Introduced by Ethel Merman in the musical *Red, Hot and Blue* (1936).

Down on the Farm, words by Raymond A. Browne, music by Harry von Tilzer (1902). The first of several songs with a similar title to come out of Tin Pan Alley.

Down the Old Ox Road, words by Sam Coslow, music by Arthur Johnston (1933). Introduced by Bing Crosby in the motion-picture musical *College Humor* (Paramount, 1933). Crosby explained in his autobiography that "an old ox road [is] a petting pit or a smooching station on any campus. . . . The song still means something special to many a balding ex-Joe College and former Betty Co-Ed of the Scott Fitzgerald age."

Down Went McGinty, words and music by Joseph Flynn (1889). One of the most celebrated comic songs of the 1890s. It told the saga of an accident-prone Irishman who was continually falling down from high walls into coal chutes, and so forth.

Flynn, an Irish stage comedian, wrote the song while appearing with Frank B. Sheridan with the Muldoon Variety Players. Muldoon did not permit Flynn to use the song in their act. After Flynn and Sheridan left Muldoon to set off on their own in vaudeville, they introduced the number at Hyde and Behman's Adams Street Theatre in Brooklyn, in 1889. Sheridan sang the verse and chorus, then Flynn repeated them while accompanying his rendition with rowdy gestures. The audience went into an uproar. The song was further popularized by Maggie Cline, who made it a staple in her vaudeville act.

Down Where the Cotton Blossoms Grow, words by Andrew B. Sterling, music by Harry von Tilzer (1901).

Down Where the Sil'vry Mohawk Flows, words by Monroe H. Rosenfeld, music by John and Otto Heinzman (1905). This was Rosenfeld's last song, thus ending his songwriting career with a hit.

Down Where the Wurzburger Flows, words by Vincent P. Bryan, music by Harry von Tilzer (1902). Introduced by Nora Bayes at the Orpheum Theatre in Brooklyn in 1902. The first time she tried to sing the number, Nora Bayes broke down. Von Tilzer, seated in a box, hurriedly took over the singing until she could regain her composure. This collaboration made such an impression on the audience, that the management urged von Tilzer to serve as Miss Bayes' stooge for the rest of the week. The song became one of her greatest successes (even without von Tilzer's subsequent participation), so much so that for many years she was often identified as "The Wurzburger Girl." In 1903 von Tilzer wrote a successful sequel to his song hit, entitled "Under the Anheuser Bush," with words by Andrew B. Sterling.

Down Yonder, words and music by L. Wolfe Gilbert (1922). Introduced by L. Wolfe Gilbert at the Orpheum Theatre in New Orleans. It was subsequently sung in vaudeville by such headliners as Al Jolson, Belle Baker, Eddie Cantor and Sophie Tucker. Nevertheless, when Gilbert founded his own publishing house and issued the song it proved a dud. The song remained forgotten for thirty years. Then, in 1952, Dell Wood recorded it for a small outfit in Nashville, Tennessee. This recording sold about a million disks and was responsible for bringing "Down Yonder" to the Hit Parade for eighteen weeks. Twenty other recording companies also issued it.

Do You Know What It Means to Miss New Orleans?, words by Edgar Leslie, music by Louis Alter (1946). Introduced by Billie Holiday and Louis Armstrong in the motion picture *New Orleans* (United Artists, 1947). Several jazz night spots in New Orleans have since adopted it as their theme song.

Do You Love Me?, words and music by Berry Gordy, Jr. (1962). Popularized by the Contours in a Gordy recording.

Do You Love Me?, words and music by Harry Ruby (1946). Popularized by

Dick Haymes in the motion picture of the same name (20th Century-Fox, 1946).

Do You Remember Love?, words by Harry B. Smith, music by Reginald de Koven (1897). Introduced by Joseph O'Mara and Hilda Clarke in the operetta *The Highwayman* (1897).

Dream, words and music by Johnny Mercer (1944). First used as the closing theme for Mercer's CBS Chesterfield radio program in 1945. It was subsequently popularized by the Pied Pipers in a Capitol recording. It was also interpolated in the motion picture *Mother Is a Freshman,* starring Loretta Young (20th Century-Fox, 1949).

Dream a Little Dream of Me, words by Gus Kahn, music by W. Schwandt and F. Andree (1931). Popularized by Kate Smith, who featured it on her first CBS radio program on May 1, 1931.

Dream Along with Me (I'm on My Way to a Star), words and music by Carl Sigman (1955). It was adopted by Perry Como as the theme song for his television programs.

Dream, Dream, Dream, words by Mitchell Parish, music by Jimmy McHugh (1954). Popularized by Fred Waring and his Pennsylvanians, who made it their theme song.

A Dream Is a Wish Your Heart Makes, words and music by Mack David, Al Hoffman and Jerry Livingston (1948). Introduced in the Walt Disney cartoon fantasy *Cinderella* (RKO, 1949), sung on the soundtrack by Ilene Woods and popularized by Perry Como in an RCA Victor recording.

Dream Lover, words and music by Bobby Darin (1959). Introduced and popularized by Bobby Darin in a best-selling Atco recording.

Dream Lover, words by Clifford Grey, music by Victor Schertzinger (1929). Introduced in the motion-picture musical *The Love Parade* (Paramount, 1929). It was interpolated in the motion picture *Lady in the Dark* (MGM, 1944).

Dream On, Little Dreamer, Dream On,

words and music by Jon Crutchfeld and Fred Burch (1965). Popularized by Perry Como in a best-selling RCA Victor recording, Como's most successful disk release in almost a decade.

Dreamy Alabama, words and music by Robert A. King, using the pen name of Mary Earl (1919).

Dresser, Paul, composer and lyricist, born Paul Dreiser, Terre Haute, Indiana, 1857; died Brooklyn, New York, 1906.

See: The Blue and the Gray; Calling to Her Boy Just Once Again; Come Tell Me What's Your Answer, Yes or No; The Convict and the Bird; The Curse of the Dreamer; Don't Tell Her That You Love Her; Every Night There's a Light; He Brought Home Another; He Fought for a Cause He Thought Was Right; I'd Still Believe You True; If You See My Sweetheart; In Dear Old Illinois; In Good Old New York Town; In the Great Somewhere; I Wish That You Were Here Tonight; I Wonder If She'll Ever Come Back to Me; I Wonder Where She Is Tonight; Jean; Just Tell Them That You Saw Me; The Letter That Never Came; My Gal Sal; My Heart Still Clings to the Old First Love; The Old Flame Flickers; Once Ev'ry Year; On the Banks of the Wabash; Our Country, May She Always Be Right; The Outcast Unknown; The Pardon Came Too Late; She Went to the City; Sweet Savannah; Take a Seat, Old Lady; There's Where My Heart Is Tonight; The Town Where I Was Born; Way Down in Old Indiana; We Fight Tomorrow, Mother; You're Going Far Away, Lad.

For Paul Dresser's screen biography, see *My Gal Sal* (20th Century-Fox, 1942).

Drifting Along with the Tide, words by Arthur Jackson, music by George Gershwin (1921). An early Gershwin song written in his teens while he was still working as a demonstration pianist at Remick's in Tin Pan Alley. It was interpolated in the revue *George White Scandals of 1921;* it was also used in the London musical production of *Mayfair and Montmartre* (1922).

Drifting and Dreaming, words by Haven Gillespie, music by Egbert Van Alstyne (1925).

Drill, Ye Tarriers, Drill, author of words and music not known (1888). Thomas Casey, a vaudeville actor who had once been employed as a blaster and driller in street excavations, often claimed writing this number. It was introduced by a trio dressed up as tarriers in Charles H. Hoyt's musical farce *A Brass Monkey* (1888). J. W. Kelly and Maggie Cline used it in their respective vaudeville acts and helped make it popular.

Drinking Song (or, Drink, Drink, Drink), words by Dorothy Donnelly, music by Sigmund Romberg (1924). A toast to romance and drink by the students of Heidelberg. It was introduced by Raymond Marlowe and a male chorus in the operetta *The Student Prince* (1924). In the motion-picture adaptation of the operetta (MGM, 1954), it was sung on the soundtrack by Mario Lanza (with chorus) and was recorded by him in a best-selling RCA Victor release.

The Drummer Boy of Shiloh, words and music by Will S. Hays (1862). A Civil War song favored by both the Confederate and the Union armies. The drummer boy was a favorite subject for Civil War ballads. Most of them described the drummer boy marching unarmed into battle only to meet death. "The Drummer Boy of Nashville" and "The Drummer Boy of Vicksburg" are two other Civil War ballads on the same theme.

Drums in My Heart, words by Edward Heyman, music by Vincent Youmans (1931). Introduced in the musical *Through the Years* (1931).

Du Barry Was a Lady, a musical comedy with book by Bud De Sylva and Herbert Fields. Lyrics and music by Cole Porter. Starring Ethel Merman and Bert Lahr (1939).

The motion-picture adaptation starred Red Skelton and Lucille Ball (MGM, 1934). Only three Cole Porter songs were retained. New songs were contributed by Lew Brown, Ralph Freed and Roger Edens; and Lew Brown, Ralph Freed and Burton Lane, among others.

See: But in the Morning; Do I Love You?; Friendship; Katie Went to Haiti; Well, Did You Evah?

Dubin, Al, lyricist, born Zurich, Switzerland, 1891; died New York City, 1945.

See: Burke, Joseph A.; Warren, Harry.

See also: A Cup of Coffee, a Sandwich and You; Feudin' and Fightin'; Indian Summer; Nobody Knows What a Red Headed Mama Can Do; South American Way; Tripoli; Where Was I?

Duke, Vernon, composer and lyricist, born Vladimir Dukelsky, Pskov, Russia, 1903.

See (Lyrics by E. Y. Harburg): April in Paris; I Like the Likes of You; I'm Only Human After All; What Is There to Say?

See (Lyrics by John Latouche): Cabin in the Sky; Honey in the Honeycomb; Taking a Chance on Love.

See also: Autumn in New York; I Can't Get Started with You; The Love I Long For; Roundabout; Suddenly.

Duke of Earl, words and music by Earl Edwards, Bernie Williams and Eugene Dixon (1962). Popularized by the Duke of Earl and by Gene Chandler, each in a best-selling Vee-Jay recording.

Dum Dum, words and music by Sharon Sheely and Jackie Deshannon (1961). Popularized by Brenda Lee in a Decca recording.

Dungaree Doll, words by Ben Raleigh, music by Sherman Edwards (1955). Popularized by Eddie Fisher in an RCA Victor recording.

Durante, Jimmy, composer and lyricist, born James Francis Durante, New York City, 1893.

See: Can Broadway Do Without Me?; Inka Dinka Doo; I Ups to Him; Jimmy the Well Dressed Man; The Man Who Found the Lost Chord; Umbriago.

D'ye Love Me?, words by Oscar Hammerstein II, music by Jerome Kern (1926). Introduced by Marilyn Miller in the musical *Sunny* (1926). In the first motion-picture adaptation of the musical (First National, 1930), it was sung by Marilyn Miller; in the second (RKO, 1941), by Anna Neagle.

E

Eadie Was a Lady, words by Bud De Sylva, music by Richard A. Whiting and Nacio Herb Brown (1932). This song was originally intended for a musical called *Humpty Dumpty,* starring Ethel Merman. When this production proved a dud during out-of-town tryouts, lyricist and composer decided to scrap it and start writing an altogether new show. Vincent Youmans was now called in to provide some new songs, and the rewritten musical was renamed *Take a Chance.* There "Eadie Was a Lady" was introduced by Ethel Merman in 1932. The song made such a hit that during the first week after the New York opening, the *New York Times* reprinted the lyrics. Of Miss Merman's rendition, Percy Hammond wrote: "She sings it in an ante-prohibition New Orleans supper club where, surrounded by chorus girls disguised as amorous sailors from the U.S. battleship *Tampico,* she mourns the death of Eadie, a sister in sin. Ere she is through with the jocular threnody, her audience is clapping its hands and waving its handkerchiefs in deserved approval." In the motion-picture adaptation of the musical (Paramount, 1933), the song was sung by Lillian Roth.

The Eagle and Me, words by E. Y. Harburg, music by Harold Arlen (1934). Introduced by Dooley Wilson in the musical *Bloomer Girl* (1934).

The Earl Carroll Vanities, an annual lavish Broadway revue produced by Earl Carroll. The first edition (1923) had book, lyrics and music by Earl Carroll. It starred Joe Cook and Peggy Hopkins Joyce. The revue was produced annually until 1932 (except for 1929, when Carroll mounted in its place a revue called *The Sketch Book*). There were no editions between 1932 and 1940, and the 1940 one was the last. Among the stars seen in these productions were Milton Berle, Joe Cook, W. C. Fields, Ted Healey, Moran and Mack, Lillian Roth, Jimmy Savo and Sophie Tucker. The following composers wrote either the complete score, or most of it, for some of the editions: Earl Carroll (1923 and 1924), Charles Gaskill (1925), Morris Hamilton (1926) and Jay Gorney (1930).

A motion-picture musical called *Earl Carroll Vanities* (Republic, 1945) starred Dennis O'Keefe and Constance Moore. It had songs by Kim Gannon and Walter Kent, by Woody Herman and by Alfred Newman. Another motion-picture musical was called *Murder at the Vanities* (Paramount, 1934), starring Carl Brisson. Here the songs were by Sam Coslow and Arthur Johnston.

See: Cocktails for Two; I Gotta Right to Sing the Blues; March of Time; My Darling.

Early in de Mornin', words and

music by Will S. Hays (1877). One of its composer's most successful songs in a Negro dialect.

Earth Angel (or, Will You Be Mine?), words and music by Jesse Belvin (1954). This was one of the earliest rock 'n' roll song hits. It was popularized by the Penguins in a Dooto recording and by the Crew Cuts in a Mercury release.

Easier Said Than Done, words and music by Larry Huff and William Linton (1963). Popularized by Essex in a Roulette recording.

Easter Parade, words and music by Irving Berlin (1933). Introduced by Clifton Webb and Marilyn Miller in the first-act finale of the musical *As Thousands Cheer* (1933).

This melody had been used by Irving Berlin in 1917 for a lyric entitled "Smile and Show Your Dimple." That song had been a failure, and was soon forgotten. Then, in 1933, while working on the score for *As Thousands Cheer,* Berlin needed a tune for a Fifth Avenue parade scene. As Berlin told an interviewer in 1963: "I dug back into my old catalogue to 1917 and found that I had written 'Smile and Show Your Dimple.' It was a bad imitation of the sort of bad songs that civilians write for soldiers. That became 'Easter Parade.' "

Harry James' recording for Columbia in 1942 and Guy Lombardo's Decca recording in 1947 each sold over a million disks. Bing Crosby sang it in the motion-picture musical *Holiday Inn* (Paramount, 1942); Judy Garland sang it in the motion-picture musical *Easter Parade* (MGM, 1948), where it was also sung by a chorus under the titles.

This is one of five songs which Berlin regards as his special favorites among his own creations, the others being "Always," "God Bless America," "Show Business" and "White Christmas."

Easter Parade, a motion-picture musical starring Judy Garland and Fred Astaire (MGM, 1948). Songs, old and new, by Irving Berlin.

See: A Couple of Swells; Easter Parade; Everybody's Doin' It; A Fella with an Umbrella; I Love a Piano; I Want to Go Back to Michigan; Snooky Oookums.

East of St. Louis Blues, words and music by W. C. Handy (1937). A W. C. Handy jazz classic which became a specialty of Lena Horne.

East of the Sun and West of the Moon, words and music by Brooks Bowman (1935). Introduced in *Stags at Bay* (1935), a production of the Princeton University Triangle Club.

East Side, West Side, All Around the Town. *See:* The Sidewalks of New York.

Easy Come, Easy Go, words by Edward Heyman, music by John Green (1934). Introduced in the motion picture *Bachelor of Arts*, starring Tom Brown and Anita Louise (Fox, 1934).

Easy to Love, words and music by Cole Porter (1936). Introduced by Frances Langford in the motion-picture musical *Born to Dance* (MGM, 1936). It was also sung in the Cole Porter screen biography *Night and Day* (MGM, 1946).

Easy to Love, words by Leo Robin, music by Ralph Rainger (1937). Written as a title song to exploit a motion picture of the same name (Paramount, 1937). It has since become a favorite of torch singers and singing pianists in night spots.

Ebb Tide, words by Carl Sigman, music by Robert Maxwell (1953). Popularized through Vic Damone's recording for Mercury and Roy Hamilton's recording for Epic. The song was successfully revived in 1964 by Lenny Welch in a Cadence recording.

The Eddie Cantor Story, a motion-picture musical biography of Eddie Cantor, starring Keefe Brasselle as Cantor with Marilyn Erskine (Warner, 1954). The score was entirely made up of song standards, with Cantor dubbing in his song specialties on the soundtrack.

See: Bedelia; Be My Little Baby Bumble Bee; Bye, Bye, Blackbird; How Ya Gonna Keep 'Em Down on the Farm?; Ida; If I Was a Millionaire; If You Knew Susie; Love Me and the World Is Mine; Makin'

Whoopee; Margie; Meet Me Tonight in Dreamland; Now's the Time to Fall in Love; Oh, You Beautiful Doll; One Hour with You; Pretty Baby; Row, Row, Row; Will You Love Me in December?; Yes, Sir, That's My Baby; Yes, We Have No Bananas.

The Eddie Duchin Story, a motion-picture musical biography of Eddie Duchin, starring Tyrone Power as Duchin with Kim Novak (Columbia, 1956). The score was made up mainly of standards associated with Eddie Duchin, with several new songs by Paul Francis Webster and Morris Stoloff. (Chopin's Nocturne in E-flat was used as a recurrent theme.) Carmen Cavallero played the piano selections on the soundtrack.

See: Body and Soul; Brazil; Exactly Like You; I Can't Give You Anything But Love, Baby; Let's Fall in Love; Manhattan; On the Sunny Side of the Street; Sweet Sue; Whispering; You're My Everything.

Edelweiss, words by Oscar Hammerstein II, music by Richard Rogers (1959). A number in the style of an Austrian folk song, introduced by Mary Martin and Theodore Bikel in the musical play *The Sound of Music* (1959). This was the last song by Rodgers and Hammerstein. It was sung by Christopher Plummer in the motion-picture adaptation of the musical (20th Century-Fox, 1965).

Edwards, Gus, composer, born Gus Simon, Hohensalza, Germany, 1879; died Los Angeles, California, 1945.

See (Lyrics by Will D. Cobb): Goodbye, Little Girl, Goodbye; I Can't Tell Why I Love You But I Do; I Couldn't Stand to See My Baby Lose; I'd Like to See a Little More of You; If I Was a Millionaire; If a Girl Like You Loved a Boy Like Me; I Just Can't Make My Eyes Behave; I'll Be with You When the Roses Bloom Again; In Zanzibar; School Days; Sunbonnet Sue.

See (Lyrics by Edward Madden): By the Light of the Silvery Moon; Jimmy Valentine; My Cousin Carus'; Up, Up, in My Aeroplane.

See also: All I Wants Is My Black Baby Back; He's Me Pal; In My Merry Oldsmobile; In the Sweet Bye and Bye.

Eeny, Meeny, Miney Mo, words by Johnny Mercer, music by Matt Malneck (1935). Introduced by Johnny Mercer in the motion-picture musical *To Beat the Band* (RKO, 1935). The song was popularized in a Decca recording by Johnny Mercer and Ginger Rogers.

Egan, Raymond B., lyricist, born Ontario, Canada, 1890; died Westport, Connecticut, 1952.

See: Whiting, Richard A.

See also: Tell Me Why You Smile; Mona Lisa.

Egern on the Tegern See, words by Oscar Hammerstein II, music by Jerome Kern (1933). A number in the style of a German folk song, introduced in the musical *Music in the Air* (1933).

Eh, Cumpari, a traditional Italian song, adapted and transcribed by Julius La Rosa and Archie Bleyer (1953). Julius La Rosa's recording for Cadence sold a million disks.

Eighteen Yellow Roses, words and music by Bobby Darin (1963). Introduced and popularized by Bobby Darin in a Capitol recording.

Eileen, an operetta with book and lyrics by Henry Blossom, Music by Victor Herbert. Starring Walter Scanlan and Grace Breen (1917).

See: Eileen Allana Asthore; Thine Alone.

Eileen Allana Asthore, words by Henry Blossom, music by Victor Herbert (1917). Introduced by Walter Scanlan in the operetta *Eileen* (1917). This was the last piece of music Herbert wrote for his *Eileen* score; its manuscript contains the date of Saturday, December 9, 1916, with the additional phrase, "Tutto finito, VH." The song is a waltz in which the hero reflects on the loveliness of Eileen. "The refrain," explains Edward N. Waters, "is less Irish than the stanza, with its minor cadences and characteristic intervals, but the whole is a piece where beauty and popularity easily combine."

Eliscu, Edward, lyricist, born New York City, 1902.

See: Youmans, Vincent.

Ellie Rhee (or, Carry Me Back to Tennessee), words and music by Septimus Winner (1865). One of the composer's most successful ballads in the post-Civil War period.

Ellington, Duke, composer, born Edward Kennedy Ellington, Washington, D.C., 1899.

See (Lyrics by Irving Mills): I Let a Song Go Out of My Heart; It Don't Mean a Thing; The Mooche.

See (Lyrics by Paul Francis Webster): I Got It Bad and That Ain't Good; Jump for Joy.

See also: The Blues I Love to Sing; Do Nothin' Till You Hear From Me; Don't Get Around Much Anymore; I'm Beginning to See the Light; In a Sentimental Mood; Mood Indigo; Solitude; Sophisticated Lady.

Elmer's Tune, words and music by Elmer Albrecht, Sammy Gallop and Dick Jurgens (1941). Introduced by Dick Jurgens and his orchestra. It was interpolated in the motion picture *Strictly in the Groove,* starring Martha Tilton and Leon Erroll (Universal, 1942). The Bluebird recording by Glenn Miller and his orchestra (vocal by Ray Eberle and the Modernaires) was a best seller. This is the number with which Peggy Lee made her recording debut as vocalist for the Benny Goodman band.

El Paso, words and music by Marty Robbins (1959). Popularized in Marty Robbins' best-selling recording for Columbia.

Elsie from Chelsea, words and music by Harry Dacre (1896).

Embraceable You, words by Ira Gershwin, music by George Gershwin (1930). Introduced by Ginger Rogers (in her first Broadway starring role) in the musical *Girl Crazy* (1930). In the first motion-picture adaptation of the musical (RKO, 1932), it was sung by Eddie Quillan and Dixie Lee; in the second (MGM, 1943), by Judy Garland and Mickey Rooney; in the third, renamed *When the Boys Meet the Girls* (MGM, 1965), by Harve Presnell. The song was interpolated in many other motion pictures. These include the George Gershwin screen biography *Rhapsody in Blue* (Warner, 1945);

Humoresque, starring Joan Crawford and John Garfield, sung by Peg La Centra (Warner, 1947); *Always Leave Them Laughing,* in which Milton Berle made his screen debut (Warner, 1949); *An American in Paris* (MGM, 1951), sung by Gene Kelly, then danced to by Gene Kelly and Leslie Caron; the Jane Froman screen biography *With a Song in My Heart* (20th Century-Fox, 1952), sung on the soundtrack by Jane Froman.

This is one of four song lyrics Ira Gershwin regards among his best. The others are "The Babbitt and the Bromide," "It Ain't Necessarily So" and the "Saga of Jenny."

Emmet's Lullaby. *See:* Lullaby.

Emmett, Dan, composer and lyricist, born Mount Vernon, Ohio, 1815; died Mount Vernon, Ohio, 1904.

See: Blue Tail Fly; De Boatman's Dance; Dixie; Jordan Is a Hard Road to Travel; My Old Aunt Sally; Old Dan Tucker.

Empty Pockets Filled with Love, words and music by Irving Berlin (1962). A song with a contrapuntal countermelody in the chorus, introduced by Jack Haskell and Anita Gillette in the musical *Mr. President* (1962).

Empty Saddles, words and music by Billy Hill (1936). Introduced by Bing Crosby in the motion-picture musical *Rhythm on the Range* (Paramount, 1936).

Enchanted, words and music by Buck Ram (1959). Popularized by the Platters in a Mercury recording.

Enchanted Island, words by Al Stillman, music by Robert Allen (1958). Introduced by the Four Lads in a Columbia recording.

The End of a Perfect Day. *See:* A Perfect Day.

England Swings, words and music by Roger Miller (1965). Introduced and popularized by Roger Miller in a best-selling smash recording.

English Muffins and Irish Stew, words by Bob Hilliard, music by Moose Charlap (1956).

Enjoy Yourself (It's Later Than You Think), words by Herb Magidson, music by Carl Sigman (1948). One of the leading hit songs of 1950, popularized by the best-selling Decca recording of Guy Lombardo and his Royal Canadians.

Ephraham, words and music by Irving Berlin (1910). Introduced by Fanny Brice in the *Ziegfeld Follies of 1910* her Broadway stage debut.

Especially for You, words and music by Orrin Tucker and Phil Grogan (1938).

Eternally, words by Geoffrey Parsons, music by Charles Chaplin (1953). Sometimes known as the "Terry Theme," it was the recurrent melody in the background music for Charlie Chaplin's motion picture *Limelight* (United Artists, 1952). Frank Chacksfield's London recording was a best seller.

Evans, Ray, composer and lyricist, born Raymond B. Evans, New York City, 1915.
See: Livingston, Jay.

Evelina, words by E. Y. Harburg, music by Harold Arlen (1944). Introduced by Celeste Holm and David Brooks in the musical *Bloomer Girl* (1944).

Even Now, words and music by Richard Adler and Jerry Ross (1952). Popularized by Eddie Fisher in an RCA Victor recording.

Everybody Loves a Lover, words by Richard Allen, music by Robert Allen (1958). It sold half a million records in the first six weeks of publication. The most popular recording was made by Doris Day for Columbia.

Everybody Loves My Baby (But My Baby Don't Love Nobody But Me), words and music by Jack Palmer and Spencer Williams (1924). The song became a favorite in Ruth Etting's repertory—the reason why it was interpolated in her screen biography *Love Me or Leave Me* (MGM, 1955), where it was sung by Doris Day. It was also successfully presented by "Fats" Waller.

Everybody's Doin' It (Doin' What, Turkey Trot), words and music by Irving Berlin (1911). A ragtime classic that helped make the turkey trot a popular dance. The song was revived in the motion-picture musicals *Alexander's Ragtime Band* (20th Century-Fox, 1938) and *Easter Parade* (MGM, 1948).

Everybody's Got a Home But Me, words by Oscar Hammerstein II, music by Richard Rodgers (1955). Ballad introduced by Judy Tyler in the musical play *Pipe Dream* (1955). It was popularized by Eddie Fisher in an RCA Victor recording.

Everybody Has the Right to Be Wrong, words by Sammy Cahn, music by James Van Heusen (1965). Introduced by Julie Harris and Peter L. Marshall in the musical *Skyscraper* (1965) and further popularized by Frank Sinatra in a Reprise recording.

Everybody Loves Somebody, words by Irving Taylor, music by Ken Lane (1950). When first published and recorded, in 1950, this song was a failure. In 1964 the song was revived by Dean Martin in a Reprise recording which sold over a million disks, and received the Gold Record Award.

Everybody's Somebody's Fool, words by Jack Keller, music by Howard Greenfield (1960). Popularized by Connie Francis in an MGM recording.

Everybody Step, words and music by Irving Berlin (1921). Introduced by the Brox Sisters in the first edition of the *Music Box Revue* (1921), where it served as a preface to a large production number. It was sung by Bing Crosby in the motion-picture musical *Blue Skies* (MGM, 1946).

Everybody Works But Father, words and music by Jean Havez (1905). Popularized by the Lew Dockstader Minstrels. The song was inspired by the influx of women and children into factories in the early 1900s.

Every Day Is Lady's Day, words by Henry Blossom, music by Victor Herbert (1906). Comedy number introduced by Neal McCay in the operetta *The Red Mill* (1906).

Every Little Movement Has a Meaning of Its Own, words by Otto Hauerbach (Harbach), music by Karl Hoschna (1910). A suggestive number provocatively introduced by Florence Mackie and Jack Reinhard in the operetta *Madame Sherry* (1910). The song was revived for the motion-picture biography of Nora Bayes, *Shine on, Harvest Moon* (Warner, 1944), and for Judy Garland in the motion picture *Presenting Lily Mars* (MGM, 1945). It was sung by Robert Alda and chorus in the motion-picture musical *April Showers* (Warner, 1948), and by Jack Smith in the motion-picture musical *On Moonlight Bay* (Warner, 1951).

Every Night There's a Light, words and music by Paul Dresser (1898). A successful "mother ballad" introduced and popularized by Dick José.

Every Street's a Boulevard in Old New York, words by Bob Hilliard, music by Jule Styne (1953). A hymn to New York. It was introduced by Jack Whiting, in song and tap dance, in the musical *Hazel Flagg* (1953).

Everything I Have Is Yours, words by Harold Adamson, music by Burton Lane (1933). Introduced in the motion-picture musical *Dancing Lady,* in which Fred Astaire made his screen debut (MGM, 1933). The song was interpolated in the motion pictures *Strictly Dishonorable,* starring Ezio Pinza and Janet Leigh (MGM, 1951), and *Everything I Have Is Yours,* starring Marge and Gower Champion (MGM, 1952).

Everything Is Peaches Down in Georgia, words by Grant Clarke, music by Milton Ager and George W. Meyer (1918). This was Ager's first song hit. While employed in Tin Pan Alley, Ager tried to get Grant Clarke, then already a successful lyricist, to collaborate with him. He besought Clarke so persistently that in desperation the lyricist threw the title at him and remarked: "See what you can do with it." The melody Ager fashioned for the chorus impelled Clarke to write the words. George W. Meyer wrote the music for the verse, since at that time Ager was serving in the Army (in Georgia, to be sure!). Al Jolson introduced the song at a Winter Garden Sunday evening concert and was responsible for its success.

Everything Makes Music When You're in Love, words by Sammy Cahn, music by James Van Heusen (1964). Introduced by Ann-Margret in the motion-picture musical *The Pleasure Seekers* (20th Century-Fox, 1964).

Everything's Coming Up Roses, words by Stephen Sondheim, music by Jule Styne (1959). Introduced by Ethel Merman in the musical *Gypsy* (1959). In the motion-picture adaptation of the musical (Warner, 1962), it was sung on the soundtrack by Lisa Kirk (for Rosalind Russell).

Ev'rybody Ought to Know How to Do the Tickle Toe. *See:* The Tickle Toe.

Ev'rything I've Got (Belongs to You), words by Lorenz Hart, music by Richard Rodgers (1942). Introduced by Ray Bolger and Benay Venuta in the musical *By Jupiter* (1942). The song was used in the motion-picture biography of Rodgers and Hart, *Words and Music* (MGM, 1948).

Ev'rytime We Say Goodbye, words and music by Cole Porter (1944). Introduced by Nan Wynn and Jere McMahon in the revue *Seven Lively Arts* (1944).

Exactly Like You, words by Dorothy Fields, music by Jimmy McHugh (1930). Introduced by Harry Richman in Lew Leslie's *International Revue* (1930). This was one of two numbers (the other being "Little White Lies") with which Ethel Merman auditioned successfully for George Gershwin to get her first Broadway role—in *Girl Crazy*. The song was interpolated in the motion-picture musicals *The Eddie Duchin Story* (Columbia, 1956) and *The Gene Krupa Story* (Columbia, 1960).

Excelsior, words by Henry Wadsworth Longfellow, music by the Hutchinson Family (1843). Introduced and popularized by the Hutchinson Family. Longfellow himself wrote an introduction for the title page of the published song.

Exodus, words by Pat Boone, music by Ernest Gold (1961). It originated as an instrumental composition—in the background music, played under the titles and used as a recurring theme, in the motion-picture epic about Israel, *Exodus* (United Artists, 1960). Pat Boone wrote lyrics for it and recorded it for Dot. "Exodus" received a "Grammy" from the National Academy of Recording Arts and Sciences as the song of the year. A two-piano recording, by Ferrante and Teicher, for United Artists, was a best seller.

F

The Fabulous Dorseys, a motion-picture musical biography of Tommy and Jimmy Dorsey, starring them with their orchestras, with Janet Blair (United Artists, 1947). The score was made up primarily of standards, with several new songs by Don George and Allie Wrubel interpolated.

See: At Sundown; Green Eyes; The Object of My Affection.

The Face on the Dime, words and music by Harold Rome (1946). A tribute to the memory of President Franklin D. Roosevelt, introduced by Lawrence Winters in the revue *Call Me Mister* (1946).

Face the Music, a musical comedy with book by Moss Hart. Lyrics and music by Irving Berlin. Starring Mary Boland and Andrew Tombes (1932).

See: Let's Have Another Cup o' Coffee; Soft Lights and Sweet Music.

Face to Face, words by Sammy Cahn, music by Sammy Fain (1953). Introduced by Jane Powell and Gordon MacRae in the motion-picture musical *Three Sailors and a Girl* (Warner, 1954).

The Facts of Life, words and music by Johnny Mercer (1960). Title song of the motion picture starring Bob Hope and Lucille Ball (United Artists, 1960). It was sung on the soundtrack under the titles by Steve Lawrence and Eydie Gorme.

Fade Out—Fade In, a musical comedy with book and lyrics by Betty Comden and Adolph Green. Music by Jule Styne. Starring Carol Burnett and Jack Cassidy (1964). Original cast recording (Paramount-ABC).

See: Call Me Savage; I'm with You; My Fortune Is My Face; You Mustn't Be Discouraged.

Fain, Sammy, composer, born New York City, 1902.

See (Lyrics by Irving Kahal): By a Waterfall; I Can Dream, Can't I?; I'll Be Seeing You; Let a Smile Be Your Umbrella on a Rainy Day; Wedding Bells Are Breaking Up That Old Gang of Mine; When I Take My Sugar to Tea; You Brought a New Kind of Love to Me.

See (Lyrics by Paul Francis Webster): April Love; A Certain Smile; Love Is a Many Spendored Thing; Secret Love; Tender Is the Night; There's a Rising Moon; A Very Precious Love.

See (Lyrics by Jack Yellen): Are You Having Any Fun?; Something I Dreamed Last Night.

See also: Dear Hearts and Gentle People; Dickey Bird Song; Face to Face; I Just Can't Do Enough for You; Nobody Knows What a Red Headed Mama Can Do; The World Is Your Balloon; You, Dear.

Fair and Warmer, words by Al Dubin, music by Harry Warren (1934). Introduced by Dick Powell and Ginger Rogers in the motion-picture musical *Twenty Million Sweethearts* (First National, 1934).

Falling in Love Again, words by Sammy Lerner, music by Frederick Hollander (1930). Introduced by Marlene Dietrich in her first American screen success, *The Blue Angel* (Paramount, 1930).

Falling in Love with Love, words by Lorenz Hart, music by Richard Rodgers (1938). Introduced by Muriel Angelus in the musical *The Boys from Syracuse* (1938).

"I remember how . . . he [Lorenz Hart] wrote the verse for 'Falling in Love with Love,' " wrote George Abbott. "He scratched it on the back of an old piece of paper while Dick and I talked about something else."

In the motion-picture adaptation of the musical (Universal, 1940), it was sung by Allan Jones.

Fanny, words and music by Harold Rome (1954). Title song of the musical play (1954), introduced by William Tabbert.

Rome reveals that this number was particularly difficult for him to write. It was the hero's love song to a girl he was abandoning so that he might go off to sea; and as such it had to convey tenderness without pointing up the fact that the hero was actually a "heel."

In the motion-picture adaptation of the musical (Warner, 1960), the title song was used for the background music, while all the other numbers from the show were deleted.

Fanny, a musical play with book by S. N. Behrman and Joshua Logan, based on a trilogy of plays by Marcel Pagnol. Lyrics and music by Harold Rome. Starring Ezio Pinza, Walter Slezak and Florence Henderson. Original cast recording (RCA Victor).

The motion-picture adaptation starred Charles Boyer, Leslie Caron and Maurice Chevalier (Warner, 1960). It dispensed with all the songs, but used the title number as a recurring theme in the background music. Soundtrack recording (Warner).

See: Be Kind to Your Parents; Fanny; To My Wife.

The Fantasticks, a musical with book and lyrics by Tom Jones suggested by Edmond Rostand's *Les Romantiques*. Music by Harvey Schmidt.

Starring Kenneth Nelson, Jerry Orbach and Rita Gardner (1960). Original cast recording (MGM).

See: Try to Remember.

Faraway, words by Dory Langdon, music by André Previn (1960). Introduced by Judy Garland in the motion-picture musical *Pepe* (Columbia, 1960).

Far-Away Places, words and music by Joan Whitney and Alex Kramer (1948). Popularized in a best-selling recording for Decca by Bing Crosby and the Ken Darby Choir in 1949. Perry Como's recording for RCA Victor was also successful.

Fare Thee Well, Annabelle, words by Mort Dixon, music by Allie Wrubel (1934). Introduced by Rudy Valleé in the motion-picture musical *Sweet Music* (Warner, 1935).

Farewell, words by Tom Blackburn, music by George Bruns (1955). Introduced by Fess Parker in *Davy Crockett at the Alamo*, a television production by Walt Disney. The song was popularized by Tennessee Ernie Ford in a Capitol recording.

Farewell, Amanda, words and music by Cole Porter (1949). Introduced by David Wayne in the motion picture *Adam's Rib*, starring Katharine Hepburn (MGM, 1949). The script of this motion picture originally named the heroine Madeline. When Porter was contracted to do the song, he insisted he couldn't write a number about a Madeline and suggested that her name be changed to Amanda.

A Farewell to Arms, words by Paul Francis Webster, music by Mario Nascimbene (1957). Introduced as an instrumental in the motion picture of the same name starring Rock Hudson and Jennifer Jones (20th Century-Fox, 1957).

Far from the Home I Love, words by Sheldon Harnick, music by Jerry Bock (1964). Ballad introduced by Julia Migenes in the musical play *Fiddler on the Roof* (1964).

The Farmer and the Cowman, words by Oscar Hammerstein II, music by Richard Rodgers (1943). Introduced by Ralph Riggs, Betty Garde, Alfred Drake, Lee Dixon and Celeste Holm in the opening scene of the second act in the musical play *Oklahoma!* (1943). In the motion-picture adaptation of the musical (Magna Theatre, 1955), it was sung by Gordon MacRae, Charlotte Greenwood, Gene Nelson, J. C. Flippen, James Whittemore and chorus.

Fascinating Rhythm, words by Ira Gershwin, music by George Gershwin (1924). Introduced by Fred and Adele Astaire, with Cliff "Ukulele Ike" Edwards, in the musical *Lady Be Good!* (1924), where it stopped the show. The critic of the New York *Herald Tribune* reported: "When at 9:15 they sang and danced 'Fascinating Rhythm,' the callous Broadwayites cheered them as if their favorite halfback had planted the ball behind the goal posts after an eighty-yard run. Seldom has it been our pleasure to witness such a heartfelt, spontaneous and so deserved a tribute."

In his autobiography, Fred Astaire reveals that while the show was in its final rehearsals, he and his sister, Adele, felt the need in the "Fascinating Rhythm" routine for a "climax wow step to get us off." For days they were unable to concoct anything suitable. Then, at one rehearsal, George Gershwin stepped from his piano and did a dance step for the Astaires he thought might do the trick. Astaire went on to explain: "He wanted us to continue doing the last step, which started center stage, and sustain it as we traveled to the side, continuing until we were out of sight. The step was a complicated precision rhythm thing in which we kicked out simultaneously as we crossed back and forth in front of each other with arm pulled and heads back. . . . It was the perfect answer to our problem, however, this suggestion by hoofer Gershwin; and it turned out to be a knockout applause getter."

In the motion-picture adaptation of *Lady, Be Good!* (MGM, 1943), the song was sung and danced to by Eleanor Powell. The number was also interpolated in the second motion picture adaptation of *Girl Crazy* (MGM, 1943).

Fascination, words by Dick Manning, music an adaptation of *Valse tzigane* by F. D. Marchetti (1932). The song was revived in the non-musical motion picture *Love in the Afternoon,* starring Gary Cooper, Maurice Chevalier and Audrey Hepburn (Allied Artists, 1957); it was used there as a recurrent theme. Jane Morgan's recording for Kapp in 1957 sold a million disks and helped make her famous.

The Fatal Wedding, words by H. W. Windom, music by Gussie L. Davis (1893). This was the composer's first hit song (Davis being Tin Pan Alley's first successful Negro composer). The song was introduced by a minstrel-show troupe in Cincinnati in 1893. It then became popular both in minstrel shows and in vaudeville. The maudlin lyrics described a fatal wedding in which the prospective husband is confronted by his former wife and their child. The child dies in her arms, the repentant father commits suicide and the two women go off to live with one another. The melody makes an interesting quotation from Mendelssohn's *Wedding March.*

F.D.R. Jones. *See:* Franklin D. Roosevelt Jones.

Feather Your Nest, words and music by James Kendis, James Brockman and Howard Johnson (1920). A song whose materialistic approach reflected some of the cynicism of the twenties.

A Fella with an Umbrella, words and music by Irving Berlin (1947). Introduced by Peter Lawford and Judy Garland in the motion-picture musical *Easter Parade* (MGM, 1948).

A Fellow Needs a Girl, words by Oscar Hammerstein II, music by Richard Rodgers (1947). Introduced by William Ching and Annamary Dickey in the musical play *Allegro* (1947).

Ferdinand the Bull, words by Larry Morey, music by Albert Hay Malotte (1938). Theme song of the Walt Disney animated cartoon of the same name (RKO, 1938).

Feudin' and Fightin', words by Al Dubin, music by Burton Lane (1947). Introduced by Pat Brewster and chorus in the Olsen and Johnson musical extravaganza *Laffing Room Only* (1944). The song was not popular between 1944 and 1947 because it could not be heard over the radio. This was due to the fact that the producers of *Laffing Room Only* were involved in a bitter dispute with ASCAP and refused to release the broadcasting rights to their show. These rights were finally acquired in 1947 by Lane, who then gave Dorothy Shay permission to reintroduce "Feudin' and Fightin'." She did so on Bing Crosby's radio program and scored a major success. The song went on from there to become one of the leading hits in 1947, with Dorothy Shay's recording for Columbia a best seller.

Fever, words and music by John Davenport and Eddie Cooley (1956). Popularized by Little Willie John in a best-selling recording for King. Peggy Lee also recorded it successfully, for Capitol in 1958. With this number Earl Grant achieved his first success as a singer in 1959.

Fickle Finger of Fate, words by Jack Lawrence, music by Stan Freeman (1964). Introduced by Richard Kiley in the musical *I Had a Ball* (1964).

Fiddle Dee Dee, a Weber and Fields musical extravaganza with book and lyrics by Edgar Smith. Music by John Stromberg. Starring Weber and Fields, De Wolf Hopper and Fay Templeton (1900).

See: Come Back, My Honey Boy, to Me; I'm a Respectable Working Girl; Ma Blushin' Rosie.

Fiddler on the Roof, words by Sheldon Harnick, music by Jerry Bock (1964). Title song of the musical (1964), its melody playing an integral part throughout that production. The number achieved considerable popularity in 1965 through several best-selling recordings, notably those by the Barry Sisters for Ampar, the Village Stompers for Epic, Al Hirt for RCA Victor and David Rose for MGM.

Fiddler on the Roof, a musical play with book by Joseph Stein based on stories by Sholom Aleichem. Lyrics by Sheldon Harnick. Music

by Jerry Bock. Starring Zero Mostel (1964). Original cast recording (RCA Victor).

See: Far From the Home I Love; Fiddler on the Roof; Matchmaker, Matchmaker; Sunrise, Sunset; To Life.

Fidgety Feet, words by Ira Gershwin, music by George Gershwin (1926). Introduced by Harland Dixon and Marion Fairbanks (and ensemble) in the musical *Oh, Kay!* (1926).

Fields, Dorothy, lyricist, born Allenhurst, New Jersey, 1905.

See: Hague, Albert; Kern, Jerome; McHugh, Jimmy; Romberg, Sigmund; Schwartz, Arthur.

See also: Who Can Tell?

Fifteen Cents, words and music by Chris Smith (1913).

Fifty Million Frenchmen, a musical comedy with book by Herbert Fields. Lyrics and music by Cole Porter. Starring William Gaxton and Genevieve Tobin (1929).

The motion-picture adaptation starred Olsen and Johnson with William Gaxton and Helen Broderick (Warner, 1931). Six Cole Porter songs were used, with an interpolation of George M. Cohan's "You Remind Me of My Mother."

See: Find Me a Primitive Man; I'm Unlucky at Gambling; Paree, What You Do for Me; You Don't Know Paree; You Do Something to Me; You Remind Me of My Mother; You've Got That Thing.

Finding Words for Spring, words and music by Raymond Jessel and Marian Grudeff (1965). Introduced by Inga Swenson in the musical *Baker Street* (1965).

Find Me a Primitive Man, words and music by Cole Porter (1929). Introduced by Evelyn Hoey, Lou Duthers, Billy Reid and ensemble in the musical comedy *Fifty Million Frenchmen* (1929). "'Find Me a Primitive Man,'" wrote Robert Littell in the New York *World* in 1929, "is one of the best pieces of popular music I have ever heard." The lyrics also came in for praise—from George Jean Nathan. He wrote: "When it comes to lyrics, this Cole Porter is so far ahead of the other boys in

New York that there just is no race at all."

Fine and Dandy, words by Paul James, music by Kay Swift (1930). Title song of a musical comedy (1930), introduced by Joe Cook and Alice Boulden.

Fine and Dandy, a musical comedy with book by Donald Ogden Stewart. Lyrics by Paul James. Music by Kay Swift. Starring Joe Cook (1930).
See: Fine and Dandy.

A Fine Romance, words by Dorothy Fields, music by Jerome Kern, (1936). Introduced by Fred Astaire and Ginger Rogers in the motion-picture musical *Swing Time* (RKO, 1936). The song was interpolated in the Jerome Kern screen biography *Till the Clouds Roll By* (MGM, 1946).

Finger Poppin' Time, words and music by Hank Ballard (1960). Introduced and popularized by Hank Ballard and the Midnighters in a King recording.

Fingertips, words and music by Henry Cosby and Clarence Paul (1963). Popularized by Little Stevie Wonder in a Talma recording.

Finian's Rainbow, a musical play with book by E. Y. Harburg and Fred Saidy. Lyrics by E. Y. Harburg. Music by Burton Lane. Starring Ella Logan, Donald Richards and David Wayne (1947). Original cast recording (Columbia).
See: The Begat; How Are Things in Glocca Morra?; Look to the Rainbow; Old Devil Moon; Something Sort of Grandish; When I'm Not Near the Girl I Love.

Fiorello!, a musical comedy based on the career of New York's Mayor, Fiorello La Guardia, with book by Jerome Weidman and George Abbot. Lyrics by Sheldon Harnick. Music by Jerry Bock. It won the Pulitzer Prize for drama in 1960. Starring Tom Bosley as La Guardia with Patricia Wilson and Eileen Hanley (1959). Original cast recording (Capitol).
See: Little Tin Box; Politics and Poker; Till Tomorrow.

Fiorito, Ted, composer, born Newark, New Jersey, 1900.

See: Charley, My Boy; I Never Knew; Laugh, Clown, Laugh; Roll Along, Prairie Moon; Sometime.

Fire Down Below, words by Ned Washington, music by Lester Lee (1957). Title song of a motion picture starring Rita Hayworth and Robert Mitchum (Columbia, 1957).

Firefly, words by Carolyn Leigh, music by Cy Coleman (1958). Popularized by Tony Bennett in a Columbia recording.

The Firefly, an operetta with book and lyrics by Otto Hauerbach (Harbach). Music by Rudolf Friml (his first stage score). Starring Emma Trentini (1912).

The motion-picture adaptation starred Jeanette MacDonald and Allan Jones (MGM, 1937). The basic stage score was used. "The Donkey Serenade," by Robert Wright, George "Chet" Forrest, Rudolf Friml and Herbert Stothart, was written for this movie.
See: The Dawn of Love; The Donkey Serenade; Giannina Mia; Love Is Like a Firefly; Sympathy; When a Maid Comes Knocking at Your Heart.

The First Gun Is Fired, words and music by George Frederick Root (1860). Root's first war song, and the first Union song of the Civil War. It was initially issued in a broadside—only three days after the firing on Fort Sumter. The chorus called on all Northerners to "arise, arise, arise, and gird ye for the fight."

Fisher, Fred, composer and lyricist, born Cologne, Germany, 1875; died New York City, 1942.
See (Lyrics by Alfred Bryan): Come, Josephine, in My Flying Machine; Lorraine, My Beautiful Lorraine; Oui, Oui, Marie; Peg o' My Heart; When I Get You Alone Tonight; Who Paid the Rent for Mrs. Rip van Winkle?
See (Lyrics by Howard Johnson): Siam; There's a Broken Heart for Every Light on Broadway.
See (Lyrics by Joseph McCarthy): Oui, Oui, Marie; There's a Little Spark of Love Still Burning; They Go Wild, Simply Wild, Over Me.
See also: Blue Is the Night; Chi-

cago; Daddy, You've Been a Mother to Me; Dardanella; I Don't Want Your Kisses; If the Man in the Moon Were a Coon; Ireland Must Be Heaven; There's a Little Bit of Bad in Every Good Little Girl.

For Fred Fisher's screen biography, see *Oh, You Beautiful Doll* (20th Century-Fox, 1949).

Fit As a Fiddle (and Ready for Love), words by Arthur Freed and Al Hoffman, music by Al Goodhart (1932). It was revived by Donald O'Connor and Gene Kelly in the motion picture musical *Singin' in the Rain* (MGM, 1952).

Five Foot Two, Eyes of Blue, words by Sam M. Lewis and Joe Young, music by Ray Henderson (1925). This was one of Henderson's early successes before he teamed up with Bud De Sylva and Lew Brown. The song was interpolated in the motion picture *Has Anybody Seen My Gal?*, starring Piper Laurie and Rock Hudson (Columbia, 1952).

Five Minutes More, words by Sammy Cahn, music by Jule Styne (1946). It was published as an independent number, then interpolated in the motion-picture musical *The Sweetheart of Sigma Chi,* starring Phil Regan (Monogram, 1946), sung by Phil Brito. It was popularized by Frank Sinatra in a Columbia recording, reaching first place in the Hit Parade in 1946.

Flat Foot Floogie with the Floy Floy, words and music by Slim Gaillard, Slam Stewart and Bud Green (1938).

The Fleet's In, a motion-picture musical starring Dorothy Lamour and William Holden (Paramount, 1942). Songs were mainly by Johnny Mercer and Victor Schertzinger.

See: Amapola; Arthur Murray Taught Me Dancing in a Hurry; Tangerine.

Flora, the Red Menace, a musical comedy with book by George Abbott and Robert Russell based on Lester Atwell's novel *Love Is Just Around the Corner.* Lyrics by Fred Ebb. Music by John Kander. Starring Liza Minnelli in her Broadway debut (1965). Original cast recording (RCA Victor).

See: All I Need; A Quiet Thing.

Flower Drum Song, a musical comedy with book by Oscar Hammerstein II and Joseph Fields based on a novel by C. Y. Lee. Lyrics by Oscar Hammerstein II. Music by Richard Rodgers. Starring Pat Suzuki and Miyoshi Umeki (in their Broadway stage debuts) with Larry Blyden (1958). Original cast recording (Columbia).

The motion-picture adaptation (Universal, 1961) starred Nancy Kwan, Miyoshi Umeki and Jack Soo. The basic stage score was used. Soundtrack recording (Decca).

See: Don't Marry Me; A Hundred Million Miracles; I Enjoy Being a Girl; Love, Look Away; Sunday; You Are Beautiful.

A Flower from Mother's Grave, words and music by Harry Kennedy (1878). A sentimental ballad inspired by the death of an infant. It was introduced by the composer at Hyde and Behman's Adams Street Theatre in Brooklyn, New York, in 1878. The composer subsequently popularized it in his vaudeville appearances throughout the country. The New York *Herald* of November 9, 1884, remarked that this song had an extraordinary hold "among the shop girls of the city."

Flying Colors, a musical comedy with book and lyrics by Howard Dietz. Music by Arthur Schwartz. Starring Clifton Webb and Tamara Geva (1932).

See: Alone Together; Day After Day; Louisiana Hayride; Shine on Your Shoes.

Flying Down to Rio, words by Gus Kahn and Edward Eliscu, music by Vincent Youmans (1933). Title song of the motion-picture musical (RKO, 1933), introduced by Fred Astaire and Ginger Rogers.

Flying Down to Rio, a motion-picture musical starring Fred Astaire and Ginger Rogers (RKO, 1933). Songs by Gus Kahn, Edward Eliscu and Vincent Youmans. This was Youmans' first screen score.

See: The Carioca; Flying Down to Rio; Orchids in the Moonlight; Music Makes Me.

Flying High, a musical comedy with book by Bud De Sylva and John McGowan. Lyrics by Bud De Sylva and Lew Brown. Music by Ray Henderson. Starring Oscar Shaw, Bert Lahr and Grace Brinkley (1930).

The motion-picture adaptation starred Bert Lahr and Charlotte Greenwood (MGM, 1931). The stage score was completely replaced by new songs by Dorothy Fields and Jimmy McHugh.

See: Good for You, Bad for Me; Thank Your Father; Wasn't It Beautiful While It Lasted?; Without Love.

The Flying Trapeze. *See:* The Man on the Flying Trapeze.

Fly Me to the Moon (or, In Other Words), words and music by Bart Howard (1954). Originally entitled "In Other Words," it was introduced by Felicia Sanders in 1954 and recorded with no success by Kaye Ballard for Decca. The song reappeared in 1962 under the new title of "Fly Me to the Moon" (title inspired by the space program) to achieve a major success for the first time. It was now recorded over a hundred times by twenty-five different performers. The most successful of these releases was the "Fly Me to the Moon Bossa Nova" by Joe Harnell and his orchestra for Kapp. It received a "Grammy" from the National Academy of Recording Arts and Sciences as the best recording of the year by an orchestra for dancing.

A Foggy Day, words by Ira Gershwin, music by George Gershwin (1937). Introduced by Fred Astaire in the motion-picture musical *Damsel in Distress* (RKO, 1937). George and Ira Gershwin originally named the song "A Foggy Day in London Town," but permitted the title to be contracted to "A Foggy Day." In *Lyrics on Several Occasions*, Ira Gershwin returns to the longer title. The song was successfully exploited by Frank Sinatra in night clubs and in a Capitol recording.

The Folks Who Live on the Hill, words by Oscar Hammerstein II, music by Jerome Kern (1937). Introduced by Irene Dunne in the motion-picture

musical *High, Wide and Handsome* (Paramount, 1937).

Following the Sun Around, words by Joseph McCarthy, music by Harry Tierney (1926). Introduced by J. Harold Murray in the musical *Rio Rita* (1927). In the motion-picture adaptation of the musical (RKO, 1929), it was sung by John Boles.

Follow Me, words by Alan Jay Lerner, music by Frederick Loewe (1960). Introduced by Marjorie Smith in the musical play *Camelot* (1960).

Follow Me (or, Love Song from Mutiny on the Bounty), words by Paul Francis Webster, music by Bronislau Kaper (1962). Introduced by a chorus (singing both in English and Tahitian) on the soundtrack of the motion picture *Mutiny on the Bounty*, starring Marlon Brando (MGM, 1962).

Follow the Boys, an all-star motion-picture revue with a cast including W. C. Fields, Sophie Tucker, Marlene Dietrich and others (Universal, 1944). Most of the score was made up of standards, with several new numbers by Sammy Cahn and Jule Styne, and others.

See: Beyond the Blue Horizon; I Feel a Song Coming On; I'll Get By; I'll Walk Alone; Is You Is or Is You Ain't My Baby?; Some of These Days.

Follow the Fleet, a motion-picture musical starring Fred Astaire and Ginger Rogers (RKO, 1936). Songs by Irving Berlin.

See: I'm Putting All My Eggs in One Basket; Let's Face the Music and Dance; Let Yourself Go.

Follow the Girls, a musical comedy with book by Guy Bolton and Eddie Davis. Additional dialogue by Fred Thompson. Lyrics by Dan Shapiro and Milton Pascal. Music by Phil Charig. Starring Gertrude Niessen and Jackie Gleason (1944).

See: I Wanna Get Married.

Follow Thru, a musical comedy with book by Laurence Schwab and Bud De Sylva. Lyrics by Bud De Sylva and Lew Brown. Music by Ray Henderson. Starring Jack Haley and Zelma O'Neal (1929).

The motion-picture adaptation

starred Charles "Buddy" Rogers, Jack
Haley, Nancy Carroll and Zelma
O'Neal (Paramount, 1930). It used
only two songs from the stage score,
with additional numbers by Edward
Eliscu and Manning Sherwin, and
Lorenz Hart and Richard Rodgers,
among others.

See: Button Up Your Overcoat;
You Are My Lucky Star.

Fooled, words by Mann Curtis, music
by Doris Tauber, melody based on a
theme by Franz Lehár (1955).
Popularized by Perry Como in an
RCA Victor recording.

Fools Rush In, words by Johnny Mercer, music by Rube Bloom, melody
based on Bloom's "Shangri La"
(1940). Popularized in 1940 in a best-
selling Bluebird recording by Glenn
Miller and his orchestra. It was successfully revived in 1963 by Ricky
Nelson in a Decca recording.

A Fool Such As I, words and music by
Bill Trader (1952). First popularized
in 1953 by Jo Stafford's Columbia
recording. The song was revived in
1959 by Elvis Presley, whose RCA
Victor recording sold over a million
disks.

Footlight Parade, a motion-picture
musical starring James Cagney,
Joan Blondell, Ruby Keeler and
Dick Powell (Warner, 1933). Songs
by Irving Kahal and Sammy Fain,
by Al Dubin and Harry Warren.

See: By a Waterfall; Shanghai Lil.

For All We Know, words by Sam M.
Lewis, music by J. Fred Coots
(1934). Introduced by Morton
Downey on his radio program. It
was then popularized in recordings
by Kay Kyser and his orchestra and
by Guy Lombardo and his Royal
Canadians.

For Bales. See: When Johnny Comes
Marching Home.

Forever and Ever, a Swiss popular song
with music by Franz Winkler, English lyrics by Malia Rosa (1948).
Popularized in 1949 in best-selling
recordings by Perry Como for RCA
Victor and by Russ Morgan and
orchestra for Decca.

Forget Domani, words by N. Newell,
music by Riz Ortolani (1965). Introduced in the non-musical motion pic-

ture *The Yellow Rolls Royce,* starring
Rex Harrison, Ingrid Bergman and
Shirley MacLaine (MGM, 1965),
and popularized by Frank Sinatra
in a best-selling recording for Reprise.

Forgive Me, words by Jack Yellen,
music by Milton Ager (1927). Popularized by Ruth Etting in a Columbia recording. It was interpolated in
the motion picture *Bells of Capistrano,* starring Gene Autry (Republic, 1942). Eddie Fisher revived it
successfully in 1952 in an RCA Victor recording.

Forgive My Heart, words by Sammy
Gallop, music by Chester Conn
1955). Popularized by Nat King
Cole in a Capitol recording.

For He's a Jolly Good Fellow. See: We
Won't Go Home Until Morning.

For Mama, a French popular song,
music by Charles Aznavour, English
lyrics by Don Black (1964). A sentimental ballad popularized by Jerry
Vale in a Columbia recording. Other
successful recordings were then
made by Connie Francis for MGM
and Vic Damone for Warner.

For Me and My Gal, words by Edgar
Leslie and E. Ray Goetz, music by
George W. Meyer (1917). Meyer
thus described this song's origin:
"I sat down and went to work. There
was nothing remarkable about it. I
was writing songs for a living and I
needed the money, so I wrote the
ballad. When I had finished I
thought up a title and took the
music and my title to lyricists E. Ray
Goetz and Edgar Leslie. They hitched
the lyric to the title."

It was first popularized in vaudeville by such headliners as Belle
Baker, Sophie Tucker, Eddie Cantor
and George Jessel. Al Jolson sang it
at the Winter Garden. Their combined efforts resulted in a sheet-
music sale exceeding three million
copies.

The song provided the title for,
and was featured prominently in, a
motion-picture musical (MGM,
1942).

For Me and My Gal, a motion-picture
musical starring Gene Kelly (in his
screen debut) and Judy Garland

(MGM, 1942). The score was made up of standards.

See: After You've Gone; Balling the Jack; For Me and My Gal; Goodbye, Broadway, Hello, France; How You Gonna Keep 'Em Down on the Farm?; Oh, You Beautiful Doll; Over There; Where Do We Go from Here?

For My Sweetheart, words by Gus Kahn, music by Walter Donaldson (1926).

For Old Times' Sake, words and music by Charles K. Harris (1900).

Forrest, George "Chet," composer and lyricist, born Brooklyn, New York, 1915.

See (In collaboration with Robert Wright): And This Is My Beloved; Baubles, Bangles and Beads; The Donkey Serenade; If This Is Goodbye; I Love You; Little Hands; Snowflakes and Sweethearts; Strange Music; Stranger in Paradise.

For Sentimental Reasons, words by Deke Watson, music by William Best (1945). Popularized by Nat King Cole in a Capitol recording. Successful recordings were also made by Eddie Howard for Majestic and Dinah Shore for Columbia.

For the First Time (I've Fallen in Love), words by Charles Tobias, music by David Kapp (1943).

For the First Time (Panzeri). See: Come Prima.

The Fortune Teller, a comic opera with book and lyrics by Harry B. Smith. Music by Victor Herbert. Starring Alice Nielsen and Eugene Cowles (1898).

See: Gypsy Love Song.

Forty-Five Minutes from Broadway, words and music by George M. Cohan (1906). Title song of a musical comedy (1906), where it was introduced by Victor Moore and chorus. It was interpolated in George M. Cohan's screen biography *Yankee Doodle Dandy* (Warner, 1942).

Forty-Five Minutes from Broadway, a musical comedy with book, lyrics and music by George M. Cohan. Starring Fay Templeton, Victor Moore and Donald Brian (1906).

See: Forty-Five Minutes from Broadway; Mary's a Grand Old Name; So Long, Mary.

Forty-Second Street, words by Al Dubin, music by Harry Warren (1932). Title song of a motion-picture musical (Warner, 1933), introduced by Ruby Keeler.

Forty-Second Street, a motion-picture musical starring Dick Powell and Ruby Keeler (Warner, 1933). Songs by Al Dubin and Harry Warren.

See: Forty-Second Street; Shuffle Off to Buffalo; Young and Healthy; You're Getting to Be a Habit with Me.

For You, words by Al Dubin, music by Joseph A. Burke (1930). It was published independently, then interpolated in the non-musical motion picture *Holy Terror*, starring George O'Brien and Sally Eilers (Fox, 1931). It was successfully revived a quarter of a century after publication in best-selling recordings by Rosemary Clooney for Columbia and Nat King Cole for Capitol.

For You, For Me, For Evermore, words by Ira Gershwin, music by George Gershwin (1947). Introduced by Dick Haymes and Betty Grable in the motion-picture musical *The Shocking Miss Pilgrim* (20th Century-Fox, 1947). George Gershwin wrote this melody sometime in 1936 or early 1937, then put it aside. It was found after his death in a batch of manuscripts. With the help of Kay Swift, Ira Gershwin adapted some of this manuscript material into a nine-song score for *The Shocking Miss Pilgrim*, providing the tunes with lyrics.

Foster, Stephen, composer and lyricist, born Lawrenceville, Pennsylvania, 1826; died New York City, 1864.

See: Beautiful Dreamer; De Camptown Races; Come Where My Love Lies Dreaming; Hard Times, Come Again No More; Jeanie with the Light Brown Hair; Lou'siana Belle; Massa's in De Cold Ground; My Old Kentucky Home; Nelly Bly; Nelly Was a Lady; Oh, Susanna; Old Black Joe; Old Folks at Home; Old Dog Tray; Old Uncle Ned; Open Thy Lattice, Love; Under the Willow She's Sleeping; We Are Coming, Father Abraham.

For screen biographies of Stephen Foster, see *I Dream of Jeanie* and *Swanee River*.

The Fountain in the Park (or, While Strolling Through the Park One Day), words and music by Robert A. King (1884). Introduced by the Du Rell Twin Brothers at Tony Pastor's Music Hall in New York in 1884. Certain features of their vaudeville presentation became traditional with later performers, such as interpolating soft-shoe steps during the chorus, and lifting the hat at the sound of "ah" toward the end of the song. This song is sometimes credited to Ed Haley, but since King was habitually publishing songs under pen names, it was possible that he used that of Haley for this release; in any event it is now generally conceded that this is King's song.

Frankie, words by Howard Greenfield, music by Neil Sedaka (1959). Popularized by Connie Francis in an MGM recording.

Franklin D. Roosevelt Jones, words and music by Harold Rome (1938). Introduced by Hazel Scott (her first success as a singing star) in the political-conscious revue *Sing Out the News* (1938), where it regularly stopped the show. It won an ASCAP award in 1938 as one of the best songs of the year. In his description of the evacuation at Dunkirk during World War II, Quentin Reynolds noted that this was one of the songs heard most often from escaping British troops.

Freckles, words by Howard Johnson, music by Milton Ager and Cliff Hess (1919).

Free America, words by Joseph Warren (a fighting minister who died at Bunker Hill) to the melody of the English song "The British Grenadiers" (c. 1774). This was one of the most celebrated war songs of the American Revolution.

The Free and Easy, words by Roy Turk, music by Fred Ahlert (1930). Introduced in the motion picture of the same name starring Buster Keaton (MGM, 1930). It was then interpolated in the non-musical motion picture *Dance, Fools, Dance,* starring Joan Crawford (MGM, 1931).

Freed, Arthur, lyricist, born Charleston, South Carolina, 1894.
See: Brown, Nacio Herb.
See also: Fit As a Fiddle; I Cried for You; It Was So Beautiful; This Heart of Mine.

Freed, Ralph, lyricist, born Vancouver, B. C., 1907.
See: Lane, Burton.
See also: You Dear; Young Man with a Horn.

Freedom Is the Word, words by E. Y. Harburg, music by Burton Lane (1964). A song inspired by the Civil Rights movement. It was introduced by Robert Preston and a chorus of children, in the production of the same name presented by the NAACP on a closed TV circuit to thirty-five cities in May, 1964.

The French Lesson, words by Betty Comden and Adolph Green (1947). A French lesson, in verses and melody, in several easy exercises, written for the motion-picture adaptation of the Broadway musical *Good News* (MGM, 1947). It was introduced by June Allyson and Peter Lawford.

Frenesi, a popular Spanish song, music by Albert Dominguez, English lyrics by Ray Charles and S. K. Russell (1939). The song was popularized in 1940 by Artie Shaw in an RCA Victor recording that sold over a million disks.

Friend, Cliff, composer, born Cincinnati, Ohio, 1893.
See (Lyrics by Charles Tobias): Don't Sweetheart Me; Old Man Time; Time Waits for No One; We Did It Before and We'll Do It Again.
See also: Hello, Bluebird; Then I'll Be Happy; When My Dream Boat Comes Home; You Can't Stop Me From Dreaming; You Tell Her I Stutter.

The Friendliest Thing, words and music by Ervin Drake (1964). Introduced by Bernice Massi in the musical *What Makes Sammy Run?* (1964).

Friendly Persuasion (or, Thee I Love), words by Paul Francis Webster, music by Dimitri Tiomkin (1956). Introduced on the soundtrack of a motion picture of the same name starring Gary Cooper and Dorothy McGuire (Allied Artists, 1956).

The producers of the motion picture originally planned naming it *Thee I Love* and the theme song was written with that title. After the picture received the new name of *Friendly Persuasion*, the title song had to stay "Thee I Love" because it had already been written.

Tiomkin hoped to get Perry Como to sing the number on the soundtrack, but his price was too high. "I'd heard of a hillbilly song sung by a beginner who was on the Arthur Godfrey television show in New York," Tiomkin wrote in his autobiography. "He had the right voice for 'Thee I Love.' His name was Pat Boone. We got in touch with his agent, and there were no difficulties." Pat Boone was paid three thousand dollars to sing the number on the soundtrack. He also made a recording for Dot that sold a million and a half disks.

Friendship, words and music by Cole Porter (1939). Introduced by Ethel Merman and Bert Lahr in the musical *Du Barry Was a Lady* (1939). The song was revived in the musical *Three for the Money* (1955).

Friml, Rudolf, composer, born Prague, Czechoslovakia, 1879.

See (Lyrics by Otto Harbach): Allah's Holiday; The Bubble; The Dawn of Love; Giannina Mia; Katinka; Love Is Like a Firefly; Rackety-Coo; Something Seems Tingle-Ingeling; Sympathy; When a Maid Comes Knocking at Your Heart; You're in Love.

See (Lyrics by Otto Harbach and Oscar Hammerstein II): The Door of My Dreams; Indian Love Call; Rose Marie; Totem Tom Tom.

See (Lyrics by Rida Johnson Young): Any Kind of Man; Sometime.

See also: All for One; L'Amour Toujours L'Amour; Bring Back My Blushing Rose; The Donkey Serenade; Give Me One Hour; Ma Belle; March of the Musketeers; My Paradise; Only a Rose; Some Day; Song of the Vagabonds; Waltz Huguette; With Red Wine.

From Here to Eternity, words by Bob Wells, music by Fred Karger (1953). Inspired by the non-musical motion picture of the same name starring Montgomery Clift, Burt Lancaster and Deborah Kerr (Columbia, 1953). It was popularized by Frank Sinatra in a best-selling Capitol recording.

From Now On, words and music by Cole Porter (1938). Introduced by William Gaxton and Tamara in the musical *Leave It to Me* (1938).

From Russia with Love, words and music by Lionel Bart (1964). Title song of a non-musical motion picture starring Sean Connery and Daniela Bianchi (United Artists, 1964). *Variety* reported that in the first few months of the song's release it became "the most recorded tune of the year . . . with eighteen different single versions, both instrumental and vocal, as well as representations in numerous albums." The most successful vocal recordings were those by Jack Jones for Kapp and Jane Morgan on Colpix; the leading instrumental recordings were by the Village Stompers for Epic and Al Caiola for United Artists.

From the Halls of Montezuma. *See:* The Marines' Hymn.

From the Top of Your Head (to the Tip of Your Toes), words by Mack Gordon, music by Harry Revel (1935). Introduced by Bing Crosby in the motion-picture musical *Two for Tonight* (Paramount, 1935), and popularized by him in a Decca recording.

From This Day On, words by Alan Jay Lerner, music by Frederick Loewe (1947). Introduced by David Brooks and Marion Bell in the musical play *Brigadoon* (1947).

From This Moment On, words and music by Cole Porter (1950). Introduced by Priscilla Gillette and William Eythe in the musical *Out of This World* (1950), during its out-of-town tryouts; it was dropped from the show by the time the production reached New York. It was adapted for a ballet sequence in the motion-picture adaptation of the Cole Porter musical *Kiss Me, Kate* (MGM, 1953), where it was sung by Ann Miller and Tommy Rall.

Frosty the Snowman, words by Steve Nelson, music by Jack Rollins (1950). Gene Autry's recording for Columbia in 1951 sold over a million disks.

Fugue for Tinhorns (or, I've Got the Horse Right Here), words and music by Frank Loesser (1950). A three-voiced canon (sometimes referred to as "The Three-Cornered Tune") sung by horseplayers picking their day's selections. It was the opening number of the musical *Guys and Dolls* (1950), introduced by Stubby Kaye, Johnny Silver and Douglas Dean. This number was also used in the motion-picture adaptation of the musical (MGM, 1955).

Full Moon and Empty Arms, words and music by Buddy Kaye and Ted Mossman, the melody based on Rachmaninoff's Second Piano Concerto (1946). Popularized by Frank Sinatra in a Columbia recording.

Funny Face, words by Ira Gershwin, music by George Gershwin (1927). Title song of the musical (1927), where it was introduced by Fred and Adele Astaire. While doing this number in that production, Fred pulled his sister around in a toy wagon. Fred sang one verse and chorus, after which Adele delivered her version. There was an additional chorus for Adele to sing to the dog. The lyric made allusions to such screen celebrities as Gloria Swanson and Ronald Colman.

In the motion-picture adaptation of the musical (Paramount, 1957), it was sung by Fred Astaire.

Funny Face, a musical comedy with book by Paul Gerard Smith and Fred Thompson. Lyrics by Ira Gershwin. Music by George Gershwin. Starring Fred and Adele Astaire and Victor Moore (1927).

The motion-picture adaptation starred Fred Astaire and Audrey Hepburn (Paramount, 1957). A few songs from the original stage production were supplemented by new numbers by Leonard Gershe and Roger Edens. Soundtrack recording (Verve).

See: The Babbitt and the Bromide; Funny Face; He Loves and She Loves; Let's Kiss and Make Up; My One and Only; 'S Wonderful.

Funny Girl, a musical comedy based on the life of Fanny Brice, with text by Isobel Lennart. Lyrics by Bob Merrill. Music by Jule Styne. Starring Barbra Streisand as Fanny Brice with Sydney Chaplin (1964). Original cast recording (Capitol).

See: Don't Rain on My Parade; I'm the Greatest Star; The Music That Makes Me Dance; People; Who Are You Now?; You Are Woman.

A Funny Thing Happened on the Way to the Forum, a musical comedy with book by Burt Shevelove and Larry Gelbart based on the plays of Plautus. Lyrics and music by Stephen Sondheim. Starring Zero Mostel (1962). Original cast recording (Capitol).

See: Lovely.

Fun to Be Fooled, words by Ira Gershwin and E. Y. Harburg, music by Harold Arlen (1934). Introduced by Frances Williams in the revue *Life Begins at 8:40* (1934).

G

The Gaby Glide, words by Harry Pilcer, music by Louis A. Hirsch (1911). Written for the American debut of the French star Gaby Deslys. She introduced it with Harry Pilcer in the musical *Vera Violetta* (1911), and repeated the performance in the musical *The Whirl of Society* (1912).

A Gal in Calico, words by Leo Robin. music by Arthur Schwartz (1946). Introduced by Jack Carson, Dennis Morgan and Martha Vickers in the motion-picture musical *The Time, The Place and The Girl* (Warner, 1946). It was popularized by Tex Beneke and his orchestra in an RCA Victor recording.

Gallagher and Shean. *See:* Mister Gallagher and Mister Shean.

Gambler's Guitar, words and music by Jim Lowe (1953). Popularized by Rusty Draper in a Mercury recording. He sang it in the motion-picture musical *Rhythms with Rusty* (Universal, 1954).

The Game of Love, words and music by C. Ballard, Jr. (1965). Popularized by Wayne Fontana and the Mindbenders in a best-selling recording for Fonata.

Garden of My Dreams, words by Gene Buck, music by Louis A. Hirsch (1918). Introduced by Lillian Lorraine and Frank Carter in the *Ziegfeld Follies of 1918*.

The Garrick Gaieties, an intimate, sophisticated revue with sketches by various writers and songs mainly by Richard Rodgers and Lorenz Hart. This was the first successful stage score by Rodgers and Hart. Starring Sterling Holloway, Romney Brent, June Cochrane and Betty Starbuck (1925).

There were two later editions of the *Gaieties*. The second (1926) had songs mainly by Rodgers and Hart; the third (1930) had songs by various composers and lyricists including Ira Gershwin, E. Y. Harburg, and Vernon Duke.

See: I'm Only Human After All; Manhattan; Mountain Greenery; Sentimental Me.

Gaunt, Percy, composer, born Philadelphia, Pennsylvania, 1852; died Palenville, New York, 1896.

See: The Bowery; Love Me Little, Love Me Long; Push Dem Clouds Away; Reuben, Reuben.

Gay Divorce, a musical comedy with book by Dwight Taylor. Lyrics and music by Cole Porter. Starring Fred Astaire and Claire Luce (1932).

The motion-picture adaptation changed the title to *The Gay Divorcee* and starred Fred Astaire and Ginger Rogers (RKO, 1934). Only one song was used from the stage score. Other musical numbers were contributed by Herb Magidson and Con Conrad, and by Mack Gordon and Harry Revel. One of these new numbers received the Academy Award ("The Continental").

See: The Continental; Don't Let It Bother You; I've Got You on My Mind; Night and Day.

Gee, But It's Great to Meet a Friend from Your Home Town, words by William Tracey, music by James McGavisk (1910). It was revived by Jack Oakie in the motion-picture musical *Hello, Frisco, Hello* (20th Century-Fox, 1943).

The Gentleman Is a Dope, words by Oscar Hammerstein II, music by Richard Rodgers (1947). Introduced by Lisa Kirk in the musical play *Allegro* (1948), and popularized by Jo Stafford in a Capitol recording.

Gentlemen Marry Brunettes, a motion-picture musical starring Alan Young, Scott Brady, Jeanne Crain and Rudy Vallée (United Artists, 1955). Anita Ellis sang for Jeanne Crain on the soundtrack; Robert Farnon sang on the soundtrack for Scott Brady. The score was made up mainly of standards.

See: Ain't Misbehavin'; Have You Met Miss Jones?; I've Got Five Dollars; I Wanna Be Loved by You; Miss Annabelle Lee; My Funny Valentine; You're Driving Me Crazy.

Gentlemen Prefer Blondes, a musical comedy with book by Anita Loos and Joseph Fields based on the novel and Broadway stage comedy of the same name by Anita Loos. Lyrics by Leo Robin. Music by Jule Styne. Starring Carol Channing and Yvonne Adair, (1949). Original cast recording (Columbia).

The motion-picture adaptation starred Marilyn Monroe and Jane Russell (20th Century-Fox, 1953). The principal songs from the stage production were used with several new numbers by Hoagy Carmichael.

See: Bye, Bye, Baby; Diamonds Are a Girl's Best Friend; A Little Girl from Little Rock.

Georgette, words by Lew Brown, music by Ray Henderson (1922). One of Henderson's earliest song successes. It was introduced by Ted Lewis and his band in the revue *The Greenwich Village Follies of 1922.*

George Washington, Jr., a musical comedy with book, lyrics and music by George M. Cohan. Starring George M. Cohan (1906).

See: I Was Born in Virginia; You're a Grand Old Flag.

George White's Scandals, an annual lavish revue produced by George White. The first edition, in 1919, starred Ann Pennington and Lou Holtz. The score was by Arthur Jackson and Richard A. Whiting. Between 1920 and 1925 inclusive, George Gershwin wrote all the songs to words by various lyricists. De Sylva, Brown and Henderson followed Gershwin for the editions of 1925, 1926 and 1928 (there was no 1927 edition). After 1928 the songs were written by Cliff Friend (1929), Lew Brown and Ray Henderson (1931 and 1935) and Sammy Fain (1939). There were no productions in 1932, 1933, 1934; that of 1939 was the last.

Among the stars who appeared between 1920 and 1939 were W. C. Fields, Lou Holtz, Willie and Eugene Howard, Winnie Lightner, Will Mahoney, the McCarthy Sisters, Ethel Merman, Tom Patricola, Harry Richman, Rudy Vallée and Paul Whiteman and his orchestra.

Three motion-picture musicals used the name of *George White's Scandals.* The first starred Rudy Vallée, Jimmy Durante and Alice Faye and had songs by Jack Yellen, Irving Caesar and Ray Henderson. "Life Is Just a Bowl of Cherries" and "Wishing" were interpolated in the score (20th Century-Fox, 1934). The second starred James Dunn, Alice Faye and Eleanor Powell, and used the songs of various composers and lyricists (20th Century-Fox, 1935). The third starred Jack Haley and Joan Davis, with a score by Jack Yellen and Sammy Fain (RKO, 1945).

See: Are You Having Any Fun?; The Birth of the Blues; Black Bottom; The Girl Is You; I'll Build a Stairway to Paradise; I'm on the Crest of a Wave; It's an Old Southern Custom; Life Is Just a Bowl of Cherries; Lucky Day; My Song; Nasty Man; Somebody Loves Me; South Sea Isles; That's Why Darkies Were Born; This Is the Missus; The Thrill Is Gone; Wishing.

Georgia, words by Howard Johnson,

music by Walter Donaldson (1922). It was adopted as the official song of the State of Georgia.

Georgia on My Mind, words by Stuart Gorrell, music by Hoagy Carmichael (1930). Popularized in recordings by Hoagy Carmichael for Decca, "Fats" Waller for RCA Victor and Frankie Laine for Mercury. The song was revived in 1959 by Ray Charles, whose ABC-Paramount recording received a "Grammy" from the National Academy of Recording Arts and Sciences as the best male vocal recording of the year.

Gershwin, George, composer, born Brooklyn, New York, 1898; died Hollywood, California, 1937.

See (Lyrics by Bud De Sylva): Do It Again; Nobody But You.

See (Lyrics by Ira Gershwin): Aren't You Kind of Glad You Did; The Babbitt and the Bromide; Back Bay Polka; Bess, You Is My Woman Now; Bidin' My Time; Boy, What Love Has Done to Me; But Not for Me; By Strauss; Clap Yo' Hands; Could You Use Me?; Delishious; Do, Do, Do; Do It Again; Embraceable You; Fascinating Rhythm; Fidgety Feet; A Foggy Day; For You, For Me, For Evermore; Funny Face; The Half of It Dearie, Blues; He Loves and She Loves; How Long Has This Been Going On?; I Can't Be Bothered Now; I Got Rhythm; Isn't It a Pity?; I've Got a Crush on You; I Was Doing All Right; K-R-A-Z-Y for You; Let's Call the Whole Thing Off; Let's Kiss and Make Up; Liza; The Lorelei; Love Is Sweeping the Country; Love Walked In; The Man I Love; Maybe; Mine; Mischa, Jascha, Toscha, Sascha; My One and Only; Nice Work If You Can Get It; Of Thee I Sing; Oh, Lady, Be Good; Oh, So Nice; Our Love Is Here to Stay; The Real American Folk Song; A Red Headed Woman Make a Choo Choo Jump Its Track; Sam and Delilah; Shall We Dance?; Slap That Bass; So Am I; So Are You; Someone to Watch Over Me; Soon; Strike Up the Band; Stiff Upper Lip; Sweet and Low Down; 'S Wonderful; That Certain Feeling; That Lost Barber Shop Chord; There's a Boat Dat's Leavin' Soon for New York; They All Laughed; They Can't Take That Away from Me; A Typical Self-Made American; Where's the Boy?; Who?; Wintergreen for President.

See (Lyrics by Ira Gershwin and Du Bose Heyward): I Got Plenty o' Nutthin'; I Loves You, Porgy; Summertime; A Woman Is a Sometime Thing.

See also: Drifting Along with the Tide; Idle Dreams; I'll Build a Stairway to Paradise; I Was So Young; I Won't Say I Will; Making of a Girl; My Man's Gone Now; Some Wonderful Sort of Someone; Song of the Flame; South Sea Isles; Swanee; Tra-la-la; When You Want 'Em You Can't Get 'Em; Yankee Doodle Blues.

For George Gershwin's screen biography, see *Rhapsody in Blue* (Warner, 1945).

Gershwin, Ira, lyricist, born New York City, 1896.

See: Arlen, Harold; Gershwin, George; Weill, Kurt.

See also: Cheerful Little Earful; I Can't Get Started with You; I'll Build a Stairway to Paradise; I'm Only Human After All; I Won't Say I Will; Oh Me, Oh My, Oh You; Sunny Disposish; Sure Thing.

For Ira Gershwin's screen biography, see *Rhapsody in Blue* (Warner, 1945).

Gertie from Bizerte, words and music by James Cavanaugh, Walter Kent and Bob Cutter (1943). A G.I. favorite in Africa during World War II.

Get a Job, words and music by E. T. A. Beal, R. W. Edward, W. F. Horton and R. A. Lewis (1958). Popularized by the Silhouettes in an Ember recording.

Get Happy, words by Ted Koehler, music by Harold Arlen (1930). Sometimes described as a "Hallelujah number," this was Arlen's first successful song. It was introduced by Ruth Etting in the first-act finale of the *9:15 Revue* (1930).

Arlen wrote this song while working as a rehearsal pianist for the Vincent Youmans musical *Great Day.* During a break in the rehearsal he improvised a "vamp" on one of Youmans' songs. Cooke, conductor of the Negro chorus for the revue, felt Arlen's effort was good enough to become a hit song. Ted Koehler then wrote the lyrics. When George Gershwin saw the *9:15 Revue* during an out-of-town tryout, he congratulated Arlen on having written an outstanding musical number.

It was sung by Judy Garland in the motion-picture musical *Summer Stock* (MGM, 1950). It was also heard in the motion-picture biography of Jane Froman, *With a Song in My Heart* (20th Century-Fox, 1952).

Get Me to the Church on Time, words by Alan Jay Lerner, music by Frederick Loewe (1956). Humorous cockney song introduced by Stanley Holloway in the musical play *My Fair Lady* (1956). He also sang it in the motion-picture adaptation of the musical (Warner, 1964).

Get Off the Track, an Abolitionist song with words and music by Jesse Hutchinson (1844). In this number a steam car (then a novelty to New Hampshire farmers) was used as a symbol of the advancing forces of freedom. Jesse Hutchinson, a member of the famous singing Hutchinson Family, got the idea for this song at an anti-slavery meeting in Boston. He adapted his words to an old slave melody. The song was introduced by the Hutchinson Family at an anti-slavery meeting. "The enthusiasm of the audience was so great," wrote Carol Brink in *Harps in the Wind,* "that the singers could scarcely go to the end. This was the song with which the Hutchinsons' audiences were to split wide open, the abolitionist sympathizers shouting with approval, the opposition hissing and howling their derision and anger."

Get Out and Get Under. *See:* He'd Have to Get Under.

Get Out and Get Under the Moon, words by Charles Tobias and William Jerome, music by Larry Shay (1928).

Get Out of Town, words and music by Cole Porter (1938). Introduced by Tamara in the musical *Leave It to Me* (1938).

Getting to Know You, words by Oscar Hammerstein II, music by Richard Rodgers (1951). Introduced by Gertrude Lawrence and a chorus of children in the musical play *The King and I* (1951). The number was also used in the motion-picture adaptation of the musical (20th Century-Fox, 1956), sung on the soundtrack by Marni Nixon (for Deborah Kerr) and a chorus of children.

John van Druten, who directed the original stage production of *The King and I*, wrote in the *New York Times:* "Her [Gertrude Lawrence's] biggest number, 'Getting to Know You,' was added in the last week in Boston (during out-of-town tryouts). She arrived in New York with no time to become certain of her performance. Everything had been indicated. . . . On the opening night she came on the stage with a new and dazzling quality. . . . She was radiant and wonderful. . . . The opening night audience cheered her."

For several years it has been the practice of the finalists in the Miss Universe contest to sing "Getting to Know You" at the beginning of ceremonies attending the final selection.

During a concert tour of the Soviet Union in 1959, Risë Stevens, the opera star, would bring down the house by singing "Getting to Know You"—in Russian.

The Ghost of the Violin, words by Bert Kalmar, music by Ted Snyder (1912). One of Kalmar's earliest successful lyrics.

Giannina Mia, words by Otto Hauerbach (Harbach), music by Rudolf Friml (1912). Introduced by Emma Trentini in Friml's first operetta, *The Firefly* (1912). In the motion-picture adaptation of the operetta (MGM, 1937), it was sung by Jeanette MacDonald.

Gid-Ap, Garibaldi, words by Howard Johnson and Billy Moll, music by Harry Warren (1927).

Gidget, words by Patti Washington, music by Fred Karger (1959). Title song of a motion picture starring Sandra Dee (Columbia, 1959), where it was introduced by James Darren.

Gigi, words by Alan Jay Lerner, music by Frederick Loewe (1958). Title song of the motion-picture musical (MGM, 1958), where it was introduced by Louis Jourdan. It was popularized by Vic Damone in a best-selling Columbia recording. The song received the Academy Award. This lyric is one of Lerner's own favorites among his songs.

Gigi, a motion-picture musical starring Leslie Caron, Louis Jourdan and Maurice Chevalier (MGM, 1958). Lyrics by Alan Jay Lerner and music by Frederick Loewe. It received nine Academy Awards (the first time a single motion picture gathered so many), including "Oscars" for the title song and as the best picture of the year.

See: Gigi; I'm Glad I'm Not Young Anymore; I Remember It Well; The Night They Invented Champagne; Say a Prayer for Me Tonight; Thank Heaven for Little Girls.

Gilbert, L. Wolfe, lyricist, born Odessa, Russia, 1886.

See: Down Yonder; I Miss My Swiss; Jeanine, I Dream of Lilac Time; Lily of the Valley; Mama Don't Want No Peas and Rice and Cocoanut Oil; Mama Inez; Marta; My Mother's Eyes; My Own Iona; My Sweet Adair; O Katharina!; Peanut Vendor; Waiting for the Robert E. Lee.

Gimme a Little Kiss, Will Ya, Huh?, words by Roy Turk and Jack Smith, music by Maceo Pinkard (1926). Introduced by Guy Lombardo and his Royal Canadians at the Clairmont Café in Cleveland, but made famous by Whispering Jack Smith. It was interpolated in the motion-picture musical *Has Anybody Seen My Gal?*, starring Rock Hudson and Piper Laurie (Universal, 1952).

A Girl, a Girl, words and music by Bennie Benjamin, George Weiss and Al Bandini (1954). Popularized by Eddie Fisher in an RCA Victor recording.

Girl Crazy, a musical comedy with book by Guy Bolton and John Mc-Gowan. Lyrics by Ira Gershwin. Music by George Gershwin. Starring Ethel Merman (her stage debut), Willie Howard, Ginger Rogers (her first Broadway starring role) and Allen Kearns (1930).

There were three motion-picture adaptations. The first starred Bert Wheeler and Robert Woolsey (RKO, 1932). It used five songs from the stage score. The second starred Judy Garland and Mickey Rooney (MGM, 1943). It used the basic stage score. The third was renamed *When the Boys Meet the Girls* and starred Connie Francis and Harve Presnell (MGM, 1965). Five songs from the stage production were used together with several new numbers.

See: Bidin' My Time; Boy, What Love Has Done to Me; But Not for Me; Embraceable You; I Got Rhythm; Sam and Delilah; Treat Me Rough.

The Girl Friend, words by Lorenz Hart, music by Richard Rodgers (1926). Title song of the musical comedy (1926), introduced by Sam White and Eva Puck. The song became one of the leading hits of 1926, and was one of the reasons for the success of this musical comedy.

The Girl Friend, a musical comedy with book by Herbert Fields. Lyrics by Lorenz Hart. Music by Richard Rodgers. Starring Sam White and Eva Puck (1926).

See: The Blue Room; The Girl Friend; Why Do I?

The Girl from Ipanema, words and music by Antonio Carlos Jobim, De Moraes and Gimbel (1963). A Brazilian popular song introduced and popularized in the United States in 1964 by Astrud Gilberto and the Stan Getz Quartet at the Café Au Go Go in New York City. Much of the effect of the number came from Astrud Gilberto's dead-pan, small-voiced and monotoned delivery. Her recording for Verve, and the performance by Antonio Carlos Jobim on the Andy Williams television program, further helped to popularize this number.

The Girl from Utah, a musical comedy with book and lyrics by James F.

Tanner. Music by Jerome Kern. Additional music by Paul Rubens and Sydney Jones. This was Kern's first successful musical comedy. Starring Julia Sanderson and Donald Brian (1914).

See: I'd Like to Wander with Alice in Wonderland; They Didn't Believe Me.

The Girl I Left Behind Me, a colonial fife song believed to be either of Irish origin or adapted from the English song "Brighton Camp" (c. 1765). It became popular in the American colonies as a stage song, as a square dance tune and as a song of farewell among pioneers. It was also often heard on occasions of military departure. During the Civil War the melody was given with various newly improvised lyrics, including such songs as "The American Volunteer" and the comedy song "I Goes to Fight Mit Sigel." Today it is played at the graduating-class ceremonies at West Point.

The Girl Is You and the Boy Is Me, words by Bud De Sylva and Lew Brown, music by Ray Henderson (1926). Introduced by Harry Richman and Frances Williams in *George White's Scandals of 1926*.

Girl of My Dreams, words and music by Sunny Clapp (1927).

The Girl on the Magazine Cover, words and music by Irving Berlin (1915). Introduced by Joseph Stanley in the revue *Stop! Look! and Listen* (1915).

Girls of My Dreams, words and music by Irving Berlin (1920). Introduced as a production number in the *Ziegfeld Follies of 1920*.

The Girls of Phi Beta Phi, words by Bud De Sylva and Lew Brown, music by Ray Henderson (1927). Introduced by a female chorus in the musical *Good News* (1927).

The Girl That I Marry, words and music by Irving Berlin (1946). Introduced by Ray Middleton in the musical *Annie Get Your Gun* (1946). In the motion-picture adaptation of the musical (MGM, 1950), it was sung by Howard Keel.

The Girl with the Golden Braids, words and music by Stanley Kahan and Eddie Snyder (1957). Popularized by Perry Como in an RCA Victor recording.

Give a Little, Get a Little Love, words by Betty Comden and Adolph Green, music by Jule Styne (1951). Introduced by Dolores Gray in the revue *Two on the Aisle* (1951).

Give Me a Moment, Please, words by Leo Robin, music by Richard A. Whiting and W. Franke Harling (1930). Introduced by Jack Buchanan in the motion picture *Monte Carlo* (Paramount, 1930). In the early 1930s this song became the radio theme music for Dave Rubinoff and his Violin.

Give Me One Hour, words by Brian Hooker, music by Rudolf Friml (1928). One of Friml's last successful songs. It was introduced in the operetta *The White Eagle* (1928).

Give Me the Moonlight, Give Me the Girl, words by Lew Brown, music by Albert von Tilzer (1917). It was interpolated in the motion-picture musical *The Dolly Sisters* (20th Century-Fox, 1945).

Give Me the Simple Life, words by Harry Ruby, music by Rube Bloom (1945). Introduced by June Haver and John Payne in the motion-picture musical *Wake Up and Dream* (20th Century-Fox, 1945). The song was first made popular by Sammy Kaye and his orchestra.

Give Me Your Tired, Your Poor, words and music by Irving Berlin (1949). A popular-song setting of Emma Lazarus' lines inscribed on the base of the Statue of Liberty. The song was introduced by Allyn McLerie in the musical *Miss Liberty* (1949).

Give My Regards to Broadway, words and music by George M. Cohan (1904). Introduced by George M. Cohan, playing the title role in the musical *Little Johnny Jones* (1904). It was sung by Eddie Buzzell in the motion-picture adaptation of the musical (First National, 1929). The song was interpolated in several later motion pictures. Among them were: the motion-picture biography of George M. Cohan, *Yankee Doodle Dandy* (Warner, 1942), sung by James Cagney; *Jolson Sings Again*

(Columbia, 1949); the motion-picture biography of Jane Froman, *With a Song in My Heart* (20th Century-Fox, 1952). The song provided the title for a motion picture (20th Century-Fox, 1948), where it was sung by Dan Dailey and Charles Winninger, with an assist from Fay Bainter.

The melody was performed by a brass band during the funeral of the tap-dancer Bill Robinson as the hearse passed by the Palace Theatre in New York, where Robinson had often appeared as a headliner.

Give Us Back Our Old Commander (or, Little Mac, the People's Pride), words and music by Septimus Winner (1862). A Civil War song inspired by the War Department's ouster of George B. McLellan for refusing to follow up his victory at Antietam. The song expressed the sentiment of the people on behalf of General McLellan's reinstatement, and sold over one hundred thousand copies of sheet music within a few days of publication. The song's success aroused the fury of Secretary of War Edwin Stanton, who ordered that any soldier heard singing it would be court-martialed. At the same time he had Septimus Winner tried for treason. Military court proceedings against him were dropped only after he had promised to stop the further distribution of the song. It, however, remained popular and was used to help campaign for General McLellan when he ran for President against Lincoln in 1864. The melody, with improvised lyrics, was used once again as a Presidential campaign song for General Ulysses S. Grant.

Glendora, words and music by Ray Stanley (1956). Popularized by Perry Como in an RCA Victor recording.

The Glenn Miller Story, a motion-picture musical biography of the famous jazz-band leader starring James Stewart as Glenn Miller (Universal, 1953). The score was made up mainly of standards associated with Glenn Miller and his orchestra.

See: Bidin' My Time; In the Mood; Little Brown Jug; Sunrise Serenade; Tuxedo Junction.

The Glory of Love, words and music by Billy Hill (1936).

The Glow Worm, a famous German popular song ("Gluehwuermchen"), from an operetta by Paul Lincke, *Lysistrata,* introduced in 1902. The song was heard in the United States for the first time in the musical *The Girl Behind the Counter* (1907), sung by May Naudain. It became a song hit in 1952 with new witty lyrics by Johnny Mercer, a version popularized by the Mills Brothers in a Decca recording. Janet Leigh and a male chorus sang it in the motion-picture musical *Walkin' My Baby Back Home* (Universal, 1953).

Go Away, Little Girl, words and music by Gerry Goffin and Carole King (1962). Written for Steve Lawrence, whose Columbia recording in 1963 was a best seller.

God Bless America, words and music by Irving Berlin (1939). A song originally written in 1918 for a production number in the all-soldiers show produced and written by Irving Berlin at Camp Yaphank: *Yip, Yip Yaphank.* Berlin deleted it from the show. "It was painting the lily," he later explained, "to have soldiers singing 'God Bless America' as they marched down the aisle of the theatre, off to war. So I wrote a new song called 'We're on Our Way to France,' which was better for the purpose, and forgot all about 'God Bless America.'"

In 1938 Kate Smith planned a patriotic program for her radio show on Armistice Day. She asked Berlin to write an appropriate number for her. Just back from Europe, where the war clouds were beginning to gather, Berlin was eager to do a song expressing his own pride in and love of country. He failed, however, to come up with anything that satisfied him. He then remembered the song he had written in 1918 and was convinced it would fill the bill. He gave Kate Smith exclusive performing rights to it without remuneration. Kate Smith introduced the number on her radio program on November 10, 1938—the last peacetime Armistice celebrated in the

United States before World War II.

Originally there had been a line in the lyric reading "to the right with a light from above." Where in 1918 "to the right" had meant "the right path," in 1938 it had acquired a political connotation. Consequently in 1938 Berlin changed the line to read "through the night with a light from above." In 1938 he also removed the word "victorious," since he now intended his song to be a hymn for peace. Otherwise the song remained in 1938 the same as it had been in 1918.

In 1939 both major political parties used it as their key song for the Presidential nominating conventions. In 1940 the National Committee for Music Appreciation gave it a special citation. With America being drawn closer to the abyss of war, the popularity of the song grew by leaps and bounds. Kate Smith's recording for Columbia was played in theaters all over the country. The song was heard at patriotic rallies, the Presidential birthday ball and at athletic events.

Refusing to capitalize on his patriotism, Berlin had the song copyrighted in 1939 in the names of Gene Tunney, Mrs. Theodore Roosevelt, Jr., and A. L. Berman for the purpose of creating a "God Bless America" Fund. All proceeds were now assigned to the Boy and Girl Scouts. The first payment made them was $43,000. By January 1, 1960, almost $300,000 had been turned over.

On February 18, 1955, President Eisenhower, on the authority of an act of Congress, presented Berlin with a gold medal "in national recognition and appreciation of services in composing many popular songs including 'God Bless America.' " The *New York Times* commented editorially: "There couldn't be a more popular law than the one that now gives Mr. Berlin his medal."

In a national poll in the late 1950s, "God Bless America" was chosen as the second most famous American national anthem after "The Star-Spangled Banner." There have even been attempts made to replace "The Star-Spangled Banner" with "God Bless America." Berlin himself has no sympathy for such an exchange, maintaining "I think it would be a terrible mistake."

"God Bless America" is one of five numbers which its composer regards as his special favorites (the others being "Always," "Easter Parade," "Show Business" and "White Christmas"): In 1963 ASCAP selected it as one of sixteen numbers in its all-time Hit Parade during its half century of existence.

The song was interpolated for Kate Smith in the motion-picture adaptation of the World War II soldiers show *This Is the Army* (Warner, 1943).

God's Green World, words by Alan Jay Lerner, music by Frederick Loewe (1945). A ballad described as a "pseudophilosophic homily," introduced by Bill Johnson in the musical *The Day Before Spring* (1945).

Go Home and Tell Your Mother, words by Dorothy Fields, music by Jimmy McHugh (1930). Introduced by Dorothy Jordan and Robert Montgomery in the motion picture *Love in the Rough* (MGM, 1930), the first motion-picture assignment for Fields and McHugh. The song was heard again in the non-musical motion picture *Dance, Fools, Dance,* starring Joan Crawford (MGM, 1931).

Going Hollywood, a motion-picture musical starring Bing Crosby and Marion Davies (MGM, 1933). Songs by Arthur Freed and Nacio Herb Brown.

See: Temptation; We'll Make Hay While the Sun Shines.

Going My Way, words by Johnny Burke, music by James Van Heusen (1944). Title song of the Academy Award motion picture (Paramount, 1944), introduced by Bing Crosby.

Going My Way, a motion picture with songs starring Bing Crosby, Barry Fitzgerald and Risë Stevens (Paramount, 1944). Songs by Johnny Burke and James Van Heusen. Shannon's "Too-ra-loo-ra-loo-ral" was interpolated. The motion picture received the Academy Award, as did the song "Swinging on a Star."

See: Going My Way; Swinging on a Star; Too-ra-loo-ra-loo-ral.

Goin' to the River, words and music by Antoine "Fats" Domino and Dave Bartholomew (1957). Popularized in an Imperial recording by "Fats" Domino.

Gold Diggers of Broadway, a motion-picture musical starring Winnie Lightner, Ann Pennington and Conway Tearle (Warner, 1929). Songs by Al Dubin and Joe Burke.

See: Painting the Clouds with Sunshine; Tip Toe Thru the Tulips.

Gold Diggers of Broadway of 1935, a motion-picture musical starring Dick Powell and Gloria Stuart (First National, 1935). Songs by Al Dubin and Harry Warren.

See: Lullaby of Broadway; The Words Are in My Heart.

Gold Diggers of 1933, a motion-picture musical starring Dick Powell and Ruby Keeler (Warner, 1933). Songs by Al Dubin and Harry Warren.

See: Shadow Waltz; We're in the Money.

Gold Diggers of 1937, a motion-picture musical starring Dick Powell and Joan Blondell (First National, 1936). Songs by Al Dubin and Harry Warren, and by E. Y. Harburg and Harold Arlen.

See: With Plenty of Money and You.

Gold Diggers' Song. See: We're in the Money.

The Golden Apple, a musical play with book and lyrics by John Latouche. Music by Jerome Moross. Starring Kaye Ballard and Jonathan Lucas (1954). Original cast recording (Elektra).

See: Lazy Afternoon.

Golden Boy, a musical comedy with book by Clifford Odets and William Gibson based on Odets' play of the same name. Lyrics by Lee Adams. Music by Charles Strouse. Starring Sammy Davis (1964). Original cast recording (Capitol).

See: Can't You See It?; Don't Forget 127th Street; I Want to Be with

You; Night Song; This Is the Life; While the City Sleeps.

Golden Days, words by Dorothy Donnelly, music by Sigmund Romberg (1924). Nostalgic duet about the German city of Heidelberg, introduced by Howard Marsh and Greek Evans in the operetta *The Student Prince* (1924). In the motion-picture adaptation of the operetta (MGM, 1954), it was sung on the soundtrack by Mario Lanza (for Edmund Purdom).

Golden Earrings, words by Jay Livingston and Ray Evans, music by Victor Young (1946). Introduced by Marlene Dietrich in the motion picture of the same name (Paramount, 1947). It was popularized by Peggy Lee in a best-selling Capitol recording.

Golden Gate, words by Billy Rose and Dave Dreyer, music by Al Jolson and Joseph Meyer (1928). Introduced and popularized by Al Jolson during a road tour of the musical *Big Boy*.

De Golden Wedding, words and music by James A. Bland (1880). Introduced and popularized in minstrel shows.

Goldfinger, words by Anthony Newley and Leslie Bricuse, music by John Barry (1964). Title song of a nonmusical motion picture starring Sean Connery (United Artists, 1964). The song was popularized by Shirley Bassey in a United Artists recording.

Gold Record Award, an award instituted in 1958 and then made annually by the Record Industry of America to single recordings selling a million disks (also to albums registering a million dollars in factory sales). The first recipients, among the singles, were "Catch a Falling Star" (Perry Como), "Hard Headed Woman" (Elvis Presley) and "Patricia" (Perez Prado).

Since 1959 this award has gone to the following singles: "Tom Dooley" (Kingston Trio); "Calcutta" (Lawrence Welk); "Big Bad John" (Jimmy Dean); "The Lion Sleeps" (the Tokens); "Can't Help Falling in Love" (Elvis Presley); "Roses Are Red" (Bobby Vinton); "I Can't Stop Loving You" (Ray Charles); "Hey, Paula" (Paul and Paula); "Sugar Shack" (Jim Gilmer and the Fireballs); "Rag Doll" (the Four Seasons); "Everybody Loves Somebody" (Dean Martin); "Oh, Pretty Woman" (Ray Orbison).

Gold Will Buy Most Anything But a True Girl's Heart, words by Charles E. Foreman, music by Monroe H. Rosenfeld (1898).

Goldwyn Follies, a motion-picture musical starring Kenny Baker and Vera Zorina (United Artists, 1938). Songs by George and Ira Gershwin. This was George Gershwin's last score.

See: I Was Doing All Right; Our Love Is Here to Stay; Love Walked In.

Gone, words and music by Smokey Rogers (1952). Popularized in 1957 by Ferlin Husky in a Capitol recording.

Gone Fishin', words and music by Nick and Charles Kenny (1950). Popularized by Arthur Godfrey in a Columbia recording.

Go, Little Boat, words by P. G. Wodehouse, music by Jerome Kern (1917). Introduced by Ivy Sawyer and chorus in the musical Oh, My Dear (1918). It was heard in the Jerome Kern screen biography, Till the Clouds Roll By (MGM, 1946).

Good-a-Bye, John, words by Henry Blossom, music supposedly by Victor Herbert (1906). Introduced by Fred A. Stone and David Montgomery in the operetta The Red Mill (1906).

This number is a curiosity. Though included in the operetta and published as a Victor Herbert number, it was in all probability not written by Herbert at all. One year before The Red Mill was produced, on October 7, 1905, the publishing house of Remick issued a song of the same name, text by Harry Williams, music by Egbert Van Alstyne; it was interpolated in the musical The Belle of Avenue A (1905). The words of the first stanza and of

the refrain were exactly the same as those in The Red Mill song. The melodies in both places also were alike. Herbert never plagiarized anybody's work, and besides he would never have been so naïve as to lift a tune from a song issued only one year before. The mystery surrounding this coincidence increases when we realize that neither the lyricist, Williams, nor the composer, Van Alstyne, challenged Herbert's right to the song. One explanation offered was that Stone and Montgomery— the stars of The Red Mill—demonstrated to Herbert a routine they wanted to use in the operetta while singing the Williams and Van Alstyne number. Herbert probably agreed and wrote "Good-a-bye, John," patterning his own number after the piece Stone and Montgomery had sung, without realizing he was using somebody else's material.

Gonna Get Along Without You, words and music by Milton Kellen (1951). Introduced by Teresa Brewer, but popularized by Patience and Prudence in a Liberty recording. It was successfully revived in 1964 in a best-selling recording by Skeeter Davis for RCA Victor.

Goodbye, Becky Cohen, words and music by Irving Berlin (1910). A character song with which Fanny Brice made her debut in the Ziegfeld Follies—at the Jardin de Paris on June 20, 1910. This was also the first Irving Berlin song to be placed in the Ziegfeld Follies.

Goodbye, Boys, I'm Going to Be Married Tomorrow, words by Andrew B. Sterling and William Dillon, music by Harry von Tilzer (1913). Interpolated for Al Jolson in the musical The Honeymoon Express (1913).

Goodbye, Broadway, Hello, France, words by C. Francis Reisner and Benny Davis, music by Billy Baskette (1917). A production number used as the finale for The Passing Show of 1917. It became a hit song during World War I, selling about four million copies of sheet music. Jack Oakie revived it in the motion-picture musical Tin Pan Alley (20th

Century-Fox, 1940). Judy Garland sang it in the motion-picture musical *For Me and My Gal* (MGM, 1942).

Goodbye, Charlie, words by Dory Langdon, music by André Previn (1964). Introduced by Pat Boone in the motion picture of the same name starring Tony Curtis and Debbie Reynolds (20th Century-Fox, 1964). It was popularized in a Dot recording by Pat Boone and in a Capitol recording by Bobby Darin.

Goodbye, Cruel World, words and music by G. Shayne (1961). Popularized in 1962 by James Darren in a Colpix recording.

Goodbye, Dolly Gray, words by Will D. Cobb, music by Paul Barnes (1900). A marching song written in 1898 and first popularized during the Spanish-American War. It sold over a million copies of sheet music following its publication in 1900. It was revived in the motion-picture musical *Wait Till the Sun Shines, Nellie* (20th Century-Fox, 1952), sung by Jean Peters and David Wayne.

Goodbye, Eyes of Blue, words by James J. Walker, music by Harry Armstrong (1898). Inspired by the Spanish-American War, this song was James J. Walker's first published lyric. On the strength of its success, Walker received a job as staff lyricist at the publishing house of Witmark.

Goodbye, Eliza Jane, words by Andrew B. Sterling, music by Harry von Tilzer (1903). Hit ragtime tune, not to be confused with the minstrel-show classic "Goodbye, Liza Jane."

Goodbye, Flo, words and music by George M. Cohan (1904). Introduced by Ethel Levey and chorus in George M. Cohan's first successful musical, *Little Johnny Jones* (1903).

Goodbye, Girls, I'm Through, words by John Golden, music by Ivan Caryll (1914). Introduced by Fred Stone in the musical extravaganza *Chin-Chin* (1914).

The song was written while the show was in rehearsal, to allow time for costume changes. Charles Dillingham, the producer, suggested that the hero sing a number in which he bids the girls goodbye. "In less than thirty minutes," John Golden later recalled, "I had the first verse and chorus complete for 'Goodbye, Girls, I'm Through.' Ivan Caryll was called in hurriedly to set the lyric. The play opened in Philadelphia and the next day I had a wire from Dillingham saying that the song was the hit of the piece—everybody was singing it."

This song proved a turning point in John Golden's career in the theater. "Because of it I said goodbye forever to songwriting and, with one of the royalty checks it brought in, I launched into the business of producing plays."

Goodbye, Good Luck, God Bless You, words by J. Keirn Brennan, music by Ernest R. Ball (1916). Popularized in vaudeville by ballad singers.

Goodbye, Jimmie, Goodbye, words and music by Jack Vaughn (1959). Popularized by Kathy Linden in a Felsted recording.

Goodbye, Little Girl, Goodbye, words by Will D. Cobb, music by Gus Edwards (1904).

Goodbye, Liza Jane, words and music of unknown authorship (1871). First published in Philadelphia in an arrangement by Eddie Fox, it was popularized in minstrel shows.

Goodbye, Ma!, Goodbye, Pa!, Goodbye, Mule (or, Long Boy), words by William Herschell, music by Barclay Walker (1917). A goodbye song favored during World War I in the rural areas of America.

Goodbye, My Lady Love, words and music by Joe E. Howard (1904). It was interpolated in the Chicago Midway scene in the Jerome Kern-Oscar Hammerstein musical play *Show Boat* (1927), sung there by Eva Puck and Sammy White.

Goodbye, Sue, words and music by Jimmy Rule, Lou Ricca and Jules Loman (1943). Popularized by Perry Como in his first solo recording—for RCA Victor.

Goodbye to Rome. *See:* Arividerci Roma.

Good for You, Bad for Me, words by Bud De Sylva and Lew Brown, music by Ray Henderson (1930). Introduced by Pearl Osgood and Russ Brown in the musical *Flying High* (1930).

Good Luck Charm, words and music by Aaron Schroeder and Wally Gold (1962). Popularized by Elvis Presley in an RCA Victor recording.

A Good Man Is Hard to Find, words and music by Eddie Green (1918). Introduced by Alberta Hunter but popularized by Sophie Tucker. It was interpolated in the motion-picture musical *Meet Danny Wilson* (Universal, 1952).

Good Morning, words by Arthur Freed, music by Nacio Herb Brown (1939). Introduced by Judy Garland and Mickey Rooney in the motion-picture musical *Babes in Arms* (MGM, 1939). It was revived by Debbie Reynolds, Gene Kelly and Donald O'Connor in the motion-picture musical *Singin' in the Rain* (MGM, 1952).

Good Morning, Mr. Zip Zip Zip (with Your Hair Cut Just As Short As Mine), words and music by Robert Lloyd (1918).

Good News, words by Bud De Sylva and Lew Brown, music by Ray Henderson (1927). Title song of the musical (1927), introduced by Zelma O'Neal. It was sung in both motion-picture adaptations of this musical (MGM, 1930, MGM, 1947), in the latter sung by Joan McCracken.

Good News, a musical comedy with book by Laurence Schwab and Bud De Sylva. Lyrics by Bud De Sylva and Lew Brown. Music by Ray Henderson. Starring Mary Lawlor, John Price Jones and Zelma O'Neal (1927).

There were two motion-picture adaptations. The first starred Bessie Love, Mary Lawlor and Cliff Edwards (MGM, 1930). Six songs were used from the stage production together with several new numbers by Arthur Freed and Nacio Herb Brown among others. The second adaptation starred June Allyson and Peter Lawford (MGM, 1947). It used six numbers from the stage score, with new numbers by Betty Comden, Adolph Green and Roger Edens, and by Ralph Blane and Hugh Martin. Soundtrack recording (MGM).

See: The Best Things in Life Are Free; The French Lesson; Good News; Just Imagine; Lucky in Love; Pass That Peace Pipe; The Varsity Drag.

Goodnight, Irene, words and music by Huddie Ledbetter and John Lomax (1936). A folk song recorded in 1936 by Huddie Ledbetter (known as Leadbelly) while serving as a prisoner in the Louisiana State Prison in Angola. It was popularized for the general song market in 1950 in a Decca recording by Gordon Jenkins and his orchestra, in collaboration with the Weavers, a release that sold over a million disks. Successful recordings were also made by Frank Sinatra for Columbia and by Ernest Tubb and Red Foley for Decca.

Goodnight, Ladies, words by Harry H. Williams, music by Egbert Van Alstyne (1911).

Goodnight, My Love, words by Mack Gordon, music by Harry Revel (1934). Introduced by Bing Crosby in the motion-picture musical *We're Not Dressing* (Paramount, 1934). It was also sung in the motion picture *Stowaway,* starring Shirley Temple (20th Century-Fox, 1936).

Goodnight, My Someone, words and music by Meredith Willson (1957). Introduced by Barbara Cook in the musical *The Music Man* (1957). In this number the composer quotes a fragment from a second hit song from the same production, "Seventy-Six Trombones." In the motion-picture adaptation of the musical, "Goodnight, My Someone" was sung by Shirley Jones.

Goodnight, Sweetheart, words and music by Ray Noble, James Campbell and Reginald Connelly, adapted by Rudy Vallée (1931). Introduced in the Earl Carroll *Vanities of 1931.* It was popularized by Rudy Vallée—who introduced it on his radio program in 1931, then made a best-selling recording for RCA Victor. Rudy Vallée subsequently sang it in the motion picture *The Palm Beach Story* (MGM, 1942). The song was also interpolated for Gene Autry in the motion picture *Stardust of the Sage* (Republic, 1942) and was sung by a chorus in the motion-picture musical *You Were Meant for Me* (20th Century-Fox, 1948).

Goodnight, Wherever You Are, words and music by Dick Robertson, Al Hoffman and Frank Weldon (1944). Successful World War II ballad, popularized by Russ Morgan and his orchestra in a Decca recording.

The Good Old U.S.A., words by Jack Drislane, music by Theodore F. Morse (1906).

Good Timin', words and music by Clint Ballard, Jr., and Fred Tobias (1960). Popularized by Jimmy Jones in a Cub recording.

Goody, Goody, words by Johnny Mercer, music by Matt Malneck (1936). A Benny Goodman specialty in the 1930s. Benny Goodman and his orchestra played it on the soundtrack in the motion-picture musical *The Benny Goodman Story* (Universal, 1956).

Gordon, Mack, lyricist, born Warsaw, Poland, 1904; died New York City, 1959.
 See: Monaco, James; Revel, Harry; Warren, Harry.
 See also: I Just Can't Do Enough for You; Mam'selle; The River Seine; Time on My Hands; Wilhelmina; You Make Me Feel So Young; You, My Love.

Gorney, Jay, composer, born Bialistock, Russia, 1896.
 See (Lyrics by E. Y. Harburg): Ah, But Is It Love?; Brother, Can You Spare a Dime?; Moonlight and Pretzels; What Wouldn't I Do for That Man.
 See also: Baby, Take a Bow; You're My Thrill.

Got Her Off My Hands (But Can't Get Her Off My Mind), words by Sam Lewis and Joe Young, music by Fred Phillips (1951). Popularized by the Mills Brothers in a Decca recording.

Got the Bench, Got the Park, words and music by Al Lewis, Al Sherman and Fred Phillips (1931).

Go to Sleepy, Little Baby, words by

Harry Tobias and Zeke Canova, music by Henry Tobias and Judy Canova (1946). Judy Canova's radio theme song.

Graff, George, Jr., lyricist, born New York City, 1886.
 See: Ball, Ernest R.

Grafted into the Army, words and music by Henry Clay Work (1862). This was Work's first song, a humorous number about an Irish mother lamenting that her young son has been "grafted" (i.e. drafted) into the Union Army. ("I thought they would spare a lone widder's heir. But they grafted him into the Army.") There were a number of songs during the Civil War satirizing the draft, exemptions from the draft and war profiteering. "Grafted into the Army" was the most popular, probably due to its racy Irish inflections and amusing malapropisms.

Soon after the end of the Civil War, William A. Field wrote a song described as a "companion to 'Grafted into the Army.'" It was called "He's Got His Discharge from the Army," and it boasted a happy ending.

Grammy Awards. *See:* National Academy of Recording Arts and Sciences Awards.

Grandfather's Clock, words and music by Henry Clay Work (1876). This was Work's last successful song and his greatest commercial success, selling over a million copies of sheet music (a phenomenon in the 1870s). The song was introduced by Sam Lucas of the Hyer Sisters Colored Minstrels, in New Haven, Connecticut, in 1876. Sigmund Spaeth suggested that the "measured ticking of the clock" gives the song its immense effectiveness. "When the clock stops 'never to run again,' the dramatic effect of the climax, with its meticulous accenting, is worthy of the higher forms of Art Song."

Grand Knowing You, words by Sheldon Harnick, music by Jerry Bock (1963). Introduced by Jack Cassidy in the musical *She Loves Me* (1963).

Grand Old Ivy, words and music by Frank Loesser (1961). A tongue-in-cheek college song introduced by Rudy Vallée and Robert Morse in the musical *How to Succeed in Business Without Really Trying* (1961).

Grass Is Greener, words by Barry Mann, music by Mike Anthony (1963). Popularized by Brenda Lee in a Decca recording.

Great Day, words by Billy Rose and Edward Eliscu, music by Vincent Youmans (1929). Title song of a musical (1929), introduced by Lois Deppe and the Jubilee Singers.

Great Day, a musical comedy with book by W. Duncan and J. Wells. Lyrics by Billy Rose and Edward Eliscu. Music by Vincent Youmans (1929).

See: Great Day; More Than You Know; Without a Song.

The Great Pretender, words and music by Buck Ram (1956). Popularized by the Platters in a Mercury recording that sold over a million disks.

The Great Victor Herbert, a motion-picture musical biography starring Walter Connolly as Victor Herbert with Mary Martin (in her screen debut) and Allan Jones (Paramount, 1939). The score was made up of Victor Herbert standards.

See: Absinthe Frappé; Ah, Sweet Mystery of Life; All for You; I'm Falling in Love with Someone; I Love Thee, I Adore Thee; I Might Be Your Once in a While; A Kiss in the Dark; Kiss Me Again; March of the Toys; Neapolitan Love Song; Rose of the World; There Once Was an Owl; Thine Alone; To the Land of My Own Romance.

The Great Ziegfeld, a motion-picture musical biography starring William Powell as Ziegfeld with Luise Rainer as Anna Held and Myrna Loy as Billie Burke (MGM, 1936). It won the Academy Award as the best motion picture of the year, with an additional "Oscar" for Luise Rainer. Songs by Harold Adamson and Walter Donaldson. Irving Berlin's "A Pretty Girl Is Like a Melody" was interpolated.

See: A Pretty Girl Is Like a Melody; You.

Green, Adolph, lyricist, born New York City, 1915.

See: Bernstein, Leonard; Styne, Jule.

See also: The French Lesson.

The Green Door, words by Marvin Moore, music by Bob Davie (1956). Popularized by Jim Lowe in a Dot recording that sold over a million disks in 1957.

Green Eyes, words and music by Nilo Mendenez and Adolph Utrera (1929). A specialty of Jimmy Dorsey and his orchestra, who popularized it (with vocal by Helen O'Connell and Bob Eberly) in an RCA Victor recording that sold over a million disks in 1941. The song was performed by Jimmy Dorsey on the soundtrack of the motion-picture musical *The Fabulous Dorseys* (United Artists, 1947).

Green Fields, words and music by Terry Gilkyson, Richard Dehr and Frank Miller (1960). Introduced by the Easy Riders, but popularized by the Brothers Four in a Columbia recording.

Green, John (Johnny), W., composer, born New York City, 1908.

See (Lyrics by Edward Heyman): Body and Soul; Easy Go; I Cover the Waterfront; Out of Nowhere.

See (Lyrics by Paul Francis Webster): Never Till Now; Song of Raintree County.

See also: I'm Yours.

The Green Leaves of Summer, words by Paul Francis Webster, music by Dimitri Tiomkin (1960). Introduced in the motion picture *The Alamo*, starring John Wayne and Laurence Harvey (United Artists, 1960), where it was sung on the soundtrack by a chorus.

Green Onions, words and music by Steve Cropper, Al Jackson, Jr., Lewis Steinberg and T. Booker (1962). Popularized by T. Booker and the MG's in a Stax recording.

Green Up Time, words by Alan Jay Lerner, music by Kurt Weill (1948). Introduced by Nanette Fabray in the musical play *Love Life* (1948).

Greenwich Village Follies, an annual Broadway revue produced by the Shuberts. The first edition, in 1919, starred Bessie McCoy and Ted Lewis and his orchestra. Songs by Arthur

Swanstrom, J. Murray Anderson and A. Baldwin Sloane. The composers for later editions were: Sloane in 1920; Carey Morgan in 1921; Louis A. Hirsch in 1922 and 1923; Cole Porter in 1924. The score in 1925 was contributed by several different lyricists and composers. There were no editions in 1926 and 1927. The last production was mounted in 1928, with songs by Clifford Grey and Maurice Rubens. The following stars appeared after the first edition: the Dolly Sisters, Benny Fields and Blossom Seeley, Vincent Lopez and his orchestra, Grace La Rue, Moran and Mack, Don Rockwell, Savoy and Brennan.

See: Georgette; I'll See You in C-U-B-A; I'm in Love Again; Three O'clock in the Morning.

Greenwillow, a musical play with book by Lesser Samuels and Frank Loesser based on a novel by J. B. Chute. Lyrics and music by Frank Loesser. Starring Anthony Perkins (1960). Original cast recording (RCA Victor).

See: The Music of Home; Never Will I Marry; Summertime Love.

Green Years, words and music by Don Reid and Arthur Altman (1954). Popularized by Eddie Fisher in an RCA Victor recording.

Grey, Clifford, lyricist, born Birmingham, England, 1887; died Ipswich, England, 1941.

See: Kern, Jerome; Schertzinger, Victor; Stothart, Herbert.

See also: Hallelujah; If You Were the Only Girl; Ma Belle; While Hearts Are Singing.

The Grizzly Bear, words by Irving Berlin, music by George Botsford (1910). A forerunner of popular-song hits about dances with animal steps (the "bunny hug," the "turkey trot," and so forth). The grizzly-bear dance was described as follows: "Both partners hug each other with both arms, bear-fashion, rocking from side to side on the beat." The song was interpolated in the non-musical motion picture *Wharf Angel,* starring Victor McLaglen (Paramount, 1934). It was used for Alice Faye and Jack Oakie in a production number in the motion-

picture musical *Hello, Frisco, Hello* (20th Century-Fox, 1943).

Guilty, words by Gus Kahn, music by Harry Akst and Richard A. Whiting (1931).

The Guns of Navarone, words by Paul Francis Webster, music by Dimitri Tiomkin (1961). Title song of the motion picture starring Gregory Peck (Columbia, 1961), sung on the soundtrack by a chorus. The song was popularized by Mitch Miller and his orchestra and chorus in a Columbia recording.

A Guy Is a Guy, words and music by Oscar Brand (1952). Adapted from a bawdy song of unknown origin, parodied during World War II by G.I.'s as "A Gob Is a Slob." "A Guy Is a Guy" was popularized by Doris Day in a best-selling Columbia recording.

Guys and Dolls, words and music by Frank Loesser (1950). Title song of the musical (1950), introduced by Stubby Kaye and Johnny Silver. It was also sung in the motion-picture adaptation of the musical (MGM, 1955).

Guys and Dolls, a musical comedy with book by Jo Swerling and Abe Burrows based on a story and characters of Damon Runyon. Lyrics and music by Frank Loesser. Starring Isabel Bigley, Sam Levene, Robert Alda and Vivian Blaine (1950). Original cast recording (Decca).

The motion-picture adaptation starred Marlon Brando, Frank Sinatra, Jean Simmons and Vivian Blaine (MGM, 1955). The principal songs from the stage score were used, with a new Frank Loesser number, "A Woman in Love."

See: Adelaide's Lament; A Bushel and a Peck; Fugue for Tinhorns; Guys and Dolls; If I Were a Bell; I'll Know; I've Never Been in Love Before; Luck Be a Lady; More I Cannot Wish You; My Time of Day; Sit Down, You're Rockin' the Boat; Take Back Your Mink; A Woman in Love.

Gypsy, a musical comedy with book by Arthur Laurents, based on Gypsy Rose Lee's autobiography. Lyrics by Stephen Sondheim. Music by Jule

Styne. Starring Ethel Merman (1959). Original cast recording (Columbia).

The motion-picture adaptation starred Rosalind Russell, Natalie Wood and Karl Malden (Warner, 1962). Lisa Kirk sang on the soundtrack for Rosalind Russell, and Marni Nixon for Natalie Wood. Soundtrack recording (Warner).

See: Everything Is Coming Up Roses; A Small World; Some People; Together, Wherever We Go.

The Gypsy, words and music by Billy Reid (1945). An English song popularized in the United States in 1946 by Dinah Shore in a Capitol recording and by the Ink Spots in a Decca recording.

Gypsy Love Song (or, Slumber On, My Little Gypsy Sweetheart), words by Harry B. Smith, music by Victor Herbert (1898). This is a Victor Herbert favorite in which the verse is as melodious as the chorus. It is a serenade introduced by Eugene Cowles in the operetta *The Fortune Teller* (1898).

H

Hague, Albert, composer, born Berlin, Germany, 1920.

See (Lyrics by Dorothy Fields): Just for Once; Look What's in Love; Two Faces in the Dark.

See also: It Wonders Me; Plain We Live; Young and Foolish.

Hail Columbia, words by Joseph Hopkinson to the melody of "The President's March," ascribed to Philip Phile (1798). Hopkinson wrote his patriotic verses during a critical period in early American history, a time when it seemed that the young country might be drawn into a war with France.

In 1798 Gilbert Fox, an actor, came to Hopkinson requesting a song for the finale of a stage comedy, *The Italian Monk*. The production was scheduled for a benefit performance at the New Theatre in Philadelphia on April 25. Fox revealed to Hopkinson that a good many of the box seats had not yet been sold, and he was convinced that a rousing patriotic hymn interpolated in the show would help the ticket sale. "I told him," Hopkinson later recalled, "I would try what I could for him. He came the next afternoon and the song, such as it was, was ready for him. The object of the song was to get up an American spirit which should be independent of, and above the interests, passion and policy of both belligerents, and to look and feel exclusively for our honor and rights. No allusion was made either to France or to England, or to the quarrel between them, or to the question of which was at fault in their treatment of us."

The following announcement appeared in the Philadelphia newspapers: "Mr. Fox's Night on Wednesday evening, April 25. By Desire will be presented (for the second time in America) a play interspersed with songs, in three acts called *The Italian Monk*. After which an entire New Song (written by a citizen of Philadelphia) to the tune of 'The President's March' will be sung by Mr. Fox, accompanied by the full band and . . . grand chorus."

The theater was packed. In attendance were President Adams and his entire Cabinet. After Fox had sung "Hail Columbia," a number of times, the ovation was thunderous. A decision, therefore, was reached to include the patriotic song in all future performances of the play.

One week after this première, the song was heard and acclaimed in New York City, and had been published in Philadelphia under the title of "The Favorite New Federal Song." Hopkinson sent a presentation copy to George Washington, saying: "As to the song, it was a hasty composition, and can pretend to very little extrinsic merit. Yet I believe its public reception has at least equalled anything of its kind."

The song soon became popular throughout the thirteen states, a favorite of government officials. Now identified by the first two words of the chorus as "Hail Columbia," it was played and sung for a quarter of a century on every American ship at the lowering of the colors. For a quarter of a century after that, it was second in popularity among patriotic anthems only to "The Star-Spangled Banner." Charles Coffin wrote in his book on the Civil War, *Four Years of Fighting:* "Everywhere the music of the streets, vocal as well as instrumental, was 'Hail Columbia.' . . . In December 1860, Major Anderson . . . raised the American flag . . . of the still unfinished Fort Sumter. As he drew the star-spangled banner . . . the band broke out with the national air, 'Hail Columbia,' loud and exultant cheers, repeated again and again, were given by officers, soldiers and workmen."

The tune was played when the first American warship passed through the Kiel Canal in Germany; and it was heard when Thomas Edison paid a visit to the Paris Opéra in 1889.

"At last," said O. G. Sonneck, in recalling that most American national ballads had borrowed their melodies from foreign sources, " 'Hail Columbia' may claim the distinction in the history of our early national songs of being both in poetry and music a product of our soil."

Hail, Hail, the Gang's All Here, words by Theodore A. Morse, using the pen name of D. A. Esrom, to the melody of "Come, Friends, Who Plough the Sea" from *The Pirates of Penzance* by Gilbert and Sullivan (1917). A favorite during World War I.

Hajji Baba, words by Ned Washington, music by Dimitri Tiomkin (1954). Introduced by Nat King Cole in the motion picture *The Adventures of Hajji Baba,* starring John Derek and Elaine Stewart (20th Century-Fox, 1954).

Half As Much, words by Curley Williams (1951). Popularized in 1952 by Rosemary Clooney in a Columbia recording that sold a million disks. Hank Williams' recording for MGM was also a best seller.

The Half of It Dearie Blues, words by Ira Gershwin, music by George Gershwin (1924). Written for Fred Astaire, who prepared a special tap-dance routine for it—the first time in his career that Fred Astaire performed a solo tap dance in public, without the assistance of his sister and partner, Adele. Song and dance were introduced in the musical *Lady Be Good!* (1924), Fred Astaire singing the number to Kathlene Martyn before embarking on his dance. The song was published commercially as a sixteen-measure fox trot. But whenever George Gershwin played it, he invariably interpolated three 2/4 breaks reminiscent of, and derived from, his *Rhapsody in Blue.*

Hallelujah, words by Leo Robin and Clifford Grey, music by Vincent Youmans (1927). A sailors' chorus introduced by Stella Mayhew in the musical *Hit the Deck* (1927), and repeated in the motion-picture adaptation of the musical (RKO, 1930). Youmans had written the melody a decade earlier, while serving in the Navy during World War I. He showed it to the bandmaster at the Great Lakes Station where Youmans was then serving. The bandmaster liked it so well that he encouraged Youmans to consider songwriting as a career. The number soon became a favorite with Navy bands, and was often featured by John Philip Sousa on his programs.

Hallelujah Trail, words by Ernie Sheldon, music by Elmer Bernstein 1965). Title song of a motion picure starring Burt Lancaster and Lee Remick (United Artists, 1965).

Hamlet Was a Melancholy Dane, words by William Jerome, music by Jean Schwartz (1903). Introduced by Eddie Foy at the Iroquois Theatre in Chicago on the afternoon of December 30, 1903. This was the day and the performance during which the theatre caught fire and six hundred lives were lost.

The song was interpolated later

the same year by Eddie Foy in the Broadway musical extravaganza *Mr. Bluebeard* (1903).

Hammerstein, Oscar II, lyricist, born New York City, 1895; died Doylestown, Pennsylvania, 1960.

See: Friml, Rudolf; Kern, Jerome; Rodgers, Richard; Romberg, Sigmund; Youmans, Vincent.

See also: Dat's Love; Dere's a Café; Dis Flower; I Want a Man; A Kiss to Build a Dream On; I'll Take Romance; My Joe; Song of the Flame; Stan' Up and Fight.

Hands Across the Table, words by Mitchell Parish, music by Jean Delettre (1934). Introduced by Lucienne Boyer in the revue *Continental Follies* (1934).

Handy, William Christopher, composer and lyricist, born Florence, Alabama, 1873; died New York City, 1958.

See: Aunt Hagar's Blues; The Beale Street Blues; East St. Louis Blues; Joe Turner Blues; John Henry Blues; Memphis Blues; St. Louis Blues.

For W. C. Handy's screen biography, see *St. Louis Blues* (Paramount, 1958).

Handy Man, words and music by Otis Blackwell, Jimmy Jones and C. Merenstein (1960). Popularized by Jimmy Jones in a Cub recording.

The Hanging Tree, words by Mack David, music by Jerry Livingston (1958). Title song of a non-musical motion picture starring Gary Cooper (Warner, 1959). It was sung under the titles by Marty Robbins, who made a best-selling recording for Columbia.

Hans Christian Andersen, a motion-picture musical starring Danny Kaye as Hans Christian Andersen with Jeanmaire (Samuel Goldwyn, 1953). Songs by Frank Loesser.

See: Anywhere I Wander; The Inch Worm; No Two People; Thumbelina; Wonderful Copenhagen.

Happiness Is a Thing Called Joe, words by E. Y. Harburg, music by Harold Arlen (1942). Interpolated in the motion-picture adaptation of the Vernon Duke musical play *Cabin in the Sky* (MGM, 1943), where it was introduced by Ethel Waters. It was sung by Susan Hayward in the motion-picture Screen biography of Lillian Roth, *I'll Cry Tomorrow* (MGM, 1955).

Happiness Street (Corner Sunshine Square), words and music by Mack Wolfsohn and Edward R. White (1955). Popularized in 1956 by Georgia Gibbs in a Mercury recording.

Happy Birthday to You, often described as "the most frequently sung number in the world." It originated as "Good Morning, to All," words by Patty Smith Hill, music by Mildred J. Hill, published in *Song Stories for Children* (1893).

It has often been involved in court litigations for infringement of copyright, due to the general belief that it was in public domain. Irving Berlin used it in all innocence in the musical *As Thousands Cheer*, for a sketch in which John D. Rockefeller's birthday is being celebrated.

Happy Days Are Here Again, words by Jack Yellen, music by Milton Ager (1929). Written for and introduced by Charles King in the motion-picture musical *Chasing Rainbows* (MGM, 1930).

Jack Yellen has described to this editor how the song came to be written: "In the last week of production, the producer of *Chasing Rainbows* phoned me and said he wanted a song for a scene in which a group of World War I soldiers receive news of the Armistice. I relayed the message to Ager, whom I hadn't seen in weeks. He said he would stop in at my house next morning on his way to the golf course. He came in, sat down at the piano, and lighted a cigar. 'Got a title?' he asked finally. I didn't have any, but blurted out 'happy days are here again.' The first tune he played was good enough. He kept playing the melody and I scribbled off the first words that came to me and handed him the corny lyrics. His only comment was that he didn't think the lyric should start with the title. I said I thought it should, and the conversation ended. The film was in the can, and the can was in the storage vault. The picture was so mediocre the studio hesitated about releasing it. But we had been given a date in 1929 on which we, as publishers, could release the song. Ben Borenstein, in New York, had dance orchestrations printed and Irving Tanz, one of our song pluggers, took one to the Pennsylvania Hotel, where George Olsen and his band were playing. It was on the Black Thursday of the Big Depression. In the big dining room at the hotel a handful of gloom-stricken diners were feasting on gall and wormwood. Olsen looked at the title of the orchestration and passed out the parts. 'Sing it for the corpses,' he said to the soloist. After a couple of choruses, the corpses joined in sardonically, hysterically, like doomed prisoners on their way to a firing squad. Before the night was over, the hotel lobby resounded with what had become the theme song of ruined stock speculators as they leaped from hotel windows.

"Some weeks later, George Olsen and his band came to the Roosevelt Hotel in Hollywood. At the MGM table was Irving Thalberg with his studio favorites. The band broke into 'Happy Days Are Here Again' and the crowd picked up the refrain. Thalberg wanted to know why a song like this was not in an MGM picture. One of his underlings mustered the courage to tell him that the song *was* in one of his pictures. Bessie Love and Charles King, the stars in the picture, were hurried to the studio, sets were rebuilt, principals and extras reassembled, costumes remade, and the scene shot over again, with several extra choruses of the song added. Nothing helped the picture. But in the meantime our song swept the country. Without any solicitations from us or anyone else, Franklin Delano Roosevelt selected 'Happy Days Are Here Again' as his campaign song. Harry Truman and John F. Kennedy marched into the White House to it, and more recently a syndicated photograph showed President Lyndon B. Johnson leading a high school

band playing what has become the anthem of the Democratic Party."

In 1963 ASCAP selected it as one of sixteen numbers representing an all-time Hit Parade during its half century of existence. In 1963 Barbra Streisand made a highly personal and successful recording for Columbia, which first helped to bring her to the limelight.

"Happy Days Are Here Again" was interpolated in the motion-picture biography of Mayor James J. Walker, *Beau James*, starring Bob Hope (Paramount, 1957), and in the non-musical motion picture *This Earth Is Mine*, starring Rock Hudson and Gene Simmons (Universal, 1959). It was sung by a busload of American female tourists in the opening scene of the non-musical motion picture *The Night of the Iguana*, starring Richard Burton, Ava Gardner and Deborah Kerr (MGM, 1964).

Happy Feet, words by Jack Yellen, music by Milton Ager (1930). Introduced by the then still unknown Bing Crosby in the motion-picture musical *The King of Jazz*, starring Paul Whiteman and his orchestra (Universal, 1930).

Happy Go Lucky Lane, words by Sam M. Lewis and Joe Young, music by Joseph Meyer (1928).

Happy Holiday, words and music by Irving Berlin (1954). Introduced by Bing Crosby in the motion-picture musical *Holiday Inn* (Paramount, 1942). It has since become a Yuletide favorite.

Happy Hunting, a musical comedy with book by Howard Lindsay and Russel Crouse. Lyrics by Matt Dubey. Music by Harold Karr. Starring Ethel Merman and Fernando Lamas (1956). Original cast recording (RCA Victor).

See: Mutual Admiration Society.

Happy Talk, words by Oscar Hammerstein II, music by Richard Rodgers (1949). Introduced by Juanita Hall in the musical play *South Pacific* (1949). In the motion-picture adaptation of the musical (20th Century-Fox, 1958), it was sung on the soundtrack by Muriel Smith (for Juanita Hall).

Happy to Make Your Acquaintance, words and music by Frank Loesser (1956). Introduced by Robert Weede, Jo Sullivan and Susan Johnson in the musical play *The Most Happy Fella* (1956).

The Happy Wanderer (or, Val-De Ri, Val-De Ra), an Austrian popular song ("Der froehliche Wanderer"), music by Friedrich Wilhelm Moeller, English lyrics by Antonia Ridge (1954). The Austrian song was introduced by the Oberkirchen Children's Choir. The song, with English lyrics, was popularized by Henri René and his orchestra in an RCA Victor recording.

Harbach, Otto, lyricist, born Otto Hauerbach, Salt Lake City, Utah, 1873; died New York City, 1963.

See: Friml, Rudolf; Hirsch, Louis A.; Hoschna, Karl; Kern, Jerome; Romberg, Sigmund; Youmans, Vincent.

See also: The Same Old Moon; Song of the Flame.

Harbor Lights, words by Jimmy Kennedy, music by Hugh Williams, pen name for Will Grosz (1937). An English popular song, revived in the United States in 1950 to become one of the leading song hits of the year, selling over a million copies of sheet music and performed twenty-nine times on the Hit Parade. A successful recording was made by Dinah Washington for Mercury.

Harburg, E. Y. ("Yip"), lyricist, born New York City, 1898.

See: Arlen, Harold; Duke, Vernon; Gorney, Jay; Kern, Jerome; Lane, Burton.

See also: I'm Yours; The World Is Your Balloon.

Hard Hearted Hannah, words by Bob Bigelow, Charles Bates and Jack Yellen, music by Milton Ager (1929). Novelty song, a favorite in vaudeville in the 1920s. It was successfully revived more than a quarter of a century after its initial publication by Peggy Lee in a Capitol recording and by the Ray Charles Singers in a Decca recording.

Hard Headed Woman, words and music by Claude De Metrus (1958). Introduced by Elvis Presley in the motion-picture musical *King Creole* (Paramount, 1958). His RCA Victor recording sold over a million disks and received the Gold Record Award.

Hard Times Come Again No More, words and music by Stephen Foster (1854). Foster borrowed his melody from a song he had heard as a child in a Negro church in Lawrenceville, Pennsylvania. In this Negro church, wrote Morrison Foster, "he [Stephen] stored up in his mind 'many a gem of purest ray serene' drawn from these caves of Negro melody. A number of strains heard there and which, he said to me, were too good to be lost, have been perserved by him, short scraps of which were incorporated in . . . 'Hard Times Come Again No More.' "

Hard to Get, words and music by Jack Segal (1955). Introduced by Gisele MacKenzie in a television production, *Justice* (1955).

Harney, Benjamin Robertson, composer and lyricist, born place unknown in or about 1872; died Philadelphia, Pennsylvania, 1938.

See: Cakewalk in the Sky; I Love My Little Honey; Mister Johnson, Turn Me Loose; My Black Mandy; You've Been a Good Old Wagon, but You've Done Broke Down.

Harnick, Sheldon, lyricist, born New York City, 1924.

See Bock, Jerry.

Harrigan, words and music by George M. Cohan (1907). An early successful example of the spelling song ("H-A-double-R-I-G-A-N spells Harrigan"). It was introduced by James C. Marlowe in the musical *Fifty Miles from Boston* (1908). James Cagney sang it in the George M. Cohan screen biography *Yankee Doodle Dandy* (Warner, 1942).

Harrigan, Edward, lyricist, born New York City, 1845; died New York City, 1911.

See: Braham, David.

Harris, Charles K., composer and lyricist, born Poughkeepsie, New York, 1867; died New York City, 1930.

See: After the Ball; Always in the Way; Break the News to Mother; For Old Times' Sake; Hello, Central, Give Me Heaven; I've a Longing in

My Heart; I've Just Come Back to Say Goodbye; Let's Kiss and Make Up; Mid the Green Fields of Virginia; Nobody Knows, Nobody Cares; One Night in June; There'll Come a Time.

Hart, Lorenz, lyricist, born New York City, 1895; died New York City, 1943.

See: Rodgers, Richard.

For Lorenz Hart's screen biography, see *Words and Music* (MGM, 1948).

The Harvey Girls, a motion-picture musical starring Judy Garland and Ray Bolger (MGM, 1946). Songs by Johnny Mercer and Harry Warren.

See: On the Atchison, Topeka and Santa Fe.

Has Anybody Here Seen Kelly?, an English popular song with words and music by C. W. Murphy and Will Letters, adapted for the United States by William C. McKenna (1909). Introduced by Nora Bayes in the musical *The Jolly Bachelors* (1909). It became one of Nora Bayes' greatest song successes up to that time. She delivered the number with arms akimbo, as she walked up and down the stage, lapsing into comic pleading every time she was made to realize that Kelly had failed to appear. She made a historic recording of it at the time for Victor.

Originally, *The Jolly Bachelors* utilized the English version of the song which Lew Fields, producer of the show, had imported from London and which had originally been entitled "Kelly from the Isle of Man." This song proved a total failure, mainly because the lyrics dealt with local English geography and customs of which American audiences were ignorant. With the show threatened by closing, Lew Fields decided to have the "Kelly" song rewritten to make it more understandable to Americans. In McKenna's version, and as delivered by Nora Bayes, the song was a sensation, and as an immediate reaction the show started prospering at the box office.

Has Anybody Seen My Gal?, a motion picture with songs starring Piper Laurie and Rock Hudson (Universal, 1952). The score was made up mainly of standards.

See: Five Feet Two, Eyes of Blue; Gimme a Little Kiss, Will Ya, Huh?; It Ain't Gonna Rain No More; When the Red, Red Robin Comes Bob Bob Bobbin' Along.

Haunted Heart, words by Howard Dietz, music by Arthur Schwartz (1948). A torch song introduced by John Tyers and Estelle Loring in the musical *Inside U.S.A.* (1948). The song had been written in 1940.

Have a Good Time, words and music by Boudleaux and Felice Bryant (1952). Popularized by Tony Bennett in a best-selling recording for Columbia. The song was successfully revived in 1962 by Sue Thompson.

Have a Heart, words by P. G. Wodehouse, music by Jerome Kern (1916). Introduced by Thurston Hall in the musical of the same name (1916). It was also interpolated in the *Ziegfeld Follies of 1916;* this was the first time that Kern contributed a song to a *Follies* production.

Have I Told You Lately?, words and music by Harold Rome (1962). A love song from husband to wife (and vice versa) introduced by Bambi Linn and Ken Le Roy in the musical *I Can Get It For You Wholesale* (1962).

Have You Ever Been Lonely? (Have You Ever Been Blue?), words by George Brown, music by Peter De Rose (1933). Interpolated in the motion picture *Oklahoma Annie* (Republic, 1952). In the early 1960s it was successfully revived by Jerry Vale in a Columbia recording.

Have You Any Castles, Baby?, words by Johnny Mercer, music by Richard A. Whiting (1937). Introduced by Dick Powell in the motion-picture musical *Varsity Show* (Paramount, 1937).

Have You Heard?, words by Lew Douglas, Frank Lavere and Ray Rodde (1952). Popularized by Joni James in 1953 in an MGM recording.

Have You Looked into Your Heart?, words and music by Teddy Randazzo, Bobby Weinstein and Bobby Barberis (1964). Popularized by Jerry Vale in a Columbia recording.

Have You Met Miss Jones?, words

by Lorenz Hart, music by Richard Rodgers (1937). Introduced by Joy Hodges and Austin Marshall in the musical *I'd Rather Be Right* (1937). It was interpolated in the motion-picture musical *Gentlemen Marry Brunettes* (United Artists, 1955).

Have Yourself a Merry Little Christmas, words by Ralph Blane, music by Hugh Martin (1944). Introduced by Judy Garland in the motion-picture musical *Meet Me in St. Louis* (MGM, 1944).

The Hawaiian Eye, words by Mack David, music by Jerry Livingston (1959). Theme song of the television series of the same name.

The Hawaiian Wedding Song, a popular Hawaiian song ("Ke Kali Nei Au"), music by Charles E. King, American lyrics by Al Hoffman and Dick Manning (1958). Popularized by Andy Williams in a Cadence recording that sold over a million disks.

Hays, William Shakespeare, composer and lyricist, born Louisville, Kentucky, 1837; died Louisville, Kentucky, 1907.

See: Drummer Boy of Shiloh; Early in De Mornin'; Little Old Log Cabin in the Lane; Mollie Darling; Number Twenty-Nine; Roll Out, Heave Dat Cotton; Susan Jane; Walk in De Middle of De Road; We Parted by the River; Write Me a Letter.

The Hazel Dell, words and music by George Frederick Root, using the pen name of Wurzel (1853). Root's first successful ballad—a lugubrious elegy for a girl named Nelly.

He, words by Jack Mullan, music by Jack Richards (1954). Popularized by Al Hibbler in a Decca recording.

Heads Up, a musical comedy with book by John McGowan and Paul Gerard Smith. Lyrics by Lorenz Hart. Music by Richard Rodgers. Starring Jack Whiting, Barbara Newberry and Victor Moore (1929).

The motion-picture adaptation starred Charles Buddy Rogers, Helen Kane and Victor Moore (Paramount, 1930). Only two songs were used from the stage production. A new number by Victor Schertzinger was interpolated.

See: A Ship Without a Sail.

Heart, words and music by Richard Adler and Jerry Ross (1955). Introduced by Russ Brown, Jimmie Komack, Nathaniel Frey and Albert Linville, in the musical *Damn Yankees* (1955). Russ Brown also sang the number in the motion-picture adaptation of the musical (Warner, 1958). Eddie Fisher's recording for RCA Victor sold a million disks.

Heartaches, words by John Klenner, music by Al Hoffman (1931). First popularized by Ted Weems and his orchestra in two Decca recordings, first in 1932, then in 1937. In 1947 (with Ted Weems long past the height of his success) a disk jockey in Charlotte, North Carolina, came upon the old Decca recording of Ted Weems, in which Elmo Tanner did a whistling chorus, and played it on his program as a curiosity. He was deluged with requests for a repetition of this broadcast. The Ted Weems record soon became popular on radio programs, first all over the South, then throughout the country. The old Weems release, reissued in 1947, sold about three million disks. Ted Weems was now suddenly restored to big-time booking; at the same time Decca issued a new recording of the number by Ted Weems and his orchestra.

Heartaches, words and music by Jack Norworth (1919). It provided the title for a motion picture (PRC, 1947), where it was sung on the soundtrack by Chill Wills.

Heartaches by the Number, words and music by Harlan Howard (1959). Introduced by Ray Price, but popularized by Guy Mitchell's Columbia recording that sold about a million disks.

Heart and Soul, words by Frank Loesser, music by Hoagy Carmichael (1938). Written and published as an independent number, then interpolated in the motion picture *A Song Is Born* (1938).

Heartbreak Hotel, words and music by Mae Boren Axton, Tommy Durden and Elvis Presley (1956). This was the song with which Presley made his TV debut—on the Jackie Gleason "Stage Show" in 1955. His RCA Victor recording in 1956 sold over a million disks within a few weeks of its release. The song was interpolated in the motion picture *Riot in Rhythm* (Universal, 1956).

Heart of My Heart, I Love You So. *See:* The Story of a Rose.

Hearts of Stone, words and music by R. Jackson and E. Ray (1955). Popularized in a Dot recording by the Fontane Sisters and in a De Luxe recording by O. Williams and the Charms.

The Heather on the Hill, words by Alan Jay Lerner, music by Frederick Loewe (1947). Scottish ballad introduced by David Brooks and Marion Bell in the musical play *Brigadoon* (1947). In the motion-picture adaptation of the musical (MGM, 1954), it was sung by Gene Kelly.

Heat Wave, words and music by Irving Berlin (1933). Introduced by Ethel Waters in the revue *As Thousands Cheer* (1933)—José Limon, Letita Ide and the Weidman Dancers providing the choreography. The song was revived in two significant Irving Berlin screen musicals: *Blue Skies* (MGM, 1946), sung by Joan Caulfield and followed by a dance creation by Fred Astaire and Joan Caulfield; and *There's No Business Like Show Business* (20th Century-Fox, 1954), sung by Marilyn Monroe.

Heaven Can Wait, words by Eddie DeLange, music by James Van Heusen (1939). Introduced by Tommy Dorsey and his band, who popularized it in an RCA Victor recording (vocal by Jack Leonard).

Heaven in My Arms, words by Oscar Hammerstein II, music by Jerome Kern (1939). Introduced by Jack Whiting, Frances Mercer and Hollace Shaw in the musical *Very Warm for May* (1939); in this production the song was followed by a dance performed by Evelyn Thawl, Sally Craven and Kate Friedlich.

Heaven Will Protect the Working Girl, words by Edgar Smith, music by A. Baldwin Sloane (1909). A satire on the sentimental ballads of the 1890s, introduced by Marie Dressler in the Broadway production *Tillie's Nightmare* (1909). "People with good memories," wrote Sigmund Spaeth, "still enjoy quoting the couplets about 'temptations, crimes and follies, villains, taxicabs and trolleys,' and 'you may tempt the upper classes with your villainous demitasses.'" The song was interpolated in the Rodgers and Hart musical *Peggy Ann* (1926), and in the Theatre Guild musical production *Sing Out, Sweet Land* (1944).

He Brought Home Another, words and music by Paul Dresser (1896).

He'd Have to Get Under, Get Out and Get Under, words by Grant Clarke and Edgar Leslie, music by Maurice Abrahams (1913). One of the earliest song hits about the trials and tribulations of a motorist. It was introduced by Bobby North in the revue *The Pleasure Seekers* (1913), where it was an interpolation. Al Jolson then popularized it at the Winter Garden.

He Fought for a Cause He Thought Was Right, words and music by Paul Dresser (1896). Introduced and popularized by Dick José.

He Goes to Church on Sunday, words by Vincent Bryan, music by E. Ray Goetz (1907). Introduced and popularized by Eddie Foy in the musical *The Orchid* (1907).

Heidelberg Stein Song (or, Biff Bang), words by Frank Pixley, music by Gustav Luders (1902). Drinking song introduced by the chorus in the operetta *The Prince of Pilsen* (1903).

Heigh Ho, words by Larry Morey, music by Frank Churchill (1937). The song of the seven dwarfs in Walt Disney's first full-length animated cartoon, *Snow White and the Seven Dwarfs* (RKO, 1937).

The Helen Morgan Story, a motion-picture musical biography starring Ann Blyth as Helen Morgan with Paul Newman (Warner, 1957). The score was made up of standards. Gogi Grant sang on the soundtrack for Ann Blyth.

See: Bill; Breezin' Along with the Breeze; Can't Help Lovin' Dat Man; Do It Again; Do, Do, Do; I Can't

Give You Anything But Love, Baby; Love Nest; The Man I Love; My Time Is Your Time; On the Sunny Side of the Street; Sweet Georgia Brown; Why Was I Born?; You Do Something to Me.

He'll Have to Go, words and music by Joe and Audrey Allison (1959). Popularized in 1960 by Jim Reeves in an RCA Victor recording.

He'll Have to Stay, words by Charles Green and Audrey Allison, music by Joe Allison (1960). Popularized by Jeanne Black in a Capitol recording.

Hello, Bluebird, words and music by Cliff Friend (1926). Revived by Judy Garland in the motion-picture musical *I Could Go On Singing* (United Artists, 1963).

Hello, Central, Give Me Heaven, words and music by Charles K. Harris (1901). One of the earliest successful "telephone songs."

Hello, Central, Give Me No Man's Land, words by Sam M. Lewis and Joe Young, music by Jean Schwartz (1918). Introduced by Al Jolson in the musical extravaganza *Sinbad* (1918).

Hello, Dolly!, words and music by Jerry Herman (1964). Introduced by Carol Channing and David Hartmann (with chorus) in the musical of the same name (1964). This number received a "Grammy" from the National Academy of Recording Arts and Sciences as "the song of the year."

While the original cast recording of the musical (RCA Victor) sold over a million copies, and thus helped to popularize the title number, it was Louis Armstrong's recording for Kapp in 1964 (which also enjoyed a disk sale of well over a million copies) that helped to make this one of the leading song hits in several years; it received a "Grammy" from the National Academy of Recording Arts and Sciences as the best male vocal performance of the year. By 1965 over seventy different recordings of this song had been made in the United States, and over thirty-five in Europe.

The song's phenomenal success was a surprise to Jerry Herman, its creator. He had written it in a single afternoon, planning it, as he explained, as "a Lillian Russell turn-of-century production number. Believe me, it was very 1890s. . . . But Louis Armstrong recorded the song as if it were written for *him*. And it's Mr. Armstrong's version that really knocked everybody out. . . . I went to a cast party where they had the first cut of the recording. Before then I never expected it would have any popular market, but when I heard his recording and saw the way the other members of the company loved it, I began to realize that it was going to be something special."

The campaign managers of both major political parties in 1964 sought permission to use a parody of this song for their respective Presidential candidates. David Merrick, producer of the show, allowed the Democratic Party to adapt the song as "Hello, Lyndon." It was sung at the Democratic National Convention in Atlantic City, New Jersey, by Carol Channing, with Jerry Herman at the piano. Merrick, however, prohibited Barry Goldwater's supporters from using the song for their own candidate.

Jerry Herman was sued by Mack David and Paramount-Famous Music Company, who maintained that "Hello, Dolly!" was an infringement of the copyright of David's 1948 song hit "Sunflower." The suit was settled out of court early in 1966 for what is believed to be the largest payment ever made in a copyright infringement settlement—in excess of half a million dollars. Herman retained exclusive rights to his song.

Hello, Dolly!, a musical comedy with book by Michael Stewart based on Thornton Wilder's play *The Matchmaker*. Lyrics and music by Jerry Herman. Starring Carol Channing (1964). Original cast recording (RCA Victor).

See: Hello, Dolly!; It Takes a Woman; Put On Your Sunday Clothes; Ribbons Down My Back; So Long, Dearie.

Hello, Frisco, words by Gene Buck, music by Louis A. Hirsch (1915). A salute to the formal opening of transcontinental telephone service in the United States. The song was introduced by Ina Claire in the *Ziegfeld Follies of 1915*. It provided the title for the motion-picture musical (20th Century-Fox, 1943), sung first by Jack Oakie and John Payne, then (in the closing scene) by Alice Faye and John Payne. It was also interpolated in the non-musical motion picture *Wharf Angel*, starring Victor McLaglen (Paramount, 1934), and in the screen biography of Eva Tanguay, *The I Don't Care Girl* (20th Century-Fox, 1953).

Hello, Frisco, Hello, a motion-picture musical starring Alice Faye and John Payne (20th Century-Fox, 1943). The score was made up mainly of standards. "You'll Never Know," by Mack Gordon and Harry Warren (winner of the Academy Award) was an interpolation.

See: By the Watermelon Vine, Lindy Lou; Hello, Frisco; Gee, But It's Great to Meet a Friend from Your Home Town; The Grizzly Bear; Hello, Ma Baby; It's Tulip Time in Holland; Ragtime Cowboy Joe; San Francisco; Strike Up the Band, Here Comes a Sailor; They Always Pick on Me; When You Wore a Tulip; You'll Never Know."

Hello, Hawaii, How Are You?, words by Bert Kalmar and Edgar Leslie, music by Jean Schwartz (1915). A hit song that helped initiate in Tin Pan Alley a vogue for Hawaiian subjects and Hawaiian type melodies. It was introduced and popularized by Willie and Eugene Howard.

Hello, Honey, words by George V. Hobart, music by Raymond Hubbell (1913). Introduced by Elizabeth Brice in the *Ziegfeld Follies of 1913*.

Hello, Ma Baby, words and music by Joe E. Howard and Ida Emerson (1899). Howard's first song success, and one of the earliest significant ragtime numbers. It was interpolated in several motion pictures, including the Joe E. Howard screen

biography *I Wonder Who's Kissing Her Now* (20th Century-Fox, 1947) and *Hello, Frisco, Hello* (20th Century-Fox, 1943).

Hello, Mary Lou, words and music by G. Pitney (1961). Popularized by Ricky Nelson in an Imperial recording.

Hello, Young Lovers, words by Oscar Hammerstein II, music by Richard Rodgers (1951). Ballad introduced by Gertrude Lawrence in the musical play *The King and I* (1951). In the motion-picture adaptation of the musical (20th Century-Fox, 1956), it was sung on the soundtrack by Marni Nixon (for Deborah Kerr).

" 'Hello, Young Lovers,' " this editor has written in his biography of Richard Rodgers, "has caught the soaring poetic lift of the verses so wonderfully that it is more of an aria than a popular song (the delicate staccato notes that introduce the song like aural stardust!). The freshness and individuality of lyricism and harmonic background touch this number with magic."

He Loves and She Loves, words by Ira Gershwin, music by George Gershwin (1927). Introduced by Fred Astaire and Allen Kearns in the musical *Funny Face* (1927). George Gershwin here borrowed the last eight bars from an earlier song, "Something About Love," written in 1919. "He Loves and She Loves" was written during the out-of-town tryouts of *Funny Face* to replace "How Long Has This Been Going On," which had to be deleted (and which was subsequently used in *Rosalie*). It was sung by Fred Astaire in the motion-picture adaptation of *Funny Face* (Paramount, 1957).

Help Me, Rhonda, words and music by Brian Wilson (1965). Popularized by the Beach Boys in a best-selling Capitol recording.

Henderson, Ray, composer, born New York City, 1896.

See (Lyrics by Lew Brown): Don't Bring Lulu; Georgette; Let's Call It a Day; Life Is Just a Bowl of Cherries; My Song; That's Why Darkies Were Born; This Is the Missus; The Thrill Is Gone; Why

Did I Kiss That Girl? (with Robert A. King).

See (Lyrics by Lew Brown and Bud De Sylva): Annabelle; Aren't We All?; The Best Things in Life Are Free; Birth of the Blues; Black Bottom; Broken Hearted; Button Up Your Overcoat; Don't Hold Everything; The Girl Is You; The Girls of Pi Beta Phi; Good for You, Bad for Me; Good News; If I Had a Talking Picture of You; I'm on the Crest of a Wave; It All Depends on You; Just a Memory; Just Imagine; Lucky Day; Lucky in Love; My Sin; Sonny Boy; Sunny Side Up; Thank Your Father; Together; Turn on the Heat; Varsity Drag; Wasn't It Beautiful While It Lasted?; Without Love; You Try Somebody Else; You're the Cream in My Coffee.

See (Lyrics by Sam M. Lewis and Joe Young): Five Foot Two, Eyes of Blue; I'm Sitting on Top of the World.

See also: Alabamy Bound; Animal Crackers in My Soup; Bye, Bye, Blackbird; Nasty Man; That Old Gang of Mine.

For Ray Henderson's screen biography, see *The Best Things in Life Are Free* (20th Century-Fox, 1956).

Herbert, Victor, composer, born Dublin, Ireland, 1859; died New York City, 1924.

See (Lyrics by Henry Blossom): All for You; Because You're You; Eileen Allana Asthore; Every Day Is Lady's Day; Good-a-bye, John; If I Were on the Stage; The Isle of Our Dreams; I Want What I Want When I Want It; Kiss Me Again; Love Is the Best of All; The Mascot of the Troop; Moonbeams; Neapolitan Love Song; Streets of New York; Thine Alone; When You're Away.

See (Lyrics by Glen MacDonough): Absinthe Frappé; I Can't Do This Sum; Love Is Like a Cigarette; Never Mind, Bo-Peep; Rose of the World; Toyland.

See (Lyrics by H. B. Smith): The Cupid and I; Gypsy Love Song; If Only You Were Mine; I Love Thee, I Adore Thee; Love Is a Tyrant; My Angeline; Star Light, Star Bright; There Once Was an Owl; To the

Land of My Own Romance; A Woman Is Only a Woman, But a Good Cigar Is a Smoke.

See (Lyrics by R. B. Smith): The Angelus; I Might Be Your Once in a While; Pretty As a Picture; Someone Like You; Sweethearts.

See (Lyrics by Rida Johnson Young): Ah, Sweet Mystery of Life; I'm Falling in Love with Someone; Italian Street Song; My Dream Girl; Neath the Southern Moon; Tramp, Tramp, Tramp.

See also: Bagdad; Indian Summer; A Kiss in the Dark; The Love Boat.

For Victor Herbert's screen biography, see *The Great Victor Herbert* (Paramount, 1939).

Here Am I, words by Hal David, music by Burt Bacharach (1965). Introduced by Dianne Warwick in the motion-picture farce *What's New, Pussycat?* (United Artists, 1965), starring Peter Sellers, Peter O'Toole and Romy Schneider.

Here Am I, words by Oscar Hammerstein II, music by Jerome Kern (1929). Introduced by Helen Morgan and Violet Carson in the musical *Sweet Adeline* (1929). In the motion-picture adaptation of the musical (Warner, 1935), it was sung by Irene Dunne.

Here Comes Cookie, words by Mack Gordon, music by Harry Revel (1935). Introduced in the motion picture *Love in Bloom*, starring George Burns and Gracie Allen (Paramount, 1935).

Here Comes My Daddy Now (or, Oh Pop—Oh Pop—Oh Pop), words by L. Wolfe Gilbert, music by Lewis F. Muir (1912).

Here Comes Summer, words and music by Jerry Keller (1959). Popularized by Jerry Keller in a Kapp recording.

Here Comes the Groom, a motion-picture musical starring Bing Crosby and Jane Wyman (Paramount, 1951). Songs by Ray Evans and Jay Livingston, and Johnny Mercer and Hoagy Carmichael.

See: Bonne Nuit; In the Cool, Cool, Cool of the Evening; Misto Cristofo Columbo.

Here Comes the Show Boat, words by

Billy Rose, music by Maceo Pinkard (1927). Interpolated in the first motion-picture adaptation of the Jerome Kern-Oscar Hammerstein musical play *Show Boat* (Universal, 1929).

Here Come the Waves, a motion-picture musical starring Bing Crosby and Betty Hutton (Paramount, 1944). Songs by Johnny Mercer and Harold Arlen.
  See: Ac-cent-tchu-ate the Positive; Let's Take the Long Way Home.

Here I'll Stay, words by Alan Jay Lerner, music by Kurt Weill (1948). Introduced by Nanette Fabray and Ray Middleton in the musical *Love Life* (1948).

Here in My Arms, words by Lorenz Hart, music by Richard Rodgers (1925). Introduced by Helen Ford and Charles Purcell in the first successful book musical by Rodgers and Hart, *Dearest Enemy* (1925).

Here in My Heart, words and music by Pat Genaro, Lou Levinson and Bill Borrelli (1952). Popularized by Al Martino in a BBS recording (Martino's last hit record for a decade).

Here Is My Heart, a motion-picture musical starring Bing Crosby and Kitty Carlisle (Paramount, 1934). Songs mainly by Leo Robin and Ralph Rainger.
  See: June in January; Love Is Just Around the Corner.

Here's Love, words and music by Meredith Willson (1963). Title song of the musical comedy (1963), introduced by Laurence Naismith, Craig Stevens and chorus.

Here's Love, a musical comedy with book, lyrics and music by Meredith Willson based on the motion picture *The Miracle on 34th Street.* Starring Janis Page and Craig Stevens (1963). Original cast recording (Columbia).
  See: Arm in Arm; Here's Love; Look, Little Girl; My Wish; Pine Cones and Holly Berries.

Here's to Romance, words by Herb Magidson, music by Con Conrad (1935). Introduced by Nino Martini in the motion-picture musical of the same name (20th Century-Fox, 1935).

Her Eyes Don't Shine Like Diamonds, words and music by Dave Marion (1894). Sentimental ballad introduced in vaudeville by John Russell of the Russell Brothers. Though the Russell Brothers were essentially a comedy team, Dave Marion prevailed on John Russell to use the song in their act, where it scored a major success.

Herman, Jerry, composer and lyricist, born New York City, 1932.
  See: Hello, Dolly!; It Only Takes a Moment; It Takes a Woman; Milk and Honey; Put on Your Sunday Clothes; Ribbons Down My Back; Shalom; So Long, Dearie.

Hernando's Hideaway, words and music by Richard Adler and Jerry Ross (1954). Tango introduced by John Raitt and Carol Haney in the musical *The Pajama Game* (1954). They repeated their performance in the motion-picture adaptation of the musical comedy (Warner, 1957). The song was further popularized in 1954 in a best-selling recording by Archie Bleyer and his orchestra for Cadence.

He's a Cousin of Mine, words by Cecil Mack, music by Chris Smith and Silvio Hein (1906). Introduced by Marie Cahill in the musical *Marrying Mary* (1906).

He's a Devil in His Own Home Town, words by Grant Clarke and Irving Berlin, music by Irving Berlin (1914).

He's So Fine, words and music by Ronnie Mack (1963). Popularized by the Chiffons in a Laurie recording.

He's Me Pal, words by Vincent P. Bryan, music by Gus Edwards (1905).

He's My Friend, words and music by Meredith Willson (1964). Introduced as a production number in the motion-picture adaptation of the musical *The Unsinkable Molly Brown* (MGM, 1964).

He Touched Me. *See:* She Touched Me.

He Walked Right In, Turned Around, and Walked Right Out Again, words by Ed Rose, music by Maxwell Silver (1906).

Hey, Baby, words by Margaret Cobb,

music by Bruce Channel (1962). Popularized by Bruce Channel in a Smash recording.

Hey, Good Lookin', words and music by Hank Williams (1951). Introduced and popularized by Hank Williams in an MGM recording. It was sung by Hank Williams, Jr., on the soundtrack (for George Hamilton) in the screen biography of Hank Williams, Sr., *Your Cheatin' Heart* (MGM, 1964).

Hey, Jealous Lover, words and music by Sammy Cahn, Kay Twomey and Bee Walker (1956). Popularized by Frank Sinatra in a Capitol recording.

Sammy Cahn wrote to this editor: "I wrote this song in collaboration with two people I never met. The song was sent in to Sinatra's publishing house and I was brought in to 'beef it up.' It turned out to be one of my most potent copyrights."

Hey, Joe, words and music by Boudleaux Bryant (1953). Popularized in best-selling recordings by Frankie Laine and Carl Smith, each for Columbia.

Hey, Look Me Over, words by Carolyn Leigh, music by Cy Coleman (1960). Introduced by Lucille Ball and Paula Stuart in the musical *Wildcat* (1960). The melody was subsequently used for the official song of the Louisiana State University under the title of "Hey, Fighting Tigers." Parodies of the song were also written to further Louis J. Lefkowitz's Mayoralty campaign in New York in 1962, and in Edward M. Kennedy's successful primary fight in Massachusetts in 1963 for the Democratic Senatorial nomination.

Heyman, Edward, lyricist, born New York City, 1907.

See: Green, John W.; Schwartz, Arthur; Youmans, Vincent; Young, Victor.

See also: My Darling; My Silent Love; The Sky Fell Down; They Say; You Oughta Be in Pictures.

Hey, Mr. Banjo, words and music by Freddy Morgan and Norman Malkin (1955). Popularized by the Sunnysiders in a Kapp recording.

Hey, Paula, words and music by Ray Hildebrand (1963). Popularized by Paul and Paula in a best-selling Mercury recording that received a Gold Record Award.

Hey, There, words and music by Richard Adler and Jerry Ross (1954). A one-man duet introduced by John Raitt in the musical *The Pajama Game* (1954). Having first sung the number into a dictaphone, Raitt then played it back and, while listening, sang pointed comments in counterpoint. Raitt also sang the number in the motion-picture adaptation of the musical (Warner, 1957). Rosemary Clooney's Columbia recording in 1954 sold about two and a half million disks. Sammy Davis' Decca recording was also a best seller.

Hey, What Did the Bluebird Say?, words by Ted Koehler, music by Jimmy McHugh. (1936). Introduced by Shirley Temple in the motion-picture musical *Dimples* (20th Century-Fox, 1936).

Hiawatha, words by James O'Dea, music by Neil Moret, pseudonym for Charles N. Daniels (1903). One of the earliest hit songs on an American-Indian subject; it helped bring about in Tin Pan Alley a vogue for Indian songs.

The "Hiawatha" in this song is not that of Longfellow's famous poem, but a little town in Kansas. Moret, who lived in Kansas City, used to visit that town regularly because his sweetheart lived there. One day, while en route by train, the melody of "Hiawatha" occurred to him and he jotted it down. He developed it first as an instrumental piece, which was published in Detroit in 1901. Later that year it was introduced by John Philip Sousa and his band. Two years later James O'Dea wrote the lyrics and the song became an immediate hit.

Hic, Haec, Hoc, words by Sidney Michaels, music by Mark Sandrich, Jr. (1964). The ebullient chorus of the monks in a monastery vineyard, in the musical *Ben Franklin in Paris* (1964).

The High and the Mighty (or, The

Whistling Song), words by Ned Washington, music by Dimitri Tiomkin (1954). Theme song from the motion picture of the same name starring John Wayne (Warner, 1954). It is known as the "whistling song" because throughout the picture the principal character whistles the melody. The number was popularized in several different instrumental recordings in 1954: those of Le Roy Holmes and his orchestra for MGM; Victor Young and his orchestra for Decca; and Les Baxter and his orchestra for Capitol.

High Button Shoes, a musical comedy with book by Stephen Longstreet based on his own novel. Lyrics by Sammy Cahn. Music by Jule Styne. Starring Phil Silvers and Nanette Fabray (1947). Original cast recording (RCA Victor).

See: I Still Get Jealous; On a Sunday by the Sea; Papa, Won't You Dance With Me?

Higher and Higher, a motion-picture musical starring Frank Sinatra (in his screen debut) with Michele Morgan and Jack Haley (RKO, 1943). Songs by Harold Adamson and Jimmy McHugh.

See: I Couldn't Sleep a Wink Last Night; A Lovely Way to Spend an Evening.

High Hopes, words by Sammy Cahn, music by James Van Heusen (1959). Introduced in the non-musical motion picture *A Hole in the Head* (Paramount, 1959) by Frank Sinatra and Eddie Hodges, whose Capitol recording was a best seller. The song received the Academy Award.

It was written as a last-minute decision, because of the sudden need for a song in an emotional scene in an otherwise non-musical motion picture. The song was used to promote John F. Kennedy's presidential campaign in 1960.

High Is Better Than Low, words by Howard Dietz, music by Arthur Schwartz (1963). Introduced by Mary Martin in the musical *Jennie* (1963).

High Noon (or, Do Not Forsake Me), words by Ned Washington, music by Dimitri Tiomkin (1952). Introduced (on the soundtrack) by Tex Ritter, a singer of cowboy ballads, in the non-musical motion picture *High Noon,* starring Gary Cooper and Grace Kelly (United Artists, 1952). The song received the Academy Award.

The song was not originally in the motion picture. When *High Noon* had its first run-through for producer and director, the overall feeling was that the picture was a dud. Tiomkin was convinced, however, that the film had many strong assets and suggested that a theme song, that would tell the plot before the picture got under way, was all that was needed to translate a failure into success. He wrote in his autobiography: "The rule book says that in movies you can't have singing while there's dialogue; but I convinced Stanley Kramer that it might be a good idea to have the song sung, whistled, and played by the orchestra. A melody came to me, I played it on the piano at home and developed it until I thought it was right."

At a preview of *High Noon* in a theater outside Los Angeles, the picture was a dismal failure—in spite of the interpolated theme song. Tiomkin now asked for, and received, the publication and recording rights to his song. Since Tex Ritter refused to record it (he did so at a later date after the song had become a success), Tiomkin persuaded Frankie Laine to do it for Columbia. This recording and the song itself became such tremendous successes by the time the motion picture was released throughout the country (four months after the Columbia recording had appeared), that they aroused considerable interest and curiosity in the picture. Eventually *High Noon* became a profitable motion-picture venture, achieving the status of a classic among Westerns.

High Society, a motion-picture musical based on Philip Barry's stage play *Philadelphia Story,* starring

Bing Crosby, Grace Kelly and Frank Sinatra (MGM, 1956). Songs by Cole Porter. Soundtrack recording (Capitol).

See: True Love; Well, Did You Evah?; You're Sensational.

High Spirits, a musical comedy based on Noel Coward's stage play *Blithe Spirit.* Book, lyrics and music by Timothy Gray and Hugh Martin. Starring Beatrice Lillie (1964). Original cast recording (Paramount).

See: Home, Sweet Heaven; If I Gave You; Talking to You; Where Is the Man I Married?

The Highwayman, an operetta with book and lyrics by Harry B. Smith. Music by Reginald de Koven. Starring Joseph O'Mara and Hilda Clarke (1897).

See: Do You Remember Love?; Moonlight Song.

High, Wide and Handsome, words by Oscar Hammerstein II, music by Jerome Kern (1937). Title song of the motion-picture musical (Paramount, 1937), sung by Irene Dunne.

High, Wide and Handsome, a motion-picture musical starring Irene Dunne (Paramount, 1937). Songs by Oscar Hammerstein II and Jerome Kern.

See: Can I Forget You?; Folks Who Live on the Hill; High, Wide and Handsome.

Hi Lili, Hi Lo, words by Helen Deutsch, music by Bronislau Kaper (1952). Introduced by Leslie Caron and Mel Ferrer in the motion picture *Lili* (MGM, 1953). It was interpolated as a piano episode in the non-musical motion picture *Rogue Cop*, starring Robert Taylor (MGM, 1954). The song was successfully revived in 1964 in conjunction with the re-release of the motion picture *Lili*.

Hill, Billy, composer and lyricist, born William Joseph Hill, Boston, Massachusetts, 1899; died New York City, 1940.

See: Call of the Canyon; Empty Saddles; The Glory of Love; In the Chapel in the Moonlight; The Last Roundup; Lights Out; The Old Spinning Wheel; Wagon Wheels.

Hilliard Bob, composer and lyricist,

born New York City, 1918.

See: Styne, Jule.

See also: Be My Life's Companion; Bouquet of Roses; Boutonniere; Careless Hands; Civilization; The Coffee Song; Dear Hearts and Gentle People; Dearie; English Muffins and Irish Stew; Moonlight Gambler; My Little Corner of the World; Sailor Boys Have Talk to Me in English; Shanghai; Somebody Bad Stole De Wedding Bell; Wee Small Hours.

Hindustan, words and music by Oliver G. Wallace and Harold Weeks (1918). Successfully revived more than half a century after publication, by Bing Crosby and Rosemary Clooney in a best-selling Decca recording.

Hinky Dinky Parlay Voo, words by Al Dubin and Irving Mills, music by Jimmy McHugh and Irwin Dash (1924). The full title of this song is "What's Become of Hinky Dinky Parlay Voo." This number should not be confused with the song favorite of doughboys during World War I, "Mad'moiselle from Armentieres," though obviously it was inspired by it. The Dubin-Mills-McHugh-Dash song was first popularized by the original Happiness Boys (Billy Jones and Ernie Hare). It was later interpolated in the non-musical motion picture *The Cockeyed World*, starring Edmund Lowe and Victor McLaglen (Fox, 1929).

Hirsch, Louis A., composer, born New York City, 1887; died New York City, 1924.

See (Lyrics by Gene Buck): Garden of My Dreams; Hello, Frisco.

See (Lyrics by Gene Buck, music in collaboration with Dave Stamper): My Rambler Rose, Neath the South Sea Moon; Some Sweet Day.

See (Lyrics by Otto Harbach): Love Nest; Mary; Tickle Toe.

See also: The Gaby Glide.

His Last Thoughts Were of You, words by Edward B. Marks, music by Joseph W. Stern (1894). Introduced by Minnie Schulte at George Huber's Prospect Garden Music Hall in New York. It was then popularized in vaudeville by Lottie Gilson.

Hitchy Koo, words by L. Wolfe Gilbert, music by Lewis F. Muir and Maurice Abrahams (1912). A ragtime hit whose title was appropriated by Raymond Hitchock for an annual Broadway revue.

Hitchy Koo, an annual Broadway revue produced by Raymond Hitchock. The first edition, mounted in 1917, had book and lyrics by Harry Grattan and Glen MacDonough, and music by E. Ray Goetz. It starred Raymond Hitchock, Irene Bordoni and Grace La Rue. There were three more editions after that (1918, 1919 and 1920). In 1918 book, lyrics and music were provided mainly by Glen MacDonough and E. Ray Goetz, though songs by other lyricists and composers were interpolated. The 1919 edition had a score by Cole Porter, while the 1920 edition boasted music by Jerome Kern to lyrics by Glen MacDonough. The principal performers between 1918 and 1920 were Irene Bordoni, Joe Cook, Leon Erroll, Raymond Hitchock, Florence O'Denishawn and Julia Sanderson.

See: I May Be Gone for a Long, Long Time; Old-Fashioned Garden; M-i-s-s-i-s-s-i-p-p-i.

The Hit Parade, a weekly radio (subsequently television) program sponsored by Lucky Strike cigarettes for over a quarter of a century. It was devoted to the ten leading popular songs of the week—based on sheet music and record sales and number of performances on juke boxes. Through the years the orchestra was conducted by Mark Warnow and, after Warnow's death, by his brother, Raymond Scott (born Harry Warnow); the principal singers included Dorothy Collins, Snooky Lanson, Russell Arms, Gisele MacKenzie and Lawrence Tibbett.

The first program was broadcast on April 20, 1935. The "Number One" hit that evening was "Lovely to Look At" by Dorothy Fields and Jerome Kern, followed by "Lullaby of Broadway" by Al Dubin and Harry Warren, and "Soon" by George

and Ira Gershwin. For the next quarter of a century and more, the program served as a valuable barometer of the nation's preferences in popular music.

The song most often represented on the Hit Parade was Irving Berlin's "White Christmas" (thirty-two times). "People Will Say We're in Love" by Rodgers and Hammerstein appeared thirty times; "Harbor Lights" by Jimmy Kennedy and Hugh Williams, twenty-nine times; "I'll Be Seeing You" by Irving Kahal and Sammy Fain, twenty-four times; and "You'll Never Know" by Mack Gordon and Harry Warren, twenty-two times.

The song most often featured in the Number One spot was "Too Young" by Sylvia Dee and Sid Lippman (twelve times). "Because of You," by Arthur Hammerstein and Dudley Wilkinson, reached the first spot eleven times, and "I'll Be Seeing You," ten times. Two songs by Richard Rodgers were heard seven times, each in the Number Two place: "Bewitched, Bothered and Bewildered," lyrics by Lorenz Hart, and "No Other Love," lyrics by Oscar Hammerstein II.

The program expired on television in 1959, mainly due to the overwhelming preponderance of rock 'n' roll songs in the weekly hit category, thus making a well-balanced and varied program impossible to devise.

Hit the Deck, a musical comedy with book by Herbert Fields based on Hubert Osborne's play *Shore Leave*. Lyrics by Leo Robin and Clifford Grey. Music by Vincent Youmans. Starring Louise Groody and Charles King (1927).

The motion-picture adaptation starred Jack Oakie and Polly Walker (RKO, 1930). It used only two songs from the stage production. A third number, "Keepin' Myself for You," by Sidney Clare and Vincent Youmans, was interpolated.

See: Hallelujah; Keepin' Myself for You; Sometimes I'm Happy.

Hit the Road to Dreamland, words by Johnny Mercer, music by Harold

Arlen (1942). Introduced by Mary Martin, Dick Powell and the Golden Gate Quartet in the motion-picture musical *Star-Spangled Rhythm* (Paramount, 1942).

Hoity Toity, a Weber and Fields musical extravaganza, with book and lyrics by Edgar Smith, music by John Stromberg. Starring Weber and Fields, De Wolf Hopper, Sam Bernard, Lillian Russell, Fay Templeton and Bessie Clayton (1901).

See: De Pullman Porters' Ball.

Hold Everything, a musical comedy with book by Bud De Sylva and John McGowan. Lyrics by Bud De Sylva and Lew Brown. Music by Ray Henderson. Starring Bert Lahr (in his first leading role in a Broadway musical comedy), Jack Whiting, Ona Munson and Victor Moore (1928).

The motion-picture adaptation starred Joe E. Brown and Winnie Lightner (Warner, 1930). It completely dispensed with the De Sylva, Brown and Henderson stage score, substituting a new one by Al Dubin and Joe Burke.

See: Don't Hold Everything; You're the Cream in My Coffee.

Hold Me, words by Art Hickman and Ben Black (1920). Introduced in the *Ziegfeld Follies of 1920*.

Hold Me, Hold Me, Hold Me, words by Betty Comden and Adolph Green, music by Jule Styne (1951). Introduced by Dolores Gray in the revue *Two on the Aisle* (1951). It was sung by Marilyn Monroe in the non-musical motion picture *Niagara* (20th Century-Fox, 1952).

Hold Me, Thrill Me, Kiss Me, words and music by Harry Noble (1952). Popularized in 1953 by Karen Chandler's recording for Coral.

Hold My Hand, words and music by Richard Myers (1950). Interpolated in the motion picture *Susan Slept Here,* starring Dick Powell and Debbie Reynolds (RKO, 1954), and popularized in a Coral recording by Don Cornell.

Holiday Inn, a motion-picture musical starring Bing Crosby and Fred Astaire (Paramount, 1942). Songs by Irving Berlin.

See: Be Careful, It's My Heart; Easter Parade; Happy Holiday; Lazy; White Christmas.

Hollander, Frederick, composer, born London, England, 1896.

See: Falling in Love Again; See What the Boys in the Back Room Will Have; True Confession; Whispers in the Dark.

Hollywood Canteen, an all-star motion picture with Jack Benny, Eddie Cantor, Joan Crawford, Bette Davis and others (Warner, 1944). Songs by various composers and lyricists, including Cole Porter.

See: Don't Fence Me In; Sweet Dreams, Sweetheart; Tumbling Tumbleweeds.

Hollywood Revue, an all-star motion-picture musical with Marion Davies, Norma Shearer, Jack Benny, Joan Crawford, Charles King and others (MGM, 1929). Songs by various composers and lyricists including Joe Goodwin and Gus Edwards, and Arthur Freed and Nacio Herb Brown.

See: Singing in the Rain; You Were Meant for Me.

Home for the Holidays, words by Al Stillman, music by Robert Allen (1954). Popularized by Perry Como in an RCA Victor recording. It has since become a Yuletide favorite.

Home on the Range, words usually ascribed to Brewster (Bruce) Higley, music to Daniel E. Kelly (1904). Higley, a homesteader, is said to have written his lyrics in his cabin near Beaver Creek, Kansas, in 1873. Dan Kelly, a guitar player who lived in Gaylord, a Smith County trading post twenty miles from Beaver Creek, fitted tune to words.

The words were first published in *The Smith County Pioneer,* in Kansas, in December of 1873 under the title "Oh, Give Me a Home Where the Buffalo Roam." It was then reprinted as "Western Home" in the *Kirwin Chief,* in Kansas, on March 21, 1874. Words and music were issued together for the first time in 1904, the title now being "Arizona Home." On this publication, William Goodwin is credited as lyricist and composer. The song's popularity began with a republication in Alan Lomax's anthology *Cowboy Songs* (1910), where the number was described as "the cowboy's national anthem," and through David Guion's skillful arrangement. Its fame was further enhanced through a newspaper story in which it was singled out as President Franklin D. Roosevelt's favorite song (undoubtedly a legend).

The song has been involved in litigations to determine its real authors. In 1934 William Goodwin and his wife, of Temple, Arizona, sued several defendants for a million dollars, insisting that the song was theirs. The court dismissed their claim. Another law action, no more successful, tried to pinpoint the writing of the song to the year of 1885, while maintaining that its authors were C. O. Swartz, Bingham Graves, Bill McCabe and somebody identified merely as "Jim." There is no convincing proof, however, that Bruce Higley and Daniel E. Kelly really wrote the song, though they are now generally given the credit. The song has become the official one of the State of Kansas.

Home, Sweet Heaven, words and music by Timothy Graves and Hugh Martin (1964). Introduced by Tammy Grimes in the musical *High Spirits* (1964).

Home, Sweet Home, words by John Howard Payne, music by Sir Henry Rowley Bishop (1823). Payne, an American—descendant of Robert Treat Paine, one of the signers of the Declaration of Independence— had come to London in early manhood. There he acted in, wrote, and produced, plays. With Sir Henry Rowley Bishop as his composer, he wrote the text for an opera, *Clari*, introduced at Covent Garden, London, on May 8, 1823. "Home, Sweet Home" was part of this score, sung by Maria Tree (in the title role) at the end of the first act. The number brought down the house and became instantly popular, first in London, then throughout England, and finally throughout the Western world. The reviewer of the *Quarterly Musi-*

cal Magazine and Review in London said: "To 'Home, Sweet Home' the most unqualified approbation must be given. It is simple, sweet and touching, beyond any air we almost ever heard. Never was any ballad so immediately and deservedly popular." In writing his lyrics, Payne was giving voice to his own homesickness. While working on *Clari* he wrote to his brother on December 31, 1822: "My yearnings towards home become stronger as the term of my exile lengthens. . . . I long to see all of your faces and hear all your voices."

Bishop's melody was long erroneously believed to be an adaptation of a Sicilian folk song. This was because Bishop had published two volumes of national airs (1821 and 1822). Here, for those countries for which he could not find suitable material, he invented melodies of his own. To represent Sicily in the second volume he created a tune which he named "A Sicilian air." The long-held belief that this melody was a folk song in the public domain was responsible for its worldwide use in pirated publications for a number of years. However, in time, Bishop received full recognition as the composer of the melody. In fact it was primarily for "Home, Sweet Home" that he was knighted in 1842 by Queen Victoria —the first musician to be thus honored.

Kitty Stephens was the first outstanding successful performer of "Home, Sweet Home," creating a furor when she presented it at the York and Birmingham Festivals, in England, in 1832. Mme. Anne Bishop, wife of the composer—and a noted concert singer—then represented it frequently on her programs through the years. But the song's universal fame came mainly through the efforts of two world-famous singers—Jenny Lind and Adelina Patti. In her concerts in the United States, Jenny Lind liked featuring it as her closing number. For forty years Adelina Patti used it as one of her favorite encores, accompanying herself on the piano. As for *Clari*—its American première took place at the Park Theatre, New York, on November 12, 1823. The year of 1823 also saw the first American publication of "Home, Sweet Home" —in Philadelphia.

John Howard Payne did not profit from the worldwide success of his song. "How often have I been in the heart of Paris, Berlin, London or some other city," he once lamented, "and have heard persons singing or hand organs playing 'Home, Sweet Home' without having a shilling to buy the next meal, or a place to lay my head." Yet, like Bishop, he was also a recipient of honors. In 1850 he was a guest at a Jenny Lind concert at the White House, in Washington, D. C., attended by President Fillmore, Henry Clay, Daniel Webster and other American notables. At the conclusion of her program, Jenny Lind turned to Payne and sang to him his "Home, Sweet Home."

Two benefit preformances of *Clari*, in Brooklyn, New York, helped raise funds for the erection of Payne's statue in Prospect Park on September 27, 1873. When the statue was unveiled, one thousand voices sang "Home, Sweet Home."

Honey, words by Seymour Simons and Haven Gillespie, music by Richard A. Whiting (1928). Introduced and popularized by Rudy Vallée on his radio program and in an RCA Victor recording. Over a million copies of sheet music were sold by 1930. The song was interpolated into the non-musical motion picture *Her Highness and the Bellboy*, starring Robert Walker and Hedy Lamarr (MGM, 1945).

Honey Babe, words by Paul Francis Webster, music by Max Steiner, the melody based on a traditional air (1954). A marching song, introduced in the non-musical motion picture *Battle Cry*, starring Van Heflin and Mona Freeman (Warner, 1955). It was popularized by Art Mooney in an MGM recording.

Honey Boy, words by Jack Norworth, music by Albert von Tilzer (1907).

Popularized by Sophie Tucker in vaudeville. The song was a tribute to the celebrated minstrel, George "Honey Boy" Evans. However, the sobriquet of "Honey Boy" was pinned to Evans years before this song was written. (See "I'll Be True to My Honey Boy.")

Honey Bun, Words by Oscar Hammerstein II, music by Richard Rodgers (1949). Introduced by Mary Martin and Myron McCormick in the musical play *South Pacific* (1949). In the motion-picture adaptation of the musical (20th Century-Fox, 1958), it was sung by Mitzi Gaynor.

Honeycomb, words and music by Bob Merrill (1954). Popularized in 1957 by Jimmie Rodgers in a Roulette recording that sold over a million disks.

Honey Gal, words and music by Shelton Brooks (1910). Introduced by Al Jolson at a Winter Garden concert in New York.

Honey in the Honeycomb, words by John Latouche, music by Vernon Duke (1940). Introduced by Katherine Dunham in the musical fantasy *Cabin in the Sky* (1940). In the motion-picture adaptation of the musical (MGM, 1943), it was sung by Lena Horne.

Honey Love, words by Jack Drislane, music by George W. Meyer (1911).

Honeysuckle Rose, words by Andy Razaf, music by Thomas "Fats" Waller (1929). Introduced in the musical production *Land of Coal* (1929). The song later became a specialty of Benny Goodman and his orchestra, and of Lena Horne. Betty Grable sang it in the motion-picture musical *Tin Pan Alley* (20th Century-Fox, 1940). The song was also interpolated in the motion-picture musical *Thousands Cheer* (MGM, 1943), sung by Lena Horne.

Honky Tonk, words by Henry Glover, music by Bill Doggett, Billy Butler, Shep Sheppard and Clifford Scott (1956). Popularized in a King recording by Bill Doggett.

La Hoola Boola, words and music by Bob Cole and Billy Johnson (1897). An early Hawaiian-type popular song that helped to popularize the word "boola." Its melody was appropriated in 1901 for the Yale University song "Boola Boola."

Hoop-Dee-Doo, words by Frank Loesser, music by Milton DeLugg (1950). Popularized by Perry Como in an RCA Victor recording.

Hooray for Captain Spalding, words by Bert Kalmar, music by Harry Ruby (1928). A paean to Captain Spalding in the musical *Animal Crackers* (1928), introduced by Groucho Marx, Robert Grieg, Margaret Dumont and ensemble. It was also sung by Groucho Marx and others in the motion-picture adaptation of the musical (Paramount, 1930). It subsequently became Groucho Marx's theme song on TV.

Hooray for Love, words by Leo Robin, music by Harold Arlen (1948). Introduced by Tony Martin in the motion picture *Casbah,* starring Yvonne De Carlo (Universal, 1948).

Hooray for Love, words by Dorothy Fields, music by Jimmy McHugh (1935). Title song of a motion picture starring Ann Sothern (RKO, 1935), sung by Gene Raymond.

Horses, words by Byron Gay, music by Richard A. Whiting (1926).

Horseshoes Are Lucky, words by Johnny Mercer, music by Robert Emmett Dolan (1949). Introduced by Mary Hatcher and Danny Scholl in the musical *Texas Li'l Darlin'* (1949). This is Dolan's own favorite among his songs.

Hoschna, Karl, composer, born Kuschwarda, Bohemia, 1877; died New York City, 1911.

See (Lyrics by Otto Harbach): The Birth of Passion; Cuddle Up a Little Closer; Every Little Movement Has a Meaning of Its Own.

See also: The Yama Yama Man.

The Hostess with the Mostes' on the Ball, words and music by Irving Berlin (1950). Introduced by Ethel Merman in the musical *Call Me Madam* (1950). She also sang it in the motion-picture adaptation of the musical (20th Century-Fox, 1953).

The Hot Canary, a novelty instrumental for violin and piano, music by Paul Nero, a jazz adaptation of a Belgian popular instrumental, "Le

Canari" by F. Poliakin (1948). Ray Gilbert provided lyrics for this melody in 1949.

Hot Chocolates. *See:* Connie's Hot Chocolates.

Hot Diggity, words by Al Hoffman and Dick Manning, melody adapted from a theme from Chabrier's *España* (1956). Perry Como's RCA Victor recording sold over a million disks.

Hot Tamale Alley, words and music by George M. Cohan (1895). Cohan's first song hit, introduced in vaudeville by May Irwin.

A Hot Time in the Old Town, words by Joe Hayden, music by Theodore M. Metz (1896). Metz was a bandleader with the McIntyre and Heath Minstrels which was traveling across Louisiana in 1886. When the train stopped at Old Town, Metz noticed several Negro children putting out a fire. One of the minstrels remarked: "There'll be a hot time in Old Town tonight." Metz saw in this comment the makings of a song, had Joe Hayden write the lyrics while he himself fashioned the melody. At first the music was used as a march for the McIntyre and Heath Minstrels parading the streets before curtain time. Later on, the number, with the words, was used as the opening chorus of the minstrel show.

While Metz is always credited as the composer, there is reason to believe he might have lifted his tune from a song he had heard Mama Lou sing at Babe Connors' place in St. Louis. Some of his contemporaries insist that they had heard the song there long before Metz published it.

A good deal of the early popularity of this song is due to Josephine Sabel's effective rendition in vaudeville. Then, during the Spanish-American War, the song became a prime favorite with American soldiers in Cuba. The Rough Riders, under Theodore Roosevelt, adopted it as their song. A French newspaper account of the victory of the Rough Riders at San Juan Hill told, on July 1, 1899, how Americans gathered around the campfire after the battle to sing *"Il fera chaud dans la vieille ville ce soir."* Theodore Roosevelt, himself, disliked the tune because it was in ragtime and he often maintained it did not deserve its widespread popularity.

A recording of the song was made as early as 1897 by the ragtime singer Len Spencer. The recording outfit was the Universal Phonograph Company, founded as a subsidiary of the Tin Pan Alley firm of Joseph W. Stern as a means of plugging its songs.

Hound Dog, words and music by Jerry Leiber and Mike Stoller (1956). Introduced by Willie Mae Thornton in 1953 but published in 1956 and popularized that year by Elvis Presley in an RCA Victor recording that sold over two million disks.

The House I Live In, words by Lewis Allen, music by Earl Robinson (1942). A hymn in praise of America and democracy, introduced in the WPA revue *Let Freedom Ring* (1942). It was introduced by Earl Robinson. The song was first popularized by Frank Sinatra in a movie short built around this number, which received an Academy Award.

House of Flowers, a musical comedy with book and lyrics by Truman Capote. Music by Harold Arlen. Starring Pearl Bailey, Juanita Hall and Diahann Carroll (1954). Original cast recording (Columbia).

See: I Never Has Seen Snow; A Sleepin' Bee; Two Ladies in de Shade of de Banana Tree.

Houston, words and music by Lee Hazlewood (1965). In the style of a Western ballad. It was introduced and popularized by Dean Martin in a Reprise recording.

How About You?, words by Ralph Freed, music by Burton Lane (1941). The lyric is one of the rare instances in which one songwriter pays a tribute to another ("I Like a Gershwin tune, how about you?"). The song was introduced by Mickey Rooney and Judy Garland in the motion-picture musical *Babes on Broadway* (MGM, 1941). It was subsequently interpolated in the non-musical motion picture *Don't Bother*

to Knock, starring Marilyn Monroe and Richard Widmark (20th Century-Fox, 1952).

Howard, Joseph E., composer and lyricist, born New York City, 1867; died Chicago, Illinois, 1961.

See: Blow the Smoke Away: Goodbye, My Lady Love; Hello, Ma Baby; I Wonder Who's Kissing Her Now; When You First Kissed the Last Girl You Loved.

For Joe E. Howard's screen biography, see *I Wonder Who's Kissing Her Now* (20th Century-Fox, 1947).

How Are Things in Glocca Morra?, words by E. Y. Harburg, music by Burton Lane (1946). Irish ballad introduced by Ella Logan in the musical play *Finian's Rainbow* (1947). It was further popularized by Dick Haymes in a Decca recording.

How Blue the Night, words by Harold Adamson, music by Jimmy McHugh (1944). Introduced by Dick Haymes in the motion picture *Four Jills and a Jeep,* starring Kay Francis and Carole Lombard (20th Century-Fox, 1944).

How Can I Wait?, words by Alan Jay Lerner, music by Frederick Loewe (1951). Introduced by Olga San Juan in the musical play *Paint Your Wagon* (1951).

How Come You Do Me Like You Do?, words and music by Gene Austin and Roy Bergere (1924). Popularized by Gene Austin. It was interpolated in the motion-picture musical *That's the Spirit,* starring Peggy Ryan and Jack Oakie (Universal, 1945), sung by Peggy Ryan and Jimmy Coy. Betty Grable sang it in the motion-picture musical *Three for the Show* Columbia, 1955).

How Could You Believe Me When I Said I Loved You? (When You Know I've Been a Liar All My Life), words by Alan Jay Lerner, music by Burton Lane (1950). The title is probably one of the longest ever concocted for a popular song. The song was introduced by Fred Astaire, Jane Powell and Nick Castle in the motion-picture musical *The Royal Wedding* (MGM, 1951).

How Deep Is the Ocean?, words and music by Irving Berlin (1932). It was written several years before its publication, the delay due to the fact that Berlin did not consider it top-drawer. Nevertheless, it went on to become one of the leading song hits of 1932. It was later interpolated in several motion pictures. Among them were *Alexander's Ragtime Band* (20th Century-Fox, 1938); *Blue Skies* (MGM, 1946), sung by Bing Crosby and a female chorus; and *Meet Danny Wilson* (Universal, 1952), sung by Frank Sinatra.

How Do You Speak to an Angel?, words by Bob Hilliard, music by Jule Styne (1952). Introduced by John Howard in the musical *Hazel Flagg* (1953). It was interpolated in the motion picture *Living It Up* (Paramount, 1954), sung by Dean Martin.

How Dry I Am, a perennial favorite of people in the happy state of inebriation. The author of the ribald verses is not known. The melody comes from (of all places!) a religious hymn, "Happy Day," music by an English scholar, Edward F. Rimbault; it was first published in 1891.

How'd You Like to Be My Daddy?, words by Sam M. Lewis and Joe Young, music by Ted Snyder (1918). Interpolated by Al Jolson in the Winter Garden extravaganza *Sinbad* (1918).

How'd You Like to Spoon with Me?, words by Edward Laska, music by Jerome Kern (1905). Kern's first American song hit (though he had previously written a song hit in London). It was interpolated in the musical *The Earl and the Girl* (1905), sung by Georgia Caine and Victor Morley, supported by six girls swinging on flower-decorated swings. The number stopped the show; the *Dramatic Mirror* called it "the most successful . . . ever produced here; it was demanded again and again." The song was revived in the Jerome Kern screen biography *Till the Clouds Roll By* (MGM, 1946), sung by Angela Lansbury.

How High the Moon, words by Nancy Hamilton, music by Morgan Lewis (1940). Introduced by Frances Com-

stock and Alfred Drake in the revue *Two for the Show* (1940). It was popularized by Benny Goodman and his orchestra (vocal by Helen Forrest) in a best-selling Columbia recording. It was subsequently revived in a Capitol recording by Les Paul and Mary Ford that sold over a million disks. Ella Fitzgerald's recording for Decca was also a best seller. In this version she presented it as a fast scat number; but she also recorded it as a ballad, for Verve.

How I Love My Lou, words by Joseph Herbert, music by John Stromberg (1897). Introduced in the Weber and Fields extravaganza *Glad Hand* (1897), then repeated the same year in the Weber and Fields extravaganza *Pousse Café*.

How Important Can It Be?, words and music by Bennie Benjamin and Georgia Weiss (1955). Popularized in two best-selling recordings: Joni James for MGM and Sarah Vaughan for Mercury.

How Little It Matters, How Little We Know, words by Carolyn Leigh, music by Philip Springer (1956). Introduced and popularized by Frank Sinatra in a Capitol recording. The release in the chorus is of harmonic interest because of unusual chord progressions.

How Little We Know, words by Johnny Mercer, music by Hoagy Carmichael (1944). Introduced by Hoagy Carmichael in the non-musical motion picture *To Have and Have Not*, starring Humphrey Bogart (Warner, 1944). It was later interpolated in the non-musical motion picture *Dark Passage*, starring Humphrey Bogart and Lauren Bacall (Warner, 1947).

How Long Has This Been Going On?, words by Ira Gershwin, music by George Gershwin (1928). Introduced by Bobbe Arnst in the musical *Rosalie* (1928). The song had been written for the musical *Funny Face*, but was dropped from that show during out-of-town tryouts, to be replaced by "He Loves and She Loves." This is one of many lyrics by Ira Gershwin in which he exploits some popular expression of the day. The song was interpolated in the motion-picture adaptation of *Funny Face* (Paramount, 1957), sung by Audrey Hepburn.

How Many Hearts Have You Broken?, words by Marty Symes, music by Al Kaufman (1943). Introduced and popularized in 1944 by the Three Sons in a Hit recording.

How Many Times Have I Said I Love You?, words and music by Irving Berlin (1926). Popularized in vaudeville by Lillian Roth. It was interpolated in the motion-picture musical *The Time, The Place and The Girl* (Warner, 1929).

How Much Is That Doggie in the Window?, words and music by Bob Merrill (1953). Popularized by Patti Page in a Mercury recording that sold over a million disks.

How Sweet You Are, words by Frank Loesser, music by Arthur Schwartz (1943). Introduced in the motion-picture musical *Thank Your Lucky Stars* (Warner, 1943) by Dinah Shore.

How the West Was Won, words by Ken Darby, music by Alfred Newman (1963). Title song of the motion-picture spectacle starring Henry Fonda, James Stewart, Debbie Reynolds among others (MGM, 1963), where it was used in the background music as a recurrent theme.

How to Handle a Woman, words by Alan Jay Lerner, music by Frederick Loewe (1960). Introduced by Richard Burton in the musical *Camelot* (1960).

How to Succeed in Business Without Really Trying, a musical comedy with book by Abe Burrows, Jack Weinstock and Willie Gilbert based on Shepherd Mead's book of the same name. Lyrics and music by Frank Loesser. It received the Pulitzer Prize in drama. Starring Robert Morse and Rudy Vallée (1961). Original cast recording (RCA Victor).
See: Brotherhood of Man; Grand Old Ivy; I Believe in You.

How Ya Gonna Keep 'em Down on the Farm? (After They've Seen Paree), words by Sam M. Lewis and Joe Young, music by Walter Donaldson (1919). Comedy song popularized in vaudeville by Sophie Tucker and

by Eddie Cantor. It was interpolated in the motion-picture musicals *For Me and My Gal* (MGM, 1942), in which it was sung by Judy Garland, and *The Eddie Cantor Story* (Warner, 1954), in the latter sung on the soundtrack by Cantor.

A Hubba Hubba Hubba (or, Dig You Later), words by Harold Adamson, music by Jimmy McHugh (1945). Introduced by Perry Como in the motion-picture musical *Doll Face* (20th Century-Fox, 1945). Como's RCA Victor recording (in collaboration with the Satisfiers) sold over a million disks.

Huguette Waltz. *See:* Waltz Huguette.

Humming Bird, words and music by Don Robertson (1955). Introduced by Lou Robertson in an Epic recording and popularized in a Capitol recording by Les Paul and Mary Ford.

A Hundred Million Miracles, words by Oscar Hammerstein II, music by Richard Rodgers (1958). Introduced by Miyoshi Umeki, Conrad Yama, Keye Luke, Juanita Hall and Rose Quong in the musical *Flower Drum Song* (1958). Miyoshi Umeki and others sang it in the motion-picture adaptation of the musical (Universal, 1961).

The Hunters of Kentucky, words by Samuel Woodworth to the melody of "Miss Bailey's Ghost," also known as "Miss Bailey" (1826). The words were written in 1815 to honor the riflemen of Kentucky at the Battle of New Orleans. Words and music were introduced in 1826 by a singer known simply as "Yankee Hill." It became a campaign song for the Presidential election of Andrew Jackson.

Hupfeld, Herman, composer and lyricist, born Montclair, New Jersey, 1894.
See: Are You Makin' Any Money?; As Time Goes By; Let's Put Out the Lights; Sing Something Simple; When Yuba Plays the Rumba on His Tuba.

Hurly Burly, a Weber and Fields musical extravaganza, with book and lyrics by Edgar Smith, music by John Stromberg. Starring Weber and

Fields, David Warfield and Fay Templeton (1898).

See: Kiss Me, Honey, Do; Life Is Only What You Make It.

Hurray for Baffin's Bay, words by Vincent Bryan, music by Charles Zimmerman (1903). Comedy number interpolated in the musical extravaganza *The Wizard of Oz* (1903), introduced by David Montgomery and Fred Stone.

Hurry! It's Lovely Up Here, words by Alan Jay Lerner, music by Burton Lane (1965). Introduced by Barbara Harris in the musical *On a Clear Day You Can See Forever* (1965).

Hurt, words and music by Jimmie Crane and Al Jacobs (1953). It was introduced in an Epic recording by Roy Hamilton, but it became popular a decade later, in 1962, in a Liberty recording by Timi Yuro.

Hush, Hush, Sweet Charlotte, words by Mack David, music by Frank De Vol (1965). Title song of a non-musical motion picture starring Bette Davis (20th Century-Fox, 1965), sung on the soundtrack by Al Martino. The song was further popularized by Patti Page in a best-selling Columbia recording.

Hut Sut Song words and music by Leo V. Killian, Ted McMichael and Jack Owens (1939). Nonsense song with lyrics supposedly utilizing Swedish double talk. It was popularized by Freddy Martin and his orchestra. It was interpolated in the motion picture *San Antonio Rose,* starring Jane Frazee (Universal, 1941), where it was sung by the Merry Macs. It was also heard in the non-musical motion picture *From Here to Eternity,* starring Burt Lancaster, Frank Sinatra and Montgomery Clift (Columbia, 1953).

I

I Ain't Down Yet, words and music by Meredith Willson (1960). Introduced by Tammy Grimes and a male quartet in the opening scene of the musical *The Unsinkable Molly Brown* (1960). In the motion-picture adaptation of the musical (MGM, 1964), it was sung by Debbie Reynolds and a male quartet.

I Ain't Got Nobody, words by Roger Graham, music by Spencer Williams and Dave Peyton (1916). A standard in Bert Williams' repertory. It was also featured successfully by Sophie Tucker in vaudeville. It was revived successfully in 1928, then was interpolated into the motionpicture musical *Atlantic City* (Republic, 1944).

I Ain't Nobody's Darling, words by Elmer Hughes, music by Robert A. King (1921). It subsequently became popular in various parodies.

I Almost Lost My Mind words and music by Ivory Joe Hunter (1950). Introduced by Ivory Joe Hunter and first popularized by him in 1950 in an MGM recording. It was revived in 1956 by Pat Boone in a Dot recording that sold a million disks.

I Am Loved, words and music by Cole Porter (1950). Introduced by Patricia Gillette in the musical *Out of This World* (1950).

I Apologize, words and music by Al Hoffman, Al Goodhart and Ed Nelson (1931). Revived in 1951 by Billy Eckstein in a best-selling MGM recording.

I Believe, words and music by Ervin Drake, Irvin Graham, Jimmy Shirl and Al Stillman (1952). Introduced in the TV production *USA Canteen* by Jane Froman, whose Capitol recording in 1953 was a best seller. It was further popularized in 1953 by Frankie Laine in a Columbia recording. According to statistics compiled by the makers of Lucky Strike cigarettes, sponsors of the Hit Parade, "I Believe" was the most successful song of 1953.

I Believe in You, words and music by Frank Loesser (1961). A hymn of self-confidence introduced by Robert Morse (with the assistance of Paul Reed, Charles Nelson Reilly and ensemble) in the musical *How to Succeed in Business Without Really Trying* (1961).

I Caint Say No, words by Oscar Hammerstein II, music by Richard Rodgers (1943). Ado Annie's sad lament over her lack of resistance to the opposite sex in the musical play *Oklahoma!* (1943), where it was introduced by Celeste Holm. In the motion-picture adaptation of the musical (Magna Theatre, 1955), it was sung by Gloria Grahame.

I Can Dance with Everyone But My Wife, words by Joseph Cawthorn and John Golden, music by John Golden (1916). Introduced by Joseph Cawthorn in the musical *Sybil* (1916). Daniel Frohman, producer of the show, maintained that this song was responsible for transforming the musical comedy from a failure to a success.

I Can Dream, Can't I?, words by Irving Kahal, music by Sammy Fain (1937). Introduced by Tamara in the musical *Right This Way* (1938). The Decca recording by the Andrews Sisters in 1949 sold a million disks.

I Can Get It for You Wholesale, a musical comedy with book by Jerome Weidman based on his own novel of the same name. Lyrics and music by Harold Rome. Starring Barbra Streisand (in her Broadway debut), Lillian Roth and Harold Lang 1962). Original cast recording (Columbia).

See: Have I Told You Lately?; The Sound of Money.

I Can't Be Bothered Now, words by Ira Gershwin, music by George Gershwin (1937). Introduced by Fred Astaire in the motion-picture musical *Damsel in Distress* (RKO, 1937.).

I Can't Begin to Tell You, words by Mack Gordon, music by James V. Monaco (1945). Introduced by Betty Grable in the motion-picture musical *The Dolly Sisters* (20th Century-Fox, 1945), and reprised in the final scene by Miss Grable and John Payne. It was popularized by Bing Crosby in a Decca recording.

I Can't Believe That You're in Love with Me, words by Clarence Gaskill, music by Jimmy McHugh (1926). Introduced by Aida Ward at the Cotton Club in Harlem, New York. It was revived in and became the theme song of the non-musical motion picture *The Caine Mutiny*, starring Humphrey Bogart (Columbia, 1954). Connie Francis sang it in the motion-picture musical *Looking for Love* (MGM, 1964).

I Can't Do This Sum, words by Glen MacDonough, music by Victor Herbert (1903). Introduced by Mable Barrison and a chorus of children (the children tapping out the rhythm of the chorus with chalk on slates) in the musical extravaganza *Babes in Toyland* (1903). In the motion-picture adaptation of the musical (MGM, 1934), the number was done by Charlotte Henry and a group of children.

I Can't Escape from You, words by Leo Robin, music by Richard A. Whiting (1936). Introduced by Bing Crosby in the motion-picture musical *Rhythm on the Range* (Paramount, 1936).

I Can't Get Started with You, words by Ira Gershwin, music by Vernon Duke (1936). Introduced by Bob Hope and Eve Arden in the revue *Ziegfeld Follies of 1936*.

In *Have Tux, Will Travel* Bob Hope wrote: " 'I Can't Get Started with You' put me in pictures. Mitchell Leisen and Harlan Thompson (two Hollywood workers who were preparing a script for the *Big Broadcast of 1936* for Paramount) saw me do the number with Eve and hired me."

Variety singled out the song, and its rendition, as the "standout ditty" of the *Follies* that year. The song was subsequently popularized by Bunny Berrigan—first in an Okeh recording where he both played and sang, and later in a best-selling RCA Victor release—to become one of the standout numbers in his repertory.

I Can't Get You Out of My Heart (or, Ti Amo, Ti Voglio Amor), words and music by Danny DiMinno and Jimmy Crane (1958). Popularized in 1959 by Al Martino in a 20th Century-Fox recording.

I Can't Give You Anything But Love, Baby, words by Dorothy Fields, music by Jimmy McHugh (1928). Introduced by Patsy Kelly in the revue *Delmar's Revels* (1927). This show closed within two weeks. When Lew Leslie's *Blackbirds of 1928* was being mounted, the song was interpolated in that show for Aida Ward, in her Broadway debut. She sang it in collaboration with Willard MacLean and Bill Robinson. Later, during the run of the show, the song was taken over by Adelaide Hall.

The idea for this song came to the writers one day when they stopped outside of Tiffany's on Fifth Avenue, in New York, and overheard a young man tell his girl, "Gee, honey, I can't give you nothin' but love."

The success of this number was

advanced through remarkable jazz performances on disks by Louis Armstrong for Decca, Benny Goodman for RCA Victor, and "Fats" Waller for RCA Victor. By 1965 this song had almost four hundred and fifty different recordings, and had sold well over two and one half million disks in all. Katharine Hepburn sang it briefly in the non-musical motion picture *Bringing Up Baby* (Columbia, 1938). It was heard in and gave the title to a motion picture starring Broderick Crawford and Peggy Moran (Universal, 1940). It was also heard in several later movies. These include *Seven Sinners,* starring John Wayne and Marlene Dietrich (Universal, 1940); *True to the Army,* starring Judy Canova and Allan Jones (Paramount, 1942), sung by Allan Jones; *Stormy Weather* (20th Century-Fox, 1943), sung by Lena Horne; *Jam Session* (Universal, 1944); *So This Is Paris* starring Tony Curtis (Universal, 1955), sung by Gloria De Haven with French lyrics; *The Eddy Duchin Story* (Columbia, 1956); *The Helen Morgan Story* (Warner, 1957), sung on the soundtrack by Gogi Grant (for Ann Blyth).

I Can't Go On, words and music by Antoine "Fats" Domino and Dave Bartholomew (1955). Popularized by "Fats" Domino in an Imperial recording.

I Can't Help It If I'm Still in Love with You, words and music by Hank Williams (1951). Introduced and popularized by Hank Williams in an MGM recording. It was sung on the soundtrack by Hank Williams, Jr. (for George Hamilton) in the screen biography of Hank Williams, Sr., *Your Cheatin' Heart* (MGM, 1964).

I Can't Stop Loving You, words and music by Don Gibson (1958). Introduced by Don Gibson and popularized by Kitty Wells in a Decca recording. It was revived in 1962 by the Ray Charles Singers in a best-selling ABC-Paramount recording that received the Gold Record Award.

I Can't Tell Why I Love You, But I Do, words by Will D. Cobb, music by Gus Edwards (1900). The first hit song by the then newly founded songwriting team of Cobb and Edwards. It was revived in several motion pictures, including *The Belle of the Yukon,* starring Randolph Scott and Gypsy Rose Lee (RKO, 1944); *In Old Sacramento,* starring Bill Elliott (Republic, 1946); and *Somebody Loves Me* (Paramount, 1952).

Ice Cream, words by Sheldon Harnick, music by Jerry Bock (1963). A mock aria in pseudo-operatic style introduced by Barbara Cook in the musical *She Loves Me* (1963).

I Concentrate on You, words and music by Cole Porter (1939). Introduced by Douglas MacPhail in the motion-picture musical *The Broadway Melody of 1940.*

I Could Go On Singing, words by E. Y. Harburg, music by Harold Arlen (1963). Title song of a motion-picture musical (United Artists, 1963), introduced by Judy Garland.

I Could Have Danced All Night, words by Alan Jay Lerner, music by Frederick Loewe (1956). Introduced by Julie Andrews in the musical play *My Fair Lady* (1956), and further popularized by Sylvia Syms in a Decca recording. In the motion-picture adaptation of the musical (Warner, 1964), it was sung on the soundtrack by Marni Nixon (for Audrey Hepburn).

I Could Have Told You, words by Carl Sigman, music by James Van Heusen (1954). Popularized by Frank Sinatra in a Capitol recording.

I Couldn't Sleep a Wink Last Night, words by Harold Adamson, music by Jimmy McHugh (1943). Introduced by Frank Sinatra in his screen debut in *Higher and Higher* (RKO, 1943). It was interpolated in the motion picture *The Blue Veil,* starring Jane Wyman and Charles Laughton (RKO, 1951).

I Couldn't Stand to See My Baby Lose, words by Will D. Cobb, music by Gus Edwards (1899). The first collaborative effort of the songwriting team of Cobb and Edwards. It was introduced in vaudeville by May Irwin.

I Could Write a Book, words by Lorenz

Hart, music by Richard Rodgers (1940). Introduced by Gene Kelly and Leila Ernst in the musical *Pal Joey* (1940). In the motion-picture adaptation of the musical (Columbia, 1957), it was sung by Frank Sinatra.

I Cover the Waterfront, words by Edward Heyman, music by John Green (1933). Written to exploit the motion picture of the same name, starring Claudette Colbert and Ben Lyon (United Artists, 1933). The picture was completed before the song was written; and the song was not included on the soundtrack of the original first-release print of the film. But after being introduced over the radio by Ben Bernie and his orchestra, the song became such a hit that subsequent prints of the movie were rescored to include the melody. Among those who helped to popularize the number were Frank Sinatra in a Columbia recording and Artie Shaw and his orchestra for RCA Victor.

I Cried a Tear, words and music by Al Julia and Fred Jay (1958). Popularized in 1959 by Lavern Baker in an Atlantic recording.

I Cried for You, words by Arthur Freed, music by Gus Arnheim and Abe Lyman (1923). One of Arthur Freed's earliest lyrics. The song was introduced by Abe Lyman and his orchestra, but was popularized by Glen Gray and his Casa Loma Orchestra. The first Glen Gray recording of this song had vocals by Kenny Sargent, who helped create a vogue for boy singers before Frank Sinatra. The song was revived in several motion pictures, including the musicals *Babes in Arms* (MGM, 1939), sung by Judy Garland, and *Somebody Loves Me* (Paramount, 1952).

Ida, Sweet As Apple Cider, words and music by Eddie Leonard (1903). Eddie Leonard, the last of the great minstrels, wrote the song while appearing with the Primose and West company. The manager of this minstrel troupe permitted Leonard to introduce this number in 1903 only because he planned on firing Leonard anyway. The song brought down the house. At the same time it saved Leonard's job. Eddie Leonard sang it again in the Broadway musical written for him, *Roly Boly Eyes* (1919).

This song is also intimately associated with Eddie Cantor, who used to sing it as a personal tribute to his wife, Ida, whom he married in 1914. Cantor sang it for the first time in 1912 as a boy performer with Gus Edwards in the vaudeville revue *Kid Kabaret;* here Cantor did an impersonation of Eddie Leonard. The song was interpolated in the motion-picture musical *The Eddie Cantor Story* (Warner, 1954), Cantor singing it on the soundtrack. It was also interpolated in the screen biography of Texas Guinan, *Incendiary Blonde* (Paramount, 1945).

The 1927 Brunswick recording by Red Nichols and the Five Pennies was a best seller—indeed, one of the few popular disks up to then to sell over a million copies.

I'd Climb the Highest Mountain, words by Lew Brown, music by Sidney Clare (1926). Popularized in vaudeville by Sophie Tucker and by Lillian Roth.

I'd Do It Again, words and music by Raymond Jessel and Marian Grudeff (1965). Introduced by Inga Swenson in the musical *Baker Street* (1965).

I Didn't Know What Time It Was, words by Lorenz Hart, music by Richard Rodgers (1939). Introduced by Marcy Westcott and Dick Kollmar in the musical *Too Many Girls* (1939). It was sung by Frances Langford (for Lucille Ball) on the soundtrack in the motion-picture adaptation of the musical (RKO, 1940). It was interpolated for Frank Sinatra in the motion-picture adaptation of the Rodgers and Hart musical *Pal Joey* (Columbia, 1957).

I Didn't Raise My Boy to Be a Soldier, words by Alfred Bryan, music by Al Piantadosi (1915). Its success reflected the anti-war sentiment in the United States during the early years of World War I. The sheet-music cover depicted a gray-haired old woman protecting her son while shells burst all around them. When pacifism died down in America, and a war spirit was rapidly being generated, numerous songs were written to reply to the sentiments expressed in this number. These included "I Did Not Raise My Boy to Be a Coward," and "I Didn't Raise My Boy to be a Soldier, But I'll Send My Girl to Be a Nurse." When the United States finally declared war on Germany, these song replies multiplied. Some of the most popular were "I Didn't Raise my Boy to Be a Molly Coddle," "I Didn't Raise My Boy to Be a Soldier But He'll Fight for the U.S.A." and "I Didn't Raise My Boy to Be a Slacker."

In or about 1916 "I Didn't Raise My Boy to Be a Soldier" was involved in a plagiarism suit. A composer by the name of Cohalin claimed that Piantadosi had lifted his melody from Cohalin's far less successful number "How Much I Really Cared." Since the melodies of these two songs were similar—and since Piantadosi had once worked for Cohalin's publisher before writing his own song, and thus had come into direct association with the earlier published number—the court ruled in Cohalin's favor.

I Didn't Slip, I Wasn't Pushed, I Fell, words and music by Eddie Pola and George Wyle (1950). Popularized by Doris Day in a Columbia recording.

I'd Leave My Happy Home for You, words by Will A. Heelan, music by Harry von Tilzer (1899). A novelty coon song with a popular "oo-oo" refrain. Though introduced in vaudeville by Annette Flagler, it was popularized by Blanche Ring, who sang it for the first time in 1899 at Tony Pastor's Music Hall in New York. Her first major success on the stage came with this performance.

Harry von Tilzer once revealed to Sigmund Spaeth the circumstances surrounding the writing of this ballad. "In 1897 Harry von Tilzer was pianist for a show, *The Prodigal Father,* playing in Hartford, Con-

necticut. After the first performance, a girl stopped von Tilzer and told him of her ambition to go on the stage. He did not take her seriously, and lightly advised her to come along with him after the show's run was over. To his surprise, when the show closed on Saturday night, he found the girl waiting for him at the stage door with packed valise. He also discovered then that she was the daughter of one of the city's wealthiest families." Von Tilzer then tried convincing her she was making a grave mistake, but she replied: "I'd leave my happy home for you." Her remark sparked him into writing his song.

Idle Dreams, words by Arthur Jackson, music by George Gershwin (1920). The most significant of Gershwin's songs in the first of his scores for *George White's Scandals,* in 1920. It was introduced there by Lloyd Garrett.

I'd Like to See a Little More of You, words by Will D. Cobb, music by Gus Edwards (1906). Introduced by a bevy of girls undressing—in a trick stage effect that made them finally seem to be nude—in the Anna Held musical *A Parisian Model* (1906).

I'd Like to See the Kaiser with a Lily in His Hand, words by Henry Leslie and Howard Johnson, music by Billy Frisch (1918). One of the more popular anti-Kaiser songs during World War I. It was interpolated in the Sigmund Romberg musical *Doing Our Bit* (1917).

I'd Like to Wander with Alice in Wonderland, words by James F. Tanner, music by Jerome Kern (1914). Introduced in Jerome Kern's first successful musical, *The Girl from Utah* (1914).

I'd Love to Live in Loveland (with a Girl Like You), words and music by W. R. Williams (1910). A favorite with barber-shop quartets.

I, Don Quixote. *See:* Man of La Mancha.

I Don't Care, words by Jean Lenox, music by Harry O. Sutton (1905). A song made famous in vaudeville by Eva Tanguay and which, in turn, brought her outstanding success. Her loud, brassy, boisterous delivery —as she strutted up and down the stage—became so much of a trademark that henceforth she became identified as the "I Don't Care Girl." The song was revived for Judy Garland in the motion-picture musical *In the Good Old Summertime* (MGM, 1949). It was sung by Mitzi Gaynor in Eva Tanguay's screen biography *The I Don't Care Girl* (20th Century-Fox, 1953).

The I Don't Care Girl, a motion-picture musical biography of Eva Tanguay, starring Mitzi Gaynor as Miss Tanguay (20th Century-Fox, 1953). The score was made up of standards.

See: Hello, Frisco; I Don't Care; On the Mississippi; Pretty Baby.

I Don't Care If the Sun Don't Shine, words and music by Mack David (1949).

I Don't Care If You Never Come Back, words and music by Monroe H. Rosenfeld (1897). Popularized in vaudeville by Bert Williams, then a member of the team of Williams and Walker.

I Don't Hurt Anymore, words by Jack Rollins, music by Don Robertson (1954). Leading song of the year in the country field. It was popularized in recordings by Dinah Washington for Mercury and Hank Snow for RCA Victor.

I Don't Know Enough About You, words and music by Peggy Lee and David Barbour (1946). This number started singer Peggy Lee on a successful songwriting career. It was popularized by her recording for Capitol.

I Don't Know Where I'm Going, But I'm On My Way, words and music by George Fairman (1917). World War I hit song inspired by the draft.

I Don't Know Why I Love You Like I Do, words by Roy Turk, music by Fred E. Ahlert (1931).

I Don't Want to Get Well, words by Howard Johnson and Harry Pease, music by Harry Jentes (1917). World War I lament of a doughboy in love with a beautiful nurse.

I Don't Want to Play in Your Yard, words by Philip Wingate, music by H. W. Petrie (1894). A child's song, the lyrics imitating children's talk. Petrie's sequel, "You Can't Play in Our Yard Any More," published later in 1894, was a failure.

I Don't Want to Set the World On Fire, words and music by Eddie Seiler, Sol Marcus, Bennie Benjamin and Eddie Durham (1941). Though Bennie Benjamin spent three years trying to find a publisher for this song, it became one of the year's leading song hits, following its belated publication. It was introduced by Harlan Leonard and his Kansas City Rockets in a Bluebird recording and popularized by the Mills Brothers in a Decca release. It was interpolated in the British-made motion picture *Passport to Pimlico*.

I Don't Want to Walk Without You, words by Frank Loesser, music by Jule Styne (1941). Introduced by Johnnie Johnston in the motion-picture musical *Sweater Girl*, starring Eddie Bracken (Paramount, 1942). It was popularized in recordings by Harry James and his orchestra for Columbia, and by Bing Crosby for Decca.

I Don't Want Your Kisses, words and music by Fred Fisher and M. M. Broones (1929). Introduced in the motion picture *So This Is College*, starring Elliott Nugent and Cliff Edwards (MGM, 1929).

I'd Rather Be Right, a political-conscious musical comedy with book by George S. Kaufman and Moss Hart. Lyrics by Lorenz Hart. Music by Richard Rodgers. Starring George M. Cohan as President Franklin D. Roosevelt (1937).

See: Have You Met Miss Jones?

I Dream of Jeanie, a motion-picture musical biography of Stephen Foster, starring Ray Middleton as Foster with Muriel Lawrence (Republic, 1952). The score was made up of Stephen Foster songs.

See: De Camptown Races; Come Where My Love Lies Dreaming; Jeanie with the Light Brown Hair; My Old Kentucky Home; Oh, Susanna; Old Dog Tray; Old Folks at Home.

I Dream of Jeanie with the Light

Brown Hair. *See:* Jeanie with the Light Brown Hair.

I Dream Too Much, words by Dorothy Fields, music by Jerome Kern (1935). Introduced by Lily Pons in the motion-picture musical of the same name (RKO, 1935). This song is of special musical interest for its chromatic harmonies and for the leap of a minor ninth in the melody.

I Dream Too Much, a motion-picture musical starring Lily Pons and Henry Fonda (RKO, 1935). Songs by Dorothy Fields and Jerome Kern.
    See: I Dream Too Much; Jockey on the Carousel.

I'd Still Believe You True, words and music by Paul Dresser (1900). Ballad popularized by Charles Kent.

I Enjoy Being a Girl, words by Oscar Hammerstein II, music by Richard Rodgers (1958). Introduced by Pat Suzuki (in her Broadway stage debut) in the musical *Flower Drum Song* (1958). In the motion-picture adaptation of the musical (Universal, 1961), it was sung by Nancy Kwan.

If a Girl Like You Loved a Boy Like Me, words by Will D. Cobb, music by Gus Edwards (1905).

I Fall in Love Too Easily, words by Sammy Cahn, music by Jule Styne (1944). Introduced by Frank Sinatra in the motion-picture musical *Anchors Aweigh* (MGM, 1945).

If a Man Answers, words and music by Bobby Darin (1962). Introduced by Bobby Darin in the motion picture of the same name (Universal, 1962), and popularized by him in a Capitol recording.

If Dreams Come True, words by Al Stillman, music by Robert Allen (1958). Popularized by Pat Boone in a Dot recording.

I Feel a Song Comin' On, words by Dorothy Fields and George Oppenheim, music by Jimmy McHugh (1935). Introduced by Frances Langford in the motion picture *Every Night at Eight,* starring Alice Faye and George Raft (Paramount, 1935). It was interpolated in the motion-picture musical *Follow the Boys* (Universal, 1944).

I Feel At Home with You, words by Lorenz Hart, music by Richard Rodgers (1927). Introduced by Jack Thompson and June Cochrane in the musical *A Connecticut Yankee* (1927). It was also sung in the motion-picture adaptation of the musical (Fox, 1931).

I Feel Like a Feather in the Breeze, words by Mack Gordon, music by Harry Revel (1936). Introduced in the motion-picture musical *Collegiate,* starring Jack Penner and Betty Grable (Paramount, 1936).

I Feel Pretty, words by Stephen Sondheim, music by Leonard Bernstein (1957). Introduced by Carol Lawrence in the musical play *West Side Story* (1957). In the motion-picture adaptation of the musical (Mirisch, 1961), it was sung on the soundtrack by Marni Nixon (for Natalie Wood).

If Ever I Would Leave You, words by Alan Jay Lerner, music by Frederick Loewe (1960). Introduced by Robert Goulet in the musical play *Camelot* (1960), and popularized by him in a Columbia recording.

If He Can Fight Like He Can Love, Good Night Germany, words by Grant Clarke and Howard E. Rogers, music by George W. Meyer (1918). Comedy hit song of World War I popularized by Rae Samuels.

If He Comes In, I'm Going Out, words by Richard C. McPherson, using the pen name of Cecil Mack, music by Chris Smith (1910).

If I Could Be with You One Hour Tonight, words and music by Henry Creamer and Jimmy Johnson (1926). Interpolated by Lillian Roth in the motion picture *Ladies They Talk About* (Paramount, 1930). It was subsequently heard in the non-musical motion picture *Flamingo Road,* starring Joan Crawford (Warner, 1949), in which it was briefly sung by Miss Crawford and used as a recurrent theme, and was sung by Danny Thomas in the motion-picture musical *The Jazz Singer* (Warner, 1953).

If I Didn't Care, words and music by Jack Lawrence (1939). Popularized by the Ink Spots, whose Decca recording was the most successful they had made up to then.

If I Didn't Have a Dime, words and music by Bert Russell and Phil Medley (1962). Popularized by Gene Pitney in a Musicor recording.

If I Forget You, words and music by Irving Caesar (1933). Popularized in vaudeville and over the radio by James Melton, and by Frank Sinatra in a Columbia recording.

If I Gave You, words and music by Timothy Gray and Hugh Martin (1964). Introduced by Louise Troy and Edward Woodward in the musical *High Spirits* (1964).

If I Give My Heart to You, words and music by Jimmie Crane, Al Jacobs and Jimmy Brewster (1954). Popularized by Doris Day in a Columbia recording.

If I Had a Hammer, words and music by Lee Hays and Pete Seeger (1963). Popularized by Trini Lopez in a Reprise recording.

If I Had a Talking Picture of You, words by Bud De Sylva and Lew Brown, music by Ray Henderson (1929). Introduced by Janet Gaynor and Charles Farrell in the motion-picture musical *Sunny Side Up* (Fox, 1929).

If I Had My Life to Live Over, words by Henry Tobias, Larry Vincent and Moe Jaffe (1939). Waltz popularized by Kate Smith over radio and in a Columbia recording.

If I Had My Way, words by Lou Klein, music by James Kendis (1913). Popularized by barber-shop quartets. It provided the title for and was featured in a motion picture starring Bing Crosby (Universal, 1940). It was sung by Gail Storm and Phil Regan in the motion-picture musical *Sunbonnet Sue* (Monogram, 1946).

If I Had You, words and music by Ted Shapiro, Jimmy Campbell and Reginald Connelly (1928). Introduced and popularized by Rudy Vallée. It was revived by Dan Dailey in the motion-picture musical *You Were Meant for Me* (20th Century-Fox, 1948).

If I Knew You Were Comin' I'd 'Ave Baked a Cake, words and music by Al Hoffman, Bob Merrill and Clem Watts (1950). Popularized by Eileen Barton, whose National recording sold over a million disks.

If I Loved You, words by Oscar Hammerstein II, music by Richard Rodgers (1945). Introduced by John Raitt and Jan Clayton in the musical play *Carousel* (1945). In the motion-picture adaptation of the musical (20th Century-Fox, 1956), it was sung by Gordon MacRae and Shirley Jones. Chad and Jeremy made a best-selling recording for World Artists in 1965.

If I May, words and music by Charles Singleton and Rose Marie McCoy (1955). Popularized by Nat King Cole in a Capitol recording.

If I Should Lose You, words by Leo Robin, music by Ralph Rainger (1936). Introduced by Gladys Swarthout in the motion-picture musical *Rose of the Rancho* (Paramount, 1936).

If I Was a Millionaire, words by Will D. Cobb, music by Gus Edwards (1910). Introduced in 1910 in a vaudeville revue written, produced and starred in by Gus Edwards; the rest of the cast was made up of child performers. The song was revived in the motion-picture musical *The Eddie Cantor Story* (Warner, 1954).

If I Were a Bell, words and music by Frank Loesser (1950). Introduced by Isabel Bigley in the musical *Guys and Dolls* (1950). In the motion-picture adaptation of the musical (MGM, 1955), it was sung by Jean Simmons.

If I Were on the Stage, words by Henry Blossom, music by Victor Herbert (1905). An extended song sequence introduced by Fritzi Scheff in the operetta *Mlle. Modiste* (1905). In it, the heroine, Fifi, tries to demonstrate her versatility as a singer by performing various types of songs—a gavotte, a polonaise, a dreamy waltz, and so forth. Originally, the hit waltz from this production, "Kiss Me Again," was part of this sequence.

If Only You Were Mine, words by Harry B. Smith, music by Victor Herbert (1899). Hit song from the operetta *The Singing Girl* (1899).

I Found a Million-Dollar Baby in a Five and Ten Cent Store, words by Mort Dixon and Billy Rose, music by Harry Warren (1931). Introduced by

Ted Healey, Phil Baker, Fanny Brice, Lew Brice and Betty Jane Watson in Billy Rose's revue *Crazy Quilt* (1931). It was interpolated in the motion-picture musical *Million Dollar Baby*, starring Arline Judge and Jimmy Fay (Monogram, 1935).

If the Man in the Moon Were a Coon, words and music by Fred Fisher (1906). Fisher's first outstanding hit, selling over three million copies of sheet music. Since it was published by a house founded that year by Fisher, this number helped to establish him not only as a songwriter but also as a publisher.

If There Is Someone Lovelier Than You, words by Howard Dietz, music by Arthur Schwartz (1934). Written in 1933 for a radio serial, *The Gibson Family*, then sung by Georges Metaxa in the musical play *Revenge with Music* (1934).

Arthur Schwartz told an interviewer: "It was originally called 'If There Is Someone Lovelier Than You, Then I Am Blind." I thought it was wonderful. I brought the melody back a few days later but told Dietz, who gave me the title, it should be shortened. He agreed." Of all his own songs, Schwartz regards this as his favorite.

If the Waters Could Speak As They Flow, words and music by Charles Graham (1887). Graham's first successful ballad.

If This Is Goodbye, words and music by Robert Wright and George Forrest, melody based on a theme from Rachmaninoff's Second Piano Concerto (1965). Introduced by Constance Towers and Michael Kermoyan in the musical *Anya* (1965).

If You Cared for Me, words by Ed Rose, music by Ted Snyder (1908). One of Ted Snyder's earliest song hits, and one of the first publications of the then recently founded firm of Ted Snyder Company.

If You Could Care for Me, words and music by Cole Porter (1920). An early Cole Porter song, introduced by Irene Bordoni in the musical *As You Were* (1920).

If You Feel Like Singing, Sing, words by Mack Gordon, music by Harry Warren (1950). Introduced by Judy Garland in the motion-picture musical *Summer Stock* (MGM, 1950).

If You Hadn't, But You Did, words by Betty Comden and Adolph Green, music by Jule Styne (1951). Introduced by Dolores Gray in the revue *Two on the Aisle* (1951).

If You Knew Susie, Like I Know Susie, words and music by Bud De Sylva and Joseph Meyer (1925). It was written for Al Jolson, who introduced it in the musical *Big Boy* (1925), where it proved a failure. Jolson then turned the number over to Eddie Cantor, saying: "I think this would fit you better than it does me." Eddie Cantor sang it for the first time at a benefit show in New York, where he brought down the house. Jolson, who was on the same bill, now told him: "Eddie, if I'd known that the song was *that* good, you dirty dog, you'd never have gotten it." The song became Eddie Cantor's specialty. He sang it on the soundtrack of the motion-picture musical *The Eddie Cantor Story* (Warner, 1954). He also sang it on the soundtrack under the titles of the motion-picture musical of the same name in which he starred and which he produced (RKO, 1948).

If You'll Be My Eve, words by James Weldon Johnson, music by J. Rosamond Johnson (1912). Introduced by Alice Lloyd in the musical *Little Miss Fix It* (1912).

If You See My Sweetheart, words and music by Paul Dresser (1897).

If You Were the Only Girl in the World, words by Clifford Grey, music by Nat D. Ayer (1925). Interpolated for Rudy Vallée in his first starring role in motion pictures, in *The Vagabond Lover* (RKO, 1929). It was successfully revived a quarter of a century later by Perry Como in a best-selling RCA Victor recording. Doris Day and Gordon MacRae sang it in the motion-picture musical *By the Light of the Silvery Moon* (Warner, 1953).

I Gave You Up Just Before You Threw Me Down, words by Bert Kalmar, music by Harry Ruby and Fred E.

Ahlert (1922). Popularized in vaudeville in the early 1920s by ballad singers.

I Get a Kick Out of You, words and music by Cole Porter (1934). Introduced by Ethel Merman and William Gaxton in the musical *Anything Goes* (1934). The song was heard only three minutes after the rise of the first-act curtain. This was most unusual, since musical comedies rarely offer an important song so early. But as Maurice Zolotow explained in *There's No People Like Show People:* "Miss Merman was equal to the situation. . . . She knocked the audience, totally unprepared, for a 'loop.'" Russel Crouse recalled that "after she finished 'I Get a Kick Out of You' she just couldn't do anything wrong for that audience."

Part of the impact of Merman's rendition came from the way in which she split the word "terrifically." She herself explained in her autobiography: "I paused in the song after the syllable 'rif.' It was just a way of phrasing, of breaking a word into syllables, and holding on to one syllable longer than I ordinarily would, but for some reason the pause killed the people."

Ethel Merman also sang "I Get a Kick Out of You" (with Bing Crosby) in the first motion-picture adaptation of the musical (Paramount, 1936). In the second (Paramount, 1956), it was sung by Mitzi Gaynor and Bing Crosby. The song was also interpolated in the Cole Porter screen biography *Night and Day* (Warner, 1946), where it was sung by Ginny Simms, and in the screen musical *On the Sunny Side of the Street* (Columbia, 1951).

I Get Along Without You Very Well (Except Sometimes), words by Jane Brown Thompson, music by Hoagy Carmichael (1939). This song has a curious history. At Indiana University, one of Carmichael's friends gave him a poem he thought might be suitable for a song. Carmichael wrote a melody for it, then forgot all about it. But a number of years later he came upon this song and

decided it was good enough to get published. However, before he could do so he had to identify the lyricist. Carmichael recruited Walter Winchell's assistance. The columnist read the opening lines of the poem during his radio broadcast, asking the audience to name the author if it could. Forty-eight people claimed the honor, but all proved fakes. Further investigation yielded the information that the poem had once been published in the old *Life* magazine, over the initials "J.B." At long last the authorship was traced to Mrs. Jane Brown Thompson of Philadelphia. The song was officially introduced by Dick Powell over the radio on January 19, 1940. Mrs. Brown, however, never heard the song. She died one day earlier—on January 18.

The song was interpolated in the motion picture *Las Vegas Story* (RKO, 1952), sung by Jane Russell and Hoagy Carmichael.

I Get Carried Away, words by Betty Comden and Adolph Green, music by Leonard Bernstein (1944). Comedy number introduced by Betty Comden and Adolph Green in Leonard Bernstein's first musical, *On the Town* (1944).

I Get Around, words and music by Brian Wilson (1964). Popularized by the Beach Boys in a Capitol recording.

I Get Ideas, an Argentine popular tango ("Adios Muchachos"), music by Sanders, English lyrics by Dorcas Cochran (1951). The song, with English lyrics, was popularized by Tony Martin in an RCA Victor recording.

I Got a Song, words by E. Y. Harburg, music by Harold Arlen (1944). Introduced by Richard Huey, a onetime redcap, in the musical *Bloomer Girl* (1944). He stopped the show regularly with this number. As Edward Jablonski revealed in his biography of Harold Arlen, *Happy with the Blues,* Huey had a difficult time mastering the rhythms of this song. "At one dress rehearsal, the night before opening, Huey simply walked off the stage without finishing the song. Arlen then decided perhaps they should write a new song for the spot, but Harburg refused; they had worked hard on the song and it must remain. Remain it did." In his rendition Huey was assisted by Dooley Wilson, Hubert Dilworth and chorus.

I Got a Woman (1954). Introduced and popularized in 1955 by Ray Charles in an Atlantic release, his first best seller.

I Got Everything I Want, words by Jack Lawrence, music by Stan Freeman (1964). Introduced by Karen Morrow in the musical *I Had a Ball* (1964).

I Got It Bad, and That Ain't Good, words by Paul Francis Webster, music by Duke Ellington (1941). Introduced by Ivie Anderson in *Jump for Joy* (1941), a Negro revue produced on the West Coast by the American Revue Theatre. The number was subsequently popularized by outstanding recordings by Duke Ellington and his orchestra for RCA Victor (with Ivie Anderson, vocalist) and by Ella Fitzgerald for Decca; the former is regarded by some jazz critics as Ivy Anderson's finest recorded performance.

I Got Lucky in the Rain, words by Harold Adamson, music by Jimmy McHugh (1948). Introduced by Bill Calhoun and Fran Warren (and danced to by Bill Calhoun and Kathryn Lee) in the musical *As the Girls Go* (1949).

I Got Plenty o' Nuthin', words by Ira Gershwin and Du Bose Heyward, music by George Gershwin (1935). Introduced by Todd Duncan in the folk opera *Porgy and Bess* (1935). In the motion-picture adaptation of the opera (Columbia, 1959), it was sung on the soundtrack by Robert McFerrin (for Sidney Poitier). The song was interpolated in the George Gershwin screen biography *Rhapsody in Blue* (Warner, 1945).

I Got Rhythm, words by Ira Gershwin, music by George Gershwin (1930). Introduced by Ethel Merman (in her Broadway debut) in the musical *Girl Crazy* (1930).

George Gershwin had written the melody some years earlier—in a slow tempo. But with new lyrics for *Girl Crazy* the tempo was speeded up and energized. This is one of three songs with which Ethel Merman hit the American theater for the first time with the force of a cyclone (the other two being "Sam and Delilah" and "Boy, What Love Has Done to Me"). If any single song can be said to have inaugurated her reign as queen of musical comedy, this is the one. She has since used it from time to time as her musical signature; and she lifted one of its phrases ("who can ask for anything more") for the title of her autobiography. Singing "I Got Rhythm," her "brassy voice struck on the consciousness of the audience like a sledge hammer," this editor wrote in his biography of George Gershwin. "She threw her voice across the footlights the way Louis Armstrong does the tones of his trumpet. When, in the second chorus, she held a C for sixteen bars, while the orchestra continued with the melody, the theatre was hers; not only the Alvin Theatre, but the musical theatre as well."

In *Lyrics on Several Occasions*, Ira Gershwin points out that one of the singular features about his lyric is that the phrase "who could ask for anything more" occurred four times. "Ordinarily and unquestionably," said Ira Gershwin, "[that] should make the phrase the title. Somehow, the first line of the refrain sounded more arresting and provocative. Therefore, 'I Got Rhythm.'" He might have added that he used the phrase "who could ask for anything more" in two later songs: "I'm About to Become a Mother" in *Of Thee I Sing* and "Nice Work If You Can Get It" in *Damsel in Distress*.

The song was interpolated in several motion pictures, including all screen adaptations of *Girl Crazy* (RKO, 1932; RKO, 1943; MGM, 1965). In the second, it was sung by Judy Garland. In the third, renamed *When the Boys Meet the Girls*, it was used for a production number. The song was also heard in the George Gershwin screen biography *Rhapsody in Blue* (Warner, 1945), and was sung by Gene Kelly and a chorus of Parisian urchins in the motion-picture musical *An American in Paris* (MGM, 1951).

George Gershwin used the basic melody of "I Got Rhythm" for a serious concert work—the *Variations on I Got Rhythm,* for piano and orchestra. It was introduced in Boston on January 14, 1934, Charles Previn conducting the Leo Reisman Orchestra, and the composer at the piano. Morton Gould made a symphonic adaptation of "I Got Rhythm," which he introduced with his orchestra over the CBS radio network in 1944.

I **Got Stung,** words and music by Aaron Schroeder and David Hill (1958). Popularized by Elvis Presley in an RCA Victor recording.

I **Gotta Right to Sing the Blues,** words by Ted Koehler, music by Harold Arlen (1932). One of the few Arlen songs that is in an authentic blues style. It was interpolated in the *Earl Carroll Vanities* (1932), introduced by Lillian Shade. When Jack Teagarden, jazz trombonist, toured with his band from 1939 to 1947 he used it as his theme song.

I **Got the Sun in the Morning.** *See:* Sun in the Morning.

I **Guess I'll Have to Change My Plan,** words by Howard Dietz, music by Arthur Schwartz (1929). Introduced by Clifton Webb in the revue *The Little Show* (1929).

Schwartz originally wrote the melody while working as a counselor in a boys' summer camp, long before he became a professional songwriter. At that time the young (and still unknown) Lorenz Hart wrote the lyric. The song was then called "I Love to Lie Awake in Bed." When Schwartz decided to use the melody for *The Little Show,* Howard Dietz provided new lyrics. The song was revived by Fred Astaire and Jack Buchanan in the motion-picture musical *The Band Wagon* (MGM, 1953). It was also interpolated as an instrumental in the non-musical motion picture *The Breaking Point,* starring John Garfield (Warner, 1950), and was used as a recurrent theme in the background music for the non-musical motion picture *Goodbye, My Fancy*

(Warner, 1951), starring Joan Crawford.

I **Guess I'll Have to Telegraph My Baby,** words and music by George M. Cohan (1898). A coon song popularized by Ethel Levey. It was Cohan's first major song success as well as the first popular song hit about telegraphy.

I **Had a Ball,** words by Jack Lawrence, music by Stan Freeman (1964). Title song of a musical (1964), introduced by Karen Morrow and ensemble.

I **Had a Ball,** a musical comedy with book by Jerome Chodorov. Lyrics by Jack Lawrence. Music by Stan Freeman. Starring Buddy Hackett (1964). Original cast recording (Mercury).
   See: Almost; Can It Be Possible?; Fickle Finger of Fate; I Got Everything I Want; I Had a Ball; The Other Half of Me.

I **Had the Craziest Dream,** words by Mack Gordon, music by Harry Warren (1942). Introduced by Harry James and his orchestra in the motion-picture musical *Springtime in the Rockies* (20th Century-Fox, (1942). Harry James' recording for Columbia (vocal by Helen Forrest) sold over a million disks.

I **Hate Men,** words and music by Cole Porter (1948). Introduced by Patricia Morison in the musical play *Kiss Me, Kate* (1948). In the motion-picture adaptation of the musical (MGM, 1953), it was sung by Kathryn Grayson.

I **Hate to Lose You,** words by Grant Clarke, music by Archie Gottler (1918). It was revived in the motion-picture musical *The Merry Monahans* (Universal, 1944).

I **Have Dreamed,** words by Oscar Hammerstein II, music by Richard Rodgers (1951). Introduced by Doretta Morrow and Larry Douglas in the musical play *The King and I* (1951). It was also sung in the motion-picture adaptation of the musical (20th Century-Fox, 1956).

I **Hear a Rhapsody,** words and music by George Fragos, Jack Baker and Dick Gasparre (1940). It was interpolated in several non-musical motion pictures, including *Casa Manana,* starring Robert Clarke and

Virginia Welles (Monogram, 1951), and *Clash by Night,* starring Barbara Stanwyck (RKO, 1952). It was popularized in a best-selling recording by Jimmy Dorsey and his orchestra for Decca.

I Heard You Cried Last Night (and So Did I), words by Jerry Kruger, music by Ted Grouya (1943). It was introduced in the motion picture *Cinderella Swings It,* starring Guy Kibbe and Gloria Warren (RKO, 1943). Popularized by Harry James and his orchestra (vocal by Helen Forrest) in a Columbia recording.

I Hear Music, words by Frank Loesser, music by Burton Lane (1940). Interpolated in the motion picture *Dancing on a Dime,* starring Grace McDonald and Robert Paige (Paramount, 1941), in which it was introduced by Peter Lind Hayes, Eddie Quillan, Frank Jenks and Robert Paige.

I Hear You Knockin', words and music by Dave Bartholomew and Pearl King (1955). Popularized by Smiley Lewis' recording for Imperial in 1955 and Gale Storm's recording for Dot in 1956.

I Hit a New High, words by Harold Adamson, music by Jimmy McHugh (1937). Introduced by Lily Pons in the motion-picture musical *Hitting a New High* (RKO, 1937). In this production the orchestra conductor for Lily Pons for this number was her then husband, André Kostelanetz.

I Just Can't Do Enough for You, words by Mack Gordon, music by Sammy Fain (1951). Introduced by Betty Grable in the motion-picture musical *Call Me Mister* (20th Century-Fox, 1951).

I Just Can't Make My Eyes Behave, words by Will D. Cobb, music by Gus Edwards (1906). Introduced by Anna Held in the musical *A Parisian Model* (1906), where it was an interpolation. This was one of Anna Held's greatest song successes. Song and singer became so inextricably associated with each other that henceforth it almost seemed inconceivable to hear the number sung without a French accent.

I Just Can't Wait, words by Betty Comden and Adolph Green, music by Jule Styne (1961). Introduced by Orson Bean in the musical *Subways Are for Sleeping* (1961).

I Just Roll Along, Havin' My Ups and Downs, words by Jo Trent, music by Peter De Rose (1927).

I Kiss Your Hand, Madame, a European popular song, music by Ralph Erwin, English lyrics by Sam M. Lewis and Joe Young (1929). The American version was introduced and popularized by Rudy Vallée. It was interpolated for Bing Crosby in the motion-picture musical *The Emperor Waltz* (Paramount, 1948). It was used in the background music as a recurrent theme for the non-musical motion picture *Baby Face,* starring Barbara Stanwyck (Warner, 1933).

I Know Now, words by Al Dubin, music by Harry Warren (1937). Introduced by Dick Powell in the motion-picture musical *The Singing Marine* (Warner, 1937).

I Know That You Know, words by Anne Caldwell, music by Vincent Youmans (1926). Introduced by Beatrice Lillie and Charles Purcell in the musical *Oh, Please* (1926). It was interpolated in the motion-picture musical *Tea for Two* (Warner, 1950), sung by Doris Day and Gordon MacRae, then danced to by Doris Day and Gene Nelson.

I Left My Heart at the Stage Door Canteen, words and music by Irving Berlin (1942). Introduced in the all-soldiers' revue *This Is the Army* (1942) and repeated in the motion-picture adaptation of the musical (Warner, 1943).

I Left My Heart in San Francisco, words and music by Douglass A. Cross and George Cory (1954). The melody had been written ten years before its publication and had been introduced by Claramae Turner. Then with new lyrics it was reissued in 1962 to become one of the leading song hits of the year, popularized by Tony Bennett. He introduced it at the Fairmont Hotel in San Francisco in 1962. His Columbia recording sold about three million disks, and received two "Grammy" Awards from the National Academy of Recording Arts and Sciences as the best popular record of the year and as the best vocal performance by a male soloist.

Tony Bennett revealed to an interviewer that this song, and this recording, was an important turning point in his career. "Rock 'n' roll all but ruined me. It seemed that any singer over twenty-five who couldn't play a steel guitar was in trouble. The Sinatras and the Crosbys had become institutions, but I wasn't anchored yet. Also, I lacked poise and experience. Then I had a date at the Fairmont Hotel in San Francisco, and I thought this may be my last. I wanted some special material and against the advice of my cohorts took a ten-year-old song that had new lyrics about San Francisco. I recorded the song—also against managerial advice—and the last I heard it had sold more than three million, and I'm still working."

I Let a Song Go Out of My Heart, words by Henry Nemo and Irving Mills, music by Duke Ellington (1938). The song started out as an instrumental, and was first popularized in a Columbia recording by Duke Ellington and his orchestra.

I Like It, I Like It, words by Mann Curtis, music by Vic Mizzy (1951). Popularized by Jane Turzy in an MGM recording.

I Like the Likes of You, words by E. Y. Harburg, music by Vernon Duke (1933). Introduced by Jack Pepper and Judith Barron in the *Ziegfeld Follies of 1934.*

I Lived My Life, words and music by Antoine "Fats" Domino and Dave Bartholomew (1954). Popularized by "Fats" Domino in an Imperial recording.

I'll Always Be in Love with You, words and music by Bud Green, Herman Ruby and Sam H. Stept (1929). Introduced in the motion-picture musical *Stepping High* (FBO Release, 1928), and interpolated in the motion-picture musical *Syncopation,* starring Fred Waring and his Pennsylvanians (RKO, 1929).

I'll Always Love You ("Querida Mia"), words and music by Jay Livingston

and Ray Evans (1950). Introduced by Dean Martin and the Guadalajara Trio in the motion picture *My Friend Irma Goes West* (Paramount, 1950), and popularized by Dean Martin's best-selling recording for Capitol.

I'll Be Happy When the Preacher Makes You Mine, words by Sam M. Lewis and Joe Young, music by Walter Donaldson (1919).

I'll Be Rich, words and music by Ferdinand Washington and Stan Lewis (1956). Popularized by Pat Boone, whose Dot recording sold a million disks. The Checker recording by the Flamingos was also a best seller.

I'll Be Home for Christmas (Though Just in Memory), words and music by Walter Kent, Kim Gannon and Buck Ram (1943). Introduced and popularized by Bing Crosby in a Decca recording that sold over a million disks.

I'll Be Seeing You, words by Irving Kahal, music by Sammy Fain (1938). Introduced by Tamara in the musical *Right This Way* (1938), where it was a failure. Freddie Martin and his orchestra wanted to record it at that time but were unable to do so because of a musicians' strike. The song then lay forgotten for five years. It was revived in 1943 and became one of the most successful ballads of World War II. Its popularity was greatly enhanced through performances and recordings by Hildegarde and Frank Sinatra. The song made twenty-four appearances on the Hit Parade in 1944, ten times in the Number One spot. It provided the title for and was used as a recurrent theme in the background music of a motion picture starring Ginger Rogers and Joseph Cotten (United Artists, 1944).

I'll Be True to My Honey Boy, words and music by George Evans (1894). Introduced by George Evans, one of the greatest minstrels of all time. He achieved such success with this number that from this time on he came to be known as George "Honey Boy" Evans.

I'll Be with You in Apple Blossom Time, words by Neville Fleeson, music by Albert von Tilzer (1920). Popularized in vaudeville by Nora Bayes.

I'll Be with You When the Roses Bloom Again, words by Will D. Cobb, music by Gus Edwards (1901). An early Gus Edwards hit song. It subsequently became a favorite of hillbilly performers.

I'll Build a Stairway to Paradise, words by Bud De Sylva and Arthur Francis (pen name for Ira Gershwin), music by George Gershwin (1922). George Gershwin's first song classic. It was introduced by Winnie Lightner in *George White's Scandals of 1922* (and danced to by Pearl Regay). Paul Whiteman conducted the pit orchestra.

As originally written by George and Ira Gershwin, the song was called "A New Step Every Day." Bud De Sylva suggested revisions in the lyrics, entered as Ira Gershwin's collaborator and proposed changing the title to "I'll Build a Stairway to Paradise."

The melody is distinguished by its unexpected intrusions of flatted thirds and sevenths, subtle enharmonic changes and daring accentuations.

The song was interpolated in the George Gershwin screen biography *Rhapsody in Blue* (Warner, 1945) and in the motion-picture musical *An American in Paris* (MGM, 1951), where it was sung by George Guetary.

I'll Cry Tomorrow, a screen biography of Lillian Roth starring Susan Hayward as Miss Roth (MGM, 1955). The score was made up of standards.

See: Happiness Is a Thing Called Joe; Sing, You Sinners; When the Red, Red Robin Comes Bob, Bob, Bobbin' Along.

I'll Dance at Your Wedding, words by Herb Magidson, music by Ben Oakland (1947).

I'll Forget You, words by Annelu Burns, music by Ernest R. Ball (1921). Dick Haymes sang it in Ernest R. Ball's screen biography *When Irish Eyes Are Smiling* (20th Century-Fox, 1944).

I'll Get By (As Long As I Have You), words by Roy Turk, music by Fred E. Ahlert (1928). It was one of the lead-ing song hits of the late 1920s, selling over a million copies of sheet music and about a million disks in various recordings. It was revived in 1943, and achieved hit status a second time. It was used as a recurring background theme in the non-musical motion picture *A Guy Named Joe,* starring Spencer Tracy and Irene Dunne (MGM, 1943), and was interpolated in the all-star motion-picture musical *Follow the Boys* (Universal, 1944). Dan Dailey sang it and danced to it in the motion-picture musical *You Were Meant for Me* (20th Century-Fox, 1948); and it was a part of the extended song sequence "Born in a Trunk," which Judy Garland sang in the motion-picture musical *A Star Is Born* (Warner, 1953). The song provided the title for a motion-picture musical (20th Century-Fox, 1950), where it was played under the titles and in the opening scene by Harry James and his orchestra, was sung in the picture by Dennis Day, June Haver and Gloria De Haven, and appeared in the background music throughout the film as a recurrent theme.

I'll Get By, a motion-picture musical starring June Haver and William Lundigan (20th Century-Fox, 1950). The score was made up mainly of standards.

See: Deep in the Heart of Texas; I'll Get By; It's Been a Long, Long Time; I've Got the World on a String; Once in a While; Taking a Chance on Love; There'll Never Be Another You; Yankee Doodle Blues; You Make Me Feel So Young.

I'll Go Home with Bonnie Jean, words by Alan Jay Lerner, music by Frederick Loewe (1947). Introduced by Lee Sullivan and chorus in the musical play *Brigadoon* (1947). In the motion-picture adaptation of the musical (MGM, 1954), it was sung on the soundtrack by John Gustafson (for Jimmy Thompson).

I'll Know, words and music by Frank Loesser (1950). Ballad introduced by Isabel Bigley and Robert Alda in the musical *Guys and Dolls* (1950).

I'll Never Be Free, words and music by Bennie Benjamin and George Weiss

(1950). Popularized by Tennessee Ernie Ford and Kay Starr in a best-selling Capitol recording; this was Tennessee Ernie Ford's first successful disk.

I'll Never Say No, words and music by Meredith Willson (1960). Introduced by Harve Presnell in the musical *The Unsinkable Molly Brown* (1960). In the motion-picture adaptation of the musical (MGM, 1964), it was sung by Debbie Reynolds and Harve Presnell.

I'll Never Smile Again, words and music by Ruth Lowe (1939). Ruth Lowe, pianist with the Ray Hutton all-girl orchestra, was inspired to write this ballad upon the death of her husband, Harold Cohen, only a few months after their marriage. Tommy Dorsey tried to interest Glenn Miller in it. When Miller turned it down, Tommy Dorsey recorded it with his orchestra (and with Frank Sinatra doing the vocal) for RCA Victor and made the song into an outstanding hit.

I'll Never Stop Loving You, words by Sammy Cahn, music by Nicholas Brodszky (1955). Introduced by Doris Day in the motion-picture biography of Ruth Etting, *Love Me or Leave Me* (MGM, 1955).

I'll Only Miss Her When I Think of Her, words by Sammy Cahn, music by James Van Heusen (1965). Introduced by Peter L. Marshall in the musical *Skyscraper* (1965).

I'll Remember April (and Be Glad), words and music by Don Raye, Gene de Paul and Pat Johnston (1941). It was introduced by Dick Foran in the motion picture *Ride 'Em Cowboy,* starring Abbott and Costello (Universal, 1942), and was popularized by Woody Herman and his orchestra in a Decca recording.

I'll Say She Does, words by Bud De Sylva and Gus Kahn, music by Al Jolson (1918). Introduced by Al Jolson in the Winter Garden extravaganza *Sinbad* (1918).

I'll See You in C-U-B-A, words and music by Irving Berlin (1919). Inspired by the passing of the Volstead Act. It was introduced by Ted Lewis and his band in the *Greenwich Vil-*

lage Follies of 1919. It was then interpolated in the Ziegfeld production of *Midnight Frolics of 1920.* It was revived in the motion-picture musical *Blue Skies* (MGM, 1946).

I'll See You in My Dreams, words by Gus Kahn, music by Isham Jones (1924). Introduced and popularized by Isham Jones and his band. It provided the title for and was used prominently in the motion-picture biography of Gus Kahn (Warner, 1951), played under the titles on the soundtrack, sung in the movie by Doris Day and presented by a chorus in the closing scene.

I'll See You in My Dreams, a motion-picture musical biography of Gus Kahn, starring Danny Thomas as Kahn with Doris Day (Warner, 1951). The score was made up of standards, all of them (with the exception of a single number) with lyrics by Kahn.

See: Ain't We Got Fun?; Carolina in the Morning; I'll See You in My Dreams; I'm Just Wild About Harry; I Never Knew; It Had to Be You; I Wish I Had a Girl; Love Me or Leave Me; Makin' Whoopee; Memories; My Buddy; Nobody's Sweetheart; No, No, Norah; The One I Love Belongs to Somebody Else; Pretty Baby; Swingin' Down the Lane; Toot, Toot, Tootsie; Ukulele Lady; Yes, Sir, That's My Baby; Your Eyes Have Told Me So.

I'll Sing You a Thousand Love Songs, words by Al Dubin, music by Harry Warren (1936). Introduced by Bob Page in the motion picture *Cain and Mabel,* starring Clark Gable and Marion Davies (Warner, 1936).

I'll String Along with You, words by Al Dubin, music by Harry Warren (1934). Introduced by Dick Powell and Ginger Rogers in the motion-picture musical *Twenty Million Sweethearts* (First National, 1934). It was interpolated in the non-musical motion picture *The Hard Way,* starring Ida Lupino and Joan Leslie (Warner, 1942) and in the motion-picture musical *My Dream Is Yours* (Warner, 1949), sung by Doris Day. It was sung by Danny Thomas in the motion-picture musical *The Jazz*

Singer (Warner, 1953), and was used as a recurring theme in the background music for the non-musical motion picture *Battle Cry*, starring Van Heflin and Mona Freeman (Warner, 1954).

I'll Take Romance, words by Oscar Hammerstein II, music by Ben Oakland (1937). Introduced by Grace Moore in the motion-picture musical of the same name (Columbia, 1937) and subsequently further popularized by Tony Martin. It was interpolated in several subsequent motion pictures, including *Good Girls Go to Paris,* starring Melvyn Douglas and Joan Blondell (Columbia, 1939); *Holiday in Havana,* starring Desi Arnaz (Columbia, 1949); and *Manhattan Angel,* starring Gloria Jean (Columbia, 1949).

I'll Take You Home Again, Kathleen, words and music by Thomas P. Westendorf (1876). For many years it was believed that this sentimental ballad had been inspired by the serious illness of Westendorf's wife, caused by the death of their son. But recent research has proved all this false. We now know that the song was Westendorf's expression of loneliness while his wife was visiting relatives out of town. The composer had been stimulated by another popular ballad of the day, "Barney, Take Me Home Again" by Arthur W. French and George W. Brown.

"I'll Take You Home Again, Kathleen" was introduced in 1876 by a local performer at the Town Hall in Plainfield, Indiana.

I'll Tell the Man in the Street, words by Lorenz Hart, music by Richard Rodgers (1938). Introduced by Vivienne Segal and Walter Slezak in the musical *I Married an Angel* (1938). In the motion-picture adaptation of the musical (MGM, 1942), it was sung by Jeanette MacDonald and Nelson Eddy. The song was successfully revived in 1963 by Barbra Streisand in a Columbia recording.

I'll Walk Alone, words by Sammy Cahn, music by Jule Styne (1944). Introduced by Dinah Shore in the motion-picture musical *Follow the Boys* (Universal, 1944). Her recording for RCA Victor and Frank Sinatra's for Capitol helped make it one of the most successful ballads of World War II. This is the only song by Cahn to sell over a million copies of sheet music. Jane Froman sang it (for Susan Hayward) on the soundtrack of Miss Froman's screen biography *With a Song in My Heart* (20th Century-Fox, 1952). Don Cornell's recording for Coral in 1952 was a best seller.

I'll Walk with God, words by Paul Francis Webster, music by Nicholas Brodszky (1952). Inspirational song, introduced by Mario Lanza on the soundtrack of the motion-picture adaptation of the Sigmund Romberg operetta *The Student Prince* (MGM, 1952). The song subsequently became a favorite at Sunday services in churches around the country.

Ill Wind, words by Ted Koehler, music by Harold Arlen (1934). Introduced by Adelaide Hall in the Cotton Club revue *Parade in Harlem,* in Harlem, New York (1934).

I Long to See the Girl I Left Behind, words and music by John T. Kelly (1893). Kelly wrote the song one day aboard a train while touring in *You and I,* a musical in which he was then starring.

I Love a Parade, words by Ted Koehler, music by Harold Arlen (1931). An early Harold Arlen success, introduced by Cab Calloway at the Cotton Club in Harlem, New York, in 1930.

Ted Koehler told an interviewer how it came to be written: "Harold liked to walk, I didn't. However, he used to talk me into walking and I remember one day it was cold out and to pep me he started to hum an ad lib marching tune. I guess I started to fall into step and got warmed up." Along the route, Koehler asked him: "Why don't you join the army if you love to walk so much?" Arlen said nothing, but kept on humming, and the two continued walking. "When we got down to 47th Street, 'I Love a Parade' was almost written."

It was interpolated in the motion picture *Manhattan Parade,* starring

Winnie Lightner (Warner, 1932).

I Love a Piano, words and music by Irving Berlin (1915). Introduced by Harry Fox and ensemble in the musical *Stop, Look and Listen* (1915). Judy Garland and Fred Astaire revived it in the motion-picture musical *Easter Parade* (MGM, 1948).

I Love, I Love, I Love My Wife, But Oh You Kid, words by Jimmy Lucas, music by Harry von Tilzer (1909). Written to capitalize on the success of "I Love My Wife, But Oh You Kid" by Harry Armstrong and Billy Clark, published earlier the same year.

I Love Life, words by Irwin M. Cassell, music by Mana Zucca (1923). An art song introduced by the concert singer Charles Hackett during an Australian tour in 1923. It was then popularized by John Charles Thomas in his song recitals in the United States. The song entered the popular repertory through repeated performances in all the popular media.

I Love Louisa, words by Howard Dietz, music by Arthur Schwartz (1931). Introduced as a production number for the first-act finale in the revue *The Band Wagon* (1931). This was the first time that a Broadway musical utilized a revolving stage, the scene being a gay Bavarian setting dominated by a merry-go-round. In the motion-picture musical *Dancing in the Dark* (20th Century-Fox, 1949), it was sung by Betsy Drake; in the motion-picture musical *The Band Wagon* (MGM, 1953), it appeared as a comedy number for Fred Astaire, with the assistance of Oscar Levant.

I Love My Baby, My Baby Loves Me, words by Bud Green, music by Harry Warren (1925). Introduced and popularized by Fred Waring and his Pennsylvanians.

I Love My Little Honey, words and music by Ben Harney (1897). A coon shout, an early example of ragtime song, introduced by Ben Harney in vaudeville.

I Love My Wife, But Oh You Kid, words and music by Harry Armstrong and Billy Clark (1909). The title became a catch phrase for young blades throughout the country in the early 1910s. A competitive song by Jimmy Lucas and Harry von Tilzer, published the same year, was also successful; it was called "I Love, I Love, I Love My Wife, But Oh You Kid."

I Love Paris, words and music by Cole Porter (1953). A hymn to the city of cafés and boulevards, introduced by Lilo in her American stage debut in the musical *Can-Can* (1953). In the motion-picture adaptation of the musical (20th Century-Fox, 1960), it was sung by Frank Sinatra and Maurice Chevalier. Porter was inspired to write this number, and include it in the score of *Can-Can*, by a stunning set design by Jo Mielziner depicting Parisian roof tops. The song was popularized in 1953 by Les Baxter and his orchestra.

I Loves You, Porgy, words by Ira Gershwin and Du Bose Heyward, music by George Gershwin (1935). Introduced by Todd Duncan and Anne Brown in the folk opera *Porgy and Bess* (1935). In the motion-picture adaptation of the opera (Columbia, 1959), it was sung on the soundtrack by Robert McFerrin (for Sidney Poitier) and Adele Addison (for Dorothy Dandridge). Nina Simone made a successful recording for Bethlehem in 1959.

I Love Thee, I Adore Thee, words by Harry B. Smith, music by Victor Herbert (1897). Introduced by W. H. MacDonald and Jessie Bartlett Davis in the operetta *The Serenade* (1897). This serenade plays such a prominent role in the operetta in developing the story line that it is sometimes called the show's "main character." It is heard for the first time as the second part of a duet in which the two principals explain how they met. The serenade is then sung by the hero, with the heroine making comments as she listens. After that the melody recurs throughout the operetta in many different guises— as a parody on grand opera, a monk's chant, a parrot's call, a song of brigands. It is heard for the last time as a love duet. It was revived as a love song in the motion-picture musical *The Great Victor Herbert* (Paramount, 1939), sung by Allan Jones.

I Love the Ladies, words by Grant Clarke, music by Jean Schwartz (1914). Introduced by Florenz Tempest in the musical *Our American Boy* (1914), where it was an interpolation.

I Love to Go Swimmin with Wimmen, words by Ballard MacDonald, music by Sigmund Romberg (1921). Comedy song introduced during the out-of-town tryouts of the musical *Love Birds* (1921), sung by Pat Rooney and a female chorus. It was revived in Romberg's screen biography *Deep in My Heart* (MGM, 1954), sung by Gene and Fred Kelly.

I Love to Walk in the Rain, words by Walter Bullock, music by Harold Spina (1938). Introduced by Shirley Temple in the motion-picture musical *Just Around the Corner* (20th Century-Fox, 1938).

I Love You, words by Harlan Thompson, music by Harry Archer (1923). Introduced by Nan Halperin and Allen Kearns in the musical *Little Jesse James* (1923). The success of this song is believed to have been responsible for making the show a major box-office attraction.

I Love You, words and music by Cole Porter (1943). Introduced by Wilbur Evans in the musical *Mexican Hayride* (1944). In *The Nine Lives of Michael Todd*, Art Cohn describes the unusual circumstances surrounding the writing of this song. "Cole Porter was unhappy about the score; he had not come up with a hit song. 'What's the most cliché title in the world?' Mike [Todd] asked him. 'I love you, of course,' Porter replied. 'I love you,' Mike repeated slowly. 'I'll bet you can take that title, use only three notes—one for each word —improvise a two-finger exercise and come up with a smash hit.'" Porter took the wager, wrote the number and saw it become the leading song hit of the show.

The song was popularized by Bing Crosby in a best-selling recording for Decca.

I Love You, words and music by Rob-

ert Wright and George Forrest (1944). Introduced by Helena Bliss in the operetta based on the life of Edvard Grieg, *The Song of Norway* (1944). The melody comes from Grieg's famous *lied* "Ich liebe dich."

I Love You in the Same Old Way, Darling Sue, words by Walter H. Ford, music by John W. Bratton (1896). Introduced and popularized in vaudeville by Dick José.

I Love You This Morning, words by Alan Jay Lerner, music by Frederick Loewe (1945). Introduced by Bill Johnson and Irene Manning in the musical *The Day Before Spring* (1945), the first stage success by Lerner and Loewe.

I Love You Truly, words and music by Carrie Jacobs Bond (1901). An art song which entered the popular repertory by virtue of repeated performances in vaudeville. This song appeared in the composer's first publication—*Seven Songs*, issued in 1901. It was reprinted as a separate number in 1906, and achieved a sheet-music sale second only to that enjoyed by the same composer's "Perfect Day."

I'm a Dreamer. *See:* Aren't We All?

I'm Afraid to Go Home in the Dark, words by Harry H. Williams, music by Egbert Van Alstyne (1907). O. Henry is reputed to have quoted the title of this song just before his death.

Imagination, words by Johnny Burke, music by James Van Heusen (1940). Introduced by Fred Waring and his Pennsylvanians, but popularized by Glenn Miller and his orchestra in a best-selling Bluebird recording. The RCA Victor recording by Tommy Dorsey and his orchestra and that of Kate Smith for Columbia were also best sellers.

I'm Always Chasing Rainbows, words by Joseph McCarthy, music by Harry Carroll, the melody taken from Chopin's *Fantaisie Impromptu* in C-sharp minor (1918). Introduced by Harry Fox in the musical *Oh, Look* (1918), where it scored a major success, the song went on to sell over a million copies of sheet music and over a million disks in various recordings.

This was the first time that a success of such proportions came to a popular tune with a melody lifted from the classics. Perry Como revived it successfully in an RCA Victor recording in 1946. The song appeared in a number of motion-picture musicals. Among them were *Rose of Washington Square* (20th Century-Fox, 1939); *Ziegfeld Girl,* starring James Stewart and Judy Garland (MGM, 1941); *The Merry Monahans* (Universal, 1944); and *The Dolly Sisters* (20th Century-Fox, 1945), sung by John Payne and used in the background music as a recurrent theme.

I'm an Old Cowhand, words and music by Johnny Mercer (1936). Introduced by Bing Crosby in the motion-picture musical *Rhythm on the Range* (Paramount, 1936), and further popularized by him in a Decca recording. The song was revived by Roy Rogers in the motion picture *King of the Cowboys* (Republic, 1943).

I'm a Popular Man, words and music by George M. Cohan (1907). Introduced by George M. Cohan in the musical *The Honeymooners* (1907).

I'm a Respectable Working Girl, words by Edgar Smith, music by John Stromberg (1900). Introduced by Fay Templeton in the Weber and Fields extravaganza *Fiddle-Dee-Dee* (1900). In his book on Weber and Fields, Felix Isman wrote: "Miss Templeton did not fancy the song, and was so certain that it would not go over that she memorized but one verse. The first-nighters made her respond to four encores. At each she could only sing the first verse over. The following night she knew the entire song. She had few more popular ones."

I Married an Angel, words by Lorenz Hart, music by Richard Rodgers (1938). Title song of a musical (1938), introduced by Dennis King. In the motion-picture adaptation of the musical (MGM, 1942), it was sung by Nelson Eddy. The song was interpolated in the screen biography of Rodgers and Hart, *Words and Music* (MGM, 1948).

I Married an Angel, a musical comedy with book by Richard Rodgers and Lorenz Hart adapted from a play by John Vaszary. Lyrics by Lorenz Hart. Music by Richard Rodgers. Starring Vera Zorina, Dennis King and Vivienne Segal (1938).

The motion-picture adaptation starred Jeanette MacDonald and Nelson Eddy (MGM, 1942). It used six numbers from the stage score. Additional songs were provided by George Forrest, Robert Wright and Herbert Stothart.

See: I'll Tell the Man in the Street; I Married an Angel; Spring Is Here.

I'm a Vamp from East Broadway, words and music by Bert Kalmar, Harry Ruby and Irving Berlin (1920). A Fanny Brice specialty which she introduced in the *Ziegfeld Follies of 1920.*

I'm Awfully Glad I Met You, words by Jack Drislane, music by George W. Meyer (1909).

I May Be Crazy But I Ain't No Fool, words and music by Alex Rogers (1904). Introduced and popularized in vaudeville by Bert Williams, then appearing with the act of Williams and Walker.

I May Be Gone for a Long, Long Time, words by Lew Brown, music by Albert von Tilzer (1917). World War I ballad, introduced by Grace La Rue in the revue *Hitchy Koo* (1917).

I May Be Wrong But I Think You're Wonderful, words by Harry Ruskin, music by Henry Sullivan (1929). Introduced by Jimmy Savo in the revue *Murray Anderson's Almanac* (1929). It was interpolated in several motion pictures. Among them were *Swingtime Johnny,* starring the Andrews Sisters (Universal, 1944); *Wallflower,* starring Joyce Reynolds and Robert Hutton (Warner, 1947); *You're My Everything* (20th Century-Fox, 1949), sung by Dan Dailey; *Young Man with a Horn,* starring Kirk Douglas (Warner, 1950), sung by Doris Day; *On the Sunny Side of the Street* (Columbia, 1951); and *Starlift* (Warner, 1951), sung by Jane Wyman.

I'm Beginning to See the Light, words and music by Don George, Johnny

Hodges, Duke Ellington and Harry James (1945). Introduced by Harry James and his orchestra. Connie Francis revived it successfully in the early 1960s in a best-selling MGM recording.

I'm Building Up to an Awful Let Down, words by Johnny Mercer, music by Fred Astaire (1935). Successfully revived in 1938, when it was represented on the Hit Parade.

I'm Falling in Love with Someone, words by Rida Johnson Young, music by Victor Herbert (1910). Introduced by Orville Harrold in the operetta *Naughty Marietta* (1910). In the motion-picture adaptation of the operetta (MGM, 1935), it was sung by Nelson Eddy; in the screen biography *The Great Victor Herbert* (Paramount, 1939), it was sung by Allan Jones. This song is unusual for the chromaticism of the opening bars and for the unusual leap of a ninth in the refrain.

I'm Forever Blowing Bubbles, words by Jean Kenbrovin (pen name for James Kendis, James Brockman and Nat Vincent), music by John William Kellette (1919). Introduced by June Caprice in *The Passing Show of 1918*. The song sold over two and a half million copies of sheet music, to become one of the leading song hits of 1918 and 1919. The first recording made of this song was a best seller, that of Ben Selvin and his Novelty Orchestra for Victor, in 1919. The song was heard as a piano instrumental in the non-musical motion pictures *Stella Dallas*, starring Barbara Stanwyck (Samuel Goldwyn, 1934), and *Men with Wings*, starring Fred MacMurray and Ray Milland (Paramount, 1938). It was also interpolated in the motion-picture musical *On Moonlight Bay* (Warner, 1951), sung by Jack Smith.

I'm Glad I'm Not Young Anymore, words by Alan Jay Lerner, music by Frederick Loewe (1958). Introduced by Maurice Chevalier in the motion-picture musical *Gigi* (MGM, 1958).

In his autobiography, Maurice Chevalier revealed how this song came to be written. Chevalier was disclosing to Lerner how glad he was that his involvements in romance had become a thing of the past. Lerner expressed surprise, but Chevalier insisted that the advancing years had their advantage. "He said no more at the time, but later gave me a nice tune to sing, inspired by our conversation—'I'm Glad I'm Not Young Anymore.'"

I'm Gettin' Sentimental Over You, words by Ned Washington, music by George Bassman (1932). Theme song of Tommy Dorsey and his orchestra, whose RCA Victor recording was a best seller.

I'm Goin' South, words by Abner Silver, music by Harry Woods (1923). Introduced by Al Jolson in the musical extravaganza *Bombo* (1921). Eddie Cantor then interpolated it in the musical *Kid Boots* (1923).

I'm Gonna Sit Right Down and Write Myself a Letter, words by Joe Young, music by Fred E. Ahlert (1935). Though a leading hit song in 1935 it was revived in 1956, to become an even greater success, Billy Williams's MGM recording selling over two million disks.

I'm Gonna Wash That Man Right Outa My Hair, words by Oscar Hammerstein II, music by Richard Rodgers (1949). Introduced by Mary Martin in the musical play *South Pacific* (1949). This song was included in that production at the suggestion of its star, Mary Martin, who thought it might be a good idea for her to wash her hair on the stage. Rodgers and Hammerstein proceeded to write an appropriate number for such a scene. In the motion-picture adaptation of the musical (20th Century-Fox, 1958), it was sung by Mitzi Gaynor.

I Might Be Your "Once in a While," words by Robert B. Smith, music by Victor Herbert (1919). Introduced by John E. Young and Ada Meade in the musical *Angel Face* (1919). It was interpolated in the motion-picture biography *The Great Victor Herbert* (Paramount, 1939), sung by Mary Martin.

I'm in Love Again, words and music by Antoine "Fats" Domino and Dave Bartholomew (1956). Popularized by

"Fats" Domino in an Imperial recording.

I'm in Love Again, words and music by Cole Porter (1925). An early Cole Porter song, introduced by the Dolly Sisters in *The Greenwich Village Follies of 1924.* It was sung by Ginny Simms in the Cole Porter screen biography *Night and Day* (Warner, 1946) and was successfully revived in 1951.

I'm in Love with a Wonderful Guy, words by Oscar Hammerstein II, music by Richard Rodgers (1949). Introduced by Mary Martin in the musical play *South Pacific* (1949). In the motion-picture adaptation of the musical (20th Century-Fox, 1958), it was sung by Mitzi Gaynor.

It was Rodgers who suggested to Hammerstein the effective repetition of the phrase "I'm in love" five times in the closing line of the chorus. The first time Mary Martin tried out the song was two in the morning at Joshua Logan's apartment. "I almost passed out, I was so excited," she later recalled. "I fell off the piano bench and I remember that the management had to call up to complain of the noise."

I'm in the Mood for Love, words by Dorothy Fields, music by Jimmy McHugh (1935). Introduced by Alice Faye in the motion picture *Every Night at Eight* (Paramount, 1935). It was interpolated in several motion pictures, including *Between Two Women,* starring Van Johnson and Lionel Barrymore (MGM, 1944), sung by Gloria De Haven; *The Big Clock,* starring Ray Milland and Charles Laughton (Paramount, 1948); *That's My Boy,* starring Dean Martin and Jerry Lewis (Paramount, 1951); *Ask Any Girl,* starring Shirley MacLaine and David Niven (MGM, 1959); and *The Misfits,* starring Clark Gable and Marilyn Monroe (United Artists, 1961). By 1965 this song had received over four hundred recordings, with a combined sale exceeding three million disks.

I Miss My Swiss, words by L. Wolfe Gilbert, music by Abel Baer (1925). Written for Nikita Balieff, master of ceremonies of the Russian revue *Chauve Souris,* while visiting the United States. Due to internal dissension in the company, the song was never introduced in the United States. But the company did present it in Paris, where it became an immediate hit. In America the song was frequently heard in vaudeville.

I'm Just a Lonely Boy, words and music by Paul Anka (1958). Anka's recording for ABC Paramount in 1959 sold a million disks. The song was interpolated in the motion picture *Girlstown,* starring Mamie van Doren and Mel Torme (MGM, 1959).

I'm Just a Vagabond Lover, words and music by Rudy Vallée and Leon Zimmerman (1929). Introduced and popularized by Rudy Vallée over the radio and in a best-selling RCA Victor recording. He sang it in the motion-picture musical *Glorifying the American Girl,* starring Mary Eaton, Eddie Cantor and Helen Morgan (Paramount, 1929). Vallée's success with this number led to the filming of a motion-picture musical entitled *Vagabond Lover* in which he was starred (RKO, 1929).

This song was involved in several plagiarism suits in which various people, from different parts of the country, claimed to have written it. Vallée insisted that he wrote it one Sunday morning at the Palace Theatre in New York where he was then appearing. All the suits were discredited.

I'm Just Wild About Harry, words and music by Noble Sissle and Eubie Blake (1921). Introduced by Florence Mills and chorus in the all-Negro revue *Shuffle Along* (1921). She repeated her performance in London in the musical *Dover Street to Dixie* (1923). The song was interpolated in several motion pictures, including the musical *Rose of Washington Square* (20th Century-Fox, 1939), sung by Alice Faye; *Broadway,* starring George Raft and Pat O'Brien (Universal, 1942); the Ted Lewis screen biography *Is Everybody Happy?* (Columbia, 1943); *Jolson Sings Again* (Columbia, 1949), sung by Jolson on the soundtrack; and

Gus Kahn's screen biography *I'll See You in My Dreams* (Warner, 1951).

I'm Looking Over a Four Leaf Clover, words by Mort Dixon, music by Harry Woods (1927). One of the leading song hits of the late 1920s. It was revived in 1948 by the band-leader Art Mooney in an MGM recording. A disk jockey in a Salt Lake station, Albert Jazzbo Collins, played it on his broadcast in 1948. When he was deluged with requests for replaying this record, he announced that he would play it all afternoon. This extended listening session brought on a storm of protest from listeners, reported by the wire services to newspapers throughout the country. This publicity led to a demand for the Art Mooney recording, which forthwith became a national best seller in the million-disk class.

The song was interpolated in the motion-picture musical *Jolson Sings Again* (Columbia, 1949), sung by Jolson on the soundtrack. It was also sung by Danny Thomas in the motion-picture musical *The Jazz Singer* (Warner, 1953).

I'm Making Believe, words by Mack Gordon, music by James V. Monaco (1944). Introduced in the motion picture *Sweet and Low Down*, starring Linda Darnell and Lynn Bari (20th Century-Fox, 1944). It was popularized by Ella Fitzgerald and the Ink Spots in a Decca recording.

I'm Nobody's Baby, words by Benny Davis, music by Milton Ager and Lester Santly (1921). A favorite of female singers in vaudeville in the early 1920s, it sold over a million copies of sheet music. Judy Garland sang it in the motion picture *Andy Hardy Meets a Debutante*, starring Mickey Rooney (MGM, 1940).

I'm Old Fashioned, words by Johnny Mercer, music by Jerome Kern (1942). Introduced by Fred Astaire in the motion-picture musical *You Were Never Lovelier* (Columbia, 1942).

I'm One of God's Children, words by Oscar Hammerstein II, music by Louis Alter (1931). Introduced in the musical *Ballyhoo* (1931).

I'm Only Human After All, words by Ira Gershwin and E. Y. Harburg, music by Vernon Duke (1930). This was Duke's first American popular song. It was introduced by James Norris, Velma Vavra and Imogene Coca in the *Garrick Gaieties of 1930*. Duke had previously contributed this number to the *9:15 Revue* but it was dropped from that production even before rehearsals.

I'm on the Crest of a Wave, words by Bud De Sylva and Lew Brown, music by Ray Henderson (1927). Introduced by Harry Richman in *George White's Scandals of 1927* —the last edition for which De Sylva, Brown and Henderson provided a complete score.

I'm on the Water Wagon Now, words by Paul West, music by John W. Bratton (1903). Interpolated in, and the hit song of, the musical *The Office Boy* (1903).

The Impatient Years, words by Sammy Cahn, music by James Van Heusen (1955). Introduced in the TV musical production of Thornton Wilder's play *Our Town* (1955).

The Impossible Dream (The Quest), words by Joe Darion, music by Mitch Leigh (1965). Introduced by Richard Kiley in the musical *Man of La Mancha* (1965).

I'm Putting All My Eggs in One Basket, words and music by Irving Berlin (1936). Introduced by Fred Astaire in the motion-picture musical *Follow the Fleet* (RKO, 1936).

I'm Shooting High, words by Ted Koehler, music by Jimmy McHugh (1935). Introduced by Alice Faye in the motion picture *King of Burlesque*, starring Warner Baxter (20th Century-Fox, 1935).

I'm Sitting on Top of the World, words by Sam M. Lewis and Joe Young, music by Ray Henderson (1925). Popularized by Al Jolson. He sang it in the motion-picture musical *The Singing Fool* (Warner, 1929) and on the soundtrack of *The Jolson Story* (Columbia, 1946); his Decca recording was a best seller.

I'm Sorry, words and music by Ronnie Self and Dub Albritton (1960). Popularized by Brenda Lee in a Decca recording.

I'm Sorry I Made You Cry, words and music by N. J. Clesi (1918). One of the most successful ballads of the late 1910s. It was interpolated in the motion-picture musicals *Rose of Washington Square* (20th Century-Fox, 1939), where it was sung by Alice Faye, and *Somebody Loves Me* (Paramount, 1952).

I'm Stepping Out with a Memory Tonight, words by Herb Magidson, music by Allie Wrubel (1940). Introduced by Kate Smith. It was interpolated in the motion-picture musical *Footlight Serenade,* starring John Payne and Betty Grable (20th Century-Fox, 1942). The Bluebird recording of Glenn Miller and his orchestra was a best seller.

I'm the Greatest Star, words by Bob Merrill, music by Jule Styne (1964). Introduced by Barbra Streisand in the musical *Funny Girl* (1964).

I'm the Last of the Red Hot Mamas, words by Jack Yellen, music by Milton Ager (1929). It was written as a specialty number for Sophie Tucker, who featured it in her vaudeville act in the late 1920s. She also sang it in her debut in talking pictures, in *Honky Tonk* (Warner, 1929).

I'm the Lonesomest Gal in Town, words by Lew Brown, music by Albert von Tilzer (1912). A hit ballad of the early 1910s. It was revived a generation later by Kay Starr, whose Capitol recording was a best seller, and helped to establish her as a star. It was interpolated in several motion pictures, including *Make Believe Ballroom,* starring Ruth Warwick (RKO, 1949), and *South Sea Sinner,* starring MacDonald Carey and Shelley Winters (Universal, 1950).

I'm Through with Love, words and music by Matty Malneck and Jerry Livingston (1931). Interpolated in the motion picture *Honeymoon Lodge,* starring Rod Cameron and June Vincent (Universal, 1943). It was also sung by Bobbie Van in the motion picture *The Affairs of Dobie Gillis* (MGM, 1953), and by Marilyn Monroe in the motion-picture musical *Some Like It Hot* (United Artists, 1959).

I'm Tired, words by William Jerome, music by Jean Schwartz (1901). Introduced and popularized by Eddie Foy in the musical *The Strollers* (1901). It was revived by Bob Hope in the motion-picture musical *The Seven Little Foys* (Paramount, 1955).

I'm Unlucky, words by William Jerome, music by Jean Schwartz (1902). Introduced in the musical *The Wild Rose* (1902).

I'm Unlucky at Gambling, words and music by Cole Porter (1929). Introduced by Evelyn Hoey in the musical *Fifty Million Frenchmen* (1929). It was revived in the Cole Porter screen biography *Night and Day* (Warner, 1946), sung by Eve Arden.

I Must Love You, words by Lorenz Hart, music by Richard Rodgers (1928). Introduced by Helen Ford and William Williams in the musical *Chee Chee* (1928).

I'm Walkin', words and music by Antoine "Fats" Domino and Dave Bartholomew (1957). Popularized in an Imperial recording by "Fats" Domino. It was sung by Ricky Nelson on his TV program *The Adventures of Ozzie and Harriet* in 1957 —his singing debut. His recording for Verve sold over a million disks and was his first song hit.

I'm Walking Behind You, words and music by Billy Reid (1953). An English popular song that became a hit in the United States in 1954 mainly through Eddie Fisher's recording for RCA Victor, which sold about a million disks.

I'm with You, words by Betty Comden and Adolph Green, music by Jule Styne (1964). Introduced by Carol Burnett and Jack Cassidy (then danced to by Don Crichton) in the musical *Fade Out—Fade In* (1964).

I'm Yours, words and music by Robert Mellin (1952). Popularized by Don Cornell in a Coral recording. Eddie Fisher's recording for RCA Victor was also a best seller.

In a Little Spanish Town, words by Sam M. Lewis and Joe Young, music by Mabel Wayne (1926). Popularized by Jimmy Carr, "the doctor of melody," and his orchestra. Its success started a vogue in Tin Pan

Alley for Spanish-type popular songs; at the same time it launched Mabel Wayne on her career as a successful popular composer. The song was interpolated in the motion picture *Ridin' Down the Canyon,* starring Roy Rogers (Republic, 1942).

In a Sentimental Mood, words and music by Duke Ellington (1935). Ellington's first recording for RCA Victor, in 1935, was made with this hit song.

In a Shanty in Old Shanty Town, words and music by Joe Young, John Siros and Little Jack Little (1933). Popularized during the depression of the early 1930s. It was introduced by Little Jack Little. Johnny Long's recording for Decca in 1940 was a best seller. The song was interpolated in the motion-picture musical *Lullaby of Broadway* (Warner, 1951).

Incendiary Blonde, a motion-picture musical biography of Texas Guinan, starring Betty Hutton as Miss Guinan (Paramount, 1945). The score was made up mainly of standards.

　See: Darktown Strutters' Ball; Ida; It Had To Be You; Margie; Oh, by Jingo; Ragtime Cowboy Joe; Row, Row, Row; What Do You Want to Make Those Eyes at Me For?

The Inch Worm, words and music by Frank Loesser (1951). Introduced by Danny Kaye in the motion picture *Hans Christian Andersen* (Samuel Goldwyn, 1953). This song is one of Loesser's favorites among his own creations.

In Dear Old Illinois, words and music by Paul Dresser (1902).

Indiana, words by Ballard MacDonald, music by James F. Hanley (1917). It was interpolated in the screen biography of Jane Froman, *With a Song in My Heart* (20th Century-Fox, 1952).

Indiana Moon, words by Benny Davis, music by Isham Jones (1923). Introduced and popularized by Isham Jones and his orchestra.

The Indian Hunter, words and music by Henry Russell (1837). One of the earliest American popular songs about the American Indian. It was introduced by the singing Hutchinson Family.

Indian Love Call, words by Otto Harbach and Oscar Hammerstein II, music by Rudolf Friml (1924). Introduced by Dennis King and Mary Ellis in the operetta *Rose Marie* (1924). It was sung in both motion-picture adaptations of the operetta (MGM, 1936, and MGM, 1954), in the first by Nelson Eddy and Jeanette MacDonald, whose recording for RCA Victor in 1936 was a best seller. It provided the title for, was used as a recurrent theme, and was sung by Jeanette MacDonald in a motion-picture musical (MGM, 1936). Slim Whitman's Imperial recording in 1954 was a best seller.

Indian Summer, words by Al Dubin, music by Victor Herbert (1939). It originated in 1919 as a piano composition described by the composer as "an American idyll." (Herbert also transcribed it for orchestra.) With Dubin's lyrics it became a hit song in 1939 and was represented on the Hit Parade.

Indiscreet, words by Sammy Cahn, music by James Van Heusen (1958). Written as the title song for a motion picture starring Cary Grant and Ingrid Bergman (Warner, 1958); the song was based on the instrumental love theme in the background music. Much of the song's popularity was due to Frank Sinatra's successful recording for Columbia.

I Need You Now, words and music by Jimmie Crane and Al Jacobs (1953). Popularized by Eddie Fisher in an RCA Victor recording.

I Never Drank Behind the Bar, words by Edward Harrigan, music by Dave Braham. (1882). Introduced in the Harrigan and Hart extravaganza *The McSorleys* (1882).

I Never Felt More Like Falling in Love, words by Ralph Freed, music by Robert Allen (1954). Revived and popularized in 1957 in a best-selling recording by Tony Bennett for Columbia.

I Never Has Seen Snow, words by Truman Capote and Harold Arlen, music by Harold Arlen (1954). Introduced by Diahann Carroll in her first Broadway starring role, in the musical *House of Flowers* (1954). In the release of the chorus, Arlen combines a melody from the verse with one from the chorus. "What results," explains Edward Jablonski, "is a trio with the voice carrying the melody and, under that, two counter melodies."

I Never Knew I Could Love Anyone Like I'm Loving You, words and music by Tom Pitts, Ray Egan and Roy Marsh (1920). It was successfully revived in 1941, and was interpolated in the motion pictures *Strictly in the Groove*, starring Martha Tilton (Universal, 1942), and *Honeymoon Lodge*, starring David Bruce and June Vincent (Universal, 1943).

I Never Knew That Roses Grew, words by Gus Kahn, music by Ted Fiorito (1925). Introduced by Ted Fiorito and his orchestra. It was interpolated in Gus Kahn's screen biography *I'll See You in My Dreams* (Warner, 1951).

I Never Was Born, words by E. Y. Harburg, music by Harold Arlen (1944). Introduced by Joan McCracken in the musical *Bloomer Girl* (1944).

In Good Old New York Town, words and music by Paul Dresser (1899). Popularized in vaudeville by Lottie Gilson.

Inka Dinka Doo, words by Ben Ryan, music by Jimmy Durante (1933). Introduced by Jimmy Durante in the motion picture *Palooka* (United Artists, 1934). Since then it has become a Durante specialty.

This is an "interrupted song"—a Durante invention. "Jimmy enters and begins singing 'Inka Dinka Doo,'" explains Maurice Zolotow. "After the introduction and a few bars of the chorus, he stops singing and begins telling a joke, while the orchestra keeps playing in the background. . . . The jokes have no connection with the music."

Jimmy Durante sang it again in the motion picture *This Time for Keeps*, starring Esther Williams (MGM, 1947).

In Love in Vain, words by Leo Robin,

music by Jerome Kern (1946). Introduced on the soundtrack by Louanne Hogan (for Jeanne Crain) in the motion-picture musical *Centennial Summer* (20th Century-Fox, 1946).

In My Arms, words by Frank Loesser, music by Ted Grouya (1943). Introduced in the motion picture *See Here, Private Hargrove*, starring Robert Walker (MGM, 1944). It was popularized by Dick Haymes in a Decca recording.

In My Merry Oldsmobile, words by Vincent P. Bryan, music by Gus Edwards (1905). Inspired by the first cross-continental trip ever attempted by automobile. Two Oldsmobiles made the journey from Detroit to the Lewis and Clark Exposition in Portland, Oregon, in forty-four days. The song was presented by Donald O'Connor, Jack Oakie and Peggy Ryan in the motion-picture musical *The Merry Monihans* (Universal, 1944).

In My Own Little Corner, words by Oscar Hammerstein II, music by Richard Rodgers (1957). Introduced by Julie Andrews in the TV "special" *Cinderella* (1957).

In My Sweet Little Alice Blue Gown, words by Joseph McCarthy, music by Harry Tierney (1919). Introduced by Adele Rowland in the musical *Irene* (1919). The song took cognizance of the fact that the color of light blue had come into vogue in 1919 through the wardrobe then favored so greatly by Alice Roosevelt Longworth, daughter of Theodore Roosevelt. The song went on to become one of America's most celebrated waltzes. In the motion-picture adaptation of the musical (RKO, 1940), it was first danced to by Anna Neagle and Ray Milland, and later sung by Anna Neagle.

Innamorata (or, Sweetheart), words by Jack Brooks, music by Harry Warren (1955). Introduced by Dean Martin in the motion-picture musical *Artists and Models* (Warner, 1955), then further popularized by him in a best-selling Capitol recording.

Innocents of Paris, a motion-picture

musical starring Maurice Chevalier in his American screen debut (Paramount, 1929). Songs by Leo Robin and Richard A. Whiting.

See: Louise.

In Old Chicago, words by Mack Gordon, music by Harry Revel (1938). Title song of a motion-picture musical starring Alice Faye and Tyrone Power (20th Century-Fox, 1938).

In Old New York. *See:* Streets of New York.

In Other Words. *See:* Fly Me to the Moon.

International Rag, words and music by Irving Berlin (1913). Berlin wrote this number for his appearances at the Hippodrome Theatre in London, in 1913, where he was billed as "The Ragtime King." In America it was popularized by Sophie Tucker. The song was revived in the motion-picture musical *Alexander's Ragtime Band* (20th Century-Fox, 1938).

In the Baggage Coach Ahead, words and music by Gussie L. Davis (1896). This sentimental ballad was the most celebrated song by Tin Pan Alley's first successful Negro composer. It was introduced by Imogene Comer at Howard's Athenaeum Theatre in Boston in 1896. She scored such a success with it there that she kept it in her vaudeville act for the next three years, and was largely responsible for its immense success.

Davis drew material for his ballad from an actual episode witnessed by him when he had worked as a Pullman porter. A weeping child, on one of his trains, revealed to him that her mother was in the baggage coach ahead—in a coffin. Davis described his poignant incident to another Pullman porter, Frank Archer, who wrote a poem about it entitled "Mother." Several years later, after he had become a songwriter, Davis came upon the poem and forthwith recognized its potential as a sentimental ballad. He wrote words and music and sold his song outright to the publishers Howley and Haviland for a few dollars. Thus he never actually profited from the song's formidable sheet-music sales.

In the Chapel in the Moonlight, words and music by Billy Hill (1936).

In the Cool, Cool, Cool of the Evening, words by Johnny Mercer, music by Hoagy Carmichael (1951). Introduced by Bing Crosby and Jane Wyman in the motion-picture musical *Here Comes the Groom* (Paramount, 1951). The song received the Academy Award.

In the Evening by the Moonlight, words and music by James Bland (1879). Introduced by James Bland and Callender's Original Georgia Minstrels.

Bland completed his ballad after visiting a plantation on the James River, in the Tidewater section of Virginia, near Williamsburg. That peaceful setting—and the picture of Negroes sitting in front of their cabins, some of them strumming on banjos—was his immediate stimulus.

In the Garden of My Heart, words by Caro Roma, music by Ernest R. Ball (1908).

In the Good Old Summertime, words by Ren Shields, music by George Evans (1902). One of the earliest song hits about a season of the year.

One Sunday, during the summer of 1902, George Evans, the famous minstrel, dined with Ren Shields and Blanche Ring at the Brighton Beach Hotel in Brooklyn. Evans happened to remark how some people liked the winter, but how he himself preferred the good old summertime. Blanche Ring suggested he write a song on the subject, and Shields consented to do the lyrics. The song was completed in a few days, and was tried out on a piano in the lobby of the Union Square Hotel in New York City. The song was introduced by Blanche Ring in the musical *The Defender* (1902), a performance that helped lift her to stardom. (When *The Defender* opened in Boston, Blanche Ring sang it on a runway. The first ten rows in the auditorium were occupied by students from Harvard University, who joined her in singing the chorus.)

Despite Blanche Ring's success

with the number, publishers were reluctant to issue it. They were violently opposed to seasonal songs. They argued that performers in vaudeville and elsewhere would be reluctant to sing about the summer in winter, and thus the song could at best have only a three-month-sale period. All such prejudice against seasonal songs, however, was permanently dispelled by the meteoric success of this song, which sold well over a million copies of sheet music, and which maintained its popularity not only through all the months of the year, but through several years.

The song provided the title and background music for a motion-picture musical (MGM, 1949).

In 1903 Ren Shields and George Evans produced a sequel which they called "In the Merry Month of June."

In the Good Old Summertime, a motion-picture musical based on Miklos Laszlo's play *The Little Shop Around the Corner*, (MGM, 1949). Starring Judy Garland and Van Johnson. The score was made up mainly of standards.

See: I Don't Care; In the Good Old Summertime; Meet Me Tonight in Dreamland; Play That Barber Shop Chord; Put Your Arms Around Me, Honey.

In the Great Somewhere, words and music by Paul Dresser (1901).

In the Heart of the Dark, words by Oscar Hammerstein II, music by Jerome Kern (1939). Introduced by Hollace Shaw in the musical *Very Warm for May* (1939).

In the Land of Harmony, words by Bert Kalmar, music by Ted Snyder (1911).

In the Merry Month of May, words by Ren Shields, music by George Evans (1903). Introduced in vaudeville by Ren Shields. This is the sequel to a successful seasonal ballad, "In the Good Old Summertime," written one year earlier by Shields and Evans.

In the Middle of an Island, words and music by Joe Garland (1939). It Varnick (1957). Popularized by Tony Bennett in a Columbia recording.

In the Middle of the Night, words by Billy Rose, music by Walter Donaldson (1925).

In the Mood, words by Andy Razaf, music by Joe Garland (1939). It became a specialty of Glenn Miller and his orchestra, recorded by them in a best-selling Bluebird disk that was responsible for bringing Glenn Miller his first success as bandleader. The song was interpolated for Glenn Miller and his orchestra in the motion-picture musical *Sun Valley Serenade*, starring Sonja Henie (20th Century-Fox, 1941). In the motion-picture biography *The Glenn Miller Story* (Universal, 1953), it was presented by Joseph Gershenson's Orchestra imitating the Glenn Miller sound.

In the Morning by the Bright Light, words and music by James A. Bland (1879). Introduced in and a favorite of minstrel shows. This number has sometimes been mistaken for a Negro spiritual.

In the Park in Paree, words by Leo Robin, music by Ralph Rainger (1933). Introduced by Maurice Chevalier in the motion-picture musical *A Bedtime Story* (Paramount, 1933). It was revived by Chevalier in the motion picture *A New Kind of Love* (Paramount, 1963).

In the Shade of the Old Apple Tree, words by Harry H. Williams, music by Egbert Van Alstyne (1905). The song is believed to have been inspired by a visit to Central Park (which has no apple trees!). Williams and van Alstyne wrote the ballad while employed as song pluggers for the publishing house of Remick, and achieved with it their first major success as songwriters.

In the Shade of the Pyramids, words by Richard C. McPherson, using the pen name of Cecil Mack, music by Ernest R. Ball (1904). Ball's first ballad, introduced by May Irwin in the musical *Miss Black Is Back* (1904).

In the Still of the Night, words and music by Cole Porter (1937). Introduced by Nelson Eddy in the motion-picture musical *Rosalie* (1937). It was interpolated in the Cole Porter screen biography *Night and Day* (Warner, 1946), sung by Ginny Simms and chorus. Della Reese's first successful recording (for Jubilee) came with this number.

In the Sweet Bye and Bye, words by Vincent P. Bryan, music by Harry von Tilzer (1902). Not to be confused with a religious hymn of the same name.

Invitation, words by Paul Francis Webster, music by Bronislau Kaper (1956). Instrumental theme from the non-musical motion picture of the same name starring Dorothy McGuire and Van Johnson (MGM, 1952) to which Webster added lyrics. The song was popularized in recordings by Rosemary Clooney for Columbia and Jack Jones for Kapp.

In Zanzibar (or, My Little Chimpanzee), words by Will D. Cobb, music by Gus Edwards (1904). Introduced in the musical *The Medal and the Maid* (1904).

I Only Have Eyes for You, words by Al Dubin, music by Harry Warren (1934). Introduced by Dick Powell in the motion-picture musical *Dames* (First National, 1934). It was subsequently interpolated in several motion pictures. These included *The Girl from Jones Beach* (Warner, 1949); *My Dream Is Yours,* starring Doris Day and Jack Carson (Warner, 1949); and *Tea for Two* (Warner, 1950), sung by Doris Day and Gordon MacRae. Al Jolson sang it on the soundtrack of the motion-picture musical *Jolson Sings Again* (Columbia, 1959).

I Poured My Heart into a Song, words and music by Irving Berlin (1939). Introduced by Rudy Vallée in the motion-picture musical *Second Fiddle* (20th Century-Fox, 1939).

I Ran All the Way Home, words and music by Bennie Benjamin and George Weiss (1951). Popularized by Eddy Howard in a Mercury recording.

I Really Don't Want to Know, words by Howard Barnes, music by Don Robertson (1953). Its composer's first hit song. It was popularized by Les Paul and Mary Ford in a Capitol recording and by Eddy Arnold in an RCA Victor release.

Ireland Must Be Heaven, For My Mother Came from There, words by Joe McCarthy and Howard Johnson, music by Fred Fisher (1916). It was interpolated in Fred Fisher's screen biography *Oh, You Beautiful Doll* (20th Century-Fox, 1949).

I Remember It Well, words by Alan Jay Lerner, music by Frederick Loewe (1958). Introduced by Maurice Chevalier and Hermione Gingold in the motion-picture musical *Gigi* (MGM, 1958).

I Remember You, words by Johnny Mercer, music by Victor Schertzinger (1942). Introduced by Dorothy Lamour in the motion-picture musical *The Fleet's In* (Paramount, 1942).

Irene, words by Joseph McCarthy, music by Harry Tierney (1919). Title song of a musical comedy (1919), where it was introduced by Edith Day and ensemble. In the motion-picture adaptation of the musical (RKO, 1940), it was sung by a chorus.

Irene, a musical comedy with book by James Montgomery. Lyrics by Joseph McCarthy. Music by Harry Tierney. Starring Edith Day (1919).

The motion-picture adaptation starred Anna Neagle and Ray Milland (RKO, 1940). It used much of the stage score as background music. "You've Got Me Out on a Limb" was written for this movie.

See: Castle of Dreams; In My Sweet Little Alice Blue Gown; Irene; You've Got Me Out on a Limb.

Irene's Lullaby. *See:* Sleep, Baby, Sleep.

The Irish Jubilee, words by James Thornton, music by Charles Lawlor (1890). One of Thornton's earliest song successes, and one of the few by him that was not a sentimental ballad. It was introduced in vaudeville by the song-and-dance team of Lawlor and Thornton, its creators. Sigmund Spaeth revealed that this song "contains some of the worst rhymes and puns in history, but it packed a tremendous amount of obvious comedy into its four long stanzas, to which a strain of 'Auld Lang Syne' was regularly added as a tag."

Irma La Douce, a French popular song, music by Marguerite Monnot, introduced in 1956 by Colette Renard in the Paris production of the musical of the same name. English lyrics by Julian More, David Heneker and Monty Norman. The song, with English lyrics, was introduced in the United States by Elizabeth Seal in the American production of the musical (1960). It was used in the background music of the motion-picture adaptation of the musical starring Shirley MacLaine and Jack Lemmon (Universal, 1963).

Irresistible You, words by Don Raye, music by Gene de Paul (1944). Introduced in the motion-picture musical *Broadway Rhythm,* starring George Murphy (MGM, 1944), sung by Ginny Simms.

I Said My Pajamas (and Put On My Prayers), words and music by Eddie Pola and George Wyle (1950). Popularized by Fran Warren and Tony Martin, with Henri René and his orchestra, in an RCA Victor recording.

I Saw Mommy Kissing Santa Claus, words and music by Tommie Connor (1952). Popularized by the Columbia recording of twelve-year-old Jimmy Boyd, which sold a million and three quarter disks in the first year of its release, and about two and a half million disks since then.

I See Your Face Before Me, words by Howard Dietz, music by Arthur Schwartz (1937). Introduced by Jack Buchanan, Evelyn Laye and Adele Dixon in the musical *Between the Devil* (1937).

Ise Gwine Back to Dixie, words and music by C. A. White (1874). A Negro dialect song popularized in minstrel shows. It was revived by Ann Sheridan and a girls' chorus in the nonmusical motion picture *Dodge City,* starring Errol Flynn (Warner, 1939). It was also interpolated in the Western motion picture *Overland Telegraph,* starring Tim Holt (RKO, 1951).

Is Everybody Happy?, the title of two different motion-picture musicals, both starring Ted Lewis and his orchestra. The title is a catch phrase used by Ted Lewis in his act and identified with him. The first screen musical starred him with Ann Pennington (Warner, 1929). It had songs by Grant Clarke and Harry Akst. The jazz classic "Tiger Rag" and W. C. Handy's "St. Louis Blues" were interpolated. The second screen musical was a motion-picture biography of Ted Lewis (Columbia, 1943). He was starred with Nan Wynn and Bob Haymes. Various standards were used in the score.

See: I'm Just Wild About Harry; It Had to Be You; On the Sunny Side of the Street; St. Louis Blues; Way Down Yonder in New Orleans.

Is He the only Man in the World?, words and music by Irving Berlin (1962). Introduced by Nanette Fabray in the musical *Mr. President* (1962).

I Should Care, words and music by Sammy Cahn, Axel Stordahl and Paul Weston (1944). Introduced by Robert Allen in the motion-picture musical *Thrill of a Romance,* starring Van Johnson and Esther Williams (MGM, 1945).

Is It Really Me?, words and music by Tom Jones and Harvey Schmidt (1963). Introduced by Inga Swenson in the musical *110 in the Shade* (1963).

Is It True What They Say About Dixie?, words by Sammy Lerner and Irving Caesar, music by Gerald Marks (1936). Popularized by Rudy Vallée and by Al Jolson over the radio and in recordings.

Isle d'Amour, words by Earl Carroll, music by Leo Edwards (1913). Interpolated in the *Ziegfeld Follies of 1913,* sung by Jose Collins, imported from the London stage. It was sung by Ann Blyth in the motion-picture musical *The Merry Monihans* (Universal, 1944).

Isle o' Dreams, words by George Graff, Jr., and Chauncey Olcott, music by Ernest R. Ball (1912). Introduced by Chauncey Olcott in the musical *The Isle o' Dreams* (1912).

Isle of Capri, words by Jimmy Kennedy, music by Will Grosz (1934). An English poplar song that became one of the leading hit tunes in the

United States in 1934 and 1935. It was successfully performed by Xavier Cugat and his orchestra in night clubs and recordings. The song sold over a million copies of sheet music and three million disks in various recordings. A swing version by Joe "Wingy" Manone became that jazz artist's first big record—a Vocalian release in 1935.

Isle of Dreams. *See:* Isle o' Dreams.

The Isle of Our Dreams, words by Henry Blossom, music by Victor Herbert (1906). Love duet introduced by Joseph M. Ratliff and Augusta Greenleaf in the operetta *The Red Mill* (1906).

Is Mother Thinking of Her Boy?, words by George Cooper, music by Joseph P. Skelly (1899). Popularized by Julius P. Witmark (a member of the publishing firm of M. Witmark and Sons) in performances all over the country as a minstrel with Thatcher, Primrose and West, and later with the Billy Emerson Minstrels.

Isn't It a Pity?, words by Ira Gershwin, music by George Gershwin (1933). Introduced by George Givot and Josephine Huston in the musical (George Gershwin's last) *Pardon My English* (1933). This lyric is unusual in that it places the song's title in the verse. In both verse and chorus the song gives the effect of rhymed conversation and has sprinklings of colloquial phrases.

Isn't It Romantic?, words by Lorenz Hart, music by Richard Rodgers (1932). Introduced by Maurice Chevalier and Jeanette MacDonald in the motion-picture musical *Love Me Tonight* (Paramount, 1932).

Isn't Love the Grandest Thing?, words by Jack Scholl, music by Louis Alter (1935). Introduced in the motion picture *The Rain Makers,* starring Bert Wheeler and Robert Woolsey (RKO, 1935).

Isn't This a Lovely Day to Be Caught in the Rain?, words and music by Irving Berlin (1935). Introduced by Fred Astaire in the motion-picture musical *Top Hat* (1935).

I Speak to the Stars, words by Paul Francis Webster, music by Sammy Fain (1954). Introduced by Doris Day in the motion-picture musical *Lucky Me* (Warner, 1954).

Is That You, Mr. Riley?, words and music probably by Pat Rooney (1883). During World War I a controversy erupted over the authorship of this comedy song. Several different people claimed to have written it. When originally published, the sheet music not only credited Pat Rooney but also used his picture on the title page. Pat Rooney introduced the song in vaudeville, accompanying it with a soft-shoe stint; this rendition marked the beginning of his success as a performer. The song and dance continued to be a basic part of his vaudeville routine for many years. This song was also responsible for initiating in Tin Pan Alley a vogue for Reilly and O'Reilly songs.

Istanbul, Not Constantinople, words by Jimmy Kennedy, music by Nat Simon (1953). Popularized by the Four Lads in a Columbia recording.

I Still Get a Thrill, words by Benny Davis, music by J. Fred Coots (1930). Introduced by Hal Kemp and his orchestra at the Hotel Taft in New York, a performance that was broadcast. The song was further popularized by Bing Crosby in a Decca recording.

Coots described to this editor how the song came to be written: "During a conference about new titles and ideas, Davis mentioned a couple of dozen potential song titles. When the session closed we decided to go over to Lindy's for coffee. On the way over to Lindy's, Davis remembered a phrase he thought had a good sound to it, and mentioned the title 'I Still Get a Thrill.' I became so excited, I made Davis return to the studios, and after a three-hour session we completed the entire song."

I Still Get Jealous, words by Sammy Cahn, music by Jule Styne (1947). Introduced by Nanette Fabray and Jack McCauley in the musical *High Button Shoes* (1947).

I Still Look at You That Way, words by Howard Dietz, music by Arthur Schwartz (1963). Introduced by

Mary Martin in the musical *Jennie* (1963).

I **Still See Elisa,** words by Alan Jay Lerner, music by Frederick Loewe (1951). Introduced by James Barton in the musical play *Paint Your Wagon* (1951).

I **Surrender, Dear,** words by Gordon Clifford, music by Harry Barris (1932). This number played a significant part in Bing Crosby's early career. Crosby introduced it in 1930 during a personal appearance at the Cocoanut Grove in Los Angeles, using a fine arrangement by Jimmie Greer. Crosby later explained: "Dance bands usually played a number in straight tempo, but ours . . . had changes of tempo and modulations and vocal touches in several spots. This had much to do with the popularity of the song. Week after week, people demanded that we sing it; we couldn't get off without singing it several times a night."

Signed to appear in six "shorts" for Mack Sennett in 1930—this was before Crosby had appeared in a full-length movie—Crosby initiated the series with *I Surrender*, built around the song. This "short" came to the attention of William S. Paley, president of CBS, who was so impressed by Crosby's performance that he signed him to a CBS contract. This marked the beginning of Crosby's successful radio career. At that time Crosby also made a successful recording of the song.

"I Surrender, Dear" was also a specialty of Kate Smith. She featured it on her first CBS radio program on May 1, 1931.

The song provided the title for and was interpolated in a full-length motion-picture musical starring Gloria Jean (Columbia, 1948). It was also used in the background music for the non-musical motion picture *Battleground*, starring Van Johnson and John Hodiak (MGM, 1949).

Benny Carter's trumpet solo in a Capitol recording of this song is a favorite of many jazz aficionados.

Is You Is, or Is You Ain't, Ma Baby?, words by Billy Austin, music by Louis Jordan (1943). Interpolated in the motion-picture musical *Follow the Boys* (Universal, 1944), in which it was sung by Louis Jordan. The Delta Rhythm Boys sang it in the motion-picture musical *Easy To Look At,* starring Gloria Jean (Universal, 1945).

It, words by Otto Harbach and Oscar Hammerstein II, music by Sigmund Romberg (1926). Introduced by Eddie Buzzell and Nellie Breen in the operetta *The Desert Song* (1926). It was revived in Romberg's screen biography *Deep in My Heart* (MGM, 1954), sung by Ann Miller.

It Ain't Gonna Rain No Mo', words and music by Wendell Hall (1923). Introduced and popularized by Wendell Hall. The copyright entry, and the first edition of the sheet music, maintains that the song was a modern version of an old Southern melody. "It Ain't Gonna Rain No Mo' " was interpolated in the motion-picture musical *Has Anybody Seen My Gal?* (Columbia, 1952).

It Ain't Necessarily So, words by Ira Gershwin, music by George Gershwin (1935). Sportin' Life's cynical philosophy of life and religion introduced by John Bubbles in the folk opera *Porgy and Bess* (1935). In the motion-picture adaptation (Columbia, 1959), it was sung by Sammy Davis.

John Bubbles had considerable difficulty mastering the slow triplets in this number during the rehearsals of *Porgy and Bess*. Alexander Steinert, the coach for the singers, hit upon the happy idea of tap-dancing the rhythm for Bubbles, and only then did Bubbles understand what was wanted from him.

The number was interpolated in George Gershwin's screen biography *Rhapsody in Blue* (Warner, 1945). This song is one of Ira Gershwin's favorite lyrics among his own creations, together with "Embraceable You," "The Babbitt and the Bromide" and "The Saga of Jenny."

Italian Street Song, words by Rida Johnson Young, music by Victor Herbert (1910). A nostalgic recollection of the city of Naples, introduced by Emma Trentini and chorus in the operetta *Naughty Marietta* (1910). In the motion-picture adaptation of the operetta (MGM, 1935), it was sung by Jeanette MacDonald. Jane Powell sang it in the motion-picture musical *Holiday in Mexico,* starring Walter Pidgeon and José Iturbi (MGM, 1946).

I Talk to the Trees, words by Alan Jay Lerner, music by Frederick Loewe (1951). Introduced in song and dance by Tony Bavaar in the musical play *Paint Your Wagon* (1951).

It All Depends on You, words by Bud De Sylva and Lew Brown, music by Ray Henderson (1926). Interpolated by Al Jolson in the musical *Big Boy* (1925) and in the motion-picture musical *The Singing Fool* (Warner, 1929). He later recorded it successfully for Decca. Since this song was also a Ruth Etting favorite, it was interpolated in her screen biography *Love Me or Leave Me* (MGM, 1955), sung by Doris Day.

It Amazes Me, words by Carolyn Leigh, music by Cy Coleman (1958). Introduced and popularized by Tony Bennett in a Columbia recording.

It Can't Be Wrong, words by Kim Gannon, music by Max Steiner (1942). Introduced in the non-musical motion picture *Now, Voyager,* starring Bette Davis and Paul Henreid (Warner, 1942). It was popularized by Dick Haymes in a Decca recording.

It Could Happen to You, words by Johnny Burke, music by James Van Heusen (1944). Introduced by Dorothy Lamour and Fred MacMurray in the motion picture *And the Angels Sing* (Paramount, 1944).

It Don't Mean a Thing (If It Ain't Got That Swing), words by Irving Mills, music by Duke Ellington (1932). First conceived as an intrumental, then published as a song with lyrics. This is one of the earliest usages in popular music of the term "swing." With this number, in February of 1932, Ivie Anderson made her first recording with Duke Ellington—for Brunswick

It Doesn't Cost You Anything to

Dream, words by Dorothy Fields, music by Sigmund Romberg (1945). Introduced by Maureen Cannon and Wilbur Evans in the musical *Up in Central Park* (1945).

It Doesn't Seem Like the Same Old Smile, words and music by James Thornton (1896). One of four successful songs written and published by Thornton in the single year of 1896. It was introduced in vaudeville by Helene Mora.

It Had Better Be Tonight, words by Johnny Mercer, music by Henry Mancini (1964). Introduced by Fran Jeffries in the non-musical motion picture *The Pink Panther,* starring Peter Sellers and David Niven (United Artists, 1964).

It Had to Be You, words by Gus Kahn, music by Isham Jones (1924). Introduced and popularized by Isham Jones and his band. It was successfully revived in 1944, then interpolated in several motion pictures. These included the Ted Lewis screen biography *Is Everybody Happy?* (Columbia, 1943), sung by Nan Wynn; *Show Business,* starring Eddie Cantor (RKO, 1944); the screen biography of Texas Guinan, *The Incendiary Blonde,* (Paramount, 1945), sung by Betty Hutton; *South Sea Sinner,* starring Macdonald Carey and Shelley Winters (Universal, 1950); and the screen biography of Gus Kahn, *I'll See You in My Dreams* (Warner, 1951), where it was sung by Danny Thomas and used as a recurrent theme. It also provided the title for and was played under the titles of a non-musical motion picture starring Ginger Rogers and Cornel Wilde (Columbia, 1947).

It Happened in Monterey, words by Billy Rose, music by Mabel Wayne (1930). Introduced in the motion-picture musical *The King of Jazz* (Universal, 1930).

It Happened in Nordland, a comic opera with book and lyrics by Glen MacDonough. Music by Victor Herbert. Starring Marie Cahill and Lew Fields (1904).
See: Absinthe Frappé.

I Think of You, words and music by

Jack Elliott and Don Marcotte, melody based on a theme from the first movement of Rachmaninoff's Second Piano Concerto (1941). Interpolated in the motion-picture musical *Holiday in Mexico*, starring Walter Pidgeon and José Iturbi (MGM, 1946), in which it was sung by Jane Powell, accompanied by the famous concert pianist José Iturbi. The song, however, was introduced on an RCA Victor recording by Tommy Dorsey and his orchestra (vocal by Frank Sinatra).

I Thought About You, words by Johnny Mercer, music by James Van Heusen (1939). Introduced and first popularized in a Columbia recording by Benny Goodman and his band, with vocal by Mildred Bailey.

I Threw a Kiss in the Ocean, words and music by Irving Berlin (1942). Written during World War II for the benefit of Navy Relief. It was introduced by Kate Smith.

It Is No Secret, words and music by Stuart Hamblen (1950). Popularized in 1951 in a Capitol recording by Jo Stafford.

It Isn't Fair, words and music by Richard Himber (1933). Introduced and popularized by Richard Himber and his orchestra. It was revived in 1952 in a best-selling recording by Don Cornell for Coral.

It Looks to Me Like a Big Night Tonight, words by Harry H. Williams, music by Egbert Van Alstyne (1908).

It Might As Well Be Spring, words by Oscar Hammerstein II, music by Richard Rodgers (1945). Introduced by Luanne Hogan singing on the soundtrack (for Jeanne Crain) in the motion-picture musical *State Fair* (20th Century-Fox, 1945). It received the Academy Award.

In trying to write the lyrics for "It Might As Well Be Spring," Hammerstein was for a long time stymied. The song was intended for the heroine of the movie, Margy, a young girl with the blues, even though she is about to have a good time at a state fair. "Hammerstein felt that her mood required a song," this editor wrote in his biography of

Richard Rodgers, "and in thinking the matter over it seemed to him that Margy's temper resembled spring fever. But state fairs are held in the fall and not in the spring. He consulted Rodgers and asked if it was possible to have a lyric in which Margy opines that it might be autumn but that the way she feels it might as well be spring. 'That's it,' Rodgers said: 'That's just it.' Hammerstein recalls: 'All my doubts were gone. I had a partner behind me.' Hammerstein completed his lyric in about one week. . . . One day, in their office at the RKO building, Hammerstein handed this lyric over to Rodgers. He then stepped down the corridor to talk to Max Dreyfus. When he returned, about an hour later, Rodgers had completed his melody in its final form."

In the motion-picture remake of *State Fair* (20th Century-Fox, 1962), it was sung on the soundtrack by Anita Gordon (for Pamela Tiffin).

It Never Entered My Mind, words by Lorenz Hart, music by Richard Rodgers (1940). Introduced by Shirley Ross in the musical *Higher and Higher* (1940).

It Never Was You, words by Maxwell Anderson, music by Kurt Weill (1938). Introduced by Richard Kollmar and Jeanne Madden in the musical *Knickerbocker Holiday* (1938). Judy Garland sang it in the motion-picture musical *I Could Go On Singing* (United Artists, 1963).

It Only Hurts for a Little While, words by Mack David, music by Fred Spielman (1956). Popularized by the Ames Brothers in an RCA Victor release.

It Only Takes a Moment, words and music by Jerry Herman (1964). Introduced by Eileen Brennan and Charles Nelson Reilly in the musical *Hello, Dolly!* (1964).

It's a Big, Wide Wonderful World, words and music by John Rox (1940). Introduced by Wynn Murray, Walter Cassell and company in the revue *All in Fun* (1940). It was interpolated in the motion-picture musical *Rhythm Inn*, starring Jane

Frazee (Monogram, 1951), and in the non-musical motion picture *Sweet Bird of Youth,* starring Paul Newman and Geraldine Page (MGM, 1962).

It's a Cute Little Way of My Own, words by Robert B. Smith, music by Harry Tierney (1916). Introduced by Anna Held and chorus in the musical *Follow Me* (1916).

It's a Good Day, words and music by Peggy Lee and Dave Barbour (1946). Popularized by Peggy Lee in a Capitol recording. Jane Froman sang it on the soundtrack of her motion-picture biography *With a Song in My Heart* (20th Century-Fox, 1952).

It's a Grand Night for Singing, words by Oscar Hammerstein II, music by Richard Rodgers (1945). Introduced by the ensemble in the motion-picture musical *State Fair* (20th Century-Fox, 1945). In the remake of this movie (20th Century-Fox, 1962), it was sung by Pat Boone, Anita Gordon (singing on the soundtrack for Pamela Tiffin) and Bobby Darin.

It's All in the Game, words by Carl Sigman, music by Charles Gates Dawes, based on an instrumental composition (*Melody*) written and published in 1912 by the then General Dawes, who later became Vice-President of the United States. The song (1951) was popularized in 1951 and 1958 by Tommy Edwards in MGM recordings, and revived in 1963 by Cliff Edwards in a best-selling Epic recording.

It's All Right with Me, words and music by Cole Porter (1953). Introduced by Peter Cookson in the musical *Can-Can* (1953). In the motion-picture adaptation of the musical (20th Century-Fox, 1960), it was sung by Frank Sinatra.

In *Show* magazine, Richard Rodgers singled out this song as his favorite among all of Porter's numbers. The lyrics, Rodgers said, "present a basic reaction that all of us have experienced at one time or another—one of almost rueful pleasure. It's all simple and direct, but there's a fairly intellectual concept accompanying the emotion that

makes for something refreshing and moving." As for the tune, said Rodgers, "it's criss-crossing of minor to major and the insistence of its rhythm make it just about irresistible. With this song, Cole Porter was never better, and there is no higher praise."

Peter Nero's recording for RCA Victor makes effective use of thematic material from Beethoven's *Appassionata Sonata.*

It's Almost Tomorrow, words by Wade Buff, music by Eugene H. Adkinson (1955). Popularized by the Dream Weavers in a Decca recording.

It's a Lovely Day Today, words and music by Irving Berlin (1950). Introduced by Galina Talva and Russell Nype in the musical *Call Me Madam* (1950). It was also sung in the motion-picture adaptation of the musical (20th Century-Fox, 1953).

It's a Lovely Day Tomorrow, words and music by Irving Berlin (1939). Introduced by Irene Bordoni in the musical *Louisiana Purchase* (1940). In the motion-picture adaptation of the musical (Paramount, 1941), it was sung by a chorus (with amusing asides by Bob Hope).

It's Always You, words by Johnny Burke, music by James Van Heusen (1941). Introduced by Bing Crosby in the motion-picture musical *The Road to Zanzibar* (Paramount, 1941). His performance of this number over the radio and in a Decca recording helped to popularize the song. The RCA Victor recording by Tommy Dorsey and his orchestra (with Frank Sinatra doing the vocal) was also a best seller.

It's a Mad, Mad, Mad, Mad World, words by Mack David, music by Ernest Gold (1963). Theme song of the motion picture of the same name with an all-star comedy cast (United Artists, 1963).

It's a Most Unusual Day, words by Harold Adamson, music by Jimmy McHugh (1948). Introduced by Jane Powell in the motion-picture musical *A Date with Judy* (MGM, 1948).

It's an Old Southern Custom, words by Jack Yellen, music by Joseph Meyer (1935). Introduced by Alice

Faye in the motion-picture musical *George White's Scandals* (20th Century-Fox, 1935).

It's a Woman's World, words by Sammy Cahn, music by Cyril Mockridge (1954). Introduced in the non-musical motion picture *Woman's World*, starring Fred MacMurray, June Allyson, Lauren Bacall and Van Heflin (20th Century-Fox, 1954), where it was sung on the soundtrack under the titles by the Four Aces.

It's a Wonderful World, words and music by Sid Tepper and Roy C. Bennett (1964). Introduced by Elvis Presley in the motion-picture musical *The Roustabout* (Paramount, 1964), and further popularized by him in a best-selling RCA Victor recording.

It's Been a Long, Long Time, words by Sammy Cahn, music by Jule Styne (1945). Introduced over the radio by Phil Brito. It was sung and danced to by Dan Dailey, June Haver and Gloria De Haven in the motion-picture musical *I'll Get By* (20th Century-Fox, 1950). A best-selling recording was made for Columbia by Harry James and his orchestra (vocal by Kitty Kallen).

It's Delightful to Be Married, a French popular song ("La petite Tonkinoise"), words by Anna Held, music by Vincent Scotto (1907). Anna Held made it famous in the United States after interpolating it with new English lyrics in the musical *A Parisian Model* (1907).

It's De-Lovely, words and music by Cole Porter (1936). Introduced by Ethel Merman and Bob Hope in the musical *Red, Hot and Blue* (1936). In verse and four choruses, the song traces a boy and girl from the time they fall in love, through marriage, to the birth of their first child. The song was interpolated in the second screen adaptation of the musical *Anything Goes* (Paramount, 1956), sung by Donald O'Connor and Mitzi Gaynor.

It's Easy to Remember (and So Hard to Forget), words by Lorenz Hart, music by Richard Rodgers (1935). Introduced by Bing Crosby in the motion-picture musical *Mississippi* (Paramount, 1935). It was interpolated in the non-musical motion picture *The Blue Dahlia*, starring Veronica Lake and Alan Ladd (20th Century-Fox, 1946).

It Seems Like Old Times, words and music by Charles Tobias and Sam H. Stept (1937). Introduced by Guy Lombardo and his Royal Canadians. Arthur Godfrey was doing an early-morning radio show from New York when the Guy Lombardo recording was first released. On Godfrey's way home from the studio he heard the disk from a loudspeaker and it caught his fancy. He played it on his program, raved about it and helped to popularize it. He subsequently used the number as his theme song.

It's Getting Dark on Old Broadway, words by Gene Buck, music by Dave Stamper (1922). A show-stopping number in the *Ziegfeld Follies of 1922,* in which Gilda Gray performed the "shimmy."

It's Good to Be Alive, words and music by Bob Merrill (1957). Introduced by Gwen Verdon in the musical *New Girl in Town* (1957).

It's Good to Be Alive, words and music by Harold Rome (1965). Introduced by Menashe Skulnik and Louis Gossett in the play *The Zulu and the Zayda (1965).*

It's in the Book, words and music by Art Thorsen and John Standly (1952). Popularized by John Standly in a Capitol recording.

It's Just a Matter of Time, words by Brook Benton, Belford Hendricks and Clyde Otis (1958). Popularized in 1959 by Brook Benton in a Mercury recording.

It's Love, Love, Love, words by Mack David, music by Joan Whitney and Alex Kramer (1943). It was popularized by Guy Lombardo and his Royal Canadians (vocal by Skip Nelson and the Lombardo Trio) in a recording for Decca.

It's Magic, words by Sammy Cahn, music by Jule Styne (1948). Introduced by Jack Carson and Doris Day in the motion-picture musical *Romance on the High Seas* (Warner, 1948). Doris Day's Columbia recording sold over a million disks.

Sammy Cahn wrote to this editor: "The song was written for Doris Day, then still unknown. Jule Styne and I brought her to the attention of Mike Curtiz at Warner's, who gave her her first important chance in the movies which catapulted her to stardom. Another interesting fact about this song is that Jule Styne had played the melody for me for two years, and I kept passing it by because it had a slightly Spanish flavor. Only after I had seen the script for *Romance on the High Seas,* and saw the song as a number for Doris Day and Jack Carson in a Latin night-club scene, did the song come into focus for me and I was able to do the lyrics."

Gene Nelson, Janice Rule and chorus sang it in the motion-picture musical *Starlift* (Warner, 1951).

It's Moving Day Way Down in Jungle Town *See:* Moving Day in Jungle Town.

It's My Party, words and music by Herb Wiener, Wally Gold and John Gluck (1963). Popularized by Lesley Gore in a Mercury recording.

It's Nobody's Business But My Own, words and music by Will E. Skidmore and Marshall Walker (1919). A ragtime tune introduced by Bert Williams in the *Ziegfeld Follies of 1919.*

It's Not for Me to Say, words by Al Stillman, music by Robert Allen (1957). Introduced by Johnny Mathis in the non-musical motion picture *Lizzie,* starring Eleanor Parker and Richard Boone (MGM, 1956). The song was popularized in 1957 in a Columbia recording by Johnny Mathis that sold a million disks.

It's Now or Never, words and music by Aaron Schroeder and Wally Gold, melody based on the Neapolitan folk song "O Sole Mio" (1960). Popularized by Elvis Presley in a best-selling RCA Victor recording.

It's Only a Paper Moon, words by Billy Rose and E. Y. Harburg, music by Harold Arlen (1933). Interpolated in the Broadway non-musical play *The Great Magoo* (1932); at that time the song was called "If You Believe

in Me" and it served as a recurring theme throughout the play. After acquiring a new and definitive title, the song was interpolated in the motion-picture musical *Take a Chance* (Paramount, 1933). It was subsequently heard in the non-musical motion picture *Too Young to Know,* starring Joan Leslie (Warner, 1945). Nat King Cole made a best-selling recording for Capitol.

It's So Nice to Have a Man Around the House, words by Jack Elliott, music by Harold Spina (1950). Popularized by Dinah Shore in a Columbia recording.

It's the Darndest Thing, words by Dorothy Fields, music by Jimmy McHugh (1931). Introduced in the motion-picture musical *Singing the Blues* (MGM, 1931).

It's the Talk of the Town, words and music by Marty Symes and Al J. Neiburg, music by Jerry Livingston (1933). Popularized by Glen Gray and the Casa Loma orchestra.

It's Tulip Time in Holland, words by Dave Radford, music by Richard A. Whiting (1915). Whiting's first song hit, selling over a million and a half copies of sheet music.

When he wrote this song, Whiting's great ambition was to own a Steinway grand piano. In selling his song to Remick, the publisher, Whiting made a deal that he thought was both profitable and shrewd—since all his earlier songs had sold so poorly. He accepted a Steinway grand piano in lieu of royalties. His royalties from "It's Tulip Time in Holland" could have bought him a carload of Steinways.

The song was interpolated for a production number in the motion-picture musical *Hello, Frisco, Hello* (20th Century-Fox, 1943), and it was sung in the motion-picture musical *April Showers* (Warner, 1948).

Itsy Bitsy Teenie Weenie Yellow Polka Dot Bikini, words and music by Paul J. Vance and Lee Pockriss (1960). Popularized by Bryan Hyland in a Kapp recording.

It's You I Love, words and music by Antoine "Fats" Domino and Dave Bartholomew (1957). Popularized by

"Fats" Domino in an Imperial recording.

It Takes a Woman, words and music by Jerry Herman (1964). Comedy number detailing the virtues of the female sex, introduced by David Burns and company in the musical *Hello, Dolly!* (1964).

It Takes Two to Tango. *See:* Takes Two to Tango.

It Was a Very Good Year, words and music by Ervin Drake (1961). Written for the Kingston Trio, who recorded it in 1961 in their album "Goin' Places." For the next few years it was recorded by numerous "folk" artists without attracting much interest. Frank Sinatra recorded it for Reprise in an album entitled "September of My Years" in 1965, in an effective arrangement by Gordon Jenkins. The number was then featured prominently on the television program "Sinatra," over the CBS network in November of 1965 in honor of Sinatra's fiftieth birthday. There was an immediate impact and Reprise rushed out a "single" which became a best seller.

It Was So Beautiful, words by Arthur Freed, music by Harry Barris (1932). Published as an independent number, and introduced and popularized by Harry Richman in night clubs and other personal appearances. The song was interpolated in the motion-picture musicals *The Big Broadcast* (Paramount, 1932) and *Blondie of the Follies,* starring Marion Davies and Robert Montgomery (MGM, 1932).

It Was Written in the Stars, words by Leo Robin, music by Harold Arlen (1948). Introduced in the motion picture *Casbah,* starring Yvonne De Carlo (Universal, 1948), sung by Tony Martin. It was successfully revived a decade later by Ella Fitzgerald for Verve in a Harold Arlen album; at that time Ella Fitzgerald told Arlen that this song was her Arlen favorite.

It Wonders Me, words by Arnold B. Horwitt, music by Albert Hague (1955). Introduced by Gloria Marlowe in the musical *Plain and Fancy* (1955).

I Understand Just How You Feel, words and music by Pat Best (1953). Popularized in 1954 by the Four Tunes in a Jubilee recording. The song was revived in 1961 by the G-Clefs in a best-selling Terrance recording.

I Ups to Him, words and music by Jimmy Durante (1929). A comedy number introduced by Durante in night clubs to become one of his specialties. He sang it in the musical *Show Girl* (1929).

I Used to Be Color Blind, words and music by Irving Berlin (1938). Introduced by Fred Astaire and Ginger Rogers in the motion-picture musical *Carefree* (RKO, 1938).

For this number, Astaire created what he described as a "dream dance, partly in slow motion." This is the first number in which Astaire kissed a heroine in any of his movies. To answer those critics who criticized Astaire for refusing to permit a kissing scene, Astaire decided once and for all to give his heroine a kiss of kisses—for all to see. "At the end of the slow motion of the 'I Used to Be Color Blind' dance," Fred Astaire wrote in his autobiography, "I installed a slow motion kiss that figures to make up for all the kisses I had not given Ginger Rogers all these years. . . . The slow motion dance went through nicely. . . . We were holding that kiss for about four minutes."

I Used to Love You But It's All Over, words by Lew Brown, music by Albert von Tilzer (1920).

I've a Longing in My Heart for You, Louise, words and music by Charles K. Harris (1900).

I've a Shooting Box in Scotland, words by T. Lawrason Riggs, music by Cole Porter (1915). One of Cole Porter's earliest commercial songs. It was introduced in his first Broadway musical *See America First* (1915). The show was a dismal failure, lasting less than two weeks. But the song was saved from extinction by Fred and Adele Astaire, who included it in their vaudeville act in 1915 and 1916.

I've Been Floating Down the Old Green

River, words by Bert Kalmar, music by Joe Cooper (1915). Interpolated in the musical *Maid in America* (1915).

I've Been Kissed Before, words and music by Lester Lee and Bob Russell (1952). Introduced by Rita Hayworth in the non-musical motion picture *Affair in Trinidad* (Columbia, 1952).

I've Got a Crush on You, words by Ira Gershwin, music by George Gershwin (1928). It originated in the musical *Treasure Girl* (1928), introduced by Clifton Webb and Mary Hay. Later it was interpolated in the musical *Strike Up the Band!* (1930), sung and danced to by Gordon Smith and Doris Carson. The publisher failed to issue it as a separate number, and the song was soon forgotten. Then Lee Wiley revived it. She was the first to sing it in the slow, sentimental style which is now so familiar. (It had formerly been done in a quick tempo.) She further increased the effectiveness of the song by expanding the phrase "I've got a crush" to "I have got a crush." The young Frank Sinatra made one of his first successful recordings with this number; he subsequently sang it in the motion-picture musical *Meet Danny Wilson* (Universal, 1952). The song was sung by Betty Grable and Jack Lemmon (and, in the closing scene, by Grable, Lemmon, and Marge and Gower Champion) in the motion-picture musical *Three for the Show* (Columbia, 1955).

I've Got a Feelin' for You (or, Way Down in My Heart), words by Edward Madden, music by Theodore F. Morse (1904).

I've Got a Feeling I'm Falling, words by Billy Rose, music by Harry Link and Thomas "Fats" Waller (1929). Introduced in the motion-picture musical *Applause* (Paramount, 1929).

I've Got a Feeling You're Fooling, words by Arthur Freed, music by Nacio Herb Brown (1935). Introduced by Robert Taylor in the motion-picture musical *Broadway Melody of 1936* (MGM, 1935). It was subsequently sung by Jane Fro-

man on the soundtrack of her screen biography *With a Song in My Heart* (20th Century-Fox, 1952). It was also heard in the motion-picture musical *Singin' in the Rain* (MGM, 1952).

I've Got a Heart Full of Music, words by Johnny Mercer, music by Richard A. Whiting (1938). Whiting's last song hit, introduced by Dick Powell in the motion-picture musical *The Cowboy from Brooklyn* (Warner, 1938).

I've Got a Pocketful of Dreams, words by Johnny Burke, music by James V. Monaco (1938). Introduced by Bing Crosby in the motion-picture musical *Sing, You Sinners* (Paramount, 1938), and further popularized by him in a best-selling Decca recording.

I've Got Five Dollars, words by Lorenz Hart, music by Richard Rodgers (1931). Introduced by Jack Whiting and Harriet Lake (Ann Sothern) in the musical *America's Sweetheart* (1931). It became popular as a depression song. It was interpolated in the revue *The Show Is On* (1936). It was sung by Jane Russell and Scott Brady in the motion-picture musical *Gentlemen Marry Brunettes* (United Artists, 1955).

I've Got My Captain Working for Me Now, words and music by Irving Berlin (1919). Comedy song, revived by Bob Hope and Bing Crosby in the motion-picture musical *Blue Skies* (MGM, 1946).

I've Got My Eyes on You, words and music by Cole Porter (1939). Introduced by Fred Astaire in the motion-picture musical *Broadway Melody of 1940*. It was sung by Kathryn Grayson in the non-musical motion picture *Andy Hardy's Private Secretary,* starring Mickey Rooney (MGM, 1941).

I've Got My Love to Keep Me Warm, words and music by Irving Berlin (1937). Introduced by Dick Powell in the motion-picture musical *On the Avenue* (20th Century-Fox, 1937). It was revived in 1958 in a best-selling recording by Les Brown and his orchestra for Coral.

I've Got Rings on My Fingers (or,

Mumbo Jumbo Jijiboo J. O'Shea), words by Weston and Barnes, music by Maurice Scott (1909). Introduced by Blanche Ring in the musical *The Midnight Sons* (1909). She made the song famous, and it was henceforth identified with her. She also sang it in the musical *The Yankee Girl* (1910), and in 1910 she made a historic recording of it for Victor.

I've Gotta Crow, words by Carolyn Leigh, music by Mark Charlap (1954). Introduced by Mary Martin and Kathy Nolan in the 1954 Broadway production of *Peter Pan.*

I've Got the Horse Right Here. *See:* Fugue for Tinhorns.

I've Got the Sun in the Morning. *See:* Sun in the Morning.

I've Got the World on a String, words by Ted Koehler, music by Harold Arlen (1932). Introduced by Aida Ward at the Cotton Club in Harlem, New York. It was sung by June Haver and Gloria De Haven in the motion-picture musical *I'll Get By* (20th Century-Fox, 1950).

I've Got You on My Mind, words and music by Cole Porter (1932). Introduced by Fred Astaire and Claire Luce in the musical *The Gay Divorce* (1932).

I've Got You Under My Skin, words and music by Cole Porter (1936). Introduced by Virginia Bruce in the motion-picture musical *Born to Dance* (MGM, 1936). It was sung by Ginny Simms in the Cole Porter screen biography *Night and Day* (Warner, 1946). It was also used for a comedy sequence for Tony Randall and Debbie Reynolds in the non-musical motion picture *The Mating Game* (MGM, 1959).

I've Grown Accustomed to Her Face, words by Alan Jay Lerner, music by Frederick Loewe (1956). The closing number in the musical play *My Fair Lady* (1956), introduced by Rex Harrison. He also sang it in the motion-picture adaptation of the musical (Warner, 1964).

I've Heard That Song Before, words by Sammy Cahn, music by Jule Styne (1942). This was the first number on which Cahn and Styne collaborated, initiating a successful song partnership that lasted for years and produced numerous hits. This number was introduced by Bob Crosby and his orchestra in the motion-picture musical *Youth on Parade* (Republic, 1942). Harry James and his orchestra recorded it for Columbia in 1943 (vocal by Helen Forrest), a release that sold a million disks.

I've Just Come Back to Say Goodbye, words and music by Charles K. Harris (1897).

I've Lost My Teddy Bear, words by Bob Cole, music by Bob Cole and J. Rosamond Johnson (1908). Introduced and popularized by Anna Held in the musical *Miss Innocence* (1908).

I've Never Been in Love Before, words and music by Frank Loesser (1950). Introduced by Robert Alda and Isabel Bigley in the musical *Guys and Dolls* (1950).

I've Taken Quite a Fancy to You, words by Edward Madden, music by Theodore F. Morse (1908).

I've Told Ev'ry Little Star, words by Oscar Hammerstein II, music by Jerome Kern (1932). Introduced by Walter Slezak and Katherine Carrington in the musical *Music in the Air* (1932), where it served as a recurring theme. In the motion-picture adaptation of the musical (Fox, 1934), it was sung by Gloria Swanson.

Kern derived this melody from the song of a finch. This happened in Nantucket in 1932 when he was awakened late one night by the bird's refrain. The next morning Kern tried to remember the bird's song, but was unable to do so; he was also unable to identify the bird. He stayed up late for the next few nights, hoping to hear the finch sing again. He finally did, and when this occurred Kern put the motive down on paper. From one of his friends, an ornithologist, Kern now discovered that the bird was a finch.

Ivory Tower, words and music by Jack Fulton and Lois Steele (1956). Popularized in recordings by Otis Williams and the Charms for De Luxe, by Gale Storm for Dot, and by Cathy Carr for Fraternity.

Ivy, words and music by Hoagy Carmichael (1947). Title song of a nonmusical motion picture starring Joan Fontaine (Universal, 1947). The song was popularized in recordings by Dick Haymes for Decca and Vic Damone for Mercury.

I Walk the Line, words and music by John R. Cash (1956). Popularized by John Cash in a Sun recording.

I Wanna Be Around, words and music by Johnny Mercer and Sadie Vimmerstedt (1959). The idea for this song was sent to Mercer by Sadie Vimmerstedt, a housewife in Youngstown, Ohio. He was impressed by it and offered to collaborate with her. The song was popularized in 1963 by Tony Bennett in a Columbia recording.

I Wanna Be Loved, words by Billy Rose and Edward Heyman, music by John Green (1933). Introduced in 1932 in Billy Rose's Casino de Paree in New York. It was popularized in a recording by the Andrews Sisters and was successfully revived in the early 1960s by Jan and Dean in a Liberty recording.

I Wanna Be Loved by You, words by Bert Kalmar, music by Herbert Stothart and Harry Ruby (1928). Introduced by Helen Kane (the "boop a-doop girl") in the musical *Good Boy* (1928). It was revived in the motion-picture biography of Ruby and Kalmar, *Three Little Words* (MGM, 1950), with Helen Kane's voice dubbed in on the soundtrack. (The part of Helen Kane in the movie was played by Debbie Reynolds in one of her first motion-picture appearances.) Marilyn Monroe sang this number in the motion-picture musical *Some Like It Hot* (United Artists, 1959). The song was also interpolated in the motion-picture musical *Gentlemen Marry Brunettes* (United Artists, 1955), sung by Rudy Vallée, Jane Russell and Anita Ellis; Anita Ellis' voice was dubbed in on the soundtrack for Jeanne Crain.

I Wanna Get Married, words by Dan Shapiro and Milton Pascal, music by Phil Charig (1944). Introduced by Gertrude Niesen in the musical *Follow the Girls* (1944).

I Wanna Go Where You Go. *See:* Then I'll Be Happy.

I Want a Girl Just Like the Girl That Married Dear Old Dad, words by William Dillon, music by Harry von Tilzer (1911). One of von Tilzer's most successful "mother" songs. It was revived in the motion-picture musical *The Jolson Story* (Columbia, 1946).

I Want a Man, words by Oscar Hammerstein II, music by Vincent Youmans (1928). Introduced by Libby Holman in the musical play *Rainbow* (1928). It was in this production, and primarily with this song, that Libby Holman first attracted attention as an interpreter of torch songs.

I Want to Be Evil, words and music by Raymond Taylor and Lester Judson (1952). Popularized by Eartha Kitt in an RCA Victor recording.

I Want to Be Good But My Eyes Won't Let Me, words by Robert B. Smith, music by Sigmund Romberg (1916). Introduced by Anna Held in the musical *Follow Me* (1916), in which she made a successful return to the Broadway stage after an absence of several years.

I Want to Be Happy, words by Irving Caesar, music by Vincent Youmans (1924). Introduced by Charles Winninger, Louise Groody and ensemble in the musical *No, No, Nanette* (1924). In the motion-picture adaptation of the musical (RKO, 1940), it was sung by Anna Neagle. The song was interpolated in the motion-picture musical *Tea for Two* (Warner, 1950), sung by Doris Day and Gordon MacRae. It was interpolated in the background music for the non-musical motion picture *The Dark at the Top of the Stairs*, starring Robert Preston and Dorothy McGuire (Warner, 1960).

I Want to Be Wanted, an Italian popular song ("Per tutta la vita"), music by Pino Spotti, English lyrics by Kim Gannon (1960). The song, with English lyrics, was popularized by Brenda Lee in a Decca recording.

I Want to Be with You, words by Lee Adams, music by Charles Strouse (1964). Introduced by Sammy Davis and Paula Wayne in the musical *Golden Boy* (1964).

I Want to Go Back to Michigan (Down on the Farm), words and music by Irving Berlin (1914). Hit song of the middle 1910s, revived by Judy Garland in the motion-picture musical *Easter Parade* (MGM, 1948).

I Want to Ring Bells, words by Maurice Sigler, music by J. Fred Coots (1933). Introduced by Guy Lombardo and his Royal Canadians. This was the first number rendered by Carmen Lombardo as soloist with this orchestra.

I Want What I Want When I Want It, words by Henry Blossom, music by Victor Herbert (1905). Comedy song introduced by William Pruette in the operetta *Mlle. Modiste* (1905).

I Want You, words and music by George M. Cohan (1907). Introduced in the musical *The Talk of the Town* (1907).

I Want You, I Need You, I Love You, words by Maurice Mysels, music by Ira Kosloff (1956). Popularized by Elvis Presley in a best-selling RCA Victor recording.

I Was a Shoo In, words by Betty Comden and Adolph Green, music by Jule Styne (1961). Introduced by Phyllis Newman and Orson Bean in the musical *Subways Are for Sleeping* (1961).

I Was Born in Virginia, words and music by George M. Cohan (1906). Introduced by Ethel Levey in the musical *George Washington, Jr.* (1906). Her rendition was so successful that this number subsequently came to be known as "Ethel Levey's Virginia Song."

I Was Doing All Right, words by Ira Gershwin, music by George Gershwin (1938). One of George Gershwin's last songs, introduced by Ella Logan in the motion-picture musical *The Goldwyn Follies* (United Artists, 1938).

I Was So Young (You Were So Beautiful), words by Irving Caesar and Al Bryan, music by George Gershwin (1919). An early George Gershwin song, interpolated in the musical *Good Morning Judge* (1919), sung by Charles and Molly King. This was the first Gershwin song to become known outside professional Tin Pan Alley circles; it was also the first Gershwin song in which, in the final bars, he used the device of a protracted sequence.

I Watch the Love Parade, words by Otto Harbach, music by Jerome Kern (1931). Introduced by George Meader and Flora Le Breton in the musical *The Cat and the Fiddle* (1931). It was also sung in the motion-picture adaptation of the musical (MGM, 1934).

I Went to Your Wedding, words and music by Jessie Mae Robinson (1952). Popularized by Patti Page in a Mercury recording that sold a million disks.

I Whistle a Happy Tune, words by Oscar Hammerstein II, music by Richard Rodgers (1951). Introduced by Gertrude Lawrence and Sandy Kennedy in the musical play *The King and I* (1951). In the motion-picture adaptation of the musical (20th Century-Fox, 1956), it was sung on the soundtrack by Marni Nixon (for Deborah Kerr).

I Wished on the Moon, words by Dorothy Parker, music by Ralph Rainger (1935). Introduced in the motion-picture musical *Big Broadcast of 1936.*

I Wish I Could Shimmy Like My Sister Kate, words and music by Armand J. Piron (1922). It helped promote the shimmy, a dance made famous by Gilda Gray, Bee Palmer and Ann Pennington. The number was revived in the opening scene of the motion-picture musical *The Girl Can't Help It,* starring Jayne Mansfield (20th Century-Fox, 1956).

I Wish I Didn't Love You So, words and music by Frank Loesser (1947). Introduced by Betty Hutton in the motion picture *Perils of Pauline* (Paramount, 1947). It was popularized in best-selling recordings by Dinah Shore for Columbia and Vaughn Monroe and his orchestra for RCA Victor.

I Wish I Had a Girl, words by Gus Kahn, music by Grace Le Boy (1907). Gus Kahn's first published song. It was popularized in burlesque by Mollie Williams. It was sung by Doris Day in Gus Kahn's screen biography *I'll See You in My Dreams* (Warner, 1951).

I Wish I Knew, words by Mack Gordon, music by Harry Warren (1945). Introduced by Dick Haymes in the motion-picture musical *Diamond Horseshoe,* starring Betty Grable (20th Century-Fox, 1945).

I Wish I Were In Love Again, words by Lorenz Hart, music by Richard Rodgers (1937). Introduced by Grace MacDonald and Rolly Pickert in the musical *Babes in Arms* (1937). Judy Garland and Mickey Rooney sang it in the screen biography of Rodgers and Hart, *Words and Music* (MGM, 1948).

I Wish I Were Twins, words by Frank Loesser and Eddie De Lange, music by Joseph Meyer (1934). Loesser's first hit song. It was introduced in 1934 by "Fats" Waller and his orchestra. Their recording for RCA Victor helped to popularize it.

I Wish That You Were Here Tonight, words and music by Paul Dresser (1896).

I Wish We Didn't Have to Say Goodbye, words by Harold Adamson, music by Jimmy McHugh (1944). Introduced by Perry Como in his screen debut in the motion-picture musical *Something for the Boys* (20th Century-Fox, 1944).

I Wish You Love, a French popular song ("Que reste-t'il de nos amours"), music by Charles Trenet, English lyrics by Albert A. Beach using the pen name of Lee Wilson (1955). The song, with English lyrics, was introduced by Keely Smith. It then received over fifty different recordings, the most popular being those of Gloria Lynne for Everest and Felicia Sanders for Time in 1964.

I Wonder If She'll Ever Come Back to Me, words and music by Paul Dresser (1896).

I Wonder If You Still Care for Me, words by Harry B. Smith and Francis Wheeler, music by Ted Snyder (1921).

I Wonder What's Become of Sally, words by Jack Yellen, music by Milton Ager (1924). Yellen described to this editor how this million-copy song hit came into being: "It was written to be a 'counter-seller'—a 'counter-seller' being a ballad not plugged professionally, but which the girls behind the music counters plugged at their pianos through friendship for favored song salesmen. I had friends among such girls in various cities around the country. So one evening we wrote 'I Wonder What's Become of Sally.' It was strictly an ear of corn, but when I left Ager's apartment, I had a feeling that we had written something more than a 'counter-seller.' My test of a song was the reaction I got after singing it for a performer. I was in our office early next morning waiting for an actor on whom I could try out 'Sally.' 'Black Face' Eddie Nelson came in. I hustled him into a piano room, sang him the chorus, noticed his reaction. I then rushed to the Pennsylvania Station for a train to Philadelphia, where Gus Van and Joe Schenck were appearing as vaudeville headliners. Schenck was in my opinion the greatest ballad singer in show business. His peculiar half-tenor, half-soprano voice sold millions and millions of copies of sheet music. I sang the song for Schenck just once. The following Monday, Van and Schenck headlined the bill at the Palace in New York and 'I Wonder What's Become of Sally' made its public debut. Within a week our professional offices were jammed with vaudevillians waiting to rehearse. Even Al Jolson sang and recorded it."

"I Wonder What's Become of Sally" was interpolated in Cole Porter's screen biography *Night and Day* (Warner, 1946), sung by Ginny Simms.

I Wonder Where My Lovin' Man Has Gone, words by Earle C. Jones, music by Richard A. Whiting and Charles L. Cooke (1914). Whiting's first published song.

I Wonder Where She Is Tonight, words and music by Paul Dresser (1899). Introduced and popularized by Dick José.

I Wonder Who's Kissing Her Now, words by Will M. Hough and Frank R. Adams, music by Joseph E. Howard and Harold Orlob (1909). Introduced by Joseph E. Howard in the musical *The Prince of Tonight* (1909), produced in Chicago, where it was a failure. It was then interpolated in the musical *Miss Nobody from Starland* (1910) in Milwaukee.

This was Howard's most successful song, selling over three million copies of sheet music. From 1909 until his death in 1961 he was always asked to sing this number whenever he appeared on stage, over radio and TV. In 1947, when his screen biography was filmed (20th Century-Fox, 1947), it was called after the ballad, which, of course, was prominently featured.

During the last years of Howard's life, however, the law courts disclosed the startling information that this song had not been written by Howard after all. What had happened was that in 1909 Howard employed an arranger and songwriter by the name of Harold Orlob. As part of his job, Orlob wrote "I Wonder Who's Kissing Her Now" for a Joseph E. Howard production. Since Orlob had been compensated for this chore—and since the practice was standard procedure at the time—Howard published the song as his own. Once it became a tremendous hit he jealously maintained the fiction that he had written it.

During the filming of the Joseph E. Howard biography, *I Wonder Who's Kissing Her Now*, Orlob went to the courts to set the record straight once and for all—almost forty years after the song's first publication. He was not seeking any financial redress. All he now wanted was official recognition that this hit

song was his. He proved his case. However, a compromise was worked out whereby Howard was not required to pay Orlob anything. In return, Howard willingly acknowledged Orlob as his collaborator in the writing of the melody.

The song was interpolated in the motion-picture musical *The Time, The Place and The Girl* (Warner, 1929).

ASCAP selected it in 1963 as one of sixteen numbers in its all-time Hit Parade during its half century of existence.

I Wonder Who's Kissing Her Now, a motion-picture musical biography of Joseph E. Howard, starring Mark Stevens as Howard with June Haver (20th Century-Fox, 1947). The score was made up of Howard song hits.

See: Hello, My Baby; I Wonder Who's Kissing Her Now.

I Won't Cry Any More, words by Fred Wise, music by Al Frisch (1951). Popularized by Tony Bennett in a Columbia recording.

I Won't Dance, words by Otto Harbach and Oscar Hammerstein II, music by Jerome Kern (1935). This song was written for the motion-picture adaptation of the musical *Roberta* (RKO, 1935), where it was introduced by Fred Astaire.

In working out a dance routine for this picture, Astaire asked Kern to write him a rhythmic high-voltage number. He told Kern that what he was looking for was something like this—and he proceeded to perform a dynamic tap dance. Kern understood, went to work and produced in "I Won't Dance" one of his finest rhythmic numbers.

The song was interpolated in the Jerome Kern screen biography *Till the Clouds Roll By* (MGM, 1946), sung by Van Johnson and Lucille Bremer. It was also used in the screen remake of *Roberta*, retitled *Lovely to Look At* (MGM, 1952).

I Won't Say I Will (But I Won't Say I Won't), words by Bud De Sylva and Arthur Francis, the latter Ira Gershwin's pen name, music by George

Gershwin (1922). Introduced by Irene Bordoni in the musical *Miss Bluebeard* (1922). The song was then interpolated in the revue *Nifties of 1923*. This melody is interesting for its octave leaps and hesitations in the rhythm.

I Yust Go Nuts at Christmas, words and music by Harry Stewart (1949). Comedy song in Swedish dialect now a Yuletide favorite, popularized in 1950 by Yogi Yorgesson in a Capitol recording.

J

Ja Da, words and music by Bob Carleton (1918). Nonsense song popular in the early 1920s. It was interpolated in the motion-picture musical *Rose of Washington Square* (20th Century-Fox, 1939), sung by Alice Faye.

Jailhouse Rock, words and music by Jerry Leiber and Mike Stoller (1957). Introduced by Elvis Presley in the motion-picture musical of the same name (20th Century-Fox, 1957). His recording for RCA Victor sold over a million disks.

Jamaica, a musical comedy with book by E. Y. Harburg and Fred Saidy. Lyrics by E. Y. Harburg. Music by Harold Arlen. Starring Lena Horne (in her first Broadway leading role) and Ricardo Montalban (1957). Original cast recording (RCA Victor).

See: Cocoanut Sweet; Take It Slow, Joe.

Jambalaya (or, On the Bayou), words and music by Hank Williams (1952). Popularized by Hank Williams in an MGM recording. Jo Stafford's recording for Columbia was also a best seller. The number was sung by Hank Williams, Jr. (for George Hamilton) on the soundtrack of the motion-picture musical biography of Hank Williams, Sr., *Your Cheatin' Heart* (MGM, 1964). This is the number that helped make Brenda Lewis a recording star in 1956, in a Decca release.

Jamboree Song, words and music by Johnny Mercer (1936). A narrative song popularized by Johnny Mercer in a Capitol recording.

Jam Session, a motion-picture musical starring Ann Miller, and featuring the Pied Pipers and various notable jazz bands including those of Louis Armstrong and Glen Gray (Columbia, 1944). The score was made up primarily of standards.

See: Brazil; Cherokee; I Can't Give You Anything But Love, Baby; St. Louis Blues.

The Japanese Sandman, words by Raymond B. Egan, music by Richard A. Whiting (1920). Popularized by Nora Bayes in vaudeville. It went on to sell over a million copies of sheet music. It was interpolated in the motion-picture musical *Rose of Washington Square* (20th Century-Fox, 1939).

The Jazz Singer, the first feature-length motion picture utilizing speech and sound (though most of the film was silent). Thus it ushered in the new age of talking pictures (Warner, 1928). Starring Al Jolson. It received a special award from the Academy of Motion Picture Arts and Sciences founded that same year. The score was made up of standards.

See: Blue Skies; Dirty Hands, Dirty Face; My Mammy; Toot, Toot, Tootsie.

The story was refilmed a quarter of a century later, starring Danny Thomas and Peggy Lee (Warner, 1953). The score once again was made up primarily of standards, though several new numbers were written by Jerry Seelen and Sammy Fain.

See: Birth of the Blues; Breezin' Along with the Breeze; If I Could Be with You One Hour Tonight; I'll String Along with You; I'm Looking Over a Four Leaf Clover; Just One of Those Things; Lover.

Jealous, words by Tommie Malie and and Dick Finch, music by Jack Little (1924). Successfully revived in the 1940s, then interpolated in the non-musical motion picture *Don't Trust Your Husband,* starring Fred MacMurray and Madeleine Carroll, (United Artists, 1948), and the motion-picture musical *Somebody Loves Me* (Paramount, 1952).

Jean, words and music by Paul Dresser (1895).

Jeanie with the Light Brown Hair, words and music by Stephen Foster (1854). Foster wrote this love ballad while temporarily separated from his wife, Jane, believed to have been the inspiration for the song. The Fosters were reconciled just about the time that the ballad was published.

When a bitter altercation between ASCAP and the radio networks removed all ASCAP music from the airwaves in 1941, "Jeanie with the Light Brown Hair" became one of the most frequently played and sung numbers over the radio for a period of several months.

Jeannine, I Dream Of Lilac Time, words by L. Wolfe Gilbert, music by Nathaniel Shilkret (1928). Theme song of the motion picture *Lilac Time* (1928), where it was introduced by Dolores del Rio.

Jeepers, Creepers, words by Johnny Mercer, music by Harry Warren (1938). Introduced by Dick Powell and Louis Armstrong in the motion-picture musical *Going Places,* starring Dick Powell and Anita Louise (Warner, 1938). Louis Armstrong and his orchestra recorded it for Capitol, and it has become one of his standards. The song was interpolated in the motion-picture musical *My Dream Is Yours* (Warner,

1949). It was heard as an instrumental in the background music for the non-musical motion picture *Onionhead,* starring Andy Griffith (Warner, 1958).

Jefferson and Liberty, a political song, author of words not known, adapted to the melody of "To Anacreon in Heaven" (1803). The song hails Jefferson as a champion of liberty and derides the Alien and Sedition Acts. It then became one of America's earliest successful Presidential campaign songs, promising the emergence of a new democracy through Jefferson's election.

Jenny. *See:* The Saga of Jenny.

Jericho, words by Leo Robin, music by Richard Myers (1929). Introduced by Fred Waring and his Pennsylvanians in the motion-picture musical *Syncopation,* starring Morton Downey and Dorothy Lee (RKO, 1929). It was interpolated in the motion picture *I Dood It,* starring Red Skelton (MGM, 1943).

Jerome, William, lyricist, born Cornwall on the Hudson, New York, 1865; died New York City, 1932.

See: Schwartz, Jean; Von Tilzer, Harry.

See also: Back Home in Tennessee; Get Out and Get Under the Moon; My Pearl's a Bowery Girl; Row, Row, Row.

Jersey Bounce, originally a successful instrumental composition by Bobby Plater, Tiny Brandshaw, Edward Johnson and Robert B. Wright (1941). Buddy Feyne and Robert B. Wright added lyrics in 1946, when the number became equally successful as a song. As an instrumental it was popularized by Benny Goodman and his orchestra for Okeh and by Glenn Miller and his orchestra for Bluebird. It was interpolated in the motion-picture musical *The Benny Goodman Story* (Universal, 1956).

The Jersey Lily, a musical comedy with book and lyrics by George Hobart. Music by Reginald De Koven. Starring Blanche Ring in her first leading Broadway role. Four songs were interpolated in the production.

See: Bedelia.

Jezebel, words and music by Wayne Shanklin (1950). Frankie Laine's recording for Columbia in 1951 sold a million disks.

Jim, words by Nelson Shawn, music by Caesar Petrillo and Edward Ross (1941). Introduced by Dinah Shore and popularized by Jimmy Dorsey and his orchestra (vocal by Bob Eberly and Helen O'Connell) in a Decca recording. It was interpolated in the motion picture *Yokel Boy*, starring Joan Davis (Republic, 1942).

Jim Crack Corn. *See:* The Blue Tail Fly.

Jim Crow, a popular song-and-dance routine written and devised by Thomas "Daddy" Rice in 1828. It helped establish a characterization of the Negro, in song and dance, on the American stage. This number, published in or about 1830, is often regarded as the beginning of the minstrel show.

Rice was a stage performer. While appearing in Baltimore, one day in 1828, he noticed an old, deformed Negro stumbling along, moving his body with absurd contortions. As he made his halting progress, the Negro chanted to himself a foolish ditty with gibberish verses. This episode so impressed Rice that he decided to include it in his act. Wearing tattered clothes, Rice danced with a halting, cumbersome gait. As he did so, he sang gibberish verses beginning with the lines:

"Wheel about an turn about
    An' do jis so;
 Eb'ry time I wheel about,
    I jump Jim Crow."

"While singing the first four measures of the song in a narrative melodic style," explains Hans Nathan in *Emmett*, "he moved cautiously along the footlights. In the refrain, however, to clear-cut accentuations, he began to dance grotesque postures and movements. On the words 'jis so' he jumped high. While doing this, he rolled his left hand in half seductive, half waggishly admonishing manner."

This act proved such a hit that before the year was over, blackface performers all over the country were doing Jump Jim Crow acts of their own. Impersonations of the Negro (up to now comparatively rare in the American theater) thus acquired a permanent vogue.

Joseph Jefferson, one of the greatest actors of all time, made his stage debut with this Jump Jim Crow routine. He was then a child of four, and he was a member of Rice's act. When Rice had finished his own performance of this routine, the child Jefferson appeared in a costume similar to that worn by Rice and imitated him.

The term "Jim Crow," designating segregation, became a part of the American language by virtue of its use in this famous song.

Sigmund Romberg used the phrase "Jim Crow" in the song-and-dance number "Jump Jim Crow" in his operetta *Maytime* (1917).

Jim Dandy, words and music by Lincoln Chase (1957). Popularized by La Vern Baker in an Atlantic recording in 1960.

Jim Fisk, a ballad with words and music believed to have been written by William J. Scanlan in or about 1872. Fisk was a corrupt New York politician involved in all kinds of shady deals both in Tammany Hall and in Wall Street. In 1872 he was murdered outside the Grand Central Hotel by Edward Stokes. Fisk's career as a "robber baron" was immortalized in this now famous ballad in which he was elevated to heroic status to become a kind of Robin Hood who stole from the rich to give to the poor. Sigmund Spaeth pointed out that when this ballad was first published, the sheet music identified composer and lyricist merely by the initials of "J.S." Later editions, however, used Scanlan's name in full. However, Spaeth also noted that serious doubts have since arisen as to whether Scanlan actually wrote the ballad; some are now inclined to place it within the category of American folk music.

Jimmy, the Well Dressed Man, words

and music by Jimmy Durante (1929). A comedy number performed by Durante in the musical *Show Girl* (1929). It has since become one of his famous routines.

Jimmy Valentine, words by Edward Madden, music by Gus Edwards (1911). Introduced in vaudeville by Gus Edwards and his company in his famous schoolchildren act.

Jingle Bells (or, The One Horse Open Sleigh), words and music by J. S. Pierpont (1857). One of the most popular songs ever written about the winter season, and a Yuletide classic. It was written for a local Sunday school entertainment in Boston. The Decca recording by Bing Crosby and the Andrews Sisters in 1943 sold over a million disks.

Jingle, Jangle, Jingle, words by Frank Loesser, music by Joseph J. Lilley (1942). Introduced by an ensemble on horseback in the non-musical motion picture *The Forest Rangers*, starring Fred MacMurray and Paulette Goddard (Paramount, 1942). Though the motion picture was not released until October, 1942, the song achieved top place in the nation's sheet music and record sales, and in juke-box performances, by mid-July. The Columbia recording by Kay Kyser and his orchestra sold over a million disks. During World War II, General Elliott Roosevelt named his Flying Fortress the "Jingle Jangle" and used the number as the theme song of his squadron.

Joan of Arc, They Are Calling You, words by Alfred Bryan and Willie Weston, music by Jack Wells (1917). A World War I song favorite, America's tribute to her French ally.

The Jockey on the Carousel, words by Dorothy Fields, music by Jerome Kern (1935). Introduced by Lily Pons in the motion-picture musical *I Dream Too Much* (RKO, 1935).

Joe Turner Blues, words and music by W. C. Handy (1916). The hero in this blues is the man assigned by his brother (the Governor of Tennessee) to escort gangs of convicts from the jail in Memphis to the penitentiary in Nashville.

Joey, words and music by Herb Wiener, James J. Kriegsman and Salmirs-Bernstein (1954). Popularized by Betty Madigan in an MGM recording.

Joey, Joey, Joey, words and music by Frank Loesser (1956). Introduced by Art Lund in the musical play *The Most Happy Fella* (1956).

John Brown's Body, words attributed either to Charles S. Hall, or Henry Howard Brownell, or Thomas Brigham Bishop (1861). The melody was the popular Southern camp-meeting tune "Say, Brothers, Will You Meet Us?" that was also used for the Civil War ballad "The Battle Hymn of the Republic." Union Army soldiers often amused themselves by improvising lyrics to this robust melody.

One of the members of the 21st Massachusetts Regiment, stationed at Fort Warren, was a Scottish sergeant named John Brown. He was always the victim of pranks and practical jokes. The fact that he bore the same name as that of the fanatic abolitionist who led his anti-slavery zealots on the quickly suppressed attack at Harper's Ferry, led the members of Brown's battalion to concoct lyrics taunting him by identifying him with the abolitionist.

"John Brown's Body" became a favored marching song of the regiment. It sang it upon receiving colors on the Boston Common on July 18, 1861, and a week later in New York en route to the battlefields of Virginia. On March 1, 1862, the regiment sang it in Charleston, Virginia, on the same spot where the abolitionist John Brown had been executed for his insurrection.

When Oliver Ditson published this number in 1861, the title of "Glory, Hallelujah" was used. The song also appeared that same year in Root and Cady's *Collection of Popular Songs by Various Composers.*

John Henry Blues, words and music by W. C. Handy (1922). The hero here is the legendary Negro giant capable of driving more rivets by hand than any four men, but who in the end lost his championship to an automatic riveter.

Johnny Angel, words by Lyn Duddy, music by Lee Pockriss (1962). Popularized by Shelley Fabares in a Colpix recording.

Johnny, Get Your Gun, words and music by Monroe H. Rosenfeld (1886). This was Rosenfeld's most successful song, its melody borrowed from an earlier number called "Johnny, Get Your Hair Cut." In 1917 George M. Cohan borrowed Rosenfeld's title for the opening line of his verse to "Over There."

Johnny Guitar. *See:* My Restless Love.

Johnny One Note, words by Lorenz Hart, music by Richard Rodgers (1937). Introduced by Wynn Murray and chorus in the musical *Babes in Arms* (1937). Judy Garland sang it in the Rodgers and Hart screen biography *Words and Music* (MGM, 1948).

Johnson, Howard, lyricist, born Waterbury, Connecticut, 1887; died New York City, 1941.

See: Fisher, Fred.

See also: Feather Your Nest; Ireland Must Be Heaven; Just Like Washington Crossed the Delaware; M-O-T-H-E-R; Sweet Lady; What Do We Do on a Dew-Dew-Dewy Day?; What Do You Want to Make Those Eyes at Me For?; When the Moon Goes Over the Mountain; Where Do We Go From Here?

Johnston, Arthur James, composer, born New York City, 1898.

See (Lyrics by Johnny Burke): The Moon Got in My Eyes; One, Two, Button My Shoe; Pennies from Heaven.

See (Lyrics by Sam Coslow): Cocktails for Two; Down the Old Ox Road; Just One More Chance; My Old Flame.

See also: Thanks a Million.

The Joker Is Wild, a motion-picture musical biography of Joe E. Lewis, starring Frank Sinatra as Lewis with Mitzi Gaynor (Paramount, 1957). Songs by Sammy Cahn and James Van Heusen.

See: All the Way.

Jolson, Al, composer and lyricist, born Washington, D. C., 1886; died San Francisco, California, 1950.

See: Anniversary Song; Avalon; Back in Your Own Back Yard; Bagdad; California, Here I Come; Golden Gate; I'll Say She Does; Keep Smiling at Trouble; Me and My Shadow; Sonny Boy; There's a Rainbow Round My Shoulder; Yoo Hoo; You Ain't Heard Nothin' Yet.

For Al Jolson's screen biographies, see *The Jolson Story* (Columbia, 1946) and *Jolson Sings Again* (Columbia, 1949).

Jolson Sings Again, a motion-picture musical biography of Al Jolson, a sequel to *The Jolson Story* (Columbia, 1946), starring Larry Parks as Jolson with Barbara Hale (Columbia, 1949). The score was made up of standards, sung on the soundtrack by Al Jolson.

See: April Showers; Anniversary Waltz; Baby Face; Back in Your Own Back Yard; California, Here I Come; Carolina in the Morning; Chinatown, My Chinatown; Give My Regards to Broadway; I'm Just Wild About Harry; I'm Looking Over a Four Leaf Clover; I Only Have Eyes for You; Ma Blushin' Rosie; Pretty Baby; Swanee.

The Jolson Story, a motion-picture musical biography of Al Jolson starring Larry Parks as Jolson with Evelyn Keyes (Columbia, 1946). The score was made up principally of standards, sung on the soundtrack by Jolson. "Anniversary Song" was written for this movie.

See: About a Quarter to Nine; Anniversary Song; April Showers; Blue Bell; By the Light of the Silvery Moon; California, Here I Come; I Want a Girl Just Like the Girl That Married Dear Old Dad; Liza; My Mammy; On the Banks of the Wabash Far Away; Rock-a-bye Your Baby with a Dixie Melody; Sitting on Top of the World; The Spaniard That Blighted My Life; Swanee; There's a Rainbow Round My Shoulder; You Made Me Love You; Waiting for the Robert E. Lee; When You Were Sweet Sixteen.

Jones, Isham, composer, born Coalton, Ohio, 1894; died Hollywood, California, 1956.

See (Lyrics by Gus Kahn): I'll See You in My Dreams; It Had to Be

You; The One I Love Belongs to Somebody Else; On the Alamo; Swingin' Down the Lane; Spain.

See also: Indiana Moon; There Is No Greater Love.

The Jones Boy, words by Mann Curtis, music by Vic Mizzy (1953). Popularized by the Mills Brothers in a Decca recording.

Jordan Is a Hard Road to Travel, words and music by Dan Emmett (1853). A favorite in minstrel shows and in concerts by the singing Hutchinson Family. Joshua Hutchinson revealed in *A Brief Narrative of the Hutchinson Family* that "its rendering to thousands of audiences did much to disgust the American people with the 'peculiar institution' [slavery]." He further points to the intimate relationship between this number and the religious music of the Negro. "Both the predominant motive of the first section of the tune and that of the refrain are strongly reminiscent of early Negro spirituals."

Joy of Living, a motion-picture musical starring Irene Dunne and Douglas Fairbanks (RKO, 1938). Songs by Dorothy Fields and Jerome Kern.

See: Just Let Me Look at You; You Couldn't Be Cuter.

Jubilation T. Cornpone, words by Johnny Mercer, music by Gene de Paul (1956). Introduced by Stubby Kaye and the "Dogpatchers" in the musical *Li'l Abner* (1956). It was also sung by Stubby Kaye in the motion-picture adaptation of the musical (Paramount, 1959). This lyric is one of Mercer's favorites among his own creations.

Jubilee, a musical comedy with book by Moss Hart. Lyrics and music by Cole Porter. Starring Mary Boland and Melville Cooper (1935).

See: Begin the Beguine; Just One of Those Things; A Picture of Me Without You; Why Shouldn't I?

Juke Box Baby, words and music by Joe Sherman and Noel Sherman (1956). Popularized by Perry Como in an RCA Victor recording.

Jumbo, a musical extravaganza with book by Ben Hecht and Charles MacArthur. Lyrics by Lorenz Hart. Music by Richard Rodgers. Starring Gloria Grafton, Jimmy Durante, Donald Novis and Paul Whiteman and his orchestra (1935).

The motion-picture adaptation starred Doris Day, Stephen Boyd, Martha Raye and Jimmy Durante (MGM, 1962). Principal numbers were used from the Broadway score. "This Can't Be Love" from *The Boys from Syracuse* was interpolated. Soundtrack recording (Columbia).

See: Little Girl Blue; The Most Beautiful Girl in the World; My Romance; This Can't Be Love.

Jump for Joy, words by Paul Francis Webster, music by Duke Ellington (1941). Title song of a West Coast musical production (1941), introduced by Herb Jeffries. It was popularized by Herb Jeffries with Duke Ellington and his orchestra in an RCA Victor recording.

June in January, words by Leo Robin, music by Ralph Rainger (1934). Introduced by Bing Crosby in the motion-picture musical *Here is My Heart* (Paramount, 1934). This was the first song recorded by Crosby for the then newly formed company of American Decca, or Decca as it soon came to be known.

June Is Bustin' Out All Over, words by Oscar Hammerstein II, music by Richard Rodgers (1945). Introduced by Christine Johnson, Jean Darling and ensemble in the musical play *Carousel* (1945). In the motion-picture adaptation of the musical (20th Century-Fox, 1956), it was sung by Claramae Turner, Barbara Ruick and chorus.

Just a Dream, words and music by Jimmy Clanton and Cosmo A. Matassa (1958). Popularized by Jimmy Clanton in an Ace recording.

Just a Gigolo, a Viennese popular song ("Schoener Gigolo") with music by Leonello Casucci and English lyrics by Irving Caesar (1930). The song was first popularized in the United States by Vincent Lopez and his orchestra. Bing Crosby then made a highly successful recording for Decca. The song was interpolated in the motion picture *Lover, Come Back*, starring George Brent and Lucille Ball (Universal, 1946).

Just a Little Bit South of North Carolina, words and music by Sunny Skylar, Bette Cannon and Arthur Shaftel (1940). Introduced over the radio by Sunny Skylar, a vocalist with the Vincent Lopez orchestra. The song was then successfully recorded by Glenn Miller and his orchestra for RCA Victor and by Gene Krupa and his orchestra (vocal by Anita O'Day) for Okeh.

Just a Little Lovin' Will Go a Long Way, words and music by Eddy Arnold and Zeke Clements (1948). Introduced by Eddy Arnold, but popularized in 1952 by Eddie Fisher in a best-selling RCA Victor recording.

Just a Memory, words by Bud De Sylva and Lew Brown, music by Ray Henderson (1926). Published as an independent number, then interpolated in the musical *Manhattan Mary* (1927). It was heard in the motion-picture biography of Marilyn Miller, *Look for the Silver Lining* (Warner, 1949). Sheree North and a female chorus sang it in the motion-picture biography of De Sylva, Brown and Henderson, *The Best Things in Life Are Free* (20th Century-Fox, 1956).

Just an Old Love of Mine, words and music by Peggy Lee and Dave Barbour (1947). Introduced and popularized by Peggy Lee.

Just Another Day Wasted Away, words by Charles Tobias, music by Roy Turk (1927).

Just Another Polka, words and music by Frank Loesser and Milton De Lugg (1953). Popularized by Jo Stafford in a Columbia recording.

Just Around the Corner, words by Dolf Singer, music by Harry von Tilzer (1925). Harry von Tilzer's last song hit. Before writing this number, he had suffered numerous song failures. Elizabeth Marbury, former Broadway producer, wrote him a consoling note telling him that "just around the corner the sun will shine for you." That letter provided von Tilzer with material for a new song —the biggest hit he had enjoyed in several years. It was popularized by Ted Lewis and his orchestra, who performed it in his motion-picture musical biography *Is Everybody Happy?* (Columbia, 1943).

Just A-Wearyin' for You, words by Frank Stanton, music by Carrie Jacobs Bond (1901). An art song which has entered the popular repertory by virtue of performances in vaudeville in the early 1900s. This song appeared in Mrs. Bond's first publication, *Seven Songs,* in 1901, and then was reprinted as a separate number.

Just Before the Battle, Mother, words and music by George Frederick Root (1863). One of the most widely heard songs of the Civil War; it is reputed to have sold over a million copies of sheet music. It first appeared in the Christmas issue of *The Song Messenger,* the house organ of the publishing house of Root and Cady in Chicago. The song described the feelings of young soldiers on the eve of battle, and it excoriates those Northern copperheads who "in every battle kill our soldiers, by the help they give the foe." Reference was made in the song to the fact that Root's "The Battle Cry of Freedom" was sung by troops marching into battle.

Just for Once, words by Dorothy Fields, music by Albert Hague (1959). Introduced by Richard Kiley, Gwen Verdon and Leonard Stone in the musical *Redhead* (1959).

Just for the Sake of Our Daughter, words and music by Monroe H. Rosenfeld (1897).

Just Imagine, words by Bud De Sylva and Lew Brown, music by Ray Henderson (1927). Introduced by Shirley Vernon, Mary Lawlor, Ruth Mayon and girls in the musical *Good News* (1927). In the second motion-picture adaptation of the musical (MGM, 1947), it was sung by June Allyson.

Just in Time, words by Betty Comden and Adolph Green, music by Jule Styne (1956). Introduced by Sydney Chaplin and Judy Holliday in the musical *Bells Are Ringing* (1956). In the motion-picture adaptation of the musical (MGM, 1960), it was sung by Dean Martin. This is one of the two favorites of Styne among his own creations, the other being "Never Never Land."

Just Let Me Look at You, words by Dorothy Fields, music by Jerome Kern (1938). Introduced in the motion-picture musical *Joy of Living* (RKO, 1938).

Just Like a Butterfly That's Caught in the Rain, words by Mort Dixon, music by Harry Woods (1927).

Just Like a Gypsy, words and music by Seymour B. Simons and Nora Bayes (1919). Introduced by Nora Bayes in the musical *Ladies First* (1919). In the motion-picture biography of Nora Bayes, *Shine On, Harvest Moon* (Warner, 1944), it was sung by Ann Sheridan.

Just Like a Melody Out of the Sky, words and music by Walter Donaldson (1928).

Just Like Washington Crossed the Delaware, General Pershing Will Cross the Rhine, words by Howard Johnson, music by George W. Meyer (1918). Hit song anticipating American victory in World War I.

Just One Girl, words by Karl Kennett, music by Lyn Udall (1898). It was revived in the motion-picture musical *By the Light of the Silvery Moon* (Warner, 1953), sung by Gordon MacRae.

Just One More Chance, words by Sam Coslow, music by Arthur Johnston (1931). Introduced in the Marx Brothers' extravaganza *Monkey Business* (Paramount, 1931).

Just One of Those Things, words and music by Cole Porter (1935). Introduced by June Knight and Charles Walters in the musical *Jubilee* (1935).

The song was written while *Jubilee* was trying out in Ohio. Moss Hart came to Porter, suggesting an important new song for the second act. Porter agreed. "I made a mental note that with luck we might have the song for the third week of rehearsal," Hart later recalled. "But the next morning Cole called me into the living room and closed the doors. He placed a scribbled sheet of note paper on the music rack of the piano and then played and sang the verse and chorus of 'Just One of Those Things.' " Hart then adds: "No word was ever altered. It has been played and sung through the years exactly as I heard it on Sunday morning in Ohio, a song written overnight."

Frank Sinatra sang it in the motion picture *Young at Heart* (Warner, 1955); Maurice Chevalier, in the motion-picture adaptation of the musical *Can-Can* (20th Century-Fox, 1960). Other motion pictures in which it was interpolated included the screen biography of Cole Porter, *Night and Day* (Warner, 1946), where it was sung by Ginny Simms; *Lullaby of Broadway* (Warner, 1951), sung by Doris Day; and *The Jazz Singer* (Warner, 1953), sung by Peggy Lee.

Just Tell Them That You Saw Me, words and music by Paul Dresser (1895). Ballad based on a story Dresser had read in the newspaper about a woman ruined by a reckless love. Theodore Dreiser, the distinguished novelist (and the composer's brother), recalled that when Paul Dresser first sang him this ballad the "tears stood in his eyes and he wiped them away." The title of the song became a popular form of salutation throughout the United States in the mid-1890s—so much so that an enterprising manufacturer reaped a harvest selling buttons on which the title was printed.

Just Try to Picture Me Down Home in Tennessee. *See:* Back Home in Tennessee.

Just Walking in the Rain, words and music by Johnny Bragg and Robert S. Riley (1953). Introduced in 1953 in a Sun recording by the Prisonaires (inmates of the Tennessee State Penitentiary). It was popularized in 1956 by Johnnie Ray in a best-selling Columbia recording.

K

Kahal, Irving, lyricist, born Houtzdale, Pennsylvania, 1903; died New York City, 1942.

    See: Fain, Sammy.

    See also: The Night Is So Young and You Are So Beautiful; Three's a Crowd.

Kahn, Gus, lyricist, born Coblenz, Germany, 1886; died Beverly Hills, California, 1941.

    See: Donaldson, Walter; Jones, Isham; Schertzinger, Victor; Van Alstyne, Egbert; Whiting, Richard; Youmans, Vincent.

    See also: All God's Chillun Got Rhythm; Charley, My Boy; Coquette; Dream a Little Dream of Me; I'll Say She Does; I Never Knew; I Wish I Had a Girl; Liza; My Isle of Golden Dreams; Nobody's Sweetheart; San Francisco; Thanks a Million; Toot, Toot, Tootsie; Where the Shy Little Violets Grow; With All My Heart; You Ain't Heard Nothin' Yet; Your Eyes Have Told Me So; You Stepped Out of a Dream.

    For Gus Kahn's screen biography, see *I'll See You in My Dreams* (Warner, 1952).

Kalmar, Bert, lyricist, born New York City, 1884; died Los Angeles, California, 1947.

    See: Ruby, Harry.

    See also: The Ghost of the Violin; Hello, Hawaii; I've Been Floating Down the Old Green River; Moonlight on the Rhine; Oh, What a Pal Was Mary; Since Maggie Learned the Hooley Hooley; Where Did You Get That Girl?

    For Bert Kalmar's screen biography, see *Three Little Words* (MGM, 1950).

Ka-lu-a, words by Anne Caldwell, music by Jerome Kern (1921). Introduced by Oscar Shaw and girls in the musical *Good Morning, Dearie* (1921).

    "Ka-lu-a" was involved in a plagiarism suit in 1921, instituted by Fred Fisher, the composer of "Dardanella." Fisher claimed that Kern had appropriated the use of a repetitive rolling bass from "Dardanella." This put the suit in a class by itself, the first such of any importance where the infringement involved the bass part of a popular song rather than the basic melody. During the court proceedings, such distinguished musical authorities as Artur Bodanzky, Leopold Stokowski and Victor Herbert testified that the way the bass had been used in "Dardanella" was not original with that number, that there were numerous examples of similar usages in classical literature. With the case seemingly going against Fisher, he offered to settle the dispute with Kern for the price of two suits of clothes. Kern refused defiantly. The court finally decided in favor of Fisher, maintaining that "the bass materially qualified if it does not dominate the melody." Damages were set at $250, with the judge, Learned Hand, commenting acidly that the whole litigation had been "a trivial pother of scarcely more than irritation and a waste of time for everyone concerned." In all probability, the only reason Kern lost the case and had to pay damages was because he had proved himself to be such a hostile and sarcastic witness that he had prejudiced the court against him.

Kansas City, words by Mike Stoller, music by Jerry Leiber (1959). It was originally (1952) called "K. C. Loving." "Kansas City" was popularized by Wilbert Harrison's recording for Fury in 1959.

Kansas City, words by Oscar Hammerstein II, music by Richard Rodgers (1943). Introduced by Lee Dixon, Betty Garde and chorus in the musical play *Oklahoma!* (1943). In the motion-picture adaptation of the musical (Magna Theatre, 1955), it was sung by Gene Nelson, Charlotte Greenwood and male chorus.

Kansas City Kitty, words by Edgar Leslie, music by Walter Donaldson (1929). It was revived by Bob Crosby in a motion-picture musical of the same name starring Joan Davis (Columbia, 1944).

Kaper, Bronislau, composer, born Warsaw, Poland, 1902.

See (Lyrics by Paul Francis Webster): Follow Me; Invitation.

See also: All God's Chillun Got Rhythm; Cosi Cosa; Don't Go Near the Water; Hi Lili, Hi Lo; San Francisco; Take My Love.

Kathleen, words and music by Helene Mora (1894). Introduced and popularized in vaudeville by Helene Mora, "the female baritone."

Katie Went to Haiti, words and music by Cole Porter (1939). Introduced by Ethel Merman in the musical *Du Barry Was a Lady* (1939). It was also sung in the motion-picture adaptation of the musical (MGM, 1943). Porter is believed to have found material for this esoteric number in a perform-

ance by a native band in Haiti.

Katinka, words by Otto Hauerbach (Harbach), music by Rudolf Friml (1916). Title song of an operetta (1916), introduced by Samuel Ash and a male chorus.

Katinka, an operetta with book and lyrics by Otto Hauerbach (Harbach). Music by Rudolf Friml. Starring Franklyn Ardell and Adele Rowland (1915).

See: Allah's Holiday; Katinka; My Paradise; Rackety Coo.

Keep a Little Cozy Corner in Your Heart for Me, words by Jack Drislane, music by Theodore F. Morse (1905).

Keep Away from Emmaline, words by Edgar Smith, music by John Stromberg (1898). Introduced by Fay Templeton in the Weber and Fields extravaganza *Hurly Burly* (1898). This was Fay Templeton's debut in a Weber and Fields Music Hall production. Together with "Kiss Me, Honey, Do" from the same production, "Keep Away from Emmaline" was the first hit song to come out of a Weber and Fields extravaganza.

Keepin' Myself for You, words by Sidney Clare, music by Vincent Youmans (1929). Written for and introduced in the motion-picture adaptation of the musical *Hit the Deck* (RKO, 1930).

Keep It Gay, words by Oscar Hammerstein II, music by Richard Rodgers (1953). Introduced by Mark Dawson and Bob Fortier in the musical *Me and Juliet* (1953).

Keep It a Secret, words and music by Jessie Mae Robinson (1952). Popularized by Slim Whitman in an Imperial recording and by Jo Stafford in a Columbia recording.

Keep On Doin' What You're Doin', words by Bert Kalmar, music by Harry Ruby (1934). Introduced in the motion-picture musical *Hips, Hips, Hooray,* starring Bert Wheeler and Robert Woolsey (RKO, 1934).

Keep on the Sunny Side, words by Jack Drislane, music by Theodore F. Morse (1906).

Keep Smiling at Trouble, words by Al Jolson and Bud De Sylva, music by

Lewis Gensler (1925). Introduced by Al Jolson in the musical *Big Boy* (1925).

Keep Sweepng the Cobwebs Off the Moon, words by Sam M. Lewis and Joe Young, music by Oscar Levant (1927).

Keep Young and Beautiful, words by Al Dubin, music by Harry Warren (1933). Introduced by Eddie Cantor in the motion-picture musical *Roman Scandals* (United Artists, 1933).

Keep Your Hands Off My Baby, words and music by Gerry Goffin and Carole King (1962).

Keep Your Sunny Side Up. *See:* Sunny Side Up.

Kentucky Babe, words by Richard Buck, music by Adam Geibel (1896). Popularized by Bessie Davis, then became a favorite of male quartets and glee clubs.

Kentucky Sue, words by Lew Brown, music by Albert von Tilzer (1912).

Kern, Jerome, composer, born New York City, 1885; died New York City, 1943.

See (Lyrics by Dorothy Fields): Bojangles of Harlem; A Fine Romance; I Dream Too Much; Jockey on the Carousel; Just Let Me Look at You; Remind Me; Waltz in Swing Time; The Way You Look Tonight; You Couldn't be Cuter.

See (Lyrics by Otto Harbach): I Watch the Love Parade; I Won't Dance; Lovely to Look At; The Night Was Made for Love; Poor Pierrot; She Didn't Say Yes; Smoke Gets in Your Eyes; The Touch of Your Hand; Try to Forget; Yesterdays; You're Devastating.

See (Lyrics by Oscar Hammerstein II): All in Fun; All the Things You Are; All Through the Day; Can I Forget You?; Can't Help Lovin' Dat Man; Don't Ever Leave Me; D'ye Love Me?; Egern on the Tegern See; The Folks Who Live on the Hill; Here Am I; Heaven in My Arms; High, Wide and Handsome; In the Heart of the Dark; I've Told Ev'ry Little Star; I Won't Dance; The Last Time I Saw Paris; Life upon the Wicked Stage; No One But Me; Ol'

Man River; Only Make Believe; The Song Is You; Sunny; Twas Not So Long Ago; Who?; Why Do I Love You?; Why Was I Born?; You Are Love.

See (Lyrics by Johnny Mercer): Dearly Beloved; I'm Old Fashioned; Two Hearts Are Better Than One; You Were Never Lovelier.

See (Lyrics by P. G. Wodehouse): Before I Met You; Bill; Cleopatterer; Go, Little Boat; Have a Heart; The Land Where Good Songs Go; Leave It to Jane; The Little Church Around the Corner; Mr. Chamberlain; An Old Fashioned Wife; Oh, Lady, Lady; Our Little Love Nest; Rolled into One; The Siren's Song; Till the Clouds Roll By; You Never Knew About Me.

See also: Babes in the Wood; Can't Help Singing; How'd You Like to Spoon with Me?; I'd Like to Wander with Alice in Wonderland; In Love in Vain; Ka-lu-a; Long Ago and Far Away; Look for the Silver Lining; The Magic Melody; More and More; Nodding Roses; Once in a Blue Moon; Raggedy Ann; Sally; Some Sort of Somebody; Sure Thing; They Didn't Believe Me; Whip-poor-will; Whose Baby Are You?; Wild Rose; You Know and I Know; You're Here and I'm Here.

For Jerome Kern's screen biography, see *Till the Clouds Roll By* (MGM, 1946).

Kewpie Doll, words and music by Sid Tepper and Roy C. Bennett (1958). Popularized by Perry Como in an RCA Victor recording.

Kids, words by Lee Adams, music by Charles Strouse (1960). The older generation's disparaging appraisal of the younger set, introduced by Paul Lynde and Marijane Maricle in the musical *Bye Bye Birdie* (1960). In the motion-picture adaptation of the musical (Columbia, 1963), it was sung by Dick Van Dyke, Paul Lynde, Maureen Stapleton and Bryan Russell.

King, Robert A. (Bobo), composer and lyricist, born New York City, 1862; died New York City, 1932.

See: Anona; Beautiful Ohio;

Dreamy Alabama; Fountain in the Park; I Ain't Nobody's Darling; Lafayette, We Hear You Calling; Moonlight on the Colorado; Why Did I Kiss That Girl?

The King and I, a musical play with book by Oscar Hammerstein II based on Margaret Landon's novel *Anna and the King of Siam.* Lyrics by Oscar Hammerstein II. Music by Richard Rodgers. Starring Gertrude Lawrence and Yul Brynner (1951). Original cast recording (Decca).

The motion-picture adaptation starred Deborah Kerr and Yul Brynner (20th Century-Fox, 1956). Marnie Nixon sang on the soundtrack for Deborah Kerr. Virtually the entire stage score was used. Soundtrack recording (Capitol).

See: Getting to Know You; Hello, Young Lovers; I Have Dreamed; I Whistle a Happy Tune; A Puzzlement; Shall We Dance?; We Kiss in the Shadow.

Kingdom Coming (or, The Year of Jubilo), words and music by Henry Clay Work (1862). Famous Civil War ballad, and Work's first song about the Negro.

George Root, of Root and Cady, the publishers of this number, wrote in his autobiography: "One day early in the war a quiet and rather solemn-looking young man, poorly clad, was sent up to my room from the store with a song for me to examine. I looked at it and then at him in astonishment. It was 'Kingdom Coming'—full of bright good sense and comical situations in its darky dialect, the words fitting the melody almost as patly and neatly as Gilbert fits Sullivan—the melody decidedly good and taking, and the whole exactly suited to the times. . . . He needed some musical help that I could give him, and we needed just such songs as he could write."

Root and Cady preceded the publication of the song with a week of advertising in Chicago. The song was introduced in Chicago by the Christy Minstrels on April 23, 1862. It caught on immediately, became a prime favorite with minstrel shows

and the inspiration for numerous parodies and sequels; of the latter, the most successful was Work's "Babylon Is Fallen" in 1863.

The song was used in the Jerome Kern Broadway musical *Good Morning, Dearie* (1921). It was also heard in the motion-picture musical *Meet Me in St. Louis* (MGM, 1944).

The King of Jazz, a motion-picture musical starring Paul Whiteman and his orchestra (Universal, 1930). Songs by Jack Yellen and Milton Ager. Several standards were interpolated.

See: Aba Daba Honeymoon; A Bench in the Park; Happy Feet; It Happened in Monterey.

King of the Road, words and music by Roger Miller (1965). Introduced and popularized by Roger Miller in a best-selling recording for Smash. It received six "Grammy" Awards. *See also:* Queen of the House.

King of the Whole Wide World, words and music by R. Batchelor and B. Roberts (1962). Introduced by Elvis Presley in the motion-picture musical *Kid Galahad* (20th Century-Fox, 1962), and popularized by him in a best-selling RCA Victor recording.

Kismet, a musical extravaganza with book by Charles Lederer and Luther Davis based on Edward Knoblock's play of the same name. Lyrics by George "Chet" Forrest and Robert Wright. Music by Forrest and Wright based on the works of Alexander Borodin. Starring Alfred Drake and Doretta Morrow (1953). Original cast recording (Columbia).

See: And This Is My Beloved; Baubles, Bangles and Beads; Stranger in Paradise.

Kiss and Let's Make Up, words and music by Charles K. Harris (1891).

Kisses Sweeter Than Wine, words by Paul Campbell, music by Joel Newman, adapted from the Irish folk song "Drimmer's Cow" (1951). "Paul Campbell" is the pseudonym for the Weavers (Pete Seeger, Lee Hays, Fred Hellerman and Ronnie Gilbert); "Joel Newman" for Huddie Ledbetter. The song was introduced by the Weavers in a Decca recording. It was revived in 1957 by Jimmie Rodgers in a best-selling Roulette recording.

A Kiss in the Dark, words by Bud De Sylva, music by Victor Herbert (1922). Introduced by Edith Day in the musical *Orange Blossoms* (1922). Edward N. Waters described this number as "one of the best in all Herbert literature."

Mary Martin sang it in the motion-picture musical *The Great Victor Herbert* (Paramount, 1939). The song was also interpolated in the screen biography of Marilyn Miller, *Look for the Silver Lining* (Warner, 1949).

Kissin' Time, words and music by Leonard and James Frazier (1959). Popularized by Bobby Rydell, whose Cameo recording was his first major best seller.

Kiss Me Again, words by Henry Blossom, music by Victor Herbert (1905). One of Herbert's most celebrated waltzes, introduced by Fritzi Scheff in the operetta *Mlle. Modiste* (1905). She scored such a triumph with this number that from then on, and for the remainder of her life, she and the song became inextricably associated with one another.

A number of different stories were circulated in the early 1900s, describing how the waltz came to be written. One of these described how the idea was born backstage after the opening performance of Herbert's operetta *Babette:* When Herbert kissed Fritzi Scheff, the star of that production, she was reputed to have remarked lightly, "Kiss me again." Another story had Herbert overhear the remark "Kiss me again" at the Grand Union Hotel in Saratoga Springs, New York. Both tales are apocryphal.

Herbert had written the melody of "Kiss Me Again" two years before he used it in *Mlle. Modiste.* In this operetta, one of the scenes showed Fritzi Scheff displaying her vocal gifts by singing various song styles —a gavotte, polonaise, waltz and so forth. The whole routine was entitled "If I Were on the Stage," and

each segment was in fact a travesty or caricature of a different musical style. For the waltz section, Herbert used the melody he had written two years earlier, presenting it as a parody of waltz music. But this part of "If I Were on the Stage" created such a profound impression on the opening night of *Mlle. Modiste,* that Herbert decided to write a special new verse for it and to use verse and chorus within the operetta as a sentimental waltz. When Herbert first played the new number for Fritzi Scheff, she did not favor it, feeling the register was too low for her vocal range, and that it was not *her* kind of song. Herbert, however, insisted she sing it, and she finally complied.

Susanna Foster sang it in the motion-picture musical *The Great Victor Herbert* (Paramount, 1939). It provided the title for and was used as a recurrent theme in the motion-picture adaptation of *Mlle. Modiste* (First National, 1931).

Kiss Me, Honey, Do (or, Dinah), words by Edgar Smith, music by John Stromberg (1898). Introduced by Peter F. Dailey in the Weber and Fields extravaganza *Hurly Burly* (1898). Together with "Keep Away from Emmaline" from the same production, "Kiss Me, Honey, Do" was the first hit song to come out of a Weber and Fields Music Hall production.

Kiss Me, Kate, a musical comedy with book by Bella and Samuel Spewack based on Shakespeare's *The Taming of the Shrew.* Lyrics and music by Cole Porter. Starring Alfred Drake, Patricia Morison, Lisa Kirk and Harold Lang (1948). Original cast recording (Columbia).

The motion-picture adaptation starred Howard Keel, Ann Miller and Kathryn Grayson (MGM, 1953). Virtually the entire stage score was used. Soundtrack recording (MGM).

See: Always True to You in My Fashion; Another Op'nin', Another Show; Brush Up Your Shakespeare; I Hate Men; So in Love; Were Thine That Special Face; Where Is the Life

That Late I Led?; Why Can't You Behave?; Wunderbar.

Kiss Me, My Honey, Kiss Me, words by Irving Berlin, music by Ted Snyder (1910).

Kiss of Fire, words and music by Lester Allen and Robert Hill, the melody adapted from an Argentine tango, A. G. Villoldo's "El Choclo" (1952). Popularized by Georgia Gibbs in a Mercury recording that sold over a million disks. The song stayed on top of the Hit Parade for several weeks. It provided the title for and was used in a motion picture (Universal, 1955).

Kiss the Boys Goodbye, words by Frank Loesser, music by Victor Schertzinger (1941). Title song of a motion picture (Paramount, 1941), in which it was sung by Mary Martin. The song was popularized by Tommy Dorsey and his orchestra (vocal by Connie Haines) in an RCA Victor recording.

Kiss Them for Me, words by Carroll Coates, music by Lionel Newman (1957). Title song of a motion picture starring Cary Grant (20th Century-Fox, 1957), introduced on the soundtrack by the McGuire Sisters.

A Kiss to Build a Dream On, words by Bert Kalmar and Oscar Hammerstein II, music by Harry Ruby (1951). It originated as a song called "Moonlight on the Meadows" by Kalmar and Ruby. When it proved a failure, Oscar Hammerstein II was called in to revise the lyrics and provide a new title. As "A Kiss to Build a Dream On" it was introduced by Kay Brown and Louis Armstrong in the motion picture *The Strip,* starring Mickey Rooney and Sallie Forrest (MGM, 1951). Louis Armstrong's recording helped to make the song popular.

The Kiss Waltz, words by Al Dubin, music by Joe Burke (1930). Introduced in the motion picture *Dancing Sweeties,* starring Sue Carol and Grant Withers (Warner, 1930).

Kiss Waltz, words by Henry Morton, music by Ivan Caryll (1911). Introduced by Alice Dovey in the operetta *The Pink Lady* (1911) as she

teaches men the art and science of kissing.

K-K-K-Katy, words and music by Geoffrey O'Hara (1918). Subtitled the "stammering song," it became one of the most successful humorous songs of World War I. Jack Oakie revived it in the motion-picture musical *Tin Pan Alley* (20th Century-Fox, 1940).

Knickerbocker Holiday, a musical comedy with book and lyrics by Maxwell Anderson (his first musical comedy). Music by Kurt Weill. Starring Walter Huston and Ray Middleton (1930).

The motion-picture adaptation starred Nelson Eddy (United Artists, 1944). Three songs were used from the stage production. Several new numbers were contributed by various lyricists and composers, including Sammy Cahn and Jule Styne.

See: It Never Was You; September Song.

Knock on Wood, words and music by Sylvia Fine (1954). Introduced by Danny Kaye in the motion picture of the same name (Paramount, 1954).

Koehler, Ted, lyricist, born Washington, D. C., 1894.

See: Arlen, Harold; McHugh, Jimmy.

See also: Animal Crackers in My Soup; Some Sunday Morning; Stop, You're Breaking My Heart; Sweet Dreams; Sweetheart; Truckin'.

Ko Ko Mo (I Love You So), words and music by Forest Wilson, Jake Porter and Eunice Levy (1955). It was featured in Edward R. Murrow's documentary film *Ambassador Satchmo.* A rhythm and blues version was recorded by Combo 64, Gene and Eunice for Combo. The song was popularized by Perry Como in an RCA Victor recording.

Kookie, Kookie (Lend Me Your Comb), words and music by Irving Taylor (1959). Inspired by and introduced in the television series 77 *Sunset Strip.* The Warner recording by Connie Stevens (her first successful disk) and Edward Byrnes sold a million disks.

K-r-a-z-y for You, words by Ira Gershwin, music by George Gershwin (1928). Introduced by Clifton Webb and Mary Hay in the musical *Treasure Girl* (1928).

Kwamina, a musical play with book by Robert Alan Aurthur. Lyrics and music by Richard Adler. Starring Sally Ann Howes and Terry Carter (1961). Original cast recording (Capitol).

See: Another Time, Another Place; Cocoa Bean Song; Nothing More to Look Forward To; Ordinary People.

L

Lady, Be Good. *See:* Oh, Lady, Be Good.

Lady, Be Good!, a musical comedy with book by Guy Bolton and Fred Thompson. Lyrics by Ira Gershwin. Music by George Gershwin. This was the first musical for which Ira Gershwin wrote all the lyrics for George Gershwin's songs. Starring Fred and Adele Astaire (1924).

The motion-picture adaptation starred Eleanor Powell, Ann Sothern and Robert Young (MGM, 1941). Only three songs were used from the stage production. Among the interpolated new numbers was "The Last Time I Saw Paris" by Oscar Hammerstein II and Jerome Kern, which received the Academy Award. *See:* Fascinating Rhythm; The Half of It, Dearie, Blues; The Last Time I Saw Paris; Oh, Lady, Be Good; So Am I.

The Lady in Ermine, words by Cyrus Wood, music by Alfred Goodman (1922). Title song of a musical comedy (1922), introduced by Harry Fender, Gladys Walton and Helen Shipman.

The Lady in Ermine, a musical comedy with book by Cyrus Wood and Frederick Lonsdale. Lyrics by Cyrus Wood and Harry Graham. Music by Alfred Goodman and Jean Gilbert. Starring Wilda Bennett and Walter Woolf (1922).

See: The Lady in Ermine; When Hearts Are Young.

The Lady in Red, words by Mort Dixon, music by Allie Wrubel (1935). Introduced in the motion picture *In Caliente,* starring Dolores del Rio (First National, 1935).

Lady in the Dark, a musical play with book by Moss Hart. Lyrics by Ira Gershwin. Music by Kurt Weill. Starring Gertrude Lawrence, Danny Kaye (in his musical comedy debut) and Victor Mature (1941).

The motion-picture adaptation starred Ginger Rogers and Ray Milland (Paramount, 1944). Six songs were used from the stage production. "Suddenly It's Spring" by Johnny Burke and James Van Heusen and "Dream Lover" by Clifford Grey and Victor Schertzinger were interpolated.

See: Dream Lover; Jenny; My Ship; Saga of Jenny; Suddenly It's Spring; Tschaikowsky; This Is Now.

The Lady Is a Tramp, words by Lorenz Hart, music by Richard Rodgers (1937). Introduced by Mitzi Green in the musical *Babes in Arms* (1937). It was sung by Judy Garland in the motion-picture adaptation of the musical (MGM, 1939). Lena Horne sang it in the screen biography of Rodgers and Hart, *Words and Music* (MGM, 1948). The song was interpolated in the motion-picture adaptation of the musical *Pal Joey* (Columbia, 1957), sung by Frank Sinatra.

Lady of Spain, words by Erell Reaves,

music by Tolchard Evans (1931). It was successfully revived in 1952 by Eddie Fisher in a best-selling recording for RCA Victor.

Lady of the Evening, words and music by Irving Berlin (1922). Introduced by John Steel in the second edition of the *Music Box Revue* (1922).

Lady, Play Your Mandolin, words by Irving Caesar, music by Oscar Levant (1930). Introduced in vaudeville by Blossom Seeley.

Lafayette, We Hear You Calling, words and music by Robert A. King, using the pseudonym of Mary Earl (1918). Hit song of World War I.

Lah Dee Dah, words by Frank Slay, music by Bob Crewe (1960). Popularized by Lillie and Billie in a Swan recording.

La, La, Lucille, a musical comedy with book by Fred Jackson. Lyrics by Arthur Jackson, and additional lyrics by Bud De Sylva. Music by George Gershwin. This was George Gershwin's first Broadway score. Starring Janet Velie and Jack Hazard (1919).
See: Nobody But You.

Lamb, Arthur J., lyricist, born Somerset, England, 1870; died Providence, Rhode Island, 1928.
See: Von Tilzer, Harry.
See also: Any Old Port in a Storm; Asleep in the Deep; The Bird on Nellie's Hat; A Picnic for Two.

The Lamp Is Low, words by Mitchell Parish, music by Peter De Rose and Bert Shefter, the melody derived from Maurice Ravel's *Pavane pour une Infante défunte* (1939).

The Lamplighter's Serenade, words by Paul Francis Webster, music by Hoagy Carmichael (1942). This number marked Frank Sinatra's debut as a solo performer on records —for Bluebird. However, the most successful recording of this song was not by Sinatra but by Glenn Miller and his orchestra (vocal by Ray Eberle and the Modernaires) for Bluebird.

The Land Where Good Songs Go, words by P. G. Wodehouse, music by Jerome Kern (1917). Introduced by Elizabeth Brice and Charles King in the first-act finale of the musical *Miss 1917.* In this production, the song served to revive several old-time tune favorites, together with impersonations of those who helped make them famous, including "Under the Bamboo Tree," "Yama Yama Man," "Kiss Me Again," "Be My Little Baby Bumble Bee" and "In the Good Old Summertime."

Lane, Burton, composer, born New York City, 1912.
See (Lyrics by Ralph Freed): How About You?; Swing High, Swing Low.
See (Lyrics by E. Y. Harburg): The Begat; Freedom Is the Word; How Are Things in Glocca Mora?; Look to the Rainbow; Old Devil Moon; Something Sort of Grandish; There's a Great Day, Mañana; When I'm Not Near the Girl I Love.
See (Lyrics by Alan Jay Lerner): Come Back to Me; Hurry, It's Lovely Up Here; On a Clear Day; Melinda; She Wasn't You; What Did I Have That I Don't Have?
See (Lyrics by Frank Loesser): I Hear Music; Says My Heart.
See also: Everything I Have Is Yours; Feudin' and Fightin'; How Could You Believe Me?; Stop, You're Breakin' My Heart.

Langdon, Dory, lyricist, born New Jersey, 1929.
See: Previn, André.
See also: The Morning After; So Long, Big Time.

La Seine. See: The River Seine.

Last Night on the Back Porch I Loved Her Best of All, words by Lew Brown, music by Carl Schraubstader (1923).

Last Night Was the End of the World, words by Andrew B. Sterling, music by Harry von Tilzer (1912). Structurally and stylistically, this is one of Harry von Tilzer's most ambitious efforts. The celebrated prima donna Lina Cavalieri sang it at some of her concerts during her American tour in 1912–1913.

Last Night When We Were Very Young, words by E. Y. Harburg, music by Harold Arlen (1936). Published as an independent number. Lawrence Tibbett wanted the song for his motion picture *Metropolitan,* but when it was dropped from the final print he recorded it for RCA Victor. Judy Garland happened to find this recording "in a pile of old records in a record shop," as she later recalled. "I was about sixteen years old when I first heard it. It was my favorite song then. I recorded it for Capitol. . . . I think that lyrically and melodically it is one of the great love songs of all time." She tried to get it into her motion-picture musical *In the Good Old Summertime.* She almost succeeded—but in the end it was dropped. Then Frank Sinatra, who also regarded the number with considerable favor, tried unsuccessfully to put it into his motion-picture musical *Take Me Out to the Ball Game.*

Harburg regards this as one of his finest lyrics; Arlen, as one of his two best songs, the other being "One for My Baby."

The Last of the Hogans, words by Edward Harrigan, music by David Braham (1891). Introduced in the Harrigan and Hart musical extravaganza of the same name (1891).

The Last Roundup, words and music by Billy Hill (1933). A popular song in the style of a cowboy ballad, introduced in 1933 by Joe Morrison at the Paramount Theatre in New York. Don Ross (supported by Willie and Eugene Howard and Jack Pepper) then sang it in the *Ziegfeld Follies of 1934.* This song was one of Bing Crosby's earliest successful recordings—for Brunswick. Even more successful was Roy Rogers' recording, which was largely responsible for landing him a motion-picture contract with Republic. He sang it in the motion picture *Don't Fence Me In* (Republic, 1945). The song was also interpolated for Gene Autry in the motion pictures *The Singing Hill* (Republic, 1941) and *The Last Roundup* (Columbia, 1947).

The Last Time I Saw Paris, words by Oscar Hammerstein II, music by Jerome Kern (1940). A ballad inspired by the Nazi occupation of Paris in June of 1940. This song is unique for Kern in that it is his only one where the lyric came before the music, and which was written without any stage or screen production in mind.

Hammerstein, who had known Paris from his boyhood days on and had always loved it dearly, felt impelled to write his lyric as an emotional release from the heartache of seeing Paris occupied by the Nazis. He asked Kern to write the music, which Kern did in a single day, most of it at a single sitting.

The song was introduced in 1940 by Kate Smith on her CBS radio program. Since she had a six-week option on the song, nobody else could perform it during this period. When the option period ended, the song was kept off the airwaves by virtue of the bitter contractual dispute between ASCAP and the radio networks in which songs by ASCAP members were barred from the air channels. "The Last Time I Saw Paris," however, was quickly popularized through other media, mainly in recordings and in night clubs, by such performing favorites as Hildegarde, Noel Coward and Sophie Tucker. Hildegarde's recording was of particular interest since it was personally supervised by Kern himself.

The song was interpolated in the motion-picture musical *Lady, Be Good!* (MGM, 1941), where it was sung by Ann Sothern. Though it was the only song by Kern in this production (three other numbers were by the Gershwins, taken from the Broadway musical comedy of the same name), it received the Academy Award. Kern himself objected severely to the award, maintaining that his song had *not* been written for motion pictures and consequently should not have been eligible; besides, he felt that the honor should have gone to Harold Arlen for "That Old Black Magic." Feeling as he did, Kern went to work to get the rules of the Academy Award changed, with the result that from that time on only songs written expressly for motion pictures were eligible.

The ballad was sung by Dinah Shore in the screen biography of Jerome Kern, *Till the Clouds Roll By* (MGM, 1946). The song title was used for a non-musical motion picture starring Elizabeth Taylor and Van Johnson (MGM, 1954), where the melody was used in the background as a recurrent theme, both as an instrumental and (in French) as a vocal.

Latouche, John, lyricist, born Richmond, Virginia, 1917; died Calais, Vermont, 1956.

See: Duke, Vernon.

See also: Lazy Afternoon.

Laugh, Clown, Laugh, words by Sam M. Lewis and Joe Young, music by Ted Fiorito (1928). A popular-song version of the old Pagliacci theme introduced by Ted Fiorito.

Laughing on the Outside, Crying on the Inside, words by Ben Raleigh, music by Bernie Wayne (1946). Introduced by Sammy Kaye and his orchestra. It was popularized by Dinah Shore in a Columbia recording.

The Laugh Parade, a musical comedy with book by Ed Wynn and Ed Prebee. Lyrics by Mort Dixon and Joe Young. Music by Harry Warren. Starring Ed Wynn (1931).

See: Ooh, That Kiss; The Torch Song; You're My Everything.

Laura, words by Johnny Mercer, music by David Raksin (1945). Theme song of the non-musical motion picture *Laura,* starring Gene Tierney and Dana Andrews (20th Century-Fox, 1944), where it appeared as a recurrent theme in the background music. Lyrics were added several months after the picture was released, by which time the melody had become popular. The song was introduced over the radio by Johnny Johnston. Woody Herman's recording for Columbia in 1945 sold a million disks.

Lavender Blue (Dilly Dilly), words by Larry Morey, music by Eliot Daniel, melody based on a seventeenth-century English folk song (1948). Introduced by Dinah Shore (then sung by Burl Ives) in the Walt Disney motion-picture production *So Dear to My Heart* (RKO, 1948). The song was revived in 1959 by Sammy Turner in a successful Big Top recording.

La Vie En Rose, a French popular song,

music by Louiguy, English lyrics by Mack David (1950). The French song was introduced in Paris, and was popularized by and has become identified by Edith Piaf. The song, with English lyrics, was popularized in the United States by Tony Martin in a recording for RCA Victor.

Lazy, words and music by Irving Berlin (1924). One of Berlin's most remarkable lyrics. Popularized by Blossom Seeley in vaudeville and in a Columbia recording. The song was interpolated in a number of motion-picture musicals, including *Alexander's Ragtime Band* (20th Century-Fox, 1938); *Holiday Inn* (Paramount, 1942), sung by Bing Crosby; *There's No Business Like Show Business* (20th Century-Fox, 1954), sung by Marilyn Monroe. It was also interpolated in the non-musical motion picture *Belles on Their Toes,* starring Myrna Loy and Jeanne Crain (20th Century-Fox, 1952), where it was sung by Jeanne Crain, Hoagy Carmichael and a children's chorus.

Lazy Afternoon, words by John Latouche, music by Jerome Moross (1954). Introduced by Kaye Ballard in the musical *The Golden Apple* (1954).

Lazybones, words by Johnny Mercer, music by Hoagy Carmichael (1933). The melody had been previously used by Carmichael for "Washboard Blues." The song, with Mercer's lyrics, was first popularized by Rudy Vallée and Ben Bernie over radio, in night-club appearances and in recordings. Ben Bernie used to sing it with a strong Negro inflection.

Lazy, Hazy Days of Summer. *See:* Those Lazy, Hazy Days of Summer.

Lazy Moon, words by Bob Cole, music by J. Rosamond Johnson (1903). Introduced and popularized by the minstrel George Primrose, who would follow his rendition with a soft-shoe dance. The song was revived in the motion picture *Here Comes Cookie,* starring George Burns and Gracie Allen (Paramount, 1935).

Lazy River, words and music by Sidney Arodin and Hoagy Carmichael (1931). Popularized in a celebrated jazz recording for RCA Victor by

Hoagy Carmichael and a band that included such all-time jazz greats as the Dorseys, Jack Teagarden, Gene Krupa, Benny Goodman, Bud Freeman, Joe Venuti and Bix Beiderbecke. The song was further popularized in a Decca recording by the Mills Brothers and in a Capitol recording by Benny Goodman.

It was interpolated in several motion pictures, including *Cowboy Canteen,* starring June Frazee (Columbia, 1944), and *The Best Years of Our Lives,* starring Fredric March and Myrna Loy (RKO, 1946); in the latter it was sung by Hoagy Carmichael.

The song was revived in two successful recordings in 1961. One was by Bobby Darin for Atco. The other was by Si Zentner for Liberty, which received a "Grammy" Award from the National Academy of Recording Arts and Sciences as the best performance on disks that year by an orchestra for dancing; this Liberty release marked the beginning of Si Zentner's success in recording.

The Leader of the German Band, words by Edward Madden, music by Theodore F. Morse (1905).

Learnin' the Blues, words and music by Dolores Vicki Silvers (1955). Popularized by Frank Sinatra in a Capitol recording.

Leave It to Jane, words by P. G. Wodehouse, music by Jerome Kern (1917). Title song of a musical (1917), introduced by Edith Hallor. In Jerome Kern's screen biography *Till the Clouds Roll By* (MGM, 1946), it was sung by June Allyson.

Leave It to Jane, a musical comedy with book by Guy Bolton based on George Ade's play *The College Widow.* Lyrics by P. G. Wodehouse. Music by Jerome Kern. Starring Edith Hallor and Oscar Shaw (1917).

See: Cleopatterer; Leave It to Jane; The Siren's Song.

Leave It to Me, a musical comedy with book by Bella and Samuel Spewack based on their play *Clear All Wires.* Lyrics and music by Cole Porter. Starring William Gaxton, Mary Martin (in her Broadway debut), Victor Moore and Sophie Tucker (1938).

See: From Now On; Get Out of Town; My Heart Belongs to Daddy.

Left, Right, Out of Your Heart (or, Hi Lee, Hi Lo, Hi Lup-Up-Up), words by Earl Shuman, music by Mort Garson (1958). Popularized by Patti Page in a Mercury recording.

Legalize My Name, words by Johnny Mercer, music by Harold Arlen (1946). Introduced by Pearl Bailey in the musical play *St. Louis Woman* (1946).

Leigh, Carolyn, lyricist, born New York City, 1926.

See: Coleman, Cy.

See also: How Little It Matters, How Little We Know; I've Gotta Crow; Never Never Land.

A Lemon in the Garden of Love, words by M. E. Rourke, music by Richard Carle (1906). Comedy number introduced by Richard Carle in the musical *The Spring Chicken* (1906). It was revived in the motion picture *Ma, He's Making Eyes at Me,* starring Constance Moore and Tom Brown (Universal, 1940).

Lena Is the Queen of Palesteena. *See:* Palesteena.

Lerner, Alan Jay, lyricist, born New York City, 1918.

See: Lane, Burton; Loewe, Frederick; Weill, Kurt.

See also: How Could You Believe Me?

Les Girls, a motion-picture musical starring Gene Kelly, Kay Kendall and Mitzi Gaynor (MGM, 1957). Songs by Cole Porter.

See: Ça C'est L'amour.

Leslie, Edgar, lyricist, born Stamford, Connecticut, 1885.

See: Ahlert, Fred E.; Burke, Joseph A.; Donaldson, Walter; Meyer, George W.; Ruby, Harry; Warren, Harry.

See also: America, I Love You; Among My Souvenirs; Dirty Hands, Dirty Face; He'd Have to Get Under; Hello, Hawaii; Moonlight on the Rhine; Oh, What a Pal Was Mary; Sadie Salome.

Let a Smile Be Your Umbrella on a Rainy Day, words by Irving Kahal and Francis Wheeler, music by Sammy Fain (1927). Interpolated in the motion picture *It's a Great Life.*

starring the Duncan Sisters (MGM, 1929). It was revived by Dan Dailey and Charles Winninger in the motion-picture musical *Give My Regards to Broadway* (20th Century-Fox, 1948).

Let Bygones Be Bygones, words by Charles Shackford, music by Kerry Mills (1897).

Let 'Em Eat Cake, a musical-comedy sequel to *Of Thee I Sing!,* with book by Morrie Ryskind and George S. Kaufman. Lyrics by Ira Gershwin. Music by George Gershwin. Starring William Gaxton and Victor Moore (1933).

See: Mine.

Let It Alone, words by Alex Rogers, music by Bert Williams (1906). Introduced and popularized by Bert Williams in the musical *Abyssinia* (1906). The sheet music described this number as "a ragtime philosophical song."

Let It Be, a French popular song ("Je t'appartiens"), music by Gilbert Becaud, English lyrics by Mann Curtis (1957). Introduced in Paris by Gilbert Becaud. The song, with English lyrics, was introduced by Jill Corey over TV in the dramatic series *Climax.* It was popularized in 1960 by the Everly Brothers in a Cadence recording.

Let It Snow, Let It Snow, Let It Snow, words by Sammy Cahn, music by Jule Styne (1945). Popularized by Vaughn Monroe in an RCA Victor recording in 1946.

Let Me Call You Sweetheart, words by Beth Slater Whitson, music by Leo Friedman (1910). One of the most successful love ballads of the decade, selling about five million copies of sheet music.

Whitson and Friedman had written a major hit song in 1909, "Meet Me Tonight in Dreamland," which was published in Chicago by Will Rossiter. They had sold their rights to it for a small consideration, thus failing to profit from its two-million-copy sheet-music sale. When Will Rossiter's brother Harold went into the publishing business in 1910, and stood ready to pay Whitson and Friedman royalties, they turned over to him their latest song, which was "Let Me Call You Sweetheart." This was Harold Rossiter's first publication and it brought him a fortune.

Let Me Go, Lover, words and music by Jenny Lou Carson, with special lyrics by Al Hill (1954). It originated in 1953 as "Let Me Go, Devil" and was then successfully recorded by George Shaw for Decca. Joan Weber then sang it in the Studio One TV production of the same name in 1954. Her Columbia recording sold over a million disks.

Let Me Sing and I'm Happy, words and music by Irving Berlin (1930). Introduced by Al Jolson in the motion-picture musical *Mammy* (Warner, 1930). Jolson sang it again on the soundtrack of *The Jolson Story* (Columbia, 1946).

Let's Be Buddies, words and music by Cole Porter (1940). Introduced by Ethel Merman and little Joan Carroll in the musical *Panama Hattie* (1940).

Cole Porter told an interviewer: "There was a spot where Joan Carroll, who is eight years old, and Ethel Merman, who is more than sixteen, had to sing and dance a duet. The spot required it. The law forbade it. The spot also stipulated that the song—as Ethel sang it— must be boozily sentimental, in, of course, a ladylike way. So I wrote it that way, boozily sentimental . . . and in rhythm that can be walked to, in order to compensate for Joan having been prevented by law from dancing, and with a patter in between so that Joan could recite instead of court jail by singing. Also, I put in an A-natural for Ethel because while all her notes are extraordinarily good, A-natural is her best and the C above is a good finish for her. The finished product . . . became the hit of the show." Brooks Atkinson said of it in the *New York Times:* "Gruff old codgers are going to choke a little this winter when tot and temptress sing 'Let's Be Buddies' and bring down the house."

In the motion-picture adaptation of the musical (MGM, 1942), it was sung by Ann Sheridan.

Let's Call It a Day, words by Lew Brown, music by Ray Henderson (1932). Introduced by Carolyn Nolte and Milton Watson in the musical *Strike Me Pink* (1933).

Let's Call the Whole Thing Off, words by Ira Gershwin, music by George Gershwin (1937). Introduced by Fred Astaire and Ginger Rogers in the motion-picture musical *Shall We Dance?* (RKO, 1937), followed by a dance routine on roller skates. The lyric mocked at affected usages of London pronunciations.

Let's Dance, words by Fanny Baldridge, music by Joseph Bonime and Gregory Stone (1935). Popularized in a best-selling Columbia recording by Benny Goodman and his orchestra, and then became his theme music. It was interpolated in the motion-picture musical *The Benny Goodman Story* (Universal, 1956). It was also heard in several other motion pictures, including *The Powers Girl,* starring Anne Shirley and George Murphy (United Artists, 1942); *The Gang's All Here,* starring Alice Faye and Carmen Miranda (20th Century-Fox, 1943); and *Sweet and Low Down,* starring Linda Darnell (20th Century-Fox, 1944).

Let's Dance, words and music by Jim Lee (1962). Popularized by Chris Montez in a Monogram recording.

Let's Do It, words and music by Cole Porter (1928). Introduced by Irene Bordoni and Arthur Margetson in the Broadway musical *Paris* (1928). Jessie Matthews and Sonnie Hale sang it in the London revue *Wake Up and Dream* (1929). Described by Stanley Green as a "zoological survey," this song goes on to describe the "amatory habits" of "bluebirds, bluebells, sponges, oysters, clams, jellyfish, electric eels, shad, sole, goldfish, dragonflies, centipedes, mosquitoes . . . in a manner that immediately established Cole Porter as one of the most ingenious creators of sly and imaginative lyrics."

This song was one of Cole Porter's own favorites among his own creations. It was interpolated in his screen biography *Night and Day* (Warner, 1946), sung by Ginny Simms, and in the motion-picture adaptation of the musical *Can-Can* (20th Century-Fox, 1960), sung by Frank Sinatra and Shirley MacLaine.

Let's Face It, a musical comedy with book by Herbert and Dorothy Fields, adapted from *Cradle Snatchers,* a play by Russel Medcraft and Norma Mitchell. Lyrics and music by Cole Porter. Starring Danny Kaye (1941).

The motion-picture adaptation starred Bob Hope and Betty Hutton (Paramount, 1943). Only two Cole Porter numbers were used from the stage score, with new songs contributed by Sammy Cahn and Jule Styne.

See: Ace in the Hole; Let's Not Talk About Love.

Let's Face the Music and Dance, words and music by Irving Berlin (1936). Introduced by Fred Astaire and Ginger Rogers in the motion-picture musical *Follow the Fleet* (RKO, 1936).

For the dance routine that followed the song, Ginger Rogers wore a beaded dress that weighed a ton. Each time she did a quick turn, Astaire tried to avoid being hit by her flying sleeve. As the song and dance were being filmed, the sleeve actually did hit him in the eye and mouth. Though made groggy by the blow, Astaire continued dancing without losing a step. In spite of the accident, which somehow eluded the cameras, the take was perfect.

Let's Fall in Love, words by Ted Koehler, music by Harold Arlen (1933). Introduced in the motion-picture musical of the same name starring Ann Sothern (Columbia, 1934); this was Harold Arlen's first screen assignment.

Arlen and Koehler wrote the number aboard The Chief bound for Hollywood. The composer tried out his melody for the first time with the aid of the musical chimes used by the diner to announce mealtime.

The song was interpolated in several motion pictures, including *Slightly French* (Columbia, 1949), sung by Don Ameche and Dorothy Lamour; *Tell It to the Judge,* starring Rosalind Russell (Columbia, 1949), in which it was used as a recurrent theme and sung by Robert Cummings; *On the Sunny Side of the Street* (Columbia, 1951); *It Should Happen to You* (Columbia, 1954), sung by Judy Holliday and Jack Lemmon; and *The Eddie Duchin Story* (Columbia, 1956), played on the soundtrack by Carmen Cavallero.

Let's Get Lost, words by Frank Loesser, music by Jimmy McHugh (1943). Introduced by Mary Martin in the motion-picture musical *Happy Go Lucky,* starring Dick Powell (Paramount, 1943).

Let's Have Another Cup o' Coffee, words and music by Irving Berlin (1932). Introduced by Katherine Carrington and J. Harold Murray in the musical *Face the Music* (1932). In the early 1930s it became one of the theme songs of the depression. It was revived in the motion-picture musical *There's No Business Like Show Business* (20th Century-Fox, 1954), sung by Ethel Merman.

Let's Kiss and Make Up, words by Ira Gershwin, music by George Gershwin (1927). Introduced by Fred and Adele Astaire in the musical *Funny Face* (1927). This song developed out of an earlier (unused) number called "Come, Come, Come Closer." Fred Astaire sang it in the motion-picture adaptation of the musical *Funny Face* (Paramount, 1957).

Let's Misbehave, words and music by Cole Porter (1928). Written for Irene Bordoni for the musical *Paris* (1928), but deleted from that show before it reached New York. Detailing the love life of various members of the animal kingdom, this song was issued as an independent number.

Let's Not Talk About Love, words and music by Cole Porter (1941). Introduced by Danny Kaye and Eve Arden in the musical *Let's Face It* (1941). In the motion-picture adaptation of the musical (Paramount, 1943), it was sung by Betty Hutton.

Let's Put Out the Lights (and Go to Bed), words and music by Herman Hupfeld (1932). A song favorite of the depression years. It was introduced by Rudy Vallée at the Atlantic City Steel Pier in 1932. "I did several

vocal choruses and, by God, the audience broke into applause, something they had done for no other number all afternoon," Vallée later recalled. Vallée then sang it on his radio program over NBC. The network however insisted that he change the word "bed" to "sleep." The song was interpolated in the stage musical *George White's Music Hall Varieties* (1932), sung in the final scene by Harry Richman, Lili Damita, Bert Lahr and ensemble.

Let's Take an Old Fashioned Walk, words and music by Irving Berlin (1948). Introduced by Allyn McLerie and Eddie Albert in the musical *Miss Liberty* (1949).

Let's Take the Long Way Home, words by Johnny Mercer, music by Harold Arlen (1944). Introduced by Bing Crosby and Betty Hutton in the motion-picture musical *Here Come the Waves* (Paramount, 1944).

Let's Twist Again, words and music by Mann and Appell (1961). Successor to "The Twist," it further established the popularity of that dance and solidified Chubby Checker as its "king." Chubby Checker's recording for Parkway received the "Grammy" from the National Academy of Recording Arts and Sciences as the best rock 'n' roll disk of the year.

Letters, words and music by Raymond Jessel and Marian Grudeff (1965). Introduced by Inga Swenson in the musical *Baker Street* (1965).

Letter Song, words by William Le Baron, music by Fritz Kreisler (1919). Introduced in the operetta *Apple Blossoms* (1919).

The Letter That Never Came, words and music by Paul Dresser (1886). Dresser's first hit ballad. It was written while Dresser was appearing in blackface as Mr. Bones with the Billy Rice Minstrels in Brooklyn, New York. The song was introduced by that company in Brooklyn in 1886 and proved such a hit that Dresser decided to give up the stage for good and devote himself to songwriting. The ballad was subsequently popularized by May Howard in burlesque.

Let the Rest of the World Go By, words by J. Keirn Brennan, music by Ernest

R. Ball (1919). Originally a failure, it was plugged to a three-million-copy success by Julius Witmark and by intensified promotion by the publishing house of Witmark. The ballad was sung by Dick Haymes, supported by a male quartet, in the Ernest R. Ball screen biography *When Irish Eyes Are Smiling* (20th Century-Fox, 1944).

Let Yourself Go, words and music by Irving Berlin (1936). Introduced by Fred Astaire in the motion-picture musical *Follow the Fleet* (RKO, 1936).

Lewis, Sam M., lyricist, born New York City, 1885.

See: Akst, Harry; Coots, J. Fred; Henderson, Ray; Meyer, George W.; Schwartz, Jean.

See also: Arrah Go On; Cryin' for the Carolines; Daddy Long Legs; Got Her Off My Hands; Happy Go Lucky; How'd You Like to Be My Daddy?; I Kiss Your Hand, Madame; In a Little Spanish Town; Keep Sweeping the Cobwebs Off the Moon; Laugh, Clown, Laugh; Lord, You Made the Night Too Long.

The Liberty Song (or, In Freedom We're Born), words by John Dickinson, to the English melody "Heart of Oak" by William Boyce (1768). America's first significant political song, inspired by the refusal of the Massachusetts Legislature to rescind the Circular Letter of February 11, 1768, imposing duties and taxes on the Colonies. Dickinson's words appeared for the first time with Boyce's melody in Bickerstaff's *Boston Almanac*, in 1769. In short order, "The Liberty Song" became the favorite anthem of the Sons of Liberty. Because of this number's tremendous popularity with the so-called radicals, parodies were concocted by the Tories in which the "hotheads" were mocked and warned that their "houses and stores will come tumbling down."

Lida Rose, words and music by Meredith Willson (1957). Introduced by Bill Spagenberg, Wayne Ward, Al Shea and Vern Reed (the Buffalo Bills) in the musical *The Music Man* (1957).

Lies, words by George W. Springer, music by Harry Barris (1931).

Life Can Be Beautiful, words by Harold Adamson, music by Jimmy McHugh (1946). Introduced by Susan Hayward in the non-musical motion picture *Smash Up* (Universal, 1946).

Life Is Just a Bowl of Cherries, words by Lew Brown, music by Ray Henderson (1931). Introduced by Ethel Merman in *George White's Scandals of 1931.* Together with other hit numbers from this edition of the *Scandals,* this song was recorded by Bing Crosby and the Boswell Sisters on both sides of a twelve-inch Brunswick record—one of the earliest attempts to reproduce the basic score of a Broadway musical on disks. The song was popularized by Ethel Merman in a Decca recording and by Rudy Vallée in a recording for RCA Victor. It was interpolated in the motion-picture musical *George White's Scandals of 1945,* starring Jack Haley and Joan Davis (RKO, 1945).

Life Is Only What You Make It, After All, words by Edgar Smith, music by A. Baldwin Sloane (1910). Introduced by Octavia Broske and a male chorus in the Broadway production *Tillie's Nightmare* (1910).

A Life on the Ocean Wave, words by Epes Sargent, music by Henry Russell (1838). Introduced and popularized by the singing Hutchinson Family at their concerts. In 1889 the song was made the official march of the English Royal Marines.

Life's a Funny Proposition After All, words and music by George M. Cohan (1904). Introduced by George M. Cohan in his first successful musical, *Little Johnny Jones* (1904).

Life's Full of Consequence, words by E. Y. Harburg, music by Harold Arlen (1943). Introduced by Lena Horne and Eddie "Rochester" Anderson in the motion-picture adaptation of the musical *Cabin in the Sky* (MGM, 1943).

Life upon the Wicked Stage, words by Oscar Hammerstein II, music by Jerome Kern (1927). Introduced by Eva Puck and a male chorus in the musical play *Show Boat* (1927). In the 1936 motion-picture adaptation of the musical (Universal), it was sung by Queenie Smith; in the 1951 version (MGM), by Marge Champion. Virginia O'Brien sang it in the Jerome Kern screen biography *Till the Clouds Roll By* (MGM, 1946).

The Lighthouse by the Sea, words and music by Gussie L. Davis (1886). The first song by Tin Pan Alley's earliest successful Negro composer, a former janitor and Pullman porter. It was published by a small Cincinnati printer. When the sheet music was displayed in the shop window, Davis would stand otuside the store day after day, stop passers-by, and tell them: "See *that*—that's *me.*"

Lights Out, words and music by Billy Hill (1935).

Like Love, words by Dory Langdon, music by André Previn (1962). Previn wrote the melody as an instrumental, in 1961. With lyrics, it was first recorded successfully by Jack Jones for Kapp.

Like Young, words by Paul Francis Webster, music by André Previn (1958). Popularized in an instrumental recording by André Previn with David Rose's orchestra in an MGM recording.

Li'l Abner, a musical comedy with book by Norman Panama and Melvin Frank based on cartoon characters created by Al Capp. Lyrics by Johnny Mercer. Music by Gene de Paul. Starring Edith Adams, Peter Palmer and Stubby Kaye (1956). Original cast recording (Columbia).

Motion-picture adaptation starred Peter Palmer, Julie Newmar and Stubby Kaye (Paramount, 1959). Virtually the entire stage score was used. Soundtrack recording (Columbia).

See: Jubilation T. Cornpone; Namely You.

Lilacs in the Rain, words by Mitchell Parish, music by Peter De Rose (1939).

Li'l Liza Jane, words and music by Countess Ada De Lachau (1916). A song in Negro dialect which became a favorite of members of the Rotary and Kiwanis.

Lily Dale, words and music by H. S. Thompson (1852). Sentimental ballad which Sigmund Spaeth regarded as the forerunner of the present-day torch song. The distinguished piano virtuoso, Sigismond Thalberg, used this melody for a series of piano variations which he featured in his American recitals.

Lily of the Valley, words by L. Wolfe Gilbert, music by Anatol Friedland (1917). Nonsense song popularized by Adele Rowland in vaudeville.

Linda, words and music by Jack Lawrence and Ann Ronell (1944). Introduced in the non-musical motion picture *The Story of G. I. Joe,* starring Burgess Meredith (United Artists, 1945).

Linger Awhile, words by Harry Owens, music by Vincent Rose (1923). Introduced by Paul Whiteman and his orchestra, then became one of their specialties; their Victor recording sold about two million disks. It was used as a recurrent theme in the background music for the non-musical motion picture *Belles on Their Toes,* starring Myrna Loy and Jeanne Crain (20th Century-Fox, 1952).

The Lion Sleeps Tonight (or, Wimoweh), words and music by Hugo Peretti, Luigi Creatore, George Weiss and Albert Stanton, based on Paul Campbell's song "Wimoweh, Hey Up Joe"; new English lyrics by Roy Ilene, and a new musical arrangement and adaptation by Paul Campbell (1951). The song was successfully revived in 1961 in a best-selling RCA Victor recording by the Tokens that received the Gold Record Award.

Lipstick on Your Collar, words by Edna Lewis, music by George Goehring (1959). Popularized by Connie Francis in an MGM recording.

Lisbon Antigua (or, In Old Lisbon), a Portuguese popular song, ("Lisboa Antigua"), music by Raul Portela, English lyrics by Harry Dupree (1954). The song was popularized by Nelson Riddle and his orchestra in a Capitol recording in 1956 that sold over a million disks.

Listen to My Tale of Woe, words by Eugene Field, music by Hubert F. Smith (1884). Popularized by Francis Wilson. The words first appeared in "Sharps and Flats," Eugene Field's celebrated column in the Chicago *Morning News*.

Listen to the Mocking Bird, words and music by Septimus Winner, using the pseudonym of Alice Hawthorne (1855). Described on the sheet music as "a sentimental Ethiopian ballad." Winner revealed that his melody came from a song he heard a little colored boy (named Richard Milburn) sing.

In half a century this song sold about twenty million copies of sheet music in the United States and abroad. Since Winner had sold out his rights for $50 he never profited from this formidable success; nor did he approach anything like it with any of his later songs. The number became popular with performers adept at interpolating either whistling or bird calls in their renditions.

Little Alabama Coon, words and music by Hattie Starr (1893). One of the most popular coon songs of the early 1890s, and one of the foremost successes by Tin Pan Alley's first important woman composer. The high regard which serious musicians held for this number was proved a quarter of a century after its publication when opera stars Mabel Garrison and Frieda Hempel recorded it for Victor and Edison, respectively. The song was interpolated in the stage extravaganza *Aladdin, Jr.* (1895), sung by Frankie Raymond.

Little Birdies Learning How to Fly, words by Hugh Morton, music by Gustave Kerker (1898). Introduced in the musical *The Telephone Girl* (1898).

A Little Bird Told Me, words and music by Harvey O. Brooks (1947). Introduced by Paula Watson in a Supreme recording but popularized by Evelyn Knight in a Decca recording.

A Little Bit Independent, words by Edgar Leslie, music by Joseph A. Burke (1935). It was successfully revived in the 1950s by Nat King Cole for Capitol and Eddie Fisher for RCA Victor.

A Little Bit of Heaven (and They Called It Ireland), words by J. Keirn Brennan, music by Ernest R. Ball (1914). Introduced by Chauncey Olcott in the musical *The Heart of Paddy Whack* (1914). It gave the title to and was featured prominently in a motion picture starring Gloria Jean (Universal, 1940). It was also interpolated in Ernest R. Ball's screen biography, *When Irish Eyes Are Smiling* (20th Century-Fox, 1944), and in Chauncey Olcott's screen biography, *My Wild Irish Rose* (Warner, 1947); in the latter it was sung by Dennis Morgan.

A Little Boy Called "Taps," words by Edward Madden, music by Theodore F. Morse (1904).

The Little Brown Jug, words and music by J. E. Winner, using the pseudonym of R. A. Eastburn (1869). It was revived in 1939 by Glenn Miller and his orchestra, whose Bluebird recording sold over a million disks. It was sung by Ann Sheridan and a girls' chorus in the non-musical motion picture *Dodge City* (Warner, 1930). It was interpolated for a male chorus in the motion-picture biography *The Glenn Miller Story* (Universal, 1953).

A Little Bunch of Shamrocks, words by William Jerome and Andrew B. Sterling, music by Harry von Tilzer (1913).

The Little Church Around the Corner, words by P. G. Wodehouse, music by Jerome Kern (1920). Introduced by Mary Hay and Walter Catlett in the finale of the musical *Sally* (1920). P. G. Wodehouse had written these lyrics for an earlier (unproduced) musical called *The Little Thing*.

Little Darlin', words and music by Maurice Williams (1957). Popularized by the Diamonds in a Mercury recording.

Little Girl, words by Madeline Hyde, music by Francis "Muff" Henry (1931). Muff Henry was a guitar player with Guy Lombardo and his Royal Canadians, who introduced and popularized the song.

Little Girl Blue, words by Lorenz Hart, music by Richard Rodgers (1935).

Introduced by Gloria Grafton in the musical extravaganza *Jumbo* (1935). In the motion-picture adaptation of this musical (MGM, 1962), it was sung by Doris Day. The song was successfully featured by Mabel Mercer in intimate night clubs and boîtes.

A Little Girl from Little Rock, words by Leo Robin, music by Jule Styne (1949). Introduced by Carol Channing in the musical *Gentlemen Prefer Blondes* (1949). This was one of two numbers which helped elevate Carol Channing to stardom for the first time (the other being "Diamonds Are a Girl's Best Friend"). In the motion-picture adaptation of the musical (20th Century-Fox, 1953), it was sung by Marilyn Monroe and Jane Russell.

Little Girls, Goodbye, words by William Le Baron, music by Victor Jacobi (1919). Introduced by John Charles Thomas in the operetta *Apple Blossoms* (1919).

Little Hands, words and music by Robert Wright and George "Chet" Forrest, melody based on Rachmaninoff's "Vocalise" (1965). Introduced by Constance Towers and Lillian Gish in the musical *Anya* (1965).

The Little House upon the Hill, words by Ballard MacDonald and Joe Goodwin, music by Harry Puck (1915).

Little Johnny Jones, a musical comedy with text, lyrics and music by George M. Cohan. This was George M. Cohan's first successful musical comedy. Starring George M. Cohan, supported by the three other Cohans (1904).

The motion-picture adaptation starred Eddie Buzzell and Alice Day (First National, 1929). Two songs were used from the stage score. New numbers by various composers and lyricists, and several standards, were interpolated.

See: Give My Regards to Broadway; Goodbye, Flo; Life's a Funny Proposition After All; Painting the Clouds with Sunshine; The Yankee Doodle Boy.

A Little Kiss Each Morning (A Little Kiss Each Night), words and music by Harry Woods (1929). Introduced by Rudy Vallée in his first motion-picture starring role, in *The Vagabond Lover* (RKO, 1929). The song was revived about a quarter of a century later by Bing Crosby in a best-selling Decca recording.

Little Liza Jane. *See:* Li'l Liza Jane.

Little Man, You've Had a Busy Day, words by Maurice Sigler and Al Hoffman, music by Mabel Wayne (1934).

Little Mother of Mine, words by Walter H. Brown, music by H. T. Burleigh (1917). An art song popularized by Frank Munn in a Brunswick recording—Munn's disk debut. It was also the first song presented by Frank Munn over the radio in his Brunswick Hour of Music.

The Little Lost Child, words by Edward B. Marks, music by Joseph W. Stern (1894). One of the most popular sentimental ballads of the 1890s. It successfully launched both the songwriting team of Stern and Marks and the publishing house of Joseph W. Stern & Co.

Marks was a salesman of buttons, notions and novelties, who liked writing lyrics; Stern was a necktie salesman with the hobby of writing melodies. They were rooming in a hotel in Mamaroneck, New York, when they came upon a news item describing the plight of a lost child. Wandering aimlessly about in the city streets, this child was picked up by a policeman who turned out to be her long-separated father. Feeling that this story was material for a ballad, Stern and Marks made for the hotel parlor, which boasted a piano, and went to work writing words and music.

To publish their song, they opened an office in the basement of a building on 14th Street and 2nd Avenue, in 1894. Their total capital was $100, which was expended in the purchase of a desk and chair and in putting down a deposit for a printing order. The new publishing firm was called Joseph W. Stern & Co.; Marks' name was omitted because he did not wish to jeopardize his job as salesman.

The day after the printer delivered the copies of "The Little Lost Child," Della Fox—noted star of Broadway musicals—came into the Stern office in search of new song material. She liked their ballad, and introduced it in vaudeville in 1894. Then Lottie Gilson included it in her vaudeville act; the first time she did so, the audience proved so enthusiastic that it started joining her in singing the refrain.

"The Little Lost Child" became the first popular song to be exploited through the use of song slides; and it was through this exploitation that the ballad went on to become one of the best sheet-music sellers of the decade, in excess of two million copies. George H. Thomas, an electrician in a Brooklyn theater, was the one who first conceived the idea of combining suitable slides with the singing of "The Little Lost Child." Stern and Marks provided the funds with which to engage a photographer to take pictures in a Brooklyn police station. Episodes from the ballad were enacted, with Thomas' wife portraying the little child's mother; a child actress portrayed the little lost girl; and an actual policeman played himself. Marks then tried to interest George Primrose of the Primrose and West Minstrels to allow Allan May to sing the ballad while the scenes were flashed on a screen by the slides. Primrose was opposed to such an innovation. Marks then arranged for Allan May to sing it with slides at a Wednesday matinee performance at the Grand Opera House on 23rd Street and 8th Avenue. So inexperienced were the operators of the slides that at first the pictures were seen upside down. Nevertheless the novelty proved a sensation. It made the ballad one of the greatest hits of the decade, and started a vogue for song slides which persisted for the next twenty years.

Little Old Lady, words by Stanley Adams, music by Hoagy Carmichael (1936). The song was written for the revue *The Show Is On* (1936).

During rehearsals the producer decided to delete it, since it did not have a suitable context. E. Y. Harburg, the lyricist, was so taken with this number that he devised a special scene in *The Show Is On,* in which Mitzi Mayfair and Charles Walters sang the ballad and then danced to it.

The Little Old Log Cabin in the Lane, words and music by Will S. Hays (1871). One of the most successful sentimental ballads of the 1870s.

The Little Show, an intimate revue with book and lyrics mainly by Howard Dietz. Music mainly by Arthur Schwartz. Additional songs by Kay Swift and Ralph Rainger, among others. Starring Clifton Webb, Libby Holman and Fred Allen. The first edition was in 1929. There were two other editions. The second (1930) had book and lyrics by Howard Dietz and music by Arthur Schwartz; it starred Al Trahan, Jay C. Flippen and Gloria Grafton. *The Third Little Show* (1931) had book and lyrics by Howard Dietz with various composers providing the music. Beatrice Lillie was the star.

See: Can't We Be Friends?; I Guess I'll Have to Change My Plan; Lucky Seven; Moanin' Low; Sing Something Simple; When Yuba Plays the Rumba on his Tuba.

Little Sister, words and music by Mort Shuman and Jerome "Doc" Pomus (1961). Popularized by Elvis Presley, whose RCA Victor recording sold over a million disks.

Little Star, words and music by Vito Picone and Arthur Venosa (1958). Popularized by the Elegants in an Apt recording.

Little Things Mean a Lot, words by Edith Lindeman and Carl Stutz (1954). Popularized by Kitty Kallen in a Decca recording.

The Little Things You Used to Do, words by Al Dubin, music by Harry Warren (1935). Introduced by Helen Morgan in the motion-picture musical *Go into Your Dance* (First National, 1935).

Little Tin Box, words by Sheldon Harnick, music by Jerry Bock (1959). A satire on political investigations and graft, introduced by Howard da Silva and male chorus in the Pulitzer Prize musical *Fiorello!* (1959).

The Little White Cloud That Cried, words and music by Johnnie Ray (1951). Popularized by Johnnie Ray in a Columbia recording.

The Little White House at the End of Honeymoon Lane, words by Eddie Dowling, music by James F. Hanley (1926). Introduced by Eddie Dowling in the musical *Honeymoon Lane* (1926). Dowling also sang it in the motion-picture adaptation of the musical (Paramount, 1931).

Little White Lies, words and music by Walter Donaldson (1930). Written for and introduced and popularized by Guy Lombardo and his Royal Canadians. Ethel Merman sang it for George Gershwin when, in 1930, she auditioned successfully for the lead in *Girl Crazy*. Tommy Dorsey and his orchestra, with Frank Sinatra doing the vocal, made a best-selling recording for RCA Victor. Dick Haymes' recording for Decca in 1948 sold over a million disks. The song was interpolated in the non-musical motion picture *Lover, Come Back,* starring George Brent and Lucille Ball (Universal, 1946).

Live and Let Live, words and music by Cole Porter (1953). Introduced by Lilo in the musical *Can-Can* (1953). It was sung by Louis Jourdan and Maurice Chevalier in the motion-picture adaptation of the musical (20th Century-Fox, 1960).

Living Simply, words and music by Walter Marks (1964). Introduced by Robert Burr, Nancy Dussault and a male trio in the gypsy musical *Bajour* (1964).

Livingston, Jay, composer and lyricist, born McDonald, Pennsylvania, 1915. Livingston's hit songs were written in collaboration with Ray Evans.

See: Almost in Your Arms; Another Time, Another Place; Bonanza; Bonne Nuit, Good Night; Buttons and Bows; Copper Canyon; Dear Heart; Golden Earrings; I'll Always Love You; Lonely Girl; Marshmallow Moon; Misto Cristofo Columbo; Mona Lisa; My Beloved; Never Let Me Go; Never Too Late; Silver Bells; Sur-prise; Tammy; To Each His Own; Warm and Willing; Whatever Will Be, Will Be.

Livingston, Jerry, composer, born Denver, Colorado, 1909.

See: Bibbidi-Bobbidi-Boo; Cat Ballou; Chi-Baba; A Dream Is a Wish Your Heart Makes; The Hanging Tree; Hawaiian Eye; It's the Talk of the Town; Mairzy Doats; The Twelfth of Never; Wake the Town and Tell the People.

Liza, words by Ira Gershwin and Gus Kahn, music by George Gershwin (1929). Introduced by Ruby Keeler —accompanied by Duke Ellington and his orchestra—in the musical *Show Girl* (1929).

During the rehearsals of *Show Girl,* George Gershwin thought it might be a novel idea for Jimmy Durante to sing the tune to Ruby Keeler—and a routine was accordingly worked out. But when the show tried out in Boston, Al Jolson, who had flown in unexpectedly from California, rose from his seat in the audience and started singing "Liza" to Ruby Keeler, whom he had married in 1928. This improvised routine brought down the house. Jolson repeated it several times more after that, not only in Boston but also in New York. Durante never sang the number to Ruby Keeler after that.

Jolson sang it on the soundtrack of the motion-picture musical *The Jolson Story* (Columbia, 1946). The song was also interpolated in the motion-picture biography of George Gershwin, *Rhapsody in Blue* (Warner, 1945); in the motion-picture musical *The Man I Love* (Warner, 1946); and was sung by Patrice Wymore in the motion-picture musical *Starlift* (Warner, 1951).

Loads of Love, words and music by Richard Rodgers (1962). Introduced by Diahann Carroll in the musical *No Strings* (1962).

Locked Out After Nine, words by Ed Harrigan, music by Dave Braham (1880). Introduced in the Harrigan and Hart musical extravaganza *The Mulligan Guards' Picnic* (1880).

Loco-Motion, words and music by

Gerry Goffin and Carole King (1962). Popularized by Little Eva in a Dimension recording.

Loesser, Frank, composer and lyricist, born New York City, 1910.

See: Lane, Burton; Schertzinger, Victor; Schwartz, Arthur.

See also: Adelaide's Lament; Anywhere I Wander; Baby, It's Cold Outside; Big D; Brotherhood of Man; A Bushel and a Peck; Can't Get Out of This Mood; Dolores; Fugue for Tinhorns; Grand Old Ivy; Guys and Dolls; Happy to Make Your Acquaintance; Heart and Soul; Hoop-Dee-Doo; I Believe in You; I Don't Want to Walk Without You, Baby; If I Were a Bell; I'll Know; In My Arms; The Inch Worm; I've Never Been in Love Before; I Wish I Didn't Love You So; I Wish I were Twins; Jingle, Jangle, Jingle; Joey, Joey, Joey; Just Another Polka; Let's Get Lost; Luck, Be a Lady; Make a Miracle; Moon of Manakoora; More I Cannot Wish You; The Most Happy Fella; The Music of Home; My Darling; Never Will I Marry; My Time of Day; The New Ashmolean Marching Society and Students Conservatory Band; No Two People; On a Slow Boat to China; Once in Love with Amy; Praise the Lord and Pass the Ammunition; Rodger Young; See What the Boys in the Back Room Will Have; Sing a Tropical Song; Sit Down, You're Rockin' the Boat; Small Fry; Spring Will Be a Little Late This Year; Standin' on the Corner; Summertime Love; Take Back Your Mink; Tallahassee; Thumbelina; Two Sleepy People; What Are You Doing New Year's Eve?; What Do You Do in the Infantry?; A Woman in Love; Wonderful Copenhagen.

Loewe, Frederick, composer, born Vienna, Austria, 1904.

See (Lyrics by Alan Jay Lerner): Almost Like Being in Love; Another Autumn; Ascot Gavotte; Before I Gaze at You Again; Come to Me, Bend to Me; Follow Me; From This Day On; Get Me to the Church on Time; God's Green World; The Heather on the Hill; How Can I Wait?; How to Handle a Woman; I Could Have Danced All Night; If Ever I Would Leave You; I'll Go Home with Bonnie Jean; I Love You This Morning; I'm Glad I'm Not Young Anymore; I Remember It Well; I Still See Elisa; I Talk to the Trees; I've Grown Accustomed to Her Face; The Love of My Life; My Love Is a Married Man; The Night They Invented Champagne; On the Street Where You Live; The Rain in Spain; Say a Prayer for Me Tonight; Show Me; Simple Joys of Maidenhood; Thank Heaven for Little Girls; There But for You Go I; They Call the Wind Maria; Waitin' for My Dearie; Wan'drin' Star; What Do Simple Folk Do?; With a Little Bit of Luck; Wouldn't It Be Loverly?

Lollipop, words and music by Beverly Ross and Julius Dixon (1958). Popularized by the Chordettes in a Cadence recording.

Lollipops and Roses, words and music by Tony Velona (1962). Introduced and popularized by Jack Jones in a Kapp release. This was Jones' first successful recording. He made it while serving in the Air Force, and not only did it lift him to success for the first time, but it also helped to establish permanently his singing style and personality. The Jack Jones disk received a "Grammy" Award from the National Academy of Recording Arts and Sciences as the best solo male recording of the year. The song points up the moral that females enjoy receiving favors and attentions whether they be fourteen years old, or forty.

Lonely Blue Boy, words by Fred Wise, music by Ben Weisman (1958). Popularized by Conway Twitty in an MGM recording.

Lonely Boy. *See:* I'm Just a Lonely Boy.

Lonely Girl (Theme from Harlow), words and music by Jay Livingston and Ray Evans (1965). Theme song from the non-musical motion picture *Harlow* (Paramount, 1965), starring Carroll Baker. It was introduced by Bobby Vinton, who popularized it in an Epic recording.

Lonely Little Robin, words and music by Cy Coben (1951). Popularized by Mindy Carson in a Columbia recording.

Lonely Street, words and music by Kenny Sowder, W. S. Stevenson and Carl Belew (1956). Popularized in 1959 by Andy Williams in a Cadence recording.

Lonely Teardrops, words and music by Berry Gordy, Jr., Gwen Gordy and Tyran Carlo (1958). Popularized in 1959 by Jackie Wilson in a Brunswick recording that sold a million disks.

Lonely Town, words by Betty Comden and Adolph Green, music by Leonard Bernstein (1945). Introduced by John Battles and chorus in Leonard Bernstein's first musical, *On the Town* (1944).

Lonesome, words by Edgar Leslie, music by George W. Meyer (1909). Meyer's first hit song. It sold over a million copies of sheet music.

Lonesome and Sorry, words by Benny Davis, music by Con Conrad (1926). A favorite of big-name bands in the late 1920s.

The Lonesome Road, words by Gene Austin, music by Nathaniel Shilkret (1928). It was interpolated in the screen adaptation of the Jerome Kern-Oscar Hammerstein musical play *Show Boat* (Universal, 1929).

Lonesome Town, words and music by Baker Knight (1958). Popularized by Ricky Nelson in an Imperial recording.

Lonesome Walls, words by Du Bose Heyward, music by Jerome Kern (1929). Interpolated for Ethel Waters in the non-musical Broadway play *Mamba's Daughters* (1929).

Long Ago and Far Away, words by Ira Gershwin, music by Jerome Kern (1944). Introduced by Gene Kelly in the motion-picture musical *Cover Girl* (Columbia, 1944). This number enjoyed the largest sheet sale (six hundred thousand copies) of any Ira Gershwin song.

Ira Gershwin had considerable difficulty writing this lyric. He worked on six versions, none of which satisfied him. Arthur Schwartz, producer of *Cover Girl*, telephoned Gershwin one day saying he needed the lyric without further delay. Gershwin read over the telephone the sixth version, even though it displeased him. Both Schwartz and Kern liked it, however, and this is the lyric that was finally used.

The song was interpolated in the Jerome Kern screen biography *Till the Clouds Roll By* (MGM, 1946).

Long Before I Knew You, words by Betty Comden and Adolph Green, music by Jule Styne (1956). Introduced by Sydney Chaplin in the musical *Bells Are Ringing* (1956). In the motion-picture adaptation of the musical (MGM, 1960), it was sung by Dean Martin.

Long Boy. *See:* Good bye, Ma! Good bye, Pa!, Good bye, Mule.

The Longest Day, words and music by Paul Anka (1962). Title song of the non-musical motion picture starring John Wayne, Henry Fonda and Robert Mitchum (20th Century-Fox, 1962), sung on the soundtrack under the titles by Paul Anka.

The Longest Walk, words by Eddie Pola, music by Fred Spielman (1955). Popularized by Jaye P. Morgan in an RCA Victor recording.

The Longest Way 'Round Is the Sweetest Way Home, words by Ren Shields, music by Kerry Mills (1908).

The Long Hot Summer, words by Sammy Cahn, music by Alex North (1957). Title song of the non-musical motion picture starring Paul Newman and Joanne Woodward (20th Century-Fox, 1957), sung under the titles on the soundtrack by Jimmie Rodgers.

Longing for You, words by Jack Drislane, music by Theodore F. Morse (1905).

Long Tall Sally, words and music by Enotris Johnson, Richard Penniman and Robert A. Blackwell (1956). Popularized by Little Richard in a Specialty recording and by Pat Boone in a Dot recording.

Long Time Ago (or, Shinbone Alley), words and music of unknown authorship. It was popularized by Thomas "Daddy" Rice in his minstrel act, in or about 1833. It was published in New York City in 1835 with a piano accompaniment by William Clifton.

Look Again, words by Dory Langdon, music by André Previn (1963). Theme song from the motion picture *Irma La Douce,* starring Shirley MacLaine and Jack Lemmon (Universal 1963). The song was popularized by Eddie Fisher in an RCA Victor recording.

Look at 'Er, words and music by Bob Merrill (1957). Introduced by George Wallace in the musical *New Girl in Town* (1957).

Look for Small Pleasures, words by Sidney Michaels, music by Mark Sandrich, Jr. (1965). Introduced by Robert Preston and Ulla Salert in the musical *Ben Franklin in Paris* (1965) and popularized by Robert Goulet in a Columbia recording.

Look for the Silver Lining, words by Bud De Sylva, music by Jerome Kern (1920). The song was written for an unproduced musical, *Brewster's Millions.* It was then interpolated in the musical *Good Morning, Dearie* (1919). It became famous in the musical *Sally* (1920), where it was sung by Marilyn Miller, with the assistance of Irving Fisher. "It was Marilyn Miller," wrote P. G. Wodehouse and Guy Bolton, "who brought a curious enchantment that no reproduction in other lands or other media ever captures." Marilyn Miller and Alexander Grey sang it in the motion-picture adaptation of the musical (First National, 1929). It was sung by Judy Garland in the Jerome Kern screen biography *Till the Clouds Roll By* (MGM, 1946). It was sung by June Haver in Marilyn Miller's screen biography, also named *Look for the Silver Lining* (Warner, 1949).

Look for the Silver Lining, a motion-picture musical biography of Marilyn Miller, starring June Haver as Marilyn Miller with Gordon MacRae and Ray Bolger (Warner, 1949). The score was made up of standards.

See: Just a Memory; A Kiss in the Dark; Look for the Silver Lining; Time on My Hands; Sunny; Whippoor-will; Who?; Wild Rose.

Looking at the World Thru Rose Colored Glasses, words and music by Tommy Malie and Jimmie Stieger (1926).

Looking for a Boy, words by Ira Gershwin, music by George Gershwin (1925). Introduced by Queenie Smith (downstage while the set was being changed behind the drop) in the musical *Tip Toes* (1925).

Looking for Love, words and music by Hank Hunter and Stan Vincent (1964). Title song of a motion-picture musical (MGM, 1964), introduced by Connie Francis.

Looking for Love, a motion-picture musical starring Connie Francis (MGM, 1964). Songs by Hank Hunter and Stan Vincent. Several standards were interpolated.

See: Be My Love; I Can't Believe That You're in Love with Me; Looking for Love.

Look, Little Girl, words and music by Meredith Willson (1963). Introduced by Craig Stevens in the musical *Here's Love* (1963).

Look to the Rainbow, words by E. Y. Harburg, music by Burton Lane (1947). Introduced by Ella Logan and Donald Richards in the musical play *Finian's Rainbow* (1947).

Look What's in Love, words by Dorothy Fields, music by Albert Hague (1959). Introduced by Gwen Verdon and Richard Kiley in the musical *Redhead* (1959).

Lord, You Made the Night Too Long, words by Sam M. Lewis, music by Victor Young (1932).

The Lorelei, words by Ira Gershwin, music by George Gershwin (1933). Introduced by Lyda Roberti (in out-of-town tryouts) and on Broadway by the team of Randall and Newberry in the musical *Pardon My English* (1933). The lyric is distinguished by its use of the skat phrase "hey! ho-de-ho," anticipating by a year a similar use in "It Ain't Necessarily So" in the Gershwin folk opera *Porgy and Bess.*

Lorena, words by H. D. L. Webster, music by J. P. Webster (1857). The lyricist and the composer were not related. This love ballad was a favorite of the Confederacy during the Civil War. So popular did this song become in the Southland, many Southern girls were named after the heroine in the ballad; so were a number of pioneer settlements and a steamship.

Lorraine, My Beautiful Alsace Lorraine, words by Alfred Bryan, music by Fred Fisher (1917). A World War I song hit.

Lost in a Fog, words by Dorothy Fields, music by Jimmy McHugh (1934). The melody was written in 1934 as a theme for the Dorsey brothers' jazz band, and was introduced during its debut at the Riviera café in New Jersey the same year, with Jimmy McHugh doing the vocal. (At this time the members of the band included Tommy and Jimmy Dorsey, Glenn Miller, Paul Weston, Alex Stordahl, Ray McKinley, Charlie Spivak and, as vocalist, Bob Crosby.) The song was then interpolated in the non-musical motion picture *Have a Heart,* starring Jean Parker and James Dunn (MGM, 1934).

Lost in Loveliness, words by Leo Robin, music by Sigmund Romberg (1954). Introduced by David Atkinson in the musical *The Girl in Pink Tights* (1954)—Romberg's last musical comedy, produced posthumously.

Lost in the Stars, words by Maxwell Anderson, music by Kurt Weill (1949). Title song of the musical play (1949), introduced by Todd Duncan and chorus.

Lost in the Stars, a musical play with book and lyrics by Maxwell Anderson based on Alan Paton's novel *Cry, the Beloved Country.* Music by Kurt Weill. Starring Todd Duncan and Inez Matthews (1949). Original cast recording (Decca).

See: Cry, the Beloved Country; Lost in the Stars.

A Lot of Livin' to Do, words by Lee Adams, music by Charles Strouse (1960). Introduced by Dick Gautier and Susan Waters in the musical *Bye Bye Birdie* (1960). In the motion-picture adaptation of the musical (Columbia, 1963), it was sung by Jessie Pearson, Ann-Margret and Bobby Rydell.

Louise, words by Leo Robin, music by Richard A. Whiting (1929). Introduced by Maurice Chevalier in his American screen debut in the motion-picture musical *Innocents of Paris* (Paramount, 1929). He revived it in the motion picture *A New Kind of Love* (Paramount, 1963). The song was interpolated in the non-musical motion picture *Halfway to Heaven,* starring Buddy Rogers and Jean Arthur (Paramount, 1929), where it appeared as an instrumental. It was also heard in the motion-picture musical *You Can't Ration Love,* starring Johnny Johnston and Betty Jane Rhodes (Paramount, 1944), and was sung by Jerry Lewis in the motion-picture farce *The Stooge,* starring Dean Martin and Jerry Lewis (Paramount, 1952).

Louisiana Hayride, words by Howard Dietz, music by Arthur Schwartz (1932). Introduced by Clifton Webb and Tamara Geva in the musical *Flying Colors* (1932); it was used here for a production number in the first-act finale, highlighting a dance sequence by Clifton Webb and featuring a trick night-ride effect. The song was revived by Nanette Fabray in the motion-picture musical *The Band Wagon* (MGM, 1953).

Louisiana Purchase, a musical comedy with book by Morrie Ryskind based on a story by Bud De Sylva. Lyrics and music by Irving Berlin. Starring William Gaxton, Vera Zorina, Irene Bordini and Victor Moore (1940).

The motion-picture adaptation starred Bob Hope, Vera Zorina, Irene Bordoni and Victor Moore (Paramount, 1941). Four songs were used from the stage score.

See: It's a Lovely Day Tomorrow.

Lou'siana Belle, words and music by Stephen Foster (1847). Foster's first published song, for which he received no payment.

L-O-V-E, words and music by Milt Gabler and Bert Kaempfert (1964). Popularized by Nat King Cole in a best-selling Capitol recording, one of his last releases.

Love, words and music by Ralph Blane and Hugh Martin (1945). Introduced by Lena Horne in the motion-picture musical *Ziegfeld Follies* (MGM, 1946).

Love and Marriage, words by Sammy Cahn, music by James Van Heusen (1955). Introduced by Frank Sinatra in the TV musical-comedy adaptation of Thornton Wilder's play *Our Town* (1955). This was the first popular song ever to win an "Emmy" Award. It also received the religious Christopher Award.

The Love Boat, words by Gene Buck, music by Victor Herbert (1920). Introduced for a production number with a Venetian setting in the *Ziegfeld Follies of 1920*.

Love for Sale, words and music by Cole Porter (1930). One of the earliest of Cole Porter's song classics— and one of the few American song standards inspired by the world's oldest profession. The song was introduced by Kathryn Crawford (with the help of June Shafer, Ida Peerson and Stella Friend) in the musical *The New Yorkers* (1930). The song was long banned from the airwaves because of its suggestive lyrics. It was interpolated orchestrally in Cole Porter's screen biography, *Night and Day* (Warner, 1946).

"Love for Sale" was one of two song favorites of Cole Porter among his own creations, the other being "Begin the Beguine."

Love Has Many Faces, words by Mack David, music by David Raksin (1964). Title song of a non-musical motion picture starring Lana Turner, Cliff Robertson and Hugh O'Brian (Columbia, 1965). It was popularized by Nancy Wilson in a Capitol recording.

The Love I Long For, words by Howard Dietz, music by Vernon Duke (1944). Introduced by June Havoc and James Newill in the musical *Sadie Thompson* (1944), and popularized in a Columbia recording by Harry James and his orchestra.

Love in Bloom, words by Leo Robin, music by Ralph Rainger (1934). Introduced by Bing Crosby in the motion-picture musical *She Loves Me Not* (Paramount, 1934), and

further popularized by him in a Decca recording.

The Paramount studio heads originally regarded this song as "too high class" for popular consumption. The song, however, went on to become one of the leading hits of 1934, selling about half a million copies of sheet music. It was interpolated by Lynn Overman in the motion picture *New York Town*, starring Fred MacMurray and Mary Martin (Paramount, 1941), and by Judy Canova in the motion picture *True to the Army* (Paramount, 1942). The song achieved its greatest public, and its prime popularity, as Jack Benny's theme song over radio and TV.

Love Is a Dancing Thing, words by Howard Dietz, music by Arthur Schwartz (1935). Introduced by James MacColl in the musical *At Home Abroad* (1935).

Love Is a Many Splendored Thing, words by Paul Francis Webster, music by Sammy Fain (1955). Theme song of the non-musical motion picture starring William Holden and Jennifer Jones (20th Century-Fox, 1955), where it was sung by a chorus in the closing scene. It received the Academy Award.

The Decca recording by the Four Aces sold over a million disks. But before this had happened, Tony Martin turned it down for recording because he regarded it as "too heavy." Several other big-name recording artists also avoided it, among them Doris Day, Eddie Fisher and Nat King Cole. However, after the song had been saved from oblivion by the Four Aces release, most of the famous artists who had originally turned it down issued successful disks.

Love Is a Simple Thing, words by June Carroll, music by Arthur Siegel (1951). Introduced by Rosemary O'Reilly, Robert Clary, Eartha Kitt and June Carroll in the revue *New Faces of 1952*.

Love Is a Tyrant, words by Harry B. Smith, music by Victor Herbert (1899). Waltz introduced by Alice

Nielsen in the operetta *The Singing Girl* (1899).

Love Is Here to Stay. *See:* Our Love Is Here to Stay.

Love Is Just Around the Corner, words by Leo Robin, music by Lewis E. Gensler (1934). Introduced by Bing Crosby in the motion-picture musical *Here Is My Heart* (Paramount, 1934), and further popularized by him in a Decca recording.

Love Is Like a Cigarette, words by Glen MacDonough, music by Victor Herbert (1908). Introduced by Frank Pollack in the operetta *The Rose of Algeria* (1909). Herbert had originally written this melody in 1905 for the operetta *It Happened in Nordland,* but it was never used there.

Love Is Like a Firefly, words by Otto Hauerbach (Harbach), music by Rudolf Friml (1912). Introduced by Emma Trentini in Friml's first operetta *The Firefly* (1912). In the motion-picture adaptation of the operetta (MGM, 1937), it was sung by Jeanette MacDonald.

Love Is Strange, words and music by Ethel Smith and Mickey Baker (1957). Popularized by Mickey and Sylvia in a Groove and Vik recording.

Love Is Sweeping the Country, words by Ira Gershwin, music by George Gershwin (1931). Introduced by George Murphy and June O'Dea in the Pulitzer Prize musical comedy *Of Thee I Sing!* (1931). The patter that follows the refrain has a Chinese character; this is because Gershwin had previously used the tune for a musical comedy with a Chinese setting, *East Is West,* which was never produced.

Love Is the Best of All, words by Henry Blossom, music by Victor Herbert (1915). Introduced by Eleanor Painter in the operetta *The Princess Pat* (1915). Edward N. Waters explains that "one stanza [has the] characteristics of the mazurka and a refrain forming one of the best waltzes Herbert ever wrote." To the distinguished melody of the waltz refrain Herbert "added choral responses and then a solo obbligato to a choral

presentation which are highly impressive."

Love Is the Reason, words by Dorothy Fields, music by Arthur Schwartz (1951). Introduced by Shirley Booth in the musical *A Tree Grows in Brooklyn* (1951).

Love Is the Sweetest Thing, words and music by Ray Noble (1932). It was interpolated in the non-musical motion picture *Confidential Agent,* starring Charles Boyer and Lauren Bacall (Warner, 1945).

Love Letters, words by Ed Heyman, music by Victor Young (1945). Title song of a non-musical motion picture starring Joseph Cotten and Jennifer Jones (Paramount, 1945). The song was successfully revived in 1962 by Kitty Lester in an Era recording.

Love Letters in the Sand, words by Nick and Charles Kenny, music by J. Fred Coots (1931). One of Coots' greatest song hits.

Coots explained to this editor how the ballad came to be written: "While traveling by train from my home in Larchmont, New York, to New York City, I happened to spot a Nick Kenny poem in the *Daily Mirror.* It struck me as a sure thing for a 'pop song.' When the train reached New York's Grand Central station, I rushed over to Nick Kenny's office and got his okay to write the music. After four different melodies, I finally hit on one that had the right treatment. I then made the rounds of all the publishers, and it was turned down by everybody except Max Winslow at the Irving Berlin Music Company. He took it, showed it to a young singer named Russ Columbo, who recorded it. Columbo at the time was a singing rival of young Bing Crosby. The record did fairly well, but it was George Hall and his orchestra, broadcasting from the Hotel Taft over the Mutual Broadcasting network, who really put the song across. Hall made it his theme and signature song, and with fourteen broadcasts weekly he put it in the 'top ten' in no time."

Pat Boone revived the song in 1957, his Dot recording selling over a million disks. The song was interpolated for him in the motion picture *Bernadine* (20th Century-Fox, 1957).

The Loveliest Night of the Year, words by Paul Francis Webster, music by Irving Aaronson, the melody adapted from Juventino Rosa's waltz "Sobre las olas" (1950). It was introduced by Ann Blyth in the motion-picture musical *The Great Caruso* (MGM, 1951). Mario Lanza's recording for RCA Victor sold over a million disks.

Love Life, a musical comedy with book and lyrics by Alan Jay Lerner. Music by Kurt Weill. Starring Ray Middleton and Nanette Fabray (1948).
See: Green Up Time; Here I'll Stay.

Love Line, words and music by Walter Marks (1964). Introduced by Chita Rivera in the gypsy musical *Bajour* (1964).

The Loveliness of You, words by Mack Gordon, music by Harry Revel (1935). Introduced in the motion-picture musical *Love in Bloom,* starring George Burns and Gracie Allen (Paramount, 1935).

Love, Look Away, words by Oscar Hammerstein II, music by Richard Rodgers (1958). Introduced by Arabella Hong in the musical *Flower Drum Song* (1958). In the motion-picture adaptation of the musical (Universal, 1961), it was sung by Reiko Sato.

Lovely, words and music by Stephen Sondheim (1962). Introduced by Brian Davies and Preshy Marker (and in the reprise, presented as a comedy number by Zero Mostel and Jack Gilford) in the musical *A Funny Thing Happened on the Way to the Forum* (1962).

Lovely Lady, words by Ted Koehler, music by Jimmy McHugh (1935). Introduced by Kenny Baker in the motion-picture musical *The King of Burlesque,* starring Warner Baxter and Alice Faye (20th Century-Fox, 1935).

Lovely to Look At, words by Dorothy Fields and Jimmy McHugh, music by Jerome Kern (1935). Written for the motion-picture adaptation of the musical *Roberta* (RKO, 1935), where it was introduced by Fred Astaire.

The producers of this movie originally felt that the song could never become popular because the refrain had only sixteen measures, and because the last four of these were unusually complex and subtle. Kern refused to make any changes. The song became such a hit (usurping first place on the Hit Parade on April 20, 1935) that when *Roberta* was filmed a second time (MGM, 1952), it was called *Lovely to Look At;* here the song was presented by Howard Keel.

Lovely to Look At (screen musical). *See: Roberta.*

A Lovely Way to Spend an Evening, words by Harold Adamson, music by Jimmy McHugh (1943). Introduced by Frank Sinatra in the motion-picture musical *Higher and Higher* (RKO, 1943), and further popularized by him in a Capitol recording. The song was interpolated in the non-musical motion picture *The Racket,* starring Robert Mitchum and Lizbeth Scott (RKO, 1951), sung by Lizbeth Scott.

Love Makes the World Go 'Round, words by Clyde Fitch, music by William Furst (1896). Introduced in the operetta *Bohemia* (1896).

Love Makes the World Go 'Round, words and music by Bob Merrill (1961). Theme song from the musical *Carnival* (1961), where it was used as a recurrent motive and introduced by Anna Maria Alberghetti.

Love Me, words by Antoine "Fats" Domino, music by Dave Bartholomew (1954). Popularized by "Fats" Domino in an Imperial recording.

Love Me and the World Is Mine, words by Dave Reed, Jr., music by Ernest R. Ball (1906). Sigmund Spaeth noted two musical "tricks" that helped make this song so popular. One is that "even though the range of the melody is a whole tone less than an octave, the scale progression makes a ringing climax of the top note, sounding much higher than it really is." The other factor is that "in the triplets of the accompaniment" the song gains a mood "of suppressed excitement, adding to the cumulative character of the melody and encouraging a freedom of harmony that inevitably appeals to any singing group, especially a male quartet or chorus."

The ballad was introduced at Proctor's Fifth Avenue Theatre in 1906, then first made successful in vaudeville by Maude Lambert (Ball's second wife). In time it sold over a million copies of sheet music. It was by virtue of the success of this one number that the publishing house of Witmark gave Ball a twenty-year contract as staff composer, with a handsome annual guarantee—the first time that a composer in Tin Pan Alley ever received such a long-term agreement.

The song was interpolated in several motion pictures. Among them was the screen musical *San Francisco* (MGM, 1936), sung by Jeanette MacDonald; *The Strawberry Blond,* starring Rita Hayworth and James Cagney (Warner, 1941); the Ernest R. Ball screen biography *When Irish Eyes Are Smiling* (20th Century-Fox, 1944); and the motion-picture musical *The Eddie Cantor Story* (Warner, 1954).

This ballad was a staple in the concert repertory of the beloved Irish tenor John McCormack.

Love Me Forever, words by Gus Kahn, music by Victor Schertzinger (1935). Title song of a motion picture (Columbia, 1935), sung by Grace Moore.

Love Me Little, Love Me Long, words and music by Percy Gaunt (1893).

Love Me or Leave Me, words by Gus Kahn, music by Walter Donaldson (1928). Interpolated for Ruth Etting (with whom this song has since been identified) in the musical *Whoopee* (1928). Ruth Etting sang it again in the musical *Simple Simon* (1930). It was sung by Doris Day in the motion-picture biography of Ruth Etting, named after the song (MGM, 1955). The song was also interpolated in the screen biography of Gus Kahn, *I'll See You in My Dreams* (Warner,

1951), sung by Patrice Wymore.

Love Me or Leave Me, a motion-picture musical biography of Ruth Etting, starring Doris Day as Ruth Etting with James Cagney (MGM, 1955). Most of the score was made up of standards. Two new numbers were interpolated, one by Sammy Cahn and Nicholas Brodzsky, the other by Chilton Price. Soundtrack recording (Columbia).

See: At Sundown; Everybody Loves My Baby; I'll Never Stop Loving You; It All Depends on You; Love Me or Leave Me; Mean to Me; Sam, the Old Accordion Man; Shaking the Blues Away; Ten Cents a Dance; You Made Me Love You.

Love Me Tender, words and music by Elvis Presley and Vera Matson, the melody based on George R. Poulton's "Aura Lee" (1956). Introduced by Elvis Presley in the motion-picture musical of the same name (20th Century-Fox, 1956). Presley's RCA Victor recording in 1956 sold over a million disks. The song was also interpolated in the motion-picture musical starring Pat Boone, *All Hands on Deck* (20th Century-Fox, 1962). The song was revived by Richard Chamberlain in a best-selling MGM recording.

Love Me Tonight, words by Lorenz Hart, music by Richard Rodgers (1932). Title song of a motion-picture musical (Paramount, 1932), sung by Jeanette MacDonald.

Love Me Tonight, a motion-picture musical starring Maurice Chevalier and Jeanette MacDonald (Paramount, 1932). Songs by Richard Rodgers and Lorenz Hart.

See: Isn't It Romantic?; Love Me Tonight; Lover; Mimi.

The Love Nest, words by Otto Harbach, music by Louis A. Hirsch (1920). Hit song from the musical *Mary* (1920), where it was introduced by Jack McGowan and Janet Velie. The song is believed to have been responsible for the box-office success of this production. A quarter of a century later it was used by Burns and Allen as their radio (and later TV) theme song. The song was interpolated in the motion-picture musical *The Helen Morgan Story* (Warner, 1957), sung on the sound-track by Gogi Grant (for Ann Blyth).

The Love of My Life, words by Alan Jay Lerner, music by Frederick Loewe (1947). Introduced by Pamela Britton in the musical play *Brigadoon* (1947).

Love of My Life, words and music by Cole Porter (1948). Introduced by Judy Garland in the motion-picture musical *The Pirate* (MGM, 1948).

The Love Parade, a motion-picture musical starring Maurice Chevalier and Jeanette MacDonald (Paramount, 1929). Songs by Clifford Grey and Victor Schertzinger.

See: Dream Lover; My Love Parade; Paris, Stay the Same.

Lover, words by Lorenz Hart, music by Richard Rodgers (1933). Introduced by Jeanette MacDonald in the motion-picture musical *Love Me To-night* (Paramount, 1932). Peggy Lee sang it in the motion-picture musical *The Jazz Singer* (Warner, 1953); her Decca recording in 1952 sold a million disks.

Lover, Come Back to Me, words by Oscar Hammerstein II, music by Sigmund Romberg, melody taken in part from Tchaikovsky's *June Barcarolle* for piano (1928). The song was introduced by Evelyn Herbert in the operetta *The New Moon* (1928). In the first motion-picture adaptation of the operetta (MGM, 1930), it was sung by Grace Moore; in the second (MGM, 1940), by Jeanette Mac-Donald. Tony Martin sang it in the Romberg screen biography *Deep in My Heart* (MGM, 1954). The song was popularized by Rudy Vallée both over the radio and in an RCA Victor recording.

Love Sends a Little Gift of Roses, words by Leslie Cooke, music by John Openshaw (1919).

Love Somebody, words and music by Joan Whitney and Alex Kramer (1947). Popularized by Doris Day (with Buddy Clark) in a best-selling Columbia recording.

Love Song from Houseboat. *See:* Almost in Your Arms.

Love Song from Mutiny on the Bounty. *See:* Follow Me.

Love Songs of the Nile, words by Arthur Freed, music by Nacio Herb Brown (1933). Theme song from the non-musical motion picture *The Barbarian* (MGM, 1933), where it was sung by Ramon Novarro.

Love Thy Neighbor, words by Mack Gordon, music by Harry Revel (1934). Introduced by Bing Crosby in the motion-picture musical *We're Not Dressing* (Paramount, 1934), and further popularized by him in a Decca recording.

Love Walked In, words by Ira Gershwin, music by George Gershwin (1938). One of George Gershwin's last songs. It was introduced by Kenny Baker in the motion-picture musical *The Goldwyn Follies* (United Artists, 1938). It was on the Hit Parade for several weeks running in 1938, one week in the Number One spot. The melody of the refrain had been written in or about 1931, the first sketch being twenty-four bars long, the first fourteen of which are exactly as they appeared in the 1938 song. George Gershwin described his melody as "Brahmsian"; Ira Gershwin called it "churchy." The song was interpolated in the George Gershwin screen biography *Rhapsody in Blue* (Warner, 1945).

Love Will Find a Way, words and music by Noble Sissle and Eubie Blake (1921). Introduced in the all-Negro revue *Shuffle Along* (1921).

Love with a Proper Stranger, words by Johnny Mercer, music by Elmer Bernstein (1964). Title song of the non-musical motion picture starring Steve McQueen and Natalie Wood (Paramount, 1964), where it was sung on the soundtrack under the titles by Jack Jones, who further popularized it in a Kapp recording.

Love Ya, words by Charles Tobias, music by Peter De Rose (1951). Introduced by Doris Day and Gordon MacRae in the motion-picture musical *On Moonlight Bay* (Warner, 1951).

Lovey Joe, words and music by Will Marion Cook and Joe Jordan (1910). A ragtime tune with which Fanny Brice made her debut in the *Ziegfeld Follies*—in the 1910 edition.

Love, Your Spell Is Everywhere, words by Elsie Janis, music by Edmund Goulding (1929). Introduced by Gloria Swanson in her talking-picture debut, in the motion picture *The Trespasser* (United Artists, 1929), where it served as the theme song.

Lovin' Sam, the Sheik of Alabam', words by Jack Yellen, music by Milton Ager (1922). Introduced by Grace Hayes in the musical *The Bunch and Judy* (1922), where it was an interpolation. It was then popularized by Anna Chandler.

Jack Yellen wrote to his editor: "Milton Ager and I finally became our own publishers because we couldn't get a break with other publishers. We scraped together a few thousand dollars, rented a couple of rooms in a dilapidated building on Broadway. We were almost broke when Max Winslow, professional manager for Waterson, Berlin and Snyder, phoned me to send over a copy of 'Lovin' Sam' to his office. He wouldn't tell me what he wanted it for. About two weeks later we heard that Grace Hayes had gone into *The Bunch and Judy,* an Otto Harbach—Jerome Kern show, and was a riot with 'Lovin' Sam' in a cabaret scene. We paid off the sheriff and were in business."

Lubly Fan (or, Buffalo Gals), words and music by Cool White (1844). Introduced by Cool White and his Serenaders in 1844 to become one of the most famous minstrel-show numbers before the Civil War. Sometimes known by its subtitle "Buffalo Gals," it was frequently referred to in different localities as "Louisiana Gals" or "Pittsburgh Gals" and so forth. The song is mentioned in Mark Twain's *Tom Sawyer.* The 1944 song hit "Dance with a Dolly" is an adaptation of "Lubly Fan."

Luck, Be a Lady, words and music by Frank Loesser (1950). Introduced by Robert Alda in the musical *Guys and Dolls* (1950). Frank Sinatra sang it in the motion-picture adaptation of the musical (MGM, 1955).

Lucky Day, words by Bud De Sylva and Lew Brown, music by Ray Henderson (1926). Introduced by Harry Richman in *George White's Scandals of 1926.* Dan Dailey sang it in the screen biography of De Sylva, Brown and Henderson, *The Best Things in Life are Free* (20th Century-Fox, 1956).

Lucky in Love, words by Bud De Sylva and Lew Brown, music by Ray Henderson (1927). Introduced by Mary Lawlor and John Price Jones in the musical *Good News* (1927). Pat Marshall, Peter Lawford and June Allyson sang it in the second motion-picture adaptation of the musical (MGM, 1947).

Lucky in the Rain. *See:* I Got Lucky in the Rain.

Lucky Seven, words by Howard Dietz, music by Arthur Schwartz (1930). Introduced in the revue *The Second Little Show* (1930).

Lucky to Be Me, words by Betty Comden and Adolph Green, music by Leonard Bernstein (1944). Introduced by John Battles and chorus in Leonard Bernstein's first musical, *On the Town* (1944).

Luders, Gustav, composer, born Bremen, Germany, 1865; died New York City, 1913.

See: Heidelberg Stein Song; Message of the Violet; Tale of a Bumble Bee; Tale of the Kangaroo; Tale of the Sea Shell; Tale of the Turtle Dove.

Lullaby (or, Emmet's Lullaby), words and music by Joseph K. Emmet (1878). Introduced in the musical *Fritz, Our Cousin German* (1878). The song is distinguished by its yodeling breaks in the chorus, whose main melody has since become famous to the words of the children's doll tune "Go to Sleep, My Baby."

Lullaby of Broadway, words by Al Dubin, music by Harry Warren (1935). Introduced by Wini Shaw in the motion-picture musical *Gold Diggers of Broadway* (First National, 1935). It received the Academy Award.

The song provided the title for a motion picture (Warner, 1951), where it was sung on the soundtrack under the titles by a chorus, and in the production-number finale was sung by Doris Day and danced to by Doris Day and Gene Nelson.

Lullaby of Broadway, a motion-picture musical starring Doris Day and Gene Nelson (Warner, 1951). The score was made up of standards.

See: Just One of Those Things; Lullaby of Broadway; Somebody Loves Me; You're Getting to Be a Habit with Me; Zing Went the Strings of My Heart.

Lullaby of the Leaves, words by Joe Young, music by Bernice Petkere (1932).

Lulu's Back in Town, words by Al Dubin, music by Harry Warren (1935). Introduced by Dick Powell and the Mills Brothers in the motion-picture musical *Broadway Gondolier,* starring Dick Powell and Joan Blondell (Warner, 1935). It was successfully revived in 1964 by Jerry Vale in a Columbia recording.

Lydia, the Tattooed Lady, words by E. Y. Harburg, music by Harold Arlen (1939). Introduced by Groucho Marx in the Marx Brothers' motion-picture extravaganza *A Day at the Circus* (MGM, 1939).

M

Ma Belle, words by Clifford Grey, music by Rudolf Friml (1928). Introduced by Dennis King in the operetta *The Three Musketeers* (1928).

Ma Blushin' Rosie (Ma Posie Sweet), words by Edgar Smith, music by John Stromberg (1900). Introduced by Fay Templeton and a chorus of girls in the Weber and Fields extravaganza *Fiddle Dee Dee* (1900).

Stromberg originally wrote this melody as a dance tune for Bessie Clayton, but she never used it. When a hurried replacement was needed for a song which had proved a dud in *Fiddle Dee Dee,* Stromberg adapted his dance tune as a song for Fay Templeton. It proved to be one of her greatest hits, and one of the most successful numbers to come out of a Weber and Fields Music Hall presentation.

The song subsequently became an Al Jolson favorite, sung by him at his Winter Garden concerts and on the soundtrack of the motion-picture musical *Jolson Sings Again* (Columbia, 1949); his Decca recording in 1946 sold over a million disks. The song was also interpolated in the motion-picture musical *Broadway to Hollywood,* starring Alice Brady and Jimmy Durante (MGM, 1933), and in the motion-picture musical *The Daughter of Rosie O'Grady,* starring June Haver and Gordon MacRae (Warner, 1950).

MacDonald, Ballard, lyricist, born Portland, Oregon, 1882; died Forest Hills, New York, 1935.

See: Carroll, Harry.

See also: Bend Down, Sister; Breeze; Bring Back Those Minstrel Days; The Little House on the Hill; I Love to Go Swimmin' with Wimmen; Indiana; Parade of the Wooden Soldiers; Rose of Washington Square; Somebody Loves Me; Three Wonderful Letters from Home.

MacDonough, Glen, lyricist, born Brooklyn, New York, 1870; died Stamford, Connecticut, 1924.

See: Herbert, Victor.

Mack, Cecil, lyricist, born Richard C. McPherson, Norfolk, Virginia, 1883; died New York City, 1944.

See: Down Among the Sugar Cane; If He Comes In, I'm Going Out; In the Shadow of the Pyramids; Shine; Teasing.

Mack the Knife (or, Moritat), new English lyrics by Marc Blitzstein, music by Kurt Weill (1956). Originally this song was named "Moritat," and had lyrics by Bertolt Brecht. As such it was introduced by Kurt Gerron in *The Three-Penny Opera* (*Die Dreigroschenoper*), at the Theater am Schiffbauerdamm in Berlin on August 31, 1928. Gerron had insisted upon a song early in the opera to set the stage for his entrance as the character Macheath. "Brecht made no comment," Lotte Lenya later recalled, "but the next morning came in with the verses for the 'Moritat' of Mack the Knife, and gave them to Kurt to set to music. . . . This . . . tune, often called the most famous . . . written in Europe during the past half century was modeled after the moritats ('mord' meaning murder, 'tat' meaning dead) sung by singers at street fairs, detailing the hideous crimes of notorious archfiends. Kurt not only produced the tune overnight, he knew the name of the hand-organ manufacturer . . . who could supply the organ on which to grind out the tune for the prologue."

Marc Blitzstein's new English words for this melody were written for a revival of Weill's *Three-Penny Opera*, with a modernized text, at the Theater de Lys, off Broadway, on March 10, 1954. It was in this production (which ran over six years before going on tour throughout the United States in two national companies) that the song, with Blitzstein's words, became one of the leading hits of the 1950s, introduced by Scott Merrill. In 1955 the song was recorded more than twenty different times and appeared in first place on the Hit Parade. In 1956 Dick Hyman's recording for MGM, entitled "Theme from the *Three-Penny Opera*," was a best seller; so was Louis Armstrong's recording for Columbia in 1957. In 1959 Bobby Darin's recording for Atco sold over two million disks and was largely responsible for first establishing the success of this young singer. Darin's recording received a "Grammy" from the National Academy of Recording Arts and Sciences in 1959 as the best popular disk of the year; Ella Fitzgerald's recording for Verve received a "Grammy" in 1960 as the year's best solo vocal female recording.

Madame Sherry, operetta with book by Otto Hauerbach (Harbach), adapted from George Edwardes' adaptation of a French vaudeville. Lyrics by Harbach. Music by Karl Hoschna. Starring Lina Abarbanell and Ralph Herz (1910).

See: The Birth of Passion; Every Little Movement Has a Meaning of Its Own.

Madden, Edward, lyricist, born New York City, 1878; died Hollywood, California, 1952.

See: Edwards, Gus; Morse, Theodore; Wenrich, Percy.

See also: The Chanticleer Rag.

Mademoiselle (Mlle.) Fifi, comic opera with book and lyrics by Henry Blossom. Music by Victor Herbert. Starring Fritzi Scheff and William Pruette (1905).

See: If I Were on the Stage; I Want What I Want When I Want It; Kiss Me Again; The Mascot of the Troop.

Motion-picture adaptation was named *Kiss Me Again* after the operetta's leading waltz. It starred Walter Pidgeon, June Collyer and Bernice Clare. The basic score was used (First National, 1931).

Mademoiselle from Armentières, author of words and music not known (1918). A song favorite of American doughboys during World War I. Alfred J. Walden, who died in 1947 and who wrote songs under the name of Harry Wincott, claimed it, but it has never been substantiated. The song has been popularized in numerous parodies.

The heroine of the song is believed to have been Marie Lecocq, a barmaid in a small French café; she died in 1945. An Associated Press dispatch from Lille, France, in 1964, reported: "A group of British Tommies of 1914 have found the grave of the woman they believe was the original 'Mademoiselle from Armentieres.' They plan to raise a monument in her honor. Coming on a pilgrimage in the fiftieth anniversary year of the bloody World War I battles along the French-Belgian border, the delegation located the grave in the Armentières cemetery."

Maggie Murphy's Home, words by Edward Harrigan, music by David Braham (1890). One of the most popular waltzes to come out of the Harrigan and Hart extravaganzas. It was introduced by Emma Pollack in *Reilly and the 400* (1890)—with such success that from then on the number became her theme song. It was further popularized in vaudeville by Ada Lewis. It is still remembered nostalgically, said Sigmund Spaeth, "as an exposition of simple New York life (the original home was in Brooklyn), and musically it was one of Braham's most effective creations."

The Magic Melody, words by Guy Bolton, music by Jerome Kern (1915). Introduced by Adele Rowland and chorus in the first Princess Theater Show, *Nobody Home* (1915). The noted musicologist Carl Engel had this to say in 1915: "Unless I am very much mistaken, 'The Magic Melody' by Mr. Jerome Kern was the opening chorus of an epoch. . . . A young man gifted with musical talent and unusual courage has dared to introduce into his tune a modulation which was nothing extraordinary in itself, but which marked a change, a new regime in American popular music. . . . The public not only liked it, but went mad over it. And well they might, for it was a relief, a liberation."

The Magic Moment, words by Howard Dietz, music by Arthur Schwartz (1961). Introduced by Barbara Cook in the musical play *Gay Life* (1961).

Magic Moments, words by Hal David, music by Burt F. Bacharach (1957). Popularized by Perry Como in an RCA Victor recording.

Magidson, Herb, lyricist, born Braddock, Pennsylvania, 1906.
See: Conrad, Con.
See also: I'll Dance at Your Wedding; I'm Stepping Out with a Memory Tonight; Music, Maestro, Please; Say a Prayer for the Boys Over There; Something I Dreamed Last Night; Twinkle, Twinkle, Little Star.

Ma, He's Making Eyes at Me, words by Sidney Clare, music by Con Conrad (1921). Comedy number written for Eddie Cantor, who introduced it in the musical *The Midnight Rounders* (1921). The song provided the title for and was featured in a motion-picture musical starring Tom Brown and Constance Moore (Universal, 1940). Judy Canova sang it in the motion picture *Singin' in the Corn* (Columbia, 1946). The song was successfully revived in 1963 by the Ray Coniff Singers in a Columbia recording.

Mah Lindy Lou, words and music by Lily Strickland (1920). Essentially an art song, which entered the popular repertory through repeated performances by ballad singers in vaudeville in the 1920s.

Maiden with the Dreamy Eyes, words by James Weldon Johnson, music by Bob Cole (1901). One of Anna Held's most successful numbers. She introduced it in the musical *The Little Duchess* (1901).

Maine Stein Song. *See:* Stein Song.

Mairzy Doats, words and music by Milton Drake, Al Hoffman and Jerry Livingston (1943). Nonsense song with gibberish lyrics introduced by Al Trace and his orchestra and popularized by the Merry Macs in a best-selling recording for Decca. For several weeks running, the song sold thirty thousand copies of sheet music a day. Grace Moore included it in her vaudeville act in the 1940s.

The idea came to Milton Drake from his four-year-old daughter Nelia, who one day came home from kindergarten, saying: "Cowzy tweet and sowzy tweet and liddle sharsky doisters." Milton Drake told an interviewer: "Kids slur their words. They talk from sound, not spelling. That's how we got 'Mairzy Doats.'"

The song was interpolated in the non-musical motion picture *A Man Called Peter,* starring Richard Todd and Jean Peters (20th Century-Fox, 1955).

Make a Miracle, words and music by Frank Loesser (1948). Introduced by Allyn McLerie in the musical *Where's Charley?* (1948). In the motion-picture adaptation of the musical (Warner, 1952), it was sung by Ray Bolger and Allyn McLerie.

Make Believe (Hammerstein–Kern). *See:* Only Make Believe.

Make Believe, words by Benny Davis, music by Jack Shilkret (1921).

Make Believe Island, words and music by Nick Kenny, Charles Kenny, Will Grosz and Sam Coslow (1940).

Popularized by Mitchell Ayres and his orchestra in a Bluebird recording.

Make Her Mine, words by Sammy Gallop, music by Chester Conn (1954). Popularized by Nat King Cole in a Capitol recording.

Make It Another Old-Fashioned, Please, words and music by Cole Porter (1940). Introduced by Ethel Merman in the musical *Panama Hattie* (1940).

Make Love to Me, words by Bill Norvas and Allan Copeland, music by Leon Rappolo, Paul Mares, Benny Pollack, George Brunes, Mel Stitzel and Walter Melrose, melody based on *Tin Roof Blues*, a jazz instrumental (1953). The song was popularized in 1954 by Jo Stafford in a Columbia recording that sold a million disks.

Make Someone Happy, words by Betty Comden and Adolph Green, music by Jule Styne (1960). Introduced by John Reardon and Nancy Dussault in the musical *Do Re Mi* (1960).

Make the Man Love Me, words by Dorothy Fields, music by Arthur Schwartz (1950). Introduced by Marcia van Dyke and Johnny Johnston in the musical *A Tree Grows in Brooklyn* (1951).

Make Yourself Comfortable, words and music by Bob Merrill (1954). Popularized by Sarah Vaughan in a best-selling Mercury recording.

Making of a Girl, words by Harold Atteridge, music by George Gershwin (1916). George Gershwin's first song heard in a Broadway show. It was interpolated in the Sigmund Romberg revue *The Passing Show of 1916*, where it was introduced by John Boyle as a preface to a parade of beautiful girls.

Makin' Whoopee, words by Gus Kahn, music by Walter Donaldson (1928). Introduced by Eddie Cantor in the musical *Whoopee* (1928). He also sang it in the motion-picture adaptation of the musical (Paramount, 1930) and on the soundtrack of the motion-picture musical *The Eddie Cantor Story* (Warner, 1954). The song was interpolated in Gus Kahn's screen biography *I'll See You in My Dreams* (Paramount, 1951), sung by Danny Thomas and Doris Day.

Both the Oxford Dictionary in England and John Moore's *English Words* credit this song title for having coined the now popular phrase "making whoopee." Actually it had been coined a few years earlier by Walter Winchell in his column in the *Daily Mirror*.

Mama Don't Want No Peas and Rice and Cocoanut Oil, popular Bahamian song, melody attributed to L. Charles, pen name for Charlie Lofthouse, a hotel keeper in Nassau, English lyrics by L. Wolfe Gilbert (1931). The song with English lyrics was interpolated in the non-musical motion picture *It Happens Every Spring*, starring Ray Milland and Jean Peters (20th Century-Fox, 1949).

Mama from the Train (or, A Kiss, a Kiss), words and music by Irving Gordon (1956). Popularized by Patti Page in a Mercury recording.

Mama Guitar, words by Budd Schulberg and Tom Glazer, music by Tom Glazer (1957). Introduced by Andy Griffith in the non-musical motion picture *A Face in the Crowd* (Warner, 1957).

Mama Inez, words by L. Wolfe Gilbert, music by Eliseo Grenet (1931). One of the earliest rhumbas in Tin Pan Alley, and one of the first to become a standard. It was popularized by Xavier Cugat.

Mama, Teach Me to Dance, words and music by Al Hoffman and Dick Manning (1956). Popularized by Eydie Gorme in an ABC Paramount recording.

Mambo Italiano, words and music by Bob Merrill (1954). Popularized by Rosemary Clooney in a Columbia recording that sold over a million disks.

Mamie, Come Kiss Your Honey, words and music by May Irwin (1893). A coon shout, introduced by May Irwin in the musical *A Country Sport* (1893).

Mammy. *See:* My Mammy.

Mammy Lou, words by Andrew B. Sterling and Edward P. Moran, music by Harry von Tilzer (1922). Popularized by ballad singers in vaudeville in the early 1920s.

Mammy's Chocolate Soldier, words by Sidney Mitchell, music by Archie Gottler (1918). One of the few successful World War I songs about the Negro doughboy.

Mammy's Little Coal Black Rose, words by Raymond Egan, music by Richard A. Whiting (1916). One of Whiting's earliest song hits.

Mam'selle, words by Mack Gordon, music by Edmund Goulding (1947). Introduced in a French café scene in the non-musical motion picture *The Razor's Edge,* starring Tyrone Power (20th Century-Fox, 1946). It was popularized by Art Lund in a best-selling MGM recording in 1947.

Mañana Is Soon Enough for Me, words by Peggy Lee, music by Dave Barbour (1948). Popularized by Peggy Lee in a Capitol recording that sold a million disks.

A Man Chases a Girl (Until She Catches Him), words and music by Irving Berlin (1954). Introduced by Donald O'Connor in the motion-picture musical *There's No Business Like Show Business* (20th Century-Fox, 1954).

Mancini, Henry, composer, born Cleveland, Ohio, 1924.
See (Lyrics by Johnny Mercer): Charade; Days of Wine and Roses; It Had Better Be Tonight; Moment to Moment; Moon River; Sweetheart Tree.
See also: Dear Heart.

Mandolins in the Moonlight, words and music by George Weiss and Aaron Schroeder (1958). Popularized by Perry Como in an RCA Victor recording.

Mandy, words and music by Irving Berlin (1918). Berlin wrote it for his all-soldier show *Yip, Yip, Yaphank* (1918). It was introduced there by Private Murphy, Private Dan Healy (as Mandy) and a chorus in a minstrel-show routine opening the first act. The song, however, became famous in the *Ziegfeld Follies of 1919,* where once again it was used for a minstrel-show routine—this time for the first-act finale, sung by

Van and Schenck with the help of Marilyn Miller (dressed up as the minstrel George Primrose) and Ray Dooley (costumed as Mandy).

The song was revived for Eddie Cantor in an elaborate production number in the motion-picture musical *Kid Millions* (United Artists, 1934). The song was also interpolated for an old-time minstrel show in the motion-picture musical *White Christmas* (Paramount, 1954).

Mandy Lee, words and music by Thurland Chattaway (1899). A favorite of barber-shop quartets. "Its natural harmonies," said Sigmund Spaeth, "are a constant urge to improvisation as well as to a variety of arrangements."

The Man from Laramie, words by Ned Washington, music by Lester Lee (1955). Introduced in the non-musical motion picture of the same name starring James Stewart (Columbia, 1955). It was popularized in a Capitol recording by the Voices of Walter Schumann.

The Man from the South, words and music by Rube Bloom and Harry Woods (1930).

Mangos, words by Sid Wayne, music by Dee Libbey (1957). Introduced by Micki Marlo in the *Ziegfeld Follies of 1957,* interpolated in the production after it had opened. The song was popularized by Rosemary Clooney in a Columbia recording.

Manhattan, words by Lorenz Hart, music by Richard Rodgers (1925). The first hit song by the songwriting team of Rodgers and Hart. It was introduced by June Cochrane and Sterling Holloway in the revue *The Garrick Gaieties* (1925). The song was subsequently interpolated in several motion pictures. These included the screen biography of Rodgers and Hart, *Words and Music* (MGM, 1948), sung by Mickey Rooney; *All About Eve,* starring Bette Davis (20th Century-Fox, 1950); the screen biography of Jane Froman, *With a Song in My Heart* (20th Century-Fox, 1952); *Don't Bother to Knock,* starring Marilyn Monroe (20th Century-Fox, 1953); *The Eddie Duchin Story* (Columbia,

1956), played on the soundtrack by Carmen Cavallero; and the screen biography of James J. Walker, *Beau James* (Paramount, 1957), where it was prominently featured on the soundtrack in the background music as a recurrent theme.

Manhattan Serenade, words by Harold Adamson, music by Louis Alter (1942). It originated as an instrumental, and in this version was first popularized by Paul Whiteman and his orchestra. It became a favorite with the orchestras of both Dorsey brothers, and was adopted as the radio theme of the program "Easy Aces."

The Man I Love, words by Ira Gershwin, music by George Gershwin (1924). The song was originally written for Adele Astaire for the opening scene of the musical *Lady, Be Good!* (1924). When the show tried out, out of town, the song was dropped because it slowed up the action. The Gershwins then tried unsuccessfully to place it first in the original version of *Strike Up the Band!* (1927) and for Marilyn Miller in *Rosalie* (1928). By the time the second version of *Strike Up the Band!* was produced in New York in 1930, the song had become too famous to be used in that show. "The Man I Love," therefore, was never heard on the Broadway stage.

The première of the song took place in Derby, Connecticut, in 1925, at a concert by Eva Gauthier, with George Gershwin as her accompanist. Meanwhile, the song was published by Harms as an independent number. Lady Louis Mountbatten took an autographed copy of the sheet music to London, where she arranged for the Berkeley Square Orchestra to introduce it. The number proved so successful that jazz orchestras throughout London began performing it. From London the song went on to conquer Paris, and only then did it return to the United States to become a hit. One of its earliest successful interpreters was Helen Morgan.

George Gershwin himself once explained that the song took so long to get appreciated in the United States because the chromaticism in the chorus made the melody difficult to be assimilated, and could not readily be sung or hummed without a piano accompaniment.

The song was interpolated in several motion pictures, including the George Gershwin screen biography *Rhapsody in Blue* (Warner, 1945); *The Man I Love* (Warner, 1946), where it served as a recurrent theme on the soundtrack and was sung by Ida Lupino; and the motion-picture musical *The Helen Morgan Story* (Warner, 1957), sung on the soundtrack by Gogi Grant (for Ann Blyth).

The Man I Love, a motion-picture musical starring Ida Lupino and Robert Alda (Warner, 1946). The score was made up mainly of standards.

See: Bill, Body and Soul; Can't We Be Friends?; The Man I Love; Why Was I Born?

Man of La Mancha (I, Don Quixote), words by Joe Darion, music by Mitch Leigh (1965). Title song of an off-Broadway musical (1965), introduced by Richard Kiley.

Man of La Mancha, a musical play with book by Dale Wasserman based on Cervantes' *Don Quixote.* Lyrics by Joe Darion. Music by Mitch Leigh. Starring Richard Kiley as Don Quixote (1965). Original cast recording (Kapp).

See: To Each His Dulcinea; The Impossible Dream; Man of La Mancha.

The Man on the Flying Trapeze, author of words and music not known (1868). First popularized in the 1870s in vaudeville by Johnny Allen.

It was revived in the Academy Award-winning motion picture *It Happened One Night,* starring Clark Gable and Claudette Colbert (Columbia, 1934). In 1939 it was presented by Walter O'Keefe on the Rudy Vallée radio program so successfully that it reached the Hit Parade—one of the rare instances in which a song almost a century old received such recognition. The song was then interpolated for Rudy Vallée in the motion-picture musical

Too Many Blondes (Universal, 1941).

In 1934 William Saroyan, the Pulitzer Prize playwright, borrowed the second line of the chorus for the title of his first published novel, *The Daring Young Man on the Flying Trapeze.*

The Mansion of Aching Hearts, words by Arthur J. Lamb, music by Harry von Tilzer (1902). The first successful publication of the then newly formed firm of Harry von Tilzer. This sentimental ballad was a sequel to von Tilzer's highly successful ballad "A Bird in a Gilded Cage," pointing up once again the moral that gold and diamonds cannot buy a happy heart. When Irving Berlin was a boy he used to sing this ballad in the streets and cafés of the Bowery district.

The Man That Got Away, words by Ira Gershwin, music by Harold Arlen (1954). Introduced by Judy Garland in the motion-picture musical *A Star Is Born* (Warner, 1953). Since then it has become one of the favorite numbers in her repertory. Of her rendition, *Time* magazine said: "Her big dark voice sobs, sighs, sulks and socks [it] out like a cross between Tara's harp and the late Bessie Smith."

When Arlen first played the refrain for Ira Gershwin, the latter was impressed by its rhythmic momentum. He forthwith suggested the title of "The Man That Got Away," to which Arlen replied simply: "I like." Both were highly pleased with the final product. The song is of unusual structure in that it extends for sixty-two measures. Though sometimes described as a "blues," this number is more a blues of the Tin Pan Alley variety than of New Orleans or Chicago.

The Man Who Found the Lost Chord, words and music by Jimmy Durante. A Jimmy Durante specialty which he popularized in the 1920s in vaudeville and night clubs. He sang it in the motion-picture musical *This Time for Keeps,* starring Esther Williams (MGM, 1947).

The Man with the Ladder and the Hose, words and music by T. Mayo Geary (1904). One of the earliest song hits inspired by a movie, in this instance a "flicker" glorifying firefighters.

Many a New Day, words by Oscar Hammerstein II, music by Richard Rodgers (1943). Introduced by Joan Roberts in the musical play *Oklahoma!* (1943), after which it was danced to by Joan McCracken, Kate Friedlich and Katharine Sergava. In the motion-picture adaptation of the musical (Magna Theatre, 1955), it was sung by Shirley Jones and a girls' chorus.

Many Tears Ago, words and music by Winfield Scott (1961). Popularized by Connie Francis in an MGM recording.

Marcheta, words and music by Victor Schertzinger (1913). A hit song of the early 1910s. It was revived a generation later in the background music for the non-musical motion picture *They Were Expendable,* starring Robert Montgomery and John Wayne (MGM, 1945).

Marching Through Georgia, words and music by Henry Clay Work (1865). Famous Civil War ballad, inspired by Sherman's historic march to the sea. Southerners were hostile to the song, referring to it as a "hymn of hate," since it recalled one of the greatest disasters of their war with the North. During the Democratic National Convention in 1916 the Southern bloc almost defected from the ranks because a misinformed bandleader had just played "Marching Through Georgia," but was finally mollified when convinced that no malice had been intended by this performance. General Sherman had also objected to the song, maintaining it deflected attention and interest from his other successful military campaigns. When General Sherman heard it played at a G.A.R. convention in Boston in 1890 he remarked wryly: "If I had thought when I made that march that it would have inspired anyone to compose a piece, I would have marched around the state."

Despite all such hostility and opposition, "Marching Through Georgia" has become one of the most famous ballads of the Civil War. It was heard at every encampment or parade of the Grand Army of the Republic. British regiments leaving England for France during World War I marched to its strains, and so did American troops when they marched into Tunis during World War II.

March of the Musketeers (or, "All For One, One For All"), words by Brian Hooker, music by Rudolf Friml (1928). Introduced by Douglas R. Dumbrille, Detmar Popper and Joseph Macauley in the operetta *The Three Musketeers* (1928).

The March of Time, words by Ted Koehler, music by Harold Arlen (1930). Introduced in the revue *The Earl Carroll Vanities* (1930).

Five years after the song was introduced, *Time* magazine purchased the rights for its use in a projected radio program series for a payment of $125 a week, with an additional $100 a week if the program was filmed. The payment was made for two years. But when *The March of Time* was finally screened, a new theme was employed, one in which Arlen's melody was revised only slightly; but because of these changes, payment was discontinued. The intimate relationship between the old Arlen tune and the new one, however, was never contested in the courts.

Margie, words by Benny Davis, music by Con Conrad and J. Russel Robinson (1920). Inspired by Marjorie Cantor—the then five-year-old daughter of Eddie Cantor. Cantor first sang it at a Sunday evening concert at the Winter Garden in New York, after which he interpolated it in the revue *The Midnight Rounders* (1921). He also sang it on the soundtrack of the motion-picture musical *The Eddie Cantor Story* (Warner, 1954).

"Margie" was one of the most significant and successful recordings by the jazz trombonist James "Trummy" Osborne, a disk which he made for Decca with Jimmie Lunceford in 1938.

The song provided the title for, and was played under the titles of, and was sung in the opening scene of, a motion picture starring Jeanne Crain (20th Century-Fox, 1946). It was interpolated in the non-musical motion picture *Stella Dallas,* starring Barbara Stanwyck (Samuel Goldwyn, 1934).

Betty Hutton sang it in the motion-picture musical biography of Texas Guinan, *Incendiary Blonde* (Paramount, 1945).

Margie, a motion-picture musical starring Jeanne Crain (20th Century-Fox, 1946). The score was made up of standards.

See: April Showers; Collegiate; Margie; My Time Is Your Time; Three O'Clock in the Morning; Wonderful One.

Marguerite, words and music by C. A. White (1883). Introduced by Denman Thompson in the non-musical play *The Old Homestead.* This is the only song by which its composer is remembered; and it is one of the earliest examples of echo effects in four-part harmony.

Maria, words by Stephen Sondheim, music by Leonard Bernstein (1957). Introduced by Larry Kert in the musical play *West Side Story* (1957); it was also sung in the motion-picture adaptation of the musical (Mirisch, 1961). The song was popularized by Johnny Mathis in a Columbia recording.

Maria, words by Oscar Hammerstein II, music by Richard Rodgers (1959). Introduced by Patricia Neway, Muriel O'Malley, Elizabeth Howell and Karen Shepard in the musical play *The Sound of Music* (1959). It was sung by a female quintet in the motion-picture adaptation of the musical (20th Century-Fox, 1965).

Maria Elena, a Mexican song, music by Lorenzo Barcelata, English lyrics by S. K. Russell (1933). The song was revived in 1941 by Lawrence Welk and his orchestra and was popularized by Jimmy Dorsey and his orchestra (with vocal by Helen O'Connell and Bob Eberle), whose Decca recording sold over a million disks. The lady in the title was the wife of the Mexican President to whom the song was originally dedicated.

Marianne, words and music by Terry Gilkyson, Frank Miller and Richard Dehr, adapted from a Bahamian folk melody (1955). It was popularized in 1957 by Terry Gilkyson and the Easy Riders in a Columbia recording and by the Hilltoppers in a Dot recording. The song was interpolated in the motion-picture spectacle *Windjammer* (National Theatre, 1958).

Marie, words and music by Irving Berlin (1928). Introduced in the motion picture *My Awakening* (United Artists, 1928), the first Berlin song to appear in a movie. "Marie" was first popularized in 1928 by Rudy Vallée over the radio and in a RCA Victor recording. In 1937 the song was revived by Tommy Dorsey and his orchestra in an RCA Victor recording that sold over a million disks and became his first major recording success; this recording was also noteworthy for Bunny Berigan's rendition of the chorus, which Leonard Feather says was "widely admired and imitated." "Marie" was interpolated in the motion-picture musical *The Fabulous Dorseys* (United Artists, 1947), where it was played by Tommy Dorsey and his orchestra.

Marie from Sunny Italy, words by Irving Berlin, music by Nick Michaelson (1907). Irving Berlin's first published song—though only the lyrics were his. Berlin's total income from this publication was thirty cents in royalties.

At the time he wrote these lyrics, Berlin was employed as a singing waiter at the Pelham Café, a saloon owned and operated by "Nigger Mike" Salter. When the employes of a competing café, Callahan's, wrote and had published a song ("My Mariuccia Take a Steamboat"), "Nigger Mike" insisted that his own men follow suit. The saloon pianist, Nick Michaelson, was recruited to do the music. Since Berlin had proved glib at doing parodies, he was asked to write the lyrics. The house of Joseph W. Stern & Co. bought the song and printed it. It was for this publication that Irving Berlin, born Israel Baline, used the name of Irving Berlin for the first time.

The Marines' Hymn (or, From the Halls of Montezuma), author of words not known, melody adapted from an air from Jacques Offenbach's opéra-bouffe *Geneviève de Brabant* (1919). Though the identity of the lyricist is unknown, he is believed to have been a Marine officer, a member of a battalion of forty men, the first to come to Mexico City in 1847 during the Mexican War. This explains the appearance of the phrase "from the halls of Montezuma." The phrase "to the shores of Tripoli" refers to the participation of the Marine Corps in the war against the Barbary pirates in 1805. The hymn became especially popular during World War II. It was sung by a chorus on the soundtrack under the titles in the non-musical motion picture *Halls of Montezuma,* starring Richard Widmark (20th Century-Fox, 1951).

The Marriage-Go-Round, words and music by Alan Bergman, Marilyn Keith and Lew Spence (1961). Title song of a non-musical motion picture starring James Mason and Susan Hayward (20th Century-Fox, 1961), where it was sung on the soundtrack under the titles by Tony Bennett.

Married I Can Always Get, words and music by Gordon Jenkins (1956). Introduced and popularized by Gordon Jenkins and his orchestra and chorus.

A Married Man, words and music by Raymond Jessel and Marian Grudeff (1965). Introduced by Peter Sallis in the musical *Baker Street* (1965). Before the show opened on Broadway the number was popularized by Richard Burton (who spoke the lyric rather than sang it) in a MGM recording.

Marshmallow Moon, words and music by Jay Livingston and Ray Evans (1951). Introduced by Dinah Shore in the motion picture *Aaron Slick from Punkin Crick* (Paramount,

1952). Dinah Shore's recording for RCA Victor was a best seller.

Marta, words by L. Wolfe Gilbert, music by Moises Simon (1931). Radio theme song of Arthur Tracy, the "Street Singer."

Martin, Hugh, composer and lyricist, born Birmingham, Alabama, 1914.
See: Blane, Ralph.
See also: Home, Sweet Heaven; If I Gave You; Where Is the Man I Married?

Mary, words by Otto Harbach, music by Louis A. Hirsch (1920). Title song of a musical (1920), introduced by Janet Velie and chorus.

Mary, a musical comedy with book and lyrics by Otto Harbach and Frank Mandel. Music by Louis A. Hirsch. Starring Jack McGowan and Janet Velie (1920).
See: The Love Nest; Mary.

Mary Blane, words by F. C. German, music arranged by J. H. Howard (1847). A Negro song popularized in minstrel shows before the Civil War, a favorite in the repertory of such troupes as the Ethiopian Serenaders, the Christy Minstrels and the Campbell Minstrels.

Maryland, My Maryland, words by James Ryder Randall, the melody being the German folk song "O Tannenbaum" (1861). A song popular with the Confederacy during the Civil War.

The author of the lyrics, a native of Maryland, was a teacher at Poydras College in Louisiana. One day in 1861 he read in the newspapers a report on how a riot had broken out in the streets of Baltimore when passing Northern troops were fired at by pro-Southern hotheads. "My Southern blood was stirred to fever heat," he later wrote. "My nerves were all unstrung. I could not dismiss what I had read from my mind. About midnight, I arose, lit a candle, and went to my desk. Some powerful spirit seemed to possess me, and almost involuntarily I proceeded to write the verses of 'My Maryland.' I remember that the ideas appeared to take shape first as music in the brain, some wild air. The whole poem was dashed off rapidly when once begun. It was not composed in cold blood, but under what may be called a conflagration of the senses. I was stirred to a desire for some way of linking my name to that of my native state."

The poem was written on April 26, 1861, and on May 1 it was printed in *Delta,* a Louisiana newspaper. It was published for the first time in Maryland in *The South,* a pro-Southern journal, on May 31. The poem was subsequently distributed in broadsides.

The Cary household was the center of pro-Confederate activities in Baltimore. At a meeting there of an amateur singing group, of which Jennie Cary was director, she sought to find some new song with which to rally the people of Baltimore to the Confederate cause. Her sister showed her Randall's poem, which impressed Jennie Cary no end. Searching for an appropriate tune she came upon "O Tannenbaum" in the Yale College song book *Lauriger Horatius*—"O Tannenbaum" being a German folk song written in 1824 and popular as a Christmas carol. She adapted Randall's words to this melody, then directed her glee club in a performance that aroused considerable enthusiasm.

A local music-publishing house released words and music in 1861. In the South the song appeared for the first time in 1862, in New Orleans. The song spread through the South like wildfire, rallying men to the Southern cause. The Cary sisters were the first ones to sing it for the Confederate troops—for General Beauregard's men in Virginia during the summer of 1861. "This I believe was the birth of the song in the Confederate army," Hetty Cary later recalled. "The refrain was speedily caught up and tossed back to us from hundreds of rebel throats. . . . There surged forth from the throng a wild shout, 'We will break her chains! Maryland will be free!'"

Originally "Maryland, My Maryland" was second in popularity only to "Dixie" in the Southland. Then, after Maryland joined the Union cause, and after General Lee's first invasion of Maryland had proved a failure, the song quickly began to lose its appeal in that state and was rarely sung. An attempt in the North to convert it into a song for the Union proved a failure.

In 1939 the State of Maryland adopted it as its official song. It has also become the anthem for the annual Preakness race at Pimlico Race Track in Maryland.

Mary Poppins, a Walt Disney screen production starring Julie Andrews (in her Academy Award-winning motion-picture debut) and Dick Van Dyke (Buena Vista, 1964). Songs by Richard M. and Robert B. Sherman. Soundtrack recording (Vista). *See:* Chim Chim Cheree; Spoonful of Sugar; Stay Awake.

Mary's a Grand Old Name, words and music by George M. Cohan (1905). Introduced by Donald Brian in the musical *Forty-Five Minutes from Broadway* (1906). James Cagney sang it in the motion-picture biography of George M. Cohan, *Yankee Doodle Dandy* (1942). It served as background music for a buck-and-wing dance by James Cagney and Bob Hope in the motion-picture musical *The Seven Little Foys* (Paramount, 1955).

The Mascot of the Troop, words by Henry Blossom, music by Victor Herbert (1905). A march introduced by Fritzi Scheff and a male chorus in the operetta *Mlle. Modiste* (1905).

Masquerade, words by Paul Francis Webster, music by John Jacob Loeb (1932). A sixty-four-measure waltz. Ferde Grofé orchestrated it for symphony orchestra, a version introduced at the Lewisohn Stadium concerts in New York, Paul Whiteman conducting.

Massa's in de Cold Ground, words and music by Stephen Foster (1852). One of Foster's most successful Negro ballads, selling almost 75,000 copies by 1854.

Matchmaker, Matchmaker, words by Sheldon Harnick, music by Jerry Bock (1964). Introduced by Joanna Merlin, Julia Migens and Tanya

Everett in the musical play *Fiddler on the Roof* (1964).

Matilda, Matilda, words and music by Harry Thomas (1953). A calypso popularized by Harry Belafonte in a best-selling RCA Victor recording.

Maverick, words by Paul Francis Webster, music by David Butolph (1958). Theme song of the TV Western dramatic series.

Maybe, words by Ira Gershwin, music by George Gershwin (1926). Introduced by Gertrude Lawrence and Oscar Shaw in the musical *Oh, Kay!* (1926).

Maybe It's Because, words by Harry Ruby, music by Johnnie Scott (1949). Popularized by Andy Russell. It was interpolated in the revue *Along Fifth Avenue* (1949). A successful recording was made by Dick Haymes for Decca.

Maybe You'll Be There, words by Sammy Gallop, music by Rube Bloom (1947). Popularized by Gordon Jenkins and his orchestra with the Weavers in a Decca recording.

May I Have the Next Romance with You?, words by Mack Gordon, music by Harry Revel (1936). Introduced in the English-produced motion-picture musical *Head Over Heels in Love* (Gaumont British, 1936), sung by Jessie Matthews and Louis Borrell.

May I Sing to You?, words by Charles Tobias, music by Harry Akst and Eddie Fisher (1954). Introduced and popularized by Eddie Fisher in an RCA Victor recording. It then became the theme song of his television program.

May the Good Lord Bless and Keep You (Till We Meet Again), words and music by Meredith Willson (1950). Introduced in 1950 as the closing number of "The Big Show," the Sunday evening NBC radio production starring Tallulah Bankhead. All the leading performers joined in singing it, each one presenting a line at a time. This procedure made such an impression that henceforth the song was featured the same way at the conclusion of each broadcast.

The song was further popularized by Frankie Laine in a Mercury recording. It went on to sell half a million copies of sheet music within the first four months of its publication. During the Korean War it was the song most often requested by G.I.'s from visiting performers.

Willson's inspiration came from a greeting his mother habitually gave every Sunday to the children in her Sunday school class in Mason City, Iowa.

Maytime, operetta with book and lyrics by Rida Johnson Young and Cyrus Wood. Music by Sigmund Romberg. Starring Peggy Wood and Charles Purcell (1917).

The motion-picture adaptation starred Nelson Eddy and Jeanette MacDonald (MGM, 1937). Three songs from the Broadway score were used, with additional new numbers by Robert Wright, George "Chet" Forrest and Herbert Stothart.

See: The Road to Paradise; Will You Remember?

May You Always, words and music by Larry Markes and Dick Charles (1958). Popularized in 1959 by the McGuire Sisters in a Coral recording.

McCarthy, Joseph, lyricist, born Summerville, Massachusetts, 1885; died New York City, 1943.

See: Fisher, Fred; Tierney, Harry.

See also: I'm Always Chasing Rainbows; Rambling Rose; Ten Pins in the Sky; What Do You Want to Make Those Eyes At Me For?; You Made Me Love You.

McHugh, Jimmy, composer, born Boston, Massachusetts, 1895.

See (Lyrics by Harold Adamson): As the Girls Go; Comin' in on a Wing and a Prayer; How Blue the Night; A Hubba Hubba Hubba; I Got Lucky in the Rain; I Hit a New High; It's a Most Unusual Day; I Wish We Didn't Have to Say Goodbye; Life Can Be Beautiful; A Lovely Way to Spend an Evening; My Own; There's Something in the Air; Where Are You?; You're a Sweetheart; You Say the Nicest Things, Baby.

See (Lyrics by Dorothy Fields): Blue Again; Cuban Love Song; Diga Diga Doo; Dinner at Eight; Don't Blame Me; Exactly Like You; Go Home and Tell Your Mother; Hooray for Love; I Can't Give You Anything But Love, Baby; I Feel a Song Comin' On; I'm in the Mood for Love; It's the Darndest Thing; Lost in a Fog; Lovely to Look At; On the Sunny Side of the Street; Singin' the Blues; You're an Angel.

See (Lyrics by Ted Koehler): Hey, What Did the Bluebird Say?; I'm Shooting High; Lovely Lady; Picture Me Without You.

See also: Can't Get Out of This Mood; Dream, Dream, Dream; Hinky Dinky Parlay Voo; I Can't Believe That You're in Love with Me; Let's Get Lost; Say a Prayer for the Boys Over There; Sing a Tropical Song; South Amercan Way; When My Sugar Walks Down the Street; With All My Heart.

Me and Juliet, a musical comedy with book and lyrics by Oscar Hammerstein II. Music by Richard Rodgers. Starring Isabel Bigley and Bill Hayes (1953). Original cast recording (RCA Victor).

See: The Big Black Giant; Keep It Gay; No Other Love.

Me and My Shadow, words by Billy Rose, music by Dave Dreyer and Al Jolson (1927). Billy Rose wrote these lyrics for Frank Fay, the vaudevillian, who introduced the song in the revue *Harry Delmar's Revels* (1927), where is was an interpolation. The song was popularized by Al Jolson, and by Ted Lewis and his band. It was subsequently interpolated in the motion picture *Feudin', Fussin' and A-Fightin',* starring Donald O'Connor (Universal, 1948).

Me and My Teddy Bear, words by J. Winters, music by J. Fred Coots (1953). Popularized by Rosemary Clooney in her first successful recording (Columbia).

Coots informed this editor: "The title was suggested to me by Leo Talent, chief executive for Mutual Music Society. He suggested I try writing a song about a Teddy bear, since all children have a strong attachment for such objects. I played around with the idea for a few weeks, and with the help of Talent, finally completed the song. We showed it to

Hecky Karasnow, head man at Columbia Records children's division. He thought it would be suitable for a young singer named Rosemary Clooney, just making her record debut at that time. The record was released and became an immediate hit—Rosemary Clooney's springboard to prominence."

Mean to Me, words by Roy Turk, music by Fred E. Ahlert (1929). A favorite in Ruth Etting's repertory, who helped make it popular. For this reason it was interpolated in her screen biography *Love Me or Leave Me* (MGM, 1955), sung by Doris Day.

Meat and Potatoes, words and music by Irving Berlin (1962). Introduced by Jack Haskell and Stanley Grover in the musical *Mr. President* (1962).

Meet Danny Wilson, a motion-picture musical starring Frank Sinatra and Shelley Winters (Universal, 1952). The score was made up mainly of standards.

See: All of Me; A Good Man Is Hard to Find; How Deep Is the Ocean; I've Got a Crush on You; She's Funny That Way; That Old Black Magic; When You're Smiling; You're a Sweetheart.

The Meeting of the Waters of Hudson and Erie, words and music by Samuel Woodworth (1825). Written and published to commemorate the opening of the Erie Canal on October 26, 1825.

Meet Me in St. Louis, Louis, words by Andrew B. Sterling, music by Kerry Mills (1904). Inspired by the St. Louis World's Fair, officially known as the Louisiana Exposition.

Mills and Sterling were in a bar, where Mills ordered an alcoholic drink then popularly known as a "Louis." As it happened the bartender's name was also Louis. When Mills wanted a refill, he called: "Another Louis, Louis." The repetition of the name amused Sterling no end. Suddenly reminded of the imminence of the St. Louis Fair, he felt that somehow, and in some way, the two Louises could be fitted into a song about the fair. He wrote a set of lyrics which Mills liked well enough to buy for $200 and to set to music.

The song proved one of the major hits of 1904.

The song was revived in the motion-picture musical *Meet Me in St. Louis,* starring Judy Garland (MGM, 1944), sung on the soundtrack under the titles and used as background music for the closing scene. It was sung by Leon Ames in the motion-picture musical *By the Light of the Silvery Moon* (Warner, 1953).

Meet Me in St. Louis, a motion-picture musical starring Judy Garland (MGM, 1944). Songs by Ralph Blane and Hugh Martin. The title song by Sterling and Mills was interpolated.

See: The Boy Next Door; Have Yourself a Merry Little Christmas; Meet Me in St. Louis, Louis; The Trolley Song.

Meet Me Tonight in Dreamland, words by Beth Slater Whitson, music by Leo Friedman (1909). One of the most successful ballads of its time, selling over two million copies of sheet music. Neither composer nor lyricist profited from this success, since their publisher, Will Rossiter, refused to pay royalties and had bought all his songs outright, usually for a pittance. When, in 1910, Will Rossiter's brother formed a publishing venture of his own and stood ready to pay royalties, Whitson and Friedman turned over to him their new ballad, "Let Me Call You Sweetheart," which proved an even greater success than "Meet Me Tonight in Dreamland," and realized a fortune both for the creators of the song and for its young publisher.

"Meet Me Tonight in Dreamland" was revived by Judy Garland in the motion-picture musical *In the Good Old Summertime* (MGM, 1949). It was also interpolated in the motion-picture musical *The Eddie Cantor Story* (Warner, 1954). Pat Boone revived it successfully in 1965 in a Dot recording.

Melancholy Baby. *See:* My Melancholy Baby.

Melancholy Rhapsody, words by Sammy Cahn, music by Ray Heindorf (1950). Introduced by Harry James on the soundtrack of the motion picture *Young Man with a Horn*, starring Kirk Douglas (Warner, 1950).

Melinda, words by Alan Jay Lerner, music by Burton Lane (1965). Waltz introduced by John Cullum in the musical *On a Clear Day You Can See Forever* (1965).

Melodie d'Amour, a French popular song ("Maladie d'Amour"), music by Henri Salvador, English lyrics by Leo Johns (1957). The song, with English lyrics, was popularized in the United States in a best-selling RCA Victor recording by the Ames Brothers.

A Melody from the Sky, words by Sidney D. Mitchell, music by Louis Alter (1936). Introduced by Fuzzy Knight in the motion picture *The Trail of the Lonesome Pine* (Paramount, 1936). In 1936 the song occupied first place in the Hit Parade for several consecutive weeks.

Melody in 4-F, words and music by Sylvia Fine and Max Liebman (1941). A tongue-twisting patter song in gibberish portraying the adventures of a G.I. conscript into the army. It was interpolated for Danny Kaye in the Cole Porter musical *Let's Face It* (1941). Danny Kaye also presented it in his motion-picture debut in *Up in Arms* (RKO, 1944). It became one of his celebrated routines.

Melody of Love, words by Tom Glazer, music based on a melody by H. Engelmann, published in 1903 and familiar to piano students in the early 1900s (1954). The melody was used for an earlier popular song with the same title, successfully recorded by Billy Vaughn and his orchestra for Dot. With new lyrics, the song became an outstanding hit in 1954–1955 through a Decca recording by the Four Aces and an RCA Victor recording by Dinah Shore and Tony Martin.

Memories, words by Gus Kahn, music by Egbert Van Alstyne (1915). One of Gus Kahn's earliest successes. It was interpolated in his screen biography *I'll See You in My Dreams* (Columbia, 1951), sung by Danny Thomas.

Memories Are Made of This, words and music by Terry Gilkyson, Richard Dehr and Frank Miller (1955). Popularized by Dean Martin, whose Capitol recording sold a million disks. It was interpolated in the motion-picture spectacle *Windjammer* (National Theatre, 1958).

Memories of You, words by Andy Razaf, music by Eubie Blake (1930). Introduced and popularized by Ethel Waters in the all-Negro revue *Blackbirds of 1930*. It then became a Benny Goodman specialty, and was played by the Benny Goodman Trio on the soundtrack of the motion-picture musical *The Benny Goodman Story* (Universal, 1956).

Memory Lane, words by Bud De Sylva, music by Larry Spier and Con Conrad (1924). It was revived in the motion picture *In Society*, starring Abbott and Costello (Universal, 1944).

The Memphis Blues, words by George A. Norton, music by W. C. Handy (1913). The first published commercial blues, and W. C. Handy's first publication.

In 1909 Handy, then a resident in Memphis, Tennessee, favored a candidate named Edward H. Crump, running for Mayor on a reform ticket. To help muster the Negro vote for Crump, Handy wrote a campaign song in a musical style familiar to Negroes—the blues, scribbling words and music at a single sitting at Pee Wee's Saloon on Beale Street. He called his piece "Mr. Crump." It grew so popular that it became a significant factor in Crump's election.

In 1912 Handy rewrote his piece as a piano blues, publishing it at his own expense. Now renamed *Memphis Blues*, it became the first commercial blues to get published. Later the same year Theron A. Bennett Company of New York purchased all the rights to *Memphis Blues* for $50. Lyrics by George A. Norton were now added. The song was reissued in New York in 1913, and enjoyed a tremendous success. Thus the "blues" came to Tin Pan Alley.

In 1931 this blues was used for still a new set of lyrics, while the melody was given a fresh adaptation. This was the work of Charles Tobias and Peter De Rose, and was issued by Joe Morris Music Company.

"The Memphis Blues," with Norton's lyrics and Handy's original melody was revived in the motion-picture musical *The Birth of the Blues* (Paramount, 1941).

Mene, Mene, Tekel, words and music by Harold Rome (1938). Introduced by Dorothy Harrison in the second edition of the social-conscious revue *Pins and Needles* (1938). The song is a popular treatment of the story of the handwriting on the wall from the Book of Daniel.

Mercer, Johnny, composer and lyricist, born Savannah, Georgia, 1909.

See: Arlen, Harold; Carmichael, Hoagy; De Paul, Gene; Kern, Jerome; Mancini, Henry; Schertzinger, Victor; Warren, Harry; Whiting, Richard A.

See also: And the Angels Sing; Autumn Leaves; Bernadine; The Big Movie Show in the Sky; The Bilboa Song; Bob White; Day In, Day Out; Dixieland Band; Dream; Eeny, Meeny, Miney Mo; The Facts of Life; Fools Rush In; The Glow Worm; Goody, Goody; Horseshoes Are Lucky; I'm an Old Cow Hand; I'm Building Up to an Awful Let Down; I Thought About You; I Wanna Be Around; Jamboree Song; Laura; Love with a Proper Stranger; On Behalf of the Visiting Firemen; P. S. I Love You; Something's Got to Give; Strip Polka; Sunday, Monday and Always; Talk to Me, Baby; When the World Was Young.

Merrill, Bob, composer and lyricist, born Atlantic City, New Jersey, 1921.

See: Styne, Jule.

See also: Belle, Belle; Candy and Cake; Did You Close Your Eyes When We Kissed?; Honeycomb; How Much Is That Doggie in the Window?; If I Knew You Were Comin' I'd 'Ave Baked a Cake; It's Good to Be Alive; Look at 'Er; Love Makes the World Go Round; Make Yourself Comfortable; Mambo Italiano; My

Truly, Truly Fair; Pittsburgh, Pa.; Promise Me a Rose; Sparrow in the Tree Top; Staying Young; Sunshine Girl; A Sweet Old Fashioned Girl; Take Me Along; Walkin' to Missouri.

The Merry Monihans, a screen musical starring Donald O'Connor and Peggy Ryan (Universal, 1944). The score was made up of standards.

See: I Hate to Lose You; In My Merry Oldsmobile; I'm Always Chasing Rainbows; Isle D'Amour; Rock-a-bye Your Baby with a Dixie Melody; What Do You Want to Make Those Eyes at Me For?; When You Wore a Tulip.

The Message of the Violet, words by Frank Pixley, music by Gustav Luders (1902). Hit song from the operetta *The Prince of Pilsen,* introduced by Albert Paar and Anna Lichter.

Me Too (or, Ho Ho, Ha Ha), words and music by Charles Tobias, Al Sherman and Harry Woods (1926). Tobias' first song hit. He was a vaudevillian at the time, with a trunkful of rejected songs. Then Shapiro, Bernstein bought and published "Me Too." Its success enabled Tobias to give up the vaudeville circuit and concentrate on writing songs. This number was successfully revived a quarter of a century after its first appearance, in a best-selling Capitol recording by Kay Starr.

Mexicali Rose, words by Helen Stone, music by Jack B. Tenny (1923). It provided the title and the principal song for a motion picture starring Gene Autry (Republic, 1939). Gene Autry sang it again in the motion picture *Barbed Wire* (Columbia, 1952); Roy Rogers, in the motion picture *Song of Texas* (Republic, 1943).

Mexican Hayride, a musical comedy with book by Herbert and Dorothy Fields. Songs by Cole Porter. Starring Bobby Clark and June Havoc (1944).

The motion-picture adaptation starred Abbott and Costello (Universal, 1948). The Cole Porter stage score was dispensed with. One new number was contributed by Jack Brooks and Walter Scharf.

See: Abracadabra; I Love You;

There Must Me Someone for Me.

Meyer, George W., composer, born Boston, Massachusetts, 1884; died New York City, 1959.

See (Lyrics by Alfred Bryan): Bring Back My Golden Dreams; Brown Eyes, Why Are You Blue?; My Song of the Nile; You Taught Me How to Love You.

See (Lyrics by Edgar Leslie): For Me and My Gal; Lonesome.

See (Lyrics by Sam M. Lewis): My Mother's Rosary; There's a Little Lane Without a Turning.

See (Lyrics by Sam M. Lewis and Joe Young): Tuck Me to Sleep in My Old 'Tucky Home; Where Did Robinson Crusoe Go with Friday on Saturday Night?

See also: Bring Back My Daddy to Me; Dear Old Rose; Everything Is Peaches Down in Georgia; Honey Love; If He Can Fight Like He Can Love, Good Night, Germany; I'm Awfully Glad I Met You; Just Like Washington Crossed the Delaware; There Are Such Things.

Meyer, Joseph, composer, born Modesto, California, 1894.

See: California, Here I Come; Crazy Rhythm; A Cup of Coffee, a Sandwich and You; Golden Gate; Happy Go Lucky Lane; If You Knew Susie; I Wish I Were Twins; It's an Old Southern Custom; My Honey's Lovin' Arms.

Mickey (Pretty Mickey), words by Harry H. Williams, music by Neil Moret (1918). The first theme song written to exploit a motion picture: *Mickey,* a silent movie starring Mabel Normand.

Midnight Flyer, words and music by Mayme Watts and Robert Mosley (1959). Popularized by Nat King Cole in a Capitol recording that received a "Grammy" Award from the National Academy of Recording Arts and Sciences as the best disk performance of the year by a "pop" single artist.

Midnight in Paris, words by Herb Magidson, music by Con Conrad (1935). Introduced by Nino Martini in the motion-picture musical *Here's to Romance* (1935).

'Mid the Green Fields of Virginia, words and music by Charles K. Harris (1898).

Mighty Lak a Rose, words by Frank L. Stanton, music by Ethelbert Nevin (1901). An art song in Negro dialect which entered the popular-song repertory by virtue of repeated performances in vaudeville in the early 1900s. It was second only to "The Rosary" among Nevin's songs in the success of its sheet-music sale. John Tasker Howard described it as "probably the simplest" of all of Nevin's songs, with "a freshness and a whimsical tenderness that makes its appeal direct and forceful."

When the publishers (John Church Co.) issued "Mighty Lak a Rose" they assumed that the composer had made the proper arrangements with his lyricist. After the song had become an outstanding success, Stanton wrote John Church that he had never granted permission for the use of his poem, and insisted upon proper compensation. Since Nevin was now dead, his widow was sent to Atlanta to discuss this matter with the lyricist. She managed to purchase the rights from Stanton for merely an immediate payment of $100, and a second payment of $100 should the sheet-music sale exceed thirty-five thousand copies in any single year. Needless to say, additional payments of $100 had to be made to Stanton (and later to Stanton's widow) on several occasions.

Military Life, words and music by Harold Rome (1946). Comedy number sometimes also known as "The Jerk Song." It was introduced by Jules Munshin, Chandler Cowles and Harry Clark in the post-World War II topical revue *Call Me Mister* (1946). It was also sung in the motion-picture adaptation of this revue (20th Century-Fox, 1951).

Milk and Honey, words and music by Jerry Herman (1961). Title song of the musical (1961), introduced by Julie Arkin, Tommy Rall and ensemble.

Milk and Honey, a musical comedy set in Israel with book by Don Appell. Lyrics and music by Jerry Herman.

Starring Robert Weede, Mimi Benzell and Molly Picon (1961). Original cast recording (RCA Victor).

See: Milk and Honey; Shalom.

Mills, Irving, composer and lyricist, born Russia, 1894.

See: Ellington, Duke.

See also: Minnie the Moocher; Mood Indigo; Moonglow; Nobody Knows What a Red Headed Mama Can Do; The Organ Grinder's Song; Riverboat Shuffle; Solitude; Straighten Up and Fly Right; When My Sugar Walks Down the Street.

Mills, Kerry, composer, born Frederick Allen Mills, Philadelphia, Pennsylvania, 1869; died Hawthorne, California, 1948.

See: Any Old Port in a Storm; At a Georgia Camp Meeting; Let Bygones Be Bygones; The Longest Way 'Round Is the Sweetest Way Home; Meet Me in St. Louis, Louis; Rastus on Parade; Whistling Rufus.

Mimi, words by Lorenz Hart, music by Richard Rodgers (1932). Introduced by Maurice Chevalier in the motion-picture musical *Love Me Tonight* (Paramount, 1932). It was revived by Maurice Chevalier in the motion picture *A New Kind of Love* (Paramount, 1963).

Mine, words by Ira Gershwin, music by George Gershwin (1933). Introduced by William Gaxton, Lois Moran and ensemble in the musical *Let 'Em Eat Cake* (1933). The chorus of this number is distinguished by its countermelody—a patter sung contrapuntally with the regular melody. The song was interpolated in a stage revival in New York of the musical *Of Thee I Sing!* in 1952.

Minnie the Moocher (or, The Ho De Ho Song), words and music by Irving Mills and Cab Calloway (1931). Introduced and popularized by Cab Calloway and his orchestra at the Cotton Club in Harlem, New York. Calloway's first recording, for Perfect in 1931, made him "a natural name as a novelty 'scat' singer, nicknamed the 'ho-de-ho man,'" notes Leonard Feather. The song has remained Cab Calloway's most famous

number. He sang it in the motion-picture musical *The Big Broadcast* (Paramount, 1932).

Minnie the Moocher's Wedding Day, words by Ted Koehler, music by Harold Arlen (1932). Written for Cab Calloway and his orchestra, who introduced it at the Cotton Club in Harlem, New York. This is a sequel to Calloway's "Minnie the Moocher," and was inspired by it.

The Minstrel's Return from the War, words and music by James Hill Hewitt (c.1827). The song was published by Hewitt's brother, who thought so little of its commercial possibilities that he failed to take out a copyright. The song went on to become one of the most successful ballads of the early 1800s, selling thousands upon thousands of sheet music in pirated editions. "It was eagerly taken up by the public," wrote the composer, "and established my reputation as a ballad composer. It was sung all over the world—and my brother, not securing the copyright, told me that he missed making at least ten thousand dollars."

Mischa, Jascha, Toscha, Sascha, words by Ira Gershwin, music by George Gershwin. An amusing ditty about violin virtuosos coming from Russia —and from the classes of Leopold Auer—to invade New York's Carnegie Hall in the 1910s. Mischa, of course, refers to Elman; Jascha, to Heifetz; Toscha, to Seidel; and Sascha, to Jacobson. The song was written in or about 1921 for private consumption. Ira Gershwin refers to it as a "party song . . . merely for our own amusement" with "no vehicle in mind." The only way the song reached publication was when Random House issued a de luxe edition of the *George Gershwin Song Book* in 1932, and used the song as a cover-insert.

Miss America, words and music by Bernie Wayne (1954). Official song of the Miss America pageant at Atlantic City, New Jersey.

Miss Annabelle Lee, words by Sidney Clare, music by Lew Pollack and Harry Richman (1927). Introduced and popularized by Harry Richman. It was revived in the motion-picture musical *Gentlemen Marry Brunettes* (United Artists, 1955).

M-i-s-s-i-s-s-i-p-p-i, words by Bert Hanlon and Benny Ryan, music by Harry Tierney (1916). A popular spelling song written for and introduced by Frances White in the Ziegfeld revue *Midnight Frolics* (1916). It was then interpolated for Grace La Rue in the revue *Hitchy Koo of 1917*.

Miss Liberty, a musical comedy with book by Robert Sherwood. Lyrics and music by Irving Berlin. Starring Eddie Albert, Mary McCarty and Allyn McLerie (1949). Original cast recording (Columbia).

See: Give Me Your Tired, Your Poor; Let's Take an Old Fashioned Walk; Paris Wakes Up and Smiles.

Miss Otis Regrets, words and music by Cole Porter (1934). A number written for the private delectation of Cole Porter's friends. He improvised it one evening in 1934 during a party at the home of a friend. Monty Woolley proceeded to borrow a morning coat and silver tray and impersonated a butler while delivering the lines to Porter's accompaniment. For the rest of that season Woolley enjoyed nothing better than to arrive at parties dressed up as a butler; always upon his entrance he would chant the first line of "Miss Otis Regrets." He sang it in the Cole Porter screen biography *Night and Day* (Warner, 1946).

√ **Missouri Waltz,** words by James Royce, using the pseudonym of J. R. Shannon, music by Frederick Knight Logan (1916). It was originally published in 1914 as a piano instrumental, the sheet music crediting Frederick Knight Logan as the "arranger" rather than "composer," explaining that the tune came "from an original melody procured by John Valentine Eppell." Logan is believed to have acquired the melody from a young Negro who sang it to him while accompanying himself on a guitar. A revised edition of the instrumental appeared later in 1914, and a vocal edition with Shannon's

words followed less than two years after that. The song became a success, selling over a million copies of sheet music and earning for Logan over $100,000. It subsequently became the official state song of Missouri. During the administration of Harry Truman it served as his unofficial theme song. The number was revived in the motion-picture musical *The Story of the Castles* (RKO, 1939), serving as the background music for an elegant dance routine by Fred Astaire and Ginger Rogers.

Miss You, words and music by Harry, Henry and Charles Tobias (1929). Popularized by Rudy Vallée over the radio and in an RCA Victor recording. The song was revived during World War II and was interpolated in the motion-picture musical *Strictly in the Groove,* starring Martha Tilton (Universal, 1942).

Mister and Mississippi, words and music by Irving Gordon (1951). Popularized by Patti Page in a Mercury recording and by Tennessee Ernie Ford in a Capitol recording.

Mister (Mr.) and Mrs., words by Cyrus Wood, music by Sigmund Romberg (1922). Introduced in the musical *The Blushing Bride* (1922). It was revived by Rosemary Clooney and José Ferrer in the Romberg screen biography *Deep in My Heart* (MGM, 1954).

Mister (Mr.) and Mrs. Is the Name, words by Mort Dixon, music by Allie Wrubel (1934). Introduced by Dick Powell and Ruby Keeler in the motion-picture musical *Flirtation Walk* (First National, 1934).

Mister (Mr.) Blue, words and music by Dewayne Blackwell (1959). Popularized by the Fleetwoods in a Dolton recording.

Mister (Mr.) Chamberlain, words by P. G. Wodehouse, music by Jerome Kern (1903). Kern's first hit song, written in London; this was also his first collaboration with P. G. Wodehouse. The Mr. Chamberlain in the song was a famous English politician of the time, the father of Neville Chamberlain, who subsequently became England's Prime

Minister. "Mister Chamberlain" was a topical song with a strong political interest.

Mister (Mr.) Dooley, words by William Jerome, music by Jean Schwartz (1902). A comedy song, Jean Schwartz's first success. The inspiration came from Finley Peter Dunn's Irish dialect sketches *Mr. Dooley.* The song was introduced by Thomas Q. Seabrooke in the musical extravaganza *A Chinese Honeymoon* (1902).

Mister (Mr.) Five by Five, words and music by Don Raye and Gene De Paul (1942). A take-off on short, corpulent jazz musicians. It was introduced by Grace McDonald and Sonny Dunham in the motion-picture musical *Behind the Eight Ball,* starring the Ritz Brothers (Universal, 1942). The song was interpolated in two other motion pictures in 1942: *Almost Married,* starring Jane Frazee (Universal), and *Who Done It?,* starring Abbott and Costello (Universal). Successful recordings were made by Freddie Slack and his orchestra for Capitol and Harry James and his orchestra for Columbia.

Mister (Mr.) Gallagher and Mister (Mr.) Shean, words by Ed Gallagher and Al Shean (1922). A comedy patter song introduced by Gallagher and Shean in the *Ziegfeld Follies of 1922.* It was interpolated for Al Shean in the motion-picture musical *The Ziegfeld Girl* (MGM, 1941), and was sung by Jack Benny and Al Shean in the motion-picture musical *Atlantic City* (Republic, 1944).

Mister (Mr.) Johnson, Turn Me Loose, words and music by Ben Harney (1896). Introduced by May Irwin in the musical *Courted into Court* (1896), where it helped to set a pattern for coon songs and a style for coon shouts. It then became one of Ben Harney's most celebrated vaudeville routines. He had a Negro named Strap Hill (one of vaudeville's first stooges) sing the verse from the front row of the balcony, after which he would repeat this verse from the stage in exact imitation of Strap Hill's delivery. Finally, Strap Hill would mount the stage

and both would present this coon shout—Strap Hill singing and Ben Harney accompanying him at the piano in ragtime style.

Mister Lonely, words and music by Gene Allan and Bobby Vinton (1964). Popularized by Bobby Vinton in a best-selling recording for Epic.

Mister (Mr.) President, a musical comedy with book by Howard Lindsay and Russel Crouse. Lyrics and music by Irving Berlin. Starring Robert Ryan and Nanette Fabray (1962). Original cast recording (Columbia).

See: Empty Pockets Filled with Love; Is He the Only Man in the World?; Meat and Potatoes; They Loved Me; This Is a Great Country.

Mister (Mr.) Sandman, words and music by Pat Ballard (1954). Popularized by the Chordettes in a Cadence recording that sold a million disks. The number subsequently became popular in a parody, as a comedy Christmas song, under the title of "Mister Santa."

Mister (Mr.) Wonderful, words by Larry Holofcener and George Weiss, music by Jerry Bock (1956). Hit song from the musical of the same name (1956), where it was introduced by Olga James.

Mister (Mr.) Wonderful, a musical comedy with book by Joseph Stein and Will Glickman. Lyrics by Larry Holofcener and George Weiss. Music by Jerry Bock. Starring Sammy Davis, Jack Carter and Olga James (1956). Original cast recording (Decca).

See: Mister Wonderful; Too Close for Comfort.

Misto Cristofo Colombo, words and music by Jay Livingston and Ray Evans (1951). Introduced by Bing Crosby (with the assistance of Dorothy Lamour, Cass Daley, Phil Harris and Louis Armstrong) in the motion-picture musical *Here Comes the Groom* (Paramount, 1951).

Misty, words by Johnny Burke, music by Erroll Garner (1955). Introduced as an instrumental by the Erroll Garner Trio in a Mercury recording in 1954. The song was popularized in 1956 in best-selling recordings by Erroll Garner and Mitch Miller and his orchestra for Columbia, and by Johnny Mathis for Columbia.

Mitchell, Sidney B., lyricist, born Baltimore, Maryland, 1888; died Los Angeles, California, 1942.

See: Alter, Louis.

See also: All My Life.

Mixed Emotions, words and music by Stuart F. Loucheim (1951). Popularized by Rosemary Clooney in a Columbia recording.

Moanin' Low, words by Howard Dietz, music by Ralph Rainger (1929). Introduced by Libby Holman in the intimate revue *The Little Show* (1929). The song used a squalid-room setting. After Libby Holman had sung the number through the first time, she repeated the chorus in a lower key, an effect that inspired an audience ovation; it was with this number that she first achieved stardom. Clifton Webb then performed a dance to it. In his review Richard Lockridge wrote: "One of the most striking things in the revue is . . . 'Moanin' Low,' which Libby Holman sings in that powerfully throbbing voice of hers while Clifton Webb dances with her in a mad grotesque."

The song was interpolated in the non-musical motion picture *Key Largo,* starring Humphrey Bogart and Lauren Bacall (Warner, 1948).

Mockin' Bird Hill, words and music by Vaughn Horton (1949). Popularized by Les Paul and Mary Ford in a Capitol recording that sold a million disks. Patti Page's Mercury recording in 1950 also sold a million disks.

Mollie Darling, words and music by Will S. Hays (1871). One of its composer's most celebrated ballads.

Molly and I and the Baby, words and music by Harry Kennedy (1892).

Molly O!, words and music by William J. Scanlan (1891). Irish ballad introduced by Scanlan in the musical *Mavourneen* (1891).

Moment to Moment, words by Johnny Mercer, music by Henry Mancini 1965). Title number, sung by a chorus under the titles, used as a recurrent theme, and resung by a

chorus in the closing scene, in the motion picture starring Jean Seberg and Sean Garrison (Universal, 1965).

Moments to Remember, words by Al Stillman, music by Robert Allen (1955). Popularized by the Four Lads in a best-selling Columbia recording.

Monaco, James (Jimmy) V., composer, born Genoa, Italy, 1885; died Beverly Hills, California, 1945.

See (Lyrics by Johnny Burke): An Apple for Teacher; I've Got a Pocketful of Dreams; Only Forever; That's for Me.

See (Lyrics by Mack Gordon): I Can't Begin to Tell You; I'm Making Believe.

See also: Dirty Hands, Dirty Face; Oh, You Circus Day; Row, Row, Row; What Do You Want to Make Those Eyes at Me For?; You Made Me Love You; You're Gonna Lose Your Girl.

Mona Lisa, words and music by Jay Livingston and Ray Evans (1949). Introduced in the motion picture *Capt. Carey of the U.S.A.* (Paramount, 1949).

Curious to note, the number was never given in its entirety in the motion picture. It was heard in fragments, and then only in Italian.

The writers induced Nat King Cole to record it for Decca, and he did so reluctantly. It sold three million disks.

The Money Song, words and music by Harold Rome (1947). Introduced in the musical *That's the Ticket* (1947), which closed in Philadelphia during out-of-town tryouts. This satire on money was first popularized by the Andrews Sisters in a Decca recording.

The Money Tree, words by Cliff Ferre, music by Mark McIntyre (1956). Popularized by Margaret Whiting in a Capitol recording.

Monotonous, words by June Carroll, with additional lyrics by Ronnie Graham, music by Arthur Siegel (1952). Introduced by Eartha Kitt in the revue *New Faces of 1952.* This song and this production helped lift Eartha Kitt to stardom. "Just before the Philadelphia closing," Leonard Sillman, producer of *New Faces,* recalled in his autobiography, "we held one last rehearsal. When Eartha Kitt came on with 'Monotonous' I stood down in the front row of the orchestra screaming at her, 'For God's sake, be a cat. . . . Spit the damned song out! . . . When you say 'Monotonous' say it between your teeth and open your eyes wide. Be a cat!' . . . She sang the song sullenly that night, hissing most of it in an absolute paralysis of boredom until the very end when she really let loose—and killed the customers."

Monte Carlo, a motion-picture musical starring Jeanette MacDonald and Jack Buchanan (Paramount, 1930). Songs by Leo Robin, W. Franke Harling and Richard A. Whiting.

See: Beyond the Blue Horizon; Give Me a Moment, Please.

The Mooche, words by Irving Mills, music by Duke Ellington (1928). A blues, one of Ellington's earliest successes, and popularized by him in a recording with his orchestra for RCA Victor in 1929.

Mood Indigo, words and music by Irving Mills, Albany Bigard and Duke Ellington (1931). Originally an instrumental, it was first recorded as such in 1930 under the title of "Dreamy Blues." With lyrics, and a change of title, "Mood Indigo" went on to become one of Ellington's first outstanding popular song hits.

Moody River, words and music by G. Bruce (1961). Popularized by Pat Boone in a best-selling Dot recording.

Moonbeams, words by Henry Blossom, music by Victor Herbert (1906). Introduced by Augusta Greenleaf in the first-act finale of the operetta *The Red Mill* (1906).

Moonglow, words and music by Will Hudson, Eddie DeLange and Irving Mills (1934). It was revived in the non-musical motion picture *Picnic,* starring Kim Novak and William Holden (Columbia, 1956). Morris Stoloff's recording with his orchestra for Decca was a best seller in

1956. The Benny Goodman Trio played it on the soundtrack of the motion-picture musical *The Benny Goodman Story* (Universal, 1956).

The Moon Got in My Eyes, words by John Burke, music by Arthur Johnston (1937). Introduced by Bing Crosby in the motion-picture musical *Double or Nothing* (Paramount, 1937).

Moon in My Window, words by Stephen Sondheim, music by Richard Rodgers (1965). Introduced by Elizabeth Allen, Carol Bruce and Julienne Marie in the musical *Do I Hear a Waltz?* (1965).

The Moon Is Low, words by Arthur Freed, music by Nacio Herb Brown (1930). Introduced by Cliff Edwards in the motion picture *Montana Moon,* starring Joan Crawford (MGM, 1930).

Moonlight and Pretzels, words by E. Y. Harburg, music by Jay Gorney (1933). Title song of a motion-picture musical (Universal, 1933).

Moonlight and Pretzels, a motion-picture musical starring Leo Carrillo and Mary Brian (Universal, 1933). Songs by E. Y. Harburg and Jay Gorney, E. Y. Harburg and Sammy Fain, and by Herman Hupfeld.

See: Ah, But Is It Love?; Are You Makin' Any Money?; Moonlight and Pretzels.

Moonlight and Roses, words and music by Ben Black and Neil Moret, the melody based on Edwin H. Lemare's *Andantino,* for organ (1925). It became one of the most successful ballads in Lanny Ross's repertory. Betty Grable sang it in the motion-picture musical *Tin Pan Alley* (20th Century-Fox, 1943). The song was also interpolated in the motion picture *Song of Texas,* starring Roy Rogers (Republic, 1943). It was successfully revived in 1965 by Vic Damone in a Dolton recording.

Moonlight and Shadows, words by Leo Robin, music by Frederick Hollander (1936). Introduced by Dorothy Lamour in the motion picture *Jungle Princess* (Paramount, 1936).

Moonlight Bay, words by Edward Madden, music by Percy Wenrich

(1912). Major hit song in the period just before World War I, popularized in vaudeville. Alice Faye revived it in the motion-picture musical *Tin Pan Alley* (20th Century-Fox, 1943). It provided the title for and was interpolated in the background music of the motion-picture musical *On Moonlight Bay* (Warner, 1951).

Moonlight Becomes You, words by Johnny Burke, music by James Van Heusen (1942). Introduced by Bing Crosby in the motion-picture musical *The Road to Morocco* (Paramount, 1942); it was further popularized by him in a Decca recording. Harry James' recording for Columbia in 1943 sold a million disks.

Moonlight Gambler, words by Bob Hilliard, music by Philip Springer (1956). Popularized by Frankie Laine, whose Columbia recording in 1957 sold a million disks.

Moonlight Love, words by Mitchell Parish, music by Domenico Savino, the melody based on Debussy's *Claire de lune,* for piano (1956). Popularized by Perry Como in an RCA Victor recording.

Moonlight on the Colorado, words by Billy Moll, music by Robert A. King (1930).

Moonlight on the Rhine, words by Bert Kalmar and Edgar Leslie, music by Ted Snyder (1914). Introduced in the musical *One Girl in a Million* (1914).

Moonlight Serenade, words by Mitchell Parish, music by Glenn Miller (1939). Introduced and popularized by Glenn Miller and his orchestra, whose Bluebird recording in 1940 was a best seller.

Moonlight Song, words by Harry B. Smith, music by Reginald de Koven (1897). Introduced by Hilda Clarke in the operetta *The Highwayman* (1897).

Moon Love, words by Mack Davis and Mack David, music by André Kostelanetz based on a theme from Tchaikovsky's Fifth Symphony (1939).

The Moon of Manakoora, words by Frank Loesser, music by Alfred Newman (1937). Introduced by Dorothy Lamour in the non-musical motion picture *The Hurricane* (United Artists, 1937).

Moon Over Miami, words by Edgar Leslie, music by Joseph A. Burke (1935).

Moon River, words by Johnny Mercer, music by Henry Mancini (1961). Introduced in the non-musical motion picture *Breakfast at Tiffany's,* starring Audrey Hepburn (Paramount, 1961), where it was sung on the soundtrack under the titles by Andy Williams. His Columbia recording sold over a million disks. Andy Williams then adopted it as the theme song for his television program. It was also released in about a hundred other recordings. It was honored with two "Grammy" Awards from the National Academy of Recording Arts and Sciences in 1961: as the best record of the year in Henry Mancini's recording for RCA Victor, and as the best song of the year. The song also received the Academy Award. Mercer regards this lyric as one of his best.

The successful songwriting team of Mercer and Mancini was born with this number.

Moonshine Lullaby, words and music by Irving Berlin (1946). Introduced by Ethel Merman in the musical *Annie, Get Your Gun* (1946). This number is one of Miss Merman's favorites. "Every time I sang it," she has explained, "there were tears in my eyes, it was that touching." The song was never able to catch on the way it deserved, probably because it was barred from the airwaves due to its references to the imbibing of liquor.

More, words by Tom Glazer, music by Alex Alstone (1956). Popularized by Perry Como in an RCA Victor recording.

More, words by N. Newell, music by Riz Ortolani (1963). Introduced in the non-musical motion picture *Mondo Cane* (Time, 1963), sung under the titles by the composer's wife, Kathina Ortolani. The song was not in this film when first released, but was interpolated in the soundtrack when *Mondo Cane* was first presented as a feature film in Los Angeles. The first recording— in April of 1963—was made by Martin Denny in a Mercury recording. In a year and a half it had received over a hundred different recordings, topped by Kai Winding's instrumental version on Verve, and including a best-selling recording by Johnny Mathis for Mercury. By 1966 it had been recorded two hundred times on fifty-six different labels.

More and More, words by E. Y. Harburg, music by Jerome Kern (1944). Introduced by Deanna Durbin in the motion-picture musical *Can't Help Singing* (Universal, 1944).

More I Cannot Wish You, words and music by Frank Loesser (1950). Ballad introduced by Pat Rooney the Third in the musical *Guys and Dolls* (1950).

The More I See of You, words by Mack Gordon, music by Harry Warren (1945). Introduced by Dick Haymes in the motion-picture musical *Diamond Horseshoe* (20th Century-Fox, 1945).

More Than You Know, words by Billy Rose and Edward Eliscu, music by Vincent Youmans (1929). Introduced by Mayo Methot in the musical *Great Day* (1929), a show that lasted only thirty-six performances. The song became one of Jane Froman's specialties.

Moritat. *See:* Mack the Knife.

The Morning After, words by Dory Langdon, music by Harold Arlen (1963). Introduced by Eileen Farrell, but popularized by Tony Bennett in a Columbia recording.

The Morningside of the Mountain, words and music by Dick Manning and Larry Stock (1951). Popularized by Tommy Edwards in an MGM recording.

Morse, Theodore F., composer, born Washington, D. C., 1873; died New York City, 1924.

See (Lyrics by Edward Madden): Blue Bell; Consolation; Daddy's Little Girl; Down in Jungle Town; I've Got a Feeling for You; I've Taken Quite a Fancy to You; A Little Boy Called Taps; Nan, Nan, Nan; Please Come and Play in My Yard; Starlight; Two Blue Eyes; Two Little Baby Shoes; When You Wore a Pinafore.

See also: Arrah Wanna; Dear Old Girl; The Good Old U.S.A.; Hail, Hail, the Gang's All Here; Keep a Little Cozy Corner in Your Heart; Keep on the Sunny Side; The Leader of the German Band; M-O-T-H-E-R; Nobody's Little Girl; One Called Mother; Where the Southern Roses Grow; Won't You Be My Honey?

The Most Beautiful Girl in the World, words by Lorenz Hart, music by Richard Rodgers (1935). Waltz introduced by Donald Novis and Gloria Grafton in the musical extravaganza *Jumbo* (1935). In the motion-picture adaptation of the musical (MGM, 1962), it was sung by Stephen Boyd, with Jimmy Durante doing a reprise.

The Most Happy Fella, words and music by Frank Loesser (1956). Title song of the musical play (1956), introduced by Robert Weede.

The Most Happy Fella, a musical play with book by Frank Loesser based on Sidney Howard's 1925 Pulitzer Prize play *They Knew What They Wanted.* Lyrics and music by Frank Loesser. Starring Robert Weede and Jo Sullivan (1956). Original cast recording (Columbia).

See: Big D; Happy to Make Your Acquaintance; Joey, Joey, Joey; The Most Happy Fella; Standin' on the Corner.

The Moth and the Flame, words by George Taggart, music by Max S. Witt (1898). Inspired by Clyde Fitch's play of the same name produced in New York in 1898. The song was introduced in 1898 by Helene Mora at the Pleasure Palace in New York City. Clyde Fitch subsequently used it frequently as background music for his play.

M-o-t-h-e-r (a Word That Means the World to Me), words by Howard Johnson, music by Theodore F. Morse (1915). A spelling mammy song, popularized in vaudeville by Sophie Tucker.

Mother Machree, words by Rida Johnson Young, music by Chauncey Olcott and Ernest R. Ball (1910). One of the most famous Irish ballads to come from Tin Pan Alley. It was introduced by Chauncey Olcott in the musical *Barry of Ballymore* (1910), and repeated by him in the musical *Isle of Dreams* (1912). It was interpolated in the motion-picture biography of Ernest R. Ball, *When Irish Eyes Are Smiling* (20th Century-Fox, 1944) and in the motion-picture biography of Chauncey Olcott, *My Wild Irish Rose* (Warner, 1947). This number was a staple in the concert repertory of the beloved Irish tenor John McCormack.

Mother Was a Lady (or, If Jack Were Only Here), words by Edward B. Marks, music by Joseph W. Stern (1896). Stimulated by an actual episode witnessed by the songwriters in a German restaurant on 21st Street in New York City. Two brash young men at a nearby table were harassing the waitress. In tears she exclaimed: "My mother was a lady!" Then she added hotly: "You wouldn't dare insult me if my brother Jack were only here!" Meyer Cohen, the singer, suggested to Stern and Marks that in this incident lay the makings of a good sentimental ballad. Marks agreed, writing the lyric for which his composing and publishing partner, Stern, provided the melody. Their song ends with the repentant young man not only begging the waitress for forgiveness but also for her hand in marriage—for he has discovered that the girl he has insulted is the sister of his best friend. The ballad was introduced by Lottie Gilson at Proctor's 58th Street Theatre in New York in 1896, a performance that helped launch a two-million-copy sheet-music sale.

Motion Picture Academy Awards ("Oscar"). *See:* Academy of Motion Picture Arts and Sciences Awards.

Mountain Greenery, words by Lorenz Hart, music by Richard Rodgers (1926). An early hit song by Rodgers and Hart, introduced by Bobbie Perkins and Sterling Holloway in the second edition of the intimate revue *The Garrick Gaieties* (1926). The song was interpolated in the screen biography of Rodgers and Hart, *Words and Music* (MGM, 1948).

The Mountains Beyond the Moon, words by Carl Sigman, music by Franz Waxman (1957). The song was adapted from Waxman's *Katusmi Love Theme* in the non-musical motion picture *Sayonara,* starring Marlon Brando (Warner, 1957).

The Mouse, words and music by Sandy Linzer and Denny Randell (1965). Comedy novelty song popularized by Soupy Sales on his television program and in an ABC-Paramount recording.

Move Over, Darling, words and music by Joe Lubin (1963). Title song of a motion picture (20th Century-Fox, 1963), introduced by Doris Day.

Moving Day in Jungle Town, words by A. Seymour Brown, music by Nat Ayer (1909). Introduced by Sophie Tucker in an elaborately mounted production number in the *Ziegfeld Follies of 1909.* The scene had been inspired by a newspaper cartoon showing jungle animals atop a tree hiding from the approaching Teddy Roosevelt—this being the time of Roosevelt's much-publicized hunting expeditions to Africa.

When the *Follies* tried out in Atlantic City, New Jersey, Sophie Tucker sang not only this song but also several popular ragtime tunes in the same scene; she brought down the house with her performance. This aroused the envy and fury of Nora Bayes, the *Follies* star, who insisted that Miss Tucker be removed from the show. A compromise was reached by having Miss Tucker delete all numbers from the scene except "Moving Day in Jungle Town." Soon after the *Follies* opened in New York, however, the scene and the song were usurped by Eva Tanguay, with the result that Sophie Tucker was permanently dropped from the show. She never again appeared in the *Follies.*

Mrs. Lofty and I, words by Mrs. Gildersleeve Longstreet, music by Judson Hutchinson (1857). Introduced in 1857 by Abby Hutchinson (of the singing Hutchinson Family) in one of her rare solo appearances. It was then popularized by the Hutchinson Family at their concerts. "The song survived the Civil War," wrote Carol Brink, "and came down through the Gibson Girl era until it touched the present generation."

Muchacha, words by Al Dubin, music by Harry Warren (1933). Introduced in the motion-picture musical *In Caliente,* starring Dolores del Rio (First National, 1933).

Muddy Water, words by Jo Trent, music by Peter De Rose and Harry Richman (1926). Introduced and popularized by Harry Richman.

Mule Train, words and music by Johnny Lange, Hy Heath and Fred Glickman (1949). Popularized by Frankie Laine, whose Mercury recording sold about a million and a half disks. This song has since become one of Laine's biggest numbers; he estimates he has sung it about four thousand times. The song provided the title for and was sung by Gene Autry in a motion picture (Columbia, 1950); in the motion picture *Singing Guns* (Republic, 1950), it was sung by Vaughn Monroe.

The Mulligan Braves, words by Edward Harrigan, music by David Braham (1880). Introduced in the Harrigan and Hart musical extravaganza *The Mulligan Guards' Nominee* (1880).

The Mulligan Guard, words by Edward Harrigan, music by David Braham (1873). Introduced by Harrigan and Hart in a vaudeville sketch at the Academy of Music in Chicago on July 15, 1873. The song was not an immediate success. Braham had to persuade William A. Pond to purchase the publication rights for $50. But the vaudeville sketch—a bitter satire on splinter military organizations then flourishing throughout the country—became a tremendous hit and soon drew the limelight to its principal song, which made fun of people who liked to wear uniforms. The song eventually spread like contagion. It was heard everywhere, as E. H. Kahn wrote. "Newsboys, policemen, hot corn vendors, the oyster sellers at their street-corner stalls and hokey pokey men who sold ice cream, whistled it as they went into their various chores. . . . Throughout America, children who in other eras might have chanted 'Ten Little Indians' could be found chanting a variation on that theme called 'Ten Little Mulligan Guards.'" The song was also popular outside the United States. In Vienna the operetta composer Karl Milloecker borrowed the melody for the first-act finale of his masterwork *The Beggar Student.* Kipling mentioned it in *Kim,* pointing up the song's popularity among the English Tommies in India.

The song, and the sketch in which it originated, became the embryo from which grew and developed the celebrated Harrigan and Hart extravaganzas, or burlesques, which flourished in the New York theater for more than a decade. It was a practice with David Braham (who was conductor of these extravaganzas as well as composer) to incorporate the tune of "The Mulligan Guard" into the overture of every new Harrigan and Hart burlesque on opening night.

Music Box Revue, an annual lavish revue with book, lyrics and music by Irving Berlin. The first edition was mounted in 1921. Four more editions were presented between then and 1924. Among the stars appearing in the various productions were Phil Baker, Fanny Brice, the Brox Sisters, Clark and McCullough, William Gaxton, Grace La Rue, Grace Moore, Oscar Shaw and Frank Tinney.

See: All Alone; Crinoline Days; Everybody Step; Lady of the Evening; Orange Grove in California; Pack Up Your Sins; Say It with Music; Tell Me a Bedtime Story; What'll I Do?

The Music Goes 'Round and 'Round, words by "Red" Hodgson, music by Edward Farley and Michael Riley (1935). A nonsense song about a French horn, introduced and first popularized by its creators in a New York night club. Michael Riley and Edward Farley recorded it in

1943 for the then newly organized recording company Decca; this release was the first with the Decca label to bring in a profit. The song was once again revived by Danny Kaye, in the motion-picture musical *The Five Pennies* (Paramount, 1959).

Music in the Air, a musical comedy with book and lyrics by Oscar Hammerstein II. Music by Jerome Kern. Starring Walter Slezak, Katherine Carrington and Tullio Carminati (1932).

The motion-picture adaptation starred John Boles and Gloria Swanson (Fox, 1934). Six songs were used from the stage score.

See: Egern on the Tegern See; I've Told Ev'ry Little Star; The Song Is You.

Music, Maestro, Please, words by Herb Magidson, music by Allie Wrubel (1938).

Music Makes Me, words by Gus Kahn and Edward Eliscu, music by Vincent Youmans (1933). Introduced by Fred Astaire and Ginger Rogers in the motion-picture musical *Flying Down to Rio* (RKO, 1933).

The Music Man, a musical comedy with book, lyrics and music by Meredith Willson. Starring Robert Preston and Barbara Cook (1957). Original cast recording (Capitol).

The motion-picture adaptation starred Robert Preston and Shirley Jones (Warner, 1962). The basic stage score was used. Soundtrack recording (Warner).

See: Goodnight, My Someone; Lida Rose; Seventy-Six Trombones; Till There Was You.

Music, Music, Music (or, Put Another Nickel In), words and music by Stephen Weiss and Bernie Baum (1950). Popularized by Teresa Brewer in a London recording that sold a million disks and became her first major success.

The Music of Home, words and music by Frank Loesser (1959). Introduced by Bruce McKay and Anthony Perkins in the musical play *Greenwillow* (1959).

The Music That Makes Me Dance, words by Bob Merrill, music by Jule Styne (1963). Introduced by Bar-

bra Streisand in the musical *Funny Girl* (1963).

Must It Be Love?, words and music by Walter Marks (1964). Introduced by Nancy Dussault in the gypsy musical *Bajour* (1964).

Mutual Admiration Society, words by Matt Dubey, music by Harold Karr (1956). Introduced by Ethel Merman and Virginia Gibson in the musical *Happy Hunting* (1956). The song was made into a hit by disk jockeys, and through juke boxes, even before the play opened.

My Angeline, words by Harry B. Smith, music by Victor Herbert (1895). Introduced in the operetta *The Wizard of the Nile* (1895).

My Baby Just Cares for Me, words by Gus Kahn, music by Walter Donaldson (1930). Introduced by Eddie Cantor in the motion-picture adaptation of the musical *Whoopee* (Paramount, 1930). It was then interpolated in the non-musical motion picture *Big City Blues*, starring Joan Blondell (Warner, 1932).

When *Whoopee* was being filmed, Samuel Goldwyn, its producer, called Kahn into his office to ask him to write a new musical number for one of the scenes. Goldwyn insisted that it be done the same day. Kahn rushed over to the golf course to get Donaldson, brought him back to the studio and worked out with him "My Baby Just Cares for Me." When they finished, Goldwyn inquired if the song was suitable for dancing. In reply, Gus Kahn started dancing with Goldwyn around the office, while humming the tune.

My Baby's Arms, words by Joseph McCarthy, music by Harry Tierney (1919). Introduced by Delyle Alda and John Steel in the *Ziegfeld Follies of 1919.*

My Baby's Coming Home, words by William G. Leavitt, John C. Grady and Sherm Feller (1952). Popularized by Les Paul and Mary Ford in a best-selling Capitol recording.

My Beautiful Lady, words by C. M. S. McLellan, music by Ivan Caryll (1911). Waltz introduced by Hazel Dawn in the operetta *The Pink Lady* (1911). Samuel Chotzinoff revealed

in *Toscanini: An Intimate Portrait*
that the Maestro was particularly
fond of this waltz, and liked to play
it on the piano "when in a reminiscent mood."

My Beloved, words and music by Jay
Livingston and Ray Evans (1951).
Introduced by Robert Merrill in the
motion picture *Aaron Slick from
Punkin Crick* (Paramount, 1952).

My Best Girl, words and music by Walter Donaldson (1924).

**My Best Girl's a New Yorker (or, My
Best Girl's a Corker),** words and
music by John Stromberg (1895).
Stromberg's first published song. It
was popularized in vaudeville by
Lottie Gilson, who insisted that it
was with this number, and with
her act, that the stooge invaded
variety entertainment. She explained
that at Hyde and Behman's Brooklyn Theatre in Adams Street, a boy
in the balcony was so taken with
her rendition of this number that
during the reprise he started to sing
along with her. His performance
brought down the house. Lottie Gilson then decided to include this
balcony-singing in her act—with a
new boy performer, since the original one (named Thomas Diamond,
aged thirteen) could not get his parents' consent to join the Gilson act.

This song made such a strong
impression on Weber and Fields
that when they planned producing
and appearing in extravaganzas in
their own Music Hall, they hired
Stromberg both as composer and as
conductor. This relationship lasted
half a dozen years and resulted in
Stromberg's best-known songs, all
of them introduced in the Weber
and Fields burlesques.

My Black Mandy, words and music by
Ben Harney (1896). Harney's first
attempt at writing ragtime tunes. He
introduced and popularized it in
vaudeville.

My Blue Heaven, words by George
Whiting, music by Walter Donaldson (1927). Written three years before its actual publication, this song
went on to become one of Donaldson's greatest hits.

Donaldson wrote his melody one

day in 1924 while waiting for a
billiard table at the Friars Club in
New York. One evening later he
played the tune to George Whiting,
then a vaudeville headliner, who
forthwith offered to write the lyrics.
Whiting introduced the number in
his act, but it failed to make an impression. The song lay in discard
until 1927, when Tommy Lyman, a
radio singer, adopted it as his theme
song. Gene Austin then made a Victor recording that sold several million disks; Austin's various Victor
recordings of this ballad are said to
have sold in excess of twelve million copies. Eddie Cantor interpolated it in the *Ziegfeld Follies of
1927*—adding several personal lines
to the lyrics about his five daughters
as "the crowd" in his own blue
heaven. It is, indeed, paradoxical
to remark that this hymn to marital
bliss was the creation of a bachelor
—Donaldson.

The song was heard in several motion pictures. It was sung by Frances
Langford in *Never a Dull Moment,*
starring the Ritz Brothers (Universal, 1943); and it was heard in
Moon Over Las Vegas, starring Anne
Gwynn and David Bruce (Universal,
1944). It provided the title for and
was sung by Betty Grable and Dan
Dailey on the soundtrack under the
titles in a motion-picture musical
(20th Century-Fox, 1949).

My Blushing Rosie. *See:* Ma Blushin'
Rosie.

My Bonnie Lies Over the Ocean. *See:*
Bring Back My Bonnie to Me.

My Buddy, words by Gus Kahn, music
by Walter Donaldson (1922). Hit
song of the early 1920s, popularized
in vaudeville by ballad singers. It
provided the title for a non-musical
motion picture starring Ruth Terry
(Republic, 1944), where it was sung
by Donald Barry. It was subsequently
interpolated in Gus Kahn's screen
biography *I'll See You in My Dreams*
(Columbia, 1951), sung by Doris
Day.

My Castle on the Nile, words by James
Weldon Johnson and Bob Cole,
music by Rosamond Johnson (1901).
Negro comedy song introduced in

vaudeville by Cole and Johnson, its creators. This was the first success of the songwriting team of Cole and the Johnsons.

My Coloring Book, words and music by John Kander and Fred Ebb (1962). This song was originally written for Kaye Ballard, who wanted to introduce it on Perry Como's TV show. The producers, however, insisted that since she was a comedienne the song would be out of character. Kaye Ballard then turned the number over to Sandy Stewart, who made it successful in a Colpix recording. Kitty Kallen's recording for RCA Victor was also a best seller.

My Country 'Tis of Thee. *See:* America.

My Cousin Carus', words by Edward Madden, music by Gus Edwards (1907). Inspired by Enrico Caruso's sensational successes at the Metropolitan Opera in New York. In his melody Edwards interpolated a strain from "Vesti la giubba," an aria from *Pagliacci* that was a Caruso tour de force. The song was interpolated in the Anna Held musical *Miss Innocence* (1908), then was sung by Arthur Deagon and chorus in the *Ziegfeld Follies of 1909*.

My Creole Sue, words and music by Gussie L. Davis (1898). Probably Davis' last ballad, and one of his best.

My Dad's Dinner Pail, words by Edward Harrigan, music by David Braham (1883). Introduced in the Harrigan and Hart musical extravaganza *Cordelia's Aspirations* (1883).

My Darlin' Eileen, words by Betty Comden and Adolph Green, music by Leonard Bernstein (1953). A parody of Irish balladry, introduced by Delbert Anderson, Edith (Edie) Adams and a chorus of police in the musical *Wonderful Town* (1953).

My Darling, words by Edward Heyman, music by Richard Myers (1932). Introduced in the Earl Carroll revue *Vanities of 1932*.

My Darling, My Darling, words and music by Frank Loesser (1948). Introduced by Doretta Morrow and Byron Palmer in the musical *Where's Charley?* (1948). For sev-

eral consecutive weeks in 1949, Frank Loesser had two songs in the first and second places of the Hit Parade—"My Darling, My Darling" alternating with "On a Slow Boat to China." Robert Shackleton and Mary Germaine sang "My Darling, My Darling" in the motion-picture adaptation of the musical (Warner, 1952). Doris Day's recording for Columbia in 1949 was a best seller.

My Dream Girl, words by Rida Johnson Young, music by Victor Herbert (1924). Introduced by Walter Woolf in the operetta *The Dream Girl* (1924), where it appeared as a recurrent theme. Edward N. Waters wrote: "The phrases of the stanza are attractively wistful, and the air of the refrain has a lilting syncopation which is gently infectious."

My Dream Is Yours, words by Ralph Freed, music by Harry Warren (1949). Title song of a motion-picture musical (Warner, 1949), introduced by Doris Day.

My Dream Is Yours, a motion-picture musical starring Doris Day (Warner, 1949). The score was made up mainly of standards. Several new numbers were contributed by Ralph Freed and Harry Warren, among others.

See: Canadian Capers; I'll String Along with You; I Only Have Eyes for You; Jeepers Creepers; My Dream Is Yours; With Plenty of Money and You; You Must Have Been a Beautiful Baby.

My Dreams Are Getting Better All the Time, words by Mann Curtis, music by Vic Mizzy (1944). Introduced in the motion picture *In Society,* starring Abbott and Costello (Universal, 1944), sung by Marion Hutton. Popularized by Les Brown and his orchestra (vocal by Doris Day) in a Columbia recording.

My Fair Lady, a musical play with book by Alan Jay Lerner adapted from Bernard Shaw's comedy *Pygmalion.* Lyrics by Lerner. Music by Frederick Loewe. Starring Rex Harrison and Julie Andrews (1956). It had the longest run of any Broadway musical (2,717 performances). Original cast recording (Columbia).

The motion-picture adaptation starred Rex Harrison and Audrey Hepburn (Warner, 1964). It received eight Academy Awards, including one as the best motion picture of the year. Marni Nixon sang on the soundtrack for Audrey Hepburn. The basic stage score was used. Soundtrack recording (Columbia).

See: Ascot Gavotte; Get Me to the Church on Time; I Could Have Danced All Night; I've Grown Accustomed to Her Face; On the Street Where You Live; The Rain in Spain; Show Me; With a Little Bit of Luck; Wouldn't It Be Loverly?

My Favorite Things, words by Oscar Hammerstein II, music by Richard Rodgers (1959). Introduced by Mary Martin and Patricia Neway in the musical play *The Sound of Music* (1959). The song was presented by Julie Andrews and a children's chorus in the motion-picture adaptation of the musical (20th Century-Fox, 1965).

My First and Last Love, words and music by Remus Harris and Marvin Fisher adapted from a theme from Rimsky-Korsakov's *Scheherazade* (1951). Popularized by Nat King Cole in a Capitol recording.

My Foolish Heart, words by Ned Washington, music by Victor Young (1949). Title song of the non-musical motion picture starring Dana Andrews and Susan Hayward (RKO, 1949), sung by Miss Hayward. It was popularized by Billy Eckstein in an MGM recording in 1950.

My Fortune Is My Face, words by Betty Comden and Adolph Green, music by Jule Styne (1964). Introduced by Jack Cassidy in the musical *Fade Out—Fade In* (1964).

My Funny Valentine, words by Lorenz Hart, music by Richard Rodgers (1937). Introduced by Mitzi Green in the musical *Babes in Arms* (1937). It was sung by Judy Garland in the motion-picture adaptation of the musical (MGM, 1939), and became one of her specialties. The song was interpolated in the motion-picture musical *Gentlemen Marry Brunettes* (United Artists, 1957) and in the motion-picture adaptation of the musical *Pal Joey* (Columbia, 1957).

My Future Just Passed, words by George Marion, Jr., music by Richard A. Whiting (1930). Introduced by Charles "Buddy" Rogers in the motion-picture musical *Safety in Numbers* (Paramount, 1930).

My Gal Is a Highborn Lady, words and music by Barney Fagan (1896). A ragtime classic of the 1890s.

Barney Fagan, one-time buck-and-wing performer in minstrel shows and vaudeville, was the stage manager of the Primrose and West Minstrels when he wrote "My Gal Is a Highborn Lady." He was cycling one day, when his attention was drawn to the peculiar rhythm produced by a broken pedal banging against the wheel. This rhythm suggested to him a syncopated tune, which he later wrote down and for which he produced lyrics. He sold words and music to the publisher Witmark for $100. Effectively arranged for the piano by Gustav Luders, this number was issued by Witmark, then introduced in 1896 by Charles Ernest Haverly of Haverly's Minstrels. It was popularized by Clara Wieland, who sang it for the first time at Koster and Bial's in New York.

My Gal Sal (or, They Called Her Frivolous Sal), words and music by Paul Dresser (1905). Dresser's last ballad, successfully introduced in vaudeville by Louise Dresser.

When he wrote his swan song, Dresser had fallen on evil times. His publishing house had gone bankrupt; his ballads were no longer selling; and the fortune he had made from his songs had been squandered. He opened a little two-room office on 28th Street, determined to rehabilitate his fortunes, insisting he was still capable of producing a major hit. His one-time friends— many of whom he had often wined and dined, and at times even supported—were skeptical. But Dresser *did* have one more best-selling ballad up his sleeve—"My Gal Sal." Unfortunately, he did not live to enjoy this success, dying just before it was on its way to become one of the great triumphs of his career, selling several million copies of sheet music.

When Paul Dresser's biography was filmed, it was called *My Gal Sal,* and it used that number as a recurrent theme (20th Century-Fox, 1942).

My Gal Sal, a motion-picture musical biography of Paul Dresser, starring Victor Mature as the songwriter with Rita Hayworth (20th Century-Fox, 1942). Three songs by Dresser were used in the score, including the title number. Several new songs were contributed by Leo Robin and Ralph Rainger.

See: Come Tell Me What's Your Answer; My Gal Sal.

My Guy, words and music by William Robinson (1964). Popularized by Mary Wells in a Motown recording.

My Happiness, words by Betty Peterson, music by Borney Bergantine (1948). It was written in 1933, but first became popular in 1948 in a best-selling recording by Jon and Sandra Steele for Damon. A decade after that Connie Francis recorded it successfully for MGM.

My Hat's on the Side of My Head, words and music by Harry Woods and Claude Hurlbert (1933). Interpolated in the British-made motion picture *Jack Ahoy* (British Gaumont, 1935).

My Heart Belongs to Daddy, words and music by Cole Porter (1938). Written to fill in a stage wait during a change of scene. It was with this number that Mary Martin, playing a minor role, made her sensational Broadway debut—in the musical *Leave It to Me* (1938). The scene was a wayside Siberian railroad station. Shedding her ermines in a simulated strip tease, Mary Martin sang the number in an innocent, quavering, babylike voice which Sophie Tucker had advised her to assume; this singing style was a delightful and provocative contradiction to the double-entendres in the lyrics. "Anyone who can keep his eyes off her while she is singing 'My Heart Belongs to Daddy,' " wrote Sidney B. Whipple in his review, "is

not a man and must hence be a mouse. She has the freshness and vitality of youth but she also has a poise and the gift of devilish humor, and I think she is a find." Brooks Atkinson reported: "There is a broad piece of ribaldry entitled 'My Heart Belongs to Daddy' which Mary Martin sings in the capital style of an inspired honky tonk."

Mary Martin sang it again in Cole Porter's screen biography *Night and Day* (Warner, 1946); Marilyn Monroe sang it in the motion picture *Let's Make Love* (20th Century-Fox, 1960).

My Heart Cries for You, words by Carl Sigman, music by Percy Faith, melody adapted from the French folk song "Chanson de Marie Antoinette" (1950). Popularized in a Columbia recording by Guy Mitchell, with Mitch Miller and his orchestra, in a release that sold over a million disks.

My Heart Has a Mind of Its Own, words by Howard Greenfield, music by Jack Keller (1960). Popularized by Connie Francis in a best-selling MGM recording.

My Heart Has Learned to Love You, Now Do Not Say Goodbye, words by Dave Reed, music by Ernest R. Ball (1910).

My Heart Is an Open Book, words by Hal David, music by Lee Pockriss (1958). Popularized in a King recording by Carl Dobkins, Jr.

My Heart Reminds Me (or, And That Reminds You), words by Al Stillman, music by Carmillo Bargoni adapted from Bargoni's *Autumn Concerto* (1957). Popularized by Kay Starr in a Capitol recording and in a Jubilee recording by Della Reese entitled "And That Reminds You."

My Heart Sings, words and music by Harold Rome, adapted from "Ma Mie," a French popular song by Jamblan and Herpin (1944). Introduced by Kathryn Grayson in the motion-picture musical *Anchors Aweigh* (MGM, 1945).

Harold Rome made this adaptation on a dare from his music publisher, Lou Levy. Rome's lyrics were completely new, bearing no relation to the French verses. The American song soon became so popular in Paris that the English lyrics were translated into French, and the song proceeded to become a hit in France all over again.

My Heart Still Clings to the Old First Love, words and music by Paul Dresser (1900).

My Heart Stood Still, words by Lorenz Hart, music by Richard Rodgers (1927). The song was originally written for the Charles B. Cochran revue in London, *One Dam Thing After Another* (1927), where it was introduced by Jessie Matthews and Sonny Hale. Convinced of its appeal, and eager to place it in a Broadway musical, Rodgers and Hart paid Cochran $5,000 for the rights to use the song in *A Connecticut Yankee* (1927). It was introduced there by William Gaxton and Constance Carpenter.

The idea for the lyrics came to Hart one day in Paris during a taxi ride with Rodgers and two girls. When their car barely avoided collision, one of the girls remarked, "My heart stood still." Hart commented that the phrase could do nicely as a song title, a fact noted down methodically by Rodgers in a little notebook. During their first evening in London, where Rodgers and Hart had come to do the score of *One Dam Thing After Another,* Rodgers came upon the title in his notebook. He sat down and wrote the entire melody. The next day, when he turned his tune over to Hart, the lyricist confessed he had completely forgotten his chance remark.

The song became a huge success in London largely through the efforts of the Prince of Wales, who fell in love with it after Rodgers himself had taught him the words and music. One evening, at the Café de Paris in London, the Prince asked the orchestra leader, Teddy Brown, to play it for him. When Brown confessed he did not know the song, the Prince proceeded to sing for him the entire number, verse as well as chorus. The band picked up the strains and finally struck up the complete melody. This incident was widely publicized.

The song was used in the motion-picture adaptation of *A Connecticut Yankee* (Fox, 1931) and was interpolated in the screen biography of Rodgers and Hart, *Words and Music* (MGM, 1948). It was also heard in several other motion pictures: as a piano episode in *Never Say Goodbye,* starring Errol Flynn (Warner, 1946); in the background music for *Humoresque,* starring John Garfield and Joan Crawford (Warner, 1947); and for *Parrish,* starring Claudette Colbert and Troy Donahue (Warner, 1951).

My Heart Tells Me, words by Mack Gordon, music by Harry Warren (1943). Introduced by Betty Grable in the motion-picture musical *Sweet Rosie O'Grady* (20th Century-Fox, 1944). It was popularized by Glen Gray and the Casa Loma Orchestra (vocal by Eugenie Baird) in a Decca recording.

My Hometown, words and music by Ervin Drake (1964). Introduced by Steve Lawrence in the musical *What Makes Sammy Run?* (1964), and further popularized by him in a Columbia recording.

My Home Town Is a One Horse Town (But It's Big Enough for Me), words by Alex Gerber, music by Abner Silver (1920).

My Honey's Lovin' Arms, words by Herman Ruby, music by Joseph Meyer (1922). Meyer's first hit song. It was successfully revived in 1963 by Barbra Streisand in a Columbia recording.

My Ideal, words by Leo Robin, music by Richard A. Whiting (1930). Introduced by Maurice Chevalier in the motion-picture musical *Playboy of Paris* (Paramount, 1930). It was sung by Charles "Buddy" Rogers in the motion-picture musical *Along Came Youth* (Paramount, 1931). This was the song with which Margaret Whiting launched her career as a recording artist—for Capitol in 1942.

My Irish Molly O, words by William Jerome, music by Jean Schwartz

(1905). Introduced by Blanche Ring in the musical *Sergeant Brue* (1905).

My Isle of Golden Dreams, words by Gus Kahn, music by Walter Blaufuss (1919).

My Joe, words by Oscar Hammerstein II, music being "Micaëla's Air" from Georges Bizet's opera *Carmen* (1943). Introduced by Carlotta Franzell in the musical play *Carmen Jones* (1943). In the motion-picture adaptation of the musical (20th Century-Fox, 1954), it was sung by Olga James.

My Kinda Love, words by Jo Trent, music by Louis Alter (1928). Introduced in the revue *Americana* (1928), but first popularized in a Decca recording by Bing Crosby— his first as a solo vocalist, and the one that helped pave his way to stardom in the recording industry.

My Kind of Girl, words and music by Leslie Bricuse (1961).

My Kind of Town (Chicago Is), words by Sammy Cahn, music by James Van Heusen (1964). Introduced by Frank Sinatra in the motion-picture musical *Robin and the Seven Hoods* (Warner, 1964), and further popularized by him in a Reprise recording. Sammy Cahn wrote a parody of this song entitled "My Kind of Guy" as a campaign song for Robert Kennedy during the Senatorial race in New York in 1964. Early in 1965 the All American Press Association, made up of thirty-one foreign and domestic periodicals, selected "My Kind of Town" as the best motion-picture song of the year.

My Lady Loves to Dance, words and music by Sammy Gallop and Milton De Lugg (1952). Popularized by Julius La Rosa in a Cadence recording.

My Landlady, words by F. E. Mierich and James T. Bryan, music by Bert Williams (1912). A ragtime comedy song introduced by Bert Williams in the *Ziegfeld Follies of 1912*.

My Last Cigar (or, 'Twas Off the Blue Canaries), words and music by James M. Hubbard (1848). A favorite with college students. Its melody was used for the University of Penn-

sylvania song, "Oh, Pennsylvania."

My Last Goodbye, words and music by Eddie Howard (1939). Popularized by Eddie Howard and his orchestra.

My Little Bimbo Down on the Bamboo Isle, words by Grant Clarke, music by Walter Donaldson (1920). Introduced by Aileen Stanley in the musical *Silks and Satins* (1920).

My Little Buckaroo, words by Jack Scholl, music by M. K. Jerome (1937). Interpolated in several motion pictures, including *The Cherokee Strip,* starring Richard Dix (Paramount, 1940); *Ridin' Down the Canyon,* starring Roy Rogers (Republic, 1942); and *Don't Fence Me In,* starring Roy Rogers (Republic, 1945).

My Little Corner of the World, words by Bob Hilliard, music by Lee Pockriss (1960).

My Little Georgia Rose, words by Robert F. Roden, music by Max S. Witt (1899).

My Little Nest of Heavenly Blue, English lyrics by Sigmund Spaeth to the melody of "Frasquita Serenade" ("Blaues Himmelbett") from Franz Lehár's operetta *Frasquita* (1923). The Lehár melody is one of its composer's most celebrated; the American song with English lyrics became a hit in the early 1920s.

My Little Red Book, words by Hal David, music by Burt Bacharach (1965). Introduced by Manfred Mann in the motion-picture farce *What's New, Pussycat?,* starring Peter Sellers, Peter O'Toole and Romy Schneider (United Artists, 1965).

My Long Blue Tail, A Negro song of unknown authorship (c. 1827). Popularized by such early minstrels as George Washington Dixon and William Pennington.

My Love Forgive Me, an Italian popular song ("Amore scusami"), music by Gino Nescoli, English lyrics by Sidney Lee (1964). Popularized in 1965 by Robert Goulet in a best-selling Columbia recording.

My Love Is a Married Man, words by Alan Jay Lerner, music by Frederick Loewe (1945). Introduced by Patricia Marshall in the first successful stage musical by Lerner and Loewe, *The Day Before Spring* (1945).

My Love, My Love, words by Bob Haymes, music by Nick Acquaviva (1952). Popularized by Joni James in an MGM recording.

My Love Parade, words by Clifford Grey, music by Victor Schertzinger (1929). Introduced by Maurice Chevalier in the motion-picture musical *The Love Parade* (Paramount, 1929).

My Lucky Star, words by Arthur Freed, music by Nacio Herb Brown (1935). Introduced by Eleanor Powell in the motion-picture musical *The Broadway Melody of 1936* (MGM, 1935). It was subsequently heard in a number of other motion-picture musicals. These included *Babes in Arms* (MGM, 1939); *Born to Sing* (MGM, 1942); and *Singin' in the Rain* (MGM, 1952). In the last-named film it was played under the titles, and was sung by Gene Kelly and Debbie Reynolds in the closing scene. It was also used as a recurrent theme in the background music for *The Stratton Story*, starring James Stewart (MGM, 1949).

My Mammy, words by Joe Young and Sam Lewis, music by Walter Donaldson (1921). Introduced in vaudeville in 1920 by Bill Frawley, but popularized by Al Jolson in the Winter Garden extravaganza *Bombo* (1921), becoming one of his prime specialties. He sang it in his first screen triumph, *The Jazz Singer* (Warner, 1928), and in the motion-picture musical *Rose of Washington Square* (20th Century-Fox, 1939); he also sang it on the soundtrack of the motion-picture musical *The Jolson Story* (Columbia, 1946). His recording for Decca in 1946 sold over a million disks.

When *Bombo* was in rehearsal, Saul Bourne, the music publisher, showed Jolson "My Mammy," which he was about to publish. Jolson looked through the number, hummed the tune and remarked: "You may have something here, Saul—depending on the man who sings it." When Al Jolson interpo-

lated it in *Bombo,* he brought down the house. As Pearl Sieben wrote: "In the sparkling new theatre which immortalized his name, he [Jolson] stood up on the stage and gave out for the first time with the heart-rending tune and lyrics of 'My Mammy.' When he sank down on one knee and beseeched his mammy to forgive him, the whole nation jumped to its feet to applaud." It was largely as a direct consequence of Jolson's triumph with this number that all subsequent performers of similar songs came to be known as "mammy singers."

My Man (or, Mon Homme), a French popular song, music by Maurice Yvain, English lyrics by Channing Pollock (1921). The French version was introduced in the United States by Irene Bordoni. The American adaptation was intended for Mistinguette's debut in America—in the *Ziegfeld Follies of 1921.* When she arrived in the United States, Ziegfeld lost all interest in her and dropped her from the production. Though up to now Fanny Brice had been famous in the *Follies* exclusively as a comedienne, she was selected by Ziegfeld to do the number. This was mainly because there was a strong parallel between the subject matter of the ballad and Fanny Brice's own unfortunate marriage to the gangster Nicky Arnstein. During rehearsals Fanny Brice sang the ballad while wearing a formal evening dress. Ziegfeld jumped on the stage and ripped off her gown, insisting she appear attired as a gamin and suggesting she deliver the number while leaning against a lamppost. That is the way Fanny Brice sang the ballad, and created a furor. Explaining her own poignant rendition, she said: "In my mind, I think of Nick leaving me, and the tears just came."

Fanny Brice sang "My Man" in her talking-picture debut—in a film entitled *My Man* (Warner, 1929). This was the first time she sang the ballad following her divorce from Nicky Arnstein. The ballad was later interpolated in her motion-picture biography, *Rose of Washington Square* (Paramount, 1939).

My Man's Gone Now, words by Du Bose Heyward, music by George Gershwin (1935). Serena's lament at the death of her husband, Robbins, in the folk opera *Porgy and Bess* (1935), introduced by Ruby Elzy. In the motion-picture adaptation of the opera (Columbia, 1959), it was sung on the soundtrack by Inez Matthews (for Ruth Attaway).

My Mariuccia Take a Steamboat, words by George Ronklyn, music by Al Piantadosi (1906). The lyricist was a waiter at Callahan's Café in downtown New York; the song's publication redounded to the credit of the saloon. This led "Nigger Mike" Salter, owner of the nearby Pelham Café, to get his own men to write and publish a song. That song was "Marie from Sunny Italy," lyrics by Irving Berlin—with which Berlin made his debut as a songwriter.

My Melancholy Baby, words by George A. Norton, music by Ernie Burnett (1912). Popularized in vaudeville in the 1910s, and in the 1930s by Paul Whiteman and his orchestra. The ballad is now most often identified with the singer Tommy Lyman, who helped to make it a standard. Bing Crosby sang it in the motion-picture musical *The Birth of the Blues* (Paramount, 1941); Benny Fields in the motion-picture musical *Minstrel Man* (PRC, 1944); and Judy Garland in the extended song sequence "Born in a Trunk" in the motion picture *A Star Is Born* (Warner, 1953). The song was also used in the background music as a recurrent theme for the non-musical motion picture *Scarlet Street*, starring Edward G. Robinson (Universal, 1945). More recently the ballad enjoyed a successful revival with Barbra Streisand in a Columbia recording.

"My Melancholy Baby" was involved in a publicized legal suit in 1940. When first written, the song had lyrics by Ernie Burnett's wife, Maybelle E. Watson, and was then called "Melancholy." This version was published in Denver in 1911.

A year later the publisher contracted with George A. Norton to revise the lyric. Now renamed "My Melancholy Baby," the song was credited on the sheet music to Norton and Burnett. In 1940 Maybelle Watson (long since divorced from Burnett) went to the courts to establish her interest in the copyright renewal. She won her case, and was awarded damages on back royalties.

The song once again made news in 1965, upon the death of a songwriter named Ben Light. The composer's son, Alan, now insisted that his father had written the music of "My Melancholy Baby" to Norton's lyrics while employed as pianist in a Denver night club. Ben Light, the son maintained, had failed to take out a copyright, with the result that before long the melody was appropriated by Ernie Burnett, who copyrighted it in his own name. Light's obituary in the *New York Times* went on to say: "No one cared particularly, the son went on, because for many years the song was unheeded by the public. . . . Mr. Light was urged by his friends to claim authorship and in the early 1940s he went on the radio with an orchestra sponsored by the Union Oil of California, was announced as the song's author, and told of the circumstances under which he had written it. Mr. Light had collected numerous affidavits attesting to his authorship of the music of 'My Melancholy Baby,' but he never brought suit in the matter, the son added. The younger Mr. Light said that Mr. Norton had died before the song became popular and so the father could not turn to him for confirmation. 'All I know is my father never received a penny from the song,' Mr. Light declared."

My Moonlight Madonna, words by Paul Francis Webster, music by William Scotti, the melody adapted from Zdenko Fibich's *Poème* (1933). Popularized in 1933 by Paul Whiteman and his orchestra in an RCA Victor recording. It was also a favorite of Rudy Vallée and of radio's "Street Singer," Arthur Tracy.

My Mother's Eyes, words by L. Wolfe Gilbert, music by Abel Baer (1928). Successfully introduced by George Jessel in vaudeville, then became his theme song. He sang it in his first starring role in talking pictures —*Lucky Boy* (Tiffany-Stahl, 1929). This number has become a Mother's Day favorite.

My Mother's Rosary (or, Ten Baby Fingers and Ten Baby Toes), words by Sam M. Lewis, music by George W. Meyer (1915). A favorite of barber-shop quartets.

My Mother Was a Lady. *See:* Mother Was a Lady.

My Mother Would Love You, words and music by Cole Porter (1940). Introduced by Ethel Merman and James Dunn in the musical *Panama Hattie* (1940).

My Nellie's Blue Eyes, words and music by William J. Scanlan (1883). Introduced by Scanlan in the musical *The Irish Minstrel* (1883). Sigmund Spaeth noted that its chorus is a note-for-note copy of the Venetian folk song "Vieni sul mar." Dennis Morgan sang "My Nellie's Blue Eyes" in the motion-picture musical biography of Chauncey Olcott, *My Wild Irish Rose* (Warner, 1947).

My Old Aunt Sally, words and music by Dan Emmett (1843). Introduced by the Virginia Minstrels in the early 1840s, then became a favorite of minstrel troupes all over the country.

My Old Flame, words by Sam Coslow, music by Arthur Johnston (1934). Interpolated in the motion-picture musical *Belle of the Nineties,* starring Mae West (Paramount, 1934). It became a specialty of Duke Ellington and his orchestra and was popularized by them in a Capitol recording.

My Old Kentucky Home, words and music by Stephen Foster (1853). Introduced in 1853 by Ed Christy and his minstrels. Within a year of publication it sold almost one hundred thousand copies of sheet music, a remarkable sales figure for that time.

The song was believed to have been written in a single morning, while Foster was visiting his cousin at Bardstown, Kentucky. His inspiration was the sound of mocking-birds there and the sight of pickaninnies at play. In 1922 a fund was raised to purchase that Bardstown mansion for $65,000, which was deeded to the State of Kentucky as a shrine.

"My Old Kentucky Home" has become the official state song of Kentucky and the anthem of the annual Kentucky Derby at Churchill Downs.

My Old New Hampshire Home, words by Andrew B. Sterling, music by Harry von Tilzer (1898). Harry von Tilzer's first song hit, selling over two million copies of sheet music.

When he wrote it, Harry von Tilzer was sharing a furnished room with Andrew B. Sterling on the top floor of an apartment house on East 14th Street, New York. Since they owed three weeks' rent, they refused to use light in their room for fear of attracting the attention of their landlord. Thus they wrote "My Old New Hampshire Home" one night by the illumination of a street lamp outside their window. When they tried to peddle the number among the publishing houses in Union Square, they found no takers. One of their friends, then, suggested they offer it to the Orphean Music Company, a small printing establishment owned by William C. Dunn. Dunn bought the song outright for $25. The song immediately became a favorite with vaudevillians throughout the country, thereby stimulating the sheet-music sales to formidable figures. When Shapiro, Bernstein bought out Dunn's catalogue, they voluntarily paid von Tilzer $4,000 as royalties even though they were not obligated to do so. They also took von Tilzer into a publishing partnership. Von Tilzer was now able to give up his job as a vaudevillian in order to concentrate on songwriting and publishing, two areas in which he forthwith achieved phenomenal success.

My One and Only, words by Ira Gershwin, music by George Gershwin (1927). Introduced by Gertrude MacDonald in the musical *Funny Face*

(1927), then danced to by Fred Astaire. The *New Republic* described this number in 1927 as "an old dark melody in despairing Polish minors."

My One and Only Highland Fling, words by Ira Gershwin, music by Harry Warren (1949). Introduced by Fred Astaire and Ginger Rogers in the motion-picture musical *The Barkleys of Broadway* (MGM, 1949). Fred Astaire has revealed in his autobiography that this is one of his favorite musical numbers.

My Own, words by Harold Adamson, music by Jimmy McHugh (1938). Introduced by Deanna Durbin in the motion-picture musical *That Certain Age* (Universal, 1938).

My Own Iona, words by L. Wolfe Gilbert, music by Anatol Friedland and Carey Morgan (1916). Popularized by Harry Owens first in Honolulu, then in vaudeville houses throughout the United States.

My Own True Love, words by Mack David, music by Max Steiner (1954). A song adapted from the instrumental "Tara's Theme" from the Max Steiner score to the motion picture *Gone with the Wind,* starring Clark Gable and Vivien Leigh (MGM, 1939).

My Paradise, words by Otto Harbach, music by Rudolf Friml (1915). Introduced by Franklyn Ardell in the operetta *Katinka* (1915).

My Pearl's a Bowery Girl, words by William Jerome, music by Andrew Mack (1894). Written in imitation of "The Bowery," it became one of the hit songs of 1894.

My Pony Boy, words by Bobby Heath, music by Charley O'Donnell (1909). Introduced by Lillian Lorraine in the Anna Held musical *Miss Innocence* (1909).

My Prayer, words and music by Jimmy Kennedy, melody based on Georges Boulanger's "Avant de mourir" (1939). It was revived in 1956 by the Platters, whose Mercury recording sold a million disks.

My Pretty Red Rose, words and music by Joseph P. Skelly (1877). Its composer's greatest commercial success.

My Rambler Rose, words by Gene Buck, music by Louis A. Hirsch and Dave Stamper (1922). Introduced by Andrew Tombes in the *Ziegfeld Follies of 1922,* then danced to by Tombes and Evelyn Law.

My Resistance Is Low, words by Harold Adamson, music by Hoagy Carmichael (1951). Introduced by Hoagy Carmichael and Jane Russell in the motion picture *Las Vegas Story* (RKO, 1952).

My Restless Love (or, Johnny Guitar), words and music by Pembroke Davenport (1954). The title originally was "Johnny Guitar," but this had to be changed to avoid confusion with a motion picture of the same name. The song was popularized in a Mercury recording by Patti Page.

My Reverie, words and music by Larry Clinton, melody adapted from Debussy's "Rêverie" (1938). The song was introduced and popularized in a recording by Larry Clinton, and was responsible for bringing Larry Clinton his first major success as a bandleader.

My Romance, words by Lorenz Hart, music by Richard Rodgers (1935). Introduced by Donald Novis and Gloria Grafton in the musical extravaganza *Jumbo* (1935). In the motion-picture adaptation of the musical (MGM, 1962), it was sung by Doris Day.

My Shining Hour, words by Johnny Mercer, music by Harold Arlen (1943). Introduced by Fred Astaire in the motion-picture musical *The Sky's the Limit* (RKO, 1943). In his autobiography, Astaire confesses that while the picture was being produced nobody suspected that "My Shining Hour" would be a hit, but "several months later . . . it became the Number One song of the day."

My Ship, words by Ira Gershwin, music by Kurt Weill (1941). Introduced by Gertrude Lawrence in the musical play *Lady in the Dark* (1941), where it served as a recurrent theme and played an important part in the development of the story. This song was written in the style of a turn-of-the-century melody, since in the play it is a tune the heroine had learned as a child. Despite the significance of the song to the plot, it was omitted when the play was adapted for motion pictures (Paramount, 1944); it was, however, mentioned several times in the script.

My Silent Love, words by Edward Heyman, music by Dana Suesse, melody adapted from Dana Suesse's instrumental *Jazz Nocturne* (1932). The song was revived more than a quarter of a century after its original publication through recordings by Eydie Gorme and Julie London.

My Sin, words by Bud De Sylva and Lew Brown, music by Ray Henderson (1929). Published as an independent number, then interpolated into the motion-picture musical *Show Girl in Hollywood,* starring Alice White (First National, 1930). More than a quarter of a century after that it was successfully revived by Patti Page in a best-selling Mercury recording.

My Song, words by Lew Brown, music by Ray Henderson (1931). Introduced by Ethel Merman and Rudy Vallée in the revue *George White's Scandals of 1931.* This and other hit songs from the 1931 *Scandals* were recorded by Bing Crosby and the Boswell Sisters on two sides of a twelve-inch Brunswick record, one of the earliest attempts to record the basic score of a Broadway show. The song was interpolated in the motion-picture musical *Chip Off the Old Block,* starring Donald O'Connor (Universal, 1944).

My Song of the Nile, words by Al Bryan, music by George W. Meyer (1929). Introduced in the non-musical motion picture *The Drag,* starring Richard Barthelmess (First National, 1929).

My Special Angel, words and music by Jimmy Duncan (1957). Popularized by Bobby Helms in a Decca recording.

My Sunny Tennessee, words by Bert Kalmar and Herman Ruby, music by Harry Ruby (1921). Introduced by Eddie Cantor in the musical *The Midnight Rounders* (1921). The number was further popularized by Sophie Tucker in vaudeville. It was interpolated in the screen biography

of Ruby and Kalmar, *Three Little Words* (MGM, 1950), sung by Fred Astaire and Red Skelton.

My Sweet Adair, words by L. Wolfe Gilbert, music by Anatol Friedland (1915). A favorite of barber-shop quartets.

My Sweeter Than Sweet, words by George Marion, Jr., music by Richard A. Whiting (1929). Introduced by Helen Kane (the boop-boop-a-doop girl) in the motion-picture musical *Sweetie,* starring Nancy Carroll (Paramount, 1929).

My Sweetheart's the Man in the Moon, words and music by James Thornton (1892). Introduced by James Thornton at the Orpheum Theatre in New York. The song was then popularized in vaudeville by Thornton's wife, Bonnie.

One evening Bonnie Thornton entreated her husband to come home straight from the theater instead of stopping off at local saloons, as was his habit. When he refused, she inquired: "Am I still your sweetheart?" He replied lightly: "My sweetheart's the man in the moon." The line pleased him and he wrote a song using it both as the title and as the first line of the chorus. The publisher, Frank Harding, bought the song outright for $25.

My Sweetie Turned Me Down (What Do I Care?), words by Gus Kahn, music by Walter Donaldson (1925).

My Time Is Your Time, words by R. S. Hooper, using the pen name of Eric Little, music by H. M. Tennant, using the pen name of Leo Dance (1925). Rudy Vallée was in London in 1925 when he heard this song and bought out the American rights. He introduced it that year with his band at the dining hall at Yale University, where he was then a student. When Vallée was contracted in 1929 to appear regularly over the radio on the Fleischman Hour, a coast-to-coast broadcast, he went in hunt of a theme song. The first suggestion was "Vagabond Lover," which he had recently popularized, but Vallée rejected it, feeling it would make him sound too egotistic. "Then a song occurred to me, a song I had brought back from London," he has revealed in his autobiography. "It was a song that had movement, being composed mostly of whole and half notes—it was a song the public had come to identify not only with the Fleischman Hour but with me, 'My Time Is Your Time.' " In fact, so intimately are this song and Rudy Vallée associated, that when the crooner wrote his autobiography in 1962 (with Gil McKean), he called it *My Time Is Your Time*.

Rudy Vallée's best-selling RCA Victor recording of "My Time Is Your Time" was heard on the soundtrack of the motion picture *Margie*, starring Jeanne Crain (20th Century-Fox, 1946). He also sang it on the soundtrack of the motion-picture musical *The Helen Morgan Story* (Warner, 1957).

My Time of Day, words and music by Frank Loesser (1950). Introduced by Robert Alda in the musical *Guys and Dolls* (1950).

My Truly, Truly Fair, words and music by Bob Merrill (1951). Popularized by Guy Mitchell (with Mitch Miller and his orchestra) in a Columbia recording that sold a million disks.

My Two Front Teeth. *See:* All I Want

for Christmas Is My Two Front Teeth.

My Wife's Gone to the Country, words by George Whiting and Irving Berlin, music by Ted Snyder (1913). Comic song that sold almost half a million copies of sheet music.

My Wild Irish Rose, words and music by Chauncey Olcott (1899). One of the earliest successful Irish ballads to come from Tin Pan Alley. It was introduced by Olcott in the musical *A Romance of Athlone* (1899). It gave the title to and was sung by Dennis Morgan in Olcott's motion-picture biography (Warner, 1947).

My Wild Irish Rose, a motion-picture musical biography of Chauncey Olcott, starring Dennis Morgan as Olcott (Warner, 1947). The score was made up of Irish standards.

See: A Little Bit of Heaven; Mother Machree; My Nellie's Blue Eyes; My Wild Irish Rose.

My Wish, words and music by Meredith Willson (1963). Introduced by Craig Stevens and Valerie Lee in the musical *Here's Love* (1963).

My Wonderful Dream Girl, words by Oliver Morosco, music by Victor Schertzinger (1913).

N

Nagasaki, words by Mort Dixon, music by Harry Warren (1928). A standard blues popularized by Bill Robinson at the Cotton Club in Harlem, New York.

Namely You, words by Johnny Mercer, music by Gene de Paul (1956). Introduced by Peter Palmer and Edith (Edie) Adams in the musical *Li'l Abner* (1956). In the motion-picture adaptation of the musical (Paramount, 1959), it was sung by Peter Palmer and Leslie Parrish.

Nancy Brown, a musical comedy with book and lyrics by Frederick Ranken. Music by Henry Hadley. Starring Marie Cahill (1903).

See: Under the Bamboo Tree; You Can't Fool All the People All the Time.

Nancy with the Laughing Face, words by Phil Silvers ("with the *sotte voce* help of Johnny Burke and Sammy Cahn"), music by James Van Heusen (1944). Written for Frank Sinatra's then two-year-old daughter. It was popularized by Sinatra in a Columbia recording.

Nan! Nan! Nan!, words by Edward Madden, music by Theodore F. Morse (1904).

National Academy of Recording Arts and Sciences Awards ("Grammy"). An award bestowed annually in various categories of recorded music by an Academy founded in 1957 by five radio executives. The aim of the Academy was to encourage and reward those who enrich the art and science of recorded music. To further this purpose, the Academy instituted in 1958 awards for every category of the recording industry, in popular and serious music. This award has been nicknamed "Grammy."

The following were among the first recipients of a "Grammy" in the initial year of these Academy Awards: "Volare," song of the year; Perry Como's release of "Catch a Falling Star," best vocal performance by a male; Ella Fitzgerald's album *The Irving Berlin Song Book,* best vocal performance by a female; the Louis Prima–Keely Smith recording of "That Old Black Magic," best vocal performance by a vocal group.

In the field of popular songs, these awards since 1958 have interest:

Record of the Year: "Mack the Knife" (Bobby Darin); "Moon River" (Henry Mancini); "I Left My Heart in San Francisco" (Tony Bennett); "The Days of Wine and Roses" (Henry Mancini); "The Girl from Ipanema" (Stan Getz and Astrud Gilberto); "A Taste of Honey" (Herb Alpert and the Tijuana Brass).

Song of the Year: "The Battle of New Orleans"; "Moon River"; "The Days of Wine and Roses"; "Hello, Dolly!"; "Shadow of Your Smile."

Best Solo Vocal Performance—Female: Ella Fitzgerald ("But Not for Me"); Ella Fitzgerald ("Mack the Knife"); Judy Garland (*Judy Garland at Carnegie Hall*); Ella Fitzgerald (*Ella Fitzgerald Swings Brightly with Nelson Riddle*); Barbra Streisand (*Barbra Streisand Album*); Barbra Streisand ("People"); Barbra Streisand ("My Name Is Barbra").

Best Solo Vocal Performance— Male: Frank Sinatra ("Come Dance with Me"); Ray Charles ("Georgia on My Mind"); Jack Jones ("Lollipops and Roses"); Tony Bennett ("I Left My Heart in San Francisco"); Jack Jones ("Wives and Lovers"); Louis Armstrong ("Hello, Dolly!"); Frank Sinatra (*September of My Years*).

Nature Boy, words and music by Eden Ahbez (1946). Introduced and popularized by Nat King Cole in a Capitol recording (distinguished by its exotic musical background) that sold half a million disks in the first month of its release in 1948, and over a million disks by the end of the year. The first appearance of this song on the Hit Parade in 1948 was in the Number One slot—the first time such a thing happened.

Ahbez, a follower of Yogi, left the manuscript of his song at the stage door of a California theater where Nat King Cole was performing. Impressed by the haunting originality of the number, Cole decided to record it; he managed to do so just before a temporary ban on all recording had been placed by the American Federation of Musicians.

The Naughty Lady of Shady Lane, words and music by Sid Tepper and Roy C. Bennett (1954). Popularized in 1955 in an RCA Victor recording by the Ames Brothers that sold a million disks.

Naughty Marietta, an operetta with book and lyrics by Rida Johnson Young. Music by Victor Herbert. Starring Emma Trentini and Orville Harrold (1910).

The motion-picture adaptation starred Jeanette MacDonald and Nelson Eddy (MGM, 1935). The principal songs from the stage score were used.

See: Ah, Sweet Mystery of Life; I'm Falling in Love with Someone; Italian Street Song; 'Neath the Southern Moon; Tramp, Tramp, Tramp

Along the Highway.

Navajo, words by Harry H. Williams, music by Egbert Van Alstyne (1903). Van Alstyne's first hit song. It was also the first successful popular song about the American Indian, initiating a vogue in Tin Pan Alley for songs on American-Indian subjects. "Navajo" was introduced by Marie Cahill in the musical *Nancy Brown* (1903)—interpolated in that show by the star after it had opened in New York.

Neapolitan Love Song, words by Henry Blossom, music by Victor Herbert (1915). A romantic ballad in Italian style introduced by Joseph R. Lertora in the operetta *The Princess Pat* (1915). It was sung by Allan Jones in the motion-picture musical *The Great Victor Herbert* (Paramount, 1939).

The Nearness of You, words by Ned Washington, music by Hoagy Carmichael (1940). Introduced by Gladys Swarthout in the motion-picture musical *Romance in the Dark* (Paramount, 1938). This is one of four Carmichael songs the composer regards as his own favorites (the other three being "Stardust," "Rockin' Chair" and "One Morning in May"). It was popularized by Glenn Miller and his orchestra in a Bluebird recording.

Near You, words by Kermit Goell, music by Francis Craig (1947). First popularized in Francis Craig's recording for Bullet, which helped draw interest both to Craig's band and to the young recording company. "Near You" became Milton Berle's theme song on his Texaco TV program.

'Neath the Southern Moon, words by Rida Johnson Young, music by Victor Herbert (1910). Introduced by Marie Duchene in the operetta *Naughty Marietta* (1910). Jeannette MacDonald and Nelson Eddy sang it in the motion-picture adaptation of the operetta (MGM, 1935). Edward N. Waters described this number as "a beautiful poem of tropical warmth of which the refrain is well known; the stanza is far less known but has a melody of strange nobility set forth over a starkly bare accompaniment—an exquisite piece of music."

'Neath the South Sea Moon, words by Gene Buck, music by Louis A. Hirsch and Dave Stamper (1922). Introduced by Gilda Gray in the *Ziegfeld Follies of 1922,* where she regularly stopped the show with it by doing the shimmy.

The Need for Love (or, The Unforgiven), words by Ned Washington, music by Dimitri Tiomkin (1960). Theme song of the motion picture of the same name starring Burt Lancaster and Audrey Hepburn (United Artists, 1960).

A Needle in a Haystack, words by Herb Magidson, music by Con Conrad (1934). Introduced by Fred Astaire in the motion-picture musical *The Gay Divorcee* (RKO, 1934).

Nel Blu, Dipinto Blu. *See:* Volare.

Nellie Kelly, I Love You, words and music by George M. Cohan (1922). Introduced by Charles King in the musical *Little Nellie Kelly* (1922).

Nelly Bly, words and music by Stephen Foster (1849). One of Foster's rare excursions into a quasi-nonsensical style.

Nelly Was a Lady, words and music by Stephen Foster (1849). Foster's first song published by Firth, Pond and Company; his payment was fifty free copies of sheet music. The song later became a favorite of barbershop quartets.

Never Be Anyone Else But You, words and music by Baker Knight (1959). Popularized by Ricky Nelson in a best-selling Imperial recording.

Never in a Million Years, words by Mack Gordon, music by Harry Revel (1937). Introduced by Alice Faye in the motion-picture musical *Wake Up and Live* (20th Century-Fox, 1937).

Never Let Me Go, words and music by Jay Livingston and Ray Evans (1956). Introduced by Nat King Cole in the motion picture *The Scarlet Hours* (Paramount, 1956), and further popularized by him in a Capitol recording.

Never Mind, Bo-Peep, words by Glen MacDonough, music by Victor Herbert (1903). Introduced by Bessie Wynn and chorus in the musical extravaganza *Babes in Toyland* (1903). It was interpolated in the motion-picture adaptation of the operetta (MGM, 1934).

Never Never Land, words by Betty Comden and Adolph Green, music by Jule Styne (1954). Introduced by Mary Martin in the Broadway musical production of *Peter Pan* (1954). This is one of two Styne songs which are the composer's own favorites, the other being "Just in Time."

Never on Sunday, a Greek popular song, music by Manos Hanjidakis, English lyrics by Billy Towne (1960). Theme song, used as an instrumental, in the Greek-made motion picture of the same name starring Melina Mercouri (Lopert, 1960). It received the Academy Award. The song was popularized by Don Costa in a United Artists recording and by the Chordettes in a Cadence recording.

Nevertheless, words by Bert Kalmar, music by Harry Ruby (1931). First popularized by both Bing Crosby and Rudy Vallée on their respective radio programs and in recordings. It was revived in the screen biography of Ruby and Kalmar, *Three Little Words* (MGM, 1950), sung by Anita Ellis, Fred Astaire and Red Skelton.

Never Till Now, words by Paul Francis Webster, music by John Green (1957). Introduced as an instrumental in the non-musical motion picture *Raintree County,* starring Elizabeth Taylor (MGM, 1957).

Never Too Late, words and music by Ray Evans, Jay Livingston and David Rose (1965). Title song of a motion picture starring Paul Ford and Connie Stevens (Warner, 1965), sung on the soundtrack by Vic Damone.

Never Will I Marry, words and music by Frank Loesser (1960). Introduced by Anthony Perkins in the musical play *Greenwillow* (1960).

The New Ashmolean Marching Society and Students Conservatory Band, words and music by Frank Loesser (1948). A marching tune introduced by the ensemble in the musical *Where's Charley?* (1948). It was also sung in the motion-picture adaptation of the musical (Warner, 1952).

New Coon in Town, words and music by Paul Allen (1883). One of the earliest published examples of a coon song. In fact, it was the word "coon" in this title that led to the identification of all similar Negro numbers as "coon songs." "New Coon in Town" was introduced in vaudeville by the team of Allen and Lester of which the composer was a member.

New Girl in Town, a musical play with book by George Abbott based on Eugene O'Neill's 1922 Pulitzer Prize play *Anna Christie*. Lyrics and music by Bob Merrill. Starring Gwen Verdon and Thelma Ritter (1957). Original cast recording (RCA Victor).

See: Did You Close Your Eyes When We Kissed?; It's Good to Be Alive; Look at 'Er; Sunshine Girl.

New Jole Blon (or, New Pretty Blonde) words and music by Sidney Nathan and Moon Mullican (1947). Popularized by Moon Mullican in a King recording.

Newman, Alfred, composer, born New Haven, Connecticut, 1901.

See: Anastasia; The Best of Everything; How the West Was Won; The Moon of Manakoora.

New Moon, an operetta with book and lyrics by Oscar Hammerstein II, Frank Mandel and Laurence Schwab. Music by Sigmund Romberg. Starring Evelyn Herbert and Robert Halliday (1928).

There were two motion-picture adaptations. The first starred Grace Moore and Lawrence Tibbett (MGM, 1930). The second starred Jeanette MacDonald and Nelson Eddy (MGM, 1940). Both utilized principal numbers from the stage score.

See: Lover, Come Back to Me; One Kiss; Softly As in a Morning Sunrise; Stout-Hearted Men; Wanting You.

A New Moon Over My Shoulder, words by Arthur Freed, music by Nacio Herb Brown (1934). Introduced in the motion-picture musical *Student Tour,* starring Jimmy Durante (MGM, 1934).

New Pretty Blonde. *See:* New Jole Blon.

New Sun in the Sky, words by Howard Dietz, music by Arthur Schwartz (1931). Introduced by Fred Astaire (as he preens himself in front of a mirror) in the revue *The Band Wagon* (1931). Jack Buchanan and Fred Astaire sang it in the motion-picture adaptation of the revue (MGM, 1953). Betsy Drake sang it in the motion-picture musical *Dancing in the Dark* (20th Century-Fox, 1949).

The New Yorkers, a musical comedy with book by Herbert Fields based on a story by Peter Arno and E. Ray Goetz. Lyrics and music by Cole Porter. Starring Charles King, Hope Williams, Ann Pennington and Clayton, Jackson and Durante (1930).

See: Love for Sale; Where Have You Been?

New York, New York, words by Betty Comden and Adolph Green, music by Leonard Bernstein (1945). Introduced by John Battles, Cris Alexander and Adolph Green in the musical *On the Town* (1944)—Leonard Bernstein's first Broadway musical. In the motion-picture adaptation of the musical (MGM, 1949), it was sung by Frank Sinatra, Gene Kelly and Jules Munshin.

Next to Your Mother Who Do You Love?, words by Irving Berlin, music by Ted Snyder (1909). An early Berlin hit song, for which he wrote only the lyrics.

Niagara Falls, words and music by Mr. Winchell, no first name known (1841). This number proved so popular that it is believed to have initiated the vogue for honeymooners' going to Niagara Falls. This song is also one of the earliest successes to exploit baby talk ("Is oo my darling?" he asks; to which she replies, "Goo, goo, goo.")

Nice Work If You Can Get It, words by Ira Gershwin, music by George Gershwin (1937). Introduced by Fred Astaire and a female trio in the motion-picture musical *A Dam-*

sel in Distress (RKO, 1937). It was interpolated in the motion-picture musical An American in Paris (MGM, 1951).

Nicodemus Johnson, words of unknown authorship, music by J. B. Murphy (1865). Comedy Negro song describing the reactions of non-secessionist landowners and slaves disinterested in the freedom of the Negro.

Night, words and music by J. Lehmann and Herb Miller (1960). Poplarized by Jackie Wilson in a Brunswick recording.

Night and Day, words and music by Cole Porter (1932). Introduced by Fred Astaire and Claire Luce in the musical Gay Divorce (1932). Fred Astaire sang it again in the motion-picture adaptation of the musical, renamed The Gay Divorcee (RKO, 1934). The song proved so popular in the stage musical that it is believed to have been responsible for the show's box-office success; in fact, that production soon became identified as the "Night and Day show." The popularity of the song was further enhanced in the early 1940s through the RCA Victor recording by Tommy Dorsey and his orchestra, with Frank Sinatra doing the vocal.

Porter's inspiration for this, one of his most famous creations, came from the hearing of rhythms of a native tune in Morocco.

The song provided the title for, was used as a recurrent theme for and was featured in the final scene of Cole Porter's screen biography (Warner, 1946). It was sung by Deanna Durbin in the motion picture Lady on a Train (Universal, 1945).

This is one of sixteen numbers selected by ASCAP in 1963 for its all-time Hit Parade during its half century of existence.

Night and Day, a motion-picture musical biography of Cole Porter starring Cary Grant, as the composer, with Alexis Smith (Warner, 1946). Ginny Simms, playing a fictional role, sang many of the Cole Porter classics which made up the score. "I Wonder What's Become of Sally"

by Jack Yellen and Milton Ager was interpolated.

See: Anything Goes; Begin the Beguine; Bulldog; Do I Love You?; Don't Fence Me In; I Get a Kick Out of You; I'm in Love Again; I'm Unlucky at Gambling; In the Still of the Night; I've Got You Under My Skin; Just One of Those Things; Let's Do It; Love for Sale; Miss Otis Regrets; My Heart Belongs to Daddy; Night and Day; Old Fashioned Garden; Rosalie; What Is This Thing Called Love?; You Do Something to Me; You're the Top; You've Got That Thing.

A Night at the Opera, a motion-picture extravaganza starring the Marx Brothers (MGM, 1935). Songs by Arthur Freed and Nacio Herb Brown, and Bronislau Kaper and Walter Jurmann.

See: Alone; Cosi Cosa.

The Night Has a Thousand Eyes, words by Buddy Bernier, music by Jerry Brainin (1948). Title song of a non-musical motion picture starring Edward G. Robinson (Paramount, 1948). It was successfully revived in 1963 by Bobby Vee in a Liberty recording.

The Night Is Filled with Music, words and music by Irving Berlin (1938). Introduced by Fred Astaire and Ginger Rogers in the motion-picture musical Carefree (RKO, 1938).

The Night Is Young and You're So Beautiful, words by Billy Rose and Irving Kahal, music by Dana Suesse (1936). Written for the Fort Worth Frontier Days Celebration in 1936, and introduced there at Billy Rose's Casa Mañana.

Night Song (or, Theme from Golden Boy), words by Lee Adams, music by Charles Strouse (1964). Introduced by Sammy Davis in the musical Golden Boy (1964).

The Night They Invented Champagne, words by Alan Jay Lerner, music by Frederick Loewe (1959). Introduced by Leslie Caron, Louis Jourdan and Hermione Gingold in the motion-picture musical Gigi (MGM, 1959).

When My Fair Lady was produced

in Moscow in December, 1964, in a Russian translation, "The Night They Invented Champagne" was interpolated for an elaborate production number.

The Night Was Made for Love, words by Otto Harbach, music by Jerome Kern (1931). A canzonetta used as a recurrent theme in the musical *The Cat and the Fiddle* (1931). It was introduced there by George Meader. Ramon Novarro sang it in the motion-picture adaptation of the musical (MGM, 1934).

Nobody, words by Alex Rogers, music by Bert Williams (1905). Comedy song made famous by Bert Williams. He introduced it in vaudeville as a member of the team of Williams and Walker, singing it (says Langston Hughes) in a "slow, sad mournful way . . . that made people laugh —and sometimes want to cry, too." Williams interpolated it in the *Ziegfeld Follies of 1910* upon making his Follies debut and becoming the first Negro performer to be starred with whites in a major Broadway musical production. The song was revived by Bob Hope in the motion-picture musical *The Seven Little Foys* (Paramount, 1955).

Nobody But You, words and music by Dee Clark (1958). Introduced and popularized by Dee Clark in an Abner recording.

Nobody But You, words by Arthur Jackson and Bud De Sylva, music by George Gershwin (1919). Introduced by Helen Clark, Orin Baker and chorus in George Gershwin's first Broadway musical, *La, La, Lucille* (1919).

Gershwin had written this song a few years before the production of *La, La, Lucille*—while still employed as a piano demonstrator at Remick's. He decided to interpolate it in his first musical comedy score, where it became the hit song.

Nobody Knows, Nobody Cares, words and music by Charles K. Harris (1909).

Nobody Knows What a Red Headed Mama Can Do, words by Irving Mills and Al Dubin, music by Sammy Fain (1925). An early Sammy Fain song hit.

Nobody Makes a Pass at Me, words and music by Harold Rome (1937). Introduced by Millie Weitz in the intimate, social-conscious revue *Pins and Needles* (1937). This is a lament of a plain girl who has tried all the advertising panaceas for beauty, without visible results. Barbra Streisand revived it in the early 1960s in a best-selling Columbia recording.

Nobody's Heart Belongs to Me, words by Lorenz Hart, music by Richard Rodgers (1942). Introduced by Constance Moore in the musical *By Jupiter* (1942), with the reprise sung by Ray Bolger.

Nobody's Little Girl, words by Jack Drislane, music by Theodore F. Morse (1907).

Nobody's Sweetheart, words and music by Gus Kahn, Ernie Erdman, Billy Meyers and Elmer Schoebel (1924). It was interpolated in several motion pictures. These included *Red Headed Woman*, starring Jean Harlow (MGM, 1932); *I'm Nobody's Sweetheart Now*, starring Dennis O'Keefe and Constance Moore (Universal, 1940); *Atlantic City* (Republic, 1944); and Gus Kahn's screen biography *I'll See You in My Dreams* (Warner, 1951), sung by Danny Thomas.

Nobody Told Me, words and music by Richard Rodgers (1962). Introduced by Diahann Carroll and Richard Kiley in the musical play *No Strings* (1962).

Nodding Roses, words by Schuyler Greene and Herbert Reynolds, music by Jerome Kern (1916). Introduced by Anna Orr and Oscar Shaw in the Princess Theatre production of *Very Good, Eddie* (1916).

No Greater Love. *See:* There Is No Greater Love.

Nola, a piano composition by Felix Arndt published as an instrumental in 1915, lyrics subsequently added by Sunny Skylar (1959). It was Arndt's musical portrait of his sweetheart, Nola Locke, a gifted singer and pianist, which he presented to her as an engagement gift. Vincent

Lopez used to play it frequently while employed as pianist and conductor at the Pekin Restaurant on Broadway in the late 1910s. When he formed his own orchestra and began his engagement at the Hotel Pennsylvania (where and when radio's first remote pickup was initiated), he began using "Nola" as his signature. He has since played it thousands of times, establishing it as an instrumental standard long before Sunny Skylar fitted it out with lyrics. As an instrumental it was interpolated in the motion picture *That's the Spirit*, starring Peggy Ryan and Jack Oakie (Universal, 1945).

No Love, No Nothin', words by Leo Robin, music by Harry Warren (1943). Introduced by Alice Faye in the motion-picture musical *The Gang's All Here* (20th Century-Fox, 1943). Popularized by Johnny Long and his orchestra (vocal by Patti Dugan) in a Decca recording.

Non Dimenticar (or, Don't Forget), an Italian popular song ("T'ho Voluto Bene"), music by P. G. Redi, English lyrics by Shelley Dobbins (1953). The song was heard in the Italian-made motion picture *Anna*, starring Silvana Mangano (Lux, 1952), and was popularized by Nat King Cole in a best-selling Capitol recording.

No, No, Nanette, a musical comedy with book by Otto Harbach and Frank Mandel. Lyrics by Irving Caesar and Otto Harbach. Music by Vincent Youmans. Starring Louise Groody, Mary Lawlor and Wellington Cross (1925).

There were three motion-picture adaptations. The first starred Alexander Gray and Bernice Claire (First National, 1930). It dispensed with the Youmans stage score, substituting songs by Grant Clarke and Harry Akst, among others. The second starred Anna Neagle (RKO, 1940). It used the hit songs from the stage score. The third, named *Tea for Two*, was only vaguely suggested by *No, No, Nanette* and starred Doris Day, Gordon MacRae and Gene Nelson (Warner, 1950). Here the prin-

cipal numbers from the Youmans stage score were used, with interpolations of several numbers by George and Ira Gershwin, Al Dubin and Harry Warren, among others.

See: Charleston; Crazy Rhythm; Do, Do, Do; I Know That You Know; I Only Have Eyes for You; I Want to Be Happy; Oh Me, Oh My, Oh You; Tea for Two.

No, No, Nora, words by Gus Kahn, music by Ted Fiorito and Ernie Erdman (1923). Introduced by Ted Fiorito and his orchestra, and interpolated in the Gus Kahn screen biography *I'll See You in My Dreams* (Warner, 1951), sung by Doris Day.

No, Not Much, words by Al Stillman, music by Robert Allen (1956). Popularized by the Four Lads in a best-selling Columbia recording.

No One But Me, words by Oscar Hammerstein II, music by Jerome Kern (1946). Kern's last song, written for the New York revival of *Show Boat* (1946), where it was introduced by Jan Clayton.

No One Ever Loved You More Than I, words by Edward B. Marks, music by Joseph W. Stern (1896).

No Other Arms, No Other Lips, words and music by Joan Whitney, Alex Kramer and Hy Zaret (1952). Revived and popularized in 1959 by the Chordettes in a best-selling Cadence recording.

No Other Love, words by Oscar Hammerstein II, music by Richard Rodgers (1953). Introduced by Bill Hayes and Isabel Bigley in the musical *Me and Juliet* (1953). The melody came from a tango in the section entitled "Beneath the Southern Cross" from *Victory at Sea*, a television documentary film in 1952–1953. The song was popularized by Perry Como in an RCA Victor recording.

North to Alaska, words by Mike Phillips (1960). Title song of a non-musical motion picture starring John Wayne and Stewart Granger (20th Century-Fox, 1960). It was popularized by Johnny Horton in a Columbia recording.

Norworth, Jack, composer and lyricist, born Philadelphia, Pennsylvania,

1879; died Laguna Beach, California, 1959.

See: Von Tilzer, Albert.

See also: Come Along, My Mandy; Heartaches; Shine On, Harvest Moon.

No Strings, words and music by Richard Rodgers (1962). Title song of a musical play (1962), introduced by Diahann Carroll and Richard Kiley.

No Strings, a musical play with book by Samuel Taylor. Lyrics and music by Richard Rodgers. This is the only stage production up to that time for which Rodgers wrote all the lyrics as well as the music. Starring Diahann Carroll and Richard Kiley (1962). Original cast recording (Capitol).

See: Loads of Love; Nobody Told Me; No Strings; The Sweetest Sounds.

Not for All the Rice in China, words and music by Irving Berlin (1933). Introduced by Marilyn Miller, Clifton Webb and ensemble in the musical *As Thousands Cheer* (1933). It was sung by Bing Crosby in the motion-picture musical *Blue Skies* (MGM, 1946).

Nothing More to Look Forward To, words and music by Richard Adler (1961). Introduced by Robert Guillaume and Ethel Ayler in the musical play *Kwamina* (1961).

No Two People, words and music by Frank Loesser (1953). Introduced by Danny Kaye and Jane Wyman in the motion-picture musical *Hans Christian Andersen* (Goldwyn, 1953).

Now, words by Ted Fetter, music by Vernon Duke (1936). Introduced by Gracie Barrie and Robert Shafer (and danced to by Paul Haakon and Evelyn Thawl) in the revue *The Show Is On* (1936).

No Wedding Bells for Me, words by E. P. Moran and Will A. Heelan, music by Seymour Furth (1906). Interpolated for Flavia Arcaro in the musical *The Orchid* (1907). This number ended with an apt quotation from Mendelssohn's *Wedding March*.

Now Hear This, words and music by Richard Adler (1951). Popularized by Tony Martin in an RCA Victor recording.

Now Is the Hour, words and music by Maewa Kaihan, Clement Scott and Dorothy Stewart (1946). This number, which had originated in Australia in 1913, came to the United States in 1946 in Dorothy Stewart's adaptation. This version was popularized by Bing Crosby in a Decca recording.

Now's the Time to Fall in Love (or, Potatoes Are Cheaper, Tomatoes Are Cheaper), words and music by Al Lewis and Al Sherman (1931). A song of the early 1930s depression, introduced over the radio in 1931 by Eddie Cantor on his Chase and Sanborn hour; it became one of his specialties. He sang it on the soundtrack of the motion-picture musical *The Eddie Cantor Story* (Warner, 1954).

Number Twenty-Nine, words and music by Will S. Hays (1871). Written to celebrate the success of the Thatcher and Perkins locomotive on the Louisville and Nashville Railroad.

O

O (or, Oh), words by Byron Gay, music by Byron Gay and Arnold Johnson (1919). Popularized in 1953 in Pee Wee Hunt's recording for Capitol.

The Object of My Affection, words and music by Pinky Tomlin, Coy Poe and Jimmie Grier (1934). It was interpolated in the non-musical motion picture *Times Square Lady,* starring Robert Taylor (MGM, 1935), and was revived in the motion-picture musical *The Fabulous Dorseys* (United Artists, 1947).

Of Thee I Sing, words by Ira Gershwin, music by George Gershwin (1931). Title song of the Pulitzer Prize musical comedy (1931), where it served as the official Presidential campaign song; it was introduced by William Gaxton and Lois Moran.

When Ira Gershwin wrote his lyrics, some of his friends felt that the juxtaposition of the dignified phrase "of thee I sing" with the word "baby" would cause some criticism. Ira Gershwin replied that if this were to prove to be the case he would make a change. But nobody seemed to mind. Ira Gershwin remarked: "Opening night, and even weeks later, one could hear a continuous, 'Of thee I sing, *baby!*' when friends and acquaintances greeted one another in the lobby at intermission time."

Of Thee I Sing!, a musical comedy with book by Morrie Ryskind and George S. Kaufman. Lyrics by Ira Gershwin. Music by George Gershwin. This was the first musical comedy to win the Pulitzer Prize for drama. It was also the first to get its text published in book form (Knopf). Starring William Gaxton, Victor Moore and Lois Moran (1931).

See: Love Is Sweeping the Country; Of Thee I Sing; Who Cares?; Wintergreen for President.

Oh, Baby Mine (I Get So Lonely), words and music by Pat Ballard (1953). Popularized in 1954 by the Four Knights in a Capitol recording.

Oh, Boy!, a musical comedy—a Princess Theatre production—with book by Guy Bolton. Lyrics by P. G. Wodehouse. Music by Jerome Kern. Starring Tom Powers and Anna Wheaton (1917).

See: An Old Fashioned Wife; Till the Clouds Roll By; Rolled into One; You Never Knew About Me.

Oh, But I Do, words by Leo Robin, music by Arthur Schwartz (1946). Introduced in the motion-picture musical *The Time, The Place and The Girl* (Warner, 1946), sung by Dennis Morgan.

Oh by Jingo, Oh by Gee (You're the Only Girl for Me), words by Lew Brown, music by Albert von Tilzer (1919). Nonsense song with gibberish lines. It was interpolated in the musical *Linger Longer, Letty* (1919), sung by Charlotte Greenwood. It was sung by Betty Hutton in the motion-picture musical biography of Texas Guinan, *Incendiary Blonde* (Paramount, 1945); it was also interpolated in the motion-picture musical *Skirts Ahoy*, starring Esther Williams (MGM, 1952).

Oh, Carol, words by Howard Greenfield, music by Neil Sedaka (1959). Popularized by Neil Sedaka in an RCA Victor recording.

Oh, Dem Golden Slippers, words and music by James Bland (1879). Introduced as a walk-around by the Original Georgia Minstrels. It soon became a favorite with minstrel troupes throughout the country. The song was revived in the motion-picture musical *Golden Girl* (20th Century-Fox, 1951), where it was sung under the titles; it was then performed in the opening scene by Mitzi Gaynor and Gale Robertson, with James Barton performing a buck-and-wing. It was also interpolated in the motion picture *Tulsa Kid*, starring Don "Red" Barry (Republic, 1940).

Oh, Didn't He Ramble?, words and music by Bob Cole and J. Rosamond Johnson, utilizing the single pen name of Will Handy (1902). Introduced by George Primrose, the famous minstrel. It soon became a favorite with minstrel troupes all over the country. Sigmund Spaeth explained that this number is "still good for a lock-step procession around a convivial table, properly situated." In the early 1900s this number was often given a vigorous performance by jazz bands in New Orleans in funeral processions.

Oh, Didn't It Rain?, words and music by Eddie Leonard (1923). One of the final song hits by the last of the great minstrels.

Oh, Frenchy!, words by Sam Ehrlich, music by Con Conrad (1918). A World War I comedy favorite inspired by the American doughboy's experiences with mademoiselles in France. It was sung by a male chorus in the motion-picture musical *The Dolly Sisters* (20th Century-Fox, 1945).

Oh, Gee, Oh, Gosh, Oh, Golly, I'm In Love, words by Olsen and Johnson, music by Ernest Breuer (1923).

Introduced by Olsen and Johnson in the *Ziegfeld Follies of 1922*.

Oh, How I Hate to Get Up in the Morning, words and music by Irving Berlin (1918). One of the most celebrated comedy songs of World War I. Irving Berlin wrote it for his first all-soldier show—*Yip, Yip, Yaphank* (1918). Supported by a male chorus, Irving Berlin himself introduced it, appearing as a sadly bedraggled rookie, roused by the bugler's morning blast and stumbling out of bed for reveille.

A generation later, during World War II, Irving Berlin revived the song in his second all-soldier show—*This Is the Army* (1942). Wearing again his old World War I uniform —and supported by a male chorus that included six alumni from *Yip, Yip, Yaphank*—Berlin sang the number in his rasping broken voice, and brought down the house. Irving Berlin also sang it with a male chorus in the motion-picture adaptation of *This Is the Army* (Warner, 1943). The song had also been interpolated in the motion-picture musical *Alexander's Ragtime Band* (20th Century-Fox, 1938).

Oh, Happy Day, words and music by Don Howard Koplow, and Nancy Binns Reed (1952). Popularized by Don Howard in an Essex-Triple A recording.

Ohio, words by Betty Comden and Adolph Green, music by Leonard Bernstein (1953). A nostalgic number with which the two heroines in Greenwich Village speak of their homesickness—in the musical *Wonderful Town* (1953). It was introduced by Rosalind Russell and Edith (Edie) Adams. Bernstein really intended "Ohio" as a parody of hometown songs; but it was taken seriously both in the theater and by radio and TV audiences, and became a hit ballad in 1953.

Oh, How She Could Yacki, Hacki, Wicki, Wacki, Woo, words by Stanley Murphy and Charles McCarron, music by Albert von Tilzer (1916). A Hawaiian-type number—a style then much in vogue in Tin Pan Alley. It was with this number that Eddie

Cantor made a sensational Broadway debut—on the Midnight Roof of the New Amsterdam Theatre in 1916, in a Ziegfeld production. Before singing it, Cantor invited three dignified men to come up on the stage from the audience. (They were William Randolph Hearst, Diamond Jim Brady and Charles B. Dillingham.) Cantor shuffled a deck of cards, then asked each of the three to draw one card and hold it over his head. They followed orders meekly. While they held the cards overhead, Cantor went through one chorus after another of "Oh, How She Could Yacki, Hacki, Wicki, Wacki, Woo." As soon as the audience started to realize that a hoax was being perpetrated on these three distinguished gentlemen, it started to let out a howl of delight. Upon completing his song, Cantor politely thanked the three men for their cooperation. Fortunately, all three enjoyed the joke as much as the audience did. With this stunt, and with the rendition of this song, Cantor stopped the show. Ziegfeld (who habitually never addressed a person face to face when he could wire him) sent Cantor the following telegram: "Enjoyed your act. You'll be here a long time."

Oh, Johnny, Oh, Johnny, Oh!, words by Ed Rose, music by Abe Olman (1917). Interpolated in the musical *Follow Me* (1916), sung by Henry Jackson. This number sold a million copies of sheet music. About twenty years later it was revived by Wee Bonnie Baker, with the Orrin Tucker orchestra, to become an even greater hit than it had originally been. Orrin Tucker's Columbia recording in 1939 (with Wee Bonnie Baker doing the vocal) sold over a million disks and helped to make the bandleader successful. The song was sung under the titles on the soundtrack of the non-musical motion picture *The Great Profile*, starring John Barrymore (20th Century-Fox, 1940).

Oh, Julie, words and music by Kenneth R. Moffitt and Noel Ball (1957). Popularized in 1958 by the Crescendos in a Nasco recording.

Oh, Katharina. *See:* O Katharina!

Oh, Kay!, a musical comedy with book by Guy Bolton and P. G. Wodehouse. Lyrics by Ira Gershwin. Music by George Gershwin. Starring Gertrude Lawrence (in her first appearance in an American musical comedy), Oscar Shaw and Victor Moore (1926).

See: Clap Yo' Hands; Do, Do, Do; Fidgety Feet; Someone to Watch Over Me.

Oh, Lady, Be Good, words by Ira Gershwin, music by George Gershwin (1924). Introduced by Walter Catlett (singing to a chorus of flappers) in the musical *Lady, Be Good!* (1924). In the production, the melody was sung slowly and gracefully, but it is now customary to speed up the tempo. Much of the appeal of the song comes from the effective use of repeated triplets in cut time in the chorus.

In planning the show, Alex Aarons, the producer of *Lady, Be Good!*, tried to sell Fred and Adele Astaire into accepting the starring roles. When they first heard the plot, they were reluctant to do so. "But when I heard the song 'Oh, Lady, Be Good,'" Fred Astaire later wrote in his autobiography, "I changed my mind."

The song was interpolated in the motion-picture adaptation of the musical (MGM, 1941) and in the George Gershwin screen biography *Rhapsody in Blue* (Warner, 1945). Lester Young's Columbia recording has become something of a jazz classic.

Oh, Lady, Lady, words by P. G. Wodehouse, music by Jerome Kern (1918). Title song of a musical (1918), introduced by Carl Randall and a female chorus. The phrase "oh, lady, lady" had been previously popularized in vaudeville by the famous Negro comedian, Bert Williams.

Oh, Lady, Lady! a musical comedy—a Princess Theatre production—with book by Guy Bolton. Lyrics by P. G. Wodehouse. Music by Jerome Kern. Starring Carl Randall and Vivienne Segal (1918).

See: Before I Met You; Oh, Lady, Lady; Our Love Nest.

Oh, Lonesome Me, words and music by Don Gibson (1958). Popularized by Don Gibson in an RCA Victor recording.

Oh, Ma-Ma (or, The Butcher Boy), words by Lew Brown, music by Rudy Valleé based on a popular Italian song ("Luna Merro Mare") with music by Paolo Citorello. Introduced and popularized by Rudy Vallée both over the radio and in an RCA Victor recording.

Oh, Marie, words by William Jerome, music by Jean Schwartz (1905). Introduced in the musical *Lifting the Lid* (1905). It was revived in the early 1950s in a successful recording by Alan Dale for Coral.

Oh Me, Oh My, Oh You, words by Ira Gershwin, using the pen name of Arthur Francis, music by Vincent Youmans (1922). This was Ira Gershwin's first song hit. It was introduced by Oscar Shaw and Marion Fairbanks in the musical *Two Little Girls in Blue* (1922)—Youmans' first successful stage score. Ira Gershwin confesses that the title was at first merely a functional one used by him to illustrate the rhythm and accent of the melody's opening bar. Youmans, however, insisted he liked it and wanted it to remain—"which," Gershwin adds, "was fine with me because I couldn't think of anything else—and the song turned out to be the most popular in the show."

It was interpolated in the motion-picture musical *Tea for Two* (Warner, 1950), sung by Doris Day and danced to by Doris Day and Gene Nelson.

Oh, My Papa, a Swiss popular song in German ("O Mein Papa"), music by Paul Burkhard, English lyrics by John Turner and Geoffrey Parsons (1953). The German-language song was introduced by Lys Assia in a Swiss musical, *Fireworks* (1948). The song, with English lyrics, was introduced and popularized in the United States in 1953 by Eddie Fisher in an RCA Victor recording that sold over a million disks.

Oh, Oh, Delphine, words by Harry Morton, using the pen name of C. M. S. McLellan, music by Ivan Caryll (1912). Title number of an operetta (1912), introduced by Frank McIntyre and Grace Edmond.

Oh, Oh, Delphine, an operetta with book and lyrics by Harry Morton, using the pen name of C. M. S. McLellan, based on a French farce. Music by Ivan Caryll. Starring Octavia Broske and Frank McIntyre (1912).

See: Oh, Oh, Delphine; Venus Waltz.

Oh, Oh, I'm Falling in Love Again, words and music by Hugo Peretti and Luigi Creatore, using the pen names of Al Hoffman, Dick Manning and Mark Markwell (1958). Popularized by Jimmie Rodgers in a best-selling Roulette recording.

Oh, Pennsylvania. *See:* My Last Cigar.

Oh, Pretty Woman, words and music by William Dees and Ray Orbison (1964). Introduced and popularized by Ray Orbison's recording for Monument, which sold a million disks and received the Gold Record Award.

Oh, Promise Me, words by Harry B. Smith, music by Reginald de Koven (1889). Introduced by Jessie Bartlett Davis in the third-act wedding scene of the operetta *Robin Hood* (1890).

This song had not originally been intended for the operetta. As Isidore Witmark revealed in his autobiography: "The song had been published independently. It had been found that *Robin Hood* needed another song; De Koven, for some reason, did not relish composing a new tune, so he brought this old one to rehearsal. He could not interest any of the singers in the song! Finally it was offered to Jessie Barlett Davis, the contralto playing Alan-a-Dale. Miss Davis, annoyed because she had not been offered the song at first, hummed it over, then disdained it. Something in the melody, however, remained. She found herself singing it an octave lower. MacDonald [the producer] happened to pass her dressing room; all who heard Jessie sing will understand why he stopped. He could not contain himself until the song was finished. 'Jessie!' he cried, bursting into her room. 'If you ever sing that song as you're singing it now, on the low octave, it will make your reputation.' She sang it, and the prophecy came true."

"Oh, Promise Me" became the hit song of *Robin Hood,* and is the main reason why this operetta is still occasionally revived. It is also the song by which its composer is most often remembered. It has become virtually a fixture at American weddings.

Oh, So Nice, words by Ira Gershwin, music by George Gershwin (1928). Introduced by Gertrude Lawrence and Paul Frawley in the musical *Treasure Girl* (1928). This is a waltz —but *not* in three-quarter time. George Gershwin explained at the time: "The waltz will always be in vogue. By that I mean music in three-four time. I find it interesting to experiment with. My number . . . is an effort to get the effect of a Viennese waltz in fox-trot time." In his lyrics, Ira Gershwin had to use clipped internal rhymes to produce a waltz effect.

Oh, Susanna, words and music by Stephen Foster (1848). The first song for which Foster received any cash payment. "Imagine my delight," he wrote, "in receiving one hundred dollars in cash! The two fifty-dollar bills I received for it had the effect of starting me on my present vocation as a songwriter." This was also the first Stephen Foster song heard in minstrel shows, where it scored a huge success. But its première performance had taken place not in a minstrel show but in an ice-cream parlor in Pittsburgh, Pennsylvania, on September 11, 1847.

"Oh, Susanna" became something of a theme song for the Forty-Niners en route to California. It was also favored by the early pioneers heading for the West. In both instances it was often given in parodies describing these experiences.

Alan Shulman made a symphonic arrangement of "Oh, Susanna" which is sometimes performed at symphony concerts. Another American composer, Lucien Cailliet, has written *Fantasia and Fugue on Oh, Susanna* for symphony orchestra.

Oh, That Beautiful Rag, words by Irving Berlin, music by Ted Snyder (1910). Interpolated in the Broadway musical *Up and Down Broadway* (1910), sung by Berlin and Snyder dressed up as men of the town.

Oh, What a Beautiful Mornin', words by Oscar Hammerstein II, music by Richard Rodgers (1943). Introduced by Alfred Drake in the musical play *Oklahoma!* (1943). It was heard in the opening scene, initially sung off-stage.

This was the first lyric completed by Hammerstein for *Oklahoma!* He has revealed that in "searching for a subject for Curly to sing about" he had been impressed by Lynn Riggs' descriptive paragraphs at the play's opening. Hammerstein decided to put some of that feeling into his song, to create "an atmosphere of relaxation and tenderness." The song thus serves "to introduce the light-hearted young man who is the center of the story."

In the motion-picture adaptation of the musical (Magna Theatre, 1955), it was sung by Gordon Mac-Rae.

In selecting his favorite Rodgers and Hammerstein song for *Show* magazine in August, 1964, Harold Arlen singled out "Oh, What a Beautiful Mornin'." "Here," wrote Arlen, "Rodgers made a sweepingly simple statement to Hammerstein's sunny lyrics with an economy of musical strokes. This could only happen to a writer of genius."

Oh, What a Pal Was Mary, words by Edgar Leslie and Bert Kalmar, music by Pete Wendling (1919).

Oh, You Beautiful Doll, words by A. Seymour Brown, music by Nat D. Ayer (1911). This number became a hit in 1911 through the song-plugging efforts of Mose Gumble of Remick's publishing house, and through subsequent performances by numerous vaudevillians. The song was interpolated in several motion pictures. These included *Wharf Angel,* starring Victor McLaglen

(Paramount, 1934); and the motion-picture musicals *The Story of the Castles* (RKO, 1939), *For Me and My Gal* (MGM, 1942) and *The Eddie Cantor Story* (Warner, 1954). It provided the title for and was heard in the screen biography of Fred Fisher (20th Century-Fox, 1949).

Oh, You Beautiful Doll, a motion-picture musical biography of Fred Fisher, starring Mark Stevens and June Haver and featuring S. Z. Sakall as Fisher (20th Century-Fox, 1949). The score was made up mainly of Fred Fisher standards.

See: Chicago; Come, Josephine, in My Flying Machine; Daddy, You've Been a Mother to Me; Dardanella; Ireland Must Be Heaven; Oh, You Beautiful Doll; Peg o' My Heart; There's a Broken Heart for Every Light on Broadway; When I Get You Alone Tonight; Who Paid the Rent for Mrs. Rip Van Winkle?

Oh, You Circus Day, words by Edith Maida Lessing, music by James V. Monaco (1911). Monaco's first hit song, introduced by Florence Moore and Billy Montgomery in the musical extravaganza *Hanky Panky* (1911).

Oh, You Crazy Moon, words by Johnny Burke, music by James Van Heusen (1939). The first collaboration of Burke and Van Heusen, introduced by Tommy Dorsey and his orchestra.

Oh, You Nasty Man, words by Jack Yellen and Irving Caesar, music by Ray Henderson (1934). Introduced by Alice Faye in the motion-picture musical *The George White Scandals* (20th Century-Fox, 1934). This song was responsible for throwing Alice Faye's Hollywood career into high gear. After seeing the rushes of Faye singing this number, George White gave her the lead in the picture.

O Katharina!, words by L. Wolfe Gilbert to a melody by Richard Fall, distinguished Austrian operetta composer (1924). "O Katharina!" was written for and introduced by Nikita Balieff, the genial, round-faced master of ceremonies of the Russian revue *Chauve souris,* imported to New York from Paris in 1924.

L. Wolfe Gilbert has explained: "My song was as timely then as it is

today. Since the American woman was diet conscious, I wrote 'O Katharina, O Katharina, to keep my love, you must be leaner.' I spent two weeks rehearsing him [Balieff]. . . . I asked one chap how Balieff sang the song. 'He didn't sing the words,' the stranger replied. 'He just kept singing the title over and over until he had most of the audience singing or whistling it."

Oklahoma!, words by Oscar Hammerstein II, music by Richard Rodgers (1943). Title number of the musical play (1943), introduced by Alfred Drake, Joan Roberts, Bette Garde, Barry Keeley and Edwin Clay. In the motion-picture adaptation of the musical (Magna Theatre, 1955), it was sung by Gordon MacRae, James Whitmore, Shirley Jones, J. C. Flippen and chorus. This number has been adopted as the official song of the State of Oklahoma.

Oklahoma!, a musical play with text by Oscar Hammerstein II adapted from Lynn Riggs' play *Green Grow the Lilacs.* Lyrics by Oscar Hammerstein II. Music by Richard Rodgers. This was the first stage collaboration of Rodgers and Hammerstein. It achieved the longest run of any musical production in Broadway history up to that time (2,248 performances), and it received a special award from the Pulitzer Prize committee. Starring Alfred Drake, Joan Roberts and Celeste Holm (1943). Original cast recording (Decca).

The motion-picture adaptation starred Gordon MacRae and Shirley Jones (Magna Theatre, 1955). It used the basic stage score. Soundtrack recording (Capitol).

See: All 'Er Nothin'; The Farmer and the Cowman; I Caint Say No; Kansas City; Many a New Day; Oh, What a Beautiful Mornin'; Oklahoma!; Out of My Dreams; People Will Say We're in Love; The Surrey with the Fringe on Top.

Olcott, Chauncey, composer, born Buffalo, New York, 1858; died Monte Carlo, Monaco, 1932.

See: Isle o' Dreams; Mother Machree; My Wild Irish Rose; When Irish Eyes Are Smiling.

For Chauncey Olcott's screen biography, see *My Wild Irish Rose* (Warner, 1947).

The Old Arm Chair, words by Eliza Cook, music by Henry Russell (1840). Sentimental ballad, sometimes described as the first mammy song in American popular music.

Old Black Joe, words and music by Stephen Foster (1860). One of the few Negro songs by Foster not in dialect. The "Joe" in the title was a servant in Jane McDowell's household, before she became Foster's wife. When, as a struggling composer, Foster would visit his sweetheart, Joe always met him at the door with a beaming smile on his face. Foster once told him: "Some day I'm going to put you in a song." He did—but Joe did not live to hear it.

Old Cape Cod, words and music by Claire Rothrock, Milt Yakus and Allan Jeffrey (1956). Popularized in 1957 by Patti Page in a best-selling Mercury recording.

Old Dan Tucker, words and music by Dan Emmett (1843). Introduced by the Virginia Minstrels on their very first program—at the Bowery Amphitheatre on February 6, 1843. At that time the song was described in the program as a "Virginian refrain in which is described the ups and downs of Negro life." It was sung by a full chorus of minstrels. Emmett got the idea for his song from an acquaintance—a ne'er-do-well who was always getting into trouble.

The song became a favorite with minstrel troupes around the country. One year after the song had been introduced, it was used by New York farmers in a parody to voice their resentment at existing feudal conditions. In our own day, the song is still popular at square dances.

Old Devil Moon, words by E. Y. Harburg, music by Burton Lane (1946). Introduced by Ella Logan and Donald Richards in the musical play *Finian's Rainbow* (1947).

Old Dog Tray, words and music by Stephen Foster (1853). One of Foster's most popular songs without

Negro interest. It is a nostalgic recollection of happy days gone by. It became one of Foster's best sellers, with almost fifty thousand copies of sheet music disposed of in less than a year.

Old-Fashioned Garden, words and music by Cole Porter (1919). Cole Porter's first hit song. It was introduced by Lillian Kemble Cooper in the revue *Hitchy-Koo of 1919.* Porter had written it some time earlier—during World War I, while he was serving in uniform at the French front; he put it down on paper within the sound of booming German cannon. Porter told an interviewer: "This is one of my favorites. I began my career with it and I still like it." It was revived in the Cole Porter screen biography *Night and Day* (Warner, 1946), sung by Cary Grant.

Old Fashioned Love, words by Cecil Mack, music by James P. Johnson (1921). Introduced in the all-Negro revue *Runnin' Wild* (1921). A generation later it became one of Lena Horne's specialties.

An Old Fashioned Wife, words by P. G. Wodehouse, music by Jerome Kern (1917). Introduced by Marie Cahill and a female chorus in the Princess Theatre production of *Oh, Boy!* (1917).

The Old Flame Flickers and I Wonder Why, words and music by Paul Dresser (1898).

Old Folks at Home (or, Swanee River), words and music by Stephen Foster (1851). Successfully introduced in 1851 by Ed Christy and his minstrels.

Interested in writing a song about a river, Stephen Foster—one day in 1851—asked his brother for suggestions. Foster rejected "Yazoo" and "Pedee" as not sufficiently euphonious. Then his brother took down an atlas, subjected the State of Florida to minute inspection and came upon "Suwanee," a river that emptied in the Gulf of Mexico. "That's it," Foster told his brother; but in writing his lyrics he contracted the name to "Swanee."

Foster submitted the song to Ed

Christy, who had written asking for a new and yet unpublished number. Christy wanted to introduce it with his minstrels; in addition, he insisted that the first edition of the sheet music identify him as creator of both the lyrics and the music. Since at that time Foster was still reluctant to achieve recognition with songs about the Negro (or "Ethiopian songs" as he described them), he agreed to give Christy "Old Folks at Home" for $500. Christy accepted the offer—but it is extremely doubtful if the minstrel ever paid Foster much more than $15.

The first edition of the sheet music described the number as an "Ethiopian melody . . . sung by Christy's Minstrels, written and composed by E. P. Christy." It became a best seller. In 1852 the *Musical World* described it as "one of the most successful songs that has ever appeared in any country. The publishers keep two presses running on it, and sometimes three; yet, they cannot supply the demand. The sale has already reached over forty thousand copies, and at the present rate will soon come up to a hundred thousand." The *Albany State Register* described how it was "on everybody's tongue, and consequently in everybody's mouth. Pianos and guitars groan with it, night and day; sentimental ladies sing it; sentimental young gentlemen warble it in midnight serenades; volatile young bucks hum it in the midst of their business and pleasures; boatmen roar it out stentorially at all times; all bands play it; amateur flute players agonize over it every spare moment; the street organs grind it out at every hour; and singing stars carol it on theatrical boards and at concerts." No less eloquent a proof of the immense popularity of the song was the fact that it was subjected so widely both to imitation and to parody. Among the songs that appeared in the early 1850s were "The Old Folks Are Gone" by George F. Root, "Young Folks at Home" by Hattie Livingston and "Young Folks From Home" by H. Craven Griffith.

By 1854 the song had sold almost 150,000 copies. Fortunately for Foster, in his arrangement with Christy he had not disposed of his rights to royalties. But in time Foster deeply regretted having allowed Christy to palm the song off as his own. Christy's name appeared on the published sheet music until 1879, when the first copyright expired.

A screen biography of Stephen Foster starring Al Jolson used the alternate title of "Old Folks at Home"—*Swanee River* (20th Century-Fox, 1939).

The Old Granite State, words by Jesse Hutchinson, the music being the melody of the old Revivalist hymn "The Old Church Yard" (1843). Introduced by the singing Hutchinson Family at a temperance meeting at the Broadway Temple in New York.

The Old Gray Mare, words of unknown authorship, music adapted by Frank Panella (1915). A song derived from "Down in Alabam'" by J. Warner, published in 1858; an instrumental version of the same melody appeared in 1860 under the title of "Get Out of the Wilderness."

The Old Lamp-Lighter, words by Charles Tobias, music by Nat Simon (1946). A leading hit song of 1946, selling about a million copies of sheet music and about two million disks. Among the best-selling recordings were those of Kay Kyser and his orchestra (vocal by Michael Douglas) for Columbia, and Sammy Kaye and his orchestra for RCA Victor (vocal by Billy Williams).

Charles Tobias got the idea for his lyrics from his childhood memories of the lamplighter in his home town of Worcester, Massachusetts.

Old Man Sunshine (Little Boy Bluebird), words by Mort Dixon, music by Harry Warren (1928). Popularized by Lee Morse, who made an outstanding Columbia recording of it in collaboration with her Blue Grass Boys.

Old Man Time, words and music by Jack Reynolds and Cliff Friend (1961). Popularized by Jimmy Durante in personal appearances and in a Warner recording.

The Old Oaken Bucket (or, The Bucket), words by Samuel Woodworth, music being the melody of "Araby's Daughter" by George Kiallmark (c. 1826). Woodworth's poem was written in 1818, and was published in 1826 in a volume entitled *Melodies, Duets, Trios, Songs and Ballads.* In 1833 these words were used for the Scottish melody, "Jessie, the Flower of Dumblane" by Robert Archibald Smith. However, it is to the melody of "Araby's Daughter" that Woodworth's lyrics are now sung.

Old Rosin the Beau (or, Old Rosin the Bow), author of words and music not known (c. 1830). Hit song in the early 1830s that stayed popular for several generations. Between 1840 and 1875 the song was four times parodied for Presidential campaigns. In 1844, when James K. Polk defeated Henry Clay, the Whigs adapted the tune for two campaign songs rhapsodizing Clay, "The Mill Boy of the Slashes" and "Old Hal of the West." The melody was once again used in 1860 for "Lincoln and Liberty," a campaign song for Abraham Lincoln. In 1872, after the Democrats had nominated Horace Greeley to oppose General Grant, a few independents of the losing party created their own ticket and tried to propagandize it with a song called "Straight-Out Democrat," the melody once again being "Rosin the Beau."

The Old Spinning Wheel, words and music by Billy Hill (1933). Hill had written this ballad several years before its publication. He finally had it published in order to capitalize on his then recent success with "The Last Round Up."

Old Uncle Ned, words and music by Stephen Foster (1848). Foster's second published song for which (like for his first) he received no payment.

Ole Buttermilk Sky, words and music by Hoagy Carmichael and Jack Brooks (1946). Introduced in the non-musical motion picture *Canyon Passage,* starring Dana Andrews and Susan Hayward (Universal, 1946), sung by Hoagy Carmichael. Popular-ized by Kay Kyser and his orchestra in a Columbia recording.

Ol' Man Mose, words and music by Louis Armstrong and Zilner Trenton Randolph (1938). First popularized by Eddie Duchin. It then became a Louis Armstrong specialty, one of the numbers with which, as Leonard Feather noted, Armstrong "began to edge out the jazz material in his repertory," and thus serving as his transition from "a musician's idol" to a "personality entertainer."

Ol' Man River, words by Oscar Hammerstein II, music by Jerome Kern (1927). A Negro work song introduced by Jules Bledsoe in the musical play *Show Boat* (1927).

In adapting Edna Ferber's *Show Boat* for the musical stage, Hammerstein felt the need of a song that would carry over to audiences the impact that the Mississippi River had in the Ferber novel. He decided to write a character song projecting the feel of the river. There was also a spot in the first act requiring a song without a situation. Hammerstein solved both problems with "Ol' Man River." Hammerstein's own interpretation of his ballad was: "It is a song of resignation with a protest implied, sung by a character who is a rugged and untutored philosopher."

In *A Peculiar Treasure,* Edna Ferber described her reaction when first she heard Kern play "Ol' Man River" for her. "Jerome Kern appeared at my apartment late one afternoon with a strange look of quiet exaltation in his eyes," she wrote. Then he sat down and played and sang "Ol' Man River." Miss Ferber continues: "The music mounted, mounted, and I give you my word my hair stood on end, the tears came to my eyes, and I breathed like a heroine in a melodrama. This was great music. It was music that would outlast Jerome Kern's day and mine."

Early in World War II, in one of his celebrated speeches, Prime Minister Winston Churchill took occasion to quote "Ol' Man River"—a fact that pleased Hammerstein no end. Churchill said: "The British Empire and the United States . . . together. . . . I do not view the process with misgiving. No one can stop it. Like the Mississippi, it just keeps rolling along. Let it roll . . . inexorable, irresistible, to broader lands and better days." This quotation appears in the published score of Jerome Kern's symphonic work *Scenario*, which is a tone poem for a large symphony orchestra built up from thematic material from the *Show Boat* score. Introduced on October 23, 1941, by the Cleveland Orchestra under Artur Rodzinski, *Scenario* has been frequently performed by America's major symphony orchestras.

In the 1936 motion-picture adaptation of *Show Boat* (Universal), "Ol' Man River" was sung by Paul Robeson; in the 1951 adaptation (MGM), by William Warfield. In the Jerome Kern screen biography *Till the Clouds Roll By* (MGM, 1946), it was sung by Frank Sinatra.

On a Bicycle Built for Two. *See:* Daisy Bell.

On a Clear Day, words by Alan Jay Lerner, music by Burton Lane (1965). Introduced by John Cullum in the musical play *On a Clear Day You Can See Forever* (1965). It was popularized by Johnny Mathis in a Mercury recording, and by Robert Goulet in a recording for Columbia.

On a Clear Day You Can See Forever, a musical play with book and lyrics by Alan Jay Lerner. Music by Burton Lane. Starring Barbara Harris and John Cullum (1965). Original cast recording (RCA Victor).

See: Come Back to Me; Hurry! It's Lovely Up Here; On a Clear Day; Melinda; She Wasn't You; What Did I Have That I Don't Have?

On a Desert Island with Thee, words by Lorenz Hart, music by Richard Rodgers (1927). Introduced by Jack Thompson and June Cochrane in the musical *A Connecticut Yankee* (1927). It was also sung in the motion-picture adaptation of the musical (Fox, 1931).

On an Evening in Roma, an Italian popular song ("Sott'er Celo de Roma"), music by S. Taccani, English lyrics by Nan Frederics (1959). The song, with English lyrics, was popularized in the United States by Dean Martin in a Capitol recording.

On a Rainy Night in Rio. *See:* Rainy Night in Rio.

On a Slow Boat to China, words and music by Frank Loesser (1948). Published as an independent number, to become one of the leading hit songs in 1948 and 1949. Kay Kyser's recording for Columbia (vocal by Harry Babbitt and Gloria Wood) sold over a million disks. The song was used as background music for a fashion show of bathing beauties in the motion-picture musical *Neptune's Daughter* (MGM, 1949). For several weeks running in 1949, Frank Loesser had two songs in the first and second places on the Hit Parade, with "On a Slow Boat to China" alternating with "My Darling."

On a Sunday Afternoon, words by Andrew B. Sterling, music by Harry von Tilzer (1902). One of von Tilzer's most successful ballads, selling almost two million copies of sheet music within a year of publication.

The idea for this song came to him one day at the beach when the line occurred to him: "People work hard on Monday, but one day that's fun day is Sunday." He persuaded Sterling to adapt his idea into a song lyric.

The song was interpolated in the motion-picture musical *Atlantic City* (Columbia, 1944), sung by Constance Moore. It was also heard in the motion picture *Naughty Nineties*, starring Abbott and Costello (Universal, 1945).

On a Sunday by the Sea, words by Sammy Cahn, music by Jule Styne (1947). Introduced by the ensemble in the musical *High Button Shoes* (1947).

On Behalf of the Visiting Firemen, words by Johnny Mercer, music by Walter Donaldson (1940). Popularized by Bing Crosby and Johnny Mercer in a Decca recording.

Once Ev'ry Year, words and music by Paul Dresser (1894).

Once in a Blue Moon, words by Anne Caldwell, music by Jerome Kern (1923). Introduced by Roy Hoyer, Evelyn Herbert, John Lambert, Lilyan and Ruth White and a female chorus in the musical *Stepping Stones* (1923).

"Once in a Blue Moon" was used by Robert Russell Bennett as a theme for a symphonic work—*Variations on a Theme by Jerome Kern* (1936).

Once in a While, words by Bud Green, music by Michael Edwards (1937). Revived by Harry James and his orchestra, in collaboration with a vocal quintet, in the motion-picture musical *I'll Get By* (20th Century-Fox, 1950).

Once in Love with Amy, words and music by Frank Loesser (1948). Hit song from the musical *Where's Charley?* (1948), introduced by Ray Bolger. He also sang it in the motion-picture adaptation of the musical (Warner, 1952).

In the stage production, Ray Bolger initiated a routine in which he would teach this song to the audience—line by line—and then urge it to sing the number along with him. A letter to this editor from Cy Feuer, the co-producer of *Where's Charley?*, explains why and how this practice was started: "My son, Robert, seven years old at the time, and a friend of his, were taken to one of the first matinees by my wife, who arranged to have them seated down front by themselves. She waited for them in the back of the house. Bobby, of course, knew Ray Bolger from having met him at home, and Bobby also knew the song. When Ray came to 'Once in Love with Amy' in the second act, he either forgot the lyrics or pretended to forget them, and as a result, stopped the music and said to himself something to the effect of 'I forgot the words' or 'What were the lyrics again?' At this point, Bobby stood up and unselfconsciously reminded Ray of the lyric. The audience laughed and Ray of course didn't know it was Bobby. In order to recover, Ray asked the little boy whether he would join him in singing. Bobby said he would, whereupon the two of them began to sing. Ray then urged the rest of the audience to join them, and so was born the community-sing spot which over a period of a couple of years evolved to about a fifteen-minute number, depending upon how long Ray felt like keeping it running."

Once Knew a Fella, words and music by Harold Rome (1959). Introduced by Andy Griffith in the musical *Destry Rides Again* (1959).

Once Upon a Time, words by Lee Adams, music by Charles Strouse (1962). Ballad introduced by Ray Bolger and Eileen Herlie in the musical *All American* (1962).

One Alone, words by Otto Harbach and Oscar Hammerstein II, music by Sigmund Romberg (1926). Love ballad introduced by Robert Halliday in the operetta *The Desert Song* (1926). In the motion-picture adaptation of the operetta (Warner, 1943), it was sung by Dennis Morgan.

One Called "Mother" and the Other "Home Sweet Home," words by William Cahill, music by Theodore F. Morse (1905).

One for My Baby (and One More for the Road), words by Johnny Mercer, music by Harold Arlen (1943). Introduced in the motion picture *The Sky's the Limit* by Fred Astaire, who regards it as "one of the best pieces of material that was written especially for me." Arlen describes the number as "a wandering song," explaining that "Johnny took it and wrote it exactly as it fell. Not only is it long—forty-eight bars—but it also changes key. Johnny made it work." This song is one of Arlen's favorites among his own creations. It was interpolated in several motion pictures, including *Roadhouse* (RKO, 1948), sung by Ida Lupino, *Macao* (RKO, 1952), sung by Jane Russell, and *Young at Heart* (Warner, 1955), sung by Frank Sinatra. Tony Bennett enjoyed his first major success with this number, which has also become one of Lena Horne's specialties.

One Horse Open Sleigh. *See:* Jingle Bells.

One Hour with You, words by Leo Robin, music by Richard A. Whiting (1932). Introduced by Maurice Chevalier in the motion-picture musical of the same name (Paramount, 1932). It became Eddie Cantor's theme song on his Chase and Sanborn radio hour; and he sang it on the soundtrack of the motion-picture musical *The Eddie Cantor Story* (Warner, 1954).

One Hour with You, a motion-picture musical starring Maurice Chevalier and Jeanette MacDonald (Paramount, 1932). Songs by Leo Robin and Richard A. Whiting, and by Oscar Straus.

    See: One Hour with You; We Will Always Be Sweethearts.

The One I Love Belongs to Somebody Else, words by Gus Kahn, music by Isham Jones (1924). Introduced by Isham Jones and his band. It was sung by Danny Thomas in the Gus Kahn screen biography *I'll See You in My Dreams* (Warner, 1951). It was recorded in best-selling disks by Bing Crosby and by Ella Fitzgerald, each for Decca.

One Kiss, words by Oscar Hammerstein II, music by Sigmund Romberg (1928). Love ballad introduced by Evelyn Herbert in the operetta *The New Moon* (1928). In the first motion-picture adaptation of the operetta (MGM, 1930), it was sung by Grace Moore; in the second (MGM, 1940), by Jeanette MacDonald.

One Little Candle, words by Jay Maloy Roach, music by George Mysels (1951). Popularized by Perry Como in an RCA Victor recording.

One Meat Ball, words by Hy Zaret, music by Lou Singer (1944). Lament of a little follow who has the price for only a single meat ball, and consequently is not entitled to bread. It was introduced by the folk singer Josh White, but was popularized by Jimmie Savo.

One Minute to One, words by Sam M. Lewis, music by J. Fred Coots (1933). Introduced by Harry Richman, to become one of his specialties.

One Morning in May, words by Mitchell Parish, music by Hoagy Carmichael (1933). One of four Carmichael songs that are the composer's own favorites. (The other three are "Stardust," "The Nearness of You" and "Rockin' Chair.")

One Night, words and music by Dave Bartholomew and Pearl King (1957). Popularized in 1958 by Elvis Presley, whose RCA Victor recording sold a million disks.

One Night in June, words and music by Charles K. Harris (1899).

One Night of Love, words by Gus Kahn, music by Victor Schertzinger (1934). Introduced by Grace Moore in her greatest screen success, a motion picture of the same name (Columbia, 1934).

One Night of Love, a motion-picture musical starring Grace Moore in her greatest screen success (Columbia, 1934). The title song was written by Gus Kahn and Victor Schertzinger.

    See: One Night of Love.

One Song, words by Larry Morey, music by Frank Churchill (1937). Introduced in the Walt Disney full-length animated cartoon *Snow White and the Seven Dwarfs* (RKO, 1937).

One Touch of Venus, a musical comedy with book by S. J. Perelman and Ogden Nash, suggested by F. Anstey's *The Tinted Venus*. Lyrics by Ogden Nash. Music by Kurt Weill. Starring Mary Martin (in her first leading role on Broadway), Kenny Baker and John Boles (1943).

    The motion-picture adaptation starred Ava Gardner and Robert Walker (Universal, 1948). Three songs were used from the stage production, with three others contributed by Ann Ronell and Kurt Weill.

    See: Speak Low; That's Him.

One, Two, Button Your Shoe, words by Johnny Burke, music by Arthur Johnston (1936). Introduced by Bing Crosby in the motion-picture musical *Pennies from Heaven* (Columbia, 1936), and further popularized by him in a Decca recording.

Only a Rose, words by Brian Hooker,

music by Rudolf Friml (1925). Love ballad introduced by Dennis King in the operetta *The Vagabond King* (1925). In the first motion-picture adaptation of the operetta (Paramount, 1930), it was once again sung by Dennis King; in the second version (Paramount, 1956), by Oreste.

Only Forever, words by Johnny Burke, music by James V. Monaco (1940). Introduced by Bing Crosby in the motion-picture musical *Rhythm on the River* (Paramount, 1940), and further popularized by him in a Decca recording.

Only Love Can Break a Heart, words by Hal David, music by Burt Bacharach (1962). Popularized by Gene Pitney in a Musicor recording.

Only Make Believe, words by Oscar Hammerstein II, music by Jerome ern (1927). Introduced by Howard Marsh and Norma Terris in the musical play *Show Boat* (1927). In the first motion-picture adaptation of the musical (Universal, 1936), it was sung by Irene Dunne and Allan Jones; in the second (MGM, 1951), by Kathryn Grayson and Howard Keel. Tony Martin and Kathryn Grayson sang it in the Jerome Kern screen biography *Till the Clouds Roll By* (MGM, 1945).

Only the Lonely Know the Way I Feel, words and music by Roy Orbison and Joe Melson (1960). Popularized by Roy Orbison in a Monument recording.

Only You, words and music by Buck Ram and Ande Rand (1955). Popularized by the Platters, whose Mercury recording sold a million disks. This recording was used on the soundtrack of the non-musical motion picture *This Angry Age,* starring Silvana Mangano (Columbia, 1958).

On Mobile Bay, words by Earl C. Jones, music by Charles N. Daniels (1910). A favorite of barber-shop quartets.

On Moonlight Bay. *See:* Moonlight Bay.

On Moonlight Bay, a motion-picture musical freely adapted from Booth Tarkington's *Penrod,* starring Doris Day and Gordon MacRae (Warner,

1951). The score was made up mainly of standards.

See: Ain't We Got Fun?; Cuddle Up a Little Closer; Every Little Movement Has a Meaning of Its Own; I'm Forever Blowing Bubbles; Love You; Moonlight Bay; Tell Me; Till We Meet Again.

On the Alamo, words by Gus Kahn, music by Isham Jones (1922). Isham Jones' first hit song, introduced by him and his band. It subsequently became a staple in Benny Goodman's repertory. It was also a Dave Brubeck specialty; he considered his Columbia recording as one of his best.

On the Atchison, Topeka and the Santa Fe, words by Johnny Mercer, music by Harry Warren (1945). Interpolated in the motion-picture musical *The Harvey Girls* (MGM, 1946), first presented by the ensemble in a production number, then sung by Judy Garland. It received the Academy Award. It was popularized further by Johnny Mercer and the Pied Pipers in a Capitol recording.

On the Avenue, a motion-picture musical starring Dick Powell and Alice Faye (20th Century-Fox, 1937). Songs by Irving Berlin.

See: I've Got My Love to Keep Me Warm; Slumming on Park Avenue; This Year's Kisses.

On the Banks of the Wabash Far Away, words and music by Paul Dresser (1897). Dresser's most celebrated ballad. Within three months of publication it was heard on the stage throughout the country, was played in the streets by barrel organs, was sung in the home, and was reprinted in many different publications. During the Spanish-American War it was a favorite with American soldiers.

In his introduction to a collection of Dresser's songs, Theodore Dreiser —the distinguished novelist and the composer's brother—insisted that it was he who had suggested to Paul that he write a song about the Wabash River in Indiana, at whose banks both of them had spent their childhood and boyhood days. Dreiser added that he had explained to his brother that songs about rivers did particularly well, and that he had helped Paul to sketch out some of the lines in the lyrics.

Max Hoffman, orchestrator for the publishing house of Witmark, who was with Dresser when this ballad was written, had a far different version of its conception; this version is now accepted as authentic. Hoffman wrote: "I went to his room in the Auditorium Hotel, where instead of a piano there was a small camp organ Paul always carried with him. It was summer. All the windows were open and Paul was mulling over a melody that was practically in finished form. But he did not have the words. So he had me play the full chorus over and over again at least for two or three hours, while he was writing the words, changing a line here and a phrase there, until the lyric suited him. . . . When Paul came to the line 'through the sycamores the candlelights are gleaming,' I was tremendously impressed. . . . I have always felt that Paul got the ideas from glancing out of the window and seeing the lights glimmering. . . . The song was published precisely as I arranged it. . . . During the whole evening we spent together, Paul made no mention of anyone's having helped him with the song."

The ballad was adopted as the state song of Indiana on March 4, 1913. It was interpolated in several motion-picture musicals, including Dresser's screen biography, *My Gal Sal* (20th Century-Fox, 1942), *The Jolson Story* (Columbia, 1946) and *Wait Till the Sun Shines, Nellie* (20th Century-Fox, 1952).

On the Benches in the Park, words and music by James Thornton (1896). Thornton's first song hit.

On the Five Fifteen (5:15), words by Stanley Murphy, music by Henry I. Marshall (1914). One of the earliest successful songs about the trials and tribulations of a commuter.

On the 'Gin, 'Gin, 'Ginny Shore, words by Edgar Leslie, music by Walter Donaldson (1922).

On the Good Ship Lollipop, words by Sidney Clare, music by Richard A. Whiting (1934). Introduced by Shirley Temple in the motion picture *Bright Eyes* (Fox, 1934).

On the Isle of May, words by Mack Davis, music by André Kostelanetz, melody based on the theme from the Andante Cantabile from Tchaikovsky's D major String Quartet (1940). Popularized by Connee Boswell in a Decca recording.

On the Mississippi, words by Ballard MacDonald, music by Harry Carroll and Arthur Fields (1912). Harry Carroll's first song hit. It was interpolated in two musical productions in 1912: *The Whirl of Society* and *Hanky Panky*. It was subsequently heard in the motion-picture musicals *The Dolly Sisters* (20th Century-Fox, 1945) and the Eva Tanguay screen biography *The I Don't Care Girl* (20th Century-Fox, 1953), in the latter sung by Mitzi Gaynor.

On the Rebound, words and music by Floyd Cramer (1961). Popularized by Floyd Cramer in an RCA Victor recording.

On the Riviera, a motion-picture musical starring Danny Kaye (20th Century-Fox, 1951). Songs by Sylvia Fine, together with the interpolation of several standards.

See: Ballin' the Jack; The Breeze and I.

On the Road to Mandalay, words by Rudyard Kipling, music by Oley Speaks (1907). An art song—a setting of Kipling's famous poem—which entered the popular repertory through performances by baritones in vaudeville. Its impact on audiences—both in vaudeville and in the concert hall—came from the rhythmic background suggesting persistent drum beats and from the effective key change from verse to chorus.

On the Street Where You Live, words by Alan Jay Lerner, music by Frederick Loewe (1956). Introduced by Michael King in the musical play *My Fair Lady* (1956). The song was further popularized in 1957 by Vic Damone in a best-selling Columbia recording. The number was sung by

Jeremy Brett in the motion-picture adaptation of the musical (Warner, 1964).

On the Sunny Side of the Street, words by Dorothy Fields, music by Jimmy McHugh (1930). Introduced by Harry Richman and Gertrude Lawrence in Lew Leslie's *International Revue* (1930). Tommy Dorsey and his orchestra recorded it successfully for RCA Victor; it became one of their specialties. The song was interpolated in the Ted Lewis screen biography *Is Everybody Happy?* (Columbia, 1943), in the motion-picture musical *Two Blondes and a Red Head,* starring Jean Porter (Columbia, 1947), and the non-musical motion picture *This Earth Is Mine,* starring Rock Hudson and Gene Simmons (Universal, 1959). It provided the title for and was sung by Frankie Lane in a motion-picture musical (Columbia, 1951); Frankie Laine's Mercury recording sold a million disks. Carmen Cavallero played it on the soundtrack of the musical *The Eddie Duchin Story* (Columbia, 1956); Benny Goodman and his orchestra on the soundtrack of the musical *The Benny Goodman Story* (Universal, 1956). Gogi Grant sang it (for Ann Blyth) on the soundtrack of the motion-picture musical *The Helen Morgan Story* (Warner, 1957).

On the Sunny Side of the Street, a motion-picture musical starring Frankie Laine, Billy Daniels and Terry Moore (Columbia, 1951). The score was made up mainly of standards.

See: I Get a Kick Out of You; I May Be Wrong But I Think You're Wonderful; Let's Fall in Love; On the Sunny Side of the Street; Too Marvelous for Words.

On the Town, a musical comedy with book and lyrics by Betty Comden and Adolph Green based on an idea by Jerome Robbins. Music by Leonard Bernstein. This was Bernstein's first musical-comedy score. Starring Sono Osato, Nancy Walker, Betty Comden and Adolph Green (1944).

The motion-picture adaptation starred Frank Sinatra, Gene Kelly, Betty Garrett and Ann Miller (MGM,

1949). The principal numbers were used from the stage score.

See: I Get Carried Away; Lonely Town; Lucky to Be Me; New York, New York.

On Top of Old Smokey, an American Southern Highlands folk song of unknown authorship. It entered the popular-song repertory in an arrangement by Pete Seeger (1951). The Decca recording by the Weavers and Gordon Jenkins and his orchestra sold over a million disks. Gene Autry sang it in the motion picture *Valley of Fire* (Columbia, 1951).

On Wisconsin, words by Carl Beck, music by W. T. Purdy (1909). A march adopted as the official state song of Wisconsin.

On Your Toes, a musical comedy with book by Richard Rodgers, Lorenz Hart and George Abbott. Lyrics by Lorenz Hart. Music by Richard Rodgers. Starring Ray Bolger and Tamara Geva (1936).

The motion-picture adaptation starred Vera Zorina and Eddie Albert (Warner, 1939). Three songs (together with the ballet score of *Slaughter on Tenth Avenue*) were used from the stage production.

See: Quiet Night; There's a Small Hotel.

Ooh, That Kiss, words by Mort Dixon and Joe Young, music by Harry Warren (1931). Introduced by Lawrence Gray and Jeanne Aubert with female chorus and dancers in the musical *The Laugh Parade* (1931).

O-oo, Ernest, Are You Earnest with Me?, words by Sidney Clare and Harry Tobias, music by Cliff Friend (1922). A comedy song popularized in vaudeville.

Open the Door, Richard!, words by "Dusty" Fletcher and John Mason, music by Jack McVea and Don Howell (1947). Novelty song inspired by a vaudeville routine popularized in the 1930s and the 1940s by Fletcher and Mason. The song was promoted by "Dusty" Fletcher in a best-selling recording for National and by Count Basie and his orchestra in a recording for RCA Victor.

Open Thy Lattice, Love, words by George P. Morris, music by Stephen Foster (1844). Foster's first published song, for which he received no payment. He dedicated it to Susan Pentland, a twelve-year-old girl living next door to him, with whom in all probability Foster was then in love.

Morris' poem first appeared in the *New Mirror* and in 1840 had been set to music by Joseph Philip Knight. A curious paradox about Foster's first publication is the fact that his name is erroneously printed on the sheet music as "L. C. Foster."

Open Up Your Heart, words and music by Stuart Hamblein (1953). A popular song with religious overtones, successfully recorded in 1955 by the Cowboy Church Sunday School for Decca.

Opera Rag, words and music by Irving Berlin (1910). Introduced by May Irwin in the musical *Getting a Polish* (1910).

Orange Blossom Special, words and music by Ervin T. Rouse (1964). Popularized by Johnny Cash in a Columbia recording.

Orange Colored Sky, words and music by Willie Stein and Milton De Lugg (1950). Introduced by Milton De Lugg and his orchestra on Jerry Lester's television program in 1950. The song was popularized by Nat King Cole and Stan Kenton's orchestra in a Capitol recording.

Orange Grove in California, words and music by Irving Berlin (1923). Introduced by Grace Moore and John Steel in the *Music Box Revue of 1923*. This was one of several songs with which Grace Moore made her Broadway debut. Robert Baral wrote: "Grace Moore and John Steel sang in the midst of a California grove, soon dissolved into a festive glow of incandescent orange-colored lights which climbed all over the stage while orange scent sprayed the audience. It was pure novelty of the highest order."

Orchids in the Moonlight, words by Gus Kahn and Edward Eliscu, music by Vincent Youmans (1933). Introduced by Fred Astaire and Ginger Rogers in their first screen musical, *Flying Down to Rio* (RKO, 1933). This score was Youmans' first for motion pictures.

Ordinary People, words and music by Richard Adler (1961). Introduced by Sally Ann Howes and Terry Carter in the musical play *Kwamina* (1961).

The Organ Grinder's Song, words by Mitchell Parish and Irving Mills, music by Will Hudson (1936).

"Oscar" Awards. *See:* Academy of Motion Picture Arts and Sciences Awards.

The Other Side of Me, words by Jack Lawrence, music by Stan Freeman (1964). Introduced by Richard Kiley in the musical *I Had a Ball* (1964).

The Other Side of the Tracks, words by Carolyn Leigh, music by Cy Coleman (1962). Introduced by Virginia Martin in the musical *Little Me* (1962).

Oui, Oui, Marie, words by Alfred Bryan and Joe McCarthy, music by Fred Fisher (1918). Comedy song of World War I inspired by the doughboys' experiences in France with mademoiselles. It was interpolated in the musical *Kissing Time* (1920). Twenty-two years later the song served as the inspiration for a comedy sketch starring Bobby Clark in the Broadway revue *Star and Garter* (1942). The number was sung by Betty Grable in the motion-picture musical *When My Baby Smiles at Me* (20th Century-Fox, 1948); it was also heard in the motion picture *What Price Glory?* (20th Century-Fox, 1952), sung in French by Corinne Calvet and in English by a male chorus.

Our Country, May She Always Be Right, words and music by Paul Dresser (1898). Patriotic hit song inspired by the Spanish-American War.

Our Lady of Fatima, words and music by Gladys Gollahon (1950). Popularized by Kitty Kallen in a Mercury recording.

Our Little Love Nest, words by P. G. Wodehouse, music by Jerome Kern (1918). Introduced by Edward Abeles and Florence Shirley in the Princess

Theatre production of *Oh, Lady, Lady!* (1918).

Our Love, words and music by Larry Clinton, Buddy Bernier and Bob Emmerich, melody adapted from a theme from Tchaikovsky's *Romeo and Juliet* (1939). Introduced and popularized by Larry Clinton and his orchestra.

Our Love Affair. *See:* An Affair to Remember.

Our Love Is Here to Stay, words by Ira Gershwin, music by George Gershwin (1938). The last piece of music written by George Gershwin. It was introduced by Kenny Baker in the motion-picture musical *The Goldwyn Follies* (United Artists, 1938). Gene Kelly and Leslie Caron sang it in the motion-picture musical *An American in Paris* (MGM, 1951).

Since the song had been left unfinished by George Gershwin's death in 1937, it had to be completed by Vernon Duke. Duke recalls: "All that could be found of 'Our Love Is Here to Stay' was a twenty-bar incomplete lead sheet; fortunately, Oscar Levant remembered the harmonies from George's frequent piano performances of the song and I was able faithfully to reconstruct it."

The Outcast Unknown, words and music by Paul Dresser (1887). It became a staple in Chauncey Olcott's repertory.

Out of My Dreams, words by Oscar Hammerstein II, music by Richard Rodgers (1943). Introduced by Joan Roberts and chorus in the musical play *Oklahoma!* (1943). The music was later used in the production as a background for a ballet sequence starring Katharine Sergava, Marc Platt, George Church and Bambi Linn. In the motion-picture adaptation of the musical (Magna Theatre, 1955), the number was sung by Shirley Jones and chorus.

Out of Nowhere, words by Edward Heyman, music by John Green (1931). Published as an independent number, and introduced by Guy Lombardo and his Royal Canadians. In a Decca release, this song became Bing Crosby's first hit recording as a solo vocalist. The song was featured in the motion picture *Dude Ranch,* starring Jack Oakie (Paramount, 1931). It enjoyed a highly successful revival in the 1940s, after being reintroduced in the non-musical motion picture *You Came Along,* starring Robert Cummings and Lizabeth Scott (Paramount, 1945).

Out of This World, a musical comedy with book by Dwight Taylor and Reginald Lawrence based on the Amphitryon legend. Lyrics and music by Cole Porter. Starring Charlotte Greenwood (1950).

See: From This Moment On; I Am Loved; Use Your Imagination.

Outside of Heaven, words by Sammy Gallop, music by Chester Conn (1952). Popularized by Eddie Fisher in an RCA Victor recording.

Overnight, words by Billy Rose and Charlotte Kent, music by Louis Alter (1930). Introduced by Fanny Brice in the revue *Sweet and Low* (1930). The song later became a hit number in Helen Morgan's night-club repertory.

Over the Rainbow, words by E. Y. Harburg, music by Harold Arlen (1939). Introduced by Judy Garland (then fourteen years old) in the motion-picture extravaganza *The Wizard of Oz* (MGM, 1939). From then on, it became her theme song. It received the Academy Award.

In an interview Judy Garland revealed: "When I first met Harold . . . the first song for the score *The Wizard of Oz* they played for me was 'Over the Rainbow.' I was terribly impressed by Mr. Arlen's genius and very much in awe of him. . . . It has become a part of my life. . . . I have sung it time and time again, and it's still the song that's closest to my heart."

In his biography of Arlen, Edward Jablonski revealed that this song came to Arlen "out of the blue." Jablonski continues: "He and Naya [Arlen's wife] had decided to drive to a movie at Graumann's Chinese Theatre. . . . They had reached the spot where the original Schwab's Drug Store was . . . when the 'broad, long-lined melody' came to Arlen; he jotted it down in the car. The next day he wrote the middle—the bridge—and the song was ready for Harburg to hear."

Arlen played it for Harburg in a slow tempo and with a rich harmonization, and Harburg did not like it. "That's for Nelson Eddy," Harburg told Arlen, "and not for a little girl in Kansas." Arlen then played the song for Ira Gershwin, who suggested a quicker tempo and a thinner harmonic texture. That did the trick. Harburg was now delighted, titled the song "Over the Rainbow" and wrote an exceptional set of lyrics.

There was not much enthusiasm for the song at the MGM studios. Three times there were attempts to delete the song from the picture. Each time the producer, Arthur Freed, stormed into the office and insisted that it be restored.

This was one of sixteen songs selected by ASCAP for its all-time Hit Parade in 1963 during its half century of existence. Irving Berlin singled it out as his favorite Harold Arlen song in *Show* magazine, in August, 1964. "I could give you many reasons for liking this wonderful song," wrote Berlin, "but they would be personal, and the opinion of a songwriter, so my best reason is that it is his most popular song—most people like it above the others, and who am I to disagree with that many people?"

The number was interpolated in the non-musical motion picture *A Patch of Blue*, starring Sidney Poitier and Shelley Winters (MGM, 1965), hummed by Elizabeth Hartman.

Over There, words and music by George M. Cohan (1917). One of America's greatest war songs, and one with which World War I is always identified.

George M. Cohan was at his home in Great Neck, Long Island, on the morning of April 6, 1917, when he read in the papers that America had declared war on Germany. "I read those war headlines," he later

revealed, "and I got to thinking and humming to myself—and for a minute I thought I was going to dance. I was all finished with the chorus and the verse by the time I got to town, and I also had a title." The opening phrase of his verse, "Johnny, get your gun," was borrowed from the title of an American popular song published in 1886.

George M. Cohan tried out his song at Fort Myers, near Washington, D. C., where he had come to entertain the troops; the reaction of the soldiers was for the most part apathetic. The first public performance of "Over There" took place at the Hippodrome Theatre in New York at a Red Cross benefit, in the fall of 1917; it was sung by Charles King. It now proved a major success. But it was Nora Bayes, in her vaudeville act, who was first responsible for making the song into a hit of fabulous proportions. Leo Feist bought the publishing rights for $25,000 and found he had made a gilt-edge investment. Within a few months of publication four hundred thousand copies of sheet music were sold; this figure passed the two-million mark by the end of the war. Over a million disks were sold; some of these were in recordings by such world-renowned opera stars as Enrico Caruso and Ernestine Schumann-Heink. President Wilson described the song as "a genuine inspiration to all American manhood." A quarter of a century later Congress authorized President Franklin Delano Roosevelt to present Cohan with the Congressional Medal of Honor "in belated recognition of his authorship of 'Over There' and 'You're a Grand Old Flag.'"

In *From Vaude to Video*, Abel Green and Joe Laurie, Jr., provide an amusing and paradoxical footnote to the history of "Over There." Practically everybody in the United States knew the words and music of "Over There" during World War I. Yet George M. Cohan himself had forgotten the lyrics when he was called upon to sing the number at a charity concert at Ebling's Casino in New York. While he was fumbling for one of the lines, Irving Berlin and Joe Laurie, Jr., jumped up from their seats in the audience, mounted the stage and helped him out with the performance.

The song was interpolated in several motion pictures with a World War I background. These included *The Cockeyed World*, starring Victor McLaglen and Edmund Lowe (Fox, 1929); *For Me and My Gal* (MGM, 1942); *Tin Pan Alley* (20th Century-Fox, 1943); and *What Price Glory?* (20th Century-Fox, 1952). The song was also interpolated in George M. Cohan's screen biography *Yankee Doodle Dandy* (Warner, 1942).

Cohan wrote a sequel to "Over There" in 1918. He called it "When You Come Back and You Will Come Back." It was a failure.

P

Pack Up Your Sins, words and music by Irving Berlin (1922). Introduced by the McCarthy Sisters in the first-act finale, "Satan's Palace," of the *Music Box Revue of 1922.*

Paddy Duffy's Cart, words by Edward Harrigan, music by David Braham (1881). Introduced in the Harrigan and Hart extravaganza *Squatter Sovereignty* (1881).

Padre, a French popular song, music by Alain Romans, English lyrics by Paul Francis Webster (1957). The song, with English lyrics, was introduced by Lola Dee in a Mercury recording, then popularized by Tony Arden.

Pagan Love Song, words by Arthur Freed, music by Nacio Herb Brown (1929). Theme song of the motion picture *The Pagan* (MGM, 1929), introduced by Ramon Novarro. It was one of the numbers in Bob Hope's act when he made his debut in vaudeville in New York at Proctor's 86th Street in 1929. He sang it straight and, as *Variety* noted, sang it well. "Pagan Love Song" gave the title to a motion picture starring Esther Williams and Howard Keel (MGM, 1950), sung by Esther Williams.

Painted, Tainted Rose, words and music by Peter de Angelis and Jean Sawyer (1963). Popularized by Al Martino in a best-selling Capitol recording.

Painting the Clouds with Sunshine, words by Al Dubin, music by Joe Burke (1929). Introduced in the motion-picture musical *Gold Diggers of Broadway* (Warner, 1929), and interpolated the same year in the motion-picture musical *Little Johnny Jones* (First National). It provided the title for a motion picture starring Dennis Morgan and Virginia Mayo (Warner, 1951), sung by Lucille Norman and Dennis Morgan.

Painting the Clouds with Sunshine, a motion-picture musical starring Dennis Morgan and Virginia Mayo (Warner, 1951). The score was made up of standards.

See: Birth of the Blues; Painting the Clouds with Sunshine; Someone Will Make You Smile; Tip Toe Through the Tulips; With a Song in My Heart; You're My Everything.

Paint Your Wagon, a musical comedy with book and lyrics by Alan Jay Lerner. Music by Frederick Loewe. Starring James Barton, Olga San Juan and Tony Bavaar. Original cast recording (RCA Victor).

See: Another Autumn; How Can I Wait?; I Talk to the Trees; I Still See Elisa; They Called the Wind Maria; Wand'rin' Star.

The Pajama Game, a musical comedy with book by George Abbott and Richard Bissell based on Bissell's novel 7½¢. Lyrics and music by Richard Adler and Jerry Ross. Starring John Raitt, Carol Haney (in her Broadway musical-comedy debut), Janis Paige and Eddie Foy, Jr. (1954). Original cast recording (Columbia).

The motion-picture adaptation of the musical starred Doris Day with most of the members of the original stage cast (Warner, 1957). The basic stage score was used. Soundtrack recording (Columbia).

See: Hernando's Hideaway; Hey, There; Steam Heat; There Once Was a Man.

The Pale Face, a motion-picture musical starring Bob Hope and Jane Russell (Paramount, 1948). Songs by Ray Evans and Jay Livingston, and others.

See: Buttons and Bows.

Palesteena (or, Lena Is the Queen of Palesteena), words by J. Russel Robinson, music by Con Conrad (1920). Written for, and introduced and popularized by, Eddie Cantor.

Palisades Park, words and music by Chuck Barris (1962). Popularized by Freddie Cannon in a Swan recording.

Pal Joey, a musical comedy with book by John O'Hara based on his short stories. Lyrics by Lorenz Hart. Music by Richard Rodgers. Starring Gene Kelly, Vivienne Segal and June Havoc (1940).

The motion-picture adaptation starred Rita Hayworth, Frank Sinatra and Kim Novak (Columbia, 1957). The principal songs from the stage score were used, with interpolations of several numbers from other Rodgers and Hart musicals. Soundtrack recording (Capitol).

See: Bewitched, Bothered and Bewildered; I Could Write a Book; I Didn't Know What Time It Was; The Lady Is a Tramp; My Funny Valentine; There's a Small Hotel; Where's that Rainbow?

Panama Hattie, a musical comedy with book by Bud De Sylva and Herbert Fields. Lyrics and music by Cole Porter. Starring Ethel Merman and James Dunn (1940).

The motion-picture adaptation starred Ann Sheridan and Red Skelton (MGM, 1942). It used only

two songs from the stage production, with other songs contributed by E. Y. Harburg and Burton Lane, and E. Y. Harburg and Walter Donaldson, among others.

See: Let's Be Buddies; Make It Another Old Fashioned; My Mother Would Love You.

Papa Loves Mambo, words by Al Hoffman, Dick Manning and Bix Reichner (1954). Popularized in an RCA Victor recording by Perry Como.

Papa, Won't You Dance with Me?, words by Sammy Cahn, music by Jule Styne (1947). A polka introduced by Nanette Fabray and Jack McCauley in the musical *High Button Shoes* (1947).

Paper Doll, words and music by Johnny S. Black (1942). Written twelve years before publication. It was interpolated in the motion picture *Hi Good Lookin'*, starring Harriet Hilliard (Universal, 1944). The Mills Brothers recording for Decca in 1948 sold a million disks.

Parade of the Wooden Soldiers, words by Ballard MacDonald, music by Leon Jessel (1922). Introduced in the *Chauve Souris* (1922), a Russian revue imported to Broadway from Paris. It originated as a German instrumental, *Die Parade der Holzsoldaten,* published in 1911.

Paradise, words and music by Gordon Clifford and Nacio Herb Brown (1931). A waltz, theme song of the non-musical motion picture *A Woman Commands,* starring Pola Negri (MGM, 1932). Belita sang it in the cabaret scene in the non-musical motion picture *The Gangster,* starring Barry Sullivan (Monogram, 1947). It was sung by Gloria Grahame in the non-musical motion picture *A Woman's Secret,* starring Melvyn Douglas and Maureen O'Hara (1949), and by Valentina Cortesa in the non-musical motion picture *Malaya,* starring Spencer Tracy and James Stewart (MGM, 1949).

The Pardon Came Too Late, words and music by Paul Dresser (1891).

Pardon My English, a musical comedy with book by Herbert Fields. Lyrics by Ira Gershwin. Music by George

Gershwin. This was the last musical comedy by George and Ira Gershwin. Starring Jack Pearl and Lyda Roberti (1933).

See: Isn't It a Pity?; The Lorelei.

Paree (What Did You Do to Me?), words and music by Cole Porter (1929). Introduced by Jack Thompson and Betty Compton in the musical *Fifty Million Frenchmen* (1929). The song was also heard in the motion-picture adaptation of the musical (Warner, 1931).

Paris, a musical comedy with book by Martin Brown. Lyrics and music by Cole Porter. This was Porter's first successful musical comedy. Starring Irene Bordoni (1928).

The motion-picture adaptation starred Irene Bordoni (First National, 1930). It dispensed completely with the stage score. New numbers were contributed by Al Bryan and Ed Ward. "Among My Souvenirs," by Edgar Leslie and Horatio Nicholls, was interpolated.

See: Among My Souvenirs; Let's Do It; Let's Misbehave; Two Little Babes in the Wood.

Parish, Mitchell, lyricist, born Shreveport, Louisiana, 1900.

See: Anderson, Leroy; Carmichael, Hoagy; De Rose, Peter.

See also: All My Love; Does Your Heart Beat for Me?; Dream, Dream, Dream; Hands Across the Table; Moonlight Love; Riverboat Shuffle; Ruby; Sophisticated Lady; Stars Fell on Alabama; Volare; Tzena, Tzena.

A Parisian Model, a musical comedy with book and lyrics by Harry B. Smith. Music by Max Hoffman. Additional songs by Will D. Cobb and Gus Edwards. Starring Anna Held (1906).

See: I'd Like to See a Little More of You; I Just Can't Make My Eyes Behave.

Paris in the Spring, words by Mack Gordon, music by Harry Revel (1935). Introduced in the motion picture of the same name starring Mary Ellis and Tullio Carminati (Paramount, 1935). It was then interpolated in the non-musical motion picture *The Princess Comes Across,* starring Carole Lombard and Fred MacMurray (Paramount, 1936).

Paris Loves Lovers, words and music by Cole Porter (1955). Introduced by Don Ameche and Hildegarde Neff in the musical *Silk Stockings* (1955). In the motion-picture adaptation of the musical (MGM, 1957), it was sung by Fred Astaire.

Paris, Stay the Same, words by Clifford Grey, music by Victor Schertzinger (1929). Introduced by Maurice Chevalier in the motion-picture musical *The Love Parade* (Paramount, 1929).

Paris Wakes Up and Smiles, words and music by Irving Berlin (1949). A Parisian lamplighter's hymn to his city, introduced by Johnny Thompson in the musical *Miss Liberty* (1949).

Parlez Moi d'Amour (Speak to Me of Love), a French popular song, music by Jean Lenoir, English lyrics by Bruce Siever (1932). The French song was introduced and popularized by Lucienne Boyer. A parody by Vandy Cape has become popular.

Party Doll, words and music by Jimmy Bowen and Buddy Knox (1957). Popularized in recordings by Buddy Knox for Roulette and by Steve Lawrence for Coral.

The Party's Over, words by Betty Comden and Adoph Green, music by Jule Styne (1956). Introduced by Judy Holliday in the musical *Bells Are Ringing* (1956). She also sang it in the motion-picture adaptation of the musical (MGM, 1960).

The Passing Show, an annual revue produced by the Shuberts at the Winter Garden in New York. The first edition (1912) had a book by Bronson Howard, lyrics by Harold Atteridge and music by Louis A. Hirsch. Willie and Eugene Howard, Jobyna Howland and Harry Fox were starred.

The Passing Show was produced annually until 1924. Sigmund Romberg wrote the music (to Atteridge's lyrics) for the editions of 1914, 1916, 1917, 1918, 1923 and 1924. Jean Schwartz wrote the scores for 1913 and 1921 (lyrics by Atteridge), while Irving Berlin did the score in 1912. Among the stars appearing in the various editions were Fred and Adele Astaire, the Avon Comedy Four, James Barton, Bessie Clayton, Irene Franklin, De Wolf Hopper, Marie Dressler, Willie and Eugene Howard, George Jessel, Marilyn Miller and Ed Wynn.

See: By the Beautiful Sea; Goodbye, Broadway, Hello, France; I'm Forever Blowing Bubbles; The Making of a Girl; Pretty Baby; Ragtime Jockey Man; Smiles; That Mysterious Rag; The Trail of the Lonesome Pine.

Pass Me By, words by Carolyn Leigh, music by Cy Coleman (1964). Introduced in the non-musical motion picture *Father Goose,* starring Cary Grant (Universal, 1964), sung on the soundtrack under the titles by Digby Wolfe. It was popularized by Peggy Lee in a Capitol recording.

Pass That Peace Pipe, words and music by Roger Edens, Ralph Blane and Hugh Martin (1943). Introduced by Joan McCracken in the motion-picture adaptation of the musical *Good News* (MGM, 1947).

Patricia (It's Patricia), words and music by Perez Prado (1958). Popularized in an RCA Victor recording by Perez Prado and his orchestra that sold a million disks and received the Gold Record Award.

The Peanut Vendor, words by L. Wolfe Gilbert and Marion Sunshine, music adapted by Moises Simons from the Latin-American popular song "El Mansiero" (1931). With English lyrics, it first became famous in the United States in an RCA Victor recording by Paul Whiteman and his orchestra. It was then further popularized by Guy Lombardo and his Royal Canadians (probably the first time that this orchestra performed a Latin-American tune). It was also performed successfully by Xavier Cugat and his orchestra. It was interpolated in the motion picture *Luxury Liner,* starring George Brent (MGM, 1948), and in the motion-picture musical *A Star Is Born* (Warner, 1953).

Peggy Ann, a musical comedy with book by Herbert Fields based on

Edgar Smith's *Tillie's Nightmare.* Lyrics by Lorenz Hart. Music by Richard Rodgers. Starring Helen Ford and Lester Cole (1926).

See: A Tree in the Park; Where's That Rainbow?

Peggy O'Neil, words and music by Harry Pease, Ed G. Nelson and Gilbert Dodge (1921). A slow waltz popularized in vaudeville in the early 1920s. It then became a favorite at community sings. Sigmund Spaeth explained: "It is also possible to sing a fast patter on the repeated chorus, very popular with service clubs."

Peggy Sue, words by Jerry Allison, Buddy Holly and Norman Petty (1957). Popularized in 1958 by Buddy Holly in a Coral recording.

Peg o' My Heart, words by Alfred Bryan, music by Fred Fisher (1913). Introduced by José Collins (imported from the London stage) in the *Ziegfeld Follies of 1913,* where it was an interpolation. The song was inspired by the successful Broadway stage comedy of the same name by J. Hartley Manners, produced in 1912; it starred Laurette Taylor, to whom the song was dedicated. The song provided the title for and was featured in a motion picture starring Marion Davies (MGM, 1933). It was also interpolated in the Fred Fisher screen biography *Oh, You Beautiful Doll* (20th Century-Fox, 1949). A recording by the Harmonicats for Mercury in 1947 sold a million disks; Peggy Lee's recording for Capitol was also a best seller.

Pennies from Heaven, words by Johnny Burke, music by Arthur Johnston (1936). Introduced by Bing Crosby in the motion-picture musical of the same name (Paramount, 1936), and further popularized by him in a Decca recording. Dick Haymes sang it in the motion-picture musical *Cruisin' Down the River* (Columbia, 1953). It was also interpolated in the non-musical motion picture *From Here to Eternity,* starring Montgomery Clift and Deborah Kerr (Columbia, 1954), and as an orchestral episode in the non-musical motion picture *Picnic*, starring Kim Novak and William Holden (Columbia, 1956).

Pennies from Heaven, a motion-picture musical starring Bing Crosby and Madge Evans (Columbia, 1936). Songs by Johnny Burke and Arthur Johnston.

See: One, Two, Button My Shoe; Pennies from Heaven; So Do I.

A Penny a Kiss, A Penny a Hug, words and music by Buddy Kaye and Ralph Care (1950). Popularized by Tony Martin and Dinah Shore in an RCA Victor recording.

People, words by Bob Merrill, music by Jule Styne (1964). Introduced by Barbra Streisand in the musical *Funny Girl* (1964), and further popularized by her in a best-selling recording for Capitol which received a "Grammy" from the National Academy of Recording Arts and Sciences.

People Will Say We're in Love, words by Oscar Hammerstein II, music by Richard Rodgers (1943). Introduced by Alfred Drake and Joan Roberts in the musical play *Oklahoma!* (1943). In the motion-picture adaptation of the musical (Magna Theatre, 1955), it was sung by Gordon MacRae and Shirley Jones.

This is the only song in *Oklahoma!* where the melody came before the lyric. Rodgers and Hammerstein discussed the kind of love song the play required. Having come upon the proper feeling and mood for his music, Rodgers went to work without waiting for Hammerstein's lyric. The song posed a problem to its creators. Though it was to be a love duet in the first act, it could not follow the customary pattern of love songs. The reason for this is that though the two main characters are in love with each other, antagonism and hostility mar their relationship. In addition, the heroine is too shy to confess the true state of her feelings. Consequently she and the hero seem incapable of speaking to one another without sooner or later lapsing into a quarrel. Rodgers and Hammerstein finally decided that the only kind of love song they could write under the circumstances was one in which the hero and heroine cautioned one another against any outward signs which outsiders might interpret as love gestures; yet beneath this warning there flowed a strong undercurrent of genuine tenderness.

Pepe, a motion-picture musical starring Cantinflas, Shirley Jones, Dan Dailey and numerous guest stars (Columbia, 1960). Songs by Dory Langdon and André Previn.

See: Faraway; That's How It Went All Right.

The Peppermint Twist, words and music by Joey Dee and Henry Glover (1961). Popularized by Joey Dee and the Starliters in a Roulette recording, and interpolated in the motion-picture musical *Hey, Let's Twist* (Paramount, 1961).

A Perfect Day, words and music by Carrie Jacobs Bond (1910). Though essentially an art song, it has entered the popular-song repertory by virtue of frequent performances in vaudeville. This is one of the most successful songs written by an American. After being introduced as an encore in a song recital in New York by David Bispham, it went on to invade the concert hall, vaudeville and every other medium of stage and musical entertainment. It was heard at weddings and funerals, in barrooms and churches, in soldiers' camps. The sheet-music sale passed the five-million mark.

The Perfect Song, words by Clarence Lucas, music by James Carl Breil (1915). Inspired by the silent motion-picture classic, D. W. Griffith's *The Birth of a Nation*. It was often heard in motion-picture theaters throughout the country in 1915 as part of the background music to this film. When Amos 'n Andy went on the air in 1928 as radio stars, they revived this melody and used it as their signature.

Personality, words and music by Harold Logan and Lloyd Price (1959). Popularized by Lloyd Price in an ABC–Paramount recording.

Personality, words by Johnny Burke, music by James Van Heusen (1945).

Introduced by Dorothy Lamour in the motion-picture musical *The Road to Utopia* (Paramount, 1945). It was popularized by Johnny Mercer in a Capitol recording—a rare instance in which one songwriter helps make a hit for a competitor. Some of this song's success was due to its provocative double-entendres, which, say Barry Ulanov, is "a neat example of the extent to which bawdy verbal humor could be introduced into a film within the canon of the producing code authority."

Pete Kelly's Blues, words by Sammy Cahn, music by Ray Heindorf (1955). Title song of a motion picture starring Jack Webb and Janet Leigh (Warner, 1955), introduced by Ella Fitzgerald.

Peter Cottontail, words by Steve Nelson, music by Jack Rollins (1950). An Easter song popularized by Gene Autry in a best-selling Columbia recording.

Piantadosi, Al, composer, born New York City, 1884; died Encino, California, 1955.
See: Baby Shoes; The Curse of an Aching Heart; I Didn't Raise My Boy to Be a Soldier; My Mariuccia Take a Steamboat; Send Me Away with a Smile.

The Piccolino, words and music by Irving Berlin (1935). Introduced by Fred Astaire and Ginger Rogers in the motion-picture musical *Top Hat* (RKO, 1935).

Picnic, words by Steve Allen, music by George W. Dunning (1955). Theme song of a non-musical motion picture starring Kim Novak and William Holden (Columbia, 1956). Morris Stoloff's Decca recording in 1956 sold a million disks.

Picture Eighty-Four (84), words by Charles B. Ward, music by Gussie Davis (1894). A successful sentimental ballad inspired by an actual occurrence: Gussie Davis and a girl friend were shown, by a Boston policeman, several pictures from the Rogues Gallery; the girl fainted, recognizing one of them as that of her own father.

Picture Me Without You, words by Ted Koehler, music by Jimmy McHugh (1936). Introduced by Shirley Temple in the motion-picture musical *Dimples* (20th Century-Fox, 1936).

A Picture of Me Without You, words and music by Cole Porter (1935). Introduced by June Knight and Charles Walters in the musical *Jubilee* (1935).

The Picture That Is Turned Toward the Wall, words and music by Charles Graham (1891). Graham's greatest hit song. It was suggested to him by a scene in Joseph Arthur's melodrama *Blue Jeans,* in which a farmer turns the picture of his wayward daughter to the wall. The publishing house of Witmark paid Graham $15 for his song. Andrew Mack, an Irish actor and tenor, found the sheet music of Graham's song at Witmark's. He introduced it in 1891 in the play *The City Directory* at the Bijou Theatre in New York. Later on, Julius Witmark —a successful performer, as well as publisher, who often did yeoman service in plugging Witmark songs —incorporated the ballad into his act, singing it to popularity from coast to coast. The formidable sheet-music sale that followed transformed a minor publishing venture into a major one. As Isidore Witmark noted in his autobiography, this number "was more than a financial success for the Witmarks. It brought them a coveted prestige. Formerly they had sold sheet music by the hundreds of copies; now they knew sales in the thousands. . . . Jobbers who scorned to deal with 'children' were camping on their doorsteps for copies. Dealers who had refused them displays now buried other songs beneath 'The Picture.' Singers whom they had been obliged to chase, now chased them."

Frank Toussey, a competing songwriter, tried to capitalize on Graham's success by writing "The Picture with Its Face Turned Toward the Wall." It was a failure, as was Graham's own sequel, "Dear Father Has Turned the Dear Picture Again."

The ballad was revived by June Haver in the motion-picture musical *The Daughter of Rosie O'Grady* (Warner, 1950).

Pillow Talk, words and music by Buddy Pepper and Inez James (1959). Introduced by Doris Day and Rock Hudson in the non-musical motion picture of the same name (Universal, 1959).

Pine Cones and Holly Berries, words and music by Meredith Willson (1963). A Christmas song introduced by Laurence Naismith, Janis Paige and Fred Gwynne in the musical *Here's Love* (1963). This number was selected in 1963 as the official song of the Christmas Seal drive.

Pink Champagne, words and music by Joe Liggins (1950). Popularized by Joe Liggins in a Specialty recording.

The Pink Lady, an operetta with book and lyrics by Harry Morton, using the pen name of C.M.S. McLellan, adapted from a French farce. Music by Ivan Caryll. Starring Hazel Dawn, William Elliott and Alice Dovey (1911).

See: By the Saskatchewan; Kiss Waltz; My Beautiful Lady.

Pink Shoelaces, words and music by Mickie Grant (1958). Popularized by Dodie Stevens in a Crystalette recording.

Pinocchio, a full-length animated cartoon produced by Walt Disney (RKO, 1940). Songs by Ned Washington and Leigh Harline.

See: When You Wish Upon a Star.

Pins and Needles, amateur political revue with book by various authors. Lyrics and music by Harold Rome. This was Harold Rome's first Broadway score. The cast was made up of members of the International Ladies Garment Workers Union. It had the longest run of any musical production on Broadway up to that time, 1108 performances (1937).

See: Mene, Mene, Tekel; Nobody Makes a Pass at Me; Sing Me a Song of Social Significance; Sunday in the Park.

Pipe Dream, a musical play with book by Oscar Hammerstein II based on John Steinbeck's novel *Sweet Thursday.* Lyrics by Hammerstein. Music by Richard Rodgers. Starring Judy Tyler, Helen Traubel and William Johnson (1955).

See: All at Once You Love Her; Everybody's Got a Home But Me.

The Pirate, a motion-picture musical starring Judy Garland and Gene Kelly (MGM, 1948). Songs by Cole Porter.

See: Be a Clown; Love of My Life; You Can Do No Wrong.

Pistol Packin' Mama, words and music by Al Dexter (1943). Introduced by Al Dexter and his Troopers in an Okeh recording, and popularized by Bing Crosby and the Andrews Sisters in a Decca recording that sold over a million disks. The song provided the title for and was featured in a motion picture starring Ruth Terry (Republic, 1943).

Pittsburgh, Pennsylvania, words and music by Bob Merrill (1952). Popularized by Guy Mitchell, with Mitch Miller and his orchestra, in a best-selling Columbia recording.

Plain and Fancy, a musical comedy with book by Joseph Stein and William Glickman suggested by a play by Marion Weaver. Lyrics by Arnold B. Horwitt. Music by Albert Hague. Starring Richard Deer, Shirl Conway and David Daniels (1955). Original cast recording (Capitol).

See: Plain We Live; Young and Foolish.

Plain We Live, words by Arnold B. Horwitt, music by Albert Hague (1955). The philosophy of the Amish people as expounded in the musical *Plain and Fancy* (1955), introduced by Stefan Schnabel and ensemble.

Play a Simple Melody, words and music by Irving Berlin (1914). Introduced by Sallie Fisher and Charles King in Irving Berlin's first musical for which he wrote the entire score, *Watch Your Step* (1914). This number is one of Berlin's—and one of Tin Pan Alley's—earliest successful attempts to combine two melodies contrapuntally, the chorus boasting an intriguing countermelody with its own lyrics. The song was revived in 1950 in a Decca recording by Bing and Gary Crosby (the label reading "Gary Crosby and a friend"); this release sold over a million disks. It was again revived by Ethel Merman and Dan Dailey in the motion-picture musical *There's No Business Like Show Business* (20th Century-Fox, 1954).

Play, Fiddle, Play, words by Jack Lawrence, music by Emery Deutsch and Arthur Altman (1932). Popularized by Emery Deutsch, gypsy violinist; it was his radio theme song with the A. & P. Gypsies.

Play, Gypsies, Dance, Gypsies, words by Harry B. Smith, music by Emmerich Kalman (1926). Introduced by Walter Woolf in the operetta *Countess Maritza* (1926).

Playmates, words and music by Harry Dacre (1889). Popularized by Eddie Leonard, the last of the great minstrels.

Play Me Hearts and Flowers (I Wanna Cry), words by Mann Curtis, music by Sanford Green (1955). Introduced by Johnny Desmond in a television dramatic production of the same name (1955).

Play That Barber Shop Chord, words by William Tracey, music by Lewis F. Muir (1910). Muir himself confessed that he had adapted his melody from an earlier published number called "Play That Fandango Rag." "Play That Barber Shop Chord" was introduced in 1910 by Bert Williams at Hammerstein's Victoria Theatre in New York, where it scored a major success. Bert Williams then included it in his act when he made his debut in the *Ziegfeld Follies*—the edition of 1910. The song subsequently became a favorite of barber-shop quartets.

This number became involved in a legal suit. Originally, Ballard MacDonald had been asked to write the lyrics, but he never completed the assignment. Muir then brought in William Tracey to do the job. After the song had been made successful by Bert Williams, and achieved a large sheet-music sale, Ballard MacDonald came out with the claim

that he had written the lyrics. Under contract at the time to Edward B. Marks, MacDonald got his employer to sue J. Fred Helf, the publisher of the Muir song. Justice Joseph E. Newberger ruled that MacDonald was entitled to damages of $37,000. This proved such a financial blow to Helf that he had to go out of business—the first time, paradoxically, that a hit song was responsible for ruining a publishing house.

The song was revived in the motion-picture musical *In the Good Old Summertime* (MGM, 1949).

Play to Me, Gypsy, a popular Czech song, music by Karel Vacek, English lyrics by Jimmy Kennedy (1934). The song became a major success in the United States in 1934, selling about a million copies of sheet music.

Please, words by Leo Robin, music by Ralph Rainger (1932). This was one of the songs with which Bing Crosby made his debut in a full-length movie—*The Big Broadcast* (Paramount, 1932). This was also the song where his interpolation of "boo-boo-boo" first became popular. The song was sung by Jack Oakie in the non-musical motion picture *From Hell to Heaven,* starring Carole Lombard (Paramount, 1933).

Please Come and Play in My Yard, words by Edward Madden, music by Theodore F. Morse (1904).

Please Don't Talk About Me When I'm Gone, words by Sidney Clare, music by Sam H. Stept (1930). Popularized in vaudeville by Bea Palmer, and over the radio by Kate Smith, who featured it on her first CBS broadcast, May 1, 1931. It was sung by Patricia Neal in the non-musical motion picture *The Breaking Point* (Warner, 1950). It was also interpolated in the motion-picture musical *Lullaby of Broadway* (Warner, 1951).

Please Go 'Way and Let Me Sleep, words and music by Harry von Tilzer (1902). When the song was introduced—in vaudeville, by the minstrel Arthur Deming—Harry von Tilzer himself plugged it, and in a novel way. Seated in the audience, he pretended to be fast asleep; all the while he was disturbing the performance with loud snoring. When Deming seemingly took von Tilzer to task, the composer-publisher rose lazily from his seat and began singing the chorus of his song, emphasizing the line, "Please go 'way and let me sleep." The routine made a strong impression on audiences and inspired a good deal of publicity— factors which undoubtedly helped to stimulate the sale of the sheet music.

Please, Mr. Sun, words by Sid Frank, music by Ray Getzov (1951). Popularized in recordings by Tommy Edwards for MGM and Johnnie Ray for Columbia.

The Pleasure Seekers, words by Sammy Cahn, music by James Van Heusen (1964). Title song of a motion picture (20th Century-Fox, 1964), where it was introduced by Ann-Margret.

The Pleasure Seekers, a motion picture with songs, starring Carol Lynley, Pamela Tiffin, Ann-Margret and Tony Franciosa (20th Century-Fox, 1964). Songs by Sammy Cahn and James Van Heusen.

See: Everything Makes Music When You're in Love; The Pleasure Seekers.

Pocketful of Miracles, words by Sammy Cahn, music by James Van Heusen (1961). Title song of a motion picture starring Bette Davis (United Artists, 1961), sung on the soundtrack under the titles by Frank Sinatra.

Pockriss, Lee, composer, born New York City, 1924.

See: Calcutta; Catch a Falling Star; Itsy Bitsy Teenie Weenie Yellow Polka Dot Bikini; Johnny Angel; My Heart Is an Open Book; My Little Corner of the World; Starlight; What Is Love?

Poison Ivy, words and music by Jerry Leiber and Mike Stoller (1959). Popularized by the Coasters in an Atco recording.

Politics and Poker, words by Sheldon Harnick, music by Jerry Bock (1959). A satirical commentary on the basic similarity between the games of politics and poker. It was introduced by Howard da Silva and a male chorus in the musical *Fiorello!* (1959).

Polka Dots and Moonbeams, words by Johnny Burke, music by James Van Heusen (1939). Introduced and popularized in 1940 in an RCA Victor recording by Tommy Dorsey and his orchestra, with Frank Sinatra doing the vocal.

Pollack, Lew, composer and lyricist, born New York City, 1896; died Hollywood, California, 1946.

See: Rapee, Erno.

See (Lyrics by Jack Yellen): Sing, Baby, Sing; Yiddishe Momme.

See also: Seventh Heaven; Toy Trumpet; Two Cigarettes in the Dark; You Do the Darnd'st Things, Baby.

Polly Wolly Doodle, a nonsense song of unknown authorship. The precise date of composition or first publication is not known; one of its early appearances in print took place in the collection *Student Songs,* edited by William H. Hills (1880). The song was popularized by the eminent minstrel Billy Emerson. It then became a favorite of minstrel troupes all over the country.

Pony Time, words and music by Don Covay and John Berry (1961). Popularized by Chubby Checker in a Cameo recording.

Poor Butterfly, words by John Golden, music by Raymond Hubbell (1916). Introduced by Haru Onuki (a Chinese-American, *not* a Japanese) in the Hippodrome extravaganza *The Big Show*. It did not at first attract attention. Only after Haru Onuki was replaced in *The Big Show* by Sophie Bernard—and only after a good dance record had been released—did the song begin to take hold. It soon became one of the greatest hit songs of its time, selling several million copies of sheet music and over a million disks in various recordings. As John Golden noted in his autobiography: "Two months later the entire country was Butterfly-mad. 'Poor Butterfly' was strummed, hummed, whistled and wept over by as many voices and hands as there are pianos, ukuleles, typewriters and tenors in the land. I think I am safe in saying that T. B. Harms, the publishers, in all their experience, never had a bigger-selling song, and I know I never had one which made more money than 'Poor Butterfly,' "

The curious part about the history of "Poor Butterfly," from the time it was written to its final dissemination throughout the country, is that its birth was due for the most part to a misunderstanding. When John Golden was told that an Oriental singer would be the star of the projected *The Big Show*, he jumped to the conclusion that she would be the Japanese prima donna Tamaki Miura, who had recently attracted attention in the role of Madame Butterfly. With this misconception in mind, he went to work and wrote, as he recalled, "a lyric embodying the story of *Butterfly*, and excused my 'borrowing' by my opening line: 'There's a story told of a little Japanese, sitting demurely 'neath the cherry blossom trees, Miss Butterfly her name.' Of course, I also had to change the title somewhat, so the song became 'Poor Butterfly.' The next day I went straight to Hubbell. . . . Hubbell . . . [played] over and over a refrain to which I took a violent dislike from the beginning. 'It's good, I tell you,' Hubbell insisted." When Golden informed Hubbell he would use his tune for a Japanese song, the composer protested that his melody was in no way Oriental. But Golden was insistent, and Hubbell permitted his creation to become Japanese. Golden was considerably put out to discover that the one assigned to introduce his number was not the Japanese prima donna after all, but a Chinese-American performer; but by then it was too late for him to do anything about it.

Russ Columbo revived "Poor Butterfly" more than a quarter of a century after its first appearance, and made it one of his specialties. It was once again revived in 1963 by the Three Suns in an RCA Victor recording, a release in which Rimsky-Korsakov's *The Flight of the Bumble Bee* was used contrapuntally with the melody of "Poor Butterfly."

The Poor Little Country Maid. *See:* The Streets of Cairo.

Poor Little Fool, words and music by Shari Sheeley (1958). Popularized by Ricky Nelson in an Imperial recording.

Poor Little Rhode Island, words by Sammy Cahn, music by Jule Styne (1944). Published as an independent number, but interpolated in the motion-picture musical *Carolina Blues*, starring Kay Kyser and his orchestra (Columbia, 1944), sung by Ann Miller. It was then adopted by Rhode Island as an official state song.

Poor Pauline, words by Charles McCarron, music by Raymond Walker (1914). One of the earliest attempts in Tin Pan Alley to create a song based on a movie—the production being Pearl White's famous serial *The Perils of Pauline*. The song was revived more than thirty years after its first appearance in the motion picture *Perils of Pauline*, starring Constance Collier (Paramount, 1947), sung by Betty Hutton.

It might be of some interest to remark that this song was indirectly responsible for Fanny Brice's creation of her successful Baby Snooks routine. At a party for a number of friends she sang "Poor Pauline" the way a child might. The laughter of her audience impelled her to include the number, and its babylike presentation, in her vaudeville act in Detroit. She brought down the house. Later on she often used the routine as an encore. "After that," she later recalled, "I knew that this was a good character this way, and I decided I wouldn't use it again until I needed it." This proved to be the beginnings of the Baby Snooks idea, which she tried out first in vaudeville and then, years later, made the staple of her radio series.

The Poor People of Paris, a French popular song ("Le Goulante de Pauvre Jean"), with music by Marguerite Monnot and English lyrics by Jack Lawrence (1956). The

French number was introduced in France by Edith Piaf. The song was popularized in the United States by Les Baxter and his orchestra in a Capitol recording that sold a million disks.

Poor Pierrot, words by Otto Harbach, music by Jerome Kern (1931). Introduced in the musical *The Cat and the Fiddle* (1931). It was also sung in the motion-picture adaptation of the musical (MGM, 1934).

Poppy, a musical comedy with book and lyrics by Dorothy Donnelly and Irving Caesar. Music by Stephen Jones and Arthur Samuels. Starring W. C. Fields (1923).

The motion-picture adaptation starred W. C. Fields (Paramount, 1936). The stage score was dispensed with. New songs were contributed by Leo Robin and Ralph Rainger, among others.

See: Someone Will Make You Smile; What Do You Do Sundays, Mary?

Porgy and Bess, a folk opera with text by Du Bose Heyward based on the play *Porgy* by Dorothy and Du Bose Heyward. Lyrics by Du Bose Heyward and Ira Gershwin. Music by George Gershwin. Starring Todd Duncan and Anne Brown (1935). Original cast recording (Decca).

The motion-picture adaptation starred Sidney Poitier, Dorothy Dandridge, Diahann Carroll, Sammy Davis and Pearl Bailey (Columbia, 1959). Robert McFerrin sang on the soundtrack for Poitier; Adele Addison for Dorothy Dandridge; and Loulie Jean Norman for Diahann Carroll. The basic stage score was used. Soundtrack recording (Columbia).

See: Bess, You Is My Woman Now; I Got Plenty o' Nuthin'; I Loves You, Porgy; It Ain't Necessarily So; My Man's Gone Now; A Red Headed Woman Makes a Choo Choo Jump Its Track; Summertime; There's a Boat Dat's Leavin' Soon for New York; A Woman Is a Sometime Thing.

Porter, Cole, composer and lyricist, born Peru, Indiana, 1891; died Santa Monica, California, 1964.

See: Abracadabra; Allez Vous En; All of You; All Through the Night; Always True to You in My Fashion; Another Op'nin', Another Show; Anything Goes; Be a Clown; Begin the Beguine; Bingo Eli Yale; Blow, Gabriel, Blow; Bridget; Brush Up Your Shakespeare; Bull Dog; But in the Morning; By the Mississinewah; Ça, C'est Amour; C'est Magnifique; Come Along with Me; Do I Love You?; Don't Fence Me In; Down in the Depths; Easy to Love; Ev'rytime We Say Goodbye; Farewell, Amanda; Find Me a Primitive Man; Friendship; From Now On; From This Moment On; Get Out of Town; I Am Loved; I Concentrate on You; If You Cared for Me; I Get a Kick Out of You; I Hate Men; I Love You; I Love Paris; I'm in Love Again; I'm Unlucky at Gambling; In the Still of the Night; It's All Right with Me; Its De-Lovely; I've a Shooting Box in Scotland; I've Got My Eyes on You; I've Got You on My Mind; I've Got You Under My Skin; Just One of Those Things; Katie Went to Haiti; Let's Be Buddies; Let's Do It; Let's Misbehave; Let's Not Talk About Love; Live and Let Live; Love For Sale; Love of My Life; Make It Another Old-Fashioned, Please; Miss Otis Regrets; My Heart Belongs to Daddy; My Mother Would Love You; Night and Day; Old-Fashioned Garden; Paree, What You Do to Me; Paris Loves Lovers; A Picture of Me Without You; So in Love; There Must Be Someone for Me; True Love; Two Little Babes in the Woods; Use Your Imagination; Well, Did You Evah?; Were Thine That Special Face; What Is This Thing Called Love?; Where Have You Been?; Where Is the Life That Late I Led?; Why Can't You Behave?; Why Shouldn't I?; Wunderbar; You Can Do No Wrong; You'd Be So Nice to Come Home To; You Don't Know Paree; You Do Something to Me; You're the Top; You're Sensational; You've Got Something; You've Got That Thing.

For Cole Porter's screen biography, see *Night and Day* (Warner, 1946).

Potatoes Are Cheaper, Tomatoes Are Cheaper. *See:* Now's the Time to Fall in Love.

Poverty's Tears Ebb and Flow, words by Edward Harrigan, music by David Braham (1885). Sentimental ballad introduced in the Harrigan and Hart extravaganza *Old Lavender* (1885).

Powder Your Face with Sunshine, words by Stanley Rochinski, music by Carmen Lombardo (1948). Rochinski, a paraplegic, came to Carmen Lombardo's hotel room in a wheel chair, bringing with him the lyric. The title so fascinated Lombardo that he helped Rochinski polish up the lyric, and then set it to music. The song was introduced by Guy Lombardo and his Royal Canadians in Washington, D.C., and then was popularized by them. A successful recording was also made by Evelyn Knight and the Starlighters for Decca. The song was interpolated for Gene Autry in the motion picture *Cow Town* (Columbia, 1950).

Praise the Lord and Pass the Ammunition, words and music by Frank Loesser (1942). This was the first hit song for which Loesser wrote both the words and the music. (Up to 1942 he had confined himself mainly to lyrics.)

He wrote the lyrics of "Praise the Lord and Pass the Ammunition" soon after Pearl Harbor, stimulated by that tragedy and by America's declaration of war. As was habitual with him, he tried out his words with a dummy tune of his own concoction. When he sang it to his friends, they insisted that the melody had a winning folklike quality and urged him to retain it for the words. Loesser, therefore, published it with his own melody. It became the first major song hit of World War II. It sold over two million records and about a million copies of sheet music in 1942. The Columbia recording of Kay Kyser and his orchestra sold over a million disks. To prevent the song from being sung and played to death, the Office of War Information requested radio stations to limit its use to no more than once every four hours.

The words "praise the lord and pass the ammunition" have been attributed to the United States Navy Chaplain William Maguire, who was believed to have spoken them during the Japanese attack on Pearl Harbor.

A Precious Little Thing Called Love, words by Lou Davis, music by J. Fred Coots (1928). Selected from 150 songs submitted to Paramount studios for use as a theme song for the motion picture *A Shopworn Angel*, starring Gary Cooper (Paramount, 1929); it was sung by Nancy Carroll. The song was further popularized by George Olsen and his orchestra, with Olsen's wife, Ethel Shutta, doing the vocal.

Present Arms, a musical comedy with book by Herbert Fields. Lyrics by Lorenz Hart. Music by Richard Rodgers. Starring Flora Le Breton and Charles King (1928).

See: You Took Advantage of Me.

Pretend, words and music by Lew Douglas, Cliff Parman and Frank Lavere (1952). Popularized in bestselling recordings by Ralph Marterie for Mercury and by Nat King Cole for Capitol.

Pretend You Don't See Her, words and music by Steve Allen (1954). Popularized in 1957 by Jerry Vale in a Columbia recording.

Pretty As a Picture, words by George Cooper, music by T. Brigham Bishop (1872). First popularized in 1872 by the famous minstrel Billy Emerson; he used to perform it with a comic swagger between verses. In 1876 the French comic opera star Mlle. Aimée made a comic specialty of imitating Billy Emerson doing this number.

Pretty As a Picture, words by Robert B. Smith, music by Victor Herbert (1913). Choral number opening the second act of the operetta *Sweetheart* (1913); it was also sung in the motion-picture adaptation of the musical (MGM, 1938).

Herbert originally planned this number as a satire on the excessive use of cosmetics by females. But within the operetta it was changed into a sweet, sentimental song.

Pretty Baby, words by Gus Kahn, music by Tony Jackson and Egbert Van Alstyne (1916). Introduced by Dolly Hackett in *The Passing Show of 1916*. This was the first real hit to come out of any of the *Passing Shows*. The song was interpolated in many motion pictures. Among them were the non-musical motion picture *Ruggles of Red Gap*, starring Charles Laughton (Paramount, 1935); the Ted Lewis screen biography *Is Everybody Happy?* (Columbia, 1943); *Broadway Rhythm* (MGM, 1944), sung by Charles Winninger; the Nora Bayes screen biography *Shine On, Harvest Moon* (Warner, 1944); *April Showers* (Warner, 1948); sung by Robert Alda and chorus; *Jolson Sings Again* (Columbia, 1949), sung on the soundtrack by Jolson; The Gus Kahn screen biography *I'll See You in My Dreams* (Warner, 1951), sung by Danny Thomas; the Eva Tanguay screen biography *The I Don't Care Girl* (20th Century-Fox, 1953); and *The Eddie Cantor Story* (Warner, 1954), sung on the soundtrack by Eddie Cantor.

A Pretty Girl, words by J. Cheever Goodwin, music by Woolson Morse (1891). Introduced by Della Fox in the extravaganza *Wang* (1891).

A Pretty Girl Is Like a Melody, words and music by Irving Berlin (1919). Introduced by John Steel in the *Ziegfeld Follies of 1919* for a lavish production number in which each of the girls is made to represent some classical composition. After 1919 "A Pretty Girl Is Like a Melody" became the theme song of the *Ziegfeld Follies*, besides serving as the song favorite of fashion shows and beauty contests the world over. The first best-selling recording was made in 1919, by Ben Selvin's Novelty Orchestra for Victor.

The song was used in the motion-picture *The Great Ziegfeld* (MGM, 1936) for an elaborate production number. Carole Landis and Anne Shirley sang it in the motion-picture musical *The Powers Girl* (Universal, 1943) and Ethel Merman and Dan Dailey in the motion-picture musical *There's No Business Like Show Busi-*

ness (20th Century-Fox, 1954).

In a communication to *Show* magazine, in August, 1964, Cole Porter singled out "A Pretty Girl Is Like a Melody" as his favorite Irving Berlin song.

Previn, André, composer, born Berlin, Germany, 1929.

See (Lyrics by Dory Langdon): Faraway; Goodbye, Charlie; Like Love; Look Again; A Second Chance; That's How It Went All Right; Yes; You're Gonna Hear From Me.

Primrose Lane, words and music by George Callender and Wayne Shanklin (1958). Popularized in 1959 by Jerry Wallace in a Challenge recording.

The Prince of Pilsen, an operetta with book and lyrics by Frank Pixley. Music by Gustav Luders. Starring John W. Ransome and Lillian Coleman (1903).

See: Heidelberg Stein Song; The Message of the Violet; The Tale of the Sea Shell.

Prisoner of Love, words by Leo Robin, music by Russ Columbo and Clarence Gaskill (1931). Introduced by Russ Columbo and his orchestra. In 1946 the song was revived by Perry Como in a best-selling RCA Victor recording.

The Prisoner's Song, words and music by Guy Massey (1924). Popularized by Vernon Dahlhart's recording for Victor in 1924 that sold over a million disks. The sheet-music sale also passed the million mark.

Guy Massey had never written a song before this smash hit—and none since. Nor had he ever been in prison—although to stimulate the sales the publishers encouraged a widely prevalent rumor that Massey had once served a prison term. The manuscript had come unsolicited into the office of Shapiro, Bernstein & Co. "I read the first line, 'I wish I had someone to love me,'" Louis Bernstein later recalled. "That's something. It breaks the heart. Maybe fifty million girls in this country wished they had someone to love them. So it was no surprise when it turned out to be something."

Promenade Walk, words and music by

Al Goodman, Maurice Rubens, Clifford Grey and J. Fred Coots (1925). Introduced by Frances Williams in the revue *Artists and Models* (1925); she scored her first major Broadway success with this number.

Promise Me a Rose, words and music by Bob Merrill (1959). Introduced by Eileen Herlie and Jackie Gleason in the musical *Take Me Along* (1959).

P. S. I Love You, words by Johnny Mercer, music by Gordon Jenkins (1934). Revived in 1957 by the Hilltoppers, whose Dot recording sold a million disks. Billy Vaughan's recording for Dot was his first success on disks.

Puppy Love, words and music by Paul Anka (1959). Popularized by Paul Anka in an ABC Paramount recording that sold a million disks.

The Purple People Eater, words and music by Sheb Wooley (1958). Popularized by Sheb Wooley in a best-selling recording for MGM.

Push Dem Clouds Away, words and music by Percy Gaunt (1892). Introduced in the musical extravaganza *A Trip to Chinatown* (1892).

Put It There, Pal, words by Johnny Burke, music by James Van Heusen (1945). Introduced by Bing Crosby and Bob Hope in the motion-picture musical *The Road to Utopia* (Paramount, 1945).

Put Me Off at Buffalo, words by Harry Dillon, music by John Dillon (1895). A comedy song introduced by the Dillon Brothers, vaudeville headliners; it was a staple in their repertory.

Put On a Happy Face, words by Lee Adams, music by Charles Strouse (1960). Introduced by Dick Van Dyke in the musical *Bye Bye Birdie* (1960). He also sang it in the motion-picture adaptation of the musical (Columbia, 1963).

Put On Your Old Gray Bonnet, words by Stanley Murphy, music by Percy Wenrich (1909). Hit song that sold over a million copies of sheet music and which has since become a favorite at community sings.

Wenrich played "Put On Your Old Gray Bonnet" for the publisher,

Remick, who, on first hearing, doubted if the song had any popular appeal. However, since he was leaving for a week-end holiday to Atlantic City, New Jersey, he took Wenrich's manuscript with him before making a final decision. Upon returning to New York he told Wenrich he had decided to publish it after all. "I can't carry a tune, but yours kept running through my head all week end," the publisher told Wenrich. "And any song that even *I* can't forget must become a hit."

Put On Your Sunday Clothes, words and music by Jerry Herman (1964). Introduced by Charles Nelson Reilly, Jerry Dodge, Carol Channing and Igor Gavon in the musical *Hello, Dolly!* (1964).

Put the Blame on Mame, words and music by Doris Fisher and Allan Roberts (1944). Popularized by Rita Hayworth in the non-musical motion picture *Gilda* (Columbia, 1946), with Anita Ellis singing for her on the soundtrack. In the same year of 1946 it was also interpolated in the motion picture *Betty Co-Ed*, starring Jean Porter (Columbia).

Puttin' On the Ritz, words and music by Irving Berlin (1929). Introduced by Harry Richman in the motion picture of the same name, in which he made his screen debut (United Artists, 1930). With new lyrics it was reintroduced by Fred Astaire in the motion-picture musical *Blue Skies* (MGM, 1946). In this production Astaire performed to this music a complicated routine, accomplished with a series of split screens to produce the effect of his dancing in front of a chorus of eight Astaire images.

Puttin' On the Ritz, a motion-picture musical starring Harry Richman in his screen debut (United Artists, 1930). The score was made up mainly of Irving Berlin's songs.

See: Puttin' On the Ritz.

Put Your Arms Around Me, Honey, words by Junie McCree, music by Albert von Tilzer (1910). Popularized by Elizabeth Murray. It then became a Blossom Seeley favorite in vaudeville. The song was interpolated in the motion picture *Louisiana Hayride,* starring Judy Canova (Columbia, 1944), and was sung by Judy Garland in the motion-picture musical *In the Good Old Summertime* (MGM, 1949). It was also used in the background music as a recurrent theme in the motion picture *In Old Oklahoma,* starring John Wayne and Martha Scott (Republic, 1943). It was successfully revived by "Fats" Domino in 1961.

Put Your Head on My Shoulder, words and music by Paul Anka (1959).

Introduced and popularized by Paul Anka in a best-selling ABC Paramount recording.

A Puzzlement, words by Oscar Hammerstein II, music by Richard Rodgers (1951). The extended narrative of the king, expressing his inability to know right from wrong, introduced by Yul Brynner in the musical play *The King and I* (1951). He also sang it in the motion-picture adaptation of the musical (20th Century-Fox, 1956).

Q

Queen High, a musical comedy with book and lyrics by Bud De Sylva and Laurence Schwab. Music by Lewis E. Gensler. Starring Charles Ruggles and Mary Lawlor (1926).

The motion-picture adaptation starred Charles Ruggles and Ginger Rogers (Paramount, 1930). Only one song was used from the Broadway score. New numbers were provided by Arthur Schwartz and Ralph Rainger, among others.

See: Cross Your Heart.

Queen of the Hop, words and music by Woody Harris (1958). Popularized in 1959 by Bobby Darin in an Atco recording.

Queen of the House, words by M. Taylor, music by Roger Miller (1965). A take-off on Roger Miller's hit song "King of the Road." It was introduced and popularized by Jody Miller in a best-selling Capitol release.

It received a "Grammy" Award.

Querida Mia. See: I'll Always Love You.

Que Sera, Sera. See: Whatever Will Be, Will Be.

The Quest. See: The Impossible Dream.

A Quiet Girl, words by Betty Comden and Adolph Green, music by Leonard Bernstein (1953). Introduced by George Gaynes in the musical Wonderful Town (1953).

Quiet Night, words by Lorenz Hart, music by Richard Rodgers (1936). Introduced by Earl MacVeigh and ensemble in the musical On Your Toes (1936). It was also sung in the motion-picture adaptation of the musical (Warner, 1939).

A Quiet Thing, words by Fred Ebb, music by John Kander (1965). Ballad introduced by Liza Minnelli in her Broadway debut in the musical Flora, the Red Menace (1965).

R

The Race Is On, words and music by D. Rollins (1965). Popularized by Jack Jones in a Kapp recording.

Rackety Coo, words by Otto Hauerbach (Harbach), music by Rudolf Friml (1916). Introduced by Adele Rowland and chorus (in a production number in which a flock of trained pigeons cavorted to the strains of the music) in the operetta *Katinka* (1916).

Rag Doll, words and music by Bob Crewe and Bob Gaudio (1964). Popularized by the Four Seasons in a Philips recording that sold a million disks and received the Gold Record Award.

A Rage to Live, words by Noel Sherman, music by Ferrante and Teicher (1965). Title song of a non-musical motion picture starring Suzanne Pleshette and Ben Gazzara (United Arists, 1965); it was played under the titles by the two-piano team of Ferrante and Teicher.

Raggedy Ann, words by Anne Caldwell, music by Jerome Kern (1923). Introduced by Fred and Dorothy Stone (with the assistance of John Lambert and the Tiller Sunshine Girls) in the musical *Stepping Stones* (1923).

Rag Mop, words and music by Johnnie Lee Wills and Deacon Anderson (1950). Popularized by the Ames Brothers in a Coral recording that sold a million disks. The song was interpolated in the motion picture *Honeychile,* starring Judy Canova (Republic, 1951).

Rags to Riches, words and music by Richard Adler and Jerry Ross (1953). Popularized by Tony Bennett in a Columbia recording that sold almost two million disks. It reached the top spot on the Hit Parade.

Ragtime Cowboy Joe, words by Grant Clarke, music by Maurice Abrahams and Lewis E. Muir (1912). A ragtime classic that became a favorite with barber-shop quartets. It was revived in the motion-picture musical *Hello, Frisco, Hello* (20th Century-Fox, 1943), sung by Alice Faye. Betty Hutton sang it in the screen biography of Texas Guinan, *Incendiary Blonde* (Paramount, 1945).

Ragtime Jockey Man, words and music by Irving Berlin (1912). Introduced by Willie Howard in the revue *The Passing Show of 1912.*

Ragtime Violin, words and music by Irving Berlin (1911). Berlin's most popular "ragtime" song before the success of "Alexander's Ragtime Band." It was revived in the motion-picture musical *Alexander's Ragtime Band* (20th Century-Fox, 1938).

Rainbow, words and music by Russ Hamilton (1957). Introduced and popularized by Russ Hamilton in a Kapp recording.

Rainbow on the River, words by Paul Francis Webster, music by Louis

Alter (1936). Introduced by Bobby Breen in the motion-picture musical of the same name (RKO, 1936). For a number of years it served as the theme song for the radio program *Dr. Christian.*

Rainger Ralph, composer, born New York City, 1901; died in an airplane crash, 1942.

See (Lyrics by Leo Robin): Blue Hawaii; If I Should Lose You; In the Park in Paree; June in January; Love in Bloom; Please; Sweet Is the Word for You; Thanks for the Memory; With Every Breath I Take; You're a Sweet Little Headache.

See also: Easy to Love; I Wished on the Moon; Moanin' Low.

The Rain in Spain, words by Alan Jay Lerner, music by Frederick Loewe (1956). Introduced by Julie Andrews, Rex Harrison and Robert Coote in the musical play *My Fair Lady* (1956). In the motion-picture adaptation of the musical (Warner, 1964), it was sung on the soundtrack by Marni Nixon (for Audrey Hepburn) in collaboration with Rex Harrison.

Rain on the Roof, words and music by Ann Ronell (1932). Introduced and popularized by Paul Whiteman and his orchestra. The eminent poets Robert Frost and Louis Untermeyer expressed enthusiasm for these lyrics.

Rain Song, words by Tom Jones, music by Harvey Schmidt (1963). Introduced by Robert Horton in the musical *110 in the Shade* (1963).

Rainy Night in Rio, words by Leo Robin, music by Arthur Schwartz (1946). Introduced in the motion-picture musical *The Time, The Place and The Girl* (Warner, 1946); it was sung there by Jack Carson, Dennis Morgan, Janis Paige and Martha Vickers.

The Ramblers, a musical comedy with book by Guy Bolton and Bert Kalmar. Lyrics by Bert Kalmar. Music by Harry Ruby. Starring Clark and McCullough with Marie Saxon (1926).

See: All Alone Monday.

Ramblin' Rose, words and music by Joe Sherman and Noel Sherman

(1962). Introduced and popularized in a best-selling Capitol recording by Nat King Cole. Nat King Cole revealed that at first he did not wish to record this number, but was prevailed upon to do so by his twelve-year-old daughter Natalie. It went on to sell almost two million disks.

Ramona, words by L. Wolfe Gilbert, music by Mabel Wayne (1927). Written to exploit the silent motion picture of the same name starring Dolores Del Rio. Weeks before the release of that film, however, the song went on to become one of the country's leading hits of the year. Paul Whiteman and his orchestra played it on a coast-to-coast radio broadcast, with Dolores Del Rio doing the vocal. What was particularly newsworthy about this broadcast was the fact that the orchestra and vocalist were separated by some three thousand miles. Whiteman and his orchestra played in a New York studio, while Dolores Del Rio sang at Joseph M. Schenck's home in Hollywood. This represented a major technological advance in broadcasting.

Dolores Del Rio also sang the number on a personal coast-to-coast tour of the country's leading motion-picture theaters. The sheet-music sale soon passed the two-million mark, and the various recordings totaled several million. The most successful was that of Gene Austin for RCA Victor, released in 1928, which sold about two million disks. The RCA Victor recording by Paul Whiteman and his orchestra was also a best seller.

The Ranger's Song (or, We're All Pals Together), words by Joseph McCarthy, music by Harry Tierney (1926). Introduced by J. Harold Murray, Harry Ratcliffe and chorus in the musical *Rio Rita* (1926). In the motion-picture adaptation of the musical (MGM, 1942), it was sung by John Carroll and chorus.

Rapee, Erno, composer, born Budapest, Hungary, 1891; died New York, 1945.

See (Lyrics by Lew Pollack): Angelia Mia; Charmaine; Diane.

Rastus on Parade, words and music by Kerry Mills (1895). A two-step march that became one of the earliest successful cakewalk tunes.

Raunchy, words by Tom Jones, music by Harvey Schmidt (1963). Introduced by Inga Swenson in the musical *110 in the Shade* (1963).

Razaf, Andy, lyricist, born Washington, D.C., 1895.

See: Ain't Misbehavin'; Memories of You; S'posin'; Twelfth Street Rag; Willow Tree; You're Lucky to Me.

Reaching for the Moon, words and music by Irving Berlin (1931). Introduced by Bing Crosby in the motion picture of the same name starring Douglas Fairbanks (United Artists, 1931).

The Real American Folk Song, words by Ira Gershwin, music by George Gershwin (1918). The first song on which George and Ira Gershwin collaborated. It was also the first time a song lyric by Ira Gershwin was performed publicly. The song was introduced by Nora Bayes in the musical *Ladies First* (1918), where it was an interpolation. Forty years after it had been written, this song was published for the first time; and soon after that it received its first recording—by Ella Fitzgerald for Verve.

Real Live Girl, words by Carolyn Leigh, music by Cy Coleman (1962). Introduced by Sid Caesar in the musical *Little Me* (1962). It was popularized by Jack Jones in a Kapp recording.

The Real McCoys, words and music by Harry Ruby (1957). Theme song of the television series of the same name.

Rebecca of Sunnybrook Farm, words by Seymour Brown, music by Albert Gumble (1914). A song inspired by the famous novel of the same name by Kate Douglas Wiggin, published in 1910. The song was interpolated in the *Ziegfeld Follies of 1913*, introduced by José Collins (an importation from the London stage).

Redhead, a musical comedy with book by Herbert and Dorothy Fields, Sidney Sheldon and David Shaw. Lyrics by Dorothy Fields. Music by Albert Hague. Starring Gwen Verdon and Richard Kiley (1959). Original cast recording (RCA Victor).

See: Just for Once; Look What's in Love; Two Faces in the Dark.

A Red Headed Woman Makes a Choo Choo Jump Its Track, words by Ira Gershwin, music by George Gershwin (1935). Crown's mocking evaluation of the female sex in the folk opera *Porgy and Bess* (1935), introduced by Warren Coleman. It was sung by Brock Peters in the motion-picture adaptation of the opera (Columbia, 1959).

Red, Hot and Blue, a musical comedy with book by Howard Lindsay and Russel Crouse. Lyrics and music by Cole Porter. Starring Ethel Merman, Jimmy Durante and Bob Hope (1936).

See: Down in the Depths; It's Delovely; You've Got Something.

The Red Mill, a comic opera with book and lyrics by Henry Blossom. Music by Victor Herbert. Starring Fred Stone and David Montgomery (1906).

See: Because You're You; Every Day Is Lady's Day; Good-a-bye, John; The Isle of Our Dreams; Moonbeams; Streets of New York.

Red Roses for a Blue Lady, words and music by Sid Tepper and Roy Brodsky (1948). First popularized by Vaughn Monroe in an RCA Victor recording and by Guy Lombardo and his Royal Canadians in a Decca release. Bert Kaempfert and his orchestra revived it in 1964 in a Decca album entitled *Midnight Blue*. Recordings by Wayne Newton for Capitol and Vic Dana for Dolton now lifted the song to a hit status.

Red Sails in the Sunset, words by Jimmy Kennedy, music by Will Grosz, using the pen name of Hugh Williams (1935). An English popular song that became a leading song hit in the United States, selling over a million copies of sheet music.

Remember, words and music by Irving Berlin (1925). One of Berlin's autobiographical love ballads inspired by his stormy courtship with Ellin Mackay, whom he married early in 1926. This ballad became a Ruth Etting specialty. The song was interpolated in the motion-picture musical *Alexander's Ragtime Band* (20th Century-Fox, 1938).

Remember, Boy, You're Irish, words and music by William J. Scanlan (1885). Introduced by Scanlan in the musical *Shane na Lawn* (1885).

Remember Me, words by Al Dubin, music by Harry Warren (1937). Introduced by Kenny Baker in the motion-picture musical *Mr. Dodd Takes the Air*, starring Jane Wyman (Warner, 1937). It was interpolated in the non-musical motion picture *Never Say Goodbye*, starring Errol Flynn (Warner, 1946).

Remember Poor Mother at Home, words and music by James Thornton (1890). Thornton's first published song, sold outright to its publisher for $2.50. It was introduced by Thornton's wife, Bonnie, at the Bal Mabile saloon on Bleecker Street in New York, where at that time Thornton was a singing waiter.

Remember You're Mine, words and music by Kal Mann and Bernie Lowe (1957). Popularized in 1958 by Pat Boone in a Dot recording.

Rememb'ring, words and music by the Duncan Sisters (1923). Introduced by the Duncan Sisters in the musical *Topsy and Eva* (1923).

Remind Me, words by Dorothy Fields, music by Jerome Kern (1940). A Latin-American type song, with an insistent rhythmic pulse, introduced by Allan Jones in the motion-picture musical *One Night in the Tropics*, starring Abbott and Costello (Universal, 1940).

Return to Me (or, Ritorna a Me), words and music by Danny Di Minno and Carmen Lombardo (1957). Popularized by Dean Martin in a best-selling Capitol recording in 1958.

Return to Paradise, words by Ned Washington, music by Dimitri Tiomkin (1953). Theme song of a nonmusical motion picture of the same name starring Gary Cooper (United Artists, 1953). The song was popularized in an instrumental recording for Columbia by Percy Faith and his orchestra.

Return to Sender, words and music by Otis Blackwell and Weinfield Scott (1962). Introduced by Elvis Presley in the motion-picture musical *Girls, Girls, Girls* (Paramount, 1962), and popularized by him in a best-selling RCA Victor recording.

Reuben and Rachel (or, Reuben, I Have Long Been Thinking), words by Harry Birch, music by William Gooch (1871). Described as a "comic musical dialogue between males and females." This song became a favorite at community sings.

Reuben, Reuben, words and music by Percy Gaunt (1893). Hit song introduced in the musical extravaganza *A Trip to Chinatown* (1893).

Revel, Harry, composer, born London, England, 1905; died New York City, 1958.

See (Lyrics by Mack Gordon): Did You Ever See a Dream Walking?; Doin' the Uptown Lowdown; Don't Let It Bother You; From the Top of Your Head to the Tip of Your Toes; Good Night, My Love; I Feel Like a Feather in the Breeze; In Old Chicago; The Loveliness of You; Love Thy Neighbor; May I Have the Next Romance with You; Never in a Million Years; Paris in the Spring; A Star Fell Out of Heaven; Stay As Sweet As You Are; There's a Lull in My Life; Underneath the Harlem Moon; Wake Up and Live; When I'm with You; With My Eyes Wide Open I'm Dreaming; Without a Word of Warning; You're My Past, Present and Future.

Revenge with Music, a musical play with book and lyrics by Howard Dietz based on Alarcon's *The Three-Cornered Hat*. Music by Arthur Schwartz. Starring Libby Holman and Georges Metaxa (1934).

See: If There Is Someone Lovelier Than You; You and the Night and the Music.

Rhapsody in Blue, a screen musical biography of George Gershwin starring Robert Alda as Gershwin with Joan Leslie (Warner, 1945). The entire score was made up of Gershwin's music, with songs represented either in part or as a whole.

See: Bidin' My Time; Clap Yo' Hands; Delishious; Do It Again; I Got Plenty o' Nuthin'; I Got Rhythm;

I'll Build a Stairway to Paradise; It Ain't Necessarily So; Liza; Love Walked In; The Man I Love; Oh, Lady, Be Good; Somebody Loves Me; Someone to Watch Over Me; Swanee; Summertime; 'S Wonderful; Yankee Doodle Blues.

Rhode Island Is Famous for You, words by Howard Dietz, music by Arthur Schwartz (1948). A catalogue of the most famous products of the various states of the Union. It was introduced by Jack Haley and Estelle Loring in the musical *Inside U.S.A.* (1948).

Rhythm on the Range, a motion-picture musical starring Bing Crosby. (Paramount, 1936). Songs by Leo Robin and Richard A. Whiting, by Billy Hill and by Johnny Mercer.

See: Empty Saddles; I'm an Old Cow Hand.

Ribbons Down My Back, words and music by Jerry Herman (1964). Introduced by Eileen Brennan in the musical *Hello, Dolly!* (1964).

Ricochet, words and music by Larry Coleman, Joe Darion and Norman Gimbel (1953). Popularized by Teresa Brewer in a Coral recording that sold a million disks. She also sang it in the motion-picture musical *Three Little Girls from Seattle.*

Riders in the Sky, words and music by Stan Jones (1949). It was introduced by Burl Ives but was popularized by Vaughn Monroe in an RCA Victor recording that sold a million disks. Gene Autry sang it in the motion picture *Riders in the Sky* (Columbia, 1949).

The Riff Song, words by Otto Harbach and Oscar Hammerstein II, music by Sigmund Romberg (1926). A riding song introduced by Robert Halliday, William O'Neal and male chorus in the opening scene of the operetta *The Desert Song* (1926). In the first motion-picture adaptation of the musical (Warner, 1929), it was sung by John Boles; in the second (Warner, 1943), by Dennis Morgan.

Right As the Rain, words by E. Y. Harburg, music by Harold Arlen (1944). Introduced by Celeste Holm and David Brooks in the musical *Bloomer Girl* (1944).

Ringo, words and music by Hal Blair and Don Robertson (1963). Introduced and popularized by Lorne Greene in a best-selling RCA Victor recording. The hero of the song is not "Ringo" of the Beatles, but a legendary outlaw of the Wild West.

Rio Rita, words by Joe McCarthy, music by Harry Tierney (1926). Title and hit song of a musical comedy (1927), introduced by Ethelind Terry and J. Harold Murray. In the first motion-picture adaptation of the musical (RKO, 1929), it was sung by John Boles; in the second (MGM, 1942), by John Carroll.

Rio Rita, a musical comedy with book by Guy Bolton and Fred Thompson. Lyrics by Joe McCarthy. Music by Harry Tierney. Starring Ethelind Terry and J. Harold Murray (1927). A Ziegfeld production that opened the then new Ziegfeld Theatre.

There were two motion-picture adaptations. The first starred John Boles and Wheeler and Woolsey (RKO, 1929). The basic stage score was used. The second starred Abbott and Costello (MGM, 1942). Only two songs from the stage score were used, with additional numbers by E. Y. Harburg and Harold Arlen, among others.

See: Following the Sun Around; The Ranger's Song; Rio Rita.

Rip Van Winkle Was a Lucky Man, words by William Jerome, music by Jean Schwartz (1901). A comedy number, one of the earliest hits of the successful songwriting team of Jerome and Schwartz. It was popularized by Harry Bolger in the musical *The Sleeping Beauty and the Beast* (1901).

Rise 'n' Shine, words by Bud De Sylva, music by Vincent Youmans (1932). A popular song in the style of a spiritual, introduced by Ethel Merman in the musical *Take a Chance* (1932). In the motion-picture adaptation of the musical (Paramount, 1933), it was sung by Lillian Roth.

Riverboat Shuffle, words by Dick Voynow, Irving Mills and Mitchell Parish, music by Hoagy Carmichael (1939). It originated as a jazz instrumental. A Gennett recording by the Wolverines attracted the interest of Irving Mills, the publisher, who issued *Riverboat Shuffle* as a piano instrumental in 1925. Lyrics were added fourteen years later.

The River Seine, a popular French song with music by Guy La Farge and English lyrics by Allan Roberts and Alan Holt (1953). A new version of the same melody—this time with lyrics by Mack Gordon—was entitled "You Will Find Your Love in Paris" (1958); it was popularized by Patti Page in a best-selling Mercury recording.

River, Stay 'Way from My Door, words by Mort Dixon, music by Harry M. Woods (1931). Popularized by Jimmy Savo in the one-man mime revue *Mum's the Word* (1931). His rendition, with accompanying pantomime, became his most celebrated routine, one which he repeated continually in later appearances.

The Road to Morocco, words by Johnny Burke, music by James Van Heusen (1942). Introduced by Bing Crosby and Bob Hope in the motion-picture musical of the same name (Paramount, 1942).

The Road to Paradise, words by Rida Johnson Young, music by Sigmund Romberg (1917). Introduced by Peggy Wood and Charles Purcell in the operetta *Maytime* (1917). In the motion-picture adaptation of the musical (MGM, 1937), it was sung by Nelson Eddy and Jeanette MacDonald. Vic Damone sang it in Romberg's screen biography *Deep in My Heart* (MGM, 1954).

The Road to Singapore, a motion-picture musical starring Bing Crosby, Bob Hope and Dorothy Lamour (Paramount, 1940). Songs by Johnny Burke and James V. Monaco, and Johnny Burke and Victor Schertzinger.

This was the first of the so-called "Road" series of motion-picture musicals produced by Paramount and starring Crosby, Hope and Miss Lamour. The most successful of these

were: *The Road to Zanzibar* (1941); *The Road to Morocco* (1942); *The Road to Utopia* (1945); *The Road to Rio* (1947); *The Road to Hong Kong* (1962). For these various productions, songs were written by Johnny Burke and James Van Heusen, and by Sammy Cahn and James Van Heusen.

See: But Beautiful; It's Always You; Moonlight Becomes You; Personality; Put It There; The Road to Morocco; Teamwork; Warmer Than a Whisper; You Don't Have to Know the Language.

Roberta, a musical comedy with book and lyrics by Otto Harbach based on *Gowns by Roberta,* a novel by Alice Duer Miller. Music by Jerome Kern. Starring Tamara, Ray Middleton, Fay Templeton and Bob Hope in his Broadway stage debut (1933).

There were two motion-picture adaptations. The first starred Irene Dunne, Fred Astaire and Ginger Rogers (RKO, 1935). The second, entitled *Lovely to Look At,* starred Kathryn Grayson, Howard Keel and Red Skelton (MGM, 1952). The principal music from the stage score was used in each of these productions, with the interpolation of "Lovely to Look At," a new number by Dorothy Fields and Jimmy McHugh.

See: I Won't Dance; Lovely to Look At; Smoke Gets in Your Eyes; The Touch of Your Hands; Yesterdays; You're Devastating.

Robin, Leo, lyricist, born Pittsburgh, Pennsylvania, 1900.

See: Rainger, Ralph; Schwartz, Arthur; Styne, Jule; Warren, Harry; Whiting, Richard A.

See also: Beyond the Blue Horizon; Hallelujah; Hooray for Love; In Love Again; It was Written in the Stars; Jericho; Lost in Loveliness; Love Is Just Around the Corner; Moonlight and Shadows; Prisoner of Love; True Blue Lou; We Will Always Be Sweethearts; Whispers in the Dark.

Robin and the Seven Hoods, a motion-picture musical starring Frank Sinatra, Sammy Davis, Dean Martin and Bing Crosby (Warner, 1964). Songs by Sammy Cahn and James Van Heusen.

See: My Kind of Town; Style.

Robin Hood, an operetta with book and lyrics by Harry B. Smith. Music by Reginald de Koven. Starring Eugene Cowles and Jessie Bartlett Davis (1891).

See: The Armorer's Song; Brown October Ale; Oh, Promise Me.

Robinson Crusoe, Jr., a musical extravaganza with book and lyrics by Harold Atteridge and Edgar Smith. Music by Sigmund Romberg and James Hanley, with various song interpolations. Starring Al Jolson (1916).

See: Where Did Robinson Crusoe Go with Friday on Saturday Night?; Yacka Hula Hickey Dula.

Rock-a-Bye, Baby, words and music by Effie I. Crockett (1887). The most famous of American lullabies, based on a familiar Mother Goose jingle. It was first included in the album of *The Old Homestead,* and was issued as a separate number for the first time in Boston in 1887.

Miss Crockett told a newspaper interviewer how she came to write the song: "I was sitting on the piazza reading when a lady put her baby in the hammock nearby and went away. I went over to the baby, and when it became restless, I remembered the old Mother Goose rhyme and began to hum it. I hummed the words to an impromptu tune, and the child went to sleep. At Christmas, I had a banjo given to me and began to take lessons from a teacher in Scollay Square, Boston. One day I strummed the tune for him, and he was so pleased he sent me to C. D. Blake, the Boston publisher. After he heard it, he asked permission to publish it. He did, after I had written three verses to go with the Mother Goose lines. I was afraid my father wouldn't approve, so instead of using my real name, Effie I. Crocket, I used the name of Canning, my grandmother's name. It was not until the song began to sweep the country that I told Father I wrote it."

On the fiftieth anniversary of the song's publication, the composer (now aged sixty-five) sang it over the radio. This was on April 14, 1938. She died two years later.

Rock-a-Bye Your Baby with a Dixie Melody, words by Sam M. Lewis and Joe Young, music by Jean Schwartz (1918). Interpolated by Al Jolson in the musical extravaganza *Sinbad* (1918), where it stopped the show. It then became a Jolson tour de force. He sang it in the motion-picture musical *Rose of Washington Square* (20th Century-Fox, 1939) and on the soundtrack of the motion-picture musical *The Jolson Story* (Columbia, 1946); his Decca recording in 1946 sold over a million disks.

The song was interpolated in several motion pictures, including the all-star screen revue *The Show of Shows* (Warner, 1929) and the motion-picture musical *The Merry Monihans* (Universal, 1944).

The Rock and Roll Waltz, words by Dick Ware, music by Shorty Allen (1955). Popularized by Kay Starr in a best-selling RCA Victor recording.

Rock Around the Clock, words and music by Max C. Freedman and Jimmy De Knight (1953). Popularized by Bill Haley and his Comets in a Decca recording that sold over a million disks. The recording was used on the soundtrack in the background music for the non-musical motion picture *The Blackboard Jungle,* starring Glenn Ford (MGM, 1955). The song provided the title for and was sung by Bill Haley and his Comets in a motion-picture musical (Columbia, 1956). The song was also interpolated in the motion-picture musical *The Girl Can't Help It,* starring Jayne Mansfield (20th Century-Fox, 1956).

Rocked in the Cradle of the Deep, words by Emma Willard, music by Joseph Philip Knight (1840). A sea lullaby introduced by Joseph Philip Knight at a "grand concert" in New York City on October 9, 1839. Its low sustained notes made the song a particular favorite with bassos—in vaudeville as well as the concert hall. This song served as a model for such later popular basso numbers as "Asleep in the Deep."

Rockin' Chair, words and music by Hoagy Carmichael (1930). One of four Carmichael songs that are the composer's favorites. (The other three are "Stardust," "One Morning in May" and "The Nearness of You.")

Rodgers, Richard, composer and lyricist, born Hammels Station, Arverne, New York, 1902.

See (Lyrics by Oscar Hammerstein II): All at Once You Love Her; All 'Er Nothin'; Bali Ha'i; The Big Black Giant; Climb Every Mountain; A Cockeyed Optimist; Do I Love You?; Don't Marry Me; Do Re Mi; Edelweiss; Everybody's Got a Home But Me; The Farmer and the Cowman; A Fellow Needs a Girl; The Gentleman Is a Dope; Getting to Know You; Happy Talk; Hello, Young Lovers; Honey Bun; A Hundred Million Miracles; I Caint Say No; I Enjoy Being a Girl; If I Loved You; I Have Dreamed; I'm Gonna Wash That Man Right Outa My Hair; I'm in Love with a Wonderful Guy; In My Own Little Corner; It Might As Well Be Spring; It's a Grand Night for Singing; I Whistle a Happy Tune; June Is Bustin' Out All Over; Kansas City; Keep It Gay; Love, Look Away; Many a New Day; Maria; My Favorite Things; No Other Love; Oh, What a Beautiful Mornin'; Oklahoma; Out of My Dreams; People Will Say We're in Love; A Puzzlement; Shall We Dance?; So Far; Soliloquy; Some Enchanted Evening; The Sound of Music; Sunday; The Surrey with the Fringe on Top; Ten Minutes Ago; That's For Me; There Is Nothin' Like a Dame; This Nearly Was Mine; We Kiss in a Shadow; What's the Use of Wond'rin'?; You Are Beautiful; You Are Sixteen; You'll Never Walk Alone; Younger Than Springtime.

See (Lyrics by Lorenz Hart): Any Old Place with You; Babes in Arms; Bewitched, Bothered and Bewildered; Blue Moon; Blue Room; Careless Rhapsody; Dancing on the Ceiling; Everything I've Got Belongs to You; Falling in Love with Love; The Girl Friend; Have You Met Miss Jones?; Here in My Arms; I Could Write a Book; I Didn't Know What Time It Was; I Feel at Home with You; I'll Tell the Man in the Street; I Married an Angel; I Must Love You; Isn't It Romantic?; It Never Entered My Mind; It's Easy to Remember; I've Got Five Dollars; I Wish I Were in Love Again; Johnny One Note; The Lady Is a Tramp; Little Girl Blue; Love Me Tonight; Lover; Manhattan; Mimi; The Most Beautiful Girl in the World; Mountain Greenery; My Funny Valentine; My Heart Stood Still; My Romance; Nobody's Heart Belongs to Me; On a Desert Island with Thee; Quiet Night; Sentimental Me; A Ship Without a Sail; Sing for Your Supper; Soon; Spring Is Here; Ten Cents a Dance; There's a Small Hotel; This Can't Be Love; Thou Swell; To Keep My Love Alive; A Tree in the Park; Wait Till You See Her; Way Out West; Where or When; Why Can't I?; Why Do I?; With a Song in My Heart; Yours Sincerely; You Took Advantage of Me.

See (Lyrics by Stephen Sondheim): Do I Hear a Waltz?; Moon in My Window; Stay; Take the Moment; Two by Two.

See also: Loads of Love; Nobody Told Me; No Strings; The Sweetest Sounds.

For the screen biography of Rodgers and Hart, see *Words and Music* (MGM, 1948).

Rodger Young, words and music by Frank Loesser (1945). Ballad glorifying the World War II American infantryman on whom the Congressional Medal of Honor was conferred posthumously.

"Rodger Young" was written at the request of the Infantry, who wanted a song glorifying that service. For his subject, Loesser chose a twenty-five-year-old soldier in the Solomons who had sacrificed his life to save his comrades by single-handedly attacking a Japanese pillbox.

Loesser's ballad was introduced in 1945 on the Meredith Willson radio show over NBC. For this première, Willson planned an elaborate arrangement calling for a huge chorus and an orchestra of seventy-six men. After the first rehearsal one of the ushers in the studio remarked to Willson: "If I'd have written the song, I know I'd rather have it sung by just one ordinary man with one ordinary guitar." This set Willson pondering. He came to the final decision to present the ballad as a simple folk song, having a single singer present it to his own guitar accompaniment. "The men and women of our big seventy-six-piece orchestra and choir just sat there listening, getting goose pimples like everybody else," Willson later recalled in *Eggs I Have Laid*. "The executives got goose pimples, too, till they got the bill for all the music and all those musicians I had hired and never used."

When Rodger Young's body was returned to the United States, and his flag-draped coffin was shown in newsreels, "Rodger Young" was sung on the soundtrack—once again by a single singer accompanying himself on the guitar.

The song was popularized in 1945 through numerous recordings, the most notable being those of Burl Ives for Decca, Nelson Eddy for Columbia, John Charles Thomas for RCA Victor.

The Rogue Song, words by Clifford Gray, music by Herbert Stothart (1930). Introduced by Lawrence Tibbett in the motion-picture musical of the same name (MGM, 1930).

The Rogue Song, a motion-picture musical starring Lawrence Tibbett (MGM, 1930). Songs mainly by Clifford Grey and Herbert Stothart.
See: The Rogue Song; Song of the Shirt; When I'm Looking at You.

Roll Along, Prairie Moon, words and music by Ted Fiorito, Cecil Mack and Albert von Tilzer (1935). Introduced in the motion-picture musical *Here Comes the Band*, starring Ted Lewis (MGM, 1935). It was subsequently interpolated in the motion picture *King of the Cowboys*, starring Roy Rogers (Republic, 1943).

Roll Dem Roly Boly Eyes, words and music by Eddie Leonard (1912). Introduced and popularized in vaudeville by Eddie Leonard, the last of the great minstrels. He henceforth became so inextricably identified with this number that all later imitations of Eddie Leonard's singing style utilized it—and the way he would pronounce "eyes" as "wa-wah-eyes." Eddie Leonard sang it in his first starring role in talking pictures, in *Melody Lane* (Universal, 1929).

Rolled into One, words by P. G. Wodehouse, music by Jerome Kern (1917). Introduced by Anna Wheaton and ensemble in the Princess Theatre production of *Oh, Boy!* (1917).

Roll Out! Heave Dat Cotton, words and music by W. S. Hays (1877). A song long mistakenly identified as a Negro spiritual, and one of its composer's most celebrated ballads in Negro dialect.

Roll Them Cotton Bales, words by James W. Johnson, music by J. Rosamond Johnson (1914). A plantation song popularized by Trixie McCoy.

Romance, words by Edgar Leslie, music by Walter Donaldson (1929). Introduced by J. Harold Murray and Norma Terris in the motion picture *Cameo Kirby* (Fox, 1929). The song was revived in the motion picture *It's a Pleasure*, starring Sonja Henie (RKO, 1945). It was then popularized in best-selling recordings by Jimmy Dorsey and his orchestra for Decca and by Mario Lanza for RCA Victor.

Romberg, Sigmund, composer, born Szeged, Hungary, 1887; died New York City, 1951.
See (Lyrics by Dorothy Donnelly): Deep in My Heart; Drinking Song; Golden Days; Serenade; Silver Moon; Song of Love; Tell Me, Daisy; Your Land and My Land.
See (Lyrics by Dorothy Fields): Carousel in the Park; Close As Pages in a Book; It Doesn't Cost You Anything to Dream.
See (Lyrics by Oscar Hammerstein II): Dance, My Darling; Lover, Come Back to Me; One Kiss; Softly As in a Morning Sunrise; Stout

Hearted Men; Wanting You; When I Grow Too Old to Dream; You Will Remember Vienna.

See (Lyrics by Oscar Hammerstein II and Otto Harbach): Blue Heaven; It; One Alone; The Riff Song.

See (Lyrics by Rida Johnson Young): Road to Paradise; Will You Remember?

See also: Auf Wiedersehen; I Love to Go Swimmin' with Wimmen; I Want to Be Good But My Eyes Won't Let Me; Lost in Loveliness; Mister and Mrs.; When Hearts Are Young; Zing, Zing, Zoom, Zoom.

For Sigmund Romberg's screen biography, see *Deep in My Heart* (MGM, 1954).

Rome Harold, composer and lyricist, born Hartford, Connecticut, 1908.

See: All of a Sudden; Along with Me; Be Kind to Your Parents; The Face on the Dime; Fanny; Franklin D. Roosevelt Jones; Have I Told You Lately?; It's Good to Be Alive; Mene, Mene, Tekel; Military Life; The Money Song; Nobody Makes a Pass at Me; Once Knew a Fella; Sing Me a Song of Social Significance: The Sound of Money; South America, Take It Away; Sunday in the Park; Take Off the Coat; To My Wife; Where Did the Night Go?; Wish You Were Here.

Ronell, Ann, composer and lyricist, born Omaha, Nebraska.

See: Baby's Birthday Party; Linda; Rain on the Roof; That's Him; Who's Afraid of the Big Bad Wolf?; Willow, Weep for Me.

Room Full of Roses, words and music by Tim Spencer (1949). Popularized by Sammy Kaye and his orchestra (vocal by Don Cornell) in an RCA Victor recording and by Dick Haymes in a Decca release. It was interpolated for Gene Autry in *Mule Train* (Columbia, 1950).

A Room Without Windows, words and music by Ervin Drake (1964). Introduced by Sally Ann Howes and Steve Lawrence in the musical *What Makes Sammy Run?* (1964).

Root, George Frederick, composer and lyricist, born Sheffield, Massachu-setts, 1820; died Bailey Island, Maine, 1895.

See: The Battle Cry of Freedom; The First Shot Is Fired; The Hazel Dell; Just Before the Battle, Mother; Rosalie, the Prairie Flower; There's Music in the Air; Tramp, Tramp, Tramp; The Vacant Chair.

Root, Hog, or Die, words and music attributed to Richard J. McGowan (1856). A song with a pronounced folk flavor popularized in minstrel shows. Various patriotic and political lyrics were subsequently adapted to this melody.

Rosalie, words and music by Cole Porter (1937). Introduced by Nelson Eddy in the motion-picture musical *Rosalie* (MGM, 1937).

"I wrote six songs under that title," Porter once revealed to an interviewer. "I handed in the sixth to Louis B. Mayer, who told me to forget Nelson Eddy and go home and write a honky-tonk song. It was a hit. I don't like it. The one he threw out was better." There is good reason to believe that the final version of "Rosalie," used in the movie was one which Porter wrote out of sheer pique—consciously employing some of the clichés and conventions of Tin Pan Alley love songs; that nobody was more amazed than Porter to see the song first accepted and then become a substantial hit.

"Rosalie" was sung by a male trio in the Cole Porter screen biography *Night and Day* (Warner, 1946).

Rosalie, a motion-picture musical starring Nelson Eddy (MGM, 1937). Songs by Cole Porter.

See: In the Still of the Night; Rosalie.

Rosalie, the Prairie Flower, words and music by George Frederick Root, using the pen name of Wurzel (1855). One of the most successful sentimental ballads in the period just preceding the Civil War. Root offered to sell the song outright to the publishers for $100, but convinced that the number had a limited sale, they insisted on a royalty arrangement. They had to pay out to the composer several thousand dollars.

The Rosary, words by Robert Cameron Rogers, music by Ethelbert Nevin (1898). An art song that entered the popular-song repertory through frequent renditions in vaudeville. It sold over two and a half million copies of sheet music between 1898 and 1928.

When Nevin had finished writing his song, he turned over his scribbled manuscript to the singer Francis Rogers, telling him: "Here is a song I have just composed. I want you to sing it at your concert next week." Then, with Nevin as accompanist, Rogers sang the song at sight. One of those present at this impromptu presentation insisted it was impossible for Rogers to memorize the number in time for his concert. Rogers insisted he could. The skeptic then promised all present a champagne supper if Rogers fulfilled his end of the bargain. Rogers did sing the number at his next concert— at the Madison Square Concert Hall. The song then became a favorite of the famous opera star Mme. Ernestine Schumann-Heink, who featured it prominently on her concert programs in Europe and America; this was one of the few songs she presented in English. She described it as follows: "The poem recites a soul tragedy to which the composer has achieved a musical setting, exquisitely conceived in the lyric mood and expressed with simplicity and directness."

The song was the inspiration for a best-selling novel, also named *The Rosary,* by Florence Barclay, published in 1910.

Rose, Billy, lyricist, born William Rose, New York City, 1899; died Jamaica, West Indies, 1966.

See: Conrad, Con; Youmans, Vincent.

See also: Back in Your Own Back Yard; Cheerful Little Earful; A Cup of Coffee, a Sandwich and You; Don't Bring Lulu; Golden Gate; Here Comes the Show Boat; I Found a Million Dollar Baby in a Five and Ten Cent Store; In the Middle of the Night; It Happened in Monterey; It's Only a Paper Moon; I've Got a Feelin' I'm Fallin'; I Wanna Be Loved; Me and My Shadow; The Night Is Young and You're So Beautiful; Overnight; Suddenly; That Old Gang of Mine; There's a Rainbow 'Round My Shoulder; Tonight You Belong to Me; Would You Like to Take a Walk?; Yours for a Song; You Tell Her I Stutter.

A Rose and a Baby Ruth, words and music by John Loudermilk (1956). Popularized in 1957 by George Hamilton IV in a best-selling ABC Paramount recording.

Rose Marie, words by Otto Harbach, and Oscar Hammerstein II, music by Rudolf Friml (1924). Title song of the operetta (1924), introduced by Dennis King and Arthur Deagon. In the first motion-picture adaptation of the operetta (MGM, 1936), it was sung by Nelson Eddy; in the second (MGM, 1954), by Howard Keel. Slim Whitman's recording for Imperial in 1954 was a best seller.

Rose Marie, an operetta with book and lyrics by Otto Harbach and Oscar Hammerstein II. Music by Rudolf Friml. Starring Dennis King and Mary Ellis (1924).

There were two-motion picture adaptations. The first starred Nelson Eddy and Jeanette MacDonald (MGM, 1936). Five numbers from the stage score were used together with several standards and some new songs. The second motion-picture adaptation starred Ann Blyth and Howard Keel (MGM, 1954). The principal numbers from the stage score were used together with two new Friml songs.

Rose O'Day (or, The Filla-Ga-Dusha Song), words and music by Al Lewis and Charles Tobias (1941). Introduced by Eddie Cantor. It was further popularized by Kate Smith in a Columbia recording in 1941 that sold a million disks.

The idea for this song came to Charles Tobias one evening while he was dining at Eddie Cantor's house. Tobias insisted that song ideas came to him continually—and everywhere. A substitute maid was just then serving the dessert. Tobias asked for her name. When she told him it was Rose O'Day, he proceeded to work out a lyric.

The Rose of Alabama (or, The Rose ob Alabama), words by S. S. Steele, composer not known (1846). A favorite in minstrel shows in the period just before the Civil War.

Rose of Killarney, words by George Cooper, music by John Rogers Thomas (1876).

The Rose of No Man's Land, words by Jack Caddingan, music by Joseph A. Brennan (1918). World War I tribute to the Red Cross nurse. The song was revived in the non-musical motion picture *The Cockeyed World,* starring Victor McLaglen and Edmund Lowe (Fox, 1929).

Rose of Rio Grande, words by Edgar Leslie, music by Harry Warren and Ross Gorman (1922). Warren's first published song—and his first success. It was introduced by Paul Whiteman and his orchestra.

Rose of the World, words by Glen Mac-Donough, music by Victor Herbert (1908). Introduced by Ida Brooks Hunt in the operetta *The Rose of Algeria* (1908). Edward N. Waters described it as "one of Herbert's best and most extended declamations of passion." The song was interpolated in the motion-picture musical *The Great Victor Herbert* (Paramount, 1939).

Rose of Washington Square, words by Ballard MacDonald, music by James F. Hanley (1920). Introduced by Fanny Brice in the Ziegfeld *Midnight Frolics of 1919;* she sang it again in the *Midnight Frolics of 1920.* It became a Brice specialty It provided the title for a screen musical (20th Century-Fox), where it was played under the titles and later sung by Alice Faye.

Rose of Washington Square, a motion-picture musical freely based on the career of Fanny Brice, starring Tyrone Power, Al Jolson and Alice Faye (20th Century-Fox, 1939). The score was made up principally of standards.

See: California, Here I Come; I'm Always Chasing Rainbows; I'm Just Wild About Harry; I'm Sorry I Made You Cry; Ja Da; Japanese Sandman; My Mammy; My Man; Rock-a-bye Your Baby with a Dixie Melody; Rose of Washington Square; Shine on, Harvest Moon; Toot, Toot, Tootsie; The Vamp; Yoo Hoo.

Rose, Rose, I Love You, words by Wilfrid Thomas, music adapted by Chris Langdon from a traditional Chinese melody (1951). Popularized by Frankie Lane in a Columbia recording and by Gordon Jenkins and his orchestra in a Decca recording.

Roses Are Red, My Love, words and music by Al Byron and Paul Evans (1961). Popularized in 1962 by Bobby Vinton in a best-selling recording for Epic that received a Gold Record Award; this was Bobby Vinton's first best seller.

Ross, Jerry, composer and lyricist, born New York City, 1926; died New York City, 1955.
See: Adler, Richard.

Roundabout, words by Ogden Nash, music by Vernon Duke (1946). Introduced by Dolores Gray in the musical *Sweet Bye and Bye* (1945), which expired during out-of-town tryouts. It was interpolated in the revue *Two's Company* (1952), where (with a new verse) it was sung by Ellen Hanley and then danced to by Nora Kaye. This is one of two Duke songs which the composer himself favors, the other one being "Autumn in New York."

Round and Round, words by Joe Shapiro, music by Lou Stallman (1956). Popularized in 1957 by Perry Como in an RCA Victor recording that sold a million disks.

Round Her Neck She Wore a Yellow Ribbon, words and music credited to George A. Norton (1917). A favorite of community sings. According to Sigmund Spaeth it traces its ancestry back to the song "All Around My Hat."

The Roving Kind, words and music by Jessie Cavanagh and Arnold Stanton, the melody based on the English folk song sometimes called "The Pirate Ship," and at other times, "The Rakish Kind" (1950). Popularized in 1951 by Guy Mitchell with Mitch Miller and his orchestra in a best-selling Columbia recording;

also by the Weavers in a Decca recording.

Row, Row, Row, words by William Jerome, music by James V. Monaco (1912). Introduced by Lillian Lorraine in the *Ziegfeld Follies of 1912.* It was interpolated in the screen biography of Texas Guinan, *Incendiary Blonde* (Paramount, 1945), sung by Betty Hutton with Maurice Rocco at the piano; in the screen musical *The Eddie Cantor Story* (Warner, 1954), sung on the soundtrack by Eddie Cantor; and in the motion-picture musical *The Seven Little Foys* (Paramount, 1955), sung by Bob Hope and seven children impersonating the Foys.

In 1920 Bert Kalmar, George Jessel and Harry Ruby wrote a comedy number based on this song. They called it "Where Do They Go When They Row, Row, Row?"

Ruby, words by Mitchell Parish, music by Heinz Roemheld (1953). Title song of the non-musical motion picture *Ruby Gentry,* starring Jennifer Jones (Bernhard Vidor Productions, 1953), based on a recurrent theme from the background music. "Ruby" was popularized by Les Baxter and his orchestra in a Capitol recording.

Ruby, Harry, composer and lyricist, born New York City, 1895.

See (Lyrics by Bert Kalmar): All Alone Monday; Hooray for Captain Spalding; I Gave You Up Just Before You Threw Me Down; I Wanna Be Loved by You; Keep on Doin' What You're Doin'; A Kiss to Build a Dream On; My Sunny Tennessee; Nevertheless; The Same Old Moon; She's Funny That Way; She's Mine, All Mine; So Long, Oo Long; Snoops the Lawyer; Thinking of You; Three Little Words; Timbuctoo; Up in the Clouds; Watching the Clouds Roll By; The Window Cleaners.

See (Lyrics by Edgar Leslie): Come On, Papa; Dixie Volunteers.

See also: And He'd Say Oo La La, Wee Wee; Daddy Long Legs; Do You Love Me? I'm the Vamp from East Broadway; Give Me the Simple Life; The Real McCoys; Who's Sorry Now?

For the screen biography of Ruby and Kalmar, see *Three Little Words* (MGM, 1950).

Rudolph, the Red Nosed Reindeer, words and music by Johnny Marks (1949). Popularized by Gene Autry's Columbia recording that sold over six million disks (one and three-quarter million in the first year, another million and a half in the second). *Variety,* on December 20, 1961, called this the second best-selling record of all time, the first being "White Christmas"; it has also been Columbia's top single seller.

It is believed that "Rudolph the Red Nosed Reindeer" has sold forty-three million disks. The sheet music has gone over the three-and-a-half-million mark. Ninety different arrangements have been made—for every possible instrument and combination of instruments, as well as for chorus. In addition, numerous commercial tieups have been made between the song and Christmas toys. In its fifteenth year (1963), fifteen new recordings were released.

ASCAP selected it in 1963 as one of sixteen numbers in its all-time Hit Parade during the half century of its existence.

Rufus Rastus Johnson Brown. *See:* What You Goin' to Do when the Rent Comes 'Round?

Rum and Coca-Cola, words by Morey Amsterdam, music by Jeri Sullavan and Paul Baron (1944). Introduced by Jeri Sullavan at the Versailles night club in New York, and popularized by the Andrews Sisters in a best-selling Decca recording.

Morey Amsterdam had heard the calypso mleody in Trinidad. Believing it to be in public domain, he had Paul Baron and Jeri Sullavan adapt it for American audiences; then he published it with his own lyrics. After the song had become a major hit, it became involved in a plagiarism suit. The plaintiff maintained that the song had been lifted from an album entitled *Songs of the Lesser Antilles,* which had been adapted, published and copyrighted by Maurice Baron. The song in dispute was proved to have been taken from "L'année passée" which Lionel

Belasco had written in 1906 when he was a boy in Trinidad. Judgment was granted to the plaintiff. All existing copies of the song and matrixes were destroyed, and heavy damages had to be paid. The defendants appealed to the Circuit Court of Appeals and lost by a unanimous decision of the judges. This case has been discussed in detail by Louis Nizer (the attorney for the plaintiff) in the best-selling book *My Life in Court,* published in 1961.

Rum Tum Tiddle, words by William Jerome, music by Jean Schwartz (1911). Introduced by Al Jolson in his first Broadway starring role— in the musical *Vera Violetta* (1911). It is with this song that Al Jolson made his debut on records—an Edison release in 1911.

Runaround Sue, words and music by Ernie Maresca and Dion Di Mucci (1961). Popularized by Mark Dinning in a Laurie recording.

Runaway, words and music by Max T. Crook and Charles Westover (1961). Popularized by Del Shannon in a Bigtop recording.

Running Bear, words and music by J. P. Richardson (1959). Popularized by Johnny Preston in a Mercury recording.

Runnin' Wild, words by Joe Gray and Leo Wood, music by A. Harrington Gibbs (1922). Hit song popularized in vaudeville . It was revived by Marilyn Monroe in the motion-picture musical *Some Like It Hot* (20th Century-Fox, 1959).

Russell Henry, composer and lyricist, born Sheerness, England, 1812; died London, England, 1900.

See: The Indian Hunter; A Life on the Ocean Wave; The Old Arm Chair; Woodman, Spare That Tree.

Russian Lullaby, words and music by Irving Berlin (1927). It was revived by Bing Crosby in the motion-picture musical *Blue Skies* (MGM, 1946).

S

Sadie Salome, Go Home, words by Edgar Leslie, music by Irving Berlin (1909). A Yiddish-type take-off on opera, introduced by Fanny Brice in 1910 in a burlesque show at Seamon's Transatlantique in New York. This is the number that transformed Fanny Brice from an interpreter of coon songs and ballads into a comedienne; it is also the number that started her off on her successful career as an interpreter of Yiddish-type comic songs.

As a member of the burlesque company, Fanny Brice was asked by its manager to do a "specialty" at a benefit performance. Fearing she would lose her job if she confessed she had no specialties in her repertory, Brice came to Irving Berlin for material. "Irving took me in the back room," Fanny Brice later recalled, "and he played 'Sadie Salome' . . . a Jewish comedy song. . . . So, of course, Irving sang 'Sadie Salome' with a Jewish accent. I had never had any idea of doing a song with a Jewish accent. I didn't even understand Jewish, couldn't speak a word of it. But, I thought, if that's the way Irving sings, that's the way I'll sing it. Well, I came out and did 'Sadie Salome,' for the first time ever doing a Jewish accent. And that starched sailor suit is killing me. And it's gathering you know where, and I'm trying to squirm it away, and singing and smiling, and the audience is loving it. They think it's an act I'm doing, so as long as they're laughing I keep it up. They start to throw roses at me."

The Saga of Jenny, words by Ira Gershwin, music by Kurt Weill (1941). Described by Ira Gershwin as "a sort of blues bordello." It was introduced by Gertrude Lawrence in the musical play *Lady in the Dark* (1941).

This song plays a significant role in the play. In this number, in one of her dream sequences, the heroine defends her actions. For this scene, Gershwin and Weill originally completed a six- or seven-minute mute "pseudo-metaphysical dissertation based on the signs of the Zodiac and their influences, all pretty fatalistic," as Ira Gershwin has explained. But the number proved too "dour and oppressive" and the authors decided to write something else. "After a week or so of experimenting with style, format and complete change of melodic mood from the Zodiac song, we started 'Jenny' and finished Liza's new defense ten days later."

The decision to use this song in the production was reached because all concerned feared that Danny Kaye's show-stopping number "Tschaikowsky" might throw too much emphasis on a minor character and thus throw the play out of focus. A big number was needed for Gertrude Lawrence, right after Danny Kaye finished his piece. At first Richard Aldrich (Gertrude Lawrence's husband) was convinced that "Jenny" was not Gertrude Lawrence's type of song and feared that coming as it did right after "Tschaikowsky" it would prove anticlimactic. Gertrude Lawrence, herself, was of a different mind. She was sure of herself, sure of the song's impact. After Danny Kaye brought down the house with his tongue-twisting Russian number, Gertrude went into "Jenny." "Suddenly, startlingly," Richard Aldrich recalled "the exquisite, glamorous Gertrude Lawrence was transformed into a tough, bawdy dive singer. As a piece of impromptu impersonation it was superb with few parallels. . . . A miracle in showmanship was accomplished that night; two tremendous hits followed each other immediately and with equal effect. The success of the Danny Kaye number did not cut down Gertrude's prestige. Instead it made possible, by its challenge, her triumph with 'Jenny.' "

Ira Gershwin's comment on Gertrude Lawrence's performance was: "She hadn't been singing more than a few lines when I realized an interpretation we'd never seen at rehearsal was materializing. Not only were there new nuances and approaches, but on top of this she 'bumped' it and 'ground' it to the complete devastation of the audience."

In the motion-picture adaptation of the musical (Paramount, 1944), the number was sung by Ginger Rogers.

Sail Along, Silvery Moon, words by Harry Tobias, music by Percy Wenrich (1937). It was revived in 1958 by Billy Vaughn's best-selling recording for Dot, his most successful disk up to that time.

Sailin' Away on the Henry Clay, words by Gus Kahn, music by Egbert Van Alstyne (1917). Introduced by Elizabeth Murray in the musical *Good Night, Paul* (1917). It was revived two decades later in the motion-picture musical *The Littlest Rebel*, starring Shirley Temple (Fox, 1935).

Sailor Boys Have Talk to Me in English, words by Bob Hilliard, music by Milton De Lugg (1955). Introduced in a night-club revue in New York, then popularized by Rosemary Clooney in a Columbia recording.

Saint (St.) Louis Blues, words and music by W. C. Handy (1914). Handy wrote his most celebrated blues song —and the most celebrated commercial blues song ever written—in order to capitalize on the success of his "The Memphis Blues," which he had sold outright for $50 and which had brought a fortune to its publisher. In search for a theme for a new number in a similar vein, Handy suddenly recalled a period in his life when he stood, as he later recalled, "unshaven, wanting even a decent meal and standing before the lighted saloon in St. Louis, without a shirt under my frayed coat." Then and there he remembered a "curious and dramatic little fragment that till now seemed to have little or no importance. While occupied with my own memories during the sojourn, I had seen a woman whose pain seemed even greater. She had tried to take the edge off her grief by heavy drinking, but it hadn't worked. Stumbling along the poorly lighted street, she muttered as she walked, 'My man's got a heart like a rock cast in the sea.'. . . By the time I had finished all this heavy thinking and remembering, I figured it was time to get something down on paper, so I wrote, 'I hate to see de evenin' sun go down.' If you ever had to sleep on the cobbles down by the river in St. Louis you'll understand the complaint." On another occasion, Handy explained to an interviewer that in writing the "St. Louis Blues," he took "the humor of the coon song, the syncopation of ragtime and the spirit of Negro folk song and called it a blues."

In 1914 W. C. Handy formed with Henry Pace a publishing partnership in Memphis, Tennessee, for the purpose of issuing the "St. Louis Blues." But the number failed to attract interest until Handy moved his publishing venture to New York. Sophie Tucker became interested in it and introduced it successfully into her vaudeville act. Victor issued an instrumental recording that did so well that competitive recording companies followed suit.

In time, the "St. Louis Blues" became one of the most successful popular songs ever written. Its record and sheet-music sales achieved astronomic figures. It was interpolated in a Broadway revue, in a movie short and in a full-length motion picture. When Handy's life was filmed in 1958, starring Nat King Cole as the composer, it was named *St. Louis Blues* (Paramount). The number has been arranged for every possible instrument and combination of instruments, and it has achieved recognition throughout the the world as an American song classic. During the first American visit of Ramsay MacDonald, then England's Prime Minister, he was welcomed with a performance of the "St. Louis Blues." Queen Elizabeth of England (mother of Elizabeth II) once described it as one of her favorite pieces of music. When Ethiopia was invaded by Italy, the Ethiopians adopted it as a war song.

Because of the "St. Louis Blues," a public park in Memphis was named after Handy, and because of it Handy was selected as one of the leading contributors to American culture at the New York World's Fair in 1939.

When Gilda Gray made her New York debut at a Winter Garden Sunday night concert, in 1919, she sang the "St. Louis Blues" and did a shimmy to it. Gilda Gray—and the shimmy—became the talk of the town—the beginnings of her great success as a dancer.

The "St. Louis Blues" was interpolated in the all-Negro revue *Change Your Life* (1930). The first time the number was interpolated in a motion picture was in 1929

(Warner) in *Is Everybody Happy?*, performed by Ted Lewis and his orchestra. Since then it has often been represented in motion-picture musicals and non-musicals. These included: *Baby Face*, starring Barbara Stanwyck (Warner, 1933), where it was used as a recurrent theme and sung; *Stella Dallas*, starring Barbara Stanwyck (Samuel Goldwyn, 1934); *St. Louis Blues* (Paramount, 1939), sung by Maxine Sullivan; *The Birth of the Blues* (Paramount, 1941), sung by Bing Crosby and chorus, accompanied by a jazz ensemble; the screen biography of Ted Lewis, *Is Everybody Happy?* (Columbia, 1943), sung by Nan Wynn, accompanied by Ted Lewis and his orchestra; *Jam Session*, starring Ann Miller with various jazz bands (Columbia, 1944); *Glory Alley*, starring Leslie Caron and Ralph Meeker (MGM, 1952); and the screen biography of W. C. Handy, *St. Louis Blues* (Paramount, 1958).

Saint (St.) Louis Blues, a motion-picture biography of W. C. Handy, starring Nat King Cole as Handy with Eartha Kitt and Pearl Bailey (Paramount, 1958). The score was made up of a number of W. C. Handy standards.
See: Saint (St.) Louis Blues.

Saint (St.) Louis Woman, a musical play with book by Arna Bontemps and Countee Cullen based on Bontemps' novel *God Sends Sunday*. Lyrics by Johnny Mercer. Music by Harold Arlen. An all-Negro cast starred Pearl Bailey, Ruby Hill and Rex Ingram (1946).
See: Any Place I Hang My Hat; Legalize My Name; A Woman's Prerogative.

Sally, words by Clifford Gray, music by Jerome Kern (1921). Title song of a musical (1920), introduced by Irving Fisher and ensemble. It was also sung in the motion-picture adaptation of the musical (First National, 1929).

Sally, a musical comedy with book by Guy Bolton. Lyrics by Clifford Grey and Bud De Sylva. Music by Jerome Kern. Starring Marilyn Miller (1920). The motion-picture adaptation starred Marilyn Miller (First National, 1929). Three songs were used from the stage score. Additional numbers were contributed by Al Dubin and Joe Burke.

See: Little Church Around the Corner; Look for the Silver Lining; Sally; Whip-poor-will; Wild Rose.

Sally, Won't You Come Back?, words by Gene Buck, music by Dave Stamper (1921). A musical tribute to Marilyn Miller introduced by Van and Schenck in the *Ziegfeld Follies of 1921.*

Sam and Delilah, words by Ira Gershwin, music by George Gershwin (1930). Introduced by Ethel Merman (in her Broadway debut)—her opening number in the musical *Girl Crazy* (1930). "When I did my first number, opened my mouth and let out 'Delilah was a floozy,'" Ethel Merman recalled in her autobiography, "everybody screamed and yelled and there was so much noise that I thought something had fallen out of the loft onto the stage." The number was used in both motion-picture adaptations of the musical (RKO, 1932, MGM, 1943); in the latter it was sung by Judy Garland.

The Same Old Moon, words by Otto Harbach and Bert Kalmar, music by Harry Ruby (1927). Introduced by Joseph Santley and Ivy Sawyer in the musical *Lucky* (1927).

Sam's Song (or, The Happy Tune), words by Jack Elliott, music by Lew Quadling (1950). The inspiration for this song was a music publisher named Sam Weiss. Bing Crosby's recording with his son Gary, for Decca (the label reading "Gary Crosby and friend"), sold over a million disks and was largely responsible for the song's success.

Sam, the Old Accordion Man, words and music by Walter Donaldson (1927). Interpolated in the motion-picture musical *Glorifying the American Girl,* starring Eddie Cantor, Mary Eaton and Rudy Vallée (Paramount, 1929). Since this song was a Ruth Etting favorite, it was interpolated in her screen biography *Love Me or Leave Me* (MGM, 1955), sung by Doris Day.

Sam, You Made the Pants Too Long, words and music by Fred Whitehouse, a parody on the hymn "Lord, You Made the Night Too Long" (1933). Introduced in night clubs by Joe E. Lewis, who made it one of his most popular routines.

Joe E. Lewis paid twenty-five dollars for this song. As Art Cohn wrote in his biography of Joe E. Lewis, its performance was "the beginning of a metamorphosis," as far as Joe E. Lewis was concerned. "It would take ten years more to complete the evolution, but gradually the bombastic buffoon . . . would emerge into a droll, Rabelaisian wit with the deft touch of a pixie. . . . 'Sam, You Made the Pants Too Long' became his trademark and his talisman."

San Antonio, words by Harry H. Williams, music by Egbert Van Alstyne (1907). A successor to Van Alstyne's first song hit, "Navajo," which in 1903 had set a vogue in Tin Pan Alley for popular songs about the American Indian.

San Antonio Rose, words and music by Bob Wills (1940). Introduced by Bob Wills in an Okeh recording, then popularized by Bing Crosby in a best-selling Decca recording. The song gave the title to and was interpolated in a motion-picture musical starring Jane Frazee and Robert Page (Universal, 1941).

San Fernando Valley, words and music by Gordon Jenkins (1943). Introduced by Roy Rogers in the motion picture of the same name (Republic, 1944), and popularized by Bing Crosby in a Decca recording.

San Francisco, words by Gus Kahn, music by Bronislau Kaper (1936). Title song of a motion picture starring Jeanette MacDonald and Clark Gable (MGM, 1936), sung on the soundtrack under the titles and used as a recurrent theme in the background music. Sung by a chorus under the titles of the non-musical motion picture *Nob Hill,* starring George Raft and Joan Bennett (20th Century-Fox, 1945) and was played on the soundtrack under the titles in the non-musical motion picture *Key* *to the City,* starring Clark Gable and Loretta Young (MGM, 1950).

Santa Baby, words and music by Joan Javits, Phil Springer and Tony Springer (1953). Popularized by Eartha Kitt in a best-selling recording for RCA Victor.

Santa Claus Is Comin' to Town, words by Haven Gillepsie, music by J. Fred Coots (1934). The song was written two years before it was published and had been turned down by most of the leading publishers, who considered it uncommercial because it was a "kiddie number." Coots, who was then writing special material for Eddie Cantor's radio show, brought the number to Cantor's attention. Cantor was not interested, but Cantor's wife, Ida, influenced him into using it on one of his programs, a week before Thanksgiving, in 1934. It became an instantaneous hit, then grew into a standard, selling over four million copies of sheet music and several million records; of the latter, the most successful was Bing Crosby's for Decca (with the Andrews Sisters) and that of Perry Como for RCA Victor.

Saskatchewan, words by Irving Caesar and Sammy Lerner, music by Gerald Marks (1936). Popularized by Dave Rubinoff and also by Rudy Vallée on their respective radio programs.

Saturday Night Is the Loneliest Night in the Week, words by Sammy Cahn, music by Jule Styne (1944). Sammy Cahn described to this editor how the song came into being: "It was written on a Saturday night in the Gotham Hotel in New York. My sister and her husband dropped by and were surprised to see me in pajamas and a robe. I told them that people in show business didn't go out on Saturday night—it belonged to The People. For show biz, Saturday night was the loneliest night in the week. Immediately after they left I went to the piano and started to improvise the song as you know it. When Styne came home I asked him what he thought, and he thought it was good enough, and we continued to write it. There was a rummy game

going on in the hotel at which Jonie Taps was present. They heard the song and Taps wanted it immediately, and so it went to the Barton Music Company. The song was introduced and popularized by Frank Sinatra."

Save the Last Dance for Me, words and music by Jerome "Doc" Pomus and Mort Shuman (1960). Popularized in 1961 by the Drifters in an Atlantic recording.

Say a Prayer for Me Tonight, words by Alan Jay Lerner, music by Frederick Loewe (1958). Introduced by Leslie Caron in the motion-picture musical *Gigi* (MGM, 1958).

Say a Prayer for the Boys Over There, words by Herb Magidson, music by Jimmy McHugh (1943). Introduced by Deanna Durbin in the motion picture *Hers to Hold* (Universal, 1943). The song was presented by Jimmy McHugh in England in a command performance for Queen Elizabeth and the Duke of Edinburgh.

Say "Au Revoir" But Not "Goodbye," words and music by Harry Kennedy (1893). One of Kennedy's most successful sentimental ballads, appealing for its effective echo effects. It came toward the end of his career, and he himself introduced it in vaudeville in 1893. Helene Mora, "the female baritone," then incorporated it into her vaudeville act a week later—opening with it at the Adams Theatre in Brooklyn, New York; she was largely responsible for the song's immense popularity. She sang it at Harry Kennedy's funeral. The song has since become a favorite of barber-shop quartets.

Say It Isn't So, words and music by Irving Berlin (1932). Berlin's first major song success after a number of frustrating years with failures; it helped restore his self-confidence. Berlin first played and sang it for Rudy Vallée; the latter "intuitively and instinctively knew it was truly an inspired melody and lyric," as Vallée revealed in his autobiography. Vallée introduced it on his radio program in 1932, which, together with his RCA Victor recording, was responsible for its initial success.

Say It with Music, words and music by Irving Berlin (1921). Introduced by Wilda Bennett and Joseph Santley in the first edition of the *Music Box Revue* (1921). Before he placed the song in the revue, Berlin tried it out with a jazz band at the Sixty Club in New York, where it was an immediate hit. Berlin had to employ drastic measures to keep the song from being played to death before its official introduction in the *Music Box Revue.* In reviewing this production, Percy Hammond described the ballad as "a molten masterpiece." The song was revived in the motion-picture musical *Alexander's Ragtime Band* (20th Century-Fox, 1938).

Sayonara, words and music by Irving Berlin (1957). Theme song of the non-musical motion picture of the same name starring Marlon Brando (Warner, 1957). It was sung under the titles and repeated intermittently in the background music. Eddie Fisher's recording for RCA Victor helped to popularize it.

Says My Heart, words by Frank Loesser, music by Burton Lane (1938). Introduced by Harriet Hilliard in the motion-picture musical *The Cocoanut Grove,* starring Fred MacMurray (Paramount, 1938). It reached the top spot in the Hit Parade in 1938.

Say You Love Me, Sue, words by Edgar Smith, music by John Stromberg (1899). Introduced by Pete Dailey in the Weber and Fields extravaganza *Whirl-i-gig* (1899).

Say You're Mine Again, words and music by Charles Nathan and Dave Heisler (1952). Popularized in 1953 by Perry Como in an RCA Victor recording.

Scandals. *See:* George White Scandals.

Scanlan William J., composer, born Springfield, Massachusetts, 1856; died White Plains, New York, 1898.

See: Jim Fisk; Molly O; My Nellie's Blue Eyes; Remember, Boy, You're Irish.

Scarlet Ribbons (for Her Hair), words by Jack Segan, music by Evelyn Danzig (1949). Introduced by Juanita Hall, and recorded by Dinah Shore

for Columbia and Jo Stafford for Decca (among others) without success. It continued to get heard in coffee houses and bistros. Then in 1956 Harry Belafonte's recording for RCA Victor made it a major success.

Scatterbrain, words by Johnny Burke, music by Keene-Bear and Frankie Masters (1939). A nonsense song introduced in the motion-picture musical *That's Right, You're Wrong,* starring Kay Kyser and his orchestra (RKO, 1939).

Schertzinger, Victor, composer, born Mahanoy City, Pennsylvania, 1890; died Hollywood, California, 1941.

See (Lyrics by Gus Kahn): Love Me Forever; One Night of Love.

See (Lyrics by Frank Loesser): Kiss the Boys Goodbye; That's How I Got My Start.

See (Lyrics by Johnny Mercer): Arthur Murray Taught Me Dancing in a Hurry; I Remember You; Tangerine.

See also: Marcheta; My Wonderful Girl.

School Day (or, Ring! Ring! Goes the Bell), words and music by Chuck Berry (1957). Introduced and popularized by Chuck Berry in a Chess recording.

School Days, words by Will D. Cobb, music by Gus Edwards (1907). Gus Edwards' greatest hit song, selling in excess of three million copies of sheet music. It was introduced by Gus Edwards and his company in a vaudeville act of the same name. This was the first edition of a revue in which Gus Edwards and his company of child stars toured the vaudeville circuit for many years. This act produced numerous song hits (some written by Edwards) besides serving as a nursery for such later stars of stage and screen as George Jessel, Eddie Cantor, Groucho Marx, Lila Lee, Georgie Price and others. "School Days" was sung by Gail Storm and Phil Regan in the motion-picture musical *Sunbonnet Sue* (Monogram, 1945).

Schwartz, Arthur, composer, born Brooklyn, New York, 1900.

See (Lyrics by Howard Dietz): Alone Together; By Myself; Dancing in the Dark; Day After Day; Haunted Heart; High Is Better Than Low; How Sweet You Are; If There Is Someone Lovelier Than You; I Guess I'll Have to Change My Plan; I Love Louisa; I See Your Face Before Me; I Still Look at You; Louisiana Hayride; Love Is a Dancing Thing; Lucky Seven; Magic Moment; New Sun in the Sky; Rhode Island Is Famous for You; A Shine on Your Shoes; Something to Remember You By; That's Entertainment; Who Can, You Can; You and the Night and the Music; Under Your Spell; Waitin' for the Evening Train.

See (Lyrics by Dorothy Fields): Love Is the Reason; Make the Man Love Me; Spring Has Sprung; This Is It.

See (Lyrics by Frank Loesser): How Sweet You Are; They're Either Too Young or Too Old.

See (Lyrics by Leo Robin): A Gal in Calico; Oh, But I Do; Rainy Night in Rio.

See also: After All, You're All I'm After; Seal It with a Kiss.

Schwartz, Jean, composer, born Budapest, Hungary, 1878; died Los Angeles, California, 1956.

See (Lyrics by William Jerome): Bedelia; Chinatown, My Chinatown; Don't Put Me Off at Buffalo Anymore; Hamlet Was a Melancholy Man; I'm Tired; I'm Unlucky; Mister Dooley; My Irish Molly O; Oh, Marie; Rip van Winkle Was a Lucky Man; Rum Tum Tiddle; When Mr. Shakespeare Comes to Town.

See (Lyrics by Sam M. Lewis and Joe Young): Hello, Central, Give Me No Man's Land; Rock-a-bye Your Baby with a Dixie Melody; Why Do They All Take the Night Boat to Albany?

See also: Au Revoir, Pleasant Dreams; Hello, Hawaii; I Love the Ladies.

Seal It with a Kiss, words by Edward Heyman, music by Arthur Schwartz (1936). Introduced by Lily Pons in the motion-picture musical *The Girl from Paris* (RKO, 1936).

Sea of Love, words and music by George Khoury and Phil Battiste (1959). Introduced and popularized by Phil Phillips' recording for Mercury.

Searchin', words and music by Jerry Leiber and Mike Stoller (1957). Popularized by the Coasters in an Atco recording.

A Second Chance, words by Dory Langdon, music by André Previn (1962). Theme song of the non-musical motion picture *Two for the Seesaw,* starring Shirley MacLaine (Seven Arts, 1962). Popularized by Sammy Davis in a Reprise recording.

Second Fiddle, a motion-picture musical starring Tyrone Power and Sonja Henie (20th Century-Fox, 1939). Songs by Irving Berlin.

See: I Poured My Heart into a Song.

Second Hand Rose, words by Grant Clarke, music by James F. Hanley (1921). Introduced by Fanny Brice in the *Ziegfeld Follies of 1921,* to become one of her specialties. She sang it in her first starring role in talking pictures, in *My Man* (Warner, 1929). It was successfully revived by Barbra Streisand in a Columbia recording.

The Second Time Around, words by Sammy Cahn, music by James Van Heusen (1961). Written for the motion picture *High Time,* starring Bing Crosby (20th Century-Fox, 1960), in which it was sung by Crosby. It was popularized by Frank Sinatra in a Capitol recording.

Secret Love, words by Paul Francis Webster, music by Sammy Fain (1953). Introduced by Doris Day in the motion picture *Calamity Jane* (Warner, 1953). It received the Academy Award. Doris Day's Columbia recording in 1954 sold over a million disks. The song was also popularized by Slim Whitman in a best-selling Imperial recording.

Send Me No Flowers, words by Hal David, music by Burt Bacharach (1964). Title song of a motion picture starring Rock Hudson and Doris Day (Universal, 1964), where it was introduced by Doris Day.

Send Me the Pillow You Dream On, words and music by Frank Locklin (1964). Introduced and popularized by Dean Martin in a best-selling Reprise recording.

Secretly, words by Al Hoffman, Dick Manning and Mark Markwell (1958). Popularized by Jimmie Rodgers in a Roulette recording.

See, Saw, Margery Daw, words and music by Arthur West (1893). A play song popular with children.

See What the Boys in the Back Room Will Have, words by Frank Loesser, music by Frederick Hollander (1939). Introduced by Marlene Dietrich in the motion picture *Destry Rides Again* (Univeral, 1939); it became one of her leading song successes.

See You Later, Alligator, words and music by Robert Guidry (1956). Introduced by Bill Haley and the Comets in the motion-picture musical *Rock Around the Clock* (Columbia, 1955). It was further popularized by them in a best-selling Decca recording.

Semper Paratus, words and music by Capt. Francis Saltus van Boskerck, USCG (1928). The song was first published in *The Coast Guard Magazine* in 1928. It was issued commercially in 1938. It has become the official march of the United States Coast Guard.

Send for Me, words and music by Ollie Jones (1957). Popularized by Nat King Cole in a Capitol recording.

Send Me Away with a Smile, words by Louis Weslyn, music by Al Piantadosi (1917). World War I ballad—a doughboy's farewell. This martial song is by the same composer who, a few years earlier, had published the pacifist song hit "I Didn't Raise My Boy to Be a Soldier."

Sentimental Journey, words and music by Bud Green, Les Brown and Ben Homer (1944). World War II ballad popularized in 1945 by Les Brown and his orchestra, with Doris Day doing the vocal, in a best-selling Columbia recording; this was the first major disk success by both Doris Day and Les Brown and his orchestra. The song provided the title for and was used prominently in the background music of a mo-

tion picture starring John Payne and Maureen O'Hara (20th Century-Fox, 1946). It was adopted by Les Brown as his theme song.

Sentimental Me, words and music by Jim Morehead and Jimmy Cassin (1950). Popularized by the Ames Brothers in a Coral recording.

Sentimental Me, words by Lorenz Hart, music by Richard Rodgers (1925). Introduced by June Cochrane, James Norris, Edith Meiser and Sterling Holloway in the sophisticated revue *The Garrick Gaieties* (1925)—the first successful Broadway production with songs by Rodgers and Hart.

September in the Rain, words by Al Dubin, music by Harry Warren (1937). Introduced by James Melton in the motion-picture musical *Stars Over Broadway* (Warner, 1935). He sang it again in the motion-picture musical *Melody for Two* (Warner, 1937). George Shearing's recording for MGM in 1949 was his first disk success.

September of My Years, words by Sammy Cahn, music by James Van Heusen (1965). Title song of a Reprise album, introduced and popularized by Frank Sinatra. The album received two "Grammy" Awards.

September Song, words by Maxwell Anderson, music by Kurt Weill (1938). Introduced by Walter Huston in the musical play *Knickerbocker Holiday* (1938). A good deal of the impact of this song came from Huston's nasal, half-recitative delivery.

When Weill first discovered that Huston was to star in *Knickerbocker Holiday,* he wired the actor in Hollywood to inquire the range of his voice. Huston replied succinctly: "No range—no voice." Later on, when Huston appeared on a coast-to-coast radio broadcast, he sang a number just to demonstrate to Weill his singing ability, such as it was. Weill heard Huston's rasping, nasal, husky voice and decided to do a special song with melodic progressions favorable to Huston's singing style.

"September Song" was one of sixteen numbers selected by ASCAP in 1963 for its all-time Hit Parade during the half century of its existence. It was sung by Nelson Eddy in the motion-picture adaptation of the musical (United Artists, 1944). Stan Kenton's recording for Capitol was a best seller, and so was Bing Crosby's for Decca.

The song was used as a recurrent theme in the background music for the non-musical motion picture *September Affair*, starring Joan Fontaine and Joseph Cotton (Paramount, 1951), with Walter Huston repeating his rendition on the soundtrack.

Serenade, words by Dorothy Donnelly, music by Sigmund Romberg (1924). Introduced by Howard Marsh, Raymond Marlowe, Paul Kleem and Frederic Wolff (with male chorus) in the operetta *The Student Prince* (1924). In the motion-picture adaptation of the operetta (MGM, 1954), it was sung on the soundtrack by Mario Lanza (for Edmund Purdom). William Olvis sang it in Romberg's screen biography *Deep in My Heart* (MGM, 1954).

The Serenade, comic opera with book and lyrics by Harry B. Smith. Music by Victor Herbert. Starring Jessie Bartlett Davis, Eugene Cowles and Alice Neilsen (1897).

See: Cupid and I; I Love Thee, I Adore Thee.

Serenade in Blue, words by Mack Gordon, music by Harry Warren (1942). Introduced by Glenn Miller and his orchestra (vocal by Ray Eberle and the Modernaires) in the motion-picture musical *Orchestra Wives* (20th Century-Fox, 1942); Glenn Miller's recording for RCA Victor was a best seller.

Seven Brides for Seven Brothers, a motion-picture musical starring Howard Keel and Jane Powell (MGM, 1954). Songs by Johnny Mercer and Gene de Paul.

See: When You're in Love.

The Seven Little Foys, a motion-picture musical biography of Eddie Foy and his children starring Bob Hope as Eddie Foy (Paramount, 1955). The score was made up of standards, some of them popularized by Foy.

See: Chinatown, My Chinatown; Mary's a Grand Old Name; Nobody; Row, Row, Row; Yankee Doodle Boy.

Seven or Eleven (My Dixie Pair o' Dice), words by Lew Brown, music by Walter Donaldson (1923). Introduced by Eddie Cantor in the musical *Make It Snappy* (1923).

Seventeen, words and music by John Young, Jr., Chuck Gorman and Boyd Bennett (1955). Popularized by Boyd Bennett and his Rockets in a King recording and by the Fontane Sisters in a Dot recording.

Seventh Heaven, words by Sidney D. Mitchell, music by Lew Pollack (1937). Theme song of the non-musical motion picture of the same name starring James Stewart (20th Century-Fox, 1937).

Seventy-Six Trombones, words and music by Meredith Willson (1957). Rousing hit song from the musical *The Music Man* (1957), introduced by Robert Preston with a children's chorus. Robert Preston and a children's chorus also sang it in the motion-picture adaptation of the musical (Warner, 1962).

Shadow of Your Smile, words by Paul Francis Webster, music by Johnny Mandel (1965). Introduced in the non-musical motion picture *The Sandpiper*, starring Richard Burton and Elizabeth Taylor (Columbia, 1965), and popularized by Tony Bennett in a Columbia recording. It received the Academy Award, and a "Grammy" as song of the year.

Shadow Waltz, words by Al Dubin, music by Harry Warren (1933). Introduced by Dick Powell and Ruby Keeler in the motion-picture musical *Gold Diggers of 1933* (Warner, 1933).

Shadrack, words and music by Robert MacGimsey (1931). Popularized in William Grant Still's orchestration, which became a specialty of Louis Armstrong and his orchestra and of several other Negro jazz musicians.

Shake, Rattle and Roll, words and music by Charles Calhoun (1954). Introduced by Joe Turner, but popularized by Elvis Presley in a best-selling RCA Victor recording and by

Bill Haley and his Comets in a Decca recording. The song was featured in the motion picture *Round Up of Rhythm* (Universal, 1955).

Shaking the Blues Away, words and music by Irving Berlin (1927). Introduced by Ruth Etting in the *Ziegfeld Follies of 1927* (her debut in the *Follies*). The song was interpolated in the Ruth Etting screen biography *Love Me or Leave Me* (MGM, 1955), sung by Doris Day.

Shall We Dance?, words by Ira Gershwin, music by George Gershwin (1937). Introduced by Fred Astaire in the motion-picture musical of the same name (RKO, 1937). The song was written to replace another number ("Wake Up, Brother, and Dance") when *Shall We Dance?* was chosen as the title of the film.

Shall We Dance?, words by Oscar Hammerstein II, music by Richard Rodgers (1951). Introduced by Yul Brynner and Gertrude Lawrence in the musical play *The King and I* (1951). In the motion-picture adaptation of the musical (20th Century-Fox, 1956), it was sung by Yul Brynner and Marni Nixon, the latter singing on the soundtrack for Deborah Kerr.

Shall We Dance?, a motion-picture muscial starring Fred Astaire and Ginger Rogers (RKO, 1937). Songs by George and Ira Gershwin.
    See: Let's Call the Whole Thing Off; Shall We Dance?; Slap That Bass; They All Laughed; They Can't Take That Away from Me.

Shalom, words and music by Jerry Herman (1961). An Israeli salutation that became the inspiration for the hit song in the musical set in Israel, *Milk and Honey* (1961), introduced by Robert Weede and Mimi Benzell.

Shanghai, words by Bob Hilliard, music by Milton De Lugg (1951). Popularized by Doris Day in a Columbia recording.

Shanghai Lil, words by Al Dubin, music by Harry Warren (1933). Introduced by James Cagney in the motion-picture musical *Footlight Parade* (Warner, 1933).

A Shanty in Old Shanty Town. *See:* In a Shanty in Old Shanty Town.

Sh-Boom (or, Life Could Be a Dream), words and music by James Keyes, Claude Feaster, Carl Feaster, Floyd F. McRae and James Edwards (1954). Popularized by the Crew Cuts in a Mercury recording and by the Chords in a Cat recording.

She Didn't Say Yes, words by Otto Harbach, music by Jerome Kern (1931). Introduced by Bettina Hall in the musical *The Cat and the Fiddle* (1931). It was also sung in the motion-picture adaptation of the musical (MGM, 1934) and in Kern's screen biography *Till the Clouds Roll By* (MGM, 1946).

The Sheik of Araby, words by Harry B. Smith and Francis Wheeler, music by Ted Snyder (1921). Inspired by the silent motion-picture classic *The Sheik,* starring Rudolph Valentino. The song was introduced in the musical *Make It Snappy* (1921). Billy Gilbert, Alice Faye and Betty Grable gave it a comedy treatment in the motion-picture musical *Tin Pan Alley* (20th Century-Fox, 1940).

She Is More to Be Pitied Than Censured, words and music by William B. Gray, date of copyright or first publication not known. A famous sentimental ballad of the 1890s. It was satirized by a chorus in a production number in the motion-picture musical *Cruisin' Down the River* (Columbia, 1953).

She Is the Belle of New York, words by Hugh Morton, music by Gustave Kerker (1898). Hit song from the musical *The Belle of New York* (1898), introduced by Edna May, whom it helped to make a star overnight.

She Loves Me, words by Sheldon Harnick, music by Jerry Bock (1963). Title song of a musical (1963), introduced by Daniel Massey.

She Loves Me, a musical comedy with book by Joe Masterhoff based on Miklos Laszlo's play *Little Shop Around the Corner.* Lyrics by Sheldon Harnick. Music by Jerry Bock. Starring Barbara Cook and Daniel Massey (1963). Original cast recording (MGM).

See: Dear Friend; Grand Knowing You; Ice Cream; She Loves Me.

She Loves Me Not, a motion-picture musical starring Bing Crosby and Miriam Hopkins (Paramount, 1934). Songs by Mack Gordon and Harry Revel, Leo Robin and Ralph Rainger and by Edward Eliscu and Arthur Schwartz.

See: Love in Bloom.

She May Have Seen Better Days, words and music by James Thornton (1894). Sentimental ballad about a fallen woman, popularized in the 1890s by W. H. Windom in a production by the Primrose and West Minstrels.

Sherman's March to the Sea, words and music by Lt. Samuel H. H. Byers (1864). A song whose title served to identify the 1864 military campaign of General Sherman when he swept across Georgia, leaving behind him a desolation from which the Confederacy never recovered. Byers, its composer, was one-time officer of an Iowa regiment who was imprisoned in a Confederate jail in Columbia, South Carolina. He was freed upon Sherman's occupation of the city, then became an aide to the General whom he honored in his song. The number sold over a million copies of sheet music, and for a while its popularity threw into the shade Work's now more famous song "Marching Through Georgia," also inspired by the Sherman campaign.

Sherry, words and music by Bob Gaudio (1962). Popularized by the Four Seasons in a Vee-Jay recording.

She's a Latin from Manhattan, words by Al Dubin, music by Harry Warren (1935). Introduced by Al Jolson in the motion-picture musical *Go into Your Dance* (First National, 1935). It was sung by Jack Carson and Joan Leslie in the non-musical motion picture *The Hard Way,* starring Ida Lupino (Warner, 1942).

She Sells Sea Shells, words by Terry Sullivan, music by Harry Gifford (1908). Interpolated in the musical *The Beauty Shop* (1911).

She's Funny That Way, words by Richard A. Whiting, music by Neil Moret (1928). One of the few songs by Whiting in which he served as lyricist to somebody else's music. The song was revived in several motion pictures, including the non-musical film *The Postman Always Rings Twice,* starring Lana Turner and John Garfield (MGM, 1946), and the screen musicals *Meet Danny Wilson* (Universal, 1952), sung by Frank Sinatra, and *Rainbow 'Round My Shoulder* (Columbia, 1952).

She's Mine, All Mine, words by Bert Kalmar, music by Harry Ruby (1921). Popularized in vaudeville in the 1920s. It was interpolated in the screen biography of Ruby and Kalmar, *Three Little Words* (MGM, 1950).

She's the Daughter of Mother Machree, words by Jeff T. Branen, using the pen name of Jeff T. Nenarb, music by Ernest R. Ball (1915). An attempt to capitalize on the success of Ball's earlier ballad "Mother Machree."

She Touched Me, words by Ira Levin, music by Milt Schafer (1965). Ballad introduced by Elliott Gould in the musical *Drat, the Cat!* (1965). As "He Touched Me" it was popularized by Barbra Streisand in a Columbia recording.

She Was Bred in Old Kentucky, words by Harry B. Berdan, using the pen name of Harry Braisted, music by Frederick J. Redcliffe, using the pen name of Stanley Carter (1898). It was written on a dare. The songwriters and some of their friends were discussing Paul Dresser's ballads when one of them insisted that creators of comedy songs were incapable of writing successful sentimental ballads. Berdan and Redcliffe, famous for their comedy number "You're Not the Only Pebble on the Beach," maintained that this was not so, and set out to write a successful ballad. "She Was Bred in Old Kentucky" proved their point, becoming a hit in 1898, plugged into a large sheet-music sale through Lottie Gilson's performances in vaudeville. The song was revived by the Klein Brothers in the revue *Gaieties of 1919.*

She Went to the City, words and music by Paul Dresser (1904). One of the last of Dresser's sentimental ballads.

Shew (or Shoo), Fly, Don't Bother Me, words by Billy Reeves, music by Frank Campbell (1869). One of the most popular nonsense ditties of its time. Though published four years after the end of the Civil War, it had become a favorite of Negro troops during that conflict. In the post-Civil War period the song was popularized by such minstrels as Cool Burgess and Rollin Howard. The song was revived in the Broadway play in which Ethel Barrymore made her American stage debut—*Captain Jinks of the Horse Marines* (1900).

Shields, Ren, composer and lyricist, born Chicago, Illinois, 1868; died Massapequa, New York, 1913.
    See: Come, Take a Trip in My Airship; In the Good Old Summertime; In the Shadow of the Pyramids; The Longest Way 'Round Is the Sweetest Way Home; Steamboat Bill; Up in a Balloon; Waltz Me Around Again, Willie.

Shinbone Alley. *See:* Long Time Ago.

S-H-I-N-E, words by Richard C. McPherson, using the pen name of Cecil Mack, music by Ford Dabney (1924). Popularized in vaudeville in the 1920s. It was revived in 1938 in Ella Fitzgerald's best-selling recording, and again in 1948 in Frankie Laine's Mercury recording that sold a million disks. It was interpolated in the motion-picture musical *Cabin in the Sky* (MGM, 1943), and played by Harry James in the motion-picture musical *The Benny Goodman Story* (Universal, 1956).

Shine On, Harvest Moon, words by Jack Norworth, music by Nora Bayes and Jack Norworth (1908). Introduced by Nora Bayes in the *Ziegfeld Follies of 1908,* and from then on her song trademark. In the same year of 1908 the song was interpolated in the musical *Miss Innocence,* starring Anna Held. Jack Norworth subsequently made the song the high spot of his vaudeville act for the remainder of his

life. Ruth Etting revived it successfully in the *Ziegfeld Follies of 1931.* The song provided the title for and was featured prominently in a motion-picture musical starring Ann Sheridan and Dennis Morgan (MGM, 1944). It was interpolated in the non-musical motion picture *Ever Since Eve,* starring Marion Davies and Robert Montgomery (Warner, 1937).

Shine on, Harvest Moon, a motion-picture musical biography of Nora Bayes, starring Ann Sheridan as Miss Bayes and Dennis Morgan as Jack Norworth (Warner, 1944). The score was made up mainly of standards popularized by Miss Bayes, but several new songs were interpolated by Cliff Friend and Charles Tobias and by Kim Gannon and M. K. Jerome among others.
    See: Breezin' Along with the Breeze; Every Little Movement Has a Meaning of Its Own; Just Like a Gypsy; Pretty Baby; Shine On, Harvest Moon; Take Me Out to the Ball Game; Time Waits for No One.

A Shine on Your Shoes, words by Howard Dietz, music by Arthur Schwartz (1932). Introduced by Vilma and Buddy Ebsen, Monette Moore and Larry Adler in the musical *Flying Colors* (1932). In the motion-picture musical *The Band Wagon* (MGM, 1953), it was sung and danced to by Fred Astaire.

A Ship Without a Sail, words by Lorenz Hart, music by Richard Rodgers (1929). Introduced by Jack Whiting in the musical *Heads Up* (1929). In the motion-picture adaptation of the musical (Paramount, 1930), it was sung by Charles "Buddy" Rogers.

The Shocking Miss Pilgrim, a motion-picture musical starring Betty Grable and Dick Haymes (20th Century-Fox, 1947). Songs by George and Ira Gershwin. George Gershwin's posthumous manuscripts provided the melodies, adapted by Kay Swift; this was the first motion picture ever to utilize a posthumous score.
    See: Aren't You Kind of Glad We Did?; Back Bay Polka; For You, For Me, For Evermore.

Shoe Shine Boy, words by Sammy Cahn, music by Saul Chaplin (1936). Written for the Cotton Club revue in Harlem, New York, where it was introduced by Louis Armstrong and his orchestra. The melody is based on a famous Louis Armstrong "riff."

In his column in the New York *Post,* Leonard Lyons revealed that "Shoe Shine Boy" was one of the first publications of the Leeds Music Corporation, a publishing firm founded in New York by Lou Levy. At that time Sammy Cahn and Lou Levy shared a $3-a-week room. Locked out for failure to pay rent, Cahn decided to sell a one-third interest in "Shoe Shine Boy" to a friend for $15; that investment yielded about $15,000. The success of "Shoe Shine Boy" established Leeds Music Corporation at once as a successful publishing venture, besides launching Sammy Cahn on his formidable career as a lyricist.

Shoo, Fly, Don't Bother Me. *See:* Shew, Fly, Don't Bother Me.

Shoofly Pie and Apple Pan Dowdy, words by Sam Gallop, music by Guy Woods (1945). Popularized in 1946 by Dinah Shore in a Columbia recording; also by Guy Lombardo and his Royal Canadians in a Decca release.

Shoo Shoo, Baby, words and music by Phil Moore (1943). Popularized in 1944 by Lena Horne.

Phil Moore was employed at the MGM studios in Hollywood, where he was in the habit of using the phrase "shoo, shoo." At a rehearsal with Lena Horne, which had gone rather badly, he kept telling her, "Shoo, shoo, Lena, take it easy, shoo, shoo." For several days he kept repeating the phrase "shoo, shoo." He then decided to improvise a lyric around it and to set it to music. Even before his song was put down on lead sheets, it was sung to popularity in night clubs and theaters by Lena Horne and Georgia Gibbs. It sold over three hundred thousand copies of sheet music following publication, and made seventeen appearances on the Hit Parade. In 1944 it was interpolated in four motion pictures: the all-star musical *Follow the Boys* (Universal); *Trocadero,* starring Rosemary Lane (Republic); *Beautiful But Broke,* starring Joan Davis (Columbia), sung by Jane Frazee and Judy Clarke; and *South of Dixie,* starring Ann Gwynne (Universal), sung by Ella Mae Morse. The Page Cavanaugh Trio sang it in the motion picture *Big City,* starring Margaret O'Brien (MGM, 1948).

Short'nin' Bread, words and music by Jacques Wolfe (1928). An art song, in the style of a Negro spiritual, that entered the popular repertory by virtue of repeated performances by baritones in vaudeville and other popular media. It is possible that this number is a transcription rather than an original composition, since a number of Negro composers have come forward with the claim of having written it. One of them is Reese d'Pree, who insisted he had written the melody in 1905. However, it is because of Wolfe that the song has become basic to the repertory of American baritones. It was introduced by Lawrence Tibbett in a concert tour of the Southern states, then was popularized by Nelson Eddy. The song was interpolated in the motion-picture musical *Louisiana Hayride,* starring Judy Canova (Columbia, 1944).

Should I?, words by Arthur Freed, music by Nacio Herb Brown (1929). Introduced by Charles Keyley in the motion-picture musical *Lord Byron of Broadway* (MGM, 1930). It was revived in the motion-picture musical *Singin' in the Rain* (MGM, 1952), sung by Debbie Reynolds.

Show Boat, a musical play with book by Oscar Hammerstein II based on the novel of the same name by Edna Ferber. Lyrics by Oscar Hammerstein II. Music by Jerome Kern. Starring Helen Morgan, Howard Marsh and Norma Terris (1927).

There were three motion-picture adaptations. The first was only a part-talking film with a synchronized musical background; it starred Laura La Plante, Joseph Schildkraut and Alma Rubens (Universal, 1929). The second starred Irene Dunne,

Allan Jones and Helen Morgan (1936). The third starred Kathryn Grayson, Howard Keel and Ava Gardner (MGM, 1951). Both the 1936 and the 1951 versions used the basic stage score.

See: Bill; Can't Help Lovin' That Man; Life Upon the Wicked Stage; Ol' Man River; Only Make Believe; No One But Me; Why Do I Love You?; You Are Love.

Show Business (or, There's No Business Like Show Business), words and music by Irving Berlin (1946). This has become the unofficial anthem of the American theatrical industry. It was introduced by William O'Neal Ray Middleton, Marty May and Ethel Merman in the musical *Annie, Get Your Gun* (1946). In the motion-picture adaptation (MGM, 1950), it was sung by Betty Hutton, Howard Keel, Louis Calhern and Keenan Wynn. The full title of the song, as well as the song itself, sung by Marilyn Monroe, was used for a motion-picture musical (20th Century-Fox, 1954). This Berlin song is one of the composer's own favorites, along with "Always," "Easter Parade," "God Bless America" and "White Christmas."

Show Girl, a musical comedy with book by William Anthony McGuire based on the J. P. McEvoy novel of the same name. Lyrics by Ira Gershwin. Music by George Gershwin. Additional lyrics by Gus Kahn. Additional songs by Jimmy Durante. Starring Ruby Keeler, Jimmy Durante and Duke Ellington (1929).

See: I Ups to Him; Jimmy the Well Dressed Man; Liza; So Are You.

Show Me, words by Alan Jay Lerner, music by Frederick Loewe (1956). Introduced by Julie Andrews in the musical play *My Fair Lady* (1956). In the motion-picture adaptation of the musical (Warner, 1964), it was sung on the soundtrack by Marni Nixon (for Audrey Hepburn).

Show Me the Way to Go Home, words and music by Irving King (1925). A favorite of the convivial set. Sigmund Spaeth maintained that this number is really "just a faster ver-

sion of a much older song beginning, 'Oh, Mister, won't you show me the right way home?' "

Shrimp Boats, words and music by Paul Mason Howard and Paul Weston (1951). Popularized by Jo Stafford in a best-selling Columbia recording.

Shuffle Along, words and music by Noble Sissle and Eubie Blake (1921). Title song of an all-Negro revue (1921), introduced by Charles Davis and "The Jimtown Pedestrians."

Shuffle Along, the first successful Broadway all-Negro revue. It first opened in Harlem, then began a successful run at the 63rd Street Music Hall on May 23, 1921. Songs by Noble Sissle and Eubie Blake. Starring Noble Sissle and Florence Mills (1921).

See: Bandana Days; I'm Just Wild About Harry; Love Will Find a Way; Shuffle Along.

Shuffle Off to Buffalo, words by Al Dubin, music by Harry Warren (1932). Introduced by Ginger Rogers and Glenda Farrell in the motion-picture musical *Forty-Second Street* (Warner, 1933). It was sung by Jack Carson and Joan Leslie in the non-musical motion picture *The Hard Way,* starring Ida Lupino (Warner, 1942).

Siam, words by Howard Johnson, music by Fred Fisher (1915).

Siboney (or, Canto Siboney), a Cuban instrumental composition by Ernesto Lecuona, English lyrics by Dolly Morse (1929). It was sung by Gloria Jean in the motion-picture musical *Get Hep to Love* (Universal, 1942).

Side by Side, words and music by Harry Woods (1927). Popularized in vaudeville in the 1920s. Kay Starr subsequently revived it successfully on records. Frankie Laine and Keefe Brasselle sang it in the motion-picture musical *Bring Your Smile Along* (Columbia, 1955).

The Sidewalks of New York, words and music by James W. Blake and Charles B. Lawlor (1894). Introduced by Lottie Gilson at the Old London Theatre in the Bowery, in 1894. It proved so successful at its première that the audience joined

Lottie Gilson in singing the refrain.

James Blake was a salesman in a hatter's shop when he collaborated with Lawlor in writing this song. Lawlor—a buck-and-wing performer in vaudeville—had come into Blake's shop humming a tune he had just concocted. Since he knew Blake was adept at writing verses, he suggested that Blake adapt his tune to some words about New York. The inspiration for Blake's lyrics was a David Braham song, "The Babies on Our Block," from a Harrigan and Hart extravaganza. Once having completed their song, and having seen it grow successful in a rendition by Lottie Gilson in vaudeville, the writers sold out all their interests in it for $5,000 to the publishers, Howley and Haviland.

During the Democratic national convention for the Presidency, in San Francisco in 1920, the band struck up "The Sidewalks of New York" after Rep. W. Bourke Cockran of New York had put into nomination the name of Alfred E. Smith. This was because the bandleader had been under the mistaken idea that this song came out of a Harrigan and Hart extravaganza, and he knew how Alfred E. Smith had been partial to these shows. Thus, through a mistake, "The Sidewalks of New York" and Alfred E. Smith became linked for the first time; as long as Smith lived the number remained his theme song. Smith adopted it as his campaign song during the 1924 Democratic convention for the Presidency. As the song was taken up lustily by the delegates, a reporter in the convention hall thought of seeking out its creators. He learned that Lawlor was dead, and that Blake was then performing in an obscure little vaudeville theater in Brooklyn, New York. When the reporter asked Blake if he had read in the newspapers that "The Sidewalks of New York" had become Smith's campaign song, the vaudevillian turned toward him a blank, expressionless face. Only then did the reporter realize that Blake was blind. In 1933, with

Blake penniless, the New York *Herald Tribune* created a fund to support him for the rest of his life, which ended two years after that.

The song gave the title to and was heard in a nostalgic musical comedy (1927). Betty Grable and June Haver sang it in the motion-picture musical *The Dolly Sisters* (20th Century-Fox, 1945), and the number was given an effective song and buck-and-wing dance treatment by Jimmy Durante and Bob Hope in the motion-picture screen biography of James J. Walker, *Beau James* (Paramount, 1957).

Sierra Sue, words and music by Joseph Buell Carey (1916). It was revised by Elliott Shapiro in 1940 when it was popularized by Bing Crosby in a Decca recording. The song provided the title for and was heard in a motion picture (Republic, 1941), sung by Gene Autry.

Sigman, Carl, composer and lyricist, born Brooklyn, New York, 1909.

See: Answer Me; Ballerina; Careless Hands; Civilization; Ebb Tide; Enjoy Yourself, It's Later Than You Think; I Could Have Told You; It's All in the Game; The Mountains Beyond the Moon; My Heart Cries for You; Till; The World Outside; Twenty-Four Hours of Sunshine.

Signed, Sealed and Delivered, words and music by Cowboy Copas and Lois Mann (1951). Popularized by Cowboy Copas in a King recording.

Silhouettes, words and music by Frank C. Shay, Jr., and Bob Crewe (1957). Popularized by the Rays in a Cameo recording.

Silk Stockings, a musical comedy with book by George S. Kaufman, Leueen MacGrath and Abe Burrows based on the motion picture *Ninotchka*. Songs by Cole Porter. Starring Don Ameche and Hildegarde Neff (1955). Original cast recording (RCA Victor).

The motion-picture adaptation of the musical starred Fred Astaire and Cyd Charisse (MGM, 1957). It utilized the basic stage score.

See: All of You; Paris Loves Lovers.

Silver, Abner, composer and lyricist, born New York City, 1895.

See: Angel Child; I'm Going South; My Home Town Is a One Horse Town; Say It Again; Say It While Dancing; There Goes My Heart; With These Hands.

Silver Bell, words by Edward Madden, music by Percy Wenrich (1910).

Silver Bells, words and music by Jay Livingston and Ray Evans (1950). Introduced by Bob Hope and Marilyn Maxwell in the motion picture *The Lemon Drop Kid* (Paramount, 1951). Bing Crosby's recording with Carol Richard for Decca was a best seller. The song has since become a Yuletide favorite, selling over a million copies of sheet music and ten million records.

Ray Evans has explained: "The main reason this song became so successful is that this is the only song . . . that's about Christmas in a big city with shop lights and shoppers and the rest. . . . We got that only because that happened to be the locale of the picture."

Silver Haired Daddy, words and music by Dan Kane (1931). Popularized by Gene Autry in a Columbia recording that sold a million disks in 1939.

Silver Moon, words by Dorothy Donnelly, music by Sigmund Romberg (1927). Introduced in the operetta *My Maryland* (1927).

Silver Threads Among the Gold, words by Eben E. Rexford, music by Hart Pease Danks (1873). One of the most successful sentimental ballads of its time. It sold over a million copies of sheet music before the end of the nineteenth century.

Danks paid Rexford three dollars for the rights to set to music a poem Rexford had published in a Wisconsin farm journal. Apparently Rexford regarded the payment as generous, for he sent Danks a batch of other poems for his use. One of these was "Silver Threads Among the Gold," which Rexford had written as a sentimental gesture to his wife. It is ironic to note that Danks divorced his wife just one year after his ballad was published.

Though extraordinarily popular in the 1870s and 1880s, the ballad entered upon a new period of success in 1907 after being revived by Richard J. José. It has since that time become one of the most successful sentimental ballads ever written. Unfortunately, since he had sold his song outright to the publishers, Danks failed to capitalize on this success. The song has become a favorite with barber-shop quartets.

The Simple Joys of Maidenhood, words by Alan Jay Lerner, music by Frederick Loewe (1960). Introduced by Julie Andrews in the musical play *Camelot* (1960).

Simple Melody. *See:* Play a Simple Melody.

Sin, words by Chester R. Shull, music by George Hoven (1951). Popularized in 1952 by Eddie Howard in a Mercury recording and by the Four Aces in a Decca recording.

Sinbad, a musical extravaganza with book and lyrics by Harold Atteridge. Music by Sigmund Romberg. Various songs by other composers and lyricists were interpolated by Al Jolson while the show was running. Starring Al Jolson (1918).

See: Bagdad; Hello, Central, Give Me No Man's Land; I'll Say She Is; My Mammy; Rock-a-bye Your Baby with a Dixie Melody; Swanee; Why Do They All Take the Night Boat to Albany?

Sincerely, words and music by Harvey Fuqua and Alan Freed (1954). Popularized in 1955 by the McGuire Sisters in a Coral recording.

Sing a Tropical Song, words by Frank Loesser, music by Jimmy McHugh (1943). One of the earliest American commercial applications of calypso music to become a success. It was introduced in the motion-picture musical *Happy Go Lucky,* starring Dick Powell and Mary Martin (Paramount, 1943), sung by Dick Powell, Eddie Bracken and Sir Lancelot. It was popularized by the Andrews Sisters in a Decca recording.

Sing, Baby, Sing, words by Jack Yellen, music by Lew Pollack (1936). Introduced by Alice Faye in the motion-picture musical of the same name (20th Century-Fox, 1936).

Sing, Baby, Sing, a motion-picture musical starring Alice Faye (20th Century-Fox, 1936). Songs by Walter Bullock and Richard A. Whiting, by Jack Yellen and Lew Pollack and by Sidney Mitchell and Louis Alter.

See: Sing, Baby, Sing; When Did You Leave Heaven?; You Turned the Tables on Me.

The Singer in the Gallery, words and music by Harry A. Mayo (1895). Inspired by the vogue in vaudeville for boy stooges during the 1890s. It is generally believed that this number's title referred to the boy Gus Edwards, who had recently enjoyed success by singing reprises while seated in the balcony. Others, however, maintain that the singer in this song refers to thirteen-year-old Thomas Dimond, who, in 1891, rose spontaneously from his seat (even though he was not part of the vaudeville act) and sang a reprise of "My Girl's a New Yorker" after it had been presented on the stage by Lottie Gilson.

Sing for Your Supper, words by Lorenz Hart, music by Richard Rodgers (1938). Introduced by Muriel Angelus, Marcy Wescott, Wynn Murray and a female chorus (then danced to by Betty Bruce and ensemble) in the musical *The Boys from Syracuse* (1938). In the motion-picture adaptation of the musical (Universal, 1940), it was sung by Martha Raye.

The Singing Fool, a motion-picture musical starring Al Jolson (Warner, 1929). Songs by De Sylva, Brown and Henderson, with an interpolation of "There's a Rainbow 'Round My Shoulder" by Billy Rose, Al Jolson and Dave Dreyer.

See: I'm Sitting on Top of the World; It All Depends on You; Sonny Boy; There's a Rainbow 'Round My Shoulder.

Singing the Blues, words and music by Melvin Endsley (1956). Popularized by Marty Robbins in a Columbia recording and in 1957 by Guy Mitchell's recording for Columbia that sold a million disks.

Singin' in the Rain, words by Arthur Freed, music by Nacio Herb Brown (1929). Introduced by Cliff Edwards (supplemented by an ensemble that included Joan Crawford, Marie Dressler and George K. Arthur) in the motion-picture musical *Hollywood Revue of 1929* (MGM, 1929). The song was interpolated for Judy Garland in the motion-picture musical *Little Nellie Kelly* (MGM, 1940). It was also the inspiration for and gave the title to a motion-picture musical (MGM, 1952); here the number was sung under the titles by Donald O'Connor, Gene Kelly and Debbie Reynolds, while Gene Kelly sang and danced to it in an extended sequence within the picture.

Singin' in the Rain, a motion-picture musical starring Gene Kelly, Donald O'Connor and Debbie Reynolds (MGM, 1952). With a single exception, the score was made up of songs by Arthur Freed and Nacio Herb Brown, many of them standards. The exception was "Moses" by Betty Comden, Adolph Green and Roger Edens.

See: All I Do Is Dream of You; Broadway Melody; Fit As a Fiddle; Good Morning; Singin' in the Rain; You Are My Lucky Star; Wedding of the Painted Doll; Would You?

Singin' the Blues, words by Dorothy Fields, music by Jimmy McHugh (1931). Title song of a motion-picture musical (MGM, 1930). It was then used as the title song of a stage musical, sung by Dinah Washington (1931).

Sing Me a Song of Social Significance, words and music by Harold Rome (1937). A social-conscious love song introduced in the topical, political revue *Pins and Needles* (1937).

Sing Something Simple, words and music by Herman Hupfeld (1930). A protest against sophisticated songs with tricky rhymes. It was introduced by Ruth Tester (with the assistance of Fay Brady, Arline Judge and a male chorus) in the *Second Little Show* (1930). In 1931 it was sung by Nelson Keys in the London revue *Folly to Be Wise*.

Sing, You Sinners, words by Sam Coslow, music by W. Franke Harling (1930). Introduced in the motion-picture musical *Honey,* starring Nancy Carroll (Paramount, 1930) The song was popularized by Lilliar Roth; and it was sung by Susan Hayward in the Lillian Roth screen biography *I'll Cry Tomorrow* (MGM, 1955). Billy Daniels sang it in the motion-picture musical *Cruisin' Down the River* (Columbia, 1953).

Sing, You Sinners, a motion-picture musical starring Bing Crosby and Fred MacMurray, with Donald O'Connor, then thirteen, making his screen debut (Paramount, 1938). Songs by Johnny Burke and James V. Monaco, and by Frank Loesser and Hoagy Carmichael.
   See: I've Got a Pocketful of Dreams; Small Fry.

Sink the Bismarck, words and music by Johnny Horton and Tillman Franks (1960). Introduced and popularized by Johnny Horton in a Columbia recording.

Sioux City Sue, words by Ray Freedman, music by Dick Thomas (1945). It provided the title for and was sung by Gene Autry in a motion picture (Republic, 1946). It was popularized by Dick Thomas in a National recording.

The Siren's Song, words by P. G. Wodehouse, music by Jerome Kern (1917). The legend of the Lorelei, introduced by Edith Hallor in the musical *Leave It to Jane* (1917).

Sit Down, You're Rockin' the Boat, words and music by Frank Loesser (1950). Introduced by Stubby Kaye in the musical *Guys and Dolls* (1950). He also sang it in the motion-picture adaptation of the musical (MGM, 1955).

Sixteen Candles, words and music by Luther Dixon and Allyson R. Khent (1959). Popularized by the Crests in a Co-Ed recording.

Sixteen Going on Seventeen. *See:* You Are Sixteen.

Sixteen Reasons, words and music by Bill and Dorce Post (1960). Popularized by Connie Stevens in a Warner recording.

Sixteen Tons, words and music by Merle Travis (1947). Introduced by Merle Travis in a Capitol recording, then popularized in 1955 by Tennessee Ernie Ford on his television show and in a Capitol recording that sold over a million disks.

The Skidmore Fancy Ball, words by Edward Harrigan, music by David Braham (1878). Introduced in the Harrigan and Hart extravaganza of the same name (1878).

The Skidmore Guard, words by Edward Harrigan, music by David Braham (1874). Introduced in the Harrigan and Hart extravaganza of the same name (1874).

The Skidmore Masquerade, words by Edward Harrigan, music by David Braham (1880). Introduced in the Harrigan and Hart extravaganza *The Mulligan Guards' Nominee* (1880).

The Sky Fell Down, words by Edward Heyman, music by Louis Alter (1940). The first song recorded by Frank Sinatra. He was then a vocalist with the Tommy Dorsey orchestra; his RCA Victor recording in 1940 was a best seller.

Skyscraper, a musical comedy with book by Peter Stone based on Elmer Rice's play *Dream Girl*. Lyrics by Sammy Cahn. Music by James Van Heusen. Starring Julie Harris (1965). Original cast recording (Capitol).
   See: Everybody Has a Right to Be Wrong; I'll Only Miss Her When I Think of Her.

Sky's the Limit, a motion-picture musical starring Fred Astaire and Joan Leslie (RKO, 1943). Songs by Johnny Mercer and Harold Arlen.
   See: One for My Baby; My Shining Hour.

Slap That Bass, words by Ira Gershwin, music by George Gershwin (1937). Introduced by Fred Astaire in the motion-picture musical *Shall We Dance?* (RKO, 1937). For this number Astaire devised an elaborate dance sequence set in the boiler room of a transatlantic steamer.

Sleep, Baby, Sleep (or, Irene's Lullaby), words and music by John J. Handley (1885).

A Sleepin' Bee, words by Truman Capote and Harold Arlen, music by Harold Arlen (1954). Introduced by Diahann Carroll, Enid Mosier, Ada Moore and Dolores Harper in the musical play *House of Flowers* (1954). Arlen originally wrote this melody a few years earlier and had planned on using it in the motion picture *A Star Is Born.* But it was not used there. With new lyrics, the melody was placed in *House of Flowers.* Edward Jablonski describes it as a "sensuous, undulating melody that rises a tenth and drops a fifth in a mere four bars," providing it with "an almost languid personality of great melodic beauty."

Sleepy Lagoon, words by Jack Lawrence, music by Eric Coates (1930). In an arrangement by Albert Sirmay it was popularized by Tommy Dorsey and his orchestra, and by Harry James and his orchestra. The song became a major hit in 1942, making seventeen appearances on the Hit Parade. The song gave the title to and was heard in a motion picture starring Judy Canova and Dennis Day (Republic, 1943).

Sleepy Time Gal, words by Joseph R. Alden and Raymond B. Egan, music by Ange Lorenzo and Richard A. Whiting (1925). Popularized by Glen Gray and his Casa Loma Orchestra. It was prominently featured in a motion picture of the same name starring Tom Brown and Judy Canova (Republic, 1942).

Sleigh Ride, words by Mitchell Parish, music by Leroy Anderson (1950). Originally an instrumental, popularized in a Decca recording by Leroy Anderson and his orchestra.

Sleigh Ride in July, words by Johnny Burke, music by James Van Heusen (1944). Introduced by Dinah Shore in the motion-picture musical *Belle of Yukon* (RKO, 1944).

Slide, Kelly, Slide, words and music by John W. Kelly (1889). Introduced by the composer in vaudeville. This was the first popular song hit about baseball, a favorite with the New York Giants in the 1890s; it was played at the opening-day ceremonies of the then newly constructed Polo Grounds, in 1889. This ballad had been inspired by Mike (King) Kelly—no relation to the composer—who is represented in Baseball's Hall of Fame in Cooperstown, New York.

Slipping Around, words and music by Floyd Tillman (1949). Popularized by Margaret Whiting and Jimmy Wakely in a Capitol recording.

Sloane, A. Baldwin, composer, born Baltimore, Maryland, 1872; died Red Bank, New Jersey, 1926.

See: Heaven Will Protect the Working Girl; Life Is Only What You Make It; When You Ain't Got No Money, Well, You Needn't Come Around.

Slowpoke, words and music by Pee Wee King, Redd Stewart and Mrs. Chilton Price (1951). Introduced and popularized by Pee Wee King's recording for RCA Victor.

This song originated with Mrs. Chilton Price—a housewife in Louisville, Kentucky; this was her maiden effort at songwriting. She submitted it to Pee Wee King, a Louisville bandleader, who collaborated with Redd Stewart in revising and polishing it.

Slumber On, My Little Gypsy Sweetheart. *See:* Gypsy Love Song.

Slumming on Park Avenue, words and music by Irving Berlin (1937). Introduced in the motion-picture musical *On the Avenue* (20th Century-Fox, 1937).

Small Fry, words by Frank Loesser, music by Hoagy Carmichael (1938). Introduced by Bing Crosby in the motion-picture musical *Sing, You Sinners* (Paramount, 1938). It was further popularized by him in a Decca recording with Johnny Mercer. The youngster to whom Crosby sang this number in the movie was the thirteen-year-old Donald O'Connor, then making his screen debut.

Small World, words by Stephen Sondheim, music by Jule Styne (1959). Introduced by Ethel Merman and Jack Klugman in the musical *Gypsy* (1959). It was popularized by Johnny Mathis in a Columbia recording. In the motion-picture adaptation of the musical (Warner, 1962), it was sung on the soundtrack by Lisa Kirk (for Rosalind Russell).

Smarty, words by Jack Norworth, music by Albert von Tilzer (1908). A song introduced and popularized in vaudeville by Jack Norworth, who made it a staple in his act.

A Smile Will Go a Long, Long Way, words by Benny Davis, music by Harry Akst (1923). Popularized by Al Jolson.

Smiles, words by J. Will Callahan, music by Lee S. Roberts (1917). Introduced by Neil Carrington and a chorus of girls in the revue *The Passing Show of 1918.*

The idea for this song came to Roberts at a convention of music dealers in Chicago. A speaker there lectured on the value of a smile in business dealings, to which Roberts remarked facetiously: "There are smiles that make us happy, and smiles that make us blue." That day he wrote a melody which he sent to Callahan with suggestions for a lyric about smiles. Callahan wrote the words in about half an hour. Having been rejected by all the principal publishers in Tin Pan Alley, "Smiles" was eventually released by a new firm, formed for this very purpose by the songwriters themselves. It was plugged by several leading dance bands until, within six months of publication, it sold in excess of two million copies of sheet music. (Eventually this sale passed the three-million mark.) It was heard in vaudeville, dance halls, restaurants; and it was released in numerous recordings and player-piano rolls. A good deal of this success stemmed from the fact that the song provided a release from war tensions—this being the period of World War I—allowing both soldiers and civilians to forget their war anxieties in a sentimental, nostalgic tune.

During radio's early history the song was used as the theme music for the Ipana Troubadours. In 1929 the song was interpolated in the motion-picture musical *Applause,* starring Helen Morgan (Paramount). It was subsequently used in several other motion-picture musicals.

These included *The Dolly Sisters* (20th Century-Fox, 1945); *What Price Glory* (20th Century-Fox, 1952), sung by a male chorus; *Wait Till the Sun Shines, Nellie* (20th-Century-Fox, 1952); and *Somebody Loves Me* (20th Century-Fox, 1952). The song was also interpolated in the background music of non-musical motion pictures. Among these were *Stella Dallas,* starring Barbara Stanwyck (Samuel Goldwyn, 1934); *Elmer Gantry,* starring Burt Lancaster (United Artists, 1960); and *Ice Palace,* starring Richard Burton (Warner, 1960), where it was used as a recurring theme.

Smilin' Through, words and music by Arthur Penn (1919). Hit song in the early 1920s. It was subsequently used as a recurrent theme in the background music for the motion picture of the same name starring Norma Shearer (MGM, 1932).

Smith, Chris, composer, born Charleston, South Carolina, 1879; died New York City, 1949.

See: All In, Down and Out; Ballin' the Jack; Beans, Beans, Beans; Down Among the Sugar Cane; Fifteen Cents; He's a Cousin of Mine; If He Comes In, I'm Going Out; You're in the Right Church But the Wrong Pew.

Smith, Edgar, lyricist, born Brooklyn, New York, 1857; died Bayside, New York, 1938.

See: Stromberg, John.

See also: Heaven Will Protect the Working Girl; Life Is Only What You Make It, After All.

Smith, Harry B., lyricist, born Buffalo, New York, 1860; died Atlantic City, New Jersey, 1936.

See: De Koven, Reginald; Herbert, Victor.

See also: I Wonder If You Still Care for Me; Play, Gypsies, Dance, Gypsies; Sheik of Araby; You're Here and I'm Here; Yours Is My Heart Alone.

Smith, Robert B., lyricist, born Chicago, Illinois, 1875; died New York City, 1951.

See: Herbert, Victor.

See also: Come Down, Ma Evenin'

Star; It's a Cute Little Way of My Own; I Want to Be Good, But My Eyes Won't Let Me.

Smoke Gets in Your Eyes, words by Otto Harbach, music by Jerome Kern (1933). Introduced by Tamara in the musical *Roberta* (1933), where it stopped the show regularly. In the first motion-picture adaptation of the musical (RKO, 1935), it was presented by Fred Astaire and Ginger Rogers in a dance that as Astaire noted in his autobiography, "has always been one of my favorites." In the second motion-picture adaptation (MGM, 1952, entitled *Lovely to Look At*), it was sung by Kathryn Grayson.

Kern originally wrote the melody as a march tune to serve as the signature music for a radio series that never materialized. When a song was needed for Stephanie in Act II of *Roberta,* Kern adapted the march tune to Harbach's lyrics by slowing up the tempo and sentimentalizing the melody.

This song has always been one of Jerome Kern's favorites among his own creations; and the lyric was regarded by Harbach as one of his best. The Kern melody is noteworthy for the diatonic skips in the broad upward sweep of the melody, and for the seductive key change in the release. The song was also interpolated in the Kern screen biography *Till the Clouds Roll By* (MGM, 1946). The song was revived in 1958 by the Platters in a Mercury recording that sold over a million disks.

Smoke, Smoke, Smoke, words and music by M. Travis and Tex Williams (1947). Popularized by Tex Williams in a Capitol recording and by Phil Harris in an RCA Victor recording.

Smoke Rings, words by Ned Washington, music by H. Eugene Gilford (1932). Introduced and popularized by Glen Gray and the Casa Loma Orchestra; it became their theme song. The composer was the arranger for this orchestra.

Smokie, words and music by William P. Black (1959, 1960). Popularized by Bill Black in two Combo recordings—"Part I" in 1959 and "Part II" in 1960.

Snooky Ookums, words and music by Irving Berlin (1913). A comedy number making effective use of baby talk, introduced and popularized by Natalie Normandie. It was revived by Fred Astaire and Judy Garland in the motion-picture musical *Easter Parade* (MGM, 1948).

Snoops the Lawyer, words by Bert Kalmar, music by Harry Ruby (1921). Popularized in vaudeville in the early 1920s. This song helped give Beatrice Lillie her start as a comedienne in England.

Snowflakes and Sweethearts (The Snowbird Song), words and music by Robert Wright and George "Chet" Forrest, melody based on three compositions by Rachmaninoff *Polka, Valse* and "Thou, My Beloved Harvest Field" (1965). Introduced by Constance Towers, Barbara Alexander, Maggie Task, Michael Quinn and chorus in the musical *Anya* (1965).

Snow White and the Seven Dwarfs, a full-length Walt Disney animated-cartoon motion picture (RKO, 1937). Songs by Larry Morey and Frank Churchill.

See: Heigh, Ho; One Song; Some Day My Prince Will Come; Whistle While You Work.

Snyder, Ted, composer, born Freeport, Illinois, 1881; died Hollywood, California, 1965.

See (Lyrics by Irving Berlin): Kiss Me, Honey, Kiss Me; My Wife's Gone to the Country; Next to Your Mother, Who Do You Love?; Oh, That Beautiful Rag; Sweet Italian Love; That Mysterious Rag.

See also: Beautiful Eyes; The Ghost of the Violin; How'd You Like to Be My Daddy?; If You Cared for Me; In the Land of Harmony; I Wonder If You Still Care for Me; Moonlight on the Rhine; The Sheik of Araby; There's a Girl in This World for Every Boy; Who's Sorry Now?

So Am I, words by Ira Gershwin, music by George Gershwin (1924). Introduced by Alan Edwards and Adele Astaire in the musical *Lady, Be Good!* (1924).

So Are You, words by Ira Gershwin, music by George Gershwin (1929). Introduced by Eddie Foy, Jr., and Kathryn Hereford in the musical *Show Girl* (1929).

So Do I, words by Johnny Burke, music by Arthur Johnston (1963). Introduced by Bing Crosby in the motion-picture musical *Pennies from Heaven* (Columbia, 1936).

So Do I, words by Bud De Sylva, music by Vincent Youmans (1932). Introduced by Jack Whiting, June Knight and chorus in the musical *Take a Chance* (1932).

So Far, words by Oscar Hammerstein II, music by Richard Rodgers (1947). Introduced by Gloria Wills in the musical play *Allegro* (1947).

Soft Lights and Sweet Music, words and music by Irving Berlin (1932). Introduced by Katherine Carrington and J. Harold Murray in the musical *Face the Music* (1932). In this production the song was cued in by a brilliant mirror scene devised by Hassard Short.

Softly, As in a Morning Sunrise, words by Oscar Hammerstein II, music by Sigmund Romberg (1928). Introduced by William O'Neal in the operetta *The New Moon* (1928). In the first motion-picture adaptation of the operetta (MGM, 1930), it was sung by Lawrence Tibbett; in the second (MGM, 1940), by Nelson Eddy. Helen Traubel sang it in the Sigmund Romberg screen biography *Deep in My Heart* (MGM, 1954).

Soft Summer Breeze, words by Judy Spencer, music by Eddie Heywood (1956). Popularized by Eddie Heywood in an instrumental recording for Mercury.

So Help Me, words by Eddie De Lange, music by James Van Heusen (1938). Introduced by Lee Wiley in a radio program, *Swing Session*. It was subsequently popularized by Russ Morgan and his orchestra.

So in Love, words and music by Cole Porter (1948). Introduced by Patricia Morison in the musical play *Kiss Me, Kate* (1948). In the motion-picture adaptation of the musical (MGM, 1953), it was sung by Kathryn Grayson and Howard Keel. Patti Page's recording for Mercury was a best seller.

So I Ups to Him. *See:* I Ups to Him.

Soldier Boy, words and music by Luther Dixon and Florence Green (1962). Popularized by the Shirelles in a Scepter recording.

Soliloquy, words by Oscar Hammerstein II, music by Richard Rodgers (1945). An extended seven-minute narrative, comprising eight different melodic fragments, in which the hero expresses his joy in discovering he is about to become a father. It was introduced by John Raitt in the musical play *Carousel* (1945). "Soliloquy" was the first number Rodgers and Hammerstein wrote for the score of *Carousel*. When they finished the narrative they knew, as Rodgers revealed, "that we had the play licked." In the motion-picture adaptation of the musical (20th Century-Fox, 1956), it was sung by Gordon MacRae.

So Little Time, words by Paul Francis Webster, music by Dimitri Tiomkin (1963). Introduced in the motion picture *55 Days at Peking*, starring Ava Gardner and Charlton Heston (Allied Artists, 1963), where it was sung under the end titles by Andy Williams.

Solitude, words by Eddie De Lange and Irving Mills, music by Duke Ellington (1934). This was Ellington's first successful song, popularized by Ellington and his orchestra first in an RCA Victor recording in 1933, and then in their recording for Brunswick in 1934. In 1934 "Solitude" received an ASCAP award of $2,500 as the best song of the year.

So Long, Big Time, words by Dory Langdon, music by Harold Arlen (1964). Introduced by Tony Bennett on television in a *20th Century* program honoring Harold Arlen.

So Long, Dearie, words and music by Jerry Herman (1964). Introduced by Carol Channing and David Burns in the musical *Hello, Dolly!* (1964).

It was popularized by Louis Armstrong and his orchestra in a Kapp recording.

So Long, Letty, words and music by Earl Carroll (1915). Opening chorus (later a duet for Charlotte Greenwood and Sydney Grant) in the musical of the same name (1916). It was also sung in the motion-picture adaptation of the musical (Warner, 1929).

So Long, Mary, words and music by George M. Cohan (1905). Introduced by Donald Brian in the musical *Forty-Five Minutes from Broadway* (1906). It was interpolated in the Cohan screen biography *Yankee Doodle Dandy* (Warner, 1942).

So Long, Oo Long, words by Bert Kalmar, music by Harry Ruby (1920). Introduced in the Palace Theatre in New York in 1920 by Bert Kalmar and Harry Ruby, as members of the House of David Band act. "We faked being in the band, pretending to play instruments, then went up and sang 'So Long, Oo Long,' which we followed with a dance routine," Ruby wrote to this editor. "We then yanked off the phony beards and the house went mad when they saw it was us." The song was revived in the screen biography of Ruby and Kalmar, *Three Little Words* (MGM, 1950), sung by Fred Astaire and Red Skelton.

So Many Ways, words and music by Bobby Stevenson (1958). Popularized by Brook Benton in a Mercury recording.

Somebody Bad Stole de Wedding Bell, words by Bob Hilliard, music by Dave Mann (1954). Popularized by Georgia Gibbs in a Mercury recording.

Somebody Bigger Than You and I, words and music by Johnny Lange, Hy Heath and Sonny Burke (1951). Introduced in the motion picture *The Old West,* starring Gene Autry (Columbia, 1952).

Somebody Else Is Taking My Place, words and music by Dick Howard, Bob Ellsworth and Russ Morgan (1937). Introduced by Russ Morgan and his orchestra. It was interpolated in two motion pictures in 1942: in the musical *Strictly in the Groove,* starring Leon Errol, Donald O'Connor and Martha Tilton (Universal, 1942), and in the *Call of the Canyon,* starring Gene Autry (Republic, 1942).

Somebody Lied, words and music by Jeff T. Brainen and Evan Lloyd, adapted by Bert Williams (1907). Ragtime comedy number introduced by Bert Williams in the musical *Bandana Land* (1907).

Somebody Loves Me, words by Bud De Sylva and Ballard MacDonald, music by George Gershwin (1924). Introduced by Winnie Lightner in the revue *George White Scandals of 1924.* This song subsequently became a favorite of Blossom Seeley. The melody is interesting for the introduction of a blue note on the word "who" in the chrous.

Lena Horne sang "Somebody Loves Me" in the motion-picture musical *Broadway Rhythm* (MGM, 1944). It was sung and danced to by Doris Day and Gene Nelson in the motion-picture musical *Lullaby of Broadway* (Warner, 1951), and it provided the title for and was heard in a motion picture starring Betty Hutton and Ralph Meeker (Paramount, 1952). The song was also interpolated in the George Gershwin screen biography *Rhapsody in Blue* (Warner, 1945) and in the screen musical *Young at Heart,* starring Doris Day and Frank Sinatra (Warner, 1955).

Somebody Loves Me, words and music by Hattie Starr (1892). Love ballad, by Tin Pan Alley's first successful woman composer. Hattie Starr brought her ballad to Josephine Sabel, singing star then appearing at Koster and Bial's. Josephine Sabel suggested revising the number from a fast to a slow waltz time. Hattie Starr complied; Josephine Sabel introduced it in vaudeville; and Joseph W. Stern & Co. in Tin Pan Alley published it.

Somebody Loves Me, a motion-picture musical biography of the vaudeville team of Blossom Seeley and Benny Fields, starring Betty Hutton as

Blossom Seeley and Ralph Meeker as Benny Fields (Paramount, 1952). The score was made up mainly of standards.

See: I Can't Tell Why I Love You; I Cried for You; I'm Sorry I Made You Cry; Jealous; Smiles; Somebody Loves Me; Wang, Wang Blues; Way Down Yonder in New Orleans.

Somebody Loves You, words by Charles Tobias, music by Peter De Rose (1932).

Somebody's Coming to My House, words and music by Irving Berlin (1913). Popularized by Sophie Tucker in vaudeville; she sang it for the first time in 1914 at Hammerstein's Victoria Theatre in New York.

Somebody Stole My Gal, words and music by Leo Wood (1918). Popularized by Ted Weems and his orchestra.

Some Day, words by Brian Hooker, music by Rudolf Friml (1925). Introduced by Carolyn Thomson in the operetta *The Vagabond King* (1925). In the first motion-picture adaptation of the operetta (Paramount, 1930), it was sung by Jeanette MacDonald; in the second screen version (Paramount, 1956), by Kathryn Grayson.

Some Day I'll Find You, words by Schuyler Greene, music by Zoel Parenteau (1921). Introduced in the cabaret scene in the Broadway play *Kiki* (1921).

Some Enchanted Evening, words by Oscar Hammerstein II, music by Richard Rodgers (1949). Introduced by Ezio Pinza in the musical play *South Pacific* (1949). In the motion-picture adaptation of the musical (20th Century-Fox, 1958), it was sung on the soundtrack by Giorgio Tozzi (for Rossano Brazzi) with Mitzi Gaynor. Successful recordings were made by Ezio Pinza for Columbia and Perry Como for RCA Victor.

Somehow I Never Could Believe, words by Langston Hughes, music by Kurt Weill (1947). Ballad of a woman's frustrations introduced by Polyna Stoska in the musical play *Street Scene* (1947).

Some Like It Hot, a motion-picture with songs starring Marilyn Monroe, Tony Curtis and Jack Lemmon (United Artists, 1959). The score was made up of standards.

See: By the Beautiful Sea; Down Among the Sheltering Palms; I'm Through with Love; I Wanna Be Loved by You; Runnin' Wild; Sweet Georgia Brown.

Some Little Bug Is Going to Find You, words by Benjamin Hapgood, Burt and Roy Atwell, music by Silvio Hein (1915). Comedy song satirizing the "flu" scare in 1915. It was interpolated in the Franz Lehár operetta *Alone at Last* (1915) and in the musical *All Over Town* (1917). Phil Harris revived it a generation later in an RCA Victor recording.

Some of These Days, words and music by Shelton Brooks (1910). Introduced by Sophie Tucker at the White City Park in Chicago in 1910; from then on it became her theme song.

Shelton was an unknown when one day in 1910 he came to a theater in Chicago, where Sophie Tucker was appearing, with the manuscript of "Some of These Days." Sophie Tucker at first refused to see him, but her maid and friend, Mollie Elkins, prevailed on her to give the young composer a hearing. "The minute I heard 'Some of These Days,'" Sophie Tucker later recalled in her autobiography, "I could have kicked myself for almost losing it. . . . It had everything. Hasn't it proved it? I've been singing it for thirty years, made it my theme. I've turned it inside out, singing it every way imaginable, as a dramatic song, as a novelty number, as a sentimental ballad, and always audiences have loved it and asked for it."

Sophie Tucker sang it in two motion-picture musicals, *Broadway Melody of 1937* (MGM, 1937) and *Follow the Boys* (Universal, 1944). The song was interpolated in the Marx Brothers' motion-picture extravaganza *Animal Crackers* (Paramount, 1930), sung by Lillian Roth. It was also heard in the motion-picture adaptation of the operetta *Rose Marie* (MGM, 1936).

Sophie Tucker's autobiography, published in 1945, was called *Some of These Days*. The melody was played on an organ at Sophie Tucker's funeral on February 11, 1966.

Someone Like You, words by Robert B. Smith, music by Victor Herbert (1919). Introduced by Richard Pyle and Mary Milburn in the operetta *Angel Face* (1919).

Someone to Watch Over Me, words by Ira Gershwin, music by George Gershwin (1926). Introduced by Gertrude Lawrence in the musical *Oh, Kay!* (1926). This was Gertrude Lawrence's first appearance in an American musical.

The song was used as a recurring theme in the non-musical motion picture *John Loves Mary*, starring Ronald Reagan and Patricia Neal (Warner, 1949), where hero and heroine identify it as "our song." The song was also interpolated in the George Gershwin screen biography *Rhapsody in Blue* (Warner, 1945); in the motion-picture musical *Young at Heart* (Warner, 1955), sung by Frank Sinatra; and in the motion-picture musical *Three for the Money* (Columbia, 1955), played under the title and used as a recurring theme. It appeared as a piano episode in the non-musical motion picture *Backfire* (Warner, 1950), starring Edmond O'Brien and Gordon MacRae.

Someone Will Make You Smile, words by Irving Caesar to the melody "Wien, du Stadt meiner Traeume" by Rudolf Siencynski (1923). Caesar wrote two different sets of lyrics for this famous Austrian song. The first version, entitled "Someone Will Make You Smile," was introduced in the Broadway musical *Poppy* (1923). The second version, named "Vienna Dreams," was published in 1937, and was interpolated a quarter of a century after that in the motion-picture musical *Painting the Clouds with Sunshine* (Warner, 1951).

Some People, words by Stephen Sondheim, music by Jule Styne (1959). Introduced by Ethel Merman in the musical *Gypsy* (1959). In the motion-picture adaptation of the musi-

cal (Warner, 1962), it was sung on the soundtrack by Lisa Kirk (for Rosalind Russell).

Some Sort of Somebody, words by Elsie Janis, music by Jerome Kern (1915). Introduced by Elsie Janis in the musical *Miss Information* (1915). It was then interpolated in and became successful in the Princess Theatre production of *Very Good, Eddie* (1915), sung by Oscar Shaw and Ann Orr.

Some Sunday Morning, words by Ted Koehler, music by J. K. Jerome and Ray Heindorf (1945). Introduced in the non-musical motion picture *San Antonio*, starring Errol Flynn (Warner, 1945), sung by Alexis Smith.

Some Sunday Morning, words by Gus Kahn and Raymond Egan, music by Richard A. Whiting (1917).

Some Sunny Day, words and music by Irving Berlin (1922). Hit song in the early 1920s. It was revived in the motion-picture musical *Alexander's Ragtime Band* (20th Century-Fox, 1938).

Some Sweet Day, words by Gene Buck, music by Dave Stamper and Louis A. Hirsch (1923). Introduced in the *Ziegfeld Follies of 1922*.

Something for the Boys, a musical comedy with book by Herbert and Dorothy Fields. Lyrics and music by Cole Porter. Starring Ethel Merman (1943).

See: But in the Morning; By the Mississinewah.

Something I Dreamed Last Night, words by Herb Magidson and Jack Yellen, music by Sammy Fain (1939). Introduced by Ella Logan in the revue *George White Scandals of 1939*. "The show died, and so did the song," Jack Yellen informed this editor. "But somehow or other the bistro torch singers managed to get copies, and every now and then I would hear it in the wee hours in some dive. Then somebody made a record, and somebody else, of no importance. Finally Peggy Lee came out with hers, and Julie London, and Johnny Mathis. And so another standard came to life."

Something Seems Tingle-Ingleing, words

by Otto Hauerbach (Harbach), music by Rudolf Friml (1913). Introduced by Burrell Barbaretto, Elaine Hammerstein and a female chorus in the musical *High Jinks* (1913).

Something's Gotta Give, words and music by Johnny Mercer (1955). Introduced by Fred Astaire in the motion-picture musical *Daddy Long Legs* (RKO, 1955). It was popularized in recordings by the McGuire Sisters for Coral and Sammy Davis for Decca.

Something Sort of Grandish, words by E. Y. Harburg, music by Burton Lane (1947). Introduced by David Wayne and Ella Logan in the musical play *Finian's Rainbow* (1947). This is one of Harburg's own favorites among his lyrics.

Something to Live For, words and music by Ervin Drake (1964). Introduced by Sally Ann Howes in the musical *What Makes Sammy Run?* (1964).

Something to Remember You By, words by Howard Dietz, music by Arthur Schwartz (1930). Introduced by Libby Holman in the revue *Three's a Crowd* (1930). She sang it to a sailor, whose back alone was visible to the audience; the part of that sailor was being performed by the then still unknown Fred MacMurray.

This song had originated as a comedy number entitled "I Have No Words" which Dietz and Schwartz had written for a London musical *Little Tommy Tucker*. Even with change of lyrics and title, Dietz still planned it as a comedy song for *Three's a Crowd*. But Libby Holman recognized its possibilities as a ballad and urged the writers to allow her to sing it with a change of tempo and mood.

"Something to Remember You By" was interpolated in the non-musical motion picture *Her Kind of Man,* starring Dane Clark and Janis Paige (Warner, 1946); in the screen musical *Dancing in the Dark* (20th Century-Fox, 1949), sung by Betsy Drake; and in the screen musical *The Band Wagon* (MGM, 1953).

Sometime, words by Rida Johnson Young, music by Rudolf Friml (1918). Introduced by Francine Larrimore in the operetta of the same name (1918).

Sometimes I'm Happy, words by Irving Caesar, music by Vincent Youmans (1927). Introduced by Louise Groody and Charles King in the musical *Hit the Deck* (1927). "If 'Sometimes I'm Happy' isn't sung all over the world until sometimes you'll be unhappy," prophesied Alan Dale, the drama critic, in reviewing *Hit the Deck,* "I'll eat my chapeau."

This Youmans melody was originally used for another song, "Come On and Pet Me," in the musical *Mary Jane McKane* (1923). It did not make much of an impression there and was taken out before the show reached New York. Then, renamed "Sometimes I'm Happy," the song was placed in the musical *A Night Out,* which never came to New York. Only after that was it placed in the score of *Hit the Deck.*

The celebrated jazz trumpeter Bunny Berigan achieved his first hit record with "Sometimes I'm Happy." The song was also a favorite with Florence Mills.

The song was heard in the motion-picture adaptation of the musical (RKO, 1930).

Somewhere Along the Way, words by Sammy Gallop, music by Kurt Adams (1952). Popularized by Nat King Cole in a Capitol recording.

Somewhere in Your Heart, words and music by Russel Faith and Clarence Kehner (1964). Popularized by Frank Sinatra in a Warner recording.

Some Wonderful Sort of Someone, words by Schuyler Greene, music by George Gershwin (1918). This was the first song by George Gershwin to be issued by Harms, his publisher from then on. It was introduced by Nora Bayes in the musical *Ladies First* (1918), where it was an interpolation. Adele Rowland sang it in the musical *The Lady in Red* (1919).

So Much in Love, words and music by William Jackson and George Williams (1963). Popularized by the

Tymes in a Parkway recording.

Sondheim, Stephen, composer and lyricist, born New York City, 1930.

See: Bernstein, Leonard; Rodgers, Richard; Styne, Jule.

See also: Lovely; With So Little to Be Sure Of.

Song for a Summer Night, words and music by Robert Allen (1956). Introduced by Mitch Miller and his orchestra in a television production of the same name, then popularized by them in a Columbia recording.

The Song from Desirée. *See:* We Meet Again.

Song from Moulin Rouge. *See:* Where Is Your Heart?

Song from Some Came Running. *See:* To Love and Be Loved.

The Song Is Ended (But the Melody Lingers On), words and music by Irving Berlin (1927).

The Song Is You, words by Oscar Hammerstein II, music by Jerome Kern (1932). Introduced by Tullio Carminati in the musical *Music in the Air* (1932). In the motion-picture adaptation of the musical (Fox, 1934), it was sung by John Boles. This number is particularly interesting for the dramatic way in which a new melodic thought unfolds in the release of the chorus, and in the way the main melody is subsequently carried to a climax.

Song of Love, words by Dorothy Donnelly, music by Sigmund Romberg, the melody based on a theme from Schubert's *Unfinished Symphony,* first movement (1921). It was introduced by Bertram Peacock, playing the role of Franz Schubert, in the operetta *Blossom Time* (1921). It has been estimated that Romberg earned over $100,000 in royalties from this song alone—a dramatic contrast to the total earnings of about $500 which Schubert is believed to have received from his total output of symphonies, songs, quartets, operas, sonatas, and so forth.

Song of Norway, an operetta based on the life of Edvard Grieg, with book by Milton Lazarus based on a play by Homer Curren. Lyrics and music by Robert Wright and George "Chet"

Forrest. Starring Lawrence Brooks as Grieg with Irra Petina (1944). Original cast recording (Decca).

See: I Love You; Strange Music.

The Song of Raintree County, words by Paul Francis Webster, music by John Green (1957). A song setting of the principal theme in Green's score for the motion picture *Raintree County,* starring Elizabeth Taylor (MGM, 1957). It was sung on the soundtrack under the titles by Nat King Cole, whose Capitol recording helped to popularize it.

Song of the Flame, words by Otto Harbach and Oscar Hammerstein II, music by George Gershwin and Herbert Stothart (1925). Introduced by Tessa Kosta, Chep Camp and the Russian Art Choir in the operetta of the same name (1925).

Song of the Islands, words and music by Charles E. King (1915). A Hawaiian song first published in Honolulu, then popularized in the United States. It was interpolated in several motion pictures. These included the screen musical *Melody Lane,* starring Eddie Leonard (Universal, 1929); the motion-picture musical *Ice-Capades Revue,* starring Ellen Drew and Richard Denning (Republic, 1942); and the non-musical motion picture *Cheaper by the Dozen,* starring Clifton Webb and Myrna Loy (20th Century-Fox, 1950).

Song of the Open Road, words and music by Albert Hay Malotte (1935). It was introduced in the motion picture *Hi, Gaucho,* starring Steffi Duna and John Carroll (RKO, 1936).

The Song of the Shirt, words by Clifford Grey, music by Herbert Stothart (1929). Introduced by Lawrence Tibbett in the motion-picture musical *The Rogue Song* (MGM, 1930).

Song of the South, the first Walt Disney motion picture with live performers, starring Ruth Warwick, Lucille Watson and Hattie McDaniel (MGM, 1946). Songs by various composers and lyricists, including Ray Gilbert and Allie Wrubel.

See: Zip-a-Dee-Doo-Dah.

Song of the Vagabonds, words by Brian Hooker, music by Rudolf Friml (1925). Rousing chorus from the operetta *The Vagabond King* (1925). It was sung in both motion-picture adaptations of the operetta (Paramount, 1930, Paramount, 1956).

Song of the Woodman, words by E. Y. Harburg, music by Harold Arlen (1936). Introduced by Bert Lahr in the revue *The Show Is On* (1936), to become one of his most celebrated routines.

The Songs That Maggie Sings, words and music by George M. Cohan (1896). An early George M. Cohan song in which he quotes a number of leading song hits, including "Sweet Rosie O'Grady," "Down in Poverty Row" and "My Mother Was a Lady." The reason for these quotations is that Cohan wanted to sell his song to the publisher, Joseph W. Stern, who had issued all the quoted hit songs. Apparently Joseph W. Stern & Company fell for the bait.

Sonny Boy, words by Al Jolson, Bud De Sylva and Lew Brown, music by Ray Henderson (1928). Introduced by Al Jolson in the motion-picture musical *The Singing Fool* (Warner, 1929). Jolson's Decca recording in 1946 sold over a million disks.

When *The Singing Fool* was being rehearsed in the Warner Brothers studios, one of its musical numbers was tried out in a local movie to get audience reaction. This reaction proved so unfavorable that the producers decided to replace this song with a new one that would play a crucial part in the story. Since shooting was about to begin, haste was imperative if a new song was to be written and used. Late that night Jolson telephoned Bud De Sylva from Hollywood to Atlantic City (where De Sylva was at work with Brown and Henderson in preparing a new show). Jolson described the kind of song he needed and how it fit into the plot. The next morning the team of De Sylva, Brown and Henderson had the song "Sonny Boy" written and ready. In the motion-picture biography of De Sylva, Brown and Henderson, *The Best Things in Life Are Free* (20th Century-Fox, 1956), the suggestion is made that the songwriters had created "Sonny Boy"

with tongue square in cheek, intending it to be a satire of sentimental ballads. In fact, when they sent their manuscript to Jolson they used for it the pen name of Elmer Colby. However, the names of De Sylva, Brown and Henderson appear on the published sheet music; and there is no record that these songwriters turned down the fabulous royalties when the song became a major success as a sentimental ballad.

Sons o' Guns, a musical comedy with book by Fred Thompson and Jack Donahue. Lyrics by Arthur Swanstrom and Benny Davis. Music by J. Fred Coots. Starring Jack Donahue and Lily Damita (1929).

See: Cross Your Fingers; Why?

Soon, words by Ira Gershwin, music by George Gershwin (1927). Introduced by Margaret Schilling and Jerry Goff in the musical *Strike Up the Band!* (1930).

Soon, words by Lorenz Hart, music by Richard Rodgers (1935). Introduced by Bing Crosby in the motion-picture musical *Mississippi* (1935).

Sophisticated Lady, words by Mitchell Parish and Irving Mills, music by Duke Ellington (1933). It originated as an instrumental composition that was recorded by Duke Ellington and his orchestra for Brunswick. When lyrics were written for this melody, "Sophisticated Lady" became one of its composer's most successful popular songs.

So Rare, words by Jack Sharpe, music by Jerry Herst (1937). Popularized in the late 1930s by Jimmy Dorsey and his orchestra. A quarter of a century later it was successfully revived by Andy Williams in a Cadence recording. The Fraternity recording by Jimmy Dorsey and his band in 1957 was also a best seller.

Sorry, I Ran All the Way Home, words and music by Harry Giosasi and Artie Zwirn (1958). Popularized in 1959 by the Impalas in a Cub recording.

So Tired, words and music by Jack Stuart and Russ Morgan (1943). This Russ Morgan specialty did not become popular until half a dozen years after its publication. In 1948 the American Federation of Musicians called a strike against the recording companies. Anticipating this move, many performers went into a recording frenzy to build up a backlog of releases before the strike went into effect. Russ Morgan and his orchestra went into an around-the-clock recording session. With one side still vacant, and nothing else in his repertory he could think of, Russ Morgan decided to revive "So Tired," which had been a failure in 1943, and forgotten since then. As Leo Walker wrote, this recording not only resurrected a song and made it a hit, but launched Russ Morgan and his orchestra on a highly successful recording career. "With the momentum from it, he [Russ Morgan] went on to become the Number One recording artist of 1949." Russ Morgan's best-selling recording was for Decca.

Sound Off, words and music by Willie Lee Duckworth (1950). Theme used by the United States Army for close-order drill training. It was originally published in *The Cadence System of Teaching Close Order Drill,* by Col. Bernard Lentz of the United States Army, in Harrisburg, Pennsylvania. The number was popularized by Vaughn Monroe in an RCA Victor recording.

The Sound of Money, words and music by Harold Rome (1962). Introduced by Elliott Gould, Sheree North, Barbara Monte, William Reilly and Edward Verso in the musical *I Can Get It for You Wholesale* (1962).

The Sound of Music, words by Oscar Hammerstein II, music by Richard Rodgers (1959). Title song of a musical play, introduced by Mary Martin (1959). In the motion-picture adaptation of the musical (20th Century-Fox, 1965), it was sung by Julie Andrews.

The Sound of Music, a musical play with text by Howard Lindsay and Russel Crouse suggested by Maria Augusta Trapp's autobiography. Lyrics by Oscar Hammerstein II. Music by Richard Rodgers. This was the last collaboration of Rodgers and Hammerstein. Starring Mary Martin,

Patricia Neway and Theodore Bikel (1959). Original cast recording (Columbia).

The motion-picture adaptation starred Julie Andrews and Christopher Plummer (20th Century-Fox, 1965). It used the basic stage score, with two new numbers by Rodgers. It received the Academy Award. Soundtract recording (RCA Victor).

See: Climb Every Mountain; Do, Re, Mi; Edelweiss; Maria; My Favorite Things; The Sound of Music; You Are Sixteen.

South American Way, words by Al Dubin, music by Jimmy McHugh (1939). A standard among rhumbas, introduced by Ramon Vinay (followed by the Hylton Sisters and Della Lind) in the revue *Streets of Paris* (1939). After a dance sequence, Carmen Miranda appeared, wearing her celebrated fruit-basket hat, and gave a rendition of the song that helped make her a star. The song was interpolated for her in the motion-picture musical *Down Argentine Way* (20th Century-Fox, 1940).

South America, Take It Away, words and music by Harold Rome (1946). A satirical number about the invasion of Latin-American songs, dances and rhythms in the United States. It was introduced by Betty Garrett in the post-World War II topical revue *Call Me Mister* (1946). The song was popularized in 1946 in a Decca recording by Bing Crosby and the Andrews Sisters in a release that sold over a million disks.

Rome had written this number a few years before he began working on his score for *Call Me Mister*, at a time when the Latin-American vogue was at a peak in the United States. Then he put it aside. When a number was needed for Betty Garrett in *Call Me Mister,* he hesitantly suggested "South America, Take It Away"—hesitantly, because he knew it did not fit into the overall theme of the revue, and because he felt that the song was now out of date. The producer, however, urged him to use it. It became the hit song of the production.

South of the Border (Down Mexico Way), words and music by Jimmy Kennedy and Michael Carr (1939). Written for Gene Autry, whose recording for Columbia sold about three million disks in two years. The song provided the title and recurrent musical theme for a motion picture starring Autry (Republic, 1939).

South Pacific, a musical play with book by Oscar Hammerstein II and Joshua Logan based on James A. Michener's Pulitzer Prize volume of stories, *Tales of the South Pacific.* Lyrics by Oscar Hammerstein II. Music by Richard Rodgers. It received the Pulitzer Prize for drama. Starring Mary Martin and Ezio Pinza (1949). Original cast recording (Columbia).

The motion-picture adaptation starred Rossano Brazzi and Mitzi Gaynor (20th Century-Fox, 1958). Giorgio Tozzi sang on the soundtrack for Rossano Brazzi. The basic stage score was used. Soundtrack recording (RCA Victor).

See: Bali Ha'i; A Cockeyed Optimist; Happy Talk; Honey Bun; I'm Gonna Wash That Man Right Outa My Hair; I'm in Love with a Wonderful Guy; Some Enchanted Evening; There Is Nothin' Like a Dame; This Nearly Was Mine; Younger Than Springtime.

South Sea Isles, words by Arthur Jackson, music by George Gershwin (1921). An early George Gershwin number, introduced by Charles King (then danced to by Ann Pennington) in the revue *George White Scandals of 1921.*

Spain, words by Gus Kahn, music by Isham Jones (1924). Introduced and popularized by Isham Jones and his band.

The Spaniard That Blighted My Life, words and music by Billy Merson (1911). Introduced and popularized by Al Jolson at the Winter Garden. Jolson sang it on the soundtrack of *The Jolson Story* (Columbia, 1946). A Decca recording by Bing Crosby and Al Jolson in the 1930s, in which they indulged in a spoof of the song with a number of ad lib side remarks, has become a collector's item.

Sparrow in the Tree Top, words and music by Bob Merrill (1951). Popularized in Columbia recordings, first by Arthur Godfrey, then by Guy Mitchell with Mitch Miller and his orchestra.

Speak Low, words by Ogden Nash, music by Kurt Weill (1943). Introduced by Mary Martin (in her first Broadway starring role) and Kenny Baker in the musical *One Touch of Venus* (1943). It was also sung in the motion-picture adaptation of the musical (Universal, 1948) in a performance by Dick Haymes with Eileen Wilson dubbing in on the soundtrack for Ava Gardner. The song was popularized further in a Decca recording by Guy Lombardo and his Royal Canadians (vocal by Billy Leach).

This is Ogden Nash's own favorite among his lyrics. He got the title and the idea from Shakespeare's line from *Much Ado About Nothing:* "Speak low, if you speak of love." Nash went on to explain: "Kurt . . . came to me with a new melody which gave me the spinal tingle that you get from 'Begin the Beguine' or 'That Old Black Magic' and Kurt's own 'September Song.' . . . If we could find the right words for it Mary Martin was willing to sing it. So it was up to me. I was a novice and in this particular crisis, the future of the show was in my hands—or in my skull."

Speak to Me of Love. *See:* Parlez-moi D'amour.

Speedy Gonzales, words and music by Buddy Kaye, David Hill and Ethel Lee (1961). Based on the character in the Warner Brothers animated cartoon. The song was popularized in 1962 by Pat Boone in a Dot recording.

Splish Splash, words and music by Bobby Darin and Jean Murray (1958). Popularized in an Atco recording by Bobby Darin—his first major recording success.

Spoonful of Sugar, words and music by Richard M. Sherman and Robert E. Sherman (1964). Introduced by Julie Andrews in the Walt Disney motion-picture production *Mary Poppins* (Buena Vista, 1964).

S'posin', words by Andy Razaf, music by Paul Denniker (1929). Popularized by Rudy Vallée in his first recording success—for RCA Victor. The song was interpolated for Donald O'Connor in the motion-picture musical *Feudin', Fussin' a-Fightin'* (Universal, 1948).

Spring Has Sprung, words by Dorothy Fields, music by Arthur Schwartz (1951). Introduced in the motion picture *Excuse My Dust,* starring Red Skelton and Monica Lewis (MGM, 1951).

Spring Is Here, words by Lorenz Hart, music by Richard Rodgers (1938). Introduced by Vivienne Segal and Dennis King in the musical *I Married an Angel* (1938). In the motion-picture adaptation of the musical (MGM, 1942), it was sung by Jeanette MacDonald and Nelson Eddy. The song was also interpolated in the screen biography of Rodgers and Hart, *Words and Music* (MGM, 1948).

Spring Is Here, a musical comedy with book by Owen Davis. Lyrics by Lorenz Hart. Music by Richard Rodgers. Starring Glenn Hunter and Lillian Taiz (1929).

The motion-picture adaptation starred Alexander Gray and Bernice Claire (First National, 1930). Five songs were used from the stage score, with an interpolation of "Crying for the Carolines" by Sam Lewis, Joe Young and Harry Warren.

See: Crying for the Carolines; Why Can't I?; With a Song in My Heart; Yours Sincerely.

Spring Will Be a Little Late This Year, words and music by Frank Loesser (1944). Introduced by Deanna Durbin in the motion picture *Christmas Holiday* (Universal, 1944).

Stagger Lee, words and music by Lloyd Price and Harold Logan (1958). Popularized in 1959 by Lloyd Price in an ABC Paramount recording.

Stamper, Dave, composer, born New York City, 1883; died Poughkeepsie, New York, 1963.

See (Lyrics by Gene Buck): Daddy Has a Sweetheart and Mother Is Her Name; It's Getting Dark on Old Broadway; My Rambler Rose; 'Neath the South Sea Moon; Sally, Won't You Come Back?; Some Sweet Day; Sweet Sixteen; Tulip Time.

Standing on the Corner, words and music by Frank Loesser (1956). A simulated hillbilly number, introduced by a male quartet (Shorty Long, Alan Gilbert, John Henson, Roy Lazarus) in the musical play *Most Happy Fella* (1956). The number was popularized in a successful Columbia recording by the Four Lads.

Stand Up and Cheer, words by Lew Brown, music by Harry Akst (1934). Introduced in the motion picture of the same name starring Shirley Temple, aged six, in her screen debut (Fox, 1934).

The Stanley Steamer, words by Ralph Blane, music by Harry Warren (1947). Introduced by Mickey Rooney and Gloria De Haven in the motion-picture musical *Summer Holiday* (MGM, 1948).

Stan' Up and Fight, words by Oscar Hammerstein II, music being "The Toreador Song" from Georges Bizet's opera *Carmen* (1943). Introduced by Glenn Bryant in the musical play *Carmen Jones* (1945). In the motion-picture adaptation of the musical (20th Century-Fox, 1954), it was sung by Joe Adams.

Stardust, words by Mitchell Parish, music by Hoagy Carmichael (1929). Carmichael was on a visit to his alma mater, the University of Indiana, in 1927, when one evening he sat on the so-called "spooning wall" there. Suddenly he recalled a girl he had once loved and lost. Then and there the melody of "Stardust" occurred to him. He went over to the university "Book Nook," which had a piano, and wrote the first version of his melody—as a piano instrumental. One of his former schoolmates, Stu Gorrell, baptized the composition "Stardust" because "it sounded like dust from stars drifting down through the summer sky." Carmichael later remarked: "I had no idea what the title meant, but I thought it was gorgeous."

As an instrumental, "Stardust" was introduced by Don Redman and his orchestra without making an impression. Jimmy Dale, an arranger, suggested to Carmichael that the piece be played in slower tempo and in a sentimental style. This is the way Isham Jones and his orchestra played it; and this is the way Emile Seidel and his orchestra recorded it, with the composer at the piano. During the playback of the latter recording, Carmichael felt for the first time that "Stardust" had the potential of a huge popular success. As he recalled in his autobiography: "This melody was bigger than I. It didn't seem a part of me. Maybe I hadn't written it at all. It didn't sound familiar even. . . . To lay my claims, I wanted to shout back at it, 'Maybe I didn't write you, but I found you!' "

At the suggestion of Irving Mills, Carmichael's publisher, lyrics were written for the melody by Mitchell Parish (then on the staff of Mills Music Company). The song was then introduced at the Cotton Club in New York, in 1929. More and more singers and popular bands started to feature it, until it became a standard. Artie Shaw's recording with his orchestra for RCA Victor in 1940 sold over two million disks. Since that time the song has been recorded almost five hundred times in forty-six different arrangements for every possible instrument or combination of instruments; the lyrics have been translated into forty languages. It is probably the only song ever recorded on both sides of the same disk in two different performances, one side in a presentation by Tommy Dorsey and his orchestra, the flip side by Benny Goodman and his band. As late as 1957 a release of "Stardust" achieved the best-seller lists, that of Billy Ward for Liberty.

"Stardust" is one of four Carmichael songs which are the composer's own favorites (the other three being "The Nearness of You," "Rockin' Chair" and "One Morning in May"). In 1963 the song was selected by ASCAP for its all-time hit parade during its half century of existence.

"Stardust" was used as a recurrent theme in the background music of the non-musical motion picture *Perfect Marriage,* starring Loretta Young and David Niven (Paramount, 1946).

A Star Fell Out of Heaven, words by Mack Gordon, music by Harry Revel (1936). Introduced in the motion picture *Poor Little Rich Girl*, starring Shirley Temple (Fox, 1936).

A Star Is Born, a motion picture with songs, starring Judy Garland and James Mason (Warner, 1953). It was based on an older non-musical motion picture starring Janet Gaynor. Songs by Ira Gershwin and Harold Arlen, with the interpolation of several standards.

See: I'll Get By; The Man That Got Away; My Melancholy Baby; Swanee; You Took Advantage of Me.

Starlift, a motion-picture musical starring Doris Day and Gordon MacRae (Warner, 1951). The score was made up mainly of standards.

See: I may Be Wrong But I Think You're Wonderful; It's Magic; Liza; 'S Wonderful; What Is This Thing Called Love?; You Do Something to Me; You Gonna Lose Your Gal; You Oughta Be in Pictures.

Starlight, words by Joe Young, music by Bernice Petkere (1931). This song was involved in a historic plagiarism suit. An amateur composer from California came forward with a dated, unpublished manuscript that proved he had written a song long before "Starlight" that had the same melody. In the court action that followed, Sigmund Spaeth was able to prove that both songs derived their melody (almost note for note) from a tune called "Violets" by Ellen Wright, published in 1900. Since the copyright on "Violets" had already expired, Bernice Petkere could have won her case if she had been willing to confess she plagiarized "Starlight" from that old number. But she insisted that her song had been original with her. As a result, Judge Alfred Coxe awarded the plaintiff damages of $10,000.

Starlight, words by Edward Madden, music by Theodore F. Morse (1905).

Starlight, words by Paul J. Vance, music by Lee Pockriss (1959). Introduced and popularized by Johnny Mathis in a Columbia recording.

Star Light, Star Bright, words by Harry B. Smith, music by Victor Herbert (1895). A waltz for vocal quintet, hit number from the operetta *The Wizard of the Nile* (1895).

Star of the Evening, words and music by James M. Sayles, arranged by Henry Tucker (1855). The song is remembered mainly through parodies. Tucker wrote an unsuccessful sequel in "Star of the Morning."

The Star-Spangled Banner, words by Francis Scott Key to the English melody "To Anacreon in Heaven" (1814).

"The Star-Spangled Banner" was written during, and inspired by, the War of 1812. This editor has told the story in his *History of Popular Music:* "During the war of 1812, Francis Scott Key, a young Baltimore lawyer, headed a commission sent out to the British fleet anchored off Fort McHenry in Baltimore. Its mission was to effect the relase of an American physician, Dr. William Beanes, captured and held prisoner by the British. Key and his party appeared on the British vessel just before the British launched an attack on Fort McHenry. During the night of September 13–14, 1814, Francis Scott Key watched the battle. When, at dawn, he saw the American flag still flying atop the fort, he spontaneously expressed his joy by writing a set of verses scribbled on an envelope."

For his melody, Key took the English song "To Anacreon in Heaven," which he himself had often previously expropriated for other verses (as other Americans had also done). On the day after the battle Key and his party returned to Baltimore, where Key's verses were published in a broadside with the title of "The Defense of Fort McHenry"; during the same evening the song was introduced by Ferdinand Durang in a Baltimore tavern. Soon afterward, on September 20, the verses without the music were published in the *Baltimore Patriot.* Words and music were published as sheet music by Carr's Music Store in Baltimore, in an arrangement by Thomas Carr. Early in 1815 the song acquired its definitive title. Its popularity was immediate. It was soon reprinted in several songsters, one of which assumed for itself the title of *The Star-Spangled Banner.*

"The Star-Spangled Banner" was accepted as America's unofficial anthem for many years. During the Civil War new martial lyrics were written for it; one set of these was the work of Oliver Wendell Holmes to express his anti-Southern sentiments. In 1889 the Secretary of the Navy ordered that this anthem be played on all naval installations both morning and evening during the flag-raising and -lowering ceremonies. In 1903 "The Star-Spangled Banner" was used by the Army as well as the Navy for specific functions—the officers of each of these two services being ordered to stand at attention while the music was being played. From 1913 a movement was launched to have "The Star-Spangled Banner" recognized as the American national anthem. Bills to this effect were written, then buried in committees. In 1928 the Veterans of Foreign Wars initiated a national campaign to interest patriotic societies throughout the country in this movement. At long last, on March 3, 1931, the bill (Public Law 823) was passed by both houses of the 71st Congress and was signed by President Hoover.

During World War II, Lucy Monroe, opera singer, became famous for her performance of the national anthem at every important public ceremony; it is believed she sang it over five thousand times during the war period.

"The Star-Spangled Banner" has been criticized through the years, and for different reasons. The New York *Herald Tribune* once condemned it for having "words nobody can remember" to a tune "nobody can sing." Some patriots felt that it celebrated too insignificant an incident in America's history to deserve the status of a national anthem. Others consider it to be offensive to a friendly power. Musicians have objected to the wide vocal range (a thirteen-step vocal span) and to its difficult rhythm. For these and sundry other reasons, attempts have been made to displace it with some other patriotic ballad—for example Irving Berlin's "God Bless America" or Katherine Lee Bates' "America the Beautiful." But all such attempts have failed.

Star Spangled Rhythm, a motion-picture musical starring Bing Crosby, Ray Milland, Bob Hope, Mary Martin and Dick Powell (Paramount, 1942). Songs by Johnny Mercer and Harold Arlen.

See: That Old Black Magic.

Stars in My Eyes. *See:* Who Can Tell?

State Fair, a motion-picture musical starring Dick Haymes and Jeanne Crain (20th Century-Fox, 1945). It was based on an older non-musical motion picture starring Will Rogers and Janet Gaynor. Luanne Hogan sang on the soundtrack for Jeanne Crain. Songs by Oscar Hammerstein II and Richard Rodgers.

This screen musical was remade, starring Pat Boone, Bobby Darin, Pamela Tiffin and Ann-Margret (Paramount, 1962). The principal songs from the 1945 production were used, with five new numbers with lyrics and music by Richard Rodgers. Anita Gordon sang on the soundtrack for Pamela Tiffin. Soundtrack recording (Dot).

See: It Might As Well Be Spring; It's a Grand Night for Singing; That's for Me.

Stay As Sweet As You Are, words by Mack Gordon, music by Harry Revel (1934). Introduced by Lanny Ross in the motion-picture musical *College Rhythm* (Paramount, 1934).

Stay Awake, words and music by Richard M. Sherman and Robert B. Sherman (1964). Introduced by Julie Andrews in the Walt Disney motion-picture production *Mary Poppins* (Buena Vista, 1964).

Staying Young, words and music by Bob Merrill (1959). Introduced by

Walter Pidgeon in the musical *Take Me Along* (1959).

Stay in Your Own Back Yard, words by Karl Kennett, music by Lyn Udall (1899). One of the first successful popular songs discussing racial problems. It stoically accepted segregation and racial discrimination as realities, and considered these problems as they affect a child. ("Now, honey, yo' stay in yo' own back yard, Don't min' what dem white chiles do.")

Steamboat Bill, words by Ren Shields, music by the Leighton Brothers (1910). A popular song hit of the early 1910s with a folk-song quality, popularized in vaudeville. It was interpolated in the motion picture *Ridin' on a Rainbow,* starring Gene Autry (Republic, 1941).

Steam Heat, words and music by Richard Adler and Jerry Ross (1954). Introduced by Carol Haney (dressed as a gamin, but with a derby and a tight-fitting man's suit), flanked by Buzz Miller and Pat Gennaro (similarly attired), in the musical *The Pajama Game* (1954). This routine—performed with hissing and other vocal sounds—helped make Carol Haney a star in this her Broadway musical comedy debut. She repeated this performance in the motion-picture adaptation of the musical (Warner, 1957).

Patti Page made a best-selling recording for Mercury.

Stein Song, words by Lincoln Colcord, music by E. A. Fenstad (1910). It originated in 1901 as an instrumental march by E. A. Fenstad. Nine years later A. W. Sprague, a student at the University of Maine, rewrote it and had his roommate, Lincoln Colcord, provide lyrics. This song version was adopted as the school number of the University of Maine. For twenty years nobody outside the university campus knew the song. So few copies of the sheet music had been sold that the university refused to buy out the rights. Then in the 1920s NBC, in testing radio as a means of plugging songs, bought it. Rudy Vallée introduced it on his radio program in 1930, then featured it the following week during a personal appearance at the Paramount Theatre in New York. In short order, the song sold over 350,000 copies of sheet music and half a million copies of Vallée's recording for RCA Victor. The song henceforth became identified with Vallée—so much so that when a bitter singing rivalry developed between Vallée and Will Osborne, the latter wrote and featured a number entitled "I'd Like to Break the Neck of the Man Who Wrote the Stein Song." The song was interpolated in the motion-picture biography of Jane Froman, *With a Song in My Heart* (20th Century-Fox, 1952).

Stella by Starlight, words by Ned Washington, music by Victor Young (1946). Theme music from the non-musical motion picture *The Uninvited,* starring Ray Milland and Ruth Hussey (Paramount, 1944). The song was introduced in a Decca recording by Victor Young and his orchestra.

Step Lively, a motion-picture musical based on the stage play *Room Service,* starring Frank Sinatra, George Murphy and Gloria De Haven (RKO, 1944). Songs by Sammy Cahn and Jule Styne.

See: And Then You Kissed Me; Come Out, Come Out, Wherever You Are.

Stepping Stones, a musical comedy with book and lyrics by W. C. Burnside and Anne Caldwell. Music by Jerome Kern. Starring Dorothy Stone, Fred Stone and Allene Stone (1923).

See: Once in a Blue Moon; Raggedy Ann.

Stept, Sam H., composer, born Odessa, Russia, 1897; died Hollywood, California, 1964.

See (Lyrics by Charles Tobias and Lew Brown): Comes Love; Don't Sit Under the Apple Tree.

See also: All My Life; I'll Always Be in Love with You; It Seems Like Old Times; Please Don't Talk About Me When I'm Gone; That's My Weakness Now.

Sterling, Andrew B., lyricist, born New York City, 1874; died Stamford, Connecticut, 1955.

See: Von Tilzer, Harry.

See also: Meet Me in St. Louis; Strike Up the Band, Here Comes a Sailor; When My Baby Smiles at Me.

Stern, Joseph W., composer, born New York City, 1870; died Brightwater, Long Island, New York, 1934.

See: His Last Thoughts Were of You; The Little Lost Child; Mother Was a Lady; No One Ever Loved You More Than I.

Stiff Upper Lip, words by Ira Gershwin, music by George Gershwin (1937). Introduced by Gracie Allen in the motion-picture musical *Damsel in Distress* (RKO, 1937). Later in the same picture the song was used for a large production number set in an English amusement park.

Stillman, Al, lyricist, born New York City, 1906.

See: Allen, Robert.

See also: The Breeze and I; I Believe; My Heart Reminds Me; Who Do You Know in Heaven?

Stood Up, words and music by Dub Dickerson and Erma Herrold (1957). Popularized in 1958 by Ricky Nelson in an Imperial recording.

Stop Dat Knocking at My Door, words and music by A. F. Winnemore (1843). A song, providing opportunities for clowning and pantomime, popularized by the Ed Christy Minstrels.

Stop in the Name of Love, words and music by Holland, Dozier and Holland (1965). Popularized by the Supremes in a best-selling Motown recording.

Stop, Look and Listen, a revue starring Gaby Deslys, Blossom Seeley and Harry Fox. Songs by Irving Berlin (1915).

See: The Girl on the Magazine Cover; I Love a Piano; Take Off a Little Bit.

Stop That Rag, words and music by Irving Berlin (1909). Introduced by Stella Mayhew in the musical *The Jolly Bachelors* (1909).

Stop, You're Breaking My Heart, words by Ted Koehler, music by Burton Lane (1937). Introduced in the motion-picture musical *Artists and Models* (Paramount, 1937), sung and danced to by Ben Blue and Judy Canova.

Stormy Weather (Keeps Rainin' All the Time), words by Ted Koehler, music by Harold Arlen (1933). Written for Cab Calloway. As Edward Jablonski reveals, this classic was "all but tossed off . . . at a party." At that time Arlen and Koehler were writing the songs for revues produced at the Cotton Club, in Harlem, New York. Since Calloway was not appearing at the Cotton Club in 1933, and since the creators of the song had come to the conclusion that it was better suited for a female singer, Cab Calloway did not introduce it. The choice of singer, as far as Arlen and Koehler were concerned, fell on Ethel Waters, and they induced her to appear in the Cotton Club revue. Meanwhile, an RCA Victor recording of the song by the Leo Reisman Orchestra, with Arlen himself doing the vocal, had become a best seller, so that by the time the Cotton Club show opened, the song was already famous. Nevertheless, it became Ethel Waters' song. She sang it under a lamppost against a log-cabin backdrop—a midnight-blue spot pointing a finger at her. Then, when her rendition ended, the song was used for an elaborate dance routine. "Stormy Weather" stopped the show, and from that first night on, Ethel Waters was compelled to give numerous encores of the number.

"Singing 'Stormy Weather' proved a turning point in my life," wrote Ethel Waters in her autobiography. "When I got out there in the middle of the Cotton Club floor . . . I was singing the story of my misery and confusion . . . the story of the wrongs and outrages done to me by people I had loved and trusted. . . . I sang 'Stormy Weather' from the depths of my private hell in which I was being crushed and suffocated."

Lena Horne is second only to Ethel Waters as a pre-eminent interpreter of this ballad. She presented it successfully in her night-club act and in an RCA Victor recording. The song was interpolated in the motion-picture musical *Swing Parade of 1946,* starring Gale Storm and Phil Regan (Monogram, 1946).

Stormy Weather, a motion-picture musical described by the producers as "a cavalcade of Negro entertainment," starring Ethel Waters, Lena Horne and Fats Waller (20th Century-Fox, 1943). The score was made up primarily of standards.

See: Ain't Misbehavin'; Diga, Diga Doo; I Can't Give You Anything But Love, Baby.

The Story of the Rose (or, Heart of My Heart, I Love You), words by "Alice," lyricist otherwise not identified, music by Andrew Mack (1899). A favorite of barber-shop quartets.

The Story of My Life, words by Hal David, music by Burt F. Bacharach (1957). Popularized by Marty Robbins in a Columbia recording.

The Story of the Castles, a motion-picture musical biography of Irene and Vernon Castle, starring Fred Astaire and Ginger Rogers as the Castles (RKO, 1939). The score was made up of standards.

See: By the Beautiful Sea; Chicago; Come, Josephine, in My Flying Machine; Cuddle Up a Little Closer; Darktown Strutters Ball; Missouri Waltz; Oh, You Beautiful Doll; Waiting for the Robert E. Lee; Yama Yama Man.

Stothart, Herbert, composer, born Milwaukee, Wisconsin, 1885; died Los Angeles, California, 1949.

See (Lyrics by Clifford Grey): The Rogue Song; Song of the Shirt.

See also: Bambalina; Cuban Love Song; The Donkey Serenade; I Wanna Be Loved by You; Song of the Flame; When I'm Looking at You; Wildflower.

Stout Hearted Men, words by Oscar Hammerstein II, music by Sigmund Romberg (1928). Introduced by Richard Halliday and a male chorus in the operetta *The New Moon* (1928). In the first motion-picture adaptation of the operetta (MGM, 1930), it was sung by Lawrence Tibbett and a male chorus; in the second screen version (MGM, 1940), by Nelson Eddy and a male chorus. Helen Traubel sang it in Romberg's screen biography *Deep in My Heart* (MGM, 1954).

Straighten Up and Fly Right, words by Irving Mills, music by Nat King Cole (1944). Popularized by the King Cole Trio, whose Capitol release in November, 1943, was that group's first hit recording. This song was based on a sermon Nat King Cole had heard in his father's church. At the time he wrote the number, Nat King Cole was so desperately in need of money that he sold all his rights to it for $50. Thus he did not profit directly from the song's success, but his career as a recording artist was given a strong boost from it for the first time, just as this recording helped to establish the then newly organized company of Capitol Records on a sound financial basis.

The song was introduced by the King Cole Trio in the motion picture *Here Comes Elmer,* starring Al Pearce and Dale Evans (Republic, 1943).

Strange Are the Ways of Love, words by Ned Washington, music by Dimitri Tiomkin (1959). Introduced by Randy Sparks in the non-musical motion picture *The Young Land,* starring Pat Wayne (Columbia, 1959).

Strange Music, words and music by Robert Wright and George "Chet" Forrest, melody based on Grieg's *Wedding Day at Troldhaugen* and *Nocturne* (1944). The popular song was introduced by Lawrence Brooks and Helena Bliss in the operetta based on Grieg's life and music, *Song of Norway* (1944).

Stranger in Paradise, words and music by Robert Wright and George "Chet" Forrest on a theme from the "Polovtsian Dances" from Borodin's opera *Prince Igor* (1953). The song was introduced by Doretta Morrow and Richard Kiley in the operetta *Kismet* (1953), whose entire score was derived from Borodin's music. The song was popularized in 1953 and 1954 through best-selling recordings by the Four Aces for Decca and Tony Bennett for Columbia.

Stranger on the Shore, words and music by Robert Mellin and Acker Bilk (1962). Popularized by Acker Bilk in an Atco recording.

The Streets of Cairo (or, The Poor Little Country Maid), words and music by James Thornton (1895). For his verse, Thornton used the melody of a hootchy-kootchy dance then popularized by Little Egypt at the Chicago Columbia Exposition.

The Streets of New York (or, In Old New York), words by Henry Blossom, music by Victor Herbert (1906). Introduced by Fred Stone and David Montgomery and chorus in the closing scene of the operetta *The Red Mill* (1906).

Strike Me Pink, a musical comedy with book and lyrics by Mack Gordon and Lew Brown. Music by Ray Henderson. Starring Jimmy Durante (1933). *See:* Let's Call It a Day.

Strike Up the Band, words by Ira Gershwin, music by George Gershwin (1930). A march introduced by Jim Townsend and Jerry Goff (with parenthetical sounds by the ensemble) in the musical of the same name (1930). George Gershwin wrote four versions of this march music before he completed the one that satisfied him; the first four had been written at the piano, the fifth in bed. In 1936 Ira Gershwin adapted the march tune as a football song for the University of California at Los Angeles. His fee: two season passes to the home football games for the remainder of his life.

The march provided the title for and was heard in a motion-picture musical starring Judy Garland and Mickey Rooney (MGM, 1940).

Strike Up the Band!, a musical comedy with book by George S. Kaufman and Morrie Ryskind. Lyrics by Ira Gershwin. Music by George Gershwin. Starring Clark and McCullough (1930).

See: Soon; Strike Up the Band; A Typical Self-Made American.

Strike Up the Band, Here Comes a Sailor, words by Andrew B. Sterling, music by Charles B. Ward (1900). A hit song popularized in vaudeville in the early 1900s. It was revived by Jack Oakie and a female chorus in the motion-picture musical *Hello,*

Frisco, Hello (20th Century-Fox, 1943). It was also heard in the motion picture *In Old Sacramento*, starring Constance Moore and Bill Elliott (Republic, 1946).

A String of Pearls, words by Eddie De Lange, music by Jerry Gray (1942). Popularized by Glenn Miller and his orchestra in a best-selling recording for Bluebird and a Columbia recording by Benny Goodman and his orchestra.

Strip Polka, words and music by Johnny Mercer (1942). Introduced by Johnny Mercer in a Capitol recording, and popularized by Kay Kyser and his band in a Columbia recording and by the Andrews Sisters in a Decca release.

The Stroll, words and music by Nancy Lee and Clyde Otis (1957). Popularized by the Diamonds in a Mercury recording.

Strolling on the Brooklyn Bridge, words by George Cooper, music by Joseph P. Skelly (1883). Hit song inspired by the opening on May 24, 1883, of the Brooklyn Bridge, spanning the East River in New York.

Stromberg, John "Honey," composer, born 1853, place not known; died New York City, 1902.

See (Lyrics by Edgar Smith): Come Back, My Honey, to Me; De Pullman Porters' Ball; I'm a Respectable Working Girl; Keep Away from Emmaline; Kiss Me, Honey, Do; Ma Blushin' Rosie; Say You Love Me, Sue; What, Marry Dat Girl; When Chloe Sings a Song.

See also: Come Down, Ma Evenin' Star; How I Love My Lou; My Best Girl's a New Yorker.

Strouse, Charles, composer, born New York City, 1928.

See (Lyrics by Lee Adams): Can't You See?; Don't Forget 127th Street; I Want to Be with You; Kids; A Lot of Livin' to Do; Once Upon a Time; This Is the Life; What a Country; While the City Sleeps.

See also: Born Too Late.

Stuck on You, words and music by Aaron Schroeder and J. Leslie McFarland (1960). Popularized by Elvis Presley in a best-selling RCA Victor recording.

The Student Prince, an operetta with book and lyrics by Dorothy Donnelly. Music by Sigmund Romberg. Starring Ilse Marvenga and Howard Marsh (1924).

The motion-picture adaptation starred Ann Blyth and Edmund Purdom (MGM, 1954). Mario Lanza sang on the soundtrack for Purdom. The basic stage score was used. "I'll Walk with God" by Paul Francis Webster and Nicholas Brodszky was interpolated. Soundtrack recording (RCA Victor).

See: Deep in My Heart; Drinking Song; Golden Days; I'll Walk with God; Serenade.

Stumbling, words and music by Zez Confrey (1922). A song commenting in lyrics and syncopated melody on the intricacy of social dances in the early 1920s.

Stupid Cupid, words by Neil Sedaka, music by Howard Greenfield (1958). Greenfield's first hit song, popularized by Connie Francis in a best-selling MGM recording.

Style, words by Sammy Cahn, music by James Van Heusen (1964). Introduced by Frank Sinatra, Bing Crosby and Dean Martin in the motion-picture musical *Robin and the Seven Hoods* (Warner, 1964).

Styne, Jule, composer, born London, England, 1905.

See (Lyrics by Betty Comden and Adolph Green): Call Me Savage; Give a Little, Get a Little; Hold Me, Hold Me, Hold Me; If You Hadn't, But You Did; I Just Can't Wait; I'm with You; Just in Time; Long Before I Knew You; Make Someone Happy; My Fortune Is My Face; Never, Never Land; The Party's Over; You Mustn't Be Discouraged.

See (Lyrics by Sammy Cahn): As Long As There Is Music; Come Out, Come Out, Wherever You Are; Five Minutes More; I Fall in Love Too Easily; I'll Walk Alone; I Still Get Jealous; It's Been a Long, Long Time; It's Magic; I've Heard That Song Before; Let It Snow, Let It Snow; On a Sunday by the Sea; Papa, Won't You Dance with Me; Pete Kelly's Blues; Pocketful of Miracles; Poor Little Rhode Island; Saturday

Night Is the Loneliest Night of the Week; Second Time Around; There Goes That Song Again; The Things We Did Last Summer; Three Coins in a Fountain.

See (Lyrics by Bob Hilliard): Every Street's a Boulevard in Old New York; How Do You Speak to an Angel?

See (Lyrics by Bob Merrill): Don't Rain on My Parade; I'm the Greatest Star; The Music That Makes Me Dance; People; Who Are You Now?; You Are Woman.

See (Lyrics by Leo Robin): Bye, Bye, Baby; Diamonds Are a Girl's Best Friend; A Little Girl from Little Rock.

See (Lyrics by Stephen Sondheim): Everything's Coming Up Roses; A Small World; Some People; Together, Wherever We Go.

See also: I Don't Want to Walk Without You.

Suddenly, words by E. Y. Harburg and Billy Rose, music by Vernon Duke (1934). Introduced by Jane Froman and Everett Marshall in the *Ziegfeld Follies of 1934*.

Suddenly It's Spring, words by Johnny Burke, music by James Van Heusen (1943). Introduced in song and dance by Ginger Rogers (accompanied by the Joseph J. Lilley Choir) in the motion-picture musical *Lady in the Dark* (Paramount, 1944). It was popularized in a Decca recording by Glen Gray and his Casa Loma Orchestra (vocal by Eugenie Baird).

Suddenly There's a Valley, words and music by Chuck Meyer and Biff Jones (1955). Popularized in recordings by Gogi Grant for Era and Jo Stafford for Columbia.

Sugar Blues, words by Lucy Fletcher, music by Clarence Williams (1923). Introduced and popularized in a Brunswick recording by Clyde McCoy in 1923. Clyde McCoy revived it in 1946 in a best-selling recording for Decca.

Sugar Shack, words and music by Keith McCormack and Faye Voss (1963). Popularized by Jim Gilmer and the Fireballs in a Dot recording that sold a million disks and received the Gold Record Award.

Sugartime, words and music by Charlie Phillips and Odis Echols (1956). Popularized in 1958 by the McGuire Sisters in a best-selling Coral recording.

Summer Holiday, a motion-picture musical (based on Eugene O'Neill's comedy *Ah, Wilderness!*) starring Mickey Rooney, Gloria De Haven and Walter Huston (MGM, 1948). Songs by Ralph Blane and Harry Warren.

See: The Stanley Steamer.

Summer Night, words by Al Dubin, music by Harry Warren (1936). Introduced by James Melton in the motion-picture musical *Sing Me a Love Song* (First National, 1936).

Summer Stock, a motion-picture musical starring Gene Kelly and Judy Garland (MGM, 1950). Songs by Mack Gordon and Harry Warren, among others.

See: If You Feel Like Singing, Sing; You Wonderful You.

Summertime, words by Du Bose Heyward, music by George Gershwin (1935). Opening number in the folk opera *Porgy and Bess,* introduced by Abbie Mitchell.

This was the first song George Gershwin completed in doing the score for *Porgy and Bess.* Rouben Mamoulian, the stage director for the opera at its première, described the composer's own reactions when this number was first tried out. "To describe George's face as he sang 'Summertime' is something beyond my capacity as a writer. 'Nirvana' might be the word. . . . George played with the most beatific smile on his face. He seemed to float on the waves of his own music with the southern sun shining on him."

In the motion-picture adaptation of the opera (Columbia, 1959), it was sung on the soundtrack by Loulie Jean Norman (for Dorothy Dandridge). Anne Brown sang it in the George Gershwin screen biography *Rhapsody in Blue* (Warner, 1945).

"Summertime" was adopted by Bob Crosby and his orchestra as a theme song.

Summertime Love, words and music by Frank Loesser (1960). Introduced by Anthony Perkins in the musical play *Greenwillow* (1960).

Sunbonnet Sue, words by Will D. Cobb, music by Gus Edwards (1906). The first number issued by the then newly formed publishing house of Gus Edwards. It sold over a million copies of sheet music. The song provided the title for and was featured in both a Broadway musical (1923) and in a motion-picture musical (Monogram, 1946); in the latter it was sung by Gale Storm and Phil Regan.

Sunbonnet Sue, a motion-picture musical starring Gail Storm and Phil Regan (Monogram, 1946). The score was made up mainly of standards by Gus Edwards.

See: By the Light of the Silvery Moon; If I Had My Way; School Days; Sunbonnet Sue.

Sunday, words by Oscar Hammerstein II, music by Richard Rodgers (1958). Introduced by Pat Suzuki and Larry Blydon in the musical *Flower Drum Song.* In the motion-picture adaptation of the musical (Universal, 1961), it was sung by Jack Soo and Nancy Kwan.

Sunday in the Park, words and music by Harold Rome (1937). A sentimental idyl of the simple pleasures of tenement dwellers in a big city. It was introduced in the social-conscious topical revue *Pins and Needles* (1937). This was Rome's first song to be represented on the Hit Parade. This number made such an impression on Max Gordon, the producer, that he forthwith contracted Rome to write the score for a new topical revue, *Sing Out the News* (1938).

Sunday, Monday, or Always, words by Johnny Burke, music by James Van Heusen (1943). Introduced by Bing Crosby in the motion-picture musical *Dixie* (Paramount, 1943). It was further popularized by him in a Decca recording. This song, however, is even more often identified with Frank Sinatra, whose Decca recording was also a best seller.

Sunflower, words and music by Mack David (1948). Popularized by Russ Morgan and his orchestra in a best-selling Decca recording in 1949. In 1966 "Sunflower" was awarded an out-of-court settlement of over half a million dollars in an infringement of copyright suit against "Hello, Dolly!"

Sun in the Mornin' and the Moon at Night, words and music by Irving Berlin (1946). Introduced by Ethel Merman and ensemble (and danced to by Lubo Roudenko and Daniel Negrin) in the musical *Annie, Get Your Gun* (1946). In the motion-picture adaptation, it was sung by Betty Hutton (MGM, 1950).

Sunny, words by Otto Harbach and Oscar Hammerstein II, music by Jerome Kern (1925). Title song of a musical (1925), introduced by Paul Frawley. It was also sung in both motion-picture adaptations of the musical (First National, 1930; RKO, 1941). In the Kern screen biography, *Till the Clouds Roll By* (MGM, 1946), it was sung by Judy Garland.

Sunny, a musical comedy with book and lyrics by Otto Harbach and Oscar Hammerstein II. Music by Jerome Kern. Starring Marilyn Miller and Jack Donahue (1925).

There were two motion-picture adaptations. The first starred Marilyn Miller (First National, 1930). Five songs were used from the stage score. The second starred Anna Neagle (RKO, 1941). Four of the stage songs were used.

See: D'ye Love Me?; Sunny; Who?

Sunny Disposish, words by Ira Gershwin, music by Phil Charig (1926). Introduced by Arline and Edgar Gardiner in the revue *Americana* (1926). It became a specialty of Frances Williams, who made an outstanding recording for Columbia in the late 1920s.

Sunny Side Up, words by Bud De Sylva and Lew Brown, music by Ray Henderson (1929). Title song of a motion-picture musical (Fox, 1929), introduced by Janet Gaynor and Charles Farrell.

Sunny Side Up, a motion-picture musical starring Janet Gaynor and Charles Farrell (Fox, 1929). Songs by De Sylva, Brown and Henderson.

See: Aren't We All?; If I Had a Talking Picture of You; Sunny Side Up; Turn on the Heat.

Sunrise Serenade, words by Jack Lawrence, music by Frankie Carle (1939). Introduced by Frankie Carle and his orchestra, and popularized by Glen Gray and the Casa Loma Orchestra and by Glenn Miller and his orchestra. The latter's recording for Bluebird sold a million disks. The song was interpolated in the motion-picture musical *The Glenn Miller Story* (Universal, 1953), where it was played on the soundtrack by Joseph Gershenson's orchestra imitating the Glenn Miller sound.

Sunrise, Sunset, words by Sheldon Harnick, music by Jerry Bock (1964). Introduced by Zero Mostel, Maria Karnilova and chorus in the musical play *Fiddler on the Roof* (1964).

Sunshine Cake, words by Johnny Burke, music by James Van Heusen (1950). Introduced by Bing Crosby in the motion-picture musical *Riding High* (Paramount, 1950), and further popularized by him in a Decca recording.

Sunshine Girl, words and music by Bob Merrill (1957). Introduced by Del Anderson, Eddie Phillips and Mike Dawson in the musical play *New Girl in Town* (1957).

The Sunshine of Paradise Alley, words by Walter H. Ford, music by John W. Bratton (1895). Paradise Alley was a nine-foot-wide thoroughfare in Philadelphia—off Cherry Street, leading into Gotham Court, and flanked by two rows of tenements. The sight there of children playing gave the songwriters the idea for this song hit. When Ford and Bratton performed their number at Witmark's, the publishers, Lottie Gilson heard it and decided to introduce it at the Casino Roof Garden in New York in 1895; she made it one of her leading song triumphs. Soon afterward Bessie Bonhill sang it successfully in the musical *1492*.

The Sunshine of Your Smile, words by Leonard Cooke, music by Lillian Ray (1915). Popularized in vaudeville in the late 1910s.

Supper Time, words and music by Irving Berlin (1933). A race-conscious ballad introduced by Ethel Waters in the revue *As Thousands Cheer* (1933). The song told of a colored woman preparing an evening meal for her husband, who has just been lynched. "In singing it," wrote Ethel Waters in her autobiography, "I was telling my comfortable, well-fed, well-dressed listeners about my people. . . . When I was through and that big, heavy curtain came down I was called back again and again. I had stopped the show with a type of song never heard before in a revue, and a number that until then had been a question mark."

Sure Thing, words by Ira Gershwin, music by Jerome Kern (1944). Described by Ira Gershwin as a "pre-World War I music hall number with a racetrack background." It was sung on the soundtrack by Nan Wynn (for Rita Hayworth) in the motion-picture musical *Cover Girl* (Columbia, 1944).

The song had been written in 1939 with different lyrics, but was not used at the time. When Gershwin and Kern began to work on the score for *Cover Girl*, Gershwin suggested using the number with new words. Kern had forgotten the song completely; he did not even have his manuscript around. His daughter, Betty, remembered the tune and hummed it to him, and with her help he rewrote it.

Surf City, words and music by Jan Berry and Brian Wilson (1963). Popularized by Jan and Dean in a Liberty recording.

Surprise, words and music by Jay Livingston and Ray Evans (1958). Introduced by Jacquelyn McKeever in the musical *Oh, Captain!* (1958).

Surrender, words and music by Jerome "Doc" Pomus and Mort Shuman (1961). Popularized by Elvis Presley in a best-selling RCA Victor recording.

The Surrey with the Fringe on Top, words by Oscar Hammerstein II, music by Richard Rodgers (1943). Introduced by Alfred Drake, Joan Roberts and Betty Garde in the musical play *Oklahoma!* (1943). In the motion-picture adaptation of the musical (Magna Theatre, 1955), it was sung by Gordon MacRae, Shirley Jones and Charlotte Greenwood.

Susan Jane, words and music by Will S. Hays (1871).

Swanee, words by Irving Caesar, music by George Gershwin (1919). The story of George Gershwin's first hit song—how it came to be written and performed—was told in this editor's biography of George Gershwin, *A Journey to Greatness.* "The idea for 'Swanee' was born during a lunch at Dinty Moore's in New York. Irving Caesar and Gershwin had met to discuss new ideas for songs. Caesar suggested that they write a one-step in the style of 'Hindustan' then in vogue. . . . They kept on discussing the idea and allowing it to acquire a definite shape as they rode atop a bus to Gershwin's apartment, then located in the Washington Heights section. By the time they reached there, much of the song was clear in the minds of both composer and lyricist. They went to the piano in the living room to work out the details. . . . On October 24, 1919, a new motion-picture palace opened in New York City, the Capitol Theatre on Broadway and 51st Street. For the opening week, Ned Wayburn prepared a sumptuous stage show prefacing the picture, and he used 'Swanee' in it. How well he thought of it can be guessed by the impressive setting he provided. After the song was introduced, sixty chorus girls, with electric lights glowing on their slippers, danced to its rhythms on an otherwise darkened stage. Since the orchestra then performing at the theatre was the famous Arthur Pryor Band, 'Swanee' was given in a band arrangement. The audience reaction was, at best, only lukewarm.

"The history of 'Swanee' might have ended at this point but for the fact that one of the most magnetic stars of the Broadway stage became interested in it—Al Jolson. . . . Jolson made the difference. . . . He introduced it at a Sunday night concert at the Winter Garden and brought down the house. He then interpolated it in the musical extravaganza *Sinbad.* The song now caught on, spreading throughout the country like contagion. In a year's time it sold two million records and one million copies of sheet music." It might be added as an interesting footnote, that though George Gershwin's magnificent career still lay well before him, he never again achieved a commercial song success of such dimensions.

"Swanee" remained a Jolson favorite. He sang it on the soundtracks of *The Jolson Story* (Columbia, 1946) and *Jolson Sings Again* (Columbia, 1949); and he sang it on the screen in the motion-picture biography of George Gershwin, *Rhapsody in Blue* (Warner, 1946). His Decca recording in 1945 sold a million disks.

The song has also become a Judy Garland specialty. She sang it as the climax of an extended song sequence entitled "Born in a Trunk" in the motion-picture musical *A Star Is Born* (Warner, 1953).

Swanee River. *See:* Old Folks at Home.

Swanee River, a motion-picture musical biography of Stephen Foster, starring Al Jolson, Don Ameche and Andrea Leeds (20th Century-Fox, 1939). The score was made up of Stephen Foster standards, including "Beautiful Dreamer," "De Camptown Races," "Jeanie with the Light Brown Hair," "Old Black Joe," "Old Folks at Home," "My Old Kentucky Home" and "Oh, Susanna."

Sweet Adeline (or, You're the Flower of My Heart, Sweet Adeline), words by Richard Gerard Husch, using the pen name of Richard H. Gerard, music by Harry Armstrong (1903). One of the most successful sentimental ballads of the early 1900s, a song most often associated with the blissful state of inebriation, and a perennial favorite of barber-shop quartets. This is also one of the most successful of the echo-type songs so popular in the early 1900s, the echo effect produced here with the words "Sweet Adeline" and "My Adeline."

Armstrong had written this melody in 1896 without any accompanying lyrics, entitling his instrumental *Down Home in New England*. Then he asked Gerard to write words for his tune. Gerard complied, now using the title of "You're the Flower of My Heart, Sweet Rosalie." When a number of publishers turned down this effort, Gerard suggested a change of title, convinced that the name of "Rosalie" had no commercial appeal. Coming upon a poster advertising one of the farewell tours of Adelina Patti, the celebrated prima donna, Gerard decided to rename the heroine of his ballad "Adeline." Witmark now bought the number, issuing it in 1903 as "one of the most charming ballads ever written." The sheet-music sale at first was nonexistent. Then Harry Ernest, manager of a singing group in vaudeville billed as the Quaker City Four, came upon "Sweet Adeline" at Witmark's and took it for his act. The Quaker City Four introduced it at Hammerstein's Victoria Theatre in New York in 1903, and from this point on, the popularity of the ballad began to soar.

In 1906 John F. "Honey" Fitzgerald used "Sweet Adeline" as his campaign song while running for Mayor in Boston. He used it again in 1910 and 1914, making it his musical identification in the same way that "The Sidewalks of New York" later served Governor Alfred E. Smith. In 1929 the title of the ballad was used to name a musical comedy by Oscar Hammerstein II and Jerome Kern.

Sweet Adeline, a musical romance with book and lyrics by Oscar Hammerstein II. Music by Jerome Kern. Starring Helen Morgan and Charles Butterworth. The cast included James Thornton, the famous songwriter of the 1890s, in his last stage appearance (1929).

The motion-picture adaptation starred Irene Dunne and Donald Woods (Warner, 1935). The principal songs from the stage score were used.

See: Don't Ever Leave Me; Here Am I; 'Twas Not So Long Ago; Why Was I Born?

Sweet and Gentle, a Cuban popular song ("Me lo Dijo Adela"), music by Otillio Portal, English lyrics by George Thorn (1955). Popularized in the United States by Alan Dale's recording for Coral and Georgia Gibbs' recording for Mercury.

Sweet and Hot, words by Jack Yellen, music by Harold Arlen (1930). Introduced by Lyda Roberti in the musical *You Said It* (1930), Arlen's first book show. It became Lyda Roberti's theme song.

Sweet and Lovely, words and music by Gus Arnheim, Harry Tobias and Jules Lemare (1931). Introduced by Gus Arnheim and his orchestra (in an effective arrangement by Jimmie Grier) at the Coconut Grove in Los Angeles in 1931. Within a few months it became one of the leading song hits throughout the country. It was revived in the motion-picture musical *Two Girls and a Sailor,* starring June Allyson and Van Johnson (MGM, 1944). It was interpolated in the non-musical motion pictures *Battleground,* starring Van Johnson and John Hodiak (MGM, 1949) and *This Earth Is Mine,* starring Rock Hudson and Jean Simmons (Universal, 1959).

Sweet and Low-Down, words by Ira Gershwin, music by George Gershwin(1925). Introduced in the musical *Tip Toes* (1925) where (as Ira Gershwin explains) it was "sung, kazooed, tromboned and danced by Andrew Tombes, Lovey Lee, Gertrude McDonald and ensemble at a party at Palm Beach." The phrase "sweet and low-down" had earlier been coined by Ira Gershwin for a discarded song, "Little Jazz Bird." This phrase was listed in *The American Thesaurus of Slang.*

Sweet Annie Moore, words and music by John H. Flynn (1901). A punning song, introduced successfully in the musical *The Casino Girl* (1901), where it was an interpolation.

Sweet Bunch of Daisies, words and music by Anita Owen (1894). A whimsical song introduced and popularized by Phyllis Allen. This was the first hit song issued by the publishing house of Remick after it had moved from Detroit to New York City.

Sweet Dreams, Sweetheart, words by Ted Koehler, music by M. K. Jerome (1944). Introduced by Joan Leslie and Kitty Carlisle in the all-star motion-picture revue *Hollywood Canteen* (Warner, 1944).

Sweet Heartaches, words and music by Nat Simon and Jimmy Kennedy (1956). Popularized by Eddie Fisher in an RCA Victor recording.

The Sweetest Sounds, words and music by Richard Rodgers (1962). Introduced by Richard Kiley and Diahann Carroll in the musical play *No Strings* (1962).

Sweet Genevieve, words by George Cooper, music by Henry Tucker (1869). Cooper had written the lyrics of this sentimental ballad upon the death of his young wife, Genevieve, soon after their marriage. Cooper sold Tucker the musical rights to his poem for five dollars. Following its publication, the song became one of the most successful sentimental ballads in the period between the end of the Civil War and 1890. It was performed extensively in minstrel shows; and it subsequently became a favorite of barber-shop quartets and community sings.

Sweet Georgia Brown, words and music by Ben Bernie, Maceo Pinkard and Kenneth Casey (1925). Introduced and popularized by Ben Bernie and his orchestra. It became a theme song for the famous Negro basketball team, the Harlem Globetrotters —the musical background for their pre-game exhibition of agility in the handling and passing of a basketball. The Tempo recording by Brother Bones was used on the soundtrack of the motion picture *The Harlem Globetrotters* (Columbia, 1951). The song was also interpolated in the non-musical motion picture *Broadway*, starring George Raft and Pat O'Brien (Universal, 1942); and in the screen musicals *The Helen Morgan Story* (Warner, 1957) and *Some Like It Hot* (United Artists, 1959).

Sweetheart. *See:* Will You Remember?

Sweetheart of All My Dreams, words and music by Art Fitch, Kay Fitch and Bert Lowe (1926). Interpolated in the motion-picture musical *Applause* (Paramount, 1929). It was revived in the non-musical motion picture *Thirty Seconds Over Tokyo*, starring Spencer Tracy and Van Johnson (MGM, 1944).

The Sweetheart of Sigma Chi, words by Byron D. Stokes, music by F. Dudleigh Vernor (1912). A song favorite in colleges. It was popularized throughout the United States in the late 1920s by Rudy Valée in night clubs, over the radio and in an RCA Victor recording. The song provided the title for and was featured in a motion picture starring Phil Regan and Elyse Knox (Monogram, 1946).

Sweethearts, words by Robert B. Smith, music by Victor Herbert (1913). A waltz introduced by Christine MacDonald in the operetta of the same name (1913). The melody of the chorus has a two-octave span and is further distinguished by its intriguing rhythmic pulse. The number was written long before the operetta was produced—a sketch of the basic melody having been found in Herbert's notebook, dated 1896. Jeanette MacDonald sang it in the motion-picture adaptation of the operetta (MGM, 1938); Dorothy Kirsten sang it in the motion-picture musical *The Great Caruso* (MGM, 1951).

Sweethearts, an operetta with book by Harry B. Smith and Fred de Gresac. Lyrics by Robert B. Smith. Music by Victor Herbert. Starring Christine MacDonald and Thomas Conkey (1913).

The motion-picture adaptation starred Nelson Eddy and Jeanette MacDonald (MGM, 1938). It utilized the basic stage score.

See: The Angelus; Pretty As a Picture; Sweethearts.

Sweethearts on Parade, words by Charles Newman, music by Carmen Lombardo (1928). Introduced by Guy Lombardo and his Royal Canadians in Chicago; within three weeks it became a nationwide hit. It was interpolated in the motion-picture musical of the same name starring Alice White and Lloyd Hughes (Columbia, 1930). The song was subsequently popularized by Guy Lombardo's best-selling Capitol recording and by Louis Armstrong in a successful Decca release.

Sweetheart Tree, words by Johnny Mercer, music by Henry Mancini (1965). Introduced by Natalie Wood in the non-musical motion picture *The Great Race,* starring Miss Wood with Jack Lemmon and Tony Curtis (Warner, 1965). An innovation in the presentation of this song came when Miss Wood, on the screen, invited the motion-picture audience to "follow the bouncing ball" and sing along with her. The song was further popularized by Johnny Mathis in a Mercury recording.

Sweet Is the Word for You, words by Leo Robin, music by Ralph Rainger (1937). Introduced by Bing Crosby in the motion-picture musical *Waikiki Wedding* (Paramount, 1937), and further popularized by him in a Decca recording.

Sweet Italian Love, words by Irving Berlin, music by Ted Snyder (1910). Interpolated in the musical *Up and Down Broadway* (1910), introduced by Irving Berlin and Ted Snyder appearing as men about town.

Sweet Lady, words by Howard Johnson, music by Frank Crumit and Dave Zoob (1921). Introduced by Julia Sanderson and Frank Crumit in the musical *Tangerine* (1921).

Sweet Leilani, words and music by Harry Owens (1937). Introduced by Bing Crosby in the motion-picture musical *Waikiki Wedding* (Paramount, 1937). The song received the Academy Award. Crosby's Decca recording in 1946 sold over a million disks.

Sweet Lorraine, words by Mitchell Parish, music by Cliff Burwell (1928). Hit song popularized in vaudeville and over the radio in the late 1920s. This was the song that transformed Nat King Cole from an instrumentalist into a singer. He was appearing with the King Cole Trio, an instrumental ensemble, at the Swanee Inn night club in Los Angeles in 1937 when an inebriated patron insisted he sing "Sweet Lorraine." Nat King Cole finally complied, though he had never before sung publicly. He proved so successful that from then on he continued doing vocals with his group—in the soft, intimate vocal style which henceforth distinguished his performances.

Sweet Madness, words by Ned Washington, music by Victor Young (1933). Introduced as a production number in the "musical mystery" *Murder at the Vanities* (1933).

Sweet Marie, words by Cy Warman, music by Raymond Moore (1893). Introduced by Raymond Moore in the minstrel show at the Euclid Opera House in Cleveland in 1893. The song's success was greatly stimulated by the promotion given it in 1893 by the New York *Sun,* which published the lyrics.

Sweet Mary Ann (or, Such an Education Has My Mary Ann), words by Edward Harrigan, music by David Braham (1878). Introduced in the Harrigan and Hart burlesque *Malone's Night Off* (1878).

A Sweet Old Fashioned Girl, words and music by Bob Merrill (1956). Popularized by Teresa Brewer in a Coral recording.

Sweet Rosie O'Grady, words and music by Maude Nugent (1896). One of the most successful waltzes of the 1890s, introduced and popularized by Maude Nugent at the Abbey, a night spot on 38th Street and 8th Avenue, New York City, where she was then appearing nightly as a featured singer. The song helped to make her a star in vaudeville, after she sang it at Tony Pastor's Music Hall in New York in 1896.

When Maude Nugent first presented the number to Edward B.

Marks, of the publishing house of Joseph W. Stern & Company, he turned it down, maintaining that popular songs with girls' names in the title were no longer commercial. She left in a huff, and proceeded in the direction of the publishing house of Howley, Haviland and Dresser. Marks, with a sudden change of heart, ran after her, caught up with her on Fifth Avenue and 20th Street and told her he was ready to buy it. He paid her a few hundred dollars for all the rights, then realized a fortune through its publication. There have been some doubts as to whether Maude Nugent wrote the song at all, since neither before nor afterward did she produce a successful number. Some insisted that the song had actually been the work of her husband, William Jerome, a successful songwriter, who had permitted her to palm it off as her own composition.

The song provided the title and inspiration for a motion-picture musical starring Betty Grable (20th Century-Fox, 1943), where it was sung by Robert Young.

Sweet Savannah, words and music by Paul Dresser (1898).

Sweet Sixteen, words by Gene Buck, music by Dave Stamper (1919). Introduced by Marilyn Miller in the *Ziegfeld Follies of 1919.*

Sweet Sue, Just You, words by Will J. Harris, music by Victor Young (1928). Written for Sue Carol (Mrs. Alan Ladd), whose portrait appears on the cover of the sheet music and to whom the song is dedicated. The song was revived by the Mills Brothers in the motion-picture musical *Rhythm Parade,* starring Gale Storm (Monogram, 1942). It was also played on the soundtrack by Carmen Cavallero in the motion-picture musical *The Eddie Duchin Story* (Columbia, 1956).

Sweet Violets, words and music by Cy Cohen and Charles Grean, adapted from a folk song (1951). Popularized by Dinah Shore in an RCA Victor recording.

Sweet Violets, words and music by Joseph K. Emmet (1882). Intro-

duced in the musical *Fritz Among the Gypsies* (1882).

De Swellest Gal in Town, words and music by Harry von Tilzer (1897). Introduced by the minstrel George H. Primrose and subsequently a favorite with minstrel troupes all over the country.

Swing High, Swing Low, words by Ralph Freed, music by Burton Lane (1937). Introduced by Dorothy Lamour in the motion-picture musical *Artists and Models* (Paramount, 1937).

Swingin' Down the Lane, words by Gus Kahn, music by Isham Jones (1923). Introduced by Isham Jones and his orchestra and subsequently popularized by Frankie Carle. Vivian Blaine, in her first featured roll in motion pictures, sang it in the screen musical *Greenwich Village,* starring Don Ameche and Carmen Miranda (20th Century-Fox, 1944). The song was also interpolated in the screen biography of Gus Kahn, *I'll See You in My Dreams* (Warner, 1951), sung by Danny Thomas and Doris Day.

Swinging on a Star, words by Johnny Burke, music by James Van Heusen (1944). Introduced by Bing Crosby and a boys' chorus in the motion picture *Going My Way* (Paramount, 1944). The song received the Academy Award (as did the motion picture). Crosby's Decca recording in 1944 sold over a million disks.

Johnny Burke and Van Heusen were dining at Bing Crosby's when one of Bing's sons misbehaved. Bing scolded him for acting like a mule. Burke, who had been worrying about a song for one of the scenes in *Going My Way,* found in this incident a suitable song subject: about somebody, stubborn as a mule, refusing to better himself. The next day Burke and Van Heusen wrote their song.

Swingin' in a Hammock, words by Tot Seymour and Charles O'Flynn, music by Pete Wendling (1930). Introduced and popularized by Guy Lombardo and his Royal Canadians.

Swingin' School, words by Karl Mann, music by Bernie Lowe and Dave

Appell (1960). Popularized by Bobby Rydell in a Camden recording.

Swing Me an Old Fashioned Song, words by Walter Bullock, music by Harold Spina (1938). Introduced by Shirley Temple in the motion-picture musical *Little Miss Broadway* (20th Century-Fox, 1938).

Swing Time, a motion-picture musical starring Fred Astaire and Ginger Rogers (RKO, 1936). Songs by Dorothy Fields and Jerome Kern.

See: Bojangles of Harlem; A Fine Romance; The Way You Look Tonight.

'S Wonderful, words by Ira Gershwin, music by George Gershwin (1927). Introduced by Allen Kearns and Adele Astaire in the musical *Funny Face* (1927). It was interpolated in the George Gershwin screen biography *Rhapsody in Blue* (Warner, 1945). Doris Day sang it in the motion-picture musical *Starlift* (Warner, 1951); Georges Guetary and Gene Kelly in the motion-picture musical *An American in Paris* (MGM, 1951); Fred Astaire and Audrey Hepburn in the motion-picture adaptation of the musical *Funny Face* (Paramount, 1957); and Dean Martin in the motion-picture musical with songs by George and Ira Gershwin, *Kiss Me Stupid* (Lopert, 1964). For the rendition in *An American in Paris,* Ira Gershwin inserted a French flavor into his lyrics with words like "'S Magnifique," and "'S Elegant" and "'Exceptionel."

Sylvia, words by Paul Francis Webster, music by David Raksin (1965). Title song of a non-musical motion picture starring Carroll Baker (Paramount, 1965), where it was sung on the soundtrack under the titles by Paul Anka.

Sylvia, words by Clinton Scollard, music by Oley Speaks (1914). An art song which entered the popular repertory through performances by tenors and male quartets in vaudeville.

Sympathy, words by Otto Hauerbach (Harbach), music by Rudolf Friml (1912). Introduced by Audrey Maple and Melville Stewart in the operetta *The Firefly* (1912). Friml's first stage score. This duet was also sung in the motion-picture adaptation of the operetta (MGM, 1937).

Syncopated Clock, words by Mitchell Parish, music by Leroy Anderson (1950). Originated as an instrumental, popularized in 1951 in a Decca recording by Leroy Anderson and his orchestra. The melody was used as the theme music for the Early and Late Shows over CBS-TV.

Syncopated Walk, words and music by Irving Berlin (1914). Introduced by Irene and Vernon Castle, and ensemble, in the musical *Watch Your Step* (1914). Irving Berlin's first stage score.

T

Take a Chance, a musical comedy with book by Bud De Sylva and Laurence Schwab. Additional dialogue by Sid Silvers. Lyrics by Bud De Sylva. Music by Vincent Youmans and Richard A. Whiting. Starring Jack Haley and Ethel Merman (1932).

The motion-picture adaptation starred James Dunn, June Knight and Charles "Buddy" Rogers (Paramount, 1933). Three songs were used from the original stage score. Additional songs by Arthur Swanstrom and Louis Alter and by Herman Hupfeld. "It's Only a Paper Moon" by Billy Rose, E. Y. Harburg and Harold Arlen was interpolated.

See: Eadie Was a Lady; It's Only a Paper Moon; Rise 'n' Shine; So Do I; Turn Out the Light.

Take a Seat, Old Lady, words and music by Paul Dresser (1894). Ballad popularized by Meyer Cohen.

Take Back Your Gold, words by Louis W. Pritzkow, music by Monroe H. Rosenfeld (1897). Though the sheet music credits Pritzkow as lyricist, the words were actually by the composer. At the time the song was written, Pritzkow was a popular minstrel. Rosenfeld bribed him into introducing the song by crediting him as the lyricist. After Pritzkow had sung the number in minstrel shows, Emma Carus plugged it consistently in vaudeville. So did Imogene Comer, who opened her vaudeville tour with a dramatic rendition of the ballad in her act at the Bowdoin Square Theater in Boston.

Take Back the Heart You Gave (or, Take Back the Heart That Thou Gavest), words and music by Mrs. Charles C. Barnard, using the pen name of Claribel (1864). One of the earliest examples of torch song, and one of its composer's greatest hits. "Its lush lines," said Sigmund Spaeth, "fitted to flowing waltz measures are still the delight of musical antiquarians."

Take Back Your Mink, words and music by Frank Loesser (1950). Introduced by Vivian Blaine in the nightclub scene in the musical *Guys and Dolls* (1950). She also sang it in the motion-picture adaptation of the musical (MGM, 1955).

Take Good Care of My Baby, words and music by Gerry Goffin and Carole King (1961). Popularized by Bobby Vee in a Liberty recording.

Take It Slow, Joe, words by E. Y. Harburg, music by Harold Arlen (1957). Introduced by Lena Horne (in her first Broadway starring role) in a dream sequence in the musical *Jamaica* (1957). "She never lets her audience down," reported Wayne Robinson in the *Evening Bulletin* of Philadelphia, "most particularly when she can coil herself around the words of 'Take It Slow, Joe,' giving this sensuous meaning beyond the lyrics." Edward Jablonski wrote: "As a song representative of Arlen's versatility, 'Take It Slow, Joe' has yet to be discovered."

Take Me Along, words and music by Bob Merrill (1959). Introduced by Walter Pidgeon and Jackie Gleason in the musical of the same name (1959).

Take Me Along, a musical comedy with book by Joseph Stein and Robert Russell based on Eugene O'Neill's stage comedy *Ah, Wilderness!*. Lyrics and music by Bob Merrill. Starring Jackie Gleason, Walter Pidgeon and Eileen Herlie (1959). Original cast recording (RCA Victor).

See: Promise Me a Rose; Staying Young; Take Me Along.

Take Me Out to the Ball Game, words by Jack Norworth, music by Albert von Tilzer (1908). The unofficial anthem of America's national game (written twenty years or so *before* Albert von Tilzer saw his first baseball game). The song was introduced in vaudeville by Albert von Tilzer. By virtue of his success with this number, he was given a contract to tour the Orpheum vaudeville circuit. The song was further popularized in vaudeville by Nora Bayes and by Sadie Jansell.

There has hardly been a motion picture about baseball that has not utilized this song in one form or another, most usually by having it played or sung on the soundtrack under the titles. The song provided the title for and was played under the titles of a motion picture starring Gene Kelly, Frank Sinatra and Esther Williams (MGM, 1949). It was sung by Ann Sheridan and Dennis Morgan in the motion-picture musical biography of Nora Bayes, *Shine On Harvest Moon* (Warner, 1944).

Take My Love, words by Helen Deutsch, music by Bronislau Kaper (1955). Introduced in the motion picture *The Glass Slipper,* starring Leslie Caron (MGM, 1954). It was popularized by Eddie Fisher in an RCA Victor recording.

Take Off a Little Bit, words and music by Irving Berlin (1915). A number

in the revue *Stop, Look and Listen* (1915) with which Gaby Deslys did what is believed to have been the first strip tease in the Broadway musical theater. She did it while reciting the lines of the Irving Berlin song, removing from time to time an article of her apparel.

Take Off the Coat, words and music by Harold Rome (1950). Introduced by Jane Harvey in the revue *Bless You All* (1950). This number is a particular favorite of its creator.

Take, Oh Take, Those Lips Away, words by Joseph McCarthy, music by Harry Tierney (1923). Introduced by Brooke Johns and Ann Pennington in the revue *Ziegfeld Follies of 1923.*

Takes Two to Tango, words and music by Al Hoffman and Dick Manning (1952). Popularized by Pearl Bailey in a Coral recording.

Take the "A" Train, words and music by Billy Strayhorn (1941). The song, described as a "swinging riff tune," was named after the subway ride on the Eighth Avenue line in New York City—an express train identified as "A." Strayhorn wrote this number for Duke Ellington and his orchestra, with whom he was employed as arranger. It became Ellington's signature music. Ellington and his orchestra introduced the song in an RCA Victor recording and presented it in the motion-picture musical *Reveille with Beverly* (1943).

Take the Moment, words by Stephen Sondheim, music by Richard Rodgers (1965). Introduced by Sergio Franchi in the musical *Do I Hear a Waltz?* (1965). It was popularized by Tony Bennett in a Columbia recording.

Take These Chains from My Heart, words and music by Fred Rose and Hy Manning (1952). Popularized in 1953 by Hank Williams in an MGM recording.

Taking a Chance on Love, words by John Latouche and Ted Fetter, music by Vernon Duke (1940). Introduced by Ethel Waters in the musical play *Cabin in the Sky* (1940), with which she regularly stopped the show. On opening night she had to sing the chorus half a dozen times. George Jean Nathan regarded it as "the finest song of the year." Ethel Waters also sang it in the motion-picture adaptation of the musical (MGM, 1943). The song was interpolated in several other motion pictures, including *I Dood It*, starring Red Skelton and Eleanor Powell (MGM, 1943), and the screen musical *I'll Get By* (20th Century-Fox, 1950), sung by June Haver and Gloria De Haven.

In his autobiography, Vernon Duke describes the writing of his hit song. "We needed a heart-warming song to put the first act over. . . . I reached for the trunk—three days before the opening—and stumbled on 'Fooling Around with Love,' a song Ted Fetter and I had written for an unproduced Abbott show. I tried it out on Latouche; he fell for the tune, but thought the title not sufficiently 'on the nose' for the dramatic situation. An afternoon's work, with an assist from Fetter, followed, and what emerged was 'Taking a Chance on Love,' one of my better-known songs, an immediate hit, and a solid standard today." When Duke first played the song for Ethel Waters, she stopped him after the first eight bars with the comment: "Mister, our troubles are over. This is it."

Taking Care of You, words by Lew Brown, music by Harry Akst (1936). Introduced by Harry Richman in the motion-picture musical *The Music Goes Round* (Columbia, 1936). It was revived in the motion-picture musical *Stars on Parade*, starring Larry Parks and Lynn Merrick (Columbia, 1944).

The Tale of a Bumble Bee, words by Frank Pixley, music by Gustav Luders (1901). Hit song from the musical *King Dodo* (1901). Pixley and Luders were partial to songs whose titles started with the words "The Tale of," and produced some of their greatest hits this way.

The Tale of the Kangaroo, words by Frank Pixley, music by Gustav Luders (1900). Hit song from the musical *The Burgomaster* (1900),

the first musical production on which Pixley and Luders collaborated. This was also the first show in which they had a hit song whose title began with the words "The Tale of."

The Tale of the Seashell, words by Frank Pixley, music by Gustav Luders (1902). Introduced by Arthur Donaldson and Lillian Coleman in the operetta *The Prince of Pilsen* (1903).

The Tale of the Turtle Dove, words by Frank Pixley, music by Gustav Luders (1904). Introduced by Margaret Sayre and company in the musical *Woodland* (1904).

Talking to Me, words and music by Timothy Gray and Hugh Martin (1964). Introduced by Beatrice Lillie (communing with a ouija board) in the musical *High Spirits* (1964).

Talk to Me, Baby, words by Johnny Mercer, music by Robert Emmett Dolan (1964). Introduced by Julienne Marie and John Davidson in the musical *Foxy* (1964).

Tallahassee, words and music by Frank Loesser (1947). Introduced in the motion-picture musical *Variety Girl*, starring Olga San Juan and De Forest Kelley (Paramount, 1947), sung by Alan Ladd and Dorothy Lamour. It was popularized by Bing Crosby and the Andrews Sisters in a Decca recording.

Tammany, words by Vincent P. Bryan, music by Gus Edwards (1905). Introduced by Lee Harrison in the musical *Fantana* (1905), where it was an interpolation. It was subsequently popularized by Jefferson de Angelis.

This song had been written for a party at the National Democratic Club in New York, where Gus Edwards served as master of ceremonies. A take-off on American Indian songs, then in vogue in Tin Pan Alley, "Tammany" was at the same time a satire on the less desirable practices of the Democratic Party in New York. To make sure he was not hurting the feelings of any of his guests, Edwards sang his number for ex-Mayor Van Wyck, Charles F. Murphy and Timothy D.

Sullivan, all of them Democratic bigwigs. They liked it, and encouraged him to use it at the party. It was acclaimed. Despite its pronounced satirical overtones, the song became the official number of of the New York Tammany Hall.

Tammy, words and music by Jay Livingston and Ray Evans (1957). Introduced by Debbie Reynolds in the motion picture *Tammy and the Bachelor* (Universal, 1957). Over ten million records were sold of this number in recordings by almost one hundred artists, the most successful being that of Debbie Reynolds for Coral, which sold over a million disks.

Tangerine, words by Johnny Mercer, music by Victor Schertzinger (1942). Introduced by the Jimmy Dorsey Orchestra (with Helen O'Connell and Bob Eberle doing the vocal) in the motion-picture musical *The Fleet's In,* starring Dorothy Lamour (Universal, 1942). The Decca recording by Jimmy Dorsey and his orchestra was a best seller.

Ta-Ra-Ra-Boom-De-Ré, words and music attributed to Henry J. Sayers (1891). One of the most successful nonsense songs of the 1890s. It is believed to have originated at Babe Connors' "maison de joie" on South Street in St. Louis, where it was introduced by Mama Lou. Some even credit Mama Lou with having created it. Ignace Jan Paderewski, on a visit to Babe Connors' night spot, was so delighted with Mama Lou's rendition of "Ta-ra-ra-boom-de-ré" that he went over to the piano and began playing it.

A publicity man named Henry J. Sayers—then handling a troupe of performers known as the Tuexdo Girls—heard the song at Babe Connors' and felt it was ideal for his company. He later explained: "I had never tried my hand at songwriting, but I thought that with a few changes I could clean up the stuff. When I showed it to the boss, he almost threw me out of the office. 'This is unprintable, unsingable, untouchable,' he shouted. I decided to

rewrite the lyrics entirely. But they fell flat and remained that way three years."

Eventually, Sayers sold his adaptation to the publishing house of Willis Woodward, who issued it in 1891, identifying Sayers as its composer and lyricist. The song's success began not in New York but in London, where it was introduced by Lottie Collins. She delivered the verse with the greatest of propriety, after which the chorus line performed the refrain with accompanying shrieks and high kicks. London went mad over the number. "Everywhere," reported a correspondent from England for the New York *Herald* on February 28, 1892, "from Belgrave and Mayfair, to Houndsditch and Whitechapel . . . one hears 'Ta-ra-ra-boom-de-ré,' and there is hardly a theatre in London in which the refrain is not alluded to at least once during the night." Sheet music of this number sold for a dollar a copy, until a competitor flooded the market with music priced at only two cents apiece. After that a copy of the song was given free with each purchase of a tin of tea.

Lottie Collins introduced the number to the United States—at Koster and Bial's Theatre in New York in 1892. The song now became the rage of New York.

A Taste of Honey, words and music by Ric Marlow and Bobby Scott (1965). Popularized by Herb Alpert and the Tijuana Brass in an A. & M. recording that received a "Grammy" Award as the record of the year.

Tchaikovsky. *See:* Tschaikowsky.

Teacher, Teacher, words by Al Stillman, music by Robert Allen (1958). Popularized by Johnny Mathis in a Columbia recording.

Teach Me Tonight, words by Sammy Cahn, music by Gene De Paul (1954). The first collaboration of Sammy Cahn and Gene De Paul. Cahn was then under contract to the Warner studios in Hollywood, who had first refusal on the song. They turned it down. Sammy Cahn goes on to explain, in a communication to this editor: "It was peddled and finally went to Hub Music, which was a company owned by six songwriters. The song had an original recording on Decca by some young lady. It sold three copies. She bought one. I bought one and Gene de Paul bought one. It wasn't until two years later that it was recorded on a small record label, Abbott Records, by the De Castro Sisters and went on to become one of the very biggest of my copyrights." The song was then further popularized by Jo Stafford in a best-selling Columbia recording.

Tea for Two, words by Irving Caesar, music by Vincent Youmans (1924). Introduced by Louise Groody and John Barker in the musical *No, No, Nanette* (1925).

Late one night, after having just completed writing the melody, Youmans played it through for Caesar. Tired and eager to get to bed, Caesar offered to produce a dummy lyric to placate the composer, intending to write the real one the following day. But the dummy lyric Caesar improvised worked out perfectly, and it was kept.

This was one of sixteen numbers selected by ASCAP in 1963 for its all-time Hit Parade during the half century of its existence. The song was interpolated in several motion pictures, including the screen adaptation of *No, No, Nanette,* renamed *Tea for Two* (Warner, 1950), sung on the soundtrack under the titles by a chorus and in the picture by Gordon MacRae and Doris Day. It was also interpolated in the Jane Froman screen biography *With a Song in My Heart* (20th Century-Fox, 1952), sung on the soundtrack by Miss Froman.

A cha-cha version was popularized in 1958 in a best-selling record release by Warren Covington for Decca.

Tea for Two (motion picture). *See: No, No, Nanette.*

Tears on My Pillow, words and music by Sylvester Bradford and Al Lewis (1958). Popularized by Little Anthony and the Imperials in an End recording.

Teasin', words by Phil Springer, music by Richard Adler (1950). Popularized by Connie Haines in an MGM recording. It then became the Number One hit song in London, England, popularized there by the Beverly Sisters; in 1951 it became the Command Performance Song.

Teasing, words by Richard C. McPherson, using the pen name of Cecil Mack, music by Albert von Tilzer (1904). Albert von Tilzer's first song success both as composer and as publisher.

Teddy, words and music by Paul Anka (1960). Popularized by Connie Francis in an MGM recording.

Teddy Bear, words and music by Kal Mann and Bernie Lowe (1957). Introduced by Elvis Presley in the motion-picture musical *Loving You* (Paramount, 1957), and popularized by him in an RCA Victor recording that sold a million disks.

Teen-Age Crush, words and music by Audrey and Joe Allison (1956). Introduced by Tommy Sands in the TV production *Singin' Idol,* and popularized by him in a best-selling Capitol recording.

A Teenager in Love, words and music by Jerome "Doc" Pomus and Mort Shuman (1959). Popularized by Dion and the Belmonts in a Laurie recording.

Teen Angel, words and music by Jean and Red Surrey (1960). Popularized by Mark Dinning in an MGM recording.

Tell Me (Why Nights Are Lonely), words by J. Will Callahan, music by Max Kortlander (1919). Hit ballad popularized in vaudeville in the early 1920s. It was interpolated in the motion-picture musical biography of Ted Lewis, *Is Everybody Happy?* (Columbia, 1943); and it was sung by Doris Day in the motion-picture musical *On Moonlight Bay* (Warner, 1951).

Tell Me a Bedtime Story, words and music by Irving Berlin (1923). The song with which Grace Moore made her debut in the Broadway musical theater—in the *Music Box Revue of 1923*. She introduced it in the opening number of the revue—seated in an enormous wicker chair, surrounded by girls dressed in their nighties. "Hats were thrown in the air and cheers resounded from one end of Broadway to the other, and a new star was born," reported Alexander Woollcott of Grace Moore's performance.

Tell Me, Daisy, words by Dorothy Donnelly, music by Sigmund Romberg, melody derived from the second-movement theme of Schubert's *Unfinished Symphony* (1921). Introduced in the operetta *Blossom Time* (1921).

Tell Me, Dusky Maiden, words by James W. Johnson and Bob Cole, music by J. Rosamond Johnson (1901). A travesty on "Tell Me, Pretty Maiden"—the celebrated sextet from the English operetta *Florodora*. It was introduced in the musical *Sleeping Beauty and the Beast* (1901).

Tell Me, Little Gypsy, words and music by Irving Berlin (1920). Introduced by John Steel in the *Ziegfeld Follies of 1920*.

Tell Me That You Love Me, a popular Italian song ("Parlami d'amore, Mariù") with music by C. A. Bixio and English lyrics by Al Silverman (1935).

Tell Me Why, words by Al Alberts, music by Marty Gold (1951). Popularized in recordings by the Four Aces for Decca and Eddie Fisher for RCA Victor.

Tell Me Why You Smile, Mona Lisa, a German popular song ("Warum laechelst du, Mona Lisa") with music by Robert Stolz and English lyrics by Raymond B. Egan (1932).

Temptation, words by Arthur Freed, music by Nacio Herb Brown (1933). Introduced by Bing Crosby in the motion-picture musical *Going Hollywood* (MGM, 1933). It was with this song, and in this movie, that Bing Crosby first joined the leading ten box-office attractions in Hollywood. He later recalled in his autobiography: " 'Temptation' was my first attempt at presenting a song

dramatically. . . . As a derelict [in Tijuana] I sang 'Temptation' to a glass of tequila, while tears dripped into my beard from the circles under my eyes. Through trick photography a dame's face appeared in the glass of tequila; then, at the end of the song, I flung the glass at the wall and staggered out into the night. It was all very Russian Art Theatre."

The song was popularized in several best-selling recordings: notably those by Bing Crosby for Decca, Perry Como for RCA Victor in 1945, and Jo Stafford and Red Ingle for Capitol in 1948. The song was interpolated in the motion picture *Malaya*, starring Spencer Tracy (MGM, 1949).

Ten Cents a Dance, words by Lorenz Hart, music by Richard Rodgers (1930). Introduced by Ruth Etting in the musical *Simple Simon* (1930). This song had been hurriedly interpolated in that production during Boston tryouts. Ziegfeld, the show's producer, informed Rodgers and Hart that he needed a new number immediately for Lee Morse, scheduled to play the female lead. Rodgers and Hart complied with "Ten Cents a Dance," which they wrote at the Hotel Ritz in less than an hour. The next day they learned that Lee Morse had suddenly been replaced by Ruth Etting, and so it was Ruth Etting who was called upon to introduce the song. Even though this lament of a "taxi dancer" was out of place within the context of *Simple Simon*, it proved to be the hit of the show. The song was interpolated in the Ruth Etting screen biography *Love Me or Leave Me* (MGM, 1955), sung by Doris Day.

Tender Is the Night, words by Paul Francis Webster, music by Sammy Fain (1961). Theme song for—and an important element in the plot of—a non-musical motion picture of the same name starring Jennifer Jones and Jason Robards (20th Century-Fox, 1961). In this motion picture it was introduced by Earl Grant; it was also sung on the soundtrack by a chorus under the main and end titles. The song was popularized by Johnny Mathis' recording for Columbia, who used its title for that of a best-selling record album.

Tenderly, words by Jack Lawrence, music by Walter Gross (1946). Introduced by Clark Dennis in a Capitol recording. It was popularized in 1955 by Rosemary Clooney in a Columbia recording. It was played under the titles of the non-musical motion picture *Torch Song,* starring Joan Crawford (MGM, 1953).

The Tender Trap, words by Sammy Cahn, music by James Van Heusen (1955). Title song of a motion picture (MGM, 1955), introduced by Frank Sinatra. It was popularized by him in a best-selling Capitol recording.

Ten Minutes Ago, words by Oscar Hammerstein II, music by Richard Rodgers (1957). Introduced by Julie Andrews in the TV musical production of *Cinderella* (1957).

Tennessee Waltz, words and music by Redd Stewart and Pee Wee King (1948). Popularized by Patti Page in a Mercury recording in which her voice was coupled contrapuntally with her own voice recorded on tape. This release sold about three million disks in 1950–1951. A King recording by Cowboy Copas in 1950 was a lesser best seller. In 1965 the waltz was chosen as the official song of the State of Tennessee.

Ten Pins in the Sky, words by Joseph McCarthy, music by Milton Ager (1938), Written for and introduced by Judy Garland in the motion-picture musical *Listen, Darling* (MGM, 1938).

Tenting on the Old Camp Ground, words and music by Walter Kittredge (1864). Ballad of the Civil War describing a soldier's moods and feelings during a lull in the battle. It was introduced in 1863 by the Hutchinson Family. Asa Hutchinson interested Oliver Ditson in publishing it several months later, sharing the royalties with the composer. In a brief period of time Asa Hutchinson and Kittredge cleared several thousand dollars in royalties, evidence of the song's successful dissemination.

Kittredge, a professional singer, wrote his ballad early in 1863, just as he was about to be drafted into the Union Army. In words and music he transferred his own feelings about leaving his wife and daughter. But Kittredge never served in the Army, having been rejected on medical grounds.

In time, Kittredge joined the Hutchinson Family in their concerts as a performer, and for about twenty years he toured with them. "Tenting on the Old Camp Ground" made frequent appearances on their programs. Kittredge and Joshua Hutchinson sang it every day during a week of anti-slavery meetings in Philadelphia in 1866 celebrating the end of the Civil War. They sang it a decade later at the Philadelphia centennial celebration, and in 1892 at a soldiers' reunion in Washington, D.C. In 1893 a chorus of five hundred presented it at the Chicago Columbia Exposition. The ballad also became a prime favorite at communal sings, picnics, campfires and parties.

Tessie, You Are the Only, Only, Only, words and music by Will R. Anderson (1902). Introduced in the musical *The Silver Slipper* (1902). Its success went into high gear in 1911, when it was adopted as a theme song by the rooters for the baseball team of the Boston Braves.

Thank Heaven for Little Girls, words by Alan Jay Lerner, music by Frederick Loewe (1958). Introduced by Maurice Chevalier in the motion-picture musical *Gigi* (MGM, 1958).

Thanks a Million, words by Gus Kahn, music by Arthur Johnston (1935). Introduced by Dick Powell in the motion-picture musical of the same name (20th Century-Fox, 1935).

Thanks for the Memory, words by Leo Robin, music by Ralph Rainger (1937). Introduced by Bob Hope (in his screen debut) and Shirley Ross in the motion-picture musical *The Big Broadcast of 1938* (Paramount, 1937); from then on it became Bob Hope's theme song.

Bob Hope recalled in his autobiography: "At Paramount I met Billy Selwyn, the assistant producer assigned to the film [*Big Broadcast of 1938*]. He greeted me with, 'You're a lucky fellow. Wait until you hear the number Leo Robin and Ralph Rainger have written for you.' . . . He took me over to the studio department and played a recording of 'Thanks for the Memory.' It sounded so beautiful. . . . 'Thanks for the Memory' was the only number that kept me in pictures when I finished work in my first film. For that matter, it was only the most important song in my life."

The song received the Academy Award. A recording by Bob Hope and Shirley Ross was a best seller in 1938. The tremendous success of this number—and Bob Hope's effective delivery—led Paramount to star Hope in a new picture, appropriately entitled *Thanks for the Memory* (Paramount, 1938).

Thank You for a Lovely Evening, words by Dorothy Fields, music by Jimmy McHugh (1934). Introduced by Leah Ray and Phil Harris (Phil Harris making his bow in big-time on Broadway) in a revue at the night club *Palais Royal,* in 1934. It was sung in the motion picture *Have a Heart,* starring Jean Parker and James Dunn (MGM, 1934), and in *Missouri,* starring Jean Harlow and Franchot Tone (MGM, 1934).

Thank Your Father, words by Bud De Sylva and Lew Brown, music by Ray Henderson (1930). Introduced by Grace Brinkley and Oscar Shaw and ensemble in the musical *Flying Colors* (1930).

Thank Your Lucky Stars, a motion-picture revue with an all-star cast that included Eddie Cantor, Bette Davis, Ann Sheridan and others (Warner, 1943). Songs by Frank Loesser and Arthur Schwartz.

See: How Sweet You Are; They're Either Too Young or Too Old.

That Certain Feeling, words by Ira Gershwin, music by George Gershwin (1925). Introduced by Allen Kearns and Queenie Smith in the musical *Tip Toes* (1925).

That Certain Party, words by Gus Kahn, music by Walter Donaldson (1925). Hit song in the 1920s. It was successfully revived a generation later by Dean Martin and Jerry Lewis in a Decca recording.

That Darn Cat, words and music by Richard M. and Robert B. Sherman (1965). Title song of the Walt Disney motion picture starring Hayley Mills (Buena Vista, 1965). It was sung on the soundtrack by Bobby Darin and was popularized by Buddy Greco in an Epic recording.

That Doggie in the Window. *See:* How Much Is That Doggie in the Window?

That Face, words by Alan Bergman and Lew Spence, music by Lew Spence (1957). Introduced and popularized by Fred Astaire.

That Funny Feeling, words and music by Bobby Darin (1965). Title song of a non-musical motion picture starring Bobby Darin and Sandra Dee (Universal, 1965), sung by Bobby Darin.

That'll Be the Day, words and music by Jerry Allison, Buddy Holly and Norman Petty (1957). Popularized by the Crickets in a Brunswick recording.

The Lost Barber Shop Chord, words by Ira Gershwin, music by George Gershwin (1926). Introduced by Louis Lazarin and the Pan American Quartet (in a barber-shop setting) in the revue *Americana* (1926).

Ira Gershwin derived his title from two earlier songs by other writers—from Sir Arthur Sullivan's "The Lost Chord" and Lewis Muir's ragtime classic, "Play that Barber Shop Chord."

The song was well liked when first heard. Charles Pike Sawyer of the New York *Post* described it as "full of melody and swinging rhythm, a perfect joy." Nevertheless, it lapsed into total obscurity after the show closed. Ira Gershwin has remarked wistfully: "Me, I haven't heard the song sung anywhere in over thirty years."

That Lovin' Rag, words by Victor H. Smalley, music by Bernie Adler

(1907). Introduced by Sophie Tucker at the Howard Atheneum, a burlesque house in Boston, in 1907. Sophie Tucker, up to now famous as a blackface "coon shouter," discarded her blackface make-up for good with this number. Her trunk and make-up kit had been delayed in coming to Boston, and she was forced to appear in white face. "I don't need blackface," she said after bringing down the house with "That Lovin' Rag." "I can hold an audience with it. I've got them eating out of my hand. I'm through with blackface. I'll never black up again."

That Lucky Old Sun, words by Haven Gillespie, music by Beasley Smith (1949). Popularized by Frankie Laine in a Mercury recording, and by Vaughn Monroe in an RCA Victor release.

That Mesmerizing Mendelssohn Tune, words and music by Irving Berlin (1909). An early Irving Berlin song success—one of the first for which he wrote both the music and the words. The melody was a ragtime treatment of Mendelssohn's *Spring Song.*

That Mysterious Rag, words by Irving Berlin, music by Ted Snyder (1911). Introduced in the revue *The Passing Show of 1912,* where it was an interpolation.

That Old Black Magic, words by Johnny Mercer, music by Harold Arlen (1942). Introduced by Johnny Johnson and danced to by Vera Zorina in a production number in the motion-picture musical *Star-Spangled Rhythm,* starring Bing Crosby, Bob Hope and Dick Powell (Paramount, 1942).

Arlen explains that one of the reasons for the success of this song is Mercer's felicitous lyrics. "The words sustain your interest, make sense, contain memorable phrases and tell a story. Without the lyric, the song would be just another song."

While this song was successfully recorded by Frank Sinatra for Decca, it is most often associated with Billy Daniels, who achieved with it his greatest success both in night clubs and on records; his Liberty recording sold well in excess of two million disks.

In the motion-picture musical *Here Come the Waves* (Paramount, 1944), the song was interpolated in order to comment upon the then current craze for Frank Sinatra, sung by Bing Crosby. Sinatra sang it in the motion-picture musical *Meet Danny Wilson* (Universal, 1952); Marilyn Monroe in the non-musical motion picture *Bus Stop* (20th Century-Fox, 1956). In 1958 the Louis Prima, Keely Smith recording for Dot received a "Grammy" from the National Academy of Recording Arts and Sciences as the best recorded performance that year by a vocal group.

That Old Feeling, words by Lew Brown, music by Sammy Fain (1937). Introduced in the motion-picture musical *Vogues of 1938,* starring Joan Bennett and Warner Baxter (United Artists, 1937). In the motion-picture biography of Jane Froman, *With a Song in My Heart* (20th Century-Fox, 1952), it was sung on the soundtrack by Miss Froman.

That Old Gang of Mine, words by Billy Rose and Mort Dixon, music by Ray Henderson (1923). One of Henderson's earliest song hits. Billy Rose (then a court stenographer) collaborated with Dixon on the lyrics, inspired by a poem entitled *Old Familiar Faces.* The first musical setting proved a dismal failure. The lyricists then asked Henderson to write a new melody. The song was placed in the *Ziegfeld Follies of 1923,* successfully introduced by Van and Schenck. For several months running the sheet-music sale topped thirty thousand copies a week.

That Old Irish Mother of Mine, words by William Jerome, music by Harry von Tilzer (1920).

That's All I Want from You, words and music by Fritz Rotter, using the pen name of M. Rotha (1954). Popularized in 1955 by Jaye P. Morgan in an RCA Victor recording.

That's All You Gotta Do, words and music by Jerry Reed (1960). Popularized by Brenda Lee in a Decca recording.

That's Amore (or, That's Love), words by Jack Brooks, music by Harry Warren (1953). Introduced by Dean Martin in the motion picture *The Caddy* (Paramount, 1953), and further popularized by him in a best-selling Capitol recording.

That's an Irish Lullaby. *See:* Too-ra-loo-ra-loo-ral.

That's Entertainment, words by Howard Dietz, music by Arthur Schwartz (1953). Introduced by Fred Astaire and Nanette Fabray (with India Adams singing on the soundtrack for Cyd Charisse) in the motion-picture musical *The Band Wagon* (MGM, 1953).

That's for Me, words by Johnny Burke, music by James V. Monaco (1940). Introduced by Bing Crosby and Mary Martin in the motion-picture musical *Rhythm on the River* (Paramount, 1940).

That's for Me, words by Oscar Hammerstein II, music by Richard Rodgers (1945). Introduced by Vivian Blaine and Dick Haymes in the motion-picture musical *State Fair* (20th Century-Fox, 1945). In the remake of this motion picture (20th Century-Fox, 1962), it was sung by Pat Boone.

That's Him, words by Ogden Nash, music by Kurt Weill (1943). A tribute to the ideal man, introduced by Mary Martin (in her first Broadway starring role) in the musical *One Touch of Venus* (1943). It was also sung (with additional lyrics by Ann Ronell) in the motion-picture adaptation of the musical (Universal, 1948)—by Olga San Juan, Eve Arden and Eileen Wilson's voice dubbed on the soundtrack for Ava Gardner.

That's How I Got My Start, words by Frank Loesser, music by Victor Schertzinger (1941). Introduced by Mary Martin in a strip-tease routine, in the motion-picture musical *Kiss the Boys Goodbye* (Paramount, 1941).

That's How It Went, All Right, words by Dory Langdon, music by André Previn (1960). Introduced by Bobby Darin in the motion-picture musical *Pepe* (Columbia, 1960).

That's My Desire, words by Carroll Loveday, music by Helmy Kresa (1931). This song went unnoticed when originally published by Irving Berlin, Inc. Sixteen years later, after the copyright had been acquired by Mills, the number was revived by Frankie Laine in his night-club act. An executive from Mercury Records heard him sing it in a night spot in Hollywood and had him record it. That recording, released in 1957, sold almost a million and a half disks. It helped make the song a major success (with top billing on the Hit Parade); it lifted Frankie Laine to recording stardom for the first time; and it helped establish Mercury as an important recording outfit.

That's My Weakness Now, words by Bud Green, music by Sam H. Stept (1928). Introduced in 1928 at the Paramount Theatre in New York by the then still unknown Helen Kane. In singing this number she interpolated several "boop-boop-a-doops" into the chorus. This performance made her a star, her name being put up in lights on the marquee of the Paramount Theatre four days after her first appearance there. From then on, for the next seven years, she became identified as the "boop-boop-a-doop" girl, and her inclusion of this exclamation in her songs became her trademark. The song was interpolated in the motion-picture musical *Applause* (Paramount, 1929).

That's the Kind of a Baby for Me, words by Alfred Harrison, music by Jack Egan (1917). Introduced by Eddie Cantor in the *Ziegfeld Follies of 1917*—his *Follies* debut. On opening night he stopped the show with this number, and had to repeat the chorus a dozen times; even then, the audience kept on shouting for more encores until Tom Richard, who was the next performer in the show, had to start his routine through the din. When Cantor finished the last of these encores, he rushed back to his dressing room, where he burst into tears. His grandmother, who had raised and supported him from his childhood on, had died a month before this, and thus had not lived to witness his triumph. Will Rogers, who found him in tears, asked: "Now, Eddie, what makes you think she didn't see you, and from a very good seat?"

Two days after Cantor had stopped the show with this song, he recorded it for Victor—his first successful disk.

That's What I Want for Christmas, words by Irving Caesar, music by Gerald Marks (1935). Introduced by Shirley Temple in the motion picture *Stowaway* (20th Century-Fox, 1936).

That's Why Darkies Were Born, words by Lew Brown, music by Ray Henderson (1931). Introduced by Everett Marshall in the *George White Scandals of 1931.* This and other song hits from the 1931 *Scandals* were recorded by Bing Crosby and the Boswell Sisters on two sides of a twelve-inch Brunswick record—one of the earliest attempts to record the basic score of a musical show on disks.

The song, used in the first-act finale, became one of the hit numbers of the *Scandals* that year. After the show closed, it entered the repertories of a number of Negro and white performers. But before long the song was given less and less performances, mainly due to the fact that many Negro groups objected to the use of the word "darky" in the song. This was also the reason why in the early 1930s the song was rarely heard over the radio.

Thee I Love. *See:* Friendly Persuasion.

Theme from Carnival. *See:* Love Makes the World Go Round.

Theme from Golden Boy. *See:* Night Song.

Theme from Harlow. *See:* Lonely Girl.

Them There Eyes, words by Maceo Pinkard, William Tracey and Doris Tauber (1930). One of Louis Armstrong's specialties.

Then I'll Be Happy (or, I Wanna Go Where You Go, Do What You Do), words by Sidney Clare and Lew Brown, music by Cliff Friend (1925).

There Are Such Things, words by Abel Baer and Stanley Adams, music by George W. Meyer (1942). One of Stanley Adams' biggest song hits. In writing the lyrics he aimed at striking a note of optimism during the World War II period. "So I started with a peaceful sky. But I decided to sick to love. It goes, 'A dream for two, there are such things, someone to whisper, you're my guiding star.' Then—and this is the philosophy I like particularly—'not caring what you own but just what you are.'"

The song was introduced and popularized by Tommy Dorsey and his orchestra (vocal by Frank Sinatra and the Pied Pipers), whose RCA Victor recording sold a million disks.

There But for You Go I, words by Alan Jay Lerner, music by Frederick Loewe (1947). Introduced by David Brooks in the musical play *Brigadoon* (1947). In the motion-picture adaptation of the musical (MGM, 1954), it was sung by Gene Kelly.

There Goes My Baby, words and music by Benjamin Nelson, Lover Patterson and George Treadwell (1959). Popularized by the Drifters in an Atlantic recording.

There Goes My Heart, words by Benny Davis, music by Abner Silver (1934). Introduced by Linay Romay and Xavier Cugat and his orchestra in the motion-picture musical *The Heat's On*, starring William Gaxton, Victor Moore and Mae West (Columbia, 1943).

There Goes That Song Again, words by Sammy Cahn, music by Jule Styne (1944). Introduced by Harry Babbitt and Kay Kyser and his orchestra in the motion-picture musical *Carolina Blues* (Columbia, 1944). In the motion-picture musical *Cruisin' Down the River* (Columbia, 1953), it was sung by Dick Haymes.

There Is a Tavern in the Town, author of words and music not known (1883). A favorite of American colleges. It made its first appearance in print in *Students' Songs,* compiled and edited by William H. Hills (1883). In this edition, in a copyright notice underneath the song—but not at the head—Hills credits himself as composer and lyricist. So does the first Tin Pan Alley publication, by Shapiro, Bernstein and Company in 1911. But it is extremely doubtful if this has any basis in fact. The song was revived in the late 1920s by Rudy Vallée and popularized by him over the radio and in a best-selling RCA Victor recording. It was interpolated as a choral episode in the non-musical motion picture *Malaya*, starring Spencer Tracy and James Stewart (MGM, 1949).

There Is No Greater Love, words by by Marty Symes, music by Isham Jones (1936). Popularized by Billie Holiday in a Decca recording.

There Is Nothin' Like a Dame, words by Oscar Hammerstein II, music by Richard Rodgers (1949). Comedy number introduced by Myron McCormick and a male chorus (dubbed on the soundtrack by the Ken Darby Singers) in the musical play *South Pacific* (1949). In the motion-picture adaptation of the musical (20th Century-Fox, 1958), it was sung by a male chorus.

There, I've Said It Again, words and music by Redd Evans and Dave Mann (1941). Redd Evans brought this song to the then young and still unknown Boston bandleader Vaughn Monroe, who recorded it for RCA Victor in 1945. The three-and-a-half-million-disk sale that followed established Monroe as a recording star of first importance. The song was revived in 1964 in a best-selling recording by Bobby Vinton for Epic.

There'll Be Some Changes Made, words and music by Billy Higgins and W. B. Overstreet (1929). The song first became popular in 1941 after BMI had acquired the catalogue of E. B. Marks and released the song for radio broadcasts during the ASCAP boycott of the airwaves. Ethel Waters' recording for Black Swan (her second performance on disks) has become a collector's item. The song has been interpolated in several non-musical motion pictures. These include *Playgirl*, starring Kay Francis (Universal, 1941); *Road-*

house, starring Ida Lupino and Richard Widmark (20th Century-Fox, 1948); *The Blue Veil*, starring Jane Wyman and Charles Laughton (RKO, 1951); and *Designing Woman*, starring Lauren Bacall and Gregory Peck (MGM, 1957), sung by Dolores Grey.

There'll Come a Time, words and music by Shelton Brooks (1911).

There'll Come a Time, words and music by Charles K. Harris (1895).

There'll Never Be Another You, words by Mack Gordon, music by Harry Warren (1942). Introduced by John Payne in the motion-picture musical *Iceland,* starring Sonja Henie (20th Century-Fox, 1942). The song was revived in the motion-picture musical *I'll Get By* (20th Century-Fox, 1950), sung by Dennis Day.

There Must Be Someone for Me, words and music by Cole Porter (1943). Introduced by June Havoc in the musical *Mexican Hayride* (1944).

There Never Was a Girl Like You, words by Harry H. Williams, music by Egbert Van Alstyne (1907).

There Once Was a Man, words and music by Richard Adler and Jerry Ross (1954). Duet in the style of a Western ballad, introduced by John Raitt and Janis Paige in the musical *The Pajama Game* (1954). In the motion-picture adaptation of the musical (Warner, 1957), it was sung by John Raitt and Doris Day.

There Once Was an Owl, words by Harry B. Smith, music by Victor Herbert (1903). Vocal sextet introduced by Josephine Bartlett, Aline Redmond, Rosa Earle, Eugene Cowles, Richie Ling and Louis Harrison in the operetta *Babette* (1903). The number was sung by Allan Jones and Mary Martin in the motion-picture musical *The Great Victor Herbert* (Paramount, 1939).

There's a Boat Dat's Leavin' Soon for New York, words by Ira Gershwin, music by George Gershwin (1935). Introduced by John Bubbles in the folk opera *Porgy and Bess* (1935). In the motion-picture adaptation of the opera (Columbia, 1959), it was sung by Sammy Davis.

There's a Broken Heart for Every Light on Broadway, words by Howard

Johnson, music by Fred Fisher (1915). Hit song popularized in vaudeville in the late 1910s. It was interpolated in the Fred Fisher screen biography *Oh, You Beautiful Doll* (20th Century-Fox, 1949).

There's a Girl in the Heart of Maryland (with a Heart That Belongs to Me), words by Ballard MacDonald, music by Harry Carroll (1913).

There's a Girl in This World for Every Boy (and a Boy for Every Girl), words by Will D. Cobb, music by Ted Snyder (1907). One of Snyder's earliest song hits—published by F. A. Mills one year before Snyder himself went into the publishing business.

There's a Gold Mine in the Sky, words and music by Charles and Nick Kenny (1937). It provided the title for and was sung by Gene Autry in the motion picture *Gold Mine in the Sky* (Republic, 1938).

There's a Great Day Coming Mañana, words by E. Y. Harburg, music by Burton Lane (1940). Introduced by Al Jolson in the musical *Hold On to Your Hats* (1940).

There's a Little Bit of Bad in Every Good Little Girl, words by Grant Clarke, music by Fred Fisher (1916).

There's a Little Lane Without a Turning (On the Way to Home Sweet Home), words by Sam M. Lewis, music by George W. Meyer (1915).

There's a Little Spark of Love Still Burning, words by Joe McCarthy, music by Fred Fisher (1914).

There's a Little Star Shining for You, words and music by James Thornton (1897).

There's a Long, Long Trail, words by Stoddard King, music by Zo Elliott (1913). A ballad favorite of World War I, written and published *before* the outbreak of that conflict.

King and Elliott were seniors at Yale, in 1913, when they wrote this ballad for a banquet held by their fraternity. When introduced, it met with little favor. All the publishers to whom the song was submitted turned it down.

In the fall of 1913 Elliott enrolled in Trinity College, Cambridge, England. Hearing of an obscure London publisher in search of songs, Elliott sent him "There's a Long, Long Trail." The song was accepted on the condition that Elliott pay the price of the initial printing, the price to be refunded if the song proved commercially successful.

When World War I broke out, Elliott was traveling in Germany. He escaped to Switzerland, where to his amazement he found a sizable sum in royalties awaiting him. Upon returning to the United States, Elliott convinced the Tin Pan Alley firm of Witmark to buy out the copyright. The song, in its American printing, did not at first move, but with America involved in the war, it started to make an impression, expressing as it did the temper and feelings of the times. In time it sold over two and a half million copies of sheet music. It was such a favorite with President Wilson that he often sang it after dinner at the White House.

The song was interpolated in a number of motion pictures with a World War I setting, including *What Price Glory?* (20th Century-Fox, 1952), sung by a male chorus.

There's a Lull in My Life, words by Mack Gordon, music by Harry Revel (1937). Introduced by Alice Faye in the motion-picture musical *Wake Up and Live* (20th Century-Fox, 1937).

There's a Rainbow 'Round My Shoulder, words by Billy Rose and Al Jolson, music by Dave Dreyer (1928). Introduced by Al Jolson in the motion-picture musical *The Singing Fool* (Warner, 1928), to become a Jolson specialty. He also sang it on the soundtrack of the motion-picture musical *The Jolson Story* (Columbia, 1946).

In his autobiography, Charles Chaplin pointed up Jolson's immense success in the rendition of this number. "When he sang . . . 'There's a Rainbow 'Round My Shoulder,' he lifted the audience by an unadulterated compulsion. He personified the poetry of Broadway, its vitality and vulgarity, its aims and dreams."

The song provided the title for

and was featured in a motion-picture musical starring Frankie Laine and Billy Daniels (Columbia, 1952).

There's a Rising Moon, words by Paul Francis Webster, music by Sammy Fain (1955). Introduced by Doris Day in the non-musical motion picture *Young at Heart,* starring Frank Sinatra (Warner, 1955).

There's a Small Hotel, words by Lorenz Hart, music by Richard Rodgers (1936). Introduced by Ray Bolger and Doris Carson in the musical *On Your Toes* (1936). It was also sung in the motion-picture adaptation of the musical (Warner, 1939). It was interpolated in the Rodgers and Hart motion-picture biography *Words and Music* (MGM, 1948), sung by Betty Garrett, and in the motion-picture adaptation of the musical *Pal Joey* (Columbia, 1957), sung by Frank Sinatra.

There's Danger in Your Eyes, Cherie, words and music by Harry Richman, Jack Meskill and Pete Wendling (1929). Introduced by Harry Richman in the motion-picture musical *Puttin' on the Ritz* (United Artists, 1930).

There's Music in the Air, words by Frances Jane Crosby, music by George Frederick Root (1854). This song, originally for vocal quartet, became a favorite in American colleges. Its chorus survives today in the refrain of a Princeton "whooper up" song, "Rah, Rah, Rah, Rah, Siss Boom Bah!"

There's No Business Like Show Business. *See:* Show Business.

There's No Business Like Show Business, a motion-picture musical starring Ethel Merman, Donald O'Connor and Marilyn Monroe (20th Century-Fox, 1954). Songs (old and new) by Irving Berlin.

See: Alexander's Ragtime Band; Heat Wave; Lazy; Let's Have Another Cup o' Coffee; A Man Chases a Girl; Play a Simple Melody; A Pretty Girl Is Like a Melody; When the Midnight Choo Choo Leaves for Alabam'; You'd Be Surprised.

There's No Tomorrow, words and music by Al Hoffman, Leo Corday and Leon Carr, melody derived from the celebrated Neapolitan folk song "O Sole mio" (1949). Popularized by Tony Martin in an RCA Victor recording.

There's Only One of You, words by Al Stillman, music by Robert Allen (1954). Revived in 1958 and popularized by the Four Lads in a Columbia recording.

There's Something About a Uniform, words and music by George M. Cohan (1908). Introduced in the musical *The Man Who Owns Broadway* (1909).

There's Something in the Air, words by Harold Adamson, music by Jimmy McHugh (1937). Introduced by Tony Martin (in his motion-picture debut) in the non-musical motion picture *Banjo on My Knee,* starring Barbara Stanwyck (20th Century-Fox, 1937).

There's Where My Heart Is Tonight, words and music by Paul Dresser (1899).

There's Yes Yes in Your Eyes, words by Cliff Friend, music by Joseph H. Santly (1924). A hit song in the 1920s that became involved in court action. A composer named Wolf insisted that one of his own songs published nine years earlier, "Without You the World Don't Seem the Same," had been plagiarized by Santly. During the legal proceedings, the testimony proved that Santly had actually served as the song plugger for Wolf's song. Judge Bondy awarded Wolf minimum damages of $250, maintaining that the publisher of Santly's hit (Remick) had, after all, been responsible for that number's success through its skillful exploitation, whereas the earlier song had been a failure.

These Boots Are Made for Walkin' words and music by Lee Hazlewood (1965). Introduced and popularized by Nancy Sinatra in a Reprise recording that sold over a million disks, her first success.

These Foolish Things Remind Me of You, words by Holt Marvell, music by Jack Strachey and Harry Link (1935). Introduced by Madge Elliott and Cyril Ritchard in the musical

Spread It Abroad (1935). The song was used as a recurrent theme in the background instrumental music for the non-musical motion picture *A Yank in the R.A.F.*, starring Tyrone Power and Betty Grable (20th Century-Fox, 1941). It was also interpolated in the non-musical motion picture *Ghost Catchers*, starring Olsen and Johnson (Universal, 1944), and *Tokyo Rose*, starring Humphrey Bogart (1949).

They All Follow Me, words by Hugh Morton, music by Gustave Kerker (1897). Introduced by Edna May in the operetta *The Belle of New York* (1897), where she became an overnight star.

They All Laughed, words by Ira Gershwin, music by George Gershwin (1937). Introduced by Fred Astaire and Ginger Rogers in the motion-picture musical *Shall We Dance?* (RKO, 1937).

The title was borrowed from—and was a take-off on—an advertisement for a correspondence school popular in the 1930s, with the following heading: "They all laughed when I sat down to play the piano."

They Always Pick on Me, words by Stanley Murphy, music by Harry von Tilzer (1911). Hit song popularized in vaudeville. It was revived by Alice Faye in the motion-picture musical *Hello, Frisco, Hello* (20th Century-Fox, 1943).

They Called Her Frivolous Sal. *See:* My Gal Sal.

They Call It Love, words by Ned Washington, music by Dimitri Tiomkin, melody based on an old Greek song, "Yala Yala" (1961). Introduced in the non-musical motion picture *The Guns of Navarone*, starring Gregory Peck (Columbia, 1961).

They Call the Wind Maria, words by Alan Jay Lerner, music by Frederick Lowe (1951). Introduced by Rufus Smith and a male chorus (and danced to by James Mitchell) in the musical play *Paint Your Wagon* (1951). This number was successfully revived a decade later by Robert Goulet over TV, in night clubs and in a Columbia recording. This was the song he used to audition

successfully for Alan Jay Lerner and Frederick Loewe for the role of Lancelot in *Camelot.*

They Can't Take That Away from Me, words by Ira Gershwin, music by George Gershwin (1937). One of many songs by Ira Gershwin in which he used a popular expression of the time both for title and subject matter. The song was introduced by Fred Astaire (singing to Ginger Rogers on a ferry to Hoboken, New Jersey) in the motion-picture musical *Shall We Dance?* (RKO, 1937). This is the only song by the Gershwins to be nominated for an Academy Award (which it failed to win). The song was interpolated for Fred Astaire in the motion-picture musical *The Barkleys of Broadway* (MGM, 1949).

They Didn't Believe Me, words by Michael E. Rourke, using the pen name of Herbert Reynolds, music by Jerome Kern (1914). Introduced by Julia Sanderson in the musical *The Girl from Utah* (1914)—Kern's first successful musical-comedy score. The song was the first by Kern to become a standard.

When Michael E. Rourke wrote the lyrics, he had in mind a song for Jolson, but Kern preferred making it into a ballad for a voice and personality like those of Julia Sanderson. Her unforgettable rendition in *The Girl from Utah* was undoubtedly a major factor in swelling the success of this song into a two-million-copy sheet-music sale.

In his biography of Jerome Kern, this editor described the structure and technique of this remarkable song as follows: "The way in which the melody of the refrain expands opulently for eight bars in simple quarter notes (with the line beginning 'your lips, your eyes, your cheeks, your hair'), the way a poignant climax is achieved through a subtle change of key—this is sheer Jerome Kern magic. Equally remarkable is the way in which, in the recapitulation of the opening section, Kern suddenly introduces a new four-bar thought before proceeding with his original intentions.

Freshness was further injected into the melody with an immediate change of rhythm for consecutive quarter and half notes to triplets in the much discussed and criticized phrase 'and I'm certainly going to tell them.' In the New York *Tribune*, F. Brock Pemberton was particularly critical of the banality of this verbal digression in the lyric. But if this is a fault, the fault is Kern's and not the lyricist's. It was Kern who suggested the insertion of this phrase to permit him greater rhythmic elasticity."

Before *The Girl from Utah* opened, Jerome Kern played his score for Victor Herbert at Max Dreyfus' office at Harms. When Kern finished playing "They Didn't Believe Me," Herbert remarked simply: "This man will inherit my mantle."

They Go Wild, Simply Wild, over Me, words by Joe McCarthy, music by Fred Fisher (1917).

They Like Ike, words and music by Irving Berlin (1950). A rousing hymn of praise to General Dwight D. Eisenhower (before he became President of the United States). It was introduced by Pat Harrington, Ralph Chambers and Jay Velie (enacting the parts of Congressmen) in the musical *Call Me Madam* (1950). The number was also used in the motion-picture adaptation of the musical (20th Century-Fox, 1953). The song was used effectively during General Eisenhower's campaign for the Presidency in 1952.

They Loved Me, words and music by Irving Berlin (1962). Introduced by Nanette Fabray (as the land's First Lady) in the musical *Mr. President* (1962).

They're Either Too Young or Too Old, words by Frank Loesser, music by Arthur Schwartz (1943). World War II lament of the females at the home front, introduced by Bette Davis in the motion-picture musical *Thank Your Lucky Stars* (Warner, 1943). It was interpolated in the motion-picture biography of Jane Froman, *With a Song in My Heart* (20th Century-Fox, 1952).

They're Wearing 'Em Higher in Hawaii, words by Joe Goodwin, music by Halsey K. Mohr (1916). Comedy number popularized in vaudeville during the vogue for Hawaiian-subject songs.

They Say, words by Edward Heyman, music by Paul Mann and Stephen Weiss (1938). Introduced by Buddy Clark.

They Say It's Wonderful, words and music by Irving Berlin (1946). Introduced by Ethel Merman and Ray Middleton in the musical *Annie, Get Your Gun* (1946). In the motion-picture adaptation of the musical (MGM, 1950), it was sung by Betty Hutton and Howard Keel. Perry Como made a successful recording for RCA Victor.

They've Got a Lot of Coffee in Brazil. *See:* The Coffee Song.

They Were Doin' the Mambo, words and music by Sonny Burke and Don Raye (1954). Popularized by Vaughn Monroe in an RCA Victor recording.

Thine Alone, words by Henry Blossom, music by Victor Herbert (1917). One of Herbert's greatest song successes and most eloquent ballads. It was introduced by Grace Breen and Walter Scanlan in the operetta *Eileen* (1917). In the motion-picture musical *The Great Victor Herbert* (Paramount, 1939), it was sung by Allan Jones and Mary Martin.

The song, suggestively Irish in melody and harmony, loses much of its impact when sung as a solo—as has now become habitual. As Edward N. Waters explains: "When the two voices sing together they are in unison, beyond question intentional; but they have characteristic individual phrases to sing separately, and the timbre of the combined voices is far different from that of one voice singing alone."

The Thing, words and music by Charles R. Grean (1950). Introduced and popularized by Phil Harris in an RCA Victor recording that sold over a million disks.

The number was published by Harry Richmond, one of the first to recognize the power of the disk jockey in promoting a song. To exploit that power, he sent out twenty-five copies of a pressing of "The Thing," which he himself had made, to disk jockeys in key cities. One of these samples went to Bob Clayton in Boston. It happened at that time that a railway strike held up all review copies of Phil Harris' RCA Victor recording, so that Clayton's pressing was an exclusive for Boston. He played it at least once an hour for several days, creating such a demand for "The Thing" that by the end of the week (with the railway strike still on), the Victor distributor in Boston had to drive his truck to New York to pick up twenty thousand records—seventeen thousand more than he had ever before ordered of any Phil Harris release.

Phil Harris sang the number in the motion picture *Wild Blue Yonder,* starring Vera Ralston and Wendell Corey (Republic, 1951).

The Things We Did Last Summer, words by Sammy Cahn, music by Jule Styne (1946). Popularized by Frank Sinatra in a Columbia recording, and by Jimmy Dorsey and his orchestra (with Bing Crosby doing the vocal) in a Decca recording.

Thinking of You, words by Bert Kalmar, music by Harry Ruby (1927). Introduced by Oscar Shaw and Mary Eaton in the musical *The Five O'Clock Girl* (1927). The song then became the theme music of Kay Kyser and his orchestra.

"Thinking of You" was interpolated in the motion-picture biography of Ruby and Kalmar, *Three Little Words* (MGM, 1950), sung by Fred Astaire and Vera Ellen.

This Can't Be Love, words by Lorenz Hart, music by Richard Rodgers (1938). Introduced by Marcy Wescott and Eddie Albert in the musical *The Boys from Syracuse* (1938). In the motion-picture adaptation of the musical (Universal, 1940), it was sung by Rosemary Lane. The song was interpolated in the Rodgers and Hart screen biography *Words and Music* (MGM, 1948); also in the motion-picture adaptation of the extravaganza *Jumbo* (MGM, 1962), sung by Doris Day.

This Heart of Mine, words by Arthur

Freed, music by Harry Warren (1943). Introduced by Fred Astaire and Lucille Bremer in the motion-picture musical *Ziegfeld Follies* (MGM, 1946).

This Is a Great Country, words and music by Irving Berlin (1962). Rousing patriotic finale for the entire ensemble in the musical *Mr. President* (1962).

This Is All I Ask, words and music by Gordon Jenkins (1958). Introduced by Danny Thomas in his television show in 1958. It was revived in 1963 by Tony Bennett in a best-selling recording for Columbia.

This Is It, words by Dorothy Fields, music by Arthur Schwartz (1939). Introduced by Ethel Merman in the musical *Stars in Your Eyes* (1939).

This Is My Beloved. *See:* And This Is My Beloved.

This Is New, words by Ira Gershwin, music by Kurt Weill (1941). Introduced in a dream sequence by Gertrude Lawrence (supported by the chorus) in the musical play *Lady in the Dark* (1941).

The song was originally intended as a duet for Gertrude Lawrence and Victor Mature. But, as Ira Gershwin has explained, neither Mature's heart nor correct key were in the song. "By cutting out the verse with its 'luckiest of men' we were able to give the song to Gertie and have it remain in the score." In the motion-picture adaptation of the musical (Paramount, 1941), it was sung by Ginger Rogers.

This Is the Army, an all-soldier revue assembled by Irving Berlin, with his own book, lyrics and music. Additional dialogue by James McColl. Starring Ezra Stone, William Horne, Julie Oshins and Irving Berlin (1942). Original cast recording (Decca).

In the motion-picture adaptation of the musical, the soldiers' cast was supplemented by various Hollywood stars, including Kate Smith, Joan Leslie, George Murphy and others (Warner, 1943). The basic stage score was used. Irving Berlin's "God Bless America" was interpolated.

See: God Bless America; I Left My

Heart at the Stage Door Canteen; Oh, How I Hate to Get Up in the Morning; This Is the Army, Mr. Jones.

This Is the Army, Mr. Jones, words and music by Irving Berlin (1942). Opening chorus in the all-soldier revue *This Is the Army* (1942). It was also sung in the motion-picture adaptation of the musical (Warner, 1943). Bing Crosby sang it in the motion-picture musical *Blue Skies* (MGM, 1945).

This Is the Life, words and music by Irving Berlin (1914). Introduced and popularized by Al Jolson at the Winter Garden.

This Is the Life, words by Lee Adams, music by Charles Strouse (1964). Introduced by Sammy Davis, Billy Daniels, Lola Falana and ensemble in the musical *Golden Boy* (1964).

This Is the Missus, words by Lew Brown, music by Ray Henderson (1931). Introduced by Rudy Vallée in the *George White Scandals of 1931*. In his autobiography, Rudy Vallée points up the irony of his performing this hit song nightly in the *Scandals*—while just being separated from his wife, Fay Webb, prior to their divorce. This and other hit songs from the 1931 *Scandals* were recorded by Bing Crosby and the Boswell Sisters on two sides of a twelve-inch Brunswick record—one of the earliest attempts to record the basic score of a musical show.

Sheree North sang it in the screen biography of De Sylva, Brown and Henderson, *The Best Things in Life Are Free* (20th Century-Fox, 1956).

This Love of Mine, words by Frank Sinatra, music by Sol Parker and Henry Sanicola (1941). Popularized by Frank Sinatra in an RCA Victor recording with the Tommy Dorsey orchestra. It was interpolated in the motion picture *Spring Reunion,* starring Betty Hutton and Dana Andrews (United Artists, 1957).

This Nearly Was Mine, words by Oscar Hammerstein II, music by Richard Rodgers (1949). Introduced by Ezio Pinza in the musical play *South Pacific* (1949). In the motion-picture adaptation of the musical (20th

Century-Fox, 1958), it was sung on the soundtrack by Giorgio Tozzi (for Rossano Brazzi).

This Ole House, words and music by Stuart Hamblen (1954). Introduced by Stuart Hamblen, but popularized by Rosemary Clooney in a Columbia recording that sold over a million disks.

This Time Next Year, words by Maxwell Anderson, music by Kurt Weill (1950). One of Weill's last songs. It was written for an opera based on Mark Twain's *Huckleberry Finn* which Weill did not live to complete. A ballad of the Negro's hope and dream of freedom, "This Time Next Year" was introduced by Thomas Carey over television in Germany in October, 1964.

This Year's Kisses, words and music by Irving Berlin (1937). Introduced by Dick Powell and Alice Faye in the motion-picture musical *On the Avenue* (20th Century-Fox, 1937).

Thornton, James, composer and lyricist, born Liverpool, England, 1861; died New York City, 1938.

See: Bridge of Sighs; Don't Give Up the Old Love for the New; The Irish Jubilee; It Don't Seem Like the Same Old Smile; My Sweetheart's the Man in the Moon; On the Benches in the Park; Remember Poor Mother at Home; She May Have Seen Better Days; The Streets of Cairo; There's a Little Star Shining for You; Upper Ten, Lower Five; When You Were Sweet Sixteen.

Those Lazy, Hazy, Crazy Days of Summer, words by Charles Tobias, music by Hans Carste (1963). Popularized by Nat King Cole in a best-selling Capitol recording.

Those Wedding Bells Shall Not Ring, words and music by Monroe H. Rosenfeld (1896). A song hit written in imitation—and in an attempt to exploit the success—of Gussie Davis' "Fatal Wedding."

Thou Swell, words by Lorenz Hart, music by Richard Rodgers (1927). Introduced by William Gaxton and Constance Carpenter in the musical *A Connecticut Yankee* (1927). It was also sung in the motion-picture adaptation of the musical (Fox,

1931). June Allyson sang it in the screen biography of Rodgers and Hart, *Words and Music* (MGM, 1948).

The Three Bells (or, While the Angelus Was Ringing), a French popular song ("Les Trois cloches"), music by Jean Villard, English lyrics by Dick Manning (1948). Introduced and popularized both in France and the United States by Edith Piaf. The song was revived in the United States in 1959 by the Browns in an RCA Victor recording.

An earlier American version of the same melody, with words by Bert Reisfeld, was called "The Three Bells" or "The Jimmy Brown Song" (1945).

Three Coins in the Fountain, words by Sammy Cahn, music by Jule Styne (1954). Theme song of the non-musical motion picture starring Rossano Brazzi, Clifton Webb, Louis Jourdan and Dorothy McGuire (20th Century-Fox, 1954). It was sung there on the soundtrack under the titles by Frank Sinatra. The inspiration for this number came from the Fountain of the Trevi in Rome, and the legend that whoever throws a coin into its waters must return to the Holy City. The song received the Academy Award. It was popularized in best-selling recordings by Frank Sinatra for Capitol and the Four Aces for Decca. The immense popularity of this song was largely responsible for making the Fountain of the Trevi a major tourist attraction for Americans in Rome after 1954.

Three for the Show, a motion-picture musical based freely on W. Somerset Maugham's play *Too Many Husbands,* starring Betty Grable and Gower Champion (Columbia, 1955). The score was made up mainly of standards by George and Ira Gershwin, Hoagy Carmichael and others.

See: How Come You Do Me Like You Do? I've Got a Crush on You; Someone to Watch Over Me.

Three Little Fishes, words and music by Saxie Dowell (1939). Popularized in 1941 by Kay Kyser and his orchestra in a Columbia recording

that sold over a million disks.

Three Little Words, words by Bert Kalmar, music by Harry Ruby (1930). One of the leading hits by the succcessful songwriting team of Ruby and Kalmar. It was introduced by Bing Crosby (backed by Duke Ellington and his orchestra) in the Amos 'n' Andy motion picture *Check and Double Check* (RKO, 1930)— the first movie with a Ruby and Kalmar score. "Everyone predicted the song would lay an egg," the composer revealed to this editor. "It was nearly dropped from the movie. But it was an overnight hit." This success began with a Decca recording by Bing Crosby with the Duke Ellington orchestra. Rudy Vallée further helped to popularize it over the radio and in an RCA Victor recording. The song was revived by Fred Astaire and Red Skelton in the motion-picture biography of Ruby and Kalmar, whose title was appropriated from that of the song (MGM, 1950). It was interpolated in the background music of the non-musical motion pictures *This Day Forward,* starring Joan Fontaine (RKO), and *This Earth Is Mine,* starring Jean Simmons and Rock Hudson (Universal, 1959).

Three Little Words, a motion-picture musical biography of the songwriting team of Bert Kalmar and Harry Ruby, starring Fred Astaire, Red Skelton and Arlene Dahl (MGM, 1950). The score was made up principally of Ruby and Kalmar standards.

See: All Alone Monday; Come On, Papa; Hooray for Captain Spalding; I Wanna Be Loved by You; My Sunny Tennesssee; Nevertheless; She's Mine, All Mine; So Long, Oo Long; Thinking of You; Three Little Words; Who's Sorry Now?

Three O'Clock in the Morning, words by Dorothy Terris, music by Julian Robledo (1922). Waltz popularized by Paul Whiteman and his orchestra, their Victor recording in 1922 selling over a million disks. The number was interpolated in the closing scene of the revue *The Greenwich Village Follies of 1921,* where Rosalind Fuller and Richard Bold sang it in front of a simple blue set, after which it was danced to by Margaret Petit and Valodia Vestoff. This was the most important song ever to come out of the *Greenwich Village Follies*.

Judy Garland sang it in the motion-picture musical *Presenting Lily Mars* (MGM, 1943), and Jeanne Crain, in the motion-picture musical *Margie* (20th Century-Fox, 1946). The song was also interpolated in the non-musical motion picture *Belles on Their Toes*, starring Jeanne Crain, Myrna Loy and Jeffrey Hunter (20th Century-Fox, 1952).

The Three Musketeers, an operetta with book by William Anthony McGuire based on Alexandre Dumas' romance. Lyrics by Clifford Grey and P. G. Wodehouse. Music by Rudolf Friml. Starring Dennis King and Vivienne Segal (1928).

See: Ma Belle; March of the Musketeers; With Red Wine.

Three's a Crowd, words by Al Dubin and Irving Kahal, music by Harry Warren (1932). Introduced by Dick Powell in the motion-picture musical *The Crooner* (First National, 1932).

Three's a Crowd, an intimate revue with book and lyrics mainly by Howard Dietz. Music mainly by Arthur Schwartz. Starring Fred Allen, Libby Holman and Clifton Webb (1930).

See: Body and Soul; Something to Remember You By.

The Three Twins, an operetta with book by Charles Dickson adapted from a farce by R. Pancheco. Lyrics by Otto Hauerbach (Harbach). Music by Karl Hoschna. Starring Bessie McCoy (1908).

See: Cuddle Up a Little Closer; The Yama Yama Man.

Three Wonderful Letters from Home, words by Joe Goodwin and Ballard MacDonald, music by James F. Hanley (1918). Popular World War I ballad.

The Thrill Is Gone, words by Lew Brown, music by Ray Henderson (1931). Introduced by Everett Marshall in the *George White Scandals*

of 1931. This and other hit songs from the 1931 *Scandals* were recorded by Bing Crosby and the Boswell Sisters on two sides of a twelve-inch Brunswick record, one of the earliest attempts to record the basic score of a musical show on disks.

Through the Years, words by Edward Heyman, music by Vincent Youmans (1931). Principal song from the musical of the same name (1931), introduced by Natalie Hall and Michael Bartlett. Though the music was a failure, the song was a major success and went on to become a standard. It was a particular favorite with the composer himself, who often singled it out as his best creation.

Throw Him Down, McCloskey, words and music by J. W. Kelly (1890). Written for and introduced by Maggie Cline—at Tony Pastor's Music Hall in New York. Her big voice, that could blast the walls of a theater, and her rough-and-tumble delivery made this Number One of her most celebrated routines. As she sang it, she would stride across the stage with athletic steps, swing her arms and hips and hitch her belt. She used the song in her act for almost a quarter of a century.

The song was written after its creator had witnessed a saloon brawl where the participants were rooting for the smaller and slighter-of-build combatant, with cries of "Throw him down, McCloskey!" Rising to the occasion, McCloskey tripped his oversized opponent and sent him flying face down to the floor.

Thumbelina, words and music by Frank Loesser (1952). Introduced by Danny Kaye in the motion-picture musical *Hans Christian Andersen* (Samuel Goldwyn, 1953).

Tickle Toe (or, Ev'rybody Ought to Know How to Do the Tickle Toe), words by Otto Harbach, music by Louis A. Hirsch (1918). Introduced by Edith Day, Allen H. Fagan and ensemble in the musical *Going Up* (1917).

Tico-Tico, a Brazilian popular song, music by Zequinha Abreu, English lyrics by Ervin Drake (1943). The

American song was introduced in the Walt Disney production *Saludos Amigos* (RKO, 1942), sung by Aloysio Oliveira. It was then popularized in night clubs and a recording by Xavier Cugat and his orchestra. The song was interpolated in the motion picture *Kansas City Kitty*, starring Joan Davis (Columbia, 1944), and was performed by Xavier Cugat and his orchestra in the motion-picture musical *Bathing Beauty*, starring Esther Williams (MGM, 1944). This number is also closely identified with the organist Ethel Smith.

Tierney, Harry, composer, born Perth Amboy, New Jersey, 1895; died New York City, 1965.

See (Lyrics by Joseph McCarthy): Castle of Dreams; Following the Sun Around; In My Sweet Little Alice Blue Gown; Irene; My Baby's Arms; The Rangers' Song; Rio Rita; Take, Oh Take, Those Lips Away; You've Got Me Out on a Limb.

See also: It's a Cute Little Way of My Own; M-i-s-s-i-s-s-i-p-p-i.

Till, a French popular song, music by Charles Danvers, English lyrics by Carl Sigman (1957). Popularized by Tony Bennett in a Columbia recording and by Roger Williams in a Kapp recording.

Tillie's Nightmare, a musical comedy with book and lyrics by Edgar Smith. Music by A. Baldwin Sloane. Starring Marie Dressler (1910).

See: Heaven Will Protect the Working Girl; Life Is Only What You Make It.

Till I Waltz Again with You, words and music by Sidney Prosen (1952). Popularized in a Coral recording by Teresa Brewer that sold a million disks.

Till the Clouds Roll By, words by P. G. Wodehouse and Jerome Kern, music by Jerome Kern (1917). Introduced by Lynn Overman and Anna Wheaton in the Princess Theatre production of *Oh, Boy!* (1917). The title was used to name the Jerome Kern screen biography (MGM, 1946), where it was sung by June Allyson.

Till the Clouds Roll By, a motion-picture musical biography of Jerome Kern, starring Robert Walker as

Kern with Kathryn Grayson and Van Heflin (MGM, 1946). The score was made up of Jerome Kern standards. Soundtrack recording (MGM).

See: All the Things You Are; Can't Help Lovin' That Man; A Fine Romance; Go, Little Boat; How'd You Like to Spoon with Me?; I Won't Dance; Land Where the Good Songs Go; The Last Time I Saw Paris; Leave It to Jane; Long Ago and Far Away; Look for the Silver Lining; Ol' Man River; Only Make Believe; She Didn't Say Yes; Smoke Gets in Your Eyes; Sunny; They Didn't Believe Me; Till the Clouds Roll By; Who?; Why Was I Born?; Yesterdays.

Till the End of Time, words by Buddy Kaye, music by Ted Mossman, melody based on Chopin's Polonaise in A-flat major, op. 53 (1945). A song inspired by the Chopin motion picture *A Song to Remember,* starring Cornel Wilde, Paul Muni and Merle Oberon (Columbia, 1945). It was popularized by Perry Como in an RCA Victor recording that sold a million disks. This number also sold over a million and a half copies of sheet music, and appeared for nineteen consecutive weeks on the Hit Parade. It provided the title, was played under the titles and was used as a recurrent theme in the motion picture starring Guy Madison and Dorothy McGuire (Vanguard, 1946).

Till Then, words and music by Eddie Seiler, Sol Marcus and Guy Wood (1944). Popularized by the Mills Brothers in a Decca recording. It was revived in 1954 by the Hilltoppers in a best-selling Dot recording.

Till There Was You, words and music by Meredith Willson (1957). Introduced by Barbara Cook and Robert Preston in the musical *The Music Man* (1957). In the motion-picture adaptation (Warner, 1962), it was sung by Shirley Jones. The song was recorded thirty-two times without making any headway. Then in 1958 it was recorded by Anita Bryant for Columbia, a release that sold a million disks and helped make Anita Bryant a recording star. In 1963 the song was successfully recorded by the Beatles for Capitol in a rock 'n' roll version.

Till the Sands of the Desert Grow Cold, words by George Graff, Jr., music by Ernest R. Ball (1911).

Till Tomorrow, words by Sheldon Harnick, music by Jerry Bock (1959). Nostalgic waltz introduced by Ellen Hanley in the musical *Fiorello!* (1959).

Till We Meet Again, words by Raymond B. Egan, music by Richard A. Whiting (1918). One of the most successful ballads of World War I, a waltz selling over three and a half million copies of sheet music. Margaret Whiting recalls: "My father wrote it in 1917, then figured it didn't have it, and tossed it into a wastebasket. My mother found it and took it to Remick, the publisher." While the song was being printed, and before its release, one of the movie theaters in Detroit held a war-song contest. Somebody entered "Till We Meet Again" and it won the first prize—the first indication of its future success. The waltz was introduced by Muriel Window.

It was sung by Gordon MacRae and Doris Day in the motion-picture musical *On Moonlight Bay* (Warner, 1951). It was also interpolated as an orchestral episode in the non-musical motion picture *Auntie Mame,* starring Rosalind Russell (Warner, 1958). It has frequently been sung in the halls of the United States Congress at adjournment.

Till We Two Are One, words by Tom Glazer, music by Larry and Billy Martin (1953). Popularized in 1954 by George Shaw in a Decca recording.

Timbuctoo, words by Bert Kalmar, music by Harry Ruby (1920). One of the earliest efforts of the successful songwriting team of Kalmar and Ruby. It was popularized in vaudeville by the Avon Comedy Four.

The Time, The Place and The Girl, a motion-picture musical starring Dennis Morgan, Janis Paige and Jack Carson (Warner, 1946). Songs by Leo Robin and Arthur Schwartz.
  See: A Gal in Calico; Oh, But I Do;

On a Rainy Night in Rio.

Time on My Hands, words by Harold Adamson and Mack Gordon, music by Vincent Youmans (1930). Introduced by Marilyn Miller and Paul Gregory in the musical *Smiles* (1930). The song was originally called "Tom, Dick and Harry," then renamed "Smiles." It was interpolated in the screen biography of Marilyn Miller, *Look for the Silver Lining* (Warner, 1949).

Time Waits for No One, words by Charles Tobias, music by Cliff Friend (1944). Introduced in the motion-picture musical biography of Nora Bayes, *Shine On, Harvest Moon* (Warner, 1944).

Time Will Tell, words by Raymond W. Klages, music by J. Fred Coots (1922). Coots' first hit song, introduced in the musical *Sally, Irene and Mary* (1922).

Tin Pan Alley, a motion-picture musical starring Alice Faye, Betty Grable and John Payne (20th Century-Fox, 1940). The score was made up of standards, with a new number contributed by Mack Gordon and Harry Revel.
  See: America, I Love You; Goodbye, Broadway, Hello, France; Honeysuckle Rose; K-K-K-Katy; Moonlight Bay; Moonlight and Roses; Over There; The Sheik of Araby.

Tiomkin, Dimitri, composer, born St. Petersburg, Russia, 1899.
  See (Lyrics by Ned Washington): Circus World; Haji Baba; The High and the Mighty; High Noon; The Need for You; Return to Paradise; Strange Are the Ways of Love; Wild Is the Wind; They Call It Love.
  See (Lyrics by Paul Francis Webster): Ballad of the Alamo; Friendly Persuasion; Green Leaves of Summer; Guns of Navarone; So Little Time; There's Never Been Anyone Else But You.

Ti-Pi-Tin, a Spanish popular song, music by Maria Grever, English lyrics by Raymond Leveen (1938). Its composer's first popular song and her greatest hit.

Tippecanoe and Tyler Too, words by Alexander C. Ross to the tune of "The Little Pigs" (1840). The song of the Whig Party during the Presidential campaign of William Henry Harrison, whose running mate was John Tyler.

Tip Toes, a musical comedy with book by Guy Bolton and Fred Thompson. Lyrics by Ira Gershwin. Music by George Gershwin. Starring Queenie Smith and Allen Kearns (1925).

See: Looking for a Boy; Sweet and Low Down; That Certain Feeling.

Tip Toe Thru the Tulips with Me, words by Al Dubin, music by Joseph A. Burke (1929). Introduced in the motion-picture musical *Gold Diggers of Broadway* (Warner, 1929). It was interpolated in the non-musical motion picture *Confidential Agent,* starring Charles Boyer and Lauren Bacall (Warner, 1945), and in the motion-picture musical *Painting the Clouds with Sunshine* (Warner, 1951).

'Tis But a Little Faded Flower, words by Frederick Enoch, music by John Rogers Thomas (1860).

T'morra', T'morra', words by E. Y. Harburg, music by Harold Arlen (1944). Introduced by Joan McCracken in the musical *Bloomer Girl* (1944).

To Anacreon in Heaven, words by Ralph Tomlinson, music generally credited to John Stafford Smith but sometimes to Samuel Arnold (c. 1780). A British popular song written in or about 1775. It is sometimes also known as "The Anacreontic Song" since it was written for the Anacreontic Society of London, a culture group meeting once every two weeks. This melody was frequently borrowed in America for its first national anthems and popular songs. Among these were "Adams and Liberty," "The Battle of the Wabash," "For the Glorious Fourth of July," "Jefferson and Liberty" and "Song for the Fourth of July." The most celebrated American use of this melody was for the national anthem "The Star-Spangled Banner."

To Be Alone with You, words by Sidney Michaels, music by Mark Sandrich, Jr. (1964). Introduced by Robert Preston and Ulla Sallert and ensemble in the musical *Ben Franklin in Paris* (1964).

Tobias, Charles, lyricist, born New York City, 1898.

See: De Rose, Peter; Friend, Cliff; Stept, Sam H.

See also: The Broken Record; For the First Time; Get Out and Get Under the Moon; It Seems Like Old Times; Just Another Day Wasted Away; May I Sing to You?; Me Too; The Old Lamp-Lighter; Rose O'Day; Sail Along, Silvery Moon; Those Lazy, Hazy, Crazy Days of Summer; Time Waits for No One; Two Tickets for Georgia; What Do We Do on a Dew Dew Dewy Day?; Zing, Zing, Zoom, Zoom.

To Each His Dulcinea, words by Joe Darion, music by Mitch Leigh (1965). Introduced by Robert Rounseville in the off-Broadway musical *Man of La Mancha* (1965).

To Each His Own, words and music by Jay Livingston and Ray Evans (1946). The first major success of the songwriting team of Livingston and Evans; it sold about a million copies of sheet music and several million disks in various recordings. It was written to publicize the non-musical motion picture of the same name starring Olivia De Havilland and John Lund (Paramount, 1946), but was not used there. The song was first popularized by Eddy Howard in a Majestic recording that sold almost two million disks. The song's success kept mounting with best-selling recordings by the Ink Spots for Decca and by Tony Martin for Mercury. It was successfully revived in 1961 by the Platters in a Mercury recording.

Together, words by Bud De Sylva and Lew Brown, music by Ray Henderson (1928). Written and published as an independent number. It became popular fifteen years later when it was interpolated in the non-musical motion picture *Since You Went Away,* starring Claudette Colbert and Joseph Cotten (MGM, 1944). It was again revived successfully in 1961 by Connie Francis in a best-selling MGM recording.

Together, Wherever We Go, words by Stephen Sondheim, music by Jule Styne (1959). Introduced by Ethel

Merman, Sandra Church and Jack Klugman in the musical *Gypsy* (1959). In the motion-picture adaptation of the musical (Warner, 1962), it was sung on the soundtrack by Lisa Kirk (for Rosalind Russell).

To Keep My Love Alive, words by Lorenz Hart, music by Richard Rodgers (1944). Written for Vivienne Segal, for the 1943 stage revival of the musical *A Connecticut Yankee,* where she introduced it.

To Know Him Is to Love Him, words and music by Phil Spector (1958). Popularized by the Teddy Bears in a Dore recording.

To Know You Is to Love You, words by Allan Roberts, music by Robert Allen (1952). Popularized by Perry Como in an RCA Victor recording.

To Love and Be Loved (or, Song from Some Came Running), words by Sammy Cahn, music by James Van Heusen (1958). Introduced in the non-musical motion picture *Some Came Running,* starring Frank Sinatra, Dean Martin and Shirley MacLaine (MGM, 1958). It was popularized by Sinatra in a Capitol recording.

Tomboy, words and music by Joe Farrell and Jim Conway (1958). Popularized in 1959 by Perry Como in an RCA Victor recording.

Tom Dooley, a popular song arranged by Dave Guard from the Blue Ridge Mountains folk tune "Tom Dula" (1958). It was popularized by the Kingston Trio in a best-selling Capitol recording that received the Gold Record Award. The success of this number helped to initiate a vogue for popular adaptations and performances of folk songs, or songs with a folklike quality.

Frank Proffitt, a folk singer, claimed that it was he who introduced the song, saying he remembered it from the way his father used to sing it and play it on the banjo; he also maintained that it was his version that the Kingston Trio used and made into a hit. Proffitt went on to explain that he gave his version to a song collector in 1938, at which time it was called "Tom

Dula." The ballad told the story of a murder in Wilkes County, North Carolina, in 1866.

To My Wife, words and music by Harold Rome (1954). Introduced by Ezio Pinza in the musical play *Fanny* (1954).

Tonight, words by Stephen Sondheim, music by Leonard Bernstein (1957). Introduced by Carol Lawrence and Larry Kert in the musical play *West Side Story* (1957). In the motion-picture adaptation of the musical (Mirisch Pictures, 1961), it was sung on the soundtrack by Marni Nixon (for Natalie Wood). "Tonight" was one of the most successful songs Bernstein had written up to this time, its popularity enhanced through a best-selling recording by the two-piano team of Ferrante and Teicher for United Artists in 1961.

Tonight We Love, words by Bobby Worth, music by Ray Austin and Freddy Martin, the melody based on a theme from Tchaikovsky's First Piano Concerto (1941). Introduced and popularized by Freddy Martin and his orchestra (vocal by Clyde Rogers) for RCA Victor, their first major disk success.

Tonight You Belong to Me, words by Billy Rose, music by Lee David (1926). It was revived in 1956 in a best-selling Liberty recording by Patience and Prudence.

Too Close for Comfort, words by Larry Holofcener and George Weiss, music by Jerry Bock (1956). Introduced by Sammy Davis in the musical *Mr. Wonderful* (1956). It was further popularized by Eydie Gorme in an ABC Paramount recording.

Too Fat Polka (or, She's Too Fat for Me), words and music by Ross MacLean and Arthur Richardson (1947). Popularized by Arthur Godfrey in a Columbia recording.

Too Many Girls, a musical comedy with book by George Marion, Jr. Lyrics by Lorenz Hart. Music by Richard Rodgers. Starring Richard Kollmar, Desi Arnaz and Eddie Bracken (1939).

The motion-picture adaptation starred Lucille Ball and Richard

Carlson (RKO, 1940). The main songs from the stage score were used.

See: I Didn't Know What Time It Was.

Too Marvelous for Words, words by Johnny Mercer, music by Richard A. Whiting (1937). Introduced by Ruby Keeler and Lee Dixon in the motion-picture musical *Ready, Willing and Able* (Warner, 1937). This is the song with which Whiting's daughter, Margaret, began her successful career as a singer of popular songs— on the Johnny Mercer NBC radio program in 1940. The song was interpolated in the non-musical motion picture *Dark Passage,* starring Humphrey Bogart and Lauren Bacall (Warner, 1947), and in the screen musical *On the Sunny Side of the Street* (Columbia, 1951).

Too Much, words and music by Lee Rosenberg and Bernard Weinman (1956). Introduced and popularized by Elvis Presley in an RCA Victor recording that sold a million disks.

Too-Ra-Loo-Ra-Loo-Ral (That's an Irish Lullaby), words and music by James Royce Shannon (1914). Introduced by Chauncey Olcott in the musical extravaganza *Shameen Dhu* (1913). It was revived in 1944 by Bing Crosby in the motion-picture musical *Going My Way* (Paramount, 1944). His Decca recording that year sold over a million disks. This number was a particular favorite of President John F. Kennedy.

Toot, Toot, Tootsie, words by Gus Kahn and Ernie Erdman, music by Dan Russo (1922). Interpolated by Al Jolson in the musical extravaganza *Bombo* (1922). It became one of his specialties, sung by him in his first talkie, *The Jazz Singer* (Warner, 1928), then in the motion-picture musical *Rose of Washington Square* (20th Century-Fox, 1939). It was also interpolated in the motion-picture biography of Gus Kahn, *I'll See You in My Dreams* (Warner, 1951), sung by Doris Day.

Too Young, words by Sylvia Dee, music by Sid Lippman (1951). Written three years before publication.

It was introduced by Johnny Desmond, then popularized by Nat King Cole, whose Capitol recording sold over a million disks. It reached the top spot on the Hit Parade a dozen times in 1951. Its success was largely responsible for a temporary vogue for the use of the word "young" in popular song titles.

Top Hat, a motion-picture musical starring Fred Astaire and Ginger Rogers (RKO, 1935). Songs by Irving Berlin.

See: Cheek to Cheek; Isn't This a Lovely Day to Be Caught in the Rain?; The Piccolino; Top Hat, White Tie and Tails.

Top Hat, White Tie and Tails, words and music by Irving Berlin (1935). Introduced by Fred Astaire in the motion-picture musical *Top Hat* (RKO, 1935).

The Torch Song, words by Mort Dixon and Joe Young, music by Harry Warren (1931). Introduced in the musical *The Laugh Parade* (1931).

Totem Tom Tom, words by Otto Harbach and Oscar Hammerstein II, music by Rudolf Friml (1924). Introduced by Pearl Regay and chorus in the operetta *Rose Marie* (1924). The music there served for a spectacular dance routine in which the chorus was dressed in costumes to appear like totem poles; Robert Benchley described it in *Life* as "one of the most effective chorus numbers we have ever seen." The song was also used in the motion-picture adaptation of the operetta (MGM, 1936).

To the Land of My Own Romance, words by Harry B. Smith, music by Victor Herbert (1911). Waltz introduced by Kitty Gordon in the operetta *The Enchantress* (1911). In the motion-picture musical *The Great Victor Herbert* (Paramount, 1939), it was sung by Susanna Foster and Allan Jones.

The Touch of Your Hand, words by Otto Harbach, music by Jerome Kern (1933). Introduced by Tamara and William Hain in the musical *Roberta* (1933). The chorus of this song has an unusual structure in that first one melody is stated, then another;

then, without repeating either subject, Kern goes on to finish his song with a seven-bar amplification of the second thought. The song was presented by Fred Astaire and Ginger Rogers in the first motion-picture adaptation of the musical (RKO, 1935). The song was also heard in the second screen adaptation of the musical, renamed *Lovely to Look At* (MGM, 1952).

The Town Where I Was Born, words and music by Paul Dresser (1905). One of Dresser's last ballads.

Toyland, words by Glen MacDonough, music by Victor Herbert (1903). Introduced by Bessie Wynn and a male chorus in the musical extravaganza *Babes in Toyland* (1903). It was also heard in the motion-picture adaptation of the musical (MGM, 1934).

Toy Trumpet, music by Raymond Scott, words by Sidney Mitchell and Lew Pollack (1938). It originated as an instrumental published in 1937. The song was introduced in the motion picture *Rebecca of Sunnybrook Farm*, starring Shirley Temple (20th Century-Fox, 1938).

The Trail of the Lonesome Pine, words by Ballard MacDonald, music by Harry Carroll (1913). A song inspired by the popular novel of John Fox, Jr. In the novel, however, the setting was the Cumberland Mountains of Kentucky, while Carroll's song refers to the Blue Ridge Mountains of Virginia. It was interpolated in *The Passing Show of 1914*, sung by Muriel Window.

Tra La La, words by Arthur Jackson, music by George Gershwin (1922). Interpolated in the musical *For Goodness Sake* (1922), introduced by John E. Hazard, Marjorie Gateson, Charles Judels and ensemble. The song was revived by Gene Kelly and Oscar Levant in the motion-picture musical *An American in Paris* (MGM, 1951).

Tramp, Tramp, Tramp (or, The Prisoner's Hope), words and music by George Frederick Root (1864). One of Root's most successful Civil War songs, inspired by the great number of Union soldiers held captive in Confederate prisons. The ballad described the feelings of a sick and lonely Union captive dreaming of liberation at the hands of victorious Northern forces.

Root wrote this ballad in 1863 because a song was needed for the Christmas issue of *The Song Messenger*, the house organ of the Chicago publishing house of Root and Cady. Root completed the required song in about two hours. When his brother saw it he said: "I confess I don't think much of it, but it may do. In fact, it *must* do. You have certainly written better numbers before." "Tramp, Tramp, Tramp" achieved immediate success, and was second only to "The Battle Cry of Freedom" among its composer's most popular war songs. In 1864 Root wrote a sequel, "On, On, On, the Boys Came Marching," but it was a failure.

Tramp, Tramp, Tramp (Along the Highway), words by Rida Johnson Young, music by Victor Herbert (1910). Introduced by Orville Harrold and a male chorus in the operetta *Naughty Marietta* (1910). This number became the prototype of numerous male-chorus marching songs in later operettas. In the motion-picture adaptation of the musical (MGM, 1935), it was sung by Nelson Eddy and a male chorus.

Travelin' Man, words and music by Ricky Nelson (1961). Introduced and popularized by Ricky Nelson in an Imperial recording.

Treasure Girl, a musical comedy with book by Vincent Lawrence and Fred Thompson. Lyrics by Ira Gershwin. Music by George Gershwin. Starring Gertrude Lawrence and Clifton Webb (1928).

See: K-razy for You; Oh, So Nice; Where's the Boy?

Treat Me Rough, words by Ira Gershwin, music by George Gershwin (1930). Introduced by William Kent in the musical *Girl Crazy* (1930). The number was used in the second motion-picture adaptation of the musical (MGM, 1943).

A Tree Grows in Brooklyn, a musical comedy with book by Betty Smith and George Abbott based on Betty Smith's novel of the same name. Lyrics by Dorothy Fields. Music by Arthur Schwartz. Starring Shirley Booth and Johnny Johnston (1951). Original cast recording (Columbia).

See: Love Is the Reason; Make the Man Love Me.

A Tree in the Meadow, words and music by Billy Reid (1948). An English popular song popularized in the United States in a best-selling Capitol recording by Margaret Whiting and Jimmie Wakely.

A Tree in the Park, words by Lorenz Hart, music by Richard Rodgers (1926). Introduced by Helen Ford and Lester Cole in the musical *Peggy-Ann* (1926).

A Trip to Chinatown, a musical extravaganza with book by Charles Hoyt. Lyrics and music mainly by Percy Gaunt. Songs by other composers were interpolated, including Charles K. Harris' "After the Ball." Starring J. Aldrich Libby (1893).

See: After the Ball; The Bowery; Push Dem Clouds Away; Reuben, Reuben.

To Life (or, L'Chaim), words by Sheldon Harnick, music by Jerry Bock (1964). Introduced by Zero Mostel, Michael Granger and male chorus in the musical play *Fiddler on the Roof* (1964).

The Trolley Song, words and music by Ralph Blane and Hugh Martin (1944). Introduced by Judy Garland in the motion-picture musical *Meet Me in St. Louis* (MGM, 1944), and further popularized by her in a best-selling Decca recording. The Capitol recording of the Pied Pipers was also a best seller.

Truckin', words by Ted Koehler, music by Rube Bloom (1935). Introduced in the night-club revue *The Cotton Club Parade,* at the Cotton Club in New York's Harlem in 1935.

True Blue Lou, words by Sam Coslow and Leo Robin, music by Richard A. Whiting (1929). Introduced by Hal Skelly in the motion picture *The Dance of Life* (Paramount, 1929).

The song was successfully revived more than a quarter of a century later by Tony Bennett in a Columbia recording.

True Confession, words by Sam Coslow, music by Frederick Hollander (1937). Title song of a non-musical motion picture starring Carole Lombard and Fred MacMurray (Paramount, 1937).

True Love, words and music by Cole Porter (1956). Introduced by Bing Crosby and Grace Kelly in the motion-picture musical *High Society* (MGM, 1956). Their Capitol recording in 1957 sold a million disks.

True Love, True Love, words and music by Jerome "Doc" Pomus and Mort Shuman (1960). Popularized by the Drifters in an Atlantic recording.

A True, True Love, words and music by Bobby Darin (1962). Introduced by Bobby Darin in the motion picture *If a Man Answers* (Universal, 1962), and further popularized by him in a Capitol recording.

Try a Little Tenderness, words and music by Harry Woods, Jimmy Campbell and Reg Connelly (1932).

Trying, words and music by Billy Vaughn (1952). Popularized by the Hilltoppers in a Dot recording.

Try to Forget, words by Otto Harbach, music by Jerome Kern (1931). Introduced by Doris Carson, Bettina Hall and Eddie Foy, Jr., in the musical *The Cat and the Fiddle* (1931). The song was also used in the motion-picture adaptation of the musical (MGM, 1934).

Try to Remember, words by Tom Jones, music by Harvey Schmidt (1960). Introduced by Jerry Orlach in the off-Broadway musical *The Fantasticks* (1960).

Tschaikowsky, words by Ira Gershwin, music by Kurt Weill (1941). Introduced by Danny Kaye in the musical play *Lady in the Dark* (1941), where he played a comparatively minor role to become a Broadway star for the first time, stopping the show at every performance. The tongue-twisting song lyric, utilizing the names of forty-nine Russian composers, was rattled off by Kaye in thirty-nine seconds. (In Madrid, Kaye broke his own record by delivering the number in thirty-one seconds.)

Ira Gershwin based this lyric on some light verse he had published in *Life* in 1924 under the pen name of Arthur Francis, for which he had been paid $12; it was then called "Music Hour."

When *Lady in the Dark* was tried out of town, there were many who feared that the success of "Tschaikowsky," as sung by Danny Kaye, would totally eclipse Gertrude Lawrence, star of the show. There were even some friends who advised the star to insist that Kaye's song be taken out of the production. "Danny is a talented performer and he's entitled to his chance," Gertrude Lawrence replied. However, to redirect the limelight on Miss Lawrence, a new special number was written for her to follow immediately after "Tschaikowsky"—"The Saga of Jenny," which provided a big hit number in its own right.

Tuck Me to Sleep in My Old 'Tucky Home, words by Sam M. Lewis and Joe Young, music by George W. Meyer (1921).

Tulip Time, words by Gene Buck, music by Dave Stamper (1919). Introduced by John Steel and Delyle Alda in the *Ziegfeld Follies of 1919*. When the Prince of Wales visited the United States in 1919, he was so enchanted with this number that Ziegfeld had the company repeat it for the Prince later the same night at the *Midnight Frolics* atop the theater.

Tumbling Tumbleweeds, words and and music by Bob Nolan (1934). Introduced by Gene Autry in the motion picture of the same name (Republic, 1935), his first appearance in a full-length movie. He sang it again in the motion picture *Don't Fence Me In* (Republic, 1945). Roy Rogers sang it in the motion picture *Silver Spurs* (Republic, 1943) and in the all-star motion-picture revue *Hollywood Canteen* (Warner, 1944). The song has become a favorite with harmonizing groups.

Turk, Roy, lyricist, born New York City, 1892; died Los Angeles, California, 1949.

See: Ahlert, Fred.

See also: Are You Lonesome Tonight?; Gimme a Little Kiss, Will Yah, Huh?; Just Another Day Wasted Away.

Turkey in the Straw. *See:* Zip Coon.

Turn Back the Universe and Give Me Yesterday, words by J. Keirn Brennan, music by Ernest R. Ball (1916). Popularized in vaudeville in the late 1910s.

Turn Me Loose, words and music by Jerome "Doc" Pomus and Mort Shuman (1959). Popularized by Fabian in a best-selling Chancellor recording.

Turn On the Heat, words by Bud De Sylva and Lew Brown, music by Ray Henderson (1929). Introduced in the motion-picture musical *Sunny Side Up* (Fox, 1929).

Turn Out the Light, words by Bud De Sylva, music by Richard A. Whiting and Nacio Herb Brown (1932). Introduced by Sid Silvers, Jack Haley, June Knight, Jack Whiting and chorus in the musical *Take a Chance* (1932). It was also sung in the motion-picture adaptation of the musical (Paramount, 1933).

Tuxedo Junction, words by Buddy Feyne, music by Erskine Hawkins, William Johnson and Julian Dash (1940). Introduced by Erskine Hawkins and his orchestra at the Savoy Ballroom in New York, but popularized by Glenn Miller and his orchestra in a Bluebird recording. It was interpolated in the motion-picture musical *The Glenn Miller Story* (Universal, 1953). Tuxedo Junction is a railroad junction in Alabama.

'Twas Not So Long Ago, words by Oscar Hammerstein II, music by Jerome Kern (1929). Introduced by Helen Morgan in the musical *Sweet Adeline* (1929). In the motion-picture adaptation of the musical (Warner, 1935), it was sung by Irene Dunne.

'Twas Off the Blue Canaries. *See:* My Last Cigar.

Tweedle Dee, words and music by

Winfield Scott (1954). Popularized in 1955 by Georgia Gibbs in a Mercury recording that sold a million disks. La Vern Baker's recording for Atlantic the same year was also a best seller.

The Twelfth of Never, words by Paul Francis Webster, music by Jerry Livingston, melody adapted from a Kentucky folk song, "The Riddle Song" (1956). Popularized by Johnny Mathis in a best-selling Columbia recording.

Twelfth Street Rag, a ragtime classic first published in 1914 as a piano rag, music by Euday L. Bowman. Lyrics by James S. Sumner were added in 1919. A new set of lyrics was written by Andy Razaf in 1942. The number was successfully revived in 1951 in a best-selling Capitol recording by Pee Wee Hunt.

Twelve Months Ago Tonight, words by J. F. Mitchell, music by Will H. Fox (1887). Mitchell wrote this lyric while hospitalized with his last fatal illness; his inspiration was the recollection of a meeting he had had with several friends one year earlier when they had pledged eternal friendship. When Frank Harding, the music publisher, visited Mitchell, the latter turned his lyric over to him, and Harding had it set to music by Will H. Fox. The song was successfully introduced by John W. Myers (one of the earliest singers to make phonograph recordings), and was then popularized by such performers as Henry Smith and Julie Mackay. Mitchell, who died in 1887, did not live to see the song become a success.

Twenty-four Hours of Sunshine, words by Carl Sigman, music by Peter De Rose (1949). Popularized by Gordon MacRae in a Capitol recording, by the Fontane Sisters in an RCA Victor recording and by Art Mooney and his orchestra in an MGM recording.

Twenty-six Miles (or, Santa Catalina), words by Bruce Belland, music by Glenn Larson (1958). Popularized by the Four Preps in a Capitol recording.

Twice As Much, words and music by Royce Swain (1953). Popularized by the Mills Brothers in a Decca recording.

Twilight on the Trail, words by Sidney D. Mitchell, music by Louis Alter (1936). Introduced by Fuzzy Knight in the motion picture *The Trail of the Lonesome Pine* (Paramount, 1936). It was then popularized by Bing Crosby in a Decca recording and by Perry Como in a recording for RCA Victor. This song was a favorite of President Franklin D. Roosevelt. For this reason, and at Mrs. Roosevelt's request, the composer presented both his manuscript and a copy of the Crosby recording to the Roosevelt Memorial Library in Hyde Park, New York. The song provided the title for and was heard in a motion picture starring Bill Boyd (Paramount, 1941).

Twilight Time, words and music by Buck Ram, Artie Dunn, Al Nevins and Morty Nevins (1944). Introduced by the Three Suns in a Hit recording. It was successfully revived in 1958 in a best-selling Mercury recording by the Platters.

Twinkle, Twinkle, Little Star, words by Herb Magidson, music by Ben Oakland (1936). Introduced in the motion picture *Hats Off,* starring John Payne and Mae Clark (First National, 1936).

Twirly Whirly, a Weber and Fields musical extravaganza with book and lyrics by Edgar Smith and Robert B. Smith. Music by John Stromberg and William T. Francis. This was Stromberg's last score. Starring Weber and Fields, Lillian Russell and Fay Templeton (1902).

See: Come Down, Ma Evenin' Star.

The Twist, words and music by Hank Ballard (1958). The number that made the twist a dance craze in 1961. The song was popularized by Chubby Checker, a twenty-year-old vocalist and dancer from South Philadelphia whose Parkway recording sold over a million disks. It was further promoted by Chubby Checker in personal appearances on the Dick Clark and Ed Sullivan television programs.

Chubby Checker explains: "There

are no basic steps in the twist. You move chest, hips and arms from side to side and balance on the balls of the feet."

Two Blue Eyes, words by Edward Madden, music by Theodore F. Morse (1907).

Two By Two, words by Stephen Sondheim, music by Richard Rodgers (1965). Introduced by Elizabeth Allen in the musical *Do I Hear a Waltz?* (1965).

Two Cigarettes in the Dark, words by Paul Francis Webster, music by Lew Pollack (1934). Introduced by Gloria Grafton in the non-musical motion picture *Kill That Story* (1934).

Two Different Worlds, words by Sid Wayne, music by Al Frisch (1956). Popularized by Don Rondo in a Jubilee recording.

Two Faces in the Dark, words by Dorothy Fields, music by Albert Hague (1958). Introduced by Bob Dixon, chorus and dancers in the musical *Redhead* (1958).

Two Girls and a Sailor, a motion-picture musical starring Van Johnson, June Allyson and Gloria De Haven (MGM, 1944). The score was made up mainly of standards. New numbers were contributed by Ralph Freed and Sammy Fain, among others.

See: A-Tisket, A-Tasket; Sweet and Lovely; You Dear; Young Man with a Horn.

Two Hearts in Three-quarter Time, a German popular waltz ("Zwei Herzen im Dreivierteltakt"), music by Robert Stolz, English lyrics by Joe Young (1930). The German song was the theme number of a German-made movie of the same name (1930).

Two Ladies in de Shade of de Banana Tree, words by Truman Capote, music by Harold Arlen (1954). Introduced by Ada Moore and Enid Mosier in the musical *House of Flowers* (1954).

This song was written while the composer was in Doctors Hospital in New York following a serious operation. "Using a tin dinner tray and a couple of spoons," Edward Jablonski reveals, "Arlen tapped out the rhythm while he and Capote worked on the lyric. As they completed a chorus they would sing it out to Arlen's tapping. . . . They kept this up until the nurses came in and put a stop to the racket."

Two Little Babes in the Wood, words and music by Cole Porter (1928). Introduced by Irene Bordoni in the musical *Paris* (1928)—Porter's first successful musical-comedy score.

Two Little Baby Shoes, words by Edward Madden, music by Theodore F. Morse (1907).

Two Little Girls in Blue, words and music by Charles Graham (1893). The creator got his idea for this hit ballad while shaving. Looking out of the bathroom window, he saw two little girls, dressed alike in blue, going to school with books under their arms. The song came to him in a flash. He had to grab a piece of soap and sketch out the title and some key words, together with several measures of the melody, on the mirror. He sold his ballad outright for $10, and thus failed to profit from its enormous sheet-music sale —after it had been popularized in vaudeville by Lottie Gilson.

Graham's ballad was unquestionably influenced by, and was in imitation of, Charles K. Harris' "After the Ball." Both ballads tell the story of a misunderstanding. In the Graham song, two sisters are married to two brothers. The couples quarrel, the sisters are separated. This is followed by a permanent breakup of the couples because each husband thinks his wife has been unfaithful. As in "After the Ball," the whole story is narrated by a heartbroken old man—to a nephew instead of a niece. Even the melody carries some reminders of "After the Ball."

Two Little Girls in Blue, a musical comedy with book by Fred Jackson. Lyrics by Ira Gershwin, using the pen name of Arthur Francis. Music by Paul Lannin and Vincent Youmans. This was the first Broadway musical for both Ira Gershwin and Vincent Youmans. Starring Oscar Shaw and the Fairbanks Twins

(1921).

See: Oh Me, Oh My, Oh You.

Two Lost Souls, words and music by Richard Adler and Jerry Ross (1955). Introduced by Gwen Verdon and Stephen Douglass and chorus in the musical *Damn Yankees* (1955). In the motion-picture adaptation of the musical (Warner, 1958), it was sung by Tab Hunter and Gwen Verdon. The song was further popularized in 1955 by Perry Como's recording for RCA Victor.

Two Sleepy People, words by Frank Loesser, music by Hoagy Carmichael (1938). Introduced by Bob Hope and Shirley Ross in the motion picture *Thanks for the Memory* (Paramount, 1938).

Two Tickets to Georgia, words by Joe Young and Charles Tobias, music by J. Fred Coots (1933). Coots played this song for Ted Lewis, then appearing with his band at the Palace Theatre in New York. Lewis introduced it the same evening, in 1933; the enthusiastic audience response compelled him to repeat it three times. Within a month the number was played and sung throughout the country.

A Typical Self-made American, words by Ira Gershwin, music by George Gershwin (1930). Introduced by Dudley Clements, Jerry Goff and chorus in the musical *Strike Up the Band!* (1930).

Tzena, Tzena, an Israeli popular tune with music by Issachar Miron (Michrovsky), adapted as an American popular song in 1950 in two versions. One had words by Gordon Jenkins and was arranged by Spencer Ross. The second version is the more familiar one, legal action having forced the earlier one out of the market. Here Julius Grossman adapted the melody (a version first published in 1947 in the anthology *Songs of Israel*); new English lyrics were written by Mitchell Parish. The song was popularized in 1950 in a best-selling Decca recording by Gordon Jenkins and the Weavers.

U

Ukulele Lady, words by Gus Kahn, music by Richard A. Whiting (1925). Revived in the screen biography of Gus Kahn, *I'll See You in My Dreams* (Warner, 1952), sung by a female chorus.

Umbriago, words by Irving Caesar, music by Jimmy Durante (1944). A Jimmy Durante specialty written for him, and introduced by him, in the motion-picture musical *Music for the Millions* (MGM, 1944). The word "umbriago" is a corruption of an Italian word meaning "a good-natured sot."

Unchained Melody, words by Hy Zaret, music by Alex North (1955). Theme song of the non-musical motion picture *Unchained*, starring Barbara Hale (Warner, 1955). The song was popularized by Al Hibbler, the blind Negro singer, in a best-selling Decca recording. A successful instrumental recording was made by Les Baxter and his orchestra for Capitol. It was successfully revived in 1965 by the Righteous Brothers in a Phillies recording.

Undecided, words by Sid Robin, music by Charles Shavers (1939). Revived in 1951 in a Coral recording by the Ames Brothers that sold a million disks.

Under a Blanket of Blue, words by Marty Symes and Al J. Neiburg, music by Jerry Levinson (1933). Popularized by Glen Gray and the Casa Loma Orchestra.

Under a Roof in Paree, a French popular song ("Sous les toits de Paris"), music by Raoul Moretti, English lyrics by Irving Caesar (1931). The French number was written for René Clair's French screen classic *Sous les toits de Paris.*

Underneath the Harlem Moon, words by Mack Gordon, music by Harry Revel (1932). Revel's first hit song; it was published as an independent number.

Under Paris Skies, a French popular song ("Sous le ciel de Paris"), music by Hubert Giraud, English lyrics by Kim Gannon (1953). The French song was introduced in the French motion picture *Sous le ciel de Paris.*

Under the Bamboo Tree, words and music by Bob Cole and J. Rosamond Johnson (1902). Described as "the king of ragtime tunes," it was one of the most significant and successful ragtime songs before 1910. Its setting is an African jungle where a Zulu and a dusky maid become convinced that two can live as cheaply as one. The song was introduced in 1902 by the vaudeville team of Cole and Johnson. At that time the title of the song was "If You Lak-a Me," the first words of the chorus. Cole's publisher suggested the change of title to "Under the Bamboo Tree." Marie Cahill, musical-comedy star, heard the song at a stage party and interpolated it in her musical *Sally in Our Alley*

(1902), where she brought down the house with it; from then on, this song became basic to her repertory. She interpolated it in 1903 in still another musical, *Nancy Brown.* The song's success was responsible for encouraging the writing in Tin Pan Alley of other numbers about animals, or numbers set in some forest primeval.

Lillian Albritton, impersonating Lillian Russell, sang it in the motion-picture musical *Bowery to Broadway,* starring Jack Oakie (Universal, 1944).

Under the Yum Yum Tree, words by Andrew B. Sterling, music by Harry von Tilzer (1910). It was revived in the non-musical motion picture *Wharf Angel,* starring Victor Mc-Laglen (Paramount, 1934).

Under Your Spell, words by Howard Dietz, music by Arthur Schwartz (1934). Title song of a motion picture (20th Century-Fox), where it was sung by Lawrence Tibbett.

Unforgettable, words and music by Irving Gordon (1951). Popularized by Nat King Cole in a best-selling Capitol recording. The song was revived in 1959 by Dinah Washington in a best-selling recording for Mercury.

The Unforgiven. *See:* The Need for Love.

The Unsinkable Molly Brown, a musical comedy with book by Richard Morris. Lyrics and music by Meredith Willson. Starring Tammy Grimes and Harve Presnell, the latter in his Broadway debut (1960). Original cast recording (Capitol).

The motion-picture adaptation starred Debbie Reynolds and Harve Presnell, the latter in his screen debut (MGM, 1964). The principal song hits from the stage score were used. A new production number, "He's My Friend," was interpolated. Soundtrack recording (MGM).

See: Dolce far niente; He's My Friend; I Ain't Down Yet; I'll Never Say No.

Unsuspecting Heart, words by Freddy James, music by Joe Beal, Bob Singer and Joe Shank (1955). Popularized by George Shaw in a Decca recording.

Up in a Balloon, words by Ren Shields, music by Percy Wenrich (1908). Waltz—one of the earliest song hits about aerial navigation—popularized by Rosie Lloyd.

Up in Central Park, a musical comedy with book and lyrics by Herbert and Dorothy Fields. Music by Sigmund Romberg. Starring Wilbur Evans and Maureen Cannon (1945).

The motion-picture adaptation starred Deanna Durbin and Dick Haymes (Universal, 1948). Three songs were used from the stage score.

See: Carousel in the Park; Close as Pages in a Book; It Doesn't Cost You Anything to Dream.

Up in the Clouds, words by Bert Kalmar, music by Harry Ruby (1927). Introduced in the musical *The Five O'Clock Girl* (1927).

Up on the Roof, words and music by Gerry Goffin and Carole King (1963). Popularized by the Drifters in an Atlantic recording.

Upper Ten, Lower Five, words and music by James Thornton (1889). An early Thornton song hit, introduced in vaudeville by Lawlor and Thornton.

Up, Up in My Aeroplane, words by Edward Madden, music by Gus Edwards (1909). An early song hit about aerial navigation, introduced by Lillian Lorraine in the *Ziegfeld Follies of 1909.* She sang this number while floating over the heads of the audience in a little flying-machine.

Use Your Imagination, words and music by Cole Porter (1950). Introduced by Priscilla Gillette and William Redfield in the musical *Out of This World* (1950).

V

The Vacant Chair (or, We Shall Meet But We Shall Miss Him), words by H. S. Washburn, music by George Frederick Root (1861). A Civil War ballad slanted at the home front. The song was inspired by the death of young Lt. John William Grout of the 15th Massachusetts Volunteer Infantry, just as he was about to come home for Thanksgiving for his first furlough. His chair at the family dinner was left vacant. Washburn, a friend of the Grout family, was so moved by this circumstance that he wrote a poem about it. It was published in the *Worcester Spy*. Several composers set it to music before Root, but Root's adaptation became the most popular. Words and music spoke the deep-felt tragedy of many a Civil War family, and for this reason the ballad met with sympathetic response both in the North and in the South.

The Vagabond King, an operetta with book and lyrics by Brian Hooker and W. H. Post based on J. H. McCarthy's romance *If I Were King*. Music by Rudolf Friml. Starring Dennis King and Carolyn Thomas (1925).

There were two motion-picture adaptations. The first starred Dennis King and Jeanette MacDonald (Paramount, 1930). The second starred Kathryn Grayson and Oreste (Paramount, 1956). Both adaptations used the principal numbers from the stage score.

See: Only a Rose; Song of the Vagabonds; Waltz Huguette.

Valencia, a popular song originally with French lyrics, music by José Padila, English lyrics by Clifford Grey (1926). The song was promoted in the United States through the efforts of Robert Benchley. It was introduced in the United States in a revue, *The Great Temptations* (1926).

Vallée, Rudy, composer, born in Island Pond, Vermont, 1901.

See: Betty Co-Ed; Deep Night; Good Night, Sweetheart; I'm Just a Vagabond Lover; Oh, Ma-Ma; Vieni, Vieni.

The Vamp, words and music by Byron Gay (1919). Inspired by the celebrated "vamp" of the silent screen —Theda Bara. The song was revived by Alice Faye and a female chorus in the motion-picture musical *Rose of Washington Square* (20th Century-Fox, 1939).

The Vamp from East Broadway. *See:* I'm the Vamp from East Broadway.

Van Alstyne, Egbert, composer and lyricist, born Chicago, Illinois, 1882; died Chicago, Illinois, 1951.

See (Lyrics by Gus Kahn): Memories; Pretty Baby; Sailin' Away on the Henry Clay.

See (Lyrics by Harry H. Williams): Back, Back, Back to Baltimore; Cheyenne; Good Night, Ladies; I'm Afraid to Go Home in the Dark; In the Shade of the Old Apple

Tree; It Looks to Me Like a Big Night Tonight; Navajo; San Antonio; There Never Was a Girl Like You; When I Was Twenty-One and You Were Sweet Sixteen; Won't You Come Over to My House?

See also: Beautiful Love; Drifting and Dreaming; Your Eyes Have Told Me So.

Van Heusen, James, composer, born Edward Chester Babock, Syracuse, New York, 1913.

See (Lyrics by Johnny Burke): Aren't You Glad You're You?; But Beautiful; Going My Way; If You Please; Imagination; It Could Happen to You; It's Always You; Moonlight Becomes You; Nancy with the Laughing Face; Oh, You Crazy Moon; Personality; Polka Dots and Moonbeams; Put It There, Pal; Road to Morocco; Sleigh Ride in July; Suddenly It's Spring; Sunshine Cake; Swinging on a Star; You Don't Have to Know the Language.

See (Lyrics by Sammy Cahn): All the Way; Call Me Irresponsible; Come Fly with Me; Everybody Has a Right to Be Wrong; Everything Makes Music When You're in Love; High Hopes; I'll Only Miss Her When I Think of Her; The Impatient Years; Indiscreet; Love and Marriage; My Kind of Town; Second Time Around; September of My Years; Style; The Tender Trap; To Love and Be Loved; Warmer Than a Whisper; Where Love Has Gone.

See (Lyrics by Eddie De Lange): All I Remember Is You; All This and Heaven Too; Darn That Dream; Deep in a Dream; Heaven Can Wait; So Help Me.

See also: I Could Have Told You; I Thought About You; You, My Love.

The Varsity Drag, words by Bud De Sylva and Lew Brown, music by Ray Henderson (1927). Introduced by Zelma O'Neal, and George Olsen and his band, in the musical *Good News* (1927). In the motion-picture adaptation of the musical (MGM, 1947), it was sung by June Allyson and Peter Lawford.

Vava Con Dios (or, May God Be with You), words and music by Larry Russell, Inez James and Buddy Pepper (1953). Introduced by Anita O'Day, and popularized by Les Paul and Mary Ford in a Capitol recording that sold a million disks.

Venus, words and music by Ed Marshall (1959). Popularized by Frankie Avalon in a Chancellor recording.

Venus Waltz, words by C. M. S. McLellan, using the pen name of Hugh Morton, music by Ivan Caryll (1912). Waltz introduced by Octavia Broske in the operetta *Oh, Oh, Delphine* (1912).

Very Good, Eddie, a musical comedy —a Princess Theatre production— with book by Philip Bartholomae and Guy Bolton based on a play by Bartholomae. Lyrics by Schuyler Greene and Elsie Janis. Music by Jerome Kern. Starring Ernest Truex, Alice Dovey and Oscar Shaw (1915).

See: Babes in the Wood; Nodding Roses; Some Sort of Somebody.

A Very Precious Love, words by Paul Francis Webster, music by Sammy Fain (1958). Introduced by Gene Kelly in the non-musical motion picture *Marjorie Morningstar,* starring Natalie Wood and Gene Kelly (Warner, 1958). The song was popularized by Doris Day in a Columbia recording.

A Very Special Love, words and music by Robert Allen (1957). Popularized by Johnny Nash in an ABC Paramount recording.

The Very Thought of You, words and music by Ray Noble (1934). It provided the title for and was used prominently in a motion picture starring Faye Emerson and Dennis Morgan (Warner, 1944). It was sung by Doris Day in the motion-picture musical *Young Man with a Horn* (Warner, 1950).

Very Warm for May, a musical comedy with book and lyrics by Oscar Hammerstein II. Music by Jerome Kern. This was Kern's last Broadway musical score. Starring Grace McDonald and Jack Whiting (1939).

The motion-picture adaptation was entitled *Broadway Rhythm* and starred George Murphy, Ginny Simms and Gloria De Haven (MGM, 1944). The only song used from the stage score was "All the Things You Are." Other songs, mostly standards, were interpolated. Several new numbers were contributed by Don Raye and Gene De Paul, Ralph Blane and Hugh Martin.

See: All the Things You Are; Irresistible You; Pretty Baby; Somebody Loves Me.

La Vie En Rose, a French popular song, music by Edith Piaf, English lyrics by Mack David (1950). The French song was introduced and popularized by Edith Piaf in Paris in 1947.

Vieni, Vieni, a popular Corsican song, music by Vincent Scotto, English lyrics by Rudy Vallée (1937). John Royal, vice-president of NBC, brought this Corsican popular tune to the attention of Rudy Vallée. Vallée introduced it over the radio on his program in 1936, then plugged it by featuring it every three or four weeks for the remainder of the year. In time the song caught on. When the publishing house of M. Witmark and Sons discovered it had owned the publication rights for years, it commissioned Vallée to prepare new English lyrics. The song reached the top spot on radio's Hit Parade in 1937.

Vienna Dreams. *See:* Someone Will Make You Smile.

The Village of St. Bernadette, words and music by Eula Parker (1960). Introduced in England by Anne Shelton. It was then popularized in the United States by Andy Williams in a Cadence recording that sold a million disks.

Violets, words by Julian Fane adapted from a poem by Heine, music by Ellen Wright (1900). Introduced by Sydney Barraclough in the operetta *The Little Duchess* (1900). The middle part of the song was appropriated by Bernice Petkere for her popular song "Starlight," which became involved in a plagiarism suit. (*See:* Starlight).

Vive La Compagnie (or, Vive L'Amour), a song favorite of college students, author of words and music not known (1844). It was first published in Baltimore. It was successfully revived in the twentieth century by the celebrated opera tenor Lauritz Melchior, who, in his American song recitals, encouraged his audiences to join him in singing the chorus.

Volare, a popular Italian song ("Nel Blu, Dipinto Blu"), music by Domenico Modugno, English lyrics by Mitchell Parish (1958). The Italian song won first prize in the song festival in San Remo, Italy. This song is a phenomenon in that it appeared in the United States under two different titles, with two different sets of lyrics, and both were major hits. First introduced as "Nel Blu, Dipinto Blu," it was sung by its composer and chief interpreter Domenico Modugno, whose Decca recording in 1958 was a best seller; it received a "Grammy" Award from the National Academy of Recording Arts and Sciences as the best popular recording of the year. The number also received a "Grammy" as the song of the year. With new lyrics by Mitchell Parish it was reintroduced as "Volare," once again achieving success, this time through Dean Martin's recording for Capitol that sold over a million disks; Bobby Rydell's recording for Cameo in 1960 was also a best seller.

Von Tilzer, Albert, composer, born Albert Gumm, Indianapolis, Indiana, 1878; died Los Angeles, California, 1956.

See (Lyrics by Lew Brown): Au Revoir, But Not Goodbye, Soldier Boy; Chili Bean; Dapper Dan; Give Me the Moonlight; I May Be Gone for a Long, Long Time; I'm the Lonesomest Gal in Town; I Used to Love You; Kentucky Sue; Oh, By Jingo.

See (Lyrics by Jack Norworth): Honey Boy; Smarty; Take Me Out to the Ball Game.

See also: Carrie; I'll Be with You in Apple Blossom Time; Oh, How She Could Yacki, Hacki, Wicki, Wacki, Woo; Put Your Arms Around Me, Honey; Roll Along, Prairie Moon; Teasing.

Von Tilzer, Harry, composer and lyricist, born Harry Gumm, Detroit,

Michigan, 1872; died New York City, 1946.

See (Lyrics by William Jerome): And the Green Grass Grew All Around; That Old Irish Mother of Mine.

See (Lyrics by Arthur J. Lamb): A Bird in a Gilded Cage; The Mansion of Aching Hearts; Where the Morning Glories Twine Around the Door.

See (Lyrics by Andrew B. Sterling): Alexander, Don't You Love Your Baby No More?; All Aboard for Blanket Bay; Coax Me; Close to My Heart; Down Where the Cotton Blossoms Grow; Goodbye, Boys, Goodbye; Eliza Jane; Last Night Was the End of the World; Mammy Lou; My Old New Hampshire Home; On a Sunday Afternoon; They're All Sweeties; Under the Yum Yum Tree; Wait Till the Sun Shines, Nellie; What You Goin' to Do When the Rent Comes 'Round?: When Kate and I Were Comin' Through the Rye; Where the Sweet Magnolias Grow; You'll Always Be the Same Sweet Girl.

See also: All Alone; The Cubanola Glide; Down on the Farm; Down Where the Wurzburger Flows; I'd Leave My Happy Home for You; I Love, I Love, I Love My Wife, But Oh You Kid; In the Sweet Bye and Bye; I Want a Girl Just Like the Girl that Married Dear Old Dad; Just Around the Corner; A Little Bunch of Shamrocks; Please Go 'Way and Let Me Sleep; De Swellest Gal in Town; They Always Pick on Me.

W

Wabash Blues, words by Dave Ringle, music by Fred Reinken (1921).

Wabash Moon, words and music by Dave Dreyer and Morton Downey (1931). Morton Downey's radio theme song.

Wagon Wheels, words by Billy Hill, music by Peter De Rose (1934). Introduced by Everett Marshall in the *Ziegfeld Follies of 1934.*

The Wah-Watusi, words by Kal Mann, music by Dave Appell (1962). Popularized by the Orlons in a Cameo recording.

Waikiki Wedding, a motion-picture musical starring Bing Crosby and Shirley Ross (Paramount, 1937). Songs by Leo Robin and Ralph Rainger, and by Harry Owens and Ralph Rainger.

    See: Blue Hawaii; Sweet Is the Word for You; Sweet Leilani.

Wait for the Wagon, author of words not known, music by George P. Knauff (1851). Knauff, whose name appears on the earliest sheet-music publications, is now generally credited as composer, though some later song publications preferred to identify the composer as R. Bishop Buckley, a member of the Buckley Serenaders.

    The melody was used for political parodies by both the Republicans and Democrats during the Presidential election of 1856—the Republicans with "We'll Give 'Em Jessie" and the Democrats with "Wait for the Wagon, the Old Democratic Wagon." The melody was again used for parodies during the Presidential election of 1864. During the Civil War the ballad, in its original form, was frequently heard at army campfires and was sung by army troops on the march.

Waitin' for My Dearie, words by Alan Jay Lerner, music by Frederick Loewe (1947). Introduced by Marion Bell and a female chorus in the musical play *Brigadoon* (1947). In the motion-picture adaptation of the musical (MGM, 1954), it was sung on the soundtrack by Carol Richards (for Cyd Charisse).

Waitin' for the Evening Star, words by Howard Dietz, music by Arthur Schwartz (1963). Introduced by Mary Martin and George Wallace in the musical *Jennie* (1963).

Waiting at the Church (or, My Wife Won't Let Me), words by Fred W. Leigh, music by Henry E. Pether (1906). Popularized by Vesta Victoria in vaudeville; she wore a dilapidated bridal veil and held a faded bunch of flowers in her hand. The song was revived for Mary Martin in the motion-picture musical *The Birth of the Blues* (Paramount, 1941).

Waiting for the Robert E. Lee, words by L. Wolfe Gilbert, music by Lewis F. Muir (1912). A ragtime classic. It was inspired by a scene on a levee in Baton Rouge, Louisiana, witnessed by the lyricist: the sight of Negroes unloading the freight from a Mississippi River boat, the *Robert E. Lee.*

When Muir first played the song for the publisher, F. A. Mills, the latter turned it down. But when, soon after that, Gilbert dropped in at Mills' office to pick up his manuscript, Mills informed him he had had a sudden change of heart and would publish it after all. Tubby Garron, a song plugger, brought the number to the attention of Al Jolson, who sang it at a Sunday evening concert at the Winter Garden; he made it one of his first big hit songs. The song was also presented successfully in vaudeville by Ruth Roye, who scored such a success with it at the Palace that because of it she was held over there for twelve weeks, the longest engagement up to then in the history of that theater. As a boy performer in the Gus Edwards school-kid revue, Eddie Cantor sang it in vaudeville.

The song was interpolated in several motion-picture musicals, including *The Story of the Castles* (RKO, 1939) and *The Jolson Story* (Columbia, 1946); in the latter it was sung on the soundtrack by Jolson.

Wait Till the Clouds Roll By, words and music by Charles E. Pratt, using the pen name of J. T. Wood for the lyrics and that of H. T. Fulmer for the music (1881).

Wait Till the Sun Shines, Nellie, words by Andrew B. Sterling, music by Harry von Tilzer (1905). A chance remark is believed to have been the inspiration for this, one of the most famous ballads of the early 1900s. Von Tilzer was standing outside a theater waiting for a sudden downpour to subside, when he happened to overhear someone near him use the phrase "wait till the sun shines." Others, however, maintain that a news item was the stimulus—an item describing the plight of a pauperized family that was comforted by the remark of a close friend, "The sun will shine after the storm."

The ballad was introduced in vaudeville by Winona Winter (daughter of the songwriter Banks Winter). It soon became a favorite both with other vaudeville headliners and with male quartets.

A jazzed-up version was presented by Mary Martin and Bing Crosby in the motion-picture musical *The Birth of the Blues* (Paramount, 1941). The song was also interpolated in the motion-picture musical *Rhythm Parade,* starring Gale Storm (Monogram, 1942); and it provided the title for and was featured in a motion picture starring Jean Peters and David Wayne (20th Century-Fox, 1952).

Wait Till the Sun Shines, Nellie, a motion-picture musical starring Jean Peters and David Wayne (20th Century-Fox, 1952). The score was made up of standards.

See: Break the News to Mother; Goodbye, Dolly Gray; On the Banks of the Wabash; Smiles; Wait Till the Sun Shines, Nellie.

Wait Till You See Her, words by Lorenz Hart, music by Richard Rodgers (1942). Introduced by Ronald Graham and chorus in the musical *By Jupiter* (1942).

Wake, Nicodemus, words and music by Henry Clay Work (1864). A ballad that became famous in minstrel shows. It told of a dead Negro slave buried in the trunk of a hollow tree who asked to be awakened at the first break of the Day of Jubilo, brought about through the Emancipation Proclamation.

Wake the Town and Tell the People, words by Sammy Gallop, music by Jerry Livingston (1954). Popularized in 1955 by Mindy Carson in a Columbia recording, and by Les Baxter and his orchestra in a recording for Capitol.

Wake Up and Dream, a musical comedy with book by J. H. Turner. Lyrics and music by Cole Porter. Starring Jack Buchanan and Jessie Matthews (1929).

See: What Is This Thing Called Love?

Wake Up and Live, words by Mack Gordon, music by Harry Revel

(1937). Title song of a motion picture (Fox, 1937), introduced by Alice Faye.

Wake Up and Live, a motion-picture musical starring Alice Faye and Patsy Kelly (20th Century-Fox, 1937). Songs by Mack Gordon and Harry Revel.

See: Never in a Million Years; There's a Lull in My Life; Wake Up and Live.

Wake Up, Little Susie, words and music by Felice and Boudleaux Bryant (1957). Popularized by the Everly Brothers in a Cadence recording.

Wal, I Swan (or, Ebenezer Frye), words and music by Benjamin Hapgood Burt (1907). A rural comedy song where the celebrated line "Giddap, Napoleon, it looks like rain" can be found. This number was interpolated for Raymond Hitchock in the musical *A Yankee Tourist* (1907).

Walk, Don't Run, words and music by Johnny Smith (1960). Popularized by the Ventures in a Dolto recording.

Walk Hand in Hand, words and music by Johnny Cowell (1956). Introduced by Denny Vaughan, but popularized by Tony Martin in an RCA Victor recording.

Walking Down Broadway, words by William Horace Lingard, music by Charles E. Pratt (1868). This is the first time that the expression "O.K." was used in a popular song. ("The O.K. thing on Saturday is walking down Broadway.") The song was introduced and popularized in 1869 by Lisa Weber in the burlesque *Ixion, Ex-King of Thessaly.*

Walk in de Middle of de Road, words and music by Will S. Hays (c. 1880). One of Hays' most popular songs in a Negro dialect. It has sometimes been erroneously classified as a Negro spiritual.

Walkin' in the Rain. *See:* Just Walking in the Rain.

Walkin' My Baby Back Home, words and music by Roy Turk, Fred E. Ahlert and Harry Richman (1930). Introduced and popularized by Harry Richman, with whom it is identified. It was revived in 1952 in a best-selling recording by Johnnie

Ray for Columbia; it was also successfully revived by Nat King Cole for Capitol. At this time the song was represented on the Hit Parade a dozen weeks. It provided the title for, was sung by a chorus under the titles of, and was presented by Donald O'Connor in a motion-picture musical (Universal, 1953).

Walkin' to Missouri, words and music by Antoine "Fats" Domino, Dave Bartholomew and F. Guidry (1960). Popularized by "Fats" Domino in an Imperial recording.

Walk Like a Man, words and music by Bob Crewe and Bob Gaudio (1963). Popularized by the Four Seasons in a Vee Jay recording.

Walk on the Wild Side, words by Mack David, music by Elmer Bernstein (1962). Theme song of a non-musical motion picture of the same name starring Laurence Harvey and Capucine (Columbia, 1962).

Walk Right In, words and music by Gus Cannon and Hosie Woods (1963). Popularized by the Rooftop Singers in a Vanguard recording.

Waller, Thomas "Fats," composer, born New York City, 1904; died Kansas City, Missouri, 1943.

See: Ain't Misbehavin'; Black and Blue; Honeysuckle Rose; I've Got a Feeling I'm Falling; Willow Tree.

The Wallflower. *See:* Dance with Me, Henry.

Waltz Huguette, words by Brian Hooker and W. H. Post, music by Rudolf Friml (1925). Introduced by Jane Carroll in the operetta *The Vagabond King* (1925). It was sung in both motion-picture adaptations of the operetta (Paramount, 1930; Paramount, 1956).

Waltz in Swing Time, words by Dorothy Fields, music by Jerome Kern (1936). Introduced in the motion-picture musical *Swing Time* (RKO, 1936).

Waltz Me Around Again, Willie (Around, Around, Around), words by Will D. Cobb, music by Ren Shields (1906). Introduced by Blanche Ring in the musical *His Honor the Mayor* (1906). It was then popularized in vaudeville by Della Fox, Willie Fitzgibbons and Willie Devere.

The Waltz You Saved for Me, words

by Gus Kahn, music by Wayne King and Emil Flindt (1930). Theme music of Wayne King and his orchestra, who introduced and popularized it.

Wanderin', words and music arranged and adapted by Sammy Kaye from a Minnesota folk song (1950). Popularized by Sammy Kaye and his orchestra in a Columbia recording.

Wand'rin Star, words by Alan Jay Lerner, music by Frederick Loewe (1951). Introduced by James Barton in the musical play *Paint Your Wagon* (1951).

Wang, a musical extravaganza with book and lyrics by J. Cheever Goodwin. Music by Woolson Morse. Starring De Wolf Hopper and Della Fox (1891).

See: Ask the Man in the Moon; A Pretty Girl.

The Wang, Wang Blues, words by Gus Mueller and "Buster" Johnson, music by Henry Busse (1921). It was revived in the motion-picture musical *Somebody Loves Me* (Paramount, 1952).

Wanted, words and music by Jack Fulton and Lois Steele (1954). Popularized by Perry Como in an RCA Victor recording.

Wanting You, words by Oscar Hammerstein II, music by Sigmund Romberg (1928). Introduced by Robert Halliday in the operetta *The New Moon* (1928). In the first motion-picture adaptation of the operetta (MGM, 1930), it was sung by Lawrence Tibbett; in the second (MGM, 1940), by Nelson Eddy.

Warm and Willing, words and music by Ray Evans, Jay Livingston and Jimmy McHugh (1959). Introduced by Gary Crosby in the motion picture *A Private's Affair*, starring Sal Mineo (20th Century-Fox, 1959).

Warmer Than a Whisper, words by Sammy Cahn, music by James Van Heusen (1962). Introduced by Dorothy Lamour in the motion-picture musical *The Road to Hong Kong* (United Artists, 1962).

Warren, Harry, composer, born Brooklyn, New York, 1893.

See (Lyrics by Al Dubin): About a Quarter to Nine; Am I in Love?;

Boulevard of Broken Dreams; Don't Give Up the Ship; Fair and Warmer; Forty-Second Street; I'll String Along with You; I Know Now; I'll Sing a Thousand Love Songs; I Love My Baby, My Baby Loves Me; I Only Have Eyes for You; Keep Young and Beautiful; The Little Things You Used to Do; Lullaby of Broadway; Lulu's Back in Town; Muchacha; Remember Me; September in the Rain; Shadow Waltz; Shanghai Lil; She's a Latin from Manhattan; Shuffle Off to Buffalo; Summer Night; Three's a Crowd; We're in the Money; Where Am I?; With Plenty of Money and You; Wonder Bar; The Words Are in My Heart; You Let Me Down; Young and Healthy; You're Getting to Be a Habit with Me.

See (Lyrics by Mort Dixon): I Found a Million-Dollar Baby; Nagasaki; Ooh, That Kiss; Old Man Sunshine; The Torch Song; Would You Like to Take a Walk?; You're My Everything.

See (Lyrics by Mack Gordon): At Last; Chattanooga Choo Choo; If You Feel Like Singing, Sing; I Had the Craziest Dream; I Wish I Knew; The More I See of You; My Heart Tells Me; Serenade in Blue; There'll Never Be Another You; You'll Never Know.

See (Lyrics by Edgar Leslie): By the River Sainte-Marie; Rose of Rio Grande.

See (Lyrics by Johnny Mercer): Jeepers, Creepers; On the Atchison, Topeka and the Santa Fe; You Must Have Been a Beautiful Baby.

See (Lyrics by Leo Robin): No Love, No Nothin'; Zing a Little Zong.

See also: An Affair to Remember; Cheerful Little Earful; Cryin' for the Carolines; Gid-ap, Garibaldi; Innamorata; My One and Only Highland Fling; The Stanley Steamer; That's Amore; This Heart of Mine; Where Do You Work-a, John; Where the Shy Little Violets Grow.

Washboard Blues, music by Hoagy Carmichael, lyrics by Fred Callahan and Mitchell Parish (1925). It originated as a jazz instrumental, a version recorded by the Wolverines, with Bix Beiderbecke, in a Gennet disk that has become a collector's item. Hoagy Carmichael subsequently recorded it successfully for Decca.

Washington, Ned, lyricist, born Scranton, Pennsylvania, 1901.

See: Tiomkin, Dimitri; Young, Victor.

See also: Cosi Cosa; Fire Down Below; The Man from Laramie; The Need for You; Smoke Rings; When You Wish Upon a Star.

Was It Rain?, words by Walter Hirsch, music by Lou Handman (1937). Introduced in the motion-picture musical *The Hit Parade,* starring Phil Regan and Frances Langford (Republic, 1937).

Wasn't It Beautiful While It Lasted?, words by Bud De Sylva and Lew Brown, music by Ray Henderson (1930). Introduced by Grace Brinkley and John Barker in the musical *Flying High* (1930).

Watching the Clouds Roll By, words by Bert Kalmar, music by Harry Ruby (1928). Introduced by Bernice Ackerman and Milton Watson in the Four Marx Brothers' musical extravaganza *Animal Crackers* (1928). It was also sung in the motion-picture adaptation of the musical (Paramount, 1930).

Watch Your Step, a musical comedy described in the program as "a syncopated musical show," with book by Harry B. Smith. Lyrics and music by Irving Berlin. This was Irving Berlin's first complete stage score. Starring Irene and Vernon Castle (1914).

See: Play a Simple Melody; Syncopated Walk.

Waterloo, words and music by John Loudermilk and Marijohn Wilkin (1959). Popularized by Stonewall Jackson in a Columbia recording.

Way Down in Old Indiana, words and music by Paul Dresser (1901).

'Way Down Yonder in New Orleans, words by Henry Creamer, music by J. Turner Layton (1922). Introduced in the revue *Spice of 1922.* It was interpolated in several motion-picture musicals, including the Ted

Lewis screen biography *Is Everybody Happy?* (Columbia, 1943) and *Somebody Loves Me* (Paramount, 1951); in the latter it was sung by Betty Hutton. The song was revived in 1960 by Freddie Cannon in a best-selling Swan recording.

Wayne, Mabel, composer, born Brooklyn, New York, 1904.

See: A Dreamer's Holiday; In a Little Spanish Town; It Happened in Monterey; Little Man, You've Had a Busy Day; Ramona.

Way Out West, words by Lorenz Hart, music by Richard Rodgers (1937). Introduced by Wynn Murray, Alex Courtney, Clifton Darling, James Gillis and Robert Rounseville in the musical *Babes in Arms* (1937). The song was revived in the screen biography of Rodgers and Hart, *Words and Music* (MGM, 1948).

The Wayward Wind, words and music by Herb Newman and Stan Lebowsky (1956). Popularized by Gogi Grant in an Era recording. The song was interpolated in the motion picture *Golden Ladder* (Universal, 1956).

The Way You Look Tonight, words by Dorothy Fields, music by Jerome Kern (1936). Introduced by Fred Astaire in the motion-picture musical *Swing Time* (RKO, 1936). It received the Academy Award.

Though it is a love ballad, and has become popular as such, "The Way You Look Tonight" was used in the motion picture as a comedy number—ridiculing Ginger Rogers, as Penny, on her unsightly appearance while shampooing her hair.

We Are Coming, Father Abraham (300,-000 More), words and music by Stephen Foster (1862). Civil War song inspired by President Lincoln's call for 300,000 volunteers—during the lowest period in the military fortunes of the Union Army.

We Are Coming, Father Abraham, words and probably the music by James Sloan Gibbons (1862). Like the Stephen Foster song listed above, this ballad was inspired by President Lincoln's call for 300,000 volunteers in 1862. Gibbons' poem, intended as a response to the President's call, was first printed anonymously in the New York *Evening Post* on July 16, 1862. Within a few weeks it was reprinted in several other publications. Several composers set these words to music, the most famous being one whose music is believed to have been the work of the poet himself. President Lincoln was reported to have been deeply moved when this number was sung to him. The song inspired numerous parodies, including several that were anti-Lincoln.

Wear My Ring Around Your Neck, words and music by Bert Carroll and Russell Moody (1958). Popularized by Elvis Presley in an RCA Victor recording that sold a million disks.

Weary River, words by Grant Clarke, music by Louis Silvers (1929). Theme song of a non-musical motion picture starring Richard Barthelemess (First National, 1929).

Webster, Paul Francis, lyricist, born New York City, 1907.

See: Carmichael, Hoagy; Ellington, Duke; Fain, Sammy; Green, John W.; Kaper, Bronislau; Tiomkin, Dimitri.

See also: Black Coffee; A Farewell to Arms; Honey Babe; I'll Walk with God; Like Young; The Loveliest Night of the Year; Masquerade; Maverick; My Moonlight Madonna; Padre; Rainbow on the River; Shadow of Your Smile; Sylvia; The Twelfth of Never; Two Cigarettes in the Dark.

We Could Make Such Beautiful Music, words by Robert Sour, music by Henry Manners (1940). It was interpolated in the non-musical motion picture *Abroad with Two Yanks,* starring William Bendix and Dennis O'Keefe (United Artists, 1944). It was popularized in 1947 in a best-selling recording for RCA Victor by Vaughn Monroe and his orchestra.

Wedding Bells Are Breaking Up That Old Gang of Mine, words by Irving Kahal and Willie Raskin, music by Sammy Fain (1929).

We Did It Before and We Can Do It Again, words by Charles Tobias, music by Cliff Friend (1941). Introduced by Eddie Cantor in the musical *Banjo Eyes* (1941), where it was an interpolation. It was introduced in the production two days after Pearl Harbor—hurriedly improvised to bring a strong martial note into the musical. It brought down the house. It was interpolated in the motion picture *Sweetheart of the Fleet,* starring Joan Davis (Columbia, 1942).

Wee Small Hours, words by Bob Hilliard, music by David Mann (1955). Popularized by Frank Sinatra in a Capitol recording.

We Fight Tomorrow, Mother, words and music by Paul Dresser (1898). Ballad inspired by and popularized during the Spanish-American War.

Weeping Sad and Lonely (or, When This Cruel War Is Over), words by Charles Carroll Sawyer, music by Henry Tucker (1863). Civil War ballad, popular both in the North and in the South. It reflected the dread of the home front awaiting news from the fields of battle. The ballad was successfully featured by the Woods Minstrels at the Woods Museum in New York. It sold about a million copies of sheet music—a phenomenon for that period.

We Got Love, words by Kal Mann, music by Bernie Lowe (1959). Popularized by Bobby Rydell in a Cameo recording.

Weill, Kurt, composer, born Dessau, Germany, 1900; died New York City, 1950.

See (Lyrics by Ira Gershwin): My Ship; The Saga of Jenny; This Is New; Tschaikowsky.

See (Lyrics by Alan Jay Lerner): Green Up Time; Here I'll Stay.

See also: The Bilboa Song; Cry, the Beloved Country; It Never Was You; Lost in the Stars; Mack the Knife; September Song; Somehow I Never Could Believe; Speak Low; That's Him; This Time Next Year.

We Kiss in a Shadow, words by Oscar Hammerstein II, music by Richard Rodgers (1951). Introduced by Doretta Morrow and Larry Douglas in the musical play *The King and I* (1951). It was also sung in the motion-picture adaptation of the musical (20th Century-Fox, 1956).

Well, Did You Evah?, words and music by Cole Porter (1939). Introduced by Betty Grable and Charles Walters in the musical *Du Barry Was a Lady* (1939). It was revived in the motion-picture musical *High Society* (MGM, 1956).

We'll Make Hay While the Sun Shines, words by Arthur Freed, music by Nacio Herb Brown (1933). Introduced by Bing Crosby in the motion-picture musical *Going Hollywood* (MGM, 1933).

We Meet Again (or, The Song from Desirée), words and music by Ken Darby and Lionel Newman (1954). Theme song from the non-musical motion picture *Desirée*, starring Marlon Brando and Jean Simmons (20th Century-Fox, 1954); it was played under the opening titles.

Wenrich, Percy, composer, born Joplin, Missouri, 1887; died New York City, 1952.

See (Lyrics by Edward Madden): Moonlight Bay; Silver Bell.

See also: Put on Your Old Gray Bonnet; Sail Along, Silvery Moon; Up in a Balloon; When You Wore a Tulip; Where Do We Go From Here?

We Parted by the River, words and music by Will S. Hays (1866). The composer's first successful ballad not inspired by the Civil War; it sold over a quarter of a million copies of sheet music.

We're in the Money (or, The Gold Diggers' Song), words by Al Dubin, music by Harry Warren (1933). Introduced by Ginger Rogers in the motion-picture musical *Gold Diggers of 1933* (Warner, 1933).

We're Off to See the Wizard of Oz, words by E. Y. Harburg, music by Harold Arlen (1939). Introduced by Judy Garland, Ray Bolger and ensemble in the motion-picture musical extravaganza *The Wizard of Oz* (MGM, 1939).

Were Thine That Special Face, words and music by Cole Porter (1948). Introduced by Alfred Drake in the musical play *Kiss Me, Kate* (1948). In the motion-picture adaptation of the musical (MGM, 1953), it was sung by Howard Keel.

We Shall Meet But We Shall Miss Him.

See: The Vacant Chair.

We Shall Overcome, music arrangement and words by Zilphia Horton, Frank Hamilton, Guy Carawan and Pete Seeger (1960). Sometimes described as "the Marseillaise of the integration movement." It originated as a religious folk song, which in 1901 was turned by C. Albert Tindley into a Baptist hymn, "I'll Overcome Some Day."

As the theme song of the integration movement in the United States, it was used for the first time in 1946 by Negro workers serving as pickets in Charleston, South Carolina. It underwent many changes in the ensuing years before receiving its final and definitive setting in 1960 by Guy Carawan, a folk singer from the West Coast; he began teaching it to Negro students in the early days of sit-in demonstrations. It soon became a practice to close civil-rights meetings and demonstrations with the singing of the hymn. "As its stately cadences are sung," Robert Shelton explained in the *New York Times* on July 23, 1963, "the participants cross arms in front of themselves, link hands with the persons on each side and sway in rhythm to the music." This style of singing the hymn, however, differs from one Southern community to the next, as Shelton went on to explain. "Sometimes it is only a verse or two, other times the singing may last as long as ten minutes. Sometimes the song is 'lined out' between leader and congregation in call and response fashion, at other times sung in unison. Improvisation of melody and lyrics is widespread."

West Side Story, a musical play with book by Arthur Laurents based on a conception by Jerome Robbins. Lyrics by Stephen Sondheim. Music by Leonard Bernstein. Starring Carol Lawrence, Larry Kert and Chita Rivera (1957). Original cast recording (Columbia).

The motion-picture adaptation starred Natalie Wood, Richard Beymer and Rita Morena (Mirisch, 1961). Marni Nixon sang on the soundtrack for Natalie Wood. The basic stage score was used. This motion picture received the Academy Award. Soundtrack recording (Columbia).

See: I Feel Pretty; Maria; Tonight.

We Will Always Be Sweethearts, words by Leo Robin, music by Oscar Straus (1932). Introduced by Jeanette MacDonald in the motion-picture musical *One Hour with You* (Paramount, 1932).

We Won't Go Home Until Morning, words by William Clifton to the tune of the French folk song "Malbrouck" (1842). The picture on the first sheet-music publication shows young collegians enjoying a drink in a tap room. This number has since become a favorite of those in the happy state of intoxication.

What a Country, words by Lee Adams, music by Charles Strouse (1962). Introduced by Ray Bolger and ensemble in the musical *All American* (1962).

What a Diff'rence a Day Made, a popular Spanish song ("Cuando vuelva a tu lado"), with music by Maria Grever, English lyrics by Stanley Adams (1934). It was successfully revived in 1958 by Dinah Washington in a Mercury recording that sold a million disks; this recording received a "Grammy" from the National Academy of Recording Arts and Sciences as the best rhythm and blues recording of the year. The number was interpolated in the non-musical motion picture *The Racers,* starring Kirk Douglas (20th Century-Fox, 1955).

What a Night This Is Going to Be, words and music by Raymond Jessel and Marian Grudeff (1965). Introduced by Fritz Weaver, Inga Swenson, Peter Sallis and Virginia Vestoff in the musical *Baker Street* (1965).

What Are You Doing New Year's Eve?, words and music by Frank Loesser (1947). Written and published as an independent number. It became a hit song in 1947–1948.

What Can I Say After I Say I'm Sorry?, words and music by Walter Donaldson and Abe Lyman (1926). Popularized by Abe Lyman and his orchestra.

What Did I Do to Be So Black and Blue? *See:* Black and Blue.

What Did I Have That I Don't Have?, words by Alan Jay Lerner, music by Burton Lane (1965). Torch song introduced by Barbara Harris in the musical *On a Clear Day You Can See Forever* (1965).

What'd I Say?, words and music by Ray Charles (1959). Popularized by the Ray Charles Singers in a best-selling Atlantic recording. It was interpolated in the motion picture *Swingin' Along,* starring Tommy Noonan and Barbara Eden (20th Century-Fox, 1962).

What Do Simple Folk Do?, words by Alan Jay Lerner, music by Frederick Loewe (1960). Introduced by Julie Andrews in the musical play *Camelot* (1960).

What Do We Do on a Dew-Dew-Dewy Day?, words by Howard Johnson and Charles Tobias, music by Al Sherman (1927).

What Do You Do in the Infantry?, words and music by Frank Loesser (1943). World War II song of the infantry, written while Loesser was serving in the armed forces. It has since become the number most often used to identify that branch of the armed services. It was introduced by Bing Crosby.

What Do You Do Sundays, Mary?, words by Irving Caesar, music by Stephen D. Jones (1923). Introduced by Robert Woolsey in the musical *Poppy* (1923).

What Do You Want to Make Those Eyes at Me For?, words by Joe McCarthy and Howard Johnson, music by James V. Monaco (1916). Interpolated in the musical *Follow Me* (1916), where it was sung by Henry Lewis to Anna Held. Emma Carus then popularized it in vaudeville. It was revived in the motion-picture musical *The Merry Monihans* (Universal, 1944) and in the screen biography of Texas Guinan, *Incendiary Blonde* (Paramount, 1945).

Whatever Lola Wants, words and music by Richard Adler and Jerry Ross (1955). Introduced by Gwen Verdon in the musical *Damn Yankees* (1955). She also presented this number in the motion-picture adaptation of the musical (Warner, 1958). Sarah Vaughan's recording for Mercury was a best seller.

Whatever Will Be, Will Be (Que Sera, Sera), words and music by Jay Livingston and Ray Evans (1956). Introduced by Doris Day in the non-musical motion picture directed by Alfred Hitchcock, *The Man Who Knew Too Much* (Paramount, 1956). It received the Academy Award. This was the first time a song was interpolated in an Alfred Hitchcock production. Doris Day's Columbia recording sold a million disks. A decade later she repeated her rendition of this number in the motion picture *The Glass Bottom Boat* (MGM, 1966).

What in the World's Come over You?, words and music by Jack Scott (1959). Popularized in 1960 by Jack Scott in a Top Rank recording.

What Is Home Without a Mother?, words and music by Septimus Winner, using the pen name of Alice Hawthorne (1854).

What Is Love?, words and music by Lee Pockriss and Lee Vance (1959). Popularized by the Playmates in a Roulette recording.

What Is There to Say?, words by E. Y. Harburg, music by Vernon Duke (1933). Written for a revue planned by Billy Rose which never materialized. It was interpolated in the *Ziegfeld Follies of 1934,* introduced by Jane Froman and Everett Marshall.

What Is This Thing Called Love?, words and music by Cole Porter (1930). Introduced by Frances Shelley (then danced to by Tillie Losch) in the musical *Wake Up and Dream* (1929). Porter is believed to have derived the basic idea for this ballad from listening to native dance music in Marrakesh. "What Is This Thing Called Love?" was interpolated by Ginny Simms in the Cole Porter screen biography *Night and Day* (Warner, 1946). It was sung by Gordon MacRae and Lucille Norman in the motion-picture musical *Starlift* (Warner, 1951).

What'll I Do?, words and music by Irving Berlin (1924). One of several autobiographical ballads inspired by the composer's turbulent love affair with Ellin Mackay, whom he married early in 1926. The ballad was interpolated in the *Music Box Revue of 1923* while that show was already running; it was sung by Grace Moore, and it helped make her an overnight star. She sang it in 1923 at a benefit performance for Equity at the Metropolitan Opera House—her first appearance in the auditorium where a number of years later she would achieve triumphs as a prima donna.

What Kind of Fool Am I?, words and music by Leslie Bricuse and Anthony Newley (1961). An English popular song introduced by Anthony Newley as the closing number in the musical *Stop the World I Want to Get Off*—a production imported from London to New York (1962). The song was popularized in America in numerous recordings, one of the most successful being that of Robert Goulet for Columbia. In the motion-picture adaptation of the musical, produced in England (Warner, 1966), it was sung by Tony Tanner.

What Makes Sammy Run?, a musical comedy with book by Budd and Stuart Schulberg, based on Budd Schulberg's novel of the same name. Lyrics and music by Ervin Drake. Starring Steve Lawrence and Sally Ann Howes (1964). Original cast recording (Columbia).

See: The Friendliest Thing; My Home Town; A Room Without Windows; Something to Live For.

What, Marry Dat Girl?, words by Edgar Smith, music by John Stromberg (1899). Introduced by Fay Templeton in the Weber and Fields musical extravaganza *Helter Skelter* (1899).

What Price Glory?, a motion picture with songs (a remake of the 1926 silent film of the same name) starring James Cagney and Corinne Calvet (20th Century-Fox, 1952). The score, with a single exception, was made up of World War I standards.

See: Charmaine; Oui, Oui, Marie;

Over There; Smiles; There's a Long, Long Trail.

What's New, Pussycat?, words by Hal David, music by Burt Bacharach (1965). Title song of a motion-picture farce (United Artists, 1965), introduced by Tom Jones and further popularized by him in a Parrot recording.

What's New, Pussycat?, a motion-picture farce with songs starring Peter Sellers, Peter O'Toole and Romy Schneider (United Artists, 1965). Songs by Hal David and Burt Bacharach. Soundtrack recording (United Artists).

See: Here Am I; My Little Red Book; What's New, Pussycat?

What's the Use of Wond'rin'?, words by Oscar Hammerstein II, music by Richard Rodgers (1945). Introduced by Jan Clayton in the musical play *Carousel* (1945). In the motion-picture adaptation of the musical (20th Century-Fox, 1956), it was sung by Shirley Jones and a girls' chorus.

When *Carousel* was revived in New York in 1954, Richard Rodgers invited Jan Clayton to attend some auditions with him at the Majestic Theatre. Since they arrived early, the theater was empty. Suddenly they recalled that it was in this very auditorium that ten years earlier *Carousel* (in which Jan Clayton had starred) had had its original run. Remembering this, Jan Clayton mounted the stage and began singing "What's the Use of Wond'rin'?" to the empty seats. Before long, Rodgers was at the piano accompanying her. When they finished, neither said a word, each trying to control tears.

What Wouldn't I Do for That Man?, words by E. Y. Harburg, music by Jay Gorney (1929). Introduced by Helen Morgan in the motion-picture musicals *Applause* (Paramount, 1929) and *Glorifying the American Girl,* starring Eddie Cantor and Rudy Vallée (Paramount, 1929). It became a specialty of Ruth Etting, who made an outstanding recording of it for Columbia.

What You Goin' to Do When the Rent Comes 'Round? (or, Rufus Rastus Johnson Brown), words by Andrew B. Sterling, music by Harry von Tilzer (1905). This song, like several others by Sterling and von Tilzer, owes its origin to a chance remark. Von Tilzer was at a railway station in Miami when he eavesdropped on a conversation between two Negroes in which a woman was berating a man for his shiftlessness. She asked him: "What you goin' to do when de rent comes 'round?" The song's alternate title is the same as the name of its protagonist. The song was successfully revived in modern times by Jimmy Durante.

Wheel of Fortune, words by George Weiss, music by Bennie Benjamin (1952). Popularized by Kay Starr in a best-selling Capitol recording. It then became a favorite in night clubs around the country.

When?, words and music by Paul Evans and Jack Reardon (1958). Popularized by the Kalin Twins in a Decca recording.

When a Fellow's on the Level with a Girl That's on the Square, words and music by George M. Cohan (1907). Interpolated in the musical *The Talk of the Town* (1907).

When a Maid Comes Knocking at Your Heart, words by Otto Hauerbach (Harbach), music by Rudolf Friml (1912). Introduced by Emma Trentini in the operetta *The Firefly* (1912), Friml's first stage score. In the motion-picture adaptation (MGM, 1937), it was sung by Jeanette MacDonald.

When Buddha Smiles, words by Arthur Freed, music by Nacio Herb Brown (1921). One of the earliest collaborations of the successful songwriting team of Freed and Brown. Published as an independent number, it was introduced and popularized by Paul Whiteman and his orchestra.

When Chloe Sings a Song, words by Edgar Smith, music by John Stromberg (1899). A coon song described on the sheet music as "a southern plantation number." Lillian Russell made with it a highly successful debut in the Weber and Fields Music

Hall—in the extravaganza *Whirl-i-gig* (1899). This was the first time that Lillian Russell ever presented a coon song.

When Day Is Done, a Viennese popular song ("Madonna"), music by Robert Katscher, English lyrics by Bud De Sylva (1926).

When Did You Leave Heaven?, words by Walter Bullock, music by Richard A. Whiting (1936). Introduced in the motion-picture musical *Sing, Baby, Sing,* starring Alice Faye (20th Century-Fox, 1936).

When Francis Dances with Me, words by Benny Ryan, music by Sol Violinsky (1921). It was revived in the motion-picture musical *Give My Regards to Broadway,* starring Dan Dailey (20th Century-Fox, 1948).

When Hearts Are Young, words by Cyrus Wood, music by Sigmund Romberg and Alfred Goodman (1922). Introduced by Wilda Bennett in the musical *The Lady in Ermine,* where it was an interpolation.

When I Dance with the Person I Love, words by Sidney Michaels, music by Mark Sandrich, Jr. (1964). Introduced by Susan Watson in the musical *Ben Franklin in Paris* (1964).

When I Fall in Love, words by Edward Heyman, music by Victor Young (1952). Introduced in the non-musical motion picture *One Minute to Zero,* starring Robert Mitchum and Ann Blyth (RKO, 1952). It was popularized by Nat King Cole in a Capitol recording. The song was successfully revived in 1962 by the Lettermen in a Capitol recording.

When I Get You Alone Tonight, words by Alfred Bryan, music by Fred Fisher (1912). It was interpolated in Fred Fisher's screen biography *Oh, You Beautiful Doll* (20th Century-Fox, 1949).

When I Grow Too Old to Dream, words by Oscar Hammerstein II, music by Sigmund Romberg (1935). One of Romberg's most celebrated waltzes. It was introduced by Evelyn Laye in the motion-picture musical *The Night Is Young* (MGM, 1935). In the Sigmund Romberg screen biog-

raphy, *Deep in My Heart* (MGM, 1954), it was sung by José Ferrer.

When I Leave the World Behind, words and music by Irving Berlin (1915). The inspiration for this ballad was a spurious will by a nonexistent lawyer named Charles Lounsberry. He was supposed to have left to his children "the dandelions of the field, and the daisies thereof . . . the long days to be merry in . . . the right to choose a star that shall be his," and so forth. This will, which Berlin took at face value, made such an impression on him that he wrote a song in a similar vein ("I'll leave the songbirds to the blind," etc.) Berlin dedicated his ballad to "the memory of Charles Lounsberry, whose will suggested the theme of the song." Only many years later did Berlin discover that there had never been any such person as Lounsberry and that the will had been the fabrication of some highly inventive imagination.

When I Lost You, words and music by Irving Berlin (1912). Irving Berlin's first successful ballad, selling about two million copies of sheet music. Like so many other and later Berlin ballads, this one was autobiographical. In 1912 Berlin had married Dorothy Goetz. They spent their honeymoon in Cuba, where Dorothy contracted typhoid fever. Soon after they had returned to New York to set up their new home, Dorothy died. Berlin sublimated his grief by writing this song.

When I'm Looking at You, words by Clifford Grey, music by Herbert Stothart (1929). Introduced in the motion-picture musical *The Rogue Song* (MGM, 1930).

When I'm Not Near the Girl I Love, words by E. Y. Harburg, music by Burton Lane (1946). Introduced by David Wayne in the musical play *Finian's Rainbow* (1947).

When I'm with You, words by Mack Gordon, music by Harry Revel (1936). Introduced in the motion-picture musical *The Poor Little Rich Girl,* starring Shirley Temple (20th Century-Fox, 1936).

When Irish Eyes Are Smiling, words

by Chauncey Olcott and George Graff, Jr., music by Ernest R. Ball (1912). One of Ball's most celebrated Irish ballads, introduced by Chauncey Olcott in the musical *The Isle o' Dreams* (1912). The ballad became a favorite in Morton Downey's radio repertory; he is believed to have sung it thousands of times. It was sung by Betty Grable and a female chorus in the motion-picture musical *Coney Island* (20th Century-Fox, 1943). It also provided the title for and was sung by Dick Haymes in the motion-picture musical biography of Ernest R. Ball (20th Century-Fox, 1944).

When Irish Eyes Are Smiling, a motion-picture musical biography of Ernest R. Ball, starring Dick Haymes and June Havoc (20th Century-Fox, 1944). The score was made up of standards, many of them by Ball.

See: Be My Little Baby Bumble Bee; Dear Little Boy of Mine; I'll Forget You; Let the Rest of the World Go By; A Little Bit of Heaven; Love Me and the World Is Mine; Mother Machree; When Irish Eyes Are Smiling.

When I Take My Sugar to Tea, words by Irving Kahal, music by Sammy Fain and Pierre Norman (1931). Interpolated in the motion-picture extravaganza starring the Marx Brothers, *Monkey Business* (Paramount, 1931). It was interpolated in the non-musical motion picture *The Mating Season,* starring Gene Tierney, Miriam Hopkins and John Lund (Paramount, 1951).

When It's Apple Blossom Time in Normandy, words and music by Mellor, Gifford and Trevor (1912). Interpolated and popularized by Nora Bayes in the Weber and Fields extravaganza *Roly Poly* (1912). It was sung by Ann Sheridan and Dennis Morgan in the motion-picture musical biography of Nora Bayes, *Shine On Harvest Moon* (Warner, 1944).

When It's Sleepy Time Down South, words and music by Leon and Otis Rene and Clarence Muse (1931). It became a Louis Armstrong specialty.

When It's Springtime in the Rockies, words by Mary Hale Woolsey and Milton Taggart, music by Robert Sauer (1929). It was revived in the motion picture *Silver Spurs,* starring Roy Rogers (Republic, 1943).

When I Was Twenty-One and You Were Sweet Sixteen, words by Harry H. Williams, music by Egbert Van Alstyne (1911). A hit song capitalizing on the sustained success of James Thornton's "When You Were Sweet Sixteen."

When Johnny Comes Marching Home, words and music by Louis Lambert, believed to be the pen name for Patrick S. Gilmore (1863). Though written and popularized during the Civil War, this song achieved its greatest success during the Spanish-American War, with which it is now most often identified. The first published sheet music stated: "Music introduced in the *Soldier's Return March* by The Gilmore Band, words and music by Louis Lambert." Nevertheless, there is good reason to believe that the ballad was the work of Patrick Gilmore, the celebrated bandmaster, while he served in that capacity for the Union Army; on one occasion Gilmore even hinted that he had lifted the tune from a traditional Negro song he had heard a Negro sing. The melody, however, sounds more Irish than Negro; as one unidentified cynic remarked: "The Negro's name must have been Pat Reilly." It is likely that Gilmore adapted his martial words to an old Irish air favored by soldiers in both camps during the Civil War.

The popularity of this song is pointed up by the fact that numerous parodies were written for it. One of the earliest was "Johnny, Fill Up the Bowl." The most popular was "For Bales," words by A. E. Blackmar, a New Orleans publisher; it was inspired by the unsuccessful Union attempt to seize the bales of cotton stored up on Red River. Blackmar's parody was published in New Orleans, the sheet music dedicated to "those pure patriots who were affiliated with cotton on the brain and who saw the elephant."

The distinguished American composer Roy Harris used the song for a symphonic overture entitled *When Johnny Comes Marching Home;* he also incorporated it in his Fourth Symphony, and John Tasker Howard quoted it in his song "The Farmer's Son." Morton Gould's adaptation was entitled *An American Salute.*

When Kate and I Were Comin' Thro' the Rye, words by Andrew B. Sterling, music by Harry von Tilzer (1902).

When Mr. Shakespeare Comes to Town, words by William Jerome, music by Jean Schwartz (1901). Jean Schwartz's first song success. It was interpolated in the Weber and Fields extravaganza *Hoity Toity* (1901).

When My Baby Smiles at Me, words by Andrew B. Sterling and Ted Lewis, music by Bill Munro (1920). Introduced by Ted Lewis and his band in a revue, *The Greenwich Village Follies of 1919.* It became Ted Lewis' theme song. It gave the title to and was sung by Dan Dailey in a motion-picture musical starring Betty Grable (20th Century-Fox, 1948).

When My Dream Boat Comes Home, words by Dave Franklin, music by Cliff Friend (1936).

When My Dreams Come True, words and music by Irving Berlin (1929). Introduced by Mary Eaton and Oscar Shaw in the motion-picture extravaganza *The Cocoanuts* (Paramount, 1929), starring the Four Marx Brothers in their screen debut. This was also the product of Irving Berlin's first screen assignment.

When My Sugar Walks Down the Street, words and music by Irving Mills, Gene Austin and Jimmy McHugh (1924). This was Jimmy McHugh's first song hit. It was written for and introduced in the Cotton Club in Harlem, New York. Gene Austin's RCA Victor recording popularized it.

When Sunny Gets Blue, words by Jack Segal, music by Marvin Fisher (1956). Popularized by Johnny Mathis in a Columbia recording.

When the Boys Meet the Girls (motion picture). *See:* Girl Crazy.

When the Leaves Begin to Turn, words and music by C. A. White (1878). A waltz-ballad featured successfully

by Frank Howard, the minstrel, whose success as a performer was launched with this number, when he appeared with Thatcher, Primrose and West.

When the Midnight Choo Choo Leaves for Alabam', words and music by Irving Berlin (1912). A major Irving Berlin hit song of the early 1910s. It was successfully revived in two motion-picture musicals with Irving Berlin scores: *Easter Parade* (MGM, 1948), sung by Judy Garland and Fred Astaire; and *There's No Business Like Show Business* (20th Century-Fox, 1954), sung by Ethel Merman and Dan Dailey.

When the Moon Comes over the Mountain, words and music by Kate Smith, Howard Johnson and Harry Woods (1931). Kate Smith's theme song. She introduced it on May 1, 1931, on her first CBS radio program. She also sang it in the motion-picture musical *The Big Broadcast* (Paramount, 1932).

"Nobody seemed to like it," Kate Smith revealed in her autobiography, discussing the number before it became her theme song. "I just carried it around with me, hoping to use it one day." When her manager, Ted Collins, planned Kate Smith's first radio broadcast, on the La Palina Hour, he selected "When the Moon Comes Over the Mountain" from a mass of music sheets for her theme song, and it has remained her theme song ever since.

When the Red, Red Robin Comes Bob, Bob, Bobbin' Along, words and music by Harry Woods (1926). Introduced by Sophie Tucker at the Woods Theatre in Chicago in 1926. It was then sung successfully by Al Jolson and by Lillian Roth; in the Lillian Roth screen biography *I'll Cry Tomorrow* (MGM, 1955), it was sung by Susan Hayward. The song was also interpolated in the motion-picture musical *Has Anybody Seen My Gal?*, starring Piper Laurie and Rock Hudson (Universal, 1952).

When the Robins Nest Again, words and music by Frank Howard (1883). Frank Howard, a successful minstrel, purchased from Barney Fagan a number called "When the Robins Nest Again." Howard then proceeded to write a completely new song—words as well as music—with the same title. He introduced it with the Thatcher, Primrose and West Minstrels in 1883 and helped to make it a huge success.

When the Saints Go Marching In, a funeral hymn and jazz classic from New Orleans, author of words and music not known. It has acquired a permanent place in the repertory of American popular songs. This was one of many numbers played by Negro bands in New Orleans to accompany parades to and from a burial. Its general popularity may be said to have begun with Louis Armstrong's Decca recording in 1930, on which he sang it and also featured his trumpet playing; this recording became a favorite on New Orleans juke boxes. The song then invaded the North through numerous and varied jazz recordings.

When the World Was Young, a French popular song ("Le Chevalier de Paris"), music by M. Philippe-Gerard, English lyrics by Johnny Mercer (1950). It was introduced and popularized by Peggy Lee.

When This Cruel War Is Over. *See*: Weeping Sad and Lonely.

When We Are M-a-double-r-i-e-d, words and music by George M. Cohan (1907). Introduced in the musical *Fifty Miles from Boston* (1907).

When Yankee Doodle Learns to Parlez Vous Français, words by William Hart, music by Ed Nelson (1917). Comedy song of World War I, inspired by the first dispatch of American troops to France.

When You Ain't Got No More Money, Well, You Needn't Come Around, words by Clarence S. Brewster, music by A. Baldwin Sloane (1898). Popularized in vaudeville, it became one of the most successful coon songs of its time.

When You and I Were Young, Maggie, words by George W. Johnson, music by J. A. Butterfield (1866). The heroine in this sentimental ballad was Maggie Clark, a young Canadian girl being courted by George W. Johnson, a schoolteacher. They would meet at a mill on the creek near her home. Johnson wrote the poem to express the permanence of his love for the girl, and published it in a book of verses entitled *Maple Leaves* (the maple, of course, being the emblem of Canada). After Johnson and Maggie Clark were married, they came to the United States and settled in Cleveland, Ohio, where Johnson found a post as teacher. Maggie died the same year; eventually her husband returned to Canada to join the faculty of the Toronto University. The composer—an Englishman by birth but a citizen of Chicago—was so deeply moved by Johnson's poem that he set it to music. The song has become a favorite at community sings.

When You Come Back (and You Will Come Back), words and music by George M. Cohan (1918). A sequel to Cohan's "Over There," written at the suggestion of Cohan's publisher.

When You First Kissed the Last Girl You Loved, words by Will M. Hough and Frank R. Adams, music by Joseph E. Howard (1908). Introduced in the musical *A Stubborn Cinderella* (1908).

When You Know You're Not Forgotten by the Girl You Can't Forget, words by Ed Gardenier, music by J. Fred Helf (1906). A hit song of the early 1900s. It was sung by Fanny Brice, aged thirteen, at an amateur contest at Kenney's Theatre in Brooklyn, New York, when she won first prize of five dollars. (An additional three dollars in coins was thrown to her by the audience.) Fanny Brice considered this appearance her "first success."

Many years after the song had been written and first published, the widow of the songwriter Fred Fisher maintained that it had been written by her late husband, who had sold his rights to the publishing firm of Helf and Heger, and that Helf has taken the credit for its composition. But she was unable to substantiate this claim in court.

When You're All Dressed Up and No

Place to Go, words by Benjamin Hapgood Burt, music by Silvio Hein (1913). Interpolated for Raymond Hitchock in the musical *The Beauty Shop* (1914).

When You're Away, words by Henry Blossom, music by Victor Herbert (1913). Waltz introduced by Wilda Bennett in the operetta *The Only Girl* (1914), where it was used as a recurrent theme. "By its avoidance of phrase repetition," writes Edward N. Waters, "and by its gradual rise to a higher melodic level, it is one of the composer's most effective and best-balanced tunes."

When You're in Love, words by Johnny Mercer, music by Gene De Paul (1954). Introduced by Jane Powell and Howard Keel in the motion-picture musical *Seven Brides for Seven Brothers* (MGM, 1954).

When You're Smiling (the Whole World Smiles with You), words and music by Mark Fisher, Joe Goodwin and Larry Shay (1928). Revived by Frank Sinatra in the motion-picture musical *Meet Danny Wilson* (Universal, 1952).

When Your Hair Has Turned to Silver (I Will Love You Just the Same), words by Charles Tobias, music by Peter De Rose (1930). Charles Tobias wrote his lyric in fifteen minutes after hearing De Rose play the melody early one morning; he never changed a single word. Rudy Vallée helped to popularize it over the radio and in an RCA Victor recording.

When You Want 'Em You Can't Get 'Em, words by Murray Roth, music by George Gershwin (1916). George Gershwin's first published song. He wrote it while employed as a piano demonstrator at Remick's in Tin Pan Alley. When he showed his song to his immediate boss, Mose Gumble, the latter said: "You're paid to play the piano and not to write songs. We've plenty of songwriters here." Sophie Tucker became interested in the number and in its composer, and brought them to the attention of Harry von Tilzer, who published the song. The sheet-music sale was so anemic that Gershwin's royalties failed to cover the advance of five dollars von Tilzer had given him. The song was recorded probably for the first time half a century after it had been published—in the Decca album *The Gershwin Years*.

When You Were Sweet Sixteen, words and music by James Thornton (1898). Thornton is believed to have been inspired to write this ballad, one of his most popular, by one of his own flippant remarks to his wife Bonnie. One day she inquired if he still loved her. He answered lightly: "I love you like I did when you were sweet sixteen." Bonnie pointed out to him that his answer had in it the makings of a good love ballad. Thornton agreed. Bonnie Thornton introduced the song in vaudeville. It became a favorite of silver-toned tenors in vaudeville and of barbershop quartets.

Thornton originally sold out all the rights to the song to Joseph W. Stern & Co. for $25. When this company filed it away without publishing it, Thornton sold it a second time—to Witmark for $15. Witmark published it and realized a sheet-music sale in excess of a million copies. With the song a major hit, the house of Stern sued Witmark, claiming prior ownership. But the case never came to court. Witmark stood ready to pay the house of Joseph W. Stern & Co. the sum of $5,000, and Stern, in turn, agreed to drop all its claims.

Shirley Temple and a male quartet sang it in the motion picture *Little Miss Broadway* (20th Century-Fox, 1938). The melody was used as a recurrent theme in the background music for the motion picture *The Strawberry Blond,* starring Rita Hayworth and James Cagney (Warner, 1941).

The ballad was revived in the motion picture *The Great John L,* starring Linda Darnell and Greg McClure (Republic, 1945); it was sung on the soundtrack by Bing Crosby. It was also interpolated in the motion-picture musical *The Jolson Story* (Columbia, 1946). Perry Como revived it in 1947 in an RCA

Victor recording that sold a million disks.

When You Wish Upon a Star, words by Ned Washington, music by Leigh Harline (1940). Introduced in the full-length Walt Disney animated motion picture *Pinocchio* (RKO, 1940), sung on the soundtrack by Cliff Edwards. It received the Academy Award.

When You Wore a Pinafore, words by Edward Madden, music by Theodore F. Morse (1908).

When You Wore a Tulip, and I Wore a Big Red Rose, words by Jack Mahoney, music by Percy Wenrich (1914). A song favorite in the years just before America's entry into World War I; it was popularized in vaudeville and burlesque.

It has been revived in numerous motion pictures, non-musical as well as musical. These include: *Larceny in Music* (Univeral, 1942), sung by Allan Jones and the King Sisters; *Hello, Frisco, Hello* (20th Century-Fox, 1943), where it was used as background music for a Dutch skating routine; *Greenwich Village* (20th Century-Fox, 1944), sung by Don Ameche, William Bendix and others; *The Merry Monihans* (Universal, 1944), sung by Ann Blyth; *Chicken Every Sunday,* starring Dan Dailey and Celeste Holm (20th Century-Fox, 1949); *Cheaper by the Dozen,* starring Clifton Webb and Myrna Loy (20th Century-Fox, 1950); *Belles on Their Toes,* starring Jeffrey Hunter, Jeanne Crain and Myrna Loy (20th Century-Fox, 1952).

When Yuba Plays the Rumba on the Tuba, words and music by Herman Hupfeld (1931). Comedy number introduced by Walter O'Keefe in the revue *The Third Little Show* (1931). Rudy Vallée helped to popularize it over the radio and in an RCA Victor recording.

Where Am I?, words by Al Dubin, music by Harry Warren (1935). Introduced by James Melton in the motion-picture musical *Stars Over Broadway* (Warner, 1935).

Where Are You?, words by Harold Adamson, music by Jimmy McHugh (1936). Introduced by George Murphy and Ella Logan in the motion-picture musical *Top of the Town* (Universal, 1937).

Where Did Our Love Go?, words and music by Eddie Holland, Lamont Dozler and Brian Holland (1964). Popularized by the Supremes in a Motown recording.

Where Did Robinson Crusoe Go with Friday on Saturday Night?, words by Sam M. Lewis and Joe Young, music by George W. Meyer (1916). Comedy number popularized by Al Jolson in the Winter Garden extravaganza *Robinson Crusoe, Jr.* (1916).

Where Did the Night Go?, words and music by Harold Rome (1952). Introduced by Jack Cassidy, Patricia Morand and ensemble in the musical *Wish You Were Here* (1952).

In working on his score for *Wish You Were Here,* Rome had a particularly hard time finding a good song idea for a spot in the show—after the dancing had ended in the social hall. He pondered the problem while entertaining some of his friends. When they rose to leave, one of them remarked: "Where did the night go?" "That's it," Rome exclaimed. He completed his song that same night.

Where Did You Get That Girl?, words by Bert Kalmar, music by Harry Puck (1913). Introduced and popularized in vaudeville in 1913. It provided the title and served as the theme song for, and was sung by Harriet Parrish in, a motion-picture musical starring Leon Errol (Universal, 1941). Fred Astaire and Anita Ellis sang it in the musical biography of Ruby and Kalmar, *Three Little Words* (MGM, 1950).

Where Did You Get That Hat?, words and music by Joseph J. Sullivan (1888). Its creator was a comedian in vaudeville and music halls. One day, while rummaging through a theatrical trunk in his father's house in Long Island, he came upon an old silk topper. He put it on and strutted up and down outside the house. A neighborhood kid asked him: "Where did you get that hat?" —and a song was born. Sullivan himself introduced the number, at

Miner's Eighth Avenue Theatre in New York in 1888. He then sang it all over the country—always wearing the topper he had found in his father's trunk. The success of the song made its title a popular expression.

The song was revived by Gene Kelly in the motion-picture musical *Take Me Out to the Ball Game,* starring Frank Sinatra and Esther Williams (MGM, 1949).

Where Do We Go from Here?, words by Howard Johnson, music by Percy Wenrich (1917). Popular World War I ditty expressing the practical viewpoint of draftees. The song was popularized in vaudeville by Jack Wise. A generation later it was revived in the motion-picture musical *For Me and My Gal* (MGM, 1942).

Where'd You Get Those Eyes?, words and music by Walter Donaldson (1926).

Where Do You Worka, John?, words by Mortimer Weinberg and Charley Marks, music by Harry Warren (1926). Comedy song popularized by Fred Waring and his Pennsylvanians.

Where Have You Been?, words and music by Cole Porter (1930). Introduced by Charles King and Hope Williams in the musical *The New Yorkers* (1930).

Where Is the Life That Late I Led?, words and music by Cole Porter (1948). Introduced by Alfred Drake in the musical play *Kiss Me, Kate* (1948). In the motion-picture adaptation of the musical (MGM, 1953), it was sung by Howard Keel.

Where Is the Man I Married?, words and music by Hugh Martin and Timothy Gray (1964). Introduced by Edward Woodward and Louise Troy in the musical play *High Spirits* (1964).

Where Is Your Heart? (or, The Song from Moulin Rouge), words by William Engvick, music by Georges Auric (1953). Theme song from the screen biography of Toulouse-Lautrec, *Moulin Rouge,* starring José Ferrer (Romulus, 1953). The song (originally entitled "Le Long de la Seine") was sung on the soundtrack (for Zsa Zsa Gabor) by Muriel Smith. The Columbia recording by Percy Faith and his orchestra, vocal by Felicia Sanders, sold a million disks.

Where Love Has Gone, words by Sammy Cahn, music by James Van Heusen (1964). Title song of a nonmusical motion picture starring Susan Hayward and Bette Davis (Paramount, 1964). It was sung under the titles by Jack Jones, who popularized it in a Kapp recording.

Where, Oh Where, Has My Little Dog Gone?, words and music by Septimus Winner, melody borrowed from the German folk song "Zu Lauterbach hab' ich mein Strumpf verlor'n" (1864). Sometimes also known as "Der Deitcher's Dog."

Where or When, words by Lorenz Hart, music by Richard Rodgers (1937). Opening song in the musical *Babes in Arms* (1937), introduced by Mitzi Green and Ray Heatherton. In the motion-picture adaptation of the musical (MGM, 1939), it was sung by Betty Jaynes and Douglas MacPhail. Lena Horne sang it in the screen biography of Rodgers and Hart, *Words and Music* (MGM, 1948). In the non-musical motion picture *Gaby,* starring Leslie Caron and John Kerr (MGM, 1956), it was played under the titles, then sung in and used as a recurrent theme for the movie.

Where's Charley?, a musical comedy with book by George Abbott based on Brandon Thomas' farce *Charley's Aunt.* Lyrics and music by Frank Loesser. This was Loesser's first Broadway stage score. Starring Ray Bolger and Allyn McLerie (1948).

The motion-picture adaptation also starred Ray Bolger and Allyn McLerie (Warner, 1952). It utilized the basic stage score.

See: Once in Love with Amy; Make a Miracle; My Darling; The New Ashmolean Marching Society and Students Conservatory Band.

Where's That Rainbow?, words by Lorenz Hart, music by Richard Rodgers (1926). Introduced by Helen Ford and Margaret Breen in the musical *Peggy Ann* (1926). Ann

Sothern sang it in the screen biography of Rodgers and Hart, *Words and Music* (MGM, 1948).

Where's the Boy?, words by Ira Gershwin, music by George Gershwin (1928). Introduced by Gertrude Lawrence in the musical *Treasure Girl* (1928).

Where the Black-Eyed Susans Grow, words by Dave Radford, music by Richard A. Whiting (1917). Interpolated in the Winter Garden extravaganza *Robinson Crusoe, Jr.* (1916), introduced by Al Jolson.

Where the Blue of the Night Meets the Gold of the Day, words by Roy Turk and Bing Crosby, music by Fred E. Ahlert (1931). Introduced by Bing Crosby in the motion-picture musical *The Big Broadcast* (Paramount, 1932)—Crosby's first major screen role. It became his theme song.

Where the Boys Are, words and music by Howard Greenfield and Neil Sedaka (1961). Title song of a motion-picture musical (MGM, 1960), introduced by Connie Francis. Her MGM recording sold a million disks.

Where the Morning Glories Grow, words by Gus Kahn and Raymond B. Egan, music by Richard A. Whiting (1917).

Where the Morning Glories Twine Around the Door, words by Andrew B. Sterling, music by Harry von Tilzer (1905).

Where the River Shannon Flows, words and music by James J. Russell (1905).

Where the Shy Little Violets Grow, words by Gus Kahn, music by Harry Warren (1928). Introduced and popularized by Guy Lombardo and his Royal Canadians.

Where the Southern Roses Grow, words by Richard H. Buck, music by Theodore F. Morse (1904).

Where the Sweet Magnolias Grow, words by Andrew B. Sterling, music by Harry von Tilzer (1899).

Where Was I?, words by Al Dubin, music by W. Franke Harling (1940). Interpolated in the non-musical motion picture *Till We Meet Again,* starring Merle Oberon and George Brent (First National, 1940). The song was popularized in a best-selling recording by Charlie Barnet and his orchestra.

The Whiffenpoof Song, words by Meade Minnigerode and George S. Pomeroy, music sometimes credited to Tod B. Galloway and now more generally credited to Guy Scull, revised and adapted by Rudy Vallée (1936). The modern version was popularized by Rudy Vallée over the radio and in an RCA Victor recording.

"The Whiffenpoof Song" originated early in 1909 with the then newly organized Whiffenpoof Society at Yale University; this group was a branch of the Yale Glee Club. The lyricists were members of the Yale class of 1910. They adapted their lines from Kipling's poem *Gentlemen Rankers.* The word "whiffenpoof," however, was taken from an imaginary character in the Victor Herbert operetta *Little Nemo,* produced in 1908.

Rudy Vallée, a member of the Yale class of 1927, had heard the song during his college days. In 1936, while appearing on a special NBC radio program called "Yale Around the World," he became reacquainted with it through a performance by the Whiffenpoof Society. He decided to feature the number on his own radio program, and did so the following Thursday. This radio presentation, and the RCA Victor recording that followed, helped build the number into a national song hit. The song was successfully revived in 1950 by Fred Waring and his Pennsylvanians in a Decca recording in which Bing Crosby collaborated; this release sold a million disks. The song was heard in the motion picture *Winged Victory,* starring Jeanne Crain and Edmond O'Brien (20th Century-Fox, 1944).

While Hearts Are Singing, words by Clifford Grey, music by Oscar Straus, melody based on one from his famous Viennese operetta *A Waltz Dream* (1931). Introduced by Claudette Colbert in the motion-picture musical *The Smiling Lieutenant* (MGM, 1931).

While Strolling Through the Park One Day. See: The Fountain in the Park.

While the Angelus Was Ringing. See: The Three Bells.

While the City Sleeps, words by Lee Adams, music by Charles Strouse (1964). Introduced by Billy Daniels (then danced to by Jaime Rogers, Lester Wilson and Mabel Robinson) in the musical *Golden Boy* (1964).

While You Danced, Danced, Danced, words and music by Stephan Weiss (1951). Popularized by Georgia Gibbs in a Mercury recording.

Whip-poor-will, words by Bud De Sylva, music by Jerome Kern (1921). The song was written for an unproduced musical, *Brewster's Millions*. It was introduced by Marilyn Miller and Irving Fisher in the musical *Sally* (1920). It was interpolated in the Marilyn Miller screen biography *Look for the Silver Lining* (Warner, 1949).

Whirl-i-gig, a Weber and Fields Music Hall extravaganza with book by Edgar B. Smith. Lyrics by Harry B. Smith. Music by John Stromberg. Starring Weber and Fields, Lillian Russell (in her Weber and Fields Music Hall debut) and Peter Dailey (1899).

See: Say You Love Me, Sue; When?; Chloe Sings a Song.

Whispering, words by Malvin Schonberger, music by John Schonberger (1920). Popularized by Paul Whiteman and his orchestra in Ferde Grofé's orchestration; their Victor recording in 1920 sold over a million disks. The song was interpolated in several motion pictures, including the screen musical *Ziegfeld Girl* (MGM, 1941); the non-musical motion picture *Belles on Their Toes*, starring Jeanne Crain and Myrna Loy (20th Century-Fox, 1952); and the screen musical *The Eddie Duchin Story* (Columbia, 1956), where it was played on the soundtrack by Carmen Cavallero.

Whispering Hope, words and music by Septimus Winner, using the pen name of Alice Hawthorne (1868). It originated as an art song, a duet for soprano and alto.

Whispers in the Dark, words by Leo Robin, music by Frederick Hollander (1937). Introduced by Connee Boswell (with André Kostelanetz and his orchestra) in the motion-picture musical *Artists and Models* (Paramount, 1937).

Whistle While You Work, words by Larry Morey, music by Frank Churchill (1937). Introduced in the full-length Walt Disney animated motion picture *Snow White and the Seven Dwarfs* (RKO, 1937).

The Whistling Coon, words and music by Sam Devere (1888). Introduced by the minstrel Sam Devere (one of the leading banjoists of his day). He first gained fame through this number, in which he invited the audience to join him in the singing.

Whistling Rufus, words by Murdock Lind, music by Kerry Mills (1899). It originated as an instrumental two-step. With lyrics it became popular in minstrel shows and vaudeville.

White Christmas, words and music by Irving Berlin (1942). A classic of the Yuletide season, grown in the United States as Christmas music second in popularity only to the traditional Austrian hymn "Silent Night." "White Christmas" was introduced by Bing Crosby (with an assist from Marjorie Reynolds) in the motion-picture musical *Holiday Inn* (Paramount, 1942). Crosby's recording for Decca, Freddy Martin's recording for RCA Victor and Frank Sinatra's recording for Columbia each sold over a million disks in 1942.

"White Christmas" is the most significant ballad to emerge from World War II. During that conflict it was a particular favorite of American troops stationed in distant bases in the Pacific, a reminder of home. Since World War II the song has become what *Variety* has described as "probably the most valuable song . . . copyright in the world." On its twentieth anniversary thirty new recordings were released, including those by Pat Boone, Paul Anka, Steve Lawrence, Peggy Lee and Ella Fitzgerald. *Variety* revealed that by December, 1965, the song had sold almost five million copies of sheet music and almost fifty million disks in more than 350 versions. Bing Crosby's version for Decca alone sold about twenty-five million disks. The song also sold well over a million copies of instrumentals, octavos and orchestrations. It has been successfully recorded in many foreign languages, including French, German, Dutch, Italian, Polish, Portuguese and Spanish.

In 1963 ASCAP selected it as one of sixteen numbers in its all-time Hit Parade during the half century of its existence. The composer himself, as might be expected, had also expressed partiality to it among his creations, picking it out as one of his five favorites (the other four being "Always," "Easter Parade," "God Bless America" and "Show Business").

It provided the title for and was featured in a motion-picture musical starring Bing Crosby and Danny Kaye (Paramount, 1954).

White Christmas, a motion-picture musical starring Bing Crosby, Danny Kaye, Vera-Ellen and Rosemary Clooney (Paramount, 1954). Songs (old and new) by Irving Berlin.

See: The Best Things Happen While You're Dancing; Blue Skies; Count Your Blessings; Mandy; White Christmas.

White Silver Sands, words and music by Charles G. "Red" Matthews (1957). Popularized by Don Rondo in a Jubilee recording. The song was revived in 1960 by Bill Black's Combo in a best-selling Hi Records release.

A White Sport Coat (and a Pink Carnation), words and music by Marty Robbins (1957). Popularized by Marty Robbins in a Columbia recording, Robbins' first major record release.

White Wings, words and music by Banks Winter (1884). The title was first used in a popular song by Joseph Gulick, who, in turn, had lifted it from that of a best-selling novel about sailing ships by William Black. Gulick introduced his own number in 1882 with the Haverly Mastodon Minstrels; it was a failure.

Banks Winter, a member of that company, bought Gulick's song for $25, then wrote new words and a new melody while retaining the title. His ballad told about a sailor's return home to his beloved after a long absence on the high seas. Banks introduced his song in 1884 at Huber's Gardens on 14th Street in New York, but it made little or no impression. J. P. O'Keefe then sang it in Boston as a member of the Thatcher, Primrose and West company. Once again the song did poorly —so poorly, in fact, that it was immediately dropped from the program. But the musical director happened to hear Winter singing it in his dressing room (Winter, by now, having joined that company). He urged Winter to use it in the minstrel show. This performance inspired such an ovation that the song was used for the remaining two weeks that the company stayed in Boston. The song was an even greater success when Banks Winter sang it at Niblo's Gardens in New York later the same year. Meanwhile, the song (having been published early in 1884) went on to become one of the leading hit ballads of the decade. It was subsequently adopted by the Young Women's Christian Association as its official song.

Whiting, Richard A., composer and lyricist, born Peoria, Illinois, 1891; died Hollywood, California, 1938.

See (Lyrics by Raymond B. Egan): Japanese Sandman; Mammy's Little Coal Black Rose; Till We Meet Again.

See (Lyrics by Raymond B. Egan and Gus Kahn): Some Sunday Morning; Where the Morning Glories Grow.

See (Lyrics by Gus Kahn): Guilty; Ukulele Lady.

See (Lyrics by Johnny Mercer): Have You Got Any Castles, Baby?; I've Got a Heart Full of Music; Too Marvelous for Words.

See (Lyrics by Leo Robin): Give Me a Moment, Please; I Can't Escape from You; My Ideal; One Hour with You.

See also: Ain't We Got Fun?; Be-

yond the Blue Horizon; Breezin'
Along with the Breeze; Eadie Was a
Lady; Honey; Horses; It's Tulip Time
in Holland; I Wonder Where My
Lovin' Man Has Gone; My Future
Just Passed; My Sweeter Than Sweet;
On the Good Ship Lollipop; She's
Funny That Way; Sleepy Time Gal;
Turn Out the Light; True Blue Lou;
When Did You Leave Heaven?;
Where the Black-Eyed Susans Grow;
You're an Old Smoothie.

Who?, words by Oscar Hammerstein II
and Otto Harbach, music by Jerome
Kern (1925). Introduced by Marilyn
Miller and Paul Frawley in the musical *Sunny* (1925). Of Marilyn
Miller's incomparable way with this
number, Kern remarked that she
was its "editor, critic, handicapper,
clocker, tout and winner." In the
first motion-picture adaptation of
the musical (First National, 1930),
it was sung by Marilyn Miller and
Lawrence Gray; in the second (RKO,
1941), by Anna Neagle.

In preparing his score for *Sunny,*
Kern had turned over to his lyricists a tune in which the refrain
started with a single note sustained
through two and a quarter measures,
or nine beats. A phrase obviously
could not be sung on one sustained
note, so the lyricists went in search
of a single word that could serve.
But that one word, they realized,
had to carry interest, since it had
to be repeated five times in the refrain—with the return of the basic
melodic phrase. Kern always said
that when his lyricists finally selected
the word "who" to solve this problem, they had hit upon the formula
that spelled sure success for the
song.

In the 1930s George Olsen and
his band recorded this number for
RCA Victor, using a vocal trio in the
chorus. This recording was so popular that a vogue was initiated
among bandleaders for the use of
vocal trios.

In the Kern screen biography *Till
the Clouds Roll By* (MGM, 1946),
"Who?" was sung by Judy Garland.
The song was also interpolated in
the Marilyn Miller screen biography
Look for the Silver Lining (Warner,
1949).

Who Are You Now?, words by Bob
Merrill, music by Jule Styne (1964).
A blues introduced by Barbra Streis-
and in the musical *Funny Girl*
(1964).

Who Can I Turn To?, words and music
by Leslie Bricuse and Anthony Newley (1964). Introduced by Anthony
Newley in the musical *The Roar of
the Greasepaint—The Smell of the
Crowd* (1965). The song was popularized before the show opened on
Broadway, in Tony Bennett's best-
selling recording for Columbia.

Who Can Tell?, words by William Le
Baron, music by Fritz Kreisler
(1919). Introduced by Wilda Bennett and a female chorus in the
operetta *Apple Blossoms* (1919).
With new lyrics by Dorothy Fields
—and under the title "Stars in My
Eyes"—this same melody was used
in the motion-picture musical *The
King Steps Out,* starring Grace
Moore (Columbia, 1936).

Who Cares?, words by Jack Yellen,
music by Milton Ager (1922). Introduced and popularized by Al Jolson in the Winter Garden extravaganza *Bombo* (1922).

Who Cares?, words by Ira Gershwin,
music by George Gershwin (1931).
Introduced by William Gaxton and
Lois Moran in the musical *Of Thee
I Sing!* (1931). During the course of
the musical, the song appears in
two different moods. At first it is
sung brightly, when President Wintergreen tries to avoid telling re-
porters what his intentions are con-
cerning the jilted Miss Devereaux.
Later on it is sung sadly and with
sentimentality, after President Wintergreen is faced with impeachment
because he refuses to renounce his
wife for Miss Devereaux.

**Who Do You Know in Heaven? (That
Made You the Angel You Are),**
words by Al Stillman, music by Peter
De Rose (1949). Popularized by Eddy
Duchin in a recording for Harmony
and by the Ink Spots in a recording
for Decca.

Who Do You Love, I Hope?, words and
music by Irving Berlin (1946). In-

troduced by Betty Nyman and Kenny Bowers in the musical *Annie, Get Your Gun* (1946).

Whole Lot-ta Shakin' Goin' On, words and music by Dave Williams and Sunny David (1957). Popularized by Jerry Lee Lewis in a Sun recording.

Who Needs You?, words by Al Stillman, music by Robert Allen (1956). Popularized by the Four Lads in a Columbia recording.

Who'll Buy My Violets?, a popular Spanish song ("La Violetera"), music by José Padilla, English lyrics by E. Ray Goetz (1923). Introduced by Irene Bordoni in the musical *Little Miss Bluebeard* (1923). Charles Chaplin borrowed the melody for his own background music to his motion picture *City Lights* (United Artists, 1931).

Whoopee, a musical comedy with book by William Anthony McGuire based on Owen Davis' play *The Nervous Wreck*. Lyrics by Gus Kahn. Music by Walter Donaldson. Starring Eddie Cantor and Ruth Etting (1928).

The motion-picture adaptation starred Eddie Cantor in his talking-picture debut (United Artists, 1930). Only three songs were used from the stage score. Several new numbers were written for this movie, including "My Baby Just Cares for Me" by Gus Kahn and Walter Donaldson.

See: Love Me or Leave Me; Makin' Whoopee; My Baby Just Cares for Me.

Who Paid the Rent for Mrs. Rip Van Winkle When Rip Van Winkle Went Away?, words by Alfred Bryan, music by Fred Fisher (1914). Comedy number introduced by Gaby Deslys in the musical *The Belle of Bond Street* (1914). It was interpolated in the Fred Fisher screen biography *Oh, You Beautiful Doll* (20th Century-Fox, 1949).

Who's Afraid of the Big Bad Wolf?, words and music by Frank E. Churchill and Ann Ronell (1933). Introduced in the Walt Disney animated cartoon *The Three Little Pigs* (1933).

Much of the success of this song in 1933 came from the fact that it helped Americans, then in the throes of the depression, to sound an optimistic note for the future while regarding the present fearlessly. The song was translated into several languages and became extremely popular abroad—probably for the very same reason. In the Soviet Union it was widely reproduced in children's books, embellished with illustrations, and identified as a Soviet folk song. "Who's Afraid of the Big Bad Wolf?" was interpolated in the motion-picture adaptation of Victor Herbert's operetta *Babes in Toyland* (MGM, 1934). Barbra Streisand made her professional debut with this song—in a Greenwich Village night spot in 1961.

Whose Baby Are You?, words by Anne Caldwell, music by Jerome Kern (1920). Introduced in the musical *The Night Boat* (1920). Clifton Webb sang it in the London revue *Fun of the Fayre* (1921).

Who's Sorry Now?, words by Bert Kalmar and Harry Ruby, music by Ted Snyder (1923). Introduced in vaudeville by Van and Schenck. It then became a hit song, selling over a million copies of sheet music. A quarter of a century later this song was remembered by the father of Connie Francis, who then was still an unknown singer. He urged her to record it and suggested she sing it with a strong beat instead of in a slow tempo. She recorded it in this way for MGM late in 1957. For several months this disk made no impression. Then it was plugged on "The American Bandstand" into a million-disk sale which started Connie Francis off on her formidable career and brought the song back to a major hit status. But before this had happened, the song had been revived in 1950 in the motion-picture biography of Ruby and Kalmar, *Three Little Words* (MGM, 1950), sung by Gloria De Haven.

Who's Your Little Whoo-Zis?, words by Walter Hirsch, music by Al Goering and Ben Bernie. Introduced by Ben Bernie and his orchestra. It was revived in the motion picture *The*

Stooge, starring Dean Martin and Jerry Lewis (Paramount, 1953).

Who Takes Care of the Caretaker's Daughter? (While the Caretaker's Busy Taking Care), words and music by Chick Endor (1925). Comedy number popularized in vaudeville. It was revived in 1963 by Bobby Darin and Johnny Mercer in a Capitol recording.

Who Threw the Overalls in Mrs. Murphy's Chowder?, words and music by George L. Giefer (1899). Comedy number (originally entitled "Who Threw the Overalls in Mistress Murphy's Chowder?") popularized by Irish comedians in vaudeville in the early 1900s. It was revived by Charles Winninger and a male chorus in the motion-picture musical *Coney Island* (20th Century-Fox, 1943).

Why?, words by Benny Davis and Arthur Swanstrom, music by J. Fred Coots (1929). Introduced by Jack Donahue and Lily Damita in the musical *Sons o' Guns* (1929).

Why, Baby, Why?, words by Luther Dixon, music by Larry Harrison (1957). Popularized by Pat Boone in a Dot recording.

Why Can't I?, words by Lorenz Hart, music by Richard Rodgers (1929). Introduced by Inez Courtney and Lillian Taiz in the musical *Spring Is Here* (1929).

Why Can't You Behave?, words and music by Cole Porter (1948). Introduced by Lisa Kirk and Harold Lang in the musical play *Kiss Me, Kate* (1948). In the motion-picture adaptation of the musical (MGM, 1953), it was sung by Ann Miller and Tommy Rall.

Why Did I Kiss That Girl?, words by Lew Brown, music by Ray Henderson and Robert A. King (1924).

Why Did Nellie Leave Home?, words and music by George M. Cohan (1891). Cohan's first published song. He was then a member of the Four Cohans, a headline act in vaudeville. The girl in the song was named after one of the Cohans, George's mother. The publishers of this number, Witmark, had Walter Ford revise Cohan's lyrics before issuing it (the last time Cohan ever permitted anybody to tamper with any of his songs). In spite of this revision, the song did poorly—so poorly in fact that the Witmarks refused to publish anything further by Cohan.

Why Did They Dig Ma's Grave So Deep?, words and music by Joseph P. Skelly (1880). One of the most successful sentimental ballads of the 1880s, popular in vaudeville and burlesque.

Why Do Fools Fall in Love?, words and music by Frankie Lymon and George Goldner (1956). Popularized by Frankie Lymon (then only fourteen) and the Teenagers in a Gee recording. A successful recording was also made by Gale Storm for Dot.

Why Do I?, words by Lorenz Hart, music by Richard Rodgers (1926). Introduced by June Cochrane and Francis K. Donegan in the musical *The Girl Friend* (1926).

Why Do I Love You?, words by Oscar Hammerstein II, music by Jerome Kern (1927). Introduced by Norma Terris, Howard Marsh, Charles Winninger and Edna May Oliver in the musical play *Show Boat* (1927). In the 1936 screen adaptation of the musical (Universal), it was sung by Irene Dunne and Allan Jones; in the 1951 screen version (MGM), by Kathryn Grayson and Howard Keel.

Why Don't They Let Me Sing a Love Song?, words by Benny Davis, music by Harry Akst (1942). Introduced in the motion-picture *This Time for Keeps,* starring Ann Rutherford (MGM, 1942). It then provided the title for and was sung by Jimmy Durante in a motion-picture musical starring Esther Williams (MGM, 1947).

Why Don't We Do This More Often?, words by Charles Newman, music by Allie Wrubel (1941). Popularized by Freddy Martin and his orchestra on the flip side of his best-selling RCA Victor disk release "Tonight We Love," with vocal by Eddie Stone; it then became a Freddy Martin specialty.

Why Don't You Believe Me?, words

and music by Lew Douglas, King Laney and Roy Rodde (1952). Popularized by Joni James in an MGM recording.

Why Do They All Take the Night Boat to Albany?, words by Joe Young and Sam M. Lewis, music by Jean Schwartz (1918). Comedy song popularized by Al Jolson at the Winter Garden.

Why Shouldn't I?, words and music by Cole Porter (1935). Introduced by Margaret Adams in the musical *Jubilee* (1935).

Why Was I Born?, words by Oscar Hammerstein II, music by Jerome Kern (1929). A blues written for and introduced by Helen Morgan in the musical *Sweet Adeline* (1929). In the motion-picture adaptation of the musical (Warner, 1935), it was sung by Irene Dunne. The song was interpolated in several other motion-picture musicals, including *The Man I Love* (Universal, 1946, sung by Ida Lupino); the Jerome Kern screen biography *Till the Clouds Roll By* (MGM, 1946), sung by Lena Horne; and *The Helen Morgan Story* (Warner, 1957), sung on the soundtrack by Gogi Grant (for Ann Blyth).

Wildflower, words by Otto Harbach and Oscar Hammerstein II, music by Vincent Youmans and Herbert Stothart (1923). Introduced by Guy Robertson in the musical of the same name (1923).

The Wildflower, a musical comedy with book and lyrics by Otto Harbach and Oscar Hammerstein II, music by Herbert Stothart and Vincent Youmans. This was Oscar Hammerstein's first successful musical. Starring Edith Day and Guy Robertson (1923).

See: Bambalina; Wildflower.

Wild Horses, words and music by Johnny Burke, using the pen name of K. C. Rogan, the melody based on Robert Schumann's "Wild Horseman" from his *Album for the Young* (1953). Popularized by Perry Como in an RCA Victor recording.

Wild is the Wind, words by Ned Washington, music by Dimitri Tiomkin (1957). Title song of a non-musical motion picture starring Anna Mag-

nani and Anthony Quinn (Paramount, 1957), where it was introduced by Johnny Mathis. Mathis' Columbia recording helped to popularize it.

Wild One, words and music by Kal Mann, Bernie Lowe and Dave Appell (1960). Popularized by Bobby Rydell in a Camden recording in 1959.

Wild Rose, words by Clifford Grey, music by Jerome Kern (1920). Introduced by Marilyn Miller and chorus in the musical *Sally* (1920). It was interpolated in the Marilyn Miller screen biography *Look for the Silver Lining* (Warner, 1949).

Wilhelmina, words by Mack Gordon, music by Josef Myrow (1950). Introduced by Betty Grable in the motion-picture musical *Wabash Avenue* (20th Century-Fox, 1950). It was popularized by Perry Como in an RCA Victor recording.

Williams, Bert, composer and lyricist, born Egbert Austin Williams, Antigua, British West Indies, 1875; died New York City, 1922.

See: Let It Alone; My Landlady; Nobody; Somebody Lied.

Williams, Harry H., lyricist, born Faribault, Minnesota, 1879; died Oakland, California, 1922.

See: Van Alstyne, Egbert.

See also: Mickey.

Willow, Weep for Me, words and music by Ann Ronell (1932). Dedicated to George Gershwin, "the only song ever dedicated to him," maintains Ann Ronell, "and the only popular publication with a dedication line, a custom never observed in the popular publishing field." It was introduced by Irene Bailey, vocalist with the Paul Whiteman Orchestra, and was popularized by Ruth Etting. This number is structurally unusual in that there is a change in rhythm notation within the refrain, a practice so unusual in Tin Pan Alley that special permission had to be obtained from the publisher (Irving Berlin) for its use in the sheet-music release. It was interpolated in the motion picture *Love Happy,* starring the Marx Brothers (United Artists, 1949).

Willson, Meredith, composer and lyricist, born Mason City Iowa, 1907.

See: Arm in Arm; Dolce Far Niente; Goodnight, My Someone; Here's Love; He's My Friend; I Ain't Down Yet; I'll Never Say No; Lida Rose; Look, Little Girl; May the Good Lord Bless and Keep You; My Wish; Pine Cones and Holly Berries; Seventy-Six Trombones; Till There Was You; You and I.

Will You Be Mine?. *See:* Earth Angel.

Will You Love Me in December As You Do in May?, words by James J. Walker, music by Ernest R. Ball (1905). This number marked Ernest R. Ball's beginnings as a composer of ballads, and was his first hit song. It was introduced by Janet Allen, a member of the vaudeville team of Allen and McShane. (She subsequently became the first wife of James J. Walker.) It was then heard throughout the country, sold several hundred thousand copies of sheet music and earned for each of its collaborators in excess of $10,-000 in royalties, a sum that at the time represented a fortune to each one. By virtue of this one song, Ernest R. Ball, up to now a $20-a-week employe in the publishing house of Witmark, found himself in a high-income bracket, where he stayed for the rest of his career.

"When I jotted down the words of my December–May song," James J. Walker later recalled, "I knew that I had something around which a capable composer could build a singable melody." And as Ernest R. Ball remembered, when Walker turned the lyric over to him, it was "scribbled on a piece of paper. I read it over. . . . I put the bit of paper in my pocket and, for the next two months, carried the scribbled lines around with me. . . . Bit by bit, I worked out a tune that somehow seemed to fit and, finally, I wrote the music to the words.

"I'll never forget the night when Ernie Ball ran his magical fingers over the keyboard," continues James J. Walker, "plucking the tune he was improvising, note by note. He finally swept both hands over the keys in the broad chords of the

finished melody and I knew that a hit had been born. I clasped Ernie around his shoulders and kissed his cheek."

The song was played when James J. Walker married Janet Allen in 1912. In 1926, when Walker became the Mayor of New York City, the ballad became his theme song; while he held office it was invariably played in his honor wherever he went. When, in 1935, he returned to New York, after his self-imposed exile abroad, the song greeted him; and when he died in 1946 it was sung and played as a final tribute.

The ballad was interpolated in the motion-picture musical *The Eddie Cantor Story* (Warner, 1954).

Will You Remember? (or, Sweetheart), words by Rida Johnson Young, music by Sigmund Romberg (1917). Waltz from the operetta *Maytime* (1917), introduced by Peggy Wood and Charles Purcell; it served throughout the production as a recurrent theme. In the motion-picture adaptation of the operetta (MGM, 1937), it was sung by Nelson Eddy and Jeanette MacDonald. Jane Powell and Vic Damone sang it in Romberg's screen biography *Deep in My Heart* (MGM, 1954).

The Window Cleaners, words by Bert Kalmar, music by Harry Ruby (1923). Introduced in the musical *The Town Clown* (1923). It was revived in the motion-picture musical *Happiness Ahead* (First National, 1934), sung by Dick Powell and Frank McHugh.

Winner, Septimus, composer and lyricist, born Philadelphia, Pennsylvania, 1847; died Philadelphia, Pennsylvania, 1902.

See: Ellie Rhee; Give Us Back Our Old Commander; Listen to the Mocking Bird; What Is Home Without a Mother?; Where, Oh Where, Has My Little Dog Gone?; Whispering Hope.

Wintergreen for President, words by Ira Gershwin, music by George Gershwin (1931). Satirical campaign song used in the torchlight parade scene, promoting the Presidential candidacy of Wintergreen—in the musical *Of Thee I Sing!* (1931); it was sung by the chorus. The melody quotes strains from "Hail, Hail, the Gang's All Here," "Tammany," "A Hot Time in the Old Town Tonight" and "The Stars and Stripes Forever." At one moment there is a suggestion in the melody of Irish and Jewish tunes to point up the fact that the candidate is loved equally by both groups. Oscar Hammerstein II once remarked that this is one of the most notable examples of a true marriage of words and music in popular-song literature, since one cannot hear the title without at once bringing the melody to mind, and vice versa.

Winter Wonderland, words by Dick Smith, music by Felix Bernard (1934). A perennial Yuletide favorite. A Decca recording by the Andrews Sisters in 1950 sold a million disks.

Wishing, words and music by Bud De Sylva. Introduced in the non-musical motion picture *Love Affair,* starring Charles Boyer and Irene Dunne (RKO, 1939). It was subsequently interpolated in the motion-picture musical *George White's Scandals of 1945* (RKO, 1945).

Wishing It Was You, words and music by Clyde Otis and Joy Byers (1965). Popularized by Connie Francis in an MGM recording.

Wish You Were Here, words and music by Harold Rome (1952). Introduced by Jack Cassidy in the musical of the same name (1952). For twenty weeks it was represented on the Hit Parade. Eddie Fisher's recording for RCA Victor sold a million disks.

Wish You Were Here, a musical comedy with book by Arthur Kober and Joshua Logan based on Kober's play *Having a Wonderful Time.* Lyrics and music by Harold Rome. Starring Jack Cassidy, Sheila Bond and Patricia Marand (1952). Original cast recording (RCA Victor).

See: Where Did the Night Go?; Wish You Were Here.

Witchcraft, words by Carolyn Leigh, music by Cy Coleman (1957). Originally written for an unproduced revue. It was introduced by Gerry Matthews in a night-club revue—Julius Monk's production *Take Five.*

It was then popularized by Frank Sinatra in a Capitol recording.

Witch Doctor, words and music by Ross Bagdasarian (1958). Popularized by Ross Bagdasarian (using the pseudonym of David Seville) in a best-selling recording for Liberty. This was the first recording in which "Seville" speeded up or slowed down the speed of his singing by manipulating the recorded tapes, an effect he finally made successful in his Chipmunk recordings (*See:* Christmas Song).

With a Little Bit of Luck, words by Alan Jay Lerner, music by Frederick Loewe (1956). Cockney song (its melody reminiscent of "Listen to the Mocking Bird"), introduced by Stanley Holloway and chorus in the musical play *My Fair Lady* (1956). He also sang it with chorus in the motion-picture adaptation of the musical (Warner, 1964).

With All Her Faults I Love Her Still, words and music by Monroe H. Rosenfeld (1888). Introduced by Dick José with the Primrose and West Minstrels in 1888. The musical director of that company, Theodore Metz, always insisted that Rosenfeld had lifted the tune from a song Metz had earlier written and published in Germany, "Mein Himmel auf Erden," and which had been introduced in America in Wilson's Harlem Pavilion.

With All My Heart, words by Gus Kahn, music by Jimmy McHugh (1935). Introduced by Peggy Conklin in the motion picture *Her Master's Voice,* starring Edward Everett Horton (Paramount, 1936).

With a Song in My Heart, words by Lorenz Hart, music by Richard Rodgers (1929). Introduced by Lillian Taiz and John Hundley in the musical *Spring Is Here* (1929). In the motion-picture adaptation of the musical (First National, 1930), it was sung by Alexander Gray and Bernice Claire.

The idea for this song first came to Rodgers while he was week-ending at Jules Glaenzer's estate in West Hampton, Long Island. After returning to New York the same day,

Rodgers wrote out the entire melody. He then proceeded to Glaenzer's apartment in New York to play it for Glaenzer's appreciative guests.

The song was such a favorite with Jane Froman that her screen biography was named after the song title (20th Century-Fox, 1952). The song itself was sung there on the soundtrack by Jane Froman (for Susan Hayward). The song was also interpolated in several other motion-picture musicals, including *This Is the Life* (Universal, 1944), sung by Donald O'Connor and Susanna Foster; the screen biography of Rodgers and Hart, *Words and Music* (MGM, 1948); and *Painting the Clouds with Sunshine* (Warner, 1951), sung by Dennis Morgan and Lucile Norman.

With a Song in My Heart, a motion-picture musical biography of Jane Froman starring Susan Hayward as Froman (20th Century-Fox, 1952). The score was made up of standards, many of them Jane Froman favorites.

See: Blue Moon; California, Here I Come; Deep in the Heart of Texas; Embraceable You; Get Happy; Give My Regards to Broadway; Indiana; I'll Walk Alone; It's a Good Day; I've Got a Feeling You're Fooling; Stein Song; Tea for Two; That Old Feeling; They're Either Too Young or Too Old; With a Song in My Heart.

With Every Breath I Take, words by Leo Robin, music by Ralph Rainger (1934). Introduced by Bing Crosby in the motion-picture musical *Here Is My Heart* (Paramount, 1934), and further popularized by him in a Decca recording.

With My Eyes Wide Open I'm Dreaming, words by Mack Gordon, music by Harry Revel (1934). Introduced in the motion-picture musical *Shoot the Works*, starring Jack Oakie and Ben Bernie and his orchestra (Paramount, 1934). It was revived by Dean Martin in the motion picture *The Stooge*, starring Dean Martin and Jerry Lewis (Paramount, 1952).

Without a Song, words by Billy Rose and Edward Eliscu, music by Vincent Youmans (1929). Introduced by Lois Deppe and the Jubilee Singers in the musical *Great Day* (1929).

Without a Word of Warning, words by Mack Gordon, music by Harry Revel (1935). Introduced by Bing Crosby in the motion-picture musical *Two for Tonight* (Paramount, 1935), and further popularized by him in a Decca recording.

Gordon and Revel instituted a plagiarism suit against a song called "Lady of Love," in which they felt that the basic melody of "Without a Word of Warning" had been used. The defendant argued that his own melody had come partly out of Johann Strauss' *Fledermaus* and partly out of Victor Herbert's *Sweethearts*—and pleaded the case so successfully that the Gordon and Revel suit was thrown out of court.

Without Love, words by Bud De Sylva and Lew Brown, music by Ray Henderson (1930). Introduced by Grace Brinkley and chorus in the musical *Flying Colors* (1930). In the screen biography of De Sylva, Brown and Henderson, *The Best Things in Life Are Free* (20th Century-Fox, 1956), it was sung by Sheree North.

With Plenty of Money and You (Oh, Baby, What I Couldn't Do), words by Al Dubin, music by Harry Warren (1937). Introduced by Dick Powell in the motion-picture musical *Gold Diggers of 1937* (First National, 1936). It was revived by Doris Day in the motion-picture musical *My Dream Is Yours* (Warner, 1949).

With Red Wine, words by Clifford Grey and P. G. Wodehouse, music by Rudolf Friml (1928). Introduced by Detmar Poppen and chorus in the operetta *The Three Musketeers* (1928).

With So Little to Be Sure Of, words and music by Stephen Sondheim (1964). Introduced by Lee Remick and Harry Guardino in the musical *Anyone Can Whistle* (1964).

With These Hands, words by Benny Davis, music by Abner Silver (1950). Introduced in 1951 by Nelson Eddy, and popularized in 1953 by Eddie

Fisher in a best-selling RCA Victor recording.

Wives and Lovers, words by Hal David, music by Burt F. Bacharach (1963). Inspired by the motion picture of the same name starring Janet Leigh and Van Johnson (Paramount, 1963). The song was popularized by Jack Jones in a Kapp recording which received a "Grammy" Award from the National Academy of Recording Arts and Sciences for the best vocal performance of the year by a male singer. This is one of the few successful popular songs that advises women how to keep their men *after* marriage rather than before it.

The Wizard of Oz, a musical extravaganza with book and lyrics by L. Frank Baum adapted from Baum's novel. Music by A. Baldwin Sloane and Paul Tietjens. Starring Fred Stone and David Montgomery (1903).
The motion-picture adaptation starred Judy Garland, then only fourteen (MGM, 1939). The entire stage score was displaced by new songs by E. Y. Harburg and Harold Arlen. Soundtrack recording (MGM).
See: Hurrah for Baffin's Bay; Over the Rainbow; We're Off to See the Wizard of Oz.

The Wizard of the Nile, an operetta with book and lyrics by Harry B. Smith. Music by Victor Herbert. This was Herbert's first successful stage score. Starring Frank Daniels and Dorothy Norton (1939).
See: My Angeline; Star Light, Star Bright.

Wodehouse, P. G., lyricist, born Pelham Grenville Wodehouse, Guildford, Surrey, England, 1881.
See: Kern, Jerome.

Wolverton Mountain, words and music by Merle Kilgore and Claude King (1962). Popularized by Claude King in a Columbia recording.

A Woman in Love, words and music by Frank Loesser (1955). Written for the motion-picture adaptation of the musical *Guys and Dolls* (MGM, 1955), where it was introduced by Marlon Brando. The song was popularized by Frankie Laine in a Columbia recording.

The Woman in the Shoe, words by Arthur Freed, music by Nacio Herb Brown (1929). Introduced in the motion-picture musical *Lord Byron of Broadway,* starring Ethelind Terry (MGM, 1930).

A Woman Is a Sometime Thing, words by DuBose Heyward, music by George Gershwin (1935). Introduced by Eddie Matthews in the folk opera *Porgy and Bess* (1935). In the motion-picture adaptation of the opera (Columbia, 1959), it was sung by Leslie Scott.

A Woman Is Only a Woman, But a Good Cigar Is a Smoke, words by Harry B. Smith, music by Victor Herbert (1905). A cynical comedy number introduced by Melville Stewart in the musical *Miss Dolly Dollars* (1905). The title, lifted from a line in Kipling's *The Betrothed,* became a catch phrase in the early 1900s.

A Woman's Prerogative, words by Johnny Mercer, music by Harold Arlen (1946). Introduced by Pearl Bailey in the musical play *St. Louis Woman* (1946).

Wonder Bar, words by Al Dubin, music by Harry Warren (1934). Introduced by Al Jolson in the motion-picture musical of the same name (Warner, 1934).

Wonderful Copenhagen, words and music by Frank Loesser (1952). Introduced by Danny Kaye in the motion-picture musical *Hans Christian Andersen* (Samuel Goldwyn, 1953).

Wonderful One, words by Dorothy Terris, music by Paul Whiteman and Ferde Grofé, the melody adapted from a theme by Marshall Nielan (1922). Introduced and popularized by Paul Whiteman and his orchestra in night clubs and other public appearances and in a Victor recording. In the non-musical motion picture, *Flight for Freedom,* starring Rosalind Russell and Fred MacMurray (MGM, 1943), it was used in the background music as a recurrent theme. It was used again as a recurrent theme in the non-musical motion picture *Thirty Seconds Over Tokyo,* starring Spencer Tracy and Van Johnson (MGM, 1944). The song was also interpolated in the motion picture *Margie,* starring

Jeanne Crain (20th Century-Fox, 1946).

A Wonderful Time Up There, words and music by L. Abernathy (1958). Popularized by Pat Boone in a best-selling Dot recording.

Wonderful Town, a musical comedy with book by Joseph Fields and Jerome Chodorov based on their play *My Sister Eileen,* in turn derived from stories by Ruth McKenney. Lyrics by Betty Comden and Adolph Green. Music by Leonard Bernstein. Starring Rosalind Russell and Edith (Edie) Adams (1953). Original cast recording (Decca).

See: My Darlin' Eileen; Ohio; A Quiet Girl.

Wonderful, Wonderful, words by Ben Raleigh, music by Sherman Edwards (1957). Popularized by Johnny Mathis in a Columbia recording, which was his first success on disks. It was revived in 1963 by the Tymes in a best-selling Parkway recording.

A Wonderful Day Like Today, words and music by Leslie Bricusse and Anthony Newley (1965). Introduced by Anthony Newley in the musical *The Roar of the Greasepaint—the Smell of the Crowd* (1965). Popularized by Sammy Davis in a Reprise recording.

Wonderland by Night, words by Lincoln Chase, music by Klauss Gunter Newman (1961). Popularized by Bert Kaempfert and his orchestra in a Decca recording.

Wonder Why, words by Sammy Cahn, music by Nicholas Brodszky (1950). Introduced by Jane Powell in the motion-picture musical *Rich, Young and Pretty* (MGM, 1951).

Won't You Be My Honey?, words by Jack Drislane, music by Theodore F. Morse (1907).

Won't You Come Over to My House?, words by Harry H. Williams, music by Egbert Van Alstyne (1906).

Woodchopper's Ball, words by Joe Bishop, music by Woody Herman (1939). A fast blues popularized by Woody Herman and his band, whose recording in April of 1939 became the group's first best-selling disk. The number was interpolated for Woody Herman and his band in the motion-picture musical *What's Cooking?,* starring the Andrews Sisters (Universal, 1942). The number was revived by Woody Herman and his band in 1947 in a best-selling recording for Decca.

Woodman, Spare That Tree, words by George Pope Morris, music by Henry Russell (1837). One of America's earliest successful sentimental ballads. It was introduced and popularized by Henry Russell in his recitals throughout the country.

The idea for the ballad came to its composer during a drive in the country with his friend George Morris, a poet. Morris told Russell about a tree which he, as a boy, had watched his father plant; Morris then suggested they drive over to see it. The two friends arrived just as a farmer-caretaker was about to cut down the tree for firewood. Morris was able to convince the farmer to spare the tree.

The impact of Russell's ballad on audiences was described by a contemporary of his, John Hill Hewitt: "He had finished the last verse. . . . The audience was spellbound for a moment, and then poured out a volume of applause that shook the building to its foundation. In the midst of this tremendous evidence of their boundless gratification, a snowy-headed gentleman with great anxiety depicted in his venerable features arose and demanded silence. He asked with tremulous voice: 'Mr. Russell, in the name of Heaven, tell me, was the tree spared?' 'It was, sir,' replied the vocalist. 'Thank God, thank God, I can breathe again,' and he sat down, perfectly overcome by emotion."

Woodman, Woodman, Spare That Tree, words and music by Irving Berlin (1911). Written for Bert Williams, who introduced it in the *Ziegfeld Follies of 1911.* It then became one of the high spots of his repertory. His delivery of this and other Bert Williams specialties was unique, as described by Langston Hughes: "A spotlight would make a great white circle against the black velvet curtains at the left of the stage, the orchestra would strike a few chords. Then out of the wings would protrude a lone hand in a white glove, then another white-gloved hand with slowly moving fingers. And just the droll motion of those two hands, before Bert Williams himself came into view, would make an audience shake with laughter. Then Williams would emerge, sing a little and talk a little, and disappear."

Woods, Harry M., composer and lyricist, born North Chelmsford, Massachusetts, 1896.

See (Lyrics by Mort Dixon): I'm Looking Over a Four Leaf Clover; Just Like the Butterfly; River, Stay Away from My Door.

See also: I'm Go'n' South; A Little Kiss Each Morning; The Man from the South; Me, Too; Side by Side; Try a Little Tenderness; When the Moon Comes Over the Mountain; When the Red, Red Robin Comes Bob, Bob, Bobbin' Along.

Woody Woodpecker, words and music by George Tibbles and Ramey Idriss (1947). Popularized in 1948 by Kay Kyser and his orchestra in a Columbia recording that sold a million disks. The song was based on the motion-picture cartoon *Wet Blanket Policy* released in 1948, whose main character was Woody Woodpecker.

Words and Music, a motion-picture musical biography of Rodgers and Hart, starring Tom Drake as Richard Rodgers and Mickey Rooney as Lorenz Hart (MGM, 1948). The all-star cast also included June Allyson, Judy Garland, Lena Horne, Gene Kelly and others. The score was made up entirely of Rodgers and Hart standards. Soundtrack recording (MGM).

See: Blue Moon; The Blue Room; Ev'rything I've Got Belongs to You; I Married an Angel; I Wish I Were in Love Again; Johnny One Note; The Lady Is a Tramp; Manhattan; Mountain Greenery; My Heart Stood Still; Spring Is Here; There's a Small Hotel; This Can't Be Love; Thou Swell; Way Out West; Where or When; Where's That Rainbow?; With a Song in My Heart; You Took Advantage of Me.

The Words Are in My Heart, words by Al Dubin, music by Harry Warren (1935). Introduced in the motion-picture musical *Gold Diggers of Broadway* (First National, 1935).

Work, Henry Clay, composer and lyricist, born Middletown, Connecticut, 1832; died Hartford, Connecticut, 1884.

See: Babylon Is Fallen; Come Home, Father; Grafted into the Army; Grandfather's Clock; Kingdom Coming; Marching Through Georgia; Wake, Nicodemus.

The World Is Waiting for the Sunrise, words by Eugene Lockhart, music by Ernest Seitz (1919). The Lockhart who is credited as the lyricist is Gene Lockhart, later famous as a motion-picture actor. The song, a hit in the 1920s, was revived in 1949 by Les Paul and Mary Ford, whose Capitol recording sold a million disks.

The World Is Your Balloon, words by E. Y. Harburg, music by Sammy Fain (1950). Introduced by Barbara Cook (in her first Broadway appearance) in the musical *Flahooley* (1950).

The World Outside, words by Carl Sigman, music by Richard Addinsell, melody based on a theme from Addinsell's *Warsaw Concerto* (1958). The song was popularized by the Four Aces in a Decca recording.

Would I Love You? (Love You, Love You), words by Bob Russell, music by Harold Spina (1951). Popularized by Patti Page in a Mercury recording.

Wouldn't It Be Loverly?, words by Alan Jay Lerner, music by Frederick Loewe (1956). Introduced by Julie Andrews in the musical play *My Fair Lady* (1956). In the motion-picture adaptation of the musical (Warner, 1964), it was sung on the soundtrack by Marni Nixon (for Audrey Hepburn).

Would You?, words by Arthur Freed, music by Nacio Herb Brown (1936). Introduced by Jeanette MacDonald in the motion picture *San Francisco* (MGM, 1936). It was revived by Debbie Reynolds in the motion-picture musical *Singin' in the Rain* (MGM, 1952).

Would You Like to Take a Walk?,

words by Mort Dixon and Billy Rose, music by Harry Warren (1930). Introduced by Ethel Norris, Tom Monroe and ensemble in the revue *Sweet and Low* (1930).

The Wreck of the Old 97, words and music by Henry Whittier, Charles W. Noell and Fred J. Lewey, based on Henry C. Work's melody for "The Ship That Never Returned" (1924). A celebrated railroad ballad inspired by the ride of a train, "de old 97," from Lynchburg to Danville, Virginia. Riding at a ninety-mile-an-hour clip, the train was wrecked; its engineer was killed at the throttle. The ballad points up the moral: "Never speak harsh words to your husband,/He may leave you and never return."

Wright, Robert, composer and lyricist, born Daytona Beach, Florida, 1914. *See:* Forrest, George "Chet."

Wringle, Wrangle, words and music by Stan Jones (1956). Introduced by Fess Parker in the Walt Disney motion picture *Westward Ho, The Wagons* (Buena Vista, 1956).

Write Me a Letter from Home, words and music by Will S. Hays (1866). One of the composer's first successful ballads not inspired by the Civil War; it sold over 350,000 copies of sheet music.

Written on the Wind, words by Sammy Cahn, music by Victor Young (1956). Introduced by the Four Aces on the soundtrack, sung under the titles of the motion picture of the same name starring Rock Hudson and Lauren Bacall (Universal, 1956).

Wunderbar, words and music by Cole Porter (1948). A take-off on "shmaltzy" Viennese waltzes. It was introduced by Alfred Drake and Patricia Morison in the musical play *Kiss Me, Kate* (1948). In the motion-picture adaptation of the musical (MGM, 1953), it was sung by Kathryn Grayson and Howard Keel.

Y

Yacka Hula Hickey Dula, words by E. Ray Goetz and Joe Young, music by Pete Wendling (1916). Introduced and popularized by Al Jolson in the Winter Garden extravaganza *Robinson Crusoe, Jr.* (1916). The song was revived in the motion-picture musical *Applause*, starring Helen Morgan (Paramount, 1929).

Yakety Yak, words and music by Jerry Leiber and Mike Stoller (1958). Popularized by the Coasters in an Atco recording.

Yale Bull Dog. *See:* Bull Dog.

The Yam, words and music by Irving Berlin (1938). Introduced by Fred Astaire and Ginger Rogers in the motion-picture musical *Carefree* (1938). "I think," wrote Fred Astaire, "we had as much fun with 'The Yam' as any number we did together. It was not exactly a dance for popular ballroom use but it made a good screen gimmick."

The Yama Yama Man, words by Collin Davis, music by Karl Hoschna (1908). Introduced by Bessie McCoy in the operetta *The Three Twins* (1908). She scored such a triumph with this number that overnight it helped make her a star; from then on she was identified as "the Yama Yama girl." Dressed in a cone-shaped cap and black velvet suit, she delivered the song with a tiny pouting mouth while performing a dance step.

"The Yama Yama Man" was not originally in the score of *The Three Twins.* While the show was trying out in Chicago, the producer expressed a need for some strong material for his star. Hoschna complied with "Yama Yama Man," which was hastily written in Chicago and just as rapidly put into rehearsal.

The song was interpolated in the motion-picture musical *The Story of the Castles* (RKO, 1939).

Yankee Doodle, the most famous popular song in the American colonies, author of words and music not known (c. 1765). Some trace this melody to a song of French vineyard workers; some, to the melody of a Spanish sword dance; some, to a German harvest tune; some, to a Dutch peasant song. The most likely source, however, was an English nursery rhyme, "Lucy Locket."

The song probably came to the colonies during the French and Indian War—and under the following circumstances. Richard Shuckburg, a British army physician, was so amused at the sight of the ragged and disheveled troops under General Braddock that he decided to mock them. In or about 1755 he improvised a set of nonsense lyrics to an English tune with which he had long been familiar; he palmed off this concoction on the colonial troops as the latest English army song. Dr. Shuckburg's nonsense song was "Yankee Doodle." It grew so popular with the British troops in the colonies that for the next two decades they used it to taunt the colonists, sometimes by singing it loudly outside church during religious services.

In 1767 the song was interpolated in an early American comic opera, *The Disappointment of Andrew Barton*. One year later the song received attention in the press for the first time when the *Journal of the Times* in Boston reported: "The British fleet was brought to anchor near Castle William. . . . Those passing in boats observed great rejoicing and that the 'Yankee Doodle' song was the capital piece of band music."

With the outbreak of the Revolution, the colonials appropriated "Yankee Doodle." It became a favorite in every camp and was frequently heard in battle, in defeat and victory. It was played at the final surrender of General Cornwallis at Yorktown on October 19, 1781.

"Yankee Doodle" retained its popularity after the Revolution. Benjamin Carr used it in an orchestral medley, *Federal Overture*, written in 1794. A century later visiting European virtuosos often wrote variations, fantasies or caprices based on "Yankee Doodle" for the delectation of American concert audiences; among them were Anton Rubinstein and Henri Vieuxtemps.

See also: The Battle of the Kegs.

Yankee Doodle Blues, words by Irving Caesar and Bud De Sylva, music by George Gershwin (1922). Interpolated in the revue *Spice of 1922*. John Howard Lawson interpolated it in his expressionist play *Processional* as a recurring musical theme. The song appeared in several motion-picture musicals, including the George Gershwin screen biography *Rhapsody in Blue* (Warner, 1945) and *I'll Get By* (20th Century-Fox, 1950); in the latter it was sung by June Haver, Gloria De Haven and chorus.

The Yankee Doodle Boy, words and music by George M. Cohan (1904). Introduced by George M. Cohan in his first full-length musical, *Little Johnny Jones* (1904). It was sung by Eddie Buzzell in the motion-picture adaptation of the musical (First National, 1929). Jimmy Cagney sang it in the screen biography of George M. Cohan, *Yankee Doodle Dandy* (Warner, 1942). In the motion-picture musical *The Seven Little Foys* (Paramount, 1955), it served as music for a buck-and-wing for Jimmy Cagney, once again enacting the part of George M. Cohan.

Yankee Doodle Dandy, a motion-picture musical biography of George M. Cohan, starring James Cagney (winner of the Academy Award) as George M. Cohan with Joan Leslie (Warner, 1942). The score was made up of George M. Cohan standards.

See: Forty-Five Minutes from Broadway; Give My Regards to Broadway; Harrigan; Mary's a Grand Old Name; Yankee Doodle Boy; You're a Grand Old Flag.

Yearning (Just for You), words by Benny Davis, music by Joe Burke (1925). Popularized by Paul Whiteman and his orchestra and by Guy Lombardo and the Royal Canadians.

Yellen, Jack, lyricist, born Poland, 1892.

See: Ager, Milton; Fain, Sammy; Pollack, Lew.

See also: At the Codfish Ball; It's an Old Southern Custom; Oh, You Nasty Man; Sweet and Hot.

Yellow Bird, words and music by Norman Luboff, Marilyn Keith and Alan Bergman adapted from a West Indian folk song (1958). Introduced by the Norman Luboff Choir, but popularized in 1961 in recordings by Arthur Lyman for Hi Fi and by Roger Williams for Kapp. This song is reported to have been one of the last pieces of music heard by President Kennedy—at his hotel suite in Fort Worth, Texas, one day before his assassination.

The Yellow Rose of Texas, a marching song, whose author is identified merely as "J.K." (1853). It was written for and became popular in minstrel shows. It then achieved considerable circulation during the Civil War, both in the North and in the

South—in its original form and in various parodies. The melody was used for "The Song of the Texas Rangers." In an adaptation by Don George (1955), the "Yellow Rose of Texas" was popularized by Mitch Miller and his orchestra and chorus in a Columbia recording that sold a million disks. A best-selling recording was also made by Johnny Desmond for Coral. The song was interpolated in the motion picture *Night Stage to Galveston,* starring Gene Autry (Columbia, 1952).

Yes, words by Dory Langdon, music by André Previn (1962). Introduced by Judy Garland, but popularized by Doris Day in a Columbia recording.

Yes Indeed!, words and music by Sy Oliver (1941). Described as a "jive spiritual." It was introduced by Tommy Dorsey and his orchestra (vocal by Jo Stafford and Sy Oliver) in an RCA Victor recording. It was popularized in a best-selling Decca recording by Bob and Bing Crosby with Connee Boswell; this was one of Bob Crosby's most successful disks.

Yes, My Darling Daughter, words and music by Jack Lawrence adapted from a Yiddish folk song (1940). Introduced by Dinah Shore, whom it launched on her meteoric career. Eddie Cantor heard her audition it and was so impressed by both the song and the singer that he bought out the rights for the one and contracted the other to appear on his radio program. Dinah Shore's recording for Columbia became her first success on disks.

Yes, Sir, That's My Baby, words by Gus Kahn, music by Walter Donaldson (1925). Written for and introduced and popularized by Eddie Cantor. He sang it on the soundtrack of the motion-picture musical *The Eddie Cantor Story* (Warner, 1954).

During one of Gus Kahn's visits to Eddie Cantor at his home in Great Neck, Long Island, he played with a mechanical pig that belonged to little Marjorie Cantor. As the animal jogged along clumsily, Kahn spontaneously improvised the lines "Yes, sir, that's my baby, no, sir, don't mean maybe" to the rhythm of the

toy's movements. Thus an idea for a song lyric was hatched. Kahn's partner, Donaldson, provided the tune, and the song was published by Irving Berlin, Inc., and introduced by Cantor. After it had become a major hit, Kahn showed his royalty check to Cantor with the wry comment: "That's a lot of money for a Jewish boy to make out of a pig."

Danny Thomas and Doris Day sang it in the Gus Kahn screen biography *I'll See You in My Dreams* (Warner, 1951). The song was also interpolated in the motion picture *Broadway,* starring George Raft and Pat O'Brien (Universal, 1942).

Yesterdays, words by Otto Harbach, music by Jerome Kern (1933). Introduced by Fay Templeton in the musical *Roberta* (1933). It was sung in both motion-picture adaptations of the musical: in *Roberta* (RKO, 1935) and in *Lovely to Look At* (MGM, 1952). It was also interpolated in the Jerome Kern screen biography *Till the Clouds Roll By* (MGM, 1946).

Yes, We Have No Bananas, words and music by Frank Silver and Irving Cohn (1923). One of the most successful nonsense songs of the 1920s. The writers got their idea by overhearing a Greek fruit peddler tell a customer: "Yes, we have no bananas." Frank Silver and Irving Cohn introduced their song in a New York restaurant, but it failed to catch fire. Then, in 1923, Eddie Cantor saw the song in manuscript while *Make It Snappy* (a revue in which Cantor was then starring) was playing in Philadelphia. Held over in that city for an extended run, the show needed some new material, since people were coming to see it a second time. Cantor decided to interpolate "Yes, We Have No Bananas" in one of his routines, one Wednesday matinee. The audience response was so enthusiastic that Cantor had to sing chorus after chorus; the show was stopped cold for over a quarter of an hour. Cantor now made the song a permanent part of his act, and he always brought down the house with it. His

Victor recording became a best seller—one of many successful releases of this number. By the end of 1923 everybody was singing "Yes, We Have No Bananas" throughout the country. In the *Music Box Revue of 1923* it was ridiculed in a performance in which it was presented in the grand-operatic manner of the Sextet from *Lucia di Lammermoor* —the performers being Grace Moore, John Steel, Joseph Santley, Frank Tinney, Florence Moore and Lora Sonderson. "Yes, We Have No Bananas" was interpolated in the motion-picture musical *Mammy*, starring Al Jolson (Warner, 1930); Eddie Cantor sang it on the soundtrack of the motion-picture musical *The Eddie Cantor Story* (Warner, 1954).

A Yiddisha Momme, words by Jack Yellen, music by Jack Yellen and Lew Pollack (1925). Yellen originally wrote the song (lyrics and music) for his own pleasure, a tribute to his mother who had died recently. Then, a few years later, he asked Lew Pollack to work over the melody with him. "On an impulse," Yellen has written to this editor, "I called up Sophie Tucker at the Claridge Hotel in New York. She bawled me out for spoiling her sleeping pill, but she listened, and when I finished singing, she was weeping. Between gulps, she asked me to send her a copy. She wrote me that her agents and friends suggested the title be changed to 'Jewish' or 'Hebrew Mama,' being afraid of the word 'Yiddish.' I told her that if she sang it, it would be 'Yiddisha Momme' or nothing at all; and what is more, I insisted that she should sing the chorus in Yiddish, the way I had written it."

Sophie Tucker introduced it at the Palace Theatre in New York in 1925, and created an instant furor. It became a Sophie Tucker specialty, second in importance in her career only to "Some of These Days." She sang "A Yiddisha Momme" not only in all of the key cities in the United States but also in the leading capitals of Europe.

As she wrote in her autobiography: "I have found whenever I have sung 'A Yiddisha Momme' in the United States or Europe, Gentiles have loved the song and have called for it. They didn't need to understand the Yiddish words. They knew by instinct what I was saying. . . . All over the Continent this is the song which has always identified me, as 'Some of These Days' is recognized as my theme song in America."

In recent years this intrinsically Jewish number has been successfully performed by many non-Jewish performers, including Connie Francis, Hazel Scott, Johnny Desmond, Vic Damone and Billy Daniels.

Yip-I-Addy-I-Ay, words by Will Cobb, music by John H. Flynn (1908). A nonsense song introduced by Blanche Ring in the musical *The Merry Widow and the Devil* (1908), to become one of her specialties; in 1908 she made a historic recording of it for Victor. The song was interpolated in the motion picture *New York Town,* starring Mary Martin and Fred MacMurray (Paramount, 1941).

Yip, Yip, Yaphank, a World War I all-soldier show with book and songs by Irving Berlin. The cast was made up principally of soldiers stationed at Camp Upton, New York, including Irving Berlin himself (1918).

See: Oh, How I Hate to Get Up in the Morning; Mandy.

Yoo Hoo, words by Bud De Sylva, music by Al Jolson (1921). Introduced by Al Jolson in the Winter Garden extravaganza *Bombo* (1921), where it was an interpolation. It was used in the motion picture *Always a Bridesmaid,* starring the Andrews Sisters (Universal, 1943).

You, words by Harold Adamson, music by Walter Donaldson (1936). Introduced in the motion picture *The Great Ziegfeld,* starring William Powell and Luise Rainer (MGM, 1936).

You Ain't Heard Nothin' Yet, words and music by Al Jolson, Gus Kahn and Bud De Sylva (1919). A song inspired by Jolson's favorite aside to his audiences. He interpolated the number in the Winter Garden extravaganza *Sinbad* (1918).

You Ain't Talking to Me, words and music by Shelton Brooks (1910). One of Al Jolson's first hit songs, introduced and popularized by him at the Winter Garden.

You Alone (or, Solo Tu), words by Al Stillman, music by Robert Allen (1953). Popularized by Perry Como in an RCA Victor recording.

You Always Hurt the One You Love, words and music by Doris Fisher and Allan Roberts (1944). Popularized by the Mills Brothers, whose Decca recording sold a million disks.

You and I, words and music by Meredith Willson (1941). Willson's first major song success. It was represented on the Hit Parade for nineteen weeks. It was popularized in a best-selling recording for Bluebird by Glenn Miller and his orchestra (vocal by Ray Eberle). It was used as the signature music for the Maxwell House radio program.

You and the Night and the Music, words by Howard Dietz, music by Arthur Schwartz (1934). Introduced by Georges Metaxa and Libby Holman in the musical play *Revenge With Music* (1934). It was interpolated in the motion-picture musical *The Band Wagon* (MGM, 1953).

You Are Beautiful, words by Oscar Hammerstein II, music by Richard Rodgers (1958). Introduced by Ed Kenny and Juanita Hall in the musical *Flower Drum Song* (1958). It was also used in the motion-picture adaptation of the musical (Universal, 1961).

You Are Free, words by William Le Baron, music by Victor Jacobi (1919). Introduced by John Charles Thomas and Wilda Bennett in the operetta *Apple Blossoms* (1919).

You Are Love, words by Oscar Hammerstein II, music by Jerome Kern (1927). Introduced by Howard Marsh and Norma Terris in the musical play *Show Boat* (1927). In the 1936 motion-picture adaptation of the musical (Universal), it was sung by Irene Dunne and Allan Jones; in the 1951 screen version (MGM), by Kathryn Grayson and Howard Keel.

You Are My Destiny, words and music by Paul Anka (1958). Introduced and popularized by Paul Anka in an ABC Paramount recording that sold a million disks.

You Are My Lucky Star. *See:* My Lucky Star.

You Are My Sunshine, words and music by Jimmie Davis and Charles Mitchell (1940). Introduced in the motion picture *Take Me Back to Oklahoma,* starring Tex Ritter (Monogram, 1940). It was then interpolated in the motion picture *In the Groove,* starring Martha Tilton and Donald O'Connor (Universal, 1942). The number served as a campaign song for its co-author, James H. (Jimmie) Davis, in his successful drive for the Governorship of the State of Louisiana in 1944.

You Are Sixteen, words by Oscar Hammerstein II, music by Richard Rodgers (1959). Introduced by Lauri Peters and Brian Davies in the musical play *The Sound of Music* (1959). In the motion-picture adaptation of the musical (20th Century-Fox, 1965), it was featured by Charmian Carr and Daniel Truhitte.

You Are Woman, words by Bob Merrill, music by Jule Styne (1964). Introduced by Barbra Streisand in the musical *Funny Girl* (1964).

You Belong to Me, words and music by Pee Wee King, Redd Stewart and Chilton Price (1952). Introduced by Joni James in her disk debut for Smash. It was then popularized by Jo Stafford in a Columbia recording and by Patti Page for Mercury. It was used as a recurrent theme in the background music for the motion picture *Forbidden,* starring Tony Curtis and Joanne Dru (Universal, 1954). It was successfully revived in 1962 by the Duprees in a best-selling recording for Coed.

You Belong to My Heart, words by Ray Gilbert, music by Augustin Lara (1944). Introduced by Dora Luz in the Walt Disney full-length animated production *Three Caballeros* (RKO, 1944). It was revived by Ezio Pinza in the motion picture

Mr. Imperium, starring Pinza and Lana Turner (MGM, 1951). The song was popularized in 1945 in a Decca recording by Bing Crosby with Xavier Cugat and his orchestra.

You Brought a New Kind of Love to Me, words by Irving Kahal, music by Pierre Norman and Sammy Fain (1930). Introduced by Maurice Chevalier in the motion-picture musical *The Big Pond* (Paramount, 1930). It was interpolated in the Marx Brothers' motion-picture extravaganza *Monkey Business* (Paramount, 1931). In 1963 it was revived in the motion picture *A New Kind of Love,* starring Paul Newman and Joanne Woodward (Paramount), where it was sung on the soundtrack, under the titles, by Frank Sinatra.

You Call Everybody Darlin', words and music by Sam Martin, Ben Trace and Clem Watts (1946). It was popularized by Al Trace and his orchestra in a Regent recording.

You Call It Madness, But I Call It Love, words by Gladys Du Bois and Paul Gregory, music by Russ Columbo and Con Conrad (1931). Introduced by Russ Columbo and his orchestra, and subsequently popularized by Tony Martin in an RCA Victor recording.

You Can Do No Wrong, words and music by Cole Porter (1948). Introduced by Judy Garland in the motion-picture musical *The Pirate,* (MGM, 1948).

You Can't Fool All the People All the Time, words by Frederick Ranken, music by Henry Hadley (1903). Introduced and popularized by Marie Cahill in the musical *Nancy Brown* (1903).

You Can't Get a Man with a Gun, words and music by Irving Berlin (1946). Comedy number introduced by Ethel Merman in the musical *Annie, Get Your Gun* (1946). In the motion-picture adaptation of the musical (MGM, 1950), it was sung by Betty Hutton.

You Can't Make Your Shimmy Shake on Tea, words and music by Irving Berlin (1919). A comedy number spoofing Prohibition, introduced by

Bert Williams in the *Ziegfeld Follies of 1919.*

You Can't Play Every Instrument in the Band, words by Joseph Cawthorn, music by John L. Golden (1912). Introduced by Joseph Cawthorn in the musical *The Sunshine Girl* (1912).

Cawthorn and Golden were one day discussing the different instruments of the orchestra and what made people begin to study some of them. One word led to another until Cawthorn said he had the idea for a song lyric; Golden offered to write the music. Golden tells the rest of the story in his autobiography: "Somehow I couldn't get a tune that satisfied me. Meanwhile, rehearsals of *The Sunshine Girl* were going on . . . and Cawthorn kept telephoning me to ask whether I had finished the song. After the fifth call I had to tell him something; so I said I had it and would deliver it in a day or so." At one of the rehearsals Golden was called upon to play his new tune. "There I was with no melody in my mind and with no notion of how to begin one. . . . I coughed and started to strum some chords. Then my fingers found a melody and to that melody Cawthorn began to sing the verses he held in his hand. When it was finished, there was a wild burst of applause and the whole company . . . assured me it was a wonderful melody. It *was,* it always *had* been, ever since Mr. Sullivan wrote it as a tenor solo in the first act of *The Mikado* and called it 'A Wandering Minstrel I.' . . . The song, known as 'You Can't Play Every Instrument in the Band,' made thousands of dollars and was one of the biggest stage successes I ever wrote. I changed the chorus before it actually went into publication, but I never had a chance to alter the verse and there it stands . . . a printed evidence of the inspiration and service which a knowledge of the great composers can be to a man in the popular music game."

You Can't Play in Our Yard Any More, words by Philip Wingate, music by H. W. Petrie (1894). A sequel to the successful "I Don't Want to Play in Your Yard," published one year earlier.

You Can't Stop Me from Dreaming, words and music by Cliff Friend and Dave Franklin (1937).

You Can't Stop Me from Loving You, words by Gerber and Murphy, music by Henry I. Marshall (1912). Revived in the late 1920s by Ethel Waters to become a staple in her repertory.

You Cheated, words and music by Don Burch (1958). Popularized by the Shields in a Dot recording.

You Couldn't Be Cuter, words by Dorothy Fields, music by Jerome Kern (1938). Introduced in the motion-picture musical *Joy of Living*, starring Irene Dunne and Douglas Fairbanks, Jr. (RKO, 1938).

You'd Be So Nice to Come Home To, words and music by Cole Porter (1942). Introduced by Janet Blair and Don Ameche in the motion-picture musical *Something to Shout About* (Columbia, 1943).

You'd Be Surprised, words and music by Irving Berlin (1919). Comedy number introduced by Eddie Cantor in the *Ziegfeld Follies* of 1919. Eddie Cantor's recording for Victor, made in 1919, was his only one to sell a million disks. The song also sold three quarters of a million copies of sheet music within a year of its publication, and almost one hundred and fifty thousand piano rolls. It was revived in the motion-picture musical *There's No Business Like Show Business* (20th Century Fox, 1954), sung by Dan Dailey.

You Dear, words by Ralph Freed, music by Sammy Fain (1944). Introduced by Buddy Moreno with Harry James and his orchestra in the motion-picture musical *Two Girls and a Sailor*, starring Van Johnson, June Allyson and Gloria De Haven (MGM, 1944).

You Didn't Have to Tell Me (I Knew It All the Time), words and music by Walter Donaldson (1931).

You Don't Have to Know the Language, words by Johnny Burke, music by James Van Heusen (1947). Introduced by Bing Crosby in the motion picture *The Road to Rio* (Paramount, 1947). It was popularized by Bing Crosby and the Andrews Sisters in a best-selling Decca recording.

You Don't Know Me, words and music by Cindy Walker and Eddy Arnold (1955). Popularized in 1956 by Eddy Arnold in an RCA Victor recording. It was revived in 1962 by Ray Charles in a best-selling recording for ABC Paramount.

You Don't Know Paree, words and music by Cole Porter (1929). Introduced by William Gaxton in the musical *Fifty Million Frenchmen* (1929).

You Do Something to Me, words and music by Cole Porter (1929). Introduced by William Gaxton and Genevieve Tobin in the musical *Fifty Million Frenchmen* (1929). In the Cole Porter screen biography *Night and Day* (Warner, 1946), it was sung by Ginny Simms and chorus. The song was also interpolated in other motion-picture musicals. These included *Starlift* (Warner, 1951), sung by Doris Day; *Because You're Mine* (MGM, 1952), sung by Mario Lanza; *The Helen Morgan Story* (Warner, 1957), sung on the soundtrack by Gogi Grant (for Ann Blyth); and the motion-picture adaptation of the musical *Can-Can* (20th Century-Fox, 1960).

You Do the Darnd'st Things, Baby, words by Sidney D. Mitchell, music by Lew Pollack (1936). Introduced in the motion-picture musical *Pigskin Parade*, starring Jack Haley and Patsy Kelly (20th Century-Fox, 1936).

You Fascinate Me So, words by Carolyn Leigh, music by Cy Coleman (1958). Introduced by Jean Arnold in a night-club revue—Julius Monk's *Demi-Dozen* (1958). It was then popularized by Peggy Lee in a Capitol recording.

You Go to My Head, words by Haven Gillespie, music by J. Fred Coots (1938). The song was written two years before its publication, but was turned down by most of the leading publishers before Remick decided to issue it. It was introduced by Glen Gray and the Casa Loma Orchestra, with Kenny Sargent doing the vocal. It was popularized by Frank Sinatra in a Capitol recording.

You Keep Coming Back Like A Song, words and music by Irving Berlin (1943). Introduced by Bing Crosby in the motion-picture musical *Blue Skies* (MGM, 1946), and further popularized by him in a Decca recording.

You Know and I Know (and We Both Understand), words by Schuyler Greene, music by Jerome Kern (1915). Introduced by Alice Dovey and George Anderson in the first Princess Theatre production, *Nobody Home* (1915).

You Let Me Down, words by Al Dubin, music by Harry Warren (1935). Introduced by Jane Froman in the motion-picture musical *Stars Over Broadway* (Warner, 1935).

You'll Always Be the Same Sweet Girl, words by Andrew B. Sterling, music by Harry von Tilzer (1915).

You'll Never Know, words by Mack Gordon, music by Harry Warren (1943). Introduced by Alice Faye (singing into the mouthpiece of a telephone) in the motion-picture musical *Hello, Frisco, Hello* (20th Century-Fox, 1943). It received the Academy Award. Dick Haymes' recording for Decca sold a million disks. Alice Faye sang it again in the motion-picture musical *Four Jills in a Jeep* (20th Century-Fox, 1944).

You'll Never Walk Alone, words by Oscar Hammerstein II, music by Richard Rodgers (1945). Inspirational song introduced by Christine Johnson in the musical play *Carousel* (1945). In the motion-picture adaptation of the musical (20th Century-Fox, 1956), it was sung by Claramae Turner.

You Made Me Love You (I Didn't Want to Do It), words by Joe McCarthy, music by James V. Monaco (1913). Introduced by Al Jolson in the Winter Garden extravaganza *The Honeymoon Express* (1913), where it was an interpolation. In this production Jolson appeared for the first time as the blackfaced character Gus, whom he would impersonate in later Winter Garden

musicals. And with this song he performed a routine that henceforth became his trademark: falling on one knee and stretching out his arms to his audience. Necessity was the mother of this invention. While performing the song, Jolson suffered a stab of pain from an ingrown toe nail. To relieve the pressure on his foot, he dropped to his knee; then, to justify this movement, he threw out his arms as if to take the whole audience in a giant embrace. Jolson sang "You Made Me Love You" on the soundtrack of the motion-picture musical *The Jolson Story* (Columbia, 1946). His recording for Decca in 1946 sold over a million disks.

"You Made Me Love You" was the first song with which Judy Garland showed her star potential. She was about eleven years old at the time, and she sang it to a photograph of Clark Gable in the motion-picture musical *The Broadway Melody of 1937* (MGM, 1937). Harry James also scored his first major success after forming his band in 1939 with this number, but in a "shmaltzy" rendition. In 1946 he recorded it again, achieving a million-disk sale in a Columbia release.

Early in her career Fanny Brice also scored successfully with this number. When she used it in her vaudeville act, in the early 1910s, she would sing the verse and first chorus seriously, then deliver the second chorus in a comic version. A decade or so after that Ruth Etting made the song one of the staples in her repertory. This is why it was interpolated in her screen biography *Love Me or Leave Me* (MGM, 1955), sung by Doris Day.

The song was interpolated in several other motion pictures. Among them were *Wharf Angel,* starring Victor McLaglen (Paramount, 1934); *Private Buckaroo,* starring the Andrews Sisters (Universal, 1942); and *Syncopation,* starring Jackie Cooper and Connee Boswell (RKO, 1942).

"You Made Me Love You" was one of sixteen numbers selected in 1963 by ASCAP for its all-time Hit Parade during the half century of its existence.

You Make Me Feel So Young, words by Mack Gordon, music by Joseph Myrow (1946). Introduced by Vera-Ellen and Frank Lattimore in the motion-picture musical *Three Little Girls in Blue* (20th Century-Fox, 1946). Frank Sinatra helped to popularize it in a best-selling Capitol recording. Dennis Day presented it as a comedy number in the motion-picture musical *I'll Get By* (20th Century-Fox, 1950). It was sung by a chorus under the titles in the non-musical motion picture *As Young As You Feel,* starring Monty Woolley (20th Century-Fox, 1951). It was also used with satiric implications as a recurrent theme in the non-musical motion picture starring Clark Gable, *But Not for Me* (Paramount, 1958).

Youmans, Vincent, composer, born New York City, 1898; died Denver, Colorado, 1946.

See (Lyrics by Irving Caesar): I Want to Be Happy; Sometimes I'm Happy; Tea for Two.

See (Lyrics by Bud De Sylva): Rise 'n Shine; So Do I.

See (Lyrics by Edward Eliscu and Gus Kahn): Carioca; Flying Down to Rio; Music Makes Me; Orchids in the Moonlight.

See (Lyrics by Edward Eliscu and Billy Rose): Great Day; More Than You Know.

See (Lyrics by Otto Harbach and Oscar Hammerstein II): Bambalina; Wildflower.

See (Lyrics by Edward Heyman): Drums in My Heart; Through the Years.

See also: The Country Cousin; Hallelujah; I Want a Man; Keepin' Myself for You; Oh Me, Oh My, Oh You; Time on My Hands.

You May Not Be an Angel. *See:* I'll String Along with You.

You Must Have Been a Beautiful Baby, words by Johnny Mercer, music by Harry Warren (1938). Introduced by Dick Powell in the motion-picture musical *Hard to Get,* starring Powell with Olivia De Havilland (Warner, 1938). Doris Day sang it in the motion-picture musical *My Dream Is Yours* (Warner, 1949). It was also interpolated in the background music of the non-musical motion picture *Mildred Pierce,* starring Joan Crawford (Warner, 1945). Bobby Darin revived it in 1961 in a best-selling recording for Atco.

You Mustn't Be Discouraged, words by Betty Comden and Adolph Green, music by Jule Styne (1964). Nostalgic ballad introduced by Carol Burnett and Jack Cassidy (followed by a soft-shoe routine) in the musical *Fade Out—Fade In* (1964).

You My Love, words by Mack Gordon, music by James Van Heusen (1955). Introduced by Frank Sinatra and Doris Day in the non-musical motion picture *Young at Heart* (Warner, 1955).

You Naughty, Naughty Men, words and music by T. Kennick and G. Bicknell (1865). Introduced by Milly Cavendish in the musical extravaganza *The Black Crook* (1865). A new kind of sex insinuation penetrated the American musical theater for the first time with this number, and the provocative way in which Milly Cavendish addressed it to the men in the audience.

You Never Knew About Me, words by P. G. Wodehouse, music by Jerome Kern (1917). Introduced by Marie Carroll and Lynn Overman in the Princess Theatre production of *Oh, Boy!* (1917).

You Never Miss the Water Till the Well Runs Dry, words and music by Rollin Howard (1874). Though some of the early published copies credit Harry Linn as the lyricist and D. Angel as the "narrator," it is now generally agreed that Howard wrote both the words and the music. This is an early successful example of a popular song pointing up a moral. It was popularized by Fred Walz with the Bryant Minstrels.

The Young Folks at Home, words by Frank Spencer, music by Hattie Livingston (1852). Inspired by, and in imitation of, Stephen Foster's "Old Folks at Home." It was written for and introduced by Wood's Minstrels in 1852.

Young, Joe, lyricist, born New York City, 1898; died Denver, Colorado, 1946.

See: Ahlert, Fred; Akst, Harry; Donaldson, Walter; Henderson, Ray; Meyer, George W.; Schwartz, Jean.

See also: Along the Rocky Road to Dublin; Annie Doesn't Live Here Any More; Cryin' for the Carolines; Daddy Long Legs; Down in Dear Old New Orleans; For All We Know; I Kiss Your Hand, Madame; In a Shanty in Old Shanty Town; Keep Sweeping the Cobwebs Off the Moon; Laugh, Clown, Laugh; Ooh, That Kiss; Starlight; The Torch Song; Two Hearts in Three-Quarter Time; Two Tickets to Georgia; Yacka Hula Hickey Dula; You're Gonna Lose Your Girl.

Young, Rida Johnson, lyricist, born Baltimore, Maryland, 1869; died Stamford, Connecticut, 1926.

See: Friml, Rudolf; Herbert, Victor; Romberg, Sigmund.

Young, Victor, composer, born Chicago, Illinois, 1900; died Palm Springs, California, 1956.

See (Lyrics by Edward Heyman): Blue Star; Love Letters; When I Fall in Love.

See (Lyrics by Ned Washington): My Foolish Heart; Stella by Starlight; Sweet Madness.

See also: Around the World; Beautiful Love; Golden Earrings; Lord, You Made the Night Too Long; Sweet Sue; Written on the Wind.

Young and Foolish, words by Arnold B. Horwitt, music by Albert Hague (1954). Introduced by David Daniels in the musical *Plain and Fancy* (1955).

Young and Healthy, words by Al Dubin, music by Harry Warren (1932). Introduced by Dick Powell in the motion-picture musical *Forty-Second Street* (Warner, 1933).

Young and Warm and Wonderful, words by Hy Zaret, music by Lou Singer (1958). Popularized by Tony Bennett in a Columbia recording.

Young at Heart, words by Carolyn Leigh, music by Johnny Richards (1954). The melody had originated with a song called "Moonbeam," which Richards had written in 1939.

With Carolyn Leigh's lyrics, this song was popularized in 1954 by Frank Sinatra in a Capitol recording that sold a million disks. The song title was then used for a motion picture starring Sinatra with Doris Day (Warner, 1955); Sinatra sang the number on the soundtrack under the titles and after that in the final scene of the film.

Young at Heart, a motion picture with songs, starring Frank Sinatra and Doris Day (Warner 1955). The score was made up mainly of standards, with a few new songs contributed by Paul Francis Webster and Sammy Fain, and by Mack Gordon and James Van Heusen.

See: Just One of Those Things; One for My Baby: Someone to Watch Over Me; There's a Rising Moon; You My Love; Young at Heart.

Younger Than Springtime, words by Oscar Hammerstein II, music by Richard Rodgers (1949). Introduced by William Tabbert in the musical play *South Pacific* (1949). It was also sung in the motion-picture adaptation of the musical (20th Century-Fox, 1958) by Bill Lee, on the soundtrack for John Kerr.

Young Love, words and music by Ric Cartey and Carole Joyner (1956). Introduced by Ric Cartey, but popularized in 1957 by Sonny James in a Capitol recording and by Tab Hunter in a Dot recording.

A Young Man's Fancy, words by John Murray Anderson and Jack Yellen, music by Milton Ager (1920). Introduced in the revue *What's In a Name?* (1920).

Young Man with a Horn, words by Ralph Freed, music by George Stoll (1944). Introduced by Harry James and his orchestra in the motion-picture musical *Two Girls and a Sailor* (MGM, 1944) with vocal by June Allyson. The song was revived by June Allyson and Harry James in the motion picture *The Opposite Sex* (MGM, 1956).

Young Man with a Horn, a motion-picture musical biography of Bix Beiderbecke, famous jazz cornetist, starring Kirk Douglas as Beiderbecke with Doris Day (Warner,

1950). The score was made up mainly of standards.

See: I May Be Wrong But I Think You're Wonderful; Melancholy Rhapsody; The Very Thought of You.

You Oughta Be in Pictures, words by Edward Heyman, music by Dana Suesse (1934). Introduced in the motion picture *New York Town,* starring Mary Martin and Fred Mac-Murray (Paramount, 1941). The song was revived in the motion-picture musical *Starlift* (Warner, 1951), sung by Doris Day.

You Planted a Rose in the Garden of Love, words by J. Will Callahan, music by Ernest R. Ball (1914).

Your Cheatin' Heart, words and music by Hank Williams (1952). Popularized in 1953 by Joni James in an MGM recording that sold a million disks. Hank Williams' recording for MGM was also a best seller. The song provided the title for and was sung on the soundtrack by Hank Williams, Jr. (for George Hamilton), in a motion-picture biography of Hank Williams (MGM, 1964).

Your Cheatin' Heart, a motion-picture musical biography of Hank Williams, starring George Hamilton as Williams (MGM, 1964). The score was made up of Hank Williams' song favorites, sung for George Hamilton on the soundtrack by Hank Williams, Jr.

See: Cold, Cold Heart; Hey, Good Lookin'; I Can't Help It; Jambalaya; Your Cheatin' Heart.

You're a Builder Upper, words by Ira Gershwin and E. Y. Harburg, music by Harold Arlen (1934). An early Arlen song hit introduced by Ray Bolger in the revue *Life Begins at 8:40* (1934).

You're a Grand Old Flag, words and music by George M. Cohan (1906). The first of Cohan's famous flag-waving routines. He introduced it in the musical *George Washington, Jr.* (1906). He also sang it in his first talking picture, *The Phantom President* (Paramount, 1932). James Cagney presented it in Cohan's screen biography *Yankee Doodle Dandy* (Warner, 1942).

Cohan's idea for this song came after talking to a G.A.R. veteran who told him he had been a color-bearer during Pickett's charge at Gettysburg. The veteran further remarked, pointing to an American flag, "She's a grand old rag." In the first version of his song, Cohan used the word "rag," instead of "flag." One day after the première of *George Washington, Jr.*, several patriotic societies denounced Cohan for referring to the flag as a "rag." Cohan always insisted that this protest had been instigated by a New York drama critic who had been denied seats to the show. Nevertheless, Cohan changed the word "rag" to "flag" and the patriotic furor died down.

You're a Million Miles from Nowhere (When You're One Little Mile from Home), words by Sam M. Lewis and Joe Young, music by Walter Donaldson (1919).

You're an Angel, words by Dorothy Fields, music by Jimmy McHugh (1935). Introduced in the motion-picture musical *Hooray for Love,* starring Ann Sothern and Gene Raymond (RKO, 1935).

You're an Old Smoothie, words by Bud De Sylva, music by Richard A. Whiting and Nacio Herb Brown (1932). Introduced by Ethel Merman and Jack Haley in the musical *Take a Chance* (1932).

This song had originally been written for a show called *Humpty Dumpty,* which proved such a dud that it closed out of town before reaching Broadway. The entire show was then rewritten, and Vincent Youmans was called in to provide some new songs. Two numbers from *Humpty Dumpty* were retained, the other being "Eadie Was a Lady."

You're a Sweetheart, words by Harold Adamson, music by Jimmy McHugh (1937). Introduced by George Murphy and Alice Faye in the motion picture of the same name (Universal, 1937). It was interpolated for Frank Sinatra in the motion-picture musical *Meet Danny Wilson* (Universal, 1952).

You're a Sweet Little Headache, words by Leo Robin, music by Ralph

Rainger (1938). Introduced by Bing Crosby in the motion-picture musical *Paris Honeymoon* (Paramount, 1938), and further popularized by him in a Decca recording.

You're Breaking My Heart, words and music by Pat Genaro and Sunny Skylar (1948). Popularized in 1949 by Vic Damone in a best-selling Mercury recording.

You're Devastating, words by Otto Harbach, music by Jerome Kern (1933). Introduced by Bob Hope in the musical *Roberta* (1933). It was sung in the second motion-picture adaptation of that musical, renamed *Lovely to Look At* (MGM, 1952).

You're Driving Me Crazy (What Did I Do?), words and music by Walter Donaldson (1930). Donaldson named this song "What Did You Do to Me?" when he turned it over to Guy Lombardo. But just before Lombardo introduced it with his Royal Canadians, Donaldson telephoned him with the revised title of "You're Driving Me Crazy." Lombardo played the song on his radio program every night for a week; within three days the sheet-music sale passed the hundred-thousand mark. The song was further popularized in best-selling recordings by Guy Lombardo and his Royal Canadians for Capitol and by Rudy Vallée for RCA Victor. The song was interpolated in the Broadway musical *Smiles* (1930), presented by Adele Astaire, Eddie Foy, Jr., and a chorus of girls. It was revived in the motion-picture musical *Gentlemen Marry Brunettes* (United Artists, 1955).

You're Getting to Be a Habit with Me, words by Al Dubin, music by Harry Warren (1932). Introduced by Bebe Daniels in the motion-picture musical *Forty-Second Street* (Warner, 1933). It was revived by Doris Day (and danced to by Miss Day and Gene Nelson) in the motion-picture musical *Lullaby of Broadway* (Warner, 1951).

You're Gonna Lose Your Girl, words by Joe Young, music by James V. Monaco (1933). It was revived by Doris Day and Gordon MacRae in the motion-picture musical *Starlift* (Warner, 1951).

You're Here and I'm Here, words by H. B. Smith, music by Jerome Kern (1914). Introduced by Venita Fitzhugh and Nigel Barrie in the musical *Laughing Husband* (1914).

You're Goin' Far Away, Lad (or, I'm Still Your Mother, Dear), words and music by Paul Dresser (1897).

You're Gonna Hear from Me, words by Dore Langdon, music by André Previn (1965). Introduced in the non-musical motion picture *Inside Daisy Clover,* starring Natalie Wood (Warner, 1965). It was popularized by Frank Sinatra in a Reprise recording, and by Barbra Streisand and Andy Williams, each in a Columbia recording.

You're in Love, words by Otto Hauerbach (Harbach) and Edward Clark, music by Rudolf Friml (1916). Introduced by Lawrence Wheat and Marie Flynn, with chorus, in the musical of the same name (1916).

You're in the Right Church, But the Wrong Pew, words by R. C. McPherson, using the pen name of Cecil Mack, music by Chris Smith (1908). Negro dialect song made famous by the vaudeville team of Williams and Walker. It became one of the most famous routines of Bert Williams (of that team) after he had interpolated it in the musical *My Landlady* (1908). He delivered it in his familiar half-comic, half-serious style that once led W. C. Fields to say: "Bert Williams was the funniest man I ever saw—and the saddest man I ever knew."

You're Just in Love, words and music by Irving Berlin (1950). A song with a two-melody chorus, with two sets of lyrics, sung contrapuntally. It was introduced by Ethel Merman and Russell Nype in the musical *Call Me Madam* (1950). In the motion-picture adaptation of the musical (20th Century-Fox, 1953), it was sung by Donald O'Connor and Ethel Merman. The song was popularized in a best-selling recording by Perry Como for RCA Victor.

The song was written during out-of-town tryouts of *Call Me Madam*. A need was felt for a strong number in the second act. George Abbott, director of the show, remembered the two-melody chorus of Berlin's "Simple Melody" and asked the composer to concoct something in a similar vein. "Irving went back to the hotel and disappeared for the day," George Abbott recalls in his autobiography. "Crouse had a room directly over Berlin's and he, therefore, would give us reports from time to time about the music which floated up to him. Two mornings later he hurried into the theatre with a big grin and said gleefully, 'I think he's got something. I keep hearing the same tune over and over.' Indeed he had something: that wonderful counterpoint melody, 'You're not sick, you're just in love,' with which Ethel Merman and Russell Nype stopped the show every night."

Berlin had planned the number to be sung straight as a sentimental love ballad. But Ethel Merman and Russell Nype managed to work out so many routines and pieces of stage business with each encore that from a tender love song it was made into something resembling a comedy routine.

You're Lucky to Me, words by Andy Razaf, music by Eubie Blake (1920). Introduced and popularized by Ethel Waters in the all-Negro revue *Blackbirds of 1930* (1930).

You Remind Me of My Mother, words and music by George M. Cohan (1922). Introduced by Elizabeth Hines and Charles King in the musical *Little Nellie Kelly* (1922). The song was interpolated in the motion-picture adaptation of the musical *Fifty Million Frenchmen* (Warner, 1931).

You're My Everything, words by Mort Dixon and Joe Young, music by Harry Warren (1931). Introduced by Jeanne Aubert and Lawrence Gray in the Ed Wynn musical *The Laugh Parade* (1931). It provided the title for and was sung by Dan Dailey in a motion-picture musical

(20th Century-Fox, 1949). It was also interpolated in two other motion-picture musicals: *Painting the Clouds With Sunshine* (Warner, 1951) and *The Eddie Duchin Story* (Columbia, 1956), played on the soundtrack by Carmen Cavallero.

You're My Everything, a motion-picture musical starring Dan Dailey (20th Century-Fox, 1949). The score was made up mainly of standards.

See: Chattanooga Choo Choo; I May Be Wrong but I Think You're Wonderful; You're My Everything.

You're My Past, Present and Future, words by Mack Gordon, music by Harry Revel (1933). Introduced in the motion-picture musical *Broadway Thru a Keyhole*, starring Texas Guinan and Russ Columbo and his orchestra (United Artists, 1933).

You're My Thrill, words by Sidney Clare, music by Jay Gorney (1933). Introduced in the motion picture *Jimmy and Sally*, starring Claire Trevor and James Dunn (Fox, 1933). The song first became popular twenty years later in recordings by Doris Day for Columbia and Harry James and his orchestra for Capitol.

You're Next, words and music by Sid Tepper and Roy C. Bennett (1964). Popularized by Jimmy Witherspoon in a Prestige recording.

You're Nobody Till Somebody Loves You, words and music by Russ Morgan, Larry Stock and James Cavanaugh (1944). When first published it was ignored. It became a hit a decade later, first popularized by Roberta Sherwood in night clubs. Dean Martin made a best-selling recording for Reprise in 1964.

This is the number Walter Winchell heard Roberta Sherwood sing in Murray Franklin's night spot in Miami in 1956, a performance that led Winchell to publicize the then unknown singer into one of the hottest properties in show business.

You're Not the Only Pebble on the Beach, words by Harry B. Berdan, using the pen name of Harry Braisted, and music by Frederick J. Redcliffe, using the pen name of

Stanley Carter (1896). A sentimental ballad introduced and popularized by Lottie Gilson at Koster and Bial's in New York in 1896. The song's success led to its title becoming a catch phrase in the 1890s. The song was interpolated in the motion picture *Trail Street*, starring Randolph Scott (RKO, 1947).

You're Sensational, words and music by Cole Porter (1955). Introduced by Frank Sinatra in the motion-picture musical *High Society* (MGM, 1956).

You're So Much a Part of Me, words and music by Richard Adler and Jerry Ross (1952). Introduced in a revue, John Murray Anderson's *Almanac* (1952), where it passed unnoticed. It was first popularized in a Philco Playhouse TV production in 1952, where it was sung by Cyril Ritchard.

You're the Cream in my Coffee, words by Bud De Sylva and Lew Brown, music by Ray Henderson (1928). Introduced by Jack Whiting in the musical *Hold Everything* (1928). It was then interpolated in the motion picture *The Cockeyed World*, starring Victor McLaglen and Edmund Lowe (Fox, 1929). It was also sung in the motion-picture biography of De Sylva, Brown and Henderson, *The Best Things in Life Are Free* (20th Century-Fox, 1956).

You're the Flower of My Heart, Sweet Adeline. *See:* Sweet Adeline.

You're the Only Star (in My Blue Heaven), words and music by Gene Autry (1938). Introduced in the motion picture *The Old Barn Dance*, starring Gene Autry (Republic, 1938).

You're the Top, words and music by Cole Porter (1934). Introduced by Ethel Merman and William Gaxton in the musical *Anything Goes* (1934). In the first motion-picture adaptation of the musical (Paramount, 1936), it was sung by Bing Crosby and Ethel Merman; in the second screen version (Paramount, 1956), by Bing Crosby and Mitzi Gaynor. Ginny Simms and Cary Grant sang it in the Cole Porter screen biography *Night and Day* (Warner, 1946).

The song idea originated a number of years before *Anything Goes* was planned—during a supper at the Boeuf sur le Toit in Paris, where Cole Porter and Mrs. Alastair Mackintosh amused themselves by trying to concoct a list of superlatives that rhymed.

Porter remembered this game when he needed a strong number in the first act of *Anything Goes*, in which the playboy and the nightclub entertainer indulge in a saucy exchange of compliments filled with all kinds of urbane allusions to subjects ranging from a Bendel bonnet to a Shakespeare sonnet, and from Mickey Mouse to a symphony by Strauss.

Your Eyes Have Told Me So, words by Gus Kahn and Egbert van Alstyne, music by Walter Blaufuss (1919). Popularized in vaudeville by Grace La Rue. It was revived for James Melton in the motion-picture musical *Sing Me a Love Song* (First National, 1936). Doris Day and Gordon MacRae sang it in the motion-picture musical *By the Light of the Silvery Moon* (Warner, 1953). It was also interpolated in Gus Kahn's screen biography *I'll See You in My Dreams* (Warner, 1951).

Your Land and My Land, words by Dorothy Donnelly, music by Sigmund Romberg (1927). Introduced by Alexander Callam and a male chorus in the musical play *My Maryland* (1927). It was revived in the Sigmund Romberg screen biography *Deep in My Heart* (MGM, 1954), sung by Howard Keel.

Yours, a Spanish popular song ("Quiérme mucho"), music by Gonzalo Roig, English lyrics by Jack Sherr (1931). The song was successfully revived in 1952.

Yours for a Song, words by Billy Rose and Ted Fetter, music by Dana Suesse (1939). Introduced at Billy Rose's Aquacade at the New York World's Fair in 1939.

Yours Is My Heart Alone, a famous German song ("Dein ist mein Ganzes Herz") from Franz Lehár's operetta *The Land of Smiles*, English lyrics by H. B. Smith (1931).

The song is inevitably identified with the eminent Austrian tenor Richard Tauber, who introduced it in Berlin at the world première of *The Land of Smiles* (*Das Land des Laechelns*) in 1929. After that Tauber rarely gave a concert without singing it either on the program itself or as an encore. He also sang it in New York in a new English adaptation of the operetta *The Land of Smiles*, produced in 1946 and renamed in honor of its main song, *Yours Is My Heart*. On the opening night of that production, the song received such an ovation that Tauber had to repeat it four times in as many different languages (English, French, Italian and German). The song was subsequently further popularized in the United States in Mario Lanza's recording for RCA Victor.

Yours Sincerely, words by Lorenz Hart, music by Richard Rodgers (1929). Introduced by Glenn Hunter and Lillian Taiz in the musical *Spring Is Here* (1929). In the motion-picture adaptation of the musical (First National, 1930), it was sung by Bernice Claire and Alexander Gray.

You Say the Nicest Things, Baby, words by Harold Adamson, music by Jimmy McHugh (1948). Introduced by Bill Callahan and Betty Jane Watson in the musical *As Girls Go* (1948). It was popularized by Jerry Wayne in a Columbia recording.

You Send Me, words and music by L. C. Cook (1957). Popularized by Sam Cooke in a Keen recording, his first successful disk.

You Stepped Out of a Dream, words by Gus Kahn, music by Nacio Herb Brown (1940). Introduced in the motion-picture musical *Ziegfeld Girl* (MGM, 1940) by Tony Martin.

You Taught Me How to Love You (Now Teach Me to Forget), words by Jack Drislane and Alfred Bryan, music by George W. Meyer (1909). One of Meyer's earliest song hits, a favorite with vaudeville tenors.

You Tell Her, I S-t-u-t-t-e-r, words by Billy Rose, music by Cliff Friend (1922). Billy Rose got the idea for this lyric from the World War I song success "K-K-K-Katy."

You Took Advantage of Me, words by Lorenz Hart, music by Richard Rodgers (1928). Introduced by Busby Berkeley and Joyce Barbour in the musical *Present Arms* (1928). This was one of Morton Downey's most successful numbers. When he made an appearance at the Café de Paris in Paris in the early 1930s, the Duke of Windsor was so delighted with his performance that he made Downey repeat the song nine times. The song was interpolated in the Rodgers and Hart screen biography *Words and Music* (MGM, 1948). It was also used in "Born in a Trunk," the extended song sequence featured by Judy Garland in the motion picture *A Star Is Born* (Warner, 1953).

You Try Somebody Else, words by Bud De Sylva and Lew Brown, music by Ray Henderson (1931). Published as an independent number. It was revived by Sheree North in the screen biography of De Sylva, Brown and Henderson, *The Best Things in Life Are Free*, (20th Century-Fox, 1956).

You Turned the Tables on Me, words by Sidney D. Mitchell, music by Louis Alter (1936). Introduced by Alice Faye in the motion-picture musical *Sing, Baby, Sing* (20th Century-Fox, 1936). This song received an award from ASCAP in 1936. It became a favorite with several notable jazz ensembles, including those of Louis Armstrong and Benny Goodman.

You've Been a Good Old Wagon But You Done Broke Down, words and music by Ben Harney (1896). Ben Harney's first published song, and an early successful example of a coon shout. It was introduced as a "stick dance specialty" by Harney himself, appearing with a minstrel company in 1896. It was then popularized by May Irwin in vaudeville. It was because of the success of this number, after its publication, that coon and ragtime songs began to flourish in Tin Pan Alley.

You've Got Me Out on a Limb, words by Joe McCarthy, music by Harry

Tierney (1940). Written for and introduced in the motion-picture adaptation of the musical *Irene* (RKO, 1940), sung and danced to by Anna Neagle.

You've Got Something, words and music by Cole Porter (1936). Introduced by Bob Hope and Ethel Merman in the musical *Red, Hot and Blue* (1936).

You've Got That Thing, words and music by Cole Porter (1929). Introduced by Jack Thompson and Betty Compton in the musical *Fifty Million Frenchmen* (1929). It was sung by a female ensemble in the Cole Porter screen biography *Night and Day* (Warner, 1946).

You've Got to See Mamma Ev'ry Night (Or You Can't See Mamma at All), words by Billy Rose, music by Con Conrad (1923).

You Were Meant for Me, words by Arthur Freed, music by Nacio Herb Brown (1929). Introduced by Charles King in the motion-picture musical *The Broadway Melody* (MGM, 1929). During that same year it was sung in two motion-picture musicals, *Hollywood Revue* (MGM, 1929) and *Show of Shows* (Warner, 1929). It provided the title for a motion-picture musical (20th Century-Fox, 1948), where it was played under the titles, was used as a recurring theme in the background music and was sung in the closing scene by Dan Dailey. It was used in the background music for the non-musical motion picture *Let's Make It Legal,* starring Claudette Colbert (20th Century-Fox, 1951). It was sung by Gene Kelly (then danced to by Kelly and Debbie Reynolds) in the motion-picture musical *Singin' in the Rain* (MGM, 1952).

You Were Meant for Me, a motion-picture musical starring Dan Dailey and Jeanne Crain (20th Century-Fox, 1948). The score was made up mainly of standards.

See: Ain't Misbehavin'; Ain't She Sweet?; Crazy Rhythm; Good Night, Sweetheart; If I Had You; I'll Get By; You Were Meant for Me.

You Were Never Lovelier, words by Johnny Mercer, music by Jerome Kern (1942). Introduced by Fred Astaire in the motion-picture musical of the same name (Columbia, 1942).

You Were Never Lovelier, a motion-picture musical starring Fred Astaire and Rita Hayworth (Columbia, 1942). Songs by Johnny Mercer and Jerome Kern.

See: Dearly Beloved; I'm Old Fashioned; You Were Never Lovelier.

You Will Find Your Love in Paris. *See:* The River Seine.

You Will Remember Vienna, words by Oscar Hammerstein II, music by Sigmund Romberg (1930). Introduced by Vivienne Segal and Alexander Gray in the motion-picture musical *Viennese Nights* (Warner, 1930). It was sung by Helen Traubel in the Romberg screen biography *Deep in My Heart* (MGM, 1954).

You, Wonderful You, words by Jack Brooks and Saul Chaplin, music by Harry Warren (1950). Introduced by Gene Kelly in the motion-picture musical *Summer Stock* (MGM, 1950).

You, You, You, a German popular song ("Du, Du, Du"), music by Lotar Olias, English words by Robert Mellin (1953). Popularized by the Ames Brothers in an RCA Victor recording.

Z

The Ziegfeld Follies, a lavish revue produced annually by Florenz Ziegfeld. The first edition was presented on the roof of the New York Theatre (Jardin de Paris) on July 8, 1907. Songs by various composers and lyricists were used; the stars included Grace La Rue, Emma Carus and Helen Broderick.

With the exceptions of 1926, 1928 and 1929, the *Ziegfeld Follies* was seen every year on Broadway until 1931. In 1908 and 1909 most of the score was done by Maurice Levi, though interpolated songs were also used. Raymond Hubbell contributed the songs for all editions between 1911 and 1914, and again in 1917; Louis A. Hirsch for 1915, 1916 and 1918; Irving Berlin for 1919 and 1927. Songs by Dave Stamper, however, were featured in most of the editions between 1912 and 1931. Songs by such outstanding composers as Jerome Kern, Gus Edwards, Rudolf Friml and Victor Herbert were interpolated in various editions.

Ziegfeld's prime aim was to glorify the American girl. Some of the most beautiful women ever to step across an American stage appeared in the chorus line of the *Follies* through the years. Out of their ranks stepped many a later star of stage and screen, including Mae Murray, Marion Davies, Lilyan Tashman, Nita Naldi and Harriet Hoctor. Among the stars who appeared in the various editions of the *Follies* were Nora Bayes, Eddie Cantor, Fanny Brice, Leon Erroll, W. C. Fields, Lillian Lorraine, Marilyn Miller, Ann Pennington, Will Rogers, Bert Williams and Ed Wynn.

The last edition produced by Ziegfeld himself was that of 1931. (Ziegfeld died in 1932.) After his death editions were mounted in 1933, 1936 and 1943. In 1945 a motion picture entitled the *Ziegfeld Follies* (MGM) starred Fred Astaire, Judy Garland and Lena Horne. The songs were by Ralph Blane and Hugh Martin, and by Arthur Freed and Harry Warren, among others; "The Babbitt and the Bromide" by George and Ira Gershwin was interpolated. The life of Florenz Ziegfeld was the basis of *The Great Ziegfeld* (MGM, 1936). The *Follies* and their girls were the subject of the screen musical *Ziegfeld Girl* (MGM, 1941).

See: Be My Little Baby Bumble Bee; Bring Back Ma Blushing Rose; By the Light of the Silvery Moon; Ephraham; Garden of My Dreams; Have a Heart; Hello, Frisco, Hello; Hello, Honey; I Can't Get Started with You; I Like the Likes of You; I'm a Vamp from East Broadway; Isle d'Amour; It's Getting Dark on Old Broadway; A Kiss in the Dark; The Last Roundup; The Love Boat;

Mandy; Mister Gallagher and Mister Shean; My Baby's Arms; My Blue Heaven; My Landlady; My Man; My Rambler Rose; 'Neath the South Sea Moon; Nobody; A Pretty Girl Is Like a Melody; Oh Gee, Oh Gosh, Oh Golly, I'm in Love; Oh, How She Could Yacki, Hacki, Wicki, Wacki, Woo; Rebecca of Sunnybrook Farm; Row, Row, Row; Rose of Washington Square; Sally, Won't You Come Back?; Second Hand Rose; Shaking the Blues Away; Shine On, Harvest Moon; Some Sweet Day; Suddenly; Sweet Sixteen; Take, Oh Take, Those Lips Away; Tell Me, Little Gypsy; That's the Kind of a Baby for Me; Tulip Time; Up, Up in My Aeroplane; Wagon Wheels; What Is There to Say?; Woodman, Woodman, Spare That Tree; You Can't Make Your Shimmy Shake on Tea; You'd Be Surprised.

Ziegfeld Girl, a motion-picture musical starring James Stewart, Lana Turner and Judy Garland (MGM, 1941). The score was made up primarily of standards. Several new songs were written by Ralph Freed and Roger Edens.

See: I'm Always Chasing Rainbows; Mister Gallagher and Mister Shean; Whispering; You Stepped Out of a Dream.

Zing a Little Zong, words by Leo Robin, music by Harry Warren (1952). Introduced by Bing Crosby and Jane Wyman in the motion-picture musical *Just for You* (Paramount, 1952).

Zing! Went the Strings of My Heart, words and music by James F. Hanley (1935). Introduced by Hal Le Roy and Eunice and Healy in the musical *Thumbs Up* (1935). Judy Garland sang it in the motion-picture musical *Listen, Darling* (MGM, 1938); Gene Nelson sang it and danced to it in the motion-picture musical *Lullaby of Broadway* (Warner, 1951). The song was also heard in the motion picture *Thumbs Up*, starring Brenda Joyce and Richard Fraser (Republic, 1943).

Zing Zing, Zoom Zoom, words by Charles Tobias, music by Sigmund Romberg (1950). Popularized by Perry Como in an RCA Victor recording. It subsequently achieved wide circulation in schools throughout the country.

Zip-A-Dee-Doo-Dah, words by Ray Gilbert, music by Allie Wrubel (1945). Introduced in the Walt Disney motion picture (his first with live actors) *Song of the South,* starring Ruth Warwick and Lucille Watson (RKO, 1946), sung by James Baskett. The song received the Academy Award. It was popularized by Johnny Mercer and the Pied Pipers in a best-selling recording for Capitol.

Zip Coon, author of words and music not known (1834). A classic of the early minstrel show and one of the earliest successful popular songs about the Negro. It was introduced by the minstrel Bob Farrell at the Bowery Theatre in New York on August 11, 1834. It subsequently became a prime favorite in minstrel shows everywhere, and particularly of the minstrel George Washington Dixon. "Zip Coon" represented the "Broadway swell" who wore swank clothes, the last word in current fashion, a silk hat, and brandished a walking stick; he pretended to be a "larned skolar." The lyrics were nonsensical, a gibberish refrain beginning with the line "Possum up a gum tree, coony on a stump."

Both Bob Farrell and George Washington Dixon claimed to have written the song, but this has never been substantiated in either case. The melody is probably derived from an old Irish tune.

Today the song is most familiar as an instrumental, under the title of *Turkey in the Straw*—a favorite at square dances. One of the most successful instrumental arrangements of this number was made by David Guion, both for the orchestra and for solo piano.

Zizzy, Ze Zum, Zum, words by Karl Kennett, music by Lyn Udall (1898). A nonsense song accompanied by absurd facial grimaces and awkward body gestures. It was popularized in vaudeville in the early 1900s.

THE ALL-TIME HIT PARADE
A Chronological Listing

---

* * * *

1765 The Girl I Left Behind Me
Yankee Doodle
1767 The Banks of the Dee
1768 The Liberty Song
1774 Free America
1775 The American Hero
1778 The Battle of the Kegs
Chester
1798 Adams and Liberty
Hail Columbia
The President's March
1800 The American Star
1803 Jefferson and Liberty
1814 The Star-Spangled Banner
1823 Home, Sweet Home
1825 The Meeting of the Waters of Hudson and Erie
1826 The Hunters of Kentucky
The Old Oaken Bucket
1827 The Coal Black Rose
The Minstrel's Return from the War
My Long Blue Tail
1830 Jim Crow
1832 America
1833 Long Time Ago
1834 Zip Coon
1835 Old Rosin the Beau
1837 Woodman, Spare That Tree
1838 A Life on the Ocean Wave
1840 The Old Arm Chair
Rocked in the Cradle of the Deep
Tippecanoe and Tyler Too
1841 Niagara Falls
1843 De Boatman's Song
Columbia, the Gem of the Ocean
Excelsior
My Old Aunt Sally

Old Dan Tucker
The Old Granite State
1844 The Blue Juniata
Vive La Compagnie
1846 The Bridge of Sighs
The Rose of Alabama
1848 Oh, Susanna
Old Uncle Ned
1849 Nelly Bly
1850 De Camptown Races
1851 Old Folks at Home
Wait for the Wagon
1852 Lily Dale
Massa's in de Cold Ground
1853 The Hazel Dell
My Old Kentucky Home
Old Dog Tray
1854 Jeanie with the Light Brown Hair
What Is Home Without a Mother?
1855 Come Where My Love Lies Dreaming
Listen to the Mocking Bird
Rosalie, the Prairie Flower
1856 Darling Nellie Gray
Root, Hog or Die
1857 Jingle Bells
Mrs. Lofty and I
1860 Annie Lisle
Dixie
Old Black Joe
'Tis But a Little Faded Flower
1861 Aura Lee
John Brown's Body
Maryland, My Maryland
The Vacant Chair
1862 Battle Hymn of the Republic
The Bonnie Blue Flag
Grafted into the Army

Kingdom Coming
We Are Coming, Father Abraham, 300,000 More
1863 Babylon Is Fallen
The Battle Cry of Freedom
Just Before the Battle, Mother
Weeping Sad and Lonely
When Johnny Comes Marching Home
1864 All Quiet Along the Potomac To-night
Beautiful Dreamer
Come Home, Father
Sherman's March to the Sea
Tenting on the Old Camp Ground
Tramp! Tramp! Tramp!
Wake, Nicodemus
Where, Oh Where, Has My Little Dog Gone?
1865 Ellie Rhee
Marching Through Georgia
1866 We Parted by the River
When You and I Were Young, Maggie
Write Me a Letter from Home
1868 The Flying Trapeze
1869 The Little Brown Jug
Shew, Fly, Don't Bother Me
Sweet Genevieve
1871 Goodbye, Liza Jane
Mollie Darling
Susan Jane
1873 The Mulligan Guard
Silver Threads Among the Gold
1874 The Skidmore Guard
1876 Grandfather's Clock
I'll Take You Home Again, Kathleen
Rose of Killarney
1877 Early in de Mornin'
Roll Out! Heave Dat Cotton
1878 Carry Me Back to Old Virginny
A Flower from Mother's Grave
Lullaby
The Skidmore Fancy Ball
1879 The Babies on Our Block
In the Morning by the Bright Light
Oh, Dem Golden Slippers
1880 Cradle's Empty, Baby's Gone
De Golden Wedding
The Mulligan Braves
The Skidmore Masquerade
Why Did They Dig Ma's Grave So Deep?
1881 Paddy Duffy's Cart

1883 Marguerite
My Dad's Dinner Pail
Strolling on the Brooklyn Bridge
There Is a Tavern in the Town
When the Robins Nest Again
1884 Always Take Mother's Advice
White Wings
1885 Poverty's Tears Ebb and Flow
Remember, Boy, You're Irish
1886 The Letter That Never Came
1887 If the Waters Could Speak As They Flow
The Outcast Unknown
1888 The Convict and the Bird
Drill, Ye Tarriers, Drill
Where Did You Get That Hat?
The Whistling Coon
With All Her Faults I Love Her Still
1889 Down Went McGinty
Oh, Promise Me
1890 The Irish Jubilee
Maggie Murphy's Home
Throw Him Down, McCloskey
1891 The Last of the Hogans
Molly O!
The Pardon Came Too Late
The Picture That Is Turned Toward the Wall
Ta-ra-ra-boom-de-ré
1892 After the Ball
The Bowery
Daddy Wouldn't Buy Me a Bow-Wow
Daisy Bell
Push Dem Clouds Away
1893 The Fatal Wedding
Little Alabama Coon
Say Au Revoir But Not Goodbye
Two Little Girls in Blue
1894 And Her Golden Hair Was Hanging Down Her Back
The Little Lost Child
She May Have Seen Better Days
The Sidewalks of New York
1895 America, the Beautiful
The Band Played On
Down in Poverty Row
Just Tell Them That You Saw Me
My Best Girl's a New Yorker
The Sunshine of Paradise Alley
1896 All Coons Look Alike to Me
A Hot Time in the Old Town
In the Baggage Coach Ahead
Mister Johnson, Turn Me Loose
Mother Was a Lady

On the Benches in the Park
Sweet Rosie O'Grady
You're Not the Only Pebble on
the Beach
1897 At a Georgia Camp Meeting
Break the News to Mother
On the Banks of the Wabash Far
Away
1898 Gold Will Buy Most Anything
But a True Girl's Heart
Gypsy Love Song
I Guess I'll have to Telegraph
My Baby
Kiss Me, Honey, Do
My Old New Hampshire Home
The Rosary
She Is the Belle of New York
She Was Bred in Old Kentucky
When You Ain't Got No Money,
Well, You Needn't Come
Around
When You Were Sweet Sixteen
Zizzy, Ze Zum, Zum
1899 The Curse of the Dreamer
Hello, Ma Baby
I'd Leave My Happy Home for
You
My Wild Irish Rose
When Chloe Sings a Song
1900 A Bird in a Gilded Cage
The Bridge of Sighs
Goodbye, Dolly Gray
Ma Blushin' Rosie
1901 Just A-Wearyin' for You
Mighty Lak a Rose
The Tale of the Bumble Bee
Way Down in Old Indiana
1902 Bill Bailey, Won't You Please
Come Home?
Come Down, Ma Evenin' Star
Down Where the Wurzburger
Flows
In the Good Old Summer Time
The Mansion of Aching Hearts
On a Sunday Afternoon
Under the Bamboo Tree
1903 Bedelia
Ida, Sweet As Apple Cider
Navajo
Sweet Adeline
Toyland
1904 Alexander, Don't You Love Your
Baby No More?
Blue Bell
Give My Regards to Broadway
Goodbye, Little Girl, Goodbye
Meet Me in St. Louis

The Tale of the Turtle Dove
The Yankee Doodle Boy
1905 Dearie
Forty-Five Minutes from Broad-
way
I Don't Care
In My Merry Oldsmobile
In the Shade of the Old Apple
Tree
Kiss Me Again
Mary's a Grand Old Name
My Gal Sal
My Irish Molly O
Nobody
So Long, Mary
Tammany
Wait Till the Sun Shines Nellie
Will You Love Me in December
As You Do in May?
1906 Anchors Aweigh
Chinatown, My Chinatown
I Love You Truly
Sunbonnet Sue
Waiting at the Church
You're a Grand Old Flag
1907 Harrigan
It's Delightful to Be Married
On the Road to Mandalay
School Days
1908 Cuddle Up a Little Closer
Shine On, Harvest Moon
Take Me Out to the Ball Game
Up in a Balloon
The Yama Yama Man
You're in the Right Church But
the Wrong Pew
1909 By the Light of the Silvery Moon
Casey Jones
The Cubanola Glide
Has Anybody Here Seen Kelly?
I've Got Rings on My Fingers
I Wonder Who's Kissing Her
Now
Meet Me Tonight in Dreamland
My Pony Boy
Put On Your Old Gray Bonnet
That Mesmerizing Mendlessohn
Tune
1910 Ah, Sweet Mystery of Life
Come, Josephine, in My Flying
Machine
Down by the Old Mill Stream
Every Little Movement
I'm Falling in Love with Some-
one
Italian Street Song
Let Me Call You Sweetheart

Mother Machree
A Perfect Day
Play That Barbershop Chord
Put Your Arms Around Me Honey
Some of These Days
Stein Song

1911 Alexander's Ragtime Band
Everybody's Doing It Now
Good Night, Ladies
I Want a Girl Just Like the Girl That Married Dear Old Dad
Jimmy Valentine
My Beautiful Lady
Oh, You Beautiful Doll
Ragtime Violin
That Mysterious Rag
Till the Sands of the Desert Grow Cold
When I Was Twenty-One and You Were Sweet Sixteen

1912 Be My Little Baby Bumble Bee
Giannina Mia
I'm the Lonesomest Gal in Town
Isle o' Dreams
Love Is Like a Firefly
The Memphis Blues
Moonlight Bay
My Melancholy Baby
Row, Row, Row
The Sweetheart of Sigma Chi
Sympathy
Waiting for the Robert E. Lee
When I Lost You
When Irish Eyes Are Smiling
When the Midnight Choo Choo Leaves for Alabam'

1913 The Angelus
Ballin' the Jack
The Curse of an Aching Heart
He'd Have to Get Under
Marcheta
My Wife's Gone to the Country
Peg o' My Heart
Something Seems Tingle-Ingle-ing
Sweethearts
There's a Long, Long Trail
The Trail of the Lonesome Pine
You Made Me Love You

1914 The Aba Daba Honeymoon
By the Beautiful Sea
Goodbye, Girls, I'm Through
I Love the Ladies
A Little Bit of Heaven
Play a Simple Melody

St. Louis Blues
Sylvia
They Didn't Believe Me
Too-ra-loo-ra-loo-ral
When You Wore a Tulip

1915 America, I Love You
Auf Wiedersehen
Babes in the Wood
Back Home in Tennessee
Down Among the Sheltering Palms
Hello, Frisco
Hello, Hawaii, How Are You?
How'd You Like to Spoon with Me?
I Didn't Raise My Boy to Be a Soldier
It's Tulip Time in Holland
My Sweet Adair
Neapolitan Love Song

1916 Goodbye, Good Luck, God Bless You
Ireland Must Be Heaven, For My Mother Came from There
M-i-s-s-i-s-s-i-p-p-i
Missouri Waltz
Poor Butterfly
Pretty Baby
Turn Back the Universe and Give Me Yesterday
What Do You Want to Make Those Eyes at Me For?
Yacka Hula Hickey Dula

1917 Beale Street Blues
The Darktown Strutters' Ball
For Me and My Gal
Goodbye, Broadway, Hello, France
Hail, Hail, the Gang's All Here
I May Be Gone for a Long, Long Time
Indiana
Leave It to Jane
Lily of the Valley
Oh, Johnny, Oh, Johnny, Oh!
Over There
Sailin' Away on the Henry Clay
Send Me Away with a Smile
The Siren's Song
Smiles
They Go Wild, Simply Wild Over Me
Till the Clouds Roll by
Where the Morning Glories Grow
Will You Remember?

1918 After You've Gone
Beautiful Ohio
The Daughter of Rosie O'Grady

Everything Is Peaches Down in
    Georgia
Hello, Central, Give Me No Man's
    Land
Hindustan
I'm Always Chasing Rainbows
Ja Da
K-K-K-Katy
Oh, How I Hate to Get Up in the
    Morning
Oui, Oui, Marie
Rock-a-bye Your Baby with a
    Dixie Melody
Tickle Toe
Till We Meet Again
1919 Castle of Dreams
Daddy Long Legs
Dardanella
How Ya Gonna Keep 'Em Down
    on the Farm?
I'm Forever Blowing Bubbles
In My Sweet Little Alice Blue
    Gown
Let the Rest of the World Go By
Mandy
Oh, What a Pal was Mary
A Pretty Girl Is Like a Melody
Smilin' Through
Swanee
Your Eyes Have Told Me So
1920 Avalon
Daddy, You've Been a Mother to
    Me
Feather Your Nest
I Used to Love You But It's All
    Over
I'll Be with You in Apple Blossom
    Time
The Japanese Sandman
Look for the Silver Lining
The Love Nest
Margie
My Mammy
When My Baby Smiles at Me
Whispering
1921 Ain't We Got Fun?
April Showers
I'm Just Wild About Harry
Ka-lu-a
Ma, He's Making Eyes at Me
My Man
My Sunny Tennessee
Sally
Say It with Music
The Sheik of Araby
Wabash Blues
Whip-poor-will

Yoo Hoo
1922 L'Amour, Toujours L'Amour
Carolina in the Morning
Chicago
Do It Again
Georgette
A Kiss in the Dark
Lovin' Sam, The Sheik of Ala-
    bam'
Mister Gallagher and Mister
    Shean
My Buddy
Runnin' Wild
Some Sunny Day
Stumbling
Three O'Clock in the Morning
Toot, Toot, Tootsie
1923 Bambalina
Barney Google
Charleston
I'm Goin' South
I Love Life
I Love You
It Ain't Gonna Rain No Mo'
Oh, Didn't It Rain
Oh, Gee, Oh, Gosh, Oh, Golly, I'm
    in Love
That Old Gang of Mine
Who's Sorry Now?
Wildflower
Yes, We Have No Bananas
1924 All Alone
Amapola
California, Here I Come
Deep in My Heart
Fascinating Rhythm
Indian Love Call
I Want to Be Happy
I'll See You in My Dreams
I Wonder What's Become of Sally
The Man I Love
O Katharina!
The Prisoner's Song
Rose Marie
Serenade
Somebody Loves Me
Tea for Two
What'll I Do?
1925 Alabamy Bound
Always
Collegiate
Dinah
Five Feet Two, Eyes of Blue
Here in My Arms
I'm Sitting on Top of the World
If You Knew Susie, Like I Know
    Susie

Manhattan
Moonlight and Roses
Remember
Sentimental Me
Sleepy Time Gal
Song of the Vagabonds
Sunny
Sweet Georgia Brown
That Certain Feeling
Waltz Huguette
Who?
Yes, Sir, That's My Baby

1926 All Alone Monday
Baby Face
The Birth of the Blues
Black Bottom
Blue Heaven
The Blue Room
Breezin' Along with the Breeze
Bye, Bye, Blackbird
Charmaine
Clap Yo' Hands
Do, Do, Do
Gimme a Little Kiss, Will Ya, Huh?
The Girl Friend
I'd Climb the Highest Mountain
In a Little Spanish Town
It All Depends on You
Mountain Greenery
One Alone
Play, Gypsies, Dance, Gypsies
Rio Rita
Somone to Watch Over Me
When the Red, Red Robin Comes Bob, Bob, Bobbin' Along

1927 At Sundown
The Best Things in Life Are Free
Bill
Blue Skies
Can't Help Lovin' Dat Man
Hallelujah
I'm Looking Over a Four Leaf Clover
Let a Smile Be Your Umbrella on a Rainy Day
Me and My Shadow
My Blue Heaven
My Heart Stood Still
Ol' Man River
Ramona
Sam, the Old Accordion Man
Side by Side
Sometimes I'm Happy
The Song Is Ended
Soon
Strike Up the Band

'S Wonderful
Thou Swell
The Varsity Drag
Why Do I Love You?

1928 Angela Mia
Button Up Your Overcoat
Carolina Moon
Diga Diga Doo
I Can't Give You Anything But Love
I'll Get By
I Wanna Be Loved by You
Let's Do It
The Lonesome Road
Love Me or Leave Me
Makin' Whoopee
One Kiss
Short'nin' Bread
Softly, As in a Morning Sunrise
Sonny Boy
Stout Hearted Men
Sweet Sue, Just You
That's My Weakness Now
There's a Rainbow 'Round My Shoulder
You're the Cream in My Coffee
You Took Advantage of Me

1929 Ain't Misbehavin'
Am I Blue?
Aren't We All?
Broadway Melody
Deep Night
Great Day
Happy Days Are Here Again
Honeysuckle Rose
If I Had a Talking Picture of You
I'm Just a Vagabond Lover
Liza
Louise
Love, Your Spell Is Everywhere
Moanin' Low
More Than You Know
Pagan Love Song
Painting the Clouds with Sunshine
Singin' in the Rain
Stardust
Sunny Side Up
Tip Toe Thru the Tulips with Me
The Wedding of the Painted Doll
Why Was I Born?
With a Song in My Heart
Without a Song
You Do Something to Me

1930 Betty Co-Ed
Beyond the Blue Horizon

Blue Again
Body and Soul
Cheerful Little Earful
Cryin' for the Carolines
Dancing on the Ceiling
Embraceable You
Fine and Dandy
Georgia on My Mind
Get Happy
I Got Rhythm
Little White Lies
Love for Sale
On the Sunny Side of the Street
Sing Something Simple
Sleepy Lagoon
Something to Remember You By
Ten Cents a Dance
Three Little Words
Time on My Hands
Walkin' My Baby Back Home
What Is This Thing Called Love?
When Your Hair Has Turned to
   Silver
You Brought a New Kind of Love
   to Me

1931 All of Me
Between the Devil and the Deep
   Blue Sea
By the River Sainte Marie
Dancing in the Dark
Drums in My Heart
Goodnight, Sweetheart
Heartaches
I Found a Million Dollar Baby
I Love a Parade
I Love Louisa
I've Got Five Dollars
Life Is Just a Bowl of Cherries
Love Letters in the Sand
Marta
Minnie the Moocher
Mood Indigo
My Song
New Sun in the Sky
The Night Was Made for Love
Of Thee I Sing
The Peanut Vendor
River Stay 'Way from My Door
She Didn't Say Yes
Singin' the Blues
Sweet and Lovely
That's Why Darkies Were Born
Through the Years
Wabash Moon
When I Take My Sugar to Tea
When the Moon Comes Over the
   Mountain

When Yuba Plays the Rumba on
   the Tuba
Where the Blue of the Night
   Meets the Gold of the Day
You're My Everything
You Try Somebody Else

1932 April in Paris
Brother, Can You Spare a Dime?
Eadie Was a Lady
Fascination
Forty-second Street
How Deep Is the Ocean?
I Gotta Right to Sing the Blues
I'm Gettin' Sentimental Over You
I Surrender, Dear
I've Told Ev'ry Little Star
Let's Have Another Cup of Coffee
Let's Put Out the Lights
Louisiana Hayride
Night and Day
Rise 'n' Shine
Shuffle Off to Buffalo
Soft Lights and Sweet Music
The Song Is You
You're an Old Smoothie
You're Getting to Be a Habit
   with Me

1933 The Boulevard of Broken Dreams
Carioca
Did You Ever See a Dream Walk-
   ing?
Don't Blame Me
Easter Parade
Flying Down to Rio
Heat Wave
It's Only a Paper Moon
The Last Round Up
Let's Fall in Love
Mine
Smoke Gets in Your Eyes
Stormy Weather
Temptation
The Touch of Your Hand
Who's Afraid of the Big Bad
   Wolf?
Yesterdays
You're My Past, Present and
   Future

1934 All I Do Is Dream of You
All Through the Night
Baby, Take a Bow
Blue Moon
Carry Me Back to the Lone
   Prairie
The Continental
Deep Purple
If There Is Someone Lovelier

Than You?
I'll String Along with You
Isle of Capri
June in January
Love in Bloom
Love Thy Neighbor
Mr. and Mrs. Is the Name
One Night of Love
Stars Fell on Alabama
Stay As Sweet As You Are
Thank You for a Lovely Evening
Tumbling Tumbleweeds
Wagon Wheels
You and the Night and the Music
You're the Top

1935 About a Quarter to Nine
Begin the Beguine
Broadway Rhythm
Cheek to Cheek
I Feel a Song Comin' On
I Got Plenty o' Nuthin
I'm in the Mood for Love
I'm Gonna Sit Right Down and
  Write Myself a Letter
In a Sentimental Mood
It Ain't Necessarily So
Just One of Those Things
Lovely to Look At
Lullaby of Broadway
The Music Goes 'Round and
  'Round
My Lucky Star
My Romance
Summertime
These Foolish Things
When I Grow Too Old to Dream
Zing Went the Strings of My
  Heart

1936 I Can't Get Started with You
I'm an Old Cowhand
Is It True What They Say About
  Dixie?
It's De-Lovely
I've Got You Under My Skin
The Night Is Young and You're
  So Beautiful
Pennies from Heaven
A Star Fell Out of Heaven
There's a Small Hotel
The Way You Look Tonight
The Whiffenpoof Song
You Turned the Tables on Me

1937 Bei Mir Bist Du Schoen
The Dipsy Doodle
The Donkey Serenade
A Foggy Day
Harbor Lights

I Can Dream, Can't I?
I Hit a New High
In the Still of the Night
I've Got My Love to Keep Me
  Warm
Johnny One Note
The Lady Is a Tramp
Let's Call the Whole Thing Off
The Moon of Manakoora
My Funny Valentine
Never in a Million Years
Nice Work If You Can Get It
One Song
Rosalie
Stop, You're Breaking My Heart
Sweet Leilani
Thanks for the Memory
That Old Feeling
Too Marvelous for Words
Where or When
Whistle While You Work

1938 A-Tisket, A-Tasket
Falling in Love with Love
The Flat Foot Floogie
Franklin D. Roosevelt Jones
Heigh Ho
I'll Be Seeing You
I Married an Angel
Jeepers Creepers
Love Walked In
Music, Maestro, Please
My Heart Belongs to Daddy
My Reverie
Ol' Man Mose
September Song
Small Fry
This Can't Be Love
Ti-Pi-Tin
Two Sleepy People
You Must Have Been a Beautiful
  Baby

1939 All the Things You Are
Beer Barrel Polka
Brazil
God Bless America
I Didn't Know What Time It Was
I'll Never Smile Again
The Lamp Is Low
Moon Love
Our Love
Over the Rainbow
South of the Border
Three Little Fishes

1940 The Breeze and I
Cabin in the Sky
How High the Moon
I Hear a Rhapsody

Imagination
It's a Big Wonderful World
The Last Time I Saw Paris
The Nearness of You
Only Forever
Taking a Chance on Love
When You Wish Upon a Star
You Are My Sunshine

1941 Bewitched, Bothered and Bewildered
Blues in the Night
Chattanooga Choo Choo
Deep in the Heart of Texas
How About You?
I Don't Want to Walk Without You
I Don't Want to Set the World on Fire
I Got It Bad and That Ain't Good
I'll Remember April
Tonight We Love

1942 Dearly Beloved
I Had the Craziest Dream
Jingle, Jangle, Jingle
Paper Doll
Praise the Lord and Pass the Ammunition
That Old Black Magic
White Christmas
You'd Be So Nice to Come Home To
You Were Never Lovelier

1943 Comin' In on a Wing and a Prayer
I Couldn't Sleep a Wink Last Night
I'll Be Seeing You
It's Love, Love, Love
I've Heard That Song Before
A Lovely Way to Spend an Evening
Mairzy Doats
Oh, What a Beautiful Mornin'
People Will Say We're in Love
Pistol Packin' Mama
Sunday, Monday or Always
They're Either Too Young or Too Old
Tico Tico
You Keep Coming Back Like a Song
You'll Never Know

1944 Ac-cent-tchu-ate the Positive
Candy
Close As the Pages of a Book
Don't Fence Me In

I'll Walk Alone
Long Ago and Far Away
Rum and Coca-Cola
Sentimental Journey
Spring Will Be a Little Late This Year
Strange Music
Swinging on a Star

1945 A Hubba Hubba Hubba
If I Loved You
It Might as Well Be Spring
It's a Grand Night for Singing
It's Been a Long, Long Time
June Is Bustin' Out All Over
Laura
Let It Snow, Let It Snow, Let It Snow
The More I See of You
On the Atchison, Topeka and the Santa Fe
Rodger Young
Till the End of Time

1946 All Through the Day
Anniversary Song
Come Rain or Come Shine
Five Minutes More
For You, For Me, For Evermore
Full Moon and Empty Arms
The Girl That I Marry
Golden Earrings
How Are Things in Glocca Morra?
It's a Good Day
Laughing on the Outside, Crying on the Inside
Ole Buttermilk Sky
South America, Take It Away
Tenderly
They Say It's Wonderful
To Each His Own
Zip-a-Dee-Doo-Dah

1947 Almost Like Being in Love
Ballerina
Civilization
Feudin' and Fightin'
The Gentleman Is a Dope
I'll Dance at Your Wedding
Papa, Won't You Dance with Me?
The Stanley Steamer
Too Fat Polka

1948 "A," You're Adorable
Baby, It's Cold Outside
Buttons and Bows
It's a Most Unusual Day
It's Magic
Mañana Is Soon Enough for Me
My Darling, My Darling
Nature Boy

On a Slow Boat to China
Once in Love with Amy
So in Love
Tennessee Waltz
A Tree in the Meadow
You're Breaking My Heart
You Say the Nicest Things

1949 Bali Ha'i
Bibbidi-Bobbidi-Boo
Careless Hands
The Cry of the Wild Goose
Dear Hearts and Gentle People
Diamonds Are a Girl's Best
   Friend
Mockin' Bird Hill
Mona Lisa
Mule Train
My Foolish Heart
Rudolph, the Red Nosed Rein-
   deer
Some Enchanted Evening

1950 Autumn Leaves
A Bushel and a Peck
Candy and Cake
C'est Si Bon
If I Knew You Were Comin I'd
   'Ave Baked a Cake
It's a Lovely Day Today
Music, Music, Music
My Heart Cries for You
Rag Mop
Sam's Song
Sunshine Cake
The Thing
Tzena, Tzena
Wilhelmina
You, Wonderful You

1951 Any Time
Be My Love
Cold, Cold Heart
Come On-a My House
Cry
Half As Much
Hello, Young Lovers
In the Cool, Cool, Cool of the
   Evening
Jezebel
Kisses Sweeter Than Wine
The Little White Cloud That Cried
The Loveliest Night of the Year
Marshmallow Moon
My Truly, Truly Fair
Shrimp Boats
Sparrow in the Tree Tops
Too Young

1952 Because You're Mine
Botch-a-Me

Don't Let the Stars Get in Your
   Eyes
High Noon
I Saw Mommy Kissing Santa
   Claus
I Went to Your Wedding
Jambalaya
Kiss of Fire
Takes Two to Tango
Thumbelina
Till I Waltz Again with You
Wheel of Fortune
Wish You Were Here
You Belong to Me
Your Cheatin' Heart
Zing a Little Zong

1953 And This Is My Beloved
April in Portugal
Baubles, Bangles and Beads
Ebb Tide
Gambler's Guitar
Hi Lili, Hi Lo
I Believe
I Love Paris
It's All Right with Me
No Other Love
Oh, My Papa
Rags to Riches
Rock Around the Clock
Secret Love
Stranger in Paradise
That Doggie in the Window
That's Amore
Where Is Your Heart?
You, You, You

1954 All of You
Cross Over the Bridge
Fanny
The Happy Wanderer
Hernando's Hideaway
Hey, There
The High and the Mighty
Home for the Holidays
Honeycomb
If I Give My Heart to You
Let Me Go, Lover
Mambo Italiano
The Man That Got Away
Mister Sandman
The Naughty Lady of Shady Lane
Papa Loves Mambo
Shake, Rattle and Roll
Sh-Boom
Teach Me Tonight
This Ole House
Three Coins in the Fountain
Young and Foolish

Young at Heart
1955 Ain't It a Shame?
All at Once You Love Her
The Ballad of Davy Crockett
Cherry Pink and Apple Blossom
　White
Cry Me a River
Dance with Me, Henry
Dungaree Doll
Love and Marriage
Love Is a Many Splendored
　Thing
Moments to Remember
Sixteen Tons
Something's Gotta Give
The Tender Trap
Tweedle Dee
Unchained Melody
Wake Up the Town and Tell the
　People
Whatever Lola Wants
The Yellow Rose of Texas
1956 Allegheny Moon
Anastasia
Around the World
Blue Suede Shoes
Blueberry Hill
Canadian Sunset
Cindy, Oh Cindy
Don't Be Cruel
Friendly Persuasion
The Great Pretender
The Green Door
Heartbreak Hotel
Hot Diggity
Hound Dog
I Could Have Danced All Night
Just in Time
Love Me Tender
Mack the Knife
Memories Are Made of This
Mister Wonderful
On the Street Where You Live
The Party's Over
The Poor People of Paris
See You Later, Alligator
Standing on the Corner
Teen Age Crush
Tonight You Belong to Me
Too Close for Comfort
True Love
Whatever Will Be, Will Be
Why Do Fools Fall in Love?
1957 All Shook Up
All the Way
April Love
Chances Are

I Feel Pretty
In the Middle of an Island
Maria
Old Cape Cod
Party Doll
A Rose and a Baby Ruth
Round and Round
Seventy-Six Trombones
Tammy
Teddy Bear
Tonight
1958 Bird Dog
Catch a Falling Star
Chanson d'Amour
The Chipmunk Song
Everybody Loves a Lover
Firefly
Gigi
I Enjoy Being a Girl
Kewpie Doll
Lollipop
Love, Look Away
The Purple People Eater
Tom Dooley
Volare
You Are Beautiful
1959 Alvin's Harmonica
The Battle of New Orleans
Climb Every Mountain
Do Re Mi
Everything's Coming Up Roses
High Hopes
Kookie Kookie
Lipstick on Your Collar
The Sound of Music
Take Me Along
1960 Calcutta
Camelot
Cathy's Clown
Dolce Far Niente
Everybody Is Somebody's Fool
I Ain't Down Yet
If Ever I Would Leave You
My Heart Has a Mind of Its Own
Never on Sunday
The Twist
1961 Big Bad John
The Bilboa Song
Exodus
Hey, Look Me Over
I Believe in You
The Lion Sleeps Tonight
Love Makes the World Go Round
Moon River
Where the Boys Are
1962 Blowin' in the Wind
Can't Help Falling in Love

Days of Wine and Roses
Do You Love Me?
Empty Pockets Filled with Love
Go Away, Little Girl
Lollipops and Roses
Roses Are Red, My Love

1963 Call Me Irresponsible
Charade
Danke Schoen
Eighteen Yellow Roses
Hey, Paula
Painted, Tainted Rose
Sugar Shack
Those Lazy, Hazy, Crazy Days of
Summer

1964 Chim Chim Cheree
Dear Heart
Fiddler on the Roof
For Mama

From Russia with Love
Hello, Dolly!
I Get Around
It's a Wonderful World
My Kind of Town
Oh, Pretty Woman
Rag Doll
Send Me the Pillow You Dream
On
Where Love Has Gone

1965 A Circus World
Hush, Hush, Sweet Charlotte
It Was a Very Good Year
King of the Road
A Married Man
Mister Lonely
Sweetheart Tree

1966 Ballad of the Green Berets

ALL-TIME BEST-SELLING

POPULAR RECORDINGS

❖

1919—1966

Only single disks are listed. A best seller is a recording that has sold half a million disks or more.

Ames Brothers
Sentimental Me (Coral, 1950)
Rag Mop (Coral, 1950)
You, You, You (RCA Victor, 1953)
Naughty Lady from Shady Lane (RCA Victor, 1954)

Anderson, Leroy
Blue Tango (Decca, 1951)
Syncopated Clock (Decca, 1951)

Andrews Sisters
Rum and Coca-Cola (Decca, 1944)
I Can Dream, Can't I? (Decca, 1949)
Winter Wonderland (Decca, 1950)

Anka, Paul
Diana (ABC Paramount, 1957)
You Are My Destiny (ABC Paramount, 1958)
I'm Just a Lonely Boy (ABC Paramount, 1959)
Puppy Love (ABC Paramount, 1960)

Armstrong, Louis
Mack the Knife (Columbia, 1957)
Hello, Dolly! (Kapp, 1964)

Arnold, Eddy
Bouquet of Roses (RCA Victor, 1957)

Austin, Gene
Ramona (RCA Victor, 1928)

Autry, Gene
Silver Haired Daddy (Columbia, 1939)
South of the Border (Columbia, 1939)
Rudolph, the Red-Nosed Reindeer (Columbia, 1950)
Frosty the Snowman (Columbia, 1950)
Peter Cottontail (Columbia, 1950)

Avalon, Frankie
Dede Dinah (Chancellor, 1958)
Venus (Chancellor, 1959)

Baker, Lavern
Tweedle Dee (Atlantic, 1955)
I Cried a Tear (Atlantic, 1959)
Jim Dandy (Atlantic, 1960)

Ballard, Hank and Midnighters
Finger Poppin' Time (King, 1960)
The Twist (King, 1962)

Barron, Blue
Cruising Down the River (MGM, 1949)

Barton, Eileen
If I Knew You Were Comin' I'd 'Ave Baked a Cake (National, 1950)

Baxter, Les
April in Portugal (Capitol, 1953)
Poor People of Paris (Capitol, 1956)

Belafonte, Harry
Matilda, Matilda (RCA Victor, 1953) (RCA Victor, 1953)
Banana Boat Song (RCA Victor, 1957)

Bennett, Tony
Because of You (Columbia, 1952)
Cold, Cold Heart (Columbia, 1952)
Rags to Riches (Columbia, 1953)
Stranger in Paradise (Columbia, 1954)
I Left My Heart in San Francisco (Columbia, 1962)
This Is a Great Country (Columbia, 1963)

Benton, Brook
It's Just a Matter of Time (Mercury, 1959)

So Many Ways (Mercury, 1959)

Benton, Brook and Dinah Washington
Baby (Mercury, 1960)

Bilk, Acker
Stranger on the Shore (Atco, 1962)

Black, Jeanne
He'll Have to Stay (Capitol, 1960)

Black's Combo, Bill
Smokie (Hi, 1959)
White Silver Sands (Hi, 1960)
Smokie, Part II (Hi, 1960)

Booker, T. and M.G.'s
Green Onions (Stax, 1962)

Boone, Pat
Ain't That a Shame (Dot, 1955)
I'll Be Home (Dot, 1956)
Friendly Persuasion (Dot, 1956)
I Almost Lost My Mind (Dot, 1956)
Love Letters in the Sand (Dot, 1957)
Don't Forbid Me (Dot, 1957)
Why, Baby, Why? (Dot, 1957)
April Love (Dot, 1957)
Remember You're Mine (Dot, 1958)
A Wonderful Time Up There (Dot, 1958)
Moody River (Dot, 1961)
Speedy Gonzales (Dot, 1962)

Boyd, Jimmy
I Saw Mommy Kissing Santa Claus (Columbia, 1952)

Brewer, Teresa
Music, Music, Music (Coral, 1950)
Till I Waltz Again with You (Coral, 1952)
Ricochet (Coral, 1953)

Brown, Les
Sentimental Journey (Columbia, 1945)
I've Got My Love to Keep Me Warm (Coral, 1958)

Browns
The Three Bells (RCA Victor, 1959)

Bryant, Anita
Till There Was You (Columbia, 1958)

Byrnes, Ed and Connie Stevens
Kookie, Kookie, Lend Me Your Comb (Warner, 1959)

Cannon, Freddie
Way Down Yonder in New Orleans (Swan, 1960)
Palisades Park (Swan, 1962)

Cantor, Eddie
You'd Be Surprised (Victor, 1919)

Yes, We Have No Bananas (Victor, 1923)

Chandler, Gene
Duke of Earl (Vee Jay, 1961)

Chandler, Karen
Hold Me, Thrill Me, Kiss Me (Coral, 1953)

Channel, Bruce
Hey, Baby (Smash, 1962)

Charles, Ray
I Can't Stop Loving You (ABC Paramount, 1962)
You Don't Know Me (ABC Paramount, 1963)

Checker, Chubby
The Twist (Parkway, 1960)
Let's Twist Again (Parkway 1961)
Pony Time (Cameo 1961)

Chordettes
Mr. Sandman (Cadence, 1954)

Clanton, Jimmy
Just a Dream (Ace, 1958)

Clooney, Rosemary
Come On-a My House (Columbia, 1951)
Half As Much (Columbia, 1952)
Hey, There (Columbia, 1954)

Coasters
Searchin' (Atco 1957)
Yakety Yak (Atco, 1958)
Charlie Brown (Atco, 1959)
Poison Ivy (Atco, 1959)

Cole, Nat King
Nature Boy (Capitol, 1948)
Mona Lisa (Capitol, 1949)
Unforgettable (Capitol, 1951)
Too Young (Capitol, 1951)
Answer Me, My Love (Capitol, 1954)
Darling, Je Vous Aime Beaucoup (Capitol, 1955)
Ramblin' Rose (Capitol, 1962)
Those Lazy, Hazy, Crazy Days of Summer (Capitol, 1963).

Como, Perry
Temptation (RCA Victor, 1945)
A Hubba Hubba Hubba (RCA Victor, 1945)
Till the End of Time (RCA Victor, 1945)
Prisoner of Love (RCA Victor, 1946)
When You Were Sweet Sixteen (RCA Victor, 1947)
Forever and Ever (RCA Victor, 1949)

Don't Let the Stars Get in Your Eyes
(RCA Victor, 1952)
Wanted (RCA Victor, 1954)
Papa Loves Mambo (RCA Victor, 1954)
Hot Diggity (RCA Victor, 1956)
Round and Round (RCA Victor, 1957)
Catch a Falling Star (RCA Victor, 1958)
Magic Moments (RCA Victor, 1958)

Contours
Do You Love Me? (Gordy, 1962)

Cooke, Sam
You Send Me (Keen, 1957)

Copas, Cowboy
Tennessee Waltz (King, 1950)
Signed, Sealed and Delivered (King, 1951)

Cornell, Don
It Isn't Fair (Coral, 1952)
I'm Yours (Coral, 1952)

Costa, Don
Never on Sunday (United Artists, 1960)

Covington, Warren
Tea for Two Cha Cha (Decca, 1958)

Crescendos
Oh, Julie (Nasco, 1958)

Crests
Sixteen Candles (Coed, 1959)

Crew Cuts
Sh-Boom (Mercury, 1954)
Earth Angel (Mercury, 1955)

Crickets
That'll Be the Day (Brunswick, 1957)

Crosby, Bing
White Christmas (Decca, 1942)
Sunday, Monday or Always (Decca, 1943)
I'll Be Home for Christmas (Decca, 1943)
Swinging on a Star (Decca, 1944)
Too-Ra-Loo-Ra-Loo-Ral (Decca, 1944)
I Can't Begin to Tell You (Decca, 1945)
Sweet Leilani (Decca, 1946)
Now Is the Hour (Decca, 1948)
Dear Hearts and Gentle People (Decca, 1949)

Crosby, Bing and Gary Crosby
Simple Melody (Decca, 1950)
Sam's Song (Decca, 1950)

Crosby, Bing and Andrews Sisters
Pistol Packin' Mama (Decca, 1943)
Jingle Bells (Decca, 1943)
Don't Fence Me In (Decca, 1944)
South America, Take It Away (Decca, 1946)

Crosby, Bing and Grace Kelly
True Love (Capitol, 1957)

Crosby, Bing and Fred Waring
Whiffenpoof Song (Decca, 1950)

Dale, Alan
Sweet and Gentle (Coral, 1956)
Cherry Pink and Apple Blossom White (Coral, 1956)

Dalhart, Vernon
Prisoner's Song (Victor, 1924)

Damone, Vic
You're Breaking My Heart (Mercury, 1949)
Again (Mercury, 1954)
On the Street Where You Live (Columbia, 1957)

Danny and Juniors
At the Hop (ABC Paramount, 1958)

Darin, Bobby
Splish Splash (Atco, 1958)
Dream Lover (Atco, 1959)
Mack the Knife (Atco, 1959)
Queen of the Hop (Atco, 1959)

Darren, James
Goodbye, Cruel World (Colpix, 1962)

Day, Doris
Love Somebody (Columbia, 1947)
It's Magic (Columbia, 1948)
A Guy Is a Guy (Columbia, 1952)
Secret Love (Columbia, 1954)
Whatever Will Be, Will Be (Columbia, 1956)

Dean, Jimmy
Big Bad John (Columbia, 1961)

Dee, Joey and Starliters
The Peppermint Twist (Roulette, 1961)

Del Vikings
Come, Go with Me (Dot, 1957)

Dexter, Al
Pistol Packin' Mama (Okeh, 1943)

Diamonds
Little Darlin' (Mercury, 1957)
The Stroll (Mercury, 1958)

Dinning, Mark
Teen Angel (MGM, 1960)

Dion
Runaround Sue (Laurie, 1961)

Dion and Belmonts
Teenager in Love (Laurie, 1959)
Dobkins, Carl
My Heart Is an Open Book (Decca, 1959)
Doggett, Bill
Honky Tonk (King, 1956)
Domino, Antoine "Fats"
Ain't It a Shame? (Imperial, 1955)
All by Myself (Imperial, 1955)
Blueberry Hill (Imperial, 1956)
Boll Weevil (Imperial, 1956)
I'm in Love Again (Imperial, 1956)
Blue Monday (Imperial, 1957)
I'm Walking (Imperial, 1957)
Whole Lotta Lovin' (Imperial, 1958)
Dorsey, Jimmy
Maria Elena (Decca, 1941)
Green Eyes (Decca, 1941)
Amapola (Decca, 1941)
So Rare (Fraternity, 1957)
Dorsey, Tommy
Marie (RCA Victor, 1937)
Imagination (RCA Victor, 1940)
The Sky Fell Down (RCA Victor, 1940)
I'll Never Smile Again (RCA Victor, 1940)
There Are Such Things (RCA Victor, 1942)
Draper, Rusty
Gambler's Guitar (Mercury, 1953)
Dream Weavers
It's Almost Tomorrow (Decca, 1951)
Drifters
There Goes My Baby (Atlantic, 1959)
True Love, True Love (Atlantic, 1960)
Save the Last Dance for Me (Atlantic, 1961)
Up on the Roof (Atlantic, 1963)
Duke of Earl
Duke of Earl (Vee Jay, 1962)
Eckstine, Billy
My Foolish Heart (MGM, 1949)
I Apologize (MGM, 1951)
Eddy, Duane
Because They're Young (Jamie, 1960)
Edwards, Tommy
It's All in the Game (MGM, 1958)
Elegants
Little Star (Apt, 1958)

Everly Brothers
Bye, Bye, Love (Cadence, 1957)
Wake Up, Little Susie (Cadence, 1957)
All I Have to Do Is Dream (Cadence, 1958)
Bird Dog (Cadence, 1958)
Devoted to You (Cadence, 1958)
Cathy's Clown (Warner, 1960)
Fabares, Shelley
Johnny Angel (Colpix, 1962)
Fabric, Bent
Alley Cat (Atco, 1962)
Faith, Percy
Where Is Your Heart?, or, The Song from Moulin Rouge (Columbia, 1953)
Ferrante and Teicher
Exodus (United Artists, 1961)
Fisher, Eddie
Any Time (RCA Victor, 1951)
Just a Little Lovin' Will Go a Long Way (RCA Victor, 1952)
I'm Walking Behind You (RCA Victor, 1953)
Oh, My Papa (RCA Victor, 1953)
I Need You Now (RCA Victor, 1954)
Fitzgerald, Ella
A-Tisket, A-Tasket (Decca, 1938)
Fleetwoods
Come Softly to Me (Dolton, 1959)
Mr. Blue (Dolton, 1959)
Foley, Red
Chattanoogie Shoe Shine Boy (Decca, 1950)
Fontane Sisters
Hearts of Stone (Dot, 1955)
Ford, Tennessee Ernie
Sixteen Tons (Capitol, 1955)
The Ballad of Davy Crockett (Capitol, 1955)
Ford, Tennessee Ernie and Kay Starr
I'll Never Be Free (Capitol, 1950)
Four Aces
Tell Me Why (Decca, 1951)
Stranger in Paradise (Decca, 1953)
Three Coins in the Fountain (Decca, 1954)
Love Is a Many Splendored Thing (Decca, 1955)
Four Lads
Moments to Remember (Columbia, 1955)
No, Not Much (Columbia, 1956)

Four Preps
Twenty-Six Miles (Capitol, 1958)
Four Seasons
Big Girls Don't Cry (Vee Jay, 1962)
Sherry (Vee Jay, 1962)
Walk Like a Man (Vee Jay, 1963)
Rag Doll (Philips, 1964)
Four Tunes
I Understand (Jubilee, 1954)
Francis, Connie
Who's Sorry Now? (MGM, 1958)
My Happiness (MGM, 1959)
Lipstick on Your Collar (MGM, 1959)
Frankie (MGM, 1959)
Among My Souvenirs (MGM, 1959)
Teddy (MGM, 1960)
Everybody Is Somebody's Fool (MGM, 1960)
My Heart Has a Mind of Its Own (MGM, 1960)
Many Tears Ago (MGM, 1961)
Together (MGM, 1961)
Where the Boys Are (MGM, 1961)
Froman, Jane
I Believe (Capitol, 1953)
Garland, Judy
The Trolley Song (Decca, 1944)
Gibbs, Georgia
Kiss of Fire (Mercury, 1952)
Tweedle Dee (Mercury, 1955)
Dance with Me, Henry (Mercury, 1955)
Gilmer, Jimmy and Fireballs
Sugar Shack (Dot, 1963)
Glahe, Will
Beer Barrel Polka (RCA Victor, 1938)
Godfrey, Arthur
Too Fat Polka (Columbia, 1947)
Gore, Lesley
It's My Party (Mercury, 1963)
Goulet, Robert
If Ever I Would Leave You (Columbia, 1960)
My Love, Forgive Me (Columbia, 1964)
Gracie, Charlie
Butterfly (Cameo, 1957)
Grant, Gogi
Suddenly There's a Valley (Era, 1955)
The Wayward Wind (Era, 1956)

Haley, Bill
Shake, Rattle and Roll (Decca, 1955)
Rock Around the Clock (Decca, 1955)
See You Later, Alligator (Decca, 1956)
Hamilton, Russ
Rainbow (Kapp, 1957)
Harmonicats
Peg o' My Heart (Mercury, 1947)
Harris, Phil
The Thing (RCA Victor, 1950)
Harrison, Wilbert
Kansas City (Fury, 1959)
Hayes, Bill
The Ballad of Davy Crockett (Cadence, 1955)
Haymes, Dick
You'll Never Know (Decca, 1943)
Little White Lies (Decca, 1948)
Heidt, Horace
Deep in the Heart of Texas (Columbia, 1941)
Helms, Bobby
My Special Angel (Decca, 1957)
Herman, Woody
Laura (Columbia, 1945)
Woodchopper's Ball (Decca, 1947)
Hilltoppers
P.S. I Love You (Dot, 1958)
Holly, Buddy
Peggy Sue (Coral, 1958)
Hollywood Argyles
Alley-Oop (Lute, 1960)
Holmes, Leroy
The High and the Mighty (MGM, 1954)
Horton, Johnny
The Battle of New Orleans (Columbia, 1959)
Howard, Eddy
To Each His Own (Majestic, 1946)
Sin (Mercury, 1951)
Hunt, Pee Wee
Twelfth Street Rag (Capitol, 1951)
Oh (Capitol, 1953)
Hunter, Tab
Young Love (Dot, 1957)
Hyland, Brian
Itsy Bitsy Teenie Weenie Yellow Polka Dot Bikini (Kapp, 1960)
Hyman, Dick
Theme from the Three Penny Opera, or Moritat (MGM, 1956)
Impalas

Sorry I Ran All the Way Home (Cub, 1959)

Ink Spots
If I Didn't Care (Decca, 1940)
To Each His Own (Decca, 1946)
The Gypsy (Decca, 1946)

Jackson, Stonewall
Waterloo (Columbia, 1959)

James, Harry
Ciribiribin (Columbia, 1939)
Easter Parade (Columbia, 1942)
I Had the Craziest Dream (Columbia, 1942)
I've Heard That Song Before (Columbia, 1943)
Moonlight Becomes You (Columbia, 1943)
You Made Me Love You (Columbia, 1946)

James, Joni
Why Don't You Believe Me? (MGM, 1952)
Your Cheatin' Heart (MGM, 1953)
Have You Heard? (MGM, 1953)
How Important Can It Be? (MGM, 1955)

James, Sonny
Young Love (Capitol, 1957)

Jan and Dean
Surf City (Liberty, 1963)

Jenkins, Gordon and Weavers
Goodnight, Irene (Decca, 1950)
Tzena, Tzena (Decca, 1950)

Jolson, Al
April Showers (Decca, 1945)
Swanee (Decca, 1945)
California, Here I Come (Decca, 1946)
Rock-a-bye Your Baby with a Dixie Melody (Decca, 1946)
You Made Me Love You (Decca, 1946)
Ma Blushin' Rosie (Decca, 1946)
Sonny Boy (Decca, 1946)
My Mammy (Decca, 1946)
The Anniversary Song (Decca, 1946)

Jones, Allan
The Donkey Serenade (RCA, 1937)

Jones, Jack
Lollipops and Roses (Kapp, 1962)
Call Me Irresponsible (Kapp, 1963)
Wives and Lovers (Kapp, 1963)

Jones, Spike and City Slickers

Der Fuehrer's Face (RCA Victor, 1942)
Chloe (RCA Victor, 1943)

Kaempfert, Bert
Wonderland by Night (Decca, 1961)
Red Roses for a Blue Lady (Decca, 1964)

Kalin Twins
When? (Decca, 1958)

Kallen, Kitty
Little Things Mean a Lot (Decca, 1954)

King, Claude
Wolverton Mountain (Columbia, 1962)

King, Pee Wee
Slow Poke (RCA Victor, 1951)

Kingston Trio
Tom Dooley (Capitol, 1958)

Knight, Evelyn
A Little Bird Told Me (Decca, 1948)

Knox, Buddy
Party Doll (Roulette, 1957)

Kyser, Kay
Three Little Fishes (Columbia, 1941)
Jingle, Jangle, Jingle (Columbia, 1942)
Praise the Lord and Pass the Ammunition (Columbia, 1942)
Strip Polka (Columbia, 1942)
Who Wouldn't Love You? (Columbia, 1942)
Woody Woodpecker (Columbia, 1948)
On a Slow Boat to China (Columbia, 1948)

Laine, Frankie
That's My Desire (Mercury, 1947)
Shine (Mercury, 1948)
Mule Train (Mercury, 1949)
Cry of the Wild Goose (Mercury, 1950)
Jezebel (Columbia, 1951)
On the Sunny Side of the Street (Columbia, 1951)
I Believe (Columbia, 1953)
Moonlight Gambler (Columbia, 1957)

La Rosa, Julius
Eh Cumpari (Cadence, 1953)

Lanza, Mario
Be My Love (RCA Victor, 1950)

Loveliest Night of the Year (RCA Victor, 1951)

Deep in My Heart (RCA Victor, 1954)

Lawrence, Steve
Go Away, Little Girl (Columbia, 1963)

Lee, Brenda
I'm Sorry (Decca, 1960)
That's All You Gotta Do (Decca, 1960)

Lee, Peggy
Peg o' My Heart (Capitol, 1947)
Golden Earrings (Capitol, 1947)
Mañana Is Soon Enough for Me (Capitol, 1948)
Lover (Capitol, 1952)
Pass Me By (Capitol, 1964)

Lester, Ketty
Love Letters (Era, 1962)

Lewis, Bobby
Tossin' and Turnin' (Beltone, 1961)

Lewis, Jerry
Rock-a-bye Your Baby with a Dixie Melody (Decca, 1956)

Lewis, Jerry Lee
Whole Lotta Shakin' Goin' On (Sun, 1957)
Breathless (Sun, 1958)

Liggins, Joe
Pink Champagne (Specialty, 1950)

Little Anthony and Imperials
Tears on My Pillow (End, 1958)

Little Eva
Loco-Motion (Dimension, 1962)

Little Richard
Long Tall Sally (Specialty, 1956)

Little Stevie Wonder
Fingertips (Tamala, 1963)

Lombardo, Guy
Easter Parade (Decca, 1947)

London, Julie
Cry Me a River (Liberty, 1955)

Long, Johnny
A Shanty in Old Shanty Town (Decca, 1940)

Lund, Art
Mam'selle (MGM, 1947)

Lymon, Frankie and Teenagers
Why Do Fools Fall in Love? (Gee, 1956)

MacDonald, Jeanette and Nelson Eddy
Indian Love Call (RCA Victor, 1935)

Maddox, Johnny
Crazy Otto (Dot, 1955)

Mantovani
Charmaine (London, 1952)

Marcels
Blue Moon (Colpix, 1961)

Martin, Dean
That's Amore (Capitol, 1953)
Innamorata (Capitol, 1955)
Memories Are Made of This (Capitol, 1955)
Return to Me (Capitol, 1958)
Volare (Capitol, 1958)
Everybody Loves Somebody (Reprise, 1964)
You're Nobody Till Somebody Loves You (Reprise, 1964)
Send Me the Pillow You Dream On (Reprise, 1964)

Martin, Freddy
White Christmas (RCA Victor, 1942)

Martin, Tony
To Each His Own (Mercury, 1946)

Martino, Al
Painted, Tainted Rose (Capitol, 1963)

Mathis, Johnny
The Twelfth of Never (Columbia, 1956)
Chances Are (Columbia, 1957)
It's Not for Me to Say (Columbia, 1957)
A Certain Smile (Columbia, 1958)

McCoy, Clyde
Sugar Blues (Brunswick, 1923)
Sugar Blues (Decca, 1946)

McGuire Sisters
Sincerel (Coral, 1955)
Sugartime (Coral, 1958)

Merry Macs
Mairzy Doats (Decca, 1944)

Miller, Glenn
In the Mood (RCA Victor, 1939)
Little Brown Jug (Bluebird, 1939)
Sunrise Serenade (Bluebird, 1939)
Moonlight Serenade (Bluebird, 1940)
Fools Rush In (Bluebird, 1940)
Tuxedo Junction (Bluebird, 1940)
Imagination (Bluebird, 1940)
Chattanooga Choo Choo (RCA Victor, 1941)

Miller, Mitch

Yellow Rose of Texas (Columbia, 1955)

Miller, Roger
King of the Road (Smash, 1965)

Mills Brothers
You Always Hurt the One You Love (Decca, 1944)
Paper Doll (Decca, 1948)
The Glow Worm (Decca, 1952)

Mitchell, Guy
My Heart Cries for You (Columbia, 1950)
My Truly, Truly Fair (Columbia, 1951)
The Roving Kind (Columbia, 1951)
Pittsburgh, Pennsylvania (Columbia, 1952)
Singing the Blues (Columbia, 1957)
Heartaches by the Number (Columbia, 1959)

Modungo, Domenico
Volare (Decca, 1958)

Monroe, Vaughn
There, I've Said It Again (RCA Victor, 1945)
Ballerina (RCA Victor, 1947)
Riders in the Sky (RCA Victor, 1949)

Montez, Chris
Let's Dance (Monogram, 1962)

Moony, Art
I'm Looking Over a Four Leaf Clover (MGM, 1948)
Baby Face (MGM, 1948)
Honey Babe (MGM, 1955)

Morgan, Jane
Fascination (Kapp, 1957)

Morgan, Russ
Cruising Down the River (Decca, 1949)

Mormon Tabernacle Choir
The Battle Hymn of the Republic (Columbia, 1959)

Morse, Ella Mae
Blacksmith Blues (Capitol, 1952)

Mullican, Moon
New Jole Blon (King, 1947)

Nelson, Ricky
I'm Walkin' (Verve, 1957)
Stood Up (Imperial, 1958)
Poor Little Fool (Imperial, 1958)
Be Bop Baby (Imperial, 1958)
Lonesome Town (Imperial, 1958)

Believe What I Say (Imperial, 1958)
Never Be Anyone Else But You (Imperial, 1959)
Travelin' Man (Imperial, 1961)
Hello, Mary Lou (Imperial, 1961)

Newton, Wayne
Danke Schoen (Capitol, 1963)
Red Roses for a Blue Lady (Capitol, 1964)

Nichols, Red and Five Pennies
Ida (Brunswick, 1927)

Orbison, Roy
Only the Lonely (Monument, 1960)
Crying (Monument, 1961)
Oh, Pretty Woman (Monument, 1964)

Orioles
Crying in the Chapel (Jubilee, 1953)

Orlons
Wah Watusi (Cameo, 1962)

Page, Patti
Mockin' Bird Hill (Mercury, 1950)
Tennessee Waltz (Mercury, 1950)
I Went to Your Wedding (Mercury, 1952)
That Doggie in the Window (Mercury, 1952)
Changing Partners (Mercury, 1953)
Cross Over the Bridge (Mercury, 1954)
Allegheny Moon (Mercury, 1956)
Old Cape Cod (Mercury, 1957)
Steam Heat (Mercury, 1957)

Parker, Fess
The Ballad of Davy Crockett (Columbia, 1955)

Patience and Prudence
Tonight You Belong to Me (Liberty, 1956)

Paul and Paula
Hey, Paula (Mercury, 1963)

Paul, Les and Mary Ford
How High the Moon (Capitol, 1947)
Mockin' Bird Hill (Capitol, 1949)
The World Is Waiting for the Sunrise (Capitol, 1949)
Vaya Con Dios (Capitol, 1953)

Peter, Paul and Mary
Blowin' in the Wind (Warner, 1963)

Penguins
Earth Angel (Dootone, 1955)

Phillips, Phil
Sea of Love (Mercury, 1959)

Pitney, Gene
Only Love Can Break a Heart (Musicor, 1962)
If I Didn't Have a Dime (Musicor, 1962)

Platters
Only You (Mercury, 1955)
The Great Pretender (Mercury, 1955)
My Prayer (Mercury, 1956)
Twilight Time (Mercury, 1958)
Smoke Gets in Your Eyes (Mercury, 1958)

Playmates
Beep Beep (Roulette, 1958)

Prado, Perez
Cherry Pink and Apple Blossom White (RCA Victor, 1955)
Patricia (RCA Victor, 1958)

Presley, Elvis
Heartbreak Hotel (RCA Victor, 1956)
I Want You, I Need You, I Love You (RCA Victor, 1956)
Love Me Tender (RCA Victor, 1956)
Anyway You Want Me (RCA Victor, 1956)
All Shook Up (RCA Victor, 1957)
Don't Be Cruel (RCA Victor, 1957)
Hound Dog (RCA Victor, 1957)
Jailhouse Rock (RCA Victor, 1957)
Too Much (RCA Victor, 1957)
Teddy Bear (RCA Victor, 1957)
Don't (RCA Victor 1958)
Wear My Ring Around Your Neck (RCA Victor, 1958)
Hard Headed Woman (RCA Victor, 1958)
I Got Stung (RCA Victor, 1958)
One Night (RCA Victor, 1958)
A Fool Such As I (RCA Victor, 1959)
A Big Hunk of Love (RCA Victor, 1959)
Stuck on You (RCA Victor, 1959)
It's Now or Never (RCA Victor, 1960)
Are You Lonesome Tonight? (RCA Victor, 1960)
Blue Moon (RCA Victor, 1961)
Little Sister (RCA Victor, 1961)
Surrender (RCA Victor, 1961)

Return to Sender (RCA Victor, 1962)
Good Luck Charm (RCA Victor, 1962)
Crying in the Chapel (RCA Victor, 1965)

Preston, Johnny
Running Bear (Mercury, 1960)

Price, Lloyd
Stagger Lee (ABC Paramount, 1959)
Personality (ABC Paramount, 1959)

Ray, Johnnie
Cry (Columbia, 1951)
The Little White Cloud That Cried (Columbia, 1951)
Just Walking in the Rain (Columbia, 1956)

Rays
Silhouettes (Cameo, 1957)

Reeves, Jim
He'll Have to Go (RCA Victor, 1960)

Reisman, Leo
Stormy Weather (RCA Victor, 1933)

Reynolds, Debbie and Carleton Carpenter
Aba Daba Honeymoon (MGM, 1951)

Reynolds, Debbie
Tammy (Coral, 1957)

Riddle, Nelson
Lisbon Antigua (Capitol, 1955)

Robbins, Marty
A White Sport Coat and a Pink Carnation (Columbia, 1957)
El Paso (Columbia, 1959)

Rodgers, Jimmie
Honeycomb (Roulette, 1957)
Kisses Sweeter Than Wine (Roulette, 1957)
Secretly (Roulette, 1958)
Oh, Oh, I'm Falling in Love Again (Roulette, 1958)

Rooftop Singers
Walk Right In (Vanguard, 1963)

Rose, David
Calypso Melody (MGM, 1957)

Rydell, Bobby
Wild One (Cameo, 1959)
Kissin' Time (Cameo, 1960)
Swingin' School (Cameo, 1960)
Volare (Cameo, 1960)

Sadler, Barry
Ballad of the Green Berets (RCA Victor, 1966)

Sands, Tommy

Teen Age Crush (Capitol, 1957)

Santo and Johnny
Sleepwalk (Can Am, 1959)

Selvin, Ben
Dardanella (Victor, 1919)

Seville, David
Witch Doctor (Liberty, 1958)
The Chipmunk Song (Liberty, 1958)
Alvin's Harmonica (Liberty, 1959)

Shannon, Del
Runaway (Bigtop, 1961)

Shaw, Artie
Begin the Beguine (RCA Victor, 1938)
Frenesi (RCA Victor, 1940)
Stardust (RCA Victor, 1940)
Dancing in the Dark (RCA Victor, 1941)

Shirelles
Soldier Boy (Scepter, 1962)

Shore, Dinah
Buttons and Bows (Columbia, 1948)

Silhouettes
Get a Job (Ember, 1958)

Sinatra, Frank
All or Nothing At All (Columbia, 1940)
White Christmas (Columbia, 1942)
The Coffee Song (Capitol, 1946)
Young at Heart (Capitol, 1954)
All the Way (Capitol, 1957)
High Hopes (Capitol, 1959)

Sinatra, Nancy
These Boots Are Made for Walkin' (Reprise, 1965)

Smith, Kate
God Bless America (Columbia, 1940)
Rose O'Day (Columbia, 1941)

Stafford, Jo
Temptation (Capitol, 1948)
Make Love to Me (Columbia, 1954)

Starr, Kay
Wheel of Fortune (Capitol, 1952)
Rock and Roll Waltz (RCA Victor, 1955)

Starr, Kay and Tennessee Ernie Ford
I'll Never Be Free (Capitol, 1950)

Steele, Jon and Sandra
My Happiness (Damon, 1948)

Stevens, Connie
Sixteen Reasons (Warner, 1960)

Stewart, Sandy
My Coloring Book (Colpix, 1962)

Stoloff, Morris

Moonglow (Decca, 1956)
Picnic (Decca, 1956)

Storm, Gale
I Hear You Knocking (Dot, 1955)

Streisand, Barbra
My Honey's Lovin' Arms (Columbia, 1963)
People (Columbia, 1964)

Teddybears
To Know Him Is to Love Him (Dore, 1958)

Thompson, Hank
Wild Side of Life (Capitol, 1960)

Todd, Art and Dotty
Chanscn D'Amour (Era, 1957)

Tokens
The Lion Sleeps Tonight (RCA Victor, 1961)

Tymes
So Much in Love (Parkway, 1963)

Vale, Jerry
For Mama (Columbia, 1964)
Have You Looked into Your Heart? (Columbia, 1964)

Valens, Ritchie
Donna (Del Fi, 1958)

Vallée, Rudy
My Time Is Your Time (RCA Victor, 1929)
I'm Just a Vagabond Lover (RCA Victor, 1930)
Stein Song (RCA Victor, 1930)
There Is a Tavern in the Town (RCA Victor, 1930)
Betty Co-Ed (RCA Victor, 1930)
Goodnight, Sweetheart (RCA Victor, 1931)

Vaughan, Sarah
Make Yourself Comfortable (Mercury, 1954)
Whatever Lola Wants (Mercury, 1958)
Broken Hearted Melody (Mercury, 1959)

Vaughn, Billy
Melody of Love (Dot, 1956)
Sail Along, Silvery Moon (Dot, 1957)

Vee, Bobby
Take Good Care of My Baby (Liberty, 1961)

Ventures
Walk, Don't Run (Dolton, 1960)

Vinton, Bobby
Roses Are Red, My Love (Epic, 1962)

There, I've Said It Again (Epic, 1963)

Mister Lonely (Epic, 1964)

Wallace, Jerry

Primrose Lane (Challenge, 1960)

Ward, Billy

Star Dust (Liberty, 1957)

Washington, Dinah

What a Diff'rence a Day Made (Mercury, 1958)

Washington, Dinah and Brook Benton

Baby, You Got What It Takes (Mercury, 1960)

Weavers

On Top of Old Smokey (Decca, 1951)

The Roving Kind (Decca, 1951)

Weber, Joan

Let Me Go, Lover (Columbia, 1954)

Weems, Ted

Heartaches (Decca, 1950)

Welk, Lawrence

Calcutta (Dot, 1961)

Whiteman, Paul

Whispering (Victor, 1920)

Three O'Clock in the Morning (Victor, 1922)

Linger Awhile (Victor, 1923)

Whiting, Margaret and Jimmie Wakely

Slipping Around (Capitol, 1948)

Whitman, Slim

Secret Love (Imperial, 1953)

Indian Love Call (Imperial, 1954)

Rose Marie (Imperial, 1954)

Williams, Andy

Canadian Sunset (Cadence, 1956)

Moon River (Columbia, 1961)

Days of Wine and Roses (Columbia, 1963)

Williams, Hank

Cold, Cold Heart (MGM, 1951)

Jambalaya (MGM, 1952)

Your Cheatin' Heart (MGM, 1953)

Williams, Otis and Charms

Hearts of Stone (De Luxe, 1955)

Ivory Tower (De Luxe, 1956)

Williams, Roger

Autumn Leaves (Kapp, 1955)

Till (Kapp, 1957)

Williams, Tex

Smoke, Smoke, Smoke (Capitol, 1947)

Wills, Bob

San Antonio Rose (Columbia, 1940)

Wilson, Jackie

Lonely Teardrops (Brunswick, 1959)

Night (Brunswick, 1960)

Winterhalter, Hugo

Canadian Sunset (RCA Victor, 1956)

Wooley, Sheb

The Purple People Eater (MGM, 1958)

Yorgeson, Yogy

I Yust Go Nuts at Christmas (Capitol, 1950)

SOME AMERICAN PERFORMERS

OF THE PAST AND PRESENT

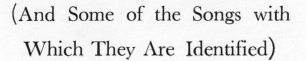

(And Some of the Songs with
Which They Are Identified)

Bernard, Sophie: Poor Butterfly

Bernie, Ben: Au Revoir, Pleasant Dreams; Lazybones; Sweet Georgia Brown

Blaine, Vivian: Adelaide's Lament; A Bushel and a Peck

Bland, James: In the Evening by the Moonlight

Bledsoe, Jules: Ol' Man River

Bolger, Harry: Rip Van Winkle Was a Lucky Man

Bolger, Ray: Once in Love with Amy; There's a Small Hotel

Boone, Pat: April Love; Friendly Persuasion; Love Letters in the Sand

Bordoni, Irene: Do It Again; Let's Do It; Who'll Buy My Violets?

Brian, Donald: Mary's a Grand Old Name; So Long, Mary

Breen, Bobby: Rainbow on the River

Brewer, Teresa: Music, Music, Music; Ricochet; Till I Waltz Again with You

Brice, Elizabeth: Do It Again

Brice, Fanny: I'm a Vamp from East Broadway; My Man; Rose of Washington Square; Second Hand Rose

Brooks, Laurence: Sweet Music

Brown, Les: Sentimental Journey

Bryant, Anita: Till There Was You

Brynner, Yul: A Puzzlement

Bubbles, John: It Ain't Necessarily So

Burgess, Cool: Shew, Fly, Don't Bother Me

Burns and Allen: Love Nest

Cahill, Marie: He's a Cousin of Mine; Navajo; You Can't Fool All the People All the Time

Calloway, Cab: Minnie the Moocher

Canova, Judy: Go to Sleep, My Baby

Cantor, Eddie: Ida; If You Knew Susie; Makin' Whoopee; Margie; My Baby Just Cares for Me; Now's the Time to Fall in Love; One Hour with You; Santa Claus Is Coming to Town; Yes, We Have No Bananas; You'd Be Surprised

Carle, Frankie: Swinging Down the Lane

Carminati, Tulio: The Song Is You

Caron, Leslie: Hi Lili, Hi Lo

Carroll, Diahann: The Sweetest Sounds

Carson, Mindy: Wake the Town and Tell the People

Carus, Emma: Alexander's Ragtime Band; Take Back Your Gold; What Do You Want to Make Those Eyes at Me For?

Castle, Irene and Vernon: Syncopated Walk

Catlett, Walter: Lady, Be Good

Cavendish, Milly: You Naughty, Naughty Men

Channing, Carol: Diamonds Are a Girl's Best Friend; Hello, Dolly!

Charles, Ray: I Can't Stop Loving You

Chase, Marian: April in Paris

Checker, Chubby: Let's Twist Again; The Twist

Chevalier, Maurice: Louise; Mimi; One Hour with You; Thank Heaven for Little Girls

Chordettes: Mr. Sandman

Christy, Ed: My Old Kentucky Home; Old Folks at Home

Claire, Ina: Hello, Frisco

Cline, Maggie: Down Went McGinty; Drill Ye Tarriers, Drill; Throw Him Down, McCloskey

Clinton, Larry: Deep Purple; My Reverie

Clooney, Rosemary: Botch-a Me; Come On-a My House; Half As Much; Mambo Italiano; This Ole House

Cohan, George M.: Give My Regards to Broadway; Yankee Doodle Boy; You're a Grand Old Flag

Cohen, Meyer: Take a Seat, Old Lady

Cole and Johnson: Under the Bamboo Tree

Cole, Nat King: Mona Lisa; Nature Boy; Non Dimenticar; Ramblin' Rose; Straighten Up and Fly Right; Sweet Lorraine; Too Young

Collins, José: Peg o' My Heart; Rebecca of Sunnybrook Farm

Como, Perry: Catch a Falling Star; Don't Let the Stars Get in Your Eyes; Dream Along with Me; Hot Diggity; A Hubba Hubba Hubba; Till the End of Time

Conor, Harry: The Bowery

Cook, Joe: Fine and Dandy

Cooke, Sam: You Send Me

Cowles, Eugene: Gypsy Love Song

Crew Cuts: Sh-Boom

Crosby, Bing: Dear Hearts and Gentle People; In the Cool, Cool, Cool of the Evening; I Surrender, Dear; Love in Bloom; Moonlight Becomes You; Pistol Packin' Mama; Small Fry; Sweet Leilani; Swinging on a Star; Temptation; True Love; Where the Blue of the Night Meets the Gold of the Day; White Christmas

Crosby Bob: Summertime

Crumit, Frank: Abdul Abulbul Amir

Cugat, Xavier: Isle of Capri; Tico Tico

Dahlhart, Vernon: The Prisoner's Song

Dailey, Peter F.: Kiss Me, Honey, Do; Say You Love Me, Sue

Dale, Alan: Cherry Pink and Apple Blossom White

Damone, Vic: Again; On the Street Where You Live; You're Breaking My Heart

Daniels, Billy: That Old Black Magic

Darin, Bobby: Dream Lover; Mack the Knife; Splish Splash

Davis, Bette: They're Either Too Young or Too Old

Davis, Jessie Bartlett: Oh, Promise Me

Davis, Sammy: Too Close for Comfort

Dawn, Hazel: My Beautiful Lady

Day, Doris: Everybody Loves a Lover; A Guy Is a Guy; It's Magic; Love Somebody; Secret Love; Sentimental Journey; Whatever Will Be, Will Be

Day, Edith: A Kiss in the Dark; Tickle Toe

De Angelis, Jefferson: Tammany

Dean, Jimmy: Big Bad John

De Haven, Gloria: The Stanley Steamer

Del Rico, Dolores: Jeanine, I Dream of Lilac Time; Ramona

Deming, Arthur: Please Go 'Way and Let Me Sleep

Deslys, Gaby: The Gaby Glide

Desmond, Johnny: Play Me Hearts and Flowers

Deutsch, Emery: Play, Fiddle, Play

Devere, Sam: The Whistling Coon

Dexter, Al: Pistol Packin' Mama

Dietrich, Marlene: Falling in Love Again; See What the Boys in the Back Room Will Have

Dillon Brothers: Do, Do, Do; Put Me Off at Buffalo

Dixon, George Washington: The Coal Black Rose; My Long Blue Tail; Zip Coon

Dolly Sisters: Be My Little Baby Bumble Bee

Domino, "Fats": Ain't It a Shame?; Blue Berry Hill; Boll Weevil; Whole Lotta Lovin'

Dorsey, Jimmy: Amapola; Green Eyes; Maria Elena; So Rare; Tangerine

Dorsey, Tommy: I'll Never Smile Again; Imagination; I'm Getting Sentimental Over You; Marie; There Are Such Things

Douglas, Mike: The Men in My Little Girl's Life

Dovey, Alice: Kiss Waltz

Downey, Morton: Carolina Moon; When Irish Eyes Are Smiling; You Took Advantage of Me

Drake, Alfred: Oh, What a Beautiful Mornin'

Draper, Rusty: Gambler's Guitar

Dresser Louise: My Gal Sal

Drifters: True, True Love

Duncan, Todd: I Got Plenty o' Nuthin'

Durante, Jimmy: Inka Dinka Doo; The Man Who Found the Lost Chord; Umbriago

Durbin, Deanna: Spring Will Be a Little Late This Year

Du Rell Twin Brothers: Fountain in the Park

Easy Aces: Manhattan Serenade.

Eberle, Bob: Green Eyes; Maria Elena; Tangerine

Eckstein, Billy: I Apologize; My Foolish Heart

Eddy, Nelson: Ah, Sweet Mystery of Life; Indian Love Call; In the Still of the Night; Rosalie; Short'nin' Bread

Edwards, Cliff: Singin' in the Rain

Ellis Mary: Indian Love Call

Emerson, Billy: The Big Sunflower; Polly Wolly Doodle; Pretty As a Picture

Emmett Dan: Dixie

Etting, Ruth: Everybody Loves My Baby; Love Me or Leave Me; Mean to Me; Remember; Ten Cents a Dance; You Made Me Love You

Evans, George "Honey Boy": I'll Be True to My Honey Boy

Everly Brothers: Bird Dog; Wake Up, Little Susie

Farrell, Charles: If I Had a Talking Picture of You; Sunny Side Up

Farrell, Glenda: Shuffle Off to Buffalo

Faye, Alice: I'm in the Mood for Love; Never in a Million Years; This Year's Kisses; You'll Never Know

Fisher, Eddie: Any Time; Cindy, Oh Cindy; May I Sing to You?; Oh, My Papa

Fitzgerald, Ella: A-Tisket, A-Tasket

Foley, Red: Chattanoogie Shoe Shine Boy

Fontane Sisters: Hearts of Stone

Ford, Tennessee Ernie: Sixteen Tons; Tell Me Why

Four Aces: Love Is a Many Splendored Thing; Melody of Love; Three Coins in a Fountain

Four Lads: Moments to Remember

Four Seasons: Big Girls Don't Cry; Rag Doll; Walk Like a Man

Fox, Della: Waltz Me Around Again, Willie

Fox, Harry: I Love a Piano; I'm Always Chasing Rainbows

Foy, Eddie: Hamlet Was a Melancholy Dane; He Goes to Church on Sunday; I'm Tired

Francis, Connie: Among My Souvenirs; Everybody's Somebody's Fool; Lipstick on Your Collar; Where the Boys Are; Who's Sorry Now?

Frawley, Paul: Sunny

Froman, Jane: I Believe; More Than You Know; That Old Feeling; With a Song in My Heart

Gallagher and Shean: Mr. Gallagher and Mr. Shean

Garrett, Betty: South America, Take It Away

Garland, Judy: Johnny One Note; The Man That Got Away; My Funny Valentine; On the Atchison, Topeka and Santa Fe; Over the Rainbow; Swanee; Trolley Song; You Made Me Love You

Gaxton, William: My Heart Stood Still; Of Thee I Sing

Gaynor, Janet: If I Had a Talking Picture of You; Sunny Side Up

Geva, Tamara: Louisiana Hayride

Gibbs, Georgia: Dance with Me, Henry; Kiss of Fire; Tweedle Dee Dee

Gilmer, Jim (and Fireballs): Sugar Shack

Gilson, Lottie: Coax Me; The Little Lost Child; Mother Was a Lady; My Best Girl's a New Yorker; She Was Bred in Old Kentucky; The Sidewalks of New York; The Sunshine of Paradise Alley; Two Little Girls in Blue

Godfrey, Arthur: It Seems Like Old Times; Too Fat Polka

Goodman, Benny: And the Angels Sing; China Boy; Goody Goody; Honeysuckle Rose; Memories of You

Gormé, Eydie: Blame It on the Bossa Nova

Goulet, Robert: If Ever I Would Leave You; They Call the Wind Maria; What Kind of Fool Am I?

Grant, Gogi: The Wayward Wind

Gray, Gilda: It's Getting Dark on Old Broadway; Near the South Sea Moon

Gray, Glen: I Cried for You; Sleepy Time Gal; Smoke Rings; Sunrise Serenade

Green, Mitzi: The Lady Is a Tramp; My Funny Valentine

Greenwood, Charlotte: Oh By Jingo, Oh By Gee

Groody, Louise: I Want to Be Happy; Sometimes I'm Happy; Tea for Two

Hackett, Dolly: Pretty Baby

Haley, Bill (and His Comets): Rock Around the Clock; See You Later, Alligator

Haley, Jack: Did You Ever See a Dream Walking?

Hall, Adelaide: Diga Diga Doo

Hall, Bettina: She Didn't Say Yes

Hall, Natalie: Through the Years

Hall, Wendell: It Ain't Gonna Rain No Mo'

Halliday, Robert: One Alone; Stout Hearted Men

Halperin, Nan: I Love You

Hamilton IV, George: A Rose and Baby Ruth

Haney, Carol: Steam Heat

Harney, Ben: Cakewalk in the Sky; My Black Mandy

Harris, Phil: Thank You for a Lovely Evening; The Thing

Harrold, Orville: I'm Falling in Love with Someone; Tramp, Tramp, Tramp Along the Highway

Haverly, Charles Ernest: My Gal Is a Highborn Lady

Hayes, Bill: The Ballad of Davy Crockett

Haymes, Dick: I Wish I Knew; Little White Lies

Hayworth, Rita: Put the Blame on Mame

Heidt, Horace: Deep in the Heart of Texas

Held, Anna: I Just Can't Make My Eyes Behave; It's Delightful to Be Married; Maiden with the Dreamy Eyes

Herbert, Evelyn: Lover, Come Back to Me

Herman, Woody: Woodchopper's Ball

Hibler, Al: Unchained Melody

Hildegarde: Darling, Je Vous Aime Beaucoup; The Last Time I Saw Paris; I'll Be Seeing You

Hilltoppers: P. S. I Love You

Hitchcock, Raymond: Wal, I Swan

Holiday, Billie: There Is No Greater Love

Holloway, Stanley: Get Me to the Church On Time; With a Little Bit of Luck

Holman, Libby: Body and Soul; Can't We Be Friends?; Moanin' Low; Something to Remember You By

Hope, Bob: Buttons and Bows; Thanks for the Memory; Two Sleepy People

Horne, Lena: East of St. Louis Blues; Honeysuckle Rose; Shoo Shoo, Baby; Stormy Weather; Take It Slow, Joe

Horton, Johnny: The Battle of New Orleans

Howard, Eddie: Mairzy Doats; My Last Goodbye; To Each His Own

Howard, Willie and Eugene: Carolina in the Morning; Hello, Hawaii, How Are You?

Howard, Joseph E.: Hello, My Baby; I Wonder Who's Kissing Her Now

Huston, Walter: September Song

Hutchinson Family: The Bridge of Sighs; Get Off the Track; Jordan Is a Hard Road to Travel; A Life upon the Ocean Wave; Mrs. Lofty and I; The Old Granite State; Tenting on the Old Camp Ground

Ink Spots: If I Didn't Care

Irwin, May: The Bully Song; You've Been a Good Old Wagon But You Done Broke Down

James, Harry: I Had the Craziest Dream; I've Heard That Song Before

Jenkins, Gordon: Goodnight, Irene; On Top of Old Smokey

Jessel, George: My Mother's Eyes

Jolson, Al: About a Quarter to Nine; Anniversary Song; April Showers; Avalon; California, Here I Come; I'm Sitting on Top of the World; Ma Blushin' Rosie; My Mammy; Rock-a-bye Your Baby with a Dixie Melody; Sonny Boy; Swanee; There's a Rainbow 'Round My Shoulder; Toot, Toot, Tootsie; Waiting for the Robert E. Lee; When the Red, Red Robin Comes Bob, Bob, Bobbin' Along; You Made Me Love You

Jones, Allan: The Donkey Serenade

Jones, Isham: I'll See You in My Dreams; The One I Love Belongs to Somebody Else

Jones, Jack: Call Me Irresponsible; Lollipops and Roses; Wives and Lovers

Jones, Spike (and City Slickers): Chloe; Der Fuehrer's Face

José, Dick: Calling to Her Boy Just Once Again; He Fought for a Cause He Thought Was Right; Silver Threads Among the Gold; With All Her Faults I Love Her Still

Kaempfert, Bert: Red Roses for a Blue Lady

Kane, Helen: I Wanna Be Loved by You; My Sweeter Than Sweet; That's My Weakness Now

Kaye, Danny: Ballin' the Jack; Melody in 4-F; Thumbelina; Tschaikowsky

Kaye, Stubby: Jubilation T. Cornpone

Kearns, Allen: That Certain Feeling

Keeler, Ruby: Forty-Second Street; Liza; Shadow Waltz; Too Wonderful for Words

Kelly, Gene: I Could Write a Book; Long Ago and Far Away

Kelly, Grace: True Love

Kiley, Richard: Stranger in Paradise; The Sweetest Sounds

King, Charles: Broadway Melody; Happy Days Are Here Again; Play a Simple Melody

King, Dennis: I Married an Angel; Indian Love Call; Only a Rose; Rose Marie

King, Wayne: The Waltz You Saved for Me

Kingston Trio: Tom Dooley

Kitt, Eartha: C'est Si Bon; Monotonous

Kyser, Kay: Jingle, Jangle, Jingle; On a Slow Boat to China; Praise the Lord and Pass the Ammunition; Three Little Fishes; Woody Woodpecker

Lahr, Bert: Song of the Woodman

Laine, Frankie: The Cry of the Wild Goose; High Noon; Jezebel; Moonlight Gambler; Mule Train; That's My Desire

Lambert, Maude: Love Me and the World Is Mine

Lamour, Dorothy: The Moon of Manakoora

Langford, Frances: I Feel a Song Coming On

Lanza, Mario: Arrividerci Roma; Be My Love

La Rosa, Julius: Eh, Cumpari

La Rue, Grace: M-i-s-s-i-s-s-i-p-p-i; Your Eyes Have Told Me So

Lawrence, Carol: I Feel Pretty; Tonight

Lawrence, Gertrude: Getting to Know You; Hello, Young Lovers; My Ship; The Saga of Jenny; Someone to Watch Over Me

Lee, Brenda: Jambalaya

Lee, Peggy: Golden Earrings; It's a Good Day; Mañana Is Good Enough for Me; Pass Me By

Leighton Brothers: Casey Jones

Leonard, Eddie: Ida; Oh, Didn't It Rain;

Roll Dem Roly Boly Eyes

Levey, Ethel: I Guess I'll Have to Telegraph My Baby; I Was Born in Virginia

Lewis, Joe E.: Sam, You Made the Pants Too Long

Lewis, Ted: Georgette; Me and My Shadow; Two Tickets to Georgia; When My Baby Smiles at Me

Libby J. Aldrich: After the Ball

Lightner, Winnie: I'll Build a Stairway to Paradise; Somebody Loves Me

Lilo: Ç'est Magnifique; I Love Paris

Lindsay, Jennie: Daisy Bell

Little Jack Little: A Shanty in Old Shanty Town

Logan, Ella: How Are Things in Glocca Morra? Something I Dreamed Last Night

Lombardo, Guy (and Royal Canadians): Boo Hoo; Little White Lies; Swingin' in a Hammock; You're Driving Me Crazy

London, Julie: Cry Me a River

Lopez, Vincent: Bell Bottom Trousers; Just a Gigolo; Nola

Lorraine, Lillian: By the Light of the Silvery Moon; Daddy Has a Sweetheart and Mother Is Her Name; My Pony Boy; Row, Row, Row; Up, Up in My Aeroplane

Lowe, Jim: Green Door

Lown, Bert: Bye, Bye, Blues

Lunceford, Jimmy: Baby, Won't You Please Come Home

Lyman Tommy: My Blue Heaven; My Melancholy Baby

MacDonald, Jeanette: Ah, Sweet Mystery of Life; Beyond the Blue Horizon; Love Me Tonight; Lover

Mack, Andrew: The Picture That Is Turned Toward the Wall

Mantovani: Charmaine

Marshall, Everett: That's Why Darkies Were Born; The Thrill Is Gone

Martin, Dean: Everybody Loves Somebody; Memories Are Made of This; That's Amore; Volare

Martin, Freddy: Hut Sut Song; Tonight We Love

Martin, Mary: I'm in Love with a Wonderful Guy; My Heart Belongs to Daddy; Speak Low

Martin, Tony: There's No Tomorrow; To Each His Own

Martini, Nino: Here's to Romance

Martino, Al: Here in My Heart;

Painted, Tainted Rose

Marx, Groucho: Hooray for Captain Spalding; Lydia, the Tattooed Lady

Mathis, Johnny: A Certain Smile; Tender Is the Night

May, Edna: She Is the Belle of New York; They All Follow Me

McCoy, Bessie: The Yama Yama Man

McDonald, Christine: Sweethearts

McGowan, Jack: Love Nest

McGuire Sisters: Sugartime

Merman, Ethel: Blow, Gabriel, Blow; Doin' What Comes Natur'lly; Eadie Was a Lady; I Got Rhythm; Katie Went to Haiti; Life Is Just a Bowl of Cherries; Rise 'n' Shine; Sam and Delilah

Merry Macs: Mairzy Doats

Middleton, Ray: Green Up Time

Miller, Glenn: At Last; Chattanooga Choo Choo; Imagination; In the Mood; The Little Brown Jug; Moonlight Serenade; Sunrise Serenade

Miller, Marilyn: Easter Parade; Look for the Silver Lining; Mandy; Time on My Hands; Whip-poor-will

Miller, Mitch: The Yellow Rose of Texas

Miller, Roger: King of the Road

Mills Brothers: Civilization; The Glow Worm; I Don't Want to Set the World on Fire; Lazy River; Paper Doll

Mills, Florence: I'm Just Wild About Harry

Miranda, Carmen: South American Way

Mitchell, Guy: Belle, Belle; Heartaches by the Number; My Heart Cries for You; My Truly, Truly Fair; Sparrow in the Tree Top

Monroe, Vaughn: Let It Snow, Let It Snow; There, I've Said it Again

Montgomery, David: Hurray for Baffin Bay; Streets of New York

Mooney, Art: I'm Lookin' Over a Four Leaf Clover

Moore, Grace: All Alone; Ciribiribin; One Night of Love; What'll I Do?

Moore, Raymond: Sweet Marie

Moore, Victor: Forty-Five Minutes from Broadway

Mora, Helene: The Moth and the Flame

Morgan, Helen: Bill; The Man I Love; Why Was I Born?

Morgan, Russ: Does Your Heart Beat for Me?; So Tired; Sunflower

Morrow, Doretta: Stranger in Paradise

Munn, Frank: Little Mother of Mine

Murray, Elizabeth: Put Your Arms

Around Me, Honey; Sailin' Away on the Henry Clay

Nelson, Ricky: I'm Walkin'; Stood Up

Newton, Wayne: Red Roses for a Blue Lady

Nielsen, Alice: Cupid and I

Novarro, Ramon: Pagan Love Song

Nugent, Maud: Sweet Rosie O'Grady

O'Connell, Helen: Green Eyes; Maria Elena; Tangerine

Olcott, Chauncey: A Little Bit of Heaven; Mother Machree; My Wild Irish Rose; The Outcast Unknown; Too-ra-loo-ra-loo-ral; When Irish Eyes Are Smiling

Olsen and Johnson: Barney Google; Oh, Gee, Oh, Gosh, Oh, Golly, I'm in Love

Orbison, Roy: Oh, Pretty Woman

Owens, Harry: My Own Iona

Page, Patti: Allegheny Moon; Cross Over the Bridge; How Much Is That Doggie in the Window?; I Went to Your Wedding; Mockin' Bird Hill; Old Cape Cod; Tennessee Waltz

Palmer, Bea: Please Don't Talk About Me When I'm Gone

Patience and Prudence: Tonight You Belong to Me

Paul, Les and Ford, Mary: How High the Moon; Mockin' Bird Hill; Vaya Con Dios

Peacock, Bertram: Song of Love

Pennington, Ann: Black Bottom

Peter, Paul and Mary: Blowin' in the Wind

Pinza, Ezio: Some Enchanted Evening; This Nearly Was Mine

Platters: The Great Pretender; My Prayer; Only You

Pollack, Emma: Maggie Murphy's Home

Powell, Dick: I'll String Along with You; I Only Have Eyes for You; I've Got My Love to Keep Me Warm; Mr. and Mrs. Is the Name; Shadow Waltz; Thanks a Million; This Year's Kisses

Powell, Eleanor: My Lucky Star

Powell, Jane: It's a Most Unusual Day

Prado, Perez: Patricia

Presley, Elvis: All Shook Up; Don't Be Cruel; A Fool Such As I; Hard Headed Woman; Heartbreak Hotel; Hound Dog; Love Me Tender

Preston, Robert: Seventy-Six Trombones

Price, George: Bye, Bye, Blackbird

Primrose, George: Carry Me Back to Old Virginny; Lazy Moon; Oh, Didn't He

Ramble?

Quaker City Four: Sweet Adeline

Raitt, John: Hey, There; Soliloquy

Ray, Johnnie: Cry; The Little White Cloud That Cried

Reynolds, Debbie: Aba Daba Honeymoon; Tammy

Rice, Thomas "Daddy": Jim Crow; Long Time Ago

Richman, Harry: The Birth of the Blues; On the Sunny Side of the Street; Walkin' My Baby Back Home

Riddle, Nelson: Lisbon Antigua

Ring, Blanche: Bedelia; Come, Josephine, in My Flying Machine; I'd Leave My Happy Home for You; In the Good Old Summertime; I've Got Rings on My Fingers; Yip-i-addy-i-ay

Robbins, Marty: The Hanging Tree; A White Sport Coat

Roberti, Lyda: Sweet and Hot

Rodgers, Jimmie: Honeycomb

Rogers, Charles "Buddy": My Future Just Passed

Rogers, Ginger: The Carioca; Cheek to Cheek; The Continental; Embraceable You; Flying Down to Rio; Shuffle Off to Buffalo

Rogers, Roy: Don't Fence Me In; The Last Round Up

Rooney, Mickey: The Stanley Steamer

Rooney, Pat (the elder): Is That You, Mr. Riley?

Rooney, Pat (the younger): The Daughter of Rosie O'Grady

Ross, Lanny: Moonlight and Roses; Stay As Sweet As You Are

Ross, Shirley: Thanks for the Memory; Two Sleepy People

Roth, Lillian: How Many Times Have I Said I Love You?; Sing, You Sinners; When the Red, Red Robin Comes Bob, Bob, Bobbin' Along

Rowland, Adele: In My Sweet Little Alice Blue Gown; Rackety Coo

Roye, Ruth: Aba Daba Honeymoon; Ain't We Got Fun?; Waiting for the Robert E. Lee

Russell, Lillian: Come Down, Ma' Evenin' Star; When Chloe Sings a Song

Rydell, Bobby: Kissin' Time

Sabel, Josephine: A Hot Time in the Old Town Tonight

Sanderson, Julia: They Didn't Believe Me

Sands, Tommy: Teen Age Crush

Santley, Joseph and Sawyer, Ivy: The Same Old Moon

Savo, Jimmy: I May Be Wrong But I Think You're Wonderful; One Meat Ball; River Stay Away from my Door

Scanlan, William J.: Molly O; My Nellie's Blue Eyes; Remember, Boy, You're Irish

Scheff, Fritzi: Kiss Me Again

Schulte, Minnie: His Last Thoughts Were of You

Scott, Hazel: Franklin D. Roosevelt Jones

Seabrook, Thomas Q.: Mister Dooley

Sedaka, Neil: Oh, Carol

Segal, Vivienne: Auf Wiedersehen; Bewitched, Bothered and Bewildered. Spring Is Here; To Keep My Love Alive

Seville, David (Ross Bagdasarian): The Chipmunk Song

Shaw, Artie: Begin the Beguine; Frenesi; Stardust

Shaw, David T.: Columbia, the Gem of the Ocean

Shaw, Oscar: Ka-lu-a

Shay, Dorothy: Feudin' and Fightin'

Sherwood, Roberta: You're Nobody Till Somebody Loves You

Shore, Dinah: Buttons and Bows; I'll Walk Alone; Shoofly Pie and Apple Pan Dowdy; Yes, My Darling Daughter

Sinatra, Frank: All or Nothing at All; All the Way; Coffee Song; Five Minutes More; High Hopes; It Was a Very Good Year; Love and Marriage; A Lovely Way to Spend an Evening; Young at Heart

Skelly, Hal: True Blue Lou

Smith, Ethel: Tico-Tico

Smith, Kate: By the River Sainte Marie; Dream a Little Dream of Me; God Bless America; I Surrender, Dear; Please Don't Talk About Me When I'm Gone; Rose O'Day; When the Moon Comes Over the Mountain

Smith, Queenie: That Certain Feeling

Smith, Whispering Jack: Gimme a Little Kiss, Will Ya, Huh?

Stafford, Jo: Make Love to Me; Shrimp Boats; Teach Me Tonight

Steel, John: A Pretty Girl Is Like a Melody; Tulip Time

Stewart, Sandy: My Coloring Book

Stoloff, Morris: Moonglow; Picnic

Stone, Fred: Hurray for Baffin Bay; Streets of New York

Streisand, Barbra: Happy Days Are Here Again; My Honey's Lovin' Arms; People

Sullivan, Joseph J.: Where Did You Get That Hat?

Suzuki, Pat: I Enjoy Being a Girl

Swanson, Gloria: Love, Your Spell Is Everywhere

Swarthout, Gladys: The Nearness of You

Tamara: Smoke Gets in Your Eyes

Tanguay, Eva: I Don't Care

Teagarden, Jack: Beale St. Blues

Temple, Shirley: Baby, Take a Bow; Hey, What Did the Bluebird Say?; On the Good Ship Lollipop

Templeton, Fay: I'm a Respectable Working Girl; Ma Blushin' Rosie; Yesterdays

Thomas, John Charles: I Love Life

Thompson, Lydia: Branigan's Band

Thornton, Bonnie: Down in Poverty Row; My Sweetheart's the Man in the Moon; Remember Poor Mother at Home

Tibbett, Lawrence: Cuban Love Song; The Rogue Song; Short'nin' Bread

Tracy, Arthur (the Street Singer): Marta

Trentini, Emma: The Dawn of Love; Giannina Mia; Italian Love Song; Love Is Like a Firefly; When a Maid Comes Knocking at Your Heart

Tucker, Sophie: The Darktown Strutters' Ball; Honey Boy; Some of These Days; A Yiddisha Momme

Vale, Jerry: For Mama; Have You Looked into Your Heart?

Vallée, Rudy: Betty Co-Ed; I'm Just a Vagabond Lover; My Time Is Your Time; Say It Isn't So; Stein Song; There Is a Tavern in the Town; The Whiffenpoof Song

Van and Schenck: I Wonder What's Become of Sally; That Old Gang of Mine

Vaughan, Sarah: Broken Hearted Melody

Vaughn, Billy: P.S. I Love You; Sail Along, Silvery Moon

Velie, Janet: Mary

Verdon, Gwen: Whatever Lola Wants

Victoria, Vesta: Daddy Wouldn't Buy Me a Bow-Wow; Waiting at the Church

Vinton, Bobby: Roses Are Red, My Love

Waller, "Fats": Ain't Misbehavin'

Ward, Aida: I've Got the World on a String

Warfield, William: Ol' Man River

Waters, Ethel: Am I Blue?; Black and Blue; Cabin in the Sky; Dinah; Happiness Is a Thing Called Joe; Heat Wave; Stormy Weather; Taking a Chance on Love; There'll Be Some Changes Made

Wayne, David: Something Sort of Grandish; When I'm Not Near the Girl I Love

Weavers: Goodnight, Irene; On Top of Old Smokey

Webb, Clifton: Easter Parade; I Guess I'll Have to Change My Plan; Louisiana Hayride

Weber, Joan: Let Me Go, Lover

Weede, Robert: Shalom

Weems, Ted: Heartaches; Somebody Stole My Gal

White, Cool: Lubly Fan

White, Francis: M-i-s-s-i-s-s-i-p-p-i

Whiteman, Paul: Linger Awhile; My Melancholy Baby; The Peanut Vendor; Three O'Clock in the Morning; Whispering

Whiting, Margaret: Slipping Around; A Tree in the Meadow

Williams, Andy: The Bilboa Song; Days of Wine and Roses; Hawaiian Wedding Song; Moon River

Williams, Bert: I Ain't Got Nobody; Let It Alone; Nobody; Somebody Lied; Woodman, Spare That Tree; You're in the Right Church But the Wrong Pew

Williams, Billy: I'm Gonna Sit Right Down and Write Myself a Letter

Williams, Frances: Sunny Disposish

Williams, Hank: Jambalaya

Williams, Hannah: Cheerful Little Earful

Williams, Roger: Autumn Leaves

Windom, W. H.: She May Have Seen Better Days

Winterhalter, Hugo: Canadian Sunset

Wilson, Dooley: As Time Goes By

Woolf, Walter: Play, Gypsies, Dance, Gypsies

Woolley, Monty: Miss Otis Regrets

Wynn, Bessie: Toyland

Yeamans, Lydia: December and May

Yorke, Alice: Cuddle Up a Little Closer

Zorina, Vera: That Old Black Magic

ABOUT THE AUTHOR

Nobody has written more books on popular music, or has enjoyed a wider circulation for them, than DAVID EWEN. His books (the serious as well as the popular) have been promoted by the leading book clubs and are basic reference works the world over.

David Ewen is the biographer of such noted composers as George Gershwin, Jerome Kern and Richard Rodgers.

His biographies on popular composers for young people have become basic to reading lists of high schools throughout the United States.

David Ewen wrote and co-produced fifty-six programs tracing the history of American popular music that were beamed all over the world for a full year by the Voice of America in more than twenty languages.